Street by St

C000092151

WES[
YORKSHIRE

Enlarged Areas Bradford, Halifax, Huddersfield, Keighley, Leeds, Wakefield

Reprinted January 2004
2nd edition January 2003

© Automobile Association Developments
Limited 2004

Original edition printed May 2001

Ordnance Survey® This product includes map data licensed from Ordnance Survey® with the permission of the Controller of Her Majesty's Stationery Office. © Crown copyright 2004. All rights reserved. Licence number 399221.

Published by AA Publishing (a trading name of Automobile Association Developments Limited, whose registered office is Millstream, Maidenhead Road, Windsor, Berkshire, SL4 5GD. Registered number 1878835).

The Post Office is a registered trademark of Post Office Ltd. in the UK and other countries.

Schools address data provided by Education Direct.

One-way street data provided by:

Tele Atlas © Tele Atlas N.V.

Mapping produced by the Cartography Department of The Automobile Association. A02097

A CIP Catalogue record for this book is available from the British Library.

Printed by in Italy by Printer Trento srl

Ref: MD017z

ii

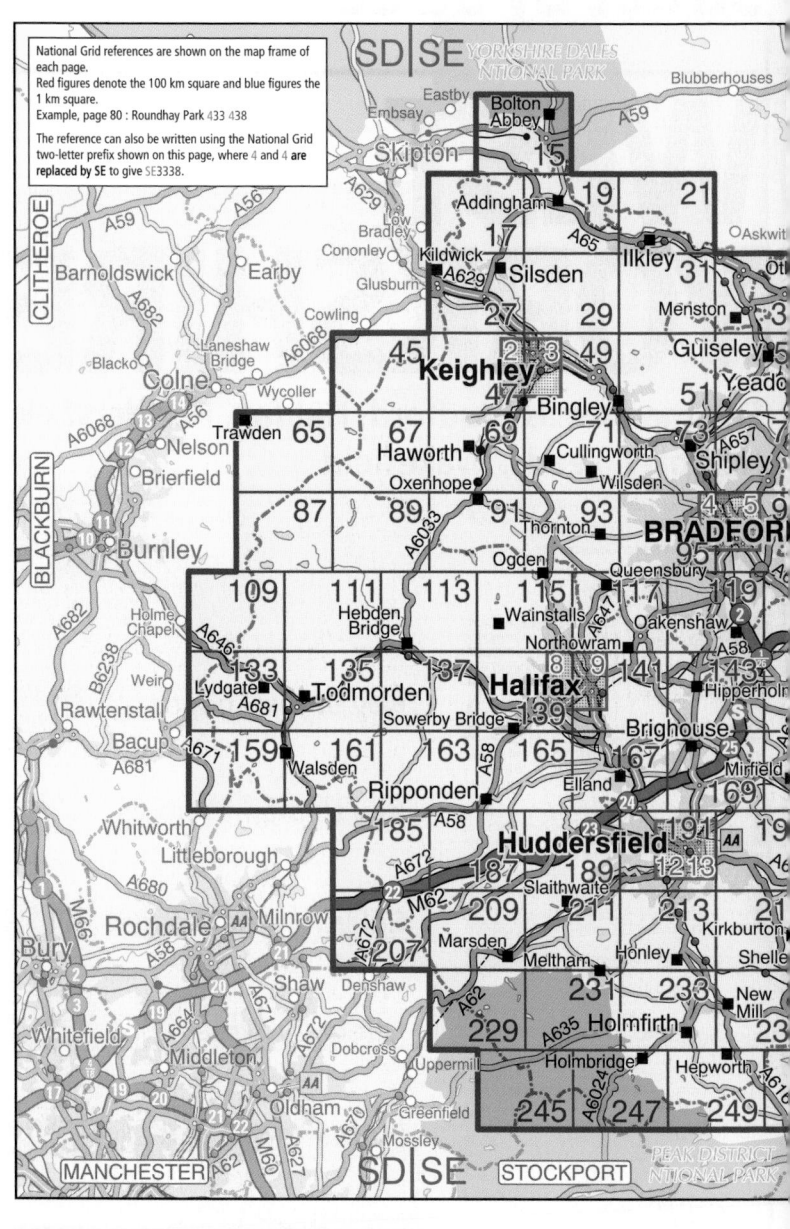

National Grid references are shown on the map frame of each page.
Red figures denote the 100 km square and blue figures the 1 km square.
Example, page 80 : Roundhay Park 433 438

The reference can also be written using the National Grid two-letter prefix shown on this page, where 4 and 4 are replaced by SE to give SE3338.

Enlarged scale pages | **1:17,500** | 3.6 inches to 1 mile

0   1/2   miles   1

0   1/2   1   kilometres   1 1/2

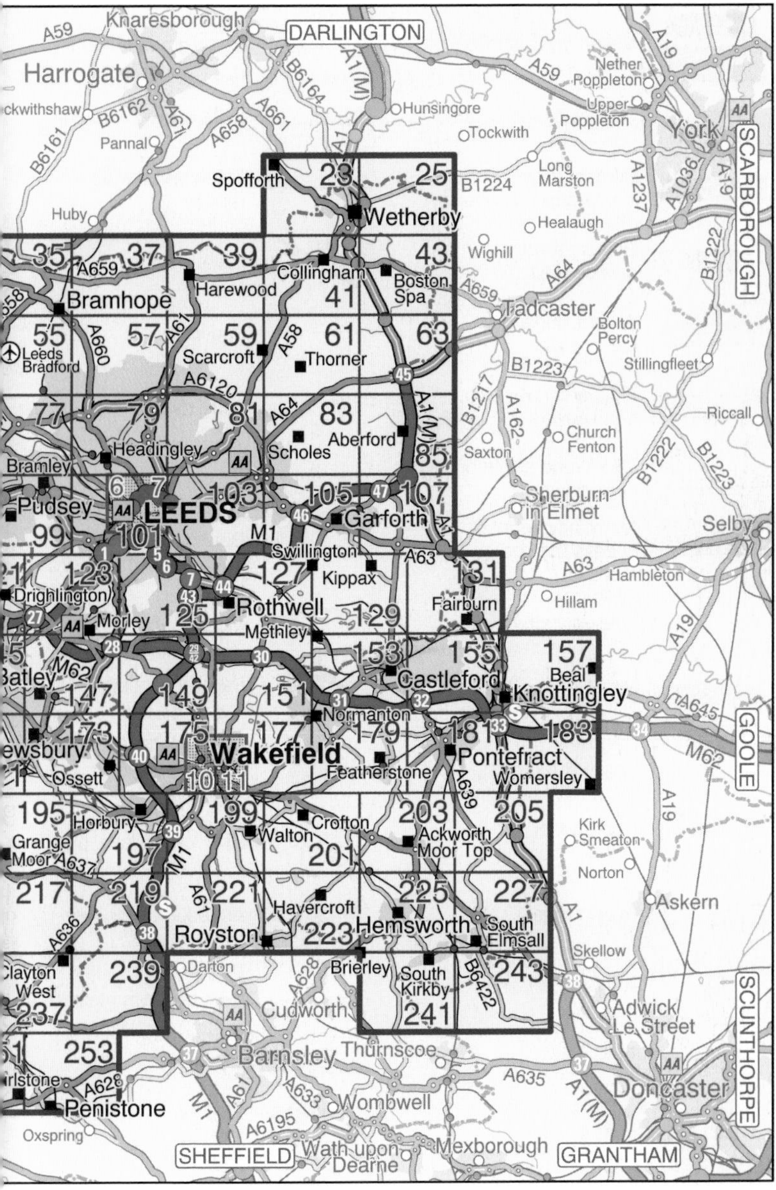

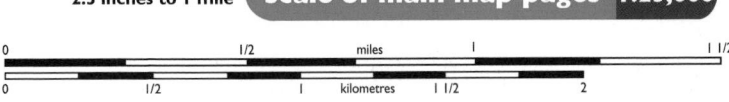

A59 Knaresborough | DARLINGTON
Harrogate
ckwithshaw B6162 A661 A658 A1 Hunsingore
B6161 Pannal A61 Tockwith
Huby
Spofforth 23 25 B1224 Long Marston
Wetherby Healaugh
35 A659 37 39 43 Wighill A64 Tadcaster
Bramhope Collingham Boston Spa
55 A660 57 59 61 63 Bolton Percy Stillingfleet
Leeds Bradford Scarcroft A58 Thorner B1223 Riccall
A6120 A64 45 Church Fenton
77 79 81 83 A1(M) 85 A162 Saxton
Headingley AA Scholes Aberford Sherburn in Elmet
Bramley 6 7 103 105 47 107 Selby
Pudsey AA LEEDS 46 Garforth A1 Hambleton
99 101 M1 Swillington A63 A63 Hillam A19
Drighlington 7 44 127 Kippax 131 Fairburn
Morley 43 Rothwell 129
Batley M62 28 125 Methley 153 155 157 Beal
147 30 149 151 31 Castleford 32 Knottingley GOOLE
Wakefield 179 Normanton 181 33 183 A645 M62
ewsbury 173 175 177 Pontefract
40 AA Wakefield Featherstone A639 Womersley
Ossett 10 11 A19
195 Horbury 199 203 205 Kirk Smeaton
Grange Moor A637 197 M1 201 Walton Crofton Ackworth Moor Top Norton SCUNTHORPE
217 219 221 Havercroft 225 227 Askern
38 Royston 223 Hemsworth South Elmsall Skellow
Clayton West 239 Darton A628 Brierley South Kirkby 243 Adwick Le Street
237 Cudworth 241 AA
253 37 Barnsley Thurnscoe A635 37 AA Doncaster
rlstone A628 A61 Wombwell A1(M)
Penistone M1 A6195
Oxspring SHEFFIELD Wath upon Dearne Mexborough GRANTHAM

2.5 inches to I mile   **Scale of main map pages   1:25,000**

0 ... 1/2 ... miles ... 1 ... 1 1/2
0 ... 1/2 ... 1 ... kilometres ... 1 1/2 ... 2

iv

Junction 9	Motorway & junction	⊖	Underground station
Services	Motorway service area	⊖	Light railway & station
	Primary road single/dual carriageway	++++++++	Preserved private railway
Services	Primary road service area	LC	Level crossing
	A road single/dual carriageway	●—●—●—	Tramway
	B road single/dual carriageway	---------	Ferry route
	Other road single/dual carriageway	....	Airport runway
	Minor/private road, access may be restricted	—·—·—·—	Boundaries - borough/district
← ←	One-way street	▼▼▼▼▼▼▼	Mounds
	Pedestrian area	93	Page continuation 1:25,000
=========	Track or footpath	7	Page continuation to enlarged scale 1:17,500
	Road under construction		River/canal, lake, pier
⊏ = = = ⊐	Road tunnel		Aqueduct, lock, weir
AA	AA Service Centre	465 ▲ Winter Hill	Peak (with height in metres)
P	Parking		Beach
P+🚌	Park & Ride		Woodland
🚌	Bus/coach station		Park
	Railway & main railway station	† † † † † † † †	Cemetery
	Railway & minor railway station		Built-up area

Map Symbols

Featured building		Abbey, cathedral or priory	
City wall		Castle	
Hospital with 24-hour A&E department		Historic house or building	
Post Office		National Trust property	Wakehurst Place NT
Public library		Museum or art gallery	
Tourist Information Centre		Roman antiquity	
Petrol station — Major suppliers only		Ancient site, battlefield or monument	
Church/chapel		Industrial interest	
Public toilets		Garden	
Toilet with disabled facilities		Arboretum	
Public house — AA recommended		Farm or animal centre	
Restaurant — AA inspected		Zoological or wildlife collection	
Theatre or performing arts centre		Bird collection	
Cinema		Nature reserve	
Golf course		Visitor or heritage centre	
Camping — AA inspected		Country park	
Caravan site — AA inspected		Cave	
Camping & caravan site — AA inspected		Windmill	
Theme park		Distillery, brewery or vineyard	

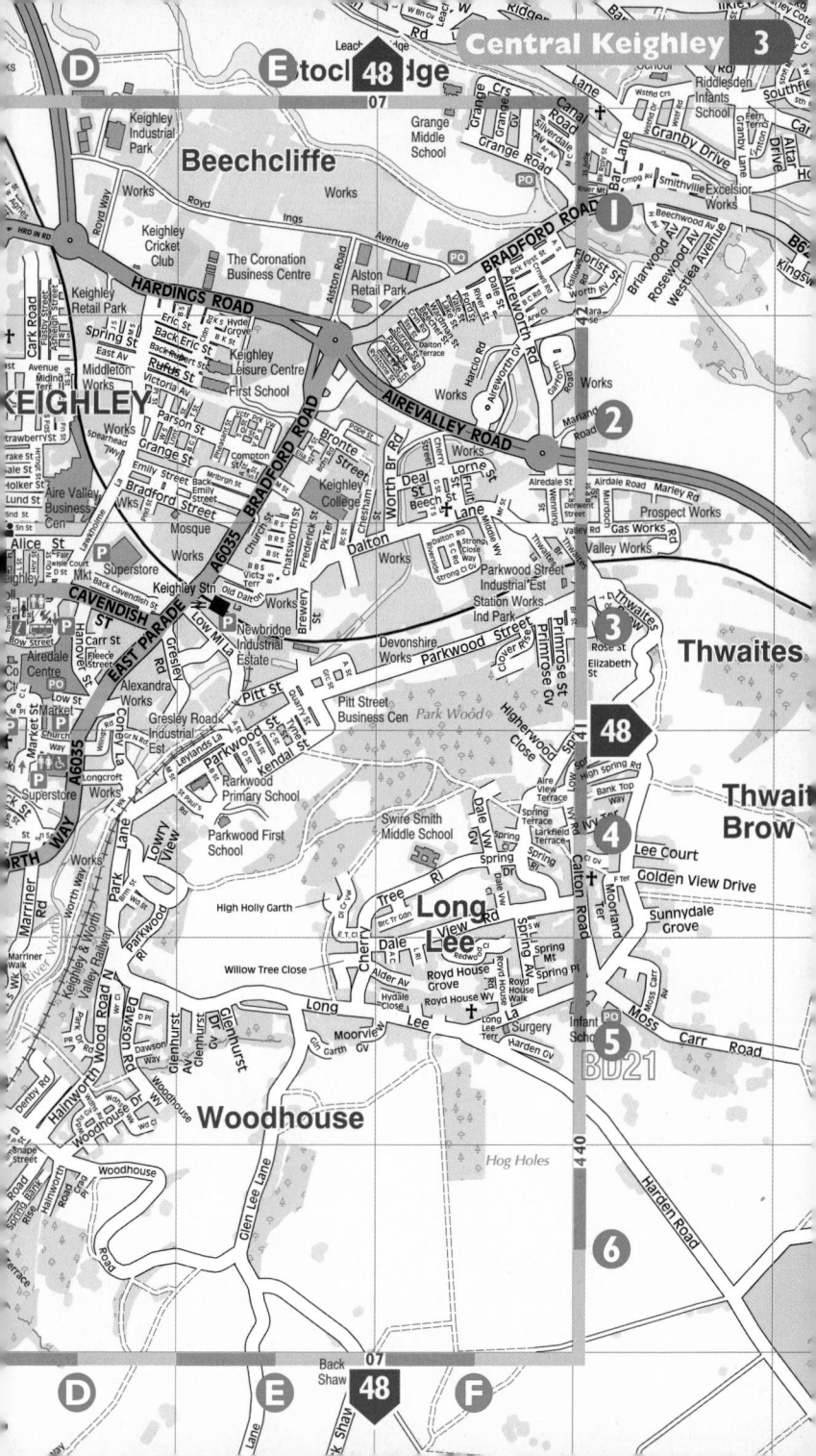

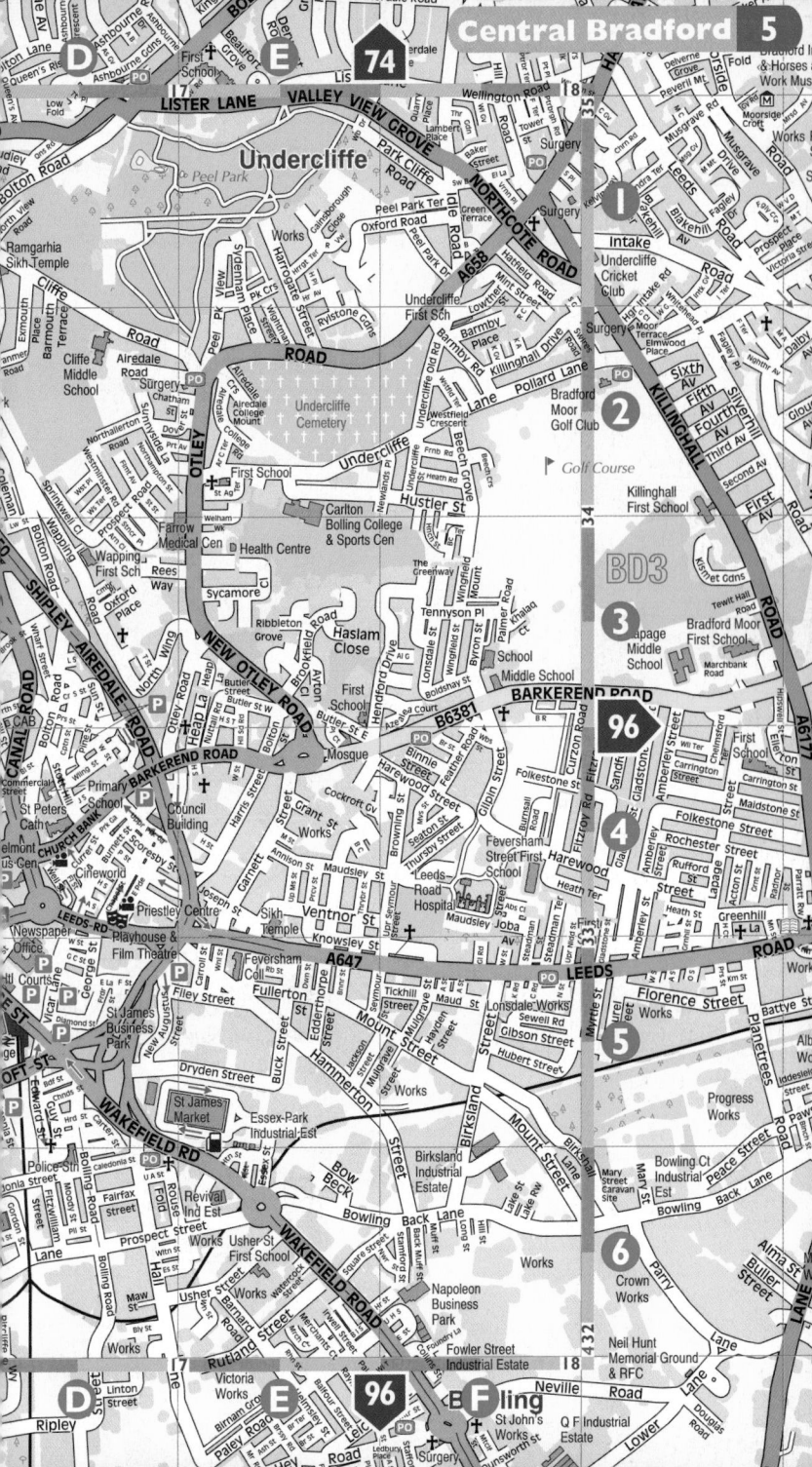

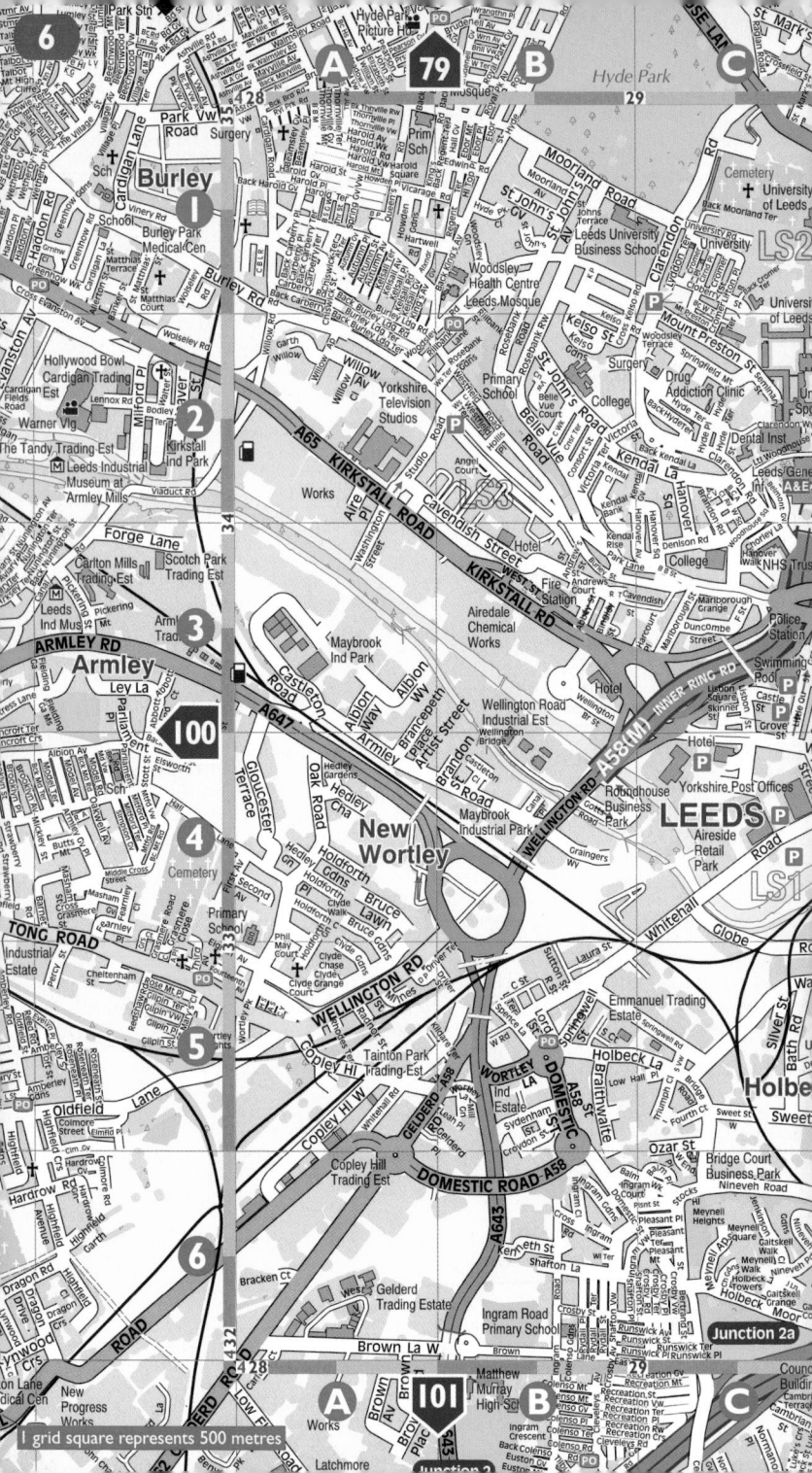

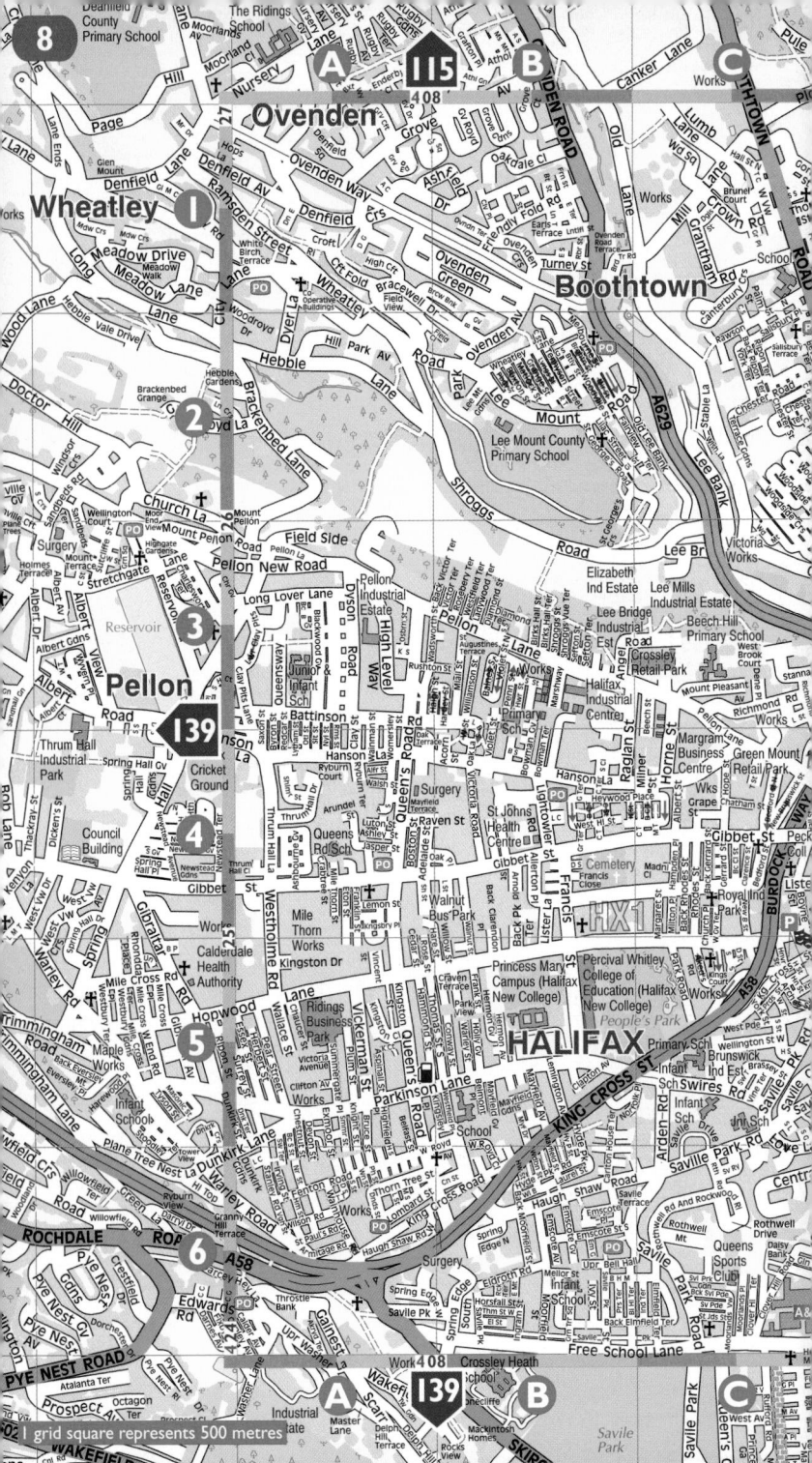

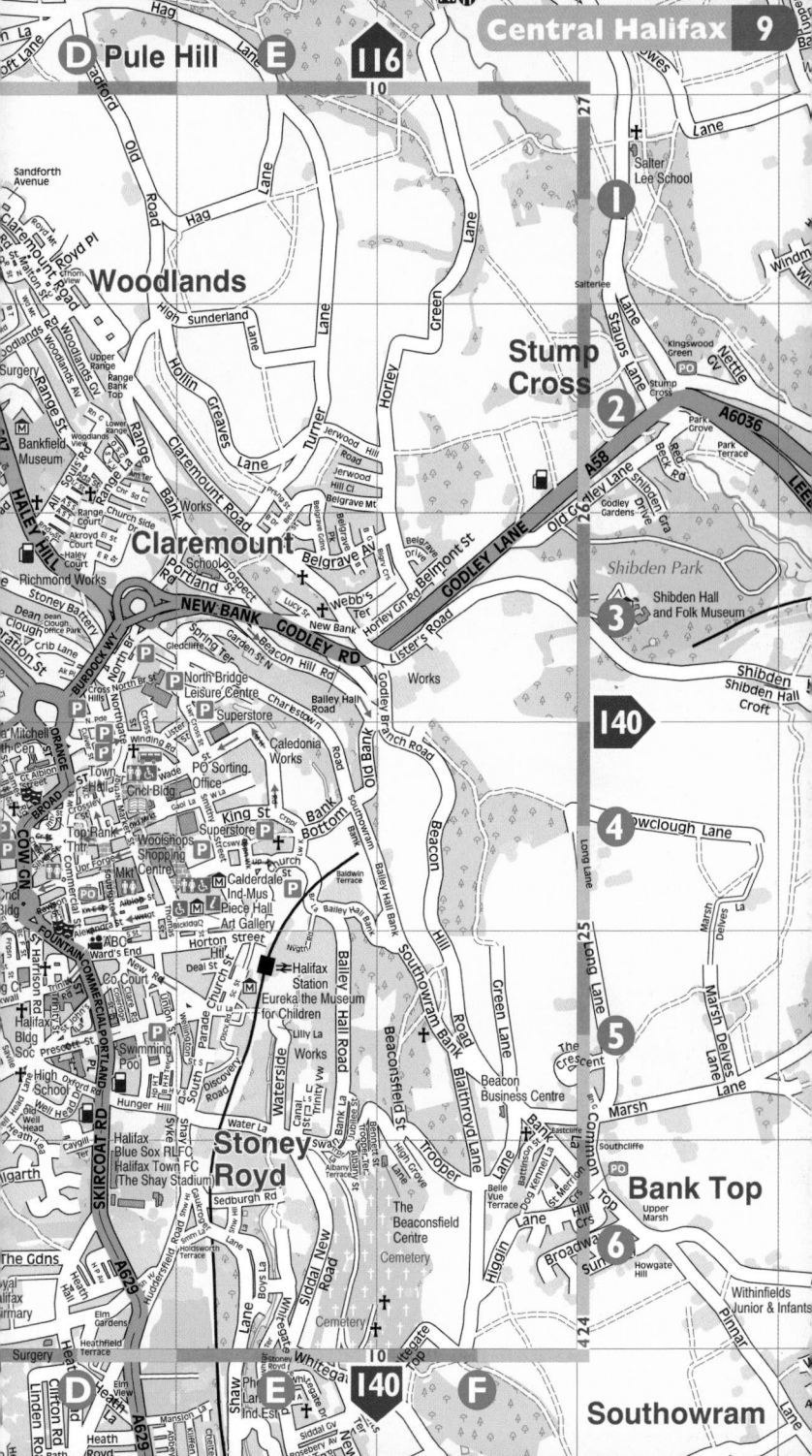

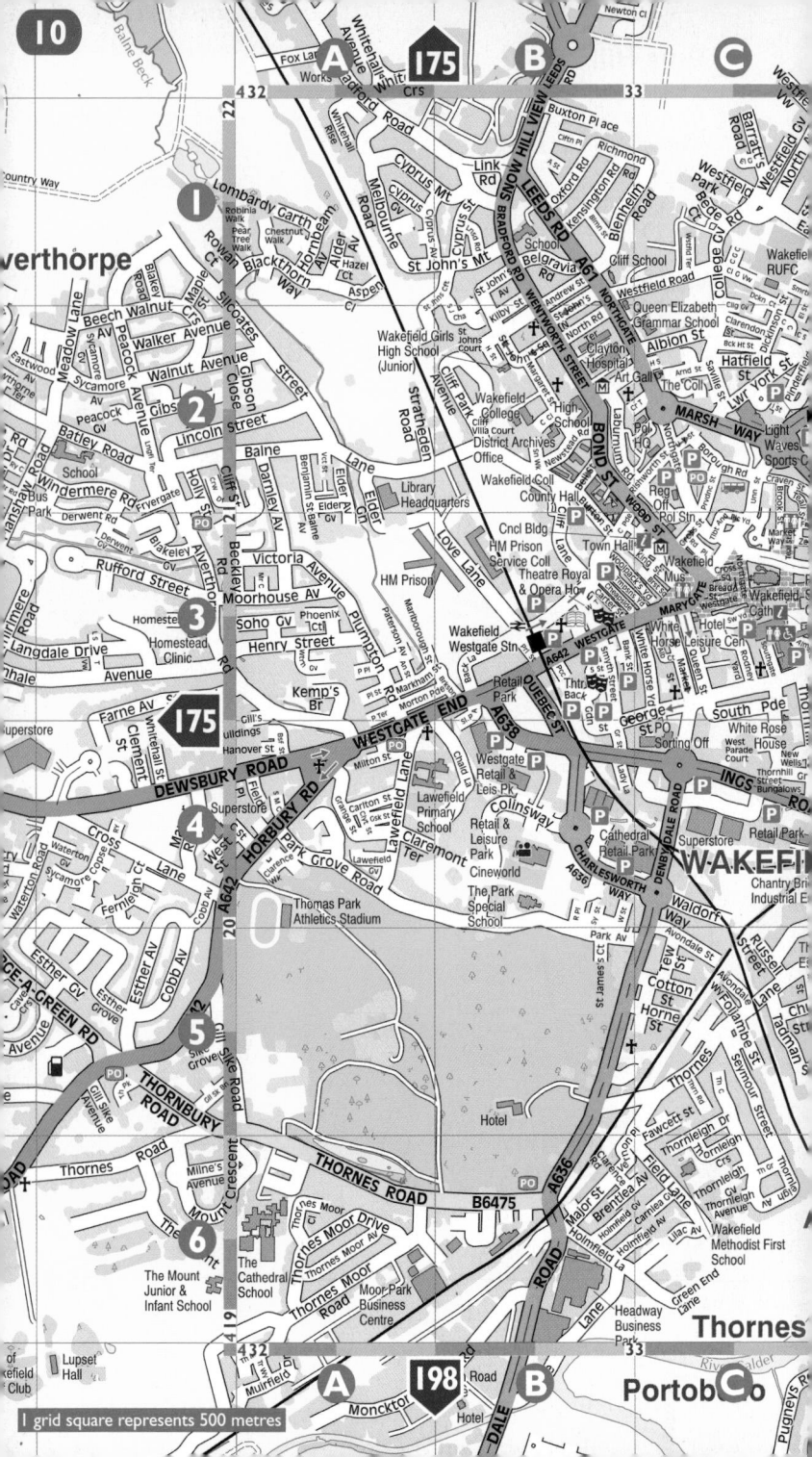

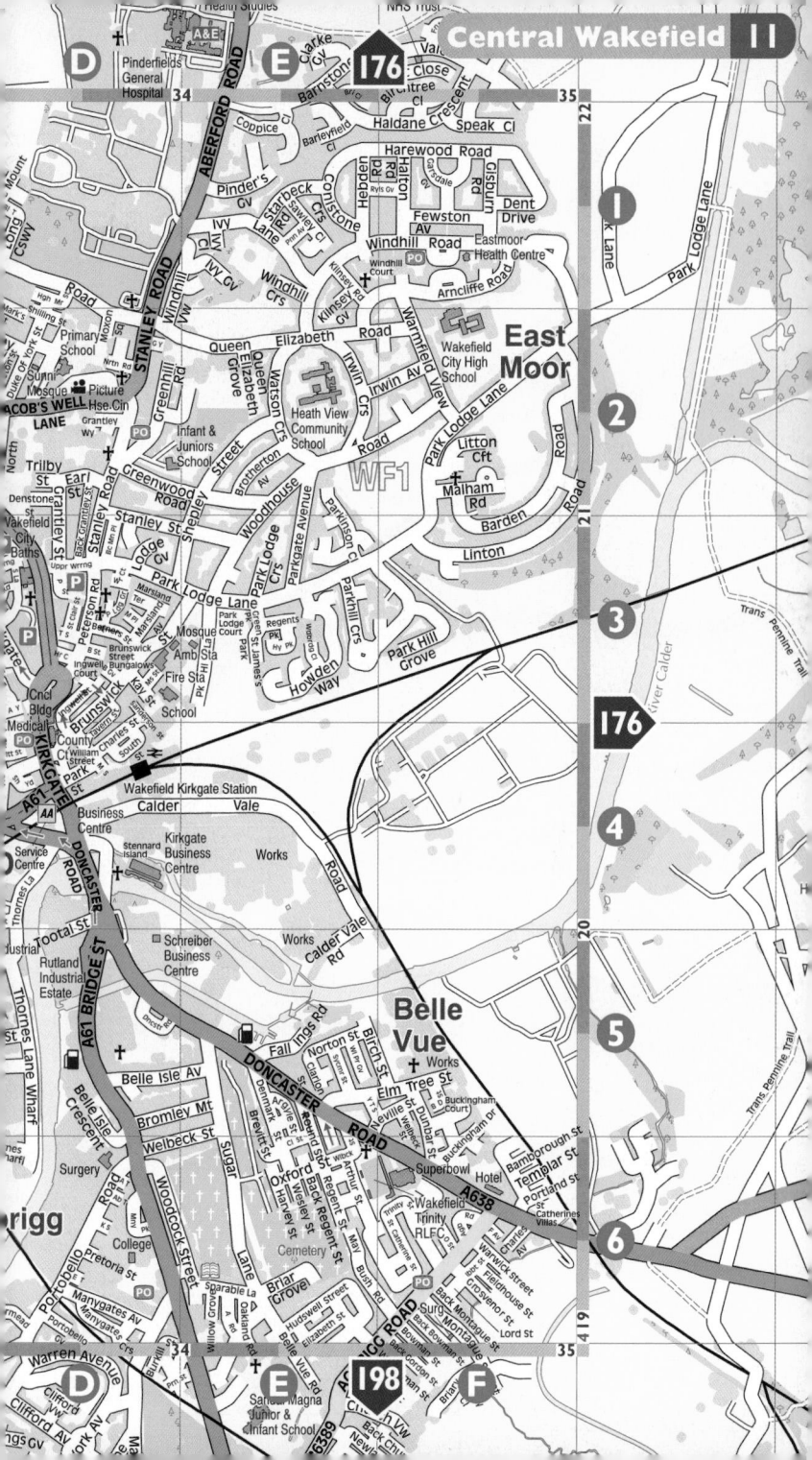

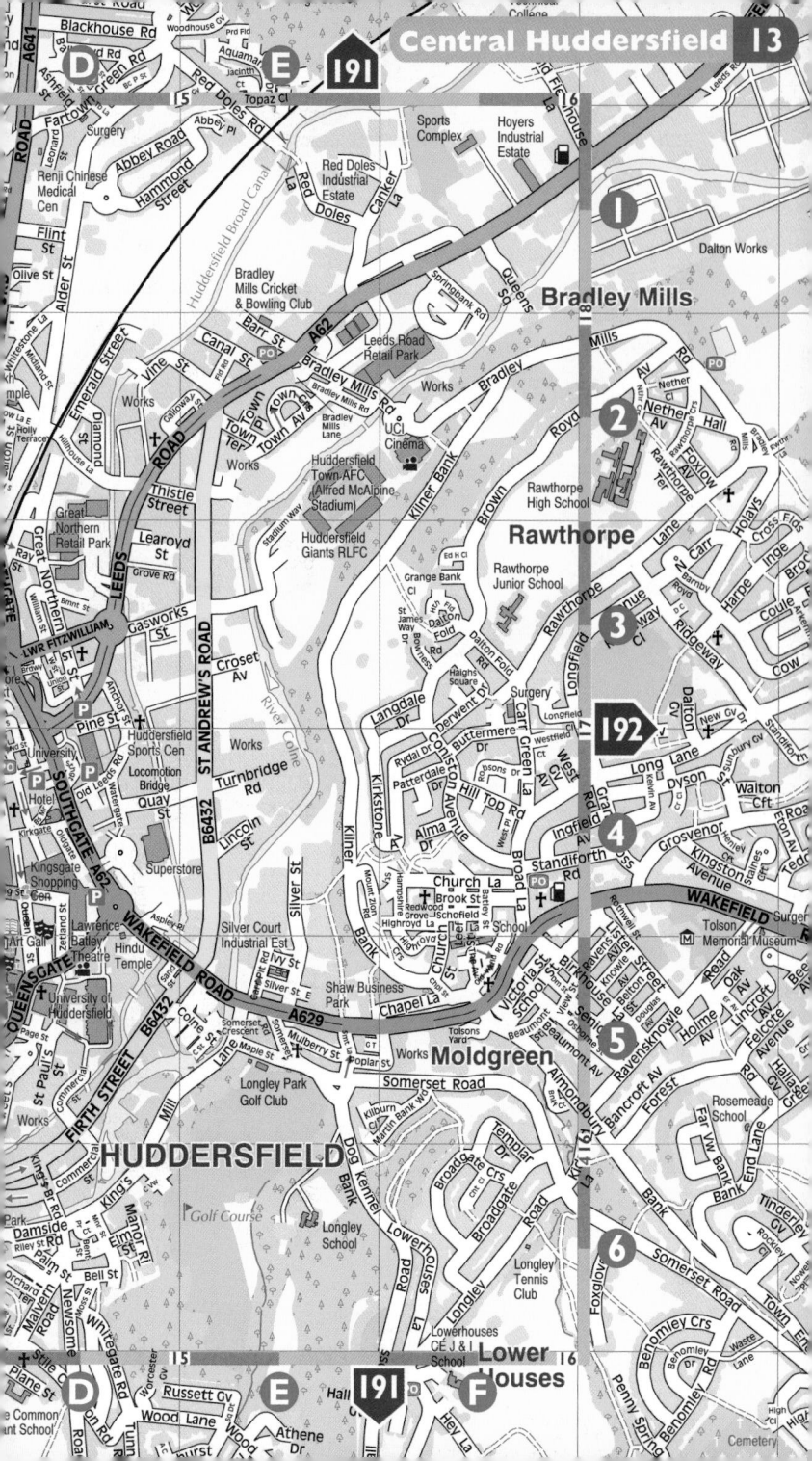

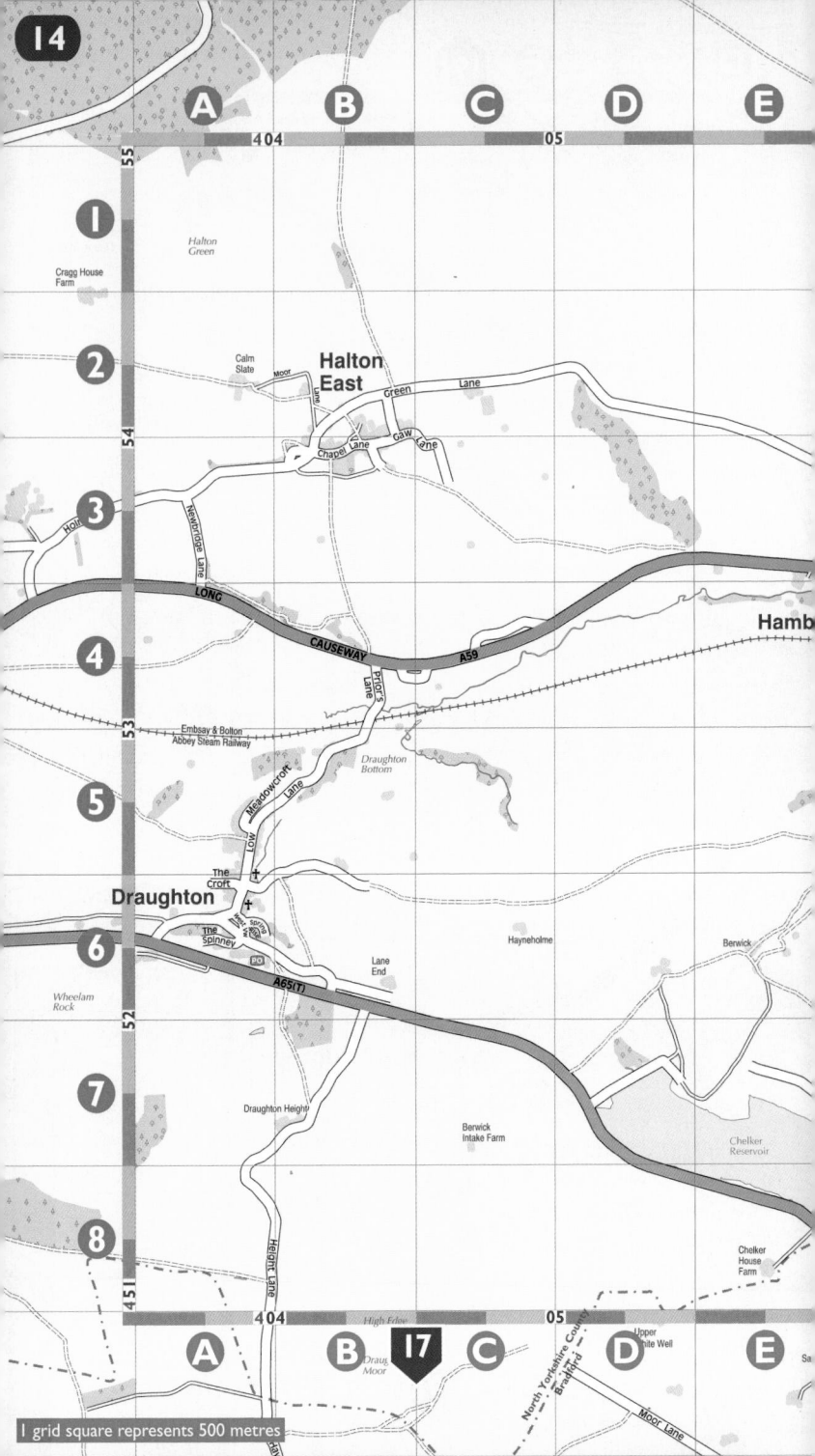

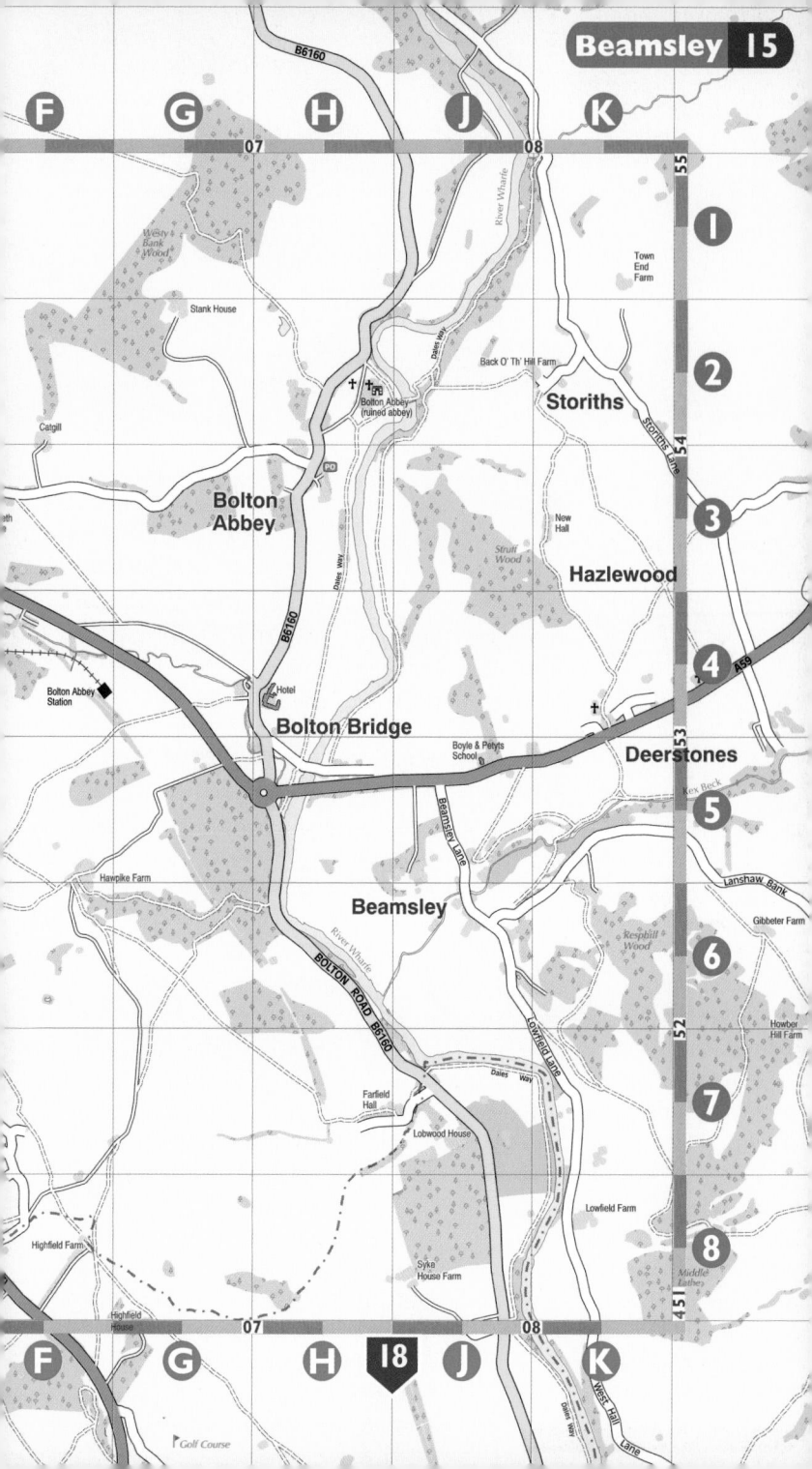

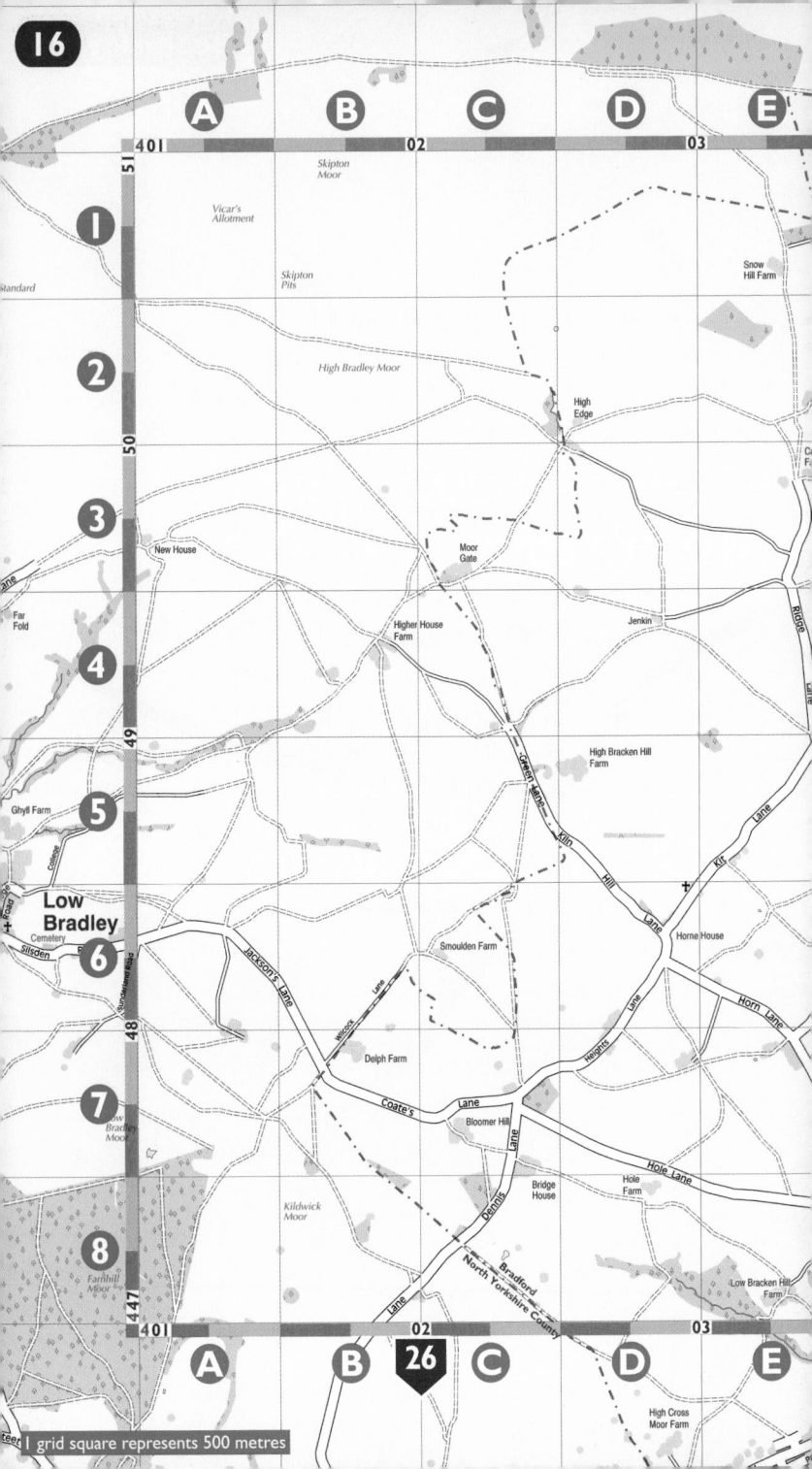

Highfield Farm

F G H **14** J Chelker House Fm K

High Edge

Draughton Moor

Upper White Well

North Yorkshire County Bradford

Moor Lane

Sandfm

I

Maygill Farm

Bank End

Cross Bank

2

Moor Lane

Addlingham Low Moor

3

Jowett's Lane

Woofa Bank Farm

Lower Marchup Farm

Bank Lane

SILSDEN ROAD

4

Cringles Lane

Walton Hole

Nudge Hill Farm

18

Silsden Moor

Middle Marchup Farm

A6034

Turner Lane

5

Foster Cliffe Farms

Old Tower

Upper Lane

Cringles

Dalesbank Farm

6

Dales Bank Holiday Park

BOLTON ROAD

Brown Bank Lane

Hayhills Lane

Sea Moor Farm

Upperside Lane

7

Hang Goose Farm

Hay Hills Farms

Fishbeck

Fishbeck

Silsden Reservoir

Crag House

Lane

8

Raikes Head

Nab End

A447

Brown Bank Lane

Light Bank Lane

F G H **27** J K

Swartha Lane

Tarn View

Works

Brown Bank Lane

Raikes House Farm

Swartha

Upper Lane

Brunthwaite Crag

1 grid square represents 500 metres

Spofforth

Sicklinghall

1 grid square represents 500 metres

40

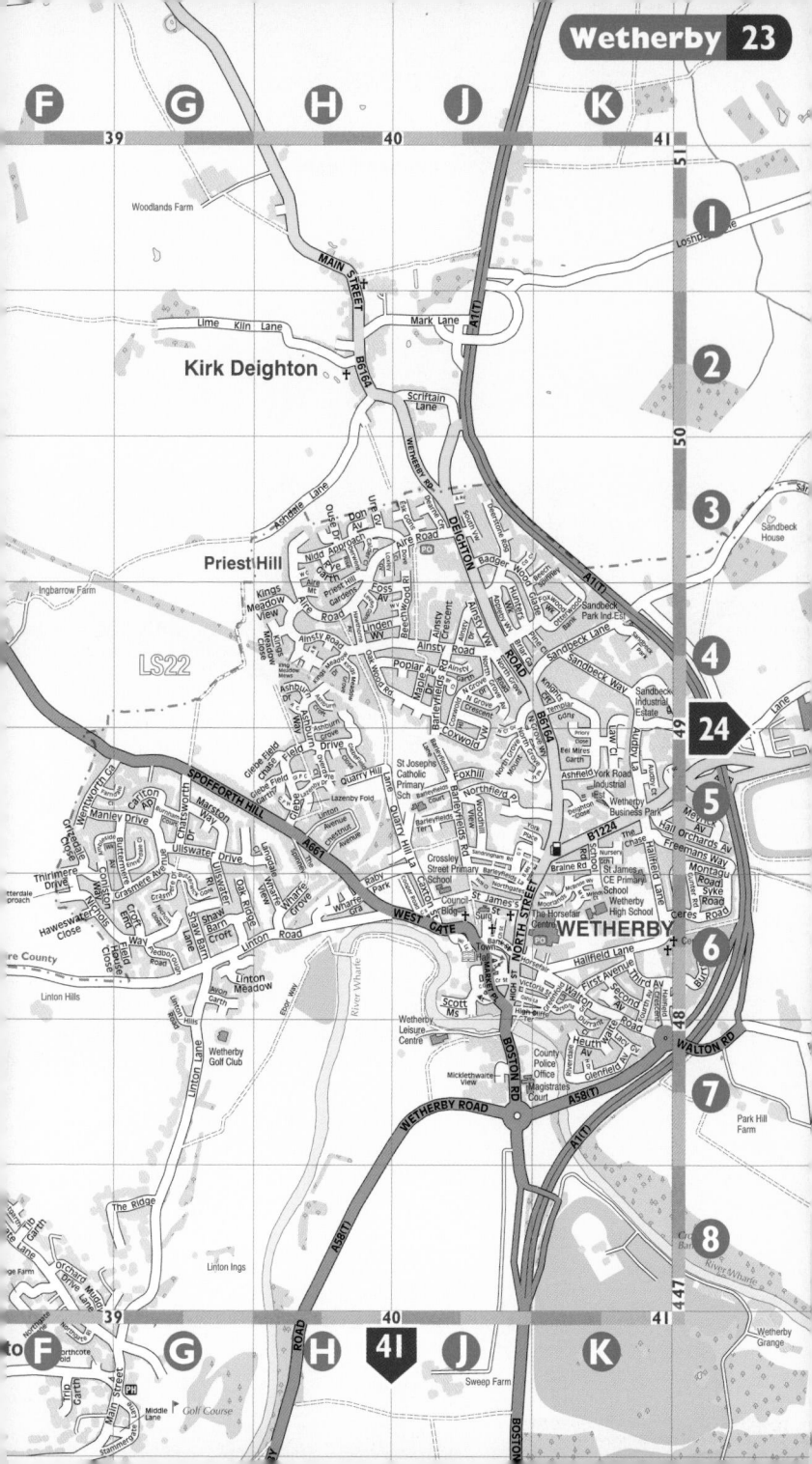

I grid square represents 500 metres

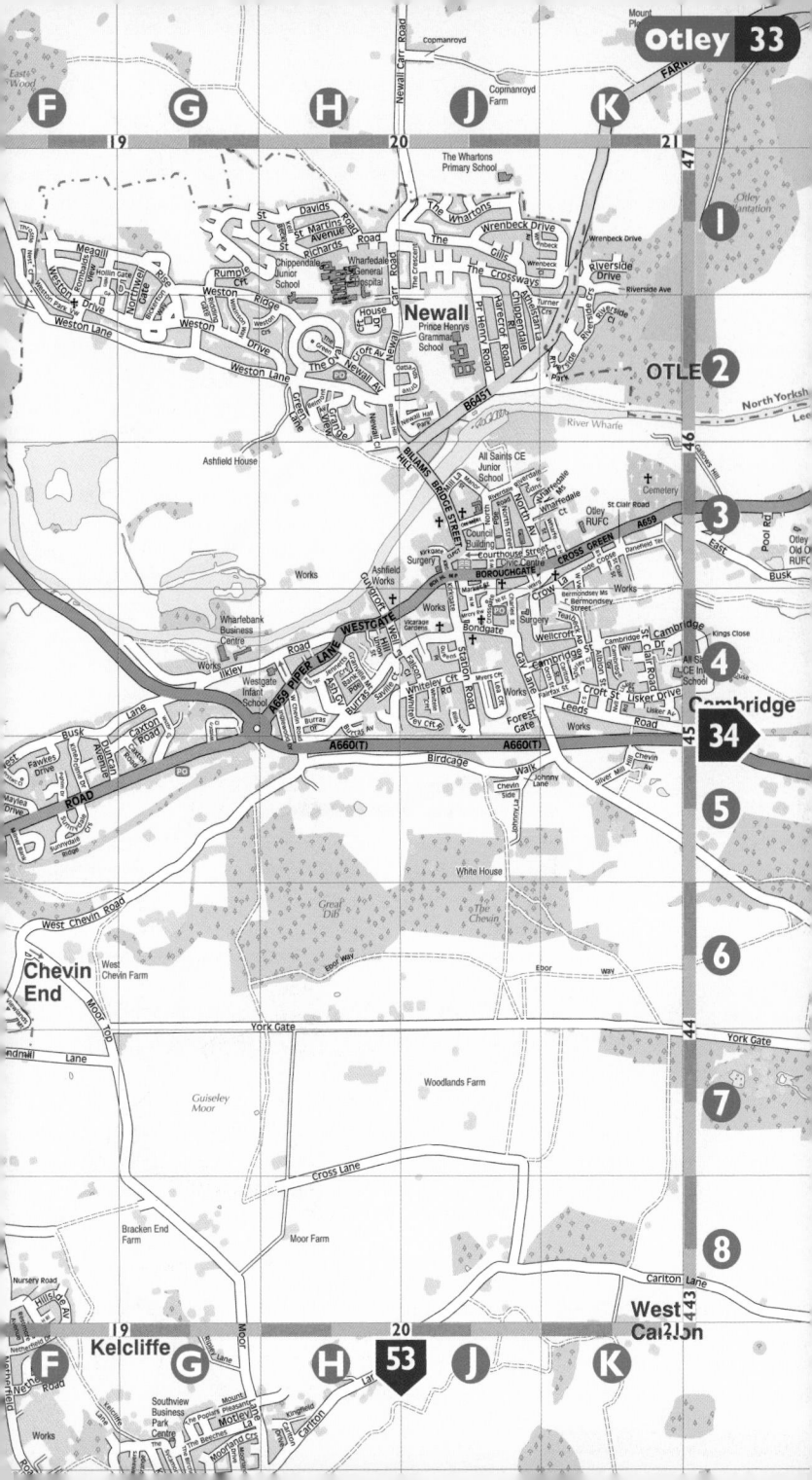

F G H J K

99 400 01

Brush

Crag
Top

New
Bridge

Clough
Head

Wood
Farm

Long House

I

Hill
Top

Start Farm

America Lane

2

High Pole Farm

3

Kid
Stone

Sutton
Moor

The New
Allotment

Long Gate

Coppy Lane

North Yorkshire County
Bradford

4

Greystones Lane

46

Slippery Ford Lane

Slippery Ford

5

Whitehill Road

6

Lower Dean
Laithe

White Hill

Keighley
Moor Reservoir

Clough
Hey

Keighley
Moor

7

Broad Head Lane

Broad Head
Farm

Clough Hey
Allotment

8

99 400 01

F G H 67 J K

Oakworth
Moor

Flask

BD22

I grid square represents 500 metres

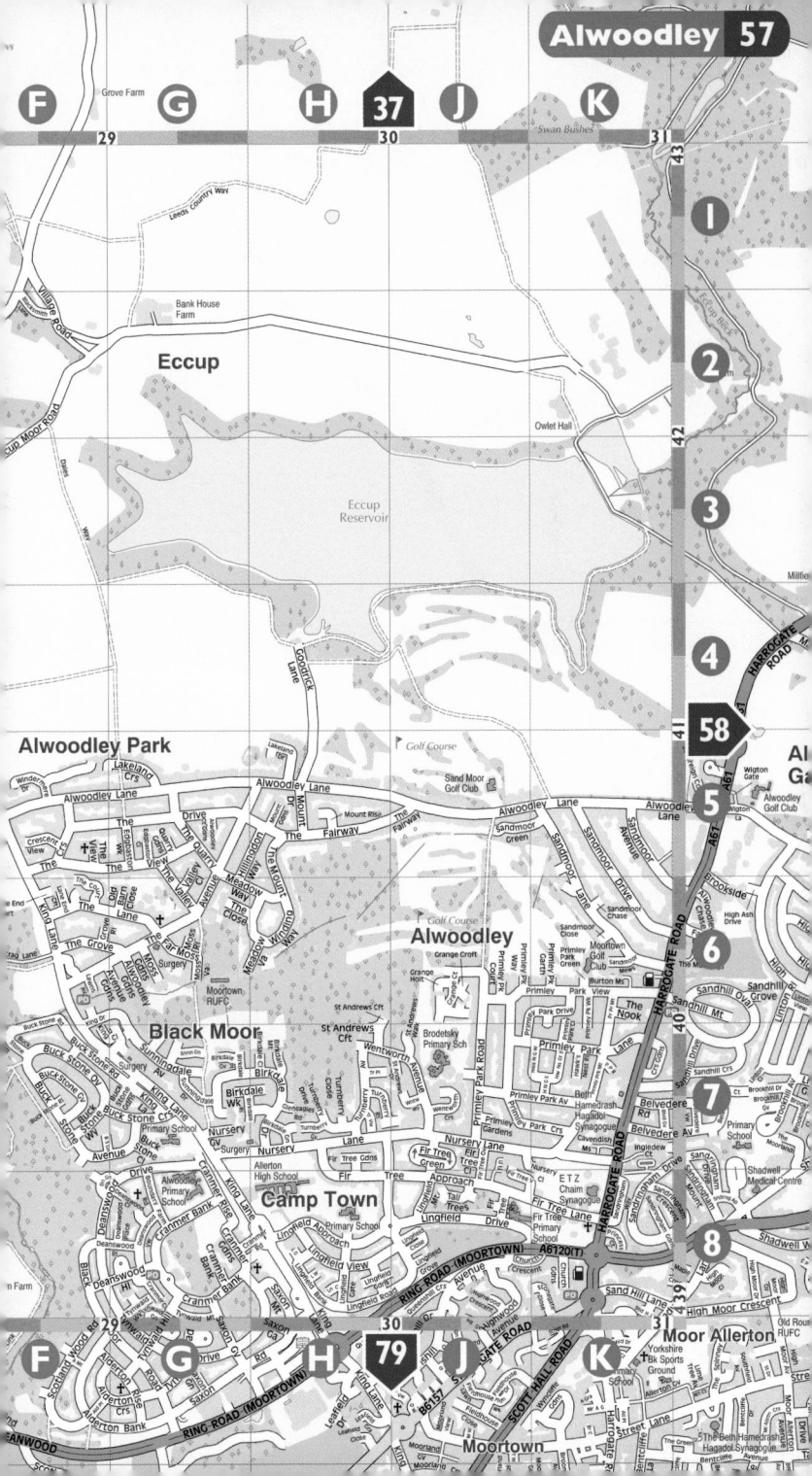

F G H 39 J K

34 35 36

1

Woodacre Crescent

Leeds Country Way

Smith Hill

Tithe Barn Lane

The Ginnel

43

Bingl

Biggin Farm

Wike Whin

Gill Beck

Spear Fir

Blackmoor Lane

Wayside Gardens

2

Wike

Manor Farm

Gill Lane

Backstone

The Village Golf Course

Glenfield Caravan Park

Moor Lodge Park

Sheepcote Farm

Scarcroft

Moss Syke

Gre

Syke Grn

42

3

Coal Road

Golf Course

Moor Allerton Golf Club

Golf Course

Scarcroft Golf Club

Syke Lane

Bracken Park

Fern Way

Heather Gardens

Man Heilwood

Brandon Lane

Bracken Park

Fern Croft

Fern Chase

The Clade

Heather Vale

Ling Lane

Ling Lane

The Firs

4

Tarn Lane

Brandon Cresc

Brandon Hall

Brandon Lodge

Brandon Lane

Bay Horse Lane

60

41

Brandon Crescent

Manor Cottage Mews

5

A58(T)

Bridle Path Road

Beech Grove

Stoney Lane

Leeds Road

6

Eltofts

Brandon Golf Club

Back Holywell Lane

Holywell Lane

Main Street

PO

Manor Court

Old

Cricket Field

Ash Hill Drive

Shadwell

Carr La

Carr Lane

40

+

Main Street

Gateland Dr

Ash Hill Gardens

Strickland Av

Strickland Cl

Chestnut

Croften

Croften Rise

Croften Dr

Birkby Grange

7

Colliers

Blind Lane

Churchfarm Garth

Main Street

Wetherby Road

Coal Rd

A58(T)

Gateland Lane

Shadwell Primary School

Charville Gdns

Hobberley

Wellington Hill

8

Elmete Lane

Whinmoor

Intake Farm

34 35 36

F G H 81 J K

Road

Seacroft

Red Hall

Hobberk

A58(T)

Coal Road

439

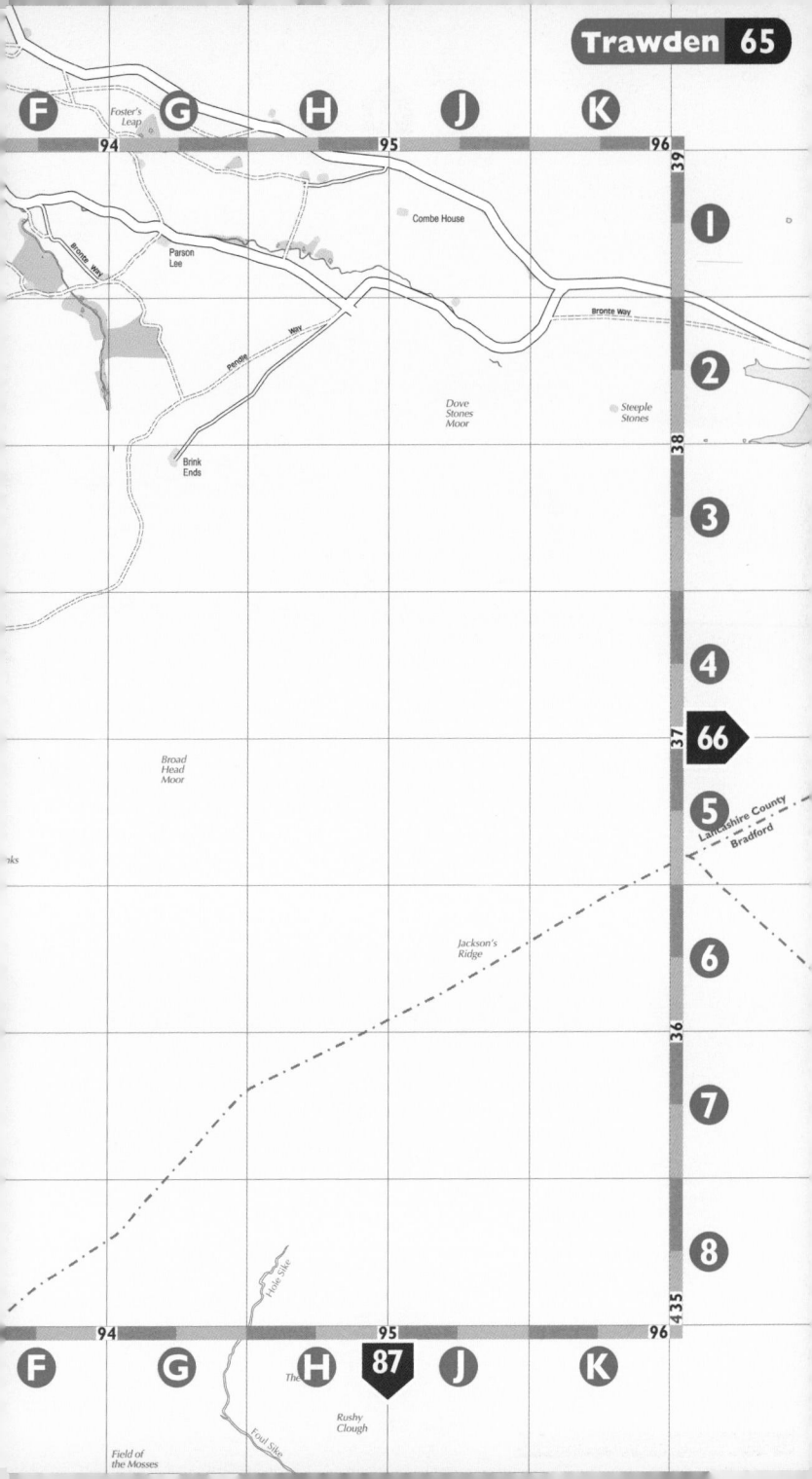

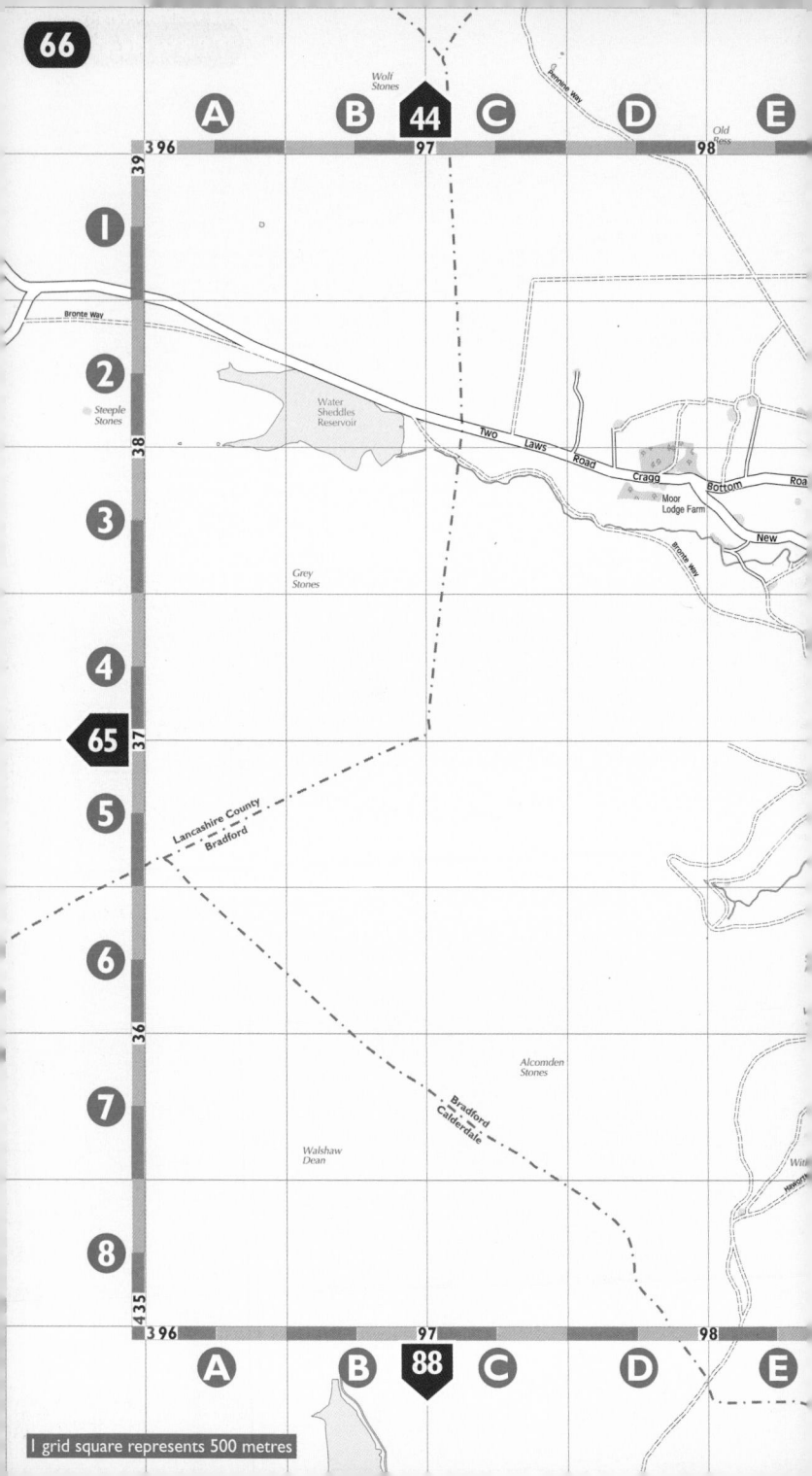

A B **44** C D E

Wolf
Stones

Avenue Way

Old
Bess

1

Bronte Way

2

Steeple
Stones

Water
Sheddles
Reservoir

38

Two Laws Road

Cragg Bottom Roa

Moor
Lodge Farm

New

Bronte Way

3

Grey
Stones

4

65 37

5

Lancashire County
Bradford

6

36

Alcomden
Stones

7

Bradford
Calderdale

Walshaw
Dean

Witl

8

435

A B **88** C D E

I grid square represents 500 metres

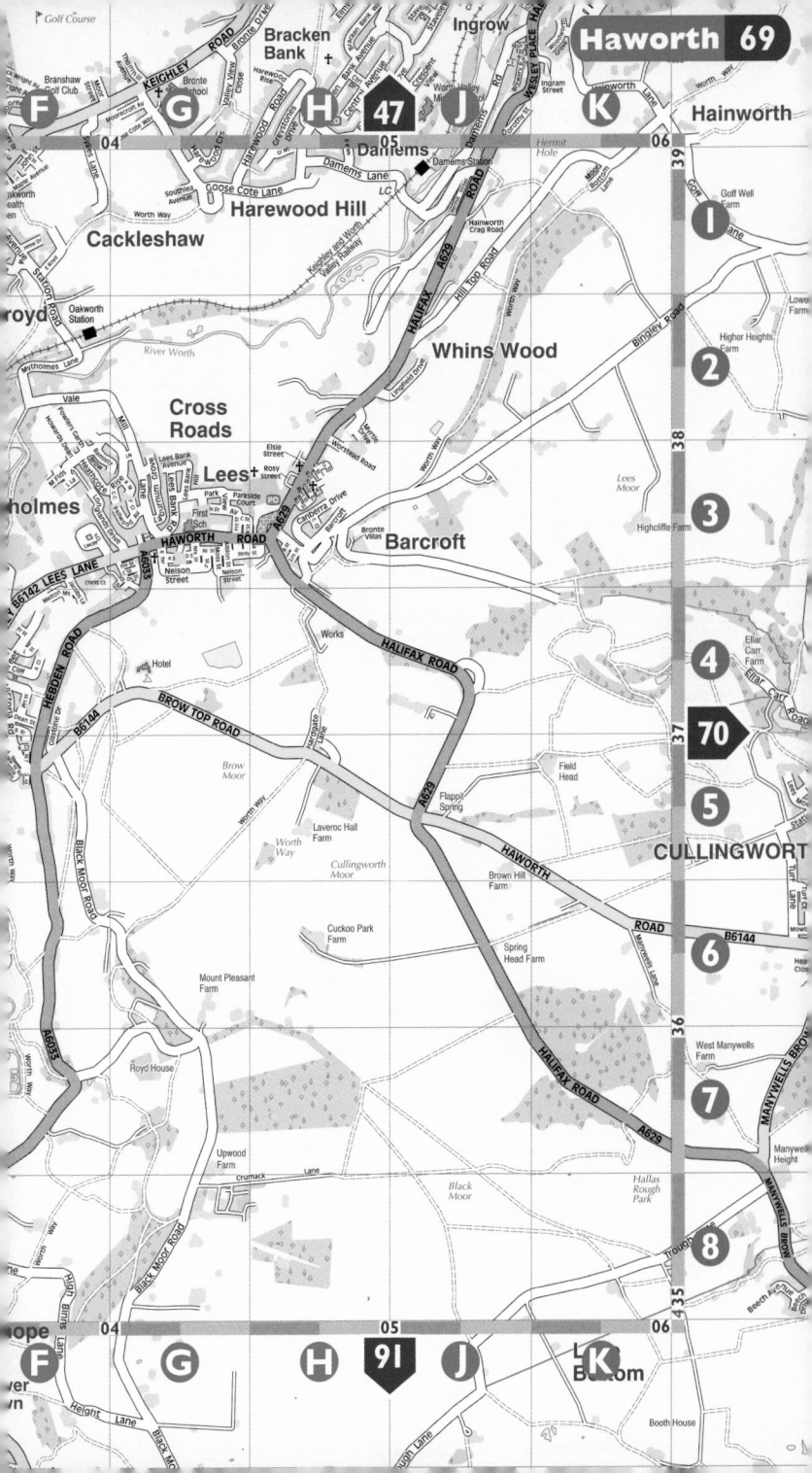

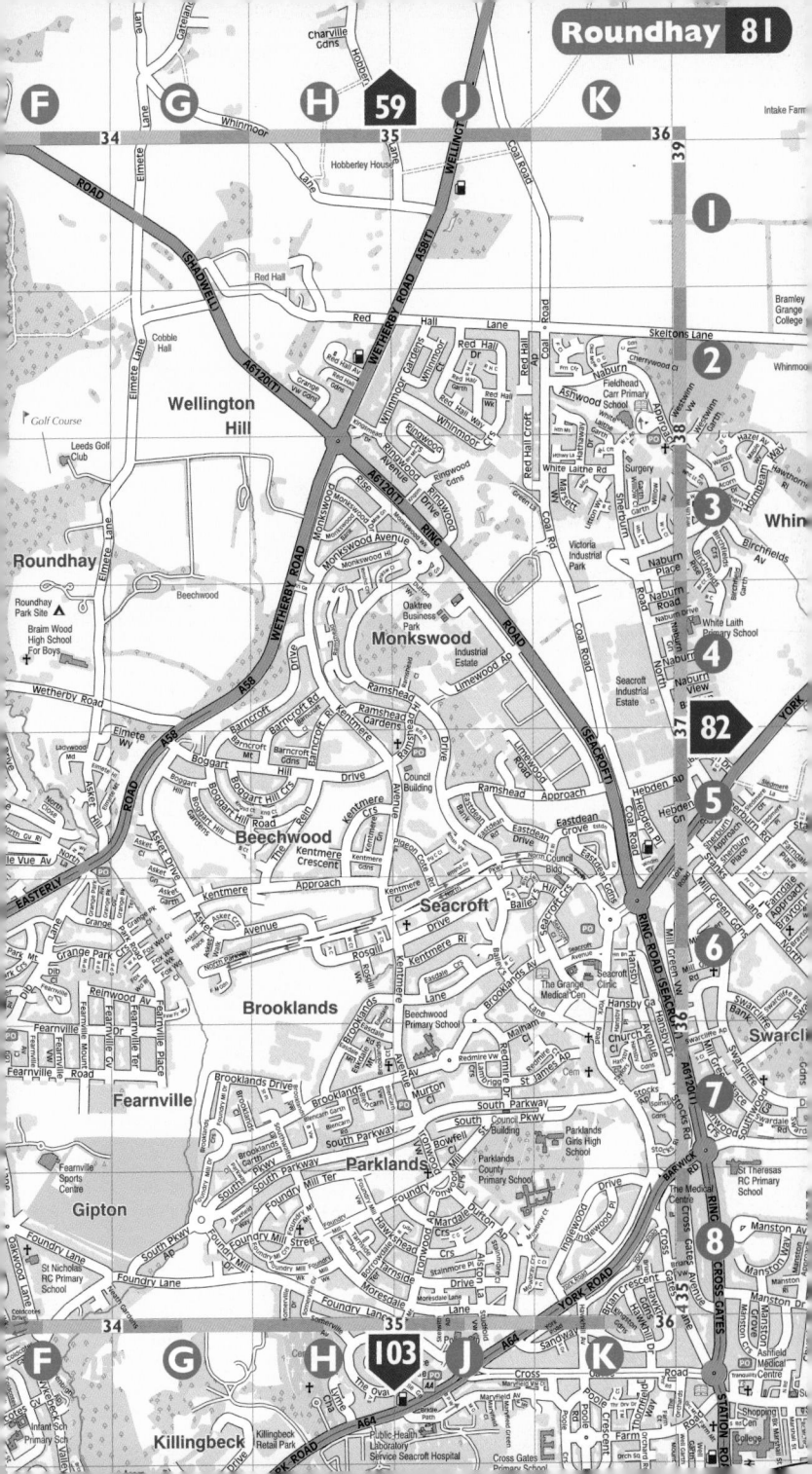

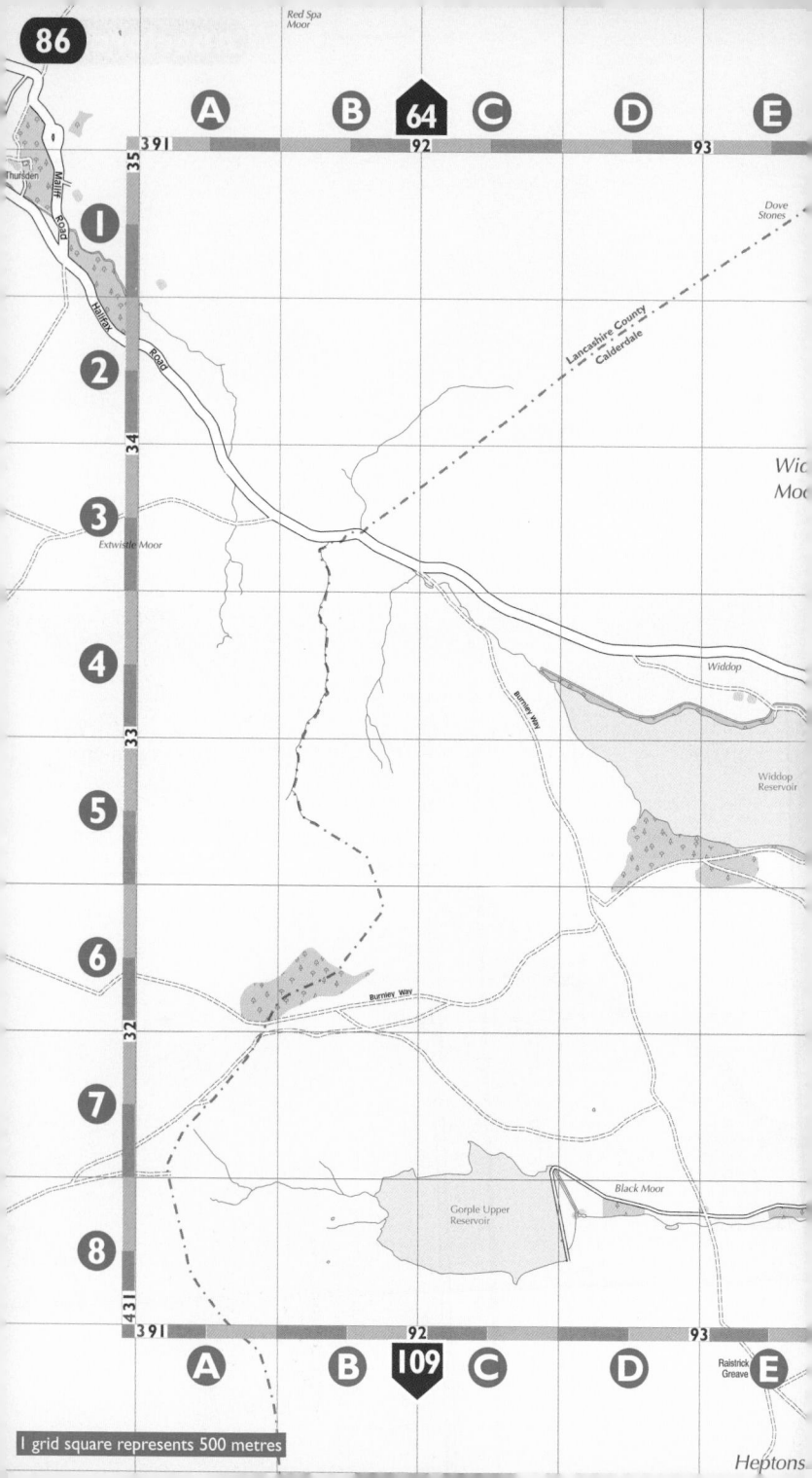

F   G   H **65** J   K

94   95   96 35

1

The Plain

Rushy Clough

Hole Sike

Foul Sike

Field of the Mosses

2

Mere Stones

34

Greave Clough

3

Pisser Clough

Pennine Way

4

op e

33 **88**

5

Flask

6

32

New Laithe Moor

Alcomden Water

7

PH

Pennine Way

Gorple Lower Reservoir

Blake Dean

8

Graining Water

94   95   96 431

F   G   H **110** J   K

Pennine Way

Coppy

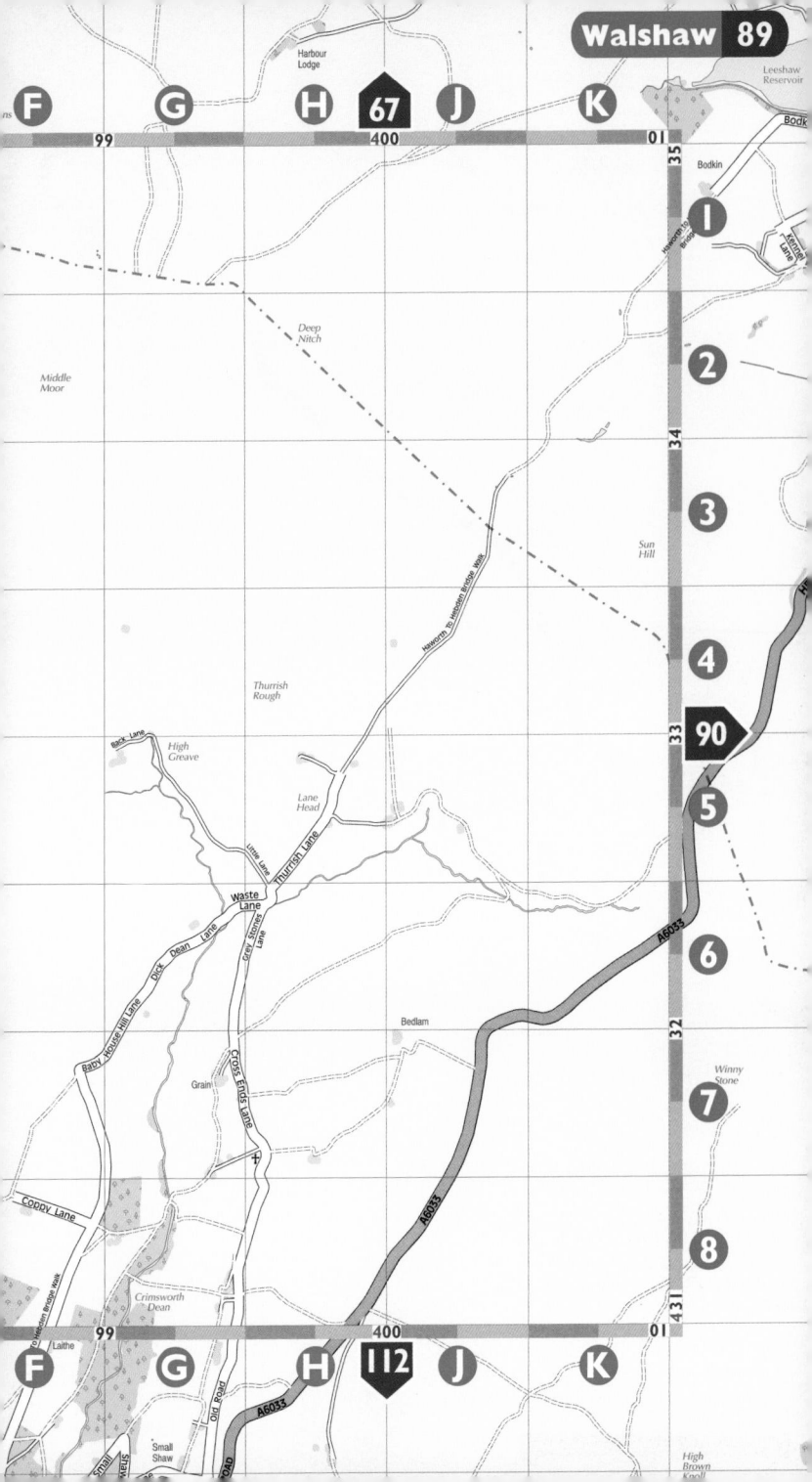

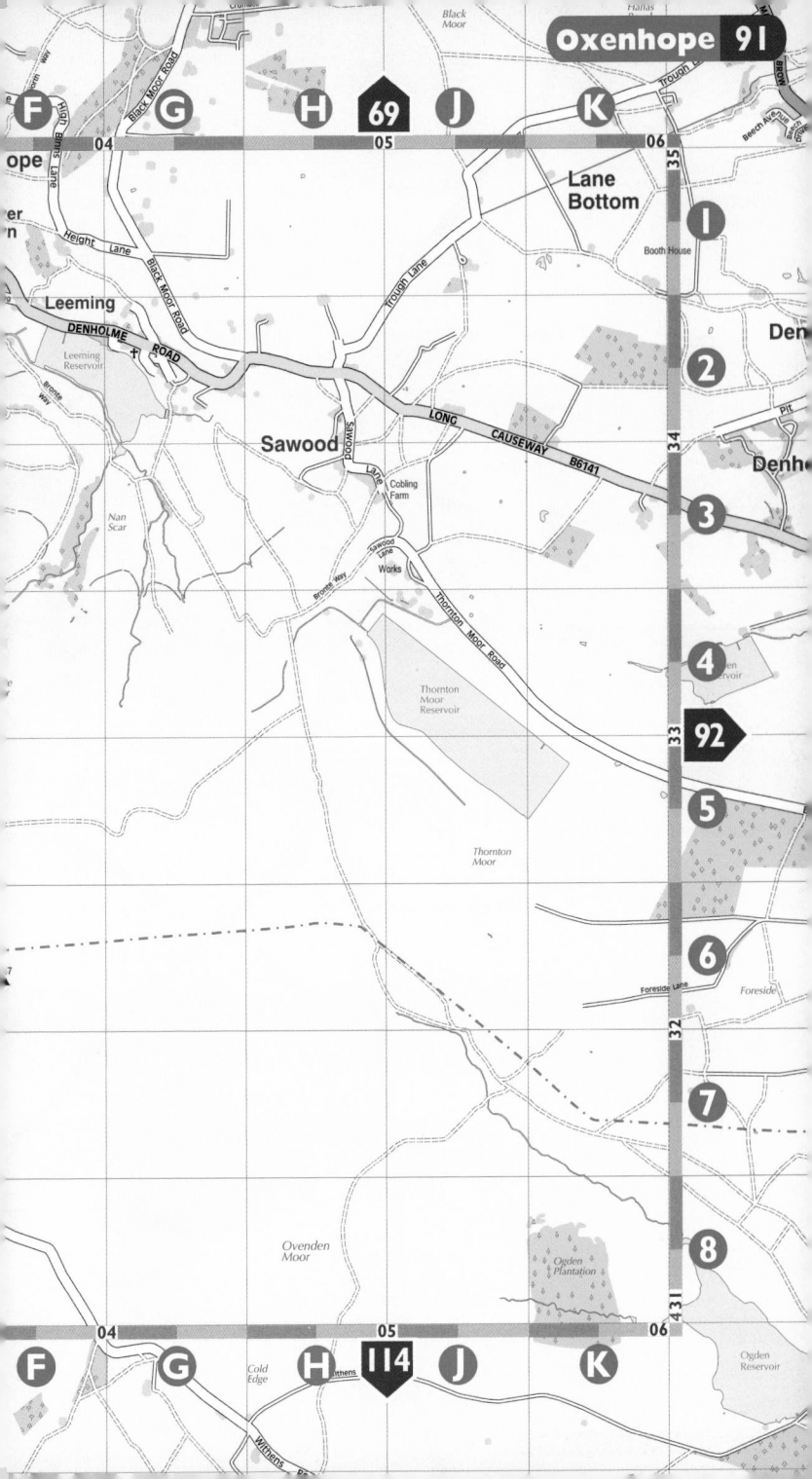

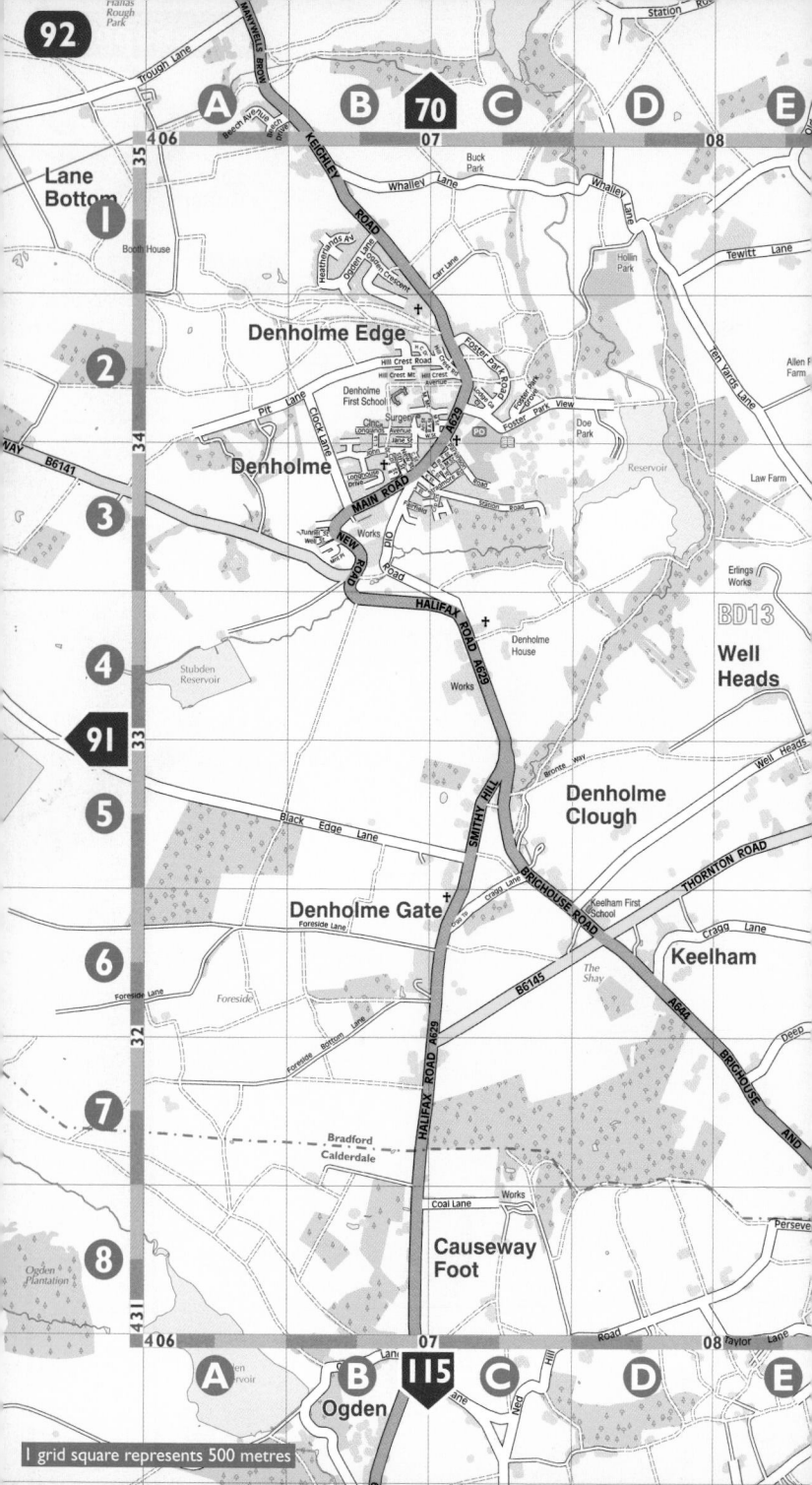

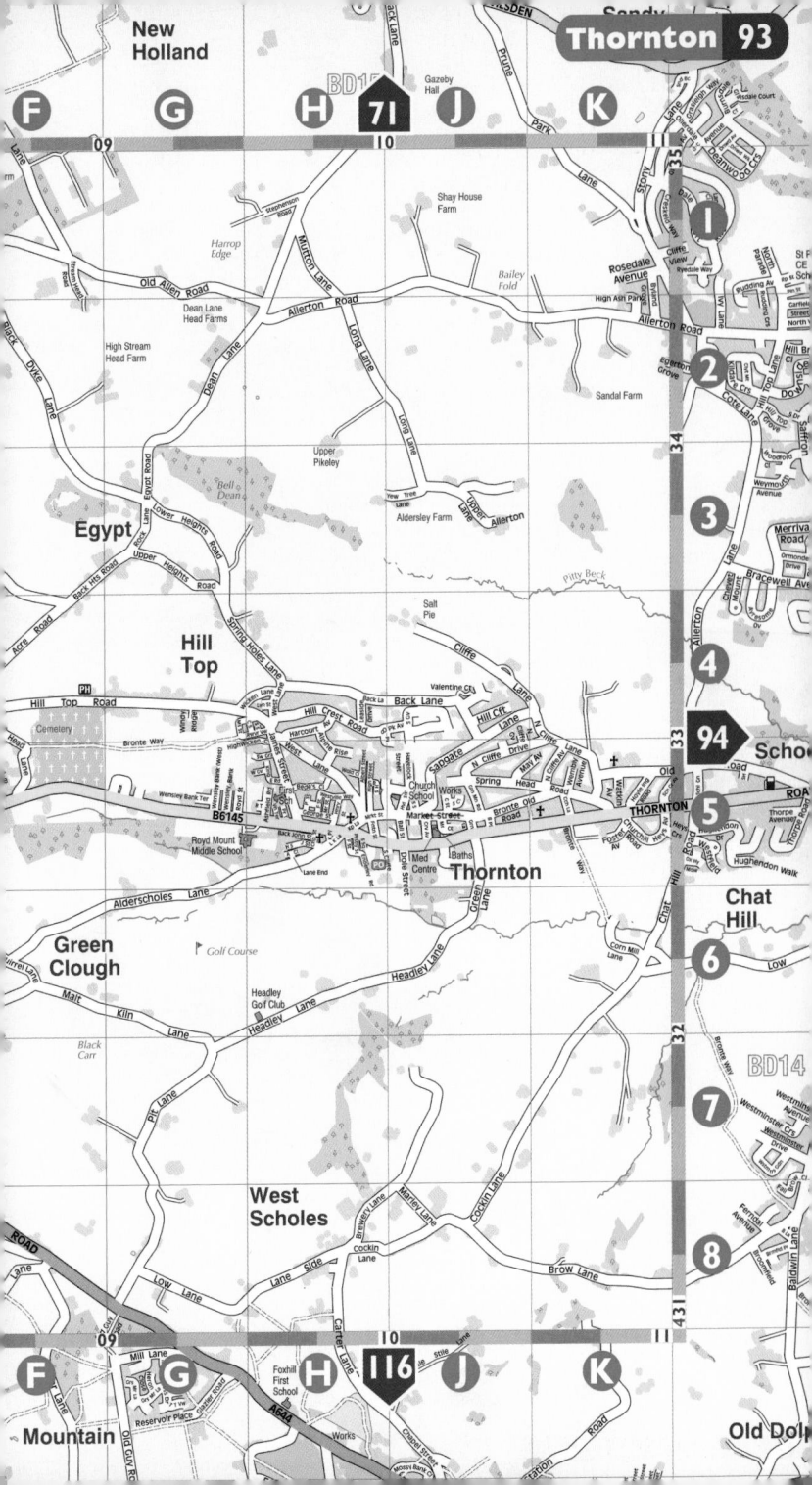

I grid square represents 500 metres

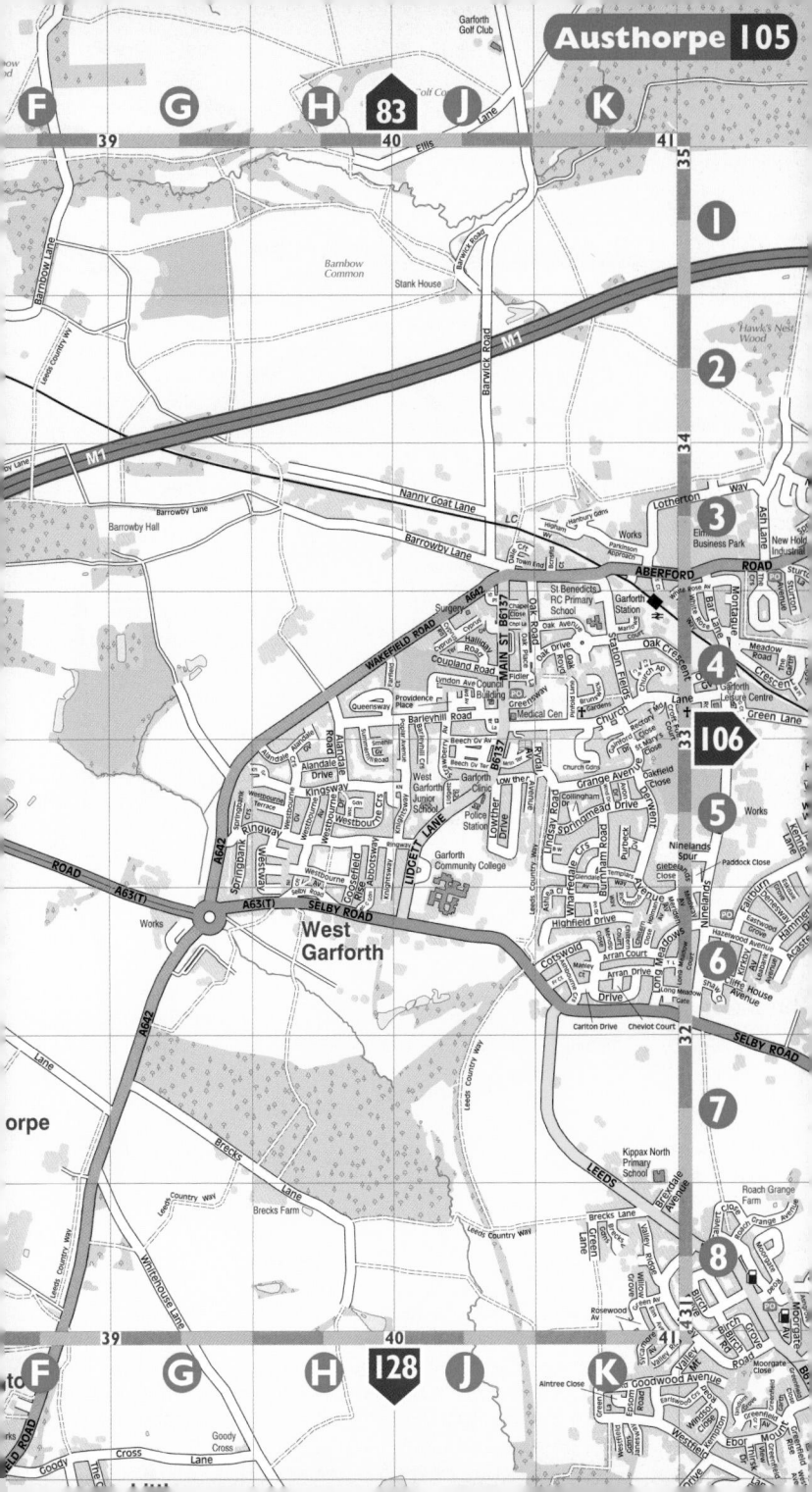

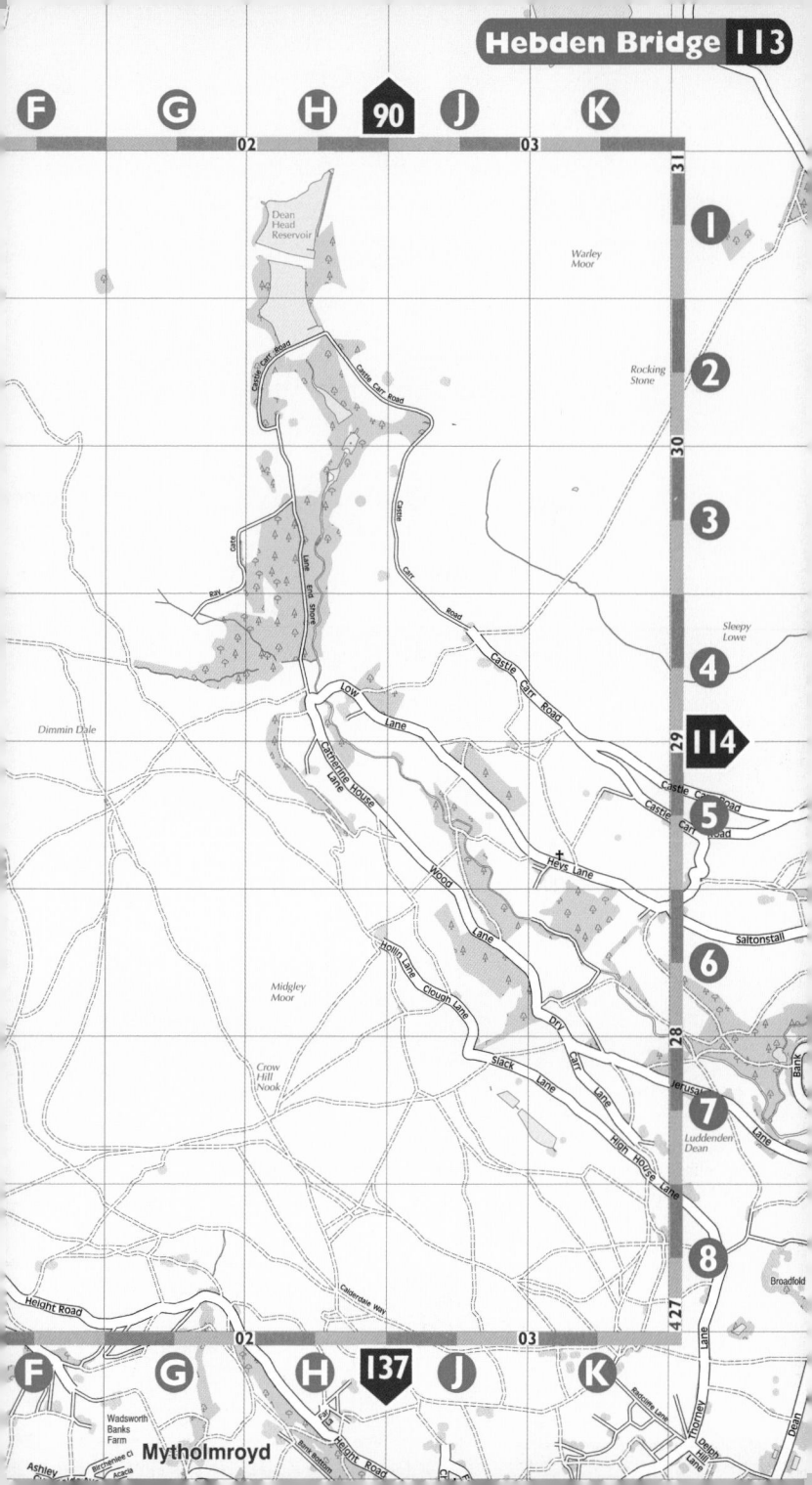

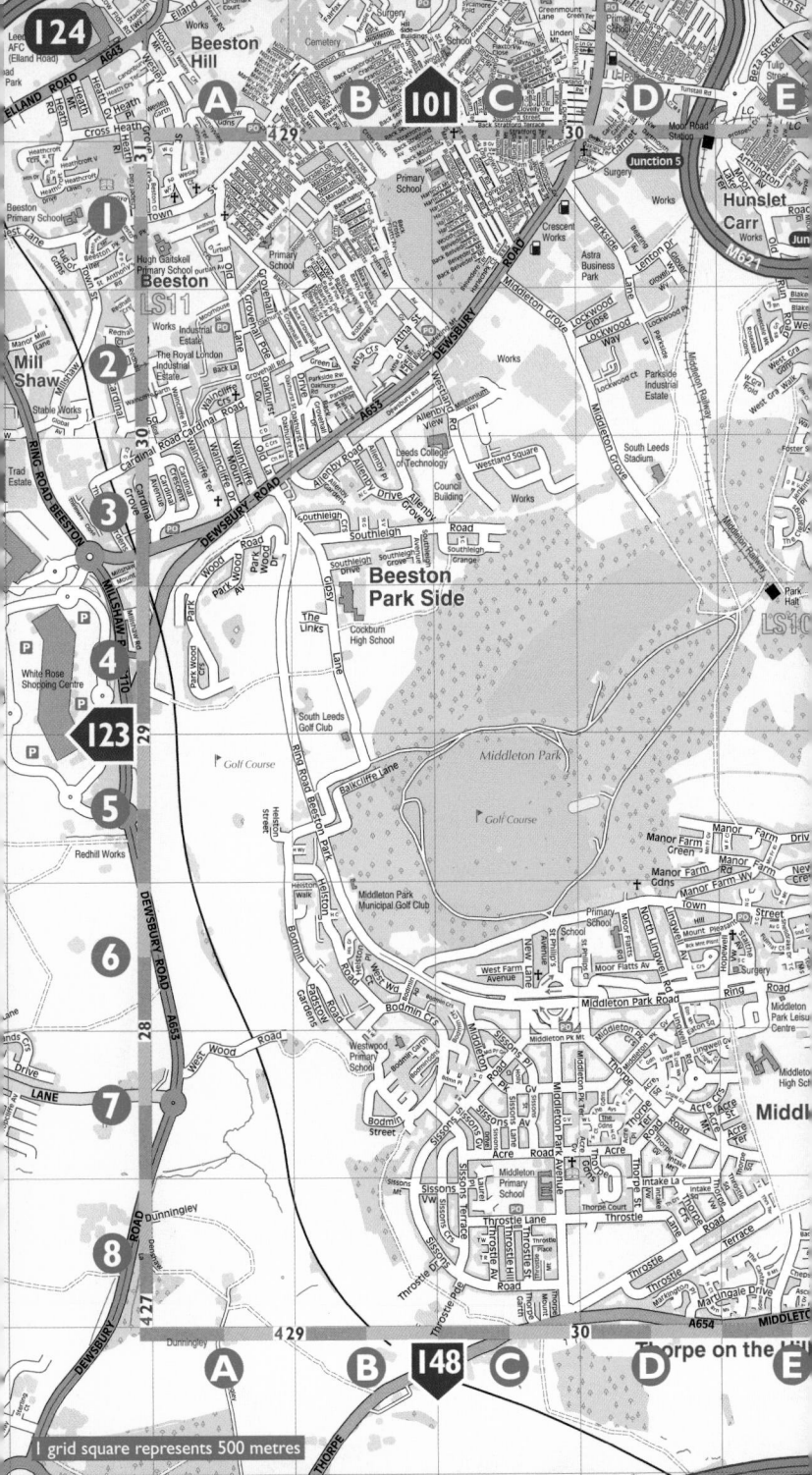

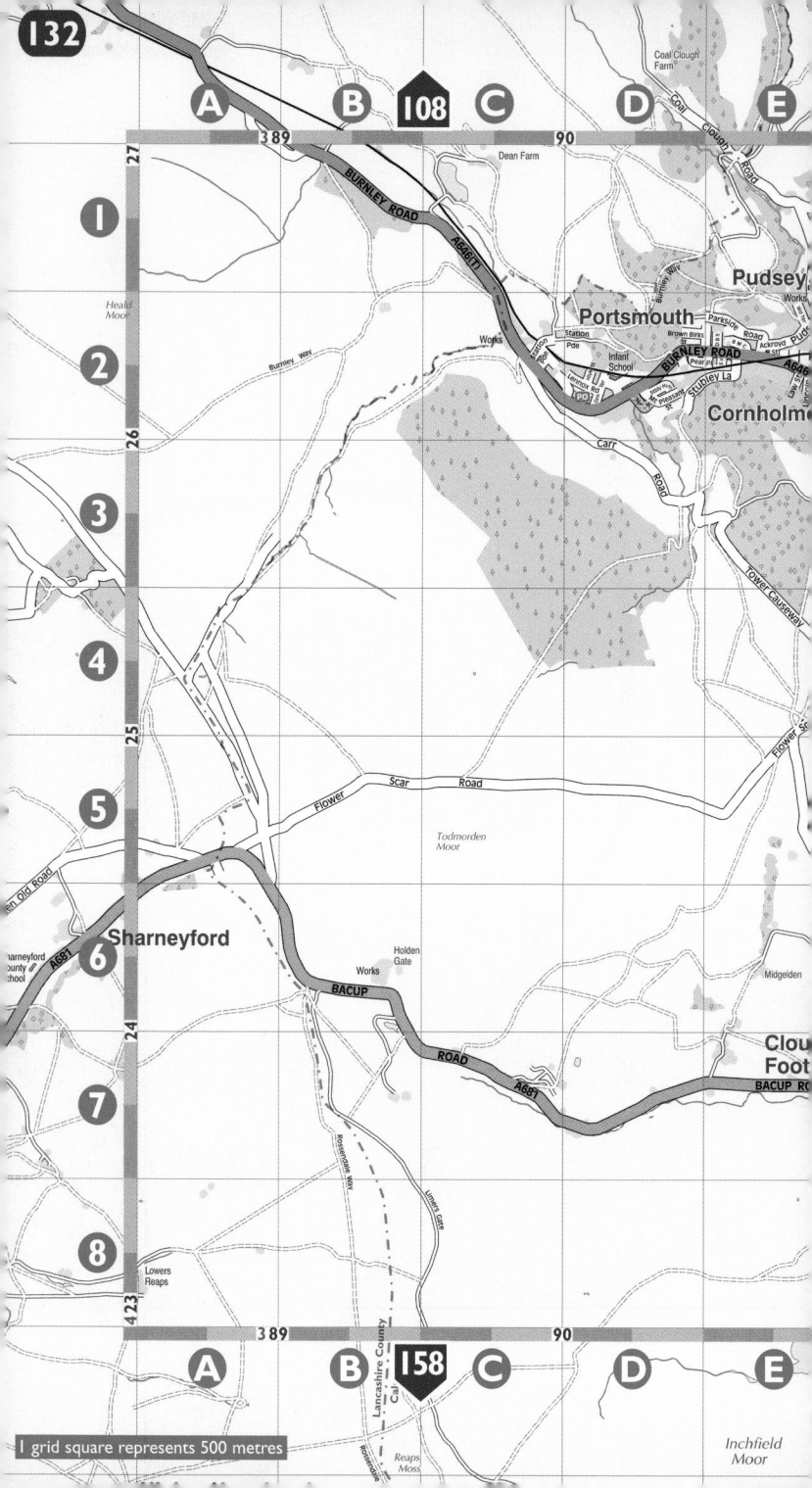

110

A **B** **C** **D** **E**

394 95

27

1

Kebs Road

Eastwood Road

Lower Lane

Staups Moor

26

2

Keelam Heights

Windy Harbour Lane

Broad Lane

Keelam Lane

Upper Lane

Eastwood Road

Calderdale Way

Crossley New Road

3

Greenhurst Hey

Whirlaw Lane

Butts Lane

Ot House Road

New Road

Great House

4

Hole Bottom

Scaitcliffe Lane

Calderdale Way

Golf Course

Hey Head Lane

Agnes Lane

Cross Stone Road

Matthew Lane

Baulk Head Lane

133

Todmorden Golf Club

Broad Gate

5

Todmorden Cricket Club

Primary & Infant Sch

The Mount

Burnt House Close

Park Rd

Stansfield Hall Rd

Pennine Gv

Keats Av

Tennyson Av

Shakespeare Av

Dover St

Castle Hill

Clinder Hl Rd

Works

HALIFAX ROAD

6

Community College

Abraham Ormerod

Health Centre

Industrial St

Cambridge St

School La

Town Hall

Sackville St

Burdale St

A646

Millwood

Commercial St

Works

Summerfield Road

Woodhouse Rd

Junior & Infant School

Castle Street

Rochdale Canal

24

Salford Industrial

OL14

Morden Station

Rose Bank Works

Longfield Way

Longfield

Kilnhurst Mt

Kilnhurst Av

Dale Rd

Glaroyd

Long Shay Lane

Lumbutts Lane

TODMORDEN

7

ROCHDALE ROAD

Shade

Calderdale Way

Lumn Hey La

Calderdale Way

Lumbutts Road

Lumbutts

Lee Lane

8

Knowl Wood

Infant School

423

Moor Lane

Lumbutts Road

Moor La

394 95

A **B** **C** **D** **E**

160

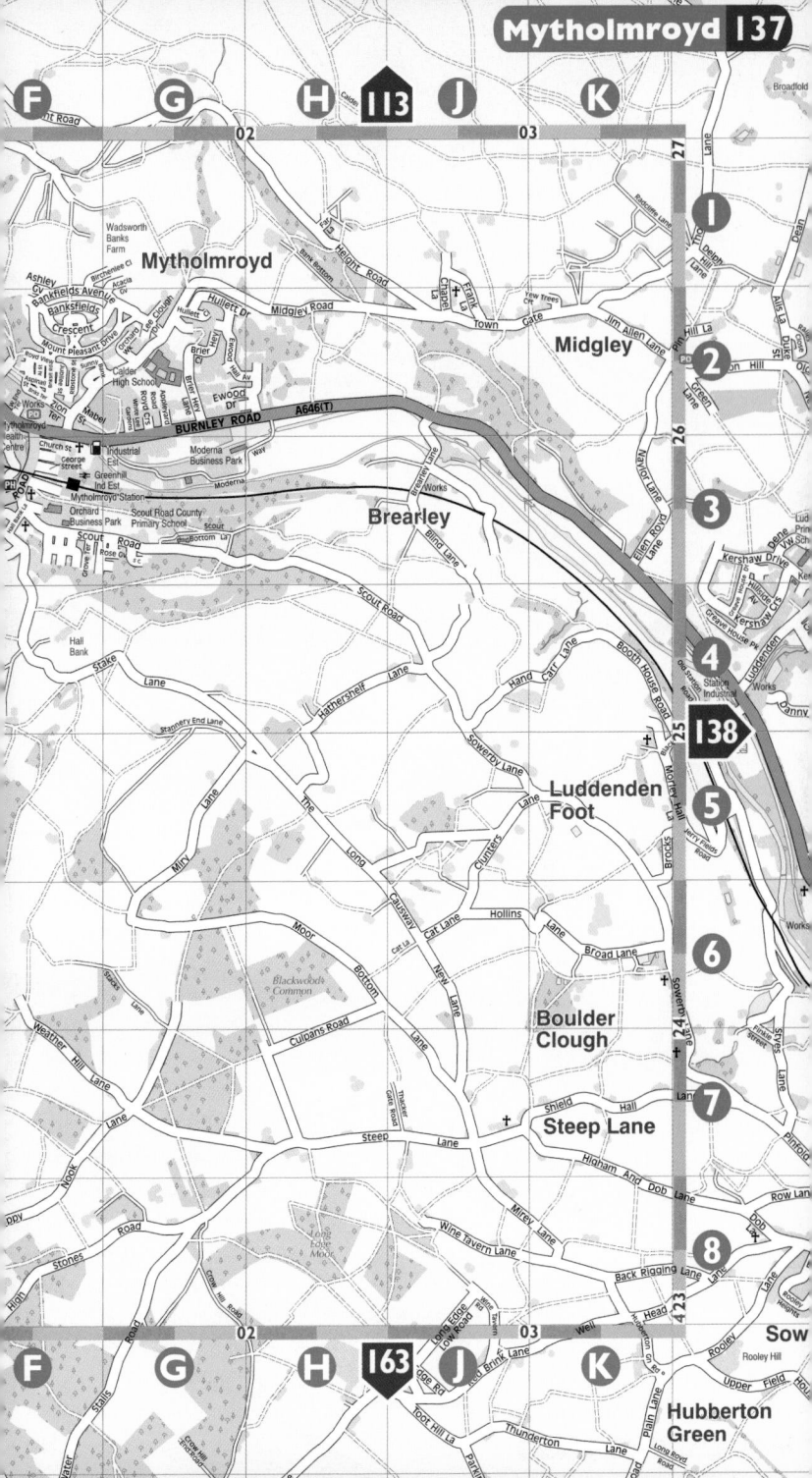

F G H 113 J K

Broadfold

02 03 27

nt Road

Wadsworth
Banks
Farm

Mytholmroyd

Ashley
Bankfields Avenue
Crescent

Mount Pleasant Drive

Calder
High School

Height Road

Banks Bottom

Brink

Midgley Road

Hullett Dr

Chapel

Frank La

Town Gate

Yew Trees

Jim Allen Lane

Pin Hill La

Green Lane

Midgley

26

Mabel

BURNLEY ROAD   A646(T)

Works

Mytholmroyd
Health
Centre

Church St
George
street

Greenhill
Ind Est

Industrial

Moderna
Business Park

Moderna

Way

Moderna

Naylor Lane

Dixon Lane

Works

3

Kershaw Drive

Kershaw

Gravel House Pl

Orchard
Business Park

Mytholmroyd Station

Scout Road County
Primary School

Scout

Rose La

Scout
Road

Bottom

Brearley

Blind Lane

Hand Carr Lane

Booth House Road

Old Stake Lane

4

Station
Industrial
Works

138

Danny

Hall
Bank

Stake

Lane

Stansey End Lane

Hathershelf
Lane

Scout Road

Sowerby Lane

Luddenden

5

The Long Causeway

Cat Lane

Cat La

Gunters

Hollins

Lane

Morten Hall

Brooks

**Luddenden
Foot**

Works

Milly
Lane

Moor

Bottom

New Lane

Broad Lane

6

Sowerby Lane

Steps Lane

Blackwood's
Common

Culpans Road

Thacker
Gate Road

**Boulder
Clough**

24

Weather Hill Lane

Lane

Steep Lane

Shield

Hall

Lane

Steep Lane

7

Pinfold

Nook Lane

ppy

Road

Stones

High

Long Edge Moor

Crow Hill Road

Wine Tavern Lane

Mirey Lane

Higham And Dob Lane

Back Rigging Lane

Row Lane

Dob Lane

8

23

Sow

Rooley Hill

F G H 163 J K

02 03

Long Edge

Low Edge

Dock Hill La

Brink Lane

Well Lane

Thunderton

Rooley

Lane

Lane

Upper
Field

Long Level

**Hubberton
Green**

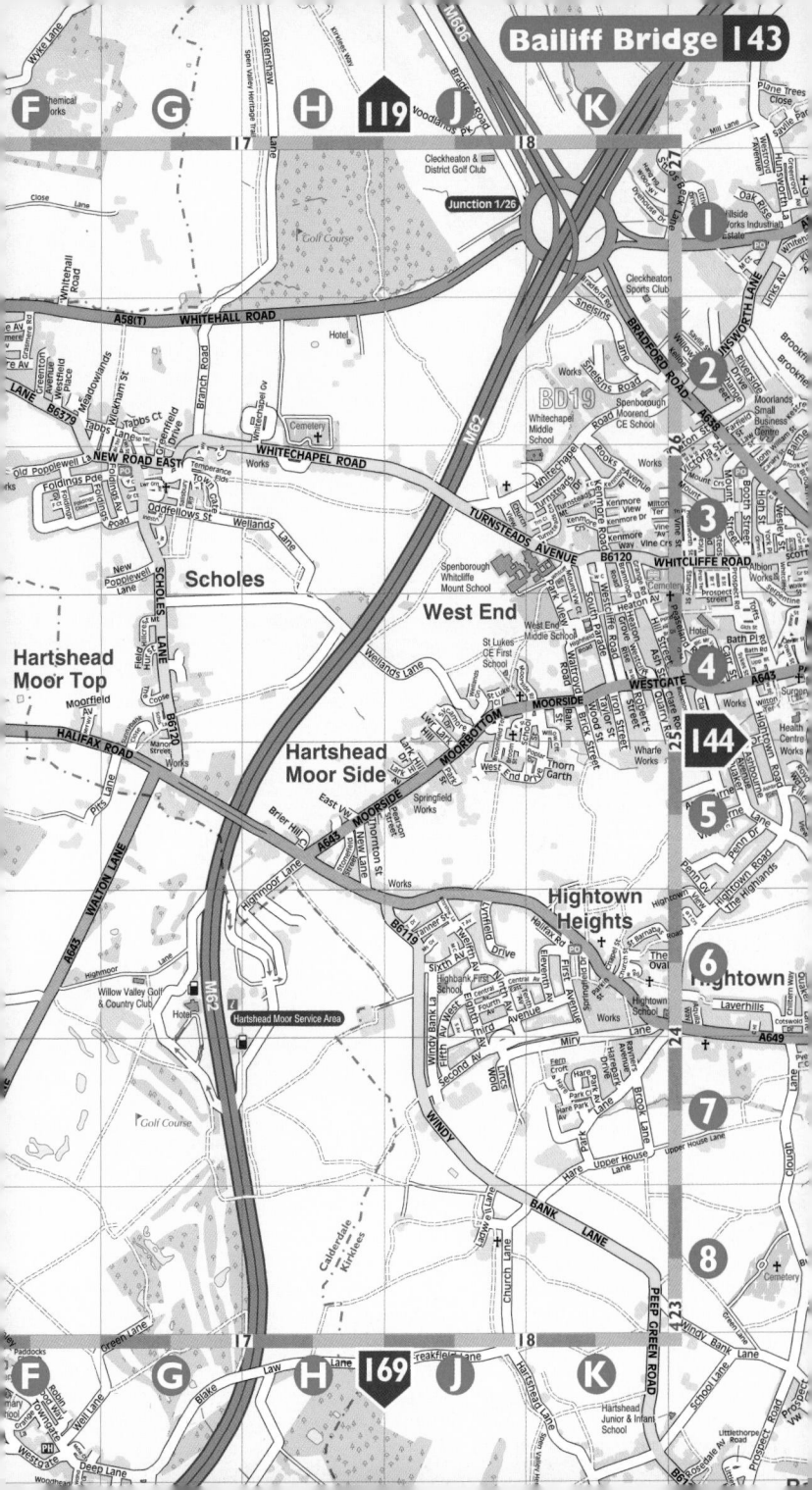

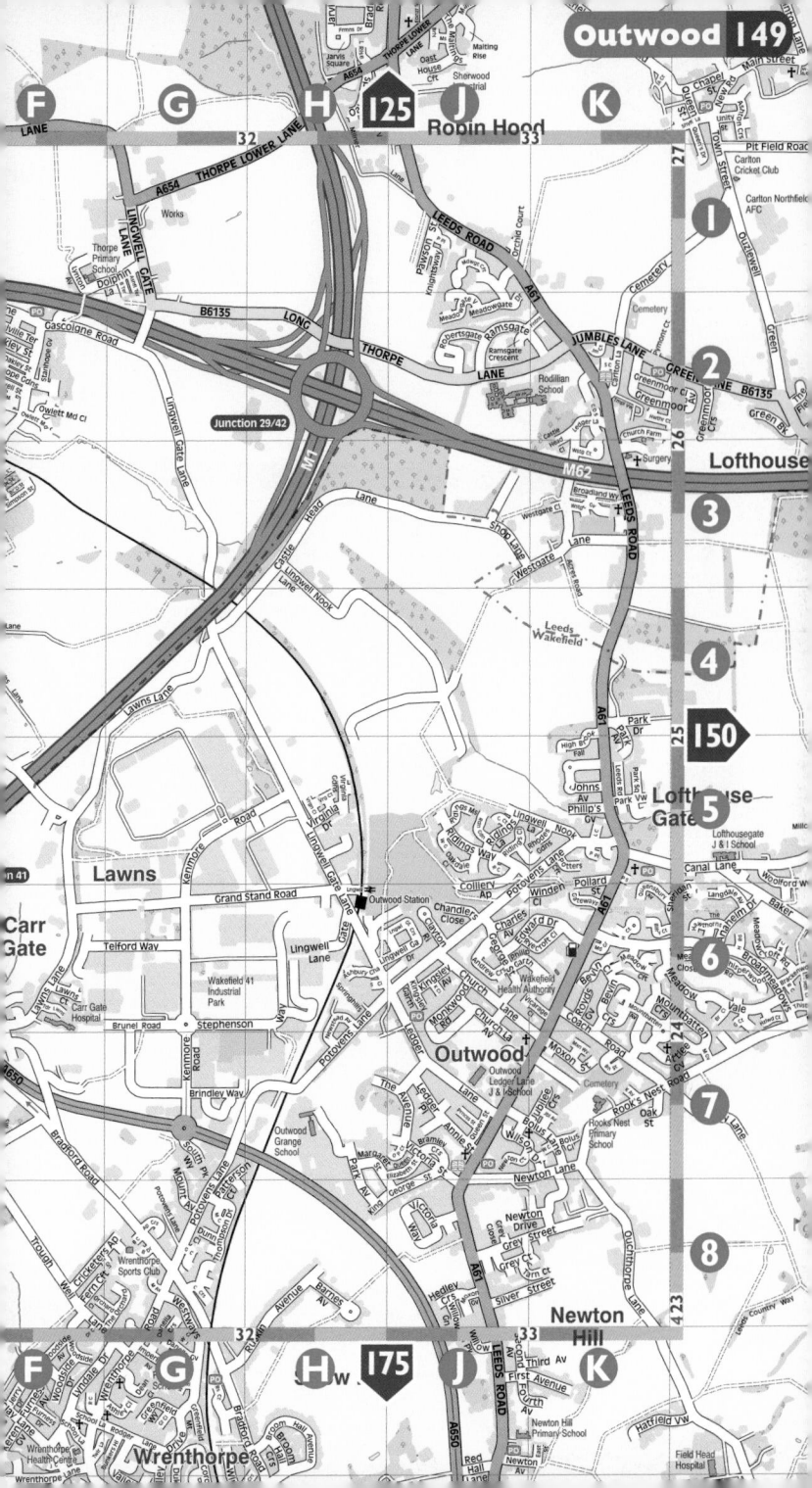

F G H **135** J K

97 98

23

1

Withins Clough Reservoir

Withins Moor

2

22

3

Turley Holes and Higher House Moor

4

Blake Moor

21 **162**▶

5

Turvin Clough

White Holme Drain

6

B6158

Light Hazzles Reservoir

20

7

White Holme Reservoir

B6158

8

Soyland Moor

419

97 98

F G H **184** J K

Turvin Road

Head Drain

162

Withens Clough Reservoir

Turley Holes Edge

Rud Lane

Withens

Market Lane

Calderdale Way

Road

A

B

136

C

D

Boyd Cragg

E

399

400

23

1

2

22

3

Turley Holes and Higher House Moor

Sykes Gate

Washfold Road

Road

Blake Moor

4

161

21

5

Turvin Clough

BLACKSTONE EDGE

B6138

6

20

STONE EDGE ROAD

7

B6138

Manshead End

Baitings Pasture

8

Moor

419

A

399

B

185

C

400

D

A58 ROCHDALE ROAD

E

Blue Ball Road

1 grid square represents 500 metres

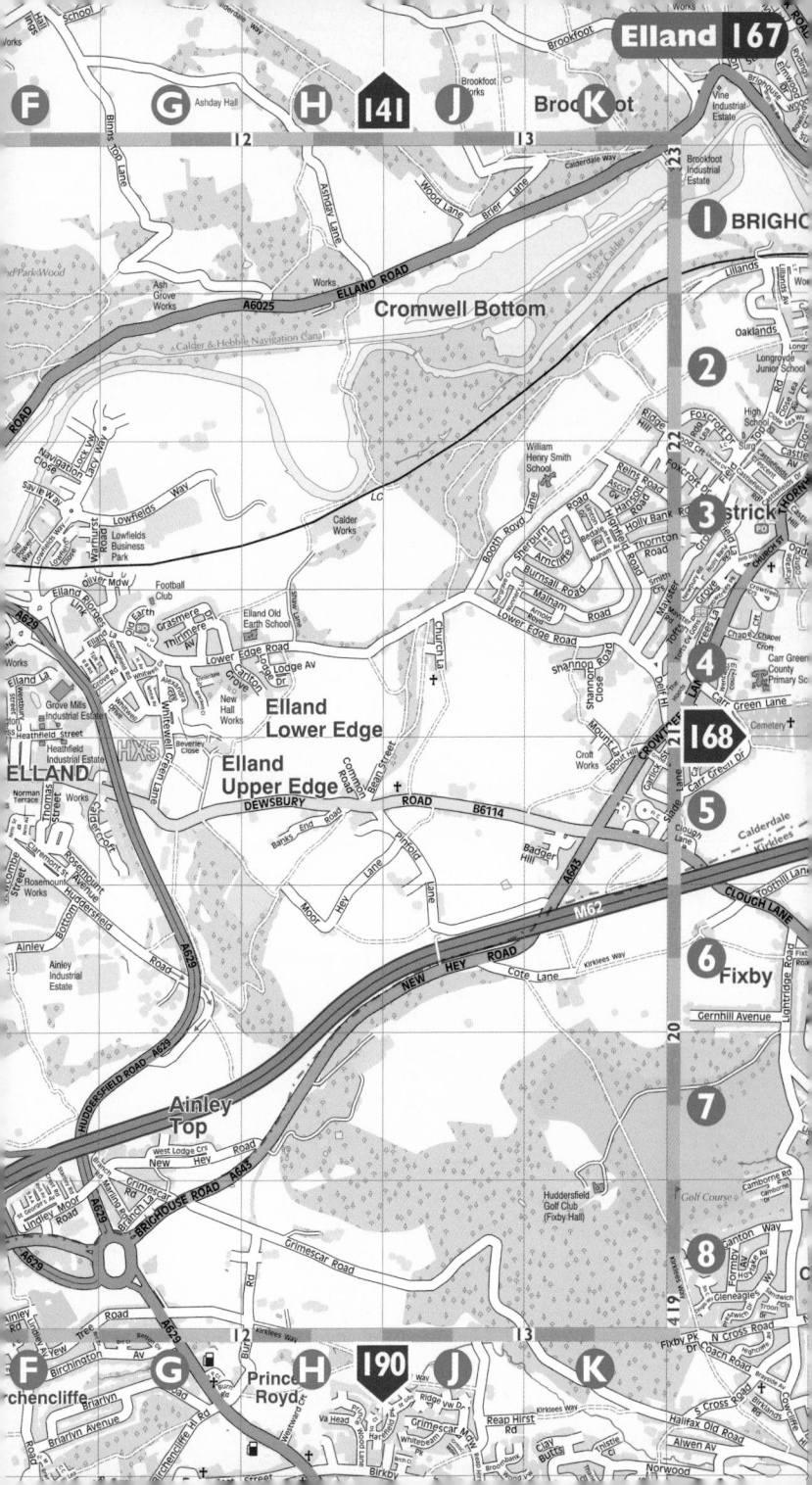

F G H 162 J K

99 400 01 19

Blue Ball Lane

Blue Ball Road

ROCHDALE ROAD

A58

Baitings
Reservoir

River Ryburn

Beck o' th' Height

DALE ROAD

1

2

18

3

Cat
Stones

Rishworth
Moor

Rishworth
Moor

Blackwood
Common

4

17 186

5

Joiner
Stones

Green Withers
Reservoir

6

OLDHAM ROAD

A672

16

7

8

A672

99 400 01 415

Moss
Moor

F M62 G H 207 J K

Junction 22

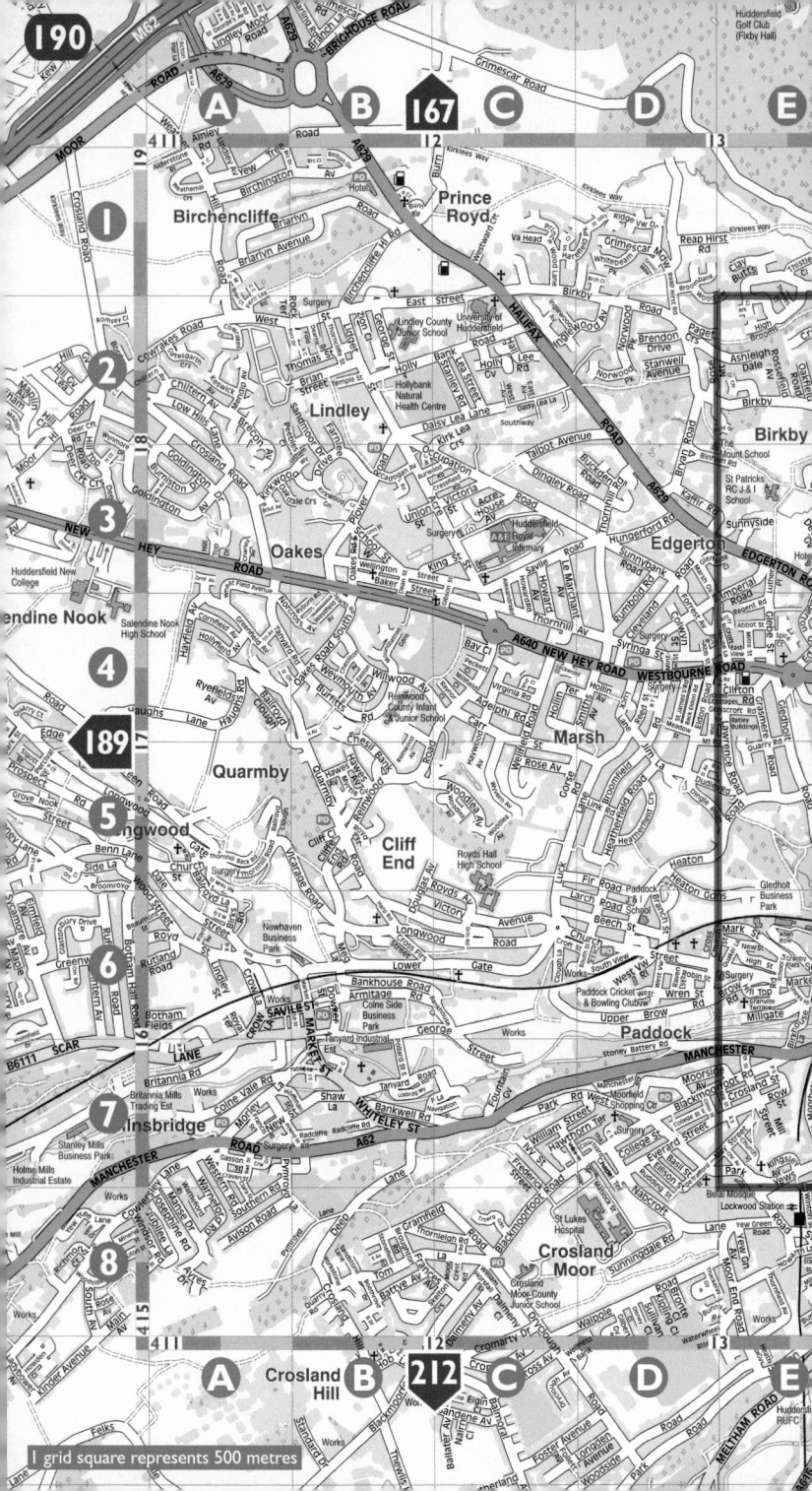

I grid square represents 500 metres

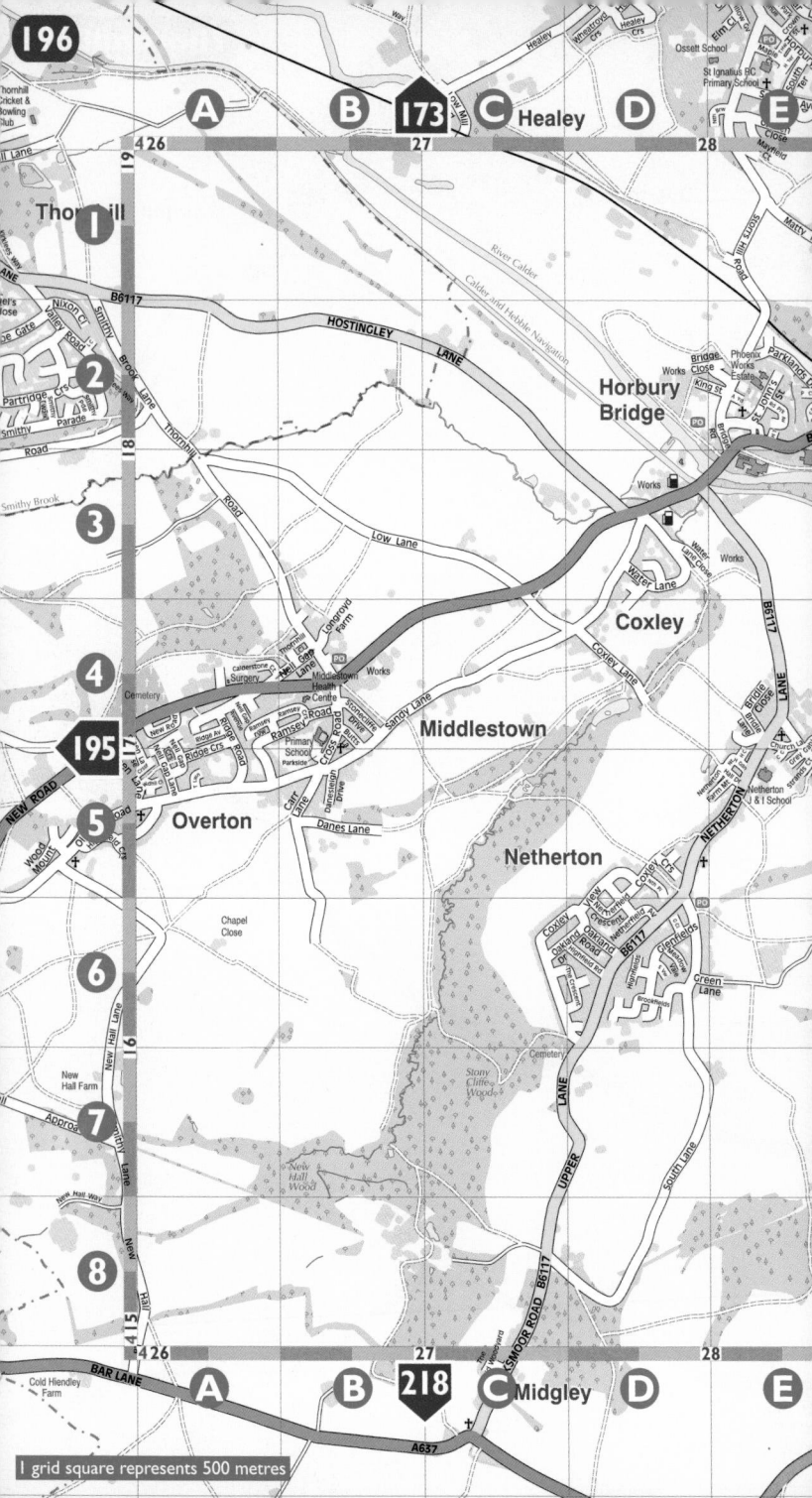

A B 181 C D E

446

9 6

HARDWICK
Water Lane
ROAD

Hundhill

1

2

18

Darrington Road
East Hardwick

3

Ackworth
Grange

WHITEGATE HILL A639

Whitegate Lane

4

Rigg Lane
Burnhill
House

River Went

203

Tan House Dike
Works

Ackworth Bridge Road

5

A639

WENTBRI

6

19

Rockingham Lane

Thorpe
Audlin

Went Vw
Surgery
Darning Lane
PO
Oakfield
Pk

DONCASTER ROAD

Watchit
Hole
Lane

7

Firthfield Lane
Owler's Lane

Hall Cl.
Hall Garth Rd
Clinton
Bridge Lane

THORPE LANE

Thorpe
Manor

Causeway

Common Lane

Grove Lane

THORPE LANE

8

High Croft
James St

15

Hotel

446

9 6

A B 226 C D E

47 48

Badsworth
CE J & I School
Surgery

New Road

Badsworth

B6474

Badsworth

F G H **185** J K

99 400 01

15

Moss Moor

I

M62

Junction 22

Way Stone Edge

Way Stone

2

Linsgreave

14

Buckstones Moss

Moss Moor

Buck Hou

3

A640

4

March Haigh

13

208

March

5

Pennine Way

Kirklees Oldham

Pennine Way

tyccon rvoir

Rapes Highway

A640 ROAD

Station To Station Walk

6

Denshaw Moor

12

7

HUDDERSFIELD ROAD

Oldham Way

8

A640

Castleshaw Moor

Kirklees Oldham

Pennine Way

4 11

F G H J K

99 400 01

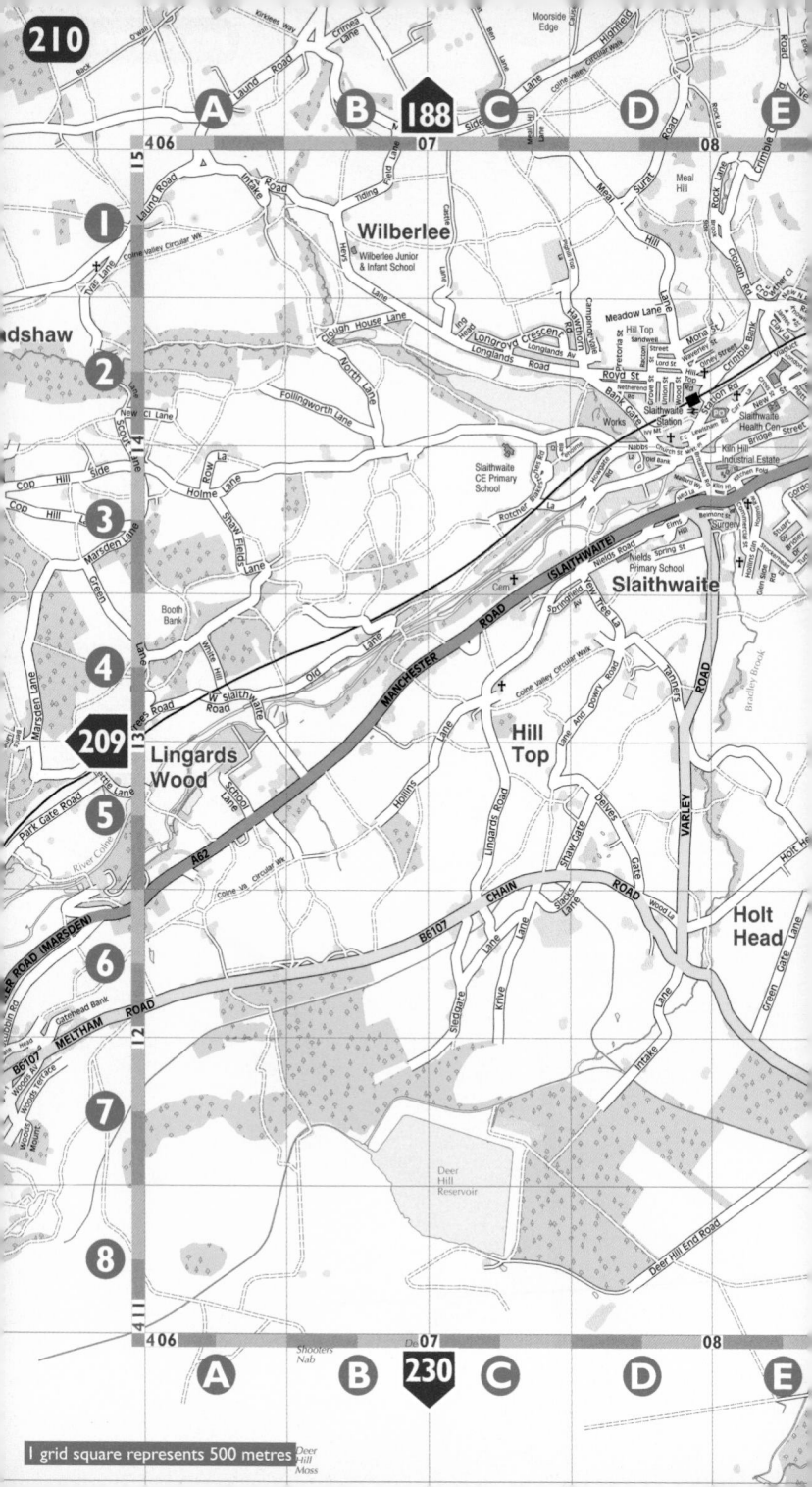

Newsome

Hall Bower

The Lumb

Farnley Bank

Lumb Head

Berry Brow

HD4

Northgate Honley Road

Hey Woods

Honley Station

Honley High School

Brockholes Station

Brockholes

WOODHEAD ROAD

HUDDERSFIELD ROAD

NEW MILL ROAD

A616

A6024

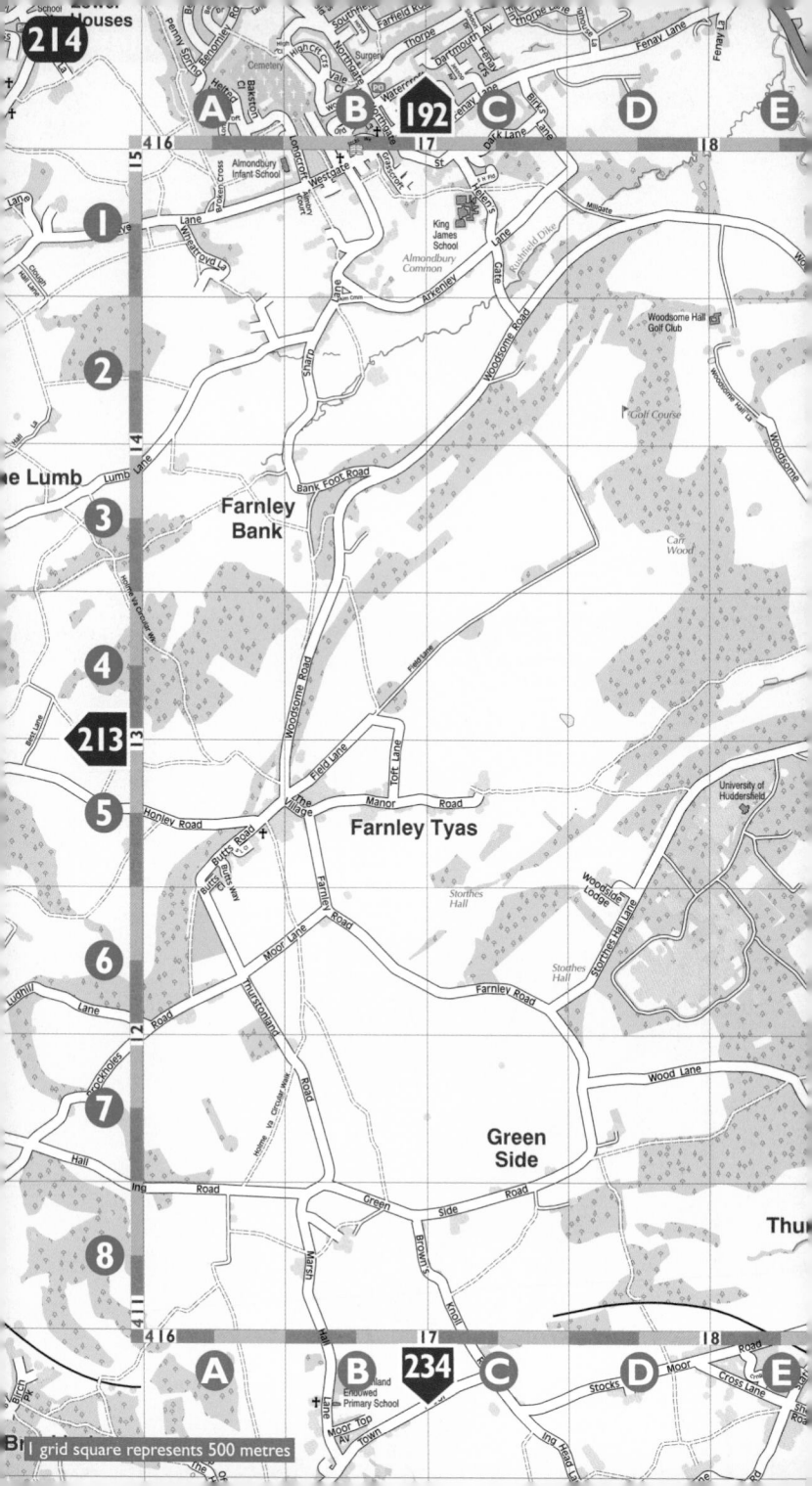

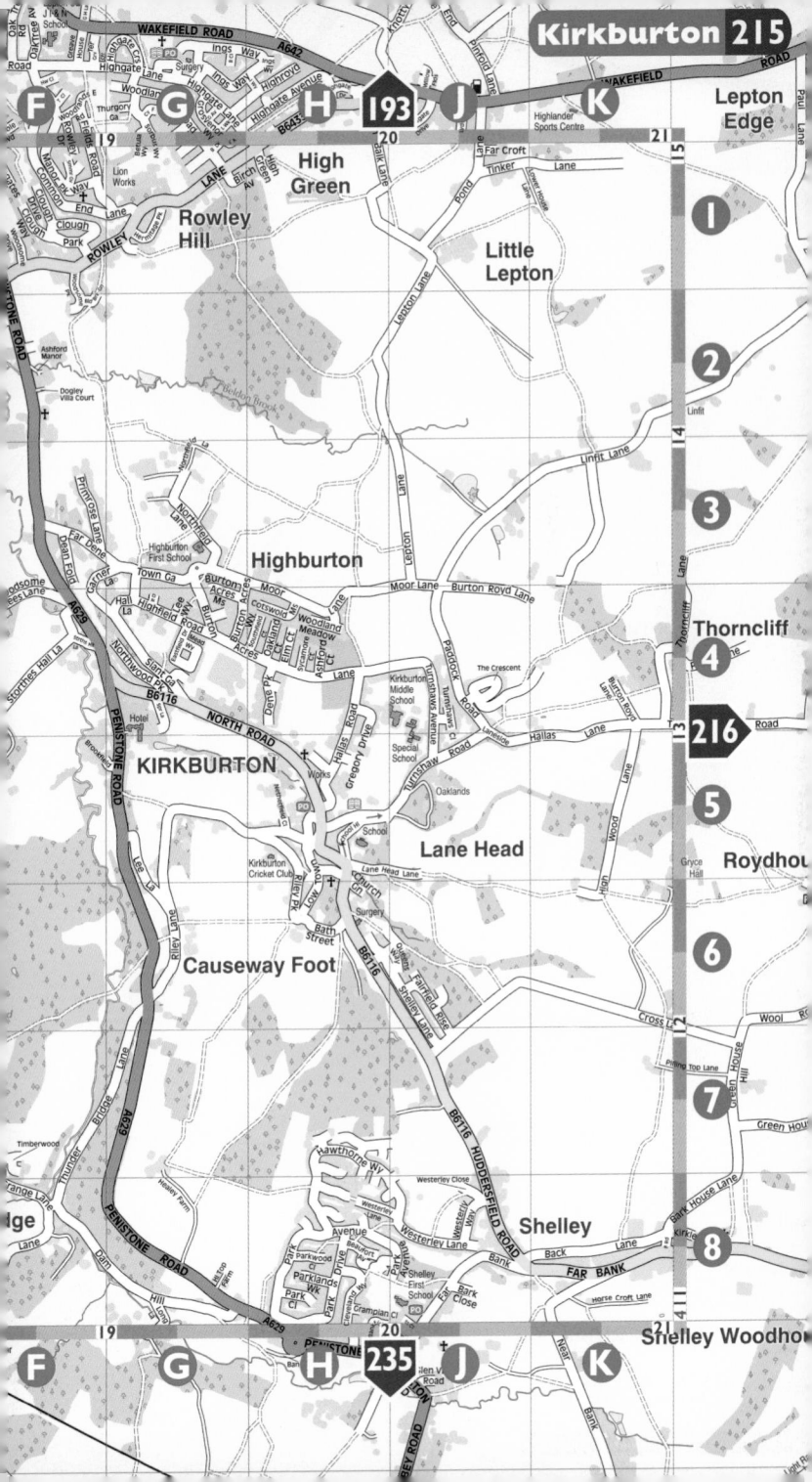

201

224

F **G** **H** **J** **K**

39 40 41

Newstead

Kinsley

Havercroft
Ryhill

South
Hiendley

Wakefield
Barnsley

Brierley

on Two Gates

F **G** **H** **J** **K**

39 40 41

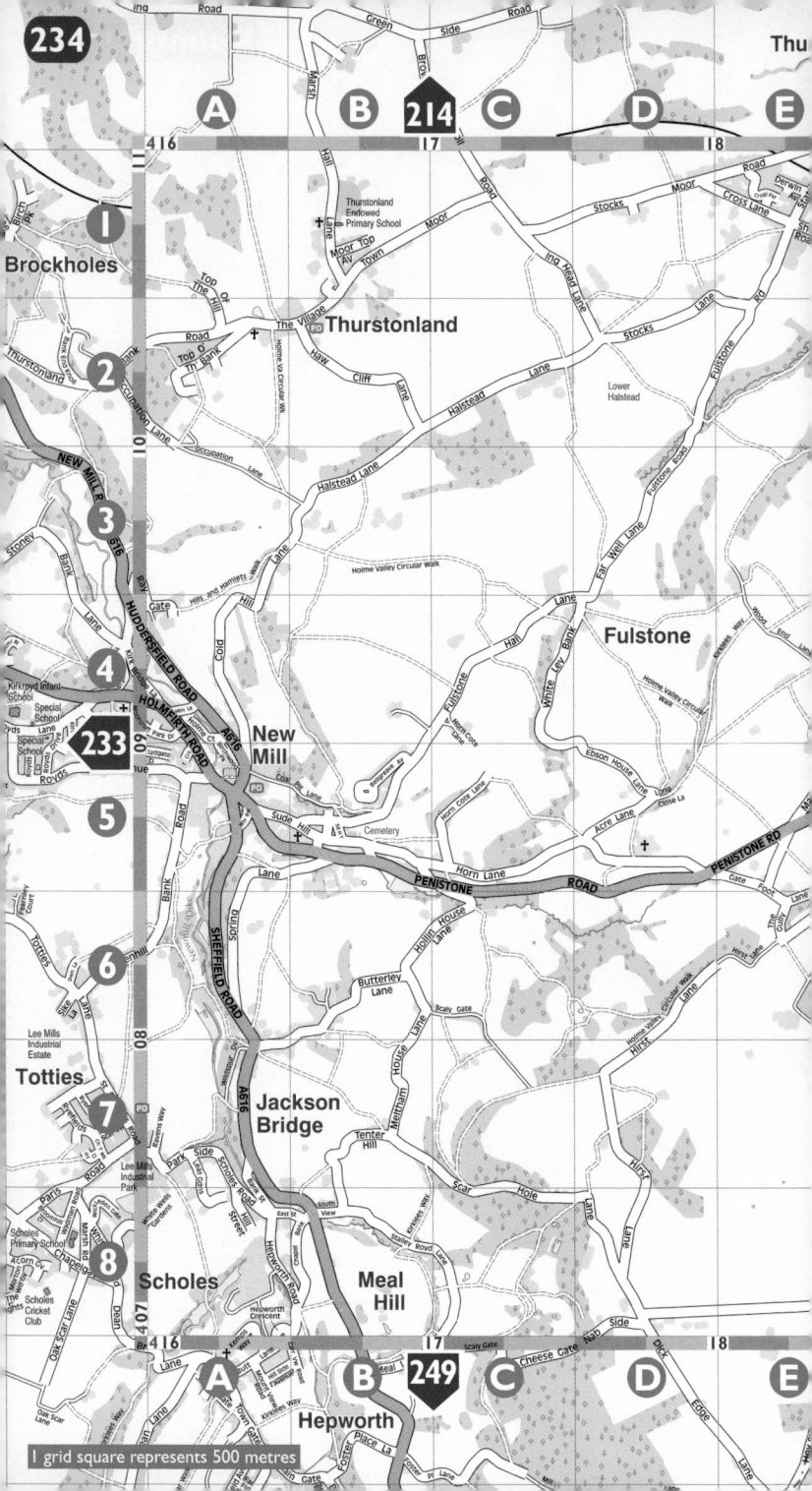

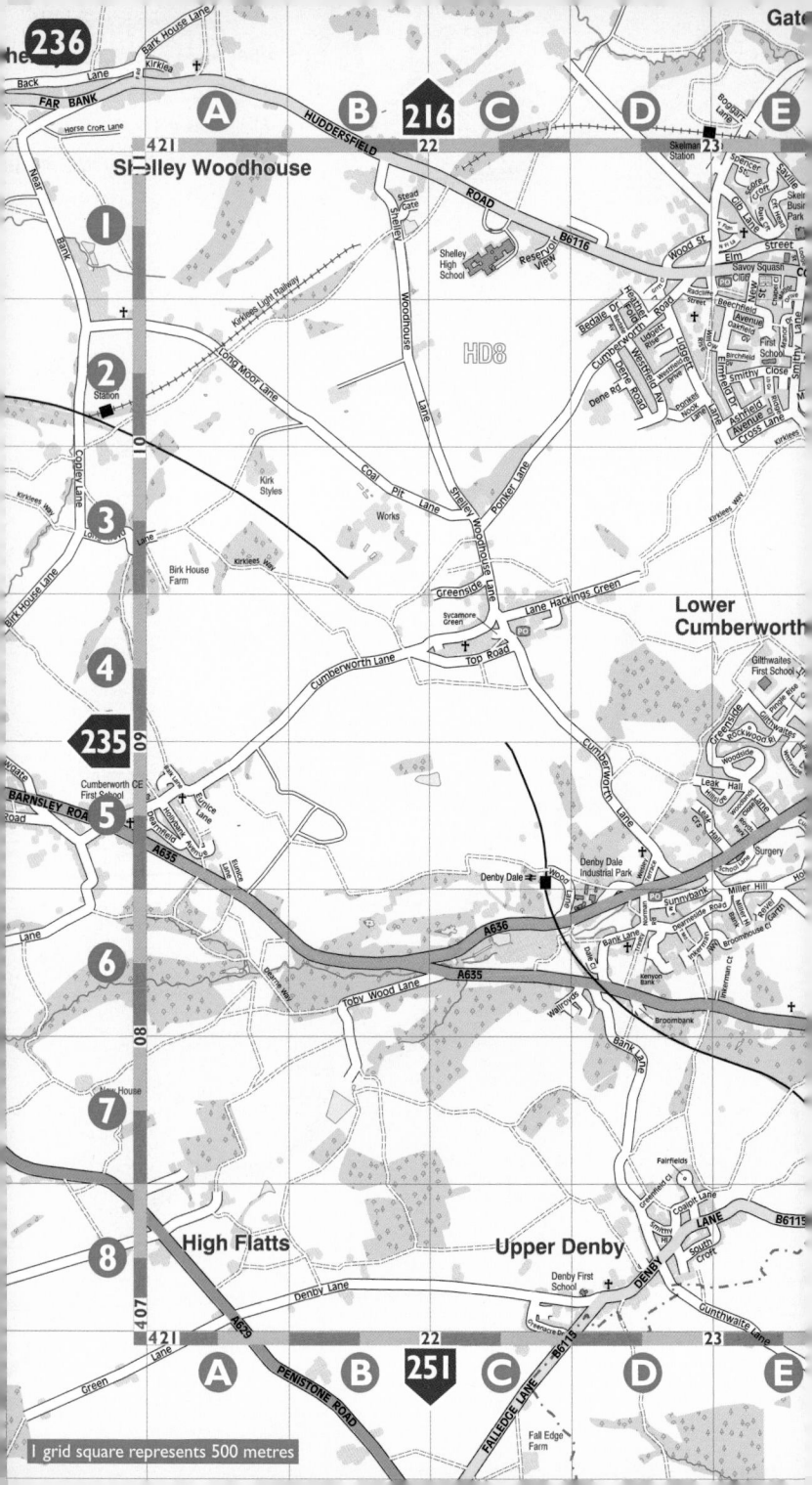

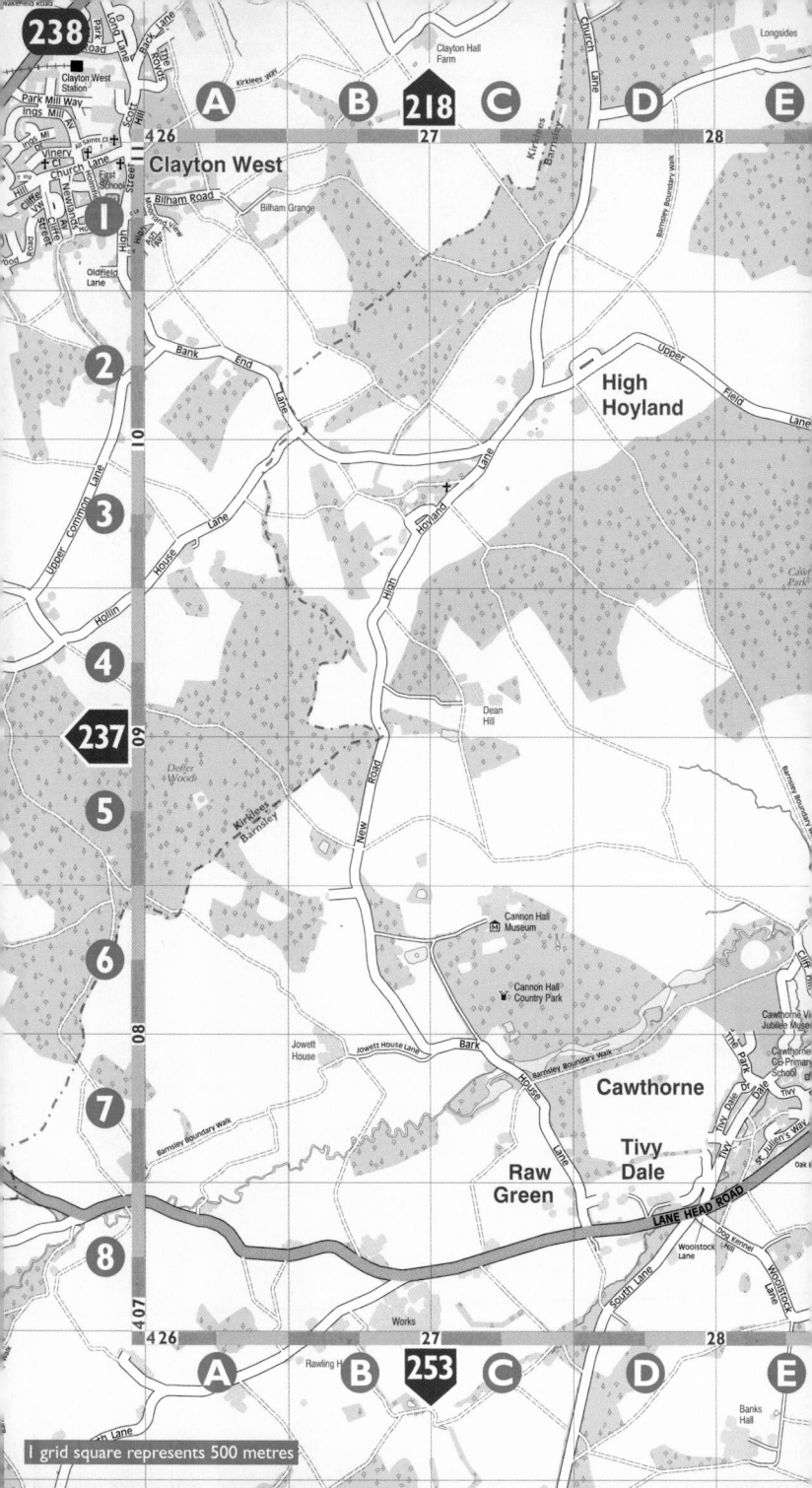

238

A B 218 C D E

426 27 28

Clayton West

Clayton West

1

Oldfield
Lane

2

Bank End Lane

High Hoyland

High Hoyland

Upper Field Lane

3

Hollin Lane

House Lane

High Hoyland Lane

4

Calf Park

237

Dean Hill

5

Kirklees Barnsley

New Road

Barnsley Boundary Walk

6

Cannon Hall Museum

Cannon Hall Country Park

Cawthorne Vi Jubilee Muse

Cawthorne CB Primar School

7

Jowett House

Jowett House Lane

Bark House Lane

Barnsley Boundary Walk

Cawthorne

Tivy Dale

Tivy Dale

St Julien's Way

Barnsley Boundary Walk

Raw Green

LANE HEAD ROAD

Dog Kennel

Oak Ri

8

407

Woolstock Lane

South Lane

WOOLSTOCK

426 27 28

A B 253 C D E

Rawling H

Works

Banks Hall

1 grid square represents 500 metres

225

242

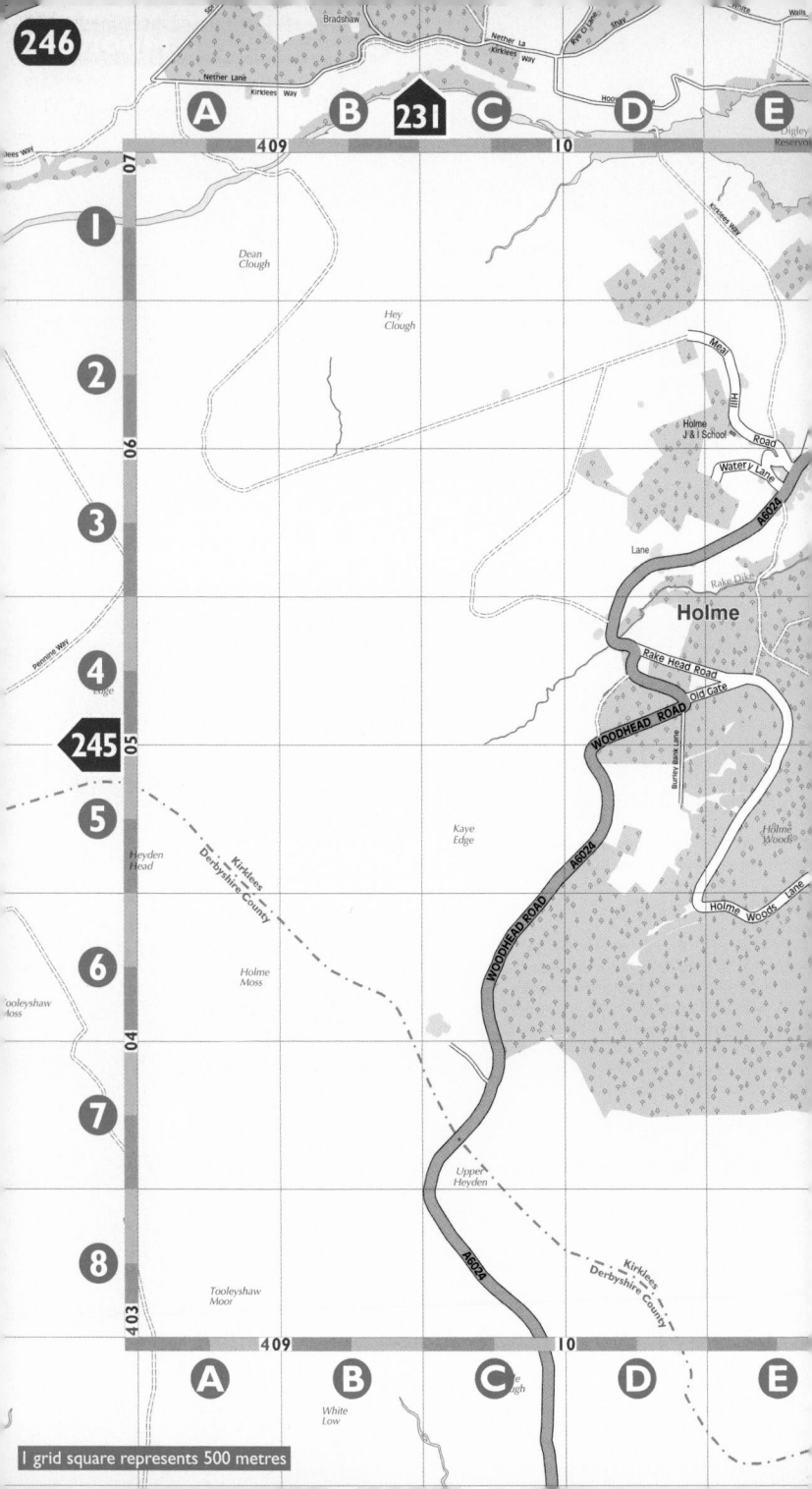

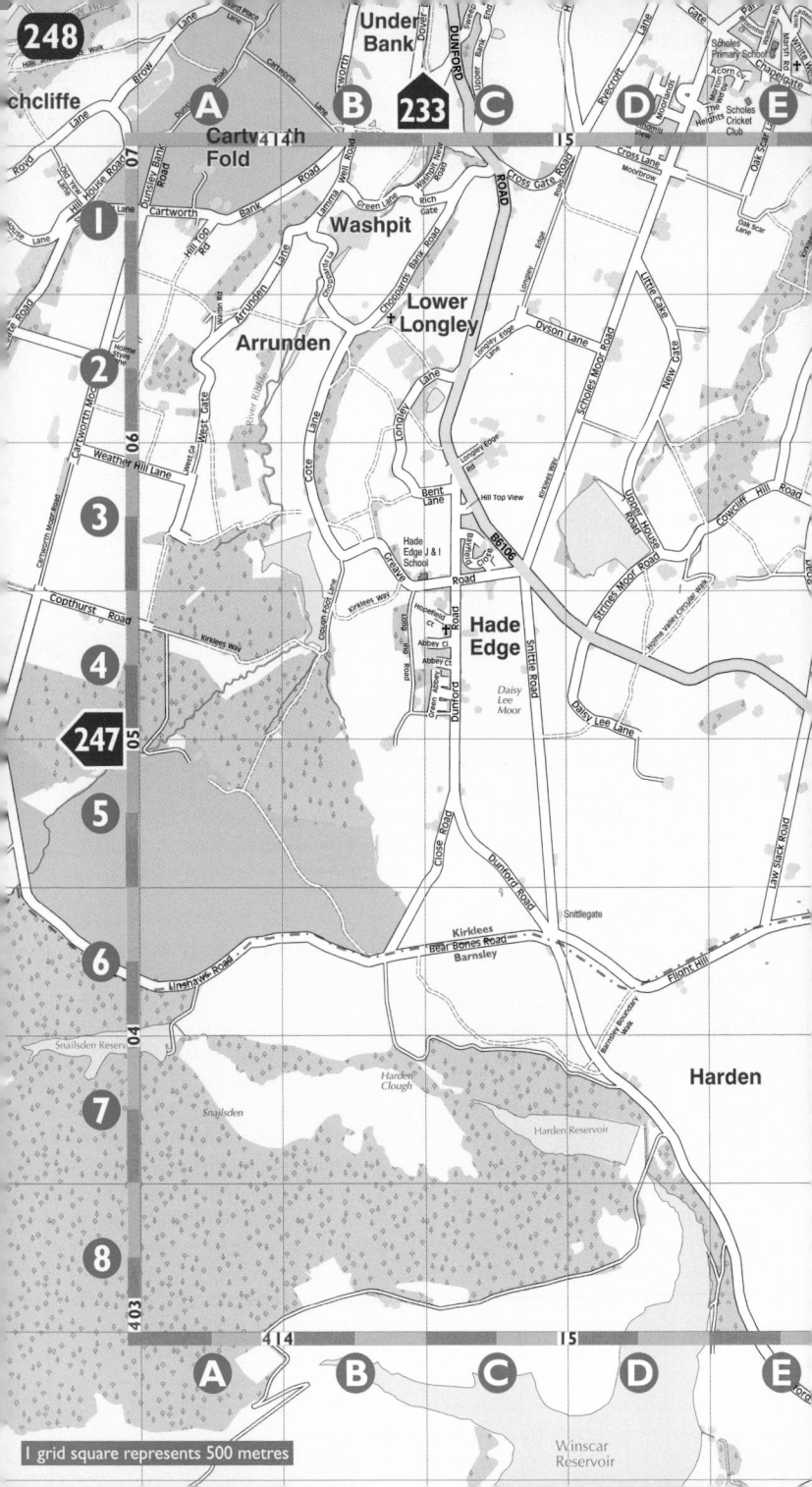

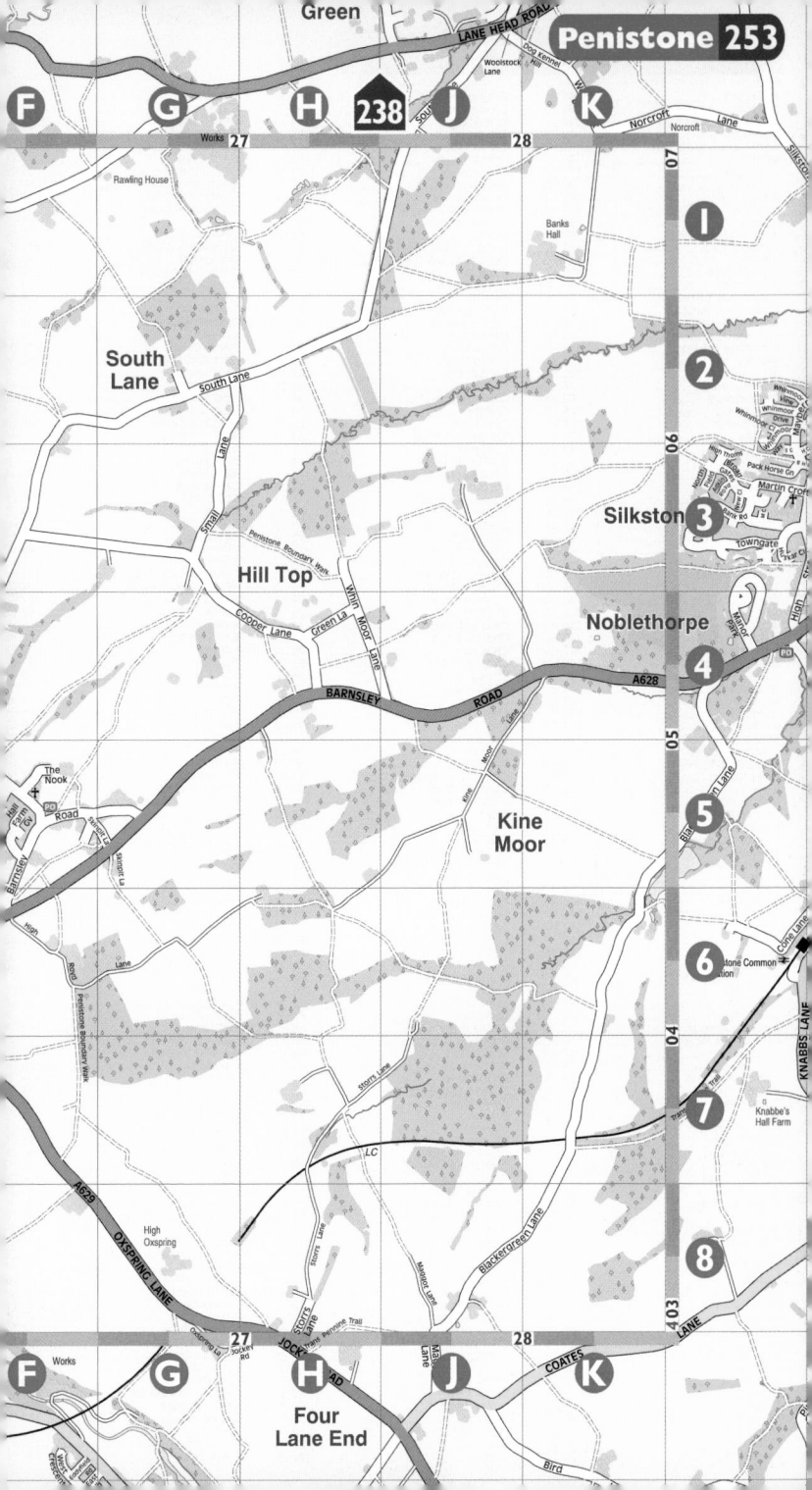

Aberford 84 D4
Ackton 179 F3
Ackworth Moor Top 202 E6
Addingham 18 C3
Addingham Moorside 18 B7
Adel 56 C7
Adwalton 121 K5
Agbrigg 10 C6
Ainley Top 167 G7
Airedale 154 C4
Allerton 94 C3
Allerton Bywater 129 H7
Almondbury 192 B7
Altofts 151 H6
Alverthorpe 175 F3
Alwoodley 57 J6
Alwoodley Gates 58 A5
Alwoodley Park 57 F5
Ambler Thorn 116 A3
Apperley Bridge 75 G2
Armitage Bridge 213 F4
Armley 100 D3
Arrunden 248 A2
Arthington 36 D5
Arthursdale 82 D3
Austhorpe 104 C3
Badsworth 225 K1
Bagley 76 C7
Baildon 51 K8
Baildon Green 73 G1
Bailiff Bridge 142 B3
Bank End 17 G2
Bank Top 74 E6
Bank Top 140 E6
Bantam Grove 123 J7
Barcroft 69 H3
Bardsey 40 A7
Barkisland 164 E7
Barnbow Carr 83 G6
Barnside 249 H3
Barwick in Elmet 83 G5
Batley 146 B7
Batley Carr 146 B8
Battyeford 170 B6
Beamsley 15 H6
Beck Bottom 148 D8
Beck Foot 71 J2
Beechcliffe 3 E1
Beechwood 81 C5
Beeston 123 K1
Beeston Hill 101 F8
Beeston Park Side 124 B3
Beeston Royds 100 B8
Beggarington Hill 147 H6
Belle Isle 125 F4
Belle Vue 11 F5
Ben Rhydding 20 E8
Berry Brow 213 F3
Bickerton 25 J1
Bierley 119 J2
Bingley 49 J8
Birchencliffe 190 A1
Birds Edge 235 J7
Birkby 12 A1
Birkenshaw 120 E5
Birkenshaw Bottoms 121 F7
Birkhouse 142 D5
Birkin 157 K1
Birks 147 F1
Birstall 145 H1
Birstall Smithies 145 H4
Black Hill 2 A1
Blackley 166 D7
Black Moor 57 C7
Blackmoorfoot 211 J4
Blackshaw Head 110 E8
Bogthorn 47 G7
Bolton 74 B7
Bolton Abbey 15 G3
Bolton Bridge 15 H4
Bolton Woods 74 A7
Booth 114 B8
Boothroyd 171 K3
Boothtown 8 B1
Booth Wood 186 E5
Boston Spa 42 C4
Bottom Boat 151 F5
Bottomley 165 G8
Boulder Clough 137 K6
Bowling 96 D7
Bracken Bank 47 H8
Brackenhall 168 C2
Bracken Hill 169 K4
Bracken Park 59 H4
Bradford 4 B4
Bradley 169 G5
Bradley Mills 13 F1
Bradshaw 115 J2
Bradshaw 209 J2
Bradup 29 F6
Braithwaite 47 F3
Brakenhill 202 C5
Bramham 42 D8
Bramhope 35 G8
Bramley 99 G2
Brandy Carr 148 E7
Brearley 137 H3
Brierley 223 K8
Briestfield 194 E4

Brighouse 168 A1
Broad Carr 166 B7
Brockholes 233 K1
Brodsworth 243 F8
Brookfoot 141 K8
Brookhouse 114 E3
Brooklands 81 G4
Brotherton 156 A3
Brown Moor 104 D4
Bruntcliffe 122 D8
Brunthwaite 27 J2
Burley 100 D1
Burley in Wharfedale 31 K3
Burley Woodhead 31 J5
Burmantofts 102 B2
Buttershaw 117 J3
Byram 156 B4
Cackleshaw 69 F1
Calder Grove 197 J5
Calverley 76 A5
Cambridge 34 A4
Camp Town 57 H8
Carlecotes 249 H8
Carleton 181 G6
Carlinghow 145 J4
Carlton 126 D8
Carr Gate 149 F6
Cartworth Fold 233 F8
Castleford 153 G4
Castleford Ings 153 K2
Castle Street 134 D6
Castley 36 B3
Catherine Slack 116 B5
Cat Hill 252 C4
Catshaw 250 E8
Causeway Foot 92 C8
Causeway Foot 215 G6
Cawthorne 238 D7
Chapel Allerton 79 J4
Chapel Allerton 79 J4
Chapelthorpe 198 C7
Chapeltown 79 J3
Charlestown 74 A1
Charlestown 111 J8
Chat Hill 94 A6
Chequerfield 181 G5
Chevin End 33 F6
Chickenley 173 G4
Chidswell 172 D6
Chiserley 112 D6
Churwell 123 H4
Claremount 9 D3
Clayton 94 C7
Clayton 241 J7
Clayton Heights 117 H1
Clayton West 238 A1
Cleckheaton 144 B3
Clerk Green 145 K7
Cliff End 190 B5
Clifford 42 D6
Clifton 168 E1
Clough Foot 132 E7
Clough Head 165 F2
Clough Head 189 F8
Cockersdale 121 J3
Cockley Hill 193 F3
Colden 111 F5
Cold Hiendley 222 B2
Coley 141 J1
Collingham 40 D4
Colne Bridge 169 H6
Colton 104 A5
Combs 173 C8
Compton 41 H5
Cookridge 55 H5
Copley 165 K1
Copley Hill 145 J1
Cornholme 132 E2
Cottingley 72 A4
Cotton Stones 163 K3
Cowcliffe 168 A8
Cowling 44 C1
Cowmes 192 E6
Coxley 196 D4
Crackenedge 172 C2
Cragg Hill 77 G3
Cragg Vale 136 E7
Crawshaw 216 E3
Cridling Stubbs 183 H4
Crigglestone 198 B5
Cringles 17 H5
Crofton 200 C3
Cromwell Bottom 167 H2
Crosland Edge 211 K6
Crosland Hill 212 A1
Crosland Moor 190 C8
Crossflatts 49 K5
Cross Gates 103 J3
Cross Green 102 B6
Crossley 170 E3
Crossley Hall 94 E4
Cross Roads 69 G2
Crow Edge 250 B5
Crow Nest 50 B8
Cullingworth 69 K5
Cutsyke 153 H6
Daisy Hill 94 D1
Daisy Hill 123 H5
Dalton 192 B5

Damems 69 H1
Dam Head 116 E8
Darrington 181 K6
Deerstones 15 K5
Deighton 169 G7
Denby Dale 237 F5
Denholme 92 A3
Denholme Clough 92 C5
Denholme Edge 92 A2
Denholme Gate 92 B6
Denton 21 G5
Dewsbury 172 B4
Dewsbury Moor 171 H2
Dockroyd 68 E2
Dogley Lane 214 E2
Drighlington 121 J5
Drub 144 C7
Dudley Hill 119 K1
Dunkeswick 37 J1
Durkar 198 C2
Earlsheaton 172 D4
East Ardsley 148 B4
East Bierley 120 C6
Eastburn 26 C5
East Carlton 34 C8
East Garforth 106 C3
East Hardwick 204 B1
East Keswick 40 A5
East Moor 11 F2
East Morton 49 J2
East Rigton 40 C6
Eastwood 135 G3
Eccleshill 74 D6
Eccup 57 G2
Edgerton 190 D3
Egypt 93 F7
Eldwick 50 D6
Elland 167 F5
Elland Lower Edge 167 H4
Elland Upper Edge 167 G5
Emley 217 G4
Esholt 52 E6
Exley 166 B1
Exley Head 2 A5
Fagley 75 F6
Fairburn 131 G6
The Fall 148 E8
Farnley 99 J8
Farnley Bank 214 A3
Farnley Tyas 214 B6
Far Royds 100 C2
Farsley 76 B3
Farsley Beck Bottom 76 C8
Fartown 191 G2
Fearnville 81 G7
Featherstone 179 H4
Felkirk 222 E5
Fell Lane 47 G5
Fenay Bridge 192 E7
Ferrybridge 155 K5
Fitzwilliam 202 A7
Five Lane Ends 74 C6
Fixby 168 A6
Flanshaw 175 F5
Flockton 195 G8
Flockton Green 195 J8
Flushdyke 174 A4
Flush House 232 B8
Foulby 201 G3
Four Lane Ends 94 E3
Fox Royd 195 F1
Friendly 138 D6
Frizinghall 73 G6
Fulneck 98 B8
Fulstone 234 D4
Gamble Hill 99 J3
Garden Village 107 F5
Garforth 106 B6
Gawthorpe 173 J2
Gawthorpe 193 F5
Gildersome 122 C3
Gildersome Street 122 C2
Gilstead 50 C8
Gipton 81 F8
Gipton Wood 80 D5
Girlington 95 G2
Glass Houghton 154 B6
Gledhow 80 C4
Golcar 189 F3
Gomersal 145 F3
Goose Eye 46 C5
Goosehill 177 G6
Grange Moor 194 D6
Great Cliff 197 J7
Great Horton 95 F2
Great Preston 128 D3
Green Clough 93 K6
Greengates 75 F5
Green Hill 85 F3
Green Side 100 C8
Green Side 214 C2
Greenside 192 B6
Greetland 165 K3
Greetland Wall Nook 165 J4
Grimethorpe 240 A4
Grove Town 181 F4
Guard House 47 G4
Guiseley 52 E3
Hade Edge 248 C5

gh	219 G7
gh Moor	148 A5
nworth	48 A8
nworth Shaw	48 B8
ifax	8 B5
l Bower	213 H2
l Green	198 B8
ton	103 G3
ton East	14 B2
ton Moor	103 F4
mbleton	14 E4
mpole	243 K2
nging Heaton	146 D8
rden	71 F2
rden	248 D7
re Croft	70 D7
rehills	102 D1
rewood	38 C4
rewood Hill	69 G1
rtshead	169 K2
rtshead Moor Side	143 H5
rtshead Moor Top	143 F4
vercroft	223 F2
wks Stones	109 H8
wksworth	52 B3
wksworth	77 H4
worth	68 D4
zlewood	15 K3
adingley	78 B6
aley	145 K6
aley	173 H8
ath Common	176 E7
aton	73 F8
aton Royds	72 E7
aton Shay	73 F6
eden Bridge	112 C8
ckmondwike	145 G7
me	211 J7
msworth	224 B4
nshaw	53 J6
ptonstall	111 K6
pworth	249 G1
ssle	202 E4
y Green	208 E6
h Ackworth	203 G3
hburton	215 H3
her Hogshead	158 A2
h Flatts	236 A8
h Green	215 H1
h Hoyland	238 D2
hroad Well Moor	138 E2
htown	144 A6
htown Heights	143 K6
foot	98 A3
Side	192 E4
Top	93 G4
Top	99 J1
Top	210 C4
Top	253 G3
chcliffe Mill	232 D8
perholme	141 G3
gley Green	232 C7
beck	6 C5
den Gate	28 B6
dsworth	116 A5
e	68 D5
e Bottom	134 A4
lingthorpe	197 K8
lin Hall	64 A2
lin Park	80 E6
linthorpe	104 E7
mbridge	247 F1
me	97 H7
me	246 D4
me Wood	97 H8
mfield	115 J6
mfirth	232 E6
t Head	210 E6
t Park	55 K6
ywell Green	166 A8
nley	212 E7
nley Moor	212 D8
o Hole	136 E4
ston Pagnell	242 E6
petown	152 C8
bury	197 F3
bury Bridge	196 D2
bury Junction	197 J3
sforth	76 D1
sforth Woodside	77 G3
gh Side	99 F3
uses Hill	193 C5
e Edge	141 K6
den Clough	146 A1
landswaine	252 D5
berton Green	163 K1
ddersfield	13 D6
gate	151 J3
slet	101 K7
slet Carr	124 E1
nsworth	120 B8
	74 D3
Moor	74 B5
ey	20 A7
gworth	115 H5
birchworth	251 H2
manthorpe	24 B1
ow	2 B6
ke	76 D8

Ireland Wood	77 K1
Jackson Bridge	234 A7
Jagger Green	166 A8
Jaw Hill	148 B7
John O'Gaunts	126 E4
Junction	26 A4
Kebroyd	164 A5
Keelham	92 D6
Keighley	3 D2
Kelcliffe	53 F1
Kellingley	157 G7
Kettlethorpe	198 C5
Kexbrough	239 J3
Kiddal Lane End	61 J7
Kildwick	26 A3
Killingbeck	103 G1
Kine Moor	253 J5
Kinsley	224 A1
Kippax	129 G5
Kirkburton	215 G5
Kirk Deighton	23 G2
Kirkhamgate	174 B1
Kirkheaton	192 E2
Kirkstall	78 A8
Kirkthorpe	177 G5
Kitchenroyd	236 E4
Knottingley	156 B7
Knowle Park	2 C5
Knowl Wood	133 K8
Knowsthorpe	102 B6
Krumlin	187 J2
Lady Wood	80 E4
Laisterdyke	97 F5
Lane Bottom	91 K1
Lane End	68 C1
Lane Ends	54 D8
Lane Head	215 J5
Lane Head	235 F5
Larkfield	54 B7
Lawns	149 F5
Lawnswood	78 A1
Laycock	46 E4
Ledsham	130 E3
Ledston	129 J5
Ledston Luck	129 J1
Leeds	6 C4
Leeming	91 F2
Lee Moor	150 B4
Lees	69 G3
Lepton Edge	194 E8
Leventhorpe	94 C5
Leymoor	189 J6
Lidget Green	95 G6
Lidgett Park	80 C3
Lightcliffe	142 A4
Lighthazles	163 H5
Lindley	190 B2
Lindwell	166 B3
Lingards Wood	210 A5
Lingbob	71 H7
Linthwaite	211 G2
Linton	40 E1
Little Horton	95 H8
Little Lepton	215 J1
Little London	53 J8
Little Preston	128 B2
Little Thorpe	170 A2
Littletown	144 D6
Liversedge	144 D7
Lockwood	190 E8
Lofthouse	150 A3
Lofthouse Gate	149 K5
Long Lee	3 F4
Longley	164 C5
Longwood	189 K5
Longwood Edge	189 J4
Loscoe	152 E8
Low Ackworth	203 J4
Lower Altofts	151 K5
Lower Clough	211 H3
Lower Cumberworth	236 D4
Lower Denby	237 F7
Lower Grange	94 C4
Lower Hopton	170 B8
Lower Houses	191 K8
Lower Longley	248 B2
Lower Maythorn	250 A4
Lower Mickletown	152 E1
Lower Soothill	146 D5
Lower Town	91 F1
Lower Wyke	142 D3
Low Fold	76 D3
Low Green	54 A8
Low Moor	118 E6
Luddenden	138 B2
Luddenden Foot	137 K5
Lumb Foot	68 B3
Lumb Head	213 J3
The Lumb	213 J3
Lumbutts	134 D7
Lupset	175 F7
Lydgate	133 H4
Mankinholes	135 F7
Manningham	4 A1
Manor Park	21 K8
Manston	104 C1
Marsden	209 G8
Marsh	68 D7
Marsh	190 C5

Meal Hill	234 B8
Meanwood	78 E3
Meltham	211 J8
Meltham Mills	231 K1
Menston	32 B8
Merchant Fields	144 B2
Methley	152 B1
Methley Junction	152 C3
Methley Lanes	151 H4
Mickletown	107 F5
Micklethwaite	49 J4
Middlestown	196 B4
Middleton	20 B4
Middleton	124 E7
Midgehole	112 B5
Midgley	137 K2
Midgley	218 C1
Miles Hill	79 G5
Mill Bank	164 A4
Millhouse Green	251 F8
Mill Shaw	123 K2
Milnsbridge	189 K7
Milnthorpe	198 E4
Minsthorpe	226 B6
Mirfield	170 D5
Mixenden	115 F6
Moldgreen	13 F5
Monkhill	180 E1
Monkswood	81 H4
Moor Allerton	79 K1
Moor End	42 B3
Moor End	114 D7
Moorhead	72 E4
Moor Head	122 B3
Moor Head	216 D5
Moorhouse	243 F2
Moor Side	68 B7
Moor Side	118 E6
Moorside	77 G7
Moorside	121 J6
Moorthorpe	241 K1
Moor Top	170 B3
Moortown	79 J1
Morley	123 G8
Mount	189 G2
Mountain	116 A1
Mount Pleasant	145 K7
Mount Tabor	114 D8
Mytholm	112 A8
Mytholmes	69 F3
Mytholmroyd	137 G1
Nab Hill	192 C2
Nab Wood	72 D3
Netherby	39 F1
Nether End	237 H6
Netherley	229 H1
Netheroyd Hill	168 B8
Netherthong	233 G3
Netherton	196 C5
Netherton	212 D5
Nether Yeadon	53 J6
Nettleton Hill	189 F4
Newall	33 J2
New Brighton	72 C5
New Brighton	122 E7
New Crofton	201 F4
New Farnley	99 J8
New Fryston	130 E8
New Holland	71 G8
New Micklefield	107 H5
New Mill	234 A4
Newmillerdam	198 E7
New Road Side	118 E7
Newsam Green	127 F2
New Scarbro	99 H1
New Sharlston	177 J6
Newsholme	46 C7
Newsome	213 G2
Newstead	223 G1
Newton Hill	149 K8
New Town	154 E7
New Wortley	6 A4
Noblethorpe	253 K4
Noon Nick	72 B7
Norland Town	165 G1
Normanton	177 J1
Norr	71 H6
Norristhorpe	170 E1
North Elmsall	226 D5
North Featherstone	179 J2
Northorpe	171 G4
Northowram	141 G1
Norwood Green	117 K8
Notton	221 H5
Oakenshaw	119 F7
Oakes	190 A3
Oakwell	121 G8
Oakwood	80 E6
Oakworth	68 D2
Odsal	119 F3
Ogden	115 G1
Old Bramhope	35 F8
Old Dolphin	117 F1
Oldfield	67 K3
Oldfield	233 F2
Old Lindley	166 C8
Old Micklefield	106 E3
Old Snydale	178 D4
Old Town	112 C6

Osmondthorpe	102 D4
Ossett	173 J5
Ossett Spa	174 B8
Ossett Street Side	173 G3
Otley	33 K2
Oulton	126 E6
Ousel Hole	49 J1
Outlane	188 E2
Outlane Moor	188 D5
Outwood	149 J7
Ouzlewell Green	150 B2
Ovenden	8 A1
Overthorpe	195 G1
Overton	196 A5
Overtown	199 J6
Owlet	73 J6
Oxenhope	90 E1
Paddock	190 D6
Painthorpe	198 A8
Park Gate	216 E7
Park Head	235 H6
Parklands	81 H7
Park Mill	218 C2
Park Villas	80 C2
Parlington	84 C6
Peas Acre	49 J3
Pecket Well	112 C3
Pellon	139 H3
Pendas Fields	82 D8
Penistone	252 A8
Penny Hill	188 A2
Pepper Hill	117 G5
Pickles Hill	68 B2
Pickwood Scar	165 H2
Pike End	186 D3
Pike Law	187 H4
Piedwick	199 F6
Pole Moor	188 B7
Pontefract	180 D3
Pool	35 G4
Portobello	198 D1
Portsmouth	132 D2
Potternewton	80 A6
Potterton	61 J8
Priest Hill	23 G3
Priesthorpe	75 J7
Priestley Green	141 J2
Priestthorpe	50 A7
Prince Royd	190 C1
Pudsey	98 B4
Pudsey	132 E1
Pule Hill	116 B8
Purston Jaglin	179 K7
Quarmby	190 A5
Queensbury	116 B2
Ramsden Wood	159 K4
Rastrick	168 A3
Ravenscliffe	75 G7
Ravensthorpe	171 H5
Rawdon	54 A8
Rawdon Carrs	76 B1
Rawfolds	144 B6
Raw Green	238 C7
Rawthorpe	13 F3
Red Hill	154 B4
Richmond Hill	102 B3
Riddlesden	48 E2
Ripponden	163 K7
Rishworth	186 D3
Roberttown	170 A2
Robin Hood	125 J8
Rodley	76 C6
Rodmer Clough	110 D4
Rothwell	126 D6
Rothwell Haigh	126 A4
Roundhay	81 F3
Rowley Hill	215 G1
Royd	251 G7
Roydhouse	216 A5
Royd Moor	225 H3
Royd Moor	251 H6
Royds Green	150 D1
Running Hill Head	228 A8
Ryecroft	70 C2
Ryhill	223 F7
St John's	84 E2
Salendine Nook	189 J4
Saltaire	73 G2
Sandal	199 F2
Sandal Magna	199 H2
Sandford	77 J6
Sandhills	60 C8
Sandy Lane	71 K8
Savile Town	172 C6
Sawood	91 H3
Scapegoat Hill	188 E5
Scarcroft	60 A2
Scholemoor	94 E6
Scholes	82 D4
Scholes	143 G3
Scholes	233 K8
Scholey Hill	151 K3
School Green	94 A5
Scissett	237 G2
Scout Dike	252 A5
Seacroft	81 J6
Shackleton	111 K3
Shade	133 K7
Shadwell	59 H7
Shafton	222 E8
Sharlston	201 F1
Sharlston Common	177 K8
Shaw	90 D1
Shaw Cross	173 F1
Shawforth	158 A6
Shay Gate	71 J7
Sheepridge	168 C8
Sheepscar	7 F1
Shelf	117 J5
Shelley	215 J8
Shelley Woodhouse	235 K1
Shepherd Hill	174 A5
Shepley	235 H3
Shibden Head	116 C5
Shipley	73 G4
Shore	133 F1
Sicklinghall	22 A5
Siddal	140 D8
Silkstone	253 K3
Silsden	27 G2
Skelmanthorpe	237 F1
Slack	111 J5
Slack	188 E3
Slaithwaite	210 D3
Slippery Ford	45 J3
Snow Hill	175 H1
Snow Lea	189 H3
Snydale	178 D6
South Crosland	212 B5
South Elmsall	226 D8
South Hiendley	223 G5
South Kirkby	241 J2
South Lane	253 G2
South Ossett	173 K7
Southowram	140 E7
Sowerby	164 A1
Sowerby Bridge	139 F8
Sowood	188 D2
Sowood Green	188 E1
Soyland Town	164 A5
Spofforth	22 B1
Spring Vale	252 D8
Staincliffe	145 K7
Stainland	165 H7
Stanbury	67 J4
Stanks	82 B8
Stanley	150 B7
Stanley Ferry	150 E8
Stanningley	98 C2
Stead	31 G2
Steep Lane	137 K7
Steeton	27 F6
Stockbridge	48 B1
Stone Chair	117 H7
Stoney Royd	9 E6
Storiths	15 K2
Stourton	125 J2
Strawberry Hill	179 K4
Streethouse	178 C6
Stump Cross	9 F2
Sutton	156 C4
Sutton-in-Craven	26 A6
Sutton Mill	26 A6
Swain House	74 B6
Swarcliffe	82 A7
Swartha	27 H1
Swillington	127 K1
Swillington Common	104 D5
Swincliffe	120 D7
Swinnow Moor	99 F3
Sympson Green	74 E2
Tandem	192 D6
Tarn	52 A7
Thackley	74 C2
Thackley End	74 B1
Thick Hollins	231 K2
Thongsbridge	233 J3
Thornbury	97 H3
Thorncliff	216 A4
Thorner	60 D6
Thornes	10 C6
Thornhill	195 K1
Thornhill Edge	195 G3
Thornhill Lees	172 B7
Thornhills	142 D7
Thornton	93 J5
Thorp Arch	42 E3
Thorpe Audlin	204 C6
Thorpe Edge	74 D5
Thorpe on The Hill	148 D1
Thunder Bridge	214 E8
Thurlstone	251 J7
Thurstonland	234 B2
Thwaites	48 D4
Thwaites Brow	48 D5
Tingley	147 K2
Tinshill	55 J8
Tivy Dale	238 D7
Todmorden	134 B7
Toftshaw	119 K3
Tong	121 H2
Tong Park	52 B7
Tong Street	120 A2
Toothill	168 B5
Totties	233 K7
Toulston	43 J6
Town End	189 G7
Town Head	27 H1
Trawden	64 A1
Triangle	164 B2
Trough Gate	158 A3
Troydale	98 E5
Tyersal	97 H6
Under Bank	233 C8
Undercliffe	5 E1
Upper Armley	100 A2
Upper Batley	146 B3
Upper Brockholes	115 F3
Upper Clough	211 G3
Upper Cumberworth	235 J5
Upper Denby	195 H6
Upper Denby	236 C5
Upper Green	147 K4
Upper Heaton	169 H8
Upper Hopton	193 G1
Upper Marsh	68 C7
Upper Maythorn	250 A3
Upper Moor Side	122 D5
Upperthong	233 G4
Upper Town	90 D1
Upton	226 E4
Upwood	29 G7
Utley	47 K1
Vale	133 F2
Victoria	249 J4
Wainstalls	114 B6
Wakefield	10 C4
Walsden	159 K2
Walshaw	88 C8
Walton	25 G7
Walton	199 K5
Warland	160 C6
Warley Town	138 E5
Warmfield	177 H5
Washpit	248 B1
Water Fryston	155 G1
Wayside Gardens	60 A2
Weardley	37 H5
Weeton	37 F1
Weetwood	78 C3
Well Heads	92 E4
Wellhouse	189 H8
Wellington Hill	81 G2
Wellroyd	76 B2
Wentbridge	204 E4
Wescoe Hill	36 C1
Wessenden	229 K5
West Ardsley	147 J5
West Bowling	96 B8
West Bretton	219 F3
West Carlton	33 K8
West End	76 C1
West End	143 J4
Westfield	53 G6
Westfield	145 G6
West Garforth	105 H6
Westgate Hill	120 D3
West Hardwick	202 B2
West Morton	48 E1
West Park	78 B3
West Royd	73 K5
West Scholes	93 H8
West Vale	166 C5
Wetherby	23 K6
Wheatley	139 G1
Wheldale	154 C2
Whinmoor	82 A3
Whins Wood	69 J2
Whitecote	77 G6
White Hill	45 K6
White Lee	145 H4
Whitkirk	104 A4
Whitley Head	26 E7
Whitley Lower	194 C3
Whitwood	152 D5
Wibsey	118 C2
Wike	59 F2
Wilberlee	210 B1
Wilsden	71 F6
Wilshaw	232 A3
Windhill	73 K4
Windmill Hill	200 E3
Wintersett	200 E7
Womersley	183 K8
Woodhall Hills	75 J8
Woodhouse	3 E5
Woodhouse	79 H6
Woodhouse	168 D3
Woodhouse	217 H4
Woodkirk	147 H4
Woodlands	9 C2
Woodlesford	127 F5
Wood Row	128 A8
Woodside	118 B9
Woolgreaves	199 F5
Woolley	220 C5
Wortley	100 A5
Wragby	202 A4
Wrangbrook	227 H4
Wrenthorpe	175 G2
Wrose	74 A5
Wyke	142 D7
Yeadon	53 K6

‍SING THE STREET INDEX

‍eet names are listed alphabetically. Each street name is followed by its postal town or area locality,
‍e Postcode District, the page number, and the reference to the square in which the name is found.

‍andard index entries are shown as follows:
‍ron Wilkinson Ct *HEM/SK/SE* WF9 ......**241** G1

‍eet names and selected addresses not shown on the map due to scale restrictions are shown in the
‍dex with an asterisk:
‍ootside CI *IDLE* * BD10 ....**74** E5

‍ENERAL ABBREVIATIONS

......ACCESS	GA......GATE	PL......PLACE
......ALLEY	GAL......GALLERY	PLN......PLAIN
......APPROACH	GDN......GARDEN	PLNS......PLAINS
......ARCADE	GDNS......GARDENS	PLZ......PLAZA
......ASSOCIATION	GLD......GLADE	POL......POLICE STATION
......AVENUE	GLN......GLEN	PR......PRINCE
......BEACH	GN......GREEN	PREC......PRECINCT
S......BUILDINGS	GND......GROUND	PREP......PREPARATORY
......BEND	GRA......GRANGE	PRIM......PRIMARY
......BANK	GRG......GARAGE	PROM......PROMENADE
......BRIDGE	GT......GREAT	PRS......PRINCESS
......BROOK	GTWY......GATEWAY	PRT......PORT
......BOTTOM	GV......GROVE	PT......POINT
......BUSINESS	HGR......HIGHER	PTH......PATH
......BOULEVARD	HL......HILL	PZ......PIAZZA
......BYPASS	HLS......HILLS	QD......QUADRANT
H......CATHEDRAL	HO......HOUSE	QU......QUEEN
......CEMETERY	HOL......HOLLOW	QY......QUAY
......CENTRE	HOSP......HOSPITAL	R......RIVER
......CROFT	HRB......HARBOUR	RBT......ROUNDABOUT
......CHURCH	HTH......HEATH	RD......ROAD
......CHASE	HTS......HEIGHTS	RDG......RIDGE
D......CHURCHYARD	HVN......HAVEN	REP......REPUBLIC
......CIRCLE	HWY......HIGHWAY	RES......RESERVOIR
......CIRCUS	IMP......IMPERIAL	RFC......RUGBY FOOTBALL CLUB
......CLOSE	IN......INLET	RI......RISE
S......CLIFFS	IND EST......INDUSTRIAL ESTATE	RP......RAMP
......CAMP	INF......INFIRMARY	RW......ROW
R......CORNER	INFO......INFORMATION	S......SOUTH
......COUNTY	INT......INTERCHANGE	SCH......SCHOOL
......COLLEGE	IS......ISLAND	SE......SOUTH EAST
......COMMON	JCT......JUNCTION	SER......SERVICE AREA
M......COMMISSION	JTY......JETTY	SH......SHORE
......CONVENT	KG......KING	SHOP......SHOPPING
......COTTAGE	KNL......KNOLL	SKWY......SKYWAY
S......COTTAGES	L......LAKE	SMT......SUMMIT
......CAPE	LA......LANE	SOC......SOCIETY
......COPSE	LDG......LODGE	SP......SPUR
......CREEK	LGT......LIGHT	SPR......SPRING
M......CREMATORIUM	LK......LOCK	SQ......SQUARE
......CRESCENT	LKS......LAKES	ST......STREET
VY......CAUSEWAY	LNDG......LANDING	STN......STATION
......COURT	LTL......LITTLE	STR......STREAM
L......CENTRAL	LWR......LOWER	STRD......STRAND
......COURTS	MAG......MAGISTRATE	SW......SOUTH WEST
D......COURTYARD	MAN......MANSIONS	TDG......TRADING
T......CUTTINGS	MD......MEAD	TER......TERRACE
......COVE	MDW......MEADOWS	THWY......THROUGHWAY
......CANYON	MEM......MEMORIAL	TNL......TUNNEL
T......DEPARTMENT	MKT......MARKET	TOLL......TOLLWAY
......DALE	MKTS......MARKETS	TPK......TURNPIKE
......DAM	ML......MALL	TR......TRACK
......DRIVE	MIL......MILL	TRL......TRAIL
......DROVE	MNR......MANOR	TWR......TOWER
......DRIVEWAY	MS......MEWS	U/P......UNDERPASS
GS......DWELLINGS	MSN......MISSION	UNI......UNIVERSITY
......EAST	MT......MOUNT	UPR......UPPER
......EMBANKMENT	MTN......MOUNTAIN	V......VALE
BY......EMBASSY	MTS......MOUNTAINS	VA......VALLEY
......ESPLANADE	MUS......MUSEUM	VIAD......VIADUCT
......ESTATE	MWY......MOTORWAY	VIL......VILLA
......EXCHANGE	N......NORTH	VIS......VISTA
Y......EXPRESSWAY	NE......NORTH EAST	VLG......VILLAGE
......EXTENSION	NW......NORTH WEST	VLS......VILLAS
......FLYOVER	O/P......OVERPASS	VW......VIEW
......FOOTBALL CLUB	OFF......OFFICE	W......WEST
......FORK	ORCH......ORCHARD	WD......WOOD
......FIELD	OV......OVAL	WHF......WHARF
S......FIELDS	PAL......PALACE	WK......WALK
......FALLS	PAS......PASSAGE	WKS......WALKS
......FLATS	PAV......PAVILION	WLS......WELLS
......FARM	PDE......PARADE	WY......WAY
......FORT	PH......PUBLIC HOUSE	YD......YARD
......FREEWAY	PK......PARK	YHA......YOUTH HOSTEL
......FERRY	PKWY......PARKWAY	

POSTCODE TOWNS AND AREA ABBREVIATIONS

Index - streets

el V BHP/TINH LS16 ....56 D7
el Wood Dr BHP/TINH LS16 ....56 D8
el Wood Gv BHP/TINH LS16 ....56 D8
el Wood Pl BHP/TINH LS16 ....56 D8
el Wood Rd BHP/TINH LS16 ....56 D8
gil Crs HIPP HX3 ....141 F7
ministration Rd DSM LS9 ....102 E8
niral St BEE/HOL LS11 ....101 J7
olphus St BFD * BD1 ....5 D5
owsley Cl FEA/AMT WF7 ....202 E5
walton Cl BIRK/DRI BD11 ....121 G6
walton Gn BIRK/DRI BD11 ....121 G6
walton Gv CUL/QBY BD13 ....116 E2
wick Gv WKFDW/WTN WF2 ....198 D6
wick Pl BULY LS4 ....100 C1
ar St GIR BD8 ....95 F3
ar Ter GIR BD8 ....95 F3
rigg Gv WKFDW/WTN WF2 ....199 G1
ncourt Dr NORM WF6 ....151 H7
nes Rd DOD/DAR S75 ....239 K3
aes St KGHY BD21 ....3 D1
La LUD/ILL HX2 ....138 A2
abry Ct HUDE HD5 ....214 D1
ley Bottom ELL HX5 ....166 E6
ley Cl HUDW HD3 ....190 A1
ley Pk MAR/SLWT HD7 ....189 J7
ley Rd HUDW HD3 ....167 F8
ley St ELL HX5 ....166 E5
sbury Av IDLE BD10 ....52 D8
sdale Gv CUL/QBY BD13 ....70 C5
sdale Rd BSLYN/ROY S71 ....221 K6
sley La MAR/SLWT HD7 ....209 F7
sty Crs WBY LS22 ....23 J4
sty Dr WBY LS22 ....23 J4
sty Garth WBY LS22 ....23 J4
sty Rd WBY LS22 ....23 H4
sty Vw WBY LS22 ....23 J4
tree Cl GFTH/SHER LS25 ....128 E1
ebank BGLY BD16 ....49 K8
e Cl BAIL BD17 ....73 H2
edale Av BGLY BD16 ....72 A5
edale College Mt BFDE BD3 ....5 E2
edale College Rd BFDE BD3 ....5 E2
edale College Ter BFDE BD3 ....5 E2
edale Ct SCFT LS14 ....81 H6
edale Crs BFDE BD3 ....5 E2
edale Cft BRAM LS13 ....76 D7
edale Dr CAS WF10 ....154 D1
FTH/SHER LS25 ....106 B5
HIPP HX3 ....117 G6
HORS LS18 ....18 D3
edale Gdns BRAM LS13 ....76 D7
edale Gv HORS LS18 ....18 D3
edale Hts WKFDW/WTN WF2 ....174 D7
edale Ms AIRE BD20 ....27 G2
edale Mt AIRE BD20 ....49 G3
edale Pl BAIL BD17 ....74 A1
edale Quay BRAM LS13 ....76 D7
edale Rd BFDE BD3 ....5 E2
AS WF10 ....154 C4
OD/DAR S75 ....239 J3
GHY BD21 ....48 D3
THW LS26 ....127 G5
edale St BGLY BD16 ....49 K8
CHL BD2 ....74 D8
GHY BD21 ....3 F2
edale Ter MOR LS27 ....123 G7
THW * LS26 ....127 G5
edale Vw RTHW * LS26 ....127 G5
edale Whf BRAM LS13 ....76 D6
AS WF10 ....153 J3
EWS WF13 ....171 J6
WTH BD22 ....69 F4
LE BD10 ....74 C2
GHY BD21 ....3 E2
NOT BD9 ....156 D6
DS LS1 ....7 D4
e Ter CAS WF10 ....153 J3
evalley Rd KGHY BD21 ....3 F2
e Vw AIRE BD20 ....27 F2
RE BD20 ....48 D1
EA LS19 ....54 A5
e View Av BGLY BD16 ....72 B3
HPY BD18 ....73 G3
eview Crs BAIL BD17 ....73 H2
e View Dr AIRE BD20 ....49 G4
e View Ter KGHY BD21 ....3 F4
HPY BD18 ....73 H6
eville Crs AIRE BD20 ....47 J1
HPY BD18 ....73 H6
eville Dr AIRE BD20 ....27 H2
TON BD9 ....73 H6
eville Gra SHPY BD18 ....73 H6
eville Gv HTON BD9 ....73 H6
eville Mt AIRE BD20 ....49 G4
eville Mouny AIRE BD20 ....27 H2
eville Rd HTON BD9 ....73 H7
ville Rd HTON BD9 ....73 H6
ville St AIRE BD20 ....47 J1

Aireville Ter ILK LS29 ....32 A2
Aire Wy BAIL BD17 ....73 G2
Aireworth Cl KGHY BD21 ....3 F2
Aireworth Gv KGHY BD21 ....3 F2
Aireworth Rd KGHY BD21 ....3 F1
Aireworth St KGHY BD21 ....2 C4
Airey St KGHY BD21 ....2 B5
Airlie Av RHAY LS8 ....80 B7
Airlie Pl RHAY LS8 ....80 B7
Akam Rd BFD BD1 ....4 B4
Aked's Rd HFAX HX1 ....8 C5
Aked St BFD BD1 ....5 D4
Aketon Dr CAS WF10 ....153 H5
Aketon Rd CAS WF10 ....153 H5
Akroyd Ct HIPP HX3 ....9 D3
Akroyd La MAR HX7 ....9 D2
Akroyd Pl HFAX HX1 ....9 D3
Akroyd Ter LUD/ILL HX2 ....8 A6
Alabama St HFAX * HX1 ....8 A4
Alan Crs MSTN/BAR LS15 ....103 J4
Alandale Crs GFTH/SHER LS25 ....105 H5
Alandale Dr GFTH/SHER LS25 ....105 H5
Alandale Gv GFTH/SHER LS25 ....105 H4
HUDN HD2 ....169 F6
Alan Rd DOD/DAR S75 ....239 K3
Alaska Pl CHAL LS7 ....80 A5
Albans Rd AL/HA/HU LS17 ....40 C5
Alban St BOW BD4 ....96 D7
Albert Av KGHY BD21 ....3 F2
PONT WF8 ....180 E4
Albany Crs HEM/SK/SE WF9 ....242 B1
Albany Dr HUDE HD5 ....192 C5
Albany Rd HUDE HD5 ....192 C5
RTHW LS26 ....126 A5
Albany Rw ILK * LS29 ....32 B7
HIPP HX3 ....9 E6
HUD HD1 ....12 B6
WBOW * BD5 ....96 A7
WBSY BD6 ....118 D2
Albany Ter HIPP HX3 ....9 G6
WOR/ARM * LS12 ....100 A4
Alberta Av CHAL LS7 ....80 A5
Albert Av IDLE BD10 ....74 E3
LUD/ILL HX2 ....139 H3
SHPY BD18 ....72 E2
Albert Cl BTLY WF17 ....172 B1
Albert Crs BIRK/DRI BD11 ....120 E7
CUL/QBY BD13 ....116 D2
Albert Dr HORS LS18 ....18 D2
MOR LS27 ....123 J6
Albert Gdns LUD/ILL HX2 ....139 H3
Albert Gv HDGY LS6 ....78 D5
Albert Pl BFDE BD3 ....97 C3
HORS LS18 ....77 G2
Albert Prom HIPP HX3 ....139 K7
Albert Rd CUL/QBY BD13 ....116 C1
KBTN HD8 ....217 J8
LUD/ILL HX2 ....139 H3
MOR LS27 ....123 G6
RPDN/SBR HX6 ....139 F6
RTHW LS26 ....127 F5
SHPY BD18 ....73 F3
Albert Sq AIRE BD20 ....27 G2
Albert St BAIL BD17 ....73 J2
BRIG HD6 ....142 D8
CAS WF10 ....153 H5
CLECK * BD19 ....144 A3
CUL/QBY BD13 ....93 H5
CUL/QBY BD13 ....116 E2
ELL HX5 ....166 E5
FEA/AMT WF7 ....179 H6
HBR * HX7 ....112 B8
HBR HX7 ....137 F2
HFAX HX1 ....8 C4
HUD HD1 ....191 F8
HWTH BD22 ....69 F4
IDLE BD10 ....74 D5
KGHY BD21 ....2 C3
LM/WK BD12 ....142 D1
LVSG WF15 ....145 F8
NORM WF6 ....152 B7
PDSY/CALV LS28 ....98 B5
WBSY BD6 ....118 C3
WIL/AL BD15 ....71 H7
Albert Ter LM/WK BD12 ....119 C6
SHPY BD18 ....73 F2
Albert Vw LUD/ILL HX2 ....139 H3
Albert Wk SHPY BD18 ....72 E2
Albert Wy BIRK/DRI BD11 ....120 E7
Albert Yd HUD HD1 ....12 C5
Albion Ar LDS LS1 ....7 D3
Albion Av WOR/ARM LS12 ....100 A4
Albion Cl BSPA/BRAM LS23 ....42 D6
Albion Ct HFAX * HX1 ....9 D4
WKFDE WF1 ....10 C3
Albion Cft OSS WF5 ....173 K5
Albion Fold WIL/AL BD15 ....71 G6
Albion Pl HEM/SK/SE WF9 ....226 C8
LDS LS1 ....7 E3
Albion Rd EARL WF12 ....195 H2
IDLE BD10 ....74 E3
PDSY/CALV LS28 ....98 C1
Albion St BFD BD1 ....4 C4
BRIG HD6 ....142 B8
BSPA/BRAM LS23 ....42 D6

BTLY WF17 ....146 C7
CAS WF10 ....153 H3
CLECK BD19 ....144 B4
CUL/QBY BD13 ....92 C3
CUL/QBY BD13 ....116 C2
DEWS * WF13 ....171 J6
DEWS WF13 ....172 D2
EARD/LOFT WF3 ....126 A8
ELL HX5 ....167 F5
HECK WF16 ....145 F7
HEM/SK/SE WF9 ....201 K8
HFAX HX1 ....9 D4
HUD HD1 ....12 C5
HWTH BD22 ....69 G3
LDS LS1 ....7 E3
LVSG WF15 ....144 D7
MOR * LS27 ....123 F7
OT LS21 ....33 K4
PDSY/CALV LS28 ....98 D4
WBSY BD6 ....117 K4
WKFDE WF1 ....10 C2
Albion Ter BSPA/BRAM LS23 ....42 D5
Albion Wy WOR/ARM LS12 ....6 A3
Alcester Garth BFDE BD3 ....5 F3
Alcester Pl RHAY * LS8 ....80 B7
Alcester Rd RHAY LS8 ....80 B7
Alcester St RHAY * LS8 ....80 B7
Alcester Ter RHAY LS8 ....80 B7
Aldams Rd EARL WF12 ....172 B4
Alden Av MOR LS27 ....147 F5
Alden Cl MOR LS27 ....147 F1
Alden Ct MOR LS27 ....147 F1
Alden Crs PONT WF8 ....180 C4
Alden Fold MOR * LS27 ....147 F1
Alder Av HOLM/MEL HD9 ....233 J3
KGHY BD21 ....3 E5
WKFDW/WTN WF2 ....10 A1
Alder Carr BAIL BD17 ....51 H8
Alder Dr PDSY/CALV LS28 ....97 J3
Alder Garth PDSY/CALV LS28 ....97 K3
Alder Gv LUD/ILL HX2 ....115 H5
NORM WF6 ....178 A4
Alder Hill Av CHAL LS7 ....79 G4
Alder Hill Gv CHAL LS7 ....79 G4
Alder Holt Dr WBSY BD6 ....118 B5
Aldermanbury BFD BD1 ....4 C5
Alderney Rd EARL WF12 ....172 E1
Alderscholes Cl CUL/QBY BD13 ....93 H5
Alderscholes La CUL/QBY BD13 ....93 G6
Alderson St WBSY BD6 ....117 K4
Alder St HUDN HD2 ....190 A1
Alderstone Ri HUDW HD3 ....190 A1
Alderston Rd HUD HD2 ....13 D2
Aldersyde BTLY WF17 ....145 H2
Alderton Bank AL/HA/HU LS17 ....79 F1
Alderton Crs AL/HA/HU LS17 ....79 F1
Alderton Mt AL/HA/HU LS17 ....79 F1
Alderton Pl AL/HA/HU LS17 ....79 F1
Alderton Ri AL/HA/HU LS17 ....79 F1
Aldonley HUDE HD5 ....192 C7
Alegar St BRIG HD6 ....168 D1
Alexander Av MSTN/BAR LS15 ....103 H4
Alexander Crs FEA/AMT WF7 ....179 J4
Alexander Rd FEA/AMT WF7 ....179 J5
Alexander Sq CLAY BD14 ....94 B7
Alexander St LDS LS1 ....7 D3
WBSY BD6 ....118 C3
Alexandra Cl RPDN/SBR HX6 ....139 F7
ILK LS29 ....20 A7
Alexandra Dr NORM WF6 ....178 A4
Alexandra Gv HDGY LS6 ....6 A1
PDSY/CALV LS28 ....98 A4
Alexandra Rd BTLY WF17 ....146 C7
ECHL BD2 ....74 E6
HBR * HX7 ....112 B8
HDGY * LS6 ....6 A1
HORS LS18 ....77 G2
HUDW HD3 ....190 C3
PDSY/CALV LS28 ....98 A3
SHPY * BD18 ....73 G4
Alexandra St CUL/QBY * BD13 ....116 D2
GTHN BD7 ....4 A6
HFAX HX1 ....9 D5
LVSG WF15 ....144 D7
Alexandra Ter ECHL BD2 ....96 E1
YEA LS19 ....54 A4
Alford Ter GTHN BD7 ....95 G4
Alfred St East HFAX * HX1 ....9 E4
Alfred St BRIG HD6 ....142 C8
BSLYN/ROY S71 ....222 C1
BTLY WF17 ....146 A7
EARL * WF12 ....172 D2
GTL/HWG HX4 ....166 C4
HECK * WF16 ....145 G8
HFAX HX1 ....8 A4
HUD HD1 ....12 C5
LVSG WF15 ....144 E7
MOR * LS27 ....123 H3
Alfreds Wy BTLY WF17 ....146 B6
Alice St CLECK BD19 ....144 A3
GIR BD8 ....4 B3
HWTH BD22 ....68 C5
KGHY BD21 ....3 D3
Alkincote St KGHY BD21 ....2 C4
All Alone Rd IDLE BD10 ....74 B4
Allanbridge Cl IDLE BD10 ....74 E4
Allandale Av WBSY BD6 ....118 B4
Allandale Rd WBSY BD6 ....118 B4
Allan Haigh Cl WKFDW/WTN WF2 ....174 E3

Allan St *BFDE* BD3 ....5 F5
Allan Ter *RPDN/SBR* HX6 ....139 F8
Allenby Cl *BEE/HOL* LS11 ....124 E5
Allenby Dr *BEE/HOL* LS11 ....124 E5
Allenby Gdns *BEE/HOL* LS11 ....124 E5
Allenby Gv *BEE/HOL* LS11 ....124 E5
Allenby Pl *BEE/HOL* LS11 ....124 E5
Allenby Rd *BEE/HOL* LS11 ....124 E5
Allenby Vw *BEE/HOL* LS11 ....124 E5
Allen Cft *BIRK/DRI* BD11 ....120 D6
Allendale Rd *DOD/DAR* S75 ....159 K5
Allen Rw *HUD* HD1 ....12 A5
Allerby Gn *WBSY* BD6 ....118 A5
Allergill Pk *HOLM/MEL* HD9 ....232 D6
Allerton Cl *WIL/AL* BD15 ....94 B2
Allerton Dr *AL/HA/HU* LS17 ....40 A5
Allerton Grange Av *AL/HA/HU* LS17 ...80 A2
Allerton Grange Cl *AL/HA/HU* LS17 ...79 J3
Allerton Grange Crs *AL/HA/HU* LS17 ...79 K3
Allerton Grange Cft *RHAY* LS8 ......80 A3
Allerton Grange Dr *AL/HA/HU* LS17 ...79 K3
WIL/AL BD15 ....94 B2
Allerton Grange Gdns
AL/HA/HU LS17 ....79 K3
Allerton Grange Ri *AL/HA/HU* LS17 ...79 K3
Allerton Grange V *AL/HA/HU* LS17 ...79 K3
Allerton Grange Wk *AL/HA/HU* LS17 ...79 K3
Allerton Grange Wy *RHAY* LS8 ......79 K3
Allerton Gv *AL/HA/HU* LS17 ....79 K1
Allerton Hl *CHAL* LS7 ....79 J4
Allerton La *WIL/AL* BD15 ....94 A4
Allerton Pk *CHAL* LS7 ....79 K4
Allerton Pl *AL/HA/HU* LS17 ....79 K1
HFAX HX1 ....8 B4
Allerton Rd *WIL/AL* BD15 ....93 H2
Allerton St *BULY* LS4 ....100 D3
Allescholes Rd *TOD* OL14 ....159 K4
Alliance St *WOR/ARM* LS12 ....100 A4
Allinson St *WOR/ARM* LS12 ....6 A5
Allison Dr *HUDN* HD2 ....168 B8
Allison La *ECHL* BD2 ....73 K7
Allison St *FEA/AMT* WF7 ....179 H6
Alloe Field Vw *LUD/ILL* HX2 ....115 H5
Allott Cl *HEM/SK/SE* WF9 ....226 B8
All Saint's Cir *RTHW* LS26 ....127 G4
All Saints Ct *KBTN* HD8 ....237 K1
All Saints Cl *KGHY* BD21 ....2 C3
All Saint's Dr *RTHW* LS26 ....127 G4
All Saints Rd *GTHN* BD7 ....4 A6
RTHW LS26 ....127 G4
All Saints Ter *KGHY* BD21 ....2 C3
All Saint's Vw *RTHW* LS26 ....127 G4
All Souls' Rd *HIPP* HX3 ....9 D2
All Souls' St *HIPP* HX3 ....9 D2
All Souls' Ter *HIPP* HX3 ....9 D2
Allums La *OT* LS21 ....36 C7
Alma Cl *PDSY/CALV* LS28 ....76 A8
Alma Cottages *HDGY* LS6 ....78 D6
Alma Dr *HUDE* HD5 ....13 F4
Alma Gv *OSM* LS9 ....102 A1
Alma La *HECK* WF16 ....145 G5
RPDN/SBR HX6 ....163 J4
Alma Pl *BFDE* BD3 ....97 F3
KGHY BD21 ....3 D5
OSM LS9 ....102 A2
Alma Rd *HDGY* LS6 ....78 D6
TOD OL14 ....134 B6
Alma St *BOW* BD4 ....96 E6
CUL/QBY BD13 ....116 C2
HWTH BD22 ....68 C3
KGHY BD21 ....3 D6
RTHW LS26 ....127 G4
SHPY BD18 ....73 J5
TOD OL14 ....159 K2
YEA LS19 ....54 A4
Alma Ter *KGHY* BD21 ....3 D6
RTHW LS26 ....126 A5
Almondbury Bank *HUDE* HD5 ....13 F5
Almondbury Cl *HUDE* HD5 ....192 C8
Almondbury Common *HUDA* HD4 ...214 B2
Almond Cl *HEM/SK/SE* WF9 ....226 C6
Almondroyd *HECK* WF16 ....145 F6
Almond St *BFDE* BD3 ....96 E5
Almond Wy *BTLY* WF17 ....145 J2
Almscliffe Av *EARL* WF12 ....172 C5
Almshouse Hl *BSPA/BRAM* LS23 .....62 D1
Almshouse La *WKFDE* WF1 ....10 C3
WKFDW/WTN WF2 ....198 D8
Alpha St *KGHY* BD21 ....3 E5
Alpine Cl *BTLY* WF17 ....146 A7
Alpine Ri *CUL/QBY* BD13 ....93 H4
Alston Cl *HTON* BD9 ....94 D1
Alston La *SCFT* LS14 ....81 J8
Alston Rd *KGHY* BD21 ....3 E1
Altar Dr *AIRE* BD20 ....48 E2
HTON BD9 ....73 G8
Altar La *BGLY* BD16 ....48 E7
Althorpe St *IDLE* BD10 ....74 C5
Altinkool St *WBOW* BD5 ....99 G1
Altofts Hall Rd *NORM* WF6 ....151 J7
Altofts La *CAS* WF10 ....152 C5
Altofts Lodge Dr *NORM* WF6 ....151 H8
Altofts Rd *NORM* WF6 ....151 K8
Alton Av *HUDE* HD5 ....192 B4
Alton Gv *HTON* BD9 ....73 F8
SHPY BD18 ....73 H6
Alum Ct *HTON* BD9 ....73 G8
Alum Dr *HTON* BD9 ....73 G8
Alvanley Ct *GIR* BD8 ....94 D3

Alverthorpe Rd *WKFDW/WTN* WF2 ...175 G5
Alwen Av *HUDN* HD2 ....191 F1
Alwoodley Cha *AL/HA/HU* LS17 .....58 A6
Alwoodley Court Gdns
AL/HA/HU LS17 ....57 G5
Alwoodley Gdns *AL/HA/HU* LS17 ...57 G6
Alwoodley La *AL/HA/HU* LS17 ......57 F5
Amberley Ct *BFDE* * BD3 ....96 E4
Amberley Gdns *WOR/ARM* LS12 ...100 C5
Amberley Rd *WOR/ARM* LS12 ....100 C5
Amberley St *BFDE* BD3 ....96 E5
WOR/ARM LS12 ....100 C5
Amber St *BTLY* WF17 ....145 K5
Amberton Ap *RHAY* LS8 ....80 E7
Amberton Crs *RHAY* LS8 ....80 E7
Amberton Dr *RHAY* LS8 ....80 E7
Amberton Garth *RHAY* LS8 ....80 E7
Amberton Gv *RHAY* LS8 ....80 E7
Amberton La *RHAY* LS8 ....80 E7
Amberton Mt *RHAY* LS8 ....80 E7
Amberton Pl *RHAY* LS8 ....80 D7
Amberton Rd *RHAY* LS8 ....80 D7
Amberton St *RHAY* LS8 ....80 E7
Amberton Ter *RHAY* LS8 ....80 E7
Ambler Gv *LUD/ILL* HX2 ....115 J3
Amblers Ct *PDSY/CALV* LS28 ....98 C5
Amblers Cft *IDLE* BD10 ....74 D1
Ambler St *HIPP* HX3 ....9 D2
KGHY BD21 ....4 A1
Ambler Wy *CUL/QBY* BD13 ....116 B4
Ambleside Av *HTON* BD9 ....94 A4
Ambleside Dr *WKFDE* WF1 ....150 A6
Ambleside Gdns *PDSY/CALV* LS28 ...98 A4
Ambleside Gv *RTHW* LS26 ....127 F5
Ambleside Rd *CAS* WF10 ....155 F2
Ambleside Wk *WBY* LS22 ....23 H5
Ambleside Wy *CUL/QBY* BD13 .....116 B3
Amelia St *SHPY* BD18 ....73 F3
HIPP HX3 ....8 B1
Anaheim Dr *WKFDE* WF1 ....150 A6
Ancaster Crs *BHP/TINH* LS16 ....78 B4
Ancaster Rd *BHP/TINH* LS16 ....78 B4
Ancaster Vw *BHP/TINH* LS16 ....78 B4
The Anchorage *BGLY* BD16 ....49 K7
Anchor Bridge Wy *EARL* WF12 ....172 B4
Anchor St *HUD* HD1 ....13 D3
TOD OL14 ....134 B6
Andersen Ct *CAS* WF10 ....154 D5
Anderson Av *RHAY* LS8 ....102 A1
Anderson Mt *RHAY* LS8 ....102 A1
Anderson St *GIR* * BD8 ....4 A2
PONT WF8 ....180 D2
WKFDW/WTN WF2 ....10 A3
Anderton St *WKFDE* * WF1 ....150 C2
Andover Gn *BOW* BD4 ....97 G7
Andrew Cl *HIPP* HX3 ....141 F7
Andrew Crs *HUDS* HD4 ....212 A2
WKFDE WF1 ....149 J6
Andrews Gv *FEA/AMT* WF7 ....203 F5
Andrew St *FEA/AMT* WF7 ....179 H7
PDSY/CALV LS28 ....76 B8
WKFDE WF1 ....10 B2
Angel Ct *BVRD* LS3 ....6 B2
Angel Pl *BGLY* BD16 ....50 A6
Angel Rd *HFAX* HX1 ....8 C3
Angel St *BAIL* BD17 ....51 K7
Angel Wy *BFD* BD7 ....4 B4
Angerton Wy *WBSY* BD6 ....118 B5
Angus Av *LM/WK* BD12 ....142 D2
Aniaby St *BOW* BD4 ....97 F6
Annat Royd La *STKB/PEN* S36 ......251 F4
Anne Crs *CUD/GR* S72 ....223 J6
Anne Ga *BFDE* * BD3 ....5 D4
Annes St *HIPP* HX3 ....141 F7
Anne St *BTLY* WF17 ....145 K4
GTHN BD7 ....4 B7
Annie St *HEM/SK/SE* WF9 ....202 A7
KGHY BD21 ....3 D1
MOR LS27 ....123 G7
RPDN/SBR HX6 ....138 E6
SHPY BD18 ....73 J5
WKFDE WF1 ....149 J7
Anning Fold *CFTH/SHER* LS25 .....106 B3
Annison St *BFDE* BD3 ....5 E4
Annottes Cft *HUDE* HD5 ....192 B4
Ann Pl *WBOW* BD5 ....4 C6
Ann St *CUL/QBY* BD13 ....92 B2
KGHY BD21 ....2 C4
Anroyd St *DEWS* WF13 ....171 K2
Anson Gv *GTHN* BD7 ....118 A1
Anston Dr *HEM/SK/SE* WF9 ....226 C6
Anthony La *BGLY* BD16 ....71 F7
Antony Cl *HUDW* HD3 ....189 H2
Anvil Ct *GIR* BD8 ....95 H2
Anvil St *BRIG* HD6 ....142 B8
GIR BD8 ....95 H2

Apex Vw *BEE/HOL* LS11 ....7 ...
Apex Wy *BEE/HOL* LS11 ....7 ...
Apperley Gdns *IDLE* BD10 ....75 ...
YEA LS19 ....53 ...
Apperley Rd *IDLE* BD10 ....74 ...
Appleby Cl *CUL/QBY* BD13 ....116 ...
Appleby La *CFTH/SHER* LS25 ....103 ...
Appleby Pl *MSTN/BAR* LS15 ....103 ...
Appleby Wk *MSTN/BAR* LS15 ....103 ...
Appleby Wy *MOR* LS27 ....123 ...
WBY LS22 ....23 ...
Apple Cl *BTLY* WF17 ....145 ...
Applegarth *RTHW* LS26 ....127 ...
WKFDW/WTN WF2 ....199 ...
Applehaigh Gv *BSLYN/ROY* S71 ...221 ...
Applehaigh La *HOR/CROF* WF4 .....221 ...
Applehaigh Vw *BSLYN/ROY* S71 ...221 ...
Appleshaw Crs *WKFDW/WTN* WF2 ...148 ...
Apple St *HWTH* BD22 ....47 ...
HWTH * BD22 ....47 ...
Appleton Cl *BGLY* BD16 ....50 ...
LM/WK BD12 ....119 ...
Appleton Gv *OSM* LS9 ....102 ...
Appleton Wy *OSM* LS9 ....102 ...
Appletree Cl *BSPA/BRAM* LS23 ......42 ...
Apple Tree Cl *EARD/LOFT* WF3 .....146 ...
PONT WF8 ....180 ...
Apple Tree Ct *EARD/LOFT* * WF3 ...148 ...
Apple Tree Gdns *ILK* LS29 ....19 ...
Apple Tree Rd *FEA/AMT* WF7 ....19 ...
Appleyard Rd *HBR* HX7 ....137 ...
The Approach *MSTN/BAR* LS15 ....83 ...
April Ct *LVSG* WF15 ....17 ...
Apsley Crs *GIR* BD8 ....4 ...
Apsley St *HWTH* BD22 ....47 ...
KGHY BD21 ....
Apsley Vls *GIR* BD8 ....
Aquamarine Dr *HUDN* HD2 ....19 ...
Aquila Wy *LVSG* WF15 ....144 ...
Arborary La *HOLM/MEL* HD9 ....211 ...
The Arbour *ILK* LS29 ....20 ...
Arcadia St *KGHY* BD21 ....
Archbell Av *BRIG* HD6 ....168 ...
Archer Rd *BRIG* HD6 ....168 ...
Archer St *CAS* WF10 ....153 ...
Archery Pl *LDSU* LS2 ....
Archery Rd *LDSU* LS2 ....
Archery St *LDSU* LS2 ....
Archery Ter *LDSU* LS2 ....
The Arches *HIPP* * HX3 ....
Arches St *HFAX* HX1 ....
Archibald St *GTHN* BD7 ....
Arctic Pde *GTHN* BD7 ....9 ...
Arctic St *HWTH* BD22 ....69 ...
KGHY BD21 ....
Arden Ct *HOR/CROF* WF4 ....197 ...
HUDE HD5 ....192 ...
Ardennes Cl *ECHL* BD2 ....74 ...
Arden Rd *GIR* BD8 ....94 ...
HFAX HX1 ....
Ardsley Cl *BOW* BD4 ....120 ...
Argent Wy *BOW* BD4 ....120 ...
Argie Av *BULY* LS4 ....78 ...
Argie Gdns *BULY* LS4 ....100 ...
Argie Rd *BULY* LS4 ....100 ...
Argyle Ms *AL/HA/HU* LS17 ....40 ...
Argyle Rd *KNOT* WF11 ....155 ...
OSM LS9 ....
Argyle St *BOW* BD4 ....96 ...
KGHY BD21 ....
MAR/SLWT HD7 ....205 ...
SHPY BD18 ....73 ...
WKFDE WF1 ....
Argyll Av *PONT* WF8 ....18 ...
Argyll Cl *BAIL* BD17 ....74 ...
HORS LS18 ....55 ...
Arkendale Ms *GTHN* * BD7 ....94 ...
Arkenley La *HUDS* HD4 ....214 ...
Arkenmore *HUDE* HD5 ....192 ...
Arksey Pl *WOR/ARM* * LS12 ....100 ...
Arksey Ter *WOR/ARM* LS12 ....100 ...
Arkwright St *BOW* BD4 ....97 ...
CLAY BD14 ....94 ...
Arkwright Wk *MOR* LS27 ....123 ...
Arlesford Rd *BOW* BD4 ....124 ...
Arley Cl *HOLM/MEL* HD9 ....23 ...
Arley Dr *WOR/ARM* LS12 ....100 ...
Arley Pl *WOR/ARM* LS12 ....100 ...
Arley Pl *WOR/ARM* LS12 ....100 ...
Arley Ter *WOR/ARM* LS12 ....100 ...
Arlington Crs *LUD/ILL* HX2 ....135 ...
Arlington Gv *CAS* * WF10 ....155 ...
RHAY LS8 ....80 ...
Arlington Rd *RHAY* LS8 ....80 ...
Arlington St *BFDE* BD3 ....5 ...
WKFDE WF1 ....
Arlington Wy *HUDE* HD5 ....19 ...
Armadale Av *BOW* BD4 ....119 ...
Armgill La *SHPY* BD18 ....73 ...
Armidale Wk *ECHL* BD2 ....74 ...
Armitage Av *BRIG* HD6 ....168 ...
Armitage Rd *HFAX* HX1 ....1 ...
HUDN HD2 ....1 ...
HUDS HD4 ....21 ...
HUDW HD3 ....196 ...
LM/WK BD12 ....11 ...
WKFDW/WTN WF2 ....17 ...

nitage Sq PDSY/CALV LS28 ....98 B5
nitage St CAS WF10 ....153 H3
EWS WF13 ....171 G6
UDS HD4 ....12 C6
THW * LS26 ....
nley Gra WOR/ARM LS12 ....99 K3
nley Grange Av WOR/ARM LS12 ....99 K3
nley Grange Crs WOR/ARM LS12 ....99 K2
nley Grange Dr WOR/ARM LS12 ....99 K3
nley Grange Mt WOR/ARM LS12 ....99 K2
nley Grange Ov WOR/ARM LS12 ....99 K2
nley Grange Ri WOR/ARM LS12 ....99 K3
nley Grange Vw WOR/ARM LS12 ....100 A3
nley Grove Pl WOR/ARM LS12 ....100 D4
nley Lodge Rd WOR/ARM LS12 ....100 C2
nley Park Rd WOR/ARM LS12 ....100 C2
nley Ridge Cl WOR/ARM LS12 ....100 A3
nley Ridge Rd WOR/ARM LS12 ....77 K8
nley Ridge Ter WOR/ARM LS12 ....100 A2
nley Rd WOR/ARM LS12 ....100 D3
nouries St HD10 ....7 F5
nouries Wy MID LS10 ....
noury Av MIRF WF14 ....170 D6
nstrong Cl NORM WF6 ....151 K7
nstrong St BOW BD4 ....97 F5
PDSY/CALV LS28 ....98 B1
nstrong Ter PONT WF8 ....180 C4
nytage Cl BRIG HD6 ....190 E8
nytage La BRIG HD6 ....168 D1
nytage Rd BRIG HD6 ....168 E2
nytage Wy BRIG HD6 ....168 E2
cliffe Av HWTH BD22 ....2 B4
cliffe Cl HUDN HD3 ....12 A3
cliffe Crs BRIG HD6 ....167 K3
MOR LS27 ....147 H1
cliffe Dr KNOT WF11 ....155 J7
cliffe Gdns BTLY WF17 ....146 A6
cliffe Garth PDSY/CALV LS28 ....98 B5
cliffe Gra AL/HA/HU LS17 ....79 K1
cliffe Gv HWTH BD22 ....2 B5
cliffe Pl HWTH * BD22 ....2 B4
cliffe Pl BHP/TINH LS16 ....78 A3
BTLY WF17 ....145 K6
WTH BD22 ....2 B5
WKFDE WF1 ....11 F1
cliffe St PDSY/CALV LS28 ....98 B1
cliffe Ter GTHN BD7 ....95 H5
dale Gv HOLM/MEL HD9 ....233 H7
nford Cl BFDE BD3 ....5 D3
old Av HUDN HD2 ....12 B1
old Pl GIR BD8 ....95 H3
old Royd BRIG HD6 ....167 K4
old St GIR BD8 ....4 A2
IFAX HX1 ....8 B4
HUDN HD2 ....12 B1
VSG WF15 ....144 D7
PPDN/SBR * HX6 ....138 E7
side Av AIRE BD20 ....3 F1
side Cl CAS WF10 ....154 E3
side Crs CAS WF10 ....154 E3
side Rd WBOW BD5 ....118 E1
an Cl MAR/SLWT HD7 ....189 H6
an Ct GFTH/SHER LS25 ....105 K6
an Dr GFTH/SHER LS25 ....105 K6
ORS LS18 ....55 F7
an Wy RTHW LS26 ....126 C6
unden La HOLM/MEL HD9 ....248 A2
hington Av MID LS10 ....124 E1
hington Dr EARD/LOFT WF3 ....147 J4
hington Garth OT LS21 ....35 K5
hington La OT LS21 ....124 E1
hington Lawns OT LS21 ....35 J5
hington Pl MID LS10 ....124 E1
hington Rd BHP/TINH LS16 ....56 C2
hington St GIR BD8 ....4 A3
MID LS10 ....124 E1
hington Ter MID LS10 ....124 E1
hington Vw MID LS10 ....124 E1
hur Av GIR BD8 ....
hur St BTLY WF17 ....145 J5
hursdale Av MSTN/BAR LS15 ....82 D4
hursdale Dr MSTN/BAR LS15 ....82 D4
hursdale Gra MSTN/BAR LS15 ....82 D4
hur St BGLY * BD16 ....49 K8
BRIG HD6 ....168 D1
IDLE BD10 ....74 D5
MAR/SLWT HD7 ....189 J7
PDSY/CALV LS28 ....98 B1
WKFDE WF1 ....11 E6
illery St HECK WF16 ....145 G8
ist St WOR/ARM LS12 ....6 A4
im St WBOW BD5 ....95 J8
undel Cl BTLY WF17 ....146 A1
undel St GFTH/SHER LS25 ....106 B3
IFAX HX1 ....8 A4
PDSY/CALV LS28 ....98 C3
WKFDE WF1 ....10 C2
undel Wk BTLY WF17 ....146 A1
cot Av GTHN BD7 ....117 K1
cot Dr WBSY BD6 ....117 K1
cot Gdns EARD/LOFT WF3 ....124 E8
GTHN BD7 ....117 K1
cot Gv BRIG HD6 ....167 K3
cot Pde GTHN BD7 ....117 K1
cot Rd GFTH/SHER LS25 ....128 E1
cot Ter OSM LS9 ....102 B4
dale Rd HOR/CROF WF4 ....198 C4

Ash Av HDGY LS6 ....78 D6
Ashbourne Av CLECK BD19 ....144 A5
ECHL BD2 ....74 B8
Ashbourne Bank ECHL BD2 ....74 B8
Ashbourne Cl ECHL BD2 ....74 B8
Ashbourne Crs CUL/QBY BD13 ....116 C2
ECHL BD2 ....74 B8
GFTH/SHER LS25 ....105 K6
Ashbourne Cft CLECK BD19 ....144 A5
Ashbourne Dr CLECK BD19 ....144 A5
ECHL BD2 ....74 B8
PONT WF8 ....180 E6
Ashbourne Gdns CLECK BD19 ....144 A5
ECHL BD2 ....74 B8
Ashbourne Garth ECHL BD2 ....74 C7
HFAX HX1 ....8 A4
Ashbourne Hvn ECHL BD2 ....74 B8
Ashbourne Mt ECHL BD2 ....74 B8
Ashbourne Ov ECHL BD2 ....74 B8
Ashbourne Ri ECHL BD2 ....74 B8
Ashbourne Rd ECHL BD2 ....74 B8
HWTH BD22 ....2 B6
Ashbourne Vw CLECK BD19 ....144 A5
Ashbourne Wy CLECK BD19 ....144 A5
ECHL BD2 ....74 B8
Ashbrook Cl OSS WF5 ....173 J5
Ashbrooke Pk BEE/HOL * LS11 ....124 D1
Ash Brow HOR/CROF WF4 ....195 G6
Ash Brow Rd HUDN HD2 ....168 C8
Ashburn Cl WBY LS22 ....23 H4
Ashburn Cft WBY LS22 ....23 H4
Ashburn Dr WBY LS22 ....23 H4
Ashburn Gv BAIL BD17 ....51 J7
WBY LS22 ....23 H5
Ashburnham Gv HTON BD9 ....73 H8
Ashburn Pl ILK LS29 ....20 A8
Ashburn Wy WBY LS22 ....23 H4
Ashbury Cha WKFDE WF1 ....149 H6
Ashby Av BRAM LS13 ....99 H1
Ashby Cl LVSG WF15 ....170 C2
Ashby Crs BRAM LS13 ....99 H1
Ashby Mt BRAM LS13 ....99 H1
Ashby Sq BOW BD4 ....96 C7
Ashby Ter BRAM LS13 ....99 H1
Ashby Vw BRAM LS13 ....99 H1
Ash Cl HIPP HX3 ....141 J3
ILK LS29 ....19 J7
Ashcombe Dr KNOT WF11 ....156 C8
Ash Ct CLECK BD19 ....143 G3
Ash Crs EARD/LOFT WF3 ....150 C7
HDGY LS6 ....78 C6
Ash Cft WBSY BD6 ....118 B3
Ashcroft Av FEA/AMT WF7 ....179 H7
Ashcroft Cl BTLY WF17 ....145 K8
Ashcroft Rd FEA/AMT WF7 ....179 H8
Ashdale WKFDW/WTN WF2 ....199 G3
Ashdale La WBY LS22 ....23 H3
Ashday La HIPP HX3 ....167 H1
Ashdene WOR/ARM LS12 ....99 H8
Ashdene Ap HOR/CROF WF4 ....200 D2
Ashdene Crs HOR/CROF WF4 ....200 D2
Ashdene Ct CUL/QBY BD13 ....70 B5
PDSY/CALV LS28 ....98 C6
Ashdene Dr HOR/CROF WF4 ....200 D2
Ashdene Garth HOR/CROF WF4 ....200 D2
Ashdene Gv PONT WF8 ....155 G7
Ashdown Rd WKFDE WF1 ....11 E6
Ashdown St BRAM LS13 ....99 H1
Ash Dyke Cl DOD/DAR S75 ....239 K4
Ashenhurst Cl HUDS HD4 ....191 J8
Ashenhurst Ri HUDS HD4 ....191 H8
TOD OL14 ....133 K4
Ashenhurst Rd HUDS HD4 ....191 H8
TOD OL14 ....133 K4
Ashes La HUDS HD4 ....213 H5
TOD OL14 ....134 C4
Ashfield BOW BD4 ....120 A2
EARL WF12 ....172 C7
WBY LS22 ....23 K5
Ashfield Av KBTN HD8 ....236 E1
MOR LS27 ....146 E1
SHPY BD18 ....73 H6
Ashfield Cl HIPP HX3 ....8 A1
MSTN/BAR LS15 ....82 B8
WOR/ARM LS12 ....99 J7
Ashfield Crs BGLY BD16 ....72 A1
PDSY/CALV LS28 ....98 B2
Ashfield Dr BAIL BD17 ....51 K7
HIPP HX3 ....8 B1
SHPY BD18 ....73 H6
Ashfield Gv PDSY/CALV * LS28 ....98 C2
SHPY BD18 ....73 G6
Ashfield Pk HDGY LS6 ....78 E6
Ashfield Pl ECHL BD2 ....97 F1
OT * LS21 ....33 H4
Ashfield Rd BTLY WF17 ....145 K1
CUL/QBY BD13 ....116 C2
GTL/HWG HX4 ....166 A4
HEM/SK/SE WF9 ....224 D6
IDLE BD10 ....74 D2
MOR LS27 ....146 E1
PDSY/CALV LS28 ....98 B3
SHPY BD18 ....72 E4
Ashfield St HUDN HD2 ....191 H1

NORM WF6 ....152 B8
Ashfield Ter EARD/LOFT WF3 ....149 G1
GTL/HWG HX4 ....166 A3
HWTH BD22 ....68 E5
MSTN/BAR LS15 ....82 B7
Ashfield Wy WOR/ARM LS12 ....99 K8
Ashford Ct BSLYN/ROY * S71 ....221 K6
KBTN HD8 ....215 H4
Ashford Dr PDSY/CALV LS28 ....98 D5
Ash Ford Gn WBSY * BD6 ....118 A2
Ashford Mnr KBTN HD8 ....215 F2
Ashford Pk MAR/SLWT HD7 ....189 H6
Ashgap La NORM WF6 ....178 A1
Ash Gdns HDGY LS6 ....78 D6
Ash Gv AIRE BD20 ....27 F6
BGLY BD16 ....72 A2
BIRK/DRI BD11 ....120 D5
BRIG HD6 ....168 D1
CLECK BD19 ....144 D2
EARD/LOFT WF3 ....176 C1
HDGY LS6 ....79 F8
HEM/SK/SE WF9 ....226 C7
HORS LS18 ....77 G1
HWTH BD22 ....2 B6
ILK LS29 ....20 C6
OT LS21 ....33 H4
PDSY/CALV LS28 ....98 C5
PONT WF8 ....181 K6
Ashgrove ECHL BD2 ....74 E8
GTHN BD7 ....4 B5
IDLE BD10 ....75 C4
Ashgrove Av HIPP * HX3 ....140 D8
Ashgrove Crs GFTH/SHER LS25 ....106 B8
Ashgrove Ms BRAM LS13 ....76 D7
Ashgrove Mt GFTH/SHER LS25 ....106 A8
Ash Grove Rd HOLM/MEL HD9 ....232 E6
Ashgrove Rd AIRE BD20 ....47 J1
HUDE HD5 ....192 B1
Ash Hall La BHP/SBR HX6 ....163 G5
Ash Hill Dr AL/HA/HU LS17 ....59 H7
Ash Hill Gdns AL/HA/HU LS17 ....59 H7
Ash Hill La AL/HA/HU LS17 ....59 H7
Ashington Cl ECHL BD2 ....75 F8
Ashlands Rd ILK LS29 ....20 C6
Ash La GFTH/SHER LS25 ....106 A3
KBTN HD8 ....217 J5
Ashlar Cl HWTH BD22 ....69 F4
Ashlar Gv CAS WF10 ....154 A5
CUL/QBY BD13 ....116 C4
Ash Lea EARD/LOFT WF3 ....176 C1
Ashlea Av BRIG HD6 ....168 C3
Ashlea Cl BRIG HD6 ....168 C3
GFTH/SHER LS25 ....105 K6
Ashlea Dr BRIG HD6 ....168 C3
Ashlea Ga BRAM LS13 ....77 G7
Ashlea Gn BRAM LS13 ....77 G8
Ashleigh CUD/OR S72 ....224 A8
Ashleigh Av PONT WF8 ....180 E4
WKFDW/WTN WF2 ....175 F6
Ashleigh Cl KBTN * HD8 ....235 H1
Ashleigh Dl HUDN HD2 ....12 A1
Ashleigh Gdns OSS WF5 ....173 H3
RTHW LS26 ....127 F5
Ashleigh Rd BHP/TINH LS16 ....78 A3
Ashleigh St KGHY BD21 ....3 D2
Ashley Av OSM LS9 ....102 C1
Ashley Cl CLECK BD19 ....144 D1
WKFDW/WTN WF2 ....175 G1
Ashley Crs HEM/SK/SE WF9 ....241 F2
Ashley Cft BSLYN/ROY S71 ....221 K7
Ashley Gv HBR HX7 ....137 F1
Ashley La BAIL BD17 ....73 G3
Ashley Park Ms GFTH/SHER LS25 ....106 B3
Ashley Rd BGLY BD16 ....72 A1
LM/WK BD12 ....142 D1
OSM LS9 ....102 C1
WOR/ARM LS12 ....100 B5
Ashley St HFAX HX1 ....8 A4
SHPY BD18 ....73 H3
Ashley Ter OSM LS9 ....102 C1
Ashmead BSPA/BRAM LS23 ....42 D6
BTLY WF17 ....145 K8
Ash Meadow Cl HUDN HD2 ....168 D8
Ashmews IDLE * BD10 ....75 G4
Ashmore Dr OSS WF5 ....173 H2
Ashmore Gdns BOW * BD4 ....119 J3
Ashmount CLAY BD14 ....94 D7
Ash Mt GTHN BD7 ....95 H6
KGHY BD21 ....2 B5
Ash Rd HDGY LS6 ....78 C6
Ashroyd RTHW LS26 ....126 C7
Ash St CLECK BD19 ....143 K4
COL BB8 ....64 A1
EARD/LOFT WF3 ....176 C1
HOR/CROF WF4 ....200 E4
HUD HD1 ....12 C2
HWTH BD22 ....68 E8
Ash Ter BGLY BD16 ....71 K1
HDGY LS6 ....78 D6
RPDN/SBR HX6 ....163 K8
Ashtofts Mt GSLY LS20 ....53 C2
Ashton Av GTHN BD7 ....94 E6
RHAY LS8 ....102 B1
Ashton Clough Rd LVSG WF15 ....144 D2
Ashton Ct RHAY LS8 ....80 C8

Ashton Crs EARD/LOFT WF3 ....126 A8
Ashton Gv OSM LS9 ....102 B1
Ashton Mt OSM LS9 ....102 B1
Ashton Pl OSM LS9 ....102 B1
Ashton Rd CAS WF10 ....153 J5
   RHAY LS8 ....80 C3
Ashton St BFD BD1 ....4 B4
   CAS WF10 ....153 J4
   RHAY LS8 ....80 B8
Ashton Ter RHAY LS8 ....102 B1
Ashton Vw OSM LS9 ....102 B1
Ashton Wk IDLE BD10 ....74 C4
Ash Tree Ap SCFT LS14 ....82 B7
Ash Tree Av CUL/QBY BD13 ....93 F5
Ash Tree Bank SCFT LS14 ....82 B6
Ash Tree Cl SCFT LS14 ....82 B6
Ash Tree Gdns LUD/ILL HX2 ....115 G3
   NORM WF6 ....151 J8
   SCFT LS14 ....82 B6
Ashtree Gv GFTH/SHER LS25 ....129 G2
   GTHN BD7 ....118 A3
Ash Tree Gv SCFT LS14 ....82 B6
Ash Tree Pk GFTH/SHER * LS25 ....129 G2
Ash Tree Rd LUD/ILL HX2 ....115 F6
Ash Tree Wk ILK LS29 ....32 A2
Ashville Av HDGY LS6 ....78 D8
Ashville Cft LUD/ILL HX2 ....139 G2
Ashville Gdns LUD/ILL HX2 ....139 G2
Ashville Gv HDGY LS6 ....78 D8
   LUD/ILL HX2 ....139 G2
Ashville Rd HDGY LS6 ....78 D8
Ashville St HIPP * HX3 ....8 B2
Ashville Ter HDGY LS6 ....78 D8
Ashville Vw HDGY LS6 ....78 D8
Ashwell Cl CUD/GR S72 ....223 G8
Ashwell St GIR BD8 ....95 H2
   HTON BD9 ....73 G7
Ashwill St GIR BD8 ....95 H2
Ashwood DEWS WF13 ....81 K2
Ashwood Cl HUDN HD2 ....168 D8
Ashwood Dr AIRE BD20 ....48 E2
   MOR LS27 ....122 A4
Ashwood Gdns MOR LS27 ....122 A4
Ashwood Gra HOR/CROF WF4 ....198 A5
Ashwood Gv CUD/GR S72 ....240 D8
   HOR/CROF WF4 ....198 A5
   MOR LS27 ....122 B4
Ashwood St BOW BD4 ....120 A2
Ashwood Ter HDGY LS6 ....79 F7
Ashwood Vls HDGY LS6 ....79 F7
Ashworth Cl DEWS WF13 ....172 B3
Ashworth Gdns DEWS WF13 ....172 B3
Ashworth Gn DEWS WF13 ....172 B3
Ashworth Pl WBSY BD6 ....118 C2
Ashworth Rd DEWS WF13 ....172 B3
   PONT WF8 ....155 F8
Askam Av PONT WF8 ....155 C7
Asket Av SCFT LS14 ....81 G6
Asket Cl SCFT LS14 ....81 G5
Asket Crs SCFT LS14 ....81 G5
Asket Dr SCFT LS14 ....81 G5
Asket Gdns RHAY LS8 ....81 F5
Asket Gn SCFT LS14 ....81 G6
Asket Hl RHAY LS8 ....81 F5
Asket Pl SCFT LS14 ....81 G6
Asket Wk SCFT LS14 ....81 G6
Askey Av MOR LS27 ....147 G1
Askey Crs MOR LS27 ....147 G1
Askham Gv HEM/SK/SE WF9 ....227 G3
Askham Rd CAS WF10 ....154 E2
Aspden St TOD OL14 ....134 A5
Aspect Gdns PDSY/CALV LS28 ....98 A3
Aspen Cl KGHY BD21 ....3 G5
   WKFDW/WTN WF2 ....10 A1
Aspen Ct EARD/LOFT WF3 ....147 H2
   KBTN HD8 ....217 G8
Aspen Dr DEWS WF13 ....172 A2
Aspen Mt BHP/TINH LS16 ....77 J1
Aspen Ri WIL/AL BD15 ....71 K7
Aspinall St HBR * HX7 ....137 F2
   HFAX HX1 ....8 A5
Aspley Pl HUD1 HD1 ....13 D4
Asprey Dr WIL/AL BD15 ....94 B3
Asquith Av WIL/AL BD15 ....94 B3
Asquith Cl MOR LS27 ....122 E5
Asquith Ct LUD/ILL * HX2 ....139 G4
Asquith Dr MOR LS27 ....122 E6
Asquith St BTLY WF17 ....146 A1
Assembly St NORM WF6 ....177 K1
Astley Av RTHW LS26 ....127 K2
Astley La RTHW LS26 ....128 A3
Astley Wy RTHW LS26 ....128 A3
Aston Av BRAM * LS13 ....99 H1
Aston Cl LVSG WF15 ....170 C1
Aston Crs BRAM LS13 ....99 J1
Aston Dr BRAM LS13 ....99 J1
Aston Gv BRAM LS13 ....99 J1
Aston Mt BRAM LS13 ....99 J1
Aston Pl BRAM LS13 ....99 J1
Aston Rd BRAM LS13 ....99 H1
   WBOW BD5 ....96 A8
Aston St BRAM LS13 ....99 H1
Aston Ter BRAM LS13 ....99 H1
Aston Vw BRAM LS13 ....99 H1
Astor Gv BRAM LS13 ....98 E1
Astor St BRAM LS13 ....98 E1
Astral Av HIPP HX3 ....141 J3

Astral Cl HIPP HX3 ....141 J3
Astral Vw WBSY BD6 ....118 B1
Astra Pk BEE/HOL * LS11 ....124 D1
Atalanta Ter LUD/ILL HX2 ....139 H7
Atha Cl BEE/HOL LS11 ....124 B2
Atha Crs BEE/HOL LS11 ....124 B2
Atha St BEE/HOL LS11 ....124 B2
Athelstan La OT LS21 ....33 J1
Athene Dr WBSY HD4 ....191 J8
Atherstone Rd WIL/AL BD15 ....94 B3
Atherton La BRIG HD6 ....168 C3
Athlone Dr EARL WF12 ....146 D8
Athlone Gv WOR/ARM LS12 ....100 C4
Athlone Ri GFTH/SHER LS25 ....106 A4
Athlone St WOR/ARM LS12 ....100 C4
Athlone Ter WOR/ARM LS12 ....100 C4
Athold Dr OSS WF5 ....174 A6
Athold St OSS WF5 ....174 A6
Athol Gdns HIPP HX3 ....115 K8
Athol Gn HIPP HX3 ....115 K8
Athol Rd HIPP HX3 ....115 K8
   HTON BD9 ....95 H1
Athol St HIPP HX3 ....115 K8
   KGHY BD21 ....3 F1
Atkinson St NORM * WF6 ....177 K2
Atkinson La PONT WF8 ....181 G1
Atkinson St MID LS10 ....102 A6
   SHPY BD18 ....73 H3
Atlanta St BRAM LS13 ....98 E1
Atlas Mill Rd BRIG HD6 ....168 B1
Atlas St GIR BD8 ....95 H2
Attlee Av HOR/CROF WF4 ....225 G2
Attlee Crs WKFDW/WTN WF2 ....199 G4
Attlee Gv WKFDE WF1 ....149 K7
Attlee St NORM WF6 ....178 A3
Auckland Rd WBSY BD6 ....118 B2
Audby Ct WBY LS22 ....23 K5
Audby La WBY LS22 ....23 K5
Audrey St OSS WF5 ....173 K7
Audsley's Yd HOR/CROF WF4 ....196 E2
Augusta St NORM WF6 ....178 C3
Austerhope Av MSTN/BAR LS15 ....104 C4
Austhorpe Dr MSTN/BAR LS15 ....104 C4
Austhorpe Dr MSTN/BAR LS15 ....104 C4
Austhorpe Gdns MSTN/BAR LS15 ....104 D5
Austhorpe Gv MSTN/BAR LS15 ....104 C5
Austhorpe La MSTN/BAR LS15 ....104 B2
Austhorpe Rd MSTN/BAR LS15 ....104 B1
Austhorpe Vw MSTN/BAR LS15 ....104 B3
Austin Av BRIG HD6 ....142 A7
Austin Rd CAS WF10 ....154 E3
Austin St KGHY BD21 ....3 E2
Authorpe Rd CHAL LS7 ....79 F5
Autumn Av HDGY LS6 ....6 A1
   WBY LS22 ....23 J3
Autumn Crs HORS LS18 ....77 H4
Autumn Gv HDGY LS6 ....6 A1
Autumn Pl HDGY LS6 ....6 A1
Autumn St HDGY LS6 ....6 A1
   HFAX * HX1 ....8 A6
Autumn Ter HDGY LS6 ....6 A1
Auty Crs EARD/LOFT WF3 ....150 C5
Auty Sq MOR LS27 ....123 G8
Avenel Rd WIL/AL BD15 ....94 B3
Avenel Ter WIL/AL BD15 ....94 B3
Avenham Wy BFDE * BD3 ....5 E3
Avens Cl PONT WF8 ....180 E4
The Avenue AL/HA/HU LS17 ....57 J7
   AL/HA/HU LS17 ....57 G6
   BGLY * BD16 ....72 B5
   BSLYN/ROY S71 ....222 C7
   BTLY WF17 ....145 H2
   BTLY WF17 ....145 K4
   CLAY BD14 ....94 B7
   DEWS WF13 ....145 J8
   EARD/LOFT WF3 ....148 B3
   HIPP HX3 ....141 J3
   HOLM/MEL HD9 ....232 B3
   HOR/CROF WF4 ....200 C2
   HORS LS18 ....76 D2
   HUDE HD5 ....58 C5
   IDLE BD10 ....53 G8
   MSTN/BAR LS15 ....82 B8
   MSTN/BAR LS15 ....82 D3
   MSTN/BAR LS15 ....127 G1
   OSM LS9 ....102 A4
   RHAY LS8 ....80 C3
   WBY LS22 ....40 E2
   WKFDE WF1 ....149 H7
Avenue A BSPA/BRAM LS23 ....25 H8
Avenue B BSPA/BRAM LS23 ....43 G2
Avenue C East BSPA/BRAM LS23 ....43 H1
Avenue Crs RHAY LS8 ....80 B7
Avenue C West BSPA/BRAM LS23 ....43 H3
Avenue D BSPA/BRAM LS23 ....43 H3
Avenue Des Hirondelles OT LS21 ....35 H5
Avenue E East BSPA/BRAM LS23 ....43 H3
Avenue E West BSPA/BRAM LS23 ....43 H5
Avenue F BSPA/BRAM LS23 ....43 J2
Avenue G BSPA/BRAM LS23 ....43 K1
Avenue Gdns AL/HA/HU LS17 ....57 F6
Avenue Hl RHAY LS8 ....80 B7
Avenue No 2 BRIG HD6 ....168 B7
Avenue Rd WBOW BD5 ....96 B8
   WKFDW/WTN WF2 ....199 G2
Avenue St BOW BD4 ....120 A2
Avenue Victoria RHAY LS8 ....80 C3
Averingcliffe Rd IDLE BD10 ....75 F5

Aviary Gv WOR/ARM LS12 100
Aviary Mt WOR/ARM LS12 100
Aviary Pl WOR/ARM LS12 100
Aviary Rd WOR/ARM * LS12 100
Aviary Rw WOR/ARM LS12 100
Aviary St WOR/ARM LS12 100
Aviary Ter WOR/ARM LS12 100
Aviary Vw WOR/ARM LS12 100
Avison Rd HUDS HD4 190
Avison Yd WKFDE WF1 11
Avocet Garth MID LS10 124
Avon Cl AL/HA/HU LS17 59
Avon Ct AL/HA/HU LS17 59
Avondale KGHY BD21 2
Avondale Crs SHPY BD18 73
Avondale Dr EARD/LOFT WF3 150
Avondale Gv SHPY BD18 73
Avondale Mt SHPY BD18 73
Avondale Pl HIPP HX3 140
Avondale Rd SHPY BD18 73
Avondale St BRAM LS13 99
   WKFDW/WTN WF2 10
Avondale Wy WKFDW/WTN WF2 10
Avon Dr GFTH/SHER LS25 105
Avon Garth WBY LS22 23
Avon Wk FEA/AMT WF7 179
Axis Ct MOR * LS27 122
Aydon Wy WBSY BD6 117
Aygill Av HTON BD9 72
Aylesbury St HWTH BD22 2
Aylesford Mt MSTN/BAR LS15 82
Aynholme Dr ILK LS29 18
Aynsley Gv WIL/AL BD15 94
Ayres Dr HUDS HD4 190
Ayresome Av RHAY LS8 80
Ayresome Ov WIL/AL BD15 94
Ayresome Ter RHAY LS8 80
Aysgarth Av BRIG HD6 142
Aysgarth Cl LM/WK BD12 142
   OSM LS9 102
   WKFDW/WTN WF2 174
Aysgarth Crs LUD/ILL HX2 114
Aysgarth Dr OSM LS9 102
   WKFDW/WTN WF2 174
Aysgarth Fold MID LS10 124
Aysgarth Pl OSM LS9 102
Aysgarth Rd BTLY WF17 145
   HUDS HD4 213
Aysgarth Wk OSM LS9 102
Ayton Cl BFDE BD3 5
Ayton Rd HUDW HD3 189
Azealea Ct BFDE BD3 5

B

Baby House Hill La HBR HX7 89
Bachelor La HORS * LS18 77
Back Ada St KGHY BD21 2
Back Aireview St AIRE * BD21 3
Back Aireville St AIRE BD20 47
Back Airlie Av RHAY * LS8 80
Back Airlie Pl RHAY LS8 80
Back Albert Gv HDGY * LS6 78
Back Albert Ter HDGY * LS6 78
Back Alcester Pl RHAY * LS8 80
Back Alcester Rd RHAY * LS8 80
Back Alcester Ter RHAY * LS8 80
Back Ann St CUL/QBY * BD13 92
Back Archery Rd LDSU * LS2 7
Back Archery St LDSU * LS2 7
Back Archery Ter LDSU * LS2 7
Back Ash Gv HDGY LS6 79
Back Ashgrove West GTHN BD7 4
Back Ashley Av OSM * LS9 102
Back Ashley St OSM LS9 102
Back Ashville Av HDGY LS6 100
Back Ashville Gv HDGY LS6 78
Back Ashville Rd HDGY LS6 78
Back Ashville Ter HDGY LS6 78
Back Ashwood Ter HDGY LS6 79
Back Aston Pl BRAM LS13 99
Back Aston St BRAM LS13 99
Back Aston Ter BRAM LS13 99
Back Aston Vw BRAM LS13 99
Back Athlone Av WOR/ARM * LS12 100
Back Athlone Gv WOR/ARM LS12 100
Back Athlone Ter WOR/ARM * LS12 100
Back Atlanta St BRAM * LS13 98
Back Austhorpe Rd
   MSTN/BAR * LS15 104
Back Autumn Rd HDGY * LS6 6
Back Aylesbury St HWTH * BD22 2
Back Baileys Pl HDGY LS6 78
Back Baker St SHPY * BD18 73
Back Baldovan Ter RHAY LS8 80
Back Balfour St BGLY BD16 71
   KGHY * BD21 2
Back Bank St CAS WF10 153
Back Bank Ter PDSY/CALV LS28 98
Back Banstead St RHAY LS8 80
Back Barden Pl WOR/ARM LS12 100
Back Barkly Av BEE/HOL LS11 124
Back Barkly Pde BEE/HOL LS11 124
Back Barkly Ter BEE/HOL LS11 124
Back Barrowby Vw
   MSTN/BAR LS15 104

ck Bath Rd *BRAM* * LS13 ....99 G1
ck Beamsley Gv *HDGY* * LS6 ....6 A1
ck Beamsley Mt *HDGY* LS6 ....78 E8
ck Beamsley Ter *HDGY* * LS6 ....6 A1
ck Beaumont St *WFDE* * WF17 .....146 B8
ck Beck La *ILK* LS29 ....18 D2
ck Beech St *BGLY* BD16 ....71 K1
ck Beech Ter *HUD* * HD1 ....13 D1
ck Beechwood Gv *BULY* LS4 ....78 D8
ck Beechwood Rd *BULY* * LS4 ....78 D8
ck Bellbrooke Av *OSM* LS9 ....102 D1
ck Bellbrooke Pl *OSM* LS9 ....102 D1
ck Bellbrooke Ter *OSM* LS9 ....102 C1
ck Belvedere Av *BEE/HOL* LS11 ...124 C1
ck Belvedere Mt *BEE/HOL* LS11 ...124 C1
ck Bentley Av *HDGY* LS6 ....79 F5
ck Bentley Gv *HDGY* LS6 ....79 F5
ck Berkeley Av *RHAY* LS8 ....80 C8
ck Berkeley Ter *RHAY* LS8 ....80 C8
ck Beverley Ter *BEE/HOL* LS11 ....101 H8
ck Blackwood Gv *HFAX* * 8 A3
ck Blenheim La *LDSU* * LS2 ....7 D1
ck Blenheim Mt *GIR* * BD8 ....4 A1
ck Blenheim Ter *LDSU* LS2 ....7 D1
ck Boundary Ter *BVRD* * LS3 ....6 A2
ck Bower Rd *ELL* HX5 ....167 F4
ck Bowling Green Rd
  GTL/HWG HX4 ....165 J8
ck Bowman St *WKFDE* WF1 ....11 D1
ck Bradshaw Rd
  HOLM/MEL HD9 ....213 F8
ck Breary Av *HORS* LS18 ....77 H2
ck Breary Ter *HORS* LS18 ....77 H2
ck Briggate *AIRE* BD20 ....27 C1
ck Broad La *BRAM* * LS13 ....77 H7
ck Broomfield Crs *HDGY* LS6 ....78 D7
ck Broomfield Pl *HDGY* LS6 ....78 D8
ck Broomfield Rd *HDGY* LS6 ....78 D8
  KGHY * BD21 ....2 C3
ck Broughton Av *OSM* LS9 ....102 C1
ck Broughton Ter *OSM* LS9 ....102 C1
ck Brudenell Gv *HDGY* LS6 ....6 B1
ck Brudenell Mt *HDGY* LS6 ....6 A1
ck Brudenell Rd *HDGY* LS6 ....6 A1
ck Brunswick St *DEWS* * WF13 .....171 K2
ck Burchett Gv *HDGY* LS6 ....79 G7
ck Burchett Pl *HDGY* LS6 ....79 G7
ck Burley Hl *BULY* LS4 ....100 C1
ck Burley Lodge Rd *HDGY* LS6 ....6 A1
ck Burley Lodge Ter *HDGY* LS6 ......6 A2
ck Burley St *BVRD* LS3 ....6 C3
ck Burlington Pl *BEE/HOL* LS11 ...124 C1
ck Burlington Rd *BEE/HOL* LS11 ...124 C1
ck Burton Crs *HDGY* * LS6 ....78 D5
ck Burton Ter *BEE/HOL* * LS11 .....10 J8
ck Buxton St *KGHY* BD21 ....3 E3
ck Byrl St *KGHY* * BD21 ....3 E3
ck Byrom St *TOD* OL14 ....134 A5
ck Caister St *KGHY* * BD21 ....2 B6
ck Caledonia St *KGHY* BD21 ....3 E1
ck Camberley Pl *BEE/HOL* * LS11 .101 J8
ck Carberry Pl *HDGY* LS6 ....6 A1
ck Carberry Rd *HDGY* LS6 ....6 A1
ck Carberry Ter *HDGY* LS6 ....6 A1
ck Carter Ter *OSM/BAR* * LS26 ....104 A2
ck Cartmel Rd *KGHY* BD21 ....2 B3
ck Castle Rd *KGHY* BD21 ....2 C2
ck Cavendish Rd *IDLE* BD10 ....74 D4
ck Cavendish St *KGHY* BD21 ....3 D3
ck Cemetery Rd *HFAX* HX1 ....8 B4
ck Cecil St *HUD* HD1 ....12 B4
ck Chapel La *BRIG* HD6 ....142 B8
ck Charles St *BRIG* HD6 ....142 B8
ck Charlton Rd *OSM* LS9 ....102 C4
ck Chatsworth Rd *RHAY* LS8 ....80 C8
ck Chestnut Av *HDGY* LS6 ....78 E8
ck *MSTN/BAR* LS15 ....104 B1
ck Chiswick St *HDGY* * LS6 ....6 A1
ck Christ Church Vw
  WOR/ARM LS12 ....100 B3
ck Church La *BHP/TINH* LS16 ....56 C1
ck Church St *KSTL* LS5 ....78 A7
ck Church Vw *WKFDE* WF1 ....199 G1
ck Claremont Av *BVRD* LS3 ....6 C2
ck Clarence Rd *HORS* LS18 ....77 F4
ck Clarendon Pl *HFAX* HX1 ....8 B4
ck Clarkson Vw *HDGY* LS6 ....79 G7
ck Clayton St *RTHW* LS26 ....126 C6
ck Cliff Mt *HDGY* LS6 ....79 G7
ck Clifton Rd *HUD* HD1 ....12 A3
ck Clifton Ter *OSM* LS9 ....102 D1
ck Clipston Av *HDGY* LS6 ....79 F5
ck Clock View St *HDGY* * BD21 ......47 K1
ck Close Lea *BRIG* HD6 ....168 B2
ck Close Lea Dr *BRIG* * HD6 ....168 B2
ck Clough *HIPP* HX3 ....141 F1
ck Coldcotes Av *OSM* LS9 ....102 D1
ck Colenso Mt *BEE/HOL* LS11 .....101 F7
ck Colenso Rd *BEE/HOL* LS11 .....101 F7
  KGHY BD21 ....3 F1
ck Colton Rd *WOR/ARM* LS12 .....100 C4
ck Colwyn Pl *BEE/HOL* * LS11 .....124 C1
ck Colwyn Vw *BEE/HOL* * LS11 ...124 C1
ck Commerical St *TOD* OL14 ....134 B6
ck Conway St *RHAY* LS8 ....80 B8
ck Cowper Gv *RHAY* * LS8 ....80 C8
ck Cowper St *CHAL* LS7 ....79 K8

Back Cranbrook Av *BEE/HOL* LS11 ...101 G8
Back Croft House La *AIRE* * BD20 .....47 J1
Back Cromer Av *KGHY* * BD21 ....2 C6
Back Cromer Gv *KGHY* * BD21 ....2 C5
Back Cromer Ter *KGHY* LS2 ....6 C1
Back Cromwell Ter *HFAX* HX1 ....8 C4
Back Cross Flatts Av
  BEE/HOL LS11 ....124 B1
Back Cross Flatts Crs
  BEE/HOL LS11 ....124 A1
Back Cross Flatts Gv
  BEE/HOL LS11 ....124 B1
Back Cross Flatts Mt
  BEE/HOL LS11 ....124 B1
Back Cross Flatts Pl *BEE/HOL* LS11 ...124 A1
Back Cross Flatts Rw
  BEE/HOL LS11 ....124 A1
Back Cross Green Crs *OSM* LS9 ......102 B5
Back Cross Green La *OSM* LS9 ....102 B5
Back Dalton Av *BEE/HOL* LS11 ......124 B1
Back Dalton Gv *BEE/HOL* LS11 ......124 B1
Back Dalton Rd *BEE/HOL* LS11 ......124 B1
Back Dargai St *CHAL* LS7 ....79 J8
Back Dawlish Mt *OSM* LS9 ....102 B4
Back De Lacy Mt *KSTL* LS5 ....78 A6
Back Delph Mt *HDGY* LS6 ....79 G7
Back Dent St *OSM* * LS9 ....102 B4
Back Der St *TOD* * OL14 ....134 B6
Back Devonshire La *RHAY* LS8 ....80 C7
Back Dorset Mt *RHAY* LS8 ....80 C7
Back Dorset Rd *RHAY* LS8 ....80 C8
Back Dorset Ter *RHAY* LS8 ....80 C8
Back Dudley Hill Rd *ECHL* * BD2 ....5 F1
Back Duke of York St *WKFDE* * WF1 ...11 D2
Back Duke St *FEA/AMT* * WF7 ....179 H5
Back Dunbar St *WKFDE* WF1 ....11 F5
Back East Park Rd *OSM* * LS9 ....102 C4
Back Eaton St *KGHY* BD21 ....3 E2
Back Eccleshurst Gv *OSM* * LS9 ....102 D4
Back Eccleshurst St *OSM* LS9 ....102 D4
Back Edensor Rd *KGHY* BD21 ....2 B5
Back Eldon Rd *HUD* HD1 ....190 D4
Back Elford Pl *RHAY* LS8 ....80 B8
Back Elizabeth St *WBOW* BD5 ....4 C6
Back Ellers Gv *RHAY* LS8 ....80 B7
Back Ellers Rd *RHAY* LS8 ....80 B7
Back Elmfield Ter *HFAX* HX1 ....8 B6
Back Elsworth St *WOR/ARM* LS12 ...100 D4
Back Emily St *KGHY* BD21 ....3 E2
  KGHY BD21 ....3 D2
Back Eshald Pl *RTHW* LS26 ....127 G5
Back Esmond Ter *WOR/ARM* LS12 ...100 B4
Back Estcourt Av *HDGY* LS6 ....78 C6
Back Eversley Mt *LUD/ILL* HX2 .....139 H5
Back Fairford Pl *BEE/HOL* * LS11 ..101 J8
Back Ferguson St *HFAX* HX1 ....9 D4
Back Field Ct *CUL/QBY* * BD13 ....93 H5
Back Fitzwilliam St *HUD* * HD1 ....12 B4
Back Florist St *KGHY* BD21 ....3 F1
Back Fold *CLAY* BD14 ....94 B6
Back Foster Rd *KGHY* * BD21 ....2 C5
Back Garden St *WKFDW/WTN* WF2 ...10 B3
Back Garton Rd *OSM* LS9 ....102 C4
Back Garton Ter *OSM* LS9 ....102 C4
Back Gathorne St *RHAY* * LS8 ....80 A8
Back Gerrard St *HFAX* HX1 ....8 C4
Back Giles St North *WBOW* * BD5 ......4 B6
Back Giles Street Sout *WBOW* BD5 .....4 B6
Back Giles St South *WBOW* * BD5 ......4 B6
Back Gillett La *RTHW* LS26 ....126 C6
Back Girlington Rd *GIR* BD8 ....4 A3
Back Gladstone St *BGLY* BD16 ....71 K1
Back Glenthorpe Ter *OSM* LS9 ....102 C3
Back Glossop St *HDGY* LS6 ....79 H7
Back Gooder La *BRIG* * HD6 ....168 C2
Back Gordon St *WKFDE* WF1 ....11 F6
Back Gordon Ter *HDGY* LS6 ....79 F5
Back Graham Gv *BULY* LS4 ....78 D8
Back Granby Gv *HDGY* LS6 ....78 D7
Back Grange Av *CHAL* LS7 ....80 A7
Back Grange Crs *CHAL* LS7 ....80 A7
Back Grange Ter *CHAL* LS7 ....79 K7
Back Grange Vw *CHAL* LS7 ....80 A7
Back Grantley St *WKFDE* WF1 ....11 J3
Back Grant St *HWTH* BD22 ....2 B3
Back Graveley St *MSTN/BAR* LS15 ...103 J5
Back Great Russell St *GTHN* BD7 ....4 A4
Back Greaves Street *WBOW* BD5 ....95 K8
Back Gn *MOR* LS27 ....123 H4
Back Greenhead Rd *HUD* HD1 ....12 C1
Back Greenmount Ter
  BEE/HOL LS11 ....101 H8
Back Greenwood Mt *HDGY* LS6 ......78 E4
Back Grosvenor Ter *HDGY* LS6 ....79 F7
  HFAX * HX1 ....8 B4
Back Grouse St *KGHY* BD21 ....3 E2
Back Grovehall Av *BEE/HOL* LS11 ..124 B2
Back Grovehall Dr *BEE/HOL* LS11 ..124 B2
Back Grove Rd *ILK* LS29 ....20 B7
Back Haigh Av *RTHW* LS26 ....126 A4
Back Haigh St *RTHW* LS26 ....125 K4
Back Haigh Vw *RTHW* LS26 ....125 K4
Back Halliday Gv *WOR/ARM* LS12 ...100 A3
Back Halliday Pl *WOR/ARM* LS12 ...100 A3
Back Hambleton St *WKFDE* * WF1 ...10 C3
Back Hamilton Av *CHAL* LS7 ....80 A7
Back Hamilton Ter *CHAL* LS7 ....80 A7

Back Harehills Av *CHAL* LS7 ....79 K7
Back Harehills Park Vw *OSM* LS9 ...102 D1
Back Harehills Pl *RHAY* * LS8 ....80 B8
Back Harehills Rd *RHAY* * LS8 ....80 B8
Back Hares Av *RHAY* LS8 ....80 B7
Back Hares Mt *RHAY* LS8 ....80 A7
Back Hares Ter *RHAY* LS8 ....80 B7
Back Hares Vw *RHAY* * LS8 ....80 B7
Back Harold Gv *HDGY* LS6 ....6 A1
Back Hartley Av *HDGY* LS6 ....79 H7
Back Hartley Gv *HDGY* LS6 ....79 G7
Back Hartley St *MOR* LS27 ....123 G8
Back Hatfield St *WKFDE* WF1 ....10 C2
Back Headingley Av *HDGY* LS6 ....78 C6
Back Headingley Mt *HDGY* LS6 ......78 C6
Back Heddon St *HDGY* LS6 ....78 E5
Back Heights Rd *CUL/QBY* BD13 ....93 F4
Back Henrietta St *BTLY* WF17 ....146 B6
Back Hessle Av *HDGY* LS6 ....78 E8
Back Hessle Mt *HDGY* * LS6 ....78 E8
Back Hessle Ter *HDGY* * LS6 ....78 E8
Back Hessle Vw *HDGY* * LS6 ....78 E8
Back Highbury Ter *HDGY* LS6 ....6 B1
Back Highfield Rd *BRAM* LS13 ....99 H1
Back High St *CUL/QBY* BD13 ....93 H5
Back Highthorne Gv
  WOR/ARM * LS12 ....100 A3
Back Highthorne St
  WOR/ARM LS12 ....100 A3
Back Hillcrest Av *CHAL* LS7 ....80 A8
Back Hillcrest Vw *CHAL* LS7 ....80 A7
Back Hill Top Av *RHAY* * LS8 ....80 B7
Back Hill Top Mt *RHAY* LS8 ....80 B7
Back Hilton Gv *RHAY* * LS8 ....80 B7
Back Hilton Pl *RHAY* LS8 ....80 B7
Back Hilton Rd *RHAY* * LS8 ....80 B7
Back Hird St *KGHY* * BD21 ....2 C4
Backhold Av *HIPP* HX3 ....166 D1
Backhold Dr *HIPP* HX3 ....166 C1
Backhold La *HIPP* HX3 ....166 C1
Backhold Rd *HIPP* HX3 ....166 D1
Back Hollyshaw Ter
  MSTN/BAR LS15 ....104 A3
Back Holywell La *AL/HA/HU* LS17 ...59 F6
Back Honoria St *HUD* HD1 ....12 C1
Back Hope Hall Ter *HFAX* HX1 ....9 D5
Backhouse La *HOR/CROF* WF4 .....220 B4
Back Hovingham Gv *RHAY* LS8 ....80 C7
Back Hovingham Mt *RHAY* LS8 ....80 C7
Back Hovingham Ter *RHAY* LS8 ......80 C8
Back Hyde Gv *KGHY* * BD21 ....3 E2
Back Hyde Ter *LDSU* LS2 ....6 C2
Back Ibbetson Pl *LDSU* * LS2 ....7 D2
Back Ingledew Crs *RHAY* LS8 ....80 D1
Back Irwell St *BOW* BD4 ....5 E6
Back Ivy Av *OSM* LS9 ....102 C3
Back Ivy Gv *OSM* * LS9 ....102 D4
Back Ivy Mt *OSM* * LS9 ....102 C3
Back Ivy St *OSM* LS9 ....102 C3
Back John St *CUL/QBY* BD13 ....93 H5
Back Karnac Rd *RHAY* LS8 ....80 B7
Back Kelso Rd *LDSU* * LS2 ....6 B1
Back Kendal La *BVRD* LS3 ....6 C2
Back Kennerleigh Wk
  MSTN/BAR LS15 ....104 A3
Back Kensington St *GIR* BD8 ....95 G2
Back Kensington Ter *HDGY* LS6 ......79 F8
Back King's Av *HDGY* LS6 ....6 B1
Back Kirby St *KGHY* BD21 ....3 E2
Back Kirkgate *SHPY* * BD18 ....73 G4
Back Kitson St *OSM* * LS9 ....102 B4
Back Knowl Rd *MIRF* WF14 ....170 C5
Back Laisteridge La *GTHN* BD7 ....4 A5
Back Lambton Gv *RHAY* * LS8 ....80 B7
Back Landseer Av *BRAM* LS13 ....77 J8
Back Landseer Gv *BRAM* LS13 ....77 J8
Back Landseer Ter *BRAM* * LS13 .....77 J8
Back La *AIRE* BD20 ....27 C1
  AIRE BD20 ....49 H2
  BEE/HOL LS11 ....124 A2
  BIRK/DRI BD11 ....121 J4
  BRAM LS13 ....99 H2
  BSPA/BRAM LS23 ....42 D8
  BTLY DN5 ....241 J7
  BTLY DN5 ....243 F6
  CAS WF10 ....129 G8
  CUL/QBY BD13 ....93 H4
  CUL/QBY BD13 ....35 J4
  CUL/QBY BD13 ....117 C1
  EARL WF12 ....194 C2
  EARL WF12 ....194 E1
  GSLY LS20 ....53 F2
  HBR HX7 ....89 G5
  HBR HX7 ....111 H5
  HBR HX7 ....112 A6
  HBR HX7 ....136 A1
  HECK WF16 ....145 G7
  HEM/SK/SE WF9 ....226 A1
  HEM/SK/SE WF9 ....235 C6
  HOLM/MEL HD9 ....233 G5
  HOR/CROF WF4 ....194 B6
  HOR/CROF WF4 ....201 G1
  HOR/CROF WF4 ....201 F7
  HOR/CROF WF4 ....220 C5
  HORS LS18 ....77 F3
  HTON BD9 ....77 J2
  HWTH BD22 ....46 D4
  HWTH BD22 ....67 J5
  IDLE BD10 ....74 C3

ILK LS29 ....32 B2
KBTN HD8 ....215 K8
KBTN HD8 ....216 K6
KBTN HD8 ....218 A8
LUD/ILL HX2 ....115 G6
MIRF WF14 ....170 B6
MIRF WF14 ....193 K4
OSS WF5 ....173 J6
PDSY/CALV LS28 ....76 B8
RPDN/SBR HX6 ....164 A7
STKB/PEN S36 ....252 C8
WIL/AL BD15 ....71 J7
WKFDW/WTN WF2 ....10 B5
WOR/ARM LS12 ....99 G8
YEA LS19 ....53 J6
Back La West *BSLYN/ROY* S71 ......221 J7
Back Langdale Gdns *HDGY* LS6 ....78 C7
Back Langdale Ter *HDGY* LS6 ....78 C7
Back Leatham St *DEWS* WF13 ....171 K2
Back Leeming *HWTH* BD22 ....91 F2
Back Lime St *KGHY* * BD21 ....47 K8
Back Lindum St *GIR* BD8 ....4 A1
Back Lodge La *BEE/HOL* LS11 ....101 H8
Back Lombard St *YEA* LS19 ....53 J7
Back Longroyd Ter *BEE/HOL* * LS11 ...101 J8
Back Lord St *HFAX* HX1 ....8 C4
Back Lucas St *HDGY* LS6 ....79 G7
Back Lunan Pl *RHAY* * LS8 ....80 D7
Back Lyon St *CUL/QBY* BD13 ....116 E2
Back Mafeking Av *BEE/HOL* * LS11 ...124 B2
Back Mafeking Mt *BEE/HOL* LS11......124 B2
Back Malt St *HWTH* BD22 ....2 B6
Back Manor Dr *HDGY* LS6 ....78 E8
Back Mannville Rd *KGHY* BD21 ....2 B4
Back Manor Dr *HDGY* LS6 ....78 E8
Back Manor St *ECHL* BD20 ....79 K5
Back Manor St *ECHL* BD20 ....98 C5
Back Manor Ter *HDGY* LS6 ....78 E7
Back Market St *WBSY* * BD6 ....118 D2
Back Markham Av *RHAY* LS8 ....80 B7
Back Marriot St *DEWS* WF13 ....172 C2
Back Marshall Dr *MSTN/BAR* LS15 ....104 A1
Back Marshall Ter *MSTN/BAR* LS15 ...104 A1
Back Mary St *EARD/LOFT* WF3 ....149 F3
Back Masham St *WOR/ARM* * LS12 ....100 D4
Back Maud Av *BEE/HOL* LS11 ....124 B1
Back Mayville Av *HDGY* LS6 ....78 E8
Back Mayville Pl *HDGY* LS6 ....78 E8
Back Mayville St *HDGY* LS6 ....78 E8
Back Mayville Ter *HDGY* LS6 ....78 E8
Back Meadow Vw *HDGY* LS6 ....78 E8
Back Melbourne Gv *BRAM* LS13 ....99 G5
Back Methley Dr *CHAL* LS7 ....79 K5
Back Mexborough Av *CHAL* LS7 ....79 K7
Back Mexborough Dr *CHAL* LS7 ....79 K7
Back Mexborough Gv *CHAL* LS7 ....79 K7
Back Mexborough St *CHAL* LS7 ....79 K7
Back Meynell Av *RTHW* LS26 ....126 B6
Back Middle Cross St
  WOR/ARM * LS12 ....100 D4
Back Middleton Vw *BEE/HOL* LS11 ....101 G8
Back Milan Av *RHAY* LS8 ....80 B8
Back Milan Rd *RHAY* LS8 ....80 B8
Back Milan St *RHAY* LS8 ....80 C8
Back Minnie St *KGHY* * BD21 ....2 C4
Back Mitchell Ter *BGLY* BD16 ....71 K1
Back Mitford Rd *WOR/ARM* LS12 ....100 A4
Back Model Rd *WOR/ARM* LS12 ....100 C4
Back Model Ter *WOR/ARM* LS12 ....100 C4
Back Model Vw *WOR/ARM* LS12 ....100 D4
Back Monk Bridge Dr *HDGY* LS6 ....79 F5
Back Montague St *WKFDE* WF1 ....11 F6
Back Moorfield St *HFAX* HX1 ....8 C2
Back Moorfield Ter *WOR/ARM* LS12...100 A3
Back Moorland Ter *LDSU* LS2 ....6 C1
Back Morning St *KGHY* * BD21 ....2 C6
Back Morritt Dr *MSTN/BAR* LS15 ....103 H3
Back Mount Pleasant *MID* LS10 ....124 D6
  WKFDE WF1 ....11 D3
Back Mount Vw *HDGY* LS6 ....79 F7
Back Muff St *BOW* BD4 ....5 F6
Back Myrtle Av *BGLY* BD16 ....71 K1
Back Nansen St *BRAM* LS13 ....98 E1
Back Newport Gdns *HDGY* LS6 ....78 D8
Back Newport Mt *HDGY* LS6 ....78 D8
Back Newport Pl *HDGY* LS6 ....78 D8
Back Newton Gv *CHAL* LS7 ....79 K7
Back Newton La *CAS* WF10 ....130 B4
Back New York St *LDS* LS2 ....7 E4
Back Nice Vw *RHAY* * LS8 ....80 B7
Back Norman Mt *KSTL* LS5 ....78 A7
Back Norman Pl *RHAY* LS8 ....80 C1
Back Norman Ter *RHAY* LS8 ....80 C1
Back Northbrook St *CHAL* LS7 ....79 K4
Back Northgate *PONT* WF8 ....180 E2
Back North Park Av *RHAY* LS8 ....80 B2
Back North St *LM/WK* * BD12 ....119 H7
Back Norwood Gv *HDGY* LS6 ....78 E8
Back Norwood Pl *HDGY* LS6 ....78 E8
Back Norwood Rd *HDGY* LS6 ....78 E8
Back Nowell Crs *OSM* LS9 ....102 D2
Back Nowell Mt *OSM* LS9 ....102 D2
Back Nowell Pl *OSM* LS9 ....102 D2
Back Nowell Ter *OSM* LS9 ....102 D2
Back Nunington St *WOR/ARM* LS12...100 D3
Back Nunington Vw
  WOR/ARM LS12 ....100 C2
Back Nunroyd Rd *AL/HA/HU* LS17 ....79 K2

Back Nursery Mt *MID* * LS10 ....125 F2
Back Oak Av *BGLY* BD16 ....71 K2
Back Oakfield Ter *HDGY* LS6 ....78 E5
Back Oakley St *EARD/LOFT* WF3 ....149 F2
Back Oak Rd *CHAL* * LS7 ....79 K6
Back Oakwood Av *RHAY* LS8 ....80 D5
Back Oakwood Dr *RHAY* LS8 ....80 D5
Back O' Dam *MAR/SLWT* * HD7 ....210 E3
Back Osmondthorpe La *OSM* LS9 ....102 E3
Back O' the MI *BGLY* BD16 ....70 E2
Back Otterburn St *KGHY* * BD21 ....3 D2
Back Outwood La *HORS* LS18 ....77 G4
Back Overdale Ter
  MSTN/BAR * LS15 ....103 J3
Back O'Wall *HUDW* HD3 ....187 K8
Back Oxford St *EARD/LOFT* WF3 ....149 F3
Back Paget St *KGHY* BD21 ....2 B3
Back Parish Ghyll Rd *ILK* LS29 ....20 B8
Back Park Crs *RHAY* LS8 ....80 D1
Back Parkfield Pl *BEE/HOL* LS11 ....101 G8
Back Parkfield Rd *BEE/HOL* LS11 ....101 G8
Back Park Ter *HFAX* HX1 ....8 B5
Back Park Vw *BEE/HOL* LS11 ....101 G8
Back Park View Av *BULY* LS4 ....78 D8
Back Parkville Rd *BRAM* * LS13 ....77 G8
Back Parnaby Av *MID* LS10 ....125 G2
Back Parnaby St *MID* LS10 ....125 G2
Back Parnaby Ter *MID* LS10 ....125 G2
Back Pasture Gv *CHAL* LS7 ....79 K4
Back Pasture Rd *RHAY* LS8 ....80 A7
Back Pawson St *EARD/LOFT* WF3 ....149 F5
Back Pleasant St *RPDN/SBR* HX6 ......139 F6
Back Pollard La *BRAM* LS13 ....77 G6
Back Pollard St *HUDN* HD2 ....191 H1
Back Poplar Av *MSTN/BAR* LS15 ....104 B1
Back Potternewton La *CHAL* LS7 ....79 J5
Back Potters St *CHAL* LS7 ....79 K5
Back Prospect Pl *KGHY* BD21 ....2 C4
Back Prospect St *OSM* * LS9 ....102 B4
Back Providence Av *HDGY* LS6 ....79 G7
Back Providence St *BTLY* * WF17 ....146 B8
Back Purlwell Hall Rd *BTLY* WF17 ....146 B8
Back Queen St *GTL/HWG* HX4 ....166 B5
  HUD * LS15 ....13 D5
Back Ravenscar Av *RHAY* LS8 ....80 C5
Back Ravens St *DEWS* WF13 ....171 K5
Back Raynville Mt *BRAM* * LS13 ....77 J8
Back Regent Park Ter *HDGY* * LS6 ....79 F7
Back Regent St *WKFDE* WF1 ....11 E6
Back Regent Ter *HDGY* LS6 ....6 B1
Back Reginald Mt *CHAL* * LS7 ....79 K7
Back Reginald Pl *CHAL* * LS7 ....79 K7
Back Reginald St *CHAL* LS7 ....79 K7
Back Rhodes St *HFAX* HX1 ....8 A4
Back Ribble St *KGHY* BD21 ....3 D5
Back Richardson St *LM/WK* BD12 ....119 H7
Back Richmond Mt *HDGY* LS6 ....78 E8
Back Ridge Mount Ter *HDGY* LS6 ....79 F7
Back Ridge St *TOD* * OL14 ....134 A6
Back Ridge Vw *CHAL* LS7 ....79 C6
Back Rigging La *RPDN/SBR* HX6 ....137 K8
Back Ripley St *BRAM* BD20 ....48 D2
Back Ripon Ter *HIPP* HX3 ....8 C2
Back River St *HWTH* BD22 ....69 F4
Back Rd *LM/WK* BD12 ....118 D7
Back Roberts St *RTHW* * LS26 ....127 F5
Back Rochester Ter *HDGY* LS6 ....78 D7
Back Rokeby Gdns *HDGY* LS6 ....78 C6
Back Roman Gv *RHAY* LS8 ....80 C1
Back Roman Pl *RHAY* LS8 ....80 C1
Back Roman St *RHAY* LS8 ....80 C1
Back Rosebank Crs *HDGY* * LS6 ....6 B1
Back Rosemont Wk *BRAM* LS13 ....99 G5
Back Rossall Rd *RHAY* * LS8 ....80 C7
Back Rossington Gv *RHAY* * LS8 ....80 A7
Back Rossington Pl *RHAY* LS8 ....80 A7
Back Roundhay Av *RHAY* LS8 ....80 B6
Back Roundhay Crs *RHAY* LS8 ....80 B6
Back Roundhay Gv *RHAY* LS8 ....80 B6
Back Roundhay Pl *RHAY* * LS8 ....80 B6
Back Roundhay Vw *RHAY* * LS8 ....80 B6
Back Rw *BEE/HOL* LS11 ....8 C6
Back Rowland Ter *BEE/HOL* * LS11 .....101 J8
Back Rowsley St *KGHY* BD21 ....3 E3
Back Rupert St *KGHY* BD21 ....3 D2
Back Russell St *WBOW* BD5 ....4 B6
Back Ruthven Vw *RHAY* LS8 ....80 C8
Back Rydal St *KGHY* * BD21 ....2 B4
Back Rylstone St *KGHY* BD21 ....3 F2
Back St Alban Crs *OSM* LS9 ....102 E2
Back St Elmo Gv *OSM* * LS9 ....102 C3
Back Saint Ives Mt *WOR/ARM* LS12 ...100 A3
Back St Luke's Crs *BEE/HOL* LS11 ......101 G7
Back St Mary's Rd *CHAL* LS7 ....79 K6
Back St Paul's Rd *SHPY* * BD18 ....73 G4
Back Salisbury Gv *WOR/ARM* LS12 ....100 C3
Back Salisbury Ter *WOR/ARM* LS12 ...100 C3
Back Salisbury Vw *WOR/ARM* LS12 ....100 C3
Back Saltaire Rd North *SHPY* BD18 ......73 G3
Back Sandhurst Gv *RHAY* LS8 ....80 C5
Back Sandhurst Pl *RHAY* LS8 ....80 C5
Back Sandhurst Rd *RHAY* LS8 ....80 C5
Back Savile Pde *HFAX* HX1 ....8 C6
Back Savile Pl *CHAL* LS7 ....79 K8
Back Savile Rd *CHAL* LS7 ....79 K8
Back School Vw *HDGY* LS6 ....78 E8
Back Seaforth Av *OSM* LS9 ....102 D1

Back Seaforth Ter *OSM* * LS9 ....80 C
Back Sefton Av *BEE/HOL* LS11 ....101 C
Back Sefton Ter *BEE/HOL* LS11 ....124 B
Back Shaftesbury Av *RHAY* LS8 ....80 C
Back Shaw La *BGLY* BD21 ....48 E
Back Shepherd's La *CHAL* LS7 ....80 A
Back Shepherd's Pl *RHAY* LS8 ....80 B
Back Sholebroke Av *CHAL* LS7 ....79 H
Back Sholebroke Mt *CHAL* LS7 ....79 H
Back Sholebroke Pl *CHAL* LS7 ....79 H
Back Sholebroke Rw *CHAL* LS7 ....79 H
Back Sholebroke Ter *CHAL* LS7 ....79 H
Back Sholebroke Vw *CHAL* LS7 ....79 H
Back Sidlaw Ter *RHAY* LS8 ....80 E
Back Simpson St *KGHY* BD21 ....2 E
Back Sladen St *KGHY* BD21 ....2 E
Back Slaithwaite Rd *EARL* WF12 ....172 E
Back Smith Rw *WBOW* * BD5 ....95 J
Back South End Gv *BRAM* LS13 ....99 G
Back South St *HUD* HD1 ....190 D
Back Springfield Mt
  WOR/ARM LS12 ....100 A
Back Springfield St *ELL* * HX5 ....167 G
Back Spring Grove Wk *HDGY* LS6 ....6 A
Back Spring St *HUD* HD1 ....12 E
Back Stanley St *OSM* * LS9 ....102 E
Back Stanmore Pl *BULY* LS4 ....78 C
Back Stanmore St *BULY* LS4 ....78 C
Back Station Rd *BTLY* * WF17 ....146 D
  MIRF WF14 ....170 D
Backstone Gill La *AL/HA/HU* LS17 ....59 F
Back Stone Hall Rd *ECHL* BD2 ....74 C
Backstone La *ILK* LS29 ....20 C
Backstone Wy *ILK* LS29 ....20 D
Back Storey Pl *SCFT* LS14 ....103 C
Back Stratford Av *BEE/HOL* LS11 ....124 D
Back Stratford St *BEE/HOL* * LS11 ......101 J
Back Stratford Ter *BEE/HOL* LS11 ....101 J
Back St *BSPA/BRAM* LS23 ....42 G
  PONT WF8 ....180 E
Back Sunnydene *SCFT* LS14 ....103 H
Back Sutton Ap *SCFT* LS14 ....103 G
Back Swinton St *HFAX* HX1 ....8 A
Back Sycamore Av *BGLY* BD16 ....71 H
Back Tamworth St *BOW* BD4 ....97 C
Back Tempest Rd *BEE/HOL* LS11 ....101 H
Back Temple Vw *BEE/HOL* * LS11 ....101 G
Back the Crs *HDGY* LS6 ....6 B
Back Thornhill St *PDSY/CALV* * LS28 ...75 H
Back Thornville Rw *HDGY* LS6 ....6 A
Back Tower Gv *WOR/ARM* LS12 ....99 H
Back Trafford Av *OSM* LS9 ....102 D
Back Trentham Pl *BEE/HOL* LS11 ....124 C
Back Trinity Ter *WBOW* BD5 ....4 B
Back Union St *HUD* * HD1 ....13 D
Back Unity St North *BGLY* BD16 ....71 J
Back Unity St South *BGLY* BD16 ....71 J
Back Vicars Rd *RHAY* * LS8 ....80 E
Back Victoria Gv *OSM* LS9 ....102 D
Back Victoria St *HFAX* HX1 ....9 C
Back Victor Ter *HFAX* HX1 ....8 B
Back Walmsley Rd *HDGY* LS6 ....78 D
Back Walnut St *KGHY* * BD21 ....47 H
Back Waverley Rd *ELL* HX5 ....166 B
Back Webster St *DEWS* * WF13 ....172 E
Back Wellfield Ter *TOD* OL14 ....134 A
Back Welton Av *HDGY* LS6 ....79 F
Back Welton Gv *HDGY* LS6 ....78 E
Back Welton Mt *HDGY* LS6 ....78 E
Back Welton Pl *HDGY* LS6 ....78 E
Back Wentworth St *HUD* HD1 ....12 C
Back Wesley St *CAS* WF10 ....153 J
Back Westbourne Ter *LDSU* LS2 ....6 C
Back Westbury St *MID* LS10 ....125 G
Back Westlock Av *OSM* LS9 ....102 D
Back Westover Rd *BRAM* LS13 ....77 G
Back West St *RPDN/SBR* HX6 ....138 D
Back Wetherby Gv *BULY* LS4 ....78 B
Back Wetherby Rd *RHAY* LS8 ....80 C
Back Wharf St *RPDN/SBR* HX6 ....139 F
Back Wickham St *BEE/HOL* LS11 ....101 G
Back William Av *MSTN/BAR* * LS15 .....103 G
Back Wilton Gv *HDGY* * LS6 ....78 E
Back Winfield Gv *LDSU* LS2 ....7 G
Back Winston Gdns *HDGY* LS6 ....78 C
Back Winterburn St *KGHY* * BD21 ....3 E
Back Wolsley Ter *HFAX* * HX1 ....8 A
Back Woodbine Ter *HDGY* LS6 ....78 E
Back Woodland Park Rd *HDGY* * LS6 ...78 E
Back Woodstock St *LDSU* * LS2 ....7 F
Back Wood St *EARD/LOFT* WF3 ....148 E
  GIR BD8 ....4 D
Back Wright Av *HWTH* BD22 ....47 H
Back York Pl *LDS* LS1 ....6 E
Back York St *LDSU* LS2 ....7 F
Bacon Av *NORM* WF6 ....152 D
Bacon St *GSLY* LS20 ....59 F
Bacup Rd *TOD* OL14 ....132 E
Baddeley Gdns *IDLE* BD10 ....74 B
Baden Powell Crs *PONT* WF8 ....180 C
Baden St *HWTH* BD22 ....68 D
Badger Brow *HOLM/MEL* HD9 ....231 H
Badger Cl *HOR/CROF* WF4 ....198 B
Badger Ga *HOLM/MEL* HD9 ....231 H
Badgergate Av *WIL/AL* BD15 ....71 F
Badger Hl *BRIG* HD6 ....167 J
Badger La *HBR* HX7 ....111 F
  HIPP HX3 ....141 G
Badgers Mt *MSTN/BAR* LS15 ....104 C

Adgers Wk HECK WF16 ....145 H8
Adgers Wy ECHL BD22 ....74 A7
Adger Wood Gld WBY LS22 ....23 J3
Adminton Dr EARD/LOFT WF3 ....124 E8
Adsworth Ct HEM/SK/SE WF9 ....204 A8
Adsworth Vw HEM/SK/SE WF9 ....226 C3
Agden La KBTN HD8 ....237 J5
Aghill Ct PONT WF8 ....181 G3
Aghill Gn EARD/LOFT WF3 ....147 J5
Aghill La PONT WF8 ....181 F2
Aghill Rd EARD/LOFT WF3 ....147 J5
Agley La PDSY/CALV LS28 ....76 B7
Agnall Ter WBSY BD6 ....118 C2
Aildon Av GFTH/SHER LS25 ....106 B8
Aildon Cl SCFT LS14 ....82 A5
Aildon Dr SCFT LS14 ....82 A5
Aildon Gn SCFT LS14 ....82 A5
Aildon Holmes BAIL BD17 ....73 J2
Aildon Pl SCFT LS14 ....82 A4
Aildon Rd BAIL BD17 ....73 J1
SCFT LS14 ....82 A4
Aildon Wood Ct BAIL BD17 ....73 J1
Ailey Crs HEM/SK/SE WF9 ....226 C7
Ailey Hall Bank HIPP HX3 ....9 E4
Ailey Hall Rd HIPP HX3 ....9 E3
Ailey Hills Rd BGLY BD16 ....49 J7
Ailey's Ct SCFT LS14 ....81 J6
Ailey's Hl SCFT LS14 ....81 J6
Aileys Lawn SCFT LS14 ....81 J6
Ailey St BOW BD4 ....5 D6
Ailey Wk HOR/CROF WF4 ....198 B8
Ailinbridge Rd HDGY LS6 ....78 D7
Aines St HFAX HX1 ....8 B3
RTHW * LS26 ....126 B6
Aird St WBOW BD5 ....96 A7
Airstow Ct LUD/ILL HX2 ....139 F5
Airstow La LUD/ILL HX2 ....139 F5
Airstow Mt LUD/ILL HX2 ....139 F6
Airstow St WIL/AL BD15 ....159 K2
Aker Crs MOR LS27 ....123 F8
Aker Fold HFAX * HX1 ....1 B4
Aker La EARD/LOFT WF3 ....150 A6
Aker Rd MOR LS27 ....123 F8
Aker's St HBR HX7 ....112 B7
Aker St ECHL BD2 ....5 F1
HUDW HD3 ....190 B3
MOR LS27 ....123 F8
SHPY BD18 ....73 G3
Aker St North LUD/ILL HX2 ....115 K6
Akes St GTHN BD7 ....95 C7
Akeston Cl HUDE HD5 ....192 A8
Albec Av HDGY LS6 ....78 E6
Albec St HDGY LS6 ....78 E6
Alderstone Hall La MIRF WF14 ......171 F5
Aldovan Mt RHAY LS8 ....80 B7
Aldovan Pl RHAY LS8 ....80 B7
Aldovan Ter RHAY LS8 ....80 B7
Aldwin La CLAY BD14 ....94 A8
Aldwin Ter HIPP HX3 ....9 E4
Alfour St BGLY BD16 ....71 K1
BOW BD4 ....96 C7
KGHY BD21 ....2 C4
Ie Balk BTLY WF17 ....146 B4
WKFDW/WTN WF2 ....199 K5
Alk Av EARD/LOFT WF3 ....176 D1
Alk Crs EARD/LOFT WF3 ....124 B5
Alk La EARD/LOFT WF3 ....176 C1
GTHN BD7 ....95 H7
Alkram Dr LUD/ILL HX2 ....114 C6
Alkram Edge LUD/ILL HX2 ....114 C6
Alkram Rd LUD/ILL HX2 ....114 E6
Alks St BTLY WF17 ....144 C7
Alks St BTLY WF17 ....146 A6
Allantyne Rd IDLE BD10 ....74 C1
Allater Av HUDS HD4 ....212 C1
Allfield La DOD/DAR S75 ....239 H2
Allroyd Clough HUDW HD3 ....190 A5
Allroyd La HUDW HD3 ....190 A5
All Royd Rd HUDN HD2 ....191 H1
St CUL/QBY BD13 ....93 J5
Alme La LM/WK BD12 ....118 E8
Alme Rd CLECK BD19 ....144 A3
Alme St BFD BD1 ....5 D4
LM/WK BD12 ....118 E8
Alme Ter HWTH * BD22 ....68 E5
Almfield LVSG WF15 ....170 D1
Almfield Crs LVSG WF15 ....170 D1
Almoral Av HUDS HD4 ....212 C1
Almoral Cl PONT WF8 ....180 C6
STKB/PEN S56 ....251 J7
Almoral Dr KNOT WF11 ....155 J7
Almoral Pl HFAX HX1 ....8 C5
Almoral St HBR HX7 ....112 B8
Almoral Wy YEA LS19 ....54 B5
Alm Pl BEE/HOL LS11 ....6 C6
Alm Rd MID LS10 ....125 F1
Alm Wk BEE/HOL LS11 ....6 B6
Alne La WKFDW/WTN WF2 ....10 A3
Alne La WKFDW/WTN WF2 ....10 A2
Amborough St WKFDE WF1 ....11 F6
Amburgh Rd MSTN/BAR LS15 ....82 C8

Bamlett Brow HWTH BD22 ....69 F3
Banbury Rd PONT WF8 ....155 F8
Bancroft Av HUDE HD5 ....192 A6
Bangor Gv WOR/ARM LS12 ....100 A7
Bangor Pl WOR/ARM LS12 ....100 A7
Bangor Ter WOR/ARM LS12 ....100 A7
Bangor Vw WOR/ARM LS12 ....100 A7
Bank IDLE BD10 ....75 F5
Bank Av HORS LS18 ....77 F3
MOR LS27 ....123 F6
Bank Bottom HBR HX7 ....137 H1
HFAX HX1 ....9 E4
Bank Bottom La LUD/ILL HX2 ......138 B2
Bank Cl IDLE BD10 ....74 E6
Bank Crest BAIL BD17 ....51 J8
Bank Crest Ri SHPY BD18 ....72 D4
Bank Edge Cl WBSY BD6 ....118 E3
Bank Edge Gdns LUD/ILL HX2 .....115 H8
Bank Edge Rd LUD/ILL HX2 ....115 G8
Bank End Knoll HOLM/MEL HD9 ...233 K2
Bank End La HUDE HD5 ....192 A7
KBTN HD8 ....236 D7
Bank End Rd MAR/SLWT HD7 ......189 F8
Banker St BULY LS4 ....100 D2
Bankfield AL/HA/HU LS17 ....40 B7
KBTN HD8 ....235 H1
MAR/SLWT * HD7 ....209 J7
Bankfield Av HUDE HD5 ....192 D3
SHPY BD18 ....72 D5
Bankfield Cl OSS WF5 ....174 A7
MIRF WF14 ....170 C6
Bankfield Ct HUDE HD5 ....13 F5
WKFDW/WTN WF2 ....149 G8
Bankfield Dr HOLM/MEL HD9 ......247 H1
HWTH BD22 ....47 G4
SHPY BD18 ....72 D4
WKFDW/WTN WF2 ....149 G8
Bankfield Flats HWTH * BD22 ....68 D1
Bankfield Gdns BULY LS4 ....100 C1
HIPP HX3 ....140 E5
Bank Field Gra GTL/HWG HX4 .....166 B4
Bankfield Gv BULY LS4 ....78 C8
Bankfield La HUDE HD5 ....192 D5
Bankfield Mt HWTH BD22 ....47 G4
Bankfield Park Av HUDS HD4 ....213 F2
Bank Field Rd BTLY WF17 ....146 B6
Bankfield Rd BULY * LS4 ....100 C1
HUD HD1 ....12 B5
HWTH BD22 ....47 G3
SHPY BD18 ....72 D4
Bankfields Av HBR HX7 ....137 F2
Bankfield St HWTH BD22 ....47 G3
Bankfield Ter BAIL BD17 ....73 K1
BULY LS4 ....100 C1
HUDS HD4 ....212 E3
Bankfield Vw HIPP HX3 ....8 C1
Bankfield Wk HWTH BD22 ....47 G4
Bankfield Yd HIPP * HX3 ....8 C2
Bankfoot HBR HX7 ....112 A8
Bank Foot La HUDS HD4 ....212 E4
Bank Foot Pl BTLY * WF17 ....146 B4
Bank Foot Rd HUDS HD4 ....214 B3
Bank Foot St BTLY * WF17 ....146 B6
Bank Ga MAR/SLWT HD7 ....210 D2
Bank Gv EARL WF12 ....173 F4
Bank Hey Bottom La
RPDN/SBR HX6 ....164 B8
Bankholme Ct BOW BD4 ....120 C1
Bankhouse PDSY/CALV LS28 ....98 B3
Bank House Cl LUD/ILL HX2 ....114 A7
Bankhouse La HIPP HX3 ....166 C1
SHPY BD18 ....190 B6
PDSY/CALV LS28 ....98 B6
Bankhouse Rd HUDW HD3 ....190 B6
Banklands AIRE BD20 ....27 G1
Banklands Av AIRE BD20 ....27 H1
Banklands La AIRE BD20 ....27 H1
Bank La AIRE BD20 ....17 G3
HOLM/MEL HD9 ....190 B8
HOLM/MEL HD9 ....233 H4
HOLM/MEL HD9 ....233 H4
KBTN HD8 ....236 D7
Bank Rd RPDN/SBR HX6 ....33 H4
Bank Royd La GTL/HWG HX4 ......187 K2
Banks Ap MAR/SLWT HD7 ....189 H6
Bank Side HORS LS18 ....77 F3
Banks Av FEA/AMT WF7 ....202 E6
MAR/SLWT HD7 ....189 H6
PONT WF8 ....180 D3
Banks Buildings FEA/AMT * WF7 ...179 J7
Banks Crs MAR/SLWT HD7 ....189 H6
Banks Dr MAR/SLWT HD7 ....189 H6
Banks End Rd ELL HX5 ....167 H5
Banksfield Av YEA LS19 ....53 K3
Banksfield Cl YEA LS19 ....53 K3
Banksfield Crs YEA LS19 ....53 K3
Banksfield Gv YEA LS19 ....53 K3
Banksfield Mt YEA LS19 ....53 K3
Banksfield Ri YEA LS19 ....53 K3
Banksfield Rd HBR HX7 ....137 F2
Banksfields Crs HBR HX7 ....137 F2
Banksfield Ter HBR HX7 ....137 F2
Banks Gv MAR/SLWT HD7 ....189 H6
Bankside KBTN HD8 ....235 H1
TOD OL14 ....134 A7
Bank Side La RHAY LS8 ....80 B8

Banks La AIRE BD20 ....28 C7
KNOT WF11 ....156 C7
Banks Mt PONT WF8 ....180 D3
Bank Sq LM/WK LS27 ....123 F6
Banks Rd HOLM/MEL HD9 ....213 H8
MAR/SLWT HD7 ....189 H6
MAR/SLWT HD7 ....211 F3
Banks Side MAR/SLWT HD7 ....189 H1
Banks St BTLY WF17 ....146 B7
Bank St BFD BD1 ....4 C4
BRIG HD6 ....168 B1
CAS WF10 ....153 J3
CLECK BD19 ....143 K4
COL BB8 ....64 A2
EARL WF12 ....172 C3
HOLM/MEL HD9 ....234 A7
HOR/CROF WF4 ....197 G2
LDS LS1 ....3 E4
MIRF WF14 ....170 B6
MOR LS27 ....123 F6
OSS WF5 ....173 J6
SHPY BD18 ....73 H3
TOD OL14 ....134 A7
WBSY * BD6 ....118 D2
WBY LS22 ....23 J6
WKFDE WF1 ....10 B3
Bank Ter HBR HX7 ....111 K8
MOR LS27 ....123 F6
Bank Top HIPP HX3 ....9 F5
Bank Top Dr AIRE BD20 ....48 D1
Bank Top La HBR HX7 ....138 A6
HOLM/MEL HD9 ....232 A8
OT LS21 ....36 D8
Bank Top Wy BGLY BD21 ....48 D5
Bank Vw BAIL BD17 ....73 H1
EARL WF12 ....173 F4
HOLM/MEL HD9 ....233 J1
Bank View Ter CHAL LS7 ....79 H4
Bank Wk BAIL BD17 ....51 J8
Bankwell Fold WBSY BD6 ....118 E2
Bankwell Rd HUDS HD4 ....190 B7
Bankwood BTLY * WF17 ....122 A7
Bank Wood Rd PONT WF8 ....182 C7
Bankwood Wy BTLY WF17 ....122 A7
Bannerman St LM/WK BD12 ....119 H6
Banner St BFDE BD3 ....5 E5
Bannockburn Ct BOW * BD4 ....119 H2
Bannockburn Wy NORM WF6 ......151 H7
Banstead St East RHAY LS8 ....80 B8
Banstead St West RHAY LS8 ....80 B8
Banstead Ter East RHAY LS8 ....80 B8
Banstead Ter West RHAY * LS8 .....80 B8
Bantam Cl MOR LS27 ....123 J7
Bantam Grove La MOR LS27 ....123 J7
Bantam Grove Vw MOR LS27 ....123 J7
Bantree Ct IDLE BD10 ....74 C2
Baptist Fold CUL/QBY BD13 ....116 D2
Baptist La OSS WF5 ....174 C7
Baptist Pl BFD BD1 ....4 B4
Baptist St BTLY WF17 ....145 K8
Barber Rw MAR/SLWT HD7 ....211 G2
Barberry Av BFDE BD3 ....97 G3
Barber Sq HECK WF16 ....145 F7
Barber St BRIG HD6 ....142 B7
Barclay Cl CUL/QBY BD13 ....70 C6
Barclay St CHAL LS7 ....7 F2
Bar Cft HUDE HD5 ....192 D2
Barcroft HWTH BD22 ....69 H3
Barcroft Gv YEA LS19 ....53 J5
Barcroft Rd HUDS HD4 ....213 F1
Barden Av WBSY BD6 ....117 J2
Barden Cl BTLY WF17 ....146 A6
WOR/ARM LS12 ....100 A4
Barden Dr BGLY BD16 ....50 C7
Barden Gn WOR/ARM LS12 ....100 A4
Barden Gv WOR/ARM * LS12 ....100 A4
Barden Mt WOR/ARM LS12 ....100 A4
Barden Pl WOR/ARM LS12 ....100 A4
Barden Rd WKFDE WF1 ....11 F3
Barden St GIR BD8 ....95 H2
Barden Ter WOR/ARM LS12 ....100 A4
Bardon Hall Ms BHP/TINH * LS16 ...78 D4
Bardsey Crs BFDE BD3 ....5 E4
Bardwell Ct EARD/LOFT WF3 ......150 B6
Bare Head La HIPP HX3 ....116 C5
Barfield Av YEA LS19 ....53 J5
Barfield Crs AL/HA/HU LS17 ....58 B6
Barfield Dr YEA LS19 ....53 J5
Barfield Cv AL/HA/HU LS17 ....58 C6
Barfield Mt AL/HA/HU LS17 ....58 C6
Barfield Rd HIPP HX3 ....141 H4
Bargate MAR/SLWT HD7 ....211 H2
Bargess Ter GFTH/SHER LS25 ......129 C2
Barge St HUD HD1 ....12 B6
Bargrange Av SHPY BD18 ....73 H5
Bargreen HUDE HD5 ....192 D2
Barham Ter IDLE BD10 ....75 F7
Bar House La AIRE BD20 ....27 H8
Baring Av BFDE BD3 ....97 F3
Bark Cl KBTN HD8 ....215 J8
Barker Ct HIPP HX3 ....140 D8
Barker Ct HUDN HD2 ....212 A1
Barkerend Rd BFDE BD3 ....5 D4
Barker Pl BRAM LS13 ....99 F1
Barker Rd HOR/CROF WF4 ....197 F1
Barker's Rd HOR/CROF WF4 ....198 A5
Barker St EARD/LOFT WF3 ....150 E5
LVSG WF15 ....144 E7
TOD OL14 ....134 A5

Barkers Well Fold *WOR/ARM* LS12 ....99 H7
Barkers Well Garth *WOR/ARM* LS12 ......99 J8
Barkers Well Ga *WOR/ARM* LS12 ....99 J8
Barkers Well Lawn *WOR/ARM* LS12 ....99 J8
Bark House La *DOD/DAR* S75 ....238 C7
  KBTN HD8 ....215 K8
Bark La *ILK* LS29 ....18 E5
Barkly Av *BEE/HOL* LS11 ....124 B2
Barkly Dr *BEE/HOL* LS11 ....124 B2
Barkly Gv *BEE/HOL* LS11 *.........................124 B2
Barkly Pde *BEE/HOL* LS11 ....124 B1
Barkly Pl *BEE/HOL* LS11 ....124 B2
Barkly Rd *BEE/HOL* LS11 ....124 A1
Barkly St *BEE/HOL* LS11 ....124 B2
Barkly Ter *BEE/HOL* LS11 ....124 B1
Bar La *AIRE* BD20 ....48 D2
  BSPA/BRAM LS23 ....43 G5
  GFTH/SHER LS25 ....106 A4
  HOR/CROF WF4 ....217 K1
  HORS LS18 ....76 C3
  RPDN/SBR HX6 ....168 E1
  WKFDE WF1 ....176 A2
Barlbro' Pl *HUDW* HD3 ....190 A7
Barlby Wy *RHAY* LS8 ....80 E5
Barleycorn Cl *WKFDE* WF1 ....176 B2
Barley Cote Av *AIRE* BD20 ....48 D1
Barley Cote La *AIRE* BD20 ....48 E1
Barley Cote Rd *AIRE* BD20 ....48 D1
Barley Cft *DEWS* WF13 ....171 J3
Barleyfield Cl *WKFDE* WF1 ....11 E1
Barley Field La *MSTN/BAR* LS15 ....103 J3
Barleyfields Cl *WBY* LS22 ....23 J4
Barleyfields Ct *WBY* LS22 ....23 J5
Barleyfields La *WBY* LS22 ....25 J5
Barleyfields Ms *WBY* LS22 ....23 J6
Barleyfields Rd *WBY* LS22 ....23 J5
Barleyfields Ter *WBY* LS22 ....23 J5
Barleyhill Crs *GFTH/SHER* LS25 ....105 J4
Barleyhill La *GFTH/SHER* LS25 ....105 J4
Barleyhill Rd *GFTH/SHER* LS25 ....105 J4
Barley Ms *EARD/LOFT* WF3 ....125 J8
Barley St *HWTH* BD22 ....2 B6
Barlow Rd *KGHY* BD21 ....2 C2
Barlow St *BFDE* BD3 ....5 H6
Barmby Crs *OSS* WF5 ....174 A7
Barmby Fold *OSS* WF5 ....174 A7
Barmby Pl *ECHL* BD2 ....5 F2
Barmby Rd *ECHL* BD2 ....5 F2
Barmby St *LM/WK* BD12 ....118 E7
Barmby Ter *ECHL* BD2 ....5 F2
The Barn *LM/WK* BD12 ....119 F5
Barnaby Rd *BGLY* BD16 ....50 C7
Barnard Cl *MSTN/BAR* LS15 ....82 C8
Barnard Rd *BOW* BD4 ....5 E6
Barnard Wy *MSTN/BAR* LS15 ....82 C8
Barnbow La *MSTN/BAR* LS15 ....83 F7
  MSTN/BAR LS15 ....83 G6
Barnbrough St *BULY* LS4 ....100 C1
Barnby Av *GIR* BD8 ....94 C4
Barnby Royd *HUDE* HD5 ....192 A4
Barncroft Cl *SCFT* LS14 ....81 H4
Barncroft Dr *SCFT* LS14 ....81 G5
Barncroft Gdns *SCFT* LS14 ....81 H5
Barncroft Mt *SCFT* LS14 ....81 G5
Barncroft Ri *SCFT* LS14 ....81 H5
Barncroft Rd *SCFT* LS14 ....81 H5
Barnes Av *WKFDE* WF1 ....149 H8
Barnes Rd *CAS* WF10 ....153 G5
  GIR BD8 ....95 F3
Barnes St *TOD* OL14 ....159 K2
Barnet Gv *MOR* LS27 ....147 F1
Barnet Rd *WOR/ARM* LS12 ....100 D4
Barnsdale Ct *CAS* WF10 ....153 G5
Barnsdale Rd *CAS* WF10 ....129 J5
  RTHW LS26 ....152 B2
Barnsdale Wy *HEM/SK/SE* WF9 ....227 G4
Barnside La *HOLM/MEL* HD9 ....249 G2
Barnsley Beck Gv *BAIL* BD17 ....51 K8
Barnsley Rd *CUD/GR* S72 ....223 K8
  FEA/AMT WF7 ....205 G7
  HEM/SK/SE WF9 ....225 K8
  HOR/CROF WF4 ....195 G8
  KBTN HD8 ....236 A5
  KBTN HD8 ....237 J2
  STKB/PEN S36 ....252 C7
  WKFDW/WTN WF2 ....198 E5
Barnstone V *WKFDE* WF1 ....11 E1
Barn St *HWTH* BD22 ....90 E1
Barnswick Cl *PONT* WF8 ....180 E5
Barnswick Vw *BHP/TINH* LS16 ....55 J7
Baron Cl *BEE/HOL* LS11 ....123 G7
Baronscourt *MSTN/BAR* LS15 ....104 B3
Baronsmead *MSTN/BAR* LS15 ....104 A3
Baronsway *MSTN/BAR* LS15 ....104 A3
Barrack Rd *CHAL* LS7 ....79 K8
Barracks Fold *HOLM/MEL* HD9 ....249 F1
Barracks St *HECK* WF16 ....145 F7
Barrack St *CHAL* LS7 ....7 F1

Barraclough Sq *LM/WK* BD12 ....118 D7
Barraclough St *LM/WK* BD12 ....118 C5
Barran St *BGLY* BD16 ....50 A8
Barras Garth Pl *WOR/ARM* LS12 ....100 B5
Barras Garth Rd *WOR/ARM* LS12 ....100 B5
Barras Pl *WOR/ARM* LS12 ....100 B5
Barras Ter *WOR/ARM* LS12.......................100 B5
Barratt's Rd *WKFDE* WF1 ....10 C1
Barrett St *AIRE* BD20 ....27 F2
Barrington Cl *HIPP* HX3 ....141 F7
Barrington Pde *CLECK* BD19 ....144 D3
Barrowby Av *MSTN/BAR* LS15 ....104 C4
Barrowby Crs *MSTN/BAR* LS15 ....104 C3
Barrowby La *MSTN/BAR* LS15 ....104 D3
Barrowby Rd *MSTN/BAR* LS15 ....104 D4
Barrows La *AIRE* BD20 ....26 E7
Barrowstead *KBTN* HD8 ....236 E2
Barr St *HUD* HD1 ....13 E2
Barr Ter *HUD* BD8 ....95 F3
Barry St *BFD* BD1 ....4 C4
Barsey Green La *GTL/HWG* HX4 ....165 F5
Barstow Fall *PONT* WF8 ....155 F8
Barstow Sq *WKFDE* WF1 ....10 C3
Bar St *BTLY* WF17 ....146 C7
  TOD OL14 ....133 K7
Barthorpe Cl *BOW* BD4 ....120 C1
Barthorpe Crs *CHAL* LS7 ....79 J3
Bartle Fold *GTHN* BD7 ....95 F8
Bartle Gil Dr *BAIL* BD17 ....52 A7
Bartle Gill Ri *BAIL* BD17 ....52 A7
Bartle Gill Vw *BAIL* * BD17 ....52 A7
Bartle Gv *GTHN* BD7 ....95 F8
Bartle La *GTHN* BD7 ....95 F8
Bartle Pl *GTHN* BD7 ....95 F8
Bartle Sq *GTHN* BD7 ....95 G7
Barton Ct *MSTN/BAR* LS15 ....104 A4
Barton Gv *BEE/HOL* LS11 ....101 G7
Barton Hl *BEE/HOL* LS11 ....101 G7
Barton Manor Cl *HUDS* HD4 ....212 B1
Barton Mt *BEE/HOL* LS11 ....101 G7
Barton Pl *BEE/HOL* LS11 ....101 G7
  BTLY WF17 ....146 B7
Barton Rd *BEE/HOL* LS11 ....101 G7
Barton St *BRIG* * HD6 ....142 B8
  WBOW BD5 ....95 H8
Barton Ter *BEE/HOL* LS11 ....101 G7
Barton Vw *BEE/HOL* LS11 ....101 G7
Barton Wy *HEM/SK/SE* WF9 ....226 C6
Barwick Gn *WBSY* BD6 ....117 H3
Barwick Rd *GFTH/SHER* LS25 ....105 J2
  SCFT LS14 ....81 K8
Basford St *WKFDW/WTN* WF2 ....10 A4
Basil St *HUDS* HD4 ....190 D7
  WBOW BD5 ....95 H8
Baslow Gv *HTON* BD9 ....95 F1
Bates Av *RPDN/SBR* HX6 ....138 C3
Bates La *PONT* WF8 ....181 G6
Bateson St *IDLE* BD10 ....75 C4
Bath Cl *BRAM* LS13 ....99 G1
Bath Gv *BRAM* * LS13 ....99 G1
Bath La *BRAM* LS13 ....99 G1
Bath Pl *CLECK* BD19 ....144 A4
  HIPP HX3 ....8 C2
Bath Rd *BEE/HOL* LS11 ....6 C5
  BRAM LS13 ....99 G1
  CLECK BD19 ....144 A4
  HECK WF16 ....145 G2
  HIPP HX3 ....140 B7
Bath St *BFDE* * BD3 ....5 E4
  BTLY WF17 ....146 C6
  DEWS WF13 ....171 J3
  ELL HX5 ....166 E5
  HFAX HX1 ....9 E5
  HUD HD1 ....12 C3
  ILK LS29 ....20 C6
  KBTN HD8 ....215 H6
  KGHY BD21 ....2 C3
  TOD OL14 ....134 A2
Batley Av *HUD* HD1 ....190 D5
Batley Buildings *HUD* HD1 ....12 A3
Batley Field Hl *BTLY* WF17 ....146 B5
Batley Fld Rd *EARD/LOFT* WF3 ....147 K6
  HECK WF16 ....145 J7
  WKFDW/WTN WF2 ....174 D2
Batley St *HIPP* HX3 ....8 B2
  HUDE HD5 ....13 H4
Batter La *YEA* LS19 ....54 A7
Battinson Rd *HFAX* HX1 ....8 A3
Battinson St *HIPP* HX3 ....9 F6
Battye Av *HUDS* HD4 ....190 B8
Battye St *BOW* BD4 ....96 E5
  EARL WF12 ....172 C5
Baulk Head La *TOD* OL14 ....134 E5
Bavaria Pl *GIR* BD8 ....95 H2
Bawn Ap *WOR/ARM* LS12 ....99 J6
Bawn Dr *WOR/ARM* LS12 ....99 J5
Bawn Av *WOR/ARM* LS12 ....99 J5
Bawn Gdns *WOR/ARM* LS12 ....99 J5
Bawn La *WOR/ARM* LS12 ....99 J5
Bawson Ct *CLECK* BD19 ....144 D2
Baxandall St *WBOW* BD5 ....95 K8
Baxtergate *PONT* WF8 ....180 E3

Baxter La *HIPP* HX3 ....117 F
Bay Cl *HUDW* HD3 ....190 C
Bayfield Cl *HOLM/MEL* HD9 ....248 C
Bay Hall Common Rd *HUDN* * HD2 ....12 C
Bay Horse La *LA/HA/HU* LS17 ....59 J
Bayldons Pl *BTLY* * WF17 ....146 B
Baylee St *HEM/SK/SE* WF9 ....224 E
Bayne Dr *BOW* BD4 ....119 J
Bay of Biscay *WIL/AL* BD15 ....72 B
Bayswater Crs *RHAY* LS8 ....80 D
Bayswater Gv *ECHL* BD2 ....97 F
  RHAY LS8 ....80 D
Bayswater Mt *RHAY* LS8 ....80 D
Bayswater Pl *RHAY* LS8 ....80 D
Bayswater Rd *RHAY* LS8 ....80 A
Bayswater Rw *RHAY* LS8 ....80 D
Bayswater Ter *HIPP* HX3 ....140 D
  RHAY LS8 ....80 D
Bayswater Vw *RHAY* LS8 ....80 D
Bayton La *YEA* LS19 ....54 C
Beacon Av *MOR* LS27 ....147 G
Beacon Brow *WBSY* BD6 117
Beacon Cl *BGLY* BD16 ....50 B
Beacon Dr *HEM/SK/SE* WF9 226
Beaconfield Rd *HEM/SK/SE* WF9 ....226 B
Beacon Gv *MOR* LS27 ....147 G
  WBSY BD6 ....118 A
Beacon Hl *HEM/SK/SE* WF9 ....226 C
Beacon Hill Rd *HIPP* HX3 ....9 G
Beacon Pl *WBSY* BD6 ....117 K
Beacon Ri *ILK* LS29 19
Beacon Rd *WBSY* BD6 ....117 K
Beaconsfield Ct *GFTH/SHER* LS25 ....105 K
Beaconsfield Rd *CLAY* BD14 ....94 C
Beaconsfield St *HIPP* HX3 ....9 F
  TOD OL14 ....134 C
Beacon St *DEWS* WF13 ....171 F
  GTHN * BD7 ....117 K
  HUDN HD2 ....12 C
  ILK LS29 ....18 E
  WBSY BD6 ....118 B
Beacon Vw *HEM/SK/SE* WF9 225
Beaden Dr *KBTN* HD8 ....215 G
Beadon Av *HUDE* HD5 ....192 D
Beagle Av *HUDS* HD4 ....212 C
Beal La *KNOT* WF11 183
Beamshaw *HEM/SK/SE* WF9 ....241 H
Beamsley Gv *BGLY* BD16 ....50 B
  HDGY LS6 9
Beamsley La *SKP/WHF* BD23 15
Beamsley Mt *HDGY* * LS6 ....6 A
Beamsley Pl *HDGY* LS6 ....6 A
Beamsley Rd *HTON* BD9 ....73 H
  HDGY LS6 95
Beamsley Ter *HDGY* * LS6 ....6 A
Beamsley Vw *ILK* LS29 19
Beancroft Rd *CAS* WF10 153
Beancroft St *CAS* WF10 153
Beanlands Pde *ILK* LS29 ....20 C
Bean St *ELL* HX5 ....167 H
Bear Pones Rd *HOLM/MEL* HD9 248
Bearing Av *BEE/HOL* LS11 ....124 C
Bear Pit Gdns *HDGY* LS6 ....78 C
Beastfair *PONT* WF8 ....180 C
Beast Market *HUD* HD1 ....13 C
Beatrice St *CLECK* BD19 ....144 F
  HWTH BD22 ....90 E
  KGHY BD21 ....3 C
Beaufort Av *KBTN* HD8 ....215 H
Beaufort Gv *ECHL* BD2 ....74 C
Beaumont Av *HEM/SK/SE* WF9 ....226 E
  HUDE HD5 13
  RHAY LS8 ....80 D
Beaumont Cl *EARD/LOFT* WF3 ....150 C
Beaumont Dr *HOR/CROF* WF4 ....219 F
Beaumont Park Rd *HUDS* HD4 ....212 C
Beaumont Pl *BTLY* WF17 ....145 J
Beaumont Rd *DOD/DAR* S75 239
  GIR BD8 ....95 F
Beaumont St *BTLY* WF17 ....146 E
  EARD/LOFT WF3 ....150 C
  HUD HD1 ....13 C
  HUDE HD5 13
  HUDS HD4 ....212 C
  HUDS HD4 ....189 H
  KBTN HD8 ....217 G
  TOD OL14 ....133 G
Beaver Dr *DEWS* WF13 171
Becca La *GFTH/SHER* LS25 ....84 C
Beck Bottom *PDSY/CALV* LS28 ....75 C
  WKFDW/WTN WF2 ....148 E
Beckbridge La *NORM* WF6 ....178 A
Beckbridge Rd *NORM* WF6 ....152 E
Beckbridge Wy *NORM* WF6 ....178 B
Beckbury Cl *PDSY/CALV* LS28 ....98 E
Beckbury St *PDSY/CALV* LS28 ....98 E
Beckenham Pl *HFAX* HX1 ....139 F
Beckers Av *BTLY* * WF17 ....146 A
Beckett Cl *HOR/CROF* WF4 197
Beckett Crs *DEWS* WF13 171
Beckett Gv *DEWS* WF13 171
Beckett La *DEWS* WF13 171
Beckett Park Campus *HDGY* LS6 77
Beckett Rd *DEWS* WF13 ....172 A
Becketts Cl *HBR* HX7 ....112 A
Beckett's Park Dr *HDGY* LS6 78
Beckett's Park Rd *HDGY* LS6 78
Beckett St *BTLY* WF17 146

OSM LS9 ......102 A2
eckett Ter OSM LS9 ......102 B2
eckett Wk DEWS WF13 ......171 J4
eckfield La KNOT WF11 ......131 F6
eckfield Rd BGLY BD16 ......71 K4
eckfoot La BGLY BD16 ......71 K2
eck Hl WBSY BD6 ......117 K4
ackhill Ap CHAL LS7 ......79 G5
ackhill Av CHAL LS7 ......79 G5
ackhill Cha CHAL LS7 ......79 G5
ackhill Cl CHAL * LS7 ......79 G5
ackhill Dr CHAL LS7 ......79 G4
ackhill Fold CHAL LS7 ......79 G4
ackhill Gdns CHAL LS7 ......79 G5
ackhill Garth CHAL LS7 ......79 G5
ackhill Ga CHAL LS7 ......79 G5
ackhill Gn CHAL LS7 ......79 G5
ackhill Gv CHAL LS7 ......79 G5
ackhill Lawn CHAL * LS7 ......79 G5
ackhill Pl CHAL LS7 ......79 G4
ackhill Rw CHAL LS7 ......79 G4
ackhill V CHAL LS7 ......79 G4
ackhill Vw CHAL LS7 ......79 G5
ackhill Wk CHAL LS7 ......79 G4
eck La BGLY BD16 ......49 K7
LVSG WF15 ......145 F8
WBY LS22 ......41 F2
eckley Rd WKFDW/WTN WF2 ......175 C5
eck Meadow MSTN/BAR LS15 ......83 J5
eck Rd BGLY BD16 ......49 J3
HUD HD1 ......12 C2
RHAY LS8 ......80 B7
acks Ct EARL WF12 ......172 E5
ack Side KGHY BD21 ......3 D4
ackside Cl ILK LS29 ......18 C3
ILK LS29 ......32 B2
ackside Gdns BHP/TINH LS16 ......78 C4
HUDE HD5 ......192 E7
ackside La BHP/TINH LS16 ......95 F6
ackside Rd GTHN BD7 ......95 G6
ackside Vw MOR LS27 ......123 H7
acks Rd HWTH BD22 ......2 B4
ack St KGHY BD21 ......2 C4
ack Vw HOR/CROF WF4 ......221 J5
active Rd WKFDW/WTN WF2 ......175 F4
edale EARD/LOFT WF3 ......147 J3
edale Av BRIG HD6 ......167 K3
KBTN HD8 ......236 D2
edale Dr KBTN HD8 ......236 D2
WBSY BD6 ......117 K2
edding Edge Rd HOLM/MEL HD9 ......249 H5
ede Ct WKFDW WF1 ......10 C1
ede's Cl CUL/QBY BD13 ......93 H5
edford Av HOR/CROF WF4 ......194 C6
edford Cl BHP/TINH LS16 ......55 J8
FEA/AMT WF7 ......179 J8
HOR/CROF WF4 ......200 E3
KBTN HD8 ......193 G8
edford Ct RHAY LS8 ......80 E5
edford Dr BHP/TINH LS16 ......55 J8
edford Fld HDGY * LS6 ......79 G7
edford Gdns BHP/TINH LS16 ......55 J8
edford Garth BHP/TINH LS16 ......55 J8
edford Gv BHP/TINH LS16 ......55 J8
edford Mt BHP/TINH LS16 ......77 J1
edford Rw MID LS10 ......101 K7
edford St BOW BD4 ......5 D5
CUD/GR S72 ......240 A6
ELL HX5 ......166 E5
HFAX HX1 ......8 C4
KGHY BD21 ......2 C3
LDS LS1 ......7 D3
TOD OL14 ......133 H4
edford St North HFAX HX1 ......8 C4
edford Vw BHP/TINH LS16 ......55 J8
edivere Rd GIR BD8 ......94 D4
ediam La OT LS21 ......37 F6
ech La CUL/QBY BD13 ......70 A8
EARD/LOFT WF3 ......150 C7
HOLM/MEL HD9 ......233 J2
HOR/CROF WF4 ......201 F4
HORS LS18 ......77 G4
HUDE HD5 ......192 B6
MAR/SLWT HD7 ......189 J6
RPDN/SBR HX6 ......138 E6
TOD OL14 ......133 K5
WKFDW/WTN WF2 ......175 G4
ech Cl CUD/GR S72 ......228 A8
HEM/SK/SE WF9 ......241 H1
HIPP HX3 ......117 J5
IDLE BD10 ......74 D1
ILK LS29 ......32 C5
OSM LS9 ......81 F8
PONT WF8 ......181 F5
ech Ct OSS WF5 ......73 H5
ech Crs BAIL BD17 ......73 F2
BFDE BD3 ......5 F2
CAS WF10 ......154 E5
PONT WF8 ......181 K6
echcroft EARD/LOFT WF3 ......150 A2
ech Cft PONT WF8 ......155 F8
WKFDW/WTN WF2 ......199 J4
echcroft Cl BEE/HOL LS11 ......123 H2
echcroft Md AL/HA/HU LS17 ......58 C7
echcroft Vw BEE/HOL LS11 ......123 H2
echdale Av BTLY WF17 ......145 K4

Beech Dr CUL/QBY BD13 ......70 A8
FEA/AMT WF7 ......203 G2
WOR/ARM LS12 ......100 C3
Beecher St HIPP HX3 ......8 C1
KGHY BD21 ......3 F1
The Beeches BAIL BD17 ......51 K7
GSLY LS20 ......53 G1
PDSY/CALV LS28 ......97 K3
WBY LS22 ......23 J3
Beeches End BSPA/BRAM LS23 ......42 E4
Beeches Rd KGHY BD21 ......3 F2
Beechfield WKFDW/WTN WF2 ......199 G2
WOR/ARM LS12 ......99 H8
Beechfield Av KBTN HD8 ......236 E2
Beechfield Dr HOR/CROF WF4 ......178 A7
Beech Gdns CAS WF10 ......154 E5
Beech Gv AIRE BD20 ......27 F2
BFDE BD3 ......5 F2
BGLY BD16 ......50 C6
CLAY BD14 ......94 C7
CLECK BD19 ......144 D2
HEM/SK/SE WF9 ......224 A1
HIPP HX3 ......142 B4
NORM WF6 ......177 K3
RTHW LS26 ......126 C5
Beech Grove Av GFTH/SHER LS25 ......105 J5
Beech Grove Ter GFTH/SHER LS25 ......105 J5
LDSU LS2 ......6 C1
Beech Hl OT LS21 ......39 J5
PONT WF8 ......181 F2
Beech La OSM LS9 ......80 E8
Beech Lees PDSY/CALV LS28 ......76 A7
Beech Mt OSM LS9 ......81 F8
Beechmount Cl BAIL BD17 ......51 K7
Beechnut La PONT WF8 ......180 D2
Beech Rd BSPA/BRAM LS23 ......42 C5
HEM/SK/SE WF9 ......226 D4
RPDN/SBR HX6 ......139 F7
WBSY BD6 ......118 D4
Beech Spinney WBY LS22 ......23 K3
Beech Sq CLAY BD14 ......94 C7
Beech St AIRE BD20 ......26 E6
BGLY BD16 ......71 K1
EARD/LOFT WF3 ......166 A3
ELL HX5 ......166 E5
GTL/HWG HX4 ......165 K7
HEM/SK/SE WF9 ......242 A2
HFAX HX1 ......8 C4
HOLM/MEL * HD9 ......233 C6
HUD HD1 ......190 D6
KGHY BD21 ......2 C3
MIRF WF14 ......170 D6
PONT WF8 ......180 E4
Beech Ter BFDE BD3 ......5 F3
Beechtree Ct BAIL BD17 ......73 G1
Beech Tree Rd FEA/AMT WF7 ......179 K7
Beech Vw GFTH/SHER LS25 ......84 D4
HOR/CROF WF4 ......198 B8
RPDN/SBR * HX6 ......138 E6
Beech Wk BHP/TINH LS16 ......78 D1
CLECK BD19 ......120 E7
OSM LS9 ......81 F8
Beech Wy BTLY WF17 ......145 K2
Beechwood PONT WF8 ......180 C4
RTHW LS26 ......127 F4
Beechwood Av AIRE BD20 ......48 D2
BIRK/DRI BD11 ......121 G4
HIPP HX3 ......117 G6
LUD/ILL HX2 ......115 K6
MIRF WF14 ......170 D6
PONT WF8 ......180 C3
RPDN/SBR HX6 ......138 C8
SHPY BD18 ......72 E4
WBSY BD6 ......118 B1
WKFDW/WTN WF2 ......174 E5
Beechwood Cl HORS LS18 ......58 E8
LUD/ILL HX2 ......115 J7
Beechwood Ct BHP/TINH LS16 ......56 B6
SCFT LS14 ......81 G5
Beechwood Crs BULY LS4 ......78 D8
HEM/SK/SE WF9 ......224 C5
PONT WF8 ......180 C4
RPDN/SBR HX6 ......138 C8
Beechwood Dr FEA/AMT WF7 ......203 H4
LUD/ILL HX2 ......115 J7
RPDN/SBR HX6 ......138 C8
WBSY BD6 ......118 C1
Beechwood Gv BIRK/DRI BD11 ......121 G4
BULY LS4 ......78 D8
HOR/CROF WF4 ......197 J2
HUDN HD2 ......168 B6
ILK LS29 ......19 K7
LUD/ILL * HX2 ......115 J7
SHPY BD18 ......72 E4
WBSY BD6 ......118 C1
Beechwood Mt BULY LS4 ......78 D8
HEM/SK/SE WF9 ......224 D5
Beechwood Pl BULY * LS4 ......78 D8
Beechwood Ri WBY LS22 ......23 J4
Beechwood Rd BULY LS4 ......78 D8
LUD/ILL HX2 ......115 J7
MIRF WF14 ......170 D5
WBSY BD6 ......118 B1
Beechwood Rw BULY LS4 ......78 D8
Beechwood St HDGY LS6 ......78 D8
PDSY/CALV LS28 ......98 A2
Beechwood Ter BULY LS4 ......78 D8
Beechwood Vw BULY LS4 ......78 D8
Beecroft St BRAM LS13 ......76 E8

Beecroft Crs BRAM LS13 ......77 F8
Beecroft Gdns BRAM LS13 ......76 E8
Beecroft Mt BRAM LS13 ......98 E1
Beecroft St KGHY BD21 ......3 E3
KSTL LS5 ......78 A8
Beehive St WBSY BD6 ......118 A4
Beehive Yd WBSY * BD6 ......118 A4
Beestonley La GTL/HWG HX4 ......165 G7
Beeston Park Cft BEE/HOL LS11 ......123 K1
Beeston Park Garth
BEE/HOL * LS11 ......123 K1
Beeston Park Pl BEE/HOL LS11 ......123 K1
Beeston Park Ter BEE/HOL LS11 ......123 K1
Beeston Rd BEE/HOL LS11 ......101 G8
Bela Av BOW BD4 ......96 E8
Belcross Dr HIPP HX3 ......8 C1
Beldon Brook Gn KBTN HD8 ......215 F2
Beldon La WBSY BD6 ......118 A2
Beldon Park Av GTHN BD7 ......118 A1
Beldon Park Cl GTHN BD7 ......118 A1
Beldon Pl ECHL BD2 ......5 F1
Beldon Rd GTHN BD7 ......95 G8
Belfast St HFAX HX1 ......A5
The Belfry YEA LS19 ......54 A5
Belfry Ct WKFDE WF1 ......149 K6
Belfry Wy NORM WF6 ......178 B2
Belgrave Av HIPP HX3 ......9 E3
OSS WF5 ......173 K7
Belgrave Cl HIPP HX3 ......9 F3
Belgrave Crs HIPP HX3 ......9 F3
Belgrave Dr HIPP HX3 ......9 F3
Belgrave Gdns HIPP HX3 ......9 E3
Belgrave Ms YEA * LS19 ......53 J7
Belgrave Mt HIPP HX3 ......9 F3
WKFDE WF1 ......11 D1
Belgrave Pk HIPP HX3 ......9 E3
Belgrave Rd BGLY BD16 ......50 A8
KGHY BD21 ......2 C2
Belgrave St LDSU LS2 ......7 E3
OSS WF5 ......173 K7
RPDN/SBR HX6 ......138 E7
Belgrave Ter HUD HD1 ......12 B3
WKFDE WF1 ......11 D1
Belgravia Gdns RHAY * LS8 ......80 C7
Belgravia Rd WKFDE WF1 ......10 B1
Belinda St MID LS10 ......102 A7
Bell Bank Vw BGLY BD16 ......49 J7
Bellbrooke Av OSM LS9 ......102 D1
Bellbrooke Gv OSM LS9 ......102 D1
Bellbrooke Pl OSM LS9 ......102 D1
Bellbrooke St OSM LS9 ......102 C1
Bell Dean Rd WIL/AL BD15 ......94 B3
Belle Isle Av WKFDE WF1 ......11 D5
Belle Isle Cl MID LS10 ......125 F3
Belle Isle Crs WKFDE WF1 ......11 D5
Belle Isle Dr WKFDE * WF1 ......11 D5
Belle Isle Pde MID LS10 ......125 F2
Belle Isle Rd HWTH BD22 ......68 E5
MID LS10 ......125 F3
Bellerby Brow WBSY BD6 ......117 J2
Belle View Ri HIPP HX3 ......117 G6
Belle Vue CUL/QBY BD13 ......116 D4
GIR BD8 ......4 B2
ILK LS29 ......20 C8
Belle Vue Av MSTN/BAR LS15 ......82 D4
RHAY LS8 ......81 F5
Belle Vue Ct BVRD LS3 ......6 B2
Belle Vue Crs HIPP HX3 ......117 G6
HUDN HD2 ......168 D8
Belle Vue Dr PDSY/CALV LS28 ......76 A8
Belle Vue Est MSTN/BAR LS15 ......82 D5
Belle Vue Pk HFAX * HX1 ......8 B4
Belle Vue Rd BVRD LS3 ......6 B2
HIPP HX3 ......117 G6
MSTN/BAR LS15 ......82 D5
WKFDE WF1 ......11 E6
Belle Vue St BTLY WF17 ......145 J6
Belle Vue Ter HIPP HX3 ......9 F6
KGHY * BD21 ......3 E4
Bellgreave Av HOLM/MEL HD9 ......234 B5
Bell Hall Mt HFAX HX1 ......8 B6
Bell Hall Ter HFAX HX1 ......8 B6
Bell House Av BOW BD4 ......119 J2
Bellhouse Crs BOW BD4 ......119 J3
Bell La BRAM LS13 ......77 G8
FEA/AMT WF7 ......203 F6
Bellmont Crs HEM/SK/SE WF9 ......224 E5
Bellmont Dr BRAM LS13 ......77 H8
Bellmont Gdns BRAM LS13 ......77 G7
Bellmont Gn BRAM LS13 ......77 H8
Bellmont Pl BRAM LS13 ......77 G7
Bellmont Vw BRAM LS13 ......77 H8
Bellioe St WBOW BD5 ......95 K7
Bell Rd BRAM LS13 ......77 G8
Bellshaw St GIR BD8 ......94 E4
Bell Sq AIRE BD20 ......27 G1
Belishaw St DEWS WF13 ......171 H6
HEM/SK/SE WF9 ......227 G3
HIPP HX3 ......9 E3
HUDS HD4 ......13 D6
LM/WK BD12 ......118 D7
OSM * LS9 ......7 F3
WKFDE WF1 ......10 B2
Bellstring La HUDE HD5 ......193 G2
Bellwood Av BSPA/BRAM LS23 ......42 D5
Belmont KNOT WF11 ......155 K2
Belmont Av BAIL BD17 ......51 H8
LM/WK BD12 ......119 F4

OT LS21 ....33 H2
Belmont Cl *BAIL* BD17 ....51 H8
  HUD HD1 ....12 C3
Belmont Crs *LM/WK* BD12 ....119 F4
  SHPY * BD18 ....73 G3
Belmont Gdns *WBSY* BD6 ....118 C4
Belmont Gv *LDSU* LS2 ....6 C2
  WBSY BD6 ....118 C4
  YEA LS19 ....54 A6
Belmont Pl *HFAX* HX1 ....8 B5
Belmont Ri *BAIL* BD17 ....51 H8
  LM/WK BD12 ....119 F4
Belmont Rd *ILK* LS29 ....20 E7
Belmont St *ECHL* BD2 ....74 E6
  FEA/AMT WF7 ....178 B6
  HIPP HX3 ....9 F3
  MAR/SLWT HD7 ....210 D3
  RPDN/SBR * HX6 ....139 F7
  WKFDE WF1 ....10 B1
Belmont Ter *EARD/LOFT* WF3 ...149 G1
  LUD/ILL HX2 ....138 B6
  SHPY * BD18 ....73 G3
Belmont Wy *HEM/SK/SE* WF9 ...226 D8
Belton Cl *GTHN* BD7 ....95 G8
Belton Gv *HUDW* HD3 ....190 B1
Belton Rd *AIRE* BD20 ....27 C3
Belton St *HUDS* HD4 ....192 A6
Belvedere Av *AL/HA/HU* LS17 ....57 K7
  BEE/HOL LS11 ....124 C1
Belvedere Ct *AL/HA/HU* LS17 .....58 A7
Belvedere Gv *AL/HA/HU* LS17 ....57 K7
Belvedere Mt *BEE/HOL* LS11 .....124 C1
Belvedere Rd *AL/HA/HU* LS17 ....57 K7
  BTLY WF17 ....146 A7
Belvedere Ter *BEE/HOL* LS11 .....124 C2
  GIR BD8 ....95 H5
Belvedere Vw *AL/HA/HU* LS17 ...58 A7
Belvoir Dr *KNOT* WF11 ....156 B7
Belvoir Gdns *HIPP* HX3 ....140 B8
Bembridge Ct *WKFDW/WTN* WF2 ...175 F6
Bempton Cl *GTHN* * BD7 ....95 H7
Bempton Gv *BTLY* WF17 ....145 J3
Bempton Pl *GTHN* * BD7 ....95 H7
Ben Booth La *HOR/CROF* WF4 ...194 C6
Benbow Av *IDLE* BD10 ....75 G6
Bence La *DOD/DAR* S75 ....259 J4
Bendigo Rd *EARL* WF12 ....172 E2
Benjamin St *LVSG* WF15 ....148 E8
Benjamin Sykes Wy *WKFDW/WTN* WF2 ....10 A2
Benn Av *GTHN* BD7 ....95 F7
Benn Crs *GTHN* BD7 ....95 F7
Bennet Ct *MSTN/BAR* LS15 ....104 B3
Bennett Av *HOR/CROF* WF4 ......197 J1
Bennett La *EARL* WF12 ....146 D8
Bennett Rd *HDGY* LS6 ....78 D6
Bennett St *HIPP* HX3 ....9 E5
  LVSG WF15 ....144 E7
Benn La *HUDW* HD3 ....189 K5
Benns La *LUD/ILL* HX2 ....138 C1
Benny La *MAR/SLWT* HD7 ....189 F8
Benny Parr Cl *BTLY* WF17 ....146 C1
Benomley Cl *HUDE* HD5 ....192 A8
Benomley Dr *HUDE* HD5 ....192 A8
Benomley Rd *HUDE* HD5 ....192 A8
Ben Rhydding Dr *ILK* LS29 ....21 F8
Ben Rhydding Rd *ILK* LS29 ....20 C8
Benson Gdns *WOR/ARM* LS12 ..100 B5
Benson La *NORM* WF6 ....152 B7
Benson St *CHAL* LS7 ....7 F2
Bentcliffe Av *AL/HA/HU* LS17 .....80 A1
Bentcliffe Cl *AL/HA/HU* LS17 .....80 A1
Bentcliffe Dr *AL/HA/HU* LS17 .....80 A1
Bentcliffe Gdns *AL/HA/HU* LS17 .80 A1
Bentcliffe Gv *AL/HA/HU* LS17 ....80 A1
Bentcliffe La *AL/HA/HU* LS17 .....79 K2
Bentcliffe Mt *AL/HA/HU* LS17 ....80 A1
Bent Close La *HBR* HX7 ....136 E8
Bentfield Cottages *CLAY* BD14 ...94 C6
Bent La *HOLM/MEL* HD9 ....248 B5
Bent Lea *HUDN* HD2 ....12 A5
Bentley Av *BRIG* HD6 ....142 B4
Bentley Cl *BAIL* BD17 ....51 H7
Bentley Gdns *CHAL* LS7 ....79 F5
Bentley Gv *HDGY* LS6 ....79 F5
Bentley La *HDGY* LS6 ....79 F5
Bentley Mt *HDGY* LS6 ....79 F5
  RPDN/SBR HX6 ....139 G6
Bentley Pde *HDGY* LS6 ....79 F5
Bent Ley Rd *HOLM/MEL* HD9 ....212 A8
Bentley Rd *WKFDW/WTN* WF2 ..175 F7
Bentley Royd Cl *RPDN/SBR* HX6 .138 D8
Bentley St *HUDS* HD4 ....190 E8
  LM/WK * BD12 ....118 E8
Benton Av *HOR/CROF* WF4 ....197 J1
Benton Park Av *YEA* LS19 ....54 A6
Benton Park Crs *YEA* LS19 ....54 A6
Benton Park Dr *YEA* LS19 ....54 A6
Benton Park Rd *YEA* LS19 ....54 A6
Bent Rd *HOLM/MEL* HD9 ....248 C4
Bents La *MAR/SLWT* HD7 ....209 K4
  WIL/AL BD15 ....70 E5
Bents Rd *STKB/PEN* S36 ....249 K7
  STKB/PEN S36 ....252 B7
Benyon Park Wy *WOR/ARM* LS12 ...100 C5
Beresford Rd *WBSY* BD6 ....118 C4
Beresford St *LM/WK* BD12 ....119 H6

Berkeley Av *RHAY* LS8 ....80 C8
Berkeley Crs *RHAY* LS8 ....80 C8
Berkeley Cft *BSLYN/ROY* S71 ...221 K7
Berkeley Gv *RHAY* LS8 ....80 C8
Berkeley Mt *RHAY* LS8 ....80 C8
Berkeley Rd *RHAY* LS8 ....80 C8
Berkeley St *RHAY* LS8 ....80 C8
Berkeley Ter *RHAY* LS8 ....80 C8
Berkeley Vw *RHAY* LS8 ....80 C8
Berking Av *OSM* LS9 ....102 B3
Bermondsey Ms *OT* LS21 ....33 K4
Bermondsey St *OT* LS21 ....33 K4
Bernard St *HUDN* HD2 ....169 F8
  RTHW LS26 ....127 G5
Berne Gv *WKFDE* WF1 ....10 C2
Berners St *WKFDE* WF1 ....11 D3
Berrington Wy *HWTH* BD22 ....46 D8
Berry Bank La *HOLM/MEL* HD9 ...233 H5
Berry Rd *HOLM/MEL* HD9 ....211 G8
Berryfield Garth *OSS* WF5 ....173 J5
Berry La *HIPP* HX3 ....9 F4
  HOR/CROF WF4 ....197 H2
  KGHY BD21 ....2 C5
  RTHW LS26 ....128 D3
Berry Moor Rd *RPDN/SBR* HX6 .165 G1
Berry Rd *HOLM/MEL* HD9 ....211 G8
Berry St *KGHY* BD21 ....3 E3
Berry's Yd *HOR/CROF* WF4 ....197 G1
Berry Vw *HUDS* HD4 ....213 F2
Bertha St *PDSY/CALV* LS28 ....98 B1
Bertie St *BOW* BD4 ....96 E8
Bertram Dr *BAIL* BD17 ....73 H1
Bertram Rd *GIR* BD8 ....4 A1
Bertrand St *BEE/HOL* LS11 ....6 C6
Berwick Av *HECK* WF16 ....145 G5
Berwick St *HFAX* * HX1 ....9 E4
Bescaby Gv *BAIL* * BD17 ....52 A8
Besha Av *LM/WK* BD12 ....118 E4
Besha Gv *LM/WK* BD12 ....118 E5
Bessingham Gdns *WBSY* BD6 ....118 A3
Best La *HUDS* HD4 ....213 K5
Beswick Cl *BFDE* BD3 ....97 F4
Beswick St *TOD* OL14 ....159 K4
Bethel Rd *SHPY* BD18 ....73 K3
Bethel St *AIRE* BD20 ....49 H5
  BRIG HD6 ....168 C1
  HIPP HX3 ....8 B1
Betula Wy *KBTN* HD8 ....215 G1
Beulah Gv *HDGY* LS6 ....79 H8
Beulah Mt *HDGY* LS6 ....79 H8
Beulah Pl *LUD/ILL* HX2 ....138 B6
Beulah St *HDGY* LS6 ....79 H7
Beulah Ter *HDGY* LS6 ....79 H8
Beulah Vw *HDGY* LS6 ....79 H8
Bevan Av *NORM* WF6 ....178 A3
Bevan Ct *GTHN* BD7 ....95 F7
Bevan Pl *WKFDW/WTN* WF2 .....174 D7
Bevedere Gdns *AL/HA/HU* LS17 ..58 A7
Beverley Av *BEE/HOL* LS11 ....101 H8
  LM/WK BD12 ....142 E1
Beverley Cl *ELL* HX5 ....167 G5
Beverley Dr *EARL* WF12 ....172 E3
  LM/WK BD12 ....142 E1
Beverley Gdns *BTLY* WF17 ....146 A1
Beverley Garth *FEA/AMT* WF7 ...203 G6
Beverley Mt *BEE/HOL* LS11 ....101 H8
Beverley Ri *ILK* LS29 ....19 J7
Beverley St *BOW* BD4 ....97 F6
Beverley Ter *BEE/HOL* LS11 ....101 H8
  HIPP HX3 ....8 C2
Beverley Vw *BEE/HOL* LS11 ....101 H8
Bevin Cl *WKFDE* WF1 ....149 K6
Bevin Crs *WKFDE* WF1 ....149 K6
Bevor Crs *HECK* WF16 ....145 G6
Bewerley Crs *LM/WK* BD12 ....118 B5
Bewick Ct *CUL/QBY* BD13 ....117 C1
Bewick Gv *RTHW* LS26 ....125 G4
Bexhill Cl *PONT* WF8 ....182 B1
Bexley Av *RHAY* LS8 ....102 B3
Bexley Gv *OSM* LS9 ....102 B3
Bexley Mt *RHAY* LS8 ....102 B3
Bexley Pl *RHAY* LS8 ....80 B8
Bexley Rd *RHAY* LS8 ....80 B8
Bexley Ter *OSM* LS9 ....102 B3
Bexley Vw *OSM* LS9 ....102 B1
Beza Rd *MID* LS10 ....101 K8
Beza St *MID* LS10 ....101 K8
Bickerton Wy *OT* LS21 ....33 G2
Biddenden Rd *MSTN/BAR* LS15 .104 D1
Bidder Dr *EARD/LOFT* WF3 ....148 D2
Bierley Hall Gv *BOW* BD4 ....119 J4
Bierley House Av *BOW* BD4 ....119 J3
Bierley La *BOW* BD4 ....119 J3
Bierley Vw *BOW* BD4 ....119 K2
Big Meadow Dr *ILK* LS29 ....18 B3
Bilberry Cl *CLAY* BD14 ....94 C8
Bilberry Ri *HWTH* BD22 ....69 F4
Bilham La *BTLY* DN5 ....242 E8
Bilham Rd *KBTN* HD8 ....238 A1
Billams Hl *OT* LS21 ....33 H2
Billey La *WOR/ARM* LS12 ....99 J7
Billingbauk Dr *BRAM* LS13 ....99 F2
Billing Ct *YEA* LS19 ....54 B8
Billing Dr *YEA* LS19 ....54 C8
Billingham Cl *WKFDW/WTN* WF2 .174 E3
Billing Vw *IDLE* BD10 ....74 E4
  YEA LS19 ....54 B8

Billingwood Dr *YEA* LS19 ....54 B7
Bill La *HOLM/MEL* HD9 ....233 J3
Billy La *HBR* HX7 ....112 D5
Bilsdale Gra *WBSY* BD6 ....118 A6
Bilsdale Wy *BAIL* BD17 ....73 F7
Bilton Pl *GIR* BD8 ....4 A4
Binbrook Vw *WIL/AL* * BD15 ....94 B3
Bingley Bank *AL/HA/HU* LS17 .....60 A7
Bingley Rd *BAIL* BD17 ....51 F7
  CUL/QBY BD13 ....70 B3
  HTON BD9 ....72 D7
  ILK LS29 ....51 H1
  KGHY BD21 ....69 K5
  SHPY BD18 ....72 D7
Bingley St *BVRD* LS3 ....6 B8
  GIR BD8 ....95 G6
Binham Rd *HUDW* HD3 ....190 C3
Binks Fold *LM/WK* BD12 ....142 E3
Binks St *WKFDE* WF1 ....149 K5
Binks Yd *OSS* * WF5 ....173 J3
Binnie St *BFDE* BD3 ....5 F2
Binn La *MAR/SLWT* HD7 ....229 J2
Binn Rd *MAR/SLWT* HD7 ....229 H4
Binns Hill La *LUD/ILL* HX2 ....138 E3
Binns La *GTHN* BD7 ....95 F7
  HOLM/MEL HD9 ....233 F7
Binns St *BGLY* BD16 ....50 A1
Binns Top La *HIPP* HX3 ....141 G3
Birch Av *KBTN* HD8 ....215 G6
  MSTN/BAR LS15 ....103 J2
  RPDN/SBR HX6 ....186 E2
  TOD OL14 ....133 C6
  WBOW BD5 ....119 G3
Birch Cliff *BAIL* BD17 ....73 H4
Birchcliffe Av *HBR* HX7 ....112 B5
Birch Cl *BRIG* HD6 ....142 D7
  WBOW BD5 ....119 G3
Birch Close La *BGLY* BD16 ....51 F2
Birch Crs *MSTN/BAR* LS15 ....103 J2
Birchdale *BGLY* BD16 ....49 K5
Birch Dr *GFTH/SHER* LS25 ....106 A3
Birchen Av *OSS* WF5 ....173 H6
Birchencliffe Hill Rd *HUDW* HD3 .190 B1
Birchenlee Cl *HBR* HX7 ....137 F2
The Birches *BHP/TINH* LS16 ....55 K5
  GSLY LS20 ....53 G3
Birchfield Av *MOR* LS27 ....122 E3
Birchfield Garth *SCFT* LS14 ....82 A4
Birchfield Gv *KBTN* HD8 ....236 E3
Birchfields Av *SCFT* LS14 ....82 A4
Birchfields Cl *SCFT* LS14 ....82 A4
Birchfields Ct *SCFT* LS14 ....82 A4
Birchfields Crs *SCFT* LS14 ....82 A4
Birchfields Ri *SCFT* LS14 ....82 A4
Birch Gv *BTLY* WF17 ....145 K3
  CAS WF10 ....154 D3
  GFTH/SHER LS25 ....129 F6
  HWTH BD22 ....2 B1
  MAR/SLWT HD7 ....189 J3
  WBOW BD5 ....119 G3
Birch Hill Ri *HORS* LS18 ....77 J1
Birchington Av *HUDW* HD3 ....190 A4
Birchington Cl *HUDW* HD3 ....190 B4
Birchington Dr *HUDW* HD3 ....190 A4
Birchlands Av *WIL/AL* BD15 ....71 F1
Birchlands Gv *WIL/AL* BD15 ....71 F1
Birch La *LUD/ILL* HX2 ....133 K2
  WBOW BD5 ....96 A4
Birch Ms *BHP/TINH* LS16 ....78 D7
Birch Pk *HBR* * HX7 ....112 B6
Birch Rd *GFTH/SHER* LS25 ....129 F6
  HUDS HD4 ....213 F7
  NORM WF6 ....178 A4
Birchroyd *RTHW* LS26 ....126 C3
Birchroyd Cl *HUDN* HD2 ....190 C3
Birch St *GIR* BD8 ....95 G6
  MOR LS27 ....147 G2
  WKFDE WF1 ....11 E1
Birchtree Cl *WKFDE* WF1 ....11 F1
Birch Tree Gdns *KGHY* BD21 ....3 F1
Birchtree Wy *BHP/TINH* * LS16 ...55 K5
Birch Wk *TOD* * OL14 ....134 C5
Birch Wy *WBOW* BD5 ....119 G3
Birchwood Av *AIRE* BD20 ....47 K1
  AL/HA/HU LS17 ....58 B1
  BTLY WF17 ....145 J3
Birchwood Ct *ILK* LS29 ....20 B7
  LVSG WF15 ....144 E7
Birchwood Dr *AIRE* BD20 ....47 K1
Birchwood Hl *AL/HA/HU* LS17 .....58 C1
Birchwood Mt *AL/HA/HU* LS17 ...58 C1
Birchwood Pk *HOLM/MEL* HD9 ..234 B1
Birchwood Rd *AIRE* BD20 ....47 K1
Birdale Field La *WBY* LS22 ....41 J1
Birdcage Hl *HIPP* HX3 ....139 J8
Birdcage La *HIPP* HX3 ....139 J8
Birdcage Wk *OT* LS21 ....33 J3
Bird Holme La *HIPP* HX3 ....141 G1
Birds Edge La *KBTN* HD8 ....235 H2
Birdsnest La *HOLM/MEL* HD9 ....249 H1
  KBTN HD8 ....250 D8
Birds Royd La *BRIG* HD6 ....168 C3
Birdswell Av *BRIG* HD6 ....142 A4
The Birdwalk *CUL/QBY* BD13 ....117 J1
Birfed Crs *BULY* LS4 ....78 E5
Birkby Brow Crs *BTLY* WF17 ......146 E2
Birkby Hall Rd *HUDN* HD2 ....12 A1
Birkby Hvn *WBSY* BD6 ....117 J6

rkby La BRIG HD6...................................142 D4
rkby Lodge Rd HUDN HD2................12 A1
rkby Rd HUDW HD3..............................190 C1
rkdale Av HUDW HD3...........................190 A3
rkdale Cl AL/HA/HU LS17.......................57 H7
CUL/QBY BD13......................................70 C5
rkdale Ct AIRE BD20.............................27 J8
rkdale Dr AL/HA/HU LS17.....................57 H7
rkdale Gn AL/HA/HU LS17.....................57 H7
rkdale La AL/HA/HU LS17.....................57 G7
DEWS WF13...171 K1
LUD/ILL HX2...115 J4
rkdale Mt AL/HA/HU LS17.....................57 H7
rkdale Pl AL/HA/HU LS17......................57 G7
rkdale Ri AL/HA/HU LS17......................57 G7
rkdale Rd BSLYN/ROY S71...................221 K6
DEWS WF13..172 A2
rkdale Wk AL/HA/HU LS17.....................57 G7
rkenshaw La BIRK/DRI BD11..............120 E6
rkett St CLECK BD19............................144 A3
rkhead St HECK WF16.........................145 H8
rkhill CAS WF10...................................154 D3
rkhill Crs BIRK/DRI BD11....................120 E6
rkhouse La BRIG HD6..........................142 C6
HUDE HD5..13 F5
rk House La KBTN HD8.......................235 K4
rkhouse Rd BRIG HD6.........................142 D4
rkin La KNOT WF11.............................157 G3
rklands Moor CLECK BD19..................120 E8
rklands Rd HUDN HD2.........................191 F1
SHPY BD18..73 G4
rklands Ter BFDE BD18.........................73 H4
rk La MOR LS27...................................122 D7
rk Lea St WBOW BD5............................96 A7
rks Av GTHN BD7..................................95 F6
STKB/PEN S36.....................................251 H8
rks Fold GTHN BD7................................95 F5
rkshall La BOW BD4................................5 F5
rks Hall St HFAX HX1...............................8 B3
rks Hall Ter HFAX HX1..............................8 B3
rksland St BOW BD4................................5 F6
rks La HUDE HD5.................................192 C6
KBTN HD8..215 F8
RPDN/SBR HX6....................................164 A3
rks Rd HUDW HD3..............................190 A6
rkwith Cl SCFT LS14.............................81 K3
rkwood Av HOR/CROF WF4.................201 F1
rkwood Rd NORM WF6.........................150 E8
rmingham La HOLM/MEL HD9............211 G8
rnam Gv BOW BD4................................96 C7
rr Rd HTON BD9....................................73 H8
rstall La BIRK/DRI BD11......................121 H6
rthwaite Rd DOD/DAR S75.................239 H3
shopdale Dr WBY BD22........................40 E2
shopdale Holme WBSY BD6...............117 K3
shopgate St LDS LS1...............................7 D4
shop St HTON BD9................................73 H8
shops Wy HOLM/MEL HD9...................231 J1
MIRF WF14...170 A4
shop Wy EARD/LOFT WF3....................148 A3
sley Cl BSLYN/ROY S71.......................222 C8
smarck Ct BEE/HOL LS11...................101 H7
smarck Dr BEE/HOL LS11...................101 H7
smarck St BEE/HOL LS11....................101 H7
cterne C CUL/QBY BD13......................117 H1
ctern Ri MOR LS27.............................123 H8
ack Aston Rd BRAM LS13......................99 J1
ackberry Wy CLAY BD14.......................94 B8
ackbird Gdns GIR BD8...........................94 C5
ack Brook Wy CTL/HWY HX4...............166 B5
ack Bull St MID LS10...............................7 F5
ackburn Ct GIR BD8..............................94 D4
HIPP HX3..115 J8
ackburn Ct RTHW LS26......................126 C6
ackburn La KNOT WF11.......................157 F8
ackburn Pl BTLY WF17.........................146 C6
ackburn Rd BRIG HD6.........................142 A7
BTLY WF17...145 H2
ack Dyke TOD * OL14...........................134 E8
ack Dyke La CUL/QBY BD13..................93 F2
ack Edge La CUL/QBY BD13..................92 A5
acker Crs HOR/CROF WF4...................196 E5
ackergreen La STKB/PEN S36.............253 J8
acker La CUD/GR S72...........................223 G8
HOR/CROF WF4...................................197 G5
acker Rd HUDN HD2.............................12 B2
acker Rd North HUDN * HD2.................12 B2
ackers Ct EARL WF12..........................171 K7
ackett St PDSY/CALV LS28...................75 K4
ack Gates Ct EARD/LOFT WF3.............148 A3
ackgates Crs EARD/LOFT WF3............147 K3
ackgates Dr EARD/LOFT WF3..............148 A3
ackgates Fold EARD/LOFT WF3...........148 A3
ack Gates Ri EARD/LOFT * WF3...........148 A3
ack Hill La AIRE BD20............................47 F2
BHP/TINH LS16.....................................56 D2
ack Hill Rd OT LS21...............................36 C6
ackhouse Rd HUDN HD2.....................191 H1
ack La MAR/SLWT HD7.........................211 J4
ackledge HFAX HX1................................9 D4
ackley Rd ELL HX5..............................166 C6
ackman La LDSY LS2...............................7 D1
ackmires LUD/ILL HX2.........................115 K6
ackmoorfoot Rd
HOLM/MEL HD9...................................211 C6
ackmoor La AL/HA/HU LS17.................59 K1
ack Moor Rd AL/HA/HU LS17................57 F8

HWTH BD22...69 F5
Blackpool Gv WOR/ARM LS12............100 A7
Blackpool Pl WOR/ARM LS12..............100 A7
Blackpool Ter WOR/ARM LS12............100 A7
Blackpool Vw WOR/ARM LS12..............99 K7
Black Rd WKFDE WF1...........................176 E8
Blackshaw Beck La HIPP HX3...............117 F4
Blackshaw Clough Rd
RPDN/SBR HX6....................................163 H5
Blackshaw Dr WBSY BD6.....................117 J3
Blackshaw St TOD OL14.......................134 C6
Blacksmith GTHN BD7............................95 G7
Blacksmith Fold GTHN BD7....................95 G7
Blacksmith La BHP/TINH LS16...............57 F2
Blacksmiths Fold HUDE HD5................192 B8
Blackstone Av BHP/TINH LS16..............55 H8
Blackstone Edge Rd
RPDN/SBR HX6....................................161 K7
Blackthorn Ct MID LS10........................124 E3
Blackthorn Wy WKFDW/WTN WF2.......10 A1
Black Wk PONT WF8.............................181 F1
Blackwall HFAX HX1................................9 D5
Blackwall La RPDN/SBR HX6................138 D6
Blackwall Ri RPDN/SBR HX6................138 E6
Blackwood Av BHP/TINH LS16...............55 H8
Blackwood Gdns BHP/TINH LS16..........55 H8
Black Wood Gv HFAX HX1.......................8 A3
Blackwood Hall La LUD/ILL HX2...........137 K5
Black Wood Mt BHP/TINH LS16.............55 H8
Black Wood Ri BHP/TINH LS16.............55 H8
Blacup Moor Vw CLECK BD19..............144 A4
Blagden La HUDS HD4..........................213 F2
Blairsville Gdns BRAM LS13...................77 C7
Blairsville Gv BRAM LS13.......................77 C7
Blaith Royd La HBR HX7.......................136 A7
Blaithroyd La HIPP HX3............................8 F5
Blake Crs GSLY LS20...............................53 H3
Blake Gv CHAL LS7.................................79 K5
Blake Hall Dr MIRF WF14......................170 E7
Blake Hall Rd MIRF WF14.....................170 E7
Blakehill Av ECHL BD2............................98 E1
Blake Hill End HIPP HX3.......................116 E7
Blakehill Ter ECHL BD2...........................98 E1
Blakeholme La MAR/SLWT HD7............210 C2
Blakelaw Dr BRIG HD6..........................142 E8
Blake Law La HIPP HX3.........................116 D8
Blake Lee La MAR/SLWT HD7...............208 D5
Blakeley Gv WKFDW/WTN WF2...........175 C5
Blakeney Gv MID LS10.........................124 E2
Blakeney Rd MID LS10.........................124 E2
Blakeridge La BTLY WF17.....................146 A6
Blakestones Rd MAR/SLWT HD7..........210 C3
Blakey Rd WKFDW/WTN WF2...............175 C3
Blamires Pl GTHN BD7............................95 F8
Blamires St GTHN BD7............................95 F8
Blanche St BOW BD4...............................97 F5
Blandford Gdns LDSU * LS2.....................7 D1
Blandford Gv LDSU * LS2.........................7 D1
Blands Av CAS WF10.............................129 F6
Bland's Cl CAS WF10.............................153 J4
Blands Gv CAS WF10............................129 F6
Blands Ter CAS WF10...........................129 F6
Bland St HFAX HX1...................................8 C4
HUD HD1..156 B6
Blantyre Rd CUL/QBY BD13....................70 B5
Blayds Garth RTHW LS26......................126 D4
Blayd's Ms LDS LS1..................................7 E4
Blayds St OSM LS9...............................102 B4
Blayd's Yd LDS LS1..................................7 E4
Bleach Mill La ILK LS29..........................32 A6
Bleakley Av HOR/CROF WF4................221 K5
Bleakley La BSLYN/ROY S71.................221 K6
Bleakley Ter HOR/CROF WF4...............221 K5
Bleak St CLECK BD19...........................145 F3
Bleak St Lower CLECK BD19.................145 F3
Bleasdale Av HUDN HD2.........................12 B1
KNOT WF11..156 B6
Blencarn Cl SCFT LS14...........................81 H7
Blencarn Garth SCFT LS14.....................81 H7
Blencarn Rd SCFT LS14..........................81 H7
Blencarn Vw SCFT LS14.........................81 H7
Blenheim Av LDSU * LS2..........................7 D1
Blenheim Cl KNOT WF11......................155 K7
Blenheim Ct HFAX * HX1..........................8 C3
LDSU LS2..7 D1
Blenheim Dr BTLY WF17.......................146 B5
DEWS WF13..171 K2
Blenheim Gv LDSU LS2............................7 D1
Blenheim Hl BTLY WF17.......................146 C4
Blenheim Mt GIR BD8..............................4 A1
Blenheim Pl IDLE BD10..........................74 D2
Blenheim Rd GIR BD8..............................4 A2
WKFDE WF1..10 B1
Blenheim Sq LDSU * LS2..........................7 D1
Blenheim St HBR HX7...........................112 B8
Blenheim Ter LDSU LS2............................7 D1
Blenheim Vw LDSU LS2...........................79 H8
Blenheim Wk LDSU LS2............................6 C1
Blind La AL/HA/HU LS17..........................59 H8
BGLY BD16...49 H8
BIRK/DRI BD11....................................121 J4
EARD/LOFT WF3..................................148 A5
LUD/ILL HX2...137 J3
TOD OL14...133 K5
Blucher St BOW BD4...............................97 F5

Blue Ball La RPDN/SBR HX6................163 F8
Blue Ball Rd RPDN/SBR HX6................163 J6
RPDN/SBR HX6....................................185 J1
Bluebell Av STKB/PEN S36...................252 B8
Bluebell Cl PONT WF8...........................180 E4
SHPY BD18..73 K6
WIL/AL * BD15......................................94 B3
Bluebell Ct BTLY WF17..........................145 H1
Blue Bell Hl HUDS HD4.........................213 F1
Blue Bell La TOD OL14..........................133 F1
Bluebell Rd DOD/DAR S75....................220 A8
Bluebell Wk LUD/ILL HX2......................138 B3
Bluebell Wy HEM/SK/SE WF9...............226 B4
Bluebird Wk BGLY BD16..........................50 C7
Blue Butts OSS WF5..............................173 J6
Blue Hill Crs WOR/ARM LS12...............100 A5
Blue Hill Gra WOR/ARM LS12...............100 A6
Blue Hill Gv WOR/ARM LS12................100 A5
Blue Hill La WOR/ARM LS12.................100 A5
Blundell St HEM/SK/SE WF9.................226 A8
LDS LS1...7 D2
Blythe Av GIR BD8..................................95 G3
Blythe St GTHN BD7................................4 A4
Boardman St TOD OL14........................134 A5
Boar La LDS LS1......................................7 E4
Boathouse La MIRF WF14.....................104 A1
Boat La RTHW LS26..............................153 F1
Bobbin Mill Cl TOD OL14......................132 E2
Bobbin Mill Ct AIRE BD20.......................26 E6
Bob La LUD/ILL HX2.............................139 G4
Bodiham Hl GFTH/SHER LS25..............106 B3
Bodkin La HWTH BD22............................68 A8
Bodley Ter BULY LS4............................100 D2
Bodmin Ap MID LS10............................124 B6
Bodmin Av SHPY BD18............................74 A4
Bodmin Crs MID LS10...........................124 B6
Bodmin Cft MID LS10............................124 C7
Bodmin Dr NORM WF6..........................152 A8
Bodmin Gdns MID LS10........................124 B7
Bodmin Garth MID LS10........................124 C7
Bodmin Pl MID LS10.............................124 C7
Bodmin Rd MID LS10............................124 A6
Bodmin St MID LS10.............................124 B7
Boggart Hl SCFT LS14.............................81 G5
Boggart Hill Crs SCFT LS14....................81 G5
Boggart Hill Dr SCFT LS14......................81 G5
Boggart Hill Gdns SCFT LS14.................81 G5
Boggart Hill Rd SCFT LS14.....................81 G5
Boggart La HIPP HX3............................141 J2
KBTN HD8...216 E8
RPDN/SBR HX6....................................138 E8
Bog Green La HUDN HD2......................169 H6
Bog La MSTN/BAR LS15..........................82 E6
Bogthorn HWTH BD22............................47 G7
Boland Crs HWTH BD22..........................47 G8
Boldgrove St EARL WF12......................173 F5
Boldmere Rd MSTN/BAR LS15..............103 G4
Boldron Holt WBSY BD6.......................118 A3
Boldshay St BFDE BD3.............................5 F3
Bolehill Pk BRIG HD6............................141 K5
Bolingbroke St WBOW BD5...................118 E1
Bolland St LM/WK BD12........................119 F6
Bolling Rd BOW BD4................................5 D6
ILK LS29..20 D7
Bolsover Cl GFTH/SHER LS25..............106 B4
Bolstermoor Rd MAR/SLWT HD7.........188 E3
Boltby La WBSY BD6............................117 K3
Bolton LUD/ILL HX2..............................115 H4
Bolton Brow RPDN/SBR HX6................139 F7
Bolton Dr ECHL BD2...............................74 D7
Bolton Gra YEA LS19...............................54 A5
Bolton Gv ECHL BD2...............................74 D7
Bolton Hall Rd SHPY BD18......................73 K6
Bolton La ECHL BD2...............................74 B8
Bolton Rd AIRE BD20..............................27 G1
BFD BD1..5 D4
ECHL BD2..74 C8
ILK LS29..18 D3
SKP/WHF BD23......................................15 H6
YEA LS19..54 A5
Bolton St BFDE BD3..................................5 E4
LM/WK BD12...118 D5
Bolton Ter AIRE BD20.............................27 G1
Bolton Wy ESPA/BRAM LS23..................42 C4
Bolus Cl WKFDE WF1............................149 K7
Bolus La WKFDE WF1............................149 J7
Bond Ct LDS * LS1...................................7 D3
Bondgate AL/HA/HU LS17........................38 C4
OT LS21...33 J4
PONT WF8..181 G1
Bond St BRIG HD6................................142 B8
BTLY WF17...145 H2
BTLY * WF17...146 B5
DEWS WF13...172 B3
HBR HX7..112 B8
LDS LS1...7 D3
PONT WF8..181 F1
TOD * OL14..134 A6
WKFDE WF1..10 B2
Bonegate Av BRIG HD6.........................142 C8
Bonegate Rd BRIG HD6........................142 B8
Bonnaccord St BTLY * WF17.................146 B7
Bonn Rd HTON BD9................................95 C1
Bonwick Ml WBSY BD6.........................117 K4
Boocock St PDSY/CALV * LS28...............98 C2
Bookers Fld CLECK BD19......................145 F4
Bootham Pk HTON BD9...........................94 D1
Booth House La HOLM/MEL HD9...........232 C7

Booth House Rd LUD/ILL HX2 .....137 K4
Boothman Wk KGHY BD21 ....2 B5
Booth Royd IDLE BD10 ....74 D2
Boothroyd Dr HDGY LS6 ....79 F6
   HUDS HD4 ....190 B8
Booth Royd Dr IDLE BD10 ....74 D2
Boothroyd Gn DEWS WF13 ....172 A3
Booth Royd La BRIG HD6 ....167 J3
Boothroyd La DEWS WF13 ....171 K3
Boothroyds Wy FEA/AMT WF7 ....179 F5
Booth St CAS WF10 ....153 J3
   CLECK BD19 ....144 A3
   IDLE BD10 ....74 D4
   ILK LS29 ....32 A1
   SHPY BD18 ....73 K4
Boothtown Rd HIPP HX3 ....116 A8
Border Cl HUDW HD3 ....189 K2
Boroughgate OT LS21 ....33 J3
Borough Market HFAX * HX1 ......9 D4
Borough Rd WKFDE WF1 ....10 C2
Borrins Wy BAIL BD17 ....51 K8
Borrough Av RHAY LS8 ....80 A3
Borrough Vw RHAY LS8 ....80 A3
Borrowdale Cl WOR/ARM LS12 ....99 K1
Borrowdale Crs WOR/ARM LS12 ..99 K1
Borrowdale Cft YEA LS19 ....53 J4
Borrowdale Dr CAS WF10 ....154 E2
Borrowdale Rd EARL WF12 ....172 D1
   WKFDW/WTN WF2 ....175 F4
Borrowdale Ter SCFT LS14 ....81 K8
Boston Av KSTL LS5 ....77 K8
Boston Rd WBY LS22 ....23 J7
Boston St CAS WF10 ....153 K3
   HFAX HX1 ....8 A4
   RPDN/SBR HX6 ....138 D8
Boston Wk WBSY BD6 ....118 A3
Bosworth Av RODW WF6 ....151 H7
Bosworth Cl WIL/AL BD15 ....94 B2
Botany Av AIRE BD20 ....49 J1
Botany La KBTN HD8 ....193 H6
Botham Flds MAR/SLWT HD7 .....189 K6
Botham Hall Rd HUDS HD4 ....189 K6
Bottom Boat Rd EARD/LOFT WF3 .150 E5
Bottom Dyke KBTN HD8 ....235 H3
Bottom La HOLM/MEL HD9 ....233 J4
Bottomley La GTL/HWG HX4 ......164 B6
Bottomley Rd TOD OL14 ....160 B5
Bottomley St BRIG HD6 ....142 C7
   WBOW BD5 ....95 K7
   WBSY BD6 ....118 A4
Bottoms HIPP HX3 ....140 C8
Bottoms La BIRK/DRI BD11 ....120 C2
The Boulevard BEE/HOL LS11 .....100 D8
   PDSY/CALV LS28 ....98 B1
Boulsworth Dr COL BB8 ....64 A2
The Boundary GIR BD8 ....94 E2
Boundary Cl BAIL BD17 ....51 K7
   MSTN/BAR LS15 ....104 C4
Boundary Dr CUD/GR S72 ....224 A8
Boundary Farm Rd AL/HA/HU LS17 .57 C8
Boundary La WKFDE WF1 ....177 J4
Boundary Rd DEWS WF13 ....171 J1
Boundary St LVSG WF15 ....145 F8
Boundary Ter * WF13 DEWS 172 A1
Bourbon Cl WBSY BD6 ....118 C3
Bourne St IDLE BD10 ....74 D1
Bourn View La HUDS HD4 ....212 D4
The Bourse LDS * LS1 ....7 G4
Bowater Ct BOW BD4 ....120 C1
Bow Beck BOW BD4 ....5 E6
Bowbridge Rd WBOW * BD5 ......96 A8
Bowcliffe Rd BSPA/BRAM LS23 ....62 C1
   MID LS10 ....102 B7
The Bower BTLY WF17 ....145 J3
Bower La DEWS WF13 ....145 J8
Bower La DEWS WF13 ....145 J8
Bower St MSTN/BAR LS15 ....82 C8
Bower Slack Rd RPDN/SBR HX6 ...163 J5
Bowers La GTL/HWG HX4 ....165 G5
Bower St WBOW * BD5 ....4 C6
Bowes Nook WBSY BD6 ....117 K4
Bowfell Cl SCFT LS14 ....81 J7
Bow Gn CLAY BD14 ....94 D3
Bowland Cl MSTN/BAR LS15 ......103 G4
Bowland St GIR BD8 ....4 B3
Bow La HBR * BD4 ....111 F7
Bowler Cl LM/WK BD12 ....118 D5
Bowling Aly BRIG HD6 ....168 B3
Bowling Av WKFDE * WF1 ....175 G1
Bowling Back La BOW BD4 ....5 E6
Bowling Ct BRIG HD6 ....142 A8
Bowling Dyke HFAX * HX1 ....9 D3
Bowling Green Ct HUDW HD3 ....189 J4
Bowling Green La GTL/HWG HX4 ..165 J8
Bowling Green Ter BEE/HOL LS11 .7 D6
Bowling Hall Rd BOW BD4 ....96 C8
Bowling Old La WBOW BD5 ....96 A4
   WBOW BD5 ....118 E1
Bowling Park Cl BOW BD4 ....96 B7
Bowling Park Dr WBOW BD5 ......96 B8
Bowling St HUDS HD4 ....190 A7
Bowman Av WBSY BD6 ....118 C4
Bowman Gv HFAX HX1 ....8 B4
Bowman La MID LS10 ....7 F4
Bowman Pl HFAX * HX1 ....8 B4
Bowman Rd WBSY BD6 ....118 C4
Bowman St HFAX HX1 ....8 B4

WKFDE WF1 ....11 F6
Bowman Ter HFAX HX1 ....8 B4
Bownas Rd BSPA/BRAM LS23 .....42 C5
Bowness Av CAS WF10 ....155 F2
   IDLE BD10 ....75 F7
Bowness Dr HUDE HD5 ....13 F5
Bowood Av CHAL LS7 ....79 G4
Bowood Crs CHAL LS7 ....79 G4
Bowood Gv CHAL LS7 ....79 G4
Bow St HD1 HD1 ....12 E5
   KGHY BD21 ....3 D3
   OSM LS9 ....102 A4
Boxwood Dr AIRE BD20 ....49 F5
Boxhill Rd ELL HX5 ....166 E4
Box La PONT WF8 ....181 F1
Box Tree Cl GIR BD8 ....94 E2
Box Tree Gv KGHY * BD21 ....3 F4
Box Trees La LUD/ILL HX2 ....115 G8
Boxwood Rd ELL HX5 ....166 E6
Boycott Dr FEA/AMT WF7 ....203 G6
Boyd Av BFDE BD3 ....97 G2
Boy La BOW BD4 ....139 G1
The Boyle MSTN/BAR LS15 ....83 H3
Boynton St WBOW BD5 ....95 K8
Boynton Ter WBOW BD5 ....96 A8
Boys La HIPP HX3 ....9 E6
Bracewell Av WIL/AL BD15 ....94 A3
Bracewell Bank HIPP HX3 ....8 A1
Bracewell Dr HIPP HX3 ....8 A1
Bracewell Gv HIPP HX3 ....8 B2
Bracewell Rd HOLM/MEL HD9 ....231 G2
Bracewell St KGHY BD21 ....3 F5
Bracken Av WIL/AL BD15 ....142 B6
Bracken Bank Av HWTH BD22 ....47 H8
Bracken Bank Crs HWTH BD22 ....47 H8
Bracken Bank Gv HWTH BD22 ....47 H8
Bracken Bank Wk HWTH BD22 ...47 H8
Bracken Bank Wy HWTH BD22 ....47 H8
Brackenbeck Rd GTHN BD7 ....95 F7
Brackenbek Gra LUD/ILL HX2 ....139 H2
Bracken La HFAX HX1 ....8 A2
Bracken Ct BRIG HD6 ....142 B6
Bracken Ct AL/HA/HU LS17 ....79 J2
   WOR/ARM LS12 ....6 A6
Brackendale IDLE BD10 ....74 C1
Brackendale Av IDLE BD10 ....74 C1
Brackendale Dr IDLE BD10 ....74 B1
Brackendale Gv IDLE BD10 ....74 B1
Brackendale Pde IDLE BD10 ......74 B1
Bracken Edge IDLE BD10 ....80 B6
   RHAY LS8 ....80 B6
Bracken Ghyll Dr AIRE BD20 ......27 F1
Bracken Gv HUDN HD2 ....168 C7
   MIRF WF14 ....170 A4
Bracken Hall Rd HUDN HD2 ......168 D8
Bracken Hl AL/HA/HU LS17 ....79 J2
   FEA/AMT WF7 ....202 D6
   HEM/SK/SE WF9 ....225 K7
   MIRF WF14 ....170 A4
Brackenhill Dr GTHN BD7 ....94 E8
Brackenholme Royd WBSY BD6 ..117 K3
Bracken Mt AIRE BD20 ....27 F1
Bracken Pk BGLY BD16 ....50 C8
Bracken Rd AIRE BD20 ....26 C6
   BRIG HD6 ....142 B6
   HWTH BD22 ....2 B6
Bracken Sq HUDN * HD2 ....168 D7
Bracken St KGHY BD21 ....2 C6
Brackenwood Cl ILK LS29 ....20 E7
   RHAY LS8 ....80 A4
Brackenwood Ct WKFDE WF1 ....150 A6
Brackenwood Dr RHAY LS8 ....80 A3
Brackenwood Gn RHAY LS8 ......80 A3
Brackenwood Rd WKFDE WF1 ....150 A6
Bradbeck Rd GTHN BD7 ....95 F4
Bradburn Rd EARD/LOFT WF3 ....125 H8
Bradbury St DEWS WF13 ....171 H6
Bradcroft HUD HD1 ....12 C1
Bradd Cl LVSG * WF15 ....144 E6
Bradfield Cl HUDN HD2 ....169 H7
Bradford & Wakefield Rd
   BOW BD4 ....121 F4
Bradford La BFDE BD3 ....97 F4
Bradford Old Rd BGLY BD16 ......116 B8
   HIPP HX3 ....116 B8
Bradford Rd BGLY BD16 ....72 A2
   BIRK/DRI BD11 ....120 D7
   BIRK/DRI BD11 ....122 A6
   BRIG HD6 ....142 C7
   BTLY WF17 ....145 G2
   CLAY BD14 ....94 D6
   CLECK BD19 ....119 J8
   CLECK BD19 ....143 K2
   DEWS WF13 ....172 B1
   EARD/LOFT WF3 ....147 K2
   EARD/LOFT WF3 ....148 C6
   GSLY LS20 ....52 E2
   HIPP HX3 ....140 E2
   HUD HD1 ....12 C2
   HUDN HD2 ....168 C7

IDLE BD10 ....74 C7
ILK LS29 ....32 B4
KGHY BD21 ....3 E1
OT LS21 ....32 E1
PDSY/CALV LS28 ....73 C7
SHPY BD18 ....73 C
WKFDW/WTN WF2 ....149 F1
Bradfords Cl BSPA/BRAM LS23 ...42 C5
Bradford St DEWS WF13 ....172 C1
   KGHY BD21 ....3 E1
Bradlaugh Rd WBSY BD6 ....118 C3
Bradlaugh Ter WBSY BD6 ....118 C3
Bradley Av AIRE BD20 ....27 F1
   CAS WF10 ....153 H2
Bradley Bvd HUDN HD2 ....168 D2
Bradley Carr Ter HEM/SK/SE WF9 .242 A1
Bradley Dr AIRE BD20 ....27 F1
Bradley Grange Gdns HUDN HD2 .169 C2
Bradley La GTL/HWG HX4 ....166 A4
   PDSY/CALV LS28 ....97 K3
Bradley Mills La HUD HD1 ....13 E5
Bradley Mills Rd HUD HD1 ....13 E5
Bradley Quarry Cl HUDN * HD2 ..169 H3
Bradley Ri AIRE BD20 ....27 F1
Bradley Rd AIRE BD20 ....27 F1
   HUDN HD2 ....168 D2
Bradley St BGLY BD16 ....49 K5
   CAS WF10 ....153 H2
   HTON BD9 ....73 K8
Bradley Vw GTL/HWG HX4 ......166 A5
Bradshaw Av HOLM/MEL HD9 ...212 E6
Bradshaw Crs HOLM/MEL HD9 ..212 E6
Bradshaw Crs HOLM/MEL * HD9 .212 E6
Bradshaw La LUD/ILL HX2 ....115 F6
   MAR/SLWT HD7 ....209 J2
Bradshaw Rd HOLM/MEL HD9 ...232 E6
   HOLM/MEL HD9 ....232 E6
Bradshaw Vw CUL/QBY BD13 ....116 A6
Bradstock Gdns MOR LS27 ....123 F7
Brae Av ECHL BD2 ....74 B2
Braemar Cft CUD/GR S72 ....223 H4
Braemar Dr GFTH/SHER LS25 ....106 C3
Braemar Ri CUD/GR S72 ....223 H4
Brafferton Arbor WBSY BD6 .....117 K3
Braine Rd WBY LS22 ....23 H6
Braithwaite Av HWTH BD22 ......2 A3
Braithwaite Crs HWTH BD22 .....2 A3
Braithwaite Dr HWTH BD22 ......2 A3
Braithwaite Edge Rd HWTH BD22 .47 F2
Braithwaite Gv HWTH BD22 ......2 A3
Braithwaite Rd HWTH BD22 ......47 F2
Braithwaite Rw MID * LS10 ......125 F1
Braithwaite St BEE/HOL LS11 ....6 E1
Braithwaite Wk HWTH BD22 .....2 A3
Braithwaite Wy HWTH BD22 .....2 A3
Bramble Av BSPA/BRAM LS23 ...42 E5
Bramble Cl CLAY BD14 ....94 B3
   PONT WF8 ....180 C2
Bramble Ct HWTH BD22 ....69 F1
The Brambles ILK LS29 ....19 J5
Bramble Wk BTLY WF17 ....145 G3
Brambling Dr CUL/QBY BD13 ....117 J2
Brambling Ms MOR LS27 ....123 F7
Bramham Dr BAIL BD17 ....51 J7
Bramham La BSPA/BRAM LS23 ...40 E7
Bramham Park Ct
   EARD/LOFT WF3 ....124 E2
Bramham Rd BGLY BD16 ....50 A5
   BSPA/BRAM LS23 ....42 E5
   CAS WF10 ....153 F1
   SCFT LS14 ....61 K7
Bramhope Old La OT LS21 ....34 C2
Bramhope Rd CLECK BD19 ....143 H8
Bramleigh Dr MOR LS27 ....123 F3
Bramleigh Gv MOR LS27 ....123 F3
Bramley Cl HOLM/MEL HD9 .....233 J4
   HWTH BD22 ....46 E4
Bramley Crs WKFDE WF1 ....149 K8
Bramley Fold HIPP HX3 ....141 J5
Bramley La HIPP HX3 ....141 J5
   HOR/CROF WF4 ....219 K2
Bramley St BRAM LS13 ....99 F4
   WBOW BD5 ....96 E4
Bramley Vw HIPP HX3 ....141 K5
Brampton Ct HEM/SK/SE WF9 ...226 C1
Bramstan Av BRAM LS13 ....76 E5
Bramstan Cl BRAM LS13 ....76 E5
Bramstan Gdns BRAM LS13 ......76 E5
Bramston Gdns BRIG HD6 ....168 B3
Bramston St BRIG HD6 ....168 B3
Brancepeth Pl WOR/ARM LS12 ..6 A8
Branch Cl WOR/ARM LS12 ....100 A7
Branch End MOR LS27 ....122 A8
Branch La HUDW HD3 ....167 K8
Branch Pl WOR/ARM LS12 ....100 A7
Branch Rd BTLY WF17 ....146 E5
   CLECK BD19 ....143 J8
   DEWS WF13 ....172 A1
   GTL/HWG HX4 ....165 G8
   HOR/CROF WF4 ....197 H5
   HUDW HD3 ....167 H1
   WOR/ARM LS12 ....100 A7
   WOR/ARM LS12 ....100 A7
Branch St HUD LS12 ....190 E1
   WOR/ARM LS12 ....100 A7
Brander Ap OSM LS9 ....102 E3
Brander Cl OSM LS9 ....102 E3
Brander Dr OSM LS9 ....102 E3
Brander Gv OSM LS9 ....102 E3

'ander Rd OSM LS9 ....102 E2
'ander St OSM LS9 ....103 F1
andfort St GTHN BD7 ....95 G6
and Hill Ap HOR/CROF WF4 ....200 C3
and Hill Dr HOR/CROF WF4 ....200 C2
andon Ct AL/HA/HU LS17 ....58 D6
andon Crs AL/HA/HU LS17 ....59 H5
andon La AL/HA/HU LS17 ....59 H4
andon Rd BVRD LS5 ....6 C2
andon St WOR/ARM LS12 ....6 B4
andon Wy CHAL LS7 ....79 K6
andy Carr Rd WKFDW/WTN WF2 ....174 C1
anksome Ct HTON * BD9 ....95 F1
anksome Crs HTON BD9 ....95 H1
anksome Dr SHPY BD18 ....72 D3
anksome Gv BGLY BD16 ....72 C3
anksome Pl HDGY LS6 ....6 A1
anksome St HDGY * LS6 ....6 A1
anksome Ter HDGY * LS6 ....6 A1
 NORM WF6 ....151 K7
ansdale Cl BAIL BD17 ....73 C1
 GSLY LS20 ....53 G5
 NORM WF6 ....151 K7
ansdale Clough WBSY BD6 ....117 K2
ansdale Gdns GSLY LS20 ....53 G5
ansdale Ms NORM WF6 ....151 K7
ansdale Mt HWTH BD22 ....47 C6
anstone Gv OSS WF5 ....173 J2
an St HWTH BD22 ....47 C6
ant Av LUD/ILL HX2 ....115 J7
ant Bank La ILK LS29 ....19 G5
antcliffe Dr BAIL BD17 ....51 H7
antdale Cl HTON BD9 ....72 C7
antdale Rd HTON BD9 ....72 C7
antford St CHAL LS7 ....79 K5
antwood Av HTON BD9 ....72 C7
antwood Crs HTON BD9 ....72 B7
antwood Dr HTON BD9 ....72 C7
antwood Gv HTON BD9 ....72 C7
antwood Ov HTON BD9 ....72 C7
antwood Rd HTON BD9 ....72 B7
antwood Vls HTON BD9 ....72 C7
anwell Av BTLY WF17 ....121 H8
anwell Ct HTON BD9 ....94 E1
anwell Dr HWTH BD22 ....68 B3
assey Rd BOW BD4 ....96 C7
assey Rd HRAX HX1 ....8 C5
assey Ter BOW BD4 ....96 C7
athay Slades SCFT LS14 ....81 J8
aybrook Ct GIR BD8 ....5 J1
ay Cl WBSY * BD6 ....117 J1
ayshaw Dr GTHN BD7 ....117 J1
ayshaw Rd EARD/LOFT WF3 ....148 D4
ayside Av HUDN HD2 ....191 F1
ayton Ap SCFT LS14 ....82 A6
ayton Cl SCFT LS14 ....82 A6
ayton Gn SCFT LS14 ....82 B6
ayton Gv SCFT LS14 ....82 A6
ayton Wk SCFT LS14 ....82 A6
azil St CAS WF10 ....153 K3
ead St WKFDE WF1 ....10 C5
eakmoor Av AIRE BD20 ....27 G1
eak Neck HIPP HX3 ....141 F8
eaks Rd LM/WK BD12 ....118 E5
earcliffe Cl WBSY BD6 ....118 B3
earcliffe Dr WBSY BD6 ....118 B3
earcliffe Gv WBSY BD6 ....118 B4
earcliffe Rd WBSY BD6 ....118 C4
earcliffe St WBSY BD6 ....118 B4
earley Gdns LVSG WF15 ....144 D8
earley La LUD/ILL HX2 ....137 J3
earley St BTLY WF17 ....146 A7
earton St BFD BD1 ....4 C5
eary Av HORS LS18 ....77 H2
eary Ct BHP/TINH LS16 ....35 J8
eary La BHP/TINH LS16 ....35 J8
eary La East BHP/TINH LS16 ....35 K8
eary La West BHP/TINH LS16 ....55 J1
eary Rd HORS LS18 ....77 H2
eary Ter HORS LS18 ....77 H2
eck Lea RPDN/SBR HX6 ....164 D1
ecks Gdns GFTH/SHER LS25 ....105 K8
ecks Rd GFTH/SHER LS25 ....105 K8
 RTHW LS26 ....105 G7
ecks Rd CLAY BD14 ....94 D6
eck Willows RPDN/SBR HX6 ....164 C1
econ Ap OSM LS9 ....105 F1
econ Av HUDW HD3 ....190 A2
econ Ct IDLE BD10 ....74 D4
edon Av SHPY BD18 ....74 B4
edon La HEM/SK/SE WF9 ....224 E3
eighton Adown WBSY BD6 ....117 J3
emner St OT LS21 ....33 K3
endon Ct BOW BD4 ....97 F8
 MIRF WF14 ....193 H1
endon Dr HUDN HD2 ....190 D2
endon Wk BOW * BD4 ....120 A1
entford Gv WOR/ARM * LS12 ....100 C4
entford Rd WBSY BD6 ....118 D4
entlea Av WKFDW/WTN WF2 ....10 B6
entwood Cl BTLY WF17 ....146 D6

 PONT WF8 ....204 C6
Brentwood Gdns WBSY BD6 ....118 D3
Brentwood St WOR/ARM * LS12 ....100 C4
Brentwood Ter WOR/ARM LS12 ....100 C4
Bretfield Ct EARL WF12 ....172 C6
Brettegate HEM/SK/SE WF9 ....224 C4
Brett Gdns BEE/HOL LS11 ....101 H7
Bretton Ct WBSY * BD6 ....118 A3
Bretton La HOR/CROF WF4 ....219 H2
Bretton Rd DOD/DAR S75 ....239 K3
Bretton St EARL WF12 ....172 C6
Brevitt St WKFDE WF1 ....11 E5
Brewerton La DEWS WF13 ....171 J1
Brewery Ct HUDW HD3 ....190 A1
Brewery La CUL/QBY BD13 ....93 H8
 CUL/QBY BD13 ....116 B4
 EARL WF12 ....172 B7
Brewery Rd HWTH BD22 ....47 J8
 ILK LS29 ....20 C7
Brewery Whf MIRF WF14 ....170 D7
Brexdale Av GFTH/SHER LS25 ....105 K8
Brian Crs MSTN/BAR LS15 ....103 K1
Brian Pl MSTN/BAR LS15 ....81 K8
Brian Royd La GTL/HWG HX4 ....165 J4
Brian St HUDW HD3 ....190 B2
Brian Vw MSTN/BAR LS15 ....81 K8
Briar Av HOLM/MEL HD9 ....211 G8
Briar Bank HEM/SK/SE WF9 ....224 A1
Briar Cl ELL HX5 ....166 D6
 HECK WF16 ....145 G6
 PDSY/CALV LS28 ....98 B1
Briar Ct HOLM/MEL HD9 ....232 D7
Briardale Rd HTON BD9 ....72 B7
Briardene RTHW * LS26 ....127 F6
Briar Dr DEWS WF13 ....171 J1
Briarfield Av IDLE BD10 ....74 C4
Briarfield Cl IDLE BD10 ....74 C4
 ILK LS29 ....20 D8
Briarfield Gdns SHPY BD18 ....74 C4
Briarfield Gv IDLE BD10 ....74 C4
Briarfield Rd HOLM/MEL HD9 ....233 J4
 SHPY BD18 ....73 J5
Briar Ga WBY LS22 ....23 J4
 WKFDE WF1 ....11 E6
Briarlea Cl LVSG WF15 ....53 H5
Briarlyn Av HUDW HD3 ....190 A1
Briarlyn Rd HUDW HD3 ....190 A1
Briarmains Rd BTLY WF17 ....145 J1
Briar Rhydding BAIL BD17 ....74 A1
Briarsdale Ct RHAY * LS8 ....80 E8
Briarsdale Cft RHAY * LS8 ....80 E8
Briarsdale Garth RHAY LS8 ....80 D8
Briarsdale Hts OSM * LS9 ....80 E8
Briarsdale Ms OSM LS9 ....80 D8
Briar Wd SHPY BD18 ....74 A4
Briarwood Av KGHY BD21 ....48 D2
Briarwood Cl WKFDE WF1 ....150 A6
Briarwood Crs WBSY BD6 ....118 C2
Briarwood Dr WBSY BD6 ....118 C2
Briarwood Gv WBSY BD6 ....118 C1
Briary Cl WKFDE WF1 ....199 H1
Brick & Tile Ter BRIG HD6 ....168 B2
Brickbank HUDE * HD5 ....192 B8
Brickfield La LUD/ILL HX2 ....115 K6
Brickfield La LUD/ILL HX2 ....115 K6
Brickfield Ter LUD/ILL HX2 ....115 K6
Brick Mill Rd PDSY/CALV LS28 ....98 C5
Brick Rw LM/WK BD12 ....118 D8
Brick St CLECK BD19 ....143 K4
 OSM * LS9 ....7 F4
 WKFDW/WTN WF2 ....174 E4
Brick Ter BRIG HD6 ....168 C2
Brickyard MIRF WF14 ....170 C6
Bride St TOD OL14 ....134 A5
Bridge Cl BSPA/BRAM LS23 ....42 E5
 HOR/CROF WF4 ....196 D2
 KBTN HD8 ....257 J1
Bridge Ct HEM/SK/SE WF9 ....202 A8
 MOR LS27 ....123 G8
Bridge Cft HUDN HD4 ....190 B7
Bridge End BRIG HD6 ....168 B2
 LDS LS1 ....7 E4
Bridge End St TOD * OL14 ....133 F2
Bridge Fold KSTL LS5 ....78 A7
Bridge Foot BSPA/BRAM LS23 ....42 E3
Bridge Garth BSPA/BRAM LS23 ....42 D5
Bridge Ga HBR HX7 ....112 B8
Bridgegate Wy IDLE BD10 ....75 F5
Bridgehouse La HWTH BD22 ....68 C5
Bridge La HIPP HX3 ....117 G4
 HOLM/MEL HD9 ....233 G5
 ILK LS29 ....20 A6
 KNOT WF11 ....156 C6
 PONT WF8 ....204 C7
 HBR HX7 ....112 A8
Bridge Rd BEE/HOL LS11 ....6 C5
 BRIG HD6 ....168 C6
 BSPA/BRAM LS23 ....42 E3
 HOR/CROF WF4 ....196 E2
 HUDN HD2 ....169 J6
 KSTL LS5 ....77 K7
Bridge St AIRE BD20 ....27 G1

 BFD BD1 ....4 C5
 BTLY WF17 ....145 H3
 BTLY WF17 ....146 C6
 CAS WF10 ....153 K3
 HECK WF16 ....145 F7
 HUD HD1 ....191 F8
 HUDS HD4 ....213 F3
 HWTH BD22 ....68 D1
 KGHY BD21 ....2 C4
 LDSU LS2 ....7 F3
 MAR/SLWT HD7 ....210 E2
 MOR LS27 ....147 G1
 NORM WF6 ....152 B8
 NORM WF6 ....178 B1
 OT LS21 ....33 J3
 PONT * WF8 ....180 E3
 STKB/PEN S36 ....252 B7
 TOD OL14 ....134 A6
 WKFDE WF1 ....11 D5
Bridge Vw BRAM LS13 ....76 C6
Bridge View Cl HORS LS18 ....77 H1
Bridgewater HDGY LS6 ....78 E5
Bridgewater Rd OSM LS9 ....102 A6
Bridgeway BOW BD4 ....119 K1
Bridgland Av ILK LS29 ....32 C6
Bridgwater Rd HTON BD9 ....95 C1
Bridle Av OSS WF5 ....173 H3
Bridle Cl HOR/CROF WF4 ....196 E4
Bridle Dene HOR/CROF WF4 ....117 H6
Bridle La HOR/CROF WF4 ....196 E4
 OSS WF5 ....173 H3
Bridle Pth MSTN/BAR LS15 ....103 J1
Bridle Path Rd AL/HA/HU LS17 ....59 F6
Bridle Path Wk MSTN/BAR LS15 ....103 J1
Bridle Pl OSS WF5 ....173 J3
Bridle Stile HIPP HX3 ....117 H6
Bridle Stile La CUL/QBY BD13 ....116 D1
Bridle St BTLY WF17 ....146 D6
Bridley Dr MAR/SLWT HD7 ....210 E3
Brierdene AIRE BD20 ....27 G1
Brierfield Gdns MOR LS27 ....122 B5
Brier Hey Cl HBR HX7 ....137 G2
Brier Hey La HBR HX7 ....137 G2
Brier Hill Cl CLECK BD19 ....143 H5
Brier Hill Vw HUDN HD2 ....168 E6
Brierlands Cl GFTH/SHER LS25 ....106 B3
Brierlands Fold GFTH/SHER LS25 ....106 B3
Brierlands La GFTH/SHER LS25 ....106 B3
Brier La ELL HX5 ....167 J1
 HOR/CROF WF4 ....223 F3
Brierley Cl SHPY BD18 ....73 J5
Brierley Crs HEM/SK/SE WF9 ....225 J8
Brierley Rd CUD/GR S72 ....223 J6
 CUD/GR S72 ....240 A3
Brier St HIPP HX3 ....8 C1
 KGHY BD21 ....2 C6
Briery Cl ILK LS29 ....19 J7
Briery Fld SHPY BD18 ....73 H6
Briery Gv MIRF WF14 ....170 D8
Briestfield Rd EARL WF12 ....194 D4
Brigate AIRE BD20 ....27 G1
 BAIL BD17 ....73 H3
 BRIG HD6 ....168 B1
 ELL HX5 ....166 E4
 LDS LS1 ....7 E4
Brigg Gdns HWTH BD22 ....2 A3
Briggland Ct WIL/AL BD15 ....71 G6
Brigglands WIL/AL * BD15 ....71 G6
Brigg's Av CAS WF10 ....153 J5
Briggs Gv WBSY BD6 ....118 B2
Briggs Pl WBSY BD6 ....118 B2
Briggs Rw FEA/AMT WF7 ....179 J2
Briggs St CUL/QBY * BD13 ....116 D7
Briggs Yd OSS * WF5 ....173 H6
Brighouse & Denholme Gate Rd HIPP HX3 ....117 F5
Brighouse & Denholme Rd CUL/QBY BD13 ....92 E7
 CUL/QBY BD13 ....92 C5
 CUL/QBY BD13 ....116 D2
Brighouse Rd CUL/QBY BD13 ....92 C5
 HIPP HX3 ....141 H4
 HUDW HD3 ....167 G8
 LM/WK BD12 ....118 E6
Brighouse Wood La BRIG HD6 ....142 A8
Brighouse Wood Rw BRIG HD6 ....142 A8
Brighton Av MOR LS27 ....122 E6
Brighton Cliff BRAM LS13 ....99 G1
Brighton Cl BTLY WF17 ....145 H5
Brighton Gv BRAM LS13 ....99 H2
 HFAX * HX1 ....8 B3
Brighton Rd ILK LS29 ....20 E8
Brighton St BAIL BD17 ....73 H3
 CUD/GR S72 ....240 A4
 HECK WF16 ....145 G6
 HIPP HX3 ....8 B2
 IDLE BD10 ....74 C2
 TOD OL14 ....133 F2
 WKFDW/WTN * WF2 ....10 A4
Brighton Ter CLECK BD19 ....143 G3
Bright St CLAY * BD14 ....94 B7
 CUL/QBY BD13 ....116 E2
 DEWS * WF13 ....172 B2
 EARD/LOFT WF3 ....148 E3
 HECK WF16 ....170 C5
 MOR LS27 ....123 G?
 PDSY/CALV LS28 ....98 D1
 RPDN/SBR HX6 ....138 E6
 TOD OL14 ....133 K8

WIL/AL BD15 .... 94 B2
Brignall Cft OSM LS9 .... 102 B2
Brignall Garth OSM LS9 .... 102 B2
Brignall Wy OSM LS9 .... 102 B2
Brigshaw Dr CAS WF10 .... 128 E4
Brigshaw La CAS WF10 .... 129 F4
Brimmy Croft La UPML OL3 .... 206 C8
Brindle Park Dr CAS WF10 .... 154 B5
Brindley Gv GIR BD8 .... 94 C4
Brindley Rd AIRE BD20 .... 27 H3
Brindley Wy EARD/WTN WF2 .... 149 G2
Brisbane Av ECHL BD2 .... 74 A8
Briscoe La GTL/HWG HX4 .... 166 A4
Bristol Av AIRE BD20 .... 49 F1
Bristol St HIPP HX3 .... 140 C8
Britannia Cl PDSY/CALV LS28 .... 98 D1
Britannia St BRAM LS13 .... 98 E3
Britannia Rd MAR/SLWT HD7 .... 189 J8
  MAR/SLWT HD7 .... 210 D3
  MOR LS27 .... 146 E1
Britannia St BGLY BD16 .... 50 A8
  LDS LS1 .... 7 D4
  PDSY/CALV LS28 .... 98 D1
  WBOW BD5 .... 5 D4
Britannia Ter CLECK BD19 .... 144 A3
Broadacre Rd OSS WF5 .... 173 K6
Broad Acres HOR/CROF WF4 .... 198 C4
Broadbent Cft HOLM/MEL HD9 .... 213 G7
Broad Carr La GTL/HWG HX4 .... 166 B7
Broadcroft Cha EARD/LOFT WF3 .... 147 K3
Broadcroft Dr EARD/LOFT WF3 .... 147 K3
Broadcroft Gv EARD/LOFT WF3 .... 147 K3
Broadcroft Wy EARD/LOFT WF3 .... 147 K3
Broadfield Cl BOW BD4 .... 120 B2
Broadfield Pk HOLM/MEL HD9 .... 247 H1
Broadfield Wy ILK LS29 .... 18 E5
Broadfolds CLAY BD14 .... 116 C3
Broadgate GTL/HWG HX4 .... 188 D1
  HUDE HD5 .... 13 F6
  OSS WF5 .... 173 K6
Broad Ga TOD OL14 .... 134 B5
  TOD OL14 .... 135 F6
Broadgate Av HORS LS18 .... 77 H2
Broadgate Crs HORS LS18 .... 77 G3
  HUDE HD5 .... 13 F6
Broadgate Dr HORS LS18 .... 77 G2
Broadgate La HORS LS18 .... 77 G2
Broadgate Ri HORS LS18 .... 77 H2
Broadgate Wk HORS LS18 .... 77 G3
Broad Head La HWTH BD22 .... 46 A7
Broad Ings Wy HIPP HX3 .... 117 H6
Broadlands BRAM LS13 .... 77 J7
Broadlea Av BRAM LS13 .... 77 J7
Broadlea Cl BRAM LS13 .... 77 J7
Broadlea Crs BRAM LS13 .... 77 J7
  WBOW BD5 .... 96 B8
Broadlea Gdns BRAM LS13 .... 77 J7
Broadlea Gv BRAM LS13 .... 77 J7
Broadlea Hl BRAM LS13 .... 77 J7
Broadlea Mt BRAM LS13 .... 77 K8
Broadlea Pl BRAM LS13 .... 77 J8
Broadlea Rd BRAM LS13 .... 77 J7
Broadlea St BRAM LS13 .... 77 J7
Broadlea Ter BRAM LS13 .... 77 J7
Broadlea Vw BRAM LS13 .... 77 H7
Broadley Av LUD/ILL HX2 .... 138 E2
Broadley Cl LUD/ILL HX2 .... 139 F2
Broadley Gv LUD/ILL HX2 .... 138 E2
Broadley Rd LUD/ILL HX2 .... 138 E2
Broadmead CAS WF10 .... 154 A3
Broadmeadows WF1 .... 150 A6
Broad Oak La HIPP HX3 .... 141 J5
  STKB/PEN S36 .... 252 C2
Broadoaks Cl EARL WF12 .... 173 F4
Broad Oak St HIPP HX3 .... 141 J5
Broadowler La OSS WF5 .... 173 K6
Broadstone Rd KBTN HD8 .... 235 H7
Broadstone St TOD OL14 .... 134 C5
Broadstone Wy BOW BD4 .... 120 B1
Broad St BFD BD1 .... 4 C4
  DEWS WF13 .... 171 K5
  HFAX HX1 .... 9 D4
  PDSY/CALV LS28 .... 76 A8
  TOD OL14 .... 134 A5
Broad Tree Rd HIPP HX3 .... 8 B1
Broad Vw OSS WF5 .... 174 A6
Broadway BFD BD1 .... 4 C4
  BGLY BD16 .... 50 A8
  GSLY LS20 .... 52 E3
  HEM/SK/SE WF9 .... 242 A2
  HIPP HX3 .... 8 B1
  HORS LS18 .... 76 D4
  HUD HD1 .... 13 D3

KSTL LS5 .... 77 J4
MSTN/BAR LS15 .... 103 H5
PONT WF8 .... 181 F4
RPDN/SBR HX6 .... 138 A8
WKFDW/WTN WF2 .... 174 D6
Broadway Av WBOW BD5 .... 118 E1
Broadway Cl WBOW BD5 .... 118 E1
Broad Way Ct EARL WF12 .... 195 J2
Broadway Dr HORS LS18 .... 77 F3
Broadwell Rd OSS WF5 .... 174 A6
Brockadale Av LUD/ILL HX2 .... 139 F2
Brockbank Av PONT WF8 .... 192 B4
Brock Bank HUDE HD5 .... 13 J1
Brockholes La HOLM/MEL HD9 .... 233 J1
Brockholes Rd HOLM/MEL HD9 .... 213 K7
Brocklesby Dr WIL/AL BD15 .... 94 B2
Brocks LUD/ILL HX2 .... 137 K5
Brockstones GTL/HWG * HX4 .... 165 J4
Brockswood Ct WKFDW/WTN WF2 .... 200 A6
Brockwell Gdns RPDN/SBR HX6 .... 138 D8
Brock Well La RPDN/SBR HX6 .... 164 C1
Brodley Cl HIPP HX3 .... 141 H3
Brodrick Ct HDGY LS6 .... 78 D6
Broken Cross HUDE HD5 .... 214 A1
Broken Wy WBOW * BD5 .... 118 E1
Bromet Pl ECHL BD2 .... 74 D7
Bromford Rd BOW BD4 .... 96 C7
Bromley Av BOW BD4 .... 96 C7
Brompton Gv BEE/HOL LS11 .... 124 C1
Brompton Mt BEE/HOL LS11 .... 124 C1
Brompton Rd BOW BD4 .... 96 C7
Brompton Rw BEE/HOL * LS11 .... 124 C1
Brompton Ter BEE/HOL LS11 .... 124 C1
Brompton Vw BEE/HOL LS11 .... 124 C1
Bronshill Gv WIL/AL BD15 .... 94 B2
Bronte Av KNOT WF11 .... 155 J7
Bronte Cl CLECK BD19 .... 144 E2
  DEWS WF13 .... 171 J1
  HTON BD9 .... 96 E1
  HUDS HD4 .... 190 D8
Bronte Ct PONT WF8 .... 180 E1
Bronte Dr HWTH BD22 .... 47 G8
Bronte Gv HEM/SK/SE WF9 .... 224 C5
  MIRF WF14 .... 171 F7
Bronte Pl CUL/QBY BD13 .... 93 J3
Bronte Ri CAS WF10 .... 154 E6
Bronte Rd BTLY WF17 .... 145 K1
Bronte St HWTH * BD22 .... 68 D4
  KGHY BD21 .... 3 G2
Bronte Vls HWTH BD22 .... 69 H3
Bronte Wy BRIG HD6 .... 142 E7
  BRIG HD6 .... 142 C3
  CUL/QBY BD13 .... 93 K5
  CUL/QBY BD13 .... 117 G2
  HWTH BD22 .... 67 H7
  HWTH BD22 .... 68 B6
  MIRF WF14 .... 171 F7
The Brook HBR HX7 .... 136 E3
Brook Cl OSS WF5 .... 174 A8
Brookdale Av OSS WF5 .... 173 H2
Brookdale Bank HUDW HD3 .... 190 A6
Brook Dr GTL/HWG HX4 .... 166 A4
Brooke Fold HOLM/MEL HD9 .... 213 F6
Brooke St BRIG HD6 .... 168 B2
  CLECK BD19 .... 144 B4
  HECK * WF16 .... 145 J4
Brookeville Av HIPP HX3 .... 141 H4
Brookfield KBTN HD8 .... 215 F5
Brook Fld MIRF WF14 .... 193 H1
Brookfield Av BRAM LS13 .... 76 B5
  CAS WF10 .... 154 A4
  CLECK BD19 .... 144 A2
  RHAY LS8 .... 80 B7
  SHPY BD18 .... 73 K3
Brookfield Ct NORM WF6 .... 178 B1
Brookfield Dr FEA/AMT WF7 .... 203 J3
Brookfield Gdns BRAM LS13 .... 76 B5
Brookfield PI BFDE BD3 .... 5 E3
  HDGY LS6 .... 78 E5
  SHPY BD18 .... 73 K3
Brookfield Rd BFDE BD3 .... 5 E3
  HDGY LS6 .... 78 E5
Brookfield St CUL/QBY BD13 .... 116 C3
  MID LS10 .... 14 E7
Brookfield Ter CLECK BD19 .... 144 A2
  MID LS10 .... 14 E6
Brookfield Vw CLECK BD19 .... 144 A2
Brookfoot Av BIRK/DRI BD11 .... 120 D6
Brookfoot La HIPP HX3 .... 141 K8
Brook Gdns HOLM/MEL HD9 .... 211 H8
Brook Grain Hl BRIG HD6 .... 168 B3
Brookhill Av AL/HA/HU LS17 .... 58 A7
Brookhill Crs AL/HA/HU LS17 .... 58 A7
Brookhill Dr AL/HA/HU LS17 .... 58 A7
Brookhill Gv AL/HA/HU LS17 .... 58 A7
Brook Hill La STKB/PEN S36 .... 249 G8
Brookhill Rd DOD/DAR S75 .... 239 H3

Brookhouse Gdns IDLE BD10 .... 75 J1
Brooklands HUDN HD2 .... 169 C
Brooklands Av GTL/HWG HX4 .... 166 A4
  SCFT LS14 .... 81 H
  WKFDW/WTN WF2 .... 199 H
Brooklands Cl SCFT LS14 .... 81 C
Brooklands Ct OSS WF5 .... 174 A
  SCFT LS14 .... 81 H
Brooklands Crs HOR/CROF WF4 .... 223 F
  SCFT LS14 .... 81 H
  YEA LS19 .... 53 K
Brooklands Dr SCFT LS14 .... 81 H
  YEA LS19 .... 53 K
Brooklands Garth SCFT LS14 .... 81 H
Brooklands La ILK LS29 .... 32 C
  SCFT LS14 .... 81 H
Brooklands Rd WKFDW/WTN WF2 ..... 199 H
Brooklands Vw SCFT LS14 .... 81 H
Brooklands Wk ILK LS29 .... 32 C
Brooklands Wy ILK LS29 .... 32 C
Brook La LVSG WF15 .... 143 H
  MAR/SLWT HD7 .... 189 H
Brooklyn Av HUDE HD5 .... 192 B
  WOR/ARM LS12 100
Brooklyn Ct CLECK BD19 .... 144 A
Brooklyn Dr CLECK BD19 .... 144 A
Brooklyn Pl WOR/ARM LS12 100
Brooklyn Rd CLECK BD19 .... 144 A
Brooklyn St AIRE BD20 27
  WOR/ARM LS12 100
Brooklyn Ter BRIG HD6 .... 141 H
  WOR/ARM LS12 100
Brook Rd DEWS WF13 .... 172 A
Brook Rw GTL/HWG * HX4 165
Brookroyd Av BRIG HD6 .... 142 C
Brookroyd Gdns BTLY WF17 145
Brookroyd La BTLY WF17 145
Brooksbank WKFDW/WTN WF2 10
Brooksbank Av GTHN BD7 94
Brooksbank Dr MSTN/BAR LS15 103
Brooksbank Gdns ELL HX5 166
Brooksfield HEM/SK/SE WF9 225
Brook Side MAR/SLWT HD7 210
Brookside AL/HA/HU LS17 58
  HBR HX7 111
  HEM/SK/SE WF9 224
  WBY LS22 41
Brookside Fold HWTH BD22 90
Brookside St HEM/SK/SE WF9 226
Brook Ter CUL/QBY BD13 117
Brook St CAS WF10 130
  DEWS WF13 171
  ELL HX5 167
  HBR HX7 112
  HUD HD1 12
  HUD HD1 12
  HUDE HD5 13
  ILK LS29 23
  KGHY BD21 2
  LM/WK BD12 119
  NORM WF6 151
  OSS WF5 173
  WKFDE WF1 10
Brooks Yd DEWS WF13 172
  HUD HD1 12
  HUD HD1 12
Brookway FEA/AMT * WF7 179
Broombank HUDN HD2 190
  KBTN HD8 236
Broom Crs MID LS10 125
Broomcroft CLAY BD14 94
Broomcroft Rd OSS WF5 173
Broom Cross MID LS10 125
Broome Cl NORM WF6 74
Broome Av ECHL BD2 74
Broome St NORM WF6 151
Broomer Cl DEWS WF13 171
Broomer St DEWS WF13 171
Broomfield BHP/TINH LS16 56
  CLAY BD14 94
  GTL/HWG HX4 166
Broomfield Av HIPP HX3 140
Broomfield Cl KBTN HD8 217
Broomfield Crs HDGY * LS6 78
Broomfield PI CLAY BD14 94
  HDGY LS6 78
  KGHY BD21 2
Broomfield Rd HDGY LS6 78
  HUD HD1 190
  HUDN HD2 168
  KGHY BD21 2
Broomfield St CUL/QBY BD13 116
  HDGY * LS6 78
  KGHY * BD21 2
Broomfield Ter CLECK BD19 143
  HDGY LS6 78
  HUD HD1 190
Broomfield Vw HDGY LS6 78
Broom Gdns MID LS10 125
Broom Garth MID LS10 125
Broom Gv MID LS10 125
Broom Hall Av WKFDE WF1 175
Broom Hall Crs WKFDE WF1 175
Broomhey Av KBTN HD8 217
Broomhill CAS WF10 154
Broomhill Av AL/HA/HU LS17 79
  KGHY BD21 2
  KNOT WF11 156
Broomhill Cl HOLM/MEL HD9 233
  KNOT WF11 156

oomhill Crs AL/HA/HU LS17 .....79 K1
KNOT WF11 .....156 E8
oomhill Dr AL/HA/HU LS17 .....79 J2
KGHY BD21 .....2 B5
KNOT WF11 .....156 E8
oomhill Gv KGHY BD21 .....2 B5
KNOT WF11 .....156 E8
oomhill Mt KGHY BD21 .....2 B5
oom Hill Rd GTL/HWG HX4 .....188 C3
oomhill Sq KNOT WF11 .....156 E8
oomhill St KGHY * BD21 .....2 B5
oomhill Wk KGHY BD21 .....2 B5
KNOT WF11 .....156 E8
oomhill Wy KGHY BD21 .....2 C5
oomhouse Cl KBTN HD8 .....236 E6
oom Nook MID LS10 .....125 G4
oomroyd HUDW HD3 .....189 K5
oomsdale Rd BTLY WF17 .....146 D6
oom St CLECK BD19 .....143 J5
KGHY BD21 .....3 D4
oom Ter MID LS10 .....125 G4
oom Vw MID LS10 .....125 G4
oomy Lea La HOLM/MEL HD9 .....233 F4
oster Av HUDW HD3 .....2 A3
otherton Av WKFDE WF1 .....11 E2
ougham Rd HIPP HX3 .....9 D2
MAR/SLWT HD7 .....209 H7
ougham St HIPP HX3 .....9 D2
ougham Ter HIPP HX3 .....9 D2
oughton Av BOW BD4 .....119 J2
OSM LS9 .....102 C1
oughton Rd HUDS HD4 .....190 B8
oughton Ter PDSY/CALV LS28 .....98 C3
ow Bottom La LUD/ILL HX2 .....114 E5
owcliff BAIL BD20 .....27 G1
owfield Vw HWTH BD22 .....47 G6
owfoot St HUD HD1 .....38 D1
owfoot Dr LUD/ILL HX2 .....139 G4
ow Foot Gate La LUD/ILL HX2 .....139 G5
owgate BAIL BD17 .....51 J8
ow Grains Rd HOLM/MEL HD9 .....230 E2
ow La CLAY BD14 .....93 K8
HIPP HX3 .....116 D8
HIPP HX3 .....117 J5
HOLM/MEL HD9 .....232 E8
KBTN HD8 .....237 H5
LUD/ILL HX2 .....115 K5
own Bank BEE/HOL LS11 .....100 E7
own Bank La AIRE BD20 .....17 H8
ownberrie Av HORS LS18 .....55 G8
ownberrie Crs HORS LS18 .....55 F8
ownberrie Gdns HORS LS18 .....55 F8
ownberrie La HORS LS18 .....54 E8
ownberrie Wk HORS LS18 .....55 G8
own Birks St TOD OL14 .....132 D2
own Hill Av OSM LS9 .....102 C1
own Hill Cl BIRK/DRI BD11 .....120 D4
ownhill Crs HEM/SK/SE WF9 .....224 A1
own Hill Crs OSM LS9 .....102 C2
own Hill La HBR HX7 .....110 C7
ownhill La HOLM/MEL HD9 .....233 F2
ownhill Rd BTLY WF17 .....145 J2
own Hill Ter OSM LS9 .....102 C1
owning Av HIPP * HX3 .....140 C8
owning Rd HUDN HD2 .....168 E8
owning St BFDE BD3 .....5 F4
MIRF WF14 .....170 C6
own La East BEE/HOL LS11 .....6 B6
own La West WOR/ARM LS12 .....6 A6
own Lea La WIL/AL BD15 .....70 E7
own Pl BEE/HOL LS11 .....100 E7
own Royd Av HUDE HD5 .....13 F3
ownroyd Hill WBSY BD6 .....118 C2
ownroyd Rd HOLM/MEL HD9 .....212 E7
ownroyd St GIR BD8 .....95 H4
ownroyd Ter WBSY BD6 .....118 C1
own's Edge Rd STKB/PEN S36 .....250 B3
own's Knoll Rd HUDS HD4 .....214 B8
own's Pl BTLY WF17 .....146 A7
own St BTLY * WF17 .....146 A7
own St KGHY * BD21 .....3 E2
ow Rd HUD HD1 .....12 A5
HWTH BD22 .....68 E5
owsfield Rd ILK LS29 .....18 B3
owsholme St KGHY * BD21 .....2 C4
ow St KGHY BD21 .....3 E4
ow Top Rd HWTH BD22 .....69 G4
ow Wood Crs ECHL BD2 .....74 A8
ow Wood La HIPP HX3 .....117 J5
ow Wood Rd BTLY WF17 .....146 A2
HIPP HX3 .....117 J5
ownwood Ter WBSY BD6 .....118 A4
uce Gdns WOR/ARM LS12 .....6 A4
uce Lawn WOR/ARM LS12 .....6 A4
uce St HFAX HX1 .....16 A3
udenell Av HDGY LS6 .....79 F8
udenell La HDGY LS6 .....79 F8
udenell Mt HDGY LS6 .....79 F8
udenell Rd HDGY LS6 .....78 E8
udenell St HDGY * LS6 .....79 F8

Brudenell Vw HDGY LS6 .....79 F8
Brunel Cl HTON BD9 .....95 G1
Brunel Ct HIPP HX3 .....8 C1
Brunel Rd WKFDW/WTN WF2 .....149 G6
Brunswick HOR/CROF WF4 .....223 F1
Brunswick Ct LDSU LS2 .....7 F2
Brunswick Dr DEWS WF13 .....171 K2
Brunswick Gdns GFTH/SHER LS25 .....105 K4
HFAX * HX1 .....8 C4
Brunswick Gv WKFDE WF1 .....11 D5
Brunswick Pl IDLE BD10 .....75 F4
Brunswick Rd IDLE BD10 .....75 F4
PDSY/CALV LS28 .....98 C3
Brunswick St BGLY BD16 .....50 B8
BTLY * WF17 .....146 B6
CUL/QBY BD13 .....70 C5
CUL/QBY BD13 .....116 E2
DEWS WF13 .....171 K2
HBR HX7 .....112 A8
HECK * WF16 .....145 G8
MOR LS27 .....123 F6
WKFDE WF1 .....11 D5
Brunswick St Bungalows
WKFDE WF1 .....11 D3
Brunswick Ter LDSU * LS2 .....7 F2
Bruntcliffe Av MOR LS27 .....122 D6
Bruntcliffe Cl MOR LS27 .....122 E7
Bruntcliffe Dr MOR LS27 .....122 E7
Bruntcliffe La MOR LS27 .....122 C7
Bruntcliffe Rd MOR LS27 .....122 D7
Bruntcliffe Wy MOR LS27 .....122 D7
Brunthwaite Br AIRE BD20 .....27 J4
Brunthwaite Bridge La AIRE BD20 .....27 H4
Brunthwaite La AIRE BD20 .....27 J3
Brussels St OSM LS9 .....15 F4
Bryan Cl CAS WF10 .....153 F5
Bryan St North PDSY/CALV LS28 .....76 B7
PDSY/CALV LS28 .....76 B7
Bryan Ter HUDW HD3 .....189 J5
Bryer St DEWS WF13 .....172 B2
Bryngate RTHW LS26 .....127 F5
Bryony Ct EARD/LOFT WF3 .....125 F6
Bubwith Gv LUD/ILL * HX2 .....139 H5
Buckden Ct AIRE BD20 .....27 G1
Buckden Rd HUDW HD3 .....190 D3
Buckfast Ct IDLE BD10 .....74 D4
Buckingham Av HDGY LS6 .....78 E8
Buckingham Ct BSLYN/ROY S71 .....221 K7
WKFDE WF1 .....11 F5
Buckingham Crs CLAY BD14 .....94 D6
Buckingham Dr HDGY LS6 .....78 E8
WKFDE WF1 .....11 F5
Buckingham Gv HDGY LS6 .....78 E7
Buckingham Mt HDGY LS6 .....78 E8
Buckingham Rd HDGY LS6 .....78 E8
Buckingham Wy BSLYN/ROY S71 .....221 K7
KNOT WF11 .....156 A4
Buckland Pl HFAX HX1 .....139 H5
Buck La BAIL BD17 .....52 B8
Buckle La ILK LS29 .....32 E7
NORM WF6 .....177 K2
Buckley Av BEE/HOL LS11 .....101 H8
Buckley La LUD/ILL HX2 .....139 F1
Buckley Vw TOD OL14 .....133 J4
Buckley Wood Bottom TOD OL14 .....134 A6
Buck Mill La IDLE BD10 .....52 C8
Buck Pk CUL/QBY * BD13 .....92 C1
Buckrose St HUD HD1 .....12 C1
Buckrose Ter HUDN * HD2 .....12 C1
Buck Stone Av AL/HA/HU LS17 .....57 F7
Buck Stone Cl AL/HA/HU LS17 .....57 G7
Buck Stone Crs AL/HA/HU LS17 .....57 F7
Buckstone Dr YEA LS19 .....53 J8
Buck Stone Gdns AL/HA/HU LS17 .....57 F7
Buckstone Garth AIRE BD20 .....49 H2
Buck Stone Gn AL/HA/HU LS17 .....57 F7
Buck Stone Gv AL/HA/HU LS17 .....57 G7
Buck Stone La HWTH BD22 .....44 E1
Buck Stone Mt AL/HA/HU LS17 .....57 F7
Buck Stone Ov AL/HA/HU LS17 .....57 F7
Buck Stone Ri AL/HA/HU LS17 .....57 F7
Buck Stone Rd AL/HA/HU LS17 .....57 F7
Buck Stone Vw AL/HA/HU * LS17 .....57 F7
Buck Stone Wy AL/HA/HU LS17 .....57 F7
Buck St BFDE BD3 .....5 E5
CUL/QBY BD13 .....92 C3
Buckthorne Cl EARD/LOFT WF3 .....148 E3
Buckthorne Ct EARD/LOFT WF3 .....148 E3
Buckthorne Dr EARD/LOFT WF3 .....148 E3
Buckthorne Fold
EARD/LOFT * WF3 .....148 E3
Buckton Cl BEE/HOL LS11 .....101 G7
Buckton Mt BEE/HOL LS11 .....101 G7
Buckton Vw BEE/HOL LS11 .....101 G7
Bude Rd BEE/HOL LS11 .....124 C1
WBOW BD5 .....119 G2
Bula Cl GFTH/SHER LS25 .....129 G1
Bulay Rd HUD HD1 .....12 B6
Bullace Trees La LVSG WF15 .....144 A8
Bull Close La HFAX HX1 .....8 C5
Bullenshaw Rd HEM/SK/SE WF9 .....224 D5
Bullenshaw Vls HEM/SK/SE * WF9 .....225 G1
Buller Cl OSM LS9 .....102 D2
Buller Ct OSM LS9 .....102 E2
Buller Gv OSM LS9 .....102 D2

Buller St BOW BD4 .....96 E6
RTHW LS26 .....127 F5
Bullerthorpe La RTHW LS26 .....127 H3
The Bullfield BGLY BD16 .....71 F2
Bullfields Cl EARL WF12 .....195 J1
Bull Gn HFAX HX1 .....9 D5
Bull Green Rd HUDW HD3 .....189 K5
Bull La HEM/SK/SE WF9 .....241 J1
HOR/CROF WF4 .....198 B6
Bullough La RTHW LS26 .....126 C4
Bull Ring WKFDE * WF1 .....10 C3
Bull Royd Av GIR BD8 .....94 E3
Bull Royd Crs GIR BD8 .....94 E3
Bull Royd Dr GIR BD8 .....94 E3
Bull Royd La GIR BD8 .....94 E3
Bullstyle Rd PONT WF8 .....180 D5
Bundria Ct GIR BD8 .....4 A1
The Bungalows FEA/AMT * WF7 .....179 J7
FEA/AMT * WF7 .....202 E5
HIPP * HX3 .....166 D1
KBTN HD8 .....237 J1
LUD/ILL * HX2 .....139 G2
NORM * WF6 .....151 K6
OSS * WF5 .....173 H5
RPDN/SBR * HX6 .....138 D7
Bunkers Hl GFTH/SHER LS25 .....84 E6
HOLM/MEL HD9 .....233 G6
WKFDW/WTN WF2 .....175 G1
Bunker's La BTLY WF17 .....145 J7
Bunny Pk HUDS HD4 .....190 D8
Bunting Dr CUL/QBY BD13 .....117 H1
Burbeary Rd HUDS HD4 .....190 E8
Burberry Ct BOW BD4 .....119 K3
Burchett Gv HDGY LS6 .....79 G7
Burchett Pl HDGY LS6 .....79 G7
Burchett Ter HDGY LS6 .....79 H7
Burcote Dr HUDW HD3 .....189 F2
Burdale Pl GTHN BD7 .....95 H5
Burdett Ter BULY LS4 .....100 C1
Burdock Wy HFAX HX1 .....8 C4
Burfitts Rd HUDW HD3 .....190 B4
Burghley Ms EARD/LOFT WF3 .....124 E8
Burgh Mill Gdns DEWS WF13 .....171 K4
Burgh Mill La DEWS WF13 .....171 J4
Burkill St WKFDE WF1 .....199 F1
Burking Rd DEWS WF13 .....172 A3
Burlees La HBR HX7 .....112 D8
Burleigh St HFAX * HX1 .....8 A6
Burley Bank La HOLM/MEL HD9 .....246 D5
Burley Ct AIRE BD20 .....26 E6
Burley Hill Crs BULY LS4 .....78 B8
Burley Hill Dr BULY LS4 .....78 B8
Burley La HORS LS18 .....77 F4
ILK LS29 .....32 B6
Burley Lodge Pl HDGY * LS6 .....6 A2
Burley Lodge Rd HDGY LS6 .....6 A1
Burley Lodge Ter HDGY LS6 .....6 A1
Burley Ms AIRE BD20 .....26 E6
Burley Rd BULY LS4 .....78 C3
ILK LS29 .....32 C5
Burley St BVRD LS3 .....6 B3
ECHL BD2 .....73 K7
ELL HX5 .....166 E5
Burley Wk BTLY WF17 .....146 A6
Burley Wood Crs BULY LS4 .....78 B8
Burley Wood La BULY LS4 .....78 C8
Burley Wood Mt BULY LS4 .....100 B1
Burley Wood Vw BULY LS4 .....78 C8
Burlington Av BFDE BD3 .....97 G2
Burlington Pl BEE/HOL LS11 .....124 C1
Burlington Rd BEE/HOL LS11 .....124 C1
Burlington St GIR BD8 .....4 B2
HFAX * HX1 .....8 A4
Burmantofts St OSM LS9 .....102 A3
Burned Gv HIPP HX3 .....117 H4
Burned Rd HIPP HX3 .....117 J4
Burneston Gdns WBSY BD6 .....117 K3
Burnett Av WBOW BD5 .....95 K8
Burnett Pl WBOW BD5 .....95 K8
Burnett Rd CUL/QBY BD13 .....116 B5
Burnett St BFD BD1 .....5 D4
Burnham Av BOW BD4 .....119 J2
Burnham Ct WBY LS22 .....23 G5
Burnham Rd GFTH/SHER LS25 .....105 K6
Burnhill La HEM/SK/SE WF9 .....204 B6
Burniston Cl WIL/AL BD15 .....71 G7
Burniston Dr HUDW HD3 .....190 A3
Burnlee Rd HOLM/MEL HD9 .....232 E7
Burnley Rd HBR HX7 .....136 C1
RPDN/SBR HX6 .....138 E6
TOD OL14 .....132 B1
Burnleys Ct RTHW LS26 .....152 C2
Burnleys Dr RTHW LS26 .....152 C2
Burnleys Ms RTHW LS26 .....152 C2
Burnleys Vw RTHW LS26 .....152 C2
Burnleyville CLECK BD19 .....144 E2
Burnley Wy BRFD/BLYE BD10 .....108 B4
HBR HX7 .....86 B6
Burn Rd HUDW HD3 .....190 C1
Burnsall Av BTLY WF17 .....145 K6
Burnsall Ct WOR/ARM LS12 .....100 B3
Burnsall Cft WOR/ARM LS12 .....100 B3
Burnsall Gdns WOR/ARM LS12 .....100 B3
Burnsall Gra WOR/ARM LS12 .....100 B3
Burnsall Ms AIRE BD20 .....27 G1
Burnsall Rd BFDE BD3 .....5 F4
BRIG HD6 .....167 J3
BTLY WF17 .....145 K6

LVSC WF15 ...144 C7
Burns Av HEM/SK/SE WF9 ...241 F2
Burns Ct BTLY WF17 ...145 C1
Burnsdale WIL/AL BD15 ...72 A8
Burnshaw Ms EARD/LOFT WF3 ...124 D8
Burns HI ILK LS29 ...18 C3
Burnside CI BTLY WF17 ...145 K2
Burnside Dr HOLM/MEL HD9 ...232 E7
Burns St HIPP HX3 ...115 K7
Burns Wy BSPA/BRAM LS23 ...42 D5
Burnt Acres La TOD OL14 ...135 G3
Burnt House CI TOD OL14 ...134 B5
Burnt Plats La MAR/SLWT HD7 ...209 J1
Burnt Side Rd ARM LS12 ...122 B1
Burntwood Av HEM/SK/SE WF9 ...241 J1
Burntwood Bank HEM/SK/SE WF9 ...224 D6
Burnt Wood Crs HEM/SK/SE WF9 ...241 J2
Burntwood Dr HEM/SK/SE WF9 ...241 H1
Burntwood Gv HEM/SK/SE WF9 ...241 J2
Burnt Wood La CUD/GR S72 ...240 E2
Burntwood Rd CUD/GR S72 ...240 B5
Burnup Gv CLECK BD19 ...143 K4
Burnwells Av IDLE BD10 ...74 C1
Burrage St BGLY BD16 ...209 J4
Burras Av OT LS21 ...33 H4
Burras Dr OT LS21 ...33 H4
Burras La OT LS21 ...33 H4
Burras Rd BOW BD4 ...119 J1
Burrel CI WBY LS22 ...24 A6
Burrell St WKFDE WF1 ...11 D3
The Burrows BTLY WF17 ...145 J4
Burrow St WBOW BD5 ...4 C5
Burr Tree Dr MSTN/BAR LS15 ...104 B4
Burr Tree Garth MSTN/BAR LS15 ...104 B4
Burr Tree Gdns MSTN/BAR LS15 ...104 B4
Burr Tree V MSTN/BAR * LS15 ...104 B4
Burrwood Wy GTL/HWG HX4 ...166 A6
Burton Acres La KBTN HD8 ...215 G4
Burton Acres Ms KBTN HD8 ...215 G3
Burton Acres Wy KBTN HD8 ...215 G4
Burton Av BEE/HOL LS11 ...101 J8
Burton Crs HDGY LS6 ...78 D5
Burton Ms AL/HA/HU LS17 ...57 K6
Burton Rw BEE/HOL LS11 ...101 J7
Burton Royd La KBTN HD8 ...215 K4
Burtons Ar LDS LS1 ...7 E4
Burton St BEE/HOL LS11 ...101 J7
  BOW BD4 ...96 C7
  HEM/SK/SE WF9 ...226 A8
  KGHY BD21 ...2 C1
  LUD/ILL HX2 ...115 K6
  PDSY/CALV LS28 ...76 B8
  WKFDE WF1 ...10 B2
Burton Ter BEE/HOL LS11 ...101 J8
Burton Wy OSM LS9 ...102 C2
Burwood Rd HUDW HD3 ...190 B3
Busely Ct MOR LS27 ...122 E6
Busfield St BGLY BD16 ...49 K8
  BOW BD4 ...96 C7
Bushill Fold CUL/QBY BD13 ...116 B1
Bush St HEM/SK/SE WF9 ...224 E5
Busker La KBTN HD8 ...237 H2
Buslingthorpe Gn CHAL LS7 ...79 J8
Buslingthorpe La CHAL LS7 ...79 J8
Bussey Ct HDGY * LS6 ...79 G8
Busy La HDGY LS6 ...74 A2
Butcher HI BHP/TINH LS16 ...77 K3
Butcher Hill Station Rd
  HEM/SK/SE WF9 ...224 E3
Butcher La RTHW LS26 ...126 B6
Butcher St BEE/HOL LS11 ...101 J7
  BFD * BD1 ...4 B4
Bute Av BRIG HD6 ...142 B6
Bute St SHPY BD18 ...73 K7
Butler St BAIL BD17 ...51 K7
Butler St BFDE BD3 ...5 E3
Butler St East BFDE BD3 ...5 E3
Butler St West BFDE BD3 ...5 E3
Butterbowl Dr WOR/ARM LS12 ...99 J6
Butterbowl Gdns WOR/ARM LS12 ...99 J6
Butterbowl Garth WOR/ARM LS12 ...99 J6
Butterbowl Gv WOR/ARM LS12 ...99 J6
Butterbowl Lawn WOR/ARM LS12 ...99 J6
Butterbowl Mt WOR/ARM LS12 ...99 J6
Butterbowl Rd WOR/ARM LS12 ...99 J6
Buttercup CI HEM/SK/SE WF9 ...226 A4
Butterfield St OSM LS9 ...102 B3
Butterley La HOLM/MEL HD9 ...234 B6
Butterley St MID LS10 ...7 F6
Buttermeade CI WBSY BD6 ...118 B4
Buttermere CI WBY LS22 ...23 G5
Buttermere Cft WKFDW/WTN WF2 ...199 J5
Buttermere Dr HUDE HD5 ...13 F4
Buttermab Rdg HUDS HD4 ...212 D3
Buttermab Rd HUDS HD4 ...212 C2
Buttershaw Dr WBSY BD6 ...117 K3
Buttershaw La LVSC WF15 ...143 J6
  WBSY BD6 ...118 C4
Butterwick Gdns WBY LS22 ...23 G6
Butterworth CI HUDS HD4 ...212 D3
Butterworth End La
  RPDN/SBR HX6 ...164 D4
Butterworth HI HUDW HD3 ...188 E4
Butterworth La RPDN/SBR HX6 ...164 B2
Butt HI GFTH/SHER LS25 ...129 F2
Buttholme Ga WBSY BD6 ...118 A3
Butt La BTLY DN5 ...245 F7
  HOLM/MEL HD9 ...249 F1
  HWTH BD22 ...68 E4

IDLE BD10 ...74 D3
  WOR/ARM LS12 ...99 H5
Button HI CHAL LS7 ...79 K7
Button Pk PONT WF8 ...180 C4
Buttress La LUD/ILL HX2 ...138 B2
Butt Rw WOR/ARM LS12 ...99 J5
The Butts PONT WF8 ...180 E2
Butts Bottom HBR HX7 ...136 B2
Butts Ct LDS LS1 ...7 E3
Butts Garth SCFT LS14 ...60 D6
Butts Green La LUD/ILL HX2 ...138 C4
Butts Green Rd LUD/ILL HX2 ...138 C4
Butts HI CLECK BD19 ...144 D1
Butts La GFTH/SHER LS25 ...131 K5
  HOR/CROF WF4 ...196 B4
Butts Mt WOR/ARM LS12 ...100 D4
Butts Rd HUDS HD4 ...214 A5
Butts Wy HUDS HD4 ...214 A5
Butts Yd CLECK BD19 ...144 A4
Buxton Av HTON * BD9 ...73 J7
Buxton HTON BD9 ...73 J7
Buxton PI WKFDE WF1 ...10 B1
Buxton St HIPP HX3 ...115 J3
  HTON BD9 ...95 H1
  KGHY BD21 ...3 E3
  WHIT OL12 ...158 A8
Buxton Wy HIPP HX3 ...115 J3
  HUD * HD1 ...12 C5
Byeway GSLY LS20 ...52 E2
Byland LUD/ILL HX2 ...115 G5
Byland CI BSPA/BRAM LS23 ...42 C4
Byland Gv WIL/AL BD15 ...93 K1
Byram Ar HUD * HD1 ...12 C4
Byram Park Av KNOT WF11 ...156 B3
Byram Park Rd KNOT WF11 ...156 B3
Byram St HUD HD1 ...12 C4
Byrl St KGHY BD21 ...3 E2
Byron Av RPDN/SBR * HX6 ...138 E6
Byron Gv DEWS WF13 ...171 H3
  EARD/LOFT WF3 ...150 B5
Byron Ms BGLY BD16 ...50 A6
Byron St BFDE BD3 ...5 F3
  HFAX HX1 ...8 A4
  LDSU LS2 ...7 F2
  RPDN/SBR HX6 ...138 E6
  TOD OL14 ...134 A6
The Byways PONT WF8 ...180 E2
Bywell CI EARL WF12 ...172 E2
Bywell Rd EARL WF12 ...172 E2

C

Cabbage HI WOR/ARM LS12 ...100 A3
Cabin Rd OT LS21 ...35 F6
Cad Beeston Ms BEE/HOL * LS11 ...101 G8
Cadogan Av HUDW HD3 ...190 B3
Caenarvon CI BTLY WF17 ...145 K2
Caernarvon Av GFTH/SHER LS25 ...106 B4
Cain CI OSM LS9 ...102 B4
Cain La HIPP HX3 ...141 F7
Cairn CI AIRE BD20 ...47 J1
Cairns CI ECHL BD2 ...74 B8
Caister CI BTLY WF17 ...145 J1
Caister Gv KGHY * BD21 ...2 B6
Caister St KGHY BD21 ...2 C6
Caister Wy KGHY BD21 ...2 C6
Calde CI LM/WK BD12 ...119 F5
Caldene Av HBR HX7 ...136 E2
  LM/WK BD12 ...119 F5
Calder Av BSLYN/ROY S71 ...222 C4
  LUD/ILL HX2 ...8 A6
Calder Bank Rd EARL WF12 ...172 A5
Calder Banks CUL/QBY BD13 ...117 F2
Caldercliffe Rd HUDS HD4 ...213 F2
Caldercroft ELL HX5 ...173 H6
Calderdale Wy BRIG HD6 ...142 D6
  ELL HX5 ...166 D4
  ELL HX5 ...167 G7
  GTL/HWG HX4 ...165 K3
  HBR HX7 ...135 K8
  HBR HX7 ...136 B3
  HIPP HX3 ...117 F6
Calder Dr HUDS HD4 ...213 F3
Calder Edge TOD * OL14 ...135 F4
Calder Gv HBR HX7 ...137 F2
Calder Island Wy
  WKFDW/WTN WF2 ...198 D1
Calder Rd DEWS WF13 ...171 H6
  MIRF WF14 ...170 D8
Calderstone Av WBSY BD6 ...117 J3
Calderstone Ct HOR/CROF WF4 ...196 A4
Calder St BRIG HD6 ...168 D2
  CAS WF10 ...153 G3
  GTL/HWG HX4 ...166 C4
  TOD OL14 ...134 A6
  WKFDE WF1 ...10 C5
Calder Ter HBR * HX7 ...112 A8
  HIPP HX3 ...165 K2
Caldervale Rd BSLYN/ROY S71 ...222 C7
Calder Vale Rd HOR/CROF WF4 ...197 J3
  WKFDE WF1 ...11 D4
Calder Vw BRIG HD6 ...168 A2
  HOR/CROF WF4 ...198 A6

OSS WF5 ...173
Caldicott CI TOD OL14 ...133
Caledonia Ct WKFDW/WTN WF2 ...174
Caledonian Rd EARL WF12 ...172
Caledonia Rd BTLY WF17 ...146
  KGHY BD21 ...3
Caledonia St BOW BD4 ...5
Calf Hey La STKB/PEN S36 ...250
Calf Hill Rd HOLM/MEL HD9 ...233
Calgary Crs EARD/LOFT WF3 ...148
Calgary PI CHAL LS7 ...79
California Dr CAS WF10 ...197
  HOR/CROF WF4 ...197
  TOD OL14 ...133
California La CLECK BD19 ...144
California Ms MOR LS27 ...123
California St MOR * LS27 ...123
Call La LDS LS1 ...7
The Calls LDS LS1 ...7
Callis La CLECK BD19 ...144
Calpin CI IDLE * BD10 ...74
Calton CI KGHY BD21 ...48
Calton Rd KGHY BD21 ...2
Calton St HUD HD1 ...13
  KGHY BD21 ...2
Calver Av KGHY BD21 ...2
Calver Gv KGHY BD21 ...2
Calverley Av BFDE BD3 ...97
  BRAM LS13 ...77
Calverley Ct BRAM LS13 ...77
  RTHW LS26 ...126
Calverley Cutting IDLE BD10 ...75
Calverley Dr BRAM LS13 ...77
Calverley Gdns BRAM LS13 ...76
Calverley Garth BRAM LS13 ...77
Calverley Green Rd NORM WF6 ...151
Calverley Gv BRAM LS13 ...77
Calverley La BRAM LS13 ...76
  HORS LS18 ...76
  PDSY/CALV LS28 ...76
Calverley Moor Av PDSY/CALV LS28 ...97
Calverley Rd RTHW LS26 ...127
Calverley St LDS LS1 ...7
Calverley Ter BRAM LS13 ...77
Calver Rd KGHY BD21 ...2
Calversyde St HWTH BD22 ...2
Calvert CI GFTH/SHER LS25 ...106
Calverts Wk OSS WF5 ...174
Camargue Fold ECHL BD2 ...74
Camberley CI PDSY/CALV LS28 ...98
Camberley Mt BOW BD4 ...97
Camberley St BEE/HOL * LS11 ...101
Camberley Wy PDSY/CALV LS28 ...98
Camborne Dr HUDN HD2 ...168
Camborne Rd HUDN HD2 ...168
Camborne Wy HWTH BD22 ...47
Cambrian Bar LM/WK BD12 ...118
Cambrian St BEE/HOL LS11 ...101
Cambrian Ter BEE/HOL LS11 ...101
Cambridge CI MOR LS27 ...123
Cambridge Ct MOR LS27 ...123
Cambridge Crs HOR/CROF WF4 ...200
Cambridge Dr BRAM LS13 ...77
  OT LS21 ...33
Cambridge Gdns BRAM LS13 ...77
Cambridge Gv GFTH/SHER LS25 ...129
  OT LS21 ...33
Cambridge PI BFDE BD3 ...5
  CUL/QBY BD13 ...116
Cambridge Rd BTLY WF17 ...145
  CHAL LS7 ...79
  HUD HD1 ...12
Cambridge St BTLY WF17 ...146
  CAS WF10 ...153
  CLAY * BD14 ...94
  CUL/QBY BD13 ...116
  GTHN BD7 ...95
  HBR HX7 ...112
  HECK WF16 ...145
  HEM/SK/SE WF9 ...226
  NORM WF6 ...151
  OT LS21 ...33
  TOD OL14 ...134
  WKFDW/WTN WF2 ...175
Cambridge Wy OT LS21 ...33
Camden Rd CAS WF10 ...154
Camden Ter GIR BD8 ...4
Camellia CI WKFDW/WTN WF2 ...174
Camellia Ct SHPY BD18 ...73
Camellia Mt GTHN BD7 ...94
Cameron Av LM/WK BD12 ...142
Cameronian Ct KGHY * BD21 ...3
Camilla Ct EARL WF12 ...172
Cam La BRIG HD6 ...142
Camm St BRIG HD6 ...142
Campbell St CUL/QBY BD13 ...116
  KGHY BD21 ...3
Campden Rd HBR HX7 ...111
Campinot V MAR/SLWT HD7 ...210
Campion La PONT WF8 ...180
Camp Mt PONT WF8 ...180
Camp Rd PONT WF8 ...180
Camp Rd BHP/TINH LS16 ...55
  HEM/SK/SE WF9 ...241
Campus Rd GTHN BD7 ...4
Camroyd St DEWS WF13 ...172
Canada Crs YEA LS19 ...54

nada Dr YEA LS19 .....54 A6
nada Rd YEA LS19 .....54 A6
nada Ter YEA LS19 .....54 A7
nal Ct EARD/LOFT * WF3 .....150 A5
nal La AIRE BD20 .....27 J4
 EARD/LOFT WF3 .....150 A5
nal Rd AIRE BD20 .....6 B4
 AIRE BD20 .....48 C1
 BFD BD1 .....5 D4
 BGLY BD16 .....49 K6
 BRAM LS13 .....76 C6
 CHL BD2 .....73 J7
 PDN/SBR HX6 .....139 H7
 WOR/ARM LS12 .....100 D3
nal St BRIG HD6 .....168 C1
 HIPP HX3 .....13 E2
 HUD HD1 .....13 E2
 WOR/ARM LS12 .....6 A3
nal Wk EARD/LOFT WF3 .....150 C5
nal Whf BEE/HOL LS11 .....7 D4
nary Dr BGLY BD16 .....50 C7
nary St CLECK BD19 .....144 A3
nberra Dr HWTH BD22 .....69 H3
nberra Dr HWTH BD22 .....69 H3
nby Gv HUDE HD5 .....192 D6
ncel St WF13 .....7 F6
nford Dr WIL/AL BD15 .....94 B2
nford Gv WIL/AL BD15 .....94 C2
nford Rd WIL/AL BD15 .....94 B2
nker La HIPP HX3 .....115 K8
NUD HD1 .....13 E1
nning Av WKFDW/WTN WF2 .....174 E3
nnon Gv HECK WF16 .....145 H6
nnon Hall La BRIG HD6 .....168 E1
nnon Hall Dr BRIG HD6 .....168 E1
nnon Mill La GTHN BD7 .....95 G7
nnon St BGLY BD16 .....72 A1
 CAS WF10 .....153 K5
 HFAX * HX1 .....8 A6
 OD OL14 .....133 K8
anon Wy EARL WF12 .....172 B4
e Canter MID LS10 .....124 E8
nterbury Av WBOW BD5 .....95 J8
nterbury Ct PONT WF8 .....155 F8
nterbury Crs HIPP HX3 .....8 C2
nterbury Dr HDGY LS6 .....78 C7
nterbury Rd EARL WF12 .....172 E2
 HDGY LS6 .....78 C7
nel Ct PDSY/CALV LS28 .....75 K5
nel St BRIG HD6 .....168 B2
 PDSY/CALV LS28 .....75 K5
pe St BFD BD1 .....5 H4
pitol Pde HDGY LS6 .....78 E4
prington Ct NORM WF6 .....178 C2
berry Pl HDGY LS6 .....6 A1
berry Rd HDGY LS6 .....6 A1
berry Ter HDGY LS6 .....6 A1
rdan Dr ILK LS29 .....20 E7
rden Av MSTN/BAR LS15 .....103 G3
rden Rd WBOW BD4 .....118 C3
rdigan Av MOR LS27 .....147 F1
rdigan Cl BTLY WF17 .....146 D6
rdigan Ct HDGY LS6 .....78 E7
rdigan Fields Rd BULY LS4 .....100 C2
rdigan La BULY LS4 .....100 D1
SS WF9 .....174 A8
rdigan St CUL/QBY BD13 .....116 D2
rdigan Ter EARD/LOFT WF3 .....149 F3
WKFDE WF1 .....10 B2
rdinal Av BEE/HOL LS11 .....124 A3
rdinal Cl HOLM/MEL HD9 .....231 J1
rdinal Crs BEE/HOL LS11 .....124 A3
rdinal Gdns BEE/HOL LS11 .....123 K3
rdinal Gv BEE/HOL LS11 .....123 K3
rdinal Rd BEE/HOL LS11 .....123 K3
rdinal Sq BEE/HOL LS11 .....123 K2
rdinal Wk BEE/HOL LS11 .....123 K2
rdwell Ter EARL WF12 .....172 B5
rforth St HUD HD1 .....13 E5
risbrooke Crs WBSY BD6 .....118 C3
risbrooke La GTHN/SHER LS25 .....106 B3
riss St MID LS10 .....101 K8
k Rd KGHY BD21 .....3 D2
rlby St HWTH BD22 .....2 B4
rlby St HWTH BD22 .....2 B4
leton Crest PONT WF8 .....181 F5
leton Dr BSPA/BRAM LS23 .....42 B4
leton Ga PONT WF8 .....180 D5
leton Gln PONT WF8 .....180 E4
leton Green Cl PONT WF8 .....181 F5
leton Park Av PONT WF8 .....180 E5
leton Park Rd PONT WF8 .....180 E5
leton Rd PONT WF8 .....180 E4
ONT WF8 .....181 H7
leton St KGHY BD21 .....3 D1
leton Vw PONT WF8 .....180 E5
sile St HOLM/MEL HD9 .....231 J1
ling Cl GTHN BD7 .....95 F8
linghow La BTLY WF17 .....146 A4
linghow La BTLY WF17 .....145 H4
isle Av YEA LS19 .....54 A5
isle Cl DEWS WF13 .....172 B1
isle Dr PDSY/CALV LS28 .....98 B5
isle Gv PDSY/CALV LS28 .....98 B5
isle Pl GIR BD8 .....4 A2

Carlisle Rd GIR BD8 .....95 H2
 MID LS10 .....7 F5
 PDSY/CALV LS28 .....98 A3
Carlisle St KGHY BD21 .....3 E4
 LUD/ILL HX2 .....139 H3
 PDSY/CALV LS28 .....98 A3
Carlisle Ter GIR BD8 .....4 A2
Carlton Ap WBY LS22 .....23 G5
Carlton Av BTLY WF17 .....146 A8
 CAS WF10 .....154 A4
 PDSY/CALV LS28 .....98 C4
 SHPY BD18 .....73 F3
Carlton Cl CHAL * LS7 .....7 E1
 HEM/SK/SE WF9 .....224 C5
 NORM WF6 .....178 A1
Carlton Ct OSS WF5 .....173 J5
 WOR/ARM LS12 .....100 E7
Carlton Cft CHAL * LS7 .....7 E1
 WKFDW/WTN WF2 .....199 F5
Carlton Dr BAIL BD17 .....51 J7
 GFTH/SHER LS25 .....105 K6
 GSLY LS20 .....53 H1
 HTON BD9 .....73 G7
Carlton Gdns CHAL LS7 .....7 E1
 HEM/SK/SE WF9 .....226 B8
 NORM WF6 .....178 B1
Carlton Garth AL/HA/HU LS17 .....58 C6
 CHAL * LS7 .....7 E1
Carlton Ga CHAL LS7 .....7 E1
Carlton Gv CHAL LS7 .....7 E1
 ELL HX5 .....167 G4
Carlton Hi CHAL LS7 .....7 E1
Carlton House Ter HFAX HX1 .....8 B6
Carlton La EARD/LOFT WF3 .....149 K2
 GSLY LS20 .....53 H1
Carlton Moor Ms EARD/LOFT WF3 .....125 G6
Carlton Mt LS19 .....54 A3
Carlton Pl HFAX HX1 .....9 D5
Carlton Ri CHAL * LS7 .....7 E1
 PDSY/CALV LS28 .....98 C4
Carlton Rd DEWS WF13 .....172 B2
 HEM/SK/SE WF9 .....226 B8
 LVSG WF15 .....144 D8
 SHPY BD18 .....72 E3
Carlton Rw WOR/ARM LS12 .....100 A4
Carlton St CAS WF10 .....153 J5
 CUD/OR S72 .....240 A5
 FEA/AMT WF7 .....179 J4
 GTHN BD7 .....4 B5
 HBR * HX7 .....112 B8
 HFAX HX1 .....9 D5
 HOR/CROF WF4 .....197 G2
 HWTH BD22 .....69 F4
 NORM WF6 .....178 A1
 OT LS21 .....33 K4
 WKFDW/WTN WF2 .....10 A4
Carlton Vw CAS WF10 .....128 E5
 CHAL LS7 .....7 E1
Carlton Wk SHPY BD18 .....73 F3
Carlyle Crs CAS WF10 .....154 B4
Carlyle Rd CAS WF10 .....154 B4
Carmel Rd HFAX HX3 .....8 C1
Carmine Cl HUDE HD5 .....192 A5
Carmona Av SHPY BD18 .....73 H6
Carmona Gdns SHPY BD18 .....73 H6
Carnaby Rd GTHN BD7 .....117 K1
Carnegie Dr SHPY BD18 .....73 J3
Carnlea Gv WKFDW/WTN WF2 .....10 C6
Carnoustie Gdns NORM WF6 .....178 C2
Carnoustie Gv BGLY BD16 .....72 A6
Carolan Ct MAR/SLWT HD7 .....189 G7
Caroline St CLECK BD19 .....144 A3
 SHPY BD18 .....73 F3
Carperley Crs CUL/QBY BD13 .....92 C3
Carr Bank WBOW BD5 .....118 C2
Carr Bottom Av WBOW BD5 .....118 C2
Carr Bottom Fold WBSY BD6 .....118 D2
Carr Bottom Gv WBSY BD6 .....118 C1
Carr Bottom Rd IDLE BD10 .....75 G5
 WBOW BD5 .....118 D1
Carr Bridge Av BHP/TINH LS16 .....55 H8
Carr Bridge Cl BHP/TINH LS16 .....55 H8
Carr Bridge Dr BHP/TINH LS16 .....55 H8
Carr Bridge Vw BHP/TINH LS16 .....55 H8
Carr Cl YEA LS19 .....54 B8
Carr Crofts WOR/ARM LS12 .....100 B4
Carr Crofts Dr WOR/ARM LS12 .....100 B4
Carrfield Cl DOD/DAR S75 .....239 K4
Carr Field Dr LUD/ILL HX2 .....138 B3
Carrfield Dr MSTN/BAR LS15 .....83 H4
Carrfield La MSTN/BAR LS15 .....83 H4
Carrfield Rd MSTN/BAR LS15 .....83 H4
Carrgate HEM/SK/SE WF9 .....224 B1
Carr Gate Crs WKFDW/WTN WF2 .....148 B5
Carr Gate Dr WKFDW/WTN WF2 .....149 F6
Carr Gate Mt WKFDW/WTN WF2 .....148 E6
Carr Green Av BRIG HD6 .....168 A5
Carr Green Cl BRIG HD6 .....168 A5
Carr Green Dr BRIG HD6 .....168 A5
Carr Green La BRIG HD6 .....168 A4
 HUDE HD5 .....13 F3
Carr Gv AIRE BD20 .....48 E2
Carr Hall La GTL/HWG HX4 .....165 K7
Carr Hall Rd LM/WK BD12 .....118 D8
Carr Hill Av PDSY/CALV LS28 .....75 J5
Carr Hill Dr PDSY/CALV LS28 .....75 J5
Carr Hill Gv PDSY/CALV LS28 .....75 J5

Carr Hill Nook PDSY/CALV * LS28 .....75 J5
Carr Hill Ri PDSY/CALV LS28 .....75 J5
Carr Hill Rd KBTN HD8 .....235 J5
 PDSY/CALV LS28 .....75 J5
Carrholm Crs CHAL LS7 .....79 H4
Carrholm Dr CHAL LS7 .....79 H4
Carrholm Gv CHAL LS7 .....79 H4
Carrholm Mt CHAL LS7 .....79 H4
Carrholm Rd CHAL LS7 .....79 H4
Carrholm Vw CHAL LS7 .....79 H4
Carr House Gv LM/WK BD12 .....118 D7
Carr House La HIPP HX3 .....117 J1
 LM/WK BD12 .....118 C6
 TOD OL14 .....134 C5
Carr House Mt LM/WK * BD12 .....118 D7
Carr House Rd HIPP HX3 .....117 J5
 HOLM/MEL HD9 .....233 G6
The Carriage Dr GTL/HWG HX4 .....165 K7
 GTL/HWG HX4 .....166 B3
 RHAY LS8 .....80 E2
Carriage Dr CLECK BD19 .....144 E1
 HUDS HD4 .....212 E3
Carricks Cl LM/WK BD12 .....119 F5
Carrington St BFDE BD3 .....96 E4
Carrington Ter GSLY LS20 .....53 F5
Carr La AIRE BD20 .....48 E2
 AL/HA/HU LS17 .....59 J7
 CAS WF10 .....153 K6
 CUL/QBY BD13 .....92 C1
 EARD/LOFT WF3 .....126 B8
 EARL WF12 .....195 F3
 HECK WF16 .....171 G2
 HEM/SK/SE WF9 .....201 K8
 HEM/SK/SE WF9 .....225 J7
 HOLM/MEL HD9 .....232 B7
 HOR/CROF WF4 .....196 B5
 KBTN HD8 .....235 H5
 LM/WK BD12 .....118 E6
 MAR/SLWT HD7 .....210 E2
 SHPY BD18 .....73 K4
 STKB/PEN S36 .....252 A4
 WBY LS22 .....24 A5
 WKFDW/WTN WF2 .....199 F4
 YEA LS19 .....54 B8
Carr Lane Av CAS WF10 .....153 K6
Carr Manor Av AL/HA/HU LS17 .....79 H3
Carr Manor Crs AL/HA/HU LS17 .....79 H2
Carr Manor Cft CHAL LS7 .....79 H4
Carr Manor Dr AL/HA/HU LS17 .....79 H3
Carr Manor Gdns AL/HA/HU LS17 .....79 H3
Carr Manor Garth AL/HA/HU LS17 .....79 H3
Carr Manor Gv AL/HA/HU LS17 .....79 H3
Carr Manor Mt AL/HA/HU LS17 .....79 H3
Carr Manor Pde AL/HA/HU LS17 .....79 H3
Carr Manor Pl AL/HA/HU LS17 .....79 H3
Carr Manor Rd AL/HA/HU LS17 .....79 H3
Carr Manor Vw AL/HA/HU LS17 .....79 H3
Carr Manor Wk CHAL LS7 .....79 H5
Carr Mill Ms HWTH BD22 .....44 C1
Carr Moor Side BEE/HOL LS11 .....101 J8
Carr Mt KBTN HD8 .....235 J5
Carroll Ct HEM/SK/SE WF9 .....226 A8
Carroll St BFDE BD3 .....5 E5
Carr Pit Rd HUD HD1 .....13 E5
Carr Rd LM/WK * BD12 .....118 D8
 PDSY/CALV LS28 .....75 H5
 TOD OL14 .....132 D3
Carr Side Crs BTLY WF17 .....146 A8
Carrs Rd MAR/SLWT HD7 .....209 J8
Carrs Side St No 2 MAR/SLWT HD7 .....209 J7
Carrs St MAR/SLWT HD7 .....209 J8
Carr St BRIG HD6 .....142 B7
 BTLY WF17 .....145 H3
 CLECK BD19 .....144 A4
 DEWS WF13 .....172 B1
 HUDW HD3 .....190 C4
 KGHY BD21 .....3 D3
 LVSG WF15 .....144 D6
 WBOW BD5 .....118 E1
Carr Top Cl DEWS WF13 .....172 A1
Carr Top La MAR/SLWT HD7 .....189 H7
Carr Vw HEM/SK/SE WF9 .....225 J7
Carr View Rd HOLM/MEL HD9 .....249 F1
Carr Wood Gdns PDSY/CALV LS28 .....75 J5
Carr Wood Rd CAS WF10 .....154 A6
Carter Av MSTN/BAR LS15 .....104 A3
Carter La CUL/QBY BD13 .....93 H8
 MSTN/BAR LS15 .....104 A2
Carter Mt MSTN/BAR LS15 .....104 A3
Carter's La ILK LS29 .....20 E5
Carter St BFD BD1 .....5 D5
 WKFDE WF1 .....10 B3
Carter Ter MSTN/BAR LS15 .....104 A3
Cartmel La AIRE BD20 .....26 E6
Cartmell Dr MSTN/BAR LS15 .....103 F5
Cartmel Rd KGHY BD21 .....2 B3
Cartworth Bank Rd HOLM/MEL HD9 .....248 A1
Cartworth La HOLM/MEL HD9 .....233 F8
Cartworth Moor Rd HOLM/MEL HD9 .....247 K3
Cartworth Rd HOLM/MEL HD9 .....233 G8
Cartwright Gdns HUDS HD4 .....190 C6
Cartwright St CLECK BD19 .....144 C5
Carver St CLECK BD19 .....144 A3
Caryl Rd BOW BD4 .....96 C8
Cashmere St HWTH BD22 .....2 B3
Casson Av EARD/LOFT WF3 .....148 C2
Casson Dr EARD/LOFT WF3 .....148 C2

Casson Gv EARD/LOFT WF3 .....148 C2
Cass Yd WKFDE * WF1 .....11 D3
Casterton Gdns SCFT LS14 .....81 K8
Castle Av BRIG HD6 .....168 A3
  HUDS HD4 .....213 G2
  WKFDW/WTN WF2 .....199 H1
Castle Carr Rd LUD/ILL HX2 .....113 K5
Castle Cl AL/HA/HU LS17 .....40 B8
  BTLY WF17 .....145 K2
Castle Crs EARL WF12 .....195 G2
  WKFDW/WTN WF2 .....199 F3
Castle Cft BGLY BD16 .....70 B2
Castlefield Ct CAS * WF10 .....153 J3
Castlefields RTHW LS26 .....125 H6
Castlefields Crs BRIG HD6 .....168 A3
Castlefields Dr BRIG HD6 .....168 A3
Castlefields La BRIG HD6 .....49 J6
Castlefields Rd BGLY BD16 .....49 H6
  BRIG HD6 .....168 A3
Castleford Br CAS WF10 .....153 K2
Castleford La FEA/AMT WF7 .....179 G1
  KNOT WF11 .....155 J6
Castleford Rd NORM WF6 .....178 A1
Castle Garth PONT WF8 .....181 F2
Castle Ga HBR HX7 .....136 D8
Castlegate HUD HD1 .....12 B5
  WBY LS22 .....23 J6
Castlegate Dr IDLE BD10 .....74 E5
  PONT WF8 .....180 C6
Castle Gra YEA * LS19 .....54 B5
Castle Gv AL/HA/HU LS17 .....40 B8
  BGLY BD16 .....70 E2
  HOR/CROF WF4 .....197 H3
Castle Grove Av HDGY LS6 .....78 D4
Castle Grove Dr HDGY LS6 .....78 D5
Castle Head Cl EARD/LOFT WF3 .....149 K2
Castle Head La EARD/LOFT WF3 .....149 H3
Castle Hi MID LS10 .....168 A3
  WKFDW/WTN WF2 .....199 F3
Castle Hill Ct HWTH * BD22 .....2 B4
Castle Hill Rd CLECK BD19 .....144 E5
Castle Hill Side HUDS HD4 .....213 J3
Castle Hill Vw HECK WF16 .....145 H8
Castle Ings Cl WOR/ARM LS12 .....99 H1
Castle Ings Dr WOR/ARM LS12 .....99 H1
Castle Ings Gdns WOR/ARM LS12 .....122 C1
Castle La MAR/SLWT HD7 .....210 C1
  RPDN/SBR HX6 .....163 K8
  TOD OL14 .....134 C5
Castle Lane Cl TOD OL14 .....134 C5
Castle Mdw HOR/CROF WF4 .....198 B8
Castlemore Rd BAIL BD17 .....73 K1
Castle Mt EARL WF12 .....195 F2
Castle Pde CAS WF10 .....154 A5
Castle Rd ILK LS29 .....20 B7
  KGHY BD21 .....2 C2
  RTHW LS26 .....126 A6
  SHPY BD18 .....73 G4
  WKFDW/WTN WF2 .....199 F3
Castle Rd West WKFDW/WTN WF2 .....199 F1
Castle Syke Hl FEA/AMT WF7 .....180 C8
Castle Syke Vw PONT WF8 .....180 D5
Castle Ter WKFDW/WTN WF2 .....199 F3
Castleton Cl WOR/ARM LS12 .....6 B4
Castleton Rd WOR/ARM LS12 .....6 A3
Castle Vw AL/HA/HU LS17 .....79 H2
  HOLM/MEL HD9 .....213 H6
  HOR/CROF WF4 .....197 J3
  MIRF WF14 .....170 E6
  WKFDW/WTN WF2 .....199 F3
Castle Wood Cl AL/HA/HU LS17 .....38 C4
Castley La AL/HA/HU LS17 .....36 B1
  OT LS21 .....35 H3
Cater St BFD * BD1 .....5 D4
Cathcart St HDGY LS6 .....79 G8
  HIPP HX3 .....8 C1
Cathedral Cl WKFDE WF1 .....10 B2
Catherine Cl HUDW HD3 .....190 A1
Catherine Gv BEE/HOL * LS11 .....101 K3
Catherine House La HBR HX7 .....113 H5
Catherine Rd HUDN HD2 .....168 C7
Catherine Slack BRIG HD6 .....142 A5
Catherine St BRIG HD6 .....142 B8
  ELL HX5 .....166 E5
  HEM/SK/SE WF9 .....202 A7
  KGHY BD21 .....2 C5
Cat Hill La STKB/PEN S36 .....252 C5
Cat La GTL/HWG HX4 .....165 H4
  LUD/ILL HX2 .....137 J6
Catlow St CAS WF10 .....153 H4
Catshaw La STKB/PEN S36 .....250 E8
Cattlelaith La KNOT WF11 .....155 K8
Cattle La GFTH/SHER LS25 .....84 E4
Cattle Market St OT LS21 .....33 J3
Caudle Hl KNOT WF11 .....131 G7
Cauldwell Gdns WBOW * BD5 .....96 A7
Caulms Wood Rd DEWS WF13 .....172 C3
Causeway GTL/HWG HX4 .....187 J1
  HFAX HX1 .....9 E4
  MAR/SLWT HD7 .....188 D3
Causeway Crs MAR/SLWT HD7 .....211 H2
Causeway Garth La PONT WF8 .....204 E7
Causeway Head RPDN/SBR * HX6 .....163 J6
Causeway Head La RPDN/SBR HX6 .....163 J7
Causeway Side MAR/SLWT HD7 .....211 H2
  TOD * OL14 .....135 F6

Causeway Wood Rd TOD OL14 .....134 D7
Cautley Rd OSM LS9 .....102 B5
Cavalier Ap OSM LS9 .....102 B5
Cavalier Cl OSM * LS9 .....102 B5
Cavalier Ct OSM LS9 .....102 B5
Cavalier Dr IDLE BD10 .....75 F4
Cavalier Gdns OSM LS9 .....102 B5
Cavalier Ga OSM LS9 .....102 B5
Cavalier Gn OSM LS9 .....102 B5
Cavalier Ms OSM LS9 .....102 B5
Cavalier Vw OSM LS9 .....102 B5
Cave Crs WKFDW/WTN WF2 .....175 H1
Cave Hl HIPP HX3 .....116 E7
Cave La EARD/LOFT WF3 .....148 A3
Cavendish Av PONT WF8 .....155 F8
Cavendish Dr BGLY BD16 .....50 B7
  GSLY LS20 .....53 F3
Cavendish Gv GSLY LS20 .....53 F3
Cavendish Pl PDSY/CALV LS28 .....98 E4
Cavendish Ri PDSY/CALV LS28 .....98 E4
Cavendish Rd GSLY LS20 .....53 F3
  IDLE BD10 .....74 D4
  LDSU LS2 .....7 D1
Cavendish St BVRD LS3 .....6 B3
  HFAX HX1 .....8 B4
  KGHY BD21 .....3 D5
  PDSY/CALV LS28 .....98 C7
  YEA LS19 .....54 A4
Cavendish Ter HFAX HX1 .....8 B4
Cavewell Cl OSS WF5 .....174 A8
Cavewell Gdns OSS WF5 .....174 A8
Cawcliffe Dr BRIG HD6 .....142 B7
Cawcliffe Rd BRIG HD6 .....142 B7
Cawley Garth HECK WF16 .....145 H4
Cawley La HECK WF16 .....145 H8
Cawood Hvn WBSY * BD6 .....117 K3
Cawthorne Av HUDN HD2 .....191 G1
Cawthorne La DOD/DAR S75 .....239 G6
Cawthorne Rd DOD/DAR S75 .....239 K7
  WKFDW/WTN WF2 .....160 E3
Cawthorne Vw STKB/PEN S36 .....252 E5
Caxton Gdns PONT WF8 .....154 E8
Caxton Rd OT LS21 .....33 G5
Caxton St WBY LS22 .....23 J6
Caygill Ter HFAX HX1 .....9 D6
Caythorne Wk IDLE BD10 .....74 E6
Caythorpe Rd BHP/TINH LS16 .....78 A3
Cecil Av BAIL BD17 .....51 J7
  GTHN BD7 .....95 H7
  HIPP HX3 .....141 K3
Cecil Gv WOR/ARM LS12 .....100 C5
Cecil Mt WOR/ARM LS12 .....100 C5
Cecil Rd WOR/ARM LS12 .....100 C5
Cecil St WOR/ARM LS12 .....100 C5
  WOR/ARM LS12 .....100 C5
Cedar Av HUD HD1 .....12 B5
  WOR/ARM LS12 .....100 C4
Cedar Cl BSLYN/ROY S71 .....221 J7
  PONT WF8 .....180 D6
  WOR/ARM LS12 .....100 C4
Cedar Ct RTHW LS26 .....127 H4
Cedar Covert WBY LS22 .....23 J5
Cedar Dr EARL WF12 .....175 G5
  LM/WG BD12 .....119 F7
Cedar Gv FEA/AMT WF7 .....179 J4
  GTL/HWG HX4 .....166 A4
Cedar Mt HUDW HD3 .....189 J8
  WOR/ARM LS12 .....100 B4
Cedar Pl WOR/ARM LS12 .....100 B4
Cedar Rdg GFTH/SHER LS25 .....106 B2
Cedar Rd EARL WF12 .....175 F5
  NORM WF6 .....178 A4
The Cedars BHP/TINH LS16 .....58 K2
Cedar St HFAX HX1 .....8 A4
  HUD * HD1 .....12 A3
  KGHY BD21 .....2 C6
  TOD OL14 .....159 K3
  WOR/ARM LS12 .....100 B4
Cedar Ter WOR/ARM LS12 .....100 B4
Cedar Wk FEA/AMT WF7 .....179 J5
Cedar Wy CLECK BD19 .....144 D3
Celandine Av HUDW HD3 .....189 J5
Celandine Cl PONT WF8 .....180 E4
Celandine Dr HUDW HD3 .....189 J5
Cemetery La AIRE BD20 .....47 K1
  EARD/LOFT WF3 .....149 K2
  RPDN/SBR HX6 .....138 D7
Cemetery Rd BEE/HOL LS11 .....101 G7
  BGLY BD16 .....49 J3
  BTLY WF17 .....146 A6
  DEWS WF13 .....171 K4
  HECK WF16 .....145 G7
  HEM/SK/SE WF9 .....
  HOLM/MEL HD9 .....233 F7
  HOR/CROF WF4 .....223 F2
  HUD HD1 .....12 B5
  HWTH BD22 .....68 C4
  NORM WF6 .....178 B1
  PDSY/CALV LS28 .....98 B3
  WBSY BD6 .....118 C4
  YEA LS19 .....54 A4
Centenary Rd BAIL BD17 .....52 B7
Centenary Sq EARL WF12 .....172 A7
  OSM * LS9 .....7 F3
Centenary Wy BTLY WF17 .....146 A5

Central Av BAIL BD17 73
  CUD/GR S72 240
  HEM/SK/SE WF9 202
  HEM/SK/SE WF9 191
  HUDN HD2 191
  HWTH BD22 47
  LVSG WF15 143
  SHPY BD18 73
  WBOW BD5 95
Central Av East LVSG WF15 143
Central Cl HUDN HD2 191
Central Dr BSLYN/ROY S71 222
  CAS WF10 152
  HUDN HD2 168
  HWTH BD22 47
Central Pde OSM LS9 102
Central Pk HFAX HX1 9
Central Rd HUDN HD2 168
Central St DEWS WF13 172
  HBR HX7 112
  HFAX HX1 9
  LDS LS1 7
Centre St HECK * WF16 145
  HEM/SK/SE WF9 224
  HEM/SK/SE WF9 226
  WBOW * BD5 95
Centuria Wk HUDW HD3 189
Century Pl GIR BD8 .....
Century Rd ELL HX5 166
Century St KGHY * BD21 2
Ceres Rd WBY LS22 23
Chaddlewood Cl HORS LS18 77
Chadwell Springs BGLY BD16 72
Chadwick Crs DEWS WF13 172
Chadwick Fold La MIRF WF14 170
Chadwick Hall Gdns MIRF WF14 170
Chadwick La MIRF WF14 170
Chadwick St MID LS10 7
Chadwick St South MID LS10 7
Chaffinch Dr GIR BD8 94
Chaffinch Wk HUDS HD4 212
Chain Rd MAR/SLWT HD7 210
Chain St BFD BD1 4
  CAS WF10 153
Chalcroft Cl HECK WF16 145
Chald La WKFDW/WTN WF2 10
Chalfont Rd BHP/TINH * LS16 78
Chalice Cl MID LS10 125
Challenge Wy BOW BD4 97
  BTLY WF17 146
Challis Gv WBOW BD5 146
Chalner Av MOR LS27 146
Chalner Cl MOR LS27 146
Chalwood HUDW HD3 169
Champion Av CAS WF10 153
Chancery La HUD HD1 12
  OSS WF5 175
  WKFDE * WF1 10
Chancery Rd EARL WF12 175
Chandler Cl BTLY WF17 145
Chandler La HOLM/MEL HD9 212
The Chandlers LDSU * LS2 7
Chandlers Cl WKFDE WF1 149
Chandos Av RHAY LS8 80
Chandos Fold RHAY LS8 80
Chandos Gdns RHAY LS8 80
Chandos Garth RHAY LS8 80
Chandos Gn RHAY LS8 80
Chandos Pl RHAY LS8 80
Chandos St BOW BD4 5
Chandos Ter RHAY LS8 80
Chandos Wk RHAY LS8 80
Changegate HWTH BD22 68
Changegate Ct HWTH BD22 68
Change La HIPP HX3 166
Channing Wy BFD BD1 4
Chantrell Ct LDSU * LS2 7
Chantry Cl PONT WF8 180
Chantry Cft MSTN/BAR LS15 104
Chantry Garth MSTN/BAR LS15 104
Chantry Rd BSLYN/ROY S71 222
Chantry La TAD LS24 63
Chantry Rd WKFDW/WTN WF2 175
Chapel Av HBR HX7 112
  HECK WF16 145
Chapel Bank HOLM/MEL HD9 234
Chapel Cl CUD/GR S72 223
  EARL WF12 195
  GFTH/SHER LS25 105
  GTL/HWG HX4 166
  HOR/CROF WF4 201
  HUDS HD4 213
  KBTN HD8 236
  WBY LS22 25
Chapel Ct MSTN/BAR LS15 103
Chapel Cft BRIG HD6 .....
Chapelfields HEM/SK/SE WF9 241
Chapel Fold BEE/HOL LS11 123
  BTLY WF17 145
  LM/WK BD12 142
  MSTN/BAR LS15 .....
  PDSY/CALV LS28 98
  WBSY BD6 118
Chapel Garth FEA/AMT WF7 203
  HOLM/MEL HD9 233
Chapelgate HOLM/MEL HD9 233
Chapel Gv BGLY BD16 49
Chapel Hl BTLY DN5 241
  HUD HD1 12

BTN HD8 ....237 J1
MAR/SLWT HD7 ....211 H3
MIRF WF14 ....193 J2
MOR LS27 ....123 F6
BY LS22 ....39 F1
EA LS19 ....53 K4
pel Hill Jct HUD HD1 ....12 C5
pel Hill La HUDW HD3 ....187 K5
T LS21 ....36 B3
pel House Rd LM/WK BD12 ....118 E4
pel La BAIL BD17 ....52 D6
SPA/BRAM LS23 ....42 D5
TLY WF17 ....145 J2
UL/OBY BD13 ....116 C2
UL/OBY BD13 ....117 G1
ARL WF12 ....195 H1
FTH/SHER LS25 ....105 J4
FTH/SHER LS25 ....129 G2
BR HX7 ....137 J1
DGY LS6 ....78 D7
ECK WF16 ....145 H7
EM/SK/SE WF9 ....226 A1
EM/SK/SE WF9 ....226 D8
IPP HX3 ....141 G7
IPP HX3 ....166 C1
UDE HD5 ....13 F5
WTH BD22 ....46 E4
BTN HD8 ....217 F4
GHY BD21 ....2 C3
MAR/SLWT HD7 ....189 H7
MSTN/BAR LS15 ....83 J4
PDN/SBR HX6 ....139 G7
VIL/AL BD15 ....14 B3
OR/ARM LS12 ....99 H6
OR/ARM LS12 ....100 C4
EA LS19 ....53 K4
pel Ms GIR * BD8 ....94 C3
pel Pl HDGY LS6 ....78 D6
pel Rd AIRE BD20 ....26 E6
GLY BD16 ....49 J6
HAL LS7 ....79 K6
M/WK BD14 ....118 C5
pel Rw WIL/AL BD15 ....71 G5
pel St South TOD OL14 ....159 K2
pel St AIRE BD20 ....27 G1
FD BD1 ....5 D4
RIG HD6 ....141 K6
UD/GR S72 ....223 G8
UD/GR S72 ....240 A5
UL/OBY BD13 ....92 B3
UL/OBY BD13 ....93 H5
UL/OBY BD13 ....116 C2
ARD/LOFT WF3 ....126 A8
ARD/LOFT WF3 ....148 A2
ARD/LOFT WF3 ....148 D4
ARD/LOFT WF3 ....150 B6
ARL WF12 ....172 B7
CHL BD2 ....75 F7
TL/HWG HX4 ....166 A7
DGY * LS6 ....78 D6
OR/CROF WF4 ....222 E2
UD HD1 ....12 C5
UDE HD5 ....13 F5
UDS HD4 ....212 C4
UDS HD4 ....218 D3
K LS29 ....18 D3
JD/ILL * HX2 ....139 H3
VSG WF15 ....143 K6
/SG WF15 ....145 F7
MAR/SLWT HD7 ....189 H7
MIRF WF14 ....170 D6
MSTN/BAR LS15 ....103 J3
SS WF15 ....174 B7
DSY/CALV LS28 ....75 K4
DSY/CALV LS28 ....98 C2
BOW * BD5 ....95 K7
VBSY BD6 ....118 D2
EA * LS19 ....53 K7
pel St North LUD/ILL HX2 ....115 J8
pel Ter HDGY LS6 ....78 D6
HOLM/MEL HD9 ....213 F7
oman St BOW BD4 ....97 F5
SM LS9 ....102 A2
KFDE WF1 ....11 F6
/KFDE WF1 ....149 J6
ries Cotton Cl
/KFDW/WTN WF2 ....174 E3
ries Ct HWTH * BD22 ....90 E1
ries Gdns BEE/HOL LS11 ....6 C6
ries Gv RTHW LS26 ....127 F5
ries Jones Ct BTLY WF17 ....146 A6
ries St BAIL BD17 ....73 H3

BFD BD1 ....5 D4
BGLY BD16 ....49 K8
BTLY WF17 ....146 B7
CAS WF10 ....153 K4
CLECK BD19 ....144 E3
CUD/GR S72 ....225 J6
CUD/GR S72 ....240 A5
DEWS WF13 ....171 H6
DEWS WF13 ....171 J3
EARL WF12 ....172 D3
ELL HX5 ....166 E5
HFAX * HX1 ....9 E4
HOR/CROF WF4 ....197 J4
HOR/CROF WF4 ....222 E2
HORS LS18 ....77 F3
HUDS HD4 ....190 D7
OSS WF5 ....174 A7
OT LS21 ....33 J4
PDSY/CALV LS28 ....76 B8
PDN/SBR HX6 ....138 E6
WKFDE WF1 ....10 B3
Charlestown Est FEA/AMT WF7 ...203 G7
Charlestown Rd HIPP HX3 ....9 E3
Charlesworth Ct EARL * WF12 .....195 H1
Charlesworth Gv LUD/ILL HX2 ....139 H3
Charlesworth Pl EARD/LOFT WF3 ..150 E5
Charlesworth Sq CLECK BD19 .....144 D3
Charlesworth St EARL WF12 ....172 B7
Charlesworth Ter LUD/ILL HX2 ....139 H3
Charlesworth Wy
WKFDW/WTN WF2 ....10 B4
Charlotte Cl RTLY WF17 ....121 J8
Charlotte Ct HWTH BD22 ....69 F5
Charlotte Gv OSS * WF5 ....174 A7
Charlotte St WKFDE WF1 ....11 D4
Charlotte WKFDE * WF1 ....11 D4
Charlton Gv AIRE BD20 ....27 H5
OSM LS9 ....102 C4
Charlton Mt OSM LS9 ....102 B4
Charlton Pl OSM LS9 ....102 B4
Charlton St OSM LS9 ....102 C4
Charney Dr CHAL LS7 ....80 A5
Charnwood Bank HECK WF16 .....145 H6
Charnwood Cl ECHL * BD2 ....96 E1
Charnwood Gv ECHL BD2 ....96 E1
Charnwood Rd ECHL BD2 ....96 E1
Charterhouse Rd IDLE BD10 ....74 D2
Charteris Rd GIR BD8 ....94 D4
Charville Gdns AL/HA/HU LS17 .....59 H8
The Chase EARD/LOFT WF3 ....150 D5
GFTH/SHER LS25 ....106 B4
KGHY BD21 ....2 A2
WBY LS22 ....23 K5
YEA LS19 ....53 J7
Chase Wy WBOW BD5 ....119 F2
Chassum Gv HTON BD9 ....95 G1
Chaster St BTLY WF17 ....145 K5
Chatham St BFDE BD3 ....5 D2
HFAX HX1 ....8 C3
RPDN/SBR HX6 ....138 E6
Chat Hill Rd CUL/OBY BD13 ....93 K6
Chatswood Av BEE/HOL LS11 .....124 A3
Chatswood Crs BEE/HOL LS11 ....124 A3
Chatswood Dr BEE/HOL LS11 .....124 A2
Chatswood Av PDSY/CALV LS28 ....97 J3
PONT WF8 ....155 F3
Chatsworth Cl HUDE HD5 ....13 F6
RHAY LS8 ....80 C8
Chatsworth Ct EARL WF12 ....172 E4
Chatsworth Crs PDSY/CALV LS28 ..97 J3
Chatsworth Dr PDSY/CALV LS28 ...97 J3
WBY LS22 ....23 C5
Chatsworth Fall PDSY/CALV LS28 ..97 J3
Chatsworth Ms MOR * LS27 ....123 H8
Chatsworth Pl GIR BD8 ....95 H1
Chatsworth Ri PDSY/CALV LS28 ...97 J3
Chatsworth Rd PDSY/CALV LS28 ...97 J3
RHAY LS8 ....80 C8
Chatsworth St KGHY BD21 ....3 E3
Chatsworth Ter EARL WF12 ....172 E4
Chatts Wood Fold LM/WK BD12 ..119 J6
Chaucer Av EARD/LOFT WF3 ....150 B5
PDSY/CALV LS28 ....98 D5
Chaucer Cl HOLM/MEL HD9 ....213 F8
Chaucer Gdns PDSY/CALV LS28 ....98 D5
Chaucer Gv PDSY/CALV LS28 ....98 D5
Chaucer St HFAX HX1 ....8 A5
Cheapside BFD BD1 ....4 C4
BTLY WF17 ....146 C6
CLECK BD19 ....144 B4
HFAX * HX1 ....9 D4
HIPP HX3 ....117 H5
NORM WF6 ....178 A1
WKFDE WF1 ....10 B3
Cheddington Gv WIL/AL BD15 ....94 B3
Cheese Gate Nab Side
HOLM/MEL HD9 ....249 H1
Cheetham St HBR HX7 ....112 B8
Chellow Gdns WIL/AL * BD15 ....94 A1
Chellow Grange Rd HTON BD9 ......72 C8
Chellow La HTON BD9 ....94 C1
Chellow St WBOW BD5 ....118 E1
Chellow Wy EARL WF12 ....172 B4
Chelmsford Rd BFD * BD3 ....96 E3
Chelmsford Ter BFDE BD3 ....96 E4
Chelsea Cl WOR/ARM LS12 ....100 C5
Chelsea Man HIPP HX3 ....141 F1

Chelsea Rd GTHN BD7 ....95 F7
Chelsea St KGHY BD21 ....2 C5
Chelsfield Wy MSTN/BAR LS15 .....82 D8
Cheltenham Av ILK LS29 ....20 E7
Cheltenham Ct HIPP * HX3 ....140 C7
Cheltenham Gdns HIPP HX3 ....140 C7
Cheltenham Pl HIPP HX3 ....140 C7
Cheltenham Rd ECHL BD2 ....74 B6
Cheltenham St WOR/ARM LS12 ..100 D5
Chelwood Av RHAY LS8 ....58 A8
Chelwood Crs RHAY LS8 ....80 B1
Chelwood Dr RHAY LS8 ....80 B1
WIL/AL BD15 ....94 B4
Chelwood Gv RHAY LS8 ....58 B8
Chelwood Mt RHAY LS8 ....58 B8
Chelwood Pl RHAY LS8 ....58 A8
Chenies Cl SCFT LS14 ....103 G2
Chepstow Cl GFTH/SHER LS25 ....106 B4
Chepstow Dr EARD/LOFT WF3 ....124 E8
Chequerfield Av PONT WF8 ....181 G4
Chequerfield Cl CAS WF10 ....183 F5
Chequerfield Dr PONT WF8 ....181 F4
Chequerfield La PONT WF8 ....181 G3
Chequerfield Mt PONT WF8 ....181 G4
Chequerfield Rd PONT WF8 ....181 F4
Chequers Cl PONT WF8 ....181 G4
Chequers St PONT WF8 ....181 G3
Cheriton Dr CUL/OBY BD13 ....116 E2
Cherry Cl BSLYN/ROY S71 ....221 J7
Cherry Ct HDGY LS6 ....79 F5
HFAX * HX1 ....8 B3
OSM LS9 ....102 A2
Cherry Flds ECHL BD2 ....74 A7
Cherry Garth HEM/SK/SE WF9 ....224 C5
Cherry Gv HDGY LS6 ....79 F5
ILK LS29 ....19 K7
Cherry La KBTN HD8 ....237 K1
LIT OL15 ....206 B8
Cherry Lea Ct YEA LS19 ....53 K7
Cherry Nook Rd HUDN HD2 ....169 F8
Cherry Pl OSM LS9 ....102 A2
Cherry Ri SCFT LS14 ....82 A3
Cherry Rw OSM LS9 ....102 A2
Cherry St HWTH BD22 ....69 G3
KGHY BD21 ....3 F2
Cherry Tree Av IDLE * BD10 ....75 F5
KNOT WF11 ....156 B8
Cherry Tree Cl MAR/SLWT HD7 ...189 J6
Cherry Tree Ct EARD/LOFT WF3 ..148 C4
Cherry Tree Crs PDSY/CALV LS28 ..76 B8
WKFDW/WTN WF2 ....199 K4
Cherry Tree Dr GTL/HWG HX4 .....166 A4
PDSY/CALV LS28 ....76 B8
WKFDW/WTN WF2
Cherry Tree Gdns SHPY BD18 ......74 B2
Cherry Tree Ri KGHY BD21 ....3 E5
Cherry Tree Rd WKFDW/WTN WF2 ..199 K4
Cherry Tree Rw BGLY BD16 ....71 F4
Cherry Tree Wk EARD/LOFT WF3 ..148 D4
HOLM/MEL HD9 ....233 K7
LDS * LS1 ....7 E4
Cherrywood Cl SCFT LS14 ....81 K2
Cherrywood Gdns SCFT LS14 ....81 K2
Chervana Ct BOW BD4 ....97 C7
Cherwell Cft GFTH/SHER LS25 .....106 B6
Cherwell Dr WBSY BD6 ....118 A4
Chesham St GTHN BD7 ....4 A5
KGHY BD21 ....3 E3
Chesil Bank HUDW HD3 ....190 B5
Chesilton Av HUDW HD3 ....190 B5
Chesney Av MID LS10 ....101 K7
Chesnut End BSPA/BRAM LS23 .....42 C4
Chessington Dr HOR/CROF WF4 ..195 H8
Chester Cl HIPP HX3 ....8 C2
Chester Gv HIPP HX3 ....8 C2
Chester Pl HIPP HX3 ....8 C2
Chester Rd HIPP HX3 ....8 C2
Chester St HIPP HX3 ....8 C2
RPDN/SBR HX6 ....138 E6
WBOW * BD5 ....4 C5
WOR/ARM LS12 ....100 C3
Chester Ter HIPP HX3 ....8 C2
Chesterton Ct HOR/CROF WF4 ....197 J1
MSTN/BAR LS15 ....104 B5
Chesterton Dr HOLM/MEL HD9 ...213 F8
Chestnut Av BSPA/BRAM LS23 .....42 C5
BTLY WF17 ....145 K7
CUD/GR S72 ....223 K8
HDGY LS6 ....78 E8
MSTN/BAR LS15 ....104 B1
TOD OL14 ....133 K4
WBY LS22 ....23 H5
WKFDW/WTN WF2 ....199 J5
Chestnut Cl FEA/AMT WF7 ....179 K3
GTL/HWG HX4 ....166 A3
HUDS HD4 ....213 G1
HWTH BD22 ....2 A4
ILK LS29 ....20 E8
Chestnut Ct SHPY BD18 ....74 E4
Chestnut Crs NORM WF6 ....177 K3
Chestnut Dr BHP/TINH LS16 ....56 B6
CUD/GR S72 ....223 H6
Chestnut Garth HUDW * HD3 ......190 B6
Chestnut Gv BSPA/BRAM LS23 .....42 C5
ECHL BD2 ....74 A7
HDGY * LS6 ....78 E8
HEM/SK/SE WF9 ....225 F6
HOR/CROF WF4 ....200 D2
PDSY/CALV LS28 ....75 K5

PONT WF8 .....180 E5
RTHW LS26 .....127 H5
Chestnut Mdw MIRF WF14 .....170 C4
Chestnut Pl HDGY * LS6 .....78 E8
Chestnut Rd WOR/ARM LS12 .....100 B5
Chestnut Rd HDGY LS6 .....78 E8
The Chestnuts PONT WF8 .....155 C7
Chestnut St CUD/GR S72 .....240 B6
HDGY * LS6 .....78 E8
HEM/SK/SE WF9 .....242 B2
HFAX HX1 .....8 A5
HUDN HD2 .....168 E8
Chestnut Ter EARL WF12 .....172 B8
Chestnut Wk WKFDW/WTN WF2 .....10 A1
Chestnut Wy BHP/TINH LS16 .....56 B6
Chevet Cft WKFDW/WTN WF2 .....199 G3
Chevet Gv WKFDW/WTN WF2 .....199 G4
Chevet La HOR/CROF WF4 .....221 K3
WKFDW/WTN WF2 .....199 G4
Chevet Mt WIL/AL BD15 .....94 A4
Chevet Park Ct WKFDW/WTN WF2 .....199 G8
Chevet Ri BSLYN/ROY S71 .....221 J7
Chevet Vw BSLYN/ROY S71 .....221 J7
Chevin Av ILK LS29 .....32 C6
OT LS21 .....33 K5
Chevin End Rd ILK LS29 .....32 E7
Chevington Ct YEA * LS19 .....53 J8
Chevins Cl BTLY WF17 .....145 J3
Chevin Side OT LS21 .....33 J5
Cheviot Av HOLM/MEL HD9 .....231 K2
Cheviot Cl HEM/SK/SE WF9 .....225 F4
Cheviot Ga GFTH/SHER LS25 .....105 K6
Cheviot Ga LM/WK BD12 .....118 C5
Cheviot Pl KNOT WF11 .....156 B7
Cheviot Wy MIRF WF14 .....193 H1
Cheyne Wk KGHY BD21 .....2 B4
Chichester St WOR/ARM * LS12 .....100 C3
Chickenley La EARL WF12 .....173 K4
Chidswell Gdns EARL WF12 .....147 G8
Chidswell La EARL WF12 .....147 F8
Child La LVSG WF15 .....170 C1
Childs La SHPY BD18 .....74 A5
Childs Rd WKFDW/WTN WF2 .....174 E3
Chiltern Av CAS WF10 .....152 E6
HUDW HD3 .....189 K2
KNOT WF11 .....156 B7
Chiltern Cl GFTH/SHER LS25 .....105 K6
GFTH/SHER LS25 .....105 K6
HEM/SK/SE WF9 .....225 F4
Chiltern Ct EARL LS13 .....76 C6
GFTH/SHER LS25 .....105 K6
Chiltern Dr FEA/AMT WF7 .....203 F6
MIRF WF14 .....193 H1
Chiltern Rd FEA/AMT WF7 .....172 E2
Chiltern Wy LVSG WF15 .....144 A6
Chilver Dr BOW BD4 .....120 D1
Chimney La KBTN HD8 .....193 F7
Chinewood Av BTLY WF17 .....146 A5
Chippendale Ri GIR BD8 .....94 D3
OT LS21 .....33 J1
Chirton Gv RHAY LS8 .....80 C6
Chiserley Gdns HBR HX7 .....112 D6
Chislehurst Pl WBOW BD5 .....95 J8
Chiswick St HDGY LS6 .....6 A2
Chiswick Ter HDGY LS6 .....6 A1
Choppards Bank Rd HOLM/MEL HD9 .....248 B2
Choppards La HOLM/MEL HD9 .....248 B2
Chorley La BVRD LS3 .....6 C3
Chrisharben Pk CLAY BD14 .....94 C7
Chrismoor IDLE BD10 .....74 C4
Christ Church Av WOR/ARM LS12 .....100 B3
Christ Church Mt WOR/ARM LS12 .....100 B3
Christ Church Pde WOR/ARM LS12 .....100 B3
Christ Church Pl WOR/ARM LS12 .....100 B3
Christ Church Ter WOR/ARM LS12 .....100 B3
Christ Church Vw WOR/ARM LS12 .....100 B3
Christopher Rd HDGY LS6 .....79 G8
Christopher St WBOW * BD5 .....95 J8
Christopher St WBOW BD5 .....95 J8
Church Ap GFTH/SHER LS25 .....105 K4
Church Av HDGY LS6 .....79 F4
HEM/SK/SE WF9 .....241 J1
HORS LS18 .....77 F2
HUDS HD4 .....12 A6
MAR/SLWT HD7 .....211 J1
MOR LS27 .....122 B3
RTHW LS26 .....127 K1
WKFDE WF1 .....177 F4
Churchbalk Dr PONT WF8 .....181 F5
Churchbalk La PONT WF8 .....181 F4
Church Bank BFD BD1 .....5 D4
LUD/ILL HX2 .....139 G5
RPDN/SBR * HX6 .....159 F7
Church Bank La HBR HX7 .....136 D8
Churchbank Wy EARL WF12 .....172 E7
Church Cswy BSPA/BRAM LS23 .....43 F2
Church Ct HECK * WF16 .....145 G7
HOR/CROF WF4 .....201 F1
KBTN HD8 .....235 G3
LUD/ILL HX2 .....115 G6
OT LS21 .....35 G4
RTHW LS26 .....127 K1
SCFT LS14 .....81 K7
Church Cts AL/HA/HU LS17 .....57 J8
HOR/CROF WF4 .....196 E5
RTHW LS26 .....128 A2

YEA LS19 .....53 J5
Church Dr AL/HA/HU LS17 .....39 K6
HEM/SK/SE WF9 .....241 J1
Church Farm SCFT LS14 .....60 D5
Church Farm Cl EARD/LOFT WF3 .....149 K2
NORM * WF6 .....151 J7
Churchfarm Garth AL/HA/HU LS17 .....59 H7
Church Farm Vw MSTN/BAR * LS15 .....83 J4
Churchfield CI DOD/DAR S75 .....239 J3
Churchfield CI DOD/DAR S75 .....239 H3
LVSG WF15 .....144 D7
Churchfield Cft NORM WF6 .....151 J7
RTHW LS26 .....126 C6
Churchfield Gv RTHW LS26 .....126 B6
Churchfield La CAS WF10 .....154 A5
DOD/DAR S75 .....239 H3
RTHW LS26 .....126 B5
Church Field Rd BTLY DN5 .....241 J7
Churchfield Rd RTHW LS26 .....126 B6
Church Flds ECHL BD2 .....97 F1
Churchfield St BTLY * WF17 .....146 B6
Church Gdns AL/HA/HU LS17 .....57 K8
GFTH/SHER LS25 .....105 K5
MOR LS27 .....122 B4
Church Garth CAS WF10 .....154 A5
OT LS21 .....35 G4
Churchgate BHP/TINH LS16 .....35 H8
Church Ga HORS LS18 .....77 F2
Churchgate MOR LS27 .....122 B4
Church Gn GIR BD8 .....95 H2
KBTN HD8 .....215 H5
LUD/ILL * HX2 .....139 H2
Church Gv HDGY LS6 .....79 F4
HEM/SK/SE WF9 .....241 J1
HORS LS18 .....77 F2
Church Hts STKB/PEN S36 .....252 E4
Church HI BAIL BD17 .....51 K7
BHP/TINH LS16 .....35 H8
BSLYN/ROY S71 .....222 B8
BSPA/BRAM LS23 .....42 D8
SCFT LS14 .....60 E5
Church Hill Gdns PDSY/CALV LS28 .....98 D1
Church Hill Gn PDSY/CALV LS28 .....98 D1
Church Hill Mt PDSY/CALV LS28 .....98 D1
Churchill Gdns LDSU * LS2 .....7 D1
Churchill Gv HECK WF16 .....145 H8
WKFDW/WTN WF2 .....199 G3
Churchill Rd St TOD OL14 .....133 H3
Churchill Wy AIRE BD20 .....26 A4
Church La AL/HA/HU LS17 .....38 B4
BAIL BD17 .....52 E6
BHP/TINH LS16 .....56 C7
BRIG HD6 .....142 B8
CHAL LS7 .....79 K5
CLECK BD19 .....145 F3
CUD/GR S72 .....222 E5
DEWS WF13 .....171 J3
DOD/DAR S75 .....218 D8
DOD/DAR S75 .....239 F7
EARD/LOFT WF3 .....147 J4
EARD/LOFT WF3 .....148 D4
EARL WF12 .....195 J1
ELL HX5 .....167 J4
FEA/AMT WF7 .....178 C3
FEA/AMT WF7 .....179 H2
GFTH/SHER LS25 .....105 K4
GFTH/SHER LS25 .....106 E4
GFTH/SHER LS25 .....129 C2
GTL/HWG HX4 .....165 K7
HBR HX7 .....111 K8
HDGY LS6 .....79 F4
HECK WF16 .....145 G7
HIPP HX3 .....141 H7
HOR/CROF WF4 .....196 E4
HOR/CROF WF4 .....198 C7
HOR/CROF WF4 .....222 C4
HORS LS18 .....77 F2
HUDE HD5 .....13 F6
HUDE HD5 .....192 D4
HUDS HD4 .....212 B5
HUDS HD4 .....213 G1
HUDW HD3 .....187 H6
KBTN HD8 .....235 G3
KBTN HD8 .....237 K1
LUD/ILL HX2 .....139 H2
LVSG WF15 .....143 J8
LVSG WF15 .....144 D6
MAR/SLWT HD7 .....209 H7
MAR/SLWT HD7 .....211 J3
MIRF WF14 .....171 F7
MSTN/BAR LS15 .....104 A1
NORM WF6 .....177 K2
OT LS21 .....32 D1
PDSY/CALV LS28 .....98 C4
PONT WF8 .....180 E3
PONT WF8 .....182 A6
RPDN/SBR HX6 .....164 A8
RTHW LS26 .....127 K2
RTHW LS26 .....152 B1
STKB/PEN S36 .....252 E4
WBSY BD6 .....116 C3
WBY LS22 .....41 F2
WKFDE WF1 .....149 J6

Church Mdw BSPA/BRAM LS23 .....42 [E7]
BTLY WF17 .....[146 A5]
Church Ms BSPA/BRAM LS23 .....42 [E7]
Church Mt HEM/SK/SE WF9 .....241 [J1]
HORS LS18 .....77 [F2]
Church Pk LVSG WF15 .....170 [C1]
Church Pl GFTH/SHER LS25 .....105 [K4]
HFAX HX1 .....[8 A6]
Church Rd BTLY WF17 .....145 [J3]
DOD/DAR S75 .....238 [E1]
EARD/LOFT WF3 .....150 [A3]
HORS LS18 .....77 [F2]
LVSG WF15 .....170 [C1]
NORM WF6 .....151 [J7]
RTHW LS26 .....127 [G5]
TOD OL14 .....133 [H3]
WBSY BD6 .....118 [A4]
WOR/ARM LS12 .....100 [B4]
Church Rw LDSU LS2 .....[7 E1]
Church Side RTHW LS26 .....152 [B1]
Church Side Cl HIPP HX3 .....[141 J6]
Church Side Dr HIPP HX3 .....[141 J6]
Churchside Vls RTHW LS26 .....152 [B1]
Church Sq GFTH/SHER LS25 .....105 [K4]
Church St BGLY BD16 .....[75 K1]
BRIG HD6 .....168 [D1]
BSLYN/ROY S71 .....222 [B8]
BSPA/BRAM LS23 .....42 [D8]
CAS WF10 .....153 [J8]
CLECK BD19 .....144 [D8]
COL BB8 .....64 [C6]
CUD/GR S72 .....223 [G4]
CUL/QBY * BD13 .....70 [D8]
DEWS WF13 .....171 [J4]
DOD/DAR S75 .....238 [E1]
EARL WF12 .....172 [C7]
ELL HX5 .....166 [E4]
GIR BD8 .....[95 H2]
GSLY LS20 .....[59 F2]
GTL/HWG HX4 .....166 [A5]
HBR HX7 .....112 [E4]
HBR HX7 .....137 [H1]
HECK WF16 .....145 [H8]
HEM/SK/SE WF9 .....242 [B2]
HFAX HX1 .....[9 F6]
HOLM/MEL * HD9 .....254 [B1]
HOR/CROF WF4 .....220 [E2]
HUD HD1 .....13 [H6]
HUDE HD5 .....13 [K6]
HUDS HD4 .....12 [C6]
HUDW HD3 .....190 [B4]
HUDW HD3 .....191 [K3]
HWTH BD22 .....68 [D6]
HWTH BD22 .....90 [E7]
ILK LS29 .....[18 D1]
KBTN HD8 .....21 [J1]
KGHY BD21 .....[3 J5]
KGHY BD21 .....[3 H3]
KNOT WF11 .....159 [F5]
KSTL LS5 .....[76 D3]
LVSG WF15 .....143 [J8]
LVSG WF15 .....144 [D6]
MAR/SLWT HD7 .....18 [E8]
MAR/SLWT HD7 .....210 [A1]
MID LS10 .....102 [C6]
MOR LS27 .....122 [C7]
MOR LS27 .....123 [J7]
OSS WF5 .....173 [G3]
RTHW LS26 .....126 [C6]
RTHW LS26 .....127 [J1]
SHPY BD18 .....[77 G4]
STKB/PEN S36 .....252 [E4]
TOD OL14 .....133 [G6]
WBSY BD6 .....116 [C3]
WBY LS22 .....[29 G3]
WKFDE WF1 .....[18 D4]
YEA LS19 .....53 [J5]
Church Ter HOLM/MEL HD9 .....231 [K2]
KBTN HD8 .....237 [K1]
LUD/ILL HX2 .....115 [H6]
Church Top HEM/SK/SE WF9 .....241 [J1]
Church Vw CLECK BD19 .....144 [D8]
GFTH/SHER LS25 .....129 [C2]
HEM/SK/SE WF9 .....225 [F4]
HOLM/MEL HD9 .....247 [K5]
HOR/CROF WF4 .....198 [C7]
KSTL LS5 .....[76 D3]
RPDN/SBR HX6 .....136 [D1]
WKFDE WF1 .....149 [G5]
Church View Cl HOR/CROF WF4 .....222 [C4]
Church View Crs STKB/PEN S36 .....252 [E4]
Church View Ms BSPA/BRAM LS23 .....42 [E7]
Church View Rd STKB/PEN S36 .....252 [E4]
Church Vis HEM/SK/SE WF9 .....241 [J1]
Churchville GFTH/SHER LS25 .....107 [F3]
Churchville Av GFTH/SHER LS25 .....107 [F3]
Churchville Dr GFTH/SHER LS25 .....107 [F3]
Churchville Ter GFTH/SHER LS25 .....107 [F3]
Church Wk BTLY WF17 .....145 [J3]
EARL WF12 .....195 [J1]
LDSU LS2 .....[14 C1]
TOD OL14 .....133 [G6]
Churchway HOR/CROF WF4 .....200 [D1]
Church Wy KGHY BD21 .....[3 G5]
MOR * LS27 .....122 [C7]
Church Wood Av BHP/TINH LS16 .....[77 F1]
Churchwood Cl MAR/SLWT HD7 .....210 [A1]
Church Wood Mt BHP/TINH LS16 .....[77 F1]

urch Wood Rd BHP/TINH LS16....78 C5
rn La LUD/ILL HX2....139 G4
rn La HIPP HX3....115 K7
rwell Av DEWS WF13....145 J8
rwell Cl CAS WF10....153 J5
rwell V EARL WF12....173 F1
der Hill Rd TOD OL14....134 D5
derhills La HIPP HX3....140 D8
der Hills Rd HOLM/MEL HD9....233 H7
der La BSPA/BRAM LS23....42 E5
AS WF10....153 H3
Circle PONT WF8....181 F4
us Vw FEA/AMT WF7....205 F6
La HIPP HX3....139 H2
Rd GIR BD8....4 A3
Sq LDS * LS1....7 D4
gate OT....33 J3
gate La RPDN/SBR HX6....164 A4
oham St CUL/QBY BD13....92 C5
oton Av HFAX HX1....8 B5
ra Dr PDSY/CALV LS28....75 H4
ra Rd ECHL BD2....74 B6
ra St BRIG HD6....168 B2
UD HD1....12 C2
UDS HD4....190 A7
DSY/CALV LS28....98 B1
e HI HUD HD1....12 C3
e Hill Rd HUD HD1....98 D4
emont Av BVRD LS3....6 C2
HPY BD18....74 A5
emont Cl HDGY LS6....78 E5
emont Crs HDGY LS6....79 F6
HPY BD18....74 A5
emont Dr HDGY LS6....78 E5
emont Gdns BGLY BD16....50 A7
emont Gv BVRD * LS3....6 C2
DSY/CALV LS28....74 A5
HPY BD18....74 A5
emont St CLECK BD19....144 A3
LL HX5....167 F5
UD HD1....12 B3
PDN/SBR * HX6....139 F6
THW * LS26....127 F1
OR/ARM LS12....100 A4
KFDW/WTN WF2....10 A4
OR/ARM LS12....100 A4
emont Vw BVRD LS3....6 C2
emont Vs BVRD * LS3....6 C2
emount HDGY LS6....78 E5
emount Rd HORS LS18....9 D1
ence Dr HORS LS18....77 F4
K LS29....32 B5
ence Gdns HORS LS18....77 F4
ence Rd HORS LS18....77 F4
ID LS10....102 A5
HPY BD18....73 F5
KFDW/WTN WF2....10 B6
ence St BRAM LS13....99 G2
TLY WF17....146 C6
LECK BD19....144 A4
OL BB8....64 A1
FAX HX1....8 C4
ence Ter PDSY/CALV LS28....98 B3
ence Wk WKFDW/WTN WF2....10 A4
endon Cl WKFDE WF1....10 C2
endon Pl CUL/QBY BD13....116 B3
FAX * HX1....8 B5
DSU LS2....6 C1
endon Rd BGLY BD16....50 A7
SPA/BRAM LS23....42 C3
DSU LS2....6 C2
endon St HBR HX7....136 E2
WTH BD22....68 E5
GHY BD21....2 C5
KFDE WF1....10 C2
endon Ter PDSY/CALV LS28....98 C5
endon Wy LDSU LS2....6 C2
e Rd CLECK BD19....143 K4
BR HX7....136 E2
FAX * HX1....9 D5
k WK BD12....142 D1
e Rd Flats HFAX * HX1....8 C4
ges St WBOW BD5....95 J8
ion St WKFDE WF1....11 E5
k Av OSM LS9....102 B4
k Ct FEA/AMT WF7....179 G2
k Crs OSM LS9....102 B4
ke Crs NORM WF6....177 K4
ke Gv WKFDE WF1....176 B3
ke Hall Rd EARD/LOFT WF3....176 B1
ke La HOLM/MEL HD9....231 J1
ke Rd EARD/LOFT WF3....147 K6
ke St DEWS WF13....171 K2
DSY/CALV LS28....75 K5
k Gv OSM LS9....102 B5
k La OSM LS9....102 B4
k Mt OSM LS9....102 B4
k Rd OSM LS9....102 B5
k Rw OSM LS9....102 B5
kson Av HECK WF16....145 H7

Clarkson Cl HECK WF16....145 H7
Clarkson Ct NORM WF6....178 B2
Clarkson St DEWS WF13....171 H5
Clarkson Vw HDGY LS6....79 G7
Clark Spring Ri MOR LS27....123 G4
Clark Ter OSM LS9....102 B4
Clark Vw OSM * LS9....102 B5
Clattering Stones Rd HBR HX7....162 E1
Clay Butts HUDN HD2....12 B2
Clayburn Vw CLECK BD19....148 A5
Clay Hill Dr LM/WK BD12....118 E8
Clay House La GTL/HWG HX4....166 C4
Clay La MAR/SLWT HD7....210 E2
Claymore Ri AIRE BD20....27 H3
Clay Pit La CHAL LS7....7 E2
Claypit La CAS WF10....130 C4
SCFT LS14....60 D6
Clay Pits La HFAX HX1....8 A3
RPDN/SBR HX6....163 J4
Clay St HFAX HX1....8 A4
RPDN/SBR HX6....139 F7
Clayton Av GFTH/SHER LS25....129 G1
HEM/SK/SE WF9....227 G3
Clayton Cl MID LS10....125 G1
Clayton Ct FEA/AMT WF7....179 H6
MID LS10....125 G1
Clayton Dr MID LS10....125 G1
Clayton Flds HUDN HD2....12 B2
Clayton Fold AIRE BD20....26 A5
Clayton Gv YEA LS19....55 K4
Clayton Hall Rd AIRE BD20....26 A5
Clayton Holt HEM/SK/SE WF9....241 H2
Clayton La BTLY DN5....242 E6
CLAY BD14....94 B8
WBOW BD5....96 A7
Clayton Ms NORM WF6....151 K7
Clayton Pl NORM WF6....151 K7
Clayton Rd KGHY BD21....2 D1
WKFDE WF1....149 J6
Clayton Rd GTHN BD7....94 E7
MID LS10....125 C1
Claytons Buildings FEA/AMT WF7....179 J3
Clayton St RTHW * LS26....126 C6
WKFDW/WTN WF2....10 A4
Clayton Vw HEM/SK/SE WF9....241 H2
Clayton Wy MID LS10....125 G1
Clayton Wood Bank BHP/TINH LS16....77 K2
Clayton Wood Cl BHP/TINH LS16....77 K2
Clayton Wood Ct BHP/TINH LS16....77 K2
Clayton Wood Ri BHP/TINH LS16....77 K2
Clayton Wood Rd BHP/TINH LS16....77 K2
Clay Well MAR/SLWT HD7....189 H7
The Clearings MID LS10....124 E3
Clear Vw CUD/QBY S72....240 A3
Cleasby Rd ILK LS29....32 C8
Cleavesty La AL/HA/HU LS17....39 K4
Cleckheaton Rd WBSY BD6....118 E4
Cleeve Hl YEA LS19....53 K7
Cleevethorpe Dr
  WKFDW/WTN WF2....199 G3
Clegg La GTL/HWG HX4....165 A4
Clement Cl NORM WF6....178 C2
Clement St GIR BD8....95 F3
HUD HD1....12 B2
HUDS HD4....190 D7
RPDN/SBR * HX6....138 E7
WKFDW/WTN WF2....175 C6
Clement Ter EARL WF12....172 B5
RTHW LS26....126 B7
Cleopatra Pl BRAM LS13....99 G2
Clerk Green St BTLY WF17....146 A7
Clevedon Pl HIPP HX3....8 B1
Clevedon Wy BSLYN/ROY S71....221 K7
Cleveland Av HIPP * HX3....140 D7
  HOLM/MEL HD9....231 K2
  KNOT WF11....156 B7
  WKFDW/WTN WF2....197 K1
Cleveland Garth WKFDW/WTN WF2....197 K1
Cleveland Gv WKFDW/WTN WF2....197 K1
Cleveland Pl HBR HX7....112 B8
Cleveland Rd HTON BD9....73 H8
  HUDW HD3....190 D4
Cleveland St TOD OL14....132 E2
Cleveland Wy KBTN HD8....235 H1
Cleveleys Av BEE/HOL LS11....101 F7
Cleveleys Ct BEE/HOL * LS11....101 F7
Cleveleys Mt BEE/HOL * LS11....101 F7
Cleveleys Rd BEE/HOL LS11....101 F7
Cleveleys St BEE/HOL * LS11....101 F7
Cleveleys Ter BEE/HOL LS11....101 F7
Cliff Cl CUD/QBY S72....223 K8
  HUDW HD3....190 B5
Cliff Ct HOR/CROF * WF4....197 K5
  LVSG WF15....144 D8
Cliff Crs GFTH/SHER LS25....129 K5
  LUD/ILL HX2....139 H6
Cliffdale Rd CHAL LS7....79 H7
Cliff Dr HOR/CROF WF4....197 K6
Cliffe Ash MAR/SLWT HD7....51 J8
Cliffe Av BAIL BD17....72 E2
  BCLY BD16....70 E2
  HIPP HX3....142 B4
Cliffe Crs GFTH/SHER LS25....129 J5
Cliffe Crest HOR/CROF WF4....197 H1
Cliffe Dr YEA LS19....53 J8
Cliffe End Rd HUDW HD3....190 B5
Cliffe House Av GFTH/SHER LS25....106 A6
Cliffe La BAIL BD17....73 J2

CLECK BD19....144 B2
CUL/QBY BD13....93 J4
YEA LS19....54 A8
Cliffe La South BAIL BD17....73 J2
Cliffe La West BAIL BD17....73 J1
Cliffe Mill Fold AIRE BD20....49 J5
Cliffe Mt CLECK BD19....144 D2
Cliffe Pk KBTN HD8....235 G3
  MOR * LS27....122 C8
Cliffe Park Cha WOR/ARM LS12....100 A5
Cliffe Park Cl WOR/ARM LS12....100 A5
Cliffe Park Crs WOR/ARM LS12....100 A6
Cliffe Park Dr WOR/ARM LS12....100 A5
Cliffe Park Mt WOR/ARM LS12....100 A5
Cliffe Park Ri WOR/ARM LS12....99 K5
Cliffe Park Wy MOR LS27....122 C8
Cliffe Rd BFDE BD3....5 D1
  BRIG HD6....168 B1
  KBTN HD8....235 G3
  KGHY BD21....3 D6
  RPDN/SBR HX6....138 D6
Cliffestone Dr AIRE BD20....49 H5
Cliffe St BTLY WF17....145 J7
  CUL/QBY BD13....93 G4
  DEWS WF13....172 C2
  HBR HX7....112 B8
  KBTN HD8....257 K1
  RPDN/SBR HX6....2 C2
Cliffe Ter BAIL BD17....73 J2
  GIR BD8....4 B2
  KGHY BD21....3 D6
  RPDN/SBR HX6....138 D6
Cliffe Vw KBTN HD8....257 J1
  MOR LS27....122 C8
  WIL/AL BD15....93 K1
Cliffe Wood Cl HTON BD9....72 E8
Cliffewood Ri KBTN HD8....257 J1
Cliff Gdns LUD/ILL HX2....139 H6
Cliff Gv HOR/CROF WF4....197 J2
Cliff Hl DOD/DAR S75....238 E6
Cliff La LUD/ILL HX2....138 E5
Cliff Hollins La LM/WK BD12....120 A5
Cliff House La HOLM/MEL HD9....233 H5
Cliff La HDGY LS6....79 F7
  HOLM/MEL HD9....233 H6
  RPDN/SBR HX6....187 F1
  WKFDE WF1....10 B1
Cliff Mt HDGY LS6....79 G7
Cliff Mount St HDGY LS6....79 G7
Clifford Av ILK LS29....20 A6
  WKFDW/WTN WF2....199 F1
Clifford Ct BSPA/BRAM * LS23....42 E6
Clifford Hodgson Pl MOR * LS27....123 G4
Clifford Moor Rd BSPA/BRAM LS23....42 B4
Clifford Rd BAIL BD17....73 J1
  BSPA/BRAM LS23....42 D8
  BSPA/BRAM LS23....42 E4
  HEM/SK/SE WF9....241 H1
  ILK LS29....20 A5
Clifford St AIRE BD20....27 F1
  HEM/SK/SE WF9....242 B1
  WBOW BD5....4 C6
Clifford Vw WKFDW/WTN WF2....199 F1
Clifford Pde WKFDE WF1....10 B3
Cliff Park Av WKFDE WF1....10 B2
Cliff Rd HDGY LS6....79 G7
  HOLM/MEL HD9....232 A7
  HOLM/MEL HD9....233 H6
  HOR/CROF WF4....197 J8
Cliff Side Gdns HDGY LS6....79 G7
Cliff St HWTH BD22....69 F4
  PONT WF8....180 D3
  WKFDW/WTN WF2....175 G4
Cliff Ter HDGY LS6....79 G7
Cliff Vale Rd SHPY BD18....73 H6
Cliff Villa Ct WKFDE WF1....10 B2
Cliff Wood Av SHPY BD18....73 H5
Clifton Av EARD/LOFT WF3....150 B6
  HFAX HX1....8 A5
  HOLM/MEL HD9....233 H6
  HOR/CROF WF4....197 G1
  OSM LS9....102 C2
  PONT WF8....180 C3
Clifton Cl HOR/CROF WF4....197 F1
Clifton Common BRIG HD6....168 D1
Clifton Ct DEWS WF13....171 J2
Clifton Crs HOR/CROF WF4....197 G1
Clifton Dr HOR/CROF WF4....197 G1
  PDSY/CALV LS28....98 C3
Clifton Gdns CUD/QR S72....223 J8
Clifton Gv OSM LS9....102 C2
Clifton Hl PDSY/CALV LS28....98 C3
Clifton La HOLM/MEL HD9....231 J1
Clifton Mt OSM LS9....102 C2
Clifton Pl PDSY/CALV LS28....98 C3
  SHPY BD18....73 H5
  WKFDE WF1....10 B1
Clifton Rd CUD/QR S72....240 A4
  HIPP HX3....140 B7
  HOR/CROF WF4....178 A8
  HOR/CROF WF4....197 G2
  HUD HD1....12 A3
  ILK LS29....20 D8
  PDSY/CALV LS28....98 C3
Clifton Side HUDN HD2....169 G5
Clifton St GIR BD8....4 B1
  HEM/SK/SE WF9....224 C5
  HIPP HX3....8 B1
  HWTH BD22....2 B4
  RPDN/SBR HX6....139 F7

Clifton Ter *BTLY* WF17 ....146 C6
 OSM LS9 ....102 C2
Clifton Vw *KBTN* HD8 ....237 K1
Clifton Vls *GIR* BD8 ....4 B2
Clipston Av *HDGY* LS6 ....79 F5
Clipston St *WBOW* BD5 ....119 F1
Clipston Ter *HDGY* LS6 ....79 F5
Clipston Ter *HDGY* * LS6 ....79 F5
Clive Pl *GTHN* BD7 ....95 H6
Clive Ter *GTHN* BD7 ....95 H6
Clock La *CUL/QBY* BD13 ....92 B2
Clock Row Av *HEM/SK/SE* WF9 ...225 K8
Clock Row La *HEM/SK/SE* WF9 ....225 K8
Clock Row Mt *HEM/SK/SE* WF9 ....225 K8
Clock View St *KGHY* BD21 ....2 C1
Clog Br *AIRE* BD20 ....27 G2
The Cloisters *HFAX* * HX1 ....8 B6
Clog Sole Rd *BRIG* HD6 ....142 A7
Close Cl *WBY* LS22 ....23 H5
Close Head Dr *CUL/QBY* BD13 .....92 E5
Close Head La *CUL/QBY* BD13 ......93 F4
Close La *HWTH* BD22 ....44 C2
Close Lea *BRIG* HD6 ....168 A2
Close Lea Av *BRIG* HD6 ....168 A2
Close Lea Dr *BRIG* HD6 ....168 A3
Close Lea Wy *BRIG* HD6 ....168 A2
Close Rd *CAS* WF10 ....154 A4
Closes Rd *BRIG* HD6 ....168 A2
Close St *HEM/SK/SE* WF9 ....224 C4
Cloth Hall St *DEWS* * WF13 ....172 C3
 HUD HD1 ....12 C4
 LDS * LS1 ....7 E4
Cloudsdale Av *WBOW* BD5 ....96 A7
The Clough *KBTN* HD8 ....193 F8
 MIRF WF14 ....170 B5
Clough Av *AIRE* BD20 ....26 E6
Clough Bank *LUD/ILL* HX2 ....114 E6
Clough Bank La *HWTH* BD22 ....46 D5
Clough Dr *BTLY* WF17 ....145 K1
 KBTN HD8 ....215 F1
 MAR/SLWT HD7 ....211 H3
Clough Foot La *HOLM/MEL* HD9 ...248 B4
Clough Ga *HOR/CROF* WF4 ....194 B6
 HWTH BD22 ....46 E8
Clough Gate Dr *HOR/CROF* WF4 ...194 B6
Clough Gn *DOD/DAR* * S75 ....238 C3
Clough Hall La *HUDS* HD4 ....213 J3
Clough Hey *MAR/SLWT* HD7 ......209 H7
Clough House La *GTL/HWG* HX4 ..164 E8
 KBTN HD8 ....237 G5
 MAR/SLWT HD7 ....210 B2
Clough La *BRIG* HD6 ....142 E6
 BRIG HD6 ....142 E6
 HBR HX7 ....113 J6
 HUDW HD3 ....190 C6
 HWTH BD22 ....46 E8
 LUD/ILL HX2 ....115 F5
 LVSG WF15 ....144 A7
Clough Lea *MAR/SLWT* HD7 ......209 H7
Clough Ml *TOD* * OL14 ....159 H4
Clough Pk *KBTN* HD8 ....215 F1
Clough Pl *LUD/ILL* HX2 ....114 E6
Clough Rd *HOR/CROF* WF4 ....217 H2
 HUDN HD2 ....191 G1
 MAR/SLWT HD7 ....188 C7
 RPDN/SBR HX6 ....165 C1
 TOD OL14 ....159 K2
Clough St *MOR* LS27 ....123 G7
 WBOW BD5 ....96 A8
Clough Wy *KBTN* HD8 ....215 F1
Clovelly Av *BEE/HOL* LS11 ....101 H8
Clovelly Gv *BEE/HOL* LS11 ....101 H8
Clovelly Pl *BEE/HOL* LS11 ....101 H8
Clovelly Rw *BEE/HOL* LS11 ....101 H8
Clovelly Ter *BEE/HOL* LS11 ....101 H8
Clover Ct *PDSY/CALV* LS28 ....75 J5
Clover Crs *PDSY/CALV* LS28 ....75 J5
Cloverdale *HIPP* HX3 ....117 J4
Clover Hl *LVSG* WF15 ....144 A6
Clover Hill Cl *HFAX* * HX1 ....8 C5
Clover Hill Rd *HFAX* HX1 ....8 C6
Clover Hill Ter *HFAX* HX1 ....8 C6
Clover Hill Vw *HFAX* * HX1 ....8 C6
Clover Ri *KGHY* BD21 ....3 F3
Clover St *GTHN* BD7 ....95 H6
Cloverville Ap *WBSY* BD6 ....118 D4
Clover Wk *HEM/SK/SE* WF9 ....226 B4
Clubhouses Cft *HOR/CROF* WF4 ..197 G2
Club La *BRAM* LS13 ....76 C6
 LUD/ILL HX2 ....115 J8
Club Rw *CHAL* LS7 ....79 J4
 YEA LS19 ....54 A4
Club St *GTHN* BD7 ....95 F5
 TOD OL14 ....132 E2
Clumber Dr *CLECK* BD19 ....144 E4

Cluntergate *HOR/CROF* WF4 ......197 H2
Clunters La *LUD/ILL* HX2 ....137 J5
Clutton St *BTLY* WF17 ....146 D6
Clyde Ap *WOR/ARM* * LS12 ....6 A5
Clyde Cha *WOR/ARM* LS12 ....6 A5
Clyde Ct *WOR/ARM* LS12 ....6 A5
Clyde Gdns *WOR/ARM* LS12 ....6 A5
Clyde Gra *WOR/ARM* LS12 ....6 A5
Clydesdale Dr *WBSY* BD6 ....118 A4
Clyde St *BGLY* BD16 ....5 K8
 RPDN/SBR HX6 ....138 E8
 WKFDE * WF1 ....11 E5
Clyde Vw *WOR/ARM* * LS12 ....6 A5
Clyde Wk *WOR/ARM* LS12 ....6 A4
Coach Gate La *STKB/PEN* S36 ....252 C1
Coach House Dr *HUD5* 192 B6
Coach La *CLECK* * BD19 ....144 B3
 PDSY/CALV BD13 ....93 K5
Coach Rd *GSLY* LS20 ....53 F4
 HIPP HX3 ....142 A4
 HEM/SK/SE WF9 ....231 K2
 HUDN HD2 ....191 F1
 RPDN/SBR HX6 ....164 A7
 WKFDE WF1 ....149 K6
 WOR/ARM LS12 ....99 J8
Coal Clough Rd *TOD* OL14 ....108 D8
Coal Ga *MAR/SLWT* HD7 ....209 H2
Coal Gate Rd *RPDN/SBR* HX6 ....163 F6
Coal Hill Dr *BRAM* LS13 ....76 D7
Coal Hill Fold *BRAM* LS13 ....76 D7
Coal Hill Gdns *BRAM* LS13 ....76 D7
Coal Hill Gn *BRAM* LS13 ....76 D7
Coal Hill La *PDSY/CALV* LS28 ....76 C7
Coala La *LUD/ILL* HX2 ....92 C8
Coal Pit La *BRIG* HD6 ....168 E2
 BTLY WF17 ....145 K5
 HEM/SK/SE WF9 ....227 J5
 HOLM/MEL HD9 ....234 A5
 KBTN HD8 ....236 B3
 MAR/SLWT HD7 ....205 H8
Coalpit La *HIPP* HX3 ....140 D7
 KBTN HD8 ....236 D8
Coal Rd *AL/HA/HU* LS17 ....59 J7
 SCFT LS14 ....83 J4
Coates Cl *EARL* WF12 ....172 D2
Coate's La *AIRE* BD20 ....16 B7
Coates St *WBOW* BD5 ....95 K7
Coates St *WBOW* BD5 ....95 K7
Cobb Av *WKFDW/WTN* WF2 ......175 G4
Cobbler Hall *HOR/CROF* WF4 ....219 F3
Cobblers La *PONT* WF8 ....181 C1
 PONT WF8 ....181 G2
Cobcroft La *KNOT* WF11 ....183 G4
Cobcroft Rd *HUDN* HD2 ....12 C1
Cobden Av *WOR/ARM* LS12 ....99 K7
Cobden Ct *HFAX* * HX1 ....8 C3
Cobden Gv *WOR/ARM* LS12 ....99 K7
Cobden Ms *MOR* LS27 ....123 F7
Cobden Pl *WOR/ARM* LS12 ....99 K7
Cobden Rd *WOR/ARM* LS12 ....99 K7
Cobden St *CLAY* BD14 ....94 B7
 CUL/QBY BD13 ....116 E2
 IDLE BD10 ....74 D4
 TOD OL14 ....134 A6
 WIL/AL BD15 ....94 B2
 WOR/ARM LS12 ....99 K7
Cobden Ter *ELL* * HX5 ....166 E6
 WOR/ARM LS12 ....99 K7
Cobham Pde *WKFDE* * WF1 ....149 J7
Cobham Wk *MSTN/BAR* LS15 ....104 D1
Cockburn Cl *BEE/HOL* LS11 ......101 J8
Cockburn Wy *BEE/HOL* LS11 .....101 J8
Cockermouth La *HOR/CROF* WF4 ...216 A1
Cock Hill La *HIPP* HX3 ....117 F5
Cocking La *ILK* LS29 ....18 A6
Cockin La *CUL/QBY* BD13 ....93 H8
Cock La *HOR/CROF* WF4 ....200 C2
Cockley Hill La *HUDE* HD5 ....192 E3
Cockley Mdw *HUDE* HD5 ....192 E2
Cock Pit La *GTL/HWG* HX4 ....187 G3
Cockroft Ga *BFDE* BD3 ....5 E4
Cockroft Cl *WOR/ARM* LS12 ....99 K7
Cockroft Dr *WOR/ARM* LS12 ....99 K2
Cockshott La *IDLE* BD10 ....74 D7
 WOR/ARM LS12 ....99 K2
Cockshott Pl *ILK* LS29 ....18 C3
Coggil St *MID* LS10 ....125 H1
Coiners Fold *HBR* HX7 ....136 D3
Colbeck Rw *BTLY* WF17 ....145 H5
Colbert Av *ILK* LS29 ....20 E6
Colby Ri *MSTN/BAR* LS15 ....103 G4
Coldbeck Dr *WBSY* BD6 ....117 K3
Coldcotes Av *OSM* LS9 ....102 D1
Coldcotes Crs *OSM* LS9 ....103 F1
Coldcotes Dr *OSM* LS9 ....102 E1
Coldcotes Garth *OSM* LS9 ....103 F1
Coldcotes Gv *OSM* LS9 ....103 F1
Coldcotes Vw *OSM* LS9 ....102 E1
Coldcotes Wk *OSM* LS9 ....103 F1
Cold Edge Rd *LUD/ILL* HX2 ....90 E6
 LUD/ILL HX2 ....114 C6
Colden Cl *HBR* * HX7 ....112 A8
Colden La *HBR* HX7 ....110 E5
Colden Rd *HBR* HX7 ....111 K7
Colders Dr *HOLM/MEL* HD9 ....231 H2
Colders Gn *HOLM/MEL* HD9 ......231 H1
Cold Hiendley Common La
 HOR/CROF WF4 ....222 A2

Cold Hill La *HOLM/MEL* HD9 234
 HUDS HD4 213
Cold Royd La *HUDE* HD5 192
Coldshaw Top *HWTH* BD22 68
Cold St *HWTH* BD22 68
Cold Well La *HOLM/MEL* HD9 232
Cold Well Rd *MSTN/BAR* LS15 ...103
Coldwells Hl *GTL/HWG* HX4 103
Cold Well Sq *MSTN/BAR* * LS15 ..103
Coldwell St *MAR/SLWT* HD7 211
Coleman St *BFDE* BD2 5
 WOR/ARM LS12 6
Colenso Gdns *BEE/HOL* LS11 101
Colenso Gv *BEE/HOL* LS11 101
 KGHY * BD21 3
Colenso Mt *BEE/HOL* LS11 101
Colenso Pl *BEE/HOL* LS11 101
Colenso Rd *BEE/HOL* LS11 101
Colenso Ter *BEE/HOL* LS11 101
Colenso Wk *KGHY* * BD21 3
Colenso Wy *KGHY* * BD21 3
Coleridge Cl *RTHW* LS26 127
Coleridge Crs *WKFDW/WTN* WF2 ..149
Coleridge Gdns *IDLE* BD10 74
Coleridge La *PDSY/CALV* LS28 98
Coleridge St *HFAX* HX1 9
Coleridge Wy *PONT* WF8 180
Coles Wy *AIRE* BD20 48
Coley Hall La *HIPP* HX3 141
Coley Rd *HIPP* HX3 112
Coley Vw *HIPP* HX3 112
Colinsway *WKFDW/WTN* WF2 112
Collbrook Av *WBSY* BD6 118
Colleen Rd *HOR/CROF* WF4 198
College Farm La *WBY* LS22 23
College Gv *CAS* WF10 153
 WKFDE WF1 ....1C
College Grove Cl *WKFDE* WF1 .....1C
College Grove Rd *WKFDE* WF1 ....1C
College Grove Vw *WKFDE* WF1 ....1C
College Lawns *WOR/ARM* LS12 ..10C
College Rd *BGLY* BD16 ....9C
 CAS WF10 154
 MOR LS27 122
College St *BTLY* WF17 145
 HUDS HD4 ....19C
 TOD OL14 133
College St East *HUDS* HD4 ....19C
College Ter *HFAX* * HX1 8
College Vw *WOR/ARM* LS12 ......10C
Collier La *BAIL* BD17 5
 GFTH/SHER LS25 85
Colliers Cl *SHPY* BD18 72
Colliers La *AL/HA/HU* LS17 59
Colliers Wy *KBTN* HD8 217
Colliery Ap *WKFDE* WF1 149
Collindale Cl *IDLE* BD10 75
Collinfield Ri *WBSY* BD6 118
Collingham Av *WBSY* BD6 117
Collingham Dr *GFTH/SHER* LS25 ..105
Collingwood Rd *NORM* WF6 177
Collin Moor La *GTL/HWG* HX4 166
Collin Rd *SCFT* LS14 103
Collins Cl *HWTH* BD22 65
Collinson St *CLECK* BD19 144
Collins St *BOW* BD4 9
 GTHN BD7 95
Colmore Gv *WOR/ARM* LS12 .....10C
Colmore Rd *WOR/ARM* LS12 .....10C
Colmore St *WOR/ARM* LS12 ......10C
Colne Hurst *HUDN* HD2 169
Colne Rd *HUD* HD1 12
Colne Rd *HUD* HD1 44
Colne Rd Goodley *HWTH* BD22 68
Colne St *HUD* HD1 12
 HUD HD1 13
Colne Vale Rd *HUDS* HD4 ....19C
Colne Valley Circular Wk
 MAR/SLWT HD7 189
 MAR/SLWT HD7 ....20S
 MAR/SLWT HD7 ....20S
Colonel's Wk *PONT* WF8 ....18C
Colorado Wy *CAS* WF10 153
Colston Cl *GIR* BD8 9
Colton Ct *MSTN/BAR* * LS15 104
Colton Cft *MSTN/BAR* LS15 104
Colton Garth *MSTN/BAR* LS15 ...104
Colton La *MSTN/BAR* LS15 104
Colton Rd *MSTN/BAR* LS15 104
 WOR/ARM LS12 ....10C
Colton Rd East *MSTN/BAR* LS15 ..10C
Colton St *WOR/ARM* * LS12 ......10C
Coltsfoot Cl *PONT* WF8 ....18C
Columbus St *HIPP* HX3 3
Colville Ter *BEE/HOL* LS11 14
 EARD/LOFT WF3 145
Colwyn Av *BEE/HOL* LS11 12
Colwyn Mt *BEE/HOL* LS11 12
Colwyn Pl *BEE/HOL* LS11 12
Colwyn Rd *BEE/HOL* LS11 12
Colwyn St *HUDW* HD3 13
Colwyn Ter *BEE/HOL* LS11 12
Colwyn Vw *BEE/HOL* LS11 12
Colyton St *WIL/AL* BD15 9
The Combs *EARL* WF12 19
Combs Rd *EARL* WF12 19
Commerce Ct *BOW* BD4 9
Commerce St *BFD* * BD1 9

Commercial Buildings
M/WK BD12.................................119 J7
mmercial Ct LDS LS1.......................7 E4
mmercial Rd DEWS WF13..............172 B2
BTN HD8.......................................236 E1
STL LS5..78 A8
mmercial St BFD BD1......................5 D4
RIG HD6..168 B1
TLY WF17.....................................146 B6
AS WF10.......................................153 J3
ECK BD19.....................................144 B4
UL/QBY BD13.................................92 B2
UL/QBY BD13..................................35 J5
ARL WF12....................................172 E4
BR HX7..112 B8
FAX HX1...9 D5
UD HD1..13 D6
DS LS1...7 E3
MAR/SLWT HD7..............................210 E3
IOR LS27..123 F7
THW LS26.....................................126 B6
HPY BD18.......................................73 H5
OD OL14..134 B6
WKFDE WF1.....................................98 D5
mmercial Vls PDSY/CALV LS28......98 B5
mmondale Wy BOW BD4..............119 H5
Common EARL WF12....................172 C8
mmon End La KBTN HD8.............215 F1
mmon Holme La ILK LS29..............19 J5
mmon Ing La HOR/CROF WF4....222 F1
TLY DN5..241 H5
ARD/LOFT WF3.............................148 D2
LE DN14.......................................157 K5
EM/SK/SE WF9..............................226 B4
IPP HX3...140 E5
OR/CROF WF4...............................216 C2
OR/CROF WF4...............................219 K3
BTN HD8.......................................216 C4
BTN HD8.......................................237 C5
VOT WF11.....................................157 G8
ONT WF8.......................................204 D7
KFDW/WTN WF2...........................199 H6
mmon Rd BTLY WF17....................145 J7
UD/GR S72.....................................224 A8
ARD/LOFT WF3..............................150 C4
LL HX5..167 H5
EM/SK/SE WF9..............................224 A1
....12 C2
M/WK BD12...................................118 D5
mmon Road Av
EM/SK/SE WF9..............................241 G2
VSG WF15......................................170 B1
mmonside BTLY WF17...................172 C1
mmon Side La FEA/AMT WF7.......179 F5
no Av GIR BD8.................................95 F2
no Dr GIR BD8.................................95 F2
no Gdns GIR BD8.............................95 F2
no Gv GIR BD8.................................95 F2
apeigne Ap AIRE BD20......................48 D2
pton Av OSM LS9...........................102 C1
pton Crs OSM LS9..........................102 C1
pton Gv OSM LS9...........................102 C1
pton La AL/HA/HU LS17...................40 D6
pton Mt OSM LS9...........................102 C1
pton Pl OSM LS9............................102 C1
pton Rd OSM LS9...........................102 C1
pton Rw OSM LS9...........................102 C1
pton St BOW BD4...........................119 K1
GHY BD21..3 E2
SM LS9...102 C1
pton Ter OSM LS9...........................102 C1
pton Vw OSM LS9...........................102 C1
cordia St BEE/HOL LS11....................7 E4
cord St HOLM/MEL HD9.................213 F7
SU LS2..7 F2
crete St HIPP * HX3............................8 B2
dor Cl WBSY BD6............................117 H2
duit St GIR BD8..................................3 D3
ey La KGHY BD21...............................3 D5
ey Moor La RTHW LS26.................128 E8
ey Wk DEWS WF13.........................171 J3
ey Warren La EARD/LOFT WF3.....150 B5
ference Mt WOR/ARM LS12...........100 A4
ference Rd WOR/ARM LS12...........100 A4
ference Ter WOR/ARM LS12...........100 A4
gress Mt WOR/ARM LS12..............100 A4
gress St WOR/ARM LS12................100 A4
greve Ap AL/HA/HU LS17.................40 C6
greve Wy AL/HA/HU LS17................40 C5
sborough La GFTH/SHER LS25.....106 B4
sston Av CUL/QBY BD13................116 C2
GY LS6..78 E6
JDE HD5..13 F4
ston Cl CUL/QBY BD13..................116 C2
L HX5..167 G4
KB/PEN S36...................................252 C7
ston Ct EARD/LOFT WF3...............149 J5
ston Dr CAS WF10.........................155 F4
stone Crs WKFDE WF1.....................11 E1
ston Gdns CAS WF10.....................155 F4
STN/BAR LS15...............................103 G5
ston Gv HTON BD9...........................95 F1
ston Rd EARL WF12........................172 E1
HN BD7..94 E8
LM/MEL HD9..................................231 J2
HW LS26..127 F4

Coniston Wy RTHW LS26................127 F4
WBY LS22...23 F5
Connaught Gdns HUDN HD2..........169 F6
Consort St BVRD LS3..........................6 B2
Consort Ter BVRD LS3........................6 B2
Consort Vw BVRD LS3.........................6 B2
Consort Wk BVRD LS3.........................6 B2
Constable Gv EARD/LOFT WF3......150 B5
Constable Rd EARD/LOFT WF3.......148 A3
ILK LS29...20 D8
Constance Gdns LDSU LS2.................7 D1
Constance St SHPY * BD18..............73 F5
Constance Wy CHAL LS7..................7 D1
Constitutional St HFAX HX1..............8 B5
Conway Av RHAY LS8.......................80 B8
Conway Crs BTLY WF17..................172 B1
HOLM/MEL HD9............................231 H2
Conway Dr RHAY LS8.......................80 B8
Conway Gv RHAY LS8......................80 B8
Conway Mt RHAY LS8......................80 B8
Conway Pl RHAY LS8........................80 B8
Conway Rd RHAY LS8......................80 B8
WKFDW/WTN WF2........................175 F4
Conway St HFAX HX1........................8 B5
PDSY/CALV LS28.............................98 B2
RHAY LS8...80 B8
Conway Ter RHAY LS8.....................80 B8
Conway Vw RHAY LS8......................80 B8
Conyers Yd OSS * WF5...................173 K4
Cooke Crs CLECK BD19..................144 D3
Cooke La KGHY BD21.........................3 D3
Cooke St KGHY BD21.........................3 D3
Cook La HECK WF16.......................145 F7
Cookridge Av BHP/TINH LS16..........55 J5
Cookridge Dr BHP/TINH LS16..........55 H5
Cookridge Gv BHP/TINH LS16..........55 J5
Cookridge La BHP/TINH LS16...........55 J4
Cookridge St LDSU LS2......................7 D3
Cooksland La FEA/AMT WF7..........178 D3
Cookson Cl CAS WF10....................154 E6
Cookson St BRIG HD6.....................142 M8
Coombe Hl CUL/QBY BD13............117 G1
Coombe Rd MAR/SLWT HD7.........189 K6
Co-operative Buildings BRIG HD6...142 C4
HIPP HX3...8 A1
Co-operative St EARD/LOFT WF3...149 K2
EARL WF12....................................173 G3
HOR/CROF WF4.............................197 G2
MIRF WF14.....................................170 B2
MOR LS27.......................................123 F7
Cooperative St TOD OL14..............134 D5
Co-operative St WKFDW/WTN * WF2..10 A1
Co-operative Ter HOLM/MEL HD9...233 J4
Cooper Bridge Rd HUDN HD2.........169 J5
Cooper Cl BOW BD4.........................50 A6
Cooperfields LUD/ILL HX2..............117 J4
Cooper La HOLM/MEL HD9.............233 G6
STKB/PEN S36...............................253 C4
WBSY BD6......................................117 J2
Cooper Rd DOD/DAR S75...............239 J3
WBY LS22...23 J6
Cooper St TOD OL14.......................134 D5
Co-op La HOLM/MEL HD9..............232 D8
Copeland St BOW BD4......................97 F6
Copeworth Dr HOR/CROF WF4......198 B9
Copgrove Cl BOW BD4.....................97 G8
Copgrove Ct BOW BD4.....................97 G8
Copgrove Rd BOW BD4....................97 G8
RHAY LS8...80 C6
Cop Hill La MAR/SLWT HD7...........209 K3
Cop Hill Side MAR/SLWT HD7........209 K3
Copley Av HOLM/MEL HD9.............231 G1
Copley Bank Rd MAR/SLWT HD7...189 C3
LUD/ILL HX2..................................139 H6
Copley Gln HIPP HX3......................166 A1
Copley Gv HIPP HX3.......................166 A1
Copley Hall St HIPP HX3................166 A1
Copley Hl BTLY WF17......................145 J2
WOR/ARM LS12................................6 A5
Copley Hill Wy WOR/ARM LS12......6 A6
Copley La EARD/LOFT WF3............125 J7
GFTH/SHER LS25.............................85 K3
HIPP HX3.......................................166 A1
KBTN HD8......................................235 K3
Copley Mt HIPP HX3.......................166 A1
Copley St BTLY WF17......................145 J2
WBOW BD5......................................95 H8
WOR/ARM * LS12.............................6 A5
Copley Ter WOR/ARM LS12...........166 A1
Copley Yd WOR/ARM LS12..............6 A5
Copperas Cl STKB/PEN S36...........251 H4
Copperas House Ter TOD OL14......159 K1
Copperas Rw GTL/HWG * HX4.......165 H4
Copper Beech Ct
WKFDW/WTN WF2.........................199 J5
Copperfield Av OSM * LS9.............102 B5
Copperfield Crs OSM LS9...............102 B5
Copperfield Dr OSM LS9................102 B5
Copperfield Gv OSM LS9................102 B5
Copperfield Mt OSM LS9................102 C5
Copperfield Pl OSM LS9.................102 B5
Copperfield Rw OSM LS9................102 B5
Copperfield Ter OSM LS9...............102 B5
Copperfield Vw OSM LS9................102 B5
Copperfield Wk OSM LS9...............102 B5
Coppertop Ms PONT WF8..............155 F8
The Coppice HFAX * HX1..................8 C6

HUDN HD2.....................................168 C7
ILK LS29..20 A5
MIRF * WF14.................................170 C3
MSTN/BAR LS15..............................83 H5
YEA LS19...53 H6
Coppice Cl WKFDE WF1..................11 E1
Coppice Dr HUDN HD4...................212 D5
Coppice Gra YEA LS19......................53 K3
Coppice Head RTHW LS26.............126 C6
Coppice Vw RHAY LS8......................80 C5
Coppice Wood Av GSLY LS20...........53 J2
GTHN BD7.......................................95 G5
Coppice Wood Cl GSLY LS20...........53 J2
Coppice Wood Crs YEA LS19............53 J3
Coppice Wood Gv GSLY LS20..........53 J3
GTHN * BD7....................................95 G5
Coppice Wood Ri YEA LS19.............53 J3
The Coppies LM/WK BD12.............118 C7
Coppin Hall Gv MIRF WF14............170 A5
Coppin Hall La MIRF WF14.............170 A5
Coppy Cl BGLY BD16........................72 A5
Coppy La BRAM LS13.......................77 C7
HBR HX7..79 F8
HWTH BD22......................................45 J4
Coppy Nook La HBR HX7................137 F8
Coppy Rd AIRE BD20.......................26 D6
ILK LS29..18 C3
Coppy Wood Dr ILK LS29.................20 B4
The Copse BGLY BD16......................50 D8
CLECK BD19...................................143 G4
FEA/AMT WF7.................................179 H2
ILK LS29..32 A3
Copthorne Gdns HUDN HD2..........169 G6
Copthurst Rd HOLM/MEL HD9.......247 K4
Copt Royd Gv YEA LS19...................53 J4
Corban St BOW BD4.........................96 E8
Corby St HUDN HD2.........................12 C1
Cordingley Cl BOW BD4.................120 B2
Cordingley St BOW BD4..................120 B2
Corfe Cl BTLY WF17........................146 A1
Corn Bank HUDS HD4.....................212 C5
Corn Ex LDS * LS1..............................7 E4
Cornfield DEWS WF13....................171 H2
Cornfield Av HUDW HD3.................190 A4
Cornfield Gv TOD * OL14...............134 C5
Cornfield St HFAX * HX1...................9 D4
Cornmarket PONT WF8..................180 D3
Corn Ml ILK LS29.............................32 D7
Cornmill Cl AL/HA/HU LS17.............40 B8
Corn Mill Ct WOR/ARM LS12.........99 H4
Cornmill Crs LVSG WF15................144 E8
Cornmill Dr LVSG WF15.................144 E8
Corn Mill La CLAY BD14..................93 K6
ILK LS29..32 C2
Cornmill La AL/HA/HU LS17.............40 B8
LVSG WF15....................................144 E8
Cornrace Vw HUD HX6...................136 C6
Cornstone Fold WOR/ARM LS12.....99 G4
Corn St HWTH BD22..........................2 B6
Cornus Gdns MID LS10...................124 E3
Cornwall Av AIRE BD20.....................26 E2
Cornwall Cl RTHW * LS26...............126 A5
Cornwall Crs BAIL BD17...................51 H7
BRIG HD6.......................................142 C5
RTHW LS26....................................126 A5
Cornwall Pl GIR BD8..........................4 B2
Cornwall Rd BGLY BD16..................72 B1
GIR BD8...4 C2
KGHY BD21.......................................3 F1
Cornwall Ter GIR BD8........................4 B2
Coronation Av CUD/GR S72...........223 F8
CUD/GR S72..................................240 H5
GFTH/SHER LS25...........................129 H2
IDLE BD10..53 F7
NORM WF6.....................................151 J8
Coronation Bungalows
GFTH/SHER LS25............................129 H2
Coronation Mt HWTH BD22...............2 A3
Coronation Pde MSTN/BAR LS15...105 J3
Coronation Rd DOD/DAR S75.........239 K7
HIPP HX3..140 B7
HOR/CROF WF4.............................178 A4
Coronation St CAS WF10................154 A2
CAS WF10......................................154 B5
EARD/LOFT * WF3.........................126 A8
ELL HX5..166 E5
GTL/HWG HX4................................166 C3
LM/WK BD12..................................119 H6
WKFDW/WTN WF2........................175 G1
Coronation Ter CAS WF10.............154 B5
RPDN/SBR HX6..............................164 B5
Coronation Wk HWTH BD22.............2 A2
Coronation Wy HWTH BD22.............47 G3
Corporal La CUL/QBY BD13............116 D5
Corporation St DEWS WF13............172 C3
ECHL BD2..74 E8
HFAX HX1...8 C3
HUD HD1...11 D5
MOR LS27.......................................122 E6
RPDN/SBR HX6..............................138 E7
Corporation Yd BTLY * WF17.........146 A6
Corrance Rd LM/WK BD12.............142 E2
Corrie St CUL/QBY BD13................116 D5
Cote Farm La SHPY BD18..................74 B3
Cotefields PDSY/CALV LS28..............76 A8
Cote Gap CUL/QBY * BD13...............93 H4
Cote La HOLM/MEL HD9.................248 B3
HUDN HD2.....................................167 J6

PDSY/CALV LS28 ....98 A1
WIL/AL BD15 ....94 A2
Cote Rd RPDN/SBR HX6 ....163 J7
Coteroyd Av MOR LS27 ....123 H3
Coteroyd Dr MOR LS27 ....123 H4
The Cote PDSY/CALV LS28 ......98 A1
Cote Wall Ms MIRF WF14 ......171 G8
Cotswold Av SHPY BD18 ....74 A4
Cotswold Cl HEM/SK/SE WF9 ...225 F4
Cotswold Dr GFTH/SHER LS25 ...105 K6
  KNOT * WF1 ....156 B7
  LVSG WF15 ....144 A6
  RTHW LS26 ....126 A5
Cotswold Ms KBTN HD8 ....215 H4
Cotswold Rd RTHW LS26 ....126 A5
  WKFDW/WTN WF2 ....174 E6
Cottage Gn GIR BD8 ....95 F3
Cottage Ms HWTH * BD22 ....68 C3
Cottage Rd HDGY LS6 ....78 D5
  IDLE BD10 ....75 F4
Cottam Av GTHN BD7 ....95 H5
Cottam Cft HEM/SK/SE WF9 ....224 E4
Cottam Ter GTHN BD7 ....95 H5
Cotterdale WIL/AL BD15 ....72 A8
Cotterdale Holt WBY LS22 ....40 E2
Cotterdale Vw MSTN/BAR LS15 ...103 G5
Cotterill Rd KNOT WF11 ....156 A8
Cottingley Cha BEE/HOL LS11 ...123 H1
Cottingley Cliffe Rd BGLY BD16 ...72 C5
Cottingley Crs BEE/HOL LS11 ...123 J2
Cottingley Dr BEE/HOL LS11 ....123 H2
  BGLY BD16 ....72 A3
Cottingley Fold BEE/HOL LS11 ...123 H1
Cottingley Gdns BEE/HOL LS11 ...123 J2
Cottingley Gn BEE/HOL LS11 ...123 J2
Cottingley Gv BEE/HOL LS11 ....123 J2
Cottingley Manor Pk BGLY BD16 ...72 B4
Cottingley New Rd BGLY BD16 ...72 A6
Cottingley Rd BEE/HOL LS11 ...123 H1
  WIL/AL BD15 ....72 A8
Cottingley Ter GIR * BD8 ....4 B2
Cottingley V BEE/HOL LS11 .....123 J2
Cotton St WKFDW/WTN WF2 .....10 C5
Couford Gv HUDN HD2 ....169 G7
Coule Royd HUDE HD5 ....192 A4
Coultas St LDS LS1 ....7 E3
County Ar LDS LS1 ....7 E3
County Cl BTLY WF17 ....146 B5
Coupe Gv NORM WF6 ....151 J6
Coupland Pl BEE/HOL LS11 ....101 H7
Coupland Rd BEE/HOL LS11 ....101 H7
  GFTH/SHER LS25 ....105 J4
Coupland St BEE/HOL LS11 .....101 H8
The Court AL/HA/HU LS17 ....57 F6
  LVSG WF15 ....144 B7
  SHPY * BD18 ....72 E4
Court Dr KSTL LS5 ....77 J5
Courtenay Cl BFDE BD3 ....97 G4
Courtenays SCFT * LS14 ....81 K1
Courthouse St OT LS21 ....33 J5
Court La LUD/ILL HX2 ....139 G4
Courts Leet LM/WK BD12 ....118 C7
The Courtyard HUDS HD4 ....190 D7
  PONT WF8 ....155 F8
  BTLY WF17 ....145 J1
The Courtyards SCFT * LS14 ......81 K4
The Court Wy FEA/AMT WF7 ....203 H3
The Covert HOR/CROF WF4 ......220 C4
Cousen Av GTHN BD7 ....95 F6
Cousen Rd GTHN BD7 ....95 H7
Cousin La LUD/ILL HX2 ....115 H7
Coustances Wy ILK LS29 ....21 G7
Coventry St BOW BD4 ....96 D7
  HFAX * HX1 ....139 H4
Coverdale Garth WBY LS22 ....40 E3
Coverdale Wy BAIL BD17 ....52 A7
Cover Dr WBY BD6 ....118 B3
Coverley Ri YEA LS19 ....53 H4
The Covet BTLY WF17 ....145 J4
The Covet IDLE BD10 ....75 F3
Covey Clough Ct MIRF * WF14 ...193 H2
Cowcliffe Hill Rd HUDN HD2 ....191 F1
Cowcliff Hill Rd HOLM/MEL HD9 ...248 E5
Cowdray St OSM LS9 ....10 A1
Cow Close Gv WOR/ARM LS12 ...100 A1
Cow Close La LM/WK BD12 ....143 F1
Cow Close Rd WOR/ARM LS12 ...99 K6
Cowdray Dr CLECK BD19 ....143 G3
Cowdry Cl EARL WF12 ....195 J1
Cowfold St TOD OL14 ....134 A3
Cow Ga HUDW HD3 ....189 K5
Cowgill St GIR BD8 ....4 A2
Cow Gn HFAX HX1 ....9 D4
Cow Hey La HBR HX7 ....88 D8
Cow Heys HUDE HD5 ....192 A4
Cow Hill Gate La LUD/ILL HX2 ...115 H5
Cowhurst Av TOD OL14 ....133 J4
Cow La AWLS/ASK DN6 ....183 K8
  HBR HX7 ....111 K4
  HIPP HX3 ....141 J7
  HIPP HX3 ....166 B1
  HOR/CROF WF4 ....177 K7
  HOR/CROF WF4 ....223 G2
  RPDN/SBR HX6 ....164 A5
Cowlersley La MAR/SLWT HD7 ...211 J1
Cowley Crs HTON BD9 ....72 C7
Cowley Rd BRAM LS13 ....76 D6
Cowling Br AIRE BD20 ....26 E3

Cowling La HIPP HX3 ....116 E6
Cowm St WHIT OL12 ....158 B6
Cowpasture Rd ILK LS29 ....20 C8
Cowper Av OSM LS9 ....102 C1
Cowper Crs OSM LS9 ....102 C1
Cowper Gv RHAY LS8 ....80 C8
Cowper Mt OSM LS9 ....80 C8
Cowper Rd OSM LS9 ....102 C1
Cowper St CHAL LS7 ....80 A8
  EARL WF12 ....172 B5
Cowper Ter OSM LS9 ....80 C8
Cowrakes Cl HUDW HD3 ....190 A2
Cowrakes Rd HUDW HD3 ....189 K2
Cowroyd Pl HIPP * HX3 ....9 E3
Cowslip St HUD * HD1 ....190 D6
Coxley Crs HOR/CROF WF4 ......196 D5
Coxley La HOR/CROF WF4 ....196 D4
Coxley Vw HOR/CROF WF4 ....196 C6
Coxwold Hl WBY LS22 ....23 J5
Coxwold Vw WBY LS22 ....23 J5
Crab Hl PONT WF8 ....180 D3
Crab La WKFDW/WTN WF2 ....198 D7
  WOR/ARM LS12 ....100 C3
Crabtree Av HECK WF16 ....145 H6
Crabtree Dr CUD/CR S72 ....240 D8
Crabtree Gn WBY LS22 ....40 E4
Crabtree Hl WBY LS22 ....41 F3
Crabtree La AL/HA/HU LS17 ....40 A4
Crab Tree La PONT WF8 ....227 K1
Crabtree Pl GTHN BD7 ....95 G7
Crabtree St GTHN BD7 ....95 G7
  HFAX HX1 ....8 A4
Crabtree Wy EARD/LOFT * WF3 ...148 A4
Crackenedge La DEWS WF13 ....172 C2
Crackenedge Ter DEWS WF13 ...172 C2
Cracoe Rd BFDE BD3 ....5 F5
The Crag BSPA/BRAM LS23 ....62 D1
Crag Cl LUD/ILL HX2 ....115 G7
Crag Gdns BSPA/BRAM LS23 ......62 D1
Cragg Av HORS LS18 ....77 F3
Cragg Bottom Rd HWTH BD22 ...66 D3
Cragg Dr ILK LS29 ....21 F8
Cragg La CUL/QBY BD13 ....92 B6
  GTHN BD7 ....95 G8
  HBR HX7 ....136 D5
Cragg Rd GTHN BD7 ....95 G8
  HBR HX7 ....136 K5
  HORS LS18 ....77 G3
Cragg Ter GTHN BD7 ....95 G8
  HORS LS18 ....77 F3
Cragg Top CUL/QBY BD13 ....92 B6
Cragg Vw AIRE BD20 ....27 G1
Cragg Wood Dr YEA LS19 ....53 J8
Craggwood Rd HORS LS18 ....77 G4
Crag Hill Av BHP/TINH LS16 ....55 J4
Crag Hill Rd IDLE BD10 ....74 C1
Crag Hill Vw BHP/TINH LS16 .....55 J4
Crag La AL/HA/HU LS17 ....57 F6
  LUD/ILL HX2 ....115 G7
Crag Mt PONT WF8 ....180 D3
Crag Pl KGHY BD21 ....3 D6
Crag Rd SHPY BD18 ....73 J5
Cragside CI KSTL LS5 ....77 J4
Cragside Crs KSTL LS5 ....77 H4
Cragside Gdns KSTL LS5 ....77 J4
Cragside Gv KSTL LS5 ....77 H4
Cragside Mt KSTL LS5 ....77 H4
Cragside PI KSTL LS5 ....77 J4
Cragside Wk KSTL LS5 ....77 J4
Crag Vw IDLE BD10 ....74 E4
Craig Ct BTLY WF17 ....146 B5
Craiglands HIPP HX3 ....141 J3
Craiglands Pk ILK LS29 ....20 C8
Craiglands Rd ILK LS29 ....20 C8
Craiglea Dr LM/WK BD12 ....142 E1
Craigmore Ct BOW BD4 ....120 C1
Craigmore Dr ILK LS29 ....20 E7
Cranberry Av TOD OL14 ....160 A4
Cranbourne Rd HTON BD9 ....94 D1
Cranbrook Av BEE/HOL LS11 ....101 G8
  WBSY BD6 ....118 D3
Cranbrook Pl WBOW BD5 ....96 A8
Cranbrook St CLAY BD14 ....116 A3
  WBOW BD5 ....96 A8
Cranbrook Vw PDSY/CALV LS28 ...98 E6
Cranewells Dr MSTN/BAR LS15 ...104 A5
Cranewells Gn MSTN/BAR LS15 ...104 A5
Cranewells Ri MSTN/BAR LS15 ...104 A5
Cranewells V MSTN/BAR LS15 ...104 A5
Cranewells Vw MSTN/BAR LS15 ...104 A4
Cranford Gdns BSLYN/ROY S71 ...221 K7
Cranford Pl WIL/AL BD15 ....71 G6
Crangle Flds HUDS HD4 ....234 E1
Cranleigh Mt KGHY BD21 ....2 B5
Cranmer Bank AL/HA/HU LS17 ...57 G8
Cranmer Cl AL/HA/HU LS17 ....57 G8
Cranmer Gdns AL/HA/HU LS17 ...57 G8
  HOLM/MEL HD9 ....231 J1
Cranmer Ri AL/HA/HU LS17 ....57 G8
Cranmer Rd AL/HA/HU LS17 ......57 G8
  BFDE BD3 ....5 D2
Cranmore Crs MID LS10 ....125 F6
Cranmore Dr MID LS10 ....125 F6
Cranmore Gdns MID LS10 ....125 F6
Cranmore Garth MID LS10 ....125 F6
Cranmore Gn MID LS10 ....125 F6
Cranmore Gv EARD/LOFT WF3 ...125 F6
Cranmore La MID LS10 ....125 G6

Cranmore Ri MID LS10 ....125 F6
Cranmore Rd MID LS10 ....125 F6
Cranwood Dr HUDE HD5 ....192 A5
Craven Av AIRE BD20 ....27 G1
  CUL/QBY BD13 ....93 K4
Craven Cl BSLYN/ROY S71 ....221 J5
  CLECK BD19 ....145 G1
Craven Ct AIRE BD20 ....27 F1
  GIR BD8 ....95 F4
  HFAX * HX1 ....8 C6
Craven Crs ILK LS29 ....18 E4
Cravendale Rd DEWS WF13 ......171 J5
Craven Dr AIRE BD20 ....27 F1
  CLECK BD19 ....145 G1
Craven Edge HFAX * HX1 ....8 B6
Craven Garth GLE DN14 ....157 G2
Craven Gv AIRE BD20 ....27 G1
Craven La CLECK BD19 ....145 G1
Craven Pk ILK LS29 ....32 C1
Craven Rd DEWS WF13 ....171 J5
  HDGY LS6 ....79 J4
  HEM/SK/SE WF9 ....224 E3
  KGHY BD21 ....3 K5
Craven St BFDE * BD3 ....5 D1
  DEWS WF13 ....171 J5
  HUDS HD4 ....190 D8
  OT LS21 ....17 G8
  WKFDE WF1 ....10 C1
Craven Ter HFAX HX1 ....8 B6
Crawford Av WBSY BD6 ....118 A4
Crawford Dr WKFDW/WTN WF2 ...175 F6
Crawford St BOW BD4 ....96 D4
Crawley Av HEM/SK/SE WF9 .....225 H3
Crawshaw Av PDSY/CALV LS28 ...98 B6
Crawshaw Gdns PDSY/CALV LS28 ...98 B6
Crawshaw Hl PDSY/CALV LS28 ...98 B6
Crawshaw La HOR/CROF WF4 ...216 A4
Crawshaw Pk PDSY/CALV LS28 ...98 B6
Crawshaw Ri PDSY/CALV LS28 ...98 B6
Crawshaw Rd PDSY/CALV LS28 ...98 B6
Crawshaw St DEWS WF13 ....171 K3
Crawthorne Crs HUDN HD2 ......169 F5
Crayford Dr HOR/CROF WF4 ....200 E5
Cray La GTL/HWG HX4 ....188 C2
The Crescent AL/HA/HU LS17 ....57 J7
  BAIL BD17 ....73 G1
  BGLY BD16 ....74 C3
  BHP/TINH LS16 ....56 E3
  BIRK/DRI BD11 ....120 D4
  CAS WF10 ....154 A1
  DEWS WF13 ....171 H4
  EARD/LOFT WF3 ....148 A3
  FEA/AMT WF7 ....178 C8
  GFTH/SHER LS25 ....106 E8
  GFTH/SHER LS25 ....107 F4
  GFTH/SHER LS25 ....129 J7
  GSLY LS20 ....52 E6
  GTL/HWG HX4 ....165 K8
  HIPP HX3 ....134 E2
  HOLM/MEL HD9 ....234 B4
  HOR/CROF WF4 ....196 E6
  ILK LS29 ....21 F1
  ILK LS29 ....32 C1
  KBTN HD8 ....215 J8
  LVSG WF15 ....144 E7
  MSTN/BAR LS15 ....103 J2
  NORM WF6 ....151 G1
  OT LS21 ....33 K5
  PDSY/CALV LS28 ....98 E5
  WBSY BD6 ....117 J6
  WBY LS22 ....23 H1
Crediton Av WIL/AL BD15 ....94 A2
Crescent Av DEWS WF13 ....171 H4
  RTHW LS26 ....126 E1
Crescent Gdns AL/HA/HU LS17 ...57 J7
  RTHW LS26 ....126 E1
Crescent Gra BEE/HOL * LS11 ...101 J8
Crescent Rd HOR/CROF WF4 ....223 J7
  HUDN HD2 ....169 J1
  HUDS HD4 ....212 A4
Crescent Royd HUDE HD5 ....192 A5
Crescent St TOD OL14 ....134 A7
Crescent Towers BEE/HOL * LS11 ...101 J8
Crescent Vw AL/HA/HU LS17 ......57 J7
  HWTH BD22 ....93 G3
Crescent Vls HEM/SK/SE * WF9 ...224 E3
Crescent Wk CLAY BD14 ....94 D3
  DEWS WF13 ....171 J5
The Cresent HIPP HX3 ....141 J3
Creskeld Crs BHP/TINH LS16 ......35 K8
Creskeld Dr BHP/TINH LS16 ....35 K8
Creskeld Gdns BHP/TINH LS16 ...35 K8
Creskeld Garth BHP/TINH LS16 ...35 K8
Creskeld La BHP/TINH LS16 ....35 J8
Creskeld Pk BHP/TINH LS16 ......35 K8
Creskeld Wy WIL/AL BD15 ....94 D3
Creskell Rd BEE/HOL LS11 ....14 B9
Cressfield Rd HUDW HD3 ....190 A2
Cresswell Mt GTHN BD7 ....116 E1
Cresswell Pl GTHN BD7 ....116 E1
Cresswell Ter GTHN BD7 ....116 E1
The Crest GFTH/SHER LS25 ......129 J7
  HUDN HD2 ....169 J1
  RTHW LS26 ....126 E1
Crest Av HUDE * HD5 ....192 D1
  LM/WK BD12 ....137 H5
Crest Dr PONT WF8 ....181 H1
Crestfield Av ELL HX5 ....164 A6
Crestfield Crs ELL HX5 ....164 A6
Crestfield Dr ELL HX5 ....164 A6

UD/ILL HX2 .....139 H6
stfield Rd ELL HX5 .....166 D6
st HI RTHW LS26 .....127 K2
st Hill Rd HUDN HD2 .....168 C8
st Rd PONT WF8 .....181 F5
st Rd HUDW HD3 .....167 F7
stville CI CLAY BD14 .....94 D6
stville Ter CLAY BD14 .....94 C6
stville Rd CLAY BD14 .....94 D6
stwood CI BOW BD4 .....119 J2
swell La DEWS WF13 .....145 J8
we Av KNOT WF11 .....155 J7
we Rd CAS WF10 .....154 D4
o La HFAX HX1 .....9 D3
Cricketers BULY LS4 .....78 B7
cketers Ap WKFDW/WTN WF2 .....149 F8
cketers CI FEA/AMT WF7 .....203 G6
FTH/SHER LS25 .....106 A5
cketers Fold AL/HA/HU LS17 .....59 G7
cketers Gn YEA LS19 .....53 K5
cketers Ter WOR/ARM LS12 .....100 C4
cketers Vw AL/HA/HU LS17 .....59 G7
cketers Wk AIRE BD20 .....27 F6
STN/BAR LS15 .....104 C4
cklegate MSTN/BAR LS15 .....103 K3
mble Bank MAR/SLWT HD7 .....210 E2
mble Clough Rd MAR/SLWT HD7 .....210 E1
mbles Ct PDSY/CALV LS28 .....98 D4
mbles CI PDSY/CALV LS28 .....98 D4
mbles Rd PDSY/CALV LS28 .....98 D4
mbles Ter PDSY/CALV LS28 .....98 D4
mea La HUDW HD3 .....188 B8
mple Gn GFTH/SHER LS25 .....106 B5
mshaw La SHPY BD18 .....73 K5
nsworth La HBR HX7 .....112 B3
han Ct NORM WF6 .....151 K7
ngles La AIRE BD20 .....17 G4
oplegate RHAY HX1 .....9 E4
dingley HOLM/MEL HD9 .....233 H3
dingley Farm Ct
HOLM/MEL HD9 .....233 H3
Croft BIRK/DRI BD11 .....121 H6
AS WF10 .....154 A5
ARD/LOFT WF3 .....147 J6
HEM/SK/SE WF9 .....203 K8
WOR/CROF WF4 .....219 F3
NOT WF11 .....156 D6
STN/BAR LS15 .....103 K2
THW LS26 .....127 F6
CFT LS14 .....60 B3
KP/WHF BD23 .....14 A6
TKB/PEN S36 .....252 E5
BY LS22 .....23 G6
ft Av BGLY BD16 .....49 H5
SLYN/ROY S71 .....221 K8
ARD/LOFT WF3 .....148 E4
NOT WF11 .....156 D6
ORM WF6 .....151 J8
ORM WF6 .....152 B8
T LS21 .....33 H2
DSY/CALV LS28 .....76 B8
ft Br RTHW LS26 .....127 F6
ft Chantry HEM/SK/SE WF9 .....224 A1
ft CI ILK LS29 .....32 B7
ft Ct HOLM/MEL HD9 .....213 F8
ORS LS18 .....77 F2
K * LS29 .....32 B7
ftdale Gv MSTN/BAR LS15 .....104 B1
ft Dr BSPA/BRAM LS23 .....42 D8
OLM/MEL HD9 .....212 E7
K LS29 .....32 C7
TKB/PEN S36 .....251 H8
ft End WBY LS22 .....23 G6
fters Gn IDLE BD10 .....74 C3
fters Lea YEA LS19 .....53 H4
ft Fld AIRE BD20 .....27 G3
ft Fold HIPP HX3 .....8 A1
ft Foulds Ct GFTH/SHER LS25 .....105 K4
ft Gdns HUDN HD2 .....12 A1
ft Head KBTN HD8 .....236 E1
ft Head La WKFDE WF1 .....177 H4
ft House Ct MOR LS27 .....123 G6
BSY BD6 .....118 C3
ft House CI PDSY/CALV * LS28 .....98 D4
ft House Dr MOR LS27 .....123 G6
T LS21 .....33 H2
ft House Fold ILK LS29 .....18 E3
ft House Gdns MOR LS27 .....123 G6
ft House Gv MOR LS27 .....123 G6
ft House La AIRE BD20 .....47 J1
UDW HD3 .....12 A5
OR LS27 .....123 G6
ft House Ms MOR LS27 .....123 G6
ft House Mt * MOR LS27 .....123 G5
ft House Ri MOR LS27 .....123 G5
ft House Rd HUDW HD3 .....188 B6
OR LS27 .....123 G6
BSY BD6 .....118 C3
ft House Vw MOR LS27 .....123 G6
ft House Vs MOR LS27 .....123 G5
ft House Wy MOR LS27 .....123 G5
ftlands BTLY WF17 .....146 E8
UDS HD4 .....213 G1
LE BD10 .....74 C3
NOT WF11 .....156 D6
ft La BSPA/BRAM LS23 .....25 K7
D LS24 .....43 K5
ton CI MAR/SLWT HD7 .....211 H3

Crofton Ri AL/HA/HU LS17 .....59 J7
Crofton Rd HTON BD9 .....73 G8
Crofton Ter AL/HA/HU LS17 .....59 J7
Croft Pk ILK LS29 .....32 B7
Croft PI BRIG HD6 .....142 C7
Croft Ri HIPP HX3 .....8 A1
ILK LS29 .....32 C7
Croft St AIRE BD20 .....49 H3
BSPA/BRAM LS23 .....42 C8
The Crofts AIRE BD20 .....26 A2
Croft's Ct LDS LS1 .....7 D5
Croftside CI SCFT LS14 .....81 K8
BTLY WF17 .....145 J7
KBTN HD8 .....217 G4
Croft St AIRE BD20 .....26 E6
BIRK/DRI BD11 .....120 D6
BRIG HD6 .....168 B1
DEWS WF13 .....172 B3
HBR * HX7 .....112 B8
HECK WF16 .....145 G8
HUDN HD3 .....190 C6
HWTH BD22 .....68 E4
IDLE BD10 .....74 E3
KGHY BD21 .....2 C4
OT LS21 .....33 K4
PDSY/CALV LS28 .....98 B8
RPDN/SBR * HX6 .....139 F7
SHPY BD18 .....73 H4
WBOW BD5 .....4 C5
WBSY BD6 .....118 D2
Croft Wy ILK LS29 .....32 C7
Croftway MSTN/BAR LS15 .....83 J4
Croisdale CI LVSG WF15 .....144 B7
Cromack Vw PDSY/CALV LS28 .....98 A4
Cromarty Av HUDS HD4 .....212 C5
Cromarty Dr HUDS HD4 .....212 C5
Cromer Av KGHY BD21 .....2 C5
Cromer Gv KGHY BD21 .....2 C5
Cromer PI LDSU LS2 .....6 C1
Cromer Rd KGHY BD21 .....2 C5
Cromer St CUD/GR S72 .....240 A4
HFAX * HX1 .....8 A6
KGHY BD21 .....2 C5
LDSU LS2 .....6 C2
Cromer Ter LDSU LS2 .....6 C2
Crompton Dr MOR LS27 .....122 E5
Cromwell Bottom Dr BRIG * HD6 .....142 B7
Cromwell CI HIPP HX3 .....141 F7
KNOT WF11 .....156 A3
Cromwell Ct BGLY BD16 .....72 B7
BIRK/DRI BD11 .....121 G6
Cromwell Crs PONT WF8 .....181 F5
Cromwell Hts OSM * LS9 .....102 A2
Cromwell Ms OSM * LS9 .....102 A2
Cromwell Mt HID LS10 .....124 E3
OSM LS9 .....102 A2
Cromwell PI OSS WF5 .....173 J4
Cromwell Rd GFTH/SHER LS25 .....129 F5
CAS WF10 .....154 D4
HIPP HX3 .....141 F7
Cromwell St OSM LS9 .....102 A3
Cromwell Ter HFAX HX1 .....8 C4
Crooked La HIPP HX3 .....116 A5
IDLE BD10 .....74 B2
Crooke La WIL/AL BD15 .....71 G7
Cropper Ga LDS * LS1 .....6 C3
Cropredy CI CUL/QBY BD13 .....116 E2
Cropstones BSPA/BRAM LS23 .....62 D1
Cropton Rd BSLYN/ROY S71 .....221 K8
Crosby Av BEE/HOL LS11 .....101 F7
Crosby PI BEE/HOL LS11 .....6 C6
Crosby Rd BEE/HOL LS11 .....6 C6
Crosby St BEE/HOL LS11 .....6 B6
KGHY BD21 .....2 C2
Crosby Ter BEE/HOL LS11 .....6 C6
Crosby Vw BEE/HOL LS11 .....6 C6
Croscombe Wk WBOW BD5 .....4 C6
Croset Av HUDE HUDE 13 E3
Crosland Ct HUDW HD3 .....189 G2
Crosland Factory La HUDS HD4 .....212 A6
Crosland Hill Rd HUDS HD4 .....190 B8
Crosland Rd HUD HD1 .....189 A1
HUDW HD3 .....189 G1
Crosland Spring Rd HUDS HD4 .....12 A6
Crosland St HUDS HD4 .....12 A6
Crosley Vw BGLY BD16 .....72 B1
Crosley Wood Rd BGLY BD16 .....72 B1
The Cross MSTN/BAR LS15 .....83 J4
Cross Albert PI WOR/ARM LS12 .....100 D5
Cross Alcester Rd RHAY LS8 .....80 B7
Cross Alma St OSM * LS9 .....102 A2
Cross Ar LDS * LS1 .....7 E3
Cross Aston Gv BRAM LS13 .....99 J1
Cross Av RTHW LS26 .....126 C4
Cross Bank Rd BTLY WF17 .....146 A5
Cross Banks SHPY BD18 .....73 H4
Cross Bank St MIRF WF14 .....170 D8
Cross Bath Rd BRAM LS13 .....99 G1
Crossbeck Ct ILK LS29 .....20 B8
Crossbeck Rd ILK LS29 .....20 B8
Cross Beck Rd RHAY * LS8 .....80 B7
Cross Belgrave St LDSU LS2 .....7 E3
Cross Bellbrooke Av OSM LS9 .....102 D1
Cross Bell St OSM * LS9 .....7 F3
Cross Bentley La HDGY LS6 .....79 F5
Cross Burley Lodge Rd HDGY LS6 .....6 A1
Cross Cardigan Mt BULY LS4 .....100 C3
Cross Cardigan Ter BULY LS4 .....100 C2

Cross Catherine St OSM LS9 .....102 A4
Cross Chancellor St HDGY LS6 .....79 H8
Cross Chapel St HDGY LS6 .....78 D6
Cross Church St HUD * HD1 .....13 D4
HUD HD1 .....190 D6
Cross Cliff Rd HDGY LS6 .....79 F7
Cross Cottages HUD HD1 .....190 D4
Cross Crown St CLECK BD19 .....144 A4
Crossdale Av WBSY BD6 .....117 J3
Cross Dawlish Gv OSM LS9 .....102 D3
Cross Dikes Rd RPDN/SBR HX6 .....163 H4
Cross Easy Rd OSM * LS9 .....102 B5
Cross Elford St RHAY * LS8 .....80 B8
Cross Emily St KGHY * BD21 .....3 D2
Cross End Fold ILK LS29 .....18 E3
Cross Ends La HBR HX7 .....89 G7
Cross Eric St BRAM LS13 .....77 G6
Cross Evanston Av BULY LS4 .....100 C1
Cross Farm Ct HWTH BD22 .....68 C8
Cross Fld GTL/HWG HX4 .....165 K7
Crossfield Ct HWTH BD22 .....68 D8
Crossfield St HOR/CROF WF4 .....195 K5
Crossfield St HWTH BD22 .....68 D8
Cross Flds HUDS HD5 .....192 A4
Cross Flatst LDSU LS2 .....79 G8
Cross Firs St HUDW HD3 .....190 B6
Cross Flatts BEE/HOL LS11 .....101 G6
Cross Flatts Av BEE/HOL LS11 .....124 B1
Cross Flatts Crs BEE/HOL LS11 .....124 B1
Cross Flatts Dr BEE/HOL LS11 .....101 F8
Cross Flatts Gv BEE/HOL LS11 .....124 B1
Cross Flatts Mt BEE/HOL LS11 .....124 B1
Cross Flatts Pde BEE/HOL LS11 .....124 A1
Cross Flatts PI BEE/HOL LS11 .....124 A1
Cross Flatts Rd BEE/HOL LS11 .....124 A1
Cross Flatts Rw BEE/HOL LS11 .....124 A1
Cross Flatts St BEE/HOL LS11 .....124 A1
Cross Flatts Ter BEE/HOL LS11 .....124 A1
Cross Foundry St DEWS * WF13 .....171 H6
Cross Francis St CHAL LS7 .....79 K8
Crossgate OT LS21 .....33 J4
Cross Gate Rd HOLM/MEL HD9 .....248 C1
Cross Gates Av MSTN/BAR LS15 .....82 A8
Cross Gates La BGLY BD16 .....49 G8
MSTN/BAR LS15 .....81 K8
Cross Gates Rd MSTN/BAR LS15 .....103 J1
Cross Glen Rd BHP/TINH LS16 .....78 C4
Cross Granby Ter HDGY * LS6 .....78 D6
Cross Grange Av RHAY LS8 .....80 A8
Cross Grasmere St WOR/ARM LS12 .....100 D4
Cross Gn OT LS21 .....33 K3
Cross Green Ap OSM * LS9 .....102 C6
Cross Green Av OSM LS9 .....102 B5
Cross Green CI OSM LS9 .....102 C6
Cross Green Ct OSM LS9 .....102 C6
Cross Green Crs OSM LS9 .....102 B5
Cross Green Dr OSM LS9 .....102 C6
Cross Green Garth OSM LS9 .....102 C6
Cross Green Gv OSM LS9 .....102 C6
Cross Green La MSTN/BAR LS15 .....103 K3
OSM LS9 .....102 B5
Cross Green Ri OSM LS9 .....102 C6
Cross Green Rd HUDE HUD5 .....192 C5
OSM LS9 .....102 B5
Cross Green Rw HDGY LS6 .....78 E4
Cross Green V OSM LS9 .....102 C7
Cross Green Wy OSM LS9 .....102 C6
Cross Grove St HUD HD1 .....12 C5
Cross Hands La HOR/CROF WF4 .....202 B5
Cross Hartley Av HDGY LS6 .....79 G7
Cross Heath Gv BEE/HOL LS11 .....100 E8
Cross Henley Rd BRAM LS13 .....99 G1
Cross HI CUD/GR S72 .....223 K8
GTL/HWG HX4 .....166 B4
HEM/SK/SE WF9 .....224 D4
HFAX * HX1 .....9 D3
KNOT WF11 .....156 D6
Cross Hill La LVSG WF15 .....169 J2
Cross Hills GFTH/SHER LS25 .....129 F2
HFAX HX1 .....9 D3
Cross Hills Dr GFTH/SHER LS25 .....129 F2
Crosshills Mt GTL/HWG HX4 .....166 B4
Cross Hilton Gv RHAY LS8 .....80 B7
Cross House Ct LM/WK * BD12 .....119 H7
Cross Ingledew Crs RHAY LS8 .....80 D1
Cross Ingram Rd BEE/HOL LS11 .....6 B6
The Crossings BTLY WF17 .....145 J3
Cross Ivy Mt OSM LS9 .....102 C3
Cross Kelso Rd LDSU LS2 .....6 B2
Cross Keys OSS WF5 .....174 B4
Cross Keys HOR/CROF WF4 .....197 H2
Crossland Ct BEE/HOL * LS11 .....6 C6
Crossland Rd MOR LS27 .....123 G4
Crossland Ter BEE/HOL LS11 .....101 J8
Cross La BGLY BD16 .....49 G8
BIRK/DRI BD11 .....120 E4
BRIG HD6 .....169 F2
BSLYN/ROY S71 .....222 C8
CUL/QBY BD13 .....116 B3
GULS HD5 .....166 D5
GSLY LS20 .....33 H8
GTHN BD7 .....95 G8
HIPP HX3 .....117 F5
HIPP HX3 .....117 G7
HOLM/MEL HD9 .....232 E1
HOLM/MEL HD9 .....248 D1
HUDS HD4 .....191 G8
HUDS HD4 .....234 E1

HWTH BD22 ..... 68 E8
KBTN HD8 ..... 215 K6
KBTN HD8 ..... 217 H3
KBTN HD8 ..... 235 G5
KBTN HD8 ..... 236 E2
STKB/PEN S36 ..... 252 E3
TOD OL14 ..... 134 E7
WIL/AL BD15 ..... 71 J4
WKFDW/WTN WF2 ..... 175 G6
WOR/ARM LS12 ..... 99 J6
WOR/ARM LS12 ..... 100 B4
Cross Lea Farm Rd KSTL LS5 ..... 77 K4
Cross Lee TOD OL14 ..... 133 J4
Cross Leeds St KGHY BD21 ..... 2 C5
Cross Lee Ga TOD OL14 ..... 133 J4
Cross Lee Rd TOD OL14 ..... 133 J4
Crossley Cl MIRF WF14 ..... 170 D3
Crossley Gdns HFAX * HX1 ..... 8 B3
Crossley Gv MIRF WF14 ..... 170 D3
Crossley Hall Ms GIR BD8 ..... 94 E4
Crossley Hall St GIR BD8 ..... 94 D4
Crossley Hl HUDE HD5 ..... 140 C8
Crossley La HUDE HD5 ..... 192 C4
MIRF WF14 ..... 170 D3
Crossley New Rd TOD OL14 ..... 134 D3
Crossley St BRIG HD6 ..... 168 C2
CUL/QBY BD13 ..... 116 C2
FEA/AMT WF7 ..... 179 J6
GTHN BD7 ..... 95 H6
HFAX HX1 ..... 9 D4
TOD OL14 ..... 134 A6
WBY LS22 ..... 23 J6
WKFDE WF1 ..... 177 J5
Crossley Ter BTLY WF17 ..... 146 B8
Crossley Ter North LUD/ILL HX2 ..... 115 K7
Crossley Ter South LUD/ILL HX2 ..... 115 K7
Crossley Vw MIRF WF14 ..... 170 E3
Cross Lidgett Pl RHAY LS8 ..... 80 B3
Cross Louis St CHAL LS7 ..... 79 K8
Crossman Dr NORM WF6 ..... 152 B8
Cross Maude St LDSU * LS2 ..... 7 F4
Cross Milan Rd RHAY LS8 ..... 80 C8
Crossmoor Cl AIRE BD20 ..... 26 E2
Crossmount St BTLY WF17 ..... 146 B8
Cross Park Av CAS WF10 ..... 154 A4
Cross Park St BTLY WF17 ..... 146 C6
EARL WF12 ..... 172 E5
HOR/CROF WF4 ..... 197 G2
MSTN/BAR LS15 ..... 103 J3
Cross Peel St MOR LS27 ..... 123 G7
Cross Pipes Rd WKFDW/WTN WF2 ..... 175 F7
Cross Quarry St HDGY * LS6 ..... 79 G7
Cross Queen St NORM 177 K1
Cross Reginald Mt CHAL * LS7 ..... 79 K7
Cross Rink St BTLY WF17 ..... 146 C8
Cross River St KGHY * BD21 ..... 3 F1
Cross Rd EARL WF12 ..... 195 G1
GIR BD8 ..... 95 H2
HOR/CROF WF4 ..... 196 B5
HOR/CROF WF4 ..... 198 B8
HORS LS18 ..... 76 E3
IDLE BD10 ..... 74 E3
LM/WK BD12 ..... 119 G6
Cross Roseville Rd RHAY * LS8 ..... 80 A3
Cross Rosse St SHPY * BD18 ..... 73 H3
Cross Roundhay Av RHAY LS8 ..... 80 B6
Cross Rydal St KGHY * BD21 ..... 2 B4
Cross Ryecroft St OSS WF5 ..... 173 J5
Cross St Michael's La KSTL * LS6 ..... 78 D7
Cross Speedwell St HDGY LS6 ..... 79 H8
Cross Sq WKFDE WF1 ..... 10 C3
Cross Stone Rd TOD * OL14 ..... 134 B8
Cross St BRIG HD6 ..... 142 B7
BTLY WF17 ..... 146 B6
CAS WF10 ..... 153 H3
CLAY BD14 ..... 94 C7
CUD/GR S72 ..... 240 B5
DOD/DAR S75 ..... 259 K7
EARD/LOFT WF3 ..... 149 F3
EARL WF12 ..... 172 C4
GTL/HWG HX4 ..... 166 A7
HEM/SK/SE WF9 ..... 224 C4
HEM/SK/SE WF9 ..... 227 J3
HFAX HX1 ..... 9 D3
HOLM/MEL HD9 ..... 213 H5
HOR/CROF WF4 ..... 197 H2
LM/WK BD12 ..... 119 H2
LVSG WF15 ..... 170 D1
MAR/SLWT HD7 ..... 210 E2
MSTN/BAR LS15 ..... 103 J3
OSS WF5 ..... 173 H2
PONT * WF8 ..... 180 E3
RTHW LS26 ..... 126 B6
WBSY * BD6 ..... 118 A4
WBY LS22 ..... 23 J6
WKFDE WF1 ..... 10 C3
Cross St West LUD/ILL * HX2 ..... 139 H3
Cross Sun St BFD BD1 ..... 5 D3
Cross Union St LDSU * LS2 ..... 7 F3
Cross Valley Dr MSTN/BAR LS15 ..... 103 J2
Crossway ED/DAR S75 ..... 71 K4
The Crossways OT LS21 ..... 33 J1
Cross Wells Rd RPDN/SBR HX6 ..... 163 J6
Cross Westfield Rd BVRD * LS3 ..... 6 B2
Cross Wingham St CHAL * LS7 ..... 7 F1
Cross York St LDSU LS2 ..... 7 F4
Crowgill Rd SHPY BD18 ..... 73 H3

Crow Hill End Rd RPDN/SBR HX6 ..... 163 G1
Crow Hill Rd HBR * HX7 ..... 137 G8
Crow La HUDW HD3 ..... 190 A7
OT LS21 ..... 33 J4
Crowlees Cl MIRF WF14 ..... 170 E6
Crowlees Gdns MIRF WF14 ..... 170 E6
Crowlees Rd MIRF WF14 ..... 170 D6
Crown & Anchor Yd PONT * WF8 ..... 180 D3
Crown Cl EARL WF12 ..... 173 F4
Crown Dr LM/WK BD12 ..... 118 D7
Crow Nest La BEE/HOL LS11 ..... 123 J1
Crow Nest La BGLY BD16 ..... 50 A7
Crow Nest Pk DEWS * WF13 ..... 171 K4
Crownest Rd BGLY BD16 ..... 50 A8
Crow Nest Rd HBR HX7 ..... 136 C1
Crow Nest Vw DEWS WF13 ..... 171 K4
Crown Flatt Wy EARL WF12 ..... 172 D2
Crown Gn HUDS HD4 ..... 190 A7
Crownlands La OSS WF5 ..... 173 J5
Crown La HOLM/MEL HD9 ..... 233 G6
Crown Point Cl OSS WF5 ..... 173 H5
Crown Point Dr OSS WF5 ..... 173 H5
Crown Point Rd MID LS10 ..... 7 F5
OSS WF5 ..... 173 H5
Crown Rd HIPP HX3 ..... 8 C1
Crown St BFD BD1 ..... 5 D5
BRIG HD6 ..... 142 B8
CLECK BD19 ..... 144 A4
ELL HX5 ..... 166 E5
HBR HX7 ..... 112 B8
HFAX HX1 ..... 9 D4
HOLM/MEL HD9 ..... 213 H6
ILK LS29 ..... 32 B2
KBTN HD8 ..... 237 H2
LDS LS1 ..... 13 E4
LM/WK BD12 ..... 118 D7
LVSG WF15 ..... 144 E7
OSS WF5 ..... 173 K8
Crown Yd HEM/SK/SE WF9 ..... 225 K8
Crowther Av MAR/SLWT HD7 ..... 210 E1
Crowther Cl MAR/SLWT HD7 ..... 210 E1
Crowther Fold BGLY BD16 ..... 71 F2
Crowther Pl CAS WF10 ..... 153 J4
HDGY LS6 ..... 79 H8
Crowther Rd HECK WF16 ..... 145 H6
MIRF WF14 ..... 170 D6
Crowther St BTLY WF17 ..... 145 J6
CAS WF10 ..... 153 H4
CLECK BD19 ..... 144 A4
HUD * HD1 ..... 13 D5
HUD * HD1 ..... 191 F8
IDLE BD10 ..... 75 F4
LM/WK BD12 ..... 118 D7
Crowther Wk WBOW * BD5 ..... 4 C5
Crow Tree Cl BAIL BD17 ..... 51 K8
Crow Tree La GIR BD8 ..... 94 E2
Crowtrees Ct YEA LS19 ..... 53 K8
Crowtrees Crs BRIG HD6 ..... 168 A3
Crowtrees La BRIG HD6 ..... 167 K5
Crowtrees Pk BRIG HD6 ..... 168 A4
Crow Trees Pk YEA LS19 ..... 53 K7
Crow Trees Rd MAR/SLWT HD7 ..... 209 K5
Crow Wood La GTL/HWG HX4 ..... 188 A3
Crow Wood Pk LUD/ILL HX2 ..... 139 G6
Croxall Dr EARD/LOFT WF3 ..... 150 B6
Croydon Rd GTHN BD7 ..... 95 F7
Croydon St BEE/HOL LS11 ..... 6 B5
Crumack La HWTH BD22 ..... 69 G8
Crystal Ct HFAX * HX1 ..... 8 B4
Crystal Pl WKFDE * WF1 ..... 11 D3
Crystal Ter BOW BD4 ..... 96 E8
Cubley Av WKFDW/WTN WF2 ..... 198 D5
Cuckoo La HOLM/MEL HD9 ..... 213 F7
Cuckstool Rd KBTN HD8 ..... 236 E5
Cudworth Vw CUD/GR S72 ..... 240 A5
Culers Wy HBR HX7 ..... 137 H7
Culver St HFAX HX1 ..... 9 D4
Cumberland Av HUDN HD2 ..... 168 B6
Cumberland Cl LUD/ILL HX2 ..... 115 H7
Cumberland Ct HDGY LS6 ..... 78 D8
Cumberland Rd CAS WF10 ..... 155 F1
GTHN BD7 ..... 95 G6
HDGY LS6 ..... 79 F7
Cumberworth La KBTN HD8 ..... 235 G6
KBTN HD8 ..... 236 B4
Cumberworth Rd KBTN HD8 ..... 236 D2
Cumbrian Wy WKFDW/WTN WF2 ..... 197 K1
Cunliffe La BAIL BD17 ..... 52 D6
Cunliffe Rd GIR BD8 ..... 4 A1
ILK LS29 ..... 20 B7
Cunliffe Ter GIR BD8 ..... 73 K8
Cunliffe Vls HTON BD9 ..... 73 K8
Cure Hl HWTH BD22 ..... 46 D8
Curlew Cl WEA WF10 ..... 153 J5
ILK LS29 ..... 19 J7
Curlew Ct AIRE BD20 ..... 26 C5
Curlew Ri MOR LS27 ..... 123 J8
Curlew St WBOW BD5 ..... 95 J4
Curly Hl ILK LS29 ..... 20 B5
Currer Av BOW BD4 ..... 119 J2
Currer St BFD BD1 ..... 5 D4
Currer Wk AIRE BD20 ..... 26 D5
Curtis Ct CUL/QBY * BD13 ..... 70 B5
Curwen Crs HECK WF16 ..... 145 G6
Curzon Rd BFDE BD3 ..... 5 F1
Curzon St HUDN HD2 ..... 169 H6
Cuthberts Cl CUL/QBY BD13 ..... 116 C3

Cutler Heights La BOW BD4 ..... 96 ...
Cutler La RTHW LS26 ..... 128 ...
Cutler Pl BOW BD4 ..... 97 ...
Cut Rd KNOT WF11 ..... 131 ...
KNOT WF11 ..... 155 ...
Cutsyke Av CAS WF10 ..... 153 ...
Cutsyke Crest CAS WF10 ..... 153 ...
Cutsyke Rd CAS WF10 ..... 153 ...
Cuttlehurst KBTN HD8 ..... 237 ...
Cutts Field Vw BSLYN/ROY * S71 ..... 221 ...
Cypress Fold KBTN HD8 ..... 199 ...
Cypress Rd NORM WF6 ..... 179 ...
Cyprus Av IDLE BD10 ..... 74 ...
WKFDE WF1 ..... 10 ...
Cyprus Crs MIRF WF14 ..... 171 ...
Cyprus Dr IDLE BD10 ..... 74 ...
Cyprus Gv GFTH/SHER LS25 ..... 105 ...
WKFDE WF1 ..... 10 ...
Cyprus Mt WKFDE WF1 ..... 10 ...
Cyprus Rd GFTH/SHER LS25 ..... 105 ...
Cyprus St OSS WF5 ..... 173 ...
WKFDE WF1 ..... 10 ...
Cyprus Ter GFTH/SHER LS25 ..... 105 ...

D

Dacre Av WKFDW/WTN WF2 ..... 174 ...
Dacre Cl LVSG WF15 ..... 144 ...
Daffels Wood Cl BOW BD4 ..... 119 ...
Daffil Av MOR LS27 ..... 123 ...
Daffil Grange Ms MOR * LS27 ..... 123 ...
Daffil Grange Wy MOR LS27 ..... 123 ...
Daffil Gv MOR LS27 ..... 123 ...
Daffil Rd MOR LS27 ..... 123 ...
Daffodil Cl WIL/AL BD15 ..... 94 ...
Dagenham Rd BOW BD4 ..... 96 ...
The Dairies NORM * WF6 ..... 152 ...
Daisy Bank HFAX HX1 ..... 8 ...
Daisy Bank St TOD OL14 ..... 132 ...
Daisy Cl BTLY WF17 ..... 146 ...
Daisy Cft AIRE BD20 ..... 27 ...
Daisyfield Rd BRAM * LS13 ..... 99 ...
Daisy Fold HEM/SK/SE WF9 ..... 226 ...
Daisy Hl AIRE BD20 ..... 27 ...
EARL WF12 ..... 172 ...
LM/WK BD12 ..... 118 ...
MOR LS27 ..... 123 ...
Daisy Hill Av MOR LS27 ..... 123 ...
Daisy Hill Back La HTON BD9 ..... 94 ...
Daisy Hill Cl MOR * LS27 ..... 123 ...
Daisy Hill Gv HTON BD9 ..... 94 ...
Daisy Hill La HTON BD9 ..... 94 ...
Daisy Lea La HUDW HD3 ..... 190 ...
Daisy Lea La HOLM/MEL HD9 ..... 248 ...
Daisy Mt RPDN/SBR HX6 ..... 136 ...
Daisy Rd BRIG HD6 ..... 168 ...
Daisy Royd HUDS HD4 ..... 213 ...
Daisy St BRIG HD6 ..... 168 ...
GTHN BD7 ..... 95 ...
HFAX HX1 ..... 8 ...
HWTH BD22 ..... 65 ...
Daisy Vale Ms EARD/LOFT WF3 ..... 149 ...
Daisy Vale Ter EARD/LOFT WF3 ..... 149 ...
Dalby Av BFDE BD3 ..... 97 ...
Dalby St BFDE * BD3 ..... 97 ...
Dalcross Gv WBOW BD5 ..... 96 ...
Dalcross St WBOW BD5 ..... 96 ...
The Dale GFTH/SHER LS25 ..... 84 ...
Dale Av TOD OL14 ..... 134 ...
Dale Cl BTLY WF17 ..... 172 ...
GSLY LS20 ..... 59 ...
KBTN HD8 ..... 236 ...
OSS WF5 ..... 173 ...
Dale Ct HOLM/MEL HD9 ..... 233 ...
OSS * WF5 ..... 9 ...
PONT WF8 ..... 180 ...
Dalecourt ILK * LS29 ..... 20 ...
Dale Crs AIRE BD20 ..... 26 ...
Dale Cft GFTH/SHER LS25 ..... 105 ...
ILK LS29 ..... 19 ...
KBTN HD8 ..... 236 ...
Dale Croft Ri WIL/AL BD15 ..... 94 ...
Dalefield Av NORM WF6 ..... 178 ...
Dalefield Rd NORM WF6 ..... 178 ...
Dalefield Wy NORM WF6 ..... 178 ...
Dale Garth BAIL BD17 ..... 52 ...
Dale Gv SHPY BD18 ..... 74 ...
Dale La HECK WF16 ..... 145 ...
HEM/SK/SE WF9 ..... 226 ...
Dale Ms PONT WF8 ..... 181 ...
Dale Park Av BHP/TINH LS16 ..... 58 ...
Dale Park Cl BHP/TINH LS16 ..... 57 ...
Dale Park Gdns BHP/TINH LS16 ..... 57 ...
Dale Park Ri BHP/TINH LS16 ..... 57 ...
Dale Park Wk BHP/TINH LS16 ..... 57 ...
Dale Rd BIRK/DRI BD11 ..... 121 ...
Dales Dr GSLY LS20 ..... 59 ...
Daleside EARL WF12 ..... 191 ...
GTL/HWG HX4 ..... 165 ...
TOD OL14 ..... 131 ...
Daleside Av HOLM/MEL HD9 ..... 233 ...
PDSY/CALV LS28 ..... 99 ...
Daleside Cl PDSY/CALV LS28 ..... 99 ...
Daleside Gv LM/WK BD12 ..... 11 ...
PDSY/CALV LS28 ..... 99 ...
Daleside Rd AIRE BD20 ..... 4 ...
BFDE BD3 ..... 9 ...

HPY BD18	...74 A2	
eside Wk WBOW BD5	...119 G1	
eson Cl HIPP HX3	...117 F8	
e Stone Cl KNOT * WF11	...155 K2	
e St BFD BD1	...4 C4	
UDW HD5	...190 A6	
GHY BD21	...3 F1	
SS WF5	...173 J5	
HX6	...138 E7	
HPY BD18	...73 H4	
DD OL14	...134 A6	
sway BGLY BD16	...50 B6	
es Wy BHP/TINH LS16	...56 E5	
HP/TINH LS16	...36 A8	
HP/TINH LS16	...56 E6	
DGY LS6	...78 E4	
T LS27	...34 D7	
e Vw AIRE BD20	...26 E6	
RE BD20	...27 G1	
EM/SK/SE WF9	...225 F5	
K LS29	...19 J7	
ONT WF8	...180 E6	
e View Cl KGHY BD21	...3 F4	
eview Ct BAIL BD17	...73 C1	
e View Gv KGHY BD21	...3 F4	
e View Rd KGHY BD21	...3 F5	
am Av SHPY BD18	...72 E3	
am Rd SHPY BD18	...72 E3	
am Wk SHPY BD18	...73 F5	
meny Av HUDS HD4	...212 C1	
meny Cl HUDS HD4	...190 C8	
meny Ter BRAM * LS13	...76 C6	
ton Av BEE/HOL LS11	...124 B1	
ton Bank Rd HUDE HD5	...192 C2	
ton Clowes HUDE HD5	...192 A4	
ton Fold HUDE HD5	...13 F1	
ton Green La HUDE HD5	...192 B5	
JDE HD5	...192 A4	
ton La BSPA/BRAM LS23	...61 J1	
GHY BD21	...3 E5	
ton Rd BEE/HOL LS11	...124 B1	
GHY BD21	...3 F5	
ton St RPDN/SBR HX6	...138 E6	
ton Ter CAS WF10	...153 J4	
R BD8	...95 H3	
GHY BD21	...3 F2	
hems La HWTH BD22	...69 H1	
hems Rd HWTH BD22	...47 J8	
hes La HWTH BD22	...69 J1	
h Head La HUDE HD5	...193 H5	
h Head Rd RPDN/SBR HX6	...139 F6	
HI KBTN HD8	...215 F8	
la YEA LS19	...54 A4	
ton Av IDLE BD10	...75 C7	
apier St TOD OL14	...159 K2	
aside KGHY BD21	...2 C4	
aside HUDS HD4	...13 D6	
son Ct CLAY BD14	...94 C8	
by Av BOW BD4	...119 J3	
by La HWTH BD22	...198 E7	
by Vw OSM LS9	...102 B4	
dy Mill Av PONT WF8	...181 G1	
dy Mill Cl PONT WF8	...181 G1	
dy Mill Vw PONT WF8	...181 G1	
ebury Rd BRIG HD6	...168 C2	
ecourt Rd BOW BD4	...97 C8	
efield Ter OT LS21	...33 K3	
e Hill Dr BOW BD4	...97 C7	
ella Crs WKFDW/WTN WF2	...175 G1	
ella Gv WKFDW/WTN WF2	...175 G1	
es La HOR/CROF WF4	...196 B5	
esleigh Dr HOR/CROF WF4	...196 B5	
iel Ct BOW BD4	...120 C1	
La CUL/QBY BD13	...117 H2	
ny La LUD/ILL HX2	...138 A4	
sk Wy ILK LS29	...20 D6	
um Dr BAIL BD17	...73 J1	
ey Hey La LUD/ILL HX2	...139 H6	
iield Av RHAY LS8	...80 C4	
iield Crs RHAY LS8	...80 C8	
iield Pl RHAY LS8	...80 C8	
iield Rd RHAY LS8	...80 C8	
iield St GIR BD8	...4 A3	
HAY LS8	...80 C8	
field La BTLY WF17	...121 J8	
LY WF17	...146 A7	
3R HX7	...111 H8	
DE HD5	...192 C8	
VTH BD22	...68 B2	
VTH BD22	...68 E8	
D/ILL HX2	...138 E5	
NT WF8	...180 D4	
wood Cl AL/HA/HU LS17	...58 C7	
wood Wy AL/HA/HU LS17	...58 C7	
ey Av MID LS10	...124 E4	
ey Rd LVSG WF15	...144 C6	
ey St BFD BD1	...4 C4	
ICK WF16	...145 C7	
HY BD21	...2 C1	
es Av LUD/ILL HX2	...139 H6	
ing La PONT WF8	...204 D6	

Darnley Av *WKFDW/WTN* WF2	...10 A2
Darnley Cl *HOLM/MEL* HD9	...231 J2
Darnley La *MSTN/BAR* LS15	...104 A4
Darren St *BOW* BD4	...97 G5
Darrington Rd *PONT* WF8	...204 A1
Darryl Dr *LUD/ILL* HX2	...139 H6
Dartmouth Av *HUDE* HD5	...192 C8
MOR LS27	...147 F1
Dartmouth Ms *MOR* LS27	...122 E8
Dartmouth Ter *GIR* BD8	...4 A1
Dartmouth Wy *BEE/HOL* LS11	...101 J8
Darton Rd *DOD/DAR* S75	...239 F6
Darwin St *WBOW* BD5	...95 J8
Davey La *HBR* HX7	...110 E8
David La *DEWS* WF13	...172 B1
David St *BEE/HOL* LS11	...7 D5
CAS WF10	...153 G4
WKFDE * WF1	...11 E5
Davies Av *CAS* WF10	...154 E5
Davis Av *CAS* WF10	...154 E5
Dawes Av *CAS* WF10	...154 E5
Daw Green Av *HOR/CROF* WF4	...198 A7
Daw La *HOR/CROF* WF4	...197 J3
HOR/CROF WF4	...197 K8
Dawlish Av *OSM* LS9	...102 D3
Dawlish Crs *OSM* LS9	...102 C3
Dawlish Gv *OSM* LS9	...102 D3
Dawlish Mt *OSM* LS9	...102 D3
Dawlish Pl *OSM* LS9	...102 D3
Dawlish Rd *OSM* LS9	...102 D3
Dawlish Rw *OSM* LS9	...102 D3
Dawlish St *OSM* LS9	...102 D3
Dawlish Ter *OSM* LS9	...102 D3
Dawnay Rd *WBOW* BD5	...95 J7
Daw Royds *HUDE* HD5	...192 C6
Dawson Av *WBSY* BD6	...118 D3
Dawson Hl *MOR* LS27	...123 F6
Dawson La *BOW* BD4	...119 K2
BOW BD4	...121 H1
Dawson Mt *BOW* BD4	...119 K2
Dawson Pl *BOW* BD4	...119 K2
KGHY BD21	...3 D5
Dawson Rd *BEE/HOL* LS11	...101 D8
HOLM/MEL HD9	...191 H8
KGHY BD21	...3 D5
Dawsons Meadow	
PDSY/CALV LS28	...98 A1
Dawson St *BOW* BD4	...119 K1
EARD/LOFT WF3	...147 J2
IDLE BD10	...74 D1
PDSY/CALV * LS28	...98 B2
Dawson Ter *BOW* BD4	...119 K2
Dawson Wy *KGHY* BD21	...3 D5
Dawtrie Cl *CAS* WF10	...154 E4
Dawtrie St *CAS* WF10	...154 E5
Daykin Cl *DOD/DAR* S75	...239 K3
Day St *DEWS* WF13	...171 H6
Deacon Cl *BFDE* * BD3	...97 F1
HOLM/MEL HD9	...231 J1
Deadmanstone *HUDS* HD4	...213 F3
Dealburn Rd *LM/WK* BD12	...118 E6
Deal St *HFAX* HX1	...9 E5
KGHY BD21	...3 F2
Dean Av *HOLM/MEL* HD9	...233 F3
RHAY LS8	...80 C5
Dean Beck Av *WBSY* BD6	...119 F3
Dean Beck Ct *WBSY* * BD6	...119 F3
Dean Bridge La *HOLM/MEL* HD9	...233 K8
Dean Brook Rd *HOLM/MEL* HD9	...233 F3
HUDS HD4	...212 E3
Dean Cl *GIR* BD8	...94 D2
WKFDW/WTN WF2	...175 C1
Dean Clough *HFAX* HX1	...9 G1
Dean Ct *HIPP* HX3	...165 K1
RHAY LS8	...80 C5
Dean Edge Rd *HWTH* BD22	...67 G3
Dean End *GTL/HWG* HX4	...166 C3
Deanery Gdns *IDLE* BD10	...74 E6
Deanfield Av *MOR* LS27	...122 E6
Dean Fold *KBTN* HD8	...215 F3
Dean Hall Cl *MOR* * LS27	...122 E7
Dean Head *HORS* LS18	...54 E3
LIT * OL15	...160 B8
Dean House La *GTL/HWG* HX4	...188 B3
LUD/ILL HX2	...138 A1
Deanhouse La *HOLM/MEL* HD9	...233 F3
Deanhurst Gdns *MOR* LS27	...122 C5
Dean La *CUL/QBY* BD13	...93 G2
GSLY LS20	...52 B3
HOLM/MEL HD9	...248 E1
HORS LS18	...54 E3
HWTH BD22	...46 B5
RPDN/SBR HX6	...164 B1
RPDN/SBR HX6	...164 B3
Dean Lane Head *CUL/QBY* BD13	...93 H2
Dean Park Av *BIRK/DRI* BD11	...121 F4
Dean Park Dr *BIRK/DRI* BD11	...121 H4
Dean Rd *HOLM/MEL* HD9	...232 D5
WBSY BD6	...118 E3
Deanroyd Rd *TOD* OL14	...160 A4
Deanstones Crs *CUL/QBY* BD13	...116 D3
Deanstones La *CUL/QBY* BD13	...116 D3
Dean St *GTL/HWG* HX4	...166 C4
HUDW HD3	...190 B4
HWTH BD22	...69 F4
ILK LS29	...20 C6
Deansway *MOR* LS27	...122 C5
Deanswood Cl *AL/HA/HU* LS17	...57 G8
Deanswood Dr *AL/HA/HU* LS17	...57 F8

Deanswood Gn *AL/HA/HU* LS17	...57 F8
Deanswood Hl *AL/HA/HU* LS17	...57 F8
Deanswood Pl *AL/HA/HU* LS17	...57 G8
Deanswood Ri *AL/HA/HU* LS17	...57 G8
Deanswood Vw *AL/HA/HU* LS17	...57 G8
Deanwood Av *WIL/AL* BD15	...94 A1
Deanwood Crs *WIL/AL* BD15	...94 A1
Deanwood Wk *WIL/AL* BD15	...94 A1
Dearden St *OSS* WF5	...173 J6
RPDN/SBR HX6	...138 E6
Dearne Cft *WBY* LS22	...23 J3
Dearne Dike La *KBTN* HD8	...235 G6
Dearne Fold *HUDW* HD3	...190 B2
Dearne Pk *KBTN* HD8	...237 J1
Dearne Royd *KBTN* HD8	...237 J1
Dearneside Rd *KBTN* HD8	...236 D6
Dearne St *HEM/SK/SE* WF9	...226 B8
Dearne Wy *DOD/DAR* S75	...219 J8
KBTN HD8	...217 J8
KBTN HD8	...235 J7
KBTN HD8	...237 G5
Dearnfield *KBTN* HD8	...236 A5
Dearnley St *DEWS* * WF13	...171 H5
Dee Ct *HWTH* BD22	...68 E1
Deep Dl *BSPA/BRAM* LS23	...42 C2
Deepdale Cl *BAIL* BD17	...73 C1
Deepdale La *BSPA/BRAM* LS23	...42 B2
Deep La *BRIG* HD6	...169 F1
CLAY BD14	...94 C6
CUL/QBY BD13	...92 E7
HUDS HD4	...190 B8
LUD/ILL HX2	...138 C4
RPDN/SBR HX6	...163 J5
Deer Croft Av *HUDW* HD3	...189 K3
Deer Croft Crs *HUDW* HD3	...189 K3
Deer Croft Rd *HUDW* HD3	...189 K2
Deer Hill Cl *MAR/SLWT* HD7	...209 H8
Deer Hill Ct *HOLM/MEL* HD9	...231 G1
Deer Hill Cft *MAR/SLWT* HD7	...209 H8
Deer Hill Dr *MAR/SLWT* HD7	...209 H8
Deer Hill End Rd *HOLM/MEL* HD9	...210 D8
Deershaw La *KBTN* HD8	...234 E6
Deershaw Sike La *KBTN* HD8	...234 E6
Deerstone Rdg *WBY* LS22	...23 J3
Defarge Ct *WBOW* BD5	...96 A3
Deffer Rd *WKFDW/WTN* WF2	...198 D5
Deganway Dr *HUDE* HD5	...192 E1
Deighton Cl *WBY* LS22	...23 K5
Deighton La *BTLY* WF17	...145 K6
Deighton Rd *HUDN* HD2	...168 E8
WBY LS22	...23 J3
De Lacey Ms *BOW* BD4	...119 J3
De Lacies Ct *RTHW* LS26	...126 D4
De Lacies Rd *RTHW* LS26	...126 D4
De Lacy Av *BOW* * BD4	...119 J3
FEA/AMT WF7	...179 H2
HUDE HD5	...192 B7
Delacy Crs *CAS* WF10	...154 E2
De Lacy Mt *KSTL* LS5	...78 A7
De Lacy Ter *PONT* WF8	...181 F5
Delamere St *WBOW* BD5	...118 E1
Delaware Ct *BOW* BD4	...119 J3
Delf Hl *BRIG* HD6	...167 K4
Delf La *HBR* HX7	...112 D3
TOD OL14	...109 G8
Delfs La *RPDN/SBR* HX6	...163 G3
Delius Av *IDLE* BD10	...75 F6
The Dell *AL/HA/HU* LS17	...40 B8
CAS WF10	...153 F6
CUL/QBY BD13	...70 C5
HUDN HD2	...168 C7
Dell Av *CUD/GR* S72	...240 A3
Dell Cft *AIRE* BD20	...26 E1
Dellside Fold *CUL/QBY* BD13	...70 B5
Delmont Cl *BTLY* WF17	...145 H5
The Delph *FEA/AMT* WF7	...180 A6
Delph Ct *HDGY* LS6	...79 G7
Delph Crs *CLAY* BD14	...94 B7
Delph Cv *KGHY* BD21	...3 E4
Delph Dr *CLAY* BD14	...94 A7
Delph Gv *CLAY* BD14	...94 B7
Delph Hl *BAIL* BD17	...51 J7
PDSY/CALV LS28	...98 C3
Delph Hill Castle *LUD/ILL* * HX2	...139 G5
Delph Hill La *LUD/ILL* HX2	...138 A1
Delph Hill Rd *LUD/ILL* HX2	...139 J7
Delph Hill Ter *LUD/ILL* HX2	...139 J7
Delph La *HUDS* HD4	...212 D4
Delph Mt *HDGY* LS6	...79 G7
Delph St *HFAX* HX1	...8 C5
Delph Ter *CLAY* BD14	...94 B7
Delph Vw *HDGY* LS6	...79 G8
Delph Wood Cl *BGLY* BD16	...50 C8
Delverne Gv *ECHL* BD2	...74 E8
Delves Ga *MAR/SLWT* HD7	...210 D5
Delves Wood Rd *HUDS* HD4	...212 C4
Denbigh Ap *OSM* LS9	...103 F1
Denbrook Av *BOW* BD4	...120 C3
Denbrook Cl *BOW* BD4	...120 C2
Denbrook Crs *BOW* BD4	...120 C2
Denbrook Wk *BOW* BD4	...120 C2
Denbrook Wy *BOW* BD4	...120 C2
Denbury Mt *BOW* BD4	...120 B1
Denby Cl *BTLY* WF17	...145 G2
LVSG WF15	...144 C6
Denby Ct *HWTH* BD22	...68 D2
Denby Crest *PONT* WF8	...181 K6
Denby Dale Rd *HOR/CROF* WF4	...218 C3
WKFDW/WTN WF2	...10 C4

Denby Dale Rd East
HOR/CROF WF4 ....198 A4
Denby Dale Rd West
HOR/CROF WF4 ....197 K5
Denby Dr *BAIL* BD17 ....73 H2
Denby Grange La *HOR/CROF* WF4 .....194 E6
Denby Hall La *KBTN* HD8 ....237 H6
Denby La *HOR/CROF* WF4 ....195 F5
KBTN HD8 ....236 B8
WIL/AL BD15 ....94 B2
Denby Mt *HWTH* BD22 ....90 E1
Denby Park Dr *HOR/CROF* WF4 ....194 C6
Denby Pl *RPDN/SBR* HX6 ....138 E6
Denby Rd *KGHY* BD21 ....5 D5
Denby St *GIR* BD8 ....181 K5
Denby Vw *EARL* WF12 ....4 A3
Dence Gn *BOW* * BD4 ....195 H2
Dence Pl *MSTN/BAR* LS15 ....97 G6
Dene House Ct *LDSU* LS2 ....103 C3
Dene Mt *WIL/AL* BD15 ....7 D1
Dene Pk *KBTN* HD8 ....94 C2
Dene Pl *HFAX* HX1 ....215 H4
Dene Rd *KBTN* HD8 ....8 C3
WBSY BD6 ....236 D2
Dene Royd Cl *GTL/HWG* HX4 ....117 J2
Dene Royd Ct *GTL/HWG* HX4 ....165 J8
Deneside *OSS* WF5 ....165 J8
Deneside Ter *WBOW* BD5 ....173 H4
Denesway *GFTH/SHER* LS25 ....118 D2
Dene Vw *LUD/ILL* HX2 ....106 A6
Denfield Av *HIPP* HX3 ....138 A3
Denfield Crs *HIPP* HX3 ....139 H1
Denfield Edge *HIPP* HX3 ....8 A1
Denfield Gdns *HIPP* HX3 ....8 A1
Denfield La *HIPP* HX3 ....8 A1
Denfield Sq *HIPP* HX3 ....139 H1
Denhale Av *MOR* LS27 ....8 A1
Denham Av *MOR* LS27 ....175 F5
Denham Dr *HOL/MEL* HD9 ....147 F1
Denham St *BRIG* HD6 ....233 F3
BTLY WF17 ....168 B2
Denholme Dr *OSS* WF5 ....145 K4
Denholme Gate Rd *HIPP* HX3 ....173 J4
Denholme Meadow
HEM/SK/SE WF9 ....141 H3
Denholme Rd *HWTH* BD22 ....226 B7
Denison Rd *BVRD* LS3 ....91 F2
Denison St *BTLY* WF17 ....6 C3
YEA LS19 ....146 B7
Denmark St *WKFDE* WF1 ....53 F7
Dennil Crs *MSTN/BAR* LS15 ....11 E5
Dennil Rd *MSTN/BAR* LS15 ....82 E7
Dennington La *HOR/CROF* WF4 ....82 B8
Dennis La *AIRE* BD20 ....197 J8
Dennison Fold *BOW* BD4 ....16 C8
Dennison Hl *OT* LS21 ....97 G6
Dennistead Crs *HDGY* LS6 ....33 K3
Denshaw Dr *MOR* LS27 ....78 D6
Denshaw Gv *MOR* LS27 ....123 J7
Denshaw La *EARD/LOFT* WF3 ....123 J7
Denstone St *WKFDE* WF1 ....123 K8
Dent Dr *WKFDE* WF1 ....11 D2
Denton Av *RHAY* LS8 ....11 F1
Denton Dr *BGLY* BD16 ....80 B3
Denton Gdns *FEA/AMT* WF7 ....50 C7
Denton Gv *RHAY* * LS8 ....203 G6
Denton Rd *ILK* LS29 ....80 B3
Denton Ter *CAS* WF10 ....20 A6
Denton St *OSM* LS9 ....153 K3
Denwell Ter *PONT* WF8 ....102 B4
Derby Pl *BFDE* * BD3 ....180 E2
Derby Rd *BFDE* BD3 ....97 F4
YEA LS19 ....97 G4
Derbyshire St *MID* LS10 ....53 K7
Derby St *CLAY* * BD14 ....102 B8
CUL/QBY BD13 ....94 B7
GTHN BD7 ....116 C2
RPDN/SBR HX6 ....95 H1
Derby Ter *MAR/SLWT* HD7 ....139 F6
Derdale St *TOD* OL14 ....209 H7
Derry Hl *ILK* LS29 ....134 B6
Derry Hill Gdns *ILK* LS29 ....32 B8
Derry La *ILK* LS29 ....32 B7
Dert St *TOD* OL14 ....32 B7
Derwent Av *GFTH/SHER* LS25 ....134 B6
RTHW LS26 ....105 K5
WIL/AL BD15 ....127 F5
Derwent Cl *HBR* HX7 ....71 G7
Derwent Dr *BHP/TINH* LS16 ....112 B7
CAS WF10 ....56 D7
HUDE HD5 ....155 F2
Derwent Gv *WKFDW/WTN* WF2 ....13 F4
KNOT WF11 ....175 G5
Derwent Pl *BEE/HOL* LS11 ....182 B1
Derwent Ri *WBY* LS22 ....6 C5
Derwent Rd *EARL* WF12 ....23 H3
ECHL BD2 ....146 E8
HOLM/MEL HD9 ....74 C8
....212 E8

HOLM/MEL HD9 ....231 J2
WKFDW/WTN WF2 ....175 G5
Derwent St *KGHY* BD21 ....3 F7
Derwentwater Gv *HDGY* LS6 ....78 C7
Derwentwater Ter *HDGY* LS6 ....78 C6
Derwin Av *HUDS* HD4 ....234 E1
De Trafford St *HUDS* HD4 ....190 D8
Detroit Av *MSTN/BAR* LS15 ....104 B3
Detroit Dr *MSTN/BAR* LS15 ....104 C3
Devon Cl *LDSU* * LS2 ....7 D1
....7 D1
Devonshire Av *RHAY* LS8 ....80 C1
Devonshire Cl *RHAY* LS8 ....80 C1
Devonshire Crs *RHAY* LS8 ....80 B2
Devonshire Gdns *LDSU* LS2 ....79 H8
Devonshire La *RHAY* LS8 ....80 C1
Devonshire St *HUDS* HD4 ....190 E8
KGHY BD21 ....2 C3
Devonshire St West *KGHY* BD21 ....2 B3
Devon St *HFAX* HX1 ....8 A5
Devon Wy *BRIG* HD6 ....142 C5
Dewar Cl *WBY* LS22 ....40 E3
Dewhirst Cl *BAIL* BD17 ....73 K1
Dewhirst Pl *BOW* BD4 ....97 F5
Dewhirst Rd *BAIL* BD17 ....73 K1
BRIG HD6 ....142 B7
Dewhurst Rd *HUD* HD2 ....191 H1
Dewsbury Gate Rd *DEWS* WF13 ....145 J8
Dewsbury Ring Rd *DEWS* WF13 ....172 B3
Dewsbury Rd *BEE/HOL* LS11 ....7 E6
CLECK BD19 ....144 B4
CLECK BD19 ....144 A4
EARD/LOFT WF3 ....147 H4
ELL HX5 ....167 H5
OSS WF5 ....173 H3
WKFDW/WTN WF2 ....174 D6
Deyne Rd *HUDS* HD4 ....212 C4
Diadem Dr *SCFT* LS14 ....103 G2
Dial St *OSM* LS9 ....102 B5
Diamond Av *HEM/SK/SE* WF9 ....226 A8
Diamond St *BFD* BD1 ....5 D5
BTLY * WF17 ....146 A5
HFAX HX1 ....8 B3
HUD HD1 ....13 D2
HUDE HD5 ....13 F5
HWTH BD22 ....2 B6
Diamond Ter *HFAX* HX1 ....8 B3
Dibb La *YEA* LS19 ....53 H4
Dib Cl *RHAY* LS8 ....81 F6
Dib La *RHAY* LS8 ....81 F6
Dick Dean La *HBR* HX7 ....89 G6
Dick Edge La *HOLM/MEL* HD9 ....249 J1
Dickens Dr *CAS* WF10 ....154 E6
Dicken's St *LUD/ILL* HX2 ....139 H4
WBOW BD5 ....96 A8
Dickin Ct *RPDN/SBR* * HX6 ....164 B7
Dickinson Ct *WKFDE* WF1 ....10 C1
Dickinson St *HORS* LS18 ....77 G1
WKFDE WF1 ....10 C2
Dickinson Ter *FEA/AMT* WF7 ....179 J5
Dick La *BOW* BD4 ....97 G6
Dick's Garth Rd *ILK* LS29 ....32 B7
Dicky Sykes La *FEA/AMT* WF7 ....202 D6
Digby Rd *ILK* LS29 ....32 C7
Digley Rd *HOLM/MEL* HD9 ....247 C1
Digley Royd La *HOLM/MEL* HD9 ....232 A8
Dimple Gdns *OSS* WF5 ....173 J7
Dimples La *AIRE* BD20 ....49 J5
....68 C4
Dimple Wells Cl *OSS* WF5 ....173 J7
Dimple Wells La *OSS* WF5 ....173 J7
Dimple Wells Rd *OSS* WF5 ....173 J7
Dineley Av *TOD* OL14 ....133 J4
Dingle Rd *HUD* HD1 ....190 D5
Dingley Rd *HUDW* HD3 ....190 C3
Dirker Av *MAR/SLWT* HD7 ....209 J6
Dirker Bank Rd *MAR/SLWT* HD7 ....209 H6
Dirker Dr *MAR/SLWT* HD7 ....209 H7
Dirkhill Rd *GTHN* BD7 ....4 A6
Dirkhill St *GTHN* BD7 ....95 H6
Discovery Rd *HFAX* HX1 ....9 E5
Disney Cl *HUDS* HD4 ....190 D8
Dispensary Wk *HFAX* HX1 ....9 E4
Disraeli Gdns *BEE/HOL* LS11 ....101 H7
Disraeli Ter *BEE/HOL* LS11 ....101 H7
Dixon Av *GTHN* BD7 ....95 F6
Dixon Cl *AIRE* BD20 ....26 E6
GTL/HWG HX4 ....165 K3
Dixon La *WOR/ARM* LS12 ....100 C6
Dixon Lane Rd *WOR/ARM* LS12 ....100 C6
Dixon St *AIRE* BD20 ....26 A6
FEA/AMT WF7 ....179 J4
Dixon's Yd *WKFDE* * WF1 ....11 D5
Dobb La *HOLM/MEL* HD9 ....247 H1
Dobb Top Rd *HOLM/MEL* HD9 ....247 G2
Dob La *RPDN/SBR* HX6 ....138 A8
Dob Royd *KBTN* HD8 ....235 F4
Dobroyd Rd *TOD* OL14 ....133 K7
Dobson Av *BEE/HOL* LS11 ....101 J8
Dobson Gv *BEE/HOL* LS11 ....101 J8
Dobson Pl *BEE/HOL* LS11 ....101 J8
Dobson Ter *BEE/HOL* LS11 ....101 J8
Dobson Vw *BEE/HOL* LS11 ....101 J8
Dockery *HUD* HD1 ....191 F8
Dockfield Pl *BAIL* BD17 ....73 J2

Dockfield Rd *BAIL* BD17 73
Dockfield Ter *BAIL* BD17 73
Dock La *BAIL* BD17 73
Dockroyd La *HWTH* BD22 68
Dock St *MID* LS10 7
Doctor Fold *HOLM/MEL* HD9 213
Doctor Hl *IDLE* BD10 74
LUD/ILL HX2 139
Doctor La *HOR/CROF* WF4 217
IDLE BD10 74
MIRF WF14 170
Doctors La *CAS* WF10 125
Dodgeholme Cl *LUD/ILL* HX2 115
Dodge Holme Gdns *LUD/ILL* HX2 115
Dodge Holme Rd *LUD/ILL* HX2 115
Dodgson Av *CHAL* LS7 ....8C
Dodgson St *ELL* HX5 166
Dodlee La *HUDW* HD3 189
Dodsworth Dr *WKFDW/WTN* WF2 198
Dog Hl *CUD/GR* S72 223
Dog Hill Dr *CUD/GR* S72 223
Doghouse La *TOD* OL14 153
Dog Kennel Bank *HUDE* HD5 13
Dog Kennel Hl *DOD/DAR* S75 238
Dog Kennel La *HIPP* HX3 6
Dog La *GTL/HWG* HX4 165
GTL/HWG HX4 188
Dogley Villa Ct *KBTN* HD8 215
Doldram La *RPDN/SBR* HX6 164
Doles Av *BSLYN/ROY* S71 22
Doles Crs *BSLYN/ROY* S71 22
Dole St *CUL/QBY* BD13 93
Dolfin Pl *HUDN* HD2 165
Doll La *CUL/QBY* BD13 107
Dolly La *OSM* LS9 102
Dolphin Ct *KBTN* HD8 102
Dolphin La *EARD/LOFT* WF3 145
Dolphin Rd *MID* LS10 121
Dolphin St *OSM* LS9 102
Dolphin Ct *BRAM* LS13 99
Dombey St *HFAX* HX1 8
Domestic Rd *BEE/HOL* LS11 7
Domestic St *BEE/HOL* LS11 7
Dominion Av *CHAL* LS7 79
Dominion Cl *CHAL* * LS7 79
Donald Av *WBSY* BD6 116
Donald St *PDSY/CALV* LS28 9
Don Av *WBY* LS22 2
Doncaster Rd *FEA/AMT* WF7 203
HEM/SK/SE WF9 226
HEM/SK/SE WF9 24
HOR/CROF WF4 200
KNOT WF11 15
PONT WF8 22
WKFDE WF1 22
Doncaster Road East *FEA/AMT* WF7 20
Doncaster St *HIPP* HX3 10
Don Ct *AIRE* BD20 9
Donisthorpe St *MID* LS10 10
WBOW BD5 9
Don Pedro Av *NORM* WF6 17
Don Pedro Cl *NORM* WF6 17
Don St *KGHY* BD21 3
Dorchester Av *PONT* WF8 18
Dorchester Ct *BOW* * BD4 9
Dorchester Crs *BAIL* BD17 5
BOW BD4 9
Dorchester Dr *LUD/ILL* HX2 11
YEA LS19 5
Dorchester Rd *HUDN* HD2 16
Dorian Cl *IDLE* BD10 9
Dorman Av *HEM/SK/SE* WF9 22
Dorothy St *KGHY* BD21 4
Dorset Av *RHAY* LS8 8
Dorset Cl *HEM/SK/SE* WF9 22
WBOW BD5 9
Dorset Gv *PDSY/CALV* * LS28 9
Dorset Mt *RHAY* LS8 8
Dorset Rd *RHAY* LS8 8
Dorset St *HUD* HD1 8
RHAY * LS8 8
WBOW BD5 8
Dorset Ter *RHAY* LS8 8
Dotterel Gln *MOR* LS27 12
Doubting La *EARL* WF12 19
Doubting Rd *EARL* WF12 19
Douglas Av *BTLY* WF17 14
HUDE HD5 19
HUDW HD3 19
Douglas Dr *BOW* * BD4 9
Douglas Rd *BOW* BD4 9
Douglas St *EARL* WF12 17
HIPP HX3 6
HWTH BD22 6
Dove Cl *WBY* LS22 2
Dovecote Cl *HOR/CROF* WF4 19
Dovecote Dr *CAS* WF10 12
Dovecote La *HOR/CROF* WF4 19
Dovedale Cl *HIPP* HX3 11
HOR/CROF WF4 20
Dovedale Gdns *MSTN/BAR* LS15 8
Dovedale Garth *MSTN/BAR* LS15 8
Dover La *HOLM/MEL* HD9 23
Dover Rd *HOLM/MEL* HD9 23
Dover St *BFDE* BD3 10
GFTH/SHER LS25 10
TOD OL14 13

vesdale Gv WBOW BD5 ....118 D1
vesdale Rd WBOW BD5 ....118 E1
ve St SHPY BD18...........................75 F3
wkell La BSPA/BRAM LS23 ....42 E2
wker St HFAX HX1 ....8 A6
MUDW HD3 ....190 B6
wley Gap La BGLY BD16 ....72 B2
wnham St BFDE BD3 ....5 E5
wning Cl BFDE * BD3 ....5 F4
wning St MAR/SLWT HD7 ....211 G3
wnland Crs KNOT WF11 ....182 E1
wnshutts La HOLM/MEL HD9 ....233 K6
wnside Crs WIL/AL BD15 ....94 A2
acup Av GTHN BD7 ....94 E6
acup Rd AIRE BD20 ....27 F2
adishaw Rd AIRE BD20 ....27 F2
agon Ct WOR/ARM * LS12 ....6 B5
agon Crs WOR/ARM LS12 ....100 D6
agon Dr WOR/ARM LS12 ....100 C6
agon La WOR/ARM LS12 ....100 C6
ake La BIRK/DRI BD11 ....121 H6
ake St BFD BD1 ....5 D5
....3 D2
aper La HBR HX7 ....111 K5
aughton Gv WBOW BD5 ....118 E2
aughton St WBOW BD5 ....118 E2
ayton Manor Yd
BEE/HOL * LS11 ....101 J7
ay Vw DEWS WF13 ....171 J1
ewry Rd KGHY BD21 ....2 C3
ewton Rd BFD BD1 ....4 B4
tholme Rd BIRK/DRI BD11 ....121 J4
I Pde GIR BD8 ....4 B2
I St HWTH BD22 ....68 E5
GHY BD21 ....3 D3
LK LS29 ....56 A7
BHP/TINH LS16 ....145 K5
FTH/SHER LS25 ....129 F2
BR HX7 ....136 E2
IPP HX3 ....141 J3
DLE BD10 ....75 F5
LK LS29 ....32 A5
MSTN/BAR LS15 ....104 B1
SM LS9 ....102 A4
HAY LS8 ....80 C3
THW LS26 ....127 K2
ver Pl WOR/ARM LS12 ....6 A5
vers Rw PONT WF8 ....180 C4
ver St WOR/ARM LS12 ....6 B5
ver Ter AIRE BD20 ....27 H1
WOR/ARM LS12 ....6 A5
WKFDE WF1 ....10 D3
r Carr La LUD/ILL HX2 ....115 K6
clough La HUDS HD4 ....212 C1
clough Cl HIPP HX3 ....140 B8
clough Cl HIPP HX3 ....140 B8
ds St CLAY BD14 ....94 B7
mmer La MAR/SLWT HD7 ....188 E8
mmond Av HDGY LS6 ....78 C5
mmond BHP/TINH LS16 ....78 C5
mmond Rd BHP/TINH LS16 ....78 C4
IR BD8 ....4 F3
ry Av HORS LS18 ....77 F3
ry Cl HORS LS18 ....77 F3
ry La GTL/HWG HX4 ....165 J7
ORS LS18 ....77 F3
ORM WF6 ....151 J8
WKFDE WF1 ....10 D3
r den St BFDE BD3 ....5 E5
GLY * BD16 ....49 K8
Hill La KBTN BD8 ....237 F6
b La BGLY BD16 ....50 A8
ckett Gv PDSY/CALV LS28 ....97 H3
ckworth Gv HTON BD9 ....95 F1
ckworth Cl HTON BD9 ....94 E2
ckworth Ter HTON BD9 ....95 F1
fleet La HOR/CROF WF4 ....197 H5
ley Av BTLY WF17 ....145 K1
UD HD1 ....190 D5
ley Crs LUD/ILL HX2 ....115 G6
ley Gv BOW BD4 ....97 G6
ley Hill Rd ECHL BD2 ....74 D8
ley Rd HUD HD1 ....190 D5
ley St BOW BD4 ....96 E8
well Av HIPP * HX3 ....166 C1
well Cl HIPP HX3 ....166 B1
well La HIPP HX3 ....166 B1
con Ap SCFT LS14 ....81 J8
ch Rd MIRF WF14 ....117 K5
nen St WBOW BD5 ....5 D6
e of York Av
KFDW/WTN WF2 ....198 E2
e of York St WKFDE WF1 ....11 D2
KFDW/WTN WF2 ....175 G1
es HI ILK * LS29 ....20 A5

Duke St BFD BD1 ....4 C4
CAS WF10 ....153 G3
CUD/OBY S72 ....240 A5
DEWS WF13 ....171 H6
ELL HX5 ....166 E5
HEM/SK/SE WF9 ....202 A8
HWTH BD22 ....69 F4
KGHY BD21 ....2 C1
LUD/ILL HX2 ....138 A2
OSM LS9 ....7 F4
Duke Wood Rd KBTN HD8 ....237 J1
Dulverton Cl BEE/HOL LS11 ....123 H1
PONT WF8 ....155 G8
Dulverton Gdns BEE/HOL LS11 ...123 H1
Dulverton Garth BEE/HOL LS11 ...123 H1
Dulverton Gn BEE/HOL LS11 ....123 J2
Dulverton Gv BEE/HOL LS11 ....123 H1
BOW BD4 ....97 F8
Dulverton Pl BEE/HOL LS11 ....123 H1
Dulverton Ri PONT WF8 ....155 G8
Dulverton Sq BEE/HOL LS11 ....123 J2
Dulverton Wy PONT WF8 ....155 G8
Dunbar St WKFDE WF1 ....11 F5
Dunbottle Cl MIRF WF14 ....170 E6
Dunbottle La MIRF WF14 ....170 E6
Dunbottle Wy MIRF WF14 ....171 F5
Duncan St OT LS21 ....33 F5
WKFDW/WTN WF2 ....199 G1
Duncan St LDS LS1 ....7 E4
WBOW BD5 ....4 C6
Dunce Park Cl ELL HX5 ....166 E6
Duncombe Rd GIR BD8 ....95 F4
Duncombe St GIR BD8 ....95 G4
LDS LS1 ....6 C3
Duncombe Wy GTHN BD7 ....95 G4
Dundas St HFAX HX1 ....8 A6
HUD HD1 ....12 C4
KGHY BD21 ....3 E4
Dundee Rd TOD OL14 ....133 G3
Dunderdale Crs CAS WF10 ....154 G3
Dunford Rd HOLM/MEL HD9 ....233 H8
HOLM/MEL HD9 ....248 D1
Dungeon La HWTH LS26 ....150 D2
Dunhill Crs OSM LS9 ....103 G3
Dunhill Ri OSM LS9 ....103 G3
Dunkhill Cft IDLE * BD10 ....74 D4
Dunkirk Crs HFAX HX1 ....139 H5
Dunkirk Gdns HFAX HX1 ....8 A6
Dunkirk La HFAX HX1 ....139 H6
Dunkirk Ri AIRE BD20 ....48 C1
Dunkirk St HFAX HX1 ....139 H5
Dunkirk Ter HFAX HX1 ....8 A5
Dunlin Cl MOR LS27 ....123 J8
Dunlin Cft MID LS10 ....124 E6
Dunlin Cft MID LS10 ....124 E6
Dunlin Dr MID LS10 ....124 E6
Dunlin Fold MID LS10 ....124 E6
Dunlin Wy GIR BD8 ....94 C4
Dunmore Av CUL/QBY BD13 ....116 B2
Dunn Cl WKFDW/WTN WF2 ....149 G8
Dunningley EARD/LOFT WF3 ....123 K8
Dunningley La EARD/LOFT WF3 ...148 A1
Dunnington Wk LM/WK BD12 ....118 B5
Dunnock Cft MOR LS27 ....123 J8
Dunrobin Av GFTH/SHER LS25 .....106 B4
Dunsford Av BOW BD4 ....119 J3
Dunsley Bank Rd HOLM/MEL HD9 233 F8
Dunsley Ter HEM/SK/SE WF9 ....241 C1
Dunsmore Dr HUDW HD3 ....189 K3
Dunstan Cl OSS WF5 ....173 K7
Dunstan Dr BHP/TINH LS16 ....56 D8
Dunstan Gdns BHP/TINH LS16 ....56 D8
Dunstarn La BHP/TINH LS16 ....78 D1
Durban Av BEE/HOL LS11 ....124 A1
Durban Crs BEE/HOL LS11 ....124 A1
Durham Rd GIR BD8 ....95 G2
Durham St CAS WF10 ....153 K5
LUD/ILL HX2 ....139 H3
Durham Ter GIR BD8 ....95 G2
Durkar Flds HOR/CROF WF4 ....198 B5
Durkar La HOR/CROF WF4 ....198 A5
Durkar Low La HOR/CROF WF4 .....198 C4
Durkar Ri HOR/CROF WF4 ....198 B5
Durkheim Ct BFDE * BD3 ....96 A3
Durley Av HTON BD9 ....73 F8
Durling Dr SHPY BD18 ....74 A4
Durlston Gv LM/WK BD12 ....118 E2
Durlston Ter LM/WK BD12 ....118 E2
Durrance St HWTH BD22 ....2 A4
Durrant Cl WBY LS22 ....23 K6
Dutton Cn SCFT LS14 ....81 J3
Dutton Wy SCFT LS14 ....81 J4
Dyehouse Dr CLECK BD19 ....143 K1
Dyehouse La BRIG HD6 ....168 D2
PDSY/CALV LS28 ....98 C7
Dye House La RPDN/SBR HX6 ....165 H2
WIL/AL BD15 ....70 E6
Dyehouse Rd LM/WK BD12 ....119 G6
Dyer La HIPP HX3 ....8 A2
Dyers Ct HDGY LS6 ....79 F7
Dyer St LDSU LS2 ....7 F3
Dyke La TOD OL14 ....135 G3
Dymond Gv LVSG * WF15 ....144 D8
Dymond Rd LVSG WF15 ....144 E8
Dymond Vw LVSG WF15 ....144 D8
Dyson La HOLM/MEL HD9 ....248 C2
RPDN/SBR HX6 ....163 K8

Dyson Pl HIPP * HX3 ....140 C8
Dyson Rd HFAX HX1 ....8 A3
Dyson's Hl HOLM/MEL HD9 ....213 F6
Dyson St BFD BD1 ....4 B4
BRIG HD6 ....142 B8
HTON BD9 ....73 G7
HUDE HD5 ....192 A5

E

Eagle Gv WKFDW/WTN WF2 ....174 E5
Eaglesfield Dr WBSY BD6 ....118 A5
Eagle St HWTH BD22 ....69 G4
KGHY BD21 ....2 C3
TOD OL14 ....134 A6
Ealand Av BTLY WF17 ....145 J6
Ealand Crs BTLY WF17 ....145 J3
Ealand Rd BTLY WF17 ....145 J3
Ealing Ct BTLY WF17 ....145 K5
Earles Av HUDE HD5 ....192 A6
Earle St FEA/AMT WF7 ....179 H5
Earismere Dr MOR LS27 ....122 E6
Earls Ter HIPP HX3 ....8 B1
Earl St EARL WF12 ....173 G4
HEM/SK/SE WF9 ....202 A8
HWTH BD22 ....68 E5
KGHY BD21 ....2 C2
WBOW BD5 ....4 C6
WKFDE WF1 ....11 D2
Earlswood LM/WK * BD12 ....118 E8
Earlswood Av RHAY LS8 ....80 B1
Earlswood Cha PDSY/CALV LS28 ...98 C5
Earlswood Crs GFTH/SHER LS25 ..128 E1
Earlswood Md PDSY/CALV LS28 ....98 C5
Earl Ter HIPP HX3 ....8 B1
Earsby Cl ILK LS29 ....19 K7
Easby Dr ILK LS29 ....19 K7
Easby Rd WBOW BD5 ....4 B6
Easdale Cl SCFT LS14 ....81 H7
Easdale Crs SCFT LS14 ....81 J6
Easdale Mt SCFT LS14 ....81 H7
Easdale Rd SCFT LS14 ....81 H7
Easingwood Dr HUDE HD5 ....192 D2
East Acres KNOT WF11 ....156 B4
East Av HEM/SK/SE WF9 ....226 C4
HOR/CROF WF4 ....197 J2
HUDW HD3 ....190 C2
KGHY BD21 ....3 D2
PONT WF8 ....180 C4
East Bath St BTLY WF17 ....146 C6
East Bolton LUD/ILL HX2 ....115 G4
Eastborough Crs DEWS WF13 ....172 C2
Eastbourne Av FEA/AMT WF7 ....179 K4
Eastbourne Cl PONT WF8 ....181 H3
Eastbourne Crs PONT WF8 ....181 H3
Eastbourne Dr PONT WF8 ....181 H3
Eastbourne Rd HTON BD9 ....73 H6
Eastbourne Ter PONT WF8 ....181 G3
Eastbourne Vw PONT WF8 ....181 G3
Eastbrook Ct BSPA/BRAM * LS23 ..62 D1
Eastbrook La BFD BD1 ....5 D5
Eastburn Br AIRE BD20 ....26 E5
Eastbury Av WBSY BD6 ....117 J2
East Busk La OT LS21 ....34 A3
East Byland LUD/ILL HX2 ....115 H5
East Cswy BHP/TINH LS16 ....56 E7
East Causeway Cl BHP/TINH LS16 ..56 D6
East Causeway Crs BHP/TINH LS16 56 E7
East Causeway V BHP/TINH LS16 ...56 E7
East Chevin Rd OT LS21 ....34 B6
Eastcliffe HIPP HX3 ....9 F5
East Cl PONT WF8 ....181 F6
East Dale CI HEM/SK/SE WF9 ....225 F4
Eastdean Bank SCFT LS14 ....81 J5
Eastdean Dr SCFT LS14 ....81 J5
Eastdean Gdns SCFT LS14 ....81 K5
Eastdean Ga SCFT LS14 ....81 K5
Eastdean Gn SCFT LS14 ....81 K5
Eastdean Ri SCFT LS14 ....81 K5
Eastdean Rd SCFT LS14 ....81 K5
East Dene AIRE BD20 ....27 G1
East Down CAS WF10 ....154 B3
East Dr GFTH/SHER LS25 ....106 B4
PONT WF8 ....181 G4
East End Crs BSLYN/ROY S71 ......222 C8
Easterly Av RHAY LS8 ....80 D7
Easterly Cl RHAY LS8 ....80 D8
Easterly Crs RHAY LS8 ....80 C7
Easterly Cross RHAY LS8 ....80 D7
Easterly Garth RHAY LS8 ....80 D7
Easterly Gv RHAY LS8 ....80 C7
Easterly Mt RHAY LS8 ....80 D7
Easterly Rd RHAY LS8 ....81 F6
Easterly Sq RHAY LS8 ....80 D7
Easterly Vw RHAY LS8 ....80 D7
Eastfield KBTN HD8 ....235 H3
Eastfield Av KNOT WF11 ....156 C8
STKB/PEN S36 ....252 C8
Eastfield Crs RTHW LS26 ....126 E5
Eastfield Dr KBTN HD8 ....215 G4
PONT WF8 ....181 G3
RTHW LS26 ....126 D5
Eastfield Gdns BOW BD4 ....97 G8
Eastfield Gv WKFD NORM WF6 .....152 B8
Eastfield La CAS WF10 ....153 K3

Eastfield Rd KNOT WF11 .....156 C8
  MIRF WF14 .....171 C5
East Field St OSM LS9 .....102 A4
East Fold KBTN HD8 .....37 C2
Eastgate BHP/TINH LS16 .....35 H8
  ELL HX5 .....166 E4
  HEM/SK/SE WF9 .....224 E5
  HOLM/MEL HD9 .....213 G7
  LDSU LS2 .....7 F3
Eastgate Cl BHP/TINH LS16 .....35 H8
East Grange Cl MID * LS10 .....125 F2
East Grange Dr MID LS10 .....125 F2
East Grange Garth MID LS10 .....125 F2
East Grange Ri MID LS10 .....125 F2
East Grange Sq MID LS10 .....125 F2
East Grange Vw MID LS10 .....125 F2
Easthorpe Ct ECHL BD2 .....153 F4
East King St OSM LS9 .....102 A4
Eastlands HUDE HD5 .....192 C7
Eastland Wk BRAM LS13 .....99 J2
East Lee La TOD OL14 .....134 E3
Eastleigh Ct EARD/LOFT WF3 .....148 B3
Eastleigh Dr EARD/LOFT WF3 .....148 B3
Eastleigh Gv WBOW BD5 .....95 K8
East Moor Crs RHAY LS8 .....80 B1
East Moor Dr RHAY LS8 .....80 B1
East Moor La BHP/TINH LS16 .....56 D7
East Moor Rd RHAY LS8 .....80 B1
East Mt BRIG HD6 .....142 B8
Easton Pl HUDW HD3 .....190 B4
East Pde AIRE BD20 .....27 F6
  BAIL BD17 .....51 K7
  BFD BD1 .....5 D4
  ILK LS29 .....20 C7
  ILK LS29 .....32 C7
  KGHY BD21 .....3 D3
  LDS LS1 .....7 D5
  RPDN/SBR HX6 .....139 C6
East Parade Wk LDS LS1 .....7 D3
East Park Dr OSM * LS9 .....102 A4
East Park Gv OSM LS9 .....102 A4
East Park Mt OSM LS9 .....102 A4
East Park Pde OSM LS9 .....102 C5
East Park Pl OSM LS9 .....102 A4
East Park Rd HIPP * HX3 .....8 B2
  OSM LS9 .....102 B4
  PBR HG5 .....22 B1
East Park St MOR LS27 .....122 E8
  OSM LS9 .....102 A4
East Park Ter OSM LS9 .....102 A4
East Park Vw OSM LS9 .....102 A4
East Pinfold BSLYN/ROY S71 .....222 A8
East Rd LM/WK BD12 .....118 C5
East Royd HWTH BD22 .....69 F1
East Side Ct PDSY/CALV LS28 .....99 F6
East Squire La GIR BD8 .....4 A1
East St BRIG HD6 .....168 B2
  BTLY WF17 .....145 H5
  CUD/OR S72 .....223 J6
  HEM/SK/SE WF9 .....226 D7
  HIPP HX3 .....142 B4
  HOLM/MEL HD9 .....234 A8
  HOR/CROF WF4 .....223 H2
  HUDW HD3 .....190 B2
  MAR/SLWT HD7 .....189 J6
  OSM LS9 .....7 F4
  RPDN/SBR HX6 .....164 B1
  WKFDE WF1 .....175 K1
East Ter HWTH BD22 .....69 G3
East Vw AIRE BD20 .....27 G1
  CAS WF10 .....153 F4
  CLECK BD19 .....143 H5
  COL BB8 .....64 A1
  GFTH/SHER LS25 .....129 G2
  HUDW HD3 .....12 A3
  KNOT WF11 .....156 D7
  LUD/ILL * HX2 .....138 B2
  MIRF WF14 .....170 C5
  MSTN/BAR * LS15 .....104 A1
  OSS WF5 .....173 K8
  PDSY/CALV LS28 .....98 C6
  RTHW LS26 .....127 F6
  WBSY BD6 .....117 H1
  YEA LS19 .....54 A5
East View Rd YEA LS19 .....54 A5
East View Ter LM/WK BD12 .....118 E7
Eastville Rd HOR/CROF WF4 .....178 A8
Eastway MIRF WF14 .....170 C4
Eastway Pk MIRF WF14 .....170 D4
Eastwick Vw WIL/AL * BD15 .....94 B2
Eastwood RPDN/SBR HX6 .....138 C8
  WKFDW/WTN WF2 .....175 F4
Eastwood Cl HOR/CROF WF4 .....198 B4
  LUD/ILL HX2 .....115 H4
Eastwood Crs SCFT LS14 .....82 B7
Eastwood Dr SCFT LS14 .....82 A6
Eastwood Gdns SCFT LS14 .....82 A7
Eastwood Garth SCFT LS14 .....82 B7
Eastwood Gv GFTH/SHER LS25 .....106 A6
  LUD/ILL HX2 .....115 H4
Eastwood La SCFT LS14 .....82 B7
  TOD OL14 .....135 F2
Eastwood Nook SCFT LS14 .....82 B7
Eastwood Rd TOD OL14 .....109 K8
Eastwood St BOW BD4 .....5 D6
  BRIG HD6 .....142 C8

Easy Rd OSM LS9 .....102 B5
Eaton Nl BHP/TINH LS16 .....55 K8
Eaton Ms MID LS10 .....124 D6
Eaton Pl HEM/SK/SE WF9 .....224 E4
Eaton Rd ILK LS29 .....20 A8
Eaton Sq MID LS10 .....124 D7
Eaton St KGHY BD21 .....2 B6
Eaton Wk HEM/SK/SE WF9 .....226 C6
Eaves Av HBR HX7 .....111 K7
Eaves Rd HBR HX7 .....111 K7
Ebberston Gv HDGY LS6 .....79 F8
Ebberston Pl HDGY LS6 .....79 F8
Ebenezer Pl GTHN BD7 .....95 G7
Ebenezer St BFD * BD1 .....5 D5
  EARD/LOFT WF3 .....125 J8
  PDSY/CALV LS28 .....76 B8
Ebor Gdns MIRF WF14 .....170 B6
Ebor La HWTH BD22 .....69 F5
Ebor Mt GFTH/SHER LS25 .....129 F1
  HDGY LS6 .....6 B1
Ebor Pl HDGY LS6 .....6 B1
Ebor St HDGY LS6 .....6 B1
Ebor Wy AL/HA/HU LS17 .....37 J7
  AL/HA/HU LS17 .....38 C3
  AL/HA/HU LS17 .....40 A3
  ILK LS29 .....31 K5
  ILK LS29 .....32 D7
  OT LS21 .....33 J6
  OT LS21 .....34 C6
Ebson House La HOLM/MEL HD9 .....234 D5
Ebury Cl BTLY WF17 .....146 C5
Ebury St BTLY WF17 .....146 C5
Ecclesburn Av OSM LS9 .....102 C4
Ecclesburn Rd OSM LS9 .....102 C4
Ecclesburn St OSM LS9 .....102 C4
Ecclesburn Ter OSM LS9 .....102 C4
Eccles Ct ECHL BD2 .....74 D7
Eccles Parlour RPDN/SBR HX6 .....163 H4
Eccup La BHP/TINH LS16 .....56 D6
  OT LS21 .....37 G7
Eccup Moor Rd BHP/TINH LS16 .....57 F5
Echo St LVSG WF15 .....170 C1
Edale Av HUDS HD4 .....213 F2
Edale Cl HUDE HD5 .....192 D3
Edale Gv CUL/QBY BD13 .....116 B3
Edale Wy BHP/TINH LS16 .....55 K8
Eddercliff Crs CLECK BD13 .....144 D5
Edderthorpe St BFDE BD3 .....6 E2
Eddison Cl BHP/TINH LS16 .....56 C6
Eddison St PDSY/CALV LS28 .....98 B1
Eddystone Ri KNOT WF11 .....156 A7
Edelshain Gv WKFDW/WTN WF2 .....199 H3
Eden Av OSS WF5 .....173 J5
  WKFDW/WTN WF2 .....174 E6
Eden Cl LM/WK BD12 .....118 E8
Eden Crs BULY LS4 .....78 B7
Edendale CAS WF10 .....154 A3
Eden Gv BULY LS4 .....78 B7
Eden Gdns BULY LS4 .....78 B8
Eden Mt BULY LS4 .....78 B8
Eden Rd BULY LS4 .....78 B8
Eden Wk BULY LS4 .....78 B8
Eden Wy BULY LS4 .....78 B8
Edensor Rd KGHY BD21 .....2 B3
Ederoyd Av PDSY/CALV LS28 .....97 K2
Ederoyd Crs PDSY/CALV LS28 .....97 K2
Ederoyd Dr PDSY/CALV LS28 .....97 K2
Ederoyd Gv PDSY/CALV LS28 .....97 K2
Ederoyd Mt PDSY/CALV LS28 .....97 J2
Ederoyd Ri PDSY/CALV LS28 .....97 J2
Edgar St CLAY BD14 .....116 B1
Edgbaston Cl AL/HA/HU LS17 .....57 G3
Edgbaston Wk AL/HA/HU LS17 .....57 G5
Edge Av EARL WF12 .....195 H2
Edgebank Av WBSY BD6 .....118 A5
Edge Cl EARL WF12 .....195 J2
  MAR/SLWT HD7 .....189 J7
Edge End Gdns WBSY BD6 .....117 K4
Edge End La HOLM/MEL HD9 .....232 A6
Edge End Rd WBSY BD6 .....117 K4
Edgehill Cl CUL/QBY BD13 .....116 E2
Edge Hill Cl HUDE HD5 .....13 F3
Edgeholme La LUD/ILL HX2 .....138 C4
Edge Jct EARL WF12 .....195 H2
Edge La EARL WF12 .....195 J2
  HBR HX7 .....110 E4
Edgemoor Cl BOW BD4 .....120 B3
  HIPP HX3 .....140 A7
Edgemoor Rd HOLM/MEL HD9 .....212 E8
  HOR/CROF WF4 .....198 B8
Edge Rd EARL WF12 .....195 J3
Edgerton Gn HUDW HD3 .....12 A3
Edgerton Grove Rd HUDW HD3 .....12 A3
Edgerton Rd BHP/TINH LS16 .....78 B4
  HUDW HD3 .....12 A2
Edge Ter HUDW HD3 .....189 K4
Edge Top Rd EARL WF12 .....195 G2
Edge Vw EARL WF12 .....195 J3
  MAR/SLWT HD7 .....189 J7
Edgeware Rd HUDE HD5 .....192 C5
Edgware Av RHAY LS8 .....102 B1
Edgware Gv RHAY LS8 .....102 B1
Edgware Mt RHAY LS8 .....102 B1
Edgware Pl RHAY LS8 .....102 B1
Edgware Rw RHAY * LS8 .....102 B1
Edgware Ter RHAY LS8 .....102 B1
Edgware Vw RHAY LS8 .....102 B1

Edinburgh Av WOR/ARM LS12 100
Edinburgh Gv WOR/ARM LS12 100
Edinburgh Pl GFTH/SHER LS25 106
  WOR/ARM LS12 100
Edinburgh Rd WOR/ARM LS12 100
Edinburgh Ter WOR/ARM LS12 100
Edlington Cl BOW BD4 97
Edmonton Pl CHAL LS7 79
Edmund St TOD OL14 159
  WBOW BD5 4
Edrich Cl LM/WK BD12 119
Edroyd Pl PDSY/CALV LS28 76
Edroyd St PDSY/CALV LS28 76
Education Rd CHAL LS7 79
Edward Cl EARL WF12 172
  HIPP HX3 141
Edward Dr WKFDE WF1 149
Edward Rd MIRF WF14 170
Edwards Rd LUD/ILL HX2 139
Edward St BOW BD4 5
  BOW BD4 120
  BRIG HD6 142
  CLECK BD19 144
  HBR HX7 112
  LDSU LS2 7
  NORM WF6 151
  RPDN/SBR HX6 138
  SHPY BD18 73
  WKFDE * WF1 11
Edward Turner Cl LM/WK BD12 118
Edwin Rd HDGY LS6 6
Eel Holme View St AIRE BD20 47
Eel Mires Garth WBY LS22 23
Effingham Rd BGLY BD16 70
Egerton Gv WIL/AL BD15 93
Egerton St RPDN/SBR HX6 138
Eggleston Dr BOW BD4 120
Eggleston Sq BSPA/BRAM LS23 42
Eggleston St BRAM LS13 76
Egremont Crs WBSY BD6 118
Egremont St RPDN/SBR HX6 138
Egypt Rd CUL/QBY BD13 93
Eiffel Buildings HBR HX7 112
Eighth Av LVSG WF15 143
  RTHW LS26 126
  WOR/ARM LS12 100
Eightlands Av BRAM LS13 99
Eightlands La BRAM LS13 99
Eightlands Rd DEWS WF13 172
Ekota Pl RHAY LS8 80
Elam Wood Rd AIRE BD20 28
Elbow La ECHL BD2 5
  LUD/ILL HX2 138
Elder Av HEM/SK/SE WF9 226
  WKFDW/WTN WF2 10
Elder Cl BTLY WF17 145
Elder Cft BRAM LS13 99
Elder Dr EARL WF12 172
  HEM/SK/SE WF9 226
Elder Garth GFTH/SHER LS25 106
Elder Gn WKFDW/WTN WF2 10
Elder Gv HUDS HD4 212
  WKFDW/WTN WF2 10
Elder Grove Ms HUDS * HD4 212
Elder La HUDN * HD2 169
Elder Lea OSS * WF5 173
Elder Mt BRAM * LS13 99
Elder Pl BRAM LS13 99
Elder Ri RTHW LS26 127
Elder Rd BRAM LS13 99
  HUDN HD2 169
Elder St AIRE BD20 47
  BRAM LS13 99
  IDLE BD10 78
Elderwood Gv IDLE BD10 78
Eldon Pl BFD BD1 5
  CLECK BD19 144
Eldon Rd HUD HD1 190
Eldon St HECK WF16 145
  HIPP HX3 9
  OSS WF5 174
  TOD OL14 134
Eldon Ter BFD BD1 5
Eldroth Mt HFAX HX1 8
Eldroth Rd HFAX HX1 8
Eldwick Cft BGLY BD16 50
Eleanor Dr PDSY/CALV LS28 75
Eleanor St BRIG HD6 168
  HUD HD1 12
Eleventh Av LVSG WF15 143
Elford Gv RHAY LS8 80
Elford Pl East RHAY LS8 80
Elford Pl West RHAY LS8 80
Elford Rd RHAY * LS8 80
Elgin Cl HUDS HD4 212
Elia St KGHY BD21 3
Eliot Gv GSLY LS20 53
Eliots Cl CAS WF10 154
Eli St WBOW BD5 96
Elizabethan Ct PONT WF8 181
Elizabeth Av CUD/OR S72 223
  LM/WK BD12 118
Elizabeth Cl LM/WK BD12 118
Elizabeth Ct CAS WF10 154
Elizabeth Crs LM/WK BD12 118
Elizabeth Dr CAS WF10 154
  KNOT WF11 155
  LM/WK BD12 118
Elizabeth Frances St ELL HX5 166

...abeth Gdns WKFDE WF1 ....10 C1
...abeth Gv MOR LS27 ....123 H6
...abeth St SCFT LS14 ....81 J6
...abeth St BGLY * BD16 ....50 A8
...UD/GR S72 ....240 A5
ELL HX5 ....166 E5
GTL/HWG HX4 ....166 C4
HDGY LS6 ....78 E8
HUDS HD4 ....191 G8
GHY BD21 ....48 D4
M/WK BD12 ....118 D7
VSG WF15 ....144 B7
VBOW BD5 ....4 C6
WKFDE WF1 ....199 C1
and Br ELL HX5 ....166 E4
and La ELL HX5 ....167 F4
and Riorges Link ELL HX5 ....167 F4
ar Rd BEE/HOL LS11 ....101 F8
RIG HD6 ....168 B1
ELL HX5 ....167 H2
PDN/SBR HX6 ....164 B7
en St CAS WF10 ....153 K2
and Wy BEE/HOL LS11 ....123 J1
and Wood Bottom ELL HX5 ....166 C2
ar Carr Rd CUL/QBY BD13 ....70 A4
DLE BD10 ....74 E1
ar Gdns ILK LS29 ....32 D6
en St HEM/SK/SE WF9 ....202 A7
en Royd La LUD/ILL HX2 ....137 K3
en Royd St HIPP HX3 ....9 D3
en St BGLY BD16 ....50 A8
enthorpe Rd BAIL BD17 ....72 E1
erby La OSM LS9 ....102 A5
erby Rd OSM LS9 ....102 A4
ercroft Av GTHN BD7 ....95 G5
ercroft Rd GTHN BD7 ....95 G5
ercroft Ter GTHN BD7 ....95 G5
rker La SCFT LS14 ....61 F6
rker Rd SCFT LS14 ....60 E5
ers Gv RHAY LS8 ....80 B7
erslie Ct HUDW HD3 ....12 A2
ers Rd RHAY LS8 ....80 B7
erton St BFDE BD3 ....96 E4
n's Ter NORM WF6 ....177 J2
anthorpe St BOW BD4 ....5 F6
ott St AIRE BD20 ....27 F2
HPY BD18 ....73 G3
s Fold WOR/ARM LS12 ....100 B4
s La GTL/HWG HX4 ....165 J3
FTH/SHER LS25 ....105 J1
s PI BEE/HOL LS11 ....101 G8
s St WBOW BD5 ....95 K8
s Ter BEE/HOL LS11 ....78 D4
stones Gdns GTL/HWG HX4 ....165 K4
stones La GTL/HWG HX4 ....165 K5
stones PI GTL/HWG HX4 ....165 K4
mont Av KBTN HD8 ....217 G5
on Gv WBSY BD6 ....118 D3
wood Cl CHAL LS7 ....79 F4
Elm Wk MSTN/BAR LS15 ....103 K6
Av EARD/LOFT WF3 ....150 C7
FTH/SHER LS25 ....105 K8
OD OL14 ....134 A4
xbridge La BSLYN/ROY S71 ....222 C8
Cl OSS WF5 ....173 K8
ONT WF8 ....181 F1
ONT WF8 ....181 K6
Ct CLECK BD19 ....120 E7
BTN HD8 ....215 H4
Crs AIRE BD20 ....49 H3
Cft SCFT LS14 ....82 A3
et Dr MSTN/BAR LS15 ....83 J4
HAY LS8 ....80 E5
ete La RHAY LS8 ....81 F5
ete Ct RHAY LS8 ....81 F5
ete Cft MSTN/BAR LS15 ....82 D5
ete Dr RHAY LS8 ....81 F4
ete La RHAY LS8 ....80 E4
ete Hl RHAY LS8 ....81 F5
ete La RHAY LS8 ....81 F5
ete Mt RHAY LS8 ....81 F5
ete Rd CAS WF10 ....154 E2
ete Wy RHAY LS8 ....81 G5
et Rd MSTN/BAR LS15 ....83 J5
field BAIL BD17 ....51 K7
field Av HUDW HD3 ....189 K6
OR LS27 ....123 F8
/BSY BD6 ....118 D3
field Dr BIRK/DRI BD11 ....120 D7
field Gv WOR/ARM * LS12 ....100 D5
field PI WOR/ARM LS12 ....100 D5
field Rd AIRE BD20 ....26 A4
UDN HD2 ....12 A1
OR LS27 ....147 G1
field Ter HFAX HX1 ....8 C6
UDE * HD5 ....13 F5
field Wy BRAM LS13 ....99 H2
Gdns CAS WF10 ....154 E6
FAX HX1 ....9 D6
Gv AIRE BD20 ....27 F2
RE BD20 ....49 H3
ECK BD19 ....144 D3
ECK WF16 ....145 F6

HEM/SK/SE WF9 ....226 B8
HIPP HX3 ....117 J5
HOR/CROF WF4 ....197 H2
HWTH BD22 ....2 B6
ILK LS29 ....32 B3
SHPY BD18 ....74 A4
Elmhurst Cl AL/HA/HU LS17 ....58 C7
Elmhurst Gdns AL/HA/HU LS17 ....58 C7
Elmhurst Gv KNOT WF11 ....156 B8
Elm Pk PONT WF8 ....180 D5
Elm PI KNOT WF11 ....156 B8
RPDN/SBR HX6 ....138 E6
Elm Rd DEWS WF13 ....171 J3
HEM/SK/SE WF9 ....224 E4
NORM WF6 ....177 K4
SHPY BD18 ....73 K4
Elmroyd RTHW LS26 ....126 C7
The Elms FEA/AMT WF7 ....203 F6
GSLY LS20 ....53 G2
Elmsall La AWLS/ASK DN6 ....226 E6
Elmsall Dr AWLS/ASK DN6 ....242 D5
Elmsall St GIR BD8 ....4 B5
Elmsall Wy HEM/SK/SE WF9 ....226 E6
Elmsdale Cl HEM/SK/SE WF9 ....242 D1
Elms Hl MAR/SLWT HD7 ....210 D3
Elmsley St AIRE BD20 ....26 E6
Elm St GTL/HWG HX4 ....165 K7
HDGY * LS6 ....79 H7
HOR/CROF WF4 ....201 F4
HUDS HD4 ....13 D6
HWTH BD22 ....90 E1
KBTN HD8 ....236 E1
Elm Wy BTLY WF17 ....145 K1
Elmwood Av MSTN/BAR LS15 ....83 H4
WKFDW/WTN WF2 ....199 K4
Elmwood Cha MSTN/BAR LS15 ....83 H4
Elmwood Cl HUD HD1 ....12 C5
MIRF WF14 ....193 H2
WKFDW/WTN WF2 ....199 K4
Elmwood Dr BRIG HD6 ....142 A8
HWTH BD22 ....2 A6
WKFDW/WTN WF2 ....199 K4
Elmwood Garth WKFDW/WTN WF2 ....199 K4
Elmwood Gv HOR/CROF WF4 ....197 J2
Elmwood La LDSU LS2 ....7 E2
MSTN/BAR LS15 ....83 H4
Elmwood PI BFDE BD3 ....96 E2
Elmwood Rd HWTH BD22 ....47 H8
LDSU LS2 ....7 E2
Elm Wood St BRIG HD6 ....142 C7
Elmwood St HFAX HX1 ....8 B6
Elmwood Ter HWTH BD22 ....2 A6
Elphaborough Cl HBR HX7 ....137 F3
Elsdon Gv WBOW BD5 ....4 C6
Elsham Ter BULY LS4 ....100 C1
Elsicker La WKFDE WF1 ....177 J5
Elsie St HWTH BD22 ....69 H3
KGHY BD21 ....47 K1
Elsinore Av ELL HX5 ....166 C5
Elsinore Ct ELL HX5 ....166 D5
Elsworth Av BFDE BD3 ....97 F3
Elsworth St WOR/ARM LS12 ....100 D4
Eltham Cl HDGY LS6 ....79 H8
Eltham Ct HDGY LS6 ....79 H8
Eltham Dr HDGY LS6 ....79 H8
Eltham Gdns HDGY LS6 ....79 H8
Eltham Gv WBSY BD6 ....118 B3
Eltham Rd HDGY LS6 ....79 H8
Elvaston Rd MOR LS27 ....147 F1
Elvey Cl ECHL BD2 ....75 F7
Elvey St WKFDE WF1 ....10 C2
Elwell Cl WBSY BD6 ....117 J4
Elwell St EARD/LOFT WF3 ....149 F2
Elwyn Gv WBOW BD5 ....96 A8
Elwyn Rd WBOW BD5 ....96 B8
Ely St GTL/HWG HX4 ....166 C5
The Embankment MIRF WF14 ....170 D6
Emblem Ter WKFDE WF1 ....11 D6
Embleton Rd RTHW LS26 ....152 B2
Emerald St BTLY WF17 ....145 K5
HUD HD1 ....13 D2
HWTH BD22 ....2 A6
Emerson Av HTON BD9 ....72 D8
Emily Hall Gdns WIL/AL BD15 ....71 G6
Emily St KGHY BD21 ....3 D1
Emmanuel Ter HUD HD4 ....213 F1
Emm La HTON BD9 ....73 G8
Emmeline Cl IDLE * BD10 ....74 D3
Emmfield Dr HTON BD9 ....73 G7
Emmott Dr YEA LS19 ....54 B8
Emmott Farm Fold HWTH BD22 ....68 E5
Emscote Av HFAX HX1 ....8 B6
Emscote Gdns HFAX HX1 ....8 B6
Emscote Gv HFAX HX1 ....8 B6
Emscote PI HFAX HX1 ....8 B6
Emscote St South HFAX HX1 ....8 B6
Emsley Cl BOW BD4 ....119 J3
Emsley PI MID LS10 ....102 A6

Emville Av AL/HA/HU LS17 ....58 E6
Enderby Cl HIPP HX3 ....115 J8
Enderley Rd CUL/QBY BD13 ....93 H5
Endor Crs ILK LS29 ....32 B4
Endor Gv ILK LS29 ....32 B4
Endsleigh PI CLAY * BD14 ....94 B7
Enfield YEA LS19 ....53 K5
Enfield Av CHAL LS7 ....102 A1
Enfield Cl BTLY WF17 ....145 J5
Enfield Dr BTLY WF17 ....145 J5
GTHN BD7 ....118 A2
Enfield Pde WBSY BD6 ....118 B2
Enfield Rd BAIL BD17 ....73 J1
Enfield Side Rd HWTH BD22 ....67 K6
Enfield St CHAL LS7 ....7 F1
KGHY BD21 ....2 C3
Enfield Ter CHAL LS7 ....102 A1
Enfield Wk WBSY BD6 ....118 B2
Engine La HOR/CROF WF4 ....197 F2
HOR/CROF WF4 ....202 A4
England La KNOT WF11 ....156 C8
Englefield Cl BOW BD4 ....120 B1
Englefield Crs BOW BD4 ....120 B1
Ennerdale Av EARL WF12 ....172 D1
Ennerdale Cl WBY LS22 ....23 G5
Ennerdale Crs EARL WF12 ....172 D1
Ennerdale Dr ECHL BD2 ....74 D8
ELL HX5 ....167 G4
Ennerdale Rd EARL WF12 ....172 D1
ECHL BD2 ....74 C8
WKFDW/WTN * WF2 ....175 G5
WOR/ARM LS12 ....122 C1
Ennerdale Wy WOR/ARM * LS12 ....122 C1
Enoch La HUDS HD4 ....191 F8
Enterprise Wy CAS WF10 ....153 H4
IDLE BD10 ....74 D5
MID LS10 ....125 G2
Envoy St BEE/HOL * LS11 ....101 J7
Epsom Rd GFTH/SHER LS25 ....128 E1
Epsom Wy HUDE HD5 ....192 E2
Epworth PI HWTH BD22 ....46 D8
MID LS10 ....102 A7
Eric St BRAM LS13 ....77 G6
HEM/SK/SE WF9 ....226 C8
KGHY BD21 ....3 D2
Ernest St DEWS WF13 ....172 C2
TOD OL14 ....133 F2
Erringden Rd HBR HX7 ....136 E2
Erringden St TOD OL14 ....134 B6
Escroft Cl LM/WK BD12 ....142 E2
Eshald La RTHW LS26 ....127 G6
Eshald PI RTHW LS26 ....127 G5
Esholt Av GSLY LS20 ....53 F4
Esholt La BAIL BD17 ....52 C7
Eshton Av LM/WK BD12 ....119 G6
Eskdale Av HIPP HX3 ....117 C6
NORM WF6 ....151 K7
Eskdale Cl EARL WF12 ....146 D8
NORM WF6 ....151 K7
Eskdale Cft NORM WF6 ....151 K7
Eskdale Gv GFTH/SHER LS25 ....106 A5
Eskdale Mt HBR HX7 ....112 B7
SCFT LS14 ....81 H7
Eskdale Ri WIL/AL BD15 ....94 B3
Eskdale Rd WKFDW/WTN WF2 ....175 F4
Esk Gdns WBY LS22 ....23 J3
Eskine Pde WBSY BD6 ....118 A5
Esmond St GTHN BD7 ....95 F8
WOR/ARM LS12 ....100 C4
Esmond Ter WOR/ARM LS12 ....100 B4
Essex St BOW BD4 ....5 E6
HFAX HX1 ....8 A5
Estcourt Av HDGY LS6 ....78 C6
Estcourt Dr PONT WF8 ....182 A7
Estcourt Gv GTHN BD7 ....95 G6
Estcourt Rd GTHN BD7 ....95 G6
PONT WF8 ....181 K6
Estcourt Ter HDGY LS6 ....78 C6
Esther Av WKFDW/WTN WF2 ....175 G7
Esther Gv WKFDW/WTN WF2 ....175 F7
Esthwaite Gdns MSTN/BAR * LS15 ....103 G5
Ethel St KGHY BD21 ....2 C1
Etna St GTHN BD7 ....95 F8
Eton Av HUDE HD5 ....192 A5
Eton St HBR HX7 ....112 A8
HFAX HX1 ....8 A4
Euden Edge Rd MAR/SLWT HD7 ....188 E8
Eunice La KBTN HD8 ....236 A5
Euston Gv BEE/HOL LS11 ....101 F7
Euston Mt BEE/HOL LS11 ....101 F7
Euston Ter BEE/HOL LS11 ....101 F7
Evanston Av BULY LS4 ....100 C2
Evelyn Av BFDE BD3 ....97 G3
Evelyn PI WOR/ARM LS12 ....100 C5
Evens Ter WBOW BD5 ....119 F1
Everard St HUDS HD4 ....190 D7
Everdale Mt HEM/SK/SE WF9 ....224 B5
HEM/SK/SE WF9 ....226 A8
Everest Av SHPY BD18 ....74 A4
Everleigh St OSM LS9 ....102 C3
Eversley Dr BOW BD4 ....97 G7
Eversley Ldg LUD/ILL * HX2 ....139 H5
Eversley Mt LUD/ILL * HX2 ....139 H5
Eversley PI LUD/ILL HX2 ....139 H5
Eversley Rd HBR HX7 ....112 B7
Every St TOD OL14 ....134 B6
Evesham Gv IDLE BD10 ....74 D4
Ewart PI GTHN BD7 ....95 G8

Ewart St CUL/QBY * BD13 .....116 D2
  GTHN BD7 .....95 C8
Ewood Dr HBR HX7 .....137 C2
Ewood Hall Av HBR HX7 .....137 C2
Ewood La TOD OL14 .....133 J5
Excelsior St RPDN/SBR HX6 .....163 K8
Exchange HOLM/MEL HD9 .....213 F7
Exchange Sq BFD * BD1 .....5 D5
Exchange St CLECK BD19 .....144 A2
  GTL/HWG HX4 .....166 C5
  HEM/SK/SE WF9 .....226 B8
  NORM WF6 .....177 K1
Exe St WBOW BD5 .....95 J8
Exeter Dr MID LS10 .....124 E4
Exeter St HIPP HX3 .....140 C8
  RPDN/SBR HX6 .....139 F7
Exhibition Rd SHPY BD18 .....73 F3
Exley Av KGHY BD21 .....2 B6
Exley Bank HIPP HX3 .....166 C1
Exley Bank Top HIPP HX3 .....166 C1
Exley Crs KGHY BD21 .....2 B5
Exley Dr KGHY * BD21 .....2 B5
Exley Gdns ELL HX5 .....166 C2
Exley Gv KGHY BD21 .....2 B6
Exley Head HWTH BD22 .....2 A5
Exley Head Vw HWTH BD22 .....47 C5
Exley La ELL HX5 .....166 D2
Exley Mt GTHN BD7 .....95 F5
  KGHY BD21 .....2 B5
Exley Rd KGHY BD21 .....2 B5
Exley St KGHY BD21 .....2 B5
Exley Wy KGHY * BD21 .....2 B6
Exmoor St HFAX HX1 .....8 A5
Exmouth Pl BFDE BD3 .....5 D2
Express Wy NORM WF6 .....152 A5
Exton Av MSTN/BAR LS15 .....105 C4
Eyres Av WOR/ARM LS12 .....100 C3
Eyres Gv WOR/ARM LS12 .....100 C3
Eyres Mill Side WOR/ARM LS12 .....100 B3
Eyres St WOR/ARM LS12 .....100 C3
Eyres Ter WOR/ARM LS12 .....100 C3
Eyre St BTLY WF17 .....146 C7
  EARL WF12 .....172 A4
Eyrie Ap MOR LS27 .....123 H8

F

Factory La BOW BD4 .....119 J1
  HUDS HD4 .....190 B7
Factory St BOW BD4 .....119 K1
Fagley Crs ECHL BD2 .....96 E1
Fagley Cft ECHL BD2 .....97 F1
Fagley Dr ECHL BD2 .....96 E1
Fagley La ECHL BD2 .....75 F8
Fagley Pl ECHL BD2 .....96 E2
Fagley Rd ECHL BD2 .....97 G1
Fagley Ter ECHL BD2 .....96 E2
Fair Bank SHPY BD18 .....73 J5
Fairbank Rd GIR BD8 .....95 C2
Fairbank Ter GIR BD8 .....95 C2
Fairbrook Rd HOR/CROF WF4 .....198 C7
Fairburn Ct HIPP * HX3 .....141 F7
Fairburn Dr GFTH/SHER LS25 .....106 A6
Fairburn Gdns ECHL BD2 .....74 E7
Fairclough Gv LUD/ILL HX2 .....115 J8
Fairfax Av BIRK/DRI BD11 .....121 K6
  BOW BD4 .....119 K2
  FEA/AMT WF7 .....179 H2
  KNOT WF11 .....156 A8
Fairfax Ct SCFT LS14 .....81 K8
Fairfax Ct BEE/HOL * LS11 .....101 G8
Fairfax Ct BOW BD4 .....119 K2
  HIPP HX3 .....141 F7
Fairfax Flats OT * LS21 .....33 K4
Fairfax Gdns ILK LS29 .....32 B6
Fairfax Gv HYS * LS19 .....53 H4
Fairfax Rd BEE/HOL LS11 .....101 G8
  BGLY BD16 .....49 K6
  CUL/QBY BD13 .....70 B4
  ILK LS29 .....32 B6
  PONT WF8 .....181 F3
Fairfax St AIRE BD20 .....27 J3
  BOW BD4 .....5 D6
  HWTH BD22 .....69 F4
  OT LS21 .....33 J4
Fairfax Vw HORS LS18 .....55 F7
Fairfield CUL/QBY BD13 .....92 B3
  KNOT WF11 .....131 H6
Fairfield Av HECK WF16 .....145 H6
  NORM WF6 .....151 H8
  OSS WF5 .....174 A7
  PDSY/CALV LS28 .....98 C3
  PONT WF8 .....180 C3
Fairfield Ct CAS WF10 .....155 F4
  LVSG WF15 .....144 C2
Fairfield Dr BRAM LS13 .....98 E1
  DEWS WF13 .....171 K2
Fairfield Dr BAIL BD17 .....52 A7
  HECK WF16 .....145 H6
  OSS WF5 .....174 A7
  RTHW LS26 .....125 J7
Fairfield Gdns OSS WF5 .....174 A7

RTHW LS26 .....125 J7
Fairfield Gv BRAM LS13 .....99 F1
  RTHW * LS26 .....125 J7
Fairfield HI BRAM LS13 .....99 F1
Fairfield La RTHW LS26 .....125 J7
Fairfield Ms DEWS WF13 .....171 K2
Fairfield Mt BRAM LS13 .....99 F1
  OSS WF5 .....174 A7
Fairfield Ri KBTN HD8 .....215 D6
Fairfield Rd BRAM LS13 .....98 E1
  GIR BD8 .....95 H2
  HECK WF16 .....145 H6
  LM/WK BD12 .....118 E8
Fairfield Sq BRAM LS13 .....77 F8
Fairfields Rd HOLM/MEL HD9 .....232 D8
Fairfields St BOW BD4 .....120 A2
  BRAM LS13 .....99 F1
Fairfield Ter BRAM LS13 .....99 F1
  EARL WF12 .....172 E3
  OSS WF5 .....173 K7
Fairfield Wk OSS WF5 .....173 K7
Fairford Av BEE/HOL LS11 .....101 J8
Fairford Ter BEE/HOL LS11 .....101 J8
Fairhaven Gn IDLE BD10 .....74 E4
Fair Isle Ct KGHY BD21 .....3 D3
Fair Lea Rd HUDS HD4 .....212 E2
Fairleigh Crs EARD/LOFT WF3 .....148 B3
Fairleigh Rd EARD/LOFT WF3 .....148 A3
Fairless Av HIPP HX3 .....142 B4
Fairmoor Wy HECK WF16 .....145 H6
Fairmount HTON BD9 .....4 A1
Fairmount Pk SHPY BD18 .....72 E4
Fairmount Ter KGHY BD21 .....48 D5
Fair Rd WBSY BD6 .....118 C2
Fair Vw LVSG WF15 .....144 C6
  PONT 181 F6
Fairview Av BTLY WF17 .....145 J5
Fairview Ct BAIL BD17 .....73 H2
Fairview Crs BTLY WF17 .....145 J5
Fairview Rd BTLY WF17 .....145 J5
Fairview Ter HIPP HX3 .....8 B1
The Fairway AL/HA/HU LS17 .....57 H5
  FEA/AMT WF7 .....179 H2
  HUDN HD2 .....168 B7
  LUD/ILL HX2 .....115 J4
  PDSY/CALV LS28 .....97 K2
Fairway GSLY LS20 .....52 E2
  IDLE BD10 .....75 H2
  NORM WF6 .....178 B2
  SHPY BD18 .....73 F4
  WBSY BD6 .....118 A2
Fairway Ap NORM WF6 .....178 B1
Fairway Av GTHN BD7 .....118 A2
  NORM WF6 .....178 B1
Fairway Cl GSLY LS20 .....52 E3
  NORM WF6 .....178 B2
  WBSY BD6 .....118 A2
Fairway Crs HWTH BD22 .....69 F5
Fairway Dr GTHN BD7 .....118 A1
  NORM WF6 .....178 B2
Fairway Gdns NORM WF6 .....178 B1
Fairway Gv GTHN BD7 .....118 A1
Fairway Mdw NORM WF6 .....178 B1
The Fairways AIRE BD20 .....27 J8
  HTON BD9 .....72 E6
Fair Ways MIRF WF14 .....193 H1
Fairway Wk GTHN BD7 .....118 A1
Fairweather Ms GIR BD8 .....94 E4
Fairy Dell BGLY BD16 .....72 A4
Fairy Hill La CAS WF10 .....154 E6
Faith St HEM/SK/SE WF9 .....225 K7
Falcon Cliffe AIRE BD20 .....26 E6
Falcon Dr CAS WF10 .....153 H5
Falconers Ride HUDS HD4 .....212 E5
Falcon Ms GIR * BD8 .....94 C3
  MOR LS27 .....123 H8
Falcon Rd BGLY BD16 .....49 K6
Falcon St EARL WF12 .....172 B5
  GTHN BD7 .....95 G6
  HIPP HX3 .....140 C8
  HUDS HD4 .....213 F2
Falhouse La EARL WF12 .....194 D3
Falkland Crs AL/HA/HU LS17 .....79 J2
Falkland Gv AL/HA/HU LS17 .....79 J2
Falkland Mt AL/HA/HU LS17 .....79 J2
Falkland Ri AL/HA/HU LS17 .....79 J2
Falkland Rd AL/HA/HU LS17 .....79 J2
  IDLE BD10 .....78 C5
Fall Brow Cl CLAY BD14 .....94 A8
Falledge La STKB/PEN S36 .....251 H1
Fall Ings Rd WKFDE WF1 .....11 E5
Fall La DEWS WF13 .....172 A5
  EARD/LOFT WF3 .....148 A3
  HIPP HX3 .....116 D7
  LVSG WF15 .....170 A2
  MAR/SLWT HD7 .....209 H8
  RPDN/SBR HX6 .....139 G8
Fallow Cft HUDN HD2 .....169 G6
Fallowfield Cl BOW BD4 .....119 K3
Fallowfield Dr BOW BD4 .....119 K3
Fallowfield Gdns BOW BD4 .....119 K2
Fallow La HWTH BD22 .....46 C1
Fall Park Ct BRAM LS13 .....77 H6
Fall Rd LVSG WF15 .....170 B2

Fall Spring Gdns GTL/HWG HX4 165
Fall Spring Gn GTL/HWG HX4 165
Fallswood Gv BRAM LS13 77
Fall Wood St HWTH BD22 69
Falmers Cottages HDGY * LS6 79
Falmouth Av BFDE BD3 5
  NORM WF6 152
Falmouth Crs NORM WF6 152
Falmouth Rd NORM WF6 152
Falsgrave Av ECHL BD2 97
Faltis IDLE BD10 78
Fanny Moor Crs HUDE HD5 213
Fanny Moor La HUDE HD5 213
Fanny St KGHY BD21 2
  SHPY BD18 73
Far Bank KBTN HD8 215
Farcliffe Pl GIR BD8 95
Farcliffe Rd GIR BD8 95
Farcliffe Ter GIR BD8 95
Far Common Rd MIRF WF14 170
Far Cft KBTN HD8 215
Far Crook IDLE BD10 74
Far Dene KBTN HD8 215
Fardene St AIRE BD20 27
Farehill Rd HUDS HD4 213
Far Field Av HOLM/MEL HD9 249
Farfield Av BTLY * WF17 145
  PDSY/CALV LS28 76
  WBSY BD6 117
Farfield Ct AL/HA/HU LS17 58
  GFTH/SHER LS25 105
Farfield Crs WBSY BD6 118
Far Field Dr HOLM/MEL HD9 249
Farfield Dr PDSY/CALV LS28 98
Farfield Gv PDSY/CALV LS28 76
  WBSY BD6 118
Far Field La HOLM/MEL HD9 249
Farfield Ri PDSY/CALV LS28 76
Farfield Rd BAIL BD17 73
  HUDE HD5 192
  SHPY BD18 73
  WBSY BD6 118
Far Fields La HOLM/MEL HD9 211
Farfield St CLECK BD19 144
  HTON BD9 95
Farfield Ter HTON BD9 95
  HTON BD9 95
Farla HBR HX7 137
  HOLM/MEL HD9 249
Farlea Dr ECHL BD2 74
Farleton Dr ECHL BD2 97
Farley Crs HWTH BD22 46
Farm Ct MSTN/BAR LS15 103
Farm Cft FEA/AMT WF7 178
Far Mead Cft ILK LS29 32
Farmfield Dr HEM/SK/SE WF9 202
Farm Gdns FEA/AMT WF7 178
Farm Hill Crs CHAL LS7 79
Farm Hill N North CHAL LS7 79
Farm Hill Ri CHAL LS7 79
Farm Hill Rd IDLE BD10 74
  MOR LS27 122
Farm Hill South CHAL LS7 79
Farm Hill Wy CHAL LS7 79
Farm La HEM/SK/SE WF9 224
Farm Mt HOR/CROF WF4 196
  MSTN/BAR LS15 104
Far Moss AL/HA/HU LS17 57
Farm Pond Dr BRIC HD6 141
Farm Rd FEA/AMT WF7 179
  MSTN/BAR LS15 103
Farmstead Rd IDLE BD10 74
Farnboro St TOD OL14 159
Farndale Ap SCFT LS14 82
  WBY LS22 23
Farndale Ct GFTH/SHER LS25 105
Farndale Garth SCFT LS14 82
Farndale Pl SCFT LS14 82
Farndale Rd BAIL BD17 73
  WIL/AL BD15 71
Farne Av WKFDW/WTN WF2 175
Farnham Cl BAIL BD17 73
  SCFT LS14 81
Farnham Cft SCFT LS14 81
Farnham Rd GTHN BD7 95
Farnham Wy HOR/CROF WF4 200
Farnlee HUDW HD3 190
Farnley Cl ILK LS29 32
Farnley Rd HUDS HD4 214
  ILK LS29 32
Farnley Vw BIRK/DRI BD11 121
Farrar Av MIRF WF14 170
Farrar Ct BRAM LS13 77
Farrar Cft BHP/TINH LS16 56
Farrar Dr MIRF WF14 170
Farrar Gv BHP/TINH LS16 56
Farrar Height La RPDN/SBR HX6 163
Farrar La BHP/TINH LS16 56
Farrar Mill La HIPP HX3 140
Far Reef Cl HORS LS18 77
Farrer La RTHW LS26 127
Far Richard Cl OSS WF5 173
Farriers Ct ECHL BD2 74
Farriers Pl CAS WF10 154
Farringdon Cl BOW BD4 98
Farringdon Dr BOW BD4 98
Farringdon Gv WBSY BD6 118
Farrow Bank WOR/ARM LS12 99
Farrow Gn WOR/ARM LS12 99

rrow HI WOR/ARM LS12 ....99 K4
rrow Rd WOR/ARM LS12 ....99 J4
rrow V WOR/ARM LS12 ....99 J4
rside Gn WBOW BD5.....................95 J8
rtown PDSY/CALV LS28 ....98 C6
rtown CI PDSY/CALV LS28 ....98 C6
rtown Green Rd HUDN HD2 ....13 D1
r View Bank HUDE HD5 ....192 A6
rway BOW BD4 ....97 G7
r Well Fold YEA * LS19 ....54 B8
r Well La HOLM/MEL HD9 ....234 D3
ugh La HBR HX7 ....111 H5
vell Av NORM WF6 ....178 A2
versham Wk BOW * 97 G7
wcett Av WOR/ARM LS12 ....100 B6
wcett Bank WOR/ARM LS12 ....100 A6
wcett CI WOR/ARM LS12 ....100 A6
wcett Dr WOR/ARM LS12 ....100 A6
wcett Gdns WOR/ARM LS12 ....100 A6
wcett La WOR/ARM LS12 ....100 A6
wcett PI BOW BD4 ....119 K3
wcett Rd WOR/ARM LS12 ....100 A6
wcett V WOR/ARM LS12 ....100 A6
wcett Wy WOR/ARM LS12 ....100 A6
wkes Dr OT LS21 ....33 F5
xfleet St WBOW BD5 ....118 E2
ye Cdns BOW BD4.....................120 A2
arnley Av OSS WF5 ....173 H4
arnley CI WOR/ARM LS12.....................100 D4
arnley Ct HOLM/MEL HD9 ....233 K6
arnley Dr OSS WF5 ....173 H4
arnley La HOLM/MEL HD9 ....233 J6
arnley PI WOR/ARM LS12 ....100 D4
arnley St DEWS WF13 ....172 A4
FEA/AMT WF7 ....179 H6
arnside CHOR/CROF * WF4 ....197 H1
arnside's CI HOR/CROF WF4 ....197 G2
arnsides St GIR BD8 ....95 H3
arnsides Ter GIR BD8 ....95 H3
arnville Av RHAY LS8 ....81 F7
arnville Cv RHAY LS8 ....81 F6
arnville Cv BSLYN/ROY S71 ....222 A8
RHAY LS8 ....81 F7
arnville Mt RHAY LS8 ....81 F6
arnville PI RHAY LS8 ....81 G6
arnville Rd RHAY LS8 ....81 F7
arnville Ter RHAY LS8 ....81 G6
arnville Vw RHAY LS8 ....81 F7
ast Fld HORS LS18 ....77 F2
atherbank Av HORS LS18 ....77 F4
atherbank Cv HORS LS18 ....77 F3
atherbank Ter HORS LS18 ....77 F4
atherbank Wk HORS LS18 ....77 F4
atherbed Ct GTL/HWG HX4 ....166 C5
ather Bed La ELL HX5 ....166 C5
atherbed La TAD LS24 ....25 K5
ather Rd BFDE BD3 ....5 F4
atherstone La FEA/AMT WF7 ....179 J3
deration St WBOW BD5.....................119 G1
brigg Av HWTH BD22 ....2 A4
court Dr BOW BD4.....................120 B1
court Fold BOW BD4 ....120 B1
kirk Dr HOR/CROF WF4 ....222 E2
kirk Vw CUD/OR S72 ....223 F8
ks Stile Rd HUDS HD4 ....211 K1
ll Greave Crs HUDN HD2 ....168 D7
ll Greave Rd HUDN HD2 ....168 C6
ll Gv HUDN HD2 ....168 C7
HWTH BD22 ....2 A4
e Fields HUDS HD4 ....212 C4
llowsides La OSS WF5 ....173 K6
side TOD OL14 ....135 C6
side CI WBOW BD5 ....119 G1
llwood Av HWTH BD22 ....69 G3
llwood CI HWTH BD22 ....69 G3
nex Crs OSM LS9 ....102 E6
nex Crs OSM LS9 ....102 E6
nex Gn OSM LS9 ....102 E6
nex Sq OSM LS9 ....102 E6
nex Wy OSM LS9 ....102 E6
nay Bankside KBTN HD8 ....193 F8
nay Bridge Rd HUDE HD5 ....192 E8
nay Crs HUDE HD5 ....192 E8
nay Dr KBTN HD8 ....192 E8
nay Lea Dr HUDE HD5 ....192 E7
nby Av BOW BD4.....................96 D7
nby CI BOW BD4 ....96 E8
nby Cv BOW BD4 ....96 E7
ncote Crs ECHL BD2 ....75 F8
nder Rd WBSY BD6 ....118 A2
nnec Rd BAIL BD17 ....52 A7
nnell Ct WKFDW/WTN WF2 ....199 F4
nton Av RTHW LS26 ....126 E4
nton CI HEM/SK/SE WF9 ....241 H2
RTHW LS26 ....126 E4
nton Dr EARD/LOFT WF3.....................150 C4
HFAX HX1 ....8 A6
HUD HD1 ....191 H8
ntongate EARD/LOFT WF3 ....149 K2
nton St EARD/LOFT WF3 ....148 A2
LK LS29 ....32 B2
MIRF WF14 ....170 D7
nwick Dr WBSY BD6 ....118 A5
rguson St HFAX HX1 ....9 D5
rn Av HOLM/MEL HD9 ....211 G8

Fernbank BRAM LS13 ....76 D8
Fernbank Av HWTH BD22 ....2 A6
Fernbank CI BRAM LS13 ....76 D8
Fernbank Dr BAIL BD17 ....73 G2
BGLY BD16 ....50 A8
BRAM LS13 ....76 D8
Fernbank Gdns BRAM LS13 ....76 D8
Fernbank PI BRAM LS13 ....76 D8
Fernbank Rd BFDE BD3 ....5 F2
BRAM LS13 ....76 D8
Fern Cha SCFT LS14 ....59 J4
Ferncliffe Dr AIRE BD20 ....47 H1
BAIL BD17 ....51 H8
Ferncliffe Rd BGLY BD16 ....50 A8
SHPY * BD18 ....73 F3
Ferncliffe Ter BRAM LS13 ....99 F1
Fern CI BTLY WF17 ....146 E6
Fern Ct AIRE BD20 ....47 J1
Fern Cft LVSG WF15 ....143 K7
WKFDW/WTN WF2 ....149 F8
Ferndale Av CLAY BD14 ....94 A8
Ferndale Gv HTON BD9 ....73 J7
Ferndale PI HEM/SK/SE WF9 ....224 C5
Ferndene BGLY BD16 ....50 B8
Ferndene Av BTLY WF17 ....121 J8
Ferndown Gn WBOW BD5 ....95 K8
Ferney Lee Rd TOD OL14 ....133 K5
Fernfield Ter HIPP * HX3 ....8 C1
Fern Gv KSTL LS5 ....78 A7
Fernhill BGLY BD16 ....50 A6
Fern Hill Av SHPY BD18 ....73 F4
Fern Hill Cv SHPY BD18 ....73 F4
Fern Hill Mt SHPY BD18 ....73 F4
Fern Hill Rd SHPY BD18 ....73 F4
Fernhurst CI MIRF WF14 ....170 D5
Fernhurst Crs MIRF WF14 ....170 E5
Fernhurst Lea MIRF WF14 ....170 E5
Fernhurst Rd MIRF WF14 ....170 D5
Fernhurst Wy MIRF WF14 ....170 D5
Fernlea RTHW LS26 ....126 C5
Fernlea CI HECK WF16 ....145 H8
HOR/CROF WF4 ....200 E2
Fernlea Gv MAR/SLWT HD7 ....189 J8
Fern Lea Rd HUDW HD3 ....190 A2
Fern Lea St RPDN/SBR HX6 ....138 E6
Fern Lea Vw PDSY/CALV LS28 ....98 C1
Fernleigh Ct WKFDW/WTN WF2 ....175 G6
Fernley Gdns LM/WK BD12 ....118 D7
Fernley Green CI KNOT WF11 ....156 E7
Fernley Green Rd KNOT WF11 ....156 E7
Fernley Hill Dr NORM WF6 ....151 J6
Fernside Av HUDE HD5 ....192 B1
Fernside CI HUDE HD5 ....192 C6
Fernside Crs HUDE HD5 ....192 B6
Fern St BOW BD4 ....97 F8
HIPP HX3 ....8 C1
HUDN HD2 ....12 C1
KGHY BD21 ....3 D2
Fern Ter AIRE BD20 ....48 D2
GIR BD8 ....4 A1
PDSY/CALV LS28 ....98 B1
Fern Wy SCFT LS14 ....59 J4
Fernwood Wal HFAX LS8 ....80 C2
Ferrand Av BOW BD4 ....119 K3
Ferrand La BGLY BD16 ....49 K8
CLECK BD19 ....144 D2
Ferrands CI BGLY BD16 ....71 F2
Ferrands Park Wy BGLY BD16 ....71 F2
Ferrand St BGLY BD16 ....50 A8
Ferriby CI WFDL BD1.....................75 F8
Ferrybridge By-Pass KNOT WF11.....................155 K5
Ferrybridge Rd CAS WF10 ....153 K3
KNOT WF11 ....156 A7
PONT WF8 ....181 F1
Ferry La EARD/LOFT WF3 ....176 C1
Ferry Top La HOR/CROF WF4 ....200 E8
Festival Av SHPY BD18 ....73 K5
Feversham St SHPY * BD18 ....73 K5
Fewson Av OSM LS9 ....102 B5
WKFDE WF1 ....11 F1
Fewston CI OSM LS9 ....102 E6
Fiddle La RPDN/SBR HX6 ....164 C7
Fidler La GFTH/SHER LS25 ....105 J4
Field CI HECK WF16 ....145 G5
HIPP HX3 ....8 B2
Fieldcroft Ct MIRF WF14 ....170 C6
Fieldedge La AIRE BD20 ....48 E1
Field End MSTN/BAR LS15 ....103 J4
Field End CI MSTN/BAR LS15 ....103 J4
Field End Crs MSTN/BAR LS15 ....103 J4
Field End Gdns MSTN/BAR LS15 ....103 J4
Field End Garth MSTN/BAR LS15 ....103 J4
Field End Gn MSTN/BAR * LS15 ....103 K3
Field End Gv MSTN/BAR * LS15 ....103 J3
Field End La HOLM/MEL HD9 ....213 G7
HOLM/MEL HD9 ....247 G1
Field End Mt MSTN/BAR LS15 ....103 J4
Field End Rd MSTN/BAR LS15 ....103 J4
Fielden PI BTLY WF17 ....134 A7
Fielden Sq TOD OL14 ....134 D5
Fieldgate Rd IDLE BD10 ....75 F4
Field Head MAR/SLWT HD7 ....189 H6
Fieldhead CI PONT WF8 ....181 G2
Fieldhead Crs BSPA/BRAM LS23 ....42 C4
Fieldhead Crs BTLY WF17 ....121 H8
Fieldhead Dr GSLY LS20 ....53 F3

MSTN/BAR LS15 ....83 K4
Fieldhead Gdns EARL WF12 ....147 G8
Field Head La BTLY WF17 ....145 H1
HBR HX7 ....136 C7
HWTH BD22 ....68 C6
LUD/ILL HX2 ....115 G4
Fieldhead La HOLM/MEL HD9 ....246 E2
Fieldhead Paddock
BSPA/BRAM LS23 ....42 C3
Fieldhead Rd GSLY LS20 ....52 E3
Fieldhead St GTHN BD7 ....4 A4
Fieldhead Wy GSLY LS20 ....145 F6
Fieldhouse CI AL/HA/HU LS17 ....79 J1
Field House CI WBY LS22 ....23 G6
Fieldhouse Dr AL/HA/HU LS17 ....79 J1
MAR/SLWT HD7 ....210 E1
Fieldhouse Gv PDSY/CALV LS28 ....98 A1
Fieldhouse Lawn AL/HA/HU LS17 ....79 J1
Fieldhouse Rd HUD HD1 ....13 E2
Fieldhouse St WKFDE WF1 ....11 F6
Fieldhouse Wk AL/HA/HU LS17 ....79 J1
Field Hurst CLECK BD19 ....143 G4
GTL/HWG HX4 ....164 E6
Fieldhurst Ct BOW BD4 ....119 J3
Fielding Ga WOR/ARM LS12 ....100 D3
Fielding Gate Ms WOR/ARM LS12 ....100 D3
Field La BRIC HD6 ....168 A3
BTLY WF17 ....146 B7
DEWS WF13 ....171 G5
GFTH/SHER LS25 ....84 E4
HEM/SK/SE WF9 ....226 C4
HEM/SK/SE WF9 ....241 F2
HUDS HD4 ....214 B5
OSS WF5 ....173 J5
WKFDW/WTN WF2 ....10 C6
Field PI WKFDW/WTN WF2.....................10 A4
Field Rd HOLM/MEL HD9 ....233 H7
Fieldshead Bungalows
MAR/SLWT HD7 ....211 G4
Fieldside CUL/QBY BD13 ....70 B5
Field Side HFAX HX1 ....8 A3
The Fields EARD/LOFT WF3 ....150 A2
Fieldside Rd HEM/SK/SE WF9 ....224 B1
Fields Ri HUDE HD5 ....192 D2
Fields Rd KBTN HD8 ....193 F8
LM/WK BD12 ....119 F6
Field St BFD BD1 ....5 D4
DEWS * WF13 ....171 H5
Fields Wy HUDE HD5 ....192 D2
Field Ter MSTN/BAR LS15 ....103 J3
Field Top Rd BRIC HD6 ....168 A3
Field Vw CAS WF10 ....153 F5
HIPP HX3 ....8 A1
Fieldway CLAY BD14 ....94 B7
ILK LS29 ....20 E7
Field Wy KBTN HD8 ....235 G3
Fieldway Av BRAM LS13 ....76 E7
Fieldway Cha RTHW LS26 ....127 G6
Fieldway CI BRAM LS13 ....76 E7
Fieldway Ri BRAM LS13 ....76 D7
Fifth Av BFDE BD3 ....96 E2
RTHW LS26 ....126 D5
Fifth Av West LVSG WF15 ....143 J7
Filbert St HUDN HD2 ....12 C1
Filey Av BSLYN/ROY S71 ....222 B7
Filey St BFD BD1 ....5 D5
Filley Royd CLECK BD19 ....144 A5
Fillingfir Dr BHP/TINH LS16 ....77 K3
Fillingfir Rd BHP/TINH LS16 ....77 K3
Fillingfir Wk BHP/TINH LS16 ....77 K3
Finch Av WKFDW/WTN WF2 ....199 F6
Finching Gv MIRF WF14 ....170 D3
Finchley St WBOW BD5 ....95 K8
Finchley Wy MOR LS27 ....123 F8
Finch St WBOW BD5 ....95 K7
Findon Ter IDLE BD10 ....75 G7
Fine Garth CI BSPA/BRAM LS23.....................42 D8
Fink HI HORS LS18 ....76 E3
Finkil St BRIC HD6 ....141 K6
Finkin Av EARD/LOFT WF3 ....176 B1
Finkin Cft EARD/LOFT WF3 ....176 B1
Finkin La EARD/LOFT WF3 ....176 B1
Finkle La MOR LS27 ....122 B5
Finkle St HOR/CROF WF4 ....220 B4
LUD/ILL HX2 ....138 A7
PONT WF8 ....180 E2
Finsbury Dr ECHL BD2 ....74 B5
Finsbury Rd LDS LS1 ....1 D2
Finthorpe La HUDE HD5 ....192 C8
Fir Av MIRF WF14 ....171 G6
Firbank Gn ECHL * BD2 ....97 F1
Firbank Gv MSTN/BAR LS15 ....103 G5
Firbeck BGLY BD16 ....71 F3
Firbeck Rd BSPA/BRAM LS23.....................42 D8
Firethorn CI GIR * BD8 ....95 G3
Firham CI BSLYN/ROY S71 ....221 J7
Fir Pde DEWS WF13 ....171 G6
Fir Rd HUDW HD3 ....190 D5
Firs La STKB/PEN S36 ....252 C4
First Av AL/HA/HU LS17 ....40 C6
BFDE BD3 ....96 E2
HEM/SK/SE WF9 ....202 A7
HEM/SK/SE WF9 ....226 C4
HEM/SK/SE WF9 ....241 F2
HIPP HX3 ....140 A7
HOR/CROF WF4 ....197 F2
HUDE HD5 ....192 B4
KGHY BD21 ....2 C4
LVSG WF15 ....143 K6

PDSY/CALV LS28	98 C2
RTHW LS26	126 C4
WBY LS22	23 K6
WKFDE WF1	175 J1
WOR/ARM LS12	100 D4
YEA LS19	54 A6
The Firs BSLYN/ROY S71	221 J7
SCFT LS14	60 A4
Fir St HWTH BD22	68 E5
KGHY BD21	2 C6
TOD OL14	159 K3
First St LM/WK BD12	119 F5
Firth Av BEE/HOL LS11	124 B1
BRIG HD6	142 E8
Firthcliffe Dr LVSG WF15	144 E6
Firthcliffe Gv LVSG WF15	144 E6
Firthcliffe La LVSG WF15	144 E6
Firthcliffe Mt LVSG WF15	144 E5
Firthcliffe Pde LVSG WF15	144 E6
Firthcliffe Pl LVSG WF15	145 F6
Firthcliffe Rd LVSG WF15	144 E6
Firthcliffe Ter LVSG WF15	144 E6
Firthcliffe Vw LVSG WF15	144 E6
Firthcliffe Wk LVSG WF15	144 E6
Firth Cl EARD/LOFT WF3	150 B6
Firthfield La HEM/SK/SE WF9	204 A7
Firthfields GFTH/SHER LS25	106 A4
Firth Gv BEE/HOL LS11	124 B1
Firth House La BRIG HD6	168 C4
GTL/HWG HX4	188 D3
Firth La WIL/AL BD15	71 G6
Firth Mt BEE/HOL LS11	124 B1
Firth Rd BEE/HOL LS11	124 B1
HTON BD9	73 G8
Firth St BRIG HD6	168 B2
CHAL LS7	7 F2
CUL/QBY BD13	93 H5
HUD HD1	13 D5
KBTN HD8	235 G3
Firths Yd DEWS * WF13	172 B1
Firth Ter OSM LS9	102 A2
Firth Vw BEE/HOL LS11	124 B1
Fir Tree Ap AL/HA/HU LS17	57 H8
Firtree Av GFTH/SHER LS25	106 B5
Fir Tree Cl AL/HA/HU LS17	57 J7
Fir Tree Gdns AL/HA/HU LS17	57 H7
IDLE BD10	75 F5
Fir Tree Gn AL/HA/HU LS17	57 J7
Fir Tree Gv AL/HA/HU LS17	57 J8
Fir Tree La AL/HA/HU LS17	57 J8
Fir Tree Ri AL/HA/HU LS17	57 J8
Fir Tree V AL/HA/HU LS17	57 J8
Fir Tree Vw RTHW LS26	128 D8
Firville Av NORM WF6	177 G2
Firville Crs NORM WF6	178 A2
Fir Wk DEWS WF13	171 G6
Firwood Cl TOD OL14	159 K2
Fishbeck La AIRE BD20	17 J7
Fishergate KNOT WF11	156 A6
Fisher Gn HOLM/MEL HD9	212 F7
Fisher Gv OSS WF5	174 A7
Fisher St KNOT WF11	156 B7
Fisher Wy HECK WF16	145 H8
Fishpond La HOR/CROF WF4	198 B6
Fishponds Dr HOR/CROF WF4	198 B6
Fish St LDS LS1	7 E3
Fitts La AL/HA/HU LS17	38 C3
Fitzgerald St WBOW BD5	4 B6
Fitzroy Dr RHAY LS8	80 C5
Fitzroy Rd BFDE BD3	5 F4
Fitzwilliam St BOW BD4	5 D6
HEM/SK/SE WF9	224 B2
HUD HD1	12 C4
Five Acres DOD/DAR S75	239 F6
Five Lane Ends BHP/TINH LS16	56 D3
HOLM/MEL * HD9	232 E6
Five Oaks BAIL BD17	73 G1
Fixby Av LUD/ILL HX2	139 H6
Fixby La EARL WF12	194 B5
Fixby Park Dr HUDN HD2	190 E1
Fixby Rd HUDN HD2	168 B6
Flagship Sq EARL WF12	173 F1
Flanshaw Av WKFDW/WTN WF2	175 F5
Flanshaw Crs WKFDW/WTN WF2	175 F5
Flanshaw Gv WKFDW/WTN WF2	175 F5
Flanshaw La WKFDW/WTN WF2	174 E5
Flanshaw Rd WKFDW/WTN WF2	175 F5
Flanshaw St WKFDW/WTN WF2	175 F5
Flanshaw Vw WKFDW/WTN WF2	175 F5
Flanshaw Wy WKFDW/WTN WF2	174 D4
Flasby St KGHY BD21	3 D2
Flash La MIRF WF14	170 E5
Flass La CAS WF10	168 C1
Flat Nook BGLY * BD16	50 B8
The Flats WF8 LS9	54 A5
Flats La MSTN/BAR LS15	83 H5
Flavell Cl HEM/SK/SE WF9	241 H2
Flawith Dr ECHL BD2	97 F1
Flaxen Ct WBSY BD6	118 E2
Flax Pl OSM LS9	102 A4
Flaxton Cl BEE/HOL LS11	101 H8
Flaxton Gdns BEE/HOL * LS11	101 H8
Flaxton Gn ECHL BD2	97 F1
Flaxton Pl GTHN BD7	117 H4
Flaxton St BEE/HOL LS11	101 H8
Flaxton Vw BEE/HOL LS11	101 H8
Fledborough Rd WBY LS22	23 G6
Fleece St KGHY BD21	3 D3
WBSY BD6	118 A4
Fleet La CUL/QBY BD13	116 C3
Fleet St KBTN HD8	237 H7
Fleet Thro Rd HORS LS18	81 F1
Fleminghouse La HUDE HD5	192 C6
Fleming St BTLY WF17	146 B6
Fletcher Av AIRE BD20	27 G1
Fletcher Crs BRIG HD6	167 K5
Fletcher La SHPY BD18	73 K8
Fletcher Rd WBSY BD6	118 C2
Fletton Ter ECHL BD2	5 F1
Flexbury Av MOR LS27	123 F8
Flight Hl HOLM/MEL HD9	248 D6
Flight House Rd RPDN/SBR HX6	165 G7
Flint La HOLM/MEL HD9	249 H6
Flintmill La BSPA/BRAM LS23	24 D8
Flinton Gv ECHL BD2	75 F8
Flint St HUDN HD2	13 D1
Flockton Av BOW BD4	96 C7
Flockton Cl BOW BD4	96 C7
Flockton Crs BOW BD4	96 C7
Flockton Dr BOW BD4	96 C7
Flockton Gv BOW BD4	96 C7
Flockton Rd BOW BD4	96 C7
KBTN HD8	215 H8
Floral Av CHAL LS7	79 J5
Floreat Cl BTLY WF17	145 K3
Florence Av OSM LS9	102 C1
WIL/AL BD15	71 F5
Florence Gv OSM LS9	102 C1
Florence Mt OSM * LS9	102 C1
Florence Pl OSM LS9	102 C1
Florence St MOR LS27	123 C7
BFDE BD3	96 C5
CAS WF10	153 J3
HFAX * HX1	8 B4
OSM LS9	102 C1
Florence Ter MOR LS27	123 C7
Florida Rd WIL/AL BD15	72 A7
Florist St KGHY BD21	3 F1
Flossmore Wy MOR LS27	122 B4
Flounders Hl FEA/AMT WF7	202 E5
Flower Acre ELL HX5	166 C5
Flower Bank ECHL BD2	74 B7
RPDN/SBR HX6	138 C8
Flower Cl YEA LS19	53 J4
Flower Ct ECHL * BD2	74 E8
Flower Cft HWTH BD22	2 A5
Flower Garth IDLE BD10	75 F5
Flower Hvn HTON BD9	72 D7
Flower Hl HTON BD9	73 F7
Flowerlands HIPP HX3	141 K2
Flower Scar Rd TOD OL14	132 B5
Floyd St WBOW BD5	95 H8
Flush LVSG WF15	144 E7
Flush House La HOLM/MEL HD9	232 A8
Fold Grassmoor HOLM/MEL HD9	213 G8
The Fold MSTN/BAR LS15	82 C7
The Foldings KBTN HD8	236 E1
Foldings Av CLECK BD19	143 G3
Foldings Cl CLECK BD19	143 F3
Foldings Ct CLECK BD19	143 F3
Foldings Pde CLECK BD19	143 F3
Foldings Pl CLECK BD19	143 F3
Fold La HBR HX7	111 F5
Foljambe St WKFDW/WTN WF2	10 C1
Folkestone St BFDE BD3	5 F4
Folkton Holme ECHL BD2	97 F1
Follett Av HUDN HD4	212 C1
Follingworth La MAR/SLWT HD7	210 A2
Follingworth Rd BTLY WF17	146 D6
Folly Hall HUD HD1	12 C6
Folly Hall Av WBSY BD6	117 H3
The Folly Hall Gdns WBSY BD6	118 C3
Folly Hall La HBR HX7	162 E1
Folly Hall Rd EARD/LOFT WF3	147 K3
Folly Hall Wk WBSY BD6	118 C3
Folly La BEE/HOL LS11	101 H7
BSPA/BRAM LS23	62 D1
STKB/PEN S36	251 J5
Folly Rd HUDN HD2	168 B8
Folly Vw BSPA/BRAM LS23	62 D1
Folly View Rd HWTH * BD22	2 A5
Fontmell Cl BOW BD4	120 B1
Football YEA LS19	54 A5
Forber Gv BOW BD4	97 G6
Forber Pl MSTN/BAR LS15	103 C4
Ford CUL/QBY BD13	116 B3
Ford Dr MIRF WF14	170 B6
Ford Hl CUL/QBY BD13	116 B3
Ford Houses BAIL * BD17	52 B8
Ford St HEM/SK/SE WF9	224 B2
KGHY BD21	2 C6
Fore La RPDN/SBR HX6	138 D8
Fore Lane Av RPDN/SBR HX6	138 C8
Foreside Bottom La CUL/QBY BD13	92 B7
Foreside La CUL/QBY BD13	91 K6
Forest Av LUD/ILL HX2	115 H8
Forest Bank MOR LS27	122 B4
Forest Cl WKFDE WF1	176 B2
Forest Crs LUD/ILL HX2	115 H7
Forest Ga OT LS21	33 J4
Forest Gn LUD/ILL HX2	115 H8
Forest Hill Gdns HUDN * HD3	188 E3
Forest Hill Rd GTL/HWG HX4	186 E8
Forest Rdg EARD/LOFT WF3	148 D2
Forest Rd HUDE HD5	192 A6
Forest Wy HOLM/MEL HD9	212 E7
Forge Hill La KNOT WF11	156 B3
Forge La AL/HA/HU LS17	59 J1
EARL WF12	172 E6
HOR/CROF WF4	197 J6
LVSG WF15	144 B1
LVSG WF15	170 C6
WOR/ARM LS12	100 A3
Forge Rw WOR/ARM LS12	99 J7
Forge Vw AIRE BD20	26 D1
Forman's Dr EARD/LOFT WF3	125 F5
Formby Av HUDN HD2	168 A8
Forrest Av HUDW HD3	190 B1
Forrester Cl HEM/SK/SE WF9	202 D7
Forster Ct BFD BD1	5 J5
Forster Dr HECK WF16	146 D8
Forster Pl WOR/ARM LS12	100 E6
Forster St MID LS10	102 C8
Forsythia Av EARD/LOFT WF3	148 C6
Fort Ann Rd BTLY WF17	146 E5
Fortis Wy HUDW HD3	189 F3
Fortshot La AL/HA/HU LS17	58 E5
Forum Vw PONT WF8	204 D4
Foss Av WBY LS22	23 J7
Fosse Wy GFTH/SHER LS25	106 E8
Foster Av AIRE BD20	27 J1
CUL/QBY BD13	116 B2
HUDS HD4	212 B4
NORM WF6	177 F1
Foster Cl ILK LS29	32 A6
MOR LS27	123 H8
Foster Crs MOR LS27	123 H8
Foster Gdns HWTH BD22	2 A1
Foster La HBR HX7	112 C5
Foster Park Gv CUL/QBY BD13	92 D1
Foster Park Rd CUL/QBY BD13	92 D1
Foster Park Vw CUL/QBY BD13	92 D1
Foster Pl HOLM/MEL HD9	200 D2
Foster Sq HUD LS10	124 B1
Foster St CUL/QBY BD13	116 B2
MOR * LS27	123 H8
Foston Cl ECHL BD2	97 F1
Foston La ECHL BD2	97 F1
Fothergill Av FEA/AMT WF7	202 E5
Foulcauseway La OT LS21	34 C1
Foul Clough Rd TOD OL14	159 G5
Foulds' Ter BGLY BD16	50 E8
Foundry Ap OSM LS9	102 E1
Foundry Av HWTH LS8	80 E3
Foundry Dr RHAY LS8	80 E3
Foundry Hl BGLY BD16	49 K3
Foundry La BOW BD4	5 K7
KNOT WF11	156 B6
OSM LS9	81 F8
PDSY/CALV LS28	98 E7
Foundry Mill Crs SCFT LS14	81 K8
Foundry Mill Dr SCFT LS14	81 K8
Foundry Mill Gdns SCFT LS14	81 K8
Foundry Mill Mt SCFT LS14	81 K8
Foundry Mill St SCFT LS14	81 K7
Foundry Mill Ter SCFT LS14	81 K8
Foundry Mill Vw SCFT LS14	81 K8
Foundry Mill Wk SCFT LS14	81 K8
Foundry Pl OSM LS9	80 E8
Foundry St BEE/HOL LS11	7 H7
BRIG HD6	168 A1
CLECK BD19	144 A3
DEWS WF13	171 K4
DEWS WF13	172 B1
HFAX * HX1	9 K3
OSM LS9	102 A4
RPDN/SBR * HX6	138 C2
Foundry St North LUD/ILL HX2	115 J1
Foundry Wk RHAY LS8	80 E3
Fountain Cl LVSG WF15	170 C6
Fountain Ct LUD/ILL * HX2	139 J2
Fountain Dr LVSG WF15	170 C6
Fountain Gv HUDN HD4	190 D8
Fountains Av BSPA/BRAM LS23	42 E8
BTLY WF17	145 J2
Fountain St BFD BD1	5 J4
CUL/QBY BD13	93 H2
CUL/QBY BD13	116 B2
HECK WF16	145 K8
HFAX HX1	8 C4
LDS LS1	9 G6
LM/WK BD12	118 B6
LVSG WF15	170 C6
MOR LS27	122 E4
RPDN/SBR * HX6	164 A5
TOD OL14	134 C7
Fountains Wy WKFDE WF1	176 C1
Fountain Ter LM/WK BD12	142 B1
Fountain Wy SHPY BD18	77 G2
Four Acres MIRF WF14	170 A8
Fourlands Ct IDLE BD10	74 D3
Fourlands Crs IDLE * BD10	74 D3
Fourlands Dr IDLE BD10	74 D3
Fourlands Gdns IDLE BD10	74 D3
Fourlands Gv IDLE BD10	74 D3
Fourlands Rd IDLE BD10	74 D3
Four Lane Ends EARL WF12	195 F6
Fourteenth Av WOR/ARM LS12	6 C7
Fourth Av BFDE BD3	6 B2
KGHY BD21	2 D1
LVSG WF15	144 E8
RTHW LS26	126 C4
WBY LS22	23 K7
WKFDE WF1	175 J1
Fourth Ct BEE/HOL LS11	6 C7

...urth St HOR/CROF WF4 .....201 F4
LM/WK BD12 .....119 F5
wlers Garth HWTH BD22 .....69 F2
wler's PI PDSY/CALV LS28 .....98 C1
xbridge St BOW * BD4 .....5 F6
xcliff KNOT WF11 .....156 A2
x CI KBTN HD8 .....217 H5
x Ct GTL/HWG HX4 .....166 C4
xcroft CI CUL/QBY BD13 .....116 B4
HDGY LS6 .....78 B6
xcroft Dr BRIG HD6 .....167 K3
xcroft Ms HDGY LS6 .....78 B6
xcroft Mt HDGY LS6 .....78 B6
xcroft Rd HDGY LS6 .....78 B6
xcroft Wk HDGY LS6 .....78 B6
xcroft Wy HDGY LS6 .....78 B6
xen La RPDN/SBR HX6 .....163 K5
xglove Av RHAY LS8 .....80 E5
xglove Folly WKFDW/WTN WF2 .....175 F3
xglove La BTLY WF17 .....145 H1
HUDE HD5 .....192 A7
xhill BAIL BD17 .....51 C8
WBY LS22 .....23 J5
xhill Av BHP/TINH LS16 .....78 C2
CUL/QBY BD13 .....116 C2
xhill CI CUL/QBY BD13 .....116 C2
xhill Ct BHP/TINH LS16 .....78 D2
xhill Crs BHP/TINH LS16 .....78 D2
CUL/QBY BD13 .....116 C2
xhill Gn BHP/TINH LS16 .....78 D2
xhill Dr CUL/QBY BD13 .....116 C2
CUL/QBY BD13 .....116 C2
e Foxhills BHP/TINH LS16 .....55 H7
xhole La PDSY/CALV LS28 .....75 K5
xholes Crs PDSY/CALV LS28 .....75 K5
x Holes Gv STKB/PEN S36 .....250 A6
xholes La NORM LS11 .....161 J6
x La HOR/CROF WF4 .....198 B4
WKFDW/WTN WF2 .....175 H2
xlow Av HUDN HD2 .....192 A3
x Royd Av MIRF WF14 .....170 C5
x Royd Dr MIRF WF14 .....170 C5
xroyd La EARL WF12 .....194 E2
x Royd La MIRF WF14 .....170 C5
xstone Rd BAIL BD17 .....52 A8
xstones La RPDN/SBR HX6 .....187 F1
ain CI BGLY BD16 .....49 K8
BTLY WF17 .....146 C7
CLECK BD19 .....143 J4
HUD HD1 .....12 C4
x Ter PONT WF8 .....181 F1
x Vw DEWS WF13 .....181 J5
x Wy MID LS10 .....102 A6
x Wood Av RHAY LS8 .....81 C6
x Wood CI RHAY LS8 .....81 C6
xwood Farm Wy RHAY LS8 .....81 C6
x Wood Gv RHAY LS8 .....81 C6
x Wood Ri RHAY LS8 .....81 C6
x Wood Rw RHAY LS8 .....81 C6
xwood Wk WBY LS22 .....23 K4
ain CI PONT WF8 .....181 F4
aisthorpe Md ECHL BD2 .....97 F1
ance Fold HOLM/MEL HD9 .....213 F6
ances Rd EARL WF12 .....172 E4
ances St BRIG * HD6 .....142 B8
KGHY BD21 .....2 B2
PDSY/CALV LS28 .....98 B1
ance La BTLY WF17 .....146 D7
ancis CI HUDS * HD4 .....190 A7
ancis CI HFAX HX1 .....8 B4
ancis Gv HUDS * HD4 .....190 A7
ancis Rd HOR/CROF WF4 .....178 A8
ancis St BFDE BD3 .....5 E6
CAS WF10 .....153 K3
CHAL LS7 .....79 K8
FEA/AMT WF7 .....202 D6
HECK WF16 .....145 H8
HFAX HX1 .....8 A4
HUDS HD4 .....190 A7
MIRF WF14 .....170 C6
ancis Vw MIRF * WF14 .....170 C6
ank CI EARL WF12 .....195 J1
ankland Gv CHAL LS7 .....80 A8
ankland PI CHAL LS7 .....80 A8
ank La EARL WF12 .....195 J1
KBTN HD8 .....217 C6
LUD/ILL HX2 .....137 J1
anklin St HFAX HX1 .....8 A4
ank Peel CI HECK WF16 .....145 C7
ank PI GTHN BD7 .....95 H7
ank St GTHN BD7 .....95 H7
HFAX HX1 .....8 B5
aser Av HORS LS18 .....76 E3
aser Rd PDSY/CALV LS28 .....75 H5
aser St GIR BD8 .....4 A3
OSM LS9 .....102 B2
eakfield La LVSG WF15 .....169 J1
ederick CI OSM LS9 .....102 C5
WKFDE WF1 .....11 F6
ederick CI IDLE BD10 .....74 B2
ederick St BFD BD1 .....5 D5
HUDS HD4 .....190 C7
KGHY BD21 .....3 E3
VSG WF15 .....144 E8
PDSY/CALV LS28 .....76 A8

WKFDE WF1 .....10 C3
Fred's PI BOW BD4 .....96 E8
Fred St KGHY BD21 .....2 C4
Freeholds Rd WHIT OL12 .....158 B5
Freely La BSPA/BRAM LS23 .....62 D1
Freeman Rd HIPP HX3 .....141 F6
Freemans Wy WBY LS22 .....23 K5
Freemont St BRAM LS13 .....98 E1
Free School La HFAX HX1 .....8 B6
Freeston Ct NORM WF6 .....152 A8
Freeston Dr NORM WF6 .....152 A8
Freestone Ms MOR/ARM LS12 .....99 G4
Freestone Wy NORM WF6 .....151 H7
Fremantle Gv BOW BD4 .....97 G6
Fremantle PI MSTN/BAR LS15 .....103 G4
Frensham Av MOR LS27 .....122 E8
GTHN BD7 .....94 D8
Frensham Dr CAS WF10 .....154 E5
GTHN BD7 .....94 D8
Frensham Gv GTHN BD7 .....117 J1
Frensham Wy GTHN BD7 .....94 D8
Freshfield Gdns WIL/AL BD15 .....94 B2
Freston Av WKFDE WF1 .....177 C5
Freston Dr WKFDE WF1 .....177 F5
Friar Ct IDLE BD10 .....74 E5
Friar PI HUDN HD2 .....169 G6
Friar's CI FEA/AMT WF7 .....179 J7
Friars Nook PONT WF8 .....181 F4
Friarwood La PONT WF8 .....180 E3
Frickley Bridge La CUD/GR S72 .....223 J7
Frickley La BTLY DN5 .....242 B5
Fieldhurst Rd TOD OL14 .....133 F2
Friendly Av RPDN/SBR HX6 .....138 D6
Friendly Fold Rd HIPP HX3 .....8 B1
Friendly St CUL/QBY BD13 .....93 H5
HIPP HX3 .....8 B1
HUD * HD1 .....13 D3
Frimley Dr WBOW BD5 .....118 D1
Frith St HWTH BD22 .....69 C3
Frizinghall Rd HTON BD9 .....73 J8
Frizley Gdns HTON BD9 .....73 J8
Frobisher Gv WKFDW/WTN WF2 .....175 F6
Frodingham Vls ECHL BD2 .....97 F1
Frogmoor La LM/WK * BD12 .....119 G6
Frontline CI RHAY LS8 .....80 C5
Front Rw BEE/HOL LS11 .....7 D5
Front St BEE/HOL LS11 .....7 D5
BSPA/BRAM LS23 .....42 C8
CAS WF10 .....154 A5
PONT WF8 .....180 D3
Frost HI LVSG WF15 .....144 E7
Fruit St KGHY BD21 .....3 F2
Fryergate WKFDW/WTN WF2 .....175 J7
Fryston La KNOT WF11 .....156 H4
Fryston Rd CAS WF10 .....154 D2
Fuchsia Cft RTHW LS26 .....127 H5
Fulford Av HUDN HD2 .....191 G1
Fulford CI NORM WF6 .....178 C2
Fulford St CAS WF10 .....153 H4
Fulford Wk ECHL BD2 .....97 F1
Fullerton St BFDE BD3 .....5 E5
Fullwood Dr MAR/SLWT HD7 .....189 F7
Fulmar Ct IDLE BD10 .....124 E6
Fulmar Ms GIR * BD8 .....94 C4
Fulmar Rd CAS WF10 .....153 H5
Fulneck PDSY/CALV LS28 .....98 C6
Fulstone CI HUDN HD2 .....168 A8
Fulstone Hall La HOLM/MEL HD9 .....234 C4
Fulstone Rd KBTN HD8 .....234 D3
Fulton St BFD * BD1 .....4 B4
Fulwood Gv WKFDW/WTN WF2 .....198 D6
Furnace CI LM/WK BD12 .....119 G6
Furnace Inn St BOW BD4 .....97 F6
Furnace La BIRK/DRI BD11 .....120 D5
Furnace Rd LM/WK BD12 .....119 G6
Furnbrook Gdns HUDE HD5 .....192 E4
Furness Av LUD/ILL HX2 .....115 G7
WKFDW/WTN WF2 .....175 F1
Furness Crs LUD/ILL HX2 .....115 G6
Furness Dr LUD/ILL HX2 .....115 G7
WKFDW/WTN WF2 .....175 F1
Furness Gdns LUD/ILL HX2 .....115 H7
Furness Gv LUD/ILL HX2 .....115 G7
Furness PI LUD/ILL HX2 .....115 H7
Fusden La CLECK BD19 .....144 D2
Fyfe Crs BAIL BD17 .....73 K1
Fyfe Gv BAIL BD17 .....74 A1
Fyfe La BAIL BD17 .....74 A1

G

The Gables BAIL BD17 .....52 A8
HWTH BD22 .....2 E8
Gadding Moor Rd STKB/PEN S36 .....252 E3
Gagewell Dr HOR/CROF WF4 .....197 H1
Gagewell La HOR/CROF WF4 .....197 H1
Gagewell Vw HOR/CROF WF4 .....197 H1
Gainest LUD/ILL HX2 .....8 A6
Gainford Dr GFTH/SHER LS25 .....105 K5
Gain La BFDE BD3 .....97 G2
Gainsborough CI BFDE BD3 .....5 E1
Gainsborough Wy EARD/LOFT WF3 .....150 B6
Gainsbro Av BHP/TINH LS16 .....56 B6
Gainsbro Dr BHP/TINH LS16 .....56 B6
Gaisby La ECHL BD2 .....73 J7

Gaisby Mt SHPY BD18 .....73 K6
Gaisby PI SHPY BD18 .....73 K5
Gaisby Ri SHPY BD18 .....73 K5
Gaitskell CI BEE/HOL LS11 .....6 C6
Gaitskell Gra BEE/HOL LS11 .....6 C6
Gaitskell Wk BEE/HOL LS11 .....6 C6
Galefield Gn WBSY BD6 .....118 A5
Gale St KGHY BD21 .....3 D2
Gall La TOD OL14 .....109 F8
Gallogate La AL/HA/HU LS17 .....37 F1
Gallon Cft HEM/SK/SE WF9 .....226 A8
Galloway Ct PDSY/CALV LS28 .....97 J3
Galloway La PDSY/CALV LS28 .....97 J2
Galloway Rd IDLE BD10 .....75 F4
Galloway St HUD HD1 .....13 D2
Gallows HI CAS WF10 .....154 D4
OT LS21 .....34 A3
Gallows La HOR/CROF WF4 .....220 B2
Galsworthy Av HTON BD9 .....72 D8
Gamble HI BRAM LS13 .....99 H3
Gamble Hill CI BRAM LS13 .....99 H3
Gamble Hill Dr BRAM LS13 .....99 H3
Gamble Hill Gn BRAM LS13 .....99 H3
Gamble Hill Lawn BRAM LS13 .....99 H3
Gamble Hill PI BRAM LS13 .....99 H3
Gamble Hill Ri BRAM LS13 .....99 H3
Gamble Hill Vw BRAM LS13 .....99 H3
Gamble La WOR/ARM LS12 .....99 G5
Camel Vw AIRE BD20 .....26 D5
Game Scar La or Goose Eye Brow HWTH BD22 .....46 D5
The Gang WOR/ARM LS12 .....100 C3
Ganners CI BRAM LS13 .....77 G7
Ganners Gn BRAM LS13 .....77 G7
Ganners Gv BRAM * LS13 .....77 H7
Ganners HI BRAM LS13 .....77 H7
Ganners La BRAM LS13 .....77 G7
Ganners Mt BRAM LS13 .....77 G7
Ganners Ri BRAM LS13 .....77 H7
Ganners Rd BRAM LS13 .....77 G7
Ganners Wk BRAM LS13 .....77 G7
Ganners Wy BRAM LS13 .....77 G7
Gannerthorpe CI LM/WK BD12 .....118 D8
Gannet CI LM/WK WF10 .....153 H5
Ganny Rd BRIG HD6 .....168 C1
Ganton CI HDGY LS6 .....79 H7
Ganton Wy HUDN HD2 .....168 A8
Gaol La HFAX HX1 .....9 D4
Garden Av CLECK BD19 .....144 D5
Garden CI CLECK BD19 .....144 D6
LM/WK BD12 .....118 D7
OSS WF5 .....173 K8
Garden Dr DEWS WF13 .....171 H5
Gardeners Ct MID LS10 .....101 K7
Gardener's Sq HIPP HX3 .....141 H3
Garden Fld LM/WK BD12 .....118 D8
Garden Fold HIPP HX3 .....141 H3
Garden House CI RTHW LS26 .....128 C8
Garden House La EARD/LOFT WF3 .....148 B3
Garden La HTON BD9 .....73 F8
KNOT WF11 .....156 D6
RPDN/SBR HX6 .....164 E4
Garden Pde CLECK BD19 .....144 D5
Garden PI DEWS WF13 .....171 J2
Garden Rd BRIG HD6 .....142 A7
The Gardens BGLY BD16 .....50 D8
Gardens Rd DEWS WF13 .....171 H5
Gardens St HTON BD9 .....73 G7
HFAX HX1 .....9 D6
MID LS10 .....124 D7
MOR LS27 .....146 E1
PDSY/CALV LS28 .....76 A8
Garden St CAS WF10 .....153 J5
CAS WF10 .....154 B5
DEWS WF13 .....171 G5
FEA/AMT WF7 .....202 D6
HECK * WF16 .....145 G8
HUD HD1 .....12 B6
HWTH BD22 .....69 H3
NORM WF6 .....151 H8
NORM * WF6 .....177 K1
TOD OL14 .....134 A5
WKFDE WF1 .....10 B4
Garden St North HIPP HX3 .....9 E3
Garden Ter HBR * HX7 .....112 B8
HOR/CROF WF4 .....197 K7
HTON BD9 .....73 G8
Garden Vw BGLY BD16 .....50 C8
CLECK BD19 .....144 D5
Garden Village GFTH/SHER LS25 .....107 G4
Garden Wk CLECK BD19 .....144 D6
Gardiner Rw BOW BD4 .....119 J1
Gare Forth Av AIRE BD20 .....26 A6
Garfield Av GIR BD8 .....95 H1
Garfield PI MAR/SLWT HD7 .....209 H7
Garfield St HIPP HX3 .....8 B2
TOD OL14 .....133 F2
WIL/AL BD15 .....94 A2
Garfit HI BTLY WF17 .....145 G3
Garforth CI NORM WF6 .....151 H8
Garforth Ct MIRF WF14 .....170 D4
Garforth Dr NORM WF6 .....151 H8
Garforth Rd KGHY BD21 .....3 F2
Garforth St HUDS HD4 .....212 C4
WIL/AL BD15 .....94 B2
Gargrave Ap OSM LS9 .....102 B3
Gargrave CI BRIG HD6 .....167 J4
Gargrave Ct OSM LS9 .....102 B2
Gargrave Crs HEM/SK/SE WF9 .....224 C5

Gargrave PI *HEM/SK/SE* WF9 ....224 C5
　OSM LS9 ....102 B2
　WKFDW/WTN WF2 ....174 D6
Garibaldi St *BFDE* BD3 ....97 G4
Garland Dr *MSTN/BAR* LS15 ....104 B4
Garlick St *BRIG* HD6 ....167 K5
Garmil Head La *HEM/SK/SE* WF9 ....201 K6
Garmont Ms *CHAL* LS7 ....79 K5
Garmont Rd *CHAL* LS7 ....79 K5
Garner La *HOLM/MEL* HD9 ....212 D7
　KBTN HD8 ....215 F4
Garnet Av *BEE/HOL* LS11 ....101 J4
Garnet Crs *BEE/HOL* LS11 ....101 J8
Garnet Cv *BEE/HOL* LS11 ....101 J8
Garnet Pde *BEE/HOL* LS11 ....101 J8
Garnet PI *BEE/HOL* LS11 ....101 J8
Garnet Rd *BEE/HOL* LS11 ....124 D1
Garnet Ter *BEE/HOL* LS11 ....124 D1
Garnett St *BFDE* BD3 ....5 F4
　DEWS WF13 ....145 J8
　HBR HX7 ....112 B8
　OT LS21 ....33 J3
Garnet Vw *BEE/HOL* LS11 ....101 J8
Garrett Cl *BTLY* BD10 ....236 D1
Garsdale Av *IDLE* BD10 ....74 E4
Garsdale Crs *BAIL* BD17 ....52 A7
Garsdale Fold *WBY* LS22 ....40 E2
Garsdale Gv *WKFDE* WF1 ....11 F1
Garsdale Rd *HUDS* HD4 ....213 H1
Garsdale Wk *KNOT* WF11 ....182 B1
The Garth *GFTH/SHER* LS25 ....106 A4
　OSM LS9 ....102 A4
　WBY LS22 ....41 F3
Garth Av *AL/HA/HU* LS17 ....79 H2
　NORM WF6 ....177 K3
　WBY LS22 ....41 F3
Garth Barn CI *HTON* BD9 ....73 C8
Garth Dr *AL/HA/HU* LS17 ....79 H2
Garth End *WBY* LS22 ....41 F3
Garth Land Wy *BOW* BD4 ....96 E8
Garth MI *GLE* DN14 ....157 K4
Garth Rectory *HEM/SK/SE* WF9 ....224 D4
Garth Rd *AL/HA/HU* LS17 ....79 H2
Garth St *CAS* WF10 ....153 H5
　KGHY BD21 ....2 B3
Garthwaite Mt *WIL/AL* BD15 ....94 B1
Garth Wk *AL/HA/HU* LS17 ....79 H2
Garth Willow *BULY* LS4 ....6 A2
Garth Willow Av *SCFT* LS14 ....81 K3
Garth Willow CI *SCFT* LS14 ....81 K3
Garton Av *OSM* LS9 ....102 C4
Garton Dr *OSM* LS9 ....102 C4
Garton Gv *OSM* LS9 ....102 C4
Garton Rd *OSM* LS9 ....102 C4
Garton Ter *OSM* LS9 ....102 C4
Garton Vw *OSM* LS9 ....102 C4
Garvey Vw *WBOW* BD5 ....96 A7
Garwick Ter *GTL/HWG* HX4 ....166 C4
Gascoigne Av *MSTN/BAR* LS15 ....83 H5
Gascoigne Cr *MSTN/BAR* LS15 ....83 H5
Gascoigne Rd *EARD/LOFT* WF3 ....149 F2
　MSTN/BAR LS15 ....83 H5
Gascoigne St *LDS* LS1 ....7 H4
Gascoigne Vw *MSTN/BAR* LS15 ....83 H5
Gashouse La *WBY* LS22 ....23 J6
Gaskell CI *HOR/CROF* WF4 ....197 G1
Gaskell St *WKFDW/WTN* WF2 ....10 A1
Gasson St *HUDS* HD4 ....190 A7
Gas St *HWTH* BD22 ....69 F4
Gas Works La *BSPA/BRAM* LS23 ....43 F4
　ELL HX5 ....166 E6
Gas Works Rd *KGHY* BD21 ....3 J4
　RPDN/SBR HX6 ....139 G7
Gasworks St *HUD* HD1 ....13 D3
　LVSG WF15 ....144 E7
Gatefield Mt *LM/WK* BD12 ....118 C5
Gate Foot La *WBOW* BD5 ....234 E5
Gate Head La *MAR/SLWT* HD7 ....209 J7
Gatehead Bank *MAR/SLWT* HD7 ....209 K6
Gate Head La *GTL/HWG* HX4 ....165 J5
　HOLM/MEL HD9 ....249 H3
Gate House Ct *RTHW* LS26 ....127 G4
Gateland Dr *AL/HA/HU* LS17 ....59 G7
Gateland La *AL/HA/HU* LS17 ....59 G8
Gateon House La *AL/HA/HU* LS17 ....39 J7
Gatesgarth Crs *HUDN* HD3 ....190 A2
Gateway *BGLY* BD16 ....70 E2
Gate Way Dr *YEA* LS19 ....53 J5
Gateways *WKFDE* WF1 ....149 K6
Gathorne CI *RHAY* LS8 ....80 A8
Gathorne Ter *RHAY* LS8 ....80 A8
Gaukroger La *HFAX* HX1 ....9 F6
Gauk St *KNOT* WF11 ....131 H7
　KNOT WF11 ....155 K3
Gavin CI *BFDE* BD3 ....97 G4
Gaw La *SKP/WHF* BD23 ....14 B3
Gawthorpe Dr *BGLY* BD16 ....49 K6
Gawthorpe Green La *HUDE* HD5 ....193 G5
Gawthorpe La *KBTN* HD8 ....193 H6
　OSS WF5 ....173 J2
Gawthorpe St *WIL/AL* BD15 ....71 F5
Gay La *OT* LS21 ....33 J4
Gayle CI *LM/WK* BD12 ....142 D1
Gaynor St *BFD* BD1 ....4 B4
Gaythorne Rd *ECHL* BD2 ....96 E1
　WBOW BD5 ....96 A8

Gaythorne Ter *CLAY* BD14 ....94 C7
Gaythorn Ter *HIPP* HX3 ....141 H2
Geary CI *WKFDW/WTN* WF2 ....174 E3
Geary Dr *WKFDW/WTN* WF2 ....174 D3
Geecroft La *WBY* LS22 ....22 A6
Geelong CI *ECHL* BD2 ....74 B8
Gelder Ct *WKFDW/WTN* WF2 ....174 E3
Gelder Cft *WKFDW/WTN* * WF2 ....174 E3
Gelderd CI *WOR/ARM* LS12 ....100 D7
Gelderd La *WOR/ARM* LS12 ....100 D7
Gelderd Rd *BTLY* WF17 ....145 J1
　MOR LS27 ....122 D4
Gelder Rd *WOR/ARM* LS12 ....100 B4
Gelder Ter *HUDE* HD5 ....13 E5
Geneva Dr *WKFDW* WF1 ....10 C2
Genista Dr *MID* LS10 ....124 E3
Gentian Ct *WKFDW/WTN* WF2 ....175 F3
George-a-Green Rd
　WKFDW/WTN WF2 ....175 F7
George & Crown Yd *WKFDE* * WF1 ....10 C5
George Av *LUD/ILL* HX2 ....12 A2
George Buckley Ct
　HEM/SK/SE WF9 ....241 G1
George La *HOR/CROF* WF4 ....221 G5
　RPDN/SBR HX6 ....137 H4
George's Sq *CUL/QBY* BD13 ....70 B5
　KGHY BD21 ....2 C4
George's Ter *LUD/ILL* HX2 ....115 J8
George St *BAIL* * BD17 ....73 J2
　BFD BD1 ....5 D5
　BRIG HD6 ....168 B1
　BTLY WF17 ....146 B7
　CLECK BD19 ....144 A3
　CUD/GR S72 ....225 H5
　CUL/QBY BD13 ....92 C2
　CUL/QBY BD13 ....98 D5
　DEWS WF13 ....171 H6
　DEWS WF13 ....171 J3
　DEWS WF13 ....172 B3
　ELL HX5 ....166 E6
　FEA/AMT WF7 ....178 C4
　FEA/AMT WF7 ....179 H6
　GTL/HWG HX4 ....166 C4
　HBR HX7 ....137 F3
　HECK WF16 ....145 C7
　HEM/SK/SE WF9 ....224 E5
　HIPP HX3 ....141 J4
　HOR/CROF WF4 ....197 H2
　HOR/CROF WF4 ....223 F2
　HUD HD1 ....12 C4
　HUDS HD4 ....12 A6
　HUDW HD3 ....190 B2
　HUDW HD3 ....190 B6
　ILK LS29 ....18 D3
　LDS LS1 ....7 E3
　LVSG WF15 ....144 D7
　NORM WF6 ....151 J8
　OSS WF5 ....173 H4
　RPDN/SBR HX6 ....138 E8
　SHPY BD18 ....77 J5
　TOD OL14 ....134 A6
　WKFDE WF1 ....10 B4
　WKFDE WF1 ....149 J6
　YEA LS19 ....53 K7
Georgia Ms *OSS* WF5 ....174 A1
Geraldton Av *ECHL* BD2 ....74 A8
Gerard Av *MOR* LS27 ....122 E7
Gernhill Av *HUDN* HD2 ....168 A6
Gerrard Av *HFAX* HX1 ....8 C4
Gervase Rd *HOR/CROF* WF4 ....197 G2
The Ghyll *HUDN* HD2 ....72 A3
　HUDN HD2 ....168 B7
Ghyllbank *AIRE* * BD20 ....27 J2
Ghyll Beck Dr *OT* LS21 ....33 F5
　YEA LS19 ....54 C8
Ghyll CI *AIRE* BD20 ....26 E6
Ghyll Dr *HWTH* BD22 ....68 C5
Ghyll Mt *YEA* LS19 ....53 H5
Ghyll Rd *HDGY* LS6 ....78 A5
Ghyll Royd *GSLY* LS20 ....53 G4
Ghyllroyd Av *BIRK/DRI* BD11 ....120 E6
Ghyllroyd Dr *BIRK/DRI* BD11 ....120 E6
Ghyll Wd *ILK* LS29 ....19 J8
Ghyll Wood Dr *BGLY* BD16 ....72 A3
Gibb La *LUD/ILL* HX2 ....114 E8
Gib La *WBY* LS22 ....236 E1
Gibraltar Av *HFAX* HX1 ....139 H5
Gibraltar Island Rd *MID* LS10 ....102 B7
Gibraltar Rd *HFAX* HX1 ....139 H4
　PDSY/CALV LS28 ....97 K4
Gibriding La *HOLM/MEL* HD9 ....231 K8
Gibson Av *WKFDW/WTN* WF2 ....175 G4
Gibson Dr *WKFDW/WTN* WF2 ....10 A2
Gibson Dr *MSTN/BAR* LS15 ....104 A4
Gibson La *GFTH/SHER* LS25 ....129 G2
Gibson St *BFDE* BD3 ....5 F5
　HUDW HD3 ....190 C4
　TOD OL14 ....134 D4
Gilbert Cha *KSTL* LS5 ....78 A8
Gilbert La *KSTL* LS5 ....78 B8
Gilbert Gv *HUDS* HD4 ....190 D8
Gilbert Mt *BULY* LS4 ....78 B8
Gilbert St *PDSY/CALV* * LS28 ....98 B1
Gilcar St *NORM* WF6 ....152 C7
Gildar Wy *NORM* WF6 ....152 B6
Gildersome Cross *MOR* * LS27 ....122 B5
Gildersome La *MOR* LS27 ....122 A3
Gildersome Sp *MOR* LS27 ....122 C6
Gilead Rd *HUDW* HD3 ....189 J4

Giles Hill La *HIPP* HX3 117
Giles St *HOLM/MEL* HD9 233
　WBOW BD5 4
　WBSY BD6 ....118 E
Gilann St *KNOT* WF11 156
Gill Bank Rd *ILK* LS29 20
Gill Beck CI *BAIL* BD17 ....52 A
Gill CI *ILK* LS29 ....18 E
Gillett Dr *RTHW* LS26 ....126 C
Gillett La *RTHW* LS26 ....126 C
Gilling Av *GFTH/SHER* LS25 ....106 A
Gillingham Gn *BOW* BD4 97
Gillion Crs *HOR/CROF* WF4 169
Gill La *HOLM/MEL* HD9 247
　HWTH BD22 46
　ILK LS29 19
　YEA LS19 53
Gillroyd La *MAR/SLWT* HD7 211
Gillroyd PI *MOR* LS27 123
Gillroyd Rd *GTHN* BD7 95
Gill's Buildings *WKFDW/WTN* WF2 10
Gill Sike Av *WKFDW/WTN* WF2 175
Gill Sike Bungalows
　WKFDW/WTN WF2 175
Gill Sike Gv *WKFDW/WTN* WF2 175
Gill Sike Rd *WKFDW/WTN* WF2 175
The Gills *OT* LS21 33
Gillstone Dr *HWTH* BD22 69
Gilt St *WKFDE* * WF1 10
Gill's Yd *WKFDE* * WF1 10
Gillygate *PONT* WF8 180
Gilmour St *HIPP* HX3 8
Gilpin PI *WOR/ARM* LS12 100
Gilpin St *BFDE* BD3 5
　WOR/ARM LS12 100
Gilpin Ter *WOR/ARM* LS12 100
Gilpin Vw *WOR/ARM* LS12 100
Gilstead Ct *BGLY* BD16 50
Gilstead Dr *BGLY* BD16 50
Gilstead La *BGLY* BD16 50
Gilstead Wy *ILK* LS29 20
Gilthwaites Crs *KBTN* HD8 236
Gilthwaites Gv *KBTN* HD8 236
Gilthwaites La *KBTN* HD8 236
Gilthwaites Top *KBTN* HD8 236
Gilynda Cl *GIR* BD8 84
Gin La *FEA/AMT* WF7 178
The Ginnel *AL/HA/HU* LS17 118
Gipsy La *BEE/HOL* LS11 124
　DOD/DAR S75 220
　RTHW LS26 126
　WKFDW/WTN WF2 199
Gipsy Md *RTHW* LS26 126
Gipsy St *BFDE* BD3 97
Gipton Ap *OSM* LS9 103
Gipton Av *RHAY* LS8 80
Gipton Ga East *OSM* LS9 80
Gipton Ga West *RHAY* LS8 80
Gipton Sq *OSM* LS9 80
Gipton St *RHAY* LS8 80
Gipton Wood Av *RHAY* LS8 80
Gipton Wood Crs *RHAY* LS8 80
Gipton Wood Gv *RHAY* LS8 80
Gipton Wood PI *RHAY* LS8 80
Gipton Wood Rd *RHAY* LS8 80
Girlington Rd *GIR* BD8 95
Girnhill La *FEA/AMT* WF7 179
Gisbourne Rd *HUDN* HD2 169
Gisburn St *KGHY* BD21 2
Gissing Rd *WKFDW/WTN* WF2 174
The Glade *PDSY/CALV* LS28 97
　SCFT LS14 59
Gladstonbury Av *WKFDE* WF1 176
Gladstone Crs *YEA* LS19 53
Gladstone Rd *HFAX* * HX1 8
Gladstone St *BFDE* BD3 96
　BGLY * BD16 71
　CLECK BD19 144
　CUL/QBY BD13 116
　FEA/AMT WF7 122
　GTL/HWG HX4 165
　KGHY BD21 3
　NORM WF6 152
　PDSY/CALV LS28 76
　TOD OL14 132
　WIL/AL BD15 94
Gladstone Ter *CAS* WF10 153
　MOR * LS27 123
Gladstone Vw *HIPP* HX3 140
Gladwin St *BTLY* WF17 146
Glaisdale CI *AIRE* BD20 27
Glaisdale Gv *WIL/AL* BD15 72
Glaisdale Gv *HIPP* HX3 141
Glamis CI *GFTH/SHER* LS25 88
Glanville Ter *RTHW* LS26 126
Glasshouse St *MID* LS10 124
Glasshouse Vw *MID* LS10 124
Glastonbury Dr *HUDW* HD3 13
Glazier Rd *CUL/QBY* BD13 116
Gleanings Av *LUD/ILL* HX2 139
Gleanings Dr *LUD/ILL* HX2 138
Glebe Av *KSTL* LS5 78
Glebe CI *KBTN* HD8 217
Glebe Field Cha *WBY* LS22 23
Glebe Field CI *WBY* LS22 23
Glebe Field Cft *WBY* LS22 23
Glebe Field Dr *WBY* LS22 23
Glebe Field Garth *WBY* LS22 23
Glebe Field Holt *WBY* LS22 23

ebe Ga EARL WF12 ...195 J2
ebelands Cl GFTH/SHER LS25 ...105 K5
ebelands Dr HDGY LS6 ...78 D5
ebe La KNOT WF11 ...156 C7
ebe Rd PDSY/CALV LS28 ...98 C5
ebe St CAS WF10 ...153 J4
HUDW HD3 ...12 A3
NORM WF6 ...178 B3
PDSY/CALV LS28 ...98 C5
ebe Ter HDGY LS6 ...78 D4
edcliffe HFAX HX1 ...9 D3
eddings Cl HIPP HX3 ...139 K8
edhill Rd BFDE BD3 ...6 A5
edhill St TOD OL14 ...134 A5
edhill Ter DEWS WF13 ...171 J3
edhow Av RHAY LS8 ...80 B3
edhow Ct CHAL LS7 ...80 A4
edhow Dr HWTH BD22 ...68 E7
edhow Grange Wk RHAY LS8 ...80 B4
edhow Grange Wk RHAY LS8 ...80 B4
edhow La CHAL LS7 ...79 K4
edhow Mt RHAY LS8 ...102 A1
edhow Park Av CHAL LS7 ...80 A5
edhow Park Crs CHAL * LS7 ...80 A5
edhow Park Dr RHAY LS8 ...79 K5
edhow Park Gv CHAL LS7 ...80 A5
edhow Park Rd CHAL LS7 ...80 A5
edhow Park Vw CHAL LS7 ...80 A5
edhow Pl RHAY LS8 ...102 A1
edhow Rd CHAL LS7 ...80 D5
edhow Rd RHAY LS8 ...102 A1
edhow Ter RHAY LS8 ...102 A1
edhow Towers RHAY LS8 ...80 A4
edhow Valley Rd CHAL LS7 ...79 K3
edhow Wood Av RHAY LS8 ...80 B4
edhow Wood Cl RHAY LS8 ...80 B4
edhow Wood Ct RHAY LS8 ...80 C6
edhow Wood Gv RHAY LS8 ...80 B5
edhow Wood Ri RHAY LS8 ...80 B5
edmow Lane End CHAL LS7 ...79 K4
e Glen TOD OL14 ...133 J4
naire SHPY BD18 ...74 A2
naire Dr BAIL BD17 ...73 C2
n Av BTLY WF17 ...146 C5
TOD OL14 ...133 J4
nbrook Dr GTHN BD7 ...94 E4
ncoe Cl GFTH/SHER LS25 ...128 E3
ncoe Cft GFTH/SHER LS25 ...128 E3
ncoe Gdns GFTH/SHER LS25 ...128 E3
ncoe Ter GFTH/SHER LS25 ...128 E3
VSG WF15 ...144 E8
n Ct CAS WF10 ...153 F5
n Di BGLY BD16 ...71 K4
ndale HOR/CROF WF4 ...197 F2
ndale Av GFTH/SHER LS25 ...105 K5
ndale Cl WBSY BD6 ...118 B4
ndale Dr WBSY BD6 ...118 B4
ndare Av GTHN BD7 ...95 F5
ndare Rd GTHN BD7 ...95 F5
ndare Ter GTHN BD7 ...95 F5
n Dene BGLY BD16 ...71 K4
EARL * WF12 ...172 E5
ILK LS29 ...32 D7
ndorne Dr HUDE HD5 ...192 E2
ndower Pk BHP/TINH LS16 ...78 D1
neagles Cl BOW BD4 ...119 J3
neagles Rd AL/HA/HU LS17 ...57 H7
EA/AMT WF7 ...179 J2
neagles Wy HUDN HD2 ...168 A8
nfield SHPY BD18 ...74 A2
n Field Av HUDN HD2 ...169 G8
nfield Av WBSY * BD6 ...118 E3
WBY LS22 ...23 K7
nfields HOR/CROF WF4 ...196 D6
nfields Cl HOR/CROF WF4 ...196 D6
n Garth KGHY BD21 ...3 E5
n Gv MOR LS27 ...125 G8
nholme SHPY BD18 ...74 A2
nholme Heath HFAX HX1 ...139 H4
nholme Rd GIR BD8 ...95 H2
PDSY/CALV LS28 ...98 A1
nholm Rd BAIL BD17 ...51 J8
nhurst BOW BD4 ...120 A2
nhurst Av KGHY BD21 ...3 E5
nhurst Dr KGHY BD21 ...3 E5
nhurst Gv KGHY BD21 ...3 E5
nhurst Rd SHPY BD18 ...72 E5
nlea Cl BRAM LS13 ...76 E8
nlea Gdns BRAM LS13 ...76 E8
nlee La KGHY BD21 ...3 E6
nlee Rd GTHN BD7 ...95 F5
nlyon Av KGHY BD21 ...2 B1
nlyon La KGHY BD21 ...2 B1
nlyon Dr KGHY BD21 ...2 B1
nmere Mt YEA LS19 ...54 B4
nmore Cl ECHL BD2 ...96 E2
nmore Ct BHP/TINH LS16 ...35 J8
nt BGLY BD16 ...71 K4
HIPP HX3 ...139 H1
K LS29 ...32 D8
OR LS27 ...123 G8
n Mount Cl HIPP HX3 ...139 H1
nn Wy HOR/CROF WF4 ...200 E4
n Ri BAIL BD17 ...73 G1
n Rd BGLY BD16 ...50 C6

BHP/TINH LS16 ...78 C4
MOR LS27 ...123 G8
Glenrose Dr GTHN BD7 ...94 E4
Glenroyal Buildings BAIL * BD17 ...73 H3
Glenroyd SHPY BD18 ...74 A2
Glenroyd Av WBSY BD6 ...118 E4
Glenroyd Cl PDSY/CALV LS28 ...98 A4
Glensdale Gv OSM LS9 ...102 B4
Glensdale Mt OSM LS9 ...102 B4
Glensdale Rd OSM LS9 ...102 B4
Glensdale St OSM LS9 ...102 B4
Glensdale Ter OSM LS9 ...102 B4
Glenside Av SHPY BD18 ...74 A2
Glenside Cl HUDW HD3 ...190 D3
Glen Side Rd MAR/SLWT HD7 ...210 E4
Glenside Rd SHPY BD18 ...74 A2
Glenstone Gv GIR BD8 ...95 F4
Glen Ter HFAX HX1 ...8 C1
Glenthorpe Av OSM LS9 ...102 C3
Glenthorpe Crs OSM LS9 ...102 C3
Glenthorpe Ter OSM LS9 ...102 C3
Glenton Sq HTON BD9 ...95 G1
Glen Vw BGLY BD16 ...71 F2
HFAX HX1 ...8 C6
Glenview Av HTON BD9 ...72 E8
Glen View St TOD OL14 ...133 F2
Glenview Ter SHPY BD18 ...73 F3
Glen Vw Dr BGLY BD16 ...50 C5
Glenwood Av BAIL BD17 ...72 E2
Global Av BEE/HOL LS11 ...123 K2
Globe Ct CUL/QBY BD13 ...144 E7
Globe Fold GIR BD8 ...4 A3
Globe Rd WOR/ARM LS12 ...6 C4
Glossop Gv HDGY LS6 ...79 H7
Glossop Mt HDGY LS6 ...79 H7
Glossop Vw HDGY * LS6 ...79 H7
Gloucester Av AIRE BD20 ...20 E2
BFDE BD3 ...97 F2
Gloucester Ct WKFDW/WTN WF2 ...149 G8
WOR/ARM * LS12 ...6 A4
Gloucester Gv WKFDW/WTN WF2 ...174 E6
Gloucester Pl WKFDW/WTN WF2 ...174 E6
Gloucester Rd BGLY BD16 ...72 B1
WKFDW/WTN WF2 ...174 D6
Gloucester Ter WOR/ARM LS12 ...6 A4
Glover Ct WBOW BD5 ...96 A7
Glovershaw La BAIL BD17 ...50 E5
Glover Wy BEE/HOL LS11 ...124 D1
Glydegate WBOW BD5 ...4 C5
Glyndon Ct BRIG HD6 ...168 C3
Glynn Ter GIR BD8 ...95 H5
Gobind Marg BFDE * BD3 ...5 E4
Godfrey Rd HIPP HX3 ...166 B1
Godfrey St GIR BD8 ...94 D4
Godley Branch Rd HIPP HX3 ...9 F3
Godley Gdns HIPP HX3 ...140 E2
Godley La HIPP HX3 ...9 F3
Godley Rd HIPP HX3 ...9 E3
Godley St BSLYN/ROY S71 ...222 B7
Godly Ct RPDN/SBR HX6 ...186 E2
Godly La RPDN/SBR HX6 ...186 E2
Godwin St BFD BD1 ...4 C4
Goff Well La KGHY BD21 ...70 A1
Goit Stock La BGLY BD16 ...71 F3
Goit Stock Ter BGLY BD16 ...71 F3
Golcar Brow Rd HOLM/MEL HD9 ...231 G1
Goldcrest Av GIR BD8 ...94 B4
Goldcrest Ct HUDS HD4 ...212 E4
Golden Butts Rd ILK LS29 ...20 C7
Golden Sq HOR/CROF WF4 ...197 H2
Golden Ter WOR/ARM LS12 ...100 A7
Golden View Dr KGHY BD21 ...48 D5
Goldfields Av GTL/HWG HX4 ...165 K3
Goldfields Cl GTL/HWG HX4 ...166 A3
Goldfields Vw GTL/HWG HX4 ...166 A3
Goldington Av HUDW HD3 ...189 K3
Goldington Dr HUDW HD3 ...190 A3
Golf Av LUD/ILL HX2 ...139 F4
Golf Crs LUD/ILL HX2 ...139 F4
Golf La MOR LS27 ...146 D3
Gomersal La CLECK BD19 ...144 D4
Gomersal Rd CLECK BD19 ...145 F5
Gondal Ct WBOW BD5 ...95 J8
Goodbard Houses LDS * LS1 ...7 D3
Gooder Av BSLYN/ROY S71 ...222 A8
Gooder La BRIG HD6 ...168 B2
Gooder St BRIG HD6 ...168 B1
Good Hope Cl NORM WF6 ...152 A1
Goodman St MID LS10 ...102 A6
Goodrick La AL/HA/HU LS17 ...57 H4
Goods La EARL WF12 ...172 C4
Goodwin Pl HUDN HD2 ...169 G6
Goodwin Rd WOR/ARM LS12 ...100 C5
Goodwood EARD/LOFT WF3 ...124 E8
Goodwood Av GFTH/SHER LS25 ...128 E1
Goody Cross La RTHW LS26 ...128 A1
Goose Cote La HWTH BD22 ...69 C1
Goose Cote Wy HWTH BD22 ...47 G8
Goosedale Ct BOW BD4 ...120 D2
Goose Eye HWTH BD22 ...46 D5
Goosefield Ri GFTH/SHER LS25 ...105 H6

Goosegate LUD/ILL * HX2 ...115 J5
Goose Gn HOLM/MEL HD9 ...233 G6
Goose HI HECK WF16 ...145 G7
Goosehill La WKFDE WF1 ...177 H4
Goosehill Rd NORM WF6 ...177 K3
Goosehole La HEM/SK/SE WF9 ...242 D2
Goose La GSLY LS20 ...51 K2
Goose West La RPDN/SBR HX6 ...164 E1
Gordale Cl BTLY WF17 ...146 A6
Gordon Av OSS * WF5 ...173 J5
Gordon Ct MIRF WF14 ...171 F5
Gordon Dr HDGY LS6 ...78 E5
Gordon Pl HEM/SK/SE WF9 ...242 B1
Gordon St CLAY * BD14 ...94 B7
EARD/LOFT WF3 ...149 F3
ELL HX5 ...166 E5
FEA/AMT WF7 ...179 J4
HIPP HX3 ...8 C1
HWTH * BD22 ...69 G3
ILK LS29 ...20 C7
KGHY BD21 ...2 C3
MAR/SLWT HD7 ...210 E3
RPDN/SBR HX6 ...138 D8
WBOW BD5 ...5 D6
WKFDE WF1 ...199 G1
Gordon Ter IDLE BD10 ...74 D2
MAR/SLWT HD7 ...211 H1
Goring Park Av OSS WF5 ...174 B7
Gorse Av BAIL BD17 ...72 E1
Gorse Lea MID LS10 ...124 E3
Gorse Rd HUDW HD3 ...190 C5
Gorton St HEM/SK/SE WF9 ...224 B2
Gosling La GTL/HWG HX4 ...187 H1
Gosport Cl HUDW HD3 ...188 E3
Gosport La GTL/HWG HX4 ...188 D2
Gosside Gv NORM WF6 ...178 C2
Gothic Mt FEA/AMT WF7 ...179 F3
Gothic St CUL/QBY BD13 ...116 D2
Gotts Park Av WOR/ARM LS12 ...99 K2
Gotts Park Crs WOR/ARM LS12 ...99 K2
Gotts Park Vw WOR/ARM LS12 ...99 K1
Gotts Rd WOR/ARM LS12 ...6 B4
Gott's Ter AIRE BD20 ...47 J1
Gott St HWTH BD22 ...69 H3
Gough La RPDN/SBR HX6 ...163 J5
Goulbourne St KGHY BD21 ...2 C4
Governor's Yd WKFDE WF1 ...11 D2
Gower St LDSU LS2 ...7 F3
WBOW BD5 ...96 A7
Gracechurch St GIR BD8 ...4 B3
Grace Leather La BTLY WF17 ...146 D6
Grace St KGHY BD21 ...3 E1
LDS LS1 ...6 C3
Gracey La WBSY BD6 ...118 A3
Grafton Cl BAIL BD17 ...51 K7
KNOT WF11 ...156 C6
Grafton Pl HIPP HX3 ...115 K8
Grafton Rd KGHY BD21 ...2 B5
Grafton St BTLY WF17 ...146 C8
CAS WF10 ...153 K5
CHAL LS7 ...7 E2
KGHY BD21 ...2 C5
WBOW BD5 ...4 C6
Cragwood Cl HORS LS18 ...77 G3
Graham Av BULY LS4 ...78 D8
HEM/SK/SE WF9 ...227 F3
Graham Dr CAS WF10 ...154 C4
Graham Gv BULY LS4 ...78 D8
Graham Mt BULY LS4 ...78 D8
Graham St BULY LS4 ...78 D8
HTON BD9 ...95 G1
Graham Ter BULY LS4 ...78 D8
Graham Vw BULY LS4 ...78 D8
Graham Wk MOR LS27 ...122 C4
Graingers Wy WOR/ARM LS12 ...6 B4
Grain St WBOW BD5 ...95 H8
Gramfield Rd HUDS HD4 ...190 B8
Grammar School St BFD BD1 ...4 C3
Grampian Av WKFDW/WTN WF2 ...175 F8
Grampian Cl WKFDE WF1 ...215 H8
Granary Ct ECHL BD2 ...74 E6
Granary Whf LDS * LS1 ...7 D4
Granby Av HDGY LS6 ...78 D6
Granby Ct HEM/SK/SE WF9 ...226 C6
Granby Dr AIRE BD20 ...48 D2
Granby Flats HDGY HD1 ...12 A5
Granby Gv HDGY LS6 ...78 D6
Granby La AIRE BD20 ...48 D2
Granby Mt HDGY LS6 ...78 D6
Granby Pl HDGY LS6 ...78 D6
Granby Rd HDGY LS6 ...78 D7
Granby St BOW * BD4 ...5 D6
CUL/QBY BD13 ...116 D2
Granby Ter HDGY LS6 ...78 D6
Granby Vw HDGY LS6 ...78 D7
Grandage Ter GIR BD8 ...95 H3
Grand Ar LDS * LS1 ...7 E3
Grand Cross Rd HUDE HD5 ...192 A5
Grandsmere Pl HIPP HX3 ...140 A7
Grand Stand MAR/SLWT HD7 ...189 F6
Grand Stand Rd EARD/LOFT WF3 ...149 G6
The Grange GFTH/SHER LS25 ...106 B4
Grange Av BFDE BD3 ...97 H3
BOW BD4 ...120 D3
BSPA/BRAM LS23 ...25 C8
BTLY * WF17 ...146 A8
CHAL LS7 ...80 A7
GFTH/SHER LS25 ...105 K5
HEM/SK/SE WF9 ...226 C8

Entry	Location	Page/Grid
	HUDN HD2	12 B1
	ILK LS29	20 D7
	ILK LS29	32 B6
	LUD/ILL HX2	115 J6
	MAR/SLWT HD7	209 J7
	SHPY BD18	72 E5
	WIL/AL BD15	94 C3
	YEA LS19	54 A5
Grange Bank	HIPP HX3	117 H5
Grange Bank Cl	HUDE HD5	13 F3
Grange Br	AIRE BD20	26 C3
Grange Castle	YEA LS19	54 B5
Grange Ct	AL/HA/HU LS17	40 B7
	CUD/GR S72	225 K8
	HEM/SK/SE WF9	226 A1
	HORS LS18	76 D3
	HUDW HD3	188 D3
	ILK LS29	20 D7
	KNOT WF11	156 A7
	MID LS10	101 K7
Grange Crs	AIRE BD20	3 F1
	CHAL LS7	80 A7
	YEA LS19	54 A5
Grange Cft	AL/HA/HU LS17	57 J6
Grange Dr	GIR BD8	94 C3
	KBTN HD8	217 H3
	OSS WF5	174 A8
Grange Est	ILK LS29	20 D7
Grangefield Av	BTLY WF17	146 A8
	ILK LS29	32 B2
Grangefield Rd	PDSY/CALV LS28	98 C2
Grange Fields Mt	RTHW LS26	125 G5
Grange Fields Rd	MID LS10	125 G5
Grange Fields Wy	RTHW LS26	125 G5
Grange Gv	AIRE BD20	3 F1
	BFDE BD3	97 H3
Grange Hts	HIPP HX3	141 F8
Grange Holt	AL/HA/HU LS17	57 J6
Grange La	BRIG HD6	169 F1
	GFTH/SHER LS25	129 G1
	HOR/CROF WF4	195 H4
	HWTH BD22	46 B8
	KBTN HD8	215 F8
Grange Mt	YEA LS19	54 A5
Grange Pk	BAIL BD17	52 A8
	HIPP HX3	140 A8
Grange Park Av	LS8	81 F6
	MSTN/BAR LS15	82 D5
Grange Park Cl	CAS WF10	129 K6
	MOR LS27	123 G4
	RHAY LS8	81 G6
Grange Park Crs	RHAY LS8	81 F6
Grange Park Dr	BGLY BD16	72 A4
	MOR LS27	123 G4
Grange Park Gv	RHAY LS8	81 F6
Grange Park Ms	MOR LS27	123 G4
Grange Park Pl	RHAY LS8	81 G6
Grange Park Ri	RHAY LS8	81 F6
Grange Park Rd	BGLY BD16	72 A4
	RHAY LS8	81 F6
Grange Park Ter	RHAY LS8	81 G6
Grange Park Wk	RHAY LS8	81 F6
Grange Park Wy	MOR * LS27	123 G4
The Grange Rd	BHP/TINH LS16	78 B2
Grange Rd	AIRE BD20	3 F1
	AIRE BD20	26 C6
	BFDE BD3	50 B7
	BSLYN/ROY S71	221 J8
	BTLY WF17	145 K8
	BTLY WF17	146 D7
	CAS WF10	154 E2
	CLECK BD19	143 K3
	EARL WF12	147 F8
	HUDW HD3	189 J5
	ILK LS29	32 B2
	MID LS10	101 K7
	WIL/AL BD15	94 C3
	YEA LS19	54 A5
Grange St	HIPP HX3	8 B2
	KGHY BD21	3 D2
	WKFDW/WTN WF2	10 A4
Grange Ter	CHAL LS7	79 K7
	MAR/SLWT HD7	209 J7
	MOR LS27	123 H3
	PDSY/CALV LS28	98 C3
	SHPY BD18	73 H5
	WIL/AL BD15	94 C3
Grange Valley Rd	BTLY WF17	146 E7
Grange Vw	BFDE * BD3	97 H3
	CHAL LS7	79 K7
	EARL WF12	195 H2
	HEM/SK/SE WF9	224 D5
	MSTN/BAR LS15	104 B5
	OT LS21	33 H2
	PDSY/CALV LS28	98 C3
Grange View Gdns	AL/HA/HU LS17	81 H2
Grangeway	GIR BD8	94 C3
	HEM/SK/SE WF9	224 D4
Grangewood Ct	WKFDE WF1	150 A6
Grangewood Gdns	BHP/TINH LS16	78 B2
Granhamthorpe	BRAM LS13	99 G1
Granny Av	MOR LS27	123 H3
Granny Hall Gv	BRIG HD6	142 A7
Granny Hall La	BRIG HD6	142 A7
Granny Hall Pk	BRIG HD6	142 A6
Granny Hill Ter	HFAX HX1	139 H6
Granny La	MIRF WF14	170 E8
	WOR/ARM LS12	100 A6
Grant Av	CHAL LS7	102 A1
Grantham Pl	GTHN BD7	4 A6
	HIPP HX3	8 C1
Grantham Rd	GTHN BD7	4 A6
	HIPP HX3	8 C1
Grantham Ter	GTHN BD7	4 A6
Grantley Pl	HUDN HD2	168 E6
Grantley St	WKFDE WF1	11 D2
Grantley Wy	WKFDE WF1	11 D2
Granton Rd	CHAL LS7	79 K6
Granton St	BFDE BD3	96 E4
Grant St	BFDE BD3	5 E4
	HWTH BD22	2 B5
	HWTH BD22	90 E1
Granville Av	PONT * WF8	180 D3
Granville Ct	OT * LS21	33 H4
Granville Mt	OT LS21	33 H4
Granville Pl	WIL/AL BD15	94 B2
	OSM LS9	102 A2
Granville Rd	HTON BD9	73 H6
	OSM LS9	102 A2
Granville St	CAS WF10	153 H6
	CLAY BD14	94 C6
	DEWS WF13	172 A3
	ELL * HX5	166 E5
	FEA/AMT WF7	179 H7
	KGHY * BD21	2 C3
	LVSG WF15	144 E8
	NORM WF6	178 A1
	PDSY/CALV LS28	98 A3
	TOD * OL14	159 K2
Granville Ter	BGLY BD16	50 A8
	HUD HD1	12 A5
	SHPY BD18	73 H5
	YEA LS19	54 A4
Grape St	HFAX HX1	8 C4
	KGHY BD21	3 F2
	MID LS10	7 F6
	WIL/AL BD15	94 C2
Grasleigh Av	WIL/AL BD15	94 A1
Grasleigh Wy	WIL/AL BD15	72 A8
Grasmere Av	WBY LS22	23 G6
Grasmere Cl	CAS WF10	155 F2
	STKB/PEN S36	252 C7
	WOR/ARM LS12	100 D5
Grasmere Ct	WOR/ARM LS12	100 D5
Grasmere Crs	DOD/DAR S75	200 C8
Grasmere Dr	EARL WF12	172 A3
	ECHL BD2	74 C8
	HOLM/MEL HD9	231 J2
	HUD HD1	12 A3
	LM/WK BD12	143 F2
	WKFDW/WTN WF2	175 F4
	WOR/ARM LS12	100 D5
Grasmere Rd	EARL WF12	172 A1
Grasscroft	HUDE HD5	214 B1
Grasscroft Av	HOLM/MEL HD9	212 E7
Grasscroft Rd	HOLM/MEL HD9	212 E7
	HUD HD1	190 D4
Gratrix La	RPDN/SBR HX6	139 F7
Grattan Rd	BFD BD1	4 B4
Graveleythorpe Ri	MSTN/BAR LS15	103 K2
Graveleythorpe Rd	MSTN/BAR LS15	103 K2
Gray Av	SHPY BD18	73 K6
Gray Ct	MSTN/BAR * LS15	104 B3
Gray Hall Cl	GTL/HWG * HX4	165 J8
Grayrigg Cl	MSTN/BAR LS15	103 G4
Grayrigg Ct	MSTN/BAR LS15	103 G4
Grayshon Dr	WBSY BD6	118 D2
Grayshon St	BIRK/DRI BD11	121 H6
Grayson Crest	BULY LS4	78 B4
Grayson Hts	BULY LS4	78 B4
Gray St	LVSG WF15	144 B7
Grayswood Crs	BOW BD4	97 F8
Grayswood Dr	BOW BD4	97 F7
Great Albion St	HFAX HX1	9 D4
Great Ben La	MAR/SLWT HD7	188 C7
Great Cross St	BFD BD7	5 D5
Great Edge Rd	LUD/ILL HX2	130 C5
Greatfield Cl	OSS WF5	173 K6
Greatfield Dr	OSS WF5	173 K6
Greatfield Gdns	OSS WF5	173 K6
Greatfield Rd	OSS WF5	173 K6
Great George St	LDS LS1	7 D3
Great Horton Rd	GTHN BD7	4 A6
Great House La	RPDN/SBR HX6	163 H8
Great House Rd	TOD OL14	134 D3
Great Northern Rd	KGHY BD21	3 D4
Great Northern St	HUD HD1	13 D3
Great North Rd	GFTH/SHER LS25	106 F1
Great Pasture	ILK LS29	32 B1
Great Pond St	DEWS * WF13	171 J6
Great Russell Ct	GTHN BD7	4 A4
Great Russell St	GTHN BD7	95 H4
Great Wilson St	BEE/HOL LS11	7 E5
Great Wood St	BTLY WF17	146 B7
	RPDN/SBR HX6	163
Greaves Av	WKFDW/WTN WF2	174
Greaves Cft	KBTN HD8	193
Greaves Fold	GTL/HWG HX4	166
Greaves Rd	DEWS WF13	172
Greaves Smithy	ILK LS29	19
Greaves St	CAS WF10	153
	WBOW BD5	95
Greave St	TOD OL14	134
Greek St	CAS WF10	153
	LDS LS1	7
The Green	AL/HA/HU LS17	79
	BGLY BD16	49
	BGLY * BD16	50
	BGLY BD16	50
	BGLY BD16	51
	BOW BD4	120
	BTLY WF17	145
	CAS WF10	154
	FEA/AMT WF7	179
	GFTH/SHER LS25	106
	GFTH/SHER LS25	129
	GSLY LS20	53
	HOR/CROF WF4	200
	HOR/CROF WF4	220
	HORS LS18	77
	HUDN HD2	168
	MAR/SLWT * HD7	209
	MIRF WF14	170
	OSS WF5	173
	OT LS21	33
	PDSY/CALV LS28	76
	WKFDW/WTN WF2	149
Green Abbey	HOLM/MEL HD9	248
Greenacre Av	LM/WK BD12	142
Green Acre Cl	BAIL BD17	51
Greenacre Cl	LM/WK BD12	142
Greenacre Ct	GFTH/SHER LS25	106
	LM/WK BD12	142
Greenacre Pk	YEA LS19	53
Greenacre Park Av	YEA LS19	53
Greenacre Park Ms	YEA LS19	54
Greenacre Park Ri	YEA LS19	53
Greenacre Rd	HEM/SK/SE WF9	226
Green Acres	FEA/AMT WF7	179
	HOR/CROF WF4	198
	STKB/PEN S36	252
	OSS WF5	173
Greenacres	HIPP HX3	117
Green Acres Cl	KBTN * HD8	217
Greenacres Ct	CAS WF10	154
Greenacres Dr	BTLY WF17	145
	HIPP HX3	117
	KGHY BD21	
Greenacres Gv	HIPP HX3	117
Greenacre Wk	HOR/CROF WF4	223
Greenacre Wy	LM/WK BD12	142
Greenaire Pl	BFD BD1	4
Green Av	AIRE BD20	27
	GFTH/SHER LS25	105
	HECK WF16	145
Green Balk La	KBTN HD8	193
Green Bank	CLECK BD19	150
	EARD/LOFT WF3	
Greenbank Cl	CAS WF10	153
Greenbank Gv	NORM WF6	151
Greenbank Rd	NORM WF6	151
	WIL/AL BD15	94
Greenbanks Av	HORS LS18	77
Greenbanks Cl	HORS LS18	77
Greenbanks Dr	HORS LS18	77
Green Cha	HDGY * LS6	78
Green Cliff	HOLM/MEL HD9	213
Greencliffe Av	BAIL BD17	51
Green Cl	AIRE BD20	26
	BTLY WF17	146
	DEWS WF13	171
	GIR BD8	94
	HDGY * LS6	
Green Ct	CLECK BD19	143
	GTHN BD7	95
	MSTN/BAR LS15	82
Green Crs	HDGY LS6	78
	MAR/SLWT HD7	189
Green Cft	HEM/SK/SE WF9	224
Greencroft Av	HIPP HX3	117
Greencroft Cl	IDLE BD10	74
Greendale Cl	HOLM/MEL HD9	213
Greendown Cl	ILK LS29	20
Green End	BRIG HD6	168
	CLAY BD14	94
Green End La	WKFDW/WTN WF2	10
Green End Rd	AIRE BD20	49
	WBSY BD6	118
Greenfell Cl	HWTH BD22	2
Greenfield Av	GFTH/SHER LS25	129
	GSLY LS20	52
	HIPP HX3	142
	HUDW HD3	190
	MOR LS27	122
	OSS WF5	173
	SHPY BD18	73
Greenfield Cl	GFTH/SHER LS25	129
	GTL/HWG HX4	188
	HIPP HX3	117
	KBTN HD8	236

OSS WF5 ....174 B7
°WKFDW/WTN WF2 ....175 G1
°eenfield Ct BHP/TINH LS16 ....56 B7
HWTH BD22..2 B3
°eenfield Crs CUL/QBY BD13............70 C5
°eenfield Dr CLECK BD19 ....143 G3
MOR LS27 ....122 A4
°eenfield Gdns AIRE BD20 ....26 B5
°eenfield Garth GFTH/SHER LS25.....129 F1
°eenfield La BOW BD4 ....93 J4
GSLY LS20 ....52 C4
°GTHN BD7 ....95 F7
IDLE BD10 ....74 D2
°eenfield Pl GIR * BD8 ....4 A2
HIPP HX3 ....142 B4
°eenfield Ri GFTH/SHER LS25..........129 F1
HOLM/MEL HD9 ....232 D6
NORM WF6 ....177 J1
OSM LS9 ....102 A4
OSS WF5 ....174 B7
°eenfields HECK WF16 ....145 F6
°eenfield Ter HUDS BD22 ....68 E3
TOD OL14..132 D2
°eenfield V GFTH/SHER LS25...........129 F1
°eenfield Vw GFTH/SHER LS25 ....129 F1
°eenfield Wy WKFDW/WTN WF2 ......175 G1
°eenfinch Gv HUDS HD4 ....212 E4
°een Gdns MAR/SLWT HD7 ....189 J6
RTHW LS26..77 F1
RTHW LS26..127 F5
°een Gate La MAR/SLWT HD7 ....210 E6
°een Gate Rd HOLM/MEL HD9 ....232 A7
°eengates Av CUL/QBY BD13 ....142 D2
°een Hall Pk HIPP HX3 ....117 J6
°een Head Av AIRE BD20 ....47 J1
°eenhead Ct HUDN HD2 ....12 A3
°een Head Dr AIRE BD20 ....47 J1
°een Head La BRIG HD6 ....167 K5
°eenhead La BRIG HD6 ....167 K5
HUDE HD5..192 B6
°een Head Rd AIRE BD20 ....47 K1
HUD HD1 ....12 B4
°een Hl HUDN HD2 ....168 C7
LUD/ILL HX2 ....138 E5
°eenhill Av PONT WF8 ....181 F5
°eenhill Bank Rd HOLM/MEL HD9 ..233 K6
°een Hill Cha WOR/ARM LS12 ....100 B5
°een Hill Cl WOR/ARM LS12 ....99 K2
°eenhill Crs WOR/ARM LS12 ....100 B5
°een Hill Crt WOR/ARM LS12 ....100 B5
°een Hill Dr BRAM LS13 ....49 J4
°een Hill Gdns WOR/ARM LS12 ......100 B5
°een Hill Gv STKB/PEN S36 ....253 F5
°een Hill Holt WOR/ARM * LS12 ....100 B5
°eenhill La BFDE BD3 ....96 E4
BGLY BD16..49 K5
°een Hill Mt WOR/ARM LS12 ....100 B6
°eenhill Mt PONT WF8 ....181 F5
°een Hill Pl BRAM LS13 ....99 J2
°een Hill Rd BRAM LS13 ....99 J2
°een Hill Rd HUDW HD3 ....189 J4
WKFDE WF1 ....11 D2
°eenhills YEA LS19 ....54 A8
°eenhills St BFDE BD3 ....96 E5
°een Hill Wy BRAM LS13 ....99 J2
°eenholme Cl ILK LS29 ....32 B1
°eenholme La HOLM/MEL HD9 ....233 K6
°een House Hl KBTN HD8 ....40 D7
°een House La KBTN HD8 ....216 A7
°eenhouse Rd HUDN HD2 ....191 G1
°eenhow Cl BULY LS4 ....100 D1
°eenhow Gdns BULY LS4 ....100 D1
°eenhow Pk ILK LS29 ....31 K2
°eenhow Wk BULY LS4 ....100 C1
°eenland Av CUL/QBY BD13 ....116 E1
°eenland Cl CUL/QBY BD13 ....116 D3
°eenland Rd HBR HX7 ....110 B5
°eenland Vls CUL/QBY BD13 ....116 E3
°een La AIRE BD20 ....26 C5
AIRE BD20 ....26 C5
BAIL BD17 ....51 G7
BAIL BD17 ....73 H2
BEE/HOL LS11..124 B2
BHP/TINH LS16 ....55 H7
BRIG HD6..141 K6
BRIG HD6..169 G1
BSPA/BRAM LS23 ....42 E4
CAS WF10..153 H6
CAS WF10..153 H6
CAS WF10..154 A1
CLECK BD19 ....144 A1
CUL/QBY BD13 ....93 F8
CUL/QBY BD13 ....93 J6
CUL/QBY BD13 ....116 D4
DEWS WF13 ....171 K2
EARD/LOFT WF3 ....149 K2
ECHL BD2 ....75 F8
FEA/AMT WF7 ....179 H5

FEA/AMT WF7 ....179 J5
FEA/AMT WF7 ....202 D5
GFTH/SHER LS25 ....105 K8
GFTH/SHER LS25 ....106 A4
GFTH/SHER LS25 ....128 E1
GIR BD8 ....4 A3
GTHN * BD7 ....95 G6
GTL/HWG HX4 ....166 B5
GTL/HWG HX4 ....187 H3
GTL/HWG HX4 ....188 D2
HBR HX7 ....111 K6
HEM/SK/SE WF9 ....226 E2
HEM/SK/SE WF9 ....241 H1
HIPP HX3 ....9 F5
HIPP HX3 ....116 D6
HIPP HX3 ....117 K6
HOLM/MEL HD9 ....231 J2
HOLM/MEL HD9 ....248 B1
HOR/CROF WF4 ....195 K5
HOR/CROF WF4 ....196 D6
HOR/CROF WF4 ....197 F5
HOR/CROF WF4 ....197 K3
HOR/CROF WF4 ....221 J5
HORS LS18..77 F4
HWTH BD22..46 B7
HWTH BD22..69 F1
IDLE BD10 ....74 C3
IDLE BD10 ....74 E3
ILK LS29 ....18 C2
ILK LS29 ....31 J5
KBTN HD8 ....250 E1
LM/WK BD12..119 G7
LM/WK BD12..142 D1
LUD/ILL HX2 ....115 H3
LUD/ILL HX2 ....138 A2
LUD/ILL HX2 ....139 H6
LVSG WF15 ....144 A8
MAR/SLWT HD7 ....209 K3
MSTN/BAR LS15 ....103 K2
OT LS21 ....33 H2
PDSY/CALV LS28 ....98 B5
PONT WF8 ....180 E4
PONT WF8 ....181 F6
RPDN/SBR HX6 ....163 J8
RTHW LS26 ....152 E2
SCFT LS14 ....81 J3
SKP/WHF BD23 ....14 B2
STKB/PEN S36 ....253 H4
WBY LS22..40 D3
WKFDW/WTN WF2 ....175 F3
WOR/ARM LS12 ....99 G6
YEA LS19 ....54 A6
Green Lane Cl HOR/CROF WF4 ....195 K4
Green Lane Ter MAR/SLWT HD7 ......189 C5
Greenlaws Cl HOLM/MEL HD9 ....232 D6
Greenlay Dr WKFDW/WTN WF2 ......174 C1
Green Lea RTHW LS26 ....127 F5
Greenlea Av YEA LS19 ....53 H5
Green Lea Cl BSPA/BRAM LS23 ....42 E4
Greenlea Cl YEA LS19 ....53 H6
Greenlea Mt YEA LS19 ....53 H5
Greenlea Rd YEA LS19 ....53 H6
Green Meadow WIL/AL BD15 ....71 H7
Greenmoor Av EARD/LOFT WF3 ......149 K2
WOR/ARM LS12 ....99 H4
Greenmoor Cl EARD/LOFT WF3 ......149 K2
Greenmoor Crs EARD/LOFT WF3 ....150 A3
Green Mt BOW * BD4 ....97 F8
HUDE * HD5 ....13 F4
OSS * WF5 ....173 J7
Greenmount Cl BEE/HOL * LS11 ....101 H8
Greenmount La BEE/HOL LS11 ....101 H8
Greenmount Pl BEE/HOL * LS11 ....101 H8
Green Mount Rd CUL/QBY BD13......93 J5
Greenmount St BEE/HOL LS11 ....101 H8
Greenmount Ter BEE/HOL LS11 ......101 H8
Greenock Pl WOR/ARM LS12 ....100 B3
Greenock Rd WOR/ARM * LS12 ......100 A3
Greenock St WOR/ARM LS12 ....100 A3
Greenock Ter WOR/ARM LS12 ....100 A3
Green Pk AL/HA/HU LS17 ....80 A1
WKFDE WF1 ....11 E3
Green Park Av HIPP HX3 ....166 B1
OSS WF5 ....173 K7
Green Park Dr HIPP HX3 ....166 B1
Green Park Rd HIPP HX3 ....166 B1
Green Park St HIPP HX3 ....140 B8
Green Pasture Cl OSM LS9 ....102 E3
Green Pl ECHL * BD2 ....5 F1
Green Rd BAIL BD17 ....73 H1
HDGY LS6..78 E3
LVSG WF15 ....144 D6
Green Rw RTHW LS26 ....152 C2
Green Royd GTL/HWG HX4 ....166 B5
Greenroyd Av CLECK BD19 ....166 B5
HIPP HX3 ....140 A8
Greenroyd Cl HIPP HX3 ....166 B1
Greenroyd Crs HFAX * HX1 ....8 A2
Greenroyd Cft PONT WF8 ....181 K6
Greenroyd La LUD/ILL HX2 ....139 H2
Greens End Rd HOLM/MEL HD9 ......231 H1
Greenside CLECK BD19 ....144 B4
CUD/GR S72 ....223 F7
HECK WF16 ....145 F7
HOR/CROF WF4 ....201 F4
KBTN HD8 ....236 C4
KBTN HD8 ....236 E5
LM/WK BD12..119 H7

PDSY/CALV LS28 ....98 B5
STKB/PEN S36 ....253 F5
WKFDW/WTN WF2 ....199 J4
WOR/ARM LS12 ....100 B6
Greenside Av HUDE HD5 ....192 C6
WOR/ARM LS12 ....100 C6
Greenside Cl WOR/ARM LS12 ....100 C6
Greenside Ct HOR/CROF WF4 ....201 F4
MOR * LS27 ....122 C4
Greenside Crs HUDE HD5..................192 C6
Greenside Dr HUDE HD5 ....192 C6
WOR/ARM LS12 ....100 C6
Greenside Gv PDSY/CALV LS28 ....98 B5
Greenside La CUL/QBY BD13 ....70 B5
GIR BD8 ....95 F4
Greenside Mt MIRF WF14 ....170 E4
Greenside Pk HOR/CROF WF4..........201 F4
Green Side Rd HUDS HD4..................214 B8
Greenside Rd MIRF WF14 ....170 E4
WOR/ARM LS12 ....100 B6
Greenside Ter WOR/ARM LS12 ......100 B6
Greenside Wk WOR/ARM LS12 ......100 B6
Green's Sq LUD/ILL HX2 ....139 H3
Green St BFD * BD1 ....5 D4
CAS WF10..153 J2
GTL/HWG HX4 ....166 A7
HUD HD1..12 C3
HWTH BD22..68 E5
HWTH BD22..90 E1
Greensway GFTH/SHER LS25............105 J4
Green Sykes Rd AIRE BD20 ....46 B3
Green Ter BEE/HOL LS11 ....101 J8
ECHL BD2 ....5 F1
Green Terrace Sq HFAX HX1 ....8 B6
Greenthorpe Hi BRAM LS13 ....99 J4
Greenthorpe Mt BRAM LS13 ....99 J3
Greenthorpe Rd WOR/ARM LS12 ....99 J4
Greenthorpe St BRAM LS13 ....99 J3
Greenthorpe Wk BRAM LS13 ....99 J3
Greenthwaite Cl KGHY BD21 ....2 B1
Greenton Av CLECK BD19..................143 F2
Greenton Crs CUL/QBY BD13 ....116 C3
Greentop HOR/CROF WF4 ....201 F4
PDSY/CALV LS28 ....98 B5
Green Top WOR/ARM LS12 ....100 B6
Green Top Gdns WOR/ARM LS12 ..100 B6
Green Top St GIR BD8 ....94 E4
Greenups Ter RPDN/SBR HX6 ....138 E7
Green Vw HDGY LS6 ....78 E4
SCFT LS14 ....60 A3
Greenview HOR/CROF WF4................201 F4
Greenview Cl OSM LS9 ....102 E1
Green View Ct RHAY LS8 ....80 C3
Greenview Mt OSM LS9 ....102 E1
The Green Vw CUD/GR S72 ....223 F7
Greenville Av WOR/ARM LS12 ....100 B6
Greenville Dr LM/WK BD12 ....119 F4
Greenville Gdns WOR/ARM LS12 ..100 B6
The Greenway BFDE BD3 ....5 F3
Green Wy LUD/ILL HX2 ....115 H3
SCFT LS14 ....52 E4
Greenway GSLY LS20 ....52 E4
HOLM/MEL HD9 ....213 F6
MAR/SLWT HD7 ....189 K6
MSTN/BAR LS15 ....104 A2
Greenway Cl MSTN/BAR LS15 ....104 A2
Greenway Dr WIL/AL BD15 ....94 B4
Greenway Rd WRDW BD5 ....119 F1
Greenwell Ct OSM LS9 ....102 E3
Greenwell Rw CLAY BD14 ....94 B7
Greenwood Av EARL WF12 ....172 E4
ECHL BD2 ....74 C6
HEM/SK/SE WF9 ....226 E3
Greenwood Cl NORM WF6..................178 A4
Greenwood Ct BFD * BD1 ....5 D5
HDGY * LS6 ....78 E4
Greenwood Dr ECHL BD2 ....74 C7
Greenwood Mt ECHL BD2 ....74 C7
HDGY LS6..78 E3
Green Wood Pk HDGY LS6 ....78 E4
Greenwood Rd BAIL BD17 ....73 H2
EARD/LOFT WF3 ....148 A3
WKFDE WF1 ....11 D2
Greenwood Rw PDSY/CALV LS28 ....98 D4
Greenwood St DEWS WF13 ....172 A3
HBR HX7 ....112 B8
HUDS HD4..12 C6
Greetland Rd GTL/HWG HX4 ....164 D6
Gregory Ct CLAY BD14 ....94 C7
Gregory Crs GTHN BD7......................117 K1
Gregory Dr KBTN HD8 ....215 H5
Gregory La HUDE HD5 ....193 J4
Gregory Rd CAS WF10 ....153 K6
Gregory Springs La MIRF WF14 ......193 K1
Gregory Springs Mt MIRF WF14 ......193 K1
Gregory Springs Rd MIRF WF14 ......170 E8
Gregory St BTLY * WF17......................146 D6
Grenfell Dr BFDE BD3 ....97 F3
Grenfell Rd BFDE BD3 ....97 F3
Grenfell Ter BFDE BD3 ....97 F3
Grenley St KNOT WF11 ....156 D7
Grenville Wk HOR/CROF WF4 ....198 B8
Gresham Av ECHL BD2 ....74 B7
Gresley Rd KGHY BD21 ....3 D3
Grey Cl WKFDE WF1 ....149 J8
Grey Crt WKFDE WF1 ....149 J8
Greycourt Cl ECHL BD2......................74 C5
Greyfriars Av HUDN HD2 ....169 F7
Greyfriar Wk GTHN BD7 ....94 E8
Grey Gables HOR/CROF WF4............196 E5

Grey Scar Rd *HWTH* BD22 ....68 C1
Greyshiels Av *HDGY* LS6 ....78 C7
Greystone Av *ELL* HX5 ....166 D6
Greystone Cl *BSPA/BRAM* LS23 ....42 E4
  ILK LS29 ....32 A1
Greystone Ct *BRIG* HD6 ....168 B4
Greystone Crs *IDLE* BD10 ....74 E5
Grey Stone La *TOD* OL14 ....134 E3
Greystone Mt *MSTN/BAR* LS15 ....103 G4
Greystone Pk *GFTH/SHER* LS25 ....84 E2
Greystones Cl *GFTH/SHER* LS25 ....84 E2
Greystones Ct *RHAY* LS8 ....80 D4
Greystones Dr *HWTH* BD22 ....47 H8
  OSS WF5 ....173 K7
Grey Stones La *HBR* HX7 ....89 H6
Greystones La *HWTH* BD22 ....69 H1
Greystones Mt *HWTH* BD22 ....69 H1
Greystones Ri *HWTH* BD22 ....47 H8
Greystones Rd *LUD/ILL* HX2 ....138 B4
Grey St *WKFDE* WF1 ....149 J8
Griffe Dr *LM/WK* BD12 ....142 D2
Griffe Gdns *HWTH* BD22 ....68 D1
Griffe Head Crs *LM/WK* BD12 ....142 D1
Griffe Head Rd *LM/WK* BD12 ....142 D1
Griffe Rd *HWTH* BD22 ....67 K5
  LM/WK BD12 ....142 D1
Griff House La *EARD/LOFT* WF3 ....148 C3
Grime La *HOLM/MEL* HD9 ....249 K2
  HOR/CROF WF4 ....178 A4
Grimescar Mdw *HUDN* HD2 ....190 D1
Grimescar Rd *HUDW* HD3 ....167 H8
Grimethorpe St *HEM/SK/SE* WF9 ....242 B1
Grimpit Hl *HOR/CROF* * WF4 ....221 J5
Grimscar Av *HUDN* HD2 ....12 B1
Grimthorpe Av *HDGY* LS6 ....78 C6
Grimthorpe Pl *HDGY* LS6 ....78 C6
Grimthorpe St *HDGY* LS6 ....78 D6
Grimthorpe Ter *HDGY* LS6 ....78 D6
Grisedale Cl *WBY* LS22 ....23 F5
Grosmont Rd *BRAM* LS13 ....99 C1
Grosmont Ter *BRAM* LS13 ....77 G8
Grosvenor Av *HEM/SK/SE* WF9 ....226 C4
  KBTN HD8 ....193 G8
  PONT WF8 ....180 B2
  SHPY BD18 ....73 F3
Grosvenor Hl *CHAL* LS7 ....79 F7
Grosvenor Mt *HDGY* LS6 ....79 F7
Grosvenor Pk *CHAL* LS7 ....79 J4
Grosvenor Park Gdns *HDGY* LS6 ....79 F7
Grosvenor Rd *BTLY* WF17 ....146 C5
  GIR BD8 ....4 B2
  HDGY LS6 ....79 F7
  HECK * WF16 ....145 G7
  HFAX HX1 ....8 B4
  WBY LS22 ....23 J5
Grosvenor St *EARL* WF12 ....172 E6
  ELL HX5 ....166 C5
  HECK WF16 ....145 H4
  WKFDE WF1 ....11 F6
Grosvenor Ter *GIR* BD8 ....4 B2
  HDGY LS6 ....79 F7
  HECK * WF16 ....145 G7
  HFAX HX1 ....8 B4
  WBY LS22 ....23 J5
Grosvenor Wy *KBTN* HD8 ....193 G8
Grouse La *CUL/QBY* BD13 ....116 B1
Grouse St *KGHY* * BD21 ....3 D2
The Grove *AL/HA/HU* LS17 ....39 K5
  AL/HA/HU LS17 ....57 F6
  BAIL BD17 ....51 J7
  BGLY BD16 ....49 J5
  BTLY WF17 ....145 K4
  EARD/LOFT WF3 ....148 C3
  GFTH/SHER LS25 ....129 F2
  HECK WF16 ....145 F5
  HEM/SK/SE WF9 ....226 B7
  HIPP HX3 ....141 H3
  HOLM/MEL HD9 ....231 K2
  HOR/CROF WF4 ....222 E2
  HORS LS18 ....77 F3
  HUDN HD2 ....191 H1
  IDLE BD10 ....74 D4
  IDLE BD10 ....75 F4
  ILK LS29 ....20 A7
  NORM * WF6 ....178 A1
  PDSY/CALV LS28 ....98 A3
  RTHW LS26 ....128 A1
  SHPY BD18 ....72 E4
  WKFDW/WTN WF2 ....199 K4
  YEA LS19 ....53 J7
  YEA LS19 ....53 K5
Grove Av *HDGY* LS6 ....78 E5
  HEM/SK/SE WF9 ....224 E5
  HIPP HX3 ....241 J1
  ILK LS29 ....19 K8
  PDSY/CALV LS28 ....98 B4
  PONT WF8 ....181 F3
  SHPY BD18 ....73 H6
Grove Cl *CLECK* BD19 ....144 E2
  ECHL BD2 ....74 C7
Grove Ct *HDGY* LS6 ....78 E5
  HIPP HX3 ....8 B1
  PDSY/CALV LS28 ....98 B4
Grove Crs *BSPA/BRAM* LS23 ....42 E4
  LUD/ILL HX2 ....138 A4
  WKFDW/WTN WF2 ....199 K4
Grove Crs South *BSPA/BRAM* LS23 ....42 E5
Grove Cft *HIPP* HX3 ....8 A1

Grove Dr *HEM/SK/SE* WF9 ....241 H1
  HIPP HX3 ....115 J8
Grove Edge *HIPP* HX3 ....8 A1
Grove Farm Cl *BHP/TINH* LS16 ....55 K7
Grove Farm Crs *BHP/TINH* LS16 ....55 J8
Grove Farm Cft *BHP/TINH* LS16 ....55 J7
Grove Farm Dr *BHP/TINH* LS16 ....55 J7
Grove Gdns *BSPA/BRAM* LS23 ....43 F4
  EARL WF12 ....173 F5
  HDGY LS6 ....78 E5
  HIPP HX3 ....8 B1
Grovehall Av *BEE/HOL* LS11 ....124 A2
Grovehall Dr *BEE/HOL* LS11 ....124 A1
Grovehall La *PONT* WF8 ....181 J5
Grovehall Pde *BEE/HOL* LS11 ....124 A2
Grovehall Rd *BEE/HOL* LS11 ....124 A2
Grove Head *HEM/SK/SE* WF9 ....241 H1
Grove House Crs *ECHL* BD2 ....74 C7
Grove House Dr *ECHL* BD2 ....74 C8
Grove House Rd *ECHL* BD2 ....74 C7
Grovelands *ECHL* BD2 ....74 C8
Grove La *CLECK* BD19 ....144 E2
  HDGY LS6 ....78 E6
  HEM/SK/SE WF9 ....204 A8
  HEM/SK/SE WF9 ....224 E5
  HEM/SK/SE WF9 ....241 H1
  KNOT WF11 ....156 B7
Grove Lea Cl *HEM/SK/SE* WF9 ....224 E5
Grove Lea Crs *PONT* WF8 ....181 F4
Grove Lea Wk *PONT* WF8 ....181 F4
Grove Marsh Lea
  HEM/SK/SE * WF9 ....225 F4
Grove Mt *HEM/SK/SE* WF9 ....241 H1
  PONT * WF8 ....181 F3
Grove Nook *HUDW* HD3 ....189 K5
Grove Pk *HIPP* HX3 ....115 J8
  HOR/CROF WF4 ....197 K5
Grove Pl *BSPA/BRAM* LS23 ....42 E4
  HEM/SK/SE WF9 ....224 E5
Grove Ri *AL/HA/HU* LS17 ....57 F6
  PONT * WF8 ....181 F3
Grove Rd *BSPA/BRAM* LS23 ....42 E4
  ELL HX5 ....167 F4
  HBR HX7 ....112 B7
  HDGY LS6 ....78 E5
  HECK WF16 ....145 H7
  HOR/CROF WF4 ....197 G2
  HORS LS18 ....77 F3
  HUD HD1 ....13 D5
  ILK LS29 ....19 J7
  ILK LS29 ....32 C7
  MID LS10 ....102 A8
  MSTN/BAR LS15 ....103 J4
  PDSY/CALV LS28 ....98 B4
  PONT WF8 ....180 E3
  SHPY BD18 ....73 H6
  WKFDE WF1 ....10 C4
Grove Royd *HIPP* HX3 ....8 B1
Groves Hall Rd *DEWS* WF13 ....171 J5
Grove Sq *CLECK* * BD19 ....144 E2
  HIPP HX3 ....8 A1
Grove St *BRIG* HD6 ....168 C1
  DEWS WF13 ....172 B3
  HECK WF16 ....145 H7
  HEM/SK/SE WF9 ....241 H1
  HUDW HD3 ....189 J3
  LDS LS1 ....6 C3
  LVSG WF15 ....170 E1
  MAR/SLWT HD7 ....210 D2
  MIRF WF14 ....170 E5
  OSS WF5 ....173 J7
  PDSY/CALV * LS28 ....98 C1
  RPDN/SBR HX6 ....139 G7
  WKFDE WF1 ....11 D4
Grove St South *HFAX* * HX1 ....8 A4
Grove Ter *GTHN* * BD7 ....4 B5
  HBR HX7 ....137 F3
  HEM/SK/SE WF9 ....224 E5
  PDSY/CALV LS28 ....98 B4
Groveville *HIPP* HX3 ....141 H2
Groveway *ECHL* BD2 ....74 C7
Grove Wy *HEM/SK/SE* WF9 ....241 H1
Grovewood *HDGY* LS6 ....78 D5
Grunberg Rd *HDGY* LS6 ....78 D6
Grunberg St *HDGY* * LS6 ....78 D6
Guard House Av *HWTH* BD22 ....2 B3
Guard House Dr *HWTH* BD22 ....2 B3
Guard House Gv *HWTH* BD22 ....2 A3
Guard House Rd *HWTH* BD22 ....2 B3
Guernsey Rd *EARL* WF12 ....172 E1
Guildford St *BSLYN/ROY* S71 ....221 K7
Guildford St *HBR* HX7 ....136 B1
  OSS WF5 ....173 J7
Guild Wy *LUD/ILL* HX2 ....138 E5
Guillemot Ap *MOR* LS27 ....123 J8
Guiseley Dr *ILK* LS29 ....52 D1
Gulley Rd *OSM* LS9 ....103 F8
The Gully *KBTN* HD8 ....234 E6
Gully Ter *HOLM/MEL* HD9 ....233 H7
Gunson Rd *OSS* WF5 ....173 J5
Gunter Rd *WBY* LS22 ....24 A5
Gunthwaite La *KBTN* HD8 ....236 B8
Gunthwaite Top *KBTN* * HD8 ....236 D8
Gurbax Ct *BFDE* BD3 ....97 G4
Gurney Rd *WBOW* BD5 ....95 K8
Guygroft *OT* LS21 ....39 J3
Guys Cft *WKFDW/WTN* WF2 ....174 D7
Guy St *BOW* BD4 ....5 D5
Gwyn Holme *DEWS* * WF13 ....171 J1

Gwynne Av *BFDE* BD3 ....97 C1
Gynn La *HOLM/MEL* HD9 ....213 G1
Gypsy Ct *CAS* WF10 ....154 D3
Gypsy La *CAS* WF10 ....154 D3
Gypsy Wood Cl *MSTN/BAR* LS15 ....104 E1
Gypsy Wood Crest *MSTN/BAR* LS15 ....104 E1

H

Hacking La *HEM/SK/SE* WF9 ....226 D1
Hadassah St *HIPP* HX3 ....140 C7
Haddingley La *KBTN* HD8 ....235 F8
Haddon Av *BULY* LS4 ....100 C3
  HIPP HX3 ....140 E7
Haddon Cl *CLECK* BD19 ....144 E1
  HEM/SK/SE WF9 ....226 D1
Haddon Pl *BULY* LS4 ....100 C3
Haddon Rd *BULY* LS4 ....100 C3
Hadfield Rd *HECK* WF16 ....145 G4
Hadleigh Ct *AL/HA/HU* LS17 ....79 K3
Hadleigh Ri *PONT* WF8 ....180 C2
Hadrian Cl *CAS* WF10 ....154 C3
Hadrian's Cl *HUDW* HD3 ....189 J1
  PONT WF8 ....204 C2
Hag Farm Rd *ILK* LS29 ....32 A1
Hagg La *MIRF* WF14 ....170 E6
Haggroyd La *HOLM/MEL* HD9 ....233 J6
Haggs Hill Rd *OSS* WF5 ....174 D3
Haggs La *WKFDW/WTN* WF2 ....174 B8
Hagg Wood Rd *HOLM/MEL* HD9 ....233 H6
Hag Hill La *KBTN* HD8 ....217 J2
Hag La *HIPP* HX3 ....116 E2
Hague Crs *HEM/SK/SE* WF9 ....224 E5
Hague Park Cl *HEM/SK/SE* * WF9 ....225 F5
Hague Park La *HEM/SK/SE* WF9 ....225 F5
Hague Park Wk *HEM/SK/SE* WF9 ....225 F5
Hague Ter *HEM/SK/SE* WF9 ....224 E5
Haigh Av *RTHW* LS26 ....126 A4
Haigh Beck Vw *IDLE* BD10 ....74 E8
Haigh Cl *STKB/PEN* S36 ....252 E5
Haigh Cnr *IDLE* BD10 ....75 F1
Haigh Cft *BSLYN/ROY* S71 ....221 K7
Haigh Cross *HUDW* * HD3 ....189 K1
Haigh Fold *ECHL* BD2 ....74 E1
Haigh Gdns *RTHW* LS26 ....125 K4
Haigh Hall *IDLE* BD10 ....75 F1
Haigh La *DOD/DAR* S75 ....219 F7
  HIPP HX3 ....140 C2
  HOLM/MEL HD9 ....233 J7
  HOR/CROF WF4 ....216 B1
  STKB/PEN S36 ....253 F5
Haigh Ms *DOD/DAR* * S75 ....219 F7
Haigh Moor Av *EARD/LOFT* WF3 ....147 K3
Haigh Moor Crs *EARD/LOFT* WF3 ....147 K4
Haigh Moor Rd *EARD/LOFT* WF3 ....147 K4
Haigh Moor St *WKFDE* WF1 ....11 D6
Haigh Moor Vw *EARD/LOFT* WF3 ....147 K4
Haigh Moor Wy *BSLYN/ROY* S71 ....221 K7
Haigh Park Rd *MID* LS10 ....125 J2
Haigh Rd *RTHW* LS26 ....126 C3
Haighside *RTHW* LS26 ....125 K4
Haighside Cl *RTHW* LS26 ....125 K4
Haighside Dr *RTHW* LS26 ....125 K4
Haighside Wy *RTHW* LS26 ....125 K5
Haighs Sq *HUDE* HD5 ....13 D1
Haigh St *BOW* BD4 ....96 C1
  BRIG HD6 ....142 E8
  GTL/HWG HX4 ....165 K6
  HFAX HX1 ....8 B4
  HUDS HD4 ....190 B1
Haigh Ter *RTHW* LS26 ....125 K4
Haigh Vw *RTHW* LS26 ....125 K5
Haigh Wood Crs *BHP/TINH* LS16 ....55 H5
Haigh Wood Gn *BHP/TINH* * LS16 ....77 H5
Haigh Wood Rd *BHP/TINH* LS16 ....55 H5
Hailhead Dr *PONT* WF8 ....181 G1
Haincliffe Rd *KGHY* BD21 ....2 C7
Haines Pk *RHAY* * LS8 ....102 A4
Hainsworth Moor Crs
  CUL/QBY BD13 ....116 C3
Hainsworth Moor Dr
  CUL/QBY BD13 ....116 C3
Hainsworth Moor Garth
  CUL/QBY BD13 ....116 C3
Hainsworth Moor Gv
  CUL/QBY BD13 ....116 C3
Hainsworth Moor Vw
  CUL/QBY BD13 ....116 C3
Hainsworth Rd *AIRE* BD20 ....27 J2
Hainsworth Sq *PDSY/CALV* LS28 ....76 E5
Hainsworth St *RTHW* LS26 ....126 E2
  WOR/ARM * LS12 ....6 A7
Hainworth Crag Rd *KGHY* BD21 ....69 J8
Hainworth La *KGHY* BD21 ....47 J4
Hainworth Rd *KGHY* BD21 ....47 K5
Hainworth Wood Rd *KGHY* BD21 ....2 E7
Hainworth Wood Rd North
  KGHY BD21 ....3 D1
Halcyon Hl *CHAL* LS7 ....79 J4
Halcyon Wy *WBOW* BD5 ....95 J7
Haldane Cl *CUD/QR* S72 ....223 K4
Haldane Crs *WKFDE* WF1 ....11 K7
Hales Rd *WOR/ARM* LS12 ....100 C8
Halesworth Crs *BOW* BD4 ....97 H5
Haley Ct *HIPP* HX3 ....9 D1
Haley Hl *HIPP* HX3 ....9 D1

alf Acre Rd CUL/QBY BD13	93 F4
alf House La BRIG HD6	141 J6
alf Mile BRAM LS13	98 C1
alf Mile Cl PDSY/CALV LS28	98 D1
alf Mile Ct PDSY/CALV LS28	98 D1
alf Mile Gdns BRAM LS13	98 D1
alf Mile Gn PDSY/CALV LS28	98 D1
alf Mile La BRAM LS13	76 D8
alf Moon La WKFDE WF1	176 E4
alfpenny La FEA/AMT WF7	180 A5
alf St KGHY BD21	2 E2
	LUD/ILL HX2	138 B3
alifax Old Rd HIPP HX3	141 G3
	HUDN HD2	191 F1
alifax Rd BRIG HD6	168 B1
	CLECK BD19	143 F4
	CUL/QBY BD13	70 B5
	CUL/QBY BD13	92 C7
	CUL/QBY BD13	116 B5
	DEWS WF13	145 J8
	ELL HX5	166 D4
	HIPP HX3	117 G7
	HUDW HD3	190 C2
	HWTH BD22	69 H4
	LUD/ILL HX2	92 B7
	LVSG WF15	143 K6
	MAR/SLWT HD7	189 F6
	RPDN/SBR HX6	164 A7
	STKB/PEN S36	252 B5
	TOD OL14	134 B6
	TOD OL14	135 C3
	WBSY BD6	118 A4
alliamshire Ms WKFDW/WTN WF2	174 D7
allas Gv HUD5	192 A6
allas La CUL/QBY BD13	70 D5
	KBTN HD8	215 J5
	KBTN HD8	215 H5
all Av HUD HD1	12 B5
DLE BD10	75 F6
allbank Cl WBOW BD5	118 E2
allbank Dr WBOW BD5	118 E2
ll Bank La HBR HX7	137 F3
ll Bower La HUDS HD4	213 H3
ll Brig BTLY DN5	241 J7
llcliffe BAIL BD17	51 K7
ll Cliffe Ct HOR/CROF WF4	197 C1
ll Cliffe Crs HOR/CROF WF4	197 C1
all Cliffe Gv HOR/CROF WF4	197 H1
ll Cliffe Ri HOR/CROF WF4	197 H1
ll Cliffe Rd HOR/CROF WF4	197 H1
ll Cl BHP/TINH LS16	35 J7
3SPA/BRAM LS23	42 E4
HIPP HX3	117 F8
HOLM/MEL HD9	231 K1
ILK LS29	31 K2
ll Ct KNOT WF11	155 K3
ll Cft HOR/CROF WF4	196 E5
llcroft Cl HOR/CROF WF4	197 H2
llcroft Dr HOR/CROF WF4	197 H3
ILK LS29	19 F4
LVSG WF15	170 E1
ll Farm Gv STKB/PEN S36	253 F5
ll Farm Pk GFTH/SHER LS25	107 F3
llfield Av GFTH/SHER LS25	107 F4
llfield Crs WBY LS22	23 K6
llfield Dr BAIL BD17	51 J8
ll Field La HOR/CROF WF4	222 E4
llfield La WBY LS22	23 K5
llfield Pl BFD BD1	4 C3
ll Field Rd GIR BD8	4 C3
llfield St BFD BD1	4 C3
llfield Ter GFTH/SHER LS25	107 F4
ll Gdns AIRE BD20	26 A2
ll Garth PONT WF8	204 C6
llgate BFD BD1	4 C3
ll Ga STKB/PEN S36	253 C8
ll Green La GTL/HWG HX4	187 F3
ILK LS29	6 B1
lliday Av WOR/ARM LS12	100 A3
lliday Dr WOR/ARM LS12	100 A3
lliday Pl WOR/ARM *LS12	100 A3
lliday Pl WOR/ARM LS12	100 A3
lliday Rd GFTH/SHER LS25	105 J4
WOR/ARM LS12	100 A3
lliday St PDSY/CALV LS28	98 C3
lliley St DEWS WF13	172 A3
l Ing La HOLM/MEL HD9	213 H6
ling Pl TOD OL14	133 K7
ll Ing Rd HOLM/MEL HD9	213 K7
ll Ings BFD BD1	4 C5
HIPP HX3	141 F8
ll La BHP/TINH LS16	55 J5
AS WF10	130 A5
CHAL LS7	79 K6
EARL WF12	195 J1
HEM/SK/SE WF9	226 D5
HIPP HX3	116 E7
OR/CROF WF4	198 B7
HORS LS18	76 E2

KBTN HD8	215 G4
MAR/SLWT HD7	188 E5
OT LS21	34 E1
SHPY BD18	73 J3
WOR/ARM LS12	99 G5
WOR/ARM LS12	100 D4
Hall Lee Rd HUDW HD3	190 C2
Hall Ms BSPA/BRAM LS23	42 E4
Hall Orchards Av WBY LS22	23 K5
Hallowes Gv CUL/QBY BD13	70 B6
Hallowes Park Rd CUL/QBY BD13	70 B6
The Hallows KGHY BD21	2 B2
Hallows Cl HUDE *HD5	192 B8
Hallows Rd KGHY BD21	3 F1
Hall Park Av HOR/CROF WF4	200 D1
HORS LS18	76 E2
LVSG WF15	170 D1
Hall Park Cl HORS LS18	76 E2
Hall Park Ct GFTH/SHER LS25	129 C3
Hall Park Cft GFTH/SHER LS25	129 C3
Hall Park Garth HORS LS18	76 E2
Hall Park Mdw GFTH/SHER LS25	129 C3
Hall Park Mt HORS * LS18	76 E2
Hall Park Orch GFTH/SHER LS25	129 F3
Hall Park Ri GFTH/SHER * LS25	129 C2
HORS LS18	76 E2
Hall Park Rd BSPA/BRAM LS23	25 H7
Hall Pl OSM LS9	102 B4
Hall Ri BHP/TINH LS16	35 J8
ILK LS29	31 K2
Hall Rise Cl BHP/TINH LS16	35 J8
Hall Rise Cft BHP/TINH LS16	35 J8
Hall Rd IDLE BD10	75 F6
RTHW LS26	128 A2
WKFDW/WTN WF2	174 E7
WOR/ARM LS12	100 C4
Hall Royd SHPY BD18	73 H4
Hallroyd Crs TOD OL14	134 B6
Hallroyd Pl TOD * OL14	134 B6
Hallroyd Rd TOD OL14	134 B5
Halls La CUL/QBY BD13	70 C6
Hall Stone Ct HIPP * HX3	117 H6
Hall St BRIG HD6	168 C1
FEA/AMT WF7	179 K7
HFAX HX1	8 C4
HUDW HD3	189 K4
HWTH BD22	47 F8
HWTH BD22	68 E5
WBSY BD6	118 D2
Hall St North HIPP HX3	8 C1
Hall Ter AIRE * BD20	48 D2
Hallwood Gn IDLE BD10	75 C6
Halstead Dr ILK LS29	32 C5
Halstead La HUDS HD4	234 B3
Halstead Pl GTHN BD7	95 C8
Halsteads Wy AIRE BD20	26 D5
Halton Cl HUDE HD5	192 B7
Halton Moor Av OSM LS9	103 F4
Halton Moor Rd OSM LS9	102 E5
Halton Pl GTHN BD7	95 H8
Halton St FEA/AMT WF7	179 J4
Hamber Cote La AIRE BD20	27 H1
Hambleden Av BOW BD4	119 J2
HOLM/MEL HD9	231 K2
Hambleton Bank LUD/ILL HX2	114 E6
Hambleton Crs LUD/ILL HX2	114 E6
Hambleton Dr LUD/ILL HX2	114 D6
Hambleton St WKFDE WF1	11 D2
The Hame GTL/HWG * HX4	165 J8
Hamel Ri HEM/SK/SE WF9	224 D5
Hamilton Av CHAL LS7	80 A7
Hamilton Ct NORM WF6	152 M6
Hamilton Gdns CHAL LS7	79 K8
Hamilton Pl CHAL LS7	80 A8
Hamilton St GIR BD8	4 B3
Hamilton Ter CHAL LS7	80 A7
Hamilton Vw CHAL LS7	80 A7
Hammer La HOR/CROF WF4	178 A7
Hammerstone Leach La ELL HX5	166 D5
Hammerstones Rd ELL HX5	166 C5
Hammerton Dr GFTH/SHER LS25	106 A6
Hammerton Farm Av	
HOR/CROF WF4	223 F2
Hammerton Gv PDSY/CALV LS28	98 B4
Hammerton Rd HUDN HD2	191 G1
Hammerton St BFDE BD3	5 E5
PDSY/CALV LS28	98 C4
Hammond Crs BIRK/DRI BD11	121 G4
Hammond Pl HTON BD9	73 C8
Hammond Rd KNOT WF11	156 A8
Hammond St HFAX HX1	8 A5
HUDN HD2	13 D1
OSM * LS9	102 A5
Hammonds Yd HUD * HD1	12 C4
Hamm Strasse BFD BD1	4 C3
Hampden Cl KNOT WF11	155 J6
Hampden Pl HFAX HX1	8 A5
WBOW BD5	95 K7
Hampden St WBOW BD5	95 K7
Hamper La STKB/PEN S36	252 E5
Hample Field La AWLS/ASK DN6	243 H2
Hampshire Cl ILK LS29	20 D7
PONT WF8	155 F8
Hampshire St HUDE HD5	13 F4
Hampson St BTLY WF17	145 K4
Hampton Pl IDLE BD10	74 D3
OSM LS9	102 B4
Hampton St HFAX HX1	8 A6
Hampton Ter OSM LS9	102 B4

Hamworth Dr HWTH BD22	69 F1
Hamza St BTLY WF17	146 A7
Hanbury Gdns GFTH/SHER LS25	105 K3
Hanby Av NORM WF6	151 J8
Hand Bank La MIRF WF14	193 J1
Hand Carr La LUD/ILL HX2	137 J4
Handel St GTHN BD7	4 A4
MAR/SLWT HD7	189 H7
Handel Ter HUDE * HD5	13 F5
Handsworth Rd WKFDW/WTN WF2	198 C7
Hanging Gate La HWTH BD22	68 C6
Hangingroyd Cl HBR HX7	112 B8
Hangingroyd La HBR HX7	112 B8
Hangingroyd Rd HBR HX7	112 B8
Hanging Stone Rd HUDS HD4	213 F4
Hangingstone Rd ILK LS29	30 D1
Hanging Stones La RPDN/SBR HX6	164 B6
Hanging Wood Wy CLECK BD19	143 K1
Hanley Rd MOR LS27	123 F8
Hannah Ct LM/WK BD12	118 D8
Hanover Av BVRD LS3	6 B2
Hanover Cl GIR BD8	95 C2
Hanover Crs PONT WF8	180 D6
Hanover Gdns DEWS WF13	172 A3
WBOW * BD5	4 B6
Hanover La BVRD * LS3	6 C3
Hanover Mt BVRD * LS3	6 B2
Hanover Pl BTLY WF17	146 C6
KNOT WF11	155 K2
Hanover Sq BFD BD1	4 B3
BVRD LS3	6 C2
Hanover St BTLY WF17	146 B6
DEWS WF13	172 A3
HFAX HX1	8 C5
KGHY BD21	3 D3
RPDN/SBR HX6	139 C6
Hanover Wk BVRD LS3	6 C3
Hanover Wy ILK LS29	32 A3
LDS * LS1	6 C3
Hansby Av SCFT LS14	81 K6
Hansby Bank SCFT LS14	81 K6
Hansby Cl SCFT LS14	81 K6
Hansby Dr SCFT LS14	81 K6
Hansby Gdns SCFT LS14	81 K7
Hansby Ga SCFT LS14	81 K6
Hansby Pl SCFT LS14	81 K7
Hanson Av NORM WF6	178 A2
Hanson Ct LM/WK BD12	142 C1
Hanson Fold LM/WK BD12	118 D8
Hanson La HFAX HX1	8 B4
HUDS HD4	212 E1
Hanson Mt LM/WK BD12	142 D1
Hanson Rd BRIG HD6	167 K3
HOLM/MEL HD9	231 G2
Hanworth Rd LM/WK BD12	118 D5
Harbeck Dr BGLY BD16	71 F3
Harbour Crs WBSY BD6	118 B3
Harbour Pk WBSY BD6	118 A4
Harbour Rd WBSY BD6	118 B4
Harclo Rd KGHY BD21	3 F2
Harcourt Av CUL/QBY BD13	93 H4
Harcourt Dr ILK LS29	18 D2
MOR LS27	122 E6
Harcourt Pl LDS LS1	9 G6
Harcourt St BOW BD4	96 D8
WKFDW/WTN * WF2	175 G6
Hardaker La BAIL BD17	73 C1
Hardakers Ap FEA/AMT WF7	203 F6
Hardaker's La FEA/AMT WF7	202 E5
Hardaker St GIR BD8	4 B3
Hardcastle Av PONT WF8	180 D2
Hardcastle La HOR/CROF WF4	195 H8
Harden Brow La BGLY BD16	70 E2
KGHY BD21	3 F5
Harden Hill Rd HOLM/MEL HD9	231 J3
Harden La BGLY BD16	71 F3
Harden Moss Rd HOLM/MEL HD9	231 H4
Harden Rd BGLY BD16	71 G2
Hardgate La HWTH BD22	69 H5
Hardie Rd HOR/CROF WF4	223 G2
Hardings La AIRE BD20	26 A4
ILK LS29	20 A3
Hard Ings Rd KGHY BD21	3 D1
Hardistry Dr PONT WF8	180 C3
Hardknot Cl GTHN BD7	94 E8
Hard Nese La HWTH BD22	90 B2
Hard Platts La GTL/HWG HX4	165 J8
Hardrow Gn WOR/ARM LS12	100 D6
Hardrow Gv WOR/ARM LS12	100 D6
Hardrow Rd WOR/ARM LS12	100 C6
Hardrow Ter WOR/ARM * LS12	100 D6
Hardwick Cl HOR/CROF WF4	222 E3
Hardwick Ct PONT WF8	180 D4
Hardwick Crs PONT WF8	180 E6
Hardwick Cft CHAL LS7	79 K5
Hardwick La HOR/CROF WF4	202 B2
Hardwick Rd FEA/AMT WF7	179 H7
PONT WF8	180 D5
PONT WF8	181 G8
Hardwick St KGHY BD21	2 B4
Hardy Av AMOR LS27	123 H3
WBSY BD6	118 D3
Hardy Ct MOR LS27	123 D7
Hardy Cft WKFDE WF1	11 D3
Hardy Gv BEE/HOL LS11	101 G8
Hardy Pl BRIG HD6	141 K6
Hardy St BEE/HOL LS11	101 G8
BOW BD4	5 D5

BRIG HD6	142 C8	
MOR LS27	123 G7	
Hardy Ter BEE/HOL LS11	101 C8	
Hardy Vw BEE/HOL LS11	101 C8	
Hareball Av WKFDW/WTN WF2	175 F4	
Harecroft Rd OT LS21	33 J2	
Hare Farm Av WOR/ARM LS12	99 H4	
Hare Farm Cl WOR/ARM LS12	99 H4	
Harefield Cl BEE BD20	26 C6	
Harefield Dr BTLY WF17	145 K2	
Harefield East MSTN/BAR LS15	103 G4	
Harefield Pl PONT WF8	181 G3	
Harefield West MSTN/BAR LS15	103 G4	
Harefield Pk HUDN HD2	190 C1	
Harehill Av TOD OL14	133 K5	
Harehill Cl IDLE BD10	74 D2	
Harehill Rd IDLE BD10	74 D2	
Harehills Av RHAY LS8	80 B7	
Harehills La HWTH BD22	67 J2	
OSM LS9	102 D1	
Harehills Park Av OSM * LS9	102 D8	
Harehills Park La OSM LS9	80 D8	
Harehills Park Vw OSM LS9	102 D1	
Harehills Pl RHAY LS8	80 B8	
Harehills Rd RHAY LS8	80 B7	
Harehills St TOD OL14	133 K5	
Hare La PDSY/CALV LS28	98 C6	
Hare Park Av LVSG WF15	143 K7	
Hare Park Cl LVSG WF15	143 K7	
Harepark Dr LVSG WF15	143 K7	
Hare Park La HOR/CROF WF4	200 D4	
LVSG WF15	143 K7	
Hare Park Vw HOR/CROF WF4	200 D3	
Hares Av RHAY LS8	80 B7	
Hares Mt RHAY LS8	80 A7	
Hares Rd RHAY LS8	80 A7	
Hares Ter RHAY LS8	80 B7	
Hare St HFAX HX1	8 A4	
Hares Vw RHAY LS8	80 B7	
Harewood Av AIRE BD20	26 C6	
AL/HA/HU LS17	38 D5	
HECK WF16	145 H4	
LUD/ILL HX2	139 G3	
NORM WF6	152 B8	
PONT WF8	181 F3	
Harewood Cl KNOT WF11	155 K7	
Harewood Crs HWTH BD22	47 G8	
Harewood Dr WKFDW/WTN WF2	174 E2	
Harewood Ga AL/HA/HU LS17	38 C4	
Harewood Gv HECK WF16	145 H4	
Harewood La HEM/SK/SE WF9	226 A5	
PONT WF8	227 H1	
Harewood Ms AL/HA/HU LS17	38 C4	
Harewood Mt HOLM/MEL HD9	231 K1	
PONT WF8	181 F3	
Harewood Pl LUD/ILL HX2	139 H5	
Harewood Ri HWTH BD22	47 G8	
Harewood Rd AL/HA/HU LS17	39 K4	
HWTH BD22	69 G1	
WKFDE WF1	11 F1	
Harewood St BFDE BD3	5 F4	
LDSU LS2	7 E3	
Harewood Vw PONT WF8	181 F3	
Harewood Wy BRAM LS13	99 F3	
Hargrave Crs ILK LS29	32 B7	
Hargreaves Av EARD/LOFT WF3	150 B6	
Hargreaves Cl MOR LS27	122 E4	
Harker Rd WBSY BD6	118 D4	
Harker St KNOT WF11	156 E7	
Harker Ter PDSY/CALV LS28	98 B2	
Harland Cl ECHL BD2	4 C1	
Harlech Av BEE/HOL LS11	124 B1	
Harlech Crs BEE/HOL LS11	124 C1	
Harlech Gv BEE/HOL LS11	124 B1	
Harlech Mt BEE/HOL LS11	124 B1	
Harlech Park Ct BEE/HOL LS11	124 C2	
Harlech Rd BEE/HOL LS11	124 C1	
Harlech St BEE/HOL LS11	124 C1	
Harlech Ter BEE/HOL LS11	124 C1	
Harlech Wy GFTH/SHER LS25	106 B4	
Harley Cl BRAM LS13	98 E3	
Harley Ct BRAM LS13	98 E3	
Harley Dr BRAM LS13	98 E3	
Harley Gdns PDSY/CALV LS28	98 E3	
Harley Gn BRAM LS13	98 E3	
Harley Ri BRAM LS13	98 E3	
Harley Rd BRAM LS13	98 E3	
Harley St BRIG HD6	168 B2	
TOD OL14	134 A5	
Harley Ter BRAM LS13	99 F3	
Harley Vw BRAM LS13	98 E3	
Harley Wk BRAM LS13	98 E3	
Harley Wd TOD OL14	133 H5	
Harlington Ct MOR LS27	147 F1	
Harlington Rd MOR LS27	147 F1	
Harlow Ct RHAY LS8	84 E4	
Harlow Rd GTHN BD7	95 C6	
Harmon Cl BOW BD4	119 K3	
Harold Av HDGY LS6	6 A1	
Harold Gdns MOR LS27	123 C7	
Harold Gv HDGY LS6	6 A1	
Harold Mt HDGY LS6	6 A1	
Harold Pl HDGY LS6	6 A1	
Harold Rd HDGY LS6	6 A1	
Harold Sq HDGY LS6	6 A1	
Harold St BGLY BD16	49 J7	
HDGY LS6	6 A1	
Harold Ter HDGY LS6	6 A1	
Harold Vw HDGY LS6	6 A1	
Harold Wk HDGY LS6	6 A1	
Harpe Inge HUDE HD5	192 A4	
Harper Av IDLE BD10	74 D2	
Harper Crs IDLE BD10	74 E2	
Harper Ga BOW BD4	97 H7	
Harper Gv IDLE BD10	74 D2	
Harper La YEA LS19	53 K5	
Harper Pl LDSU * LS2	7 F3	
Harper Royd La RPDN/SBR HX6	164 E1	
Harper St LDSU LS2	7 F4	
Harp Rd HUDW HD3	190 B6	
Harrap St WKFDW/WTN WF2	174 E5	
Harrier Cl CIR BD8	94 B4	
Harrier Wy MOR LS27	123 J7	
Harriet St BRIG HD6	142 B7	
CHAL LS7	79 K8	
GIR BD8	95 H3	
Harrington Ct HOLM/MEL HD9	231 K2	
Harris Ct GTHN BD7	95 G8	
Harris Crs OSM LS9	103 F2	
Harrison La HOLM/MEL HD9	211 J7	
Harrison Rd HFAX HX1	9 D5	
Harrisons Av PDSY/CALV LS28	98 D1	
Harrison St BGLY BD16	7 E3	
LDSU LS2	7 E3	
TOD * OL14	132 E2	
Harris St BFDE BD3	5 F1	
BGLY BD16	72 A1	
Harrogate Av BFDE BD3	5 E1	
Harrogate Pl BFDE BD3	5 E1	
Harrogate Rd AL/HA/HU LS17	57 K8	
AL/HA/HU LS17	79 K1	
CHAL * LS7	79 J5	
ECHL BD2	75 F5	
IDLE BD10	75 F5	
WBY LS22	22 D3	
YEA LS19	53 K7	
Harrogate St BFDE BD3	5 E1	
Harrogate Ter BFDE BD3	5 E1	
Harrogate Vw AL/HA/HU LS17	58 E6	
Harrop Av MOR LS27	147 G1	
Harrop Gv MOR LS27	147 G1	
Harrop La WIL/AL BD15	71 F8	
Harrop Ter MOR LS27	147 G1	
Harrop Well La PONT WF8	180 E2	
Harrowby Crs BHP/TINH LS16	78 B4	
Harrowby Rd BHP/TINH LS16	78 B4	
Harrow St HEM/SK/SE WF9	226 A8	
Harry La CLAY BD14	94 B7	
HWTH BD22	68 E8	
Harry St BOW BD4	96 E8	
Hartcliff Av STKB/PEN S36	252 B8	
Harthill MOR LS27	122 C4	
Harthill Av MOR LS27	122 C4	
Harthill Cl MOR LS27	122 C4	
Harthill La MOR LS27	122 C4	
Harthill Paddock MOR LS27	122 C4	
Harthill Ri MOR LS27	122 C4	
Hartington St BTLY WF17	146 B8	
KGHY BD21	3 D2	
Hartington Ter GTHN BD7	95 G6	
Hartland Rd BOW BD4	97 G7	
Hartley Av LVSG WF15	79 H1	
Hartley Ct LVSG WF15	144 D8	
Hartley Crs HDGY LS6	79 G7	
Hartley Gdns HDGY LS6	79 H1	
Hartley Gv HDGY LS6	79 G7	
Hartley Hl LDSU LS2	7 F2	
Hartley Park Av PONT WF8	180 C3	
Hartley Park Vw PONT WF8	180 C3	
Hartley Pl MOR * LS27	123 G7	
Hartley's Buildings MOR LS27	123 G8	
Hartley's Sq AIRE BD20	49 H2	
Hartley St BOW BD4	5 E6	
CAS WF10	153 H4	
DEWS WF13	172 B2	
HFAX HX1	8 B3	
MOR LS27	123 G4	
MOR LS27	123 G4	
Hartley Ter FEA/AMT WF7	177 J7	
Hartlington Ct BAIL * BD17	52 A8	
Hartman Pl HTON * BD9	95 F1	
Hartshead Hall La LVSG WF15	169 K3	
Hartshead La LVSG WF15	169 J1	
Hart St GTHN BD7	95 G7	
HUDS HD4	213 G1	
Hartwell Rd HDGY LS6	6 A1	
Harvelin Pk TOD OL14	135 F6	
Harvest Cl PONT WF8	155 F8	
Harvey Royd HUDE HD5	192 C7	
Harvey St WKFDE WF1	9 H5	
Harwill Ap MOR LS27	123 H4	
Harwill Av MOR LS27	123 H4	
Harwill Cft MOR LS27	123 H4	
Harwill Gv MOR LS27	123 H4	
Harwill Ri MOR LS27	123 H4	
Harwill Rd MOR LS27	123 H4	
Harwood Cl HUDE HD5	192 B6	
WKFDW/WTN WF2	199 G2	
Haselden Crs WKFDW/WTN WF2	174 D2	
Haselden Rd WKFDW/WTN WF2	174 E6	
Haslam Cl BFDE BD3	5 E3	
Haslam Gv SHPY BD18	74 A5	
Haslemere Cl BOW BD4	97 F8	
Haslewood Cl OSM LS9	102 A5	
Haslewood Ct OSM LS9	102 B3	
Haslewood Dene OSM LS9	102 B3	
Haslewood Dr OSM LS9	102 A5	
Haslewood Gdns OSM LS9	102 B3	
Haslewood Gn OSM LS9	102 B3	
Haslewood Ms OSM LS9	102 B3	
Haslewood Pl OSM LS9	102 B3	
Haslewood Sq OSM LS9	102 B3	
Haslewood Vw OSM LS9	102 B3	
Hasley Rd ILK LS29	32	
Haslingden Dr HTON BD9	95	
Hassocks La HOLM/MEL HD9	212	
Hassocks Rd HOLM/MEL HD9	211	
Haste St CAS WF10	153	
Hastings Av WBOW BD5	118	
WKFDW/WTN WF2	198	
Hastings Ct AL/HA/HU LS17	59	
NORM WF6	151	
Hastings Crs CAS WF10	154	
Hastings Gv WKFDW/WTN WF2	199	
Hastings Pl WBOW BD5	118	
Hastings St CUD/GR S72	240	
WBOW BD5	118	
Hastings Ter WBOW BD5	118	
Hastings Wk CAS WF10	154	
Hastings Wy WBY LS22	40	
Hatchet La LM/WK BD12	119	
Hatfield Gdns BSLYN/ROY S71	221	
Hatfield Pl HOR/CROF WF4	223	
Hatfield Rd ECHL BD2	5	
Hatfield St WKFDE WF1	10	
Hatfield Vw WKFDE WF1	175	
Hathaway Av HTON BD9	72	
Hathaway Dr SCFT LS14	81	
Hathaway La SCFT LS14	81	
Hathaway Ms SCFT LS14	81	
Hathershelf La LUD/ILL HX2	137	
Hatton Cl WBSY BD6	116	
Haugh End La RPDN/SBR HX6	164	
Haugh Head Rd STKB/PEN S36	252	
Haugh Rd TOD OL14	134	
Haugh Shaw Cft HFAX * HX1	8	
Haugh Shaw Rd HFAX HX1	8	
Haugh Shaw Rd West HFAX HX1	8	
Haughs La HUDW HD3	189	
Haughs Rd HUDW HD3	190	
Hauxley Ct ILK LS29	20	
Hauxwell Dr YEA LS19	53	
Havelock Sq CUL/QBY BD13	115	
Havelock St CUL/QBY BD13	115	
DEWS WF13	171	
GTHN BD7	95	
The Haven IDLE BD10	74	
MSTN/BAR LS15	104	
Haven Cha BHP/TINH LS16	55	
Haven Cl BHP/TINH LS16	55	
PONT WF8	180	
Haven Cft BHP/TINH LS16	55	
Haven Gdns BHP/TINH LS16	55	
Haven Garth BHP/TINH LS16	55	
Haven Gn BHP/TINH LS16	55	
Haven La HBR HX7	136	
Haven Mt BHP/TINH LS16	55	
Haven Ri BHP/TINH LS16	55	
Haven St TOD * OL14	134	
Haven Vw BHP/TINH LS16	55	
Havercroft OSS WF5	173	
WOR/ARM LS12	99	
Havercroft La PONT WF8	182	
Havercroft Ri BTLY WF17	223	
Havercroft Wy BTLY WF17	145	
Haverdale Rd HOR/CROF WF4	222	
The Haverlands HEM/SK/SE WF9	224	
Haveroid La HOR/CROF WF4	198	
Haveroid Wy HOR/CROF WF4	198	
Haverthwaites Dr GFTH/SHER LS25	84	
Havertop La NORM WF6	178	
Haw Av YEA LS19	54	
Hawber Cote Dr AIRE * BD20	27	
Hawber La AIRE BD20	27	
Haw Cliff La HUDS HD4	234	
Hawes Av HUDW HD3	190	
HWTH BD22	2	
Hawes Cl CAS WF10	154	
Hawes Crs WBOW BD5	118	
Hawes Dr WBOW BD5	118	
Hawes Gv WBOW BD5	118	
Hawes Mt WBOW BD5	118	
Hawes Rd WBOW BD5	118	
Hawes Ter WBOW BD5	118	
Haweswater Cl WBY LS22	23	
Haw Hill Vw NORM WF6	152	
Hawkcliffe Vw AIRE BD20	26	
Hawke Av HECK WF16	145	
Hawke Wy LM/WK BD12	119	
Hawkhill Av GSLY LS20	53	
MSTN/BAR LS15	81	
Hawkhill Dr MSTN/BAR LS15	81	
Hawkhill Gdns MSTN/BAR LS15	81	
Hawkhills CHAL LS7	80	
Hawkhurst Rd WOR/ARM LS12	100	
Hawkingcroft Rd HOR/CROF WF4	197	
Hawkins Dr CHAL LS7	7	
Hawkroyd Bank Rd HUDS HD4	212	
Hawksbridge La HWTH BD22	68	
Hawkshead Cl WBOW BD5	4	
Hawkshead Crs SCFT LS14	81	
Hawkshead Dr WBOW BD5	4	
Hawkshead Wk WBOW * BD5	4	
Hawkshead Wy WBOW * BD5	4	
Hawksley Ct MOR LS27	122	

wk's Nest Gdns East
L/HA/AD LS17 ....57 K7
wk's Nest Gdns South
L/HA/AD LS17 ....57 K7
wk's Nest Gdns West
L/HA/AD LS17 ....57 K7
wk's Nest Ri AL/HA/HU LS17 ....57 K7
wkstone Av GSLY LS20 ....52 E4
wkstone Dr BPD21 ....2 B1
wkstone Vw GSLY LS20 ....52 E4
wk St KGHY BD21 ....3 E2
wkswood Av HTON BD9 ....73 F8
STL LS5 ....77 J4
wkswood Crs KSTL LS5 ....77 J4
wkswood Gv KSTL LS5 ....77 J4
wkswood Mt KSTL LS5 ....77 J4
wkswood Pl KSTL LS5 ....77 J5
wkswood St KSTL LS5 ....77 K5
wkswood Ter KSTL LS5 ....77 K5
wksworth Av GSLY LS20 ....53 F4
wksworth Cl ILK LS29 ....32 C8
wksworth Dr ILK LS29 ....32 B7
wksworth La GSLY LS20 ....52 B3
wksworth Rd BAIL BD17 ....51 J6
ORS LS13 ....77 H4
w La YEA LS19 ....54 A3
wley Cl MOR LS27 ....146 E1
wley Ter IDLE BD10 ....75 G7
wley Wy MOR LS27 ....146 E1
worth Cl MIRF WF14 ....170 C5
worth Gv HTON BD9 ....72 E8
worth La YEA LS19 ....53 K4
worth Rd BTLY WF17 ....145 J1
UL/OBY BD13 ....69 J5
WTH BD22 ....69 G3
VIL/AL BD15 ....70 E7

worth to Hebden Bridge Wk
BR HX7 ....66 E8
BR HX7 ....89 J4
BR HX7 ....111 H1
w Park La WKFDW/WTN WF2 ....221 K1
wswater Pl KNOT WF11 ....182 B2
wthorn Av BFDE BD3 ....97 G3
TLY WF17 ....145 K8
OR/CROF WF4 ....54 B8
NOT WF11 ....156 A8
EA LS19 ....53 K4
wthorn Cl HOR/CROF WF4 ....195 H8
BTN HD8 ....193 F8
MOR LS27 ....122 C4
wthorn Ct DOD/DAR S75 ....239 F7
wthorn Ct HEM/SK/SE WF9 ....224 C5
wthorn Dr MOR LS27 ....122 C4
wthorn Gdns BHP/TINH LS16 ......56 B6
wthorn Mt NORM WF6 ....178 A4
wthorn Ri SCFT LS14 ....82 A3
wthorn St AIRE BD20 ....27 F2
UD/GR S72 ....223 G8
wthorn Vw CUD/GR S72 ....223 G8
BTN HD8 ....215 H7
LK LS29 ....32 B4
wthorn La CHAL * LS7 ....79 K4
wthorn Mt CHAL * LS7 ....79 K4
wthorn Pl TOD * OL14 ....134 A5
wthorn Rd CHAL LS7 ....79 K4
MAR/SLWT HD7 ....210 C2
EA LS19 ....53 K4
Hawthorns OSS WF5 ....173 K8
WKFDE WF1 ....150 A6
wthorn St BFDE BD3 ....97 G3
FAX HX1 ....8 B6
IPP * HX3 ....141 J3
wthorn Ter HFAX * HX1 ....1 B6
HUDS HD4 ....190 C7
SS WF5 ....173 K8
wthorn V CHAL * LS7 ....79 K4
wthorn Vw BAIL BD17 ....51 K8
HAL * LS7 ....79 K4
den St BFDE BD3 ....5 F5
dn Av EARD/LOFT WF3 ....150 A6
dn's Ter PDSY/CALV LS28 ....98 C1
field Av BSPA/BRAM LS23 ....42 C3

HUDW HD3 ....190 A4
Hayfield Cl HOLM/MEL HD9 ......233 K7
The Hayfields HWTH BD22 ....68 C5
Hayfield Ter WOR/ARM LS12 .....100 C5
Haygill Nook SKP/WHF BD23 ......17 F1
Hayhills La AIRE BD20 ....17 F1
Hayhills Rd AIRE BD20 ....27 G1
Hayleigh Av BRAM LS13 ....77 G8
Hayleigh Mt BRAM LS13 ....99 G1
Hayleigh Ter HOR/CROF WF4 ....195 J6
Haynes St KGHY BD21 ....3 E4
Hays La LUD/ILL HX2 ....114 E4
Hayson Cl EARL WF12 ....172 E2
Haythorns Av AIRE BD20 ....27 F2
Haythorns Mt AIRE BD20 ....27 F2
Hayton Dr WBY LS22 ....22 D5
Hayton Wood Vw GFTH/SHER LS25 ...84 E3
The Haywain ILK LS29 ....20 D8
Haywood Av HUDW HD3 ....190 C5
Hazel Av EARL WF12 ....173 G4
SCFT LS14 ....82 A3
Hazel Bank WKFDW/WTN WF2 ..175 F3
Hazel Beck BGLY BD16 ....71 K3
Hazel Cl BIRK/DRI BD11 ....120 D5
EARL WF12 ....173 G4
Hazel Ct RTHW LS26 ....126 C7
WKFDW/WTN WF2 ....10 A1
Hazel Crs EARL WF12 ....173 G4
Hazelcroft IDLE BD10 ....75 F7
Hazel Cft SHPY BD18 ....73 K4
Hazeldene CUL/QBY BD13 ....116 C3
Hazel Dr EARL WF12 ....173 C4
Hazel Gdns CAS WF10 ....134 E6
Hazel Gv BTLY WF17 ....145 K7
HIPP HX3 ....142 B4
HOR/CROF WF4 ....195 H8
HUDN HD2 ....168 C6
PONT WF8 ....181 F1
Hazelheads BAIL BD17 ....51 J6
Hazelhurst Av BGLY BD16 ....71 K3
Hazelhurst Brow HTON BD9 ....94 D1
Hazelhurst Ct BFDE BD3 ....96 E4
PDSY/CALV LS28 ....98 D4
Hazel Hurst Gv CUL/QBY BD13 ..116 C4
Hazel Hurst Rd CUL/QBY BD13 ..116 C4
Hazelhurst Rd HTON BD9 ....94 D1
Hazelhurst Ter HTON BD9 ....94 D1
Hazel La AWLS/ASK DN6 ....243 J2
Hazelmere Av BGLY BD16 ....72 A3
Hazel Mt SHPY BD18 ....73 J4
Hazel Ri RTHW LS26 ....152 B2
Hazel Rd KNOT WF11 ....156 B8
Hazel Wk HTON BD9 ....94 D1
Hazelwood Av AIRE BD20 ....48 D2
GFTH/SHER LS25 ....106 A6
Hazelwood Ct WKFDE WF1 ....150 A6
Hazelwood Rd HEM/SK/SE WF9 ...224 D2
HTON BD9 ....72 C8
WKFDE WF1 ....150 A6
Hazelwood St TOD OL14 ....134 A6
Headfield Rd EARL WF12 ....172 B5
HUDS HD4 ....191 G8
Headfield Vw EARL WF12 ....172 C7
Headingley Av HDGY LS6 ....78 C6
Headingley La HDGY LS6 ....78 E7
Headingley Mt HDGY LS6 ....78 C6
Headingley Vw HDGY LS6 ....78 D7
Headland Gv WBSY BD6 ....118 A2
Headland La EARL WF12 ....172 E5
Headlands Av OSS WF5 ....173 H6
Headlands Cl LVSG WF15 ....144 E8
Headlands Gv OSS WF5 ....173 H6
Headlands La KNOT WF11 ....156 B7
PONT WF8 ....180 D2
Headlands Pk OSS WF5 ....173 H6
Headlands Rd HUD HD1 ....12 C3
LVSG WF15 ....144 D7
OSS WF5 ....173 H6
Headlands St LVSG WF15 ....144 D8
Headlands Wk OSS WF5 ....173 H6
Headley La BSPA/BRAM LS23 ....62 E2
CUL/QBY BD13 ....93 H6
The Headrow LDS LS1 ....7 E3
Healdfield Rd CAS WF10 ....154 A3
Healds Av LVSG WF15 ....144 E7
Healds Rd DEWS WF13 ....171 K3
Heald St CAS WF10 ....154 A3
Healdwood Cl CAS WF10 ....154 B4
Healdwood Rd CAS WF10 ....154 B3
Healey Av BCLY BD16 ....72 A1
Healey Cl BTLY WF17 ....145 J4
Healey Crs OSS WF5 ....173 J8
Healey Croft La EARD/LOFT WF3 ..148 C3
Healey Dr OSS WF5 ....173 J8
Healey Farm KBTN HD8 ....215 G8
Healey Green La HUDE HD5 ....193 H4
Healey La BGLY BD16 ....72 A1
BTLY WF17 ....145 J7
EARL WF12 ....194 D5
Healey Ri OSS WF5 ....173 H8
Healey St BTLY WF17 ....145 J6
Healey Wood Crs BRIG HD6 ....168 B3
Healey Wood Gdns BRIG HD6 ....168 B3
Healey Wood Gv BRIG HD6 ....168 B3
Healey Wood Rd BRIG HD6 ....168 C3
Heap La BFDE BD3 ....5 E4
Heap St BFDE BD3 ....5 E4
HIPP HX3 ....9 D1

Heath Av HIPP HX3 ....140 A7
Heathcliff HWTH BD22 ....68 D4
Heathcliffe Cl BTLY WF17 ....121 J8
Heath Cl EARL WF12 ....173 G3
MAR/SLWT HD7 ....211 J4
Heathcote Ri HWTH BD22 ....69 F3
Heath Crs BEE/HOL LS11 ....100 E8
Heathcroft Crs BEE/HOL LS11 ....123 K1
Heathcroft Dr BEE/HOL LS11 .....123 K1
Heathcroft Lawn BEE/HOL LS11 ..123 K1
Heathcroft Ri BEE/HOL LS11 ......123 K1
Heathcroft V BEE/HOL LS11 ....123 K1
Heathdale Av HUDN HD2 ....12 B1
Heath Dr BSPA/BRAM LS23 ....42 B4
Heatherbank Av HWTH BD22 ....2 A6
Heather Bank Cl CUL/QBY BD13 ...70 A6
Heather Cl EARD/LOFT WF3 ....150 A6
HEM/SK/SE WF9 ....225 K8
OSS WF5 ....174 A8
Heather Ct BTLY WF17 ....145 H1
EARD/LOFT WF3 ....150 A6
HUDW HD3 ....189 K3
Heathercroft CHAL LS7 ....80 A5
Heather Cft HOR/CROF WF4 ......178 B8
Heatherdale Ct EARD/LOFT WF3 ..147 K3
Heatherdale Dr EARD/LOFT WF3 ..147 K3
Heatherdale Rd EARD/LOFT WF3 ..147 J3
Heather Dr LUD/ILL HX2 ....114 D8
Heatherfield Crs HUD HD1 ....190 D5
Heatherfield Rd HUD HD1 ....190 D5
Heather Fold KBTN HD8 ....236 D1
Heather Gdns BRAM LS13 ....99 J3
SCFT LS14 ....60 A4
Heather Gv BRAM LS13 ....99 H3
HTON BD9 ....72 B8
KGHY BD21 ....2 A2
Heathergrove Fold HUDE HD5 ......13 F3
Heatherlands WHIT OL12 ....158 A7
Heatherlands Av CUL/QBY BD13 ...92 B1
Heather Ri ILK LS29 ....32 A3
Heather Rd BAIL * BD17 ....51 K7
HOLM/MEL HD9 ....231 H2
Heather Side BAIL BD17 ....51 H7
The Heathers HOR/CROF WF4 ....178 B8
Heatherstones HIPP HX3 ....140 A7
Heather V SCFT LS14 ....59 K4
Heather Vw BGLY BD16 ....50 D6
HOR/CROF WF4 ....178 B8
OSS WF5 ....173 J6
Heathfield La BSPA/BRAM LS23 ...42 B3
Heathfield Ms MAR/SLWT HD7 ...189 J7
Heathfield Pl HIPP * HX3 ....140 B7
Heathfield Ri RPDN/SBR HX6 .....186 E2
Heathfield Rd MAR/SLWT HD7 ...189 J7
OSS WF5 ....173 H3
Heathfield St ELL HX5 ....167 F5
Heathfield Ter HDGY LS6 ....78 D5
HFAX HX1 ....9 D6
Heath Gdns HIPP HX3 ....140 B7
Heath Gv AIRE BD20 ....49 H3
BEE/HOL LS11 ....100 E8
BTLY WF17 ....146 E2
HUDS HD4 ....212 E1
PDSY/CALV LS28 ....98 A4
Heath Hall HFAX HX1 ....9 D6
Heath Hall Av BOW BD4 ....119 J2
Heath Hill Rd LUD/ILL HX2 ....138 D1
Heath House La MAR/SLWT HD7 ..189 F7
Heath House Ml MAR/SLWT * HD7 ..189 G7
Heath La HIPP HX3 ....140 B7
Heath Lea HFAX HX1 ....9 D5
Heathmoor Cl IDLE BD10 ....74 C4
LUD/ILL HX2 ....115 G5
Heathmoor Mt LUD/ILL HX2 ....115 G5
Heathmoor Park Rd LUD/ILL HX2 ..115 G5
Heathmoor Wy LUD/ILL HX2 ......115 G5
Heath Mt BEE/HOL LS11 ....100 E8
HFAX HX1 ....140 A7
Heath Mount Rd BRIG HD6 ....168 B3
Heathness Rd ILK LS29 ....18 B2
Heath Pk ILK LS29 ....19 K8
Heath Park Av HFAX HX1 ....9 D6
Heath Pl BEE/HOL LS11 ....100 E8
Heath Ri BEE/HOL LS11 ....100 E8
Heath Rd BEE/HOL LS11 ....100 E8
BFDE BD3 ....5 F2
EARL WF12 ....173 G3
HFAX HX1 ....9 D5
MAR/SLWT HD7 ....211 J3
Heath Royd HIPP HX3 ....140 B7
Heath St BFDE BD3 ....96 E4
BGLY BD16 ....50 A8
HIPP HX3 ....140 B7
LVSG WF15 ....170 D1
Heath Ter BFDE BD3 ....5 F4
Heath Vw Vw HFAX * HX1 ....9 D5
Heath View St HFAX HX1 ....9 D5
Heath Wk EARL * WF12 ....173 G3
Heathwood Dr MAR/SLWT HD7 ..189 G6
Heathy Av LUD/ILL HX2 ....115 K6
Heathy La LUD/ILL HX2 ....115 J5
Heaton Av AIRE BD20 ....49 G4

CLECK BD19............143 K4
EARL WF12............172 D3
HUDE HD5............192 E2
WOR/ARM LS12............100 C6
Heaton Cl BD16............50 B7
Heaton Crs BGLY * BD16............50 A3
Heaton Dr BAIL BD17............51 H7
  BGLY BD16............50 B7
  HUDE HD5............192 E1
Heaton Fold La HUD HD1............190 D5
Heaton Gdns HUD HD1............190 D5
Heaton Gra BTLY WF17............146 D8
Heaton Gv CLECK BD19............143 K4
  HTON BD9............73 H7
  SHPY BD18............73 J4
Heaton HI WBSY BD6............117 K4
Heaton Moor Rd HUDE HD5............192 E2
Heaton Park Dr HTON BD9............73 F8
Heaton Park Rd HTON BD9............73 F8
Heaton Rd BTLY WF17............146 B4
  HTON BD9............73 G8
  HUD HD1............190 D5
Heaton Royds SHPY * BD18............73 F6
Heaton Royds La SHPY BD18............73 F6
Heaton's Ct LDS LS1............7 E4
Heaton St BEE/HOL LS11............7 D5
  BOW BD4............5 E6
  BRIG HD6............168 B1
  CLECK BD19............144 A3
  FEA/AMT WF7............202 E6
Heator La KBTN HD8............235 J4
Hebble Brook Cl LUD/ILL HX2............115 F7
Hebble Dr HOLM/MEL HD9............233 C4
Hebble End HBR HX7............112 A8
Hebble Gdns LUD/ILL HX2............139 H2
Hebble La HFAX HX1............8 A3
  HOLM/MEL HD9............231 H5
Hebble Mt HOLM/MEL HD9............231 J2
Hebble St DEWS WF13............171 J6
  HUD HD1............13 D2
Hebble Vale Dr LUD/ILL HX2............139 H1
Hebb Vw WBSY BD6............117 K1
Hebden Ap SCFT LS14............81 K5
Hebden Bridge Rd HWTH BD22............90 A4
Hebden Cl SCFT * LS14............81 K5
Hebden Gn SCFT * LS14............81 K5
Hebden Pth SCFT LS14............81 K5
Hebden Pl SCFT LS14............81 K5
Hebden Rd HWTH BD22............69 F4
  WKFDE WF1............11 E1
Heber Cl AIRE BD20............27 H3
Heber's Ghyll Dr ILK LS29............19 J8
Heber's Gv ILK LS29............19 J8
Heber St KGHY BD21............2 C4
Heckmondwike Rd DEWS WF13............171 J2
Hector Cl WBSY BD6............118 D2
Heddon Cl WBOW * BD5............4 C6
Heddon Gv WBOW BD5............4 C6
Heddon St HDGY LS6............78 E5
Heddon Wk WBOW * BD5............4 C6
Hedge Cl GIR BD8............94 D2
Hedge Hill Rd STKB/PEN * S36............251 K8
Hedge La DOD/DAR S75............239 K4
Hedge Side GIR BD8............94 E3
Hedge Top La HIPP HX3............117 F8
Hedge Wy GIR BD8............94 E2
Hedley Cl WOR/ARM LS12............6 A4
Hedley Crs WKFDE WF1............149 J8
Hedley Gdns WOR/ARM LS12............6 A4
Hedley Gn WOR/ARM LS12............6 A4
Heeley Rd WKFDW/WTN WF2............198 C7
Heidelberg Rd HTON BD9............95 G1
The Heights HOLM/MEL HD9............233 J8
Heights Bank WOR/ARM LS12............99 J3
Heights Cl WOR/ARM LS12............99 J3
Heights Dr MAR/SLWT HD7............211 H4
  WOR/ARM LS12............99 K4
Heights Garth WOR/ARM LS12............99 J4
Heights La AIRE BD20............16 D7
  BGLY BD16............50 A4
  HECK WF16............145 H8
  HTON BD9............72 D8
  WOR/ARM LS12............99 J4
Heights Pde WOR/ARM LS12............99 J4
Heights Vw MAR/SLWT * HD7............189 F6
Heights Wy WOR/ARM LS12............99 K4
Helena Ct GFTH/SHER LS25............128 E3
Helena Pl GFTH/SHER LS25............128 E3
Helena St GFTH/SHER LS25............128 E3
Helena Wy BOW BD4............119 K3
Helene Ct HUDW HD3............189 J3
Helen Rose Ct SHPY BD18............74 A2
Helen St HUDS HD4............190 B8
  SHPY BD18............73 J5
Hellewell St WBSY BD6............118 A4
Hell La WKFDE WF1............177 G7
Hellwood La SCFT LS14............60 A4
Helme La HOLM/MEL HD9............211 J8
Helme Rk HOLM/MEL HD9............211 H8
Helmet La HOLM/MEL HD9............211 J8
Helm La HUDE HD5............169 K6
  RPDN/SBR HX6............163 K3
Helmsley Ct MID LS10............124 D1
Helmsley Dr BHP/TINH LS16............78 B4
Helmsley Rd BHP/TINH LS16............78 B4

BSPA/BRAM LS23............42 C4
  WKFDW/WTN WF2............199 G2
Helmsley St BOW BD4............96 C7
Helston Cft MID LS10............124 B6
Helston Garth MID LS10............124 B6
Helston Gv HOLM/MEL HD9............212 E7
Helston Pl MID LS10............124 B6
Helston St MID LS10............124 B5
  NORM WF6............152 A8
Helston St MID LS10............124 A6
Helston Wk MID LS10............124 A6
Helston Wy MID LS10............124 B5
Helted Wy HUDE HD5............192 A8
Hemingway Cl MID * LS10............102 A8
Hemingway Garth MID * LS10............102 A8
Hemingway Gn MID * LS10............102 A8
Hemingway Rd IDLE BD10............75 F3
Hemishor Dr RTHW LS26............128 D3
Hemsby Gv KGHY * BD21............2 B6
Hemsby Rd CAS WF10............153 H4
Hemsby St KGHY BD21............2 B6
Hemsworth La HEM/SK/SE WF9............202 A7
Hemsworth Rd HEM/SK/SE WF9............224 E6
Henacrewood Ct CUL/QBY BD13............116 D4
Henbury St CHAL * LS7............7 F2
Henconner Av CHAL LS7............79 H3
Henconner Crs CHAL LS7............79 H3
Henconner Dr CHAL LS7............79 H3
Henconner Gdns CHAL LS7............79 H3
Henconner Gv CHAL LS7............79 H3
Henconner La BRAM LS13............99 H2
  CHAL LS7............79 H3
Henconner Rd CHAL LS7............79 H3
Hendal La WKFDW/WTN WF2............198 C6
Henderson Av NORM WF6............178 A5
Henderson Pl BSLYN/ROY S71............221 J8
Henderson Pl WBSY BD6............118 D2
Hendford Dr BFDE BD3............5 E3
Hen Holme La AIRE BD20............27 G4
Henley Av BRAM LS13............99 G1
  EARL WF12............195 J1
  WBOW BD5............119 F1
  YEA LS19............54 B8
Henley Cl YEA LS19............54 B8
Henley Ct WBOW BD5............119 G1
Henley Crs BRAM LS13............99 G1
  YEA LS19............54 B8
Henley Cft HUDE HD5............192 A5
Henley Dr FEA/AMT WF7............179 J8
  YEA LS19............54 A8
Henley Gv BRAM LS13............99 G1
  WBOW BD5............119 F1
Henley HI YEA LS19............54 A8
Henley Mt YEA LS19............54 B8
Henley Pl BRAM LS13............99 G1
Henley Rd BRAM LS13............99 G1
  EARL WF12............195 J1
  WBOW BD5............119 F1
Henley St BRAM LS13............99 G1
Henley Ter BRAM LS13............99 G1
Henley Vw BRAM LS13............99 G1
Henrietta St BTLY WF17............146 B6
Henry Av HOR/CROF WF4............223 G3
Henry Cl CUL/QBY S72............223 F8
Henry Frederik Av HUDS HD4............212 C4
Henry Moore Ct CAS WF10............154 C4
Henry Ralph Av HUDS HD4............212 C4
Henry St BRIG HD6............142 B7
  BTLY WF17............172 B1
  CLAY BD14............94 C7
  CUL/QBY BD13............93 H5
  HFAX HX1............8 C5
  HUD HD1............12 C4
  KGHY BD21............3 D3
  WKFDW/WTN WF2............10 A3
Henry Ter YEA LS19............53 H4
Henshaw Av YEA LS19............53 K5
Henshaw Crs YEA LS19............53 K5
Henshaw La YEA LS19............53 K5
Henshaw Ov YEA LS19............53 K5
Henshaw Rd TOD OL14............159 K2
Henson Gv CAS WF10............154 C5
Hepton Ct OSM LS9............102 D2
Hepton Dr HBR HX7............112 A7
Heptonstall Rd HBR HX7............112 A8
Hepworth Av MOR LS27............123 G3
Hepworth Cl MIRF WF14............170 E5
Hepworth Crs HOLM/MEL HD9............234 A8
  MOR LS27............123 G3
Hepworth Dr MIRF WF14............171 F5
Hepworth La MIRF WF14............170 E5
Hepworth Rd HOLM/MEL HD9............234 A8
Hepworth St CAS WF10............154 A2
Herbalist St WOR/ARM LS12............6 A5
Herbert Pl BFDE BD3............97 G3
Herbert St BGLY BD16............50 A8
  CAS WF10............153 J4
  CLAY BD14............94 C7
  HFAX HX1............8 A5
  SHPY BD18............73 F3
  WBOW BD5............95 K7
Hereford Cl HEM/SK/SE WF9............224 D5
Hereford Wy BOW * BD4............96 C7
Heritage Ms HFAX * HX1............9 E5
Heritage Pk BGLY BD16............50 A5
Heritage Rd BTLY WF17............146 B7
Heritage Wy HWTH BD22............68 E1
Hermitage Pk KBTN HD8............215 G1
Hermit St HWTH BD22............69 J1

Hermon Av HFAX HX1............8
Hermon Gv HFAX HX1............8
Hermon Rd MSTN/BAR LS15............103
Hermon St MSTN/BAR LS15............103
Heron Cl AIRE BD20............26
  AL/HA/HU LS17............58
  CUL/QBY BD13............116
Heron Ct MOR LS27............123
Heron Dr WKFDW/WTN WF2............198
Heron Gv AL/HA/HU LS17............58
Herriot Ms CAS WF10............154
Herschel Rd GIR BD8............94
Hertford Cha MSTN/BAR LS15............104
Hertford Cl MSTN/BAR LS15............104
Hertford Cft MSTN/BAR LS15............104
Hertford Fold MSTN/BAR LS15............104
Hertford Lawn MSTN/BAR LS15............104
Heseltine La HBR HX7............136
Heshbon St BOW BD4............96
Hesketh Av EARD/LOFT WF3............147
  KSTL LS5............78
Hesketh La EARD/LOFT WF3............147
Hesketh Mt KSTL LS5............78
Hesketh Pl KSTL LS5............78
Hesketh Rd KSTL LS5............78
Hesketh Ter KSTL LS5............78
Hesley Rd WKFDW/WTN WF2............198
Hessel Ct PONT WF8............180
Hessle Av HDGY LS6............78
Hessle Common La
  HOR/CROF WF4............202
Hessle La HOR/CROF WF4............202
Hessle Mt HDGY * LS6............78
Hessle Pl HDGY LS6............78
Hessle Rd HDGY LS6............78
Hessle Ter HDGY * LS6............78
Hessle Vw HDGY * LS6............78
Hessle Wk HDGY LS6............78
Hetchell Vw AL/HA/HU LS17............60
Hetton Dr BFDE BD3............97
Hetton Rd RHAY LS8............80
Heuthwaite Av WBY LS22............23
Hever Gv HUDE * HD5............192
New Clews GTHN BD7............94
Hey Beck La EARL WF12............147
Heybeck Wk BOW BD4............120
Heycliffe Rd HOLM/MEL HD9............233
Hey Crs HOLM/MEL HD9............231
Heyford Ct ECHL BD2............73
Heygate Cl BAIL BD17............51
Heygate La BAIL BD17............51
  BSPA/BRAM LS23............43
Hey Head La TOD OL14............134
Hey La HUDE HD5............191
  HUDS HD4............188
  HUDW HD3............188
Heys Av CUL/QBY BD13............93
Heys Cl KNOT WF11............156
Heys Crs CUL/QBY BD13............94
Heys Gdns HOLM/MEL HD9............233
Heysham Dr BOW BD4............97
Hey Slack La KBTN HD8............249
Heys La LUD/ILL HX2............113
  MAR/SLWT HD7............210
  RPDN/SBR HX6............187
Heys Rd HOLM/MEL HD9............233
Hey St BRIG HD6............142
  GTHN BD7............4
Heywood Cl HIPP HX3............141
Heywood Pl HFAX HX1............8
Heywood St HFAX HX1............8
Hick La BTLY WF17............146
Hicks La RTHW LS26............128
Hick St BFD BD1............5
Higgin Farm LUD/ILL * HX2............137
Higgin La HIPP HX3............9
Higham And Dob La
  RPDN/SBR HX6............137
Higham Vw DOD/DAR S75............239
Higham Wy GFTH/SHER LS25............105
High Ash AL/HA/HU LS17............58
  SHPY BD18............74
High Ash Av AL/HA/HU LS17............58
  KBTN HD8............237
High Ash Cl HOR/CROF WF4............221
High Ash Dr AL/HA/HU LS17............58
High Ash Mt AL/HA/HU LS17............58
High Ash Pk WIL/AL BD15............93
High Bank Ap MSTN/BAR LS15............104
High Bank Cl ILK * LS29............18
  MSTN/BAR LS15............104
High Bank Gdns MSTN/BAR LS15............104
High Bank Ga MSTN/BAR * LS15............104
High Bank La SHPY BD18............72
  STKB/PEN S36............251
High Bank Pl MSTN/BAR LS15............104
High Banks Cl AIRE BD20............48
High Bank Vw MSTN/BAR LS15............104
High Bank Wy MSTN/BAR LS15............104
High Binns La HWTH BD22............69
Highbridge La KBTN HD8............237
Highbridge Ter WBOW BD5............119
High Brook La EARD/LOFT WF3............149
High Brooms HUDN HD2............12
High Bury Ct CUL/QBY BD13............116
Highbury Cl HDGY LS6............78
Highbury La HDGY LS6............78
Highbury Pl BRAM LS13............98
  HDGY LS6............78

ghbury Rd HDGY LS6 ....78 E5
ghbury St HDGY LS6 ....78 E5
gh Cliffe BULY LS4 ....78 C8
gh Busy La SHPY BD18 ....74 A3
ghcliffe Av HUDN HD2 ....191 F1
ghcliffe Dr LUD/ILL HX2 ....139 G4
ghcliffe Rd BTLY WF17 ....146 B8
MOR LS27 ....122 E7
gh Cliffe Ter WBY LS22 ....23 J6
gh Cl DOD/DAR S75 ....239 K2
GSLY LS20 ....59 J3
HUDE HD5 ....192 A8
MAR/SLWT HD7 ....211 J3
OSS WF5 ....173 J2
YEA LS19 ....53 K8
gh Ct HBR HX7 ....111 J5
LDSU LS2 ....7 F4
gh Court La LDSU LS2 ....7 F4
gh Crest MAR/SLWT HD7 ....211 J1
gh Cft CUL/QBY BD13 ....116 D2
HIPP HX3 ....8 A1
ghcroft HOLM/MEL HD9 ....232 E6
WBY LS22 ....40 E3
ghcroft Cl PDSY/CALV LS28 ....98 A3
gh Croft Crs HUDE HD5 ....192 B8
ghcroft Gdns KGHY BD21 ....48 D5
gh Croft Rd TOD OL14 ....134 B5
gh Cross La HIPP HX3 ....117 F4
ghdale EARL WF12 ....172 D1
ghdale Cft IDLE BD10 ....74 D3
gher Ashenhurst TOD OL14 ....133 K4
gher Back La HBR HX7 ....110 D7
gher Brockwell RPDN/SBR HX6 ....138 C8
gher Coach Rd BGLY BD16 ....72 D1
gher Downs GIR BD8 ....94 D3
gher Grange Rd PDSY/CALV LS28 ....98 C3
gher Intake Rd ECHL BD2 ....96 E2
gher Park Royd Dr RPDN/SBR HX6 ....164 B4
gher School St SHPY * BD18 ....73 F3
gherwood Cl KGHY BD21 ....3 F3
ghfell Ri HWTH BD22 ....47 G6
gh Fernley Ct LM/WK * BD12 ....118 D7
gh Fernley Rd LM/WK BD12 ....118 E8
ghfield BOW BD4 ....120 A2
EARD/LOFT WF3 ....147 J2
HIPP HX3 ....117 G6
ghfield Av BRIG HD6 ....142 C3
GTL/HWG HX4 ....166 A3
HIPP HX3 ....117 J4
HOLM/MEL HD9 ....211 H8
IDLE BD10 ....74 C4
KBTN HD8 ....235 J7
LVSG * WF15 ....155 H7
PONT WF8 ....180 D4
WOR/ARM LS12 ....100 D6
ghfield Cl AIRE BD20 ....49 G2
FEA/AMT WF7 ....179 J3
MOR LS27 ....122 D4
WOR/ARM LS12 ....100 D5
ghfield Ct HWTH BD22 ....68 E1
HBR HX7 ....112 B7
HOLM/MEL HD9 ....211 H8
HOR/CROF WF4 ....195 K5
HTON BD9 ....72 D7
PDSY/CALV LS28 ....98 B3
LS26 ....127 F4
WOR/ARM LS12 ....100 D5
ghfield Dr BTLY WF17 ....145 H1
CAS WF10 ....128 E6
GFTH/SHER LS25 ....105 K6
HTON BD9 ....72 D7
LVSG WF15 ....144 B7
MOR LS27 ....122 C4
WKFDW/WTN WF2 ....175 F3
YEA LS19 ....54 A8
ghfield Gdns EARL WF12 ....172 C8
HTON BD9 ....72 D8
MOR LS27 ....122 C4
ghfield Garth WOR/ARM LS12 ....100 D6
ghfield Gra HOR/CROF WF4 ....197 G2
ghfield Gn CAS WF10 ....128 E5
PDSY/CALV LS28 ....98 B3
ghfield Gv CAS WF10 ....128 E5
ILL HX5 ....166 D3
DLE BD10 ....74 C5
gh Field La HWTH BD22 ....46 E8
RPDN/SBR HX6 ....164 A5
ghfield La AIRE BD20 ....27 G1
MEWS WF13 ....145 J8
GFTH/SHER LS25 ....107 K7
HOLM/MEL HD9 ....211 H8
HUDE HD5 ....192 E6
KGHY BD21 ....2 B2
MSTN/BAR LS15 ....83 H6
MSTN/BAR LS15 ....83 J6
THW * LS26 ....127 F4
ghfield Ms AIRE BD20 ....49 G2
BAIL BD17 ....51 J7
ghfield Mt EARL WF12 ....195 F8
THW * LS26 ....127 F5
ghfield Pl CAS WF10 ....129 F5
GIR BD8 ....4 A2
HEM/SK/SE WF9 ....224 C5

HFAX HX1 ....8 A5
MOR LS27 ....125 G8
Highfield Ri WKFDW/WTN WF2 ....175 F3
Highfield Rd BRAM LS13 ....99 H1
BRIG HD6 ....167 K3
CLECK BD19 ....143 K4
ELL HX5 ....166 E5
GFTH/SHER LS25 ....84 E3
HEM/SK/SE WF9 ....224 C5
HOLM/MEL * HD9 ....211 H8
HOR/CROF WF4 ....196 D6
HOR/CROF WF4 ....197 G2
HTON BD9 ....73 J6
IDLE BD10 ....74 C5
KBTN HD8 ....215 G4
KGHY BD21 ....2 B2
LUD/ILL HX2 ....138 D7
MAR/SLWT HD7 ....188 D8
PDSY/CALV LS28 ....98 A3
PONT WF8 ....180 D5
Highfields HOR/CROF WF4 ....196 D6
HOR/CROF WF4 ....223 H1
High Flds LUD/ILL HX2 ....139 H7
Highfields STKB/PEN S36 ....252 E5
Highfields Rd DOD/DAR S75 ....239 H3
HUD HD1 ....12 B3
Highfield St BRAM * LS13 ....99 H1
KGHY BD21 ....2 C3
PDSY/CALV LS28 ....98 A3
Highfield Ter EARL WF12 ....172 C8
HFAX * HX1 ....8 A5
PDSY/CALV LS28 ....98 A3
SHPY BD18 ....72 E5
Highfield Vw MOR LS27 ....122 D4
Highfold YEA LS19 ....53 J6
High Fold La AIRE BD20 ....47 J1
Highgate HTON BD9 ....73 F7
Highgate Av KBTN HD8 ....193 F8
Highgate Cl CUL/QBY BD13 ....117 H1
Highgate Crs KBTN HD8 ....193 G8
Highgate Dr KBTN HD8 ....193 H8
Highgate Gdns LUD/ILL HX2 ....139 K3
Highgate Gv CLAY BD14 ....117 H1
Highgate La HUDE HD5 ....193 F1
KBTN HD8 ....193 F8
Highgate Rd CUL/QBY BD13 ....117 G1
EARL WF12 ....172 C8
Highgate St BTLY WF17 ....146 E8
Highgate Wk KBTN * HD8 ....193 H8
High Gn KBTN HD8 ....215 H1
High Green Dr AIRE BD20 ....27 F1
High Green Rd NORM WF6 ....151 H7
Highgrove Ct NORM WF6 ....151 J6
High Grove La HIPP HX3 ....9 F6
High Holly Garth KGHY BD21 ....3 E4
High House Av ECHL BD2 ....74 C7
High House Edge MAR/SLWT HD7 ....211 G4
High House La LUD/ILL HX2 ....113 K7
MAR/SLWT HD7 ....211 F4
High House Rd ECHL BD2 ....74 C7
High Hoyland La DOD/DAR S75 ....238 B4
High Keep Fold HOR/CROF WF4 ....198 B8
Highland Cl PONT WF8 ....155 G8
The Highlands LVSG WF15 ....144 A6
Highlands Cl GTHN BD7 ....94 E8
RTHW LS26 ....125 G4
Highlands Dr RTHW LS26 ....125 G3
RTHW LS26 ....125 G4
Highlands Gv GTHN BD7 ....94 E8
RTHW LS26 ....125 G3
Highlands La LUD/ILL HX2 ....115 J5
Highlands Wk RTHW LS26 ....125 G3
Highland Ville HIPP HX3 ....141 J3
High La HBR HX7 ....136 D3
HOLM/MEL HD9 ....233 J8
HUDS HD4 ....213 H1
HWTH BD22 ....44 B2
STKB/PEN S36 ....251 G4
High Lea MAR/SLWT HD7 ....209 H7
Highlea Cl YEA LS19 ....53 H6
Highlee La RPDN/SBR HX6 ....164 C4
High Lee La STKB/PEN S36 ....252 E6
High Lees Rd LUD/ILL HX2 ....114 E6
High Level Wy HFAX HX1 ....8 A3
Highley Hall Cft BRIG HD6 ....168 E1
Highley Pk BRIG HD6 ....169 F1
High Meadow KGHY BD21 ....2 B1
High Mdw EARL WF12 ....195 G2
GTL/HWG HX4 ....166 A4
WIL/AL BD15 ....71 F6
WKFDW/WTN WF2 ....199 K5
High Mill ILK * LS29 ....18 E2
High Mill La ILK LS29 ....18 E2
Highmoor BAIL BD17 ....51 H5
High Moor Av AL/HA/HU LS17 ....80 A1
High Moor Cl AL/HA/HU LS17 ....58 A8
High Moor Crs AL/HA/HU LS17 ....80 A1
Highmoor Crs BRIG HD6 ....142 E8
High Moor Dr AL/HA/HU LS17 ....58 A8
High Moor La BRIG HD6 ....142 E8
CLECK BD19 ....143 H6
Highmoor Wk BAIL BD17 ....51 H5
Highoak Garth HWTH BD22 ....68 E1
High Oxford St CAS WF10 ....153 H4
High Park Crs HTON BD9 ....72 E8
High Park Dr HTON BD9 ....72 D8
High Park Gv HTON BD9 ....72 E8

High Poplars ECHL BD2 ....74 B7
High Rdg HOR/CROF WF4 ....196 E5
High Ridge Av RTHW LS26 ....126 A4
High Ridge Ct RTHW LS26 ....126 B5
High Ridge Pk RTHW LS26 ....126 B4
High Ridge Wy BHP/TINH LS16 ....55 K1
High Rd EARL WF12 ....172 D4
Highroad Well La LUD/ILL HX2 ....139 F4
Highroyd KBTN HD8 ....193 H8
Highroyd Crs HUDE HD5 ....13 F5
Highroyd La HUDE HD5 ....13 F4
High Royd La STKB/PEN S36 ....253 F6
High Royds Dr ILK LS29 ....32 C8
High Spring Gardens La KGHY BD21 ....2 B1
High Spring Rd KGHY BD21 ....48 D5
High Stones Rd HBR HX7 ....137 F8
High St AIRE BD20 ....26 E6
BRIG HD6 ....142 C8
BSLYN/ROY S71 ....221 K8
BSPA/BRAM LS23 ....23 J8
BSPA/BRAM LS23 ....42 E6
BSPA/BRAM LS23 ....62 D1
BTLY WF17 ....145 H1
BTLY WF17 ....146 E8
CAS WF10 ....153 H4
CLECK BD19 ....144 A3
CUD/GR S72 ....223 J6
CUL/QBY BD13 ....93 H5
CUL/QBY BD13 ....116 D2
DEWS WF13 ....172 A4
EARL WF12 ....172 E4
EARL WF12 ....195 G2
GFTH/SHER LS25 ....129 G2
GTL/HWG * HX4 ....165 H8
HECK WF16 ....145 G8
HEM/SK/SE WF9 ....226 C4
HEM/SK/SE WF9 ....226 C4
HFAX HX1 ....8 C5
HOLM/MEL * HD9 ....213 F7
HOR/CROF WF4 ....177 H1
HOR/CROF WF4 ....197 G2
HOR/CROF WF4 ....198 A6
HOR/CROF WF4 ....200 D3
HOR/CROF WF4 ....220 B4
HUD HD1 ....12 A5
IDLE BD10 ....74 D3
KBTN HD8 ....237 K1
KGHY BD21 ....2 C3
KNOT * WF11 ....155 K6
KNOT WF11 ....155 K2
LUD/ILL HX2 ....138 D2
MAR/SLWT HD7 ....189 F6
MOR LS27 ....147 F1
NORM WF6 ....151 J8
NORM WF6 ....178 A1
OSS WF5 ....173 H2
PBR HG3 ....22 A1
PDSY/CALV LS28 ....76 B8
WBSY BD6 ....118 D2
WBY LS22 ....23 J6
YEA LS19 ....53 K4
High Street Ct LUD/ILL HX2 ....138 D2
High Sunderland La HIPP HX3 ....9 D2
Highthorne Ct AL/HA/HU LS17 ....58 B7
Highthorne La AL/HA/HU LS17 ....58 B7
Highthorne Gv AL/HA/HU LS17 ....58 A7
WOR/ARM * LS12 ....100 A3
Highthorne Mt AL/HA/HU LS17 ....58 B7
Highthorne Vw WOR/ARM * LS12 ....100 B3
Hightown La HOLM/MEL HD9 ....233 D6
Hightown Rd CLECK BD19 ....144 A4
Hightown Vw LVSG WF15 ....143 K6
High Trees La GTL/HWG HX4 ....165 G5
High Vw BSLYN/ROY S71 ....221 K8
HOR/CROF WF4 ....198 A6
Highway GSLY LS20 ....52 D2
High Ways SCFT LS14 ....103 G2
High Weardley La OT LS21 ....37 G5
High Well Hill La CUD/GR S72 ....223 G5
High Wheatley ILK LS29 ....20 E8
High Wicken Cl CUL/QBY BD13 ....93 G5
High Wd ILK LS29 ....21 F8
Highwood Av AL/HA/HU LS17 ....79 J1
Highwood Cl DOD/DAR S75 ....239 J3
Highwood Crs AL/HA/HU LS17 ....57 J8
Highwood Gv AL/HA/HU LS17 ....79 J1
High Woodlands EARD/LOFT WF3 ....148 D4
High Wood La KBTN HD8 ....215 K6
High Wood Rd BTLY WF17 ....121 K7
Higson Ct HUDE HD5 ....192 C4
Hilberoyd Rd BTLY WF17 ....146 C7
Hilda St HTON BD9 ....73 G7
OSS WF5 ....173 K7
Hillam Rd ECHL BD2 ....73 K8
Hillam St WBOW BD5 ....95 H8
Hillary Pl LDSU LS2 ....7 D1
Hillary Rd SHPY BD18 ....74 A4
Hillary St DEWS WF13 ....145 J8
Hillbro Ct BAIL * BD17 ....51 K7
Hillbrook Ri ILK LS29 ....19 K8
Hill Brow Cft WIL/AL BD15 ....94 A2
Hill Cl BAIL BD17 ....73 H1
HUDW HD3 ....189 K2
PONT WF8 ....180 E4
Hill Clough Gv HWTH BD22 ....46 E4
Hillcote Dr WBOW BD5 ....96 A7
Hillcourt Av BRAM LS13 ....77 G7

Hillcourt Cft BRAM LS13...............77 G7
Hill Court Dr BRAM LS13................77 G7
Hillcourt Gv BRAM LS13................77 G7
Hill Crs BTLY WF17......................145 K2
  HIPP HX3.................................9 F6
  ILK LS29................................32 B4
  YEA LS19................................54 A6
Hill Crest HOR/CROF WF4...............223 G2
  WBY LS22................................40 C3
Hillcrest BHP/TINH * LS16..............34 E7
  HEM/SK/SE * WF9.......................224 D5
  NORM WF6..............................151 H7
Hill Crest Av CUL/QBY BD13.............92 B2
Hillcrest Av AIRE BD20..................27 G1
  BTLY WF17.............................145 K6
  CAS WF10..............................154 E5
  CHAL LS7...............................80 A8
  CUL/QBY BD13..........................116 E3
  FEA/AMT WF7...........................179 G6
  OSS WF5...............................173 H3
Hillcrest Cl CAS WF10..................154 E5
  RTHW LS26.............................127 J2
Hill Crest Dr CUL/QBY BD13.............92 B2
Hillcrest Dr CAS WF10..................154 E5
  CUL/QBY BD13..........................116 E3
Hillcrest Mt BHP/TINH LS16.............55 J7
  CAS WF10..............................154 E5
  CLECK BD19............................143 G4
Hill Crest Mt CUL/QBY BD13.............92 B2
Hillcrest Pl CHAL LS7...................80 A7
Hillcrest Ri BHP/TINH LS16.............55 J7
Hill Crest Rd CUL/QBY BD13.............92 B2
  CUL/QBY BD13...........................93 H4
  EARL WF12.............................172 B6
Hillcrest Rd CAS WF10.................155 F5
  CUL/QBY BD13..........................116 E3
Hill Cft CUL/QBY BD13...................93 J4
Hill Croft Cl PONT WF8.................182 A6
Hill Dr FEA/AMT WF7.....................203 G3
Hill End EARL WF12.....................172 D5
Hill End Cl HIPP HX3...................142 B1
Hill End Gv GTHN BD7....................94 E8
Hill End La CUL/QBY BD13...............116 C3
  CUL/QBY BD13...........................93 H4
Hill End Rd WOR/ARM LS12................99 K3
Hillesley Rd EARL WF12.................147 F8
Hillfold HEM/SK/SE WF9.................226 E4
Hill Foot SHPY BD18.....................72 D4
Hillfoot Crs PDSY/CALV LS28............97 K3
Hillfoot Dr PDSY/CALV LS28.............97 K3
Hillfoot Ri PDSY/CALV LS28.............97 K3
Hillgarth EARL WF12....................172 C4
  KNOT WF11............................156 B8
Hill Green Ct BOW BD4..................121 H1
Hill Gv HUDW HD3.......................189 K2
Hill Grove Lea HUDW HD5...............189 K2
Hillhead Dr BTLY WF17..................145 J2
Hill House Edge La HWTH BD22............90 D3
Hill House La HOLM/MEL HD9.............247 J1
  HWTH BD22..............................90 E2
Hillhouse La HUD HD1....................12 C2
Hill House Rd HOLM/MEL HD9.............247 H1
Hillidge Rd MID LS10...................101 K7
Hillidge Sq MID LS10...................101 K7
Hillingdon Wy AL/HA/HU LS17............57 G6
Hillings La ILK LS29....................57 G6
Hill La HOLM/MEL HD9...................232 E6
Hill Mount Pleasant MID LS10...........124 D6
Hill Park Av HX3.........................8 A2
Hill Ri BTLY WF17......................146 E2
Hill Rise Av BRAM LS13..................77 G7
Hill Rise Gv BRAM LS13.................77 G7
Hill Rd CAS WF10.......................154 A4
  WKFDW/WTN WF2.......................198 E7
Hills & Hamlets Wk
  HOLM/MEL HD9.........................232 D5
  HOLM/MEL HD9.........................232 E8
  HOLM/MEL HD9.........................233 G3
  HOLM/MEL HD9.........................234 A4
Hillside GFTH/SHER LS25................106 A5
  KBTN HD8.............................236 D5
  KNOT WF11............................156 A4
Hill Side Av HOLM/MEL HD9.............249 F1
Hillside Av GSLY LS20...................33 F8
  HUDN HD2.............................191 H1
  HWTH BD22.............................68 D1
  LUD/ILL HX2............................68 A1
  RPDN/SBR HX6.........................164 B5
Hill Side Buildings BEE/HOL LS11......101 G8
Hillside Cl ILK LS29....................18 C3
  STKB/PEN S36.........................252 E5
  WKFDW/WTN WF2.......................174 E8
Hillside Ct CHAL LS7....................80 A4
  HEM/SK/SE WF9........................226 C7
  ILK LS29...............................32 B7
Hillside Crs CUD/GR S72................240 C1
  HUDS HD4.............................213 G1
Hillside Gv HWTH BD22...................68 D1
  PDSY/CALV LS28........................98 A4
Hill Side Mt CUD/GR S72................240 A1
  PDSY/CALV LS28........................98 A4
  PONT WF8.............................181 G5
Hillside Ri GSLY LS20...................53 F1
Hill Side Rd BFDE BD3....................5 E4

BGLY BD16..............................49 K8
Hillside Rd CHAL LS7....................79 K4
  FEA/AMT WF7..........................203 G5
  PONT WF8.............................181 F5
  SHPY BD18.............................73 J5
Hillside Ter BAIL * BD17................51 J7
Hill Side Ter BFDE BD3...................5 E3
Hillside Vw MAR/SLWT HD7...............211 H2
  PDSY/CALV LS28.........................98 D4
  RPDN/SBR HX6.........................158 D7
Hill St BEE/HOL LS11...................101 G8
  BOW BD4................................5 F6
  CLECK BD19...........................143 K4
  HFAX HX1................................8 C5
  HOLM/MEL HD9.........................234 A8
  HWTH BD22.............................68 C5
  OSM LS9...............................102 A2
  WBSY BD6..............................118 B2
Hillthorpe Ct MID LS10.................124 D8
Hillthorpe Dr PONT WF8.................204 C6
Hillthorpe Ri PDSY/CALV LS28...........98 C6
Hillthorpe Rd PDSY/CALV LS28...........98 C6
Hillthorpe Sq PDSY/CALV LS28...........98 B6
Hillthorpe St PDSY/CALV * LS28.........98 C6
Hillthorpe Ter PDSY/CALV * LS28........98 C6
Hilltop CUD/GR S72....................223 K8
Hill Top CAS WF10.....................152 E4
  DOD/DAR S75..........................238 E7
  HEM/SK/SE * WF9......................202 A8
  HFAX HX1.............................139 H6
  ILK LS29..............................30 A1
  ILK LS29..............................32 A2
  KNOT WF11............................156 C2
Hill Top Av RHAY LS8...................80 B7
Hilltop Cl EARD/LOFT WF3..............147 K5
  HEM/SK/SE * WF9......................202 B8
  HOR/CROF WF4.........................221 K5
  WOR/ARM LS12...........................99 K3
Hill Top Cottages HTON LS9.............94 C1
Hill Top Ct EARD/LOFT WF3.............147 K5
  WKFDW/WTN * WF2.....................198 E7
Hill Top Crs MIRF WF14.................193 G2
Hill Top Cft HUDS HD4..................212 C5
Hill Top Dr HUDW HD3..................190 A3
Hill Top Farm KBTN HD8................215 G8
Hill Top Gdns EARD/LOFT * WF3.........147 K5
Hill Top Gn EARD/LOFT WF3.............147 J5
Hill Top Gv EARD/LOFT WF3.............147 K5
  WIL/AL BD15............................94 A2
Hill Top La BGLY BD16..................49 K3
  EARD/LOFT WF3.........................147 J5
  HBR HX7..............................136 C8
  HOR/CROF WF4.........................202 C2
  WIL/AL BD15............................94 A2
Hill Top Ms KNOT WF11.................156 C2
Hill Top Mt RHAY LS8...................80 B7
Hill Top Pl HDGY LS6....................8 B1
  RHAY LS8..............................80 B7
Hill Top Rd CUL/QBY BD13...............93 F4
  HOLM/MEL HD9.........................248 A1
  HOR/CROF WF4.........................195 H8
  HUD HD1................................12 A5
  HUDE HD5...............................13 F4
  HUDW HD3.............................189 K2
  HWTH BD22.............................68 D1
  KGHY BD21..............................3 H6
  MAR/SLWT HD7.........................210 D2
  WKFDW/WTN WF2.......................198 E7
  WOR/ARM LS12...........................99 K3
Hill Top Vw EARD/LOFT WF3.............147 J5
  HOLM/MEL HD9.........................248 D3
Hill Top Wk HWTH BD22....................2 A3
Hill Top Wy HWTH * BD22..................2 A3
Hill Vw LUD/ILL HX2....................115 J4
Hillview Gdns HIPP HX3.................141 F2
Hill View Pl CHAL * LS7.................79 K4
Hill View Ter CHAL * LS7...............79 K4
Hillway GSLY LS20.......................52 E4
Hillworth Village KGHY * BD21...........2 C4
Hilmian Wy HEM/SK/SE WF9...............225 F6
Hilton Av SHPY BD18.....................73 H6
Hilton Ct BHP/TINH LS16................34 E8
Hilton Crs BAIL BD17...................73 J1
Hilton Dr SHPY BD18....................73 H6
Hilton Gra BHP/TINH LS16...............34 E7
Hilton Gv CTHN BD7......................95 G5
  RHAY LS8..............................80 B6
  SHPY BD18.............................73 H6
Hilton Ms BHP/TINH LS16................34 E8
Hilton Pl RHAY LS8.....................80 B7
Hilton Rd BGTHN BD7.....................95 G5
  RHAY LS8..............................80 B7
  SHPY BD18.............................73 H6
Hilton St RHAY * LS8...................112 B8
  RHAY * LS8.............................80 B7
Hilton Ter RHAY * LS8...................80 B7
Hinchcliffe Av OSS WF5.................174 A6
Hinchcliffe St BFDE BD3.................5 F3
Hinchliffe Av BAIL BD17................73 K1
Hind Ct HOLM/MEL HD9...................211 G8
Hindle Pl MOR * LS27...................123 G4
Hindley Rd LVSG WF15..................144 D8
Hindley Wk GTHN BD7...................117 J1
Hinds Crs HEM/SK/SE WF9...............226 E4
Hind St GIR BD8.........................4 A3
  LM/WK BD12...........................142 D1
Hinsley Ct HDGY LS6.....................78 E6
Hinton Cl PONT WF8....................155 F8

Hinton La KNOT WF11...................155 F1
Hions Cl BRIG HD6.....................168 E2
Hipswell St BFDE BD3...................96 E1
Hird Av WBSY BD6.......................118 C1
Hird Rd LM/WK BD12....................118 B4
Hird St BAIL BD17......................73 H1
  BEE/HOL LS11.........................101 C2
  KGHY BD21..............................3 G6
Hirst Av HECK WF16....................145 G6
Hirst Gv HBR HX7......................112 A4
Hirstlands Av OSS WF5..................173 H5
Hirstlands Dr OSS WF5..................173 H5
Hirst La HOLM/MEL HD9.................234 E2
  SHPY BD18.............................72 E7
Hirst Lodge Ct ECHL BD2................74 E7
Hirst Mill Crs SHPY BD18...............72 D6
Hirst Rd DEWS WF13....................172 D6
  WKFDW/WTN WF2.......................174 D1
Hirst St CAS WF10.....................128 C6
  TOD * OL14...........................132 C2
Hirst Wood Crs SHPY BD18...............72 E7
Hirst Wood Rd SHPY BD18................72 E7
Hive St HWTH BD22.......................2 C3
Hobart Rd CAS WF10....................154 E5
  EARL WF12.............................172 A6
Hobberley La AL/HA/HU LS17.............59 F5
Hob Cote La HWTH BD22..................68 D4
Hob La HUDS HD4.......................212 B6
  HWTH BD22..............................67 H6
  RPDN/SBR HX6.........................163 K4
  RPDN/SBR HX6.........................164 A5
Hockney Rd GIR BD8.....................95 H4
Hodgewood La PONT WF8.................182 A4
Hodgkinson Av STKB/PEN S36............252 C7
Hodgson Av AL/HA/HU LS17...............58 E5
  BFDE BD3..............................97 H4
Hodgson Crs AL/HA/HU LS17..............58 C7
Hodgson Fold ILK LS29..................18 C6
Hodgson La BIRK/DRI BD11..............120 C3
Hodgson St MOR LS27...................147 F1
  WKFDE WF1..............................10 D4
Hodster La CUD/GR S72.................240 D5
Hoffman St HUDS HD4...................190 A5
Hog Close La HOLM/MEL HD9.............249 G5
Hogley La HOLM/MEL HD9................232 D5
Holays HUDE HD5.......................192 A7
Holbeck La BEE/HOL LS11................6 A7
Holbeck Moor La BEE/HOL LS11...........6 D9
Holbeck Towers BEE/HOL LS11............6 B9
Holborn Ap HDGY LS6....................79 H5
Holborn Ct HDGY LS6....................79 H5
  WBSY BD6.............................118 E4
Holborn Gdns HDGY * LS6................79 H5
Holborn Gn HDGY LS6...................79 H5
Holborn Gv HDGY LS6...................79 H5
Holborn St HDGY LS6...................79 H5
Holborn Ter HDGY LS6..................79 H5
Holborn Vw HDGY LS6...................79 H5
Holborn Wk HDGY LS6..................79 H5
Holby Sq WKFDW/WTN * WF2.............174 D1
Holden Ing Wy BTLY WF17...............121 H7
Holden La AIRE BD20....................27 K3
  BAIL BD17.............................51 J6
Holderness Rd KNOT WF11..............156 A4
Holderness St TOD OL14................134 A7
Holdforth Cl WOR/ARM LS12.............6 A8
Holdforth Gdns WOR/ARM LS12...........6 A8
Holdforth Gn WOR/ARM LS12.............6 A8
Holdforth Pl WOR/ARM LS12.............6 A9
Holdsworth Av HECK WF16...............145 H6
Holdsworth Ct CLECK BD19..............144 B7
Holdsworth Rd LUD/ILL HX2.............115 J3
  CLECK BD19...........................144 B4
  SHPY BD18.............................73 G4
Holdsworth Ter HFAX HX1.................9 G1
Hole Bottom Rd TOD OL14...............134 A7
Hole La AIRE BD20.......................16 E1
Holes La KNOT WF11....................156 A4
Holgate Crs HEM/SK/SE WF9.............224 C6
Holgate Gdns HEM/SK/SE WF9............224 C6
Holgate Rd PONT WF8...................180 B4
Holgate Vw CUD/GR S72................224 C6
Holker St GIR BD8.......................95 J2
  KGHY BD21..............................3 G5
Holland Rd GFTH/SHER LS25.............129 K8
Holland St BTLY WF17..................146 E6
Hollas La RPDN/SBR HX6................116 D5
Hollerton La EARD/LOFT WF3.............148 A6
The Hollies WOR/ARM * LS12............100 C5
Hollin Av HUDW HD3....................190 A5
Hollinbank La HECK WF16...............145 H6
Hollin Brigg La HOLM/MEL HD9..........247 H5
Hollin Close La ECHL BD2...............74 C4
Hollin Ct BHP/TINH * LS16..............78 B2
Hollin Crs BHP/TINH LS16...............78 B2
Hollin Dr BHP/TINH LS16................78 B2
  HOR/CROF WF4.........................198 C5
Hollin Edge KBTN HD8..................236 E4
Hollin Gdns BHP/TINH LS16.............78 B2
Hollin Ga OT LS21.......................33 G1
Hollingbourne Rd MSTN/BAR LS15........104 C2
Hollin Greaves La HIPP HX3.............9 K6
Hollings HWTH * BD22...................68 D1
Hollings Rd GIR BD8....................95 J2
Hollings Sq GIR BD8....................95 J2
Hollings St BGLY BD16..................72 E2
  GIR BD8...............................95 J2
The Hollings RTHW LS26.................128 C1

llings Ter GIR BD8	95 H3
llingthorpe Av HOR/CROF WF4	198 A8
llingthorpe Ct HOR/CROF WF4	220 A1
llingthorpe Gv HOR/CROF WF4	198 A8
llingthorpe La HOR/CROF WF4	198 A8
llingthorpe Rd HOR/CROF WF4	198 A8
lingwood Dr GTHN BD7	94 E7
lingwood Dr GTHN BD7	94 E7
lingwood Ga GTHN BD7	19 J8
lingwood La GTHN BD7	94 E8
lingwood Mt GTHN BD7	94 E7
lingwood Ri ILK LS29	19 J8
lingworth La KNOT WF11	156 D7
TOD OL14	160 A3
llin Hall Dr ILK LS29	19 J8
llin Hall La HUDE HD5	193 F1
MAR/SLWT HD7	189 H6
llin Hall Rd SHPY BD18	72 E5
llin Hill Av RHAY LS8	80 E6
llinhirst La HOR/CROF WF4	197 F6
llin House La HOLM/MEL HD9	234 B6
CBTN HD8	237 K4
llin La BHP/TINH LS16	78 D4
HBR HX7	113 H6
HOR/CROF WF4	197 K5
llin Park Av RHAY LS8	81 F6
llin Park Cl PDSY/CALV LS28	75 J5
llin Park Crs RHAY LS8	81 F6
llin Park Dr PDSY/CALV LS28	75 J5
llin Park Mt RHAY LS8	81 F6
llin Park Pl RHAY LS8	80 E6
llin Park Rd PDSY/CALV LS28	75 J5
RHAY LS8	80 E6
llin Ri SHPY * BD18	73 J5
llin Rd BHP/TINH LS16	78 D4
SHPY BD18	73 J5
llinroyd Rd EARL WF12	172 D3
e Hollins TOD OL14	134 A5
lins Av DEWS WF13	171 J1
lins Bank La AIRE BD20	27 F7
lins Bank La RPDN/SBR HX6	138 E7
lins Beck Cl GFTH/SHER LS25	129 F3
lins La AIRE BD20	27 H8
lins Bungalows	
RPDN/SBR * HX6	138 E6
lins Cl AIRE BD20	47 H1
lins Gln MAR/SLWT HD7	210 E3
lins Gv CAS WF10	128 E5
lins Hey Rd CTL/HWG HX4	166 C7
lins Hl BAIL BD17	52 D5
LUD/ILL HX2	115 F6
UD/ILL HX2	137 J6
MAR/SLWT HD7	210 E5
lins Meadow TOD OL14	159 K2
lins Mill La RPDN/SBR HX6	138 D7
lins Pk GFTH/SHER LS25	129 F3
lins Pl HBR HX7	112 B7
TOD OL14	159 K2
lins Rd DEWS WF13	171 J1
TOD OL14	159 K1
lins Rw MAR/SLWT HD7	210 E3
lins St TOD OL14	160 A3
lins St RPDN/SBR HX6	164 B2
lin Ter HUDW HD3	190 C4
HPY * BD18	73 J5
lin Vw BHP/TINH LS16	78 D4
lin Wood Cl SHPY BD18	72 E4
linwood Vw AIRE BD20	49 H4
lis Pl BVRD LS3	6 B2
e Hollow HOLM/MEL HD9	231 G1
lowfield Cft LM/WK BD12	119 J6
lowgate HOLM/MEL HD9	233 G6
ly Ap OSS WF5	173 J3
ly Av BHP/TINH LS16	55 H8
ly Bank FEA/AMT WF7	188 A2
FTH/SHER LS25	106 B5
DGY LS6	78 D5
ly Bank Ct HUDW * HD3	190 A4
ly Bank Dr HIPP HX3	141 J3
lybank Gdns GTHN BD7	94 E8
lybank Gv GTHN BD7	94 E8
ly Bank Pk BRIC HD6	168 A3
ly Bank Rd BRIC HD6	167 K3
UDW HD3	190 B2
lybank Rd GTHN BD7	94 E8
ly Bush Cl BSPA/BRAM LS23	42 E4
lybush Gn WBY LS22	41 G3
ly Cl HEM/SK/SE WF9	242 B1
ly Ct EARD/LOFT WF3	200 C2
MID LS10	124 C7
ly Ct EARD/LOFT WF3	147 K5
YKFDE WF1	149 K6
ly Crs HOR/CROF WF4	200 C2
PDN/SBR HX6	163 K8
lycroft Ct BHP/TINH LS16	56 A8
ly Dene OSS WF5	173 J3
ly Dr BHP/TINH LS16	55 H8

Hollyfield Av HUDW HD3	190 A4
Hollygarth La GLE DN14	157 K4
Holly Gv BTLY WF17	146 A7
CUD/GR S72	224 A8
HFAX HX1	8 B5
HUDW HD3	190 C2
Holly Hall La LM/WK BD12	118 D7
Holly Mede OSS WF5	173 J3
Hollynsmith GTL/HWG HX4	166 C4
Hollyoake La MAR/SLWT HD7	211 G3
Holly Pk HORS LS18	76 D5
Holly Park Dr GTHN BD7	94 E7
Holly Park Gv GTHN * BD7	94 E7
Holly Park Mills PDSY/CALV * LS28	75 J5
PDSY/CALV * LS28	76 C7
Holly Rd BSPA/BRAM LS23	42 C3
HUD HD1	12 A6
Hollyshaw Crs MSTN/BAR LS15	104 A3
Hollyshaw Gv MSTN/BAR LS15	104 A3
Hollyshaw La MSTN/BAR LS15	104 A4
Hollyshaw St MSTN/BAR LS15	104 A3
Hollyshaw Ter MSTN/BAR LS15	104 A3
Hollyshaw Wk MSTN/BAR LS15	104 A2
Holly St HEM/SK/SE WF9	224 D4
WBSY BD6	117 J1
WKFDW/WTN WF2	175 G4
Holly Ter HUD HD1	13 D2
Holly Tree La MSTN/BAR LS15	104 D5
Hollywell Gv WOR/ARM LS12	100 B3
Hollywell La WOR/ARM LS12	100 B3
Holman Av GFTH/SHER LS25	105 K6
Holmcliffe Av HUDS HD4	213 F2
Holmclose HOLM/MEL HD9	247 G1
Holmdale Crs HOLM/MEL HD9	233 F3
Holmdene Dr NORF WF14	170 D5
Holme Av HUDE HD5	214 A2
Holmebank Ms HOLM/MEL HD9	213 H8
Holme Cl HOR/CROF WF4	194 C6
Holme Cft HOLM/MEL HD9	234 A4
Holme Cft HOR/CROF WF4	198 B4
Holme Dr LUD/ILL HX2	138 E5
Holme Farm WBSY BD6	117 J2
Holme Farm La BSPA/BRAM LS23	40 D8
Holme Farm La BSPA/BRAM LS23	40 D8
Holme Gv ILK LS29	32 B4
Holme House La HWTH BD22	46 E6
LUD/ILL HX2	114 D7
Holme House Rd TOD OL14	133 F2
Holme Ings ILK LS29	19 G4
Holme La BOW BD4	120 B2
HOLM/MEL HD9	234 A4
MAR/SLWT HD7	210 A3
WKFDW/WTN WF2	198 D1
Holme Leas Dr OSS WF5	173 H4
Holme Mill La HWTH BD22	2 A4
Holme Pk ILK LS29	32 B4
Holme Park Ct HUDS * HD4	213 F3
Holme Pl HBR HX7	112 B7
Holme Rd LUD/ILL HX2	138 E5
Holmeside Cl HUDS HD4	212 E5
Holme South HUDS HD4	144 E7
Holmes Ct RPDN/SBR HX6	139 F7
Holmes St BEE/HOL LS11	7 E5
GIR * BD8	4 B3
Holmes Ter LUD/ILL HX2	139 G3
Holme St BRIC HD6	182 B4
HBR HX7	112 B8
HWTH BD22	90 E1
LVSG WF15	144 E7
TOD OL14	133 H4
WBOW BD5	95 K7
Holme Styes La HOLM/MEL HD9	247 G2
Holme Top La WBOW BD5	95 K7
Holme Top St WBOW BD5	95 K7
Holme Valley Circular Wk	
HOLM/MEL HD9	232 E4
HOLM/MEL HD9	234 A4
HOLM/MEL HD9	234 B5
HOLM/MEL HD9	234 D7
HUDS HD4	212 E6
HUDS HD4	214 A7
Holme View Dr HOLM/MEL HD9	232 D6
Holme View Pk HECK/MEL HD9	232 E6
Holme View Rd DOD/DAR S75	239 H3
Holme Wy OSS WF5	173 H4
Holme Well Rd MID LS10	125 F6
Holme Wood Rd BOW BD4	97 F8
HWTH BD22	2 A4
Holme Woods La HOLM/MEL HD9	246 E6
Holmfield KBTN * HD8	237 K1
Holmfield Av WKFDW/WTN WF2	10 B6
Holmfield Cha EARD/LOFT WF3	150 E5
Holmfield Cl KBTN HD8	237 K1
PONT	155 G8
Holmfield Dr MAR/SLWT HD7	189 K7
RHAY LS8	80 B2
Holmfield Gv WKFDW/WTN WF2	10 B6
Holmfield La PONT WF8	155 C7
WKFDW/WTN WF2	10 B6
Holmfield Rd KBTN HD8	237 K1
Holmfield St BFD BD1	4 B4
Holmfirth Rd HOLM/MEL HD9	231 J2
HOLM/MEL HD9	233 K4
KBTN HD8	235 F5
Holmsley Av HEM/SK/SE WF9	241 G1
Holmsley Crest RTHW LS26	126 D4

Holmsley Field Ct RTHW LS26	127 F5
Holmsley Field La RTHW LS26	126 E5
Holmsley Garth RTHW LS26	126 E4
Holmsley Gv HEM/SK/SE WF9	241 G1
Holmsley La CUD/GR S72	240 E1
RTHW LS26	126 E5
Holmsley Mt HEM/SK/SE WF9	241 G1
Holmwood Av HDGY LS6	78 E3
Holmwood Cl HDGY LS6	79 F3
Holmwood Crs HDGY LS6	78 E4
Holmwood Dr HDGY LS6	78 E3
Holmwood Gv HDGY LS6	79 F3
Holmwood Mt HDGY LS6	79 F3
Holroyd Hl WBSY BD6	118 D2
Holroyd St CHAL LS7	7 F1
Holsworthy Rd BOW BD4	97 G8
The Holt SHPY BD18	73 J4
Holt Av MAR/SLWT HD7	56 C6
HUDN HD2	168 D8
Holtby Gv BRIG HD6	142 B4
Holt Cl BHP/TINH LS16	56 C7
Holt Crs BHP/TINH LS16	55 K6
Holtdale Ap BHP/TINH LS16	55 J6
Holtdale Av BHP/TINH LS16	55 K6
Holtdale Cl BHP/TINH LS16	55 K6
Holtdale Cft BHP/TINH LS16	55 K6
Holtdale Dr BHP/TINH LS16	55 K6
Holtdale Fold BHP/TINH LS16	55 K6
Holtdale Gdns BHP/TINH LS16	55 K6
Holtdale Garth BHP/TINH LS16	55 K6
Holtdale Gn BHP/TINH LS16	55 K6
Holtdale Gv BHP/TINH LS16	55 J6
Holtdale Lawn BHP/TINH LS16	55 K6
Holtdale Pl BHP/TINH LS16	55 K6
Holtdale Rd BHP/TINH LS16	55 K6
Holtdale Vw BHP/TINH LS16	55 K6
Holtdale Wy BHP/TINH LS16	55 K6
Holt Dr BHP/TINH LS16	56 A6
Holt Farm Cl BHP/TINH LS16	55 K6
Holt Farm Ri BHP/TINH LS16	55 K6
Holt Gdns BHP/TINH LS16	55 C6
IDLE BD10	74 B3
Holt Garth BHP/TINH LS16	56 A6
Holt Ga BHP/TINH LS16	56 A6
Holt La BHP/TINH LS16	56 A6
HOLM/MEL HD9	233 F5
Holt Park Ap BHP/TINH LS16	56 A6
Holt Park Av BHP/TINH LS16	56 A6
Holt Park Cl BHP/TINH LS16	56 A6
Holt Park Crs BHP/TINH LS16	56 A6
Holt Park Dr BHP/TINH LS16	56 A6
Holt Park Gdns BHP/TINH LS16	56 A6
Holt Park Ga BHP/TINH LS16	56 A6
Holt Park Grn BHP/TINH LS16	56 A6
Holt Park Gv BHP/TINH LS16	56 A6
Holt Park La BHP/TINH LS16	56 A6
Holt Park Ri BHP/TINH LS16	56 A6
Holt Park Rd BHP/TINH LS16	56 A6
Holt Park V BHP/TINH LS16	56 A6
Holt Park Wy BHP/TINH LS16	56 A6
Holt Ri BHP/TINH LS16	56 A6
Holt Rd BHP/TINH LS16	56 A6
Holts La CLAY BD14	94 B6
Holts Ter HIPP HX3	140 C7
Holt Vw BHP/TINH LS16	55 K6
Holt Wy BHP/TINH LS16	56 A6
Holybrook Av IDLE BD10	75 F5
Holycroft St KGHY BD21	2 C4
Holyoake Av BCLY BD16	71 K2
BTLY WF17	145 K6
Holyoake St TOD OL14	132 D2
Holyoake Ter HOR/CROF WF4	196 E2
MAR/SLWT HD7	211 G2
Holyrood Crs NORM WF6	151 J7
Holy Rood La GFTH/SHER LS25	131 F3
Holywell Ash La GIR BD8	4 B2
Holywell Gdns CAS WF10	154 A5
Holywell La AL/HA/HU LS17	59 F6
CAS WF10	154 C5
Holywell Mt CAS WF10	154 C5
Homefield Av MOR LS27	147 F1
Home Lea RTHW LS26	126 A4
Home Lea Dr RTHW LS26	126 A4
The Homestead HECK WF16	145 H7
Homestead Dr WKFDW/WTN WF2	175 G5
Home View Ter GIR BD8	95 H2
Honey Head La HOLM/MEL HD9	213 F8
Honey Hole Cl TOD OL14	134 A7
Honey Hole Rd TOD OL14	134 A7
Honey Pot La BAIL * BD17	51 H8
Honeysuckle Cl WKFDW/WTN WF2	175 F4
Honeysuckle Dr EARL WF12	172 C3
Honley Rd HUDS HD4	213 J5
Honley Sq HOR/CROF WF4	197 G2
Honoria St HUD HD1	12 C1
The Hoods BRIC HD6	168 A4
Hood St HEM/SK/SE WF9	242 A3
HUDS HD4	213 F3
Hooton Crs HOR/CROF WF4	222 E2
Hooton Rd BTLY DN5	243 H8
Hoowood La HOLM/MEL HD9	231 J8
Hopbine Av WBOW BD5	119 F1
Hopbine Rd WBOW BD5	119 F1
Hope Av SHPY BD18	73 K3
WBOW BD5	118 D3
Hopefield Cha EARD/LOFT WF3	125 J7
Hopefield Cl RTHW LS26	125 J7

Hopefield Ct *EARD/LOFT* WF3 ... 125 J7
  EARD/LOFT WF3 ... 148 D4
  HOLM/MEL HD9 ... 248 B4
Hopefield Crs *RTHW* LS26 ... 125 J7
Hopefield Dr *EARD/LOFT* WF3 ... 125 J7
Hopefield Gdns *EARD/LOFT* WF3 ... 125 J7
Hopefield Gn *RTHW* LS26 ... 125 J7
Hopefield Gv *EARD/LOFT* WF3 ... 125 J7
Hopefield Ms *EARD/LOFT* WF3 ... 125 J7
Hopefield Pl *RTHW* LS26 ... 125 J7
Hopefield Vw *RTHW* LS26 ... 125 J7
Hopefield Wk *RTHW* LS26 ... 125 J7
Hopefield Wy *BOW* BD4 ... 119 J2
  EARD/LOFT WF3 ... 125 J7
Hope Hall St *HFAX* HX1 ... 9 D5
Hope Hall Ter *HFAX* HX1 ... 9 D5
Hope La *BAIL* BD17 ... 51 H8
Hope Pl *KGHY* BD21 ... 2 C5
Hope Rd *LDSU* LS2 ... 7 F2
Hopes Farm Mt *RTHW* LS26 ... 125 G4
Hopes Farm Rd *RTHW* LS26 ... 125 G4
Hopes Farm Vw *RTHW* LS26 ... 125 G4
Hope St *CAS* WF10 ... 130 D8
  DEWS WF13 ... 172 B2
  HBR HX7 ... 112 B8
  HFAX HX1 ... 8 C4
  HUDW * HD3 ... 190 B6
  MOR LS27 ... 123 F7
  NORM WF6 ... 177 K3
  OSS WF5 ... 174 A7
  RPDN/SBR HX6 ... 139 F8
  WKFDE * WF1 ... 10 C2
Hope St East *CAS* * WF10 ... 153 J5
Hope St West *CAS* * WF10 ... 153 H4
Hope Vw *SHPY* BD18 ... 76 D6
Hopewell Pl *HDGY* * LS6 ... 6 A1
Hopewell Ter *GTL/SHER* LS25 ... 129 G2
Hopewell Vw *MID* LS10 ... 124 E6
Hopewell Wy *WOR/CROF* WF4 ... 198 A6
Hopkinson Dr *BOW* BD4 ... 119 K3
Hopkinson Rd *HUDN* HD2 ... 168 C7
Hopkinson Rd *LUD/ILL* HX2 ... 115 J7
Hopkin St *BOW* BD4 ... 120 B2
Hops La *HIPP* HX3 ... 139 G1
Hopton Av *BOW* BD4 ... 119 J2
  MIRF WF14 ... 193 G1
Hopton Dr *MIRF* WF14 ... 193 G1
Hopton Hall La *HUDE* HD5 ... 193 H5
Hopton La *MIRF* WF14 ... 193 G1
Hopton Ms *WOR/ARM* LS12 ... 100 B4
Hopton New Rd *MIRF* WF14 ... 170 D8
Hopwood Bank *HORS* LS18 ... 77 G1
Hopwood Gv *HORS* LS18 ... 77 G1
Hopwood Gv *CAS* WF10 ... 154 C4
Hopwood La *HORS* LS18 ... 77 G1
Horace Waller VC Pde *EARL* WF12 ... 173 F1
Horbury Ms *HOR/CROF* WF4 ... 197 F1
Horbury Rd *OSS* WF5 ... 173 K8
  WKFDW/WTN WF2 ... 10 A4
Horley Green La *HIPP* HX3 ... 9 F2
Horley Green Rd *HIPP* HX3 ... 9 E3
Hornbeam Av *WKFDW/WTN* WF2 ... 10 A1
Hornbeam Cl *WIL/AL* BD15 ... 71 K7
Hornbeam Wy *SCFT* LS14 ... 82 A3
Hornby St *HFAX* HX1 ... 8 A5
Hornby Ter *HFAX* * HX1 ... 8 A6
Horncastle St *CLECK* BD19 ... 144 B4
Horncastle Vw *HOR/CROF* WF4 ... 225 H2
Horn Cote La *KBTN* HD8 ... 234 C5
Horn Cft *DOD/DAR* S75 ... 238 E6
Horner Av *BTLY* WF17 ... 146 J5
Horner Crs *BTLY* WF17 ... 145 J5
Horne St *HFAX* HX1 ... 8 C4
  WKFDW/WTN WF2 ... 10 C5
Horn La *AIRE* BD20 ... 16 E6
  HOLM/MEL HD9 ... 234 C3
  STKB/PEN S36 ... 250 D2
Hornsea Dr *WIL/AL* BD15 ... 71 G7
Horse Bank Dr *HUDS* * HD4 ... 212 F1
Horse Croft La *KBTN* HD8 ... 215 K8
Horse Fair *PONT* WF8 ... 168 D1
Horsefair *WBY* LS22 ... 23 J6
Horsehold La *HBR* * HX7 ... 135 K1
Horsehold Rd *HBR* HX7 ... 135 K1
Horse Pond La *HUDW* HD3 ... 188 E4
Horsfall St *HFAX* HX1 ... 8 B6
  MOR LS27 ... 122 C5
  TOD OL14 ... 134 C8
Horsfall Vls *TOD* * OL14 ... 134 D5
Horsforth New Rd *BRAM* LS13 ... 76 C5
Horsham Ct *HWTH* BD22 ... 47 G6
Horsham Rd *BOW* * BD4 ... 120 B1
Horsley St *WBSY* BD6 ... 118 D2
Horsman St *BOW* BD4 ... 120 B2
Horton Cl *BRAM* LS13 ... 76 D7
Horton Garth *BRAM* * LS13 ... 76 D7
Horton Grange Rd *GTHN* BD7 ... 95 H5
Horton Hall Cl *WBOW* BD5 ... 4 B6
Horton Park Av *GTHN* BD7 ... 95 H6
Horton Ri *BRAM* LS13 ... 76 D7
Horton St *HECK* WF16 ... 145 G8
  HFAX HX1 ... 9 E5
  OSS WF5 ... 173 H5
Hospital La *BHP/TINH* LS16 ... 55 K8
Hospital Rd *AIRE* BD20 ... 21 G6
Hostingley La *EARL* WF12 ... 195 K2
Hothfield St *AIRE* BD20 ... 27 F2
Hough *HIPP* HX3 ... 141 F1

Hough End Av *BRAM* LS13 ... 99 H2
Hough End Cl *BRAM* * LS13 ... 99 H2
Hough End Ct *BRAM* LS13 ... 99 H2
Hough End Crs *BRAM* LS13 ... 99 G2
Hough End Gdns *BRAM* LS13 ... 99 G2
Hough End Garth *BRAM* LS13 ... 99 G2
Hough End La *BRAM* LS13 ... 99 G2
Hough Gv *BRAM* LS13 ... 99 G1
Hough La *BRAM* LS13 ... 99 G1
Houghley Av *WOR/ARM* LS12 ... 99 K1
Houghley Cl *BRAM* LS13 ... 99 J1
Houghley Crs *WOR/ARM* LS12 ... 99 K1
Houghley La *BRAM* LS13 ... 99 J1
Houghley Pl *WOR/ARM* LS12 ... 99 K1
Houghley Rd *WOR/ARM* LS12 ... 99 K1
Houghley Sq *WOR/ARM* LS12 ... 99 K1
Hough Side Cl *PDSY/CALV* LS28 ... 99 F4
Hough Side La *PDSY/CALV* LS28 ... 98 E4
Hough Side Rd *PDSY/CALV* LS28 ... 98 E4
Hough Ter *BRAM* LS13 ... 99 G1
Houghton Av *KNOT* WF11 ... 155 J7
Houghton Pl *BRIG* HD6 ... 4 B3
Houghton St *BRIG* HD6 ... 122 C8
Hough Top *BRAM* LS13 ... 98 E3
Hough Tree Rd *BRAM* LS13 ... 99 G3
Hoults La *GTL/HWG* HX4 ... 166 A3
Houndhill La *FEA/AMT* WF7 ... 180 A7
House Ct *KBTN* HD8 ... 237 F6
House Grove Dr *KBTN* HD8 ... 237 J1
Hovingham Av *RHAY* LS8 ... 80 C7
Hovingham Gv *RHAY* LS8 ... 80 C7
Hovingham Mt *RHAY* LS8 ... 80 C7
Hovingham Ter *RHAY* LS8 ... 80 C7
Howard Av *HUDW* HD3 ... 190 C3
  MSTN/BAR LS15 ... 103 H4
Howard Cr *MSTN/BAR* LS15 ... 103 H4
Howard Crs *HOR/CROF* WF4 ... 198 A5
Howard Dr *FEA/AMT* WF7 ... 203 F7
Howard Pl *BTLY* WF17 ... 146 B8
Howard Rd *HUDW* HD3 ... 190 C3
Howards Dean *HWTH* BD22 ... 69 F2
Howard St *BTLY* WF17 ... 146 B8
  HFAX HX1 ... 8 B3
  OSS * WF5 ... 173 J4
  WBOW * BD5 ... 4 B5
  WKFDE WF1 ... 18 D5
Howard Wy *HOLM/MEL* HD9 ... 231 J2
Howarth Av *ECHL* BD2 ... 74 C6
Howarth Crs *ECHL* * BD2 ... 74 C6
Howarth Cl *HUD4* ... 190 E8
Howarth Pl *CHAL* * LS7 ... 7 E2
Howbeck Dr *AIRE* BD20 ... 48 E3
Howbeck Rd *AIRE* BD20 ... 48 E3
Howcans La *HIPP* HX3 ... 115 K7
Howcroft Gdns *WKFDW/WTN* WF2 ... 199 G4
Howden Av *AIRE* BD20 ... 47 J1
Howdenbrook *HIPP* HX3 ... 117 J4
Howden Cl *BOW* BD4 ... 120 C1
  HUDS HD4 ... 211 K1
Howden Clough Rd *MOR* LS27 ... 122 B8
Howden Gdns *HDGY* LS6 ... 6 A1
Howden Pl *HDGY* LS6 ... 6 A1
Howden Rd *AIRE* BD20 ... 27 H2
Howden Wy *WKFDE* WF1 ... 11 E3
Howell La *CUD/GR* S72 ... 240 E5
Howes La *HIPP* HX3 ... 116 E8
Howgate *IDLE* BD10 ... 74 E3
Howgate Hl *HIPP* HX3 ... 140 E6
Howgate Rd *MAR/SLWT* HD7 ... 186 D8
Howitt *WBSY* BD6 ... 118 B5
Howley Mill La *BTLY* WF17 ... 146 C4
Howley Park Cl *MOR* LS27 ... 146 E1
Howley Park Rd *MOR* LS27 ... 146 E1
Howley Park Rd East *MOR* LS27 ... 146 E2
Howley St *BTLY* WF17 ... 146 C5
Howley Wk *BTLY* WF17 ... 146 D6
Howroyd La *EARL* WF12 ... 194 C4
  GTL/HWG HX4 ... 164 E7
Howroyd's Yd *OSS* WF5 ... 173 H2
Howson Cl *GSLY* LS20 ... 53 H3
Hoxton Mt *BEE/HOL* LS11 ... 101 F8
Hoxton St *GIR* BD8 ... 95 G3
Hoylake Av *HUDN* HD2 ... 168 A8
Hoyland Cl *STKB/PEN* S36 ... 251 G8
Hoyland Rd *WKFDW/WTN* WF2 ... 198 D6
Hoyle Court Av *BAIL* BD17 ... 52 A8
Hoyle Court Dr *BAIL* BD17 ... 52 A8
Hoyle Court Rd *BAIL* BD17 ... 52 A8
Hoyle Fold *HWTH* BD22 ... 2 A5
Hoyle House Fold *MAR/SLWT* HD7 ... 211 H2
Hoyle Ing *MAR/SLWT* HD7 ... 211 H1
Hoyle Ing Rd *CUL/QBY* BD13 ... 93 K5
Hoyle Mill Rd *HEM/SK/SE* WF9 ... 224 C2
Hoyle St *WHIT* OL12 ... 158 A8
Hubberton Green Rd
  RPDN/SBR HX6 ... 137 K8
Hubert St *BFDE* BD3 ... 5 F5
  HUDW HD3 ... 189 J2
  LUD/ILL * HX2 ... 139 G4
Huddersfield Rd *BRIG* HD6 ... 168 C1
  BTLY WF17 ... 145 H4
  DEWS WF13 ... 171 G6
  DEWS WF13 ... 171 K5
  DOD/DAR S75 ... 219 H6
  ELL HX5 ... 166 C2
  ELL HX5 ... 166 E4
  HIPP HX3 ... 140 B7
  HOLM/MEL HD9 ... 213 G6

HOLM/MEL HD9 ... 231
HOLM/MEL HD9 ... 233
HOLM/MEL HD9 ... 233
HOR/CROF WF4 ... 219
HUDW HD3 ... 167
KBTN HD8 ... 216
LM/WK BD12 ... 142
MIRF WF14 ... 170
MIRF WF14 ... 170
STKB/PEN S36 ... 251
UPML OL3 ... 207
Huddleston Ct *EARL* WF12 ... 172
Hud Hl *HIPP* HX3 ... 117
Hudroyd *HUDE* HD5 ... 192
The Hudson *LM/WK* BD12 ... 118
Hudson Av *GTHN* BD7 ... 95
  HOR/CROF WF4 ... 221
Hudson Cl *GTHN* BD7 ... 95
  WBY LS22 ... 23
Hudson Crs *GTHN* BD7 ... 95
Hudson Gdns *GTHN* BD7 ... 95
Hudson Gv *OSM* LS9 ... 102
  Hudson Ms *BSPA/BRAM* LS23 ... 42
Hudson Mill Rd *HBR* HX7 ... 111
Hudson Pl *OSM* * LS9 ... 102
Hudson Rd *OSM* LS9 ... 102
Hudson St *BFDE* BD3 ... 97
  OSM LS9 ... 102
  PDSY/CALV * LS28 ... 98
  TOD OL14 ... 133
Hudswell Rd *MID* LS10 ... 101
Hudswell St *WKFDE* WF1 ... 11
Hughenden Vw *MOR* * LS27 ... 123
Hughendon Dr *CUL/QBY* BD13 ... 94
Hughendon Wk *CUL/QBY* BD13 ... 93
Hugh St *CAS* WF10 ... 153
Hugill St *CUL/QBY* BD13 ... 93
Hulbert Cft *HUDE* HD5 ... 192
Hulbert St *BGLY* BD16 ... 72
Hullenedge Gdns *ELL* HX5 ... 166
Hullenedge La *GTL/HWG* HX4 ... 166
Hullenedge Rd *ELL* HX5 ... 166
Hullen Rd *ELL* HX5 ... 166
Hullett Cl *HBR* HX7 ... 137
Hullett Dr *HBR* HX7 ... 137
Hull St *MOR* LS27 ... 123
Hulme Sq *CAS* WF10 ... 154
Humber Cl *MAR/SLWT* HD7 ... 211
Humboldt St *BFDE* BD3 ... 5
Hume Crest *BTLY* WF17 ... 146
Humley Rd *WKFDW/WTN* WF2 ... 198
Hundhill La *PONT* WF8 ... 203
Hungate La *RTHW* LS26 ... 151
Hungerford Rd *HUDW* HD3 ... 190
Hunger Hl *HFAX* HX1 ... 9
  ILK LS29 ... 20
  MOR LS27 ... 123
Hunger Hills Av *HORS* LS18 ... 78
Hunger Hills Dr *HORS* LS18 ... 76
Hunslet Green Wy *MID* LS10 ... 101
Hunslet Hall Rd *BEE/HOL* LS11 ... 101
Hunslet La *MID* LS10 ... 7
Hunslet Rd *MID* LS10 ... 7
Hunston Av *HUDW* HD3 ... 190
Hunsworth La *BIRK/DRI* BD11 ... 140
  CLECK BD19 ... 144
Hunter Hill Rd *LUD/ILL* HX2 ... 114
Huntercombe Ct *BGLY* BD16 ... 50
Hunters Ct *HTON* BD9 ... 73
Hunters Gn *CUL/QBY* BD13 ... 70
Hunters La *TOD* OL14 ... 133
Hunters Meadow *AIRE* BD20 ... 27
Hunters Park Av *CLAY* BD14 ... 94
Hunters Wk *WBY* LS22 ... 23
Huntingdon Av *HUDN* HD2 ... 169
Huntingdon Rd *BRIG* HD6 ... 168
Huntock Pl *BRIG* HD6 ... 142
Huntsman Cl *BGLY* BD16 ... 50
Huntsman Fold *WKFDW/WTN* WF2 ... 174
  HUDS HD4 ... 212
  KGHY BD21 ... 2
Huntsmans Wy *HEM/SK/SE* WF9 ... 226
Hunt St *CAS* WF10 ... 153
  CAS WF10 ... 153
Huntwick Av *FEA/AMT* WF7 ... 179
Huntwick Crs *FEA/AMT* WF7 ... 179
Huntwick Dr *FEA/AMT* WF7 ... 179
Huntwick La *FEA/AMT* WF7 ... 178
Huntwick Rd *FEA/AMT* WF7 ... 179
Hurst Knowle *HUDE* HD5 ... 192
Hurst La *MIRF* WF14 ... 170
Hurst Rd *HBR* HX7 ... 112
Hurstville Av *BIRK/DRI* BD11 ... 120
Hurstwood *HUDN* HD2 ... 169
Husler Gv *CHAL* LS7 ... 79
Husler Pl *CHAL* LS7 ... 79
The Hustings *LVSG* * WF15 ... 144
Hustlergate *BFD* BD1 ... 4
Hustlers Rw *HDGY* LS6 ... 78
Hustler St *BFDE* BD3 ... 5
Hutchinson's Pl *KSTL* LS5 ... 78
Hutson St *WBOW* BD5 ... 5
Hutton Dr *HECK* WF16 ... 145
  HEM/SK/SE WF9 ... 226
Hutton Rd *WBOW* BD5 ... 118
Hutton Ter *IDLE* BD10 ... 75
  PDSY/CALV LS28 ... 98
Hydale Cl *KGHY* BD21 ... 3
Hydale Ct *LM/WK* BD12 ... 118

de Gv KGHY BD21 .... 3 E2
de Pk HFAX HX1 .... 8 B5
 WKFDE WF1 .... 11 E3
de Park Cl HDGY LS6 .... 6 B1
de Park Cnr HDGY LS6 .... 79 F8
de Park Rd HDGY LS6 .... 6 B1
 HFAX HX1 .... 8 B6
de Park St HFAX HX1 .... 8 B5
de Park Ter HDGY LS6 .... 79 F8
de St LDSU LS2 .... 6 C2
de St IDLE BD10 .... 74 D2
 LDSU LS2 .... 6 C2
de Ter LDSU LS2 .... 6 C2
dro Cl ILK LS29 .... 21 F8
ne Av BOW BD4 .... 119 K2
rst Garth BTLY WF17 .... 172 A1
rstlands Rd BTLY WF17 .... 146 A8
rst Wk BTLY WF17 .... 146 B8

I

etson Cl MOR LS27 .... 123 F4
etson Ct MOR LS27 .... 123 F4
etson Cft MOR LS27 .... 123 F4
etson Dr MOR LS27 .... 123 F4
etson Gv MOR LS27 .... 123 F4
etson Ri MOR LS27 .... 123 F4
etson Rd MOR LS27 .... 123 F4
otroyd Av TOD OL14 .... 133 K4
ootson Flats HUD * HD1 .... 13 D3
ottson St WKFDE WF1 .... 11 F6
st MID LS10 .... 125 H1
WBOW BD5 .... 95 J8
esleigh St BOW BD4 .... 96 E5
ecroft Rd IDLE BD10 .... 74 D3
e Rd ECHL BD2 .... 74 C6
ethorp Wy IDLE BD10 .... 74 E4
ert Av BOW BD4 .... 119 K2
ord St MOR LS27 .... 123 G7
ey Hall Ms ILK LS29 .... 20 B8
ey Hall Pk ILK LS29 .... 20 B8
ey Rd AIRE BD20 .... 48 D1
LK LS29 .... 19 F4
LK LS29 .... 21 K8
OT LS21 .... 33 C4
ngworth Av LUD/ILL HX2 .... 115 H4
NORM WF6 .... 151 H7
YEA LS19 .... 54 A6
ngworth Crs LUD/ILL HX2 .... 115 H4
ngworth Ct LUD/ILL HX2 .... 115 H4
ngworth Gdns LUD/ILL HX2 .... 115 H5
ngworth Gv LUD/ILL HX2 .... 115 H4
LUD/ILL HX2 .... 115 H4
ngworth St OSS WF5 .... 173 J6
ngworth Wy LUD/ILL HX2 .... 115 H4
perial Ar WKFDW/WTN WF2 .... 175 C1
perial Rd HUDW HD3 .... 12 A3
chfield Rd TOD OL14 .... 159 K3
dependent St WBOW BD5 .... 95 J8
tus Cl HECK WF16 .... 145 H7
ustrial Av BTLY * WF17 .... 145 G2
ustrial Rd RPDN/SBR HX6 .... 138 E7
ustrial St BGLY BD16 .... 49 K8
BRIG HD6 .... 142 C8
CLCK BD19 .... 143 G3
HOR/CROF WF4 .... 197 J3
HUDS HD5 .... 191 G8
LVSG WF15 .... 144 B7
TOD LS9 .... 102 B2
TOD OL14 .... 134 A6
ustrial Ter HFAX HX1 .... 8 C6
HUDE HD5 .... 192 C6
dustry St TOD OL14 .... 159 K2
irmary St TOD OL14 .... 159 J2
irmary St BFD BD1 .... 4 B4
LDS LS1 .... 7 D3
gbirchworth La STKB/PEN S36 .... 251 H4
gbirchworth Rd STKB/PEN S36 .... 251 K7
gdale Dr HOLM/MEL HD9 .... 233 H5
field Av HUDE HD5 .... 192 C6
g Fld LM/WK BD12 .... 119 H7
OSS WF5 .... 173 K5
jham Cl LUD/ILL HX2 .... 115 J3
jham Cft MIRF WF14 .... 171 F7
jham Garth MIRF WF14 .... 171 F6
jham La LUD/ILL HX2 .... 115 H2
jham Rd EARL WF12 .... 172 C8
jham's Av PDSY/CALV LS28 .... 97 K3
jhams Ct HIPP * HX3 .... 8 B2
jhams Ter PDSY/CALV LS28 .... 97 K3
jham St MID LS10 .... 7 F6
jham's Vw PDSY/CALV LS28 .... 97 K3
Head MAR/SLWT HD7 .... 210 C2
head Gdns HIPP HX3 .... 117 C7
Head La HUDS HD4 .... 234 C1
a La HUDS HD4 .... 213 G1
le Av HUDS HD4 .... 192 C6
jleborough Cl BOW BD4 .... 97 G8
jleborough Dr MOR LS27 .... 123 H8
leby Pl GTHN WF9 .... 95 G5
leby Rd GIR BD8 .... 95 G4
leby St GIR BD8 .... 95 G4
leby Wy MID LS10 .... 125 F4

Ingle Ct KBTN HD8 .... 193 F7
 MOR LS27 .... 122 E5
Ingle Crs BEE/HOL LS11 .... 123 F6
Ingledew Ct AL/HA/HU LS17 .... 57 K7
Ingledew Crs RHAY LS8 .... 80 D1
Ingledew Dr RHAY LS8 .... 80 D2
Ingle Gv MOR LS27 .... 122 E6
Ingle Rw CHAL LS7 .... 79 J5
Ingleton Cl BEE/HOL LS11 .... 101 H8
Ingleton Dr MSTN/BAR LS15 .... 103 G4
Ingleton Gv BEE/HOL LS11 .... 101 H8
Ingleton Pl BEE/HOL LS11 .... 101 H8
Ingleton Rd HUDS HD4 .... 213 H1
Ingleton St BEE/HOL LS11 .... 101 H8
Inglewood Av HUDW HD3 .... 190 C2
Inglewood Dr OT LS21 .... 33 H4
 SCFT LS14 .... 81 K8
Inglewood Pl SCFT LS14 .... 81 K8
Inglewood Ter HDGY LS6 .... 79 G7
Ingram Cl BEE/HOL LS11 .... 6 B6
Ingram Ct BEE/HOL LS11 .... 6 B6
Ingram Crs BEE/HOL LS11 .... 101 F7
 KNOT WF11 .... 156 A8
Ingram Gdns BEE/HOL LS11 .... 6 B6
Ingram Pde RTHW LS26 .... 126 B6
Ingram Rd BEE/HOL LS11 .... 101 F7
Ingram Row HFAX * HX1 .... 7 D5
Ingram Sq HFAX * HX1 .... 8 B6
Ingram St BEE/HOL LS11 .... 7 D5
 HFAX HX1 .... 8 B6
 KGHY BD21 .... 47 K3
Ingram Vw BEE/HOL LS11 .... 6 B6
Ingrow La HWTH BD22 .... 2 A6
The Ings BRIG HD6 .... 142 B5
 KBTN HD8 .... 237 K1
Ings Av GSLY LS20 .... 53 F1
Ings Cl HEM/SK/SE WF9 .... 225 K8
 HOR/CROF WF4 .... 223 G2
Ings Ct GSLY LS20 .... 52 E1
Ings Crs EARL WF12 .... 195 C1
 GSLY LS20 .... 52 E2
 LVSG WF15 .... 144 E2
 OSM LS9 .... 102 D4
Ings Dr RTHW LS26 .... 128 D8
Ings Holt HEM/SK/SE WF9 .... 225 K8
Ings La BSPA/BRAM LS23 .... 43 G3
 CAS WF10 .... 129 K8
 CAS WF10 .... 154 A2
 EARL WF12 .... 195 C1
 GLE DN14 .... 157 K4
 GSLY LS20 .... 52 E1
 MAR/SLWT HD7 .... 209 J7
Ings Mere Ct KNOT WF11 .... 131 H7
Ings Mill Av KBTN HD8 .... 217 K8
Ings Mill Dr KBTN HD8 .... 237 K1
Ings Rd AIRE BD20 .... 26 D4
 BTLY WF17 .... 146 A5
 EARL WF12 .... 172 C2
 HECK WF16 .... 145 G7
 HEM/SK/SE WF9 .... 224 B2
 HUDE HD5 .... 192 C7
 LVSG WF15 .... 144 E6
 OSM LS9 .... 102 D4
 WKFDW/WTN WF2 .... 10 B3
Ings St BFDE BD3 .... 97 F5
Ings Vw CAS WF10 .... 154 C3
Ings Vil LVSG WF15 .... 171 F1
Ings Wk HEM/SK/SE WF9 .... 225 K8
Ings La AIRE BD20 .... 27 H3
 GIR BD8 .... 94 E3
 KBTN HD8 .... 193 H8
 STKB/PEN S36 .... 251 F6
Ingswell Av HOR/CROF WF4 .... 221 H4
Ingswell Dr HOR/CROF WF4 .... 221 H4
Ingwell Ct WKFDE WF1 .... 11 D3
Ingwell St WKFDE WF1 .... 11 D3
Ingwell Ter CLECK BD19 .... 144 B4
Inholmes La TAD LS24 .... 25 J7
Inkerman Ct KBTN HD8 .... 236 E6
Inkerman St BOW BD4 .... 97 F7
 ECHL BD2 .... 75 F7
Inkerman Wy KBTN HD8 .... 236 D6
Inkersley Rd BFD BD1 .... 4 C3
Inner Hey MAR/SLWT HD7 .... 209 J7
The Innings IDLE BD10 .... 74 C3
Institute Rd ECHL BD2 .... 74 E6
The Intake GFTH/SHER LS25 .... 129 C2
Intake MAR/SLWT HD7 .... 180 J6
Intake Cl EARD/LOFT WF3 .... 150 C6
Intake Gv ECHL BD2 .... 96 E1
Intake La AIRE BD20 .... 26 D8
 BRAM LS13 .... 76 D3
 BTLY WF17 .... 145 J3
 EARD/LOFT WF3 .... 150 C6
 HOLM/MEL HD9 .... 210 D7
 HOR/CROF WF4 .... 219 K4
 HUDS HD4 .... 211 K4
 KNOT WF11 .... 157 K2
 MID LS10 .... 124 D8
 OSS WF5 .... 173 K6
 SCFT LS14 .... 60 B8
 YEA LS19 .... 54 B8
Intake Mt MID LS10 .... 124 D7
Intake Rd ECHL BD2 .... 96 E1
 MAR/SLWT HD7 .... 210 A1
 PDSY/CALV LS28 .... 98 E3
Intake Sq MID LS10 .... 124 D8

Intake Vw MID LS10 .... 124 D8
Intercity Wy PDSY/CALV LS28 .... 98 E2
Intermezzo Dr MID LS10 .... 125 J2
Invargarry Cl GFTH/SHER LS25 .... 106 B3
Inverness Rd GFTH/SHER LS25 .... 106 B4
Invertrees Av YEA LS19 .... 54 A7
Iona Pl HIPP HX3 .... 8 C1
Iona St HIPP HX3 .... 8 C2
Iqbal Ct BFDE * BD3 .... 97 F5
Ireland Crs BHP/TINH LS16 .... 55 K8
Ireland St BGLY BD16 .... 49 J8
Ireland Ter BGLY BD16 .... 49 J8
Ireton St GTHN BD7 .... 95 H5
Iron Rw ILK LS29 .... 32 B2
Iron St CLECK BD19 .... 143 K4
Ironwood Ap SCFT LS14 .... 81 J8
Ironwood Crs SCFT LS14 .... 81 J8
Ironwood Vw SCFT LS14 .... 81 J7
Irving St HFAX HX1 .... 8 A6
Irving Ter CLAY BD14 .... 94 C8
Irwell St BOW BD4 .... 5 E6
Irwin Ap MSTN/BAR LS15 .... 105 H4
Irwin Av WKFDE WF1 .... 11 E2
Irwin Crs WKFDE WF1 .... 11 E2
Irwin St PDSY/CALV LS28 .... 98 B1
Isaac St GIR BD8 .... 95 H3
The Island HOR/CROF * WF4 .... 196 E3
Island Dr HOLM/MEL HD9 .... 233 J1
Islay Cl RTHW LS26 .... 126 D6
Isles St GIR BD8 .... 95 F3
Ivanhoe Rd GTHN BD7 .... 95 H6
Ivegate BFD BD1 .... 4 C4
 YEA LS19 .... 53 K5
Ive House La LUD/ILL HX2 .... 138 E5
Iver Wy SHPY BD18 .... 73 G4
Iveson Ap BHP/TINH LS16 .... 77 K1
Iveson Cl BHP/TINH LS16 .... 77 K1
Iveson Ct BHP/TINH LS16 .... 77 K1
Iveson Crs BHP/TINH LS16 .... 77 K1
Iveson Dr BHP/TINH LS16 .... 77 K1
Iveson Gdns BHP/TINH LS16 .... 77 K1
Iveson Garth BHP/TINH LS16 .... 78 A1
Iveson Gn BHP/TINH LS16 .... 77 K1
Iveson Gv BHP/TINH LS16 .... 77 K1
Iveson Lawn BHP/TINH LS16 .... 78 A1
Iveson Ri BHP/TINH LS16 .... 78 A1
Iveson Rd BHP/TINH LS16 .... 77 K1
Ives St BAIL BD17 .... 73 H3
Ivory St BEE/HOL LS11 .... 7 E6
Ivy Av OSM LS9 .... 102 D3
Ivy Bank La HWTH BD22 .... 68 E5
Ivy Cha BRAM LS13 .... 99 F4
Ivy Cl HEM/SK/SE WF9 .... 242 B2
 WKFDE WF1 .... 11 E1
Ivy Crs HIPP HX3 .... 141 K4
 OSM LS9 .... 102 C3
Ivy Gdns BRAM LS13 .... 77 H7
 CAS WF10 .... 154 E6
Ivy Garth CHAL LS7 .... 79 K5
Ivy Gv OSM LS9 .... 102 D3
 SHPY BD18 .... 72 E4
 WKFDE WF1 .... 11 E1
Ivy House Rd WBOW BD5 .... 119 F2
Ivy La BSPA/BRAM LS23 .... 42 C5
 LUD/ILL HX2 .... 115 G5
 WIL/AL BD15 .... 94 A2
 WKFDE WF1 .... 11 E1
Ivy Mt MAR/SLWT HD7 .... 210 D2
 OSM LS9 .... 102 C3
Ivy Pl BRAM LS13 .... 77 H7
Ivy Rd KGHY BD21 .... 3 F4
 OSM LS9 .... 102 C4
 SHPY BD18 .... 72 E4
Ivy St BRIG HD6 .... 142 A8
 FEA/AMT WF7 .... 179 J5
 HFAX HX1 .... 8 B6
 HUD HD1 .... 13 E5
 HUDS HD4 .... 190 C7
 KGHY BD21 .... 2 C2
 OSM LS9 .... 102 C3
Ivy Ter BRIG HD6 .... 142 A8
 HEM/SK/SE WF9 .... 226 B8
 HIPP HX3 .... 141 K4
 KGHY BD21 .... 48 D5
Ivy Vw OSM LS9 .... 102 C3

J

Jacana Wy CUL/QBY BD13 .... 117 H2
Jacinth Ct HUDN HD2 .... 191 J1
Jack Br HBR HX7 .... 111 F6
Jack Close Orch BSLYN/ROY S71 .... 222 A7
Jackdaw La BSPA/BRAM LS23 .... 42 C3
Jack Hl HUDN HD2 .... 12 C1
Jackie Smart Ct CHAL LS7 .... 80 A8
Jackie Smart Rd WBOW BD5 .... 96 A7
Jack La BEE/HOL LS11 .... 7 D6
 DEWS WF13 .... 172 C1
Jackman Dr HORS LS18 .... 77 H4
Jackroyd La HUDS HD4 .... 213 G1
 MIRF WF14 .... 193 G1
Jackson Av RHAY LS8 .... 80 B4
Jackson Hill La CUL/QBY BD13 .... 116 E4
Jackson La GTL/HWG HX4 .... 164 D6
Jackson Mdw GTL/HWG HX4 .... 164 D6
Jackson Rd CHAL LS7 .... 79 J8
Jackson's La AIRE BD20 .... 16 A6

EARL WF12 ....194 E1
PONT WF8 ....205 G4
Jackson St BFDE BD3 ....5 E5
Jacky La HWTH BD22 ....68 E5
Jacobs Hall Ct DOD/DAR * S75 ....239 J3
Jacob's Rw HUDS HD4 ....191 F8
Jacob St LDSU LS2 ....7 E2
WBOW BD5 ....95 K1
Jacob's Well La WKFDE WF1 ....11 D2
Jacques Gv AIRE BD20 ....27 H2
Jaggar La HOLM/MEL HD9 ....
Jagger Green La HUDW HD3 ....189 F1
Jagger La HUDE HD5 ....192 C3
KBTN HD8 ....216 C8
Jail Rd BTLY WF17 ....145 J6
Jakeman Cl EARD/LOFT WF3 ....147 K3
Jakeman Ct EARD/LOFT WF3 ....147 K3
Jakeman Dr EARD/LOFT WF3 ....147 K3
James Av HUDS HD4 ....26 C6
RHAY LS8 ....80 B3
James Ct WBY LS22 ....41 F3
James Duggan Av FEA/AMT WF7 ....179 H5
James Ga BFD * BD1 ....5 J5
James Gibbs Cl FEA/AMT * WF7 ....179 J5
James La HUDS HD4 ....212 A5
James Mason Ct HUDW HD3 ....190 D4
James St BFD BD1 ....4 C4
BIRK/DRI * BD11 ....120 D5
BRIG HD6 ....142 B7
BTLY WF17 ....146 A7
CAS WF10 ....153 J2
CUD/GR S72 ....223 K6
CUL/QBY BD13 ....93 H4
DEWS WF13 ....172 A2
ELL HX5 ....167 F5
GTL/HWG HX4 ....166 A3
HWTH BD22 ....68 D1
LVSG WF15 ....144 E8
MAR/SLWT HD7 ....189 H7
MAR/SLWT HD7 ....210 E2
MIRF WF14 ....170 D4
WIL/AL BD15 ....94 C2
YEA LS19 ....53 K7
Jamie Cl IDLE BD10 ....75 F5
Jane St CUL/QBY BD13 ....93 H4
SHPY BD18 ....73 F3
WHIT OL12 ....158 B5
Janesway GFTH/SHER LS25 ....128 E1
Janet St WBY LS22 ....69 G3
Jardine La FEA/AMT WF7 ....179 J5
Jardine Rd BGLY BD16 ....50 A8
Jarratt St GIR BD8 ....95 H2
Jarratt St East GIR BD8 ....95 H2
Jarrom Cl BOW BD4 ....97 F7
Jarvis Wk EARD/LOFT WF3 ....125 H8
Jarvis Wk EARD/LOFT WF3 ....125 H8
Jasmin Ter GIR BD8 ....A3
Jason Ter BTLY * WF17 ....145 K1
Jasper St HFAX HX1 ....8 A4
IDLE BD10 ....74 D3
Javelin La IDLE BD10 ....74 D5
Jay House La BRIG HD6 ....142 E6
Jay St HWTH BD22 ....69 F5
Jean Av MSTN/BAR LS15 ....103 J4
Jebb La DOD/DAR S75 ....219 F7
Jenkin Dr HOR/CROF WF4 ....197 F2
Jenkin La HOR/CROF WF4 ....197 F2
Jenkin Rd HOR/CROF WF4 ....197 F2
Jenkinson Cl BEE/HOL LS11 ....6 C6
Jenkinson Lawn BEE/HOL LS11 ....6 C6
Jenkinsons Pl MID LS10 ....124 E3
Jenkyn La KBTN HD8 ....235 F5
Jennetts Crs OT LS21 ....33 H4
Jennings Cl AIRE BD20 ....27 G3
Jennings Pl GTHN BD7 ....95 G7
Jennings St GTHN BD7 ....95 G7
Jenny La BAIL BD17 ....51 K7
MIRF WF14 ....170 E4
Jensen Av DEWS WF13 ....145 J8
Jepson La ELL HX5 ....166 E5
Jeremy La HECK WF16 ....145 G7
Jer Gv WBSY BD6 ....117 K1
Jer La WBSY BD6 ....117 K1
Jermyn St BFDE BD3 ....5 D4
Jerry Clay Dr WKFDW/WTN WF2 ....175 F1
Jerry Clay La WKFDW/WTN WF2 ....148 E8
Jerry Fields Rd LUD/ILL HX2 ....138 A5
Jerry La AIRE BD20 ....28 D2
RPDN/SBR HX6 ....138 D8
Jersey Cl EARL WF12 ....172 E1
Jerusalem La LUD/ILL HX2 ....114 A7
Jerusalem Rd MAR/SLWT HD7 ....211 F4
Jervaulx Cl BSPA/BRAM LS23 ....42 C4
Jervaulx Crs GIR BD8 ....4 A3
Jerwood Hill Cl HIPP HX3 ....9 E2
Jerwood Hill Rd HIPP HX3 ....9 E2
Jesmond Av BSLYN/ROY S71 ....221 K8
HTON BD9 ....95 F1
Jesmond Gv DEWS WF13 ....172 A2
HTON BD9 ....95 F1
Jessamine Av BEE/HOL LS11 ....124 A2
Jessamine St DEWS WF13 ....171 G6
Jesse St GIR BD8 ....94 A4
WBOW BD5 ....4 C6
Jessop Av HUDE HD5 ....192 C8

Jessop Fold HOLM/MEL HD9 ....213 F6
Jessop St CAS WF10 ....153 J3
Jewitt La WBY LS22 ....41 G4
Jew La HWTH BD22 ....90 E1
Jill La MIRF WF14 ....171 F4
Jilley Royd La HUDN HD2 ....168 B7
Jim Allen La LUD/ILL HX2 ....137 K2
Jim La HUD HD1 ....190 D5
Jinnah Ct GIR * BD8 ....4 B3
Jinny Moor La RTHW LS26 ....127 H3
Jin-Whin Hl CAS WF10 ....152 E3
Joan Royd HECK WF16 ....145 G5
Joba Av BFDE BD3 ....5 F4
Joffre Av CAS WF10 ....153 K5
John Carr Av HOR/CROF WF4 ....197 G1
John Charles Wy WOR/ARM LS12 ....100 D7
John Eastwood Homes TOD * OL14 ....159 K2
John Escritt Rd BGLY BD16 ....72 A1
John Haigh Rd MAR/SLWT HD7 ....210 E3
John Naylor La LUD/ILL HX2 ....138 B6
John Nelson Cl BTLY * WF17 ....145 J2
Johnny La OT LS21 ....33 J5
John O'Gaunts Wk RTHW LS26 ....126 C5
John Ormsby Vc Wy EARL WF12 ....147 F8
Johns Av EARD/LOFT WF3 ....149 K5
John's Crs WKFDW/WTN WF2 ....175 F1
Johns Cl ELL HX5 ....166 E2
Johnson St BFDE BD3 ....97 F4
BGLY BD16 ....49 K8
MIRF WF14 ....170 C8
Johnson Ter MOR LS27 ....123 G7
Johnston St HDGY LS6 ....79 H8
WKFDE * WF1 ....11 D4
John St BFD BD1 ....4 C4
BOW BD4 ....120 B2
BRIG HD6 ....142 B8
BTLY WF17 ....145 H2
CAS WF10 ....153 H5
CLAY BD14 ....94 C7
CUL/QBY BD13 ....92 B3
CUL/QBY BD13 ....93 H5
DEWS WF13 ....171 H6
DEWS WF13 ....172 B1
ELL HX5 ....166 E5
GTL/HWG HX4 ....166 B3
HDGY LS6 ....8 E2
HECK * WF16 ....145 G8
HEM/SK/SE WF9 ....242 B1
HFAX HX1 ....9 D4
HUDS HD4 ....190 B7
HWTH BD22 ....69 F1
SHPY BD18 ....73 G3
WKFDE * WF1 ....11 D4
YEA LS19 ....53 K7
John St West RPDN/SBR HX6 ....138 E7
John William St CLECK BD19 ....144 B1
ELL HX5 ....166 E5
HUD HD1 ....12 C5
LVSG WF15 ....145 F7
Jonathan Garth ILK * LS29 ....18 C3
Jons Av HEM/SK/SE WF9 ....241 G1
Joseph Av HIPP HX3 ....141 F1
Josephine Rd HUDS HD4 ....190 A8
Joseph St BFD BD1 ....5 E4
BOW BD4 ....120 B2
CUD/GR S72 ....240 A5
MID LS10 ....102 A7
Josephs Well LDS * LS1 ....6 C3
Joshua St TOD OL14 ....134 A5
Jos La KBTN HD8 ....235 G3
Jos Wy KBTN HD8 ....235 G2
Jowett House La DOD/DAR S75 ....238 B7
Jowett Park Crs IDLE BD10 ....74 C1
Jowett's La AIRE BD20 ....17 F3
Jowett St BFD BD1 ....4 A4
Jubilee Av KBTN HD8 ....235 J1
NORM WF6 ....177 K3
WKFDE WF1 ....149 K7
Jubilee Crs SHPY * BD18 ....73 J3
Jubilee Dr HOR/CROF WF4 ....178 A8
WKFDE WF1 ....149 K7
Jubilee Gdns BSLYN/ROY S71 ....222 B7
Jubilee La HUDS HD4 ....189 K8
Jubilee Pl MOR LS27 ....123 G7
Jubilee Rd HIPP HX3 ....166 C1
HOR/CROF WF4 ....178 A8
Jubilee St HBR HX7 ....137 F2
HIPP HX3 ....9 E5
MOR LS27 ....198 B8
Jubilee St North HIPP HX3 ....115 K7
Jubilee Ter HIPP * HX3 ....9 E5
MOR LS27 ....123 G7
RPDN/SBR HX6 ....164 B5
Jubilee Trees ILK LS29 ....31 J4
Jubilee Wy PONT WF8 ....180 C5
SHPY BD18 ....73 K3
Judy Haigh La EARL WF12 ....195 H3
Judy La HUDN HD2 ....168 C8
Julian Dr CUL/QBY BD13 ....117 H1
Julian St HUDE * HD5 ....192 A6
Julie Av HOR/CROF WF4 ....198 A6
Jumb Beck Cl ILK LS29 ....32 B3
Jumble Dyke BRIG HD6 ....168 A3
Jumble Hole Rd TOD OL14 ....135 G1
Jumbles Ct EARD/LOFT WF3 ....149 K2

Jumbles La EARD/LOFT WF3 149
Jumble Wd KBTN HD8 193
Jumples LUD/ILL HX2 115
Jumples Cl LUD/ILL HX2 115
Jumps La HBR HX7 136
TOD OL14 133
Junction La OSS WF5 174
Junction Rd BAIL BD17 73
DEWS WF13 7
Junction St MID LS10 7
June St KGHY BD21 3
Juniper Av RTHW LS26 127
Juniper Cl GIR * BD8 4
Juniper Gv HUDS HD4 212
Juniper Pl OSM LS9 102
Justin Wy HUDS HD4 212

K

Kaffir Rd HUDW HD3 190
Karnac Rd RHAY LS8 80
Karon Dr HOR/CROF WF4 197
Katherine St SHPY BD18 73
Katrina Gv FEA/AMT WF7 179
Kaycell St BOW BD4 119
Kay Cl MOR LS27 122
Kaye La HUDE HD5 213
Kaye St EARL WF12 172
HECK WF16 145
Kay St HTON BD9 73
WKFDE WF1 11
Kearby Cliff WBY LS22 39
Keats Av TOD OL14 134
Keats Cl PONT WF8 180
Keats Dr HECK WF16 171
Keats Gv EARD/LOFT WF3 150
STKB/PEN S36 252
Keat St HUDS HD4 ....
Kebble Ct CLECK BD19 144
Keble Garth GFTH/SHER LS25 129
Kebroyd La RPDN/SBR HX6 164
Kebroyd Mt RPDN/SBR HX6 164
Kebs Rd HBR HX7 110
Kedleston Rd RHAY LS8 58
Keeldar Cl GTHN BD7 95
Keelham Dr YEA LS19 54
Keelham La AIRE BD20 47
TOD OL14 134
Keel Moorings BRAM LS13 76
Keenan Av HEM/SK/SE WF9 202
Keeper La BOW BD4 98
HOR/CROF WF4 221
Keeton St OSM LS9 102
Keighley Cl LUD/ILL HX2 115
Keighley Dr LUD/ILL HX2 115
Keighley Pl PDSY/CALV LS28 98
Keighley Rd AIRE BD20 27
BGLY BD16 48
BGLY BD16 49
CUL/QBY BD13 70
CUL/QBY BD13 70
HBR HX7 112
HBR HX7 112
HTON BD9 73
HWTH BD22 47
HWTH BD22 68
ILK LS29 29
LUD/ILL HX2 115
Keir Hardy Cl LVSG * WF15 144
Kelburn Gv HWTH BD22 46
Kelcliffe Av GSLY LS20 53
Kelcliffe La GSLY LS20 53
Keldholme Cl BRAM LS13 76
Keldholme Rd BRAM * LS13 76
Keldregate HUDN HD2 169
Kell Beck OT LS21 33
Kellett Av WOR/ARM LS12 100
Kellett Crs WOR/ARM LS12 100
Kellett Dr WOR/ARM LS12 100
Kellett Gv WOR/ARM LS12 100
Kellett La WOR/ARM LS12 100
Kellett Mt WOR/ARM * LS12 100
Kellett Pl WOR/ARM LS12 100
Kellett Rd WOR/ARM LS12 100
Kellett Ter WOR/ARM * LS12 100
Kellett Wk WOR/ARM LS12 100
Kell La HIPP HX3 140
LUD/ILL HX2 114
Kelloe St CLECK BD19 143
Kell St BGLY BD16 50
Kelmore Gv WBSY BD6 117
Kelmscott Av MSTN/BAR LS15 82
Kelmscott Crs MSTN/BAR LS15 82
Kelmscott Gdns MSTN/BAR LS15 82
Kelmscott Garth MSTN/BAR LS15 82
Kelmscott Gn MSTN/BAR LS15 82
Kelmscott Gv MSTN/BAR LS15 82
Kelmscott La MSTN/BAR LS15 82
Kelsall Av HDGY LS6 6
Kelsall Gv HDGY LS6 6
Kelsall Pl HDGY LS6 6
Kelsall Rd HDGY LS6 6
Kelsall Ter HDGY LS6 6
Kelsey St HFAX HX1 8
Kelso Gdns LDSU LS2 6
Kelso Gv HUDE HD5 192

...so Pl *LDSU* LS2 ....6 B1
...so Rd *LDSU* LS2 ....6 B2
...so St *LDSU* LS2 ....6 B2
...vin Av *HUDE* HD5 ....192 A5
LUD/ILL HX2 ....139 G4
...vin Crs *LUD/ILL* HX2 ....139 G5
...vin Rd *ELL* HX5 ....166 D5
...vin Wy *ECHL* BD2 ....96 E1
...np's Br *WKFDW/WTN* WF2 ....10 A3
...nps Wy *HOLM/MEL* HD9 ....82 F1
...npton Rd *GFTH/SHER* LS25 ....129 F1
...nsing Wk *MSTN/BAR* LS15 ....282 D8
...Churchill Dr *HOR/CROF* WF4 ....197 G1
...dal Bank *BVRD* LS3 ....6 B2
...dal Cl *BVRD* LS3 ....6 B2
AS WF10 ....155 F4
...dal Dr *CAS* WF10 ....155 F4
...dal Dr *CAS* WF10 ....154 E3
OR/CROF WF4 ....200 A1
MSTN/BAR LS15 ....103 G5
...dal Gdns *CAS* WF10 ....154 E4
...dal Garth *CAS* WF10 ....155 F4
...dal La *BVRD* LS3 ....6 B2
...dal La *BVRD* LS3 ....6 B2
...dall Av *SHPY* BD18 ....72 E3
...dal Mellor Cl *KGHY* BD21 ....2 C3
...dal Ri *BVRD* LS3 ....6 B2
OR/CROF WF4 ....200 A1
/KFDW/WTN WF2 ....199 J3
...dal Rd *BVRD* * LS3 ....6 C2
...dal St *KGHY* BD21 ....3 E4
...dell St *MID* LS10 ....1 E4
...ilworth Av *MOR* LS27 ....122 C5
...ilworth Dr *MIRF* WF14 ....170 C5
...ilworth Dr *BRIG* HD6 ....142 B5
...ilworth Gdns *MOR* LS27 ....122 C4
...ilworth Rd *WOR/ARM* LS12 ....100 C6
...ilworth St *BOW* BD4 ....96 C7
...ley Av *WBSY* BD6 ....118 A2
...ley Mt *WBSY* BD6 ....118 B1
...ley Pde *GTHN* BD7 ....118 A1
...more Av *CLECK* BD19 ....143 K3
...more Cl *CLECK* BD19 ....143 K3
...more Crs *CLECK* BD19 ....143 K3
/BSY BD6 ....118 B1
...more Dr *CLECK* BD19 ....143 K3
/BSY BD6 ....143 B1
...more Gv *CLECK* BD19 ....143 K3
/BSY BD6 ....118 B1
...more Rd *CLECK* BD19 ....143 K3
ARD/LOFT WF3 ....149 G6
/BSY BD6 ....118 B1
...more Vw *CLECK* BD19 ....143 K3
...more Wk *WBSY* BD6 ....118 B1
...more Wk *CLECK* BD19 ....143 K3
...nedy Av *HUDN* HD2 ....136 B1
...nedy Cl *BTLY* WF17 ....146 E8
'KB/PEN S36 ....251 G8
...nel La *HWTH* BD22 ....90 A1
...nels La *SCFT* LS14 ....60 D3
...nerleigh Av *MSTN/BAR* LS15 ....104 B2
...nerleigh Crs *MSTN/BAR* LS15 ....104 A2
...nerleigh Garth *MSTN/BAR* LS15 ...104 B2
...nerleigh Gln *MSTN/BAR* LS15 ....104 B2
...nerleigh Gv *MSTN/BAR* LS15 ....104 B2
...nerleigh Mt *MSTN/BAR* LS15 ....104 B2
...nerleigh Rd *MSTN/BAR* LS15 ....104 A2
...nerleigh Wk *MSTN/BAR* LS15 ....104 A2
...neth St *BEE/HOL* LS11 ....6 B6
...net La *GFTH/SHER* LS25 ....106 A5
...nion St *WBOW* BD5 ....4 B6
...sington Av *SCFT* LS14 ....60 E5
TKB/PEN S36 ....251 E8
...sington Cl *BTLY* WF17 ....146 A7
IPP HX3 ....139 A7
...sington Gdns *MID* LS10 ....125 G4
...sington Rd *HIPP* HX3 ....139 K7
WKFDE WF1 ....10 B1
...sington St *GIR* BD8 ....95 G2
GHY BD21 ....2 C4
...sington Ter *HDGY* LS6 ....79 F8
...stone Crs *IDLE* BD10 ....74 C4
...t Av *AIRE* BD20 ....27 F2
DSY/CALV LS28 ....98 E4
...t Cl *BSLYN/ROY* S71 ....222 A7
DSY/CALV LS28 ....98 E4
...t Crs *PDSY/CALV* LS28 ....98 E4
...t Dr *PDSY/CALV* LS28 ....98 E4
...tmere Av *SCFT* LS14 ....81 G6
...tmere Av *GFTH/SHER* LS25 ....106 B5
/W/MK BD12 ....143 F2
CFT LS14 ....81 H4
...tmere Cl *SCFT* LS14 ....81 H6
...tmere Crs *SCFT* LS14 ....81 H5
...tmere Gdns *SCFT* LS14 ....81 H5
...tmere Ga *SCFT* LS14 ....81 H4
...tmere Gn *SCFT* LS14 ....81 H5
...tmere Ri *SCFT* LS14 ....81 J6
...t Ms *BGLY* BD16 ....72 B1
...ton Dr *HOR/CROF* WF4 ....198 C4
...ton Wy *BOW* * BD4 ....97 G8
...t Rd *BGLY* BD16 ....50 B8
DSY/CALV LS28 ....98 D4
...t St *HFAX* HX1 ....8 C5
...worthy Cl *BHP/TINH* LS16 ....56 A6
...worthy Gdns *BHP/TINH* LS16 ....56 A6
...worthy Garth *BHP/TINH* LS16 ....56 A6
...worthy Ga *BHP/TINH* LS16 ....56 A6

Kenworthy La *RPDN/SBR* HX6 ....164 B5
Kenworthy Ri *BHP/TINH* LS16 ....56 A6
Kenworthy St *BHP/TINH* LS16 ....56 A6
Kenya Mt *HWTH* BD22 ....2 A7
Kenyon Bank *MSTN* HD8 ....236 D6
Kenyon La *LUD/ILL* HX2 ....139 G2
Kenyon St *HEM/SK/SE* WF9 ....226 C8
Kepler Gv *RHAY* LS8 ....102 A1
Kepler Mt *RHAY* LS8 ....102 A1
Kepler Ter *RHAY* LS8 ....102 A1
Kepstorn Cl *KSTL* LS5 ....78 A6
Kepstorn Ri *KSTL* LS5 ....78 A6
Kepstorn Rd *BHP/TINH* LS16 ....78 B4
Keren Gv *WKFDW/WTN* WF2 ....175 F1
Kerry Garth *HORS* LS18 ....77 F2
Kerry Hl *HORS* LS18 ....77 F3
Kerry St *HORS* LS18 ....77 F2
Kershaw Av *CAS* WF10 ....154 C4
Kershaw Ct *LUD/ILL* * HX2 ....138 A3
Kershaw Crs *LUD/ILL* HX2 ....138 A4
Kershaw Dr *LUD/ILL* HX2 ....138 A3
Kershaw La *KNOT* WF11 ....156 A8
Kershaw Rd *TOD* OL14 ....159 K2
Kertland St *EARL* WF12 ....172 B4
Kester Rd *BTLY* WF17 ....145 J6
Kesteven Cl *BOW* BD4 ....120 C1
Kesteven Rd *BOW* BD4 ....120 C1
Kesteven Rd *BOW* BD4 ....120 B1
Kestrel Bank *HUDS* HD4 ....212 E4
Kestrel Cl *AL/HA/HU* LS17 ....58 B7
Kestrel Dr *ECHL* BD2 ....74 C7
WKFDW/WTN WF2 ....199 F6
Kestrel Garth *MOR* LS27 ....123 J7
Kestrel Gv *AL/HA/HU* LS17 ....58 B7
Kestrel Mt *ECHL* BD2 ....74 C7
Kestrel Vw *CLECK* BD19 ....144 A2
Keswick Av *HUDN* HD3 ....190 A2
Keswick Cl *HIPP* HX3 ....140 D8
TOD OL14 ....133 J4
Keswick Dr *CAS* WF10 ....155 F1
WKFDW/WTN WF2 ....175 F4
Keswick Gra *AL/HA/HU* LS17 ....40 A6
Keswick La *AL/HA/HU* LS17 ....40 A7
Keswick St *BOW* BD4 ....97 F6
Keswick Vw *AL/HA/HU* LS17 ....40 C6
Kettle La *MAR/SLWT* HD7 ....209 K5
Kettlethorpe Hall Dr
WKFDW/WTN WF2 ....198 D1
Kettlethorpe Rd
WKFDW/WTN WF2 ....198 D6
Kew Hl *HUDW* HD3 ....166 E8
Kexbrough Dr *DOD/DAR* S75 ....239 J3
Key Hill La *CUD/CR* S72 ....223 K8
Keystone Av *CAS* WF10 ....153 K6
Key Syke La *TOD* OL14 ....134 B6
Khalaq Ct *BFDE* BD3 ....5 F3
Khus Wk *KGHY* BD21 ....3 D6
Kibroyd Dr *DOD/DAR* S75 ....239 J4
Kidacre St *BEE/HOL* LS11 ....7 E6
Kiddal La *MSTN/BAR* LS15 ....61 J8
Kidroyd La *HUDE* HD5 ....13 F6
Kilburn Cl *HUDE* HD5 ....13 E5
Kilburn La *DEWS* WF13 ....172 B2
Kilburn Rd *WOR/ARM* LS12 ....100 C4
Kilby St *WKFDE* WF1 ....10 B2
Kildare Crs *WIL/AL* BD15 ....94 A2
Kildare Ter *WOR/ARM* LS12 ....6 A5
Killingbeck Br *SCFT* LS14 ....103 G3
Killingbeck Dr *SCFT* LS14 ....103 G2
Killinghall Av *ECHL* BD2 ....5 F2
Killinghall Dr *ECHL* BD2 ....5 F2
Killinghall Gv *ECHL* BD2 ....5 F2
Killinghall Rd *BFDE* BD3 ....96 E2
Kiln Bent La *HOLM/MEL* HD9 ....247 F5
Kiln Cft *HOLM/MEL* HD9 ....247 G2
Kilner Bank *HUDE* HD5 ....13 E4
Kilner Rd *WBSY* * BD6 ....118 E2
Kilners Cft *ILK* LS29 ....18 D3
Kiln Fold *BRIG* HD6 ....142 E8
Kiln Hl *MAR/SLWT* HD7 ....210 E3
Kiln Hill La *AIRE* BD20 ....16 C5
Kilnhouse Bank La *HOLM/MEL* HD9 ..247 G2
Kilnhurst La *TOD* OL14 ....134 C7
Kilnhurst Mt *TOD* OL14 ....134 B6
Kilnhurst Rd *TOD* OL14 ....134 B6
Kiln La *HBR* HX7 ....88 C8
KBTN HD8 ....217 K6
Kilnsea Mt *BOW* BD4 ....97 G8
Kilnsey Fold *AIRE* BD20 ....27 F1
Kilnsey Gv *WKFDE* WF1 ....11 E2
Kilnsey Hl *BTLY* WF17 ....172 C1
Kilnsey Ms *BAIL* BD17 ....51 H8
Kilnsey Rd *BFDE* BD3 ....5 F5
WKFDE WF1 ....11 E1
Kilnshaw La *HBR* HX7 ....136 A3
Kilpin Hill La *DEWS* WF13 ....145 J8
Kilroyd Av *CLECK* BD19 ....144 A1
Kilroyd Dr *CLECK* BD19 ....144 B1
Kimberley Pl *HIPP* HX3 ....115 K7
OSM LS9 ....102 D1
Kimberley Rd *OSM* LS9 ....102 D1
Kimberley St *BFDE* BD3 ....96 E5
BRIG HD6 ....142 C8
FEA/AMT WF7 ....179 H5
HIPP HX3 ....115 K7
WKFDE WF1 ....11 D6
Kimberley Vw *OSM* LS9 ....102 D1

Kimberly Cl *PONT* WF8 ....204 D6
Kinder Av *HUDS* HD4 ....211 K1
Kineholme Dr *OT* LS21 ....33 F5
Kine Moor La *STKB/PEN* S36 ....253 J5
King Alfred's Dr *HDGY* LS6 ....79 G2
King Alfred's Wy *HDGY* LS6 ....79 G2
King Charles St *LDS* * LS1 ....7 E3
King Cl *AL/HA/HU* LS17 ....57 F7
King Cross Rd *HFAX* HX1 ....8 A6
King Cross St *HFAX* HX1 ....8 C5
King Dr *AL/HA/HU* LS17 ....57 F7
King Edward Av *CAS* WF10 ....128 E5
HORS LS18 ....77 F3
King Edward Crs *HORS* LS18 ....77 G2
King Edward Rd *CUL/QBY* BD13 ....93 H5
King Edward St *EARL* WF12 ....172 A8
HEM/SK/SE WF9 ....224 E5
HFAX HX1 ....9 D4
LDS LS1 ....7 E5
NORM WF6 ....177 K1
King Edwin's Ct *RHAY* LS8 ....80 D7
Kingfield *OSLY* LS20 ....53 H1
Kingfisher Cl *AL/HA/HU* LS17 ....58 B7
HOR/CROF WF4 ....198 B4
Kingfisher Ct *KGHY* * BD21 ....3 D3
Kingfisher Gv *GIR* BD8 ....94 C4
HUDS HD4 ....212 E4
WKFDW/WTN WF2 ....199 F6
Kingfisher Ms *MOR* LS27 ....123 H8
Kingfisher Reach *WBY* LS22 ....40 E2
Kingfisher Wy *AL/HA/HU* LS17 ....58 B7
King George Av *CHAL* LS7 ....79 K4
HORS LS18 ....79 K2
MOR LS27 ....123 G5
King George Cft *MOR* LS27 ....123 G6
King George Gdns *CHAL* * LS7 ....79 K4
King George Rd *HORS* LS18 ....77 G2
King George St *WKFDE* WF1 ....149 H8
King La *AL/HA/HU* LS17 ....56 E4
AL/HA/HU LS17 ....57 G7
AL/HA/HU LS17 ....79 H1
King Royd La *HOR/CROF* WF4 ....202 C5
Kings Ap *BRAM* LS13 ....99 J1
Kings Av *CAS* WF10 ....154 B4
HDGY LS6 ....6 A2
ILK LS29 ....20 A7
NORM WF6 ....151 J6
King's Bridge Rd *HUD* HD1 ....13 D6
Kingsbury Pl *HFAX* HX1 ....8 A4
Kings Cha *RTHW* LS26 ....126 C5
Kings Cl *FEA/AMT* WF7 ....202 D6
ILK LS29 ....19 J7
OSS WF5 ....173 H4
OT LS21 ....34 A4
Kings Ct *HEM/SK/SE* WF9 ....180 D4
HFAX HX1 ....8 C5
King's Crs *PONT* WF8 ....181 F4
Kings Cft *HEM/SK/SE* WF9 ....241 H1
OSS WF5 ....173 H3
King's Croft Gdns *AL/HA/HU* LS17 ....79 K2
Kingsdale Av *BIRK/DRI* BD11 ....121 H5
ECHL BD2 ....74 C8
Kingsdale Ct *SCFT* LS14 ....81 H5
Kingsdale Crs *ECHL* BD2 ....74 C8
Kingsdale Dr *ECHL* BD2 ....74 C8
Kingsdale Gdns *BIRK/DRI* BD11 ....121 H5
Kingsdale Gv *ECHL* BD2 ....74 B8
King's Dr *BTLY* WF17 ....145 H1
ECHL BD2 ....74 B5
NORM WF6 ....151 J6
Kingsfield *RTHW* LS26 ....125 J6
Kings Ga *BFDE* BD3 ....4 C2
Kings Gv *BGLY* BD16 ....50 A7
Kings Head Buildings *HUD* * HD1 ....12 C4
Kings Head Dr *MIRF* * WF14 ....170 C5
Kings Head Rd *MIRF* WF14 ....170 C5
Kings Lea *HIPP* HX3 ....166 A1
LVSG WF15 ....171 F1
OSS WF5 ....173 H3
Kingsley Av *BHP/TINH* LS16 ....56 B6
BIRK/DRI BD11 ....120 E7
ECHL BD2 ....74 A8
FEA/AMT WF7 ....179 J3
HOR/CROF WF4 ....177 H8
HUDS HD4 ....12 A6
KNOT WF11 ....155 K6
RPDN/SBR HX6 ....138 C8
WKFDE WF1 ....149 J6
WKFDW/WTN WF2 ....198 E5
Kingsley Cl *BIRK/DRI* BD11 ....120 E7
HOR/CROF WF4 ....200 C1
WKFDE WF1 ....149 J6
WKFDW/WTN WF2 ....198 E5
Kingsley Crs *BAIL* BD17 ....73 J1
BIRK/DRI BD11 ....120 E7
Kingsley Dr *BHP/TINH* LS16 ....56 B6
BIRK/DRI BD11 ....120 E7
CAS WF10 ....154 E6
Kingsley Garth *WKFDE* WF1 ....149 J6
Kingsley Pl *HFAX* HX1 ....8 A5
Kingsley Rd *BHP/TINH* LS16 ....56 B6
Kings Md *RTHW* LS26 ....126 D5
Kingsmead *OSS* WF5 ....173 H3
SCFT LS14 ....81 J3
Kingsmead Dr *SCFT* LS14 ....81 H2
Kings Meadow *OSS* WF5 ....173 H4
Kings Meadow Cl *WBY* LS22 ....23 H4
Kings Meadow Dr *WBY* LS22 ....23 H4

Kings Meadow Gv WBY LS22 ....23 H4
Kings Meadow Ms WBY LS22 ....23 H4
Kings Meadow Vw WBY LS22 ....23 H4
Kingsmill Cl MOR LS27 ....122 E6
King's Mill La HUDS HD4 ....13 D6
King's Mt CHAL LS7 ....79 J3
　KNOT LS14 ....155 J6
Kings Paddock OSS WF5 ....173 H4
King's Pl HDGY LS6 ....78 D7
King's Rd BGLY BD16 ....49 J6
　BHP/TINH LS16 ....56 A2
　ECHL BD2 ....4 C1
　ECHL BD2 ....74 A8
　HDGY LS6 ....6 A1
　ILK LS29 ....19 K7
　NORM WF6 ....151 H5
King's St CUD/GR S72 ....240 A5
Kingston Av HUDE HD5 ....192 A5
Kingston Cl HFAX HX1 ....8 A5
　WIL/AL BD15 ....71 G7
Kingston Ct HFAX HX1 ....8 A5
Kingston Dr HFAX HX1 ....8 A5
　NORM WF6 ....178 B2
Kingston Gdns MSTN/BAR LS15 ....81 K8
Kingston Gv IDLE BD10 ....74 D2
Kingston Rd IDLE BD10 ....74 D2
Kingston St HFAX HX1 ....8 A5
Kingston Ter LDSU LS2 ....7 D1
King St AIRE * BD20 ....27 G2
　AIRE BD20 ....27 G2
　BIRK/DRI BD11 ....121 J5
　BFD BD1 ....4 C4
　BRIG HD6 ....168 C1
　BTLY WF17 ....145 G2
　CAS WF10 ....153 K5
　BTLY WF17 ....146 E8
　CLECK BD19 ....144 B3
　HUD HD1 ....13 D4
　HBR HX7 ....111 K8
　LDS LS1 ....33 J3
　HBR HX7 ....137 F5
　OT LS21 ....33 J3
　HECK WF16 ....145 C7
　SHPY BD18 ....73 G4
　HEM/SK/SE WF9 ....224 B2
　WKFDE WF1 ....11 D4
　HFAX HX1 ....9 E4
Kirkgate La CUD/GR S72 ....223 G5
　HOR/CROF WF4 ....196 D2
Kirkham Rd GTHN * BD7 ....95 H5
　HUD HD1 ....13 D4
Kirkham St BRAM LS13 ....76 D6
　HUDW HD3 ....190 B3
Kirkhaw La KNOT WF11 ....155 J5
　IDLE BD10 ....74 E6
Kirk Ings Yd LDSU * LS2 ....7 F4
　KBTN HD8 ....236 E1
Kirklands HOLM/MEL HD9 ....233 J4
　KGHY BD21 ....2 C4
　LVSG WF15 ....164 D7
　LDS LS1 ....7 D4
Kirklands Av BAIL BD17 ....52 A8
　MIRF WF14 ....170 D7
Kirklands Cl BAIL BD17 ....74 A1
　MOR LS27 ....123 F8
　YEA LS19 ....53 J4
　NORM WF6 ....151 J7
Kirklands Gdns BAIL BD17 ....52 A8
　NORM WF6 ....177 K2
Kirklands La BAIL BD17 ....52 A8
　OSS WF5 ....173 K7
Kirklands Rd BAIL BD17 ....51 K8
　PDSY/CALV LS28 ....98 B2
Kirklands Vls BAIL * BD17 ....52 A8
　PONT WF8 ....180 D3
Kirk La HIPP HX3 ....141 H5
　RPDN/SBR * HX6 ....138 B8
　YEA LS19 ....53 J4
　TOD OL14 ....134 C5
Kirklea KBTN HD8 ....216 A8
　WHIT OL12 ....158 A8
Kirk Lea Crs HUDW HD3 ....190 C5
　WKFDE WF1 ....11 J3
Kirklees Cl PDSY/CALV LS28 ....76 C7
　YEA LS19 ....53 J7
Kirklees Cft PDSY/CALV LS28 ....76 B7
　YEA LS19 ....54 A4
Kirklees Dr PDSY/CALV LS28 ....76 B7
Kings Vw HIPP HX3 ....141 F7
Kirklees Garth PDSY/CALV LS28 ....76 B7
Kingsway AIRE BD20 ....48 E2
Kirklees Ri PDSY/CALV LS28 ....76 B7
　BGLY BD16 ....72 A1
Kirklees Rd WIL/AL BD15 ....94 B4
　BIRK/DRI BD11 ....121 J5
Kirklees Wy BIRK/DRI BD11 ....120 C6
　BTLY WF17 ....145 H1
　BTLY WF17 ....146 B2
　EARD/LOFT WF3 ....176 C1
　CLECK BD19 ....119 H8
　ECHL BD2 ....74 B5
　EARL WF12 ....172 D4
　GFTH/SHER LS25 ....105 H5
　HOLM/MEL HD9 ....233 J4
　MSTN/BAR LS15 ....104 A3
　HUDN HD2 ....168 A8
　NORM WF6 ....151 J7
　HUDN HD2 ....168 D7
　OSS WF5 ....173 K7
　KBTN HD8 ....234 E4
　PDSY/CALV LS28 ....98 B2
　KBTN HD8 ....235 K3
　PONT WF8 ....154 E8
　KBTN HD8 ....237 F4
Kingsway Cl OSS WF5 ....173 H4
　MAR/SLWT HD7 ....188 B6
Kingsway Ct OSS WF5 ....173 H4
　MAR/SLWT HD7 ....209 F2
Kingsway Dr ILK LS29 ....20 A7
　MAR/SLWT HD7 ....229 K5
Kingsway Garth GFTH/SHER LS25 ....105 G5
　OSS WF5 ....175 G7
Kingswear Crs MSTN/BAR LS15 ....104 B2
Kirkley Av LM/WK BD12 ....142 D2
Kingswear Garth MSTN/BAR LS15 ....104 B2
Kirkroyds La HOLM/MEL HD9 ....233 J4
Kingswear Gln MSTN/BAR LS15 ....104 B2
Kirkstall Av KSTL LS5 ....77 K8
Kingswear Gv MSTN/BAR LS15 ....104 B2
Kirkstall Cl GIR BD8 ....94 D4
Kingswear Pde MSTN/BAR LS15 ....104 B2
Kirkstall Hl BULY LS4 ....78 B8
Kingswear Ri MSTN/BAR LS15 ....104 B2
Kirkstall La KSTL LS5 ....78 B7
Kingswear Vw MSTN/BAR LS15 ....104 B2
Kirkstall Mt KSTL LS5 ....77 K8
Kingswell Av WKFDE WF1 ....149 K7
Kirkstall Rd BVRD LS6 ....6 B3
Kingswood Av RHAY LS8 ....58 C8
Kirkstone Av HUDE HD5 ....13 E4
Kingswood Crs RHAY LS8 ....58 B8
Kirkstone Dr CLECK BD19 ....144 E3
Kingswood Dr RHAY LS8 ....58 B8
　LUD/ILL HX2 ....138 C3
Kingswood Gdns RHAY LS8 ....58 B8
Kirkthorpe La WKFDE WF1 ....176 E5
Kingswood Gn HIPP HX3 ....140 E2
Kirkwall Av OSM LS9 ....102 D4
Kingswood Gv RHAY LS8 ....58 C8
Kirkwall Dr BOW BD4 ....97 G8
Kingswood Pl GTHN BD7 ....95 G7
Kirkwood Av BHP/TINH LS16 ....55 H7
Kingswood St GTHN BD7 ....95 G7
Kirkwood Cl BHP/TINH LS16 ....55 H6
Kingswood Ter GTHN * BD7 ....95 G7
Kirkwood Crs BHP/TINH LS16 ....55 H6
Kinnaird Cl BTLY WF17 ....146 D6
Kirkwood Dr BHP/TINH LS16 ....55 H6
　ELL HX5 ....166 E3
　HUDW HD3 ....190 A3
Kinsley House Crs HEM/SK/SE WF9 ....224 A1
Kirkwood Gdns BHP/TINH LS16 ....55 J6
Kinsley St HEM/SK/SE WF9 ....224 B1
Kirkwood Gn HUDW HD3 ....190 B3
Kipling Cl HUDS HD4 ....190 D8
Kirkwood Gv BHP/TINH LS16 ....55 H7
Kipling Ct IDLE BD10 ....75 F4
　EARD/LOFT WF3 ....148 A3
Kipling Gv PONT WF8 ....180 E1
Kirkwood La BHP/TINH LS16 ....55 H6
Kippax Mt OSM LS9 ....102 B4
Kirkwood Ri BHP/TINH LS16 ....55 J6
Kippax Pl OSM LS9 ....102 B4
Kirkwood Vw BHP/TINH LS16 ....55 H6
Kipping La CUL/QBY BD13 ....93 H5
Kirkwood Wy BHP/TINH LS16 ....55 J6
Kipping Pl CUL/QBY BD13 ....93 H5
Kismet Gdns BFDE BD3 ....96 E3
Kirby Cote La HBR HX7 ....136 E8
Kistyaen Gdns HOLM/MEL HD9 ....211 F8
Kirby St KGHY BD21 ....3 G1
Kitchener Av OSM LS9 ....102 D2
Kirk Beston Cl BEE/HOL LS11 ....123 K1
Kitchener Gv OSM LS9 ....102 D1
Kirkbourne Gv BAIL BD17 ....74 A1
Kitchener Mt OSM LS9 ....102 D1
Kirk Bridge La HOLM/MEL HD9 ....233 K4
Kitchener Pl OSM LS9 ....102 D2
Kirkbridge Wy HEM/SK/SE WF9 ....226 B8

Kirkburn Pl GTHN BD7 ....95 H5
Kirkby Av GFTH/SHER LS25 ....106 A6
Kirkby Cl HEM/SK/SE WF9 ....225 J8
Kirkbygate HEM/SK/SE WF9 ....224 D5
Kirkby La HOR/CROF WF4 ....217 G3
Kirkby Leas HFAX HX1 ....9 D5
Kirkby Rd HEM/SK/SE WF9 ....224 E5
Kirk Cl EARL WF12 ....173 G3
Kirkdale CAS WF10 ....154 D4
Kirkdale Av WOR/ARM LS12 ....100 B7
Kirkdale Crs WOR/ARM LS12 ....100 B8
Kirkdale Dr HOR/CROF WF4 ....197 K5
　WOR/ARM LS12 ....100 B7
Kirkdale Gdns WOR/ARM LS12 ....100 A7
Kirkdale Gv WOR/ARM LS12 ....100 A7
Kirkdale Mt WOR/ARM LS12 ....100 B8
Kirkdale Ter WOR/ARM LS12 ....100 B8
Kirkdale Vw WOR/ARM LS12 ....100 B8
Kirkfield AIRE BD20 ....26 A3
Kirkfield Av SCFT LS14 ....51 K7
Kirkfield Cl DOD/DAR S75 ....239 F7
Kirkfield Crs SCFT LS14 ....60 E5
Kirkfield Dr MSTN/BAR LS15 ....104 A4
Kirkfield Gdns MSTN/BAR LS15 ....104 B4
Kirkfield La SCFT LS14 ....60 E5
Kirkfields BAIL BD17 ....52 A7
Kirkfield Vw MSTN/BAR LS15 ....104 B4
Kitchener St LM/WK BD12 119
　OSM LS9 102
　RTHW LS26 127
Kitchen Fold MAR/SLWT HD7 210
Kite Ms GIR BD8 94
Kit La AIRE BD20 16
Kitson Cl WOR/ARM LS12 100
Kitson Gdns WOR/ARM LS12 100
Kitson Hill Crs MIRF WF14 170
Kitson Hill Rd MIRF WF14 170
Kitson La RPDN/SBR HX6 165
Kitson Rd MID LS10 7
Kitson St EARD/LOFT WF3 147
　OSM LS9 102
　SHPY BD18 73
Kitson Wood Rd TOD OL14 133
Kliffen Pl HIPP HX3 140
Knaresborough Dr HUDN HD2 191
Knavesmire RTHW LS26 125
Knightsbridge Wk BOW BD4 119
Knightsclose MSTN/BAR LS15 104
Knights Cft WBY LS22 23
Knightscroft Av RTHW LS26 126
Knightscroft Dr RTHW LS26 126
Knightscroft Pde HEM/SK/SE WF9 242
Knight's Fold GTHN BD7 95
Knightshill MSTN/BAR LS15 104
Knight St HFAX HX1 8
　HUD HD1 13
Knightsway EARD/LOFT WF3 149
　GFTH/SHER LS25 105
　MSTN/BAR LS15 104
　WKFDW/WTN WF2 198
The Knoll BSPA/BRAM LS23 42
　PDSY/CALV LS28 75
Knoll Cl OSS WF5 173
Knoll La HOLM/MEL HD9 232
Knoll Pk EARD/LOFT WF3 148
Knoll Park Dr BAIL BD17 73
Knoll Wood Pk HORS LS18 77
Knott Hill St WHIT OL12 158
Knottingley Rd PONT WF8 181
Knott La AIRE BD20 76
　YEA LS19 76
Knotts Rd TOD OL14 133
Knotty La KBTN HD8 193
The Knowle KBTN HD8 235
Knowle Av BULY LS4 78
　HUDE HD5 192
Knowle Gv BULY LS4 78
Knowle La HOLM/MEL HD9 232
　LM/WK BD12 142
Knowle Mt BULY LS4 100
Knowle Park Av KBTN HD8 235
Knowle Pl BULY LS4 78
Knowler Cl LVSG WF15 144
Knowler Hl LVSG WF15 144
Knowle Rd BULY * LS4 78
　MAR/SLWT HD7 210
Knowler Wy LVSG WF15 144
Knowles Av BOW BD4 120
Knowles Hl DEWS * WF13 171
Knowles Hill Rd DEWS WF13 171
Knowles La BOW BD4 120
　BTLY * WF17 146
　CLECK BD19 120
Knowle Spring Rd KGHY * BD21 2
Knowles Rd BRIG HD6 168
　BTLY WF17 146
Knowles St BOW BD4 119
　CUL/QBY BD13 92
Knowles Vw BOW BD4 120
Knowle Ter BULY LS4 100
Knowle Top Dr HIPP HX3 141
Knowle Top Rd HIPP HX3 141
Knowl Gv MIRF WF14 170
Knowl Rd HOLM/MEL HD9 233
　MAR/SLWT HD7 189
　MIRF WF14 170
Knowlwood Rd TOD OL14 133
Knowsley Av TOD * OL14 159
Knowsley Crs WHIT OL12 158
Knowsley St BFDE BD3 5
Knowsthorpe Crs OSM LS9 102
Knowsthorpe Ga OSM LS9 102
Knowsthorpe La OSM LS9 102
　OSM LS9 126
Knowsthorpe Rd OSM LS9 102
Knowsthorpe Wy OSM LS9 102
Knox St BRAM LS13 76
Knutsford Gv BOW BD4 120
Knutsford Ms BOW * BD4 120
Komla Cl BFD * BD1 5
Krive La MAR/SLWT HD7 210
Kyffin Av MSTN/BAR LS15 103
Kyffin Pl BOW BD4 97

L

Laburnum Cl EARD/LOFT WF3 148
Laburnum Ct HOR/CROF WF4 197
Laburnum Dr BAIL BD17 51
Laburnum Gv BRIG HD6 142
　CLECK BD19 144
　HOR/CROF WF4 197
　HWTH BD22 66

...BTN HD8	...236 E2	
MAR/SLWT HD7	...189 K6	
urnum Pl GIR BD8	...4 A2	
DLE BD10	...75 G3	
urnum Rd DEWS WF13	...171 H1	
HPY BD18	...73 K6	
urnum St GIR BD8	...4 A2	
PDSY/CALV LS28	...98 A3	
urnum Ter HUD * HD1	...13 D2	
eby Cl IDLE BD10	...74 E3	
ey St DEWS WF13	...172 A3	
y AV TOD OL14	...159 K2	
y Gv WBY LS22	...23 K7	
y St HEM/SK/SE WF9	...224 C4	
y Wy ELL HX5	...167 F3	
broke Gra BOW * BD4	...120 B2	
derbanks La BAIL BD17	...51 K7	
y Ann Rd BTLY WF17	...146 C6	
y Balk La PONT WF8	...180 E1	
y Beck Cl LDSU LS2	...7 F3	
ybower Av HUDS HD4	...211 J1	
y Cl OSS WF5	...173 H3	
y Heton Av MIRF WF14	...170 C5	
y Heton Cl MIRF * WF14	...170 B5	
y Heton Dr MIRF WF14	...170 B5	
y Heton Gv MIRF WF14	...170 B5	
y House La HUDS HD4	...213 G3	
y La BGLY BD16	...50 A5	
OSU LS2	...7 F3	
KFDE WF1	...10 B4	
y Pk AL/HA/HU LS17	...58 B7	
y Park Av BGLY BD16	...50 A5	
y Park Ct AL/HA/HU * LS17	...58 A7	
y Pit La BEE/HOL LS11	...101 H8	
yroyd St BIRK/DRI BD11	...120 B5	
ysmith Rd CUL/QBY BD13	...116 B3	
ywell Cl WBOW BD5	...96 A8	
ywell La LVSG WF15	...143 J8	
ywood Gra RHAY * LS8	...81 F5	
ywood Md RHAY LS8	...81 F5	
ywood Rd CUD/GR S72	...240 D6	
y Wood Rd RHAY LS8	...80 D4	
ywood Ter HFAX HX1	...8 B5	
ywood Wy DEWS WF13	...171 G7	
lands La HOR/CROF WF4	...222 E2	
steridge La WBOW BD5	...4 A6	
h Cl BHP/TINH LS16	...55 K8	
he Av HOLM/MEL HD9	...247 H1	
he Bank La HOLM/MEL HD9	...247 H1	
he Cl AIRE BD20	...27 F1	
he Croft Rd BTLY WF17	...146 D6	
he Gv WBSY BD6	...118 B1	
he Rd WBSY BD6	...118 C2	
hes Cha WKFDW/WTN WF2	...174 E4	
hes Cl WKFDW/WTN WF2	...174 E4	
hes Ct WKFDW/WTN WF2	...174 E4	
hes Cv WKFDW/WTN WF2	...174 E4	
hes Cft EARL WF12	...172 D4	
hes Dr WKFDW/WTN WF2	...174 E4	
hes Fold WKFDW/WTN WF2	...174 E4	
h Gdns BHP/TINH LS16	...55 K8	
h Garth BHP/TINH LS16	...55 K8	
h Gn BHP/TINH LS16	...55 K8	
h Rd BHP/TINH LS16	...55 K8	
eland Crs AL/HA/HU LS17	...57 G5	
eland Dr AL/HA/HU LS17	...57 H5	
eland Wy WKFDW/WTN WF2	...199 J5	
e Lock Dr EARD/LOFT WF3	...150 C6	
e Lock Gv EARD/LOFT WF3	...150 C6	
e Lock Rd EARD/LOFT WF3	...150 C6	
e Rw BOW BD4	...5 F6	
eside AIRE BD20	...49 J1	
eside Cha YEA LS19	...54 A7	
eside Cl ILK LS29	...20 A6	
eside Ct HUDW HD3	...190 B5	
eside Est HOR/CROF WF4	...225 F1	
eside Gdns YEA LS19	...54 A7	
eside Mdw PONT WF8	...154 E8	
eside Rd WOR/ARM LS12	...99 J5	
eside Ter YEA LS19	...54 A7	
eside Vw YEA LS19	...54 A7	
e St BOW BD4	...5 F6	
CGHY BD21	...3 F1	
e Ter MID LS10	...124 E1	
e Vw HFAX HX1	...8 C3	
PONT WF8	...154 D8	
WKFDW/WTN WF2	...198 E7	
e View Cl RHAY LS8	...80 E3	
e Yd EARD/LOFT WF3	...150 D6	
nb Cote Rd HUDN HD2	...168 A5	
nbe Flatt DOD/DAR * S75	...239 J3	
nbert Av DOD/DAR S75	...80 B5	
nbert Av CTL/HWG HX4	...166 C4	
nbert Dr RHAY LS8	...80 B5	
nbert Pl ECHL BD2	...5 F1	
nbert St COL BB8	...64 A1	
TL/HWG HX4	...166 C4	
nb Hall Rd HUDW HD3	...189 J3	
nb Hey MAR/SLWT * HD7	...211 F2	
nb Inn Rd KNOT WF11	...156 D7	
nbourne Av IDLE BD10	...75 F6	
nbrigg Crs SCFT LS14	...81 J7	
nbton Gv RHAY LS8	...80 B7	
nbton Pl RHAY LS8	...80 B7	
nbton St RHAY * LS8	...80 B7	

Lambton Ter RHAY LS8	...80 B7	
Lambton Vw RHAY * LS8	...80 B7	
Lamma Well Rd HOLM/MEL HD9	...248 B1	
Lampards Cl WIL/AL BD15	...94 A1	
Lamplands BTLY WF17	...146 C4	
Lanark Dr HORS LS18	...54 E7	
Lanark Ri HOR/CROF WF4	...200 E3	
Lancaster Cl PONT WF8	...180 E5	
Lancaster Ct KGHY BD21	...2 C5	
Lancaster Crs HUDE HD5	...192 E7	
Lancaster La HOLM/MEL HD9	...233 J2	
Lancaster St CAS WF10	...77 K8	
Lancastre Av KSTL LS5	...77 K8	
Lancastre Gv KSTL LS5	...77 K8	
Land Ga WHIT OL12	...158 B6	
Landmark Ct BEE/HOL LS11	...101 F8	
Landor St KGHY * BD21	...3 E2	
Lands Beck Wy LVSG WF15	...144 C7	
Landscove Av BOW BD4	...120 B1	
Landsdown Av HEM/SK/SE WF9	...241 G2	
Landseer Av BRAM LS13	...77 J8	
EARD/LOFT WF3	...147 K3	
Landseer Cl BRAM LS13	...77 H8	
Landseer Crs BRAM LS13	...77 H8	
Landseer Dr BRAM LS13	...77 H8	
Landseer Gdns BRAM LS13	...77 H8	
Landseer Gn BRAM LS13	...77 H8	
Landseer Gv BRAM LS13	...77 J8	
Landseer Mt BRAM LS13	...77 J8	
Landseer Ri BRAM LS13	...77 H8	
Landseer Rd BRAM LS13	...77 H8	
Landseer Ter BRAM LS13	...77 J8	
Landseer Vw BRAM LS13	...77 J8	
Lands Head La HIPP HX3	...116 E7	
Landsholme Ct BOW BD4	...120 C1	
Lands La GSLY LS20	...53 G2	
IDLE BD10	...74 E6	
LDS LS1	...7 E3	
Landsmoor Gv BGLY BD16	...50 B6	
Land St PDSY/CALV LS28	...76 B8	
The Lane AL/HA/HU LS17	...57 F6	
OSM LS9	...102 A4	
Lane & Dowry Rd MAR/SLWT HD7	...210 C5	
Lane End CUL/QBY BD13	...93 H5	
PDSY/CALV LS28	...98 D3	
Lane End Cl AL/HA/HU LS17	...57 F6	
Lane End Cft AL/HA/HU LS17	...57 F6	
Lane End Fold PDSY/CALV LS28	...98 D3	
Lane End Mt PDSY/CALV LS28	...98 D3	
Lane End Pl BEE/HOL LS11	...7 D6	
Lane Ends LUD/ILL HX2	...139 H1	
Lane Ends Cl HEM/SK/SE WF9	...201 K7	
Lane Ends Gn HIPP HX3	...141 G3	
Lane Ends La HBR HX7	...112 D7	
Lane Hackings Gn KBTN HD8	...236 C4	
Lane Head La KBTN HD8	...215 H5	
LUD/ILL HX2	...115 F3	
Lane Head Rd DOD/DAR S75	...238 D5	
DOD/DAR S75	...239 J6	
KBTN HD8	...235 J4	
RPDN/SBR HX6	...163 K6	
Lane House La COL BB8	...64 A1	
Lane Side CUL/QBY BD13	...93 H8	
WIL/AL BD15	...71 F7	
Laneside KBTN HD8	...215 J4	
MOR LS27	...123 G4	
Lane Side LM/WK BD12	...118 D7	
Laneside Cl MOR LS27	...123 G4	
Laneside Fold MOR LS27	...123 G4	
Laneside Gdns MOR LS27	...123 G5	
Lane Side La HUDE HD5	...192 E4	
The Lanes PDSY/CALV LS28	...98 D3	
Laneside St TOD OL14	...133 K7	
Lane Top BRIG * HD6	...142 E4	
Langbar Av SCFT LS14	...82 B6	
Langbar Av HTON BD9	...72 D8	
Langbar Cl SCFT LS14	...82 B5	
Langbar Garth SCFT LS14	...82 B5	
Langbar Gn SCFT LS14	...82 B6	
Langbar Gv SCFT LS14	...82 B6	
Langbar Rd ILK LS29	...20 A5	
SCFT LS14	...82 A6	
Langdale Av EARD/LOFT WF3	...150 A6	
GIR BD8	...94 B3	
HDGY LS6	...78 D8	
LM/WK BD12	...143 F2	
NORM WF6	...151 K7	
Langdale Cl CAS WF10	...155 F1	
WBY LS22	...23 H5	
Langdale Crs BGLY BD16	...50 A7	
Langdale Crs LUD/ILL HX2	...139 H2	
Langdale Dr CUL/QBY BD13	...116 C2	
FEA/AMT WF7	...203 J4	
HUDE HD5	...13 G5	
NORM WF6	...151 K6	
WKFDW/WTN WF2	...175 F5	
Langdale Gdns HDGY LS6	...78 C7	
Langdale Ms NORM * WF6	...151 K7	
Langdale Mt WKFDW/WTN WF2	...199 J5	
Langdale Rd EARL WF12	...172 E1	
IDLE BD10	...79 G7	
RTHW LS26	...126 E5	
Langdale Sq WKFDW/WTN WF2	...175 G5	
Langdale St ELL HX5	...166 E5	
Langdale Ter HDGY LS6	...78 C7	
Langford La ILK LS29	...32 B2	
Langford Ride ILK LS29	...32 B2	
Langford Rd ILK LS29	...32 A2	

Lang Kirk Cl AIRE BD20	...26 A3	
Langlands Rd BGLY BD16	...72 A4	
Lang La ECHL * BD2	...73 K7	
Langley Av BGLY BD16	...50 A7	
BOW BD4	...119 K2	
BRAM LS13	...76 E7	
Langley Cl BRAM LS13	...76 E7	
Langley Crs BAIL BD17	...52 A8	
BRAM LS13	...77 F8	
Langley Garth BRAM LS13	...76 E7	
Langley Gv BGLY BD16	...50 A7	
Langley La BAIL BD17	...52 A7	
KBTN HD8	...217 J7	
Langley Mt BRAM LS13	...76 E7	
Langley Pl BRAM LS13	...76 E7	
Langley Rd BGLY BD16	...50 A7	
BRAM LS13	...76 E7	
Langport Cl CUL/QBY BD13	...116 E2	
Langsett Cft HUDN HD2	...169 F6	
Langsett Rd WKFDW/WTN WF2	...198 D6	
Langthorne Ct MOR LS27	...147 H1	
Langthwaite La HEM/SK/SE WF9	...242 A1	
Langthwaite Rd HEM/SK/SE WF9	...241 K2	
Langton Av BOW BD4	...119 J2	
Langton Cl CLECK BD19	...144 D1	
Langton Gn WOR/ARM LS12	...100 C5	
Langton St RPDN/SBR HX6	...138 E6	
Langtons Whf MID LS10	...7 F4	
Langwith Av WBY LS22	...40 E3	
Langwith Dr WBY LS22	...40 C3	
Langwith Valley Rd WBY LS22	...40 C3	
Lansdale Ct BOW BD4	...120 C1	
Lansdowne Av CAS WF10	...154 A4	
Lansdowne Cl BAIL BD17	...52 B8	
BTLY WF17	...146 A5	
Lansdowne Crs DOD/DAR S75	...239 K4	
Lansdowne Pl WBOW BD5	...4 B5	
Lansdowne St WOR/ARM LS12	...100 C5	
Lanshaw Cl MID LS10	...125 F5	
Lanshaw Crs MID LS10	...125 F5	
Lanshaw Pl MID LS10	...125 F5	
Lanshaw Rd MID LS10	...125 F5	
Lanshaw Ter MID LS10	...125 F6	
Lanshaw Vw MID LS10	...125 F5	
Lanshaw Wk MID LS10	...125 F5	
Lapage St BFDE BD3	...96 E4	
Lapage Ter BFDE * BD3	...96 E4	
Lapwing Cl GIR BD8	...94 B3	
Larch Av HOLM/MEL HD9	...233 J3	
Larch Cl BTLY WF17	...145 K1	
HUDE * HD5	...192 D2	
HWTH BD22	...69 F1	
LVSG WF15	...145 F8	
NORM WF6	...178 A3	
Larch Dl HUDN HD2	...168 B7	
Larch Dr WBSY BD6	...116 E4	
Larchfield Rd MID LS10	...102 A6	
Larchfield Wy HOR/CROF WF4	...223 F2	
Larch Gv BGLY BD16	...49 K6	
Larch Hl WBSY BD6	...118 E4	
Larch Hill Crs WBSY BD6	...118 E3	
Larch La GFTH/SHER LS25	...106 B5	
Larchmont CLAY BD14	...94 C7	
Larch Rd HUDW HD3	...190 C6	
Larch St KGHY BD21	...2 C6	
Larch Wd SCFT LS14	...60 A4	
Larkfield Av YEA LS19	...54 A7	
Larkfield Crs YEA LS19	...54 A7	
Larkfield Dr YEA LS19	...54 A7	
Larkfield Mt YEA LS19	...54 A7	
Larkfield Rd PDSY/CALV LS28	...98 C3	
YEA LS19	...54 A7	
Larkfield Ter KGHY BD21	...3 F4	
Lark Hl BTLY WF17	...145 K2	
Lark Hill Av CLECK BD19	...143 J5	
Larkhill Cl RHAY LS8	...80 A3	
Lark Hill Dr CLECK BD19	...143 J4	
Larkhill Gn AL/HA/HU LS17	...80 A2	
Larkhill Rd AL/HA/HU LS17	...80 A2	
Larkhill Vw RHAY LS8	...80 A3	
Larkhill Wk RHAY LS8	...80 A3	
Larkhill Wy AL/HA/HU LS17	...80 A2	
Larks Hl PONT WF8	...180 C5	
Larkspur Wy WKFDW/WTN WF2	...175 F4	
Lark St BGLY BD16	...49 K8	
HWTH BD22	...69 F4	
HWTH BD22	...69 F1	
KGHY BD21	...2 C3	
Larwood Av IDLE BD10	...78 D6	
Lascelles Hall Rd HUDE HD5	...192 D4	
Lascelles Mt RHAY * LS8	...80 B8	
Lascelles Pl RHAY LS8	...80 B8	
Lascelles Rd HECK WF16	...145 H8	
Lascelles Rd East RHAY * LS8	...80 B8	
Lascelles Rd West RHAY * LS8	...80 B8	
Lascelles St RHAY LS8	...80 B8	
Lascelles Ter RHAY LS8	...80 B8	
Lascelles Vw RHAY LS8	...80 B8	
Lastingham Gn WBSY * BD6	...117 K2	
Latchmere Av BHP/TINH LS16	...77 K3	
Latchmere Cl BHP/TINH LS16	...78 A3	
Latchmere Crest BHP/TINH LS16	...77 K3	
Latchmere Cross BHP/TINH LS16	...77 K3	
Latchmere Dr BHP/TINH LS16	...77 K3	
Latchmere Gdns BHP/TINH LS16	...77 K3	
Latchmere Gn BHP/TINH LS16	...77 K3	
Latchmere Vw BHP/TINH LS16	...78 A3	
Latchmere Wk BHP/TINH LS16	...78 A3	
Latchmore Rd WOR/ARM LS12	...100 D7	
Latham Ct CLECK BD19	...144 E1	

Latham La CLECK BD19 ....120 D8
Latham Lea CLECK BD19 ....144 D2
Latimer St BFDE BD3 ....97 F5
Launceston Dr BOW BD4 ....120 B1
Laund Rd HUD3 HD3 ....189 J2
　　MAR/SLWT HD7 ....209 K1
Launton Wy WBOW BD5 ....95 K7
Laura St BRIG HD6 ....168 B2
　　HIPP HX3 ....9 D2
　　WOR/ARM LS12 ....6 B5
Laurel Bank BGLY * BD16 ....50 D7
Laurel Bank CI LUD/ILL HX2 ....115 K5
Laurel Bank Ct BULY LS17 ....78 C7
Laurel CI AL/HA/HU LS17 ....40 A6
　　ELL HX5 ....166 D5
　　HIPP HX3 ....117 H4
Laurel Ct OSS WF5 ....173 H5
Laurel Crs KGHY BD21 ....2 C1
Laurel Dr BTLY WF17 ....145 K4
Laurel Fold WOR/ARM * LS12 ....100 C4
Laurel Gv AIRE BD20 ....27 F2
　　BGLY BD16 ....49 J6
　　BTLY WF17 ....145 J4
　　KGHY BD21 ....2 C2
　　WOR/ARM LS12 ....100 C4
Laurel Hill Av MSTN/BAR LS15 ....104 B4
Laurel Hill Cft MSTN/BAR * LS15 .....104 B4
Laurel Hill Gdns MSTN/BAR LS15 ....104 B4
Laurel Hill Gv MSTN/BAR LS15 ....104 B4
Laurel Hill Vw MSTN/BAR LS15 ....104 B4
Laurel Hill Wy MSTN/BAR LS15 ....104 B5
Laurel Mt CHAL * LS7 ....79 K6
　　HFAX * HX1 ....8 B6
　　PDSY/CALV LS28 ....98 C5
Laurel Pk WIL/AL BD15 ....71 G7
Laurel PI MID LS10 ....124 C8
　　WOR/ARM LS12 ....100 C4
The Laurels BGLY * BD16 ....50 B8
　　EARL WF12 ....173 F4
　　RHAY LS8 ....80 B5
Laurel St BFDE BD3 ....96 E5
　　HFAX HX1 ....8 B6
　　WOR/ARM LS12 ....100 C4
Laurel Ter PDSY/CALV LS28 ....98 C3
Laurence Ct RTHW LS26 ....27 G4
Lavender Ct HUDS HD4 ....212 D5
Lavender Cft HECK WF16 ....145 H7
Lavender HI IDLE BD10 ....74 E6
Lavender Wk OSM LS9 ....102 B4
Laverhills LVSG WF15 ....144 A6
Laverock Crs BRIG HD6 ....142 A6
Laverock La BRIG HD6 ....142 A6
Laverton Rd BOW BD4 ....96 D7
Lavinia Ter CLAY BD14 ....94 D7
Lawcliffe Crs HWTH BD22 ....69 F3
Law CI WBY LS22 ....23 J4
Law Common Rd HOLM/MEL HD9 ....249 F6
Lawefield Av RTHW LS26 ....125 K5
Lawefield Gv WKFDW/WTN WF2 ....10 A4
Lawefield La WKFDW/WTN WF2 ......10 A4
Lawkholme Crs KGHY * BD21 ....3 D3
Lawkholme La KGHY BD21 ....3 D3
Law La HIPP HX3 ....141 F6
Lawn Av ILK LS29 ....32 B2
Lawn Rd ILK LS29 ....32 B2
The Lawns AL/HA/HU LS17 ....196 A5
Lawns Av AL/HA/HU LS17 ....57 F6
　　WOR/ARM LS12 ....99 H8
Lawns CI NORM WF6 ....151 H7
　　WOR/ARM LS12 ....99 H8
Lawns Cft WKFDW/WTN WF2 ....149 F6
Lawns Crs WOR/ARM LS12 ....99 H8
Lawns Dene WOR/ARM LS12 ....99 H8
Lawns Dr WOR/ARM LS12 ....99 H8
Lawns Gn WOR/ARM LS12 ....99 H8
Lawns Hall CI BHP/TINH LS16 ....56 B8
Lawn's La MID LS10 ....102 A8
　　WKFDW/WTN WF2 ....149 F6
　　WOR/ARM LS12 ....99 H8
Lawns Mt WOR/ARM LS12 ....99 H8
Lawns Sq WOR/ARM LS12 ....99 H8
Lawns Ter EARD/LOFT WF3 ....148 E4
　　WOR/ARM LS12 ....99 H8
Lawnswood Gdns BHP/TINH LS16 .....78 B1
Lawnswood Rd KGHY BD21 ....2 B5
Lawrence Av AL/HA/HU LS17 ....57 F6
Lawrence Crs HECK WF16 ....145 G5
　　RHAY LS8 ....80 E7
Lawrence Gdns RHAY LS8 ....80 E6
Lawrence Rd HIPP HX3 ....140 A8
　　HUD HD1 ....12 A3
　　RHAY LS8 ....80 E7
Lawrence St HIPP * HX3 ....8 B1
Lawrence Wk RHAY LS8 ....80 E7
Law Slack Rd HOLM/MEL HD9 ....248 E6
Lawson Rd BRIG HD6 ....168 C1
Lawson St BFDE BD3 ....5 D3
　　WOR/ARM * LS12 ....100 B4
Law St BOW BD4 ....119 K1
　　BTLY WF17 ....145 J3
　　CLECK BD19 ....144 A2
　　TOD OL14 ....132 E2
Lawton St HUDS HD4 ....191 G8
Laycock La HWTH BD22 ....46 B5
Laycock PI CHAL LS7 ....79 K8
Lay Garth CI RTHW * LS26 ....126 B6

Laygarth Dr HUDE HD5 ....192 E5
Lay Garth Gdns RTHW LS26 ....126 A7
Lay Garth Gn RTHW LS26 ....126 B7
Lay Garth Md RTHW LS26 ....126 B7
Lay Garth PI RTHW LS26 ....126 B7
Lay Garth Rd RTHW LS26 ....126 B7
Lay Garth Sq RTHW LS26 ....126 B7
Layton Av YEA LS19 ....54 C8
Layton CI YEA LS19 ....76 C1
Layton Crs YEA LS19 ....54 C8
Layton Dr YEA LS19 ....54 C8
Layton La YEA LS19 ....54 C8
Layton Mt YEA LS19 ....54 B8
Layton Park Av YEA LS19 ....76 C1
Layton Park CI YEA LS19 ....54 B8
Layton Park Cft YEA LS19 ....76 C1
Layton Park Dr YEA LS19 ....76 C1
Layton Ri HORS LS18 ....54 D8
Layton Rd YEA LS19 ....54 C8
Lazenby Dr WBY LS22 ....23 H5
Lazenby Fold WBY LS22 ....23 H5
The Lea GFTH/SHER LS25 ....105 K6
The Lea Av HIPP HX3 ....140 B8
Leabank Av GFTH/SHER LS25 ....106 A6
Leach Crs AIRE BD20 ....48 C1
Leache's Br AIRE BD20 ....48 B1
Leach Ri AIRE BD20 ....48 B1
Leach Rd AIRE BD20 ....48 C1
Leach Wy AIRE BD20 ....48 C1
Lea CI BRIG HD6 ....142 B7
Lea Ct GTHN BD7 ....117 K1
Lea Cft BSPA/BRAM LS23 ....42 D6
　　OT LS21 ....33 J4
Leadenhall St HFAX HX1 ....8 A6
Lea Dr KBTN HD8 ....235 H5
Leadwell La EARD/LOFT WF3 ....125 J8
Lea Farm Crs KSTL LS5 ....77 K5
Lea Farm Dr KSTL LS5 ....77 K5
Lea Farm Gv KSTL LS5 ....77 K5
Lea Farm Mt KSTL LS5 ....77 J4
Lea Farm PI KSTL LS5 ....77 J4
Lea Farm Rd KSTL LS5 ....77 J4
Lea Farm Rw KSTL LS5 ....77 K5
Lea Farm Wk KSTL LS5 ....77 K5
Leafield Av MID LS10 ....74 E8
Leafield Bank HUDW HD3 ....189 J5
Leafield CI AL/HA/HU LS17 ....79 H1
　　HUDN HD2 ....168 E7
Leafield Crs ECHL BD2 ....74 D8
Leafield Dr AL/HA/HU LS17 ....79 H1
　　ECHL BD2 ....74 E7
　　PDSY/CALV LS28 ....98 D5
Leafield Gra AL/HA/HU LS17 ....79 H1
Leafield Gv ECHL BD2 ....74 E8
Leafield Ter ECHL BD2 ....74 E8
Leafield Wy ECHL BD2 ....74 E8
Leafland St HFAX * HX1 ....8 B4
Leaf St CAS WF10 ....153 H4
　　HWTH * BD22 ....69 G3
Leafsway WBSY * BD6 ....118 A5
Lea Head KBTN HD8 ....235 G3
Leah PI WOR/ARM LS12 ....6 B5
Leake St CAS WF10 ....153 K4
Leak Hall Crs KBTN HD8 ....236 D5
Leak Hall La KBTN HD8 ....236 D5
Lea La FEA/AMT WF7 ....179 K7
　　HUDS HD4 ....212 C5
Lea Mill Park CI YEA LS19 ....53 J4
Lea Mill Park Dr YEA LS19 ....53 J4
Leamington Dr IDLE BD10 ....74 E3
Leamington St HTON BD9 ....95 H1
Leamside Wk BOW BD4 ....120 B1
Lea Park CI RTHW LS26 ....125 G4
Lea Park Cft RTHW LS26 ....125 G4
Lea Park Dr RTHW LS26 ....125 G4
Lea Park Gdns RTHW LS26 ....125 G4
Lea Park Garth RTHW * LS26 ....125 G4
Lea Park V RTHW LS26 ....125 G4
Lea Park W RTHW LS26 ....125 H4
Leapings La STKB/PEN S36 ....251 J2
Learise RTHW LS26 ....126 B7
Learoyd St HUD HD1 ....13 D3
Leas Gdns HOLM/MEL HD9 ....234 A7
Leaside Dr CUL/QBY BD13 ....93 H4
Lea Side Gdns HUDW HD3 ....189 J5
Leasowe Av MID LS10 ....125 F1
Leasowe CI MID LS10 ....125 F1
Leasowe Gdns MID LS10 ....125 F1
Leasowe Garth MID LS10 ....125 F1
Leasowe Rd MID LS10 ....125 F1
Lea St HUD HD1 ....12 C2
　　HUDW HD3 ....190 C2
Leatham Av FEA/AMT WF7 ....179 K7
Leatham Crs FEA/AMT WF7 ....179 K7
Leatham Dr FEA/AMT WF7 ....180 A7
Leatham Park Rd FEA/AMT WF7 .....179 K7
Leatham Royd MAR/SLWT * HD7 .....209 H7
Leathley Av ILK LS29 ....32 D8
Leathley Br OT LS21 ....34 E2
Leathley Crs ILK LS29 ....32 D7
Leathley La ILK LS29 ....32 D7
Leathley Rd ILK LS29 ....32 D7
　　MID LS10 ....7 E6
Leathley St MID LS10 ....7 F6
The Leavens IDLE BD10 ....75 F3
Leaventhorpe Av GIR BD8 ....94 C4
Leaventhorpe Gv CUL/QBY BD13 .....94 C5

Leaventhorpe La CUL/QBY BD13 94
Leaventhorpe Wy GIR BD8 94
Lea Vw BTLY WF17 145
Leavington CI LM/WK BD12 118
Ledbury Av MID LS10 125
Ledbury CI MID LS10 125
Ledbury Dr EARD/LOFT WF3 125
Ledbury Gn MID LS10 125
Ledbury Gv MID * LS10 125
Ledbury PI BOW BD4 125
Ledgard Dr HOR/CROF WF4 198
Ledgard Wy WOR/ARM LS12 100
Ledger La EARD/LOFT WF3 147
　　WKFDE WF1 149
Ledger PI WKFDE WF1 149
Ledston Av GFTH/SHER LS25 106
Ledston Mill La CAS WF10 129
Lee Bank HIPP HX3 8
Lee Beck Gv EARD/LOFT WF3 150
Lee Bottom Rd TOD OL14 135
Lee Br HFAX HX1 8
Lee Brig NORM WF6 151
Leech La BGLY BD16 70
Lee CI WIL/AL BD15 71
Lee Clough Dr HBR HX7 137
Lee Ct KGHY BD21 48
　　OSS WF5 174
Leeds & Bradford Rd
　　PDSY/CALV LS28 98
Leeds Barnsdale Rd CAS WF10 153
Leeds Country Wy AL/HA/HU LS17 37
　　BHP/TINH LS16 56
　　HORS LS18 54
　　MOR LS27 121
　　MOR LS27 146
　　OSS WF5 174
　　PDSY/CALV LS28 75
　　RTHW LS26 127
　　SCFT LS14 60
　　SCFT LS14 61
　　WKFDE WF1 176
Leeds La RTHW LS26 105
Leeds Old Rd BFDE BD3 97
　　HECK WF16 145
Leeds Rd AL/HA/HU LS17 40
　　BFD BD1 5
　　BHP/TINH LS16 35
　　BTLY WF17 145
　　CAS WF10 128
　　CAS WF10 153
　　EARD/LOFT WF3 149
　　EARD/LOFT WF3 149
　　EARL WF12 172
　　ECHL BD2 74
　　GFTH/SHER LS25 105
　　GSLY LS20 53
　　HIPP HX3 3
　　HIPP HX3 141
　　HUD HD1 2
　　HUDN HD2 192
　　ILK LS29 20
　　LVSG WF15 144
　　MIRF WF14 170
　　MSTN/BAR LS15 81
　　OSS WF5 173
　　OT LS21 33
　　RTHW LS26 125
　　RTHW LS26 128
　　SHPY BD18 73
　　WBY LS22 40
　　WKFDE WF1 10
　　YEA LS19 54
Leeds St KGHY BD21 2
Leefield Rd HECK WF16 145
Leef St HUDE HD5 13
Lee Gn MIRF WF14 170
Lee Head HUDN HD2 12
Leeke Rv HOR/CROF WF4 197
Lee La BGLY BD16 8
　　FEA/AMT WF7 203
　　HIPP HX3 116
　　HORS LS18 77
　　HWTH BD22 68
　　KBTN HD8 215
　　STKB/PEN S36 250
　　TOD OL14 134
　　WIL/AL BD15 71
Lee La East HORS LS18 77
Lee La West HORS LS18 76
Lee Mill Rd HBR HX7 112
Leeming St BFD BD1 5
Lee Moor La EARD/LOFT WF3 150
Lee Moor Rd EARD/LOFT WF3 150
Lee Mount Gdns HIPP HX3 8
Lee Mount Rd HIPP HX3 8
Lee Orchards BSPA/BRAM LS23 42
Lee Rd DEWS WF13 171
Lees Av EARL WF12 172
　　STKB/PEN S36 252
Lees Bank Av HWTH BD22 69
Lees Bank Dr HWTH * BD22 69
Lees Bank HI HWTH BD22 69
Lees Bank Rd HWTH BD22 69
Lees CI CUL/QBY BD13 92
　　HUDE HD5 192
Lees Crs HOR/CROF WF4 198
Lees Dr EARL * WF12 172
Lees Hall Rd EARL WF12 172
Lees Holm EARL WF12 172

es House Rd EARL WF12 ....172 B6
eside Av HUDN HD2 ....168 C7
eside Rd WKFDE WF16 ....145 H6
es La HWTH BD22 ....69 F3
PDSY/CALV LS28 ....76 B7
es Moor Rd CUL/QBY BD13 ....70 A5
es Rd HBR HX7 ....112 B7
e St BRIG HD6 ....142 B7
CUL/QBY BD13 ....116 C3
DEWS WF13 ....171 H5
LVSG WF15 ....144 D6
WKFDE * WF1 ....10 C3
esworth Ct HWTH * BD22 ....69 G3
e Wood Rd HBR HX7 ....215 G4
grams Av GTHN BD7 ....95 F6
grams La GTHN BD7 ....95 G5
grams Mill La GTHN BD7 ....95 G5
grams St GTHN BD7 ....95 H4
grams Ter GTHN BD7 ....4 A4
icester Cl LDSU LS2 ....7 D1
icester La LDSU LS2 ....7 D1
icester Pl CHAL LS7 ....7 E1
icester St BOW BD4 ....96 C7
icester Ter HIPP HX3 ....140 A7
igh Av EARD/LOFT WF3 ....148 B3
igh Rd EARD/LOFT WF3 ....148 B3
igh St FEA/AMT WF7 ....202 D6
RPDN/SBR HX6 ....139 F6
ighton La LDS LS1 ....6 C3
igh Vw EARD/LOFT WF3 ....148 A3
isure La KBTN HD8 ....217 J3
ith Ct EARL WF12 ....195 J2
ith St KGHY BD21 ....2 C2
mans Dr DEWS WF13 ....145 J8
Marchant Av HUDN HD3 ....190 C3
mington Av HFAX HX1 ....8 B5
mon St HFAX HX1 ....8 A4
WBOW BD5 ....118 D1
mon Tree Cl PONT WF8 ....180 C5
nacre La KBTN HD8 ....216 B2
nham Cl MOR LS27 ....123 F8
nhurst Av WOR/ARM LS12 ....78 A8
nnie St KGHY BD21 ....2 C4
nnon Dr GIR BD8 ....95 H2
nnox Dr WKFDW/WTN WF2 ....197 K1
nnox Gdns MSTN/BAR LS15 ....104 A4
nnox Rd BULY LS4 ....100 D3
TOD OL14 ....132 D2
nny Balk AWLS/ASK DN6 ....243 G4
ns Dr BAIL BD17 ....51 J7
ntlifield St HIPP HX3 ....8 B1
ntlifield Ter HIPP HX3 ....8 B3
nton Dr BEE/HOL LS11 ....124 D1
nton Vls IDLE BD10 ....74 D2
odis Ct BEE/HOL LS11 ....7 D5
odis Vw RTHW LS26 ....125 J3
onard's Pl BGLY BD16 ....71 K1
onard St BGLY BD16 ....72 A1
HUDN HD2 ....13 D1
LM/WK BD12 ....118 E8
opold Gdns CHAL LS7 ....80 A8
opold Gv CHAL LS7 ....79 K8
opold St CHAL LS7 ....79 K8
OSS WF5 ....174 B7
pton La KBTN HD8 ....215 J2
pton Rd MOR LS27 ....122 C4
sley Hy HUDS HD4 ....212 A2
slie St HUDN HD2 ....12 B1
slie Ter HDGY LS6 ....79 G8
smere Cir WBSY BD6 ....118 A1
ssarna Ct BOW * BD4 ....96 E6
ven Gdns WBY LS22 ....23 H4
vens Bank MSTN/BAR LS15 ....103 K5
vens Ct MSTN/BAR LS15 ....103 C5
vens Garth MSTN/BAR LS15 ....103 C5
vens Pl MSTN/BAR LS15 ....103 C5
venthorpe Ct RTHW LS26 ....127 F6
venthorpe St RTHW LS26 ....127 F6
veret Wy BTLY WF17 ....146 A2
ver St WBSY BD6 ....118 B2
vita Gv BOW BD4 ....97 F7
vita Pl BOW BD4 ....97 F7
MSTN/BAR LS15 ....103 G3
win Cl CAS WF10 ....154 E3
wis Cl CUL/QBY BD13 ....116 C2
wisham Gv MOR LS27 ....123 C7
wisham Rd MAR/SLWT HD7 ....210 D2
wisham St MOR LS27 ....122 D8
wis St HFAX HX1 ....8 C3
xington Cl BOW BD4 ....119 J3
HIPP HX3 ....141 J3
yburn Cl BOW BD4 ....119 J3
yburn Gv BGLY BD16 ....50 A7
yburne St GIR BD8 ....4 A2
yden Ri WIL/AL BD15 ....94 B3
yfield BAIL BD17 ....51 C8
yfield Bank HOLM/MEL HD9 ....233 J4
y Fleaks Rd IDLE BD10 ....74 D4
ygards La HOLM/MEL HD9 ....231 F2
yland Cft HUDN HD2 ....169 F5
yland Rd BTLY WF17 ....145 G2
CAS WF10 ....154 E3
ylands Av HTON BD9 ....73 F8
ylands Gv HTON BD9 ....73 F8
ylands La HTON BD9 ....73 F8

KGHY BD21 ....3 E4
Leylands Rd LDSU LS2 ....7 F2
Leylands Ter HTON BD9 ....73 F8
Ley La WOR/ARM LS12 ....100 D3
Leymoor Rd MAR/SLWT HD7 ....189 H6
Leys Cl IDLE BD10 ....74 C2
Leysholme Crs WOR/ARM LS12 .....100 B5
Leysholme Dr WOR/ARM LS12 ....100 B5
Leysholme Ter WOR/ARM LS12 .....100 B5
Leysholme Vw WOR/ARM LS12 .....100 A5
Leyside Dr WIL/AL BD15 ....94 B1
Leys La BSPA/BRAM LS23 ....42 B3
KBTN HD8 ....217 F5
KNOT WF11 ....182 C1
Leys Rd PONT WF8 ....182 C5
The Leys HEM/SK/SE WF9 ....241 G2
Leyton Crs IDLE * BD10 ....74 D4
Leyton Dr IDLE BD10 ....74 D4
Leyton Gdns IDLE BD10 ....74 D4
Leyton Ter IDLE BD10 ....74 D4
Ley Top La WIL/AL BD15 ....94 C3
Leywell Ter WOR/ARM LS12 ....100 A3
Libbey St GIR BD8 ....95 H2
Lichen Cl GTHN BD7 ....95 G8
Lichfield Mt ECHL BD2 ....74 A7
Lichfield Rd EARL WF12 ....172 B5
Lickless Av HORS LS18 ....77 H2
Lickless Dr HORS LS18 ....77 H2
Lickless Gdns HORS LS18 ....77 H2
Lickless Ter HORS LS18 ....77 H2
Lidgate Cl DEWS WF13 ....172 B1
Lidgate Crs HEM/SK/SE WF9 ....241 K1
Lidgate La CUD/OBY S72 ....223 F8
DEWS WF13 ....172 B1
Lidget Av GTHN * BD7 ....95 F6
Lidget Hl PDSY/CALV LS28 ....98 C3
Lidget La HOR/CROF WF4 ....201 H1
Lidget Pl GTHN BD7 ....95 F6
Lidget La HUDW HD3 ....190 B2
Lidgett Av RHAY LS8 ....80 B4
Lidgett Ct GFTH/SHER LS25 ....105 J5
Lidgett Crs RHAY LS8 ....80 B3
Lidget Gv RHAY LS8 ....80 B4
Lidget Ter CLAY BD14 ....94 D7
Lidgett Gv RHAY LS8 ....80 B4
Lidgett Hl RHAY LS8 ....80 B4
Lidgett La AL/HA/HU LS17 ....77 H2
GFTH/SHER LS25 ....105 J5
KBTN HD8 ....236 D2
Lidgett Mt RHAY LS8 ....80 B2
Lidgett Park Av RHAY LS8 ....80 B3
Lidgett Park Gdns RHAY LS8 ....80 B3
Lidgett Park Gv RHAY LS8 ....80 C2
Lidgett Park Ms RHAY LS8 ....80 C2
Lidgett Park Rd RHAY LS8 ....80 B2
Lidgett Park Vw RHAY LS8 ....80 B2
Lidgett Pl RHAY LS8 ....80 B3
Lidgett Ri KBTN HD8 ....236 D2
Lidgett Mt RHAY LS8 ....80 B4
Lidgett Wk BSLYN/ROY S71 ....222 A7
Lifton Pl LDSU LS2 ....6 C1
Light Bank La AIRE BD20 ....18 A7
Lightcliffe Rd BRIG HD6 ....142 B7
Lightcliffe Royd La GTL/HWG HX4 ..165 F5
Lightenfield La HUDS HD4 ....212 C5
Lightfoot Av CAS WF10 ....153 J5
Lightfoot Cl CAS WF10 ....153 J5
Lighthazles Chapel Rd
RPDN/SBR HX6 ....163 H5
Lighthazles Rd RPDN/SBR HX6 ....163 J4
Light La WKFDW/WTN WF2 ....175 F4
Lightowler Cl HFAX HX1 ....8 B4
Lightowler Rd HFAX HX1 ....8 B4
Lightowler St WBSY BD6 ....118 D2
Lightridge Cl HUDN HD2 ....168 A7
Lightridge Rd HUDN HD2 ....168 A6
Lilac Av WKFDW/WTN WF2 ....10 C6
Lilac Cl BRIG HD6 ....142 D8
ILK LS29 ....18 E3
Lilac Gv BOW BD4 ....97 F5
CLECK BD19 ....144 D2
SHPY BD18 ....73 K6
The Lilacs GSLY LS20 ....53 G2
Lilac St HIPP HX3 ....95 K7
Liley La HUDE HD5 ....193 H3
MIRF WF14 ....194 A5
Lilian St BOW BD4 ....96 E8
Lillands Av BRIG HD6 ....168 A1
Lillands La BRIG HD6 ....168 A1
Lillands Ter BRIG HD6 ....168 A1
Lilley St HEM/SK/SE WF9 ....224 D5
Lilley Ter HEM/SK/SE WF9 ....241 H6
Lilly La HFAX HX1 ....9 E5
Lilly St RPDN/SBR HX6 ....138 E8
Lilycroft Rd GIR BD8 ....95 G1
Lilycroft Wk HTON BD9 ....95 G1
Lily St GIR BD8 ....95 H1
TOD OL14 ....133 H5
Lilythorne Av IDLE BD10 ....74 E3
Lime Av HBR HX7 ....112 A8
HOLM/MEL HD9 ....233 J3
TOD OL14 ....133 K5
Lime Cl ILK LS29 ....18 B3
KGHY BD21 ....2 B1
Lime Crs HEM/SK/SE WF9 ....242 A1
WKFDW/WTN WF2 ....199 H2
Lime Gv HEM/SK/SE WF9 ....242 A1
MAR/SLWT HD7 ....189 J6
YEA LS19 ....53 J7

Lime Kiln La WBY LS22 ....23 G2
Lime Pit La EARD/LOFT WF3 ....150 C7
Limers Ga TOD OL14 ....132 C8
Limes Av HIPP HX3 ....140 B7
Lime St BGLY BD16 ....49 K8
GTHN BD7 ....95 G7
HUDS HD4 ....190 E8
HWTH BD22 ....68 E5
KGHY BD21 ....2 C3
OSS WF5 ....173 K7
TOD OL14 ....133 K5
Lime Tree Av AL/HA/HU LS17 ....81 J1
BSPA/BRAM LS23 ....42 D3
BTLY WF17 ....145 K7
PONT WF8 ....180 C3
Lime Tree Cl RTHW LS26 ....127 G4
HEM/SK/SE * WF9 ....224 C5
Lime-Tree Crs GFTH/SHER LS25 ......129 H2
Lime-Tree Gdns BSPA/BRAM LS23 ...42 E4
Lime Tree Gv BIRK/DRI * BD11 ....120 D4
Limetrees PONT WF8 ....155 H7
Lime Tree Sq SHPY BD18 ....72 D3
Limewood Ap SCFT LS14 ....81 J4
Limewood Rd SCFT LS14 ....81 J5
Linburn Cl BSLYN/ROY S71 ....221 J7
Lincoln Av HECK WF16 ....145 G6
LVSG WF15 ....170 C1
Lincoln Cl GIR * BD8 ....4 A2
Lincoln Ct HUDE * HD5 ....192 C4
Lincoln Crs HEM/SK/SE WF9 ....226 C7
Lincoln Dr LVSG WF15 ....170 D1
Lincoln Green Ct OSM * LS9 ....102 A2
Lincoln Green Rd OSM LS9 ....102 A2
Lincoln Gv HUDE HD5 ....192 C7
LVSG WF15 ....170 C1
Lincoln Rd EARL WF12 ....172 E2
GIR BD8 ....4 A3
OSM LS9 ....102 A2
Lincoln St CAS WF10 ....153 K3
HUD HD1 ....13 E4
TOD OL14 ....132 E2
WKFDW/WTN WF2 ....175 G4
Lincoln Wk GFTH/SHER LS25 ....129 H1
Lincoln Wy HIPP HX3 ....8 C2
Lincombe Bank RHAY LS8 ....80 A5
Lincombe Dr RHAY LS8 ....80 A4
Lincombe Mt RHAY LS8 ....80 A3
Lincombe Ri RHAY LS8 ....80 A3
Lincroft Av HUDE HD5 ....192 A6
Lincroft Crs BRAM LS13 ....77 H8
Lincs Wold LVSG WF15 ....143 J7
Lindale Av FEA/AMT WF7 ....203 J4
Lindale Cl MID LS10 ....124 E4
Lindale Garth WKFDW/WTN WF2 ....174 D1
Lindale Gv WKFDW/WTN WF2 ....174 E2
Lindale La WKFDW/WTN WF2 ....174 E2
Lindale Mt WKFDW/WTN WF2 ....174 D1
Linden Av BFDE BD3 ....97 G3
TOD OL14 ....133 K5
Linden Cl AL/HA/HU LS17 ....40 B7
BRIG HD6 ....142 D8
CAS WF10 ....154 E5
EARL WF12 ....173 G4
KNOT WF11 ....155 K7
Linden Ct BHP/TINH LS16 ....78 D4
Linden Gdns BEE/HOL LS11 ....101 J8
Linden Mt BEE/HOL LS11 ....101 J8
Linden Gv BEE/HOL LS11 ....101 J8
Linden Pl BEE/HOL LS11 ....101 J8
HBR * HX7 ....112 B7
Linden Ri KGHY BD21 ....3 F5
Linden Rd BEE/HOL LS11 ....101 H8
ELL HX5 ....166 D5
HBR HX7 ....112 B7
HIPP HX3 ....136 E2
HUDN HD2 ....12 B1
Linden St BEE/HOL LS11 ....101 J8
Linden Ter PONT WF8 ....180 D3
Linden Wy WBY LS22 ....23 H4
Lindisfarne Rd SHPY BD18 ....73 F4
Lindley Av HUDW HD3 ....167 F8
Lindley Dr GTHN BD7 ....118 A1
Lindley Moor Rd HUDW HD3 ....189 H2
Lindley Rd ELL HX5 ....166 E7
WBOW BD5 ....95 K8
Lindley St HUDW HD3 ....190 A6
Lindrick Gv LUD/ILL HX2 ....115 J4
Lindrick Wk LUD/ILL HX2 ....115 J4
Lindsay Acre EARD/LOFT WF3 ....148 B3
Lindsay Av WKFDW/WTN WF2 ....174 D6
Lindsay Rd GFTH/SHER LS25 ....105 K3
Lindsey Ct OSM LS9 ....102 A2
Lindsey Gdns OSM * LS9 ....102 A2
Lindsey Mt OSM LS9 ....102 A2
Lindsey Rd OSM LS9 ....102 A2
Lindwell Av GTL/HWG HX4 ....166 B4
Lindwell Gv GTL/HWG HX4 ....166 B4
Linefield Rd BTLY WF17 ....146 C6
Lineham Ct LVSG WF15 ....170 D1
Lineholme Av TOD OL14 ....133 H4
Lineside Cottages EARL * WF12 ....171 K8
Linfit Fold MAR/SLWT HD7 ....210 A3
Linfit La KBTN HD8 ....215 K3
MAR/SLWT HD7 ....210 E3
Lingards Rd MAR/SLWT HD7 ....210 C5
Lingards Ter MAR/SLWT * HD7 ....210 A5

Lingard St *BFD* BD1 .....5 D3
Ling Bob *LUD/ILL* HX2 .....139 G3
Ling Bob Cft *LUD/ILL* HX2 .....139 G2
Lingdale Rd *LM/WK* BD12 .....118 B5
Lingfield Ap *AL/HA/HU* LS17 .....57 H8
Lingfield Bank *AL/HA/HU* LS17 .....57 H8
Lingfield Cl *AL/HA/HU* LS17 .....57 J8
Lingfield Crs *AL/HA/HU* LS17 .....57 H8
  WBY BD6 .....117 H1
Lingfield Dr *AL/HA/HU* LS17 .....57 J8
  HWTH BD22 .....69 J2
Lingfield Gdns *AL/HA/HU* LS17 .....57 H8
Lingfield Ga *AL/HA/HU* LS17 .....57 H8
Lingfield Gn *AL/HA/HU* LS17 .....57 H8
Lingfield Gv *AL/HA/HU* LS17 .....57 J8
  WIL/AL BD15 .....71 H6
Lingfield Mt *AL/HA/HU* LS17 .....57 J8
  WIL/AL BD15 .....71 H6
Lingfield Vw *WBY* BD6 .....117 H1
Lingfield Vw *AL/HA/HU* LS17 .....57 H8
Lingfield Wk *AL/HA/HU* LS17 .....57 H8
Ling La *AL/HA/HU* LS17 .....59 H4
Ling Park Ap *WIL/AL* BD15 .....71 G7
Ling Park Av *WIL/AL* BD15 .....71 G7
Ling Royd Av *LUD/ILL* HX2 .....139 G5
Lings La *PONT* WF8 .....227 J3
  RTHW LS26 .....127 J2
The Link *PONT* WF8 .....180 D5
Link End *EARL* WF12 .....172 C4
  HUDW HD3 .....190 D5
  WKFDE WF1 .....10 B1
The Links *BEE/HOL* LS11 .....124 B4
Links Av *CLECK* BD19 .....144 A2
  FEA/AMT WF7 .....179 J2
Linkway *BGLY* BD16 .....72 A4
Linnet *GIR* * BD8 .....94 C3
  MIRF WF14 .....170 D3
Linnet Ct *MOR* LS27 .....123 J8
Linnet Gv *WKFDW/WTN* WF2 .....199 F6
Linnet St *KGHY* BD21 .....3 D2
Linnhe Av *WBY* BD6 .....118 A5
Linshaws Rd *HOLM/MEL* HD9 .....248 A6
Linton Av *AIRE* BD20 .....27 G1
  AL/HA/HU LS17 .....58 B7
  BTLY WF17 .....145 K6
  WBY LS22 .....23 H5
Linton Cl *AL/HA/HU* LS17 .....58 A7
  LVSG WF15 .....144 C6
Linton Common *WBY* LS22 .....40 E2
Linton Crs *AL/HA/HU* LS17 .....58 B7
Linton Gv *AL/HA/HU* LS17 .....58 A7
  BRIG HD6 .....167 K3
Linton Hills Rd *WBY* LS22 .....23 G6
Linton La *WBY* LS22 .....22 D4
  WBY LS22 .....23 G7
Linton Mdw *WBY* LS22 .....23 G6
Linton Ri *AL/HA/HU* LS17 .....58 A7
  NORM WF6 .....178 C2
Linton Rd *WBY* LS22 .....23 G6
  WBY LS22 .....41 F2
  WKFDE WF1 .....11 F3
Linton St *BOW* BD4 .....96 B7
  HWTH BD22 .....2 A5
Linton Vw *AL/HA/HU* LS17 .....58 A6
Lion Chambers *HUD* * HD1 .....12 C4
Lionel St *OSS* WF5 .....175 K7
Liphill Bank Rd *HOLM/MEL* HD9 .....232 C6
Lippersley La *AIRE* BD20 .....17 J5
Lipscomb St *HUDW* HD3 .....190 B6
Liquorice Wy *PONT* WF8 .....180 D3
Lisbon Sq *LDS* LS1 .....6 C3
Lisbon St *LDS* LS1 .....6 C3
Lisheen Av *CAS* WF10 .....153 K5
Lisheen Gv *CAS* WF10 .....153 K4
Lisker Av *OT* LS21 .....33 K4
Lisker Ct *OT* LS21 .....33 K4
Lisker Dr *OT* LS21 .....33 K4
Lismore Cl *RTHW* LS26 .....126 C6
Lismore Rd *KGHY* BD21 .....2 C2
Lister Av *BOW* BD4 .....96 D8
Lister Cl *FEA/AMT* WF7 .....179 H4
Lister Ct *HFAX* * HX1 .....9 D4
Listerdale *LVSG* WF15 .....144 D6
Lister Gdns *GIR* BD8 .....4 A1
Lister Hl *HORS* LS18 .....77 G1

Listerhills Rd *GTHN* BD7 .....4 A4
Lister La *ECHL* BD2 .....5 D1
  HFAX HX1 .....8 B5
Lister Rd *FEA/AMT* WF7 .....179 G6
Lister's Rd *HIPP* HX3 .....9 F5
Lister St *BOW* BD4 .....119 K1
  BRIG HD6 .....142 B8
  CAS WF10 .....153 H3
  HFAX HX1 .....9 D4
  HUDE HD5 .....192 A5
  ILK LS29 .....20 A7
  KGHY BD21 .....2 C4
Little Bankes St *HFAX* HX1 .....8 B5
Littlebeck Dr *BGLY* BD16 .....50 C8
Little Bradley *GTL/HWG* HX4 .....166 B5
Little Brunswick St *HUD* * HD1 .....12 C4
Little Cake *HOLM/MEL* HD9 .....248 D1
Little Church La *RTHW* LS26 .....152 B1
Little Cote *IDLE* BD10 .....74 C2
Little Cross St *WBOW* BD5 .....119 F1
Littlefield Gv *OSS* WF5 .....173 K5
Littlefield Rd *OSS* WF5 .....173 K6
Littlefield Wk *WBSY* BD6 .....118 C3
Little Fold *HUDS* * HD4 .....212 E5
Little Fountain St *MOR* LS27 .....123 F7
Little Green La *HECK* WF16 .....145 F6
Little Hemsworth *HEM/SK/SE* WF9 .....224 E5
Little Hew Royd *IDLE* BD10 .....74 B3
Littleholme St *TOD* OL14 .....133 K8
Little Horton Gn *WBOW* BD5 .....4 A6
Little Horton La *WBOW* BD5 .....4 C5
Little King St *LDS* LS1 .....7 D4
Littlelands *BGLY* BD16 .....72 A4
Littlelands Ct *BGLY* * BD16 .....72 A4
Little La *AIRE* BD20 .....49 J3
  EARD/LOFT WF3 .....126 B8
  FEA/AMT WF7 .....179 K7
  HBR HX7 .....89 H5
  HEM/SK/SE WF9 .....226 B8
  HEM/SK/SE WF9 .....226 D4
  HEM/SK/SE WF9 .....226 D8
  HOLM/MEL * HD9 .....233 F6
  HOLM/MEL HD9 .....233 J5
  HTON BD9 .....95 F1
  ILK LS29 .....20 C7
  MOR LS27 .....123 H3
Little Lane Ct *MOR* LS27 .....123 H5
Littlemoor Ct *PDSY/CALV* LS28 .....98 D5
Littlemoor Crs *PDSY/CALV* LS28 .....98 C6
Littlemoor Crs South
  PDSY/CALV LS28 .....98 C6
Littlemoor Gdns *LUD/ILL* HX2 .....115 H5
  PDSY/CALV LS28 .....98 C6
Littlemoor Gv *MIRF* WF14 .....170 C6
Little Moor La *SCFT* LS14 .....60 D8
Little Moor Pl *WOR/ARM* LS12 .....100 B4
Littlemoor Rd *LUD/ILL* HX2 .....115 H5
  MIRF WF14 .....170 C6
  PDSY/CALV LS28 .....98 C5
Littlemoor Vw *PDSY/CALV* LS28 .....98 D5
Little Neville St *LDS* LS1 .....7 D4
Little Pk *IDLE* BD10 .....75 G2
Little Queen St *LDS* LS1 .....6 C3
Littlethorpe Hl *LVSG* WF15 .....170 A1
Littlethorpe Rd *LVSG* WF15 .....170 A1
Little Westfields *BSLYN/ROY* * S71 .....222 A8
Littlewood Cl *WBSY* BD6 .....118 D4
Littlewood Cft *HUDS* HD4 .....213 G1
Little Wood Dr *CLECK* BD19 .....144 A1
Little Woodhouse *BRIG* HD6 .....168 B1
Little Woodhouse St *LDSU* LS2 .....6 C2
Litton Cft *WKFDE* WF1 .....11 F2
Littondale *BAIL* BD17 .....52 A7
Litton Rd *HWTH* BD22 .....2 B1
Litton Wy *SCFT* LS14 .....81 K3
Liversedge Hall La *LVSG* WF15 .....144 D8
Livingstone Cl *ECHL* BD2 .....74 B5
Livingstone Rd *SHPY* BD18 .....73 K7
Livingstone St *HIPP* HX3 .....8 B2
Livingstone St North *LUD/ILL* HX2 .....115 K6
Livinia Gv *CHAL* LS7 .....7 D1
Lloyds Dr *LM/WK* BD12 .....119 F5
Lloyd St *TOD* OL14 .....134 A3
Lobley St *HECK* WF16 .....145 H7
Locarno Av *HTON* BD9 .....94 B7
Locherbie Gn *WIL/AL* * BD15 .....94 A2
Lochy Rd *WBSY* BD6 .....118 A5
Lockbridge Wy *HUDS* HD4 .....190 B7
Lock La *CAS* WF10 .....153 J2
  NORM WF6 .....151 J5
The Locks *BGLY* BD16 .....49 K7
Locksley Rd *BRIG* HD6 .....168 A3
Lock St *EARL* WF12 .....172 C7
  HIPP HX3 .....9 E5
  TOD OL14 .....133 K8
Lock Vw *ELL* HX5 .....167 F3
Lock Wy *DEWS* WF13 .....171 H7
Lockwood Av *MIRF* WF14 .....170 A4
Lockwood Cl *BEE/HOL* LS11 .....124 C2
  HUDW HD3 .....190 B6

Lockwood Rd *HUD* HD1 .....191 F5
Lockwood Scar *HUDS* HD4 .....191 F6
Lockwood St *LM/WK* BD12 .....119 F2
  SHPY * BD18 .....73 K5
  WBSY BD6 .....118 C3
Lockwoods Yd *HUD* HD1 .....12 C4
Lockwood Wy *BEE/HOL* LS11 .....124 C2
Locomotion Br *HUD* HD1 .....13 E5
Lode Pit La *BGLY* BD16 .....50 E4
The Lodge *MAR/SLWT* HD7 .....211 K5
Lodge Av *CAS* WF10 .....154 D2
  ELL HX5 .....167 K5
Lodge Cl *HUDS* HD4 .....212 B5
Lodge Dr *ELL* HX5 .....167 K5
  MIRF WF14 .....171 F5
Lodge Farm Cl *EARL* WF12 .....172 C4
Lodge Farm Gdns *NORM* WF6 .....151 J5
Lodge Gate Cl *CUL/QBY* BD13 .....92 D2
Lodge Gv *WKFDE* WF1 .....11 D1
Lodge Hl *BAIL* BD17 .....51 J8
Lodge Hill Cl *WOR/ARM* LS12 .....99 G5
Lodge Hill Rd *OSS* WF5 .....173 J8
Lodge La *BEE/HOL* LS11 .....14 A1
  HOR/CROF WF4 .....200 C8
  LUD/ILL * HX2 .....114 B7
  LVSG WF15 .....171 G2
  WKFDW/WTN WF2 .....199 F8
Lodge Pl *ELL* * HX5 .....167 K5
Lodge Rd *PDSY/CALV* LS28 .....98 B5
Lodges Cl *HOR/CROF* WF4 .....223 K1
Lodge St *CUL/QBY* BD13 .....70 E2
  HEM/SK/SE WF9 .....224 A1
  KBTN HD8 .....236 A3
  LDS LS1 .....6 C1
Lodge Ter *BEE/HOL* * LS11 .....124 A1
Lodore Pl *ECHL* BD2 .....74 C1
Lodore Rd *ECHL* BD2 .....74 C1
Lofthouse Pl *LDSU* LS2 .....7 E1
Lofthouse Ter *CHAL* LS7 .....7 E1
Loft St *GIR* BD8 .....4 A1
Logwood St *HUD* HD1 .....12 B4
Loiner Ct *OSM* LS9 .....102 A7
Lombardi Ct *OSS* WF5 .....174 B5
Lombard St *HFAX* HX1 .....8 A3
  MSTN/BAR LS15 .....103 K4
  YEA LS19 .....59 K5
Lomond Av *HORS* LS18 .....55 F8
Londesboro Gv *OSM* LS9 .....102 B5
Londesboro Ter *OSM* LS9 .....102 A5
London La *YEA* LS19 .....53 H3
London Rd *MAR/SLWT* HD7 .....210 A1
  RPDN/SBR HX6 .....135 G2
  TOD OL14 .....135 F2
London Spring Rd *RPDN/SBR* HX6 .....163 H8
London St *YEA* LS19 .....59 K5
Longacre *CAS* WF10 .....153 F8
Longacre La *HWTH* BD22 .....69 F2
Longacres *HWTH* BD22 .....69 F2
Longbottom Av *AIRE* BD20 .....27 K5
  RPDN/SBR HX6 .....138 B6
Longbottom Ter *HIPP* * HX3 .....140 C6
Longbow Cl *HUDN* HD2 .....168 C1
The Long Cswy *BRFD/BLYE* BD10 .....108 B1
  LUD/ILL HX2 .....137 G2
Longcauseway *EARL* WF12 .....172 C6
Long Cswy *BHP/TINH* LS16 .....56 D1
  EARD/LOFT WF3 .....150 A8
  EARL WF12 .....172 B6
  HBR HX7 .....110 D5
  HWTH BD22 .....91 H8
  OSM LS9 .....102 B4
  RPDN/SBR HX6 .....186 A3
  SKP/WFD BD23 .....14 B2
  TOD OL14 .....134 B3
  WKFDE WF1 .....11 E3
Long Cl *LM/WK* BD12 .....118 C4
Long Close La *HEM/SK/SE* WF9 .....226 C8
  KBTN HD8 .....234 A3
  OSM LS9 .....102 B4
Long Crest *PONT* WF8 .....181 H4
Longcroft *HUDE* HD5 .....192 E8
  KGHY HD8 .....3 F3
Longcroft Link *BFD* * BD1 .....4 C3
Longcroft Pl *BFD* * BD1 .....4 C3
Longcroft Rd *ILK* LS29 .....20 A8
Long Croft St *MAR/SLWT* HD7 .....189 J6
Longdale Dr *HEM/SK/SE* WF9 .....226 A6
Long Dam La *HOR/CROF* WF4 .....200 C4
Longden Av *HUDS* HD4 .....212 B5
Longdike Cl *GFTH/SHER* LS25 .....129 J1
Longdike La *GFTH/SHER* LS25 .....129 J1
Longdon Av *KBTN* HD8 .....193 H8
Longdon Wk *KBTN* HD8 .....193 H8
Long Edge Low Rd *RPDN/SBR* HX6 .....163 F5
Long Edge Rd *RPDN/SBR* HX6 .....163 G5
Long Fallas Crs *BRIG* HD6 .....168 E2
Longfellow Gv *EARD/LOFT* WF3 .....150 E7
Longfield *GTL/HWG* HX4 .....166 B7
  HBR HX7 .....112 A1
Longfield Av *HIPP* HX3 .....141 H3
  HUDE HD5 .....13 K8
  MAR/SLWT HD7 .....189 G6
  PDSY/CALV LS28 .....98 A2
Longfield Cl *HUDE* HD5 .....13 K8
  TOD OL14 .....134 A4
Longfield Ct *HECK* WF16 .....145 J5
  PDSY/CALV LS28 .....98 A2
Longfield Dr *BOW* BD4 .....96 E6
  BRAM LS13 .....76 D6

EA/AMT WF7 ....203 J4
1STN/BAR LS15 ....103 J3
gfield Garth BRAM LS13 ....76 D6
gfield Gv PDSY/CALV LS28 ....98 D4
OD OL14 ....134 A7
gfield Mt PDSY/CALV LS28 ....98 D4
gfield Rd HECK WF16 ....145 G7
DSY/CALV LS28 ....98 D4
OD OL14 ....134 A6
gfield Ter PDSY/CALV LS28 ....98 C4
VKFDW/WTN WF2 ....175 G4
gfield Vw TOD OL14 ....134 A7
gford Ter GTHN BD7 ....95 F6
g Ga HWTH BD22 ....45 J4
PDN/SBR HX6 ....186 C3
g Grove Av HUDE HD5 ....192 A5
g Hey La TOD OL14 ....134 B8
g Heys GTL/HWG HX4 ....166 B5
g Hill End HWTH BD22 ....44 B8
g Hill Rd HUDE HD5 ....168 C7
ghouse Dr CUL/QBY BD13 ....92 B3
ghouse Rd CUL/QBY BD13 ....92 B3
g House Rd LUD/ILL HX2 ....115 F5
g Ing HOLM/MEL HD9 ....232 D8
g Ing Rd HOLM/MEL HD9 ....248 B4
MAR/SLWT HD7 ....210 C2
glands Bank HOLM/MEL HD9 ....233 H4
glands Cl OSS WF5 ....173 K5
glands Dr HWTH BD22 ....69 F3
glands La WBY LS22 ....22 A6
glands Rd DEWS WF13 ....171 K1
MAR/SLWT HD7 ....210 C2
SS WF5 ....173 K5
glands St BFD BD1 ....4 B4
g La BGLY BD16 ....70 E2
UL/QBY BD13 ....116 C4
ARL WF13 ....172 E5
EA/AMT WF7 ....203 H2
BR HX7 ....135 J8
BR HX7 ....135 K2
IPP HX3 ....159 H1
IPP HX3 ....159 F8
OLM/MEL HD9 ....213 F8
OR/CROF WF4 ....216 B2
TON BD9 ....72 D6
UDE HD5 ....192 A5
STN HD8 ....215 C8
STN HD8 ....217 K8
STN HD8 ....235 C7
STN/BAR LS15 ....83 H4
ONT WF8 ....181 G5
SBR HX6 ....164 D1
IL/AL DS15 ....93 H2
g Lee La KGHY BD21 ....3 E5
g Lee La KGHY BD21 ....3 F5
gley Edge La HOLM/MEL HD9 ....248 C1
gley Edge Rd HOLM/MEL HD9 ....248 C1
gley La HOLM/MEL HD9 ....248 B2
UDE HD5 ....213 J1
SBR HX6 ....164 C3
gley Rd HUDE HD5 ....13 F6
g Lover La HFAX HX1 ....8 A3
g Meadow La GFTH/SHER LS25 ....106 K6
g Meadow Vw GFTH/SHER LS25 ....105 K6
g Mdw BHP/TINH LS16 ....55 J1
HL BD2 7
K LS29 ....32 A1
FTH/SHER LS25 ....105 K6
gside La GTHN BD7 ....4 A5
g St BOW BD4 ....5 F6
g Thorpe La EARD/LOFT WF3 ....149 H2
g Tongue Scrog La HUDE HD5 ....193 F4
g Wall ELL HX5 ....166 D5
gwood Av BGLY BD16 ....49 J6
gwood Cl AL/HA/HU LS17 ....58 D6
ARD/LOFT * WF3 ....147 J3
gwood Ct EARD/LOFT WF3 ....147 K3
gwood Crs AL/HA/HU LS17 ....58 D6
gwood Edge Rd HUDW HD3 ....189 J3

Longwood Fold EARD/LOFT WF3 ....147 K3
Longwood Garth EARD/LOFT WF3 ....147 K3
Longwood Ga HUDW HD3 ....189 K5
Longwood House Rd HUDN * HD2 ....168 B8
Longwood Rd EARD/LOFT WF3 ....147 J3
HUDW HD3 ....190 B6
Longwoods Wv KNOT WF11 ....156 D6
Longwood V EARD/LOFT WF3 ....147 K3
Longwood Vw BCLY BD16 ....49 J6
Longwood Wy AL/HA/HU LS17 ....58 D6
Lonsbrough Av HECK WF16 ....145 G6
Lonsbrough Flats HUD * HD1 ....13 D4
Lonsdale Av BTLY WF17 ....145 J4
Lonsdale Cl MID LS10 ....124 E2
Lonsdale Mdw BSPA/BRAM LS23 ....42 D4
Lonsdale Ri EARD/LOFT WF3 ....147 K3
Lonsdale St BFDE BD3 ....5 F3
Lonsdale Ter LVSG * WF15 ....144 D7
Lord La HWTH BD22 ....68 D5
Lordsfield Pl BOW BD4 ....120 A2
Lord's La BRIG HD6 ....168 C2
Lord St DEWS WF13 ....145 J7
EARL * WF12 ....173 G4
HFAX HX1 3
KGHY BD21 ....3 D3
MAR/SLWT HD7 ....210 D2
RPDN/SBR HX6 ....139 F6
TOD OL14 ....159 K2
WKFDE WF1 ....11 F6
WOR/ARM LS12 ....6 B5
Lore Ter WOR/ARM LS12 ....6 B5
Loris St BOW BD4 ....120 A2
Lorne St BOW BD4 ....96 D8
HWTH BD22 ....69 H3
KGHY BD21 ....3 F2
Lorry Bank CHAL LS7 ....79 J7
Loscoe Cl NORM WF6 ....152 D8
Loscoe La NORM WF6 ....178 D1
Loshpot La WBY LS22 ....24 A1
Lotherton La GFTH/SHER LS25 ....85 F5
GFTH/SHER LS25 ....85 H6
Lotherton Wy GFTH/SHER LS25 ....105 K3
Loughrigg St WBOW BD5 ....96 A8
Loughrigg Wk FEA/AMT WF7 ....202 E6
Louisa St CAS WF10 ....153 H3
IDLE * BD10 ....74 D3
Louis Av WBOW BD5 ....95 J7
Louis Ct CHAL LS7 ....79 K8
Louis Gv CHAL LS7 ....80 A8
Louis Le Prince Ct RHAY LS8 ....80 D4
Louis St CHAL LS7 ....79 K8
Lound La BTLY DN5 ....243 H6
Lovaine Gv WKFDW/WTN WF2 ....199 F2
Love La CAS WF10 ....153 H5
HFAX HX1 ....8 C5
OSS WF5 ....173 H5
PONT WF8 ....180 C4
RTHW LS26 ....126 B6
WKFDW/WTN WF2 ....10 B3
Love Lane Ter PONT WF8 ....180 D3
Lovell Park Cl CHAL * LS7 ....7 F2
Lovell Park Ga CHAL LS7 ....7 F2
Lovell Park Gra CHAL * LS7 ....7 F2
Lovell Park Gn CHAL * LS7 ....7 F2
Lovell Park Hl CHAL LS7 ....7 F2
Lovell Park Ms CHAL * LS7 ....7 F2
Lovell Park Vw CHAL * LS7 ....7 F2
Lovell Vw HOR/CROF WF4 ....200 E3
Low Ash Av SHPY BD18 ....73 K4
Low Ash Crs SHPY BD18 ....74 A4
Low Ash Dr SHPY BD18 ....73 K4
Low Ash Gv SHPY BD18 ....73 K4
Low Ash Rd SHPY BD18 ....74 A4
Low Bank Dr HWTH BD22 ....46 D8
Low Bank La HWTH BD22 ....46 D8
Low Banks AIRE * BD20 ....20 B5
Low Bank St PDSY/CALV LS28 ....76 A8
Low Cliff Wk HECK WF16 ....171 H1
Low Cl BGLY BD16 ....72 B1
ILK LS29 ....20 B5
Low Close St LDSU * LS2 ....79 G8
Low Cft BSLYN/ROY S71 ....222 B8
Lowcroft WBY LS22 ....40 E3
Lowdale EARL WF12 ....172 D1
Lowell Av GTHN BD7 ....95 F6
Lowell Gv BRAM LS13 ....98 E3
Lowell Pl BRAM LS13 ....98 E3
Lower Asthgrove WBOW BD5 ....4 B5
Lower Back La HBR HX7 ....110 E7
Lower Bankhouse PDSY/CALV LS28 ....98 B7
Lower Bank Houses GTL/HWG * HX4 ....165 G7
Lower Basinghall St LDS LS1 7
Lower Bower La DEWS WF13 ....145 J4
Lower Brock Well La RPDN/SBR HX6 ....164 C1
Lower Brunswick St LDSU LS2 ....7 F3
Lower Cambridge St CAS WF10 ....153 J3
Lower Clay Pits HFAX HX1 ....8 A3
Lower Clifton St RPDN/SBR * HX6 ....139 F7
Lower Clyde St RPDN/SBR HX6 ....138 E8
Lower Common La KBTN HD8 ....237 J2
Lower Constable Rd ILK LS29 ....20 D1
Lower Cow Cl LM/WK * BD12 ....143 G1
Lower Cross St HFAX HX1 9
Lower Crow Nest Dr BRIG HD6 ....142 C4
Lower Denby La KBTN HD8 ....236 E8

Lower Edge Rd ELL HX5 ....167 G4
Lower Ellistones GTL/HWG * HX4 ....165 K4
Lower Ferney Lee TOD OL14 ....133 K5
Lower Finkil St BRIG HD6 ....141 K6
Lower Fitzwilliam St HUD HD1 ....13 D3
Lower Fold BRIG HD6 ....168 A5
HOLM/MEL HD9 ....213 F6
Lower Ga HUDW HD3 ....190 B6
Lower George St TOD OL14 ....134 A6
WBSY * BD6 ....118 C2
Lower Globe St GIR BD8 ....4 A3
Lower Gra HUDN HD2 ....169 F5
Lower Grattan Rd BFD BD1 ....4 B4
Lower Greave Rd HOLM/MEL HD9 ....232 B3
Lower Green Av CLECK BD19 ....143 G3
Lower Hall Cl LVSG WF15 ....144 C7
Lower Hall Crs HUDE HD5 ....192 E5
Lower Hall Dr LVSG WF15 ....144 C7
Lower Hall La LVSG WF15 ....144 C7
Lower Hall Mt LVSG WF15 ....144 C7
Lower Hall Rd HUDE HD5 ....192 E5
Lower Heights Rd CUL/QBY BD13 ....93 G3
Lower Hey HOLM/MEL HD9 ....211 H8
Lower Holme BAIL BD17 ....73 J2
Lower House Cl SHPY BD18 ....74 B2
Lower House La KBTN HD8 ....215 J1
Lowerhouses La HUDE HD5 ....13 F6
Lowerhouses Rd HUDW * HD3 ....190 B5
Lower Kipping La CUL/QBY BD13 ....93 H5
Lower Laith Av TOD OL14 ....134 B6
Lower La BIRK/DRI BD11 ....120 A6
BOW BD4 ....96 E7
CLECK BD19 ....144 E4
HBR HX7 ....110 D8
HOLM/MEL HD9 ....212 D7
Lower Langwith WBY LS22 ....40 E3
Lower Lark Hl CLECK BD19 ....143 J4
Lower Maythorn La HOLM/MEL HD9 ....249 K3
Lower Mdw HOLM/MEL HD9 ....232 D6
Lower Mickletown RTHW LS26 ....128 D8
Lower Mill Bank Rd RPDN/SBR HX6 ....164 A4
Lower Newlands BRIG HD6 ....168 C2
Lower Northcroft HEM/SK/SE WF9 ....226 C8
Lower Northfield La HEM/SK/SE WF9 ....225 J8
Lower North St BTLY WF17 ....146 A7
Lower Oxford St CAS WF10 ....153 J4
Lower Park Gn AIRE BD20 ....26 E2
Lower Park Royd Dr RPDN/SBR HX6 ....164 B4
Lower Peel St DEWS WF13 ....172 B2
Lower Quarry Rd HUDN HD2 ....169 H4
Lower Range HIPP HX3 ....9 D2
Lower Rd HUDW HD3 ....187 H5
Lower Rushton Rd BFDE BD3 ....97 G4
Lower Sandhills SCFT LS14 ....60 C8
Lower School St LM/WK BD12 ....118 D5
SHPY * BD18 ....73 F3
Lower Station Rd NORM WF6 ....177 K1
Lower Tofts Rd PDSY/CALV LS28 ....98 C4
Lowertown HWTH BD22 ....90 E1
Lower Town St BRAM LS13 ....99 H1
Lower Viaduct St HUD * HD1 ....13 D3
Lower Warrengate WKFDE WF1 ....11 D5
Lower Wellhouse Rd MAR/SLWT HD7 ....189 H8
Lower Wellington Rd ILK LS29 ....20 C7
Lower Westfield Rd GIR * BD8 ....95 G2
Lower Wortley Rd WOR/ARM LS12 ....100 B6
Lower Wyke Gn LM/WK BD12 ....142 C3
Lower Wyke La LM/WK BD12 ....142 D3
Lower York St WKFDE WF1 ....10 C2
Lowestwood La MAR/SLWT HD7 ....211 H1
Loweswater Av WBSY BD6 ....118 A5
Low Farm RTHW LS26 ....128 D3
Low Farm La FEA/AMT WF7 ....203 G5
Lowfield Cl LM/WK BD12 ....119 F6
Lowfield Crs AIRE BD20 ....27 H3
HEM/SK/SE WF9 ....224 E4
Lowfield La SKP/WHF WF23 ....15 J6
Lowfield Rd DEWS WF13 ....171 J3
HEM/SK/SE WF9 ....224 E4
Low Fields Av BEE/HOL LS11 ....100 E7
Low Fields Rd WOR/ARM LS12 ....100 D7
Lowfields Wy ELL HX5 ....167 F3
Low Fold AIRE BD20 ....26 E5
CLECK BD19 ....143 G3
ECHL BD2 ....5 D1
Low Ga HEM/SK/SE WF9 ....226 C8
HOLM/MEL HD9 ....233 H7
Low Gipton Crs OSM LS9 ....81 F8
Low Grange Crs MID LS10 ....125 F2
Low Grange Vw MID LS10 ....125 F3
Low Gn FEA/AMT WF7 ....203 H4
GTHN BD7 ....95 G8
KNOT WF11 ....154 A8
YEA LS19 ....76 B3
Low Green Ter GTHN BD7 ....95 H8
Low Hall Pl BEE/HOL LS11 ....6 B5
Low Hall Rd ILK LS29 ....32 D7
YEA LS19 ....76 B3
Low Hills La HUDW HD3 ....190 A2
Low House Dr AIRE BD20 ....27 G3
Low House Fold LVSG WF15 ....144 C7
Lowlands Rd MIRF WF14 ....170 E7

Low La AIRE BD20 ....16 E6
  AIRE BD20 ....27 H4
  BRIG HD6 ....142 D5
  BTLY WF17 ....145 H2
  CLAY BD14 ....94 A6
  CUL/QBY BD13 ....93 C8
  HBR HX7 ....113 H4
  HOR/CROF WF4 ....196 B5
  HORS LS18 ....77 H1
  SKP/WHF BD23 ....19 C4
Low Mi ILK * LS29 ....19 C4
Low Mill La DEWS WF13 ....171 C7
  ILK LS29 ....19 F3
  KGHY BD21 ....3 E5
Low Mill Rd OSS WF5 ....173 H8
Low Mills GSLY * LS20 ....53 C3
Low Mills Rd WOR/ARM LS12 ....100 B7
Low Moor Crs HOR/CROF WF4 ....198 B8
Low Moor La HOR/CROF WF4 ....219 J6
Low Moor Side WIL/AL BD15 ....99 H8
Low Moor Side Cl WOR/ARM * LS12 ..99 J8
Low Moor Side La WOR/ARM LS12 ...122 B1
Low Moor St LM/WK * BD12 ....118 E5
Low Moor Ter LUD/ILL HX2 ....139 C5
Lowood La BTLY WF17 ....121 H8
Low Park Rd ILK LS29 ....21 H6
Low Rd DEWS WF13 ....171 J5
  EARL WF12 ....172 D4
  EARL WF12 ....195 C2
  HUDS HD4 ....213 F3
  MID LS10 ....102 A7
Lowry Rd EARD/LOFT WF3 ....147 K3
Lowry Vw KGHY BD21 ....3 D4
Low Shops La RTHW LS26 ....125 K5
Low Spring Rd KGHY BD21 ....3 F4
Low St DEWS * WF13 ....172 B2
  EARD/LOFT WF3 ....147 K2
  KGHY BD21 ....3 D3
  KNOT WF11 ....155 K4
Lowswater Rd KNOT WF11 ....182 B1
Lowther Av GFTH/SHER LS25 ....105 J5
Lowther Crs RTHW LS26 ....127 J1
Lowther Dr GFTH/SHER LS25 ....105 J5
  RTHW LS26 ....127 J1
Lowther St ECHL BD2 ....5 F2
  RHAY LS8 ....80 D7
Low Town KBTN HD8 ....215 H6
Lowtown PDSY/CALV LS28 ....98 D3
Low Wy BSPA/BRAM LS23 ....42 D5
  BSPA/BRAM LS23 ....62 D1
Low Well Rd WBOW * BD5 ....95 K8
Low Wood Cl LARR * BD20 ....27 K8
Low Wood Ri ILK LS29 ....20 E8
Loxley Gv WBY LS22 ....23 H3
Loxley St BTLY WF17 ....145 K4
Lucas Ct CHAL LS7 ....79 J8
Lucas Pl HDGY LS6 ....79 G7
Lucas St HDGY LS6 ....79 G7
Luck La HDUW HD3 ....190 C5
Lucy Av MSTN/BAR LS15 ....103 G3
Lucy Hall Dr BAIL BD17 ....72 E1
Lucy La KBTN HD8 ....193 G6
Lucy St HIPP * HX3 ....9 E3
Luddenden La LUD/ILL HX2 ....138 A4
Ludhill La HOLM/MEL HD9 ....213 K6
Ludlam St WBOW BD5 ....4 C6
Ludlow Av GFTH/SHER LS25 ....106 B4
Ludolf Dr AL/HA/HU LS17 ....59 C7
Ludwell Cl EARL WF12 ....195 K2
Ludwood Cl HOLM/MEL HD9 ....213 C6
Luke La HOLM/MEL HD9 ....233 J3
Luke Rd WBOW BD5 ....95 J7
Lulworth Av MSTN/BAR LS15 ....104 B3
Lulworth Cl MSTN/BAR LS15 ....104 B3
Lulworth Crs MSTN/BAR LS15 ....104 B3
Lulworth Garth MSTN/BAR LS15 ......104 B3
Lulworth Gv BOW BD4 ....120 A1
Lulworth Vw MSTN/BAR LS15 ....104 B3
Lulworth Wk MSTN/BAR LS15 ....104 B3
Lumb Bottom BIRK/DRI BD11 ....121 J4
Lumbfoot Rd HWTH BD22 ....68 A4
Lumb Gill La ILK LS29 ....19 F5
Lumb La HBR HX7 ....4 A2
  HIPP HX3 ....8 C1
  HUDS HD4 ....213 K3
  HWTH BD22 ....44 B3
  LUD/ILL HX2 ....114 C4
  LVSG WF15 ....170 C1
  RPDN/SBR HX6 ....163 K4
Lumb Rd HBR HX7 ....111 J6
Lumbrook Cl HIPP HX3 ....117 H8
Lumbutts La TOD OL14 ....134 C7
Lumbutts Rd TOD OL14 ....134 C8
Lumby Cl PDSY/CALV LS28 ....98 D6
Lumby La AL/HA/HU LS17 ....39 J5
  PDSY/CALV LS28 ....98 D6
Lumby St IDLE * BD10 ....74 D5
Lumley Av BULY LS4 ....78 D8
  CAS WF10 ....153 F4
Lumley Gv BULY LS4 ....78 D8
Lumley Hl CAS WF10 ....153 F4
Lumley Mt BULY LS4 ....78 D8
Lumley Pl BULY LS4 ....78 D8
Lumley Rd BULY LS4 ....78 D8
  EARL WF12 ....172 D1
Lumley St BULY LS4 ....78 D8
  CAS WF10 ....153 G4
Lumley Ter BULY LS4 ....78 D8

Lumley Vw BULY LS4 ....78 D8
Lumley Wk BULY LS4 ....78 D8
Lunan Pl RHAY LS8 ....80 B7
Lund Dr HECK WF16 ....145 H8
Lund Hill La BSLYN/ROY S71 ....222 D7
Lund La HWTH BD22 ....46 D5
Lund St BGLY BD16 ....50 A8
  GIR BD8 ....94 E4
  KGHY BD21 ....3 D2
Lunnfields La KNOT WF11 ....131 J7
Lupset Crs WKFDW/WTN WF2 ....75 F8
Lupton Av OSM LS9 ....102 C3
Lupton St GIR BD8 ....4 B2
  MID LS10 ....102 A8
Lustre St KGHY BD21 ....2 B5
Luther Pl HUDW HD3 ....12 A3
Luther Wy ECHL BD2 ....74 B8
Luton St HFAX HX1 ....8 A4
  HUDS HD4 ....189 K8
  KGHY BD21 ....2 C5
Luttrell Cl BHP/TINH LS16 ....78 A1
Luttrell Crs BHP/TINH LS16 ....78 A1
Luttrell Gdns BHP/TINH LS16 ....78 A1
Luttrell Pl BHP/TINH LS16 ....78 A1
Luttrell Rd BHP/TINH LS16 ....78 A1
The Lutyens ILK LS29 ....19 K7
Luxor Av RHAY LS8 ....80 B7
Luxor Rd RHAY LS8 ....80 B7
Luxor St RHAY LS8 ....80 C7
Luxor Vw RHAY LS8 ....80 B7
Lydbrook Pk HIPP HX3 ....165 K1
Lyddon Ter LDSU LS2 ....6 C1
Lydgate HIPP HX3 ....117 F8
  KBTN HD8 ....193 J8
  OSM LS9 ....102 B2
Lydgate Cl HOLM/MEL HD9 ....234 A5
Lydgate La HOLM/MEL HD9 ....233 K4
  KBTN HD8 ....193 J8
Lydgate Pk HIPP HX3 ....141 K4
Lydgate Pl PDSY/CALV LS28 ....75 J4
Lydgate Ri HEM/SK/SE * WF9 ....225 K8
Lydgate Rd BTLY WF17 ....146 E6
  KBTN HD8 ....235 G3
Lydgate St PDSY/CALV LS28 ....75 J4
Lydget Ct AIRE BD20 ....2 B1
Lydgetts HOLM/MEL HD9 ....232 D6
Lydia St LDSU LS2 ....7 F3
Lyme Cha SCFT LS14 ....103 H1
Lymington Dr BOW BD4 ....97 G7
Lynch Av GTHN BD7 ....95 F8
Lyncroft ECHL BD2 ....74 B7
Lynda Gv OSS WF5 ....174 B7
Lyndale Gv NORM WF6 ....174 B7
Lyndale Dr SHPY BD18 ....74 B4
  WKFDW/WTN WF2 ....175 F1
Lyndale Gv NORM WF6 ....178 B2
Lyndale Ms DEWS WF13 ....145 J8
Lyndale Rd BGLY BD16 ....50 C6
Lyndean Gdns IDLE BD10 ....74 C4
Lynden Av SHPY BD18 ....74 A3
Lynden Ct WBSY BD6 ....118 B4
Lyndhurst BGLY * BD16 ....49 K7
Lyndhurst Av BRIG HD6 ....168 B4
Lyndhurst Cl MSTN/BAR LS15 ....82 C4
Lyndhurst Crs MSTN/BAR LS15 ....82 D4
Lyndhurst Gv WIL/AL BD15 ....94 C2
Lyndhurst Grove Rd BRIG HD6 ....168 B3
Lyndhurst Rd BRIG HD6 ....168 B5
  HUDW HD3 ....190 B5
  MSTN/BAR LS15 ....82 D5
Lyndhurst Vw MSTN/BAR LS15 ....82 D5
Lyndon Av BSPA/BRAM LS23 ....42 C8
  GFTH/SHER LS25 ....105 J4
Lyndon Cl BSPA/BRAM LS23 ....42 C8
Lyndon Rd BSPA/BRAM LS23 ....42 C8
Lyndon Sq BSPA/BRAM LS23 ....42 C8
Lyndon Ter BGLY BD16 ....50 A8
Lyndon Wy BSPA/BRAM LS23 ....42 C8
Lyndum Gv GFTH/SHER LS25 ....129 F1
Lynfield Dr HTON BD9 ....72 D8
  LVSG WF15 ....143 J6
Lynfield Mt SHPY BD18 ....74 A3
Lynmoor Ct IDLE BD10 ....74 B4
Lynndale Av HUDN HD2 ....12 B1
Lynnfield Gdns MSTN/BAR LS15 ....82 D5
Lynnwood Gdns PDSY/CALV LS28 .....98 A5
Lynsey Gdns BOW BD4 ....119 J4
Lynthorne Rd HTON BD9 ....73 H7
Lynton Av BSPA/BRAM LS23 ....42 D3
  EARD/LOFT WF3 ....149 F1
  HTON BD9 ....73 F8
  HUD HD1 ....12 B4
Lynton Dr AIRE BD20 ....48 D2
  HTON BD9 ....94 E1
  SHPY BD18 ....73 G4
Lynton Gv LUD/ILL HX2 ....115 J2
Lynton Pl DOD/DAR S75 ....239 K3
Lynton Ter CLECK * BD19 ....144 A3
Lynton Vls HTON BD9 ....95 F1
Lynwood Av RTHW LS26 ....127 G5
  SHPY BD18 ....74 A3
  WOR/ARM LS12 ....100 C7
Lynwood Cl BIRK/DRI BD11 ....120 E6
  FEA/AMT WF7 ....178 D7
Lynwood Ct HWTH BD22 ....47 G6
Lynwood Crs HEM/SK/SE WF9 ....201 K8
  HFAX HX1 ....8 A6

PONT WF8 180
RTHW LS26 127
WOR/ARM LS12 100
Lynwood Dr WKFDW/WTN WF2 198
Lynwood Garth WOR/ARM LS12 100
Lynwood Gv WOR/ARM LS12 100
Lynwood Ms BOW BD4 118
Lynwood Mt WOR/ARM LS12 100
Lynwood Ri WOR/ARM LS12 100
Lynwood Vw WOR/ARM LS12 100
Lyon Rd AIRE BD20 26
  PONT WF8 180
Lyon St CUL/QBY BD13 93
  CUL/QBY BD13 116
Lytham Cl NORM WF6 178
Lytham Dr CUL/QBY BD13 117
Lytham Gv WOR/ARM LS12 100
Lytham Pl WOR/ARM LS12 100
Lytham St HFAX HX1 8
Lytham Wy HUDW HD3 190
Lytton Rd GIR BD8 95
Lytton St HIPP * HX3 9
  MID LS10 101

M

Mabel Royd GTHN BD7 95
Mabel St HBR HX7 137
Mabgate Gn OSM LS9 7
Macaulay Rd HUDN HD2 12
Macaulay St OSM LS9 102
Macham St HUD HD1 12
Mackie Hill Cl HOR/CROF WF4 197
Mackingstone Dr HWTH BD22 46
Mackingstone La HWTH BD22 46
Mackinnon Av NORM WF6 152
Mackintosh Homes LUD/ILL HX2 139
Macturk Gv GIR * BD8 95
Maddocks St SHPY BD18 73
Madeley Rd HOR/CROF WF4 223
Madeley Sq CAS WF10 154
Madgin La HUDS HD4 212
Madison Av BOW BD4 120
Madni Cl HFAX HX1 8
Mafeking Av BEE/HOL LS11 124
Mafeking Gv BEE/HOL LS11 124
Mafeking Mt BEE/HOL LS11 124
Magdalene Cl BHP/TINH LS16 166
Magdalene Flds NORM WF6 178
Magdalene Rd WKFDW/WTN WF2 174
Magdalen Rd HOLM/MEL HD9 231
Maggot La STKB/PEN S36 253
Magna Gv WKFDW/WTN WF2 199
Magnolias BTLY WF17 145
Magpie Cl WBSY BD6 117
Magpie La MOR LS27 123
Maidstone St BFDE BD3 96
Maidwell Wy WBSY BD6 118
Mail Cl MSTN/BAR LS15 82
Main Av HUDS HD4 189
Main Ga HOLM/MEL HD9 249
Main Rd AIRE BD20 26
  AIRE BD20 26
  AIRE BD20 49
  CUL/QBY BD13 92
Mainspring Rd WIL/AL BD15 71
Main St AL/HA/HU LS17 37
  AL/HA/HU LS17 40
  AL/HA/HU LS17 55
  AWLS/ASK DN6 183
  AWLS/ASK DN6 222
  BAIL BD17 52
  BGLY BD16 49
  BGLY BD16 72
  BSPA/BRAM LS23 25
  CAS WF10 129
  CAS WF10 129
  CUD/GR S72 221
  EARD/LOFT WF3 126
  EARD/LOFT WF3 148
  GFTH/SHER LS25 84
  GFTH/SHER LS25 105
  GLE DN14 153
  GSLY LS20 58
  HEM/SK/SE WF9 226
  HEM/SK/SE WF9 227
  HWTH BD22 6
  HWTH BD22 6
  ILK LS29 18
  ILK LS29 32
  ILK LS29 32
  LM/WK BD12 118
  LM/WK BD12 137
  MSTN/BAR LS15 81
  MSTN/BAR LS15 83
  OT LS21 3
  RTHW LS26 126
  SCFT LS14 63
  WBY LS22 23
  WBY LS22 24
  WBY LS22 24
  WIL/AL BD15 70
Maister Pl HWTH BD22 4
Maitland Cl WIL/AL BD15 9
Maitland St TOD OL14 15
Maizebrook DEWS WF13 17

ze St HWTH BD22 ....2 B6
or St WKFDW/WTN WF2 ....10 B6
ham Av BRIG HD6 ....167 K3
TON BD9 ....72 C8
ham Cl CUD/GR S72 ....223 G8
CFT LS14 ....81 J7
ham Dr BTLY WF17 ....145 K6
VSG WF8 ....170 C2
ham Rd BRIG HD6 ....167 K4
VKFDE WF1 ....11 F2
ham Sq WKFDE * WF1 ....11 F2
in Rd EARL WF12 ....146 E8
lard Cl AV WKFDW/WTN WF2 ....198 E6
lard Cl IDLE BD10 ....74 E6
THW LS26 ....125 G4
lard Ct GIR BD8 ....94 C4
lard Rd CAS WF10 ....153 H5
Mallards AIRE BD20 ....27 G2
lard Vw HWTH BD22 ....90 E1
lard Wy MAR/SLWT HD7 ....210 D3
MOR LS27 ....123 J7
llinson St DEWS WF13 ....171 K2
iory Cl GTHN BD7 ....95 F4
mesbury Cl BOW BD4 ....120 B1
VOR/ARM LS12 ....100 C5
mesbury Gv WOR/ARM LS12 ....100 C5
mesbury Pl WOR/ARM LS12 ....100 C5
mesbury Ter WOR/ARM LS12 ....100 C5
isis Crs KGHY * BD21 ....2 B4
isis Rd KGHY BD21 ....2 B4
thouse Ct SCFT LS14 ....60 A3
tby Ct MSTN/BAR * LS15 ....104 B4
ting Cl EARD/LOFT WF3 ....125 J8
ting Rd EARD/LOFT WF3 ....125 J8
Maltings EARD/LOFT WF3 ....125 J8
DGY * LS6 ....6 A1
IRF WF14 ....170 C6
ONT WF8 ....180 E2
tings Cft BEE/HOL * LS11 ....101 J7
tings Rd BEE/HOL LS11 ....101 J7
UD/ILL HX2 ....139 G1
tkiln Cft WKFDW/WTN WF2 ....199 G2
tkiln Dr HOR/CROF WF4 ....219 F3
tkiln La CAS WF10 ....153 K3
t Kiln La CUL/QBY BD13 ....93 F6
FTH/SHER LS25 ....129 G2
ton St HIPP HX3 ....9 D1
PDN/SBR HX6 ....138 E6
t St HWTH BD22 ....2 B6
vern Brow HTON BD9 ....94 D1
vern Cl CAS WF10 ....152 E6
vern Crs AIRE BD20 ....28 B8
vern Gv BEE/HOL LS11 ....101 G8
TON BD9 ....94 D2
vern Ri BEE/HOL LS11 ....101 G8
UDS HD4 ....191 G8
vern Rd BEE/HOL LS11 ....101 G7
ARL WF12 ....172 D2
TON BD9 ....94 D2
UDS HD4 ....13 D6
vern St BEE/HOL LS11 ....101 G7
UDS HD4 ....190 D2
nchester Rd HUD * HD1 ....12 C5
MAR/SLWT HD7 ....228 C3
VBSY BD6 ....118 E3
nchester Rd Linthwaite
MAR/SLWT HD7 ....210 E3
nchester Rd Marsden
MAR/SLWT HD7 ....209 J7
nchester Rd Slaithwaite
MAR/SLWT HD7 ....210 B4
ndale Gv WBSY BD6 ....117 J3
ndale Rd WBSY BD6 ....117 J3
ndeville Crs WBSY BD6 ....118 A3
ndarin Wy RTHW LS26 ....125 G4
ngrill La BSPA/BRAM LS23 ....61 H5
nitoba Pl CHAL LS7 ....80 A5
nkinholes Bank TOD OL14 ....134 E7
nley Ct GFTH/SHER LS25 ....105 K6
nley Dr WBY LS22 ....23 F5
nley Gv ILK LS29 ....20 D7
nley Rd ILK LS29 ....20 D8
nley St BRIG HD6 ....142 B8
nnerley Gv CLECK BD19 ....95 G1
nnheim Rd HTON BD9 ....95 C1
nningham La GIR BD8 ....4 B3
nville Ho MAR/SLWT HD22 ....2 B4
nville Pl HWTH BD22 ....2 B4
nville Rd KGHY BD21 ....2 B5
nville St HWTH * BD22 ....2 B4
nville Ter GTHN BD7 ....4 B5
nville Wk HWTH * BD22 ....2 B4
nville Wy HWTH * BD22 ....2 B4
or Av HDGY LS6 ....78 E7
SS WF5 ....174 A8
or Cl BHP/TINH LS16 ....35 H8
RK/DRI BD11 ....121 H4
R BD8 ....94 D3
SM/SK/SE WF9 ....226 A1
PP HX3 ....140 A7
OR/CROF WF4 ....221 H4
SS WF5 ....174 A8
HW LS26 ....126 B5
A LS19 ....53 K4

Manor Cottage Ms SCFT LS14 ....60 A5
Manor Ct AL/HA/HU LS17 ....59 H7
BGLY * BD16 ....72 A4
KNOT WF11 ....131 H6
OSS WF5 ....174 A8
Manor Crs OT LS21 ....35 G4
RTHW LS26 ....126 A6
WKFDW/WTN WF2 ....175 F7
WKFDW/WTN WF2 ....199 J3
Manor Cft CUD/GR S72 ....223 H8
HBR HX7 ....112 C8
MSTN/BAR LS15 ....104 A4
Manorcroft NORM WF6 ....178 A1
Manor Dr BGLY BD16 ....72 A4
CUD/GR S72 ....223 G5
FEA/AMT WF7 ....179 H2
HBR HX7 ....112 C8
HDGY LS6 ....78 E8
HIPP HX3 ....140 E7
HOR/CROF WF4 ....195 H8
HOR/CROF WF4 ....200 E4
KBTN HD8 ....236 E2
MIRF WF14 ....170 A4
OSS WF5 ....174 A8
Manor Farm HEM/SK/SE * WF9 ....226 A1
Manor Farm Cl BGLY BD16 ....72 B5
MID LS10 ....124 E5
Manor Farm Crs MOR LS27 ....123 J4
Manor Farm Dr BTLY WF17 ....146 E6
MID LS10 ....124 D5
MOR LS27 ....123 H3
Manor Farm Gdns MID LS10 ....124 D5
Manor Farm Gn MID LS10 ....124 D5
Manor Farm Gv MID LS10 ....124 D5
Manor Farm Ri MID LS10 ....124 E5
Manor Farm Rd HOR/CROF WF4 ....198 A7
MID LS10 ....124 D5
Manor Farm Wy MID LS10 ....124 D6
Manorfield Dr HOR/CROF WF4 ....197 G1
Manorfields Av HOR/CROF WF4 ....200 E3
Manorfields St HOR/CROF WF4 ....200 E3
Manor Fold BGLY BD16 ....72 B5
Manor Gdns CUL/QBY BD13 ....70 B6
EARL * WF12 ....173 F1
OT LS21 ....35 G4
SCFT LS14 ....60 E5
Manor Garth GFTH/SHER LS25 ....130 E3
MSTN/BAR LS15 ....129 C1
WKFDW/WTN WF2 ....199 J3
Manor Garth Rd EARL WF12 ....172 E4
GFTH/SHER LS25 ....129 C1
Manor Gra KBTN HD8 ....235 F3
Manor Gv AIRE BD20 ....48 E3
BSLYN/ROY S71 ....221 K8
CAS WF10 ....153 K5
CHAL LS7 ....79 K5
HEM/SK/SE WF9 ....241 G2
OSS WF5 ....174 A8
Manor Haigh Rd WKFDW/WTN WF2 ....175 F8
Manor Heath Rd HIPP HX3 ....140 A7
Manor House Cft BHP/TINH LS16 ....56 B8
Manor House La AL/HA/HU LS17 ....58 B6
Manor House Rd WIL/AL BD15 ....71 G5
Manor La OSS WF5 ....174 A8
SHPY BD18 ....73 H4
UPML OL3 ....228 A3
Manorley La HIPP HX3 ....117 K5
Manor Mill La BEE/HOL LS11 ....123 K2
Manor Occupation Rd
BSLYN/ROY S71 ....221 K7
Manor Pk CAS WF10 ....129 K5
EARL WF12 ....147 C8
GIR BD8 ....94 D1
HWTH BD22 ....68 D1
MIRF WF14 ....169 K4
PONT WF8 ....182 A6
SCFT LS14 ....60 E5
Manor Park Av CAS WF10 ....129 G6
PONT WF8 ....155 G8
Manor Park Gdns CLECK BD19 ....120 D8
Manor Park Wy KBTN HD8 ....215 F1
Manor Ri HUD HD1 ....13 D6
ILK LS29 ....20 D7
KBTN HD8 ....236 E2
WKFDW/WTN WF2 ....199 J3
Manor Rd ABR BD20 ....47 J1
BEE/HOL LS11 ....7 D5
BGLY BD16 ....72 B4
BTLY WF17 ....146 E6
DEWS WF13 ....172 A4
GLE DN14 ....157 J4
HOR/CROF WF4 ....197 G2
HORS LS18 ....76 E3
HUDS HD4 ....214 D5
KBTN HD8 ....218 A7
MAR/SLWT HD7 ....189 H7
MOR LS27 ....123 H3
OSS WF5 ....174 B7
RTHW LS26 ....126 A5
WKFDW/WTN WF2 ....175 G6
WKFDW/WTN WF2 ....199 J3
Manor Rw BFD BD1 ....4 C3
WBSY BD6 ....118 D4
Manor Sq YEA LS19 ....53 K4
Manorstead KBTN HD8 ....236 E2
Manor St CHAL LS7 ....7 F1
CLECK BD19 ....143 G5
EARL WF12 ....172 E4
ECHL BD2 ....74 D8

HUDS HD4 ....13 D6
OT LS21 ....33 J3
Manor Ter ECHL BD2 ....74 D8
HDGY LS6 ....78 E7
Manor Vw CAS WF10 ....153 K6
HDGY LS6 ....78 E7
PDSY/CALV LS28 ....98 C4
Manor Wy BTLY WF17 ....145 K6
Manscombe Rd WIL/AL BD15 ....94 C2
Manse Crs ILK LS29 ....32 A2
Manse Dr HUDS HD4 ....190 A8
Mansel Ms BOW BD4 ....120 B2
Manse Rd ILK LS29 ....32 A2
Manse St BFDE BD3 ....96 E4
Mansfield Av BGLY BD16 ....50 C6
Mansfield Rd GIR BD8 ....4 A1
ILK LS29 ....32 A2
Mansion Gdns HUDS HD4 ....213 F2
Mansion Ga CHAL LS7 ....79 K5
Mansion Gate Dr CHAL LS7 ....80 A5
Mansion La HIPP HX3 ....140 B7
RHAY LS8 ....80 D2
Manston Ap MSTN/BAR LS15 ....82 A8
Manston Av MSTN/BAR LS15 ....82 A8
Manston Crs MSTN/BAR LS15 ....82 A8
Manston Dr MSTN/BAR LS15 ....82 A8
Manston Gdns MSTN/BAR LS15 ....82 B8
Manston Gv MSTN/BAR LS15 ....82 A8
Manston La MSTN/BAR LS15 ....104 C1
Manston Ri MSTN/BAR LS15 ....82 A8
Manston Wy MSTN/BAR LS15 ....82 A8
Manygates Av WKFDE WF1 ....11 D6
Manygates Ct WKFDE * WF1 ....11 D6
Manygates Crs WKFDE WF1 ....11 D6
Manygates La WKFDW/WTN WF2 ....199 F1
Manygates Pk WKFDE WF1 ....11 D6
Manywells Brow CUL/QBY BD13 ....70 A8
Manywells Crs CUL/QBY BD13 ....70 B6
Manywells Dr CUL/QBY BD13 ....69 K6
Maple Av BFDE BD3 ....97 G3
HWTH BD22 ....69 F1
MAR/SLWT HD7 ....189 K6
PONT WF8 ....180 D6
Maple Cl CAS WF10 ....153 G6
HUDE HD5 ....192 E2
Maple Ct OSS WF5 ....173 K8
Maple Cft AL/HA/HU LS17 ....58 A8
WOR/ARM LS12 ....99 H6
Maple Dr PONT WF8 ....180 D5
WBY LS22 ....23 J4
WOR/ARM LS12 ....99 H6
Maple Fold WOR/ARM LS12 ....99 H6
Maple Gdns AL/HA/HU LS17 ....40 C6
Maple Gv CLECK BD19 ....144 D3
HUDN HD2 ....168 B7
KGHY BD21 ....2 B1
PONT WF8 ....180 D6
WOR/ARM LS12 ....99 H6
Maple Ri RTHW * LS26 ....126 B7
Maple Rd EARL WF12 ....173 C4
Maple St HFAX * HX1 ....8 A6
HUD HD1 ....13 E5
TOD OL14 ....159 K4
WKFDW/WTN WF2 ....175 G3
Maple Wk EARL WF12 ....173 C4
Maple Wy SCFT LS14 ....82 A3
Maplin Av HUDW HD3 ....189 K2
Maplin Cl HUDW HD3 ....189 K2
Maplin Dr HUDW HD3 ....189 K2
Mapplewell Crs OSS WF5 ....173 K6
Mapplewell Dr OSS WF5 ....173 K6
Marbridge Ct WBSY BD6 ....118 C1
Marchant St CAS WF10 ....153 H8
Marchbank Rd BFDE BD3 ....72 A5
March Cote La BGLY BD16 ....72 A5
March St NORM WF6 ....177 K2
Marchwood Gv CLAY BD14 ....94 D4
Marcus Wy HUDW HD3 ....189 H2
Mardale Crs SCFT LS14 ....81 J8
Mardale Rd EARL WF12 ....172 D1
Margaret Av AL/HA/HU LS17 ....40 B7
Margaret Cl MOR LS27 ....123 H5
Margaret St HFAX HX1 ....8 C5
KGHY BD21 ....8 E2
WKFDE WF1 ....10 E2
WKFDE WF1 ....149 H7
Margate RTHW * LS26 ....127 F5
Margate Rd BOW BD4 ....96 C7
Margate St CUD/GR S72 ....240 A4
RPDN/SBR HX6 ....138 D8
Margerison Ct ILK LS29 ....20 E8
Margerison Rd ILK LS29 ....20 E8
Margetson Rd BIRK/DRI BD11 ....121 J6
Marian Gv BEE/HOL * LS11 ....101 H8
Marian Rd HDGY LS6 ....79 H8
Marian Ter HDGY LS6 ....79 H8
Maria St ILK LS29 ....32 A1
Marie Cl HUDE HD5 ....192 E5
Marina Crs MOR LS27 ....122 E8
Marina Ter MAR/SLWT HD7 ....189 J6
Marine Villa Rd KNOT WF11 ....156 C7
Marion Cl HEM/SK/SE WF9 ....241 G1
Marion Dr SHPY BD18 ....73 J4
Marion Gv WKFDW/WTN WF2 ....174 E3
Marion St BGLY * BD16 ....50 A8
BRIG HD6 ....142 B7
GTHN BD7 ....4 A4
Marizon Gv WKFDE * WF1 ....10 C2
Mark Bottoms La HOLM/MEL HD9 ....233 F5

Mark Cl IDLE BD10.....74 E3
Market Ar CLECK * BD19.....144 B4
Market Av HUD * HD1.....12 C4
Market Balcony HFAX * HX1.....9 D4
Market Ct CUL/QBY BD13.....93 J5
Market Pl CLECK BD19.....144 B4
 HECK WF16.....145 G8
 HUD HD1.....12 C4
 KGHY BD21.....3 D3
 MAR/SLWT HD7.....209 H7
 MAR/SLWT HD7.....210 D3
 NORM WF6.....177 K1
 OT LS21.....33 J3
 PDSY/CALV LS28.....98 C4
 PONT WF8.....180 E3
 WBY LS22.....23 J2
Market Sq SHPY BD18.....73 H3
Market St AIRE BD20.....26 E6
 BCUP OL13.....158 A4
 BFD BD1.....4 C5
 BGLY BD16.....49 K8
 BRIG HD6.....168 C1
 BTLY WF17.....145 H2
 CLECK BD19.....144 B4
 DEWS WF13.....171 C3
 FEA/AMT WF7.....179 H5
 HBR HX7.....112 A8
 HECK WF16.....145 G8
 HEM/SK/SE WF9.....224 D4
 HFAX HX1.....9 D4
 HOLM/MEL HD9.....233 G8
 HUD HD1.....12 A5
 HUD HD1.....12 C4
 HUDW HD3.....190 B6
 KGHY BD21.....3 D4
 NORM WF6.....177 K1
 OT LS21.....33 J4
 SHPY BD18.....73 H4
 STKB/PEN S36.....252 C8
 WBSY * BD6.....118 D2
 WKFDE WF1.....10 C3
Market Street Ar LDS LS1.....7 E4
Market Wk HUD * HD1.....12 C4
 MAR/SLWT * HD7.....209 H7
Market Wy WKFDE WF1.....10 C3
Markfield Av LM/WK BD12.....118 D6
Markfield Cl LM/WK BD12.....118 D6
Markfield Crs LM/WK BD12.....118 D6
Markfield Dr LM/WK BD12.....118 D6
Markham Av RHAY LS8.....80 B7
 YEA LS19.....54 A6
Markham Crs YEA LS19.....54 A6
Markham Cft YEA LS19.....54 A6
Markham St WKFDW/WTN WF2.....10 A3
Markington Pl MID LS10.....124 D8
Mark La TOD OL14.....133 J4
 WBY LS22.....23 J2
Mark St HUD HD1.....12 A5
 LVSG WF15.....146 E7
 WBOW BD5.....96 A8
 WKFDE WF1.....10 C3
Marland Rd KGHY BD21.....3 F2
Maribeck Cl HOLM/MEL HD9.....213 F8
 KNOT WF11.....156 A4
Marlborough Av HIPP HX3.....140 A7
Marlborough Cft HEM/SK/SE WF9.....226 F7
Marlborough Gdns DEWS WF13.....172 A1
 LDSU * LS2.....7 D1
Marlborough Gra LDS LS1.....6 C3
Marlborough Gv LDSU * LS2.....7 D1
Marlborough Rd GIR BD8.....4 A2
 HBR HX7.....112 B8
 HUDN * HD2.....168 C6
 SHPY BD18.....73 G4
Marlborough Sq ILK LS29.....20 D8
Marlborough St KGHY BD21.....3 C3
 LDS LS1.....6 C3
 OSS WF5.....173 H6
 WKFDW/WTN WF2.....10 A3
Marlborough Ter DEWS * WF13.....172 A1
 HBR HX7.....112 B8
Marldon Rd HIPP HX3.....141 F2
Marley Cl HUDE HD5.....192 B5
Marley Cottages KGHY * BD21.....48 E4
Marley Ct AIRE BD20.....49 H4
Marley Gv BEE/HOL LS11.....101 F3
Marley La CUL/QBY BD13.....93 J8
Marley Rd KGHY BD21.....48 D3
Marley St BEE/HOL LS11.....101 F3
 BFDE BD3.....5 E4
 KGHY BD21.....2 C4
Marley Ter BEE/HOL LS11.....101 F8
Marley Vw AIRE BD20.....49 H4
 BEE/HOL LS11.....101 F8
Marling Rd HUDW HD3.....167 G8
Marlo Rd EARL WF12.....173 F1
Marlott Rd SHPY BD18.....73 K3
Marlow Cl HUDE HD5.....192 B5
Marlowe Cl PDSY/CALV LS28.....98 D6
Marlowe Ct GFTH/SHER LS25.....105 K4
Marlow St KGHY BD21.....3 F2
Marl Pit Hl PONT WF8.....180 B5
Maripit La PONT WF8.....181 J5
Marmion Av GIR BD8.....4 A2
Marne Av CLAY BD14.....94 C8
Marne Crs IDLE BD10.....74 D4
Marquis Av LM/WK BD12.....119 J6

Mariner Rd KGHY BD21.....3 D4
Marriner's Dr HTON BD9.....75 H7
Marriner's Wk KGHY BD21.....3 D5
Marriner's Wk KGHY BD21.....3 D5
Marriott Gv WKFDW/WTN WF2.....199 H3
Marsden Ga GTL/HWG HX4.....188 C3
Marsden Mt BEE/HOL LS11.....124 B1
Marsden La MAR/SLWT HD7.....209 J6
Marsden Mt BEE/HOL LS11.....124 B1
Marsden Pl BEE/HOL LS11.....124 B1
Marsden St KBTN HD8.....216 E8
Marsden Vw BEE/HOL LS11.....124 B1
Marsett Wy SCFT LS14.....85 K3
Marsh HOLM/MEL HD9.....213 F7
 PDSY/CALV LS28.....98 A4
Marshall Av HOR/CROF WF4.....198 B8
 MSTN/BAR LS15.....104 B1
Marshall Crs MOR LS27.....147 G1
Marshall Dr HEM/SK/SE WF9.....226 A8
Marshall Mill Ct KBTN HD8.....237 H2
Marsh Ct PDSY/CALV LS28.....98 A4
Marshall St BEE/HOL LS11.....150 C6
 EARD/LOFT WF3.....2 C1
 KGHY BD21.....170 D8
 MIRF WF14.....123 F7
 MOR LS27.....123 F7
 MSTN/BAR LS15.....104 A1
 YEA LS19.....53 K6
Marshall Ter MSTN/BAR LS15.....104 A1
Marsham Gv HUDW * HD3.....190 C4
Marsh Ct PDSY/CALV LS28.....98 A4
Marsh Cft KNOT WF11.....155 K4
Marsh Delves La HIPP HX3.....140 E5
Marshfield Pl WBOW BD5.....95 K8
Marshfield St WBOW BD5.....95 K8
Marsh Gdns HOLM/MEL HD9.....213 F7
Marsh Gv WBOW BD5.....118 E1
Marsh Grove Rd HUDW * HD3.....12 A3
Marsh Hall La HUDS HD4.....214 B8
Marsh La BIRK/DRI BD11.....120 C7
 GLE DN14.....157 K4
 HBR HX7.....111 F8
 HIPP HX3.....140 E5
 HWTH BD22.....68 E7
 KBTN HD8.....234 E5
 KNOT WF11.....156 A5
 OSM LS9.....7 F4
Marsh Platt La HOLM/MEL HD9.....213 G7
Marsh Rd CAS WF10.....153 F6
 HOLM/MEL HD9.....233 K8
Marsh St CLECK BD19.....144 B5
 HDGY LS6.....79 G8
 RTHW LS26.....126 B7
 WBOW BD5.....95 K8
 WBOW BD5.....118 E1
Marsh Ter PDSY/CALV LS28.....98 A4
Marsh V HDGY LS6.....79 G8
Marshway HFAX HX1.....10 C2
Marsland Av WKFDE WF1.....11 D3
Marsland Ct CLECK BD19.....144 A1
Marsland Pl BFDE BD3.....97 K4
 WKFDE WF1.....11 D3
Marsland St WKFDE WF1.....11 D3
Marsland Ter WKFDE WF1.....11 D3
Marston Av MOR LS27.....123 F8
Marston Cl CUL/QBY BD13.....116 E2
Marston Ct CAS WF10.....153 F5
Marston Mt OSM LS9.....102 A2
Marston Wk NORM WF6.....151 H7
Marston Wy WBY LS22.....23 G5
Marten Dr HUDS HD4.....212 D4
Marten Gv HUDS HD4.....212 D4
Martin Cl MOR LS27.....123 F7
Martindale Dr BRAM LS13.....99 J2
Martin Frobisher Dr NORM WF6.....151 J8
Martingale Dr EARD/LOFT WF3.....124 D4
Martin Green La GTL/HWG HX4.....165 K4
Martin Gv WKFDW/WTN WF2.....199 G5
Martin St BRIG * HD6.....142 C8
 BTLY WF17.....145 H2
 NORM WF6.....177 K3
Martin Ter BULY LS4.....100 C1
Martlett Dr WBOW BD5.....119 G1
Marton Av HEM/SK/SE WF9.....224 C5
Marton Ct BFDE BD3.....97 F4
Marwood Rd WOR/ARM LS12.....99 H4
Maryfield Av MSTN/BAR LS15.....103 J1
Maryfield Cl MSTN/BAR LS15.....103 J1
Maryfield Ct MSTN/BAR LS15.....103 J1
Maryfield Gdns MSTN/BAR LS15.....103 J1
Maryfield Gn MSTN/BAR LS15.....103 J1
Maryfield Ms MSTN/BAR LS15.....103 J1
Maryfield V MSTN/BAR LS15.....103 J1
Margate WKFDE WF1.....10 C3
Mary St AIRE BD20.....26 A2
 BOW BD4.....96 E6
 BRIG HD6.....142 B7
 CUL/QBY BD13.....92 C2
 CUL/QBY BD13.....93 H5
 DOD/DAR S75.....239 K7
 EARD/LOFT WF3.....144 F3
 HWTH BD22.....90 E1
 LM/WK BD12.....118 D7
 PDSY/CALV LS28.....76 C7
 SHPY BD18.....73 F3

Maryville Av BRIG HD6.....142
Masefield Av HTON BD9.....72
Masefield St GSLY LS20.....53
Masham Gv WOR/ARM LS12.....100
Masham Pl HTON BD9.....100
Masham St WOR/ARM LS12.....100
Masonic St HFAX HX1.....139
Mason St HBR HX7.....112
Massey Flds HWTH BD22.....69
Master La LUD/ILL HX2.....2
Matherville KBTN HD8.....236
Matlock St HIPP HX3.....8
 HUDS HD4.....190
Matterdale Cl EARL WF12.....172
Matterdale Rd EARL WF12.....172
Matthew Cl AIRE BD20.....3
Matthew Gv HOLM/MEL HD9.....231
Matthew La HOLM/MEL HD9.....231
 TOD OL14.....134
Matty Marsden La OSS WF5.....196
Maud Av BEE/HOL LS11.....124
Maude Av BAIL BD17.....73
Maude Crs RPDN/SBR HX6.....138
Maude St GTL/HWG HX4.....166
 HIPP HX3.....115
 LDSU LS2.....7
Maud Pl BEE/HOL LS11.....101
Maudsley St BFDE BD3.....5
Maud St BFDE BD3.....5
Maufe Wy ILK LS29.....20
Maurice Av BRIG HD6.....142
Mavis Av BHP/TINH LS16.....55
 DEWS WF13.....171
Mavis Gv BHP/TINH LS16.....55
Mavis La BHP/TINH LS16.....55
Mavis Rd DEWS WF13.....145
Mavis St BFDE BD3.....5
 DEWS WF13.....171
Mawcroft Cl YEA LS19.....53
Mawcroft Grange Dr YEA LS19.....53
Mawson Ct BFD * BD1.....4
Mawson St SHPY BD18.....73
Maw St BOW BD4.....5
Maxwell Av DEWS WF13.....172
Maxwell Rd ILK LS29.....20
 WBSY BD6.....118
Maxwell St FEA/AMT WF7.....179
May Av CUL/QBY BD13.....93
Maybury Av HOR/CROF WF4.....198
May Bush Rd WKFDE WF1.....11
Mayfair WBOW BD5.....95
Mayfair Av GTL/HWG HX4.....188
Mayfair Pl HEM/SK/SE WF9.....224
Mayfair Wy BOW BD4.....97
Mayfield Av BRIG HD6.....142
 HFAX HX1.....192
 HUDE HD5.....8
 LM/WK BD12.....118
Mayfield Cl ILK LS29.....20
 OSS WF5.....173
Mayfield Dr AIRE BD20.....49
 HFAX HX1.....8
Mayfield Gdns HFAX HX1.....8
 OSS WF5.....173
Mayfield Gv BAIL BD17.....142
 BRIG HD6.....142
 HFAX HX1.....8
 HUDE HD5.....192
 WIL/AL BD15.....71
Mayfield Mt HFAX * HX1.....8
Mayfield Pl LM/WK BD12.....118
Mayfield Ri HOR/CROF WF4.....222
 LM/WK BD12.....118
Mayfield Rd HBR HX7.....112
 ILK LS29.....20
 KGHY BD21.....103
 MSTN/BAR LS15.....103
Mayfield St HFAX HX1.....8
Mayfields Wy HEM/SK/SE WF9.....241
Mayfield Ter CLAY BD14.....94
 HFAX HX1.....8
 LM/WK BD12.....118
Mayfield Ter South HFAX * HX1.....118
Mayfield Vw LM/WK BD12.....118
Mayflower St MID LS10.....125
Maylea Dr OT LS21.....33
Mayman Cl BTLY WF17.....146
Mayman La BTLY WF17.....146
Maynes Cl EARL WF12.....118
Mayo Av WBOW BD5.....118
Mayo Cl RHAY LS8.....81
Mayo Crs WBOW BD5.....119
Mayo Dr WBOW BD5.....119
Mayo Gv WBOW BD5.....119
Mayo Rd WBOW BD5.....119
Mayors Wk CAS WF10.....155
 PONT WF8.....180
Mayor's Walk Av PONT WF8.....180
Mayors Walk Cl PONT WF8.....180
Maypole Rd HUDN HD2.....168
Mayster Gv BRIG HD6.....168
Mayster Rd BRIG HD6.....167
May St CLECK BD19.....144
 HUDS HD4.....190
 HWTH BD22.....69
 KGHY BD21.....3
May Ter OSM LS9.....102
Maythorne Av BTLY WF17.....14

ythorne Crs CLAY BD14 ....94 D7
y thorne Dr CLAY BD14 ....94 E7
y Tree Cl CLAY BD14 ....94 D7
ville Av AIRE BD20 ....49 F3
DGY LS6 ....78 E8
ville Pl HDGY LS6 ....78 E8
ville Rd HDGY LS6 ....78 E8
ville St HDGY LS6 ....78 D8
ville Ter HDGY LS6 ....78 E8
eebrook Av CLECK BD19 ....144 B1
eebrook Crs CLECK BD19 ....144 B1
Bride Wy WBY LS22 ....23 K6
aren Av HEM/SK/SE WF9 ....227 F3
aren Flds BRAM LS13 ....99 H1
ahon Dr CUL/QBY BD13 ....117 H1
Millan Gdns WBSY BD6 ....118 E4
ad Cl MSTN/BAR * LS15 ....104 C5
Meade GFTH/SHER LS25 ....105 K4
ad Gv MSTN/BAR LS15 ....104 C5
adow Bank DEWS WF13 ....171 J3
EA/AMT WF7 ....203 G2
OLM/MEL HD9 ....233 J5
OR/CROF WF4 ....223 G2
adow Ct BRIC HD6 ....169 F1
SLYN/ROY S71 ....222 B8
SG WF10 ....154 E5
EM/SK/SE WF9 ....226 D8
SS WF5 ....173 H4
VIL/AL BD15 ....72 A7
adow Crs BSLYN/ROY S71 ....222 B8
adow Cft AL/HA/HU LS17 ....40 A6
adow Cft AL/HA/HU LS17 ....40 A6
EE/HOL LS11 ....7 D6
JD/GR S72 ....225 C8
L/WHX HX4 ....164 E7
EM/SK/SE WF9 ....226 D6
UDN HD2 ....169 G6
WTH BD22 ....47 C5
KFDE WF1 ....149 K6
adowcroft HOLM/MEL HD9 ....212 E7
KP/WHF BD23 ....14 A5
adow Croft Cl IDLE BD10 ....74 B3
adowcroft Cl WKFDE * WF1 ....150 A6
adowcroft Cl WKFDE * WF1 ....150 A6
adowcroft Crs CAS WF10 ....154 B3
adowcroft La RPDN/SBR HX6 ...164 B6
adowcroft Ms CAS WF10 ....154 B3
SM * LS9 ....102 A4
adowcroft Ri BOW BD4 ....119 K3
adowcroft Rd WKFDE WF1 ....150 A6
adow Dr HIPP HX3 ....139 H1
SG WF15 ....170 C2
dow End BHP/TINH LS16 ....55 J1
dowfield Cl HEM/SK/SE * WF9 ...202 A8
dowfields Cl EARD/LOFT WF3 ...150 E5
dowfields Cl HOR/CROF WF4 ...200 E3
dowfields Dr HOR/CROF WF4 ...200 E3
dow Garth BHP/TINH LS16 ....55 K1
KFDE WF1 ....149 K6
dowgate OSS WF5 ....173 H4
dowgate Cft EARD/LOFT WF3 ...149 J1
dowgate Dr EARD/LOFT WF3 ...149 J2
dowgate V EARD/LOFT WF3 .....149 J2
dowgate Gn MAR/SLWT HD7 ...211 H3
dowhurst Gdns
DSY/CALV LS28 ....98 B4
dowlands CLECK BD19 ....143 F2
dow La BEE/HOL LS11 ....7 E5
EWS WF13 ....172 B2
PP HX3 ....139 H1
SG WF15 ....170 C2
AR/SLWT HD7 ....210 D2
SG WF15 ....175 G4
dow Pk HUDE HD5 ....192 D1
dow Park Crs DSY/CALV LS28 ....97 K1
dow Park Dr PDSY/CALV LS28 ...97 K1
dow Ri HEM/SK/SE WF9 ....224 C5
dow Rd BEE/HOL LS11 ....7 D6
SLYN/ROY S71 ....222 B8
AS WF10 ....153 G6
FTH/SHER LS25 ....106 A4
LE BD10 ....75 C5
Meadows BHP/TINH LS16 ....56 C8
TN HD8 ....236 D6
SSY BD20 ....118 D2
dows Morvern
EM/SK/SE WF9 ....225 F4
dow St HUD HD1 ....190 D4
dow V HOR/CROF WF4 ....196 D6
KFDE WF1 ....149 K6
dow Va AL/HA/HU LS17 ....57 G6
dow Vw HDGY LS6 ....78 E8
TH BD22 ....69 F1
TN HD8 ....237 F2
/WK BD12 ....142 D2
STN/BAR LS15 ....83 J3
S WF5 ....173 H4

STKB/PEN S36 ....252 E5
Meadow Wk CHAL LS7 ....80 A5
HEM/SK/SE WF9 ....203 K8
HIPP HX3 ....139 H1
Meadow Wy AL/HA/HU LS17 ....57 G6
CAS WF10 ....154 B3
EARD/LOFT WF3 ....147 J4
FEA/AMT WF7 ....203 G2
Mead Rd MSTN/BAR LS15 ....104 C5
Meadstead Dr BSLYN/ROY S71 ...221 K8
Mead St HUDN HD2 ....12 C1
Mead Vw BOW * BD4 ....97 G8
Meadway FEA/AMT WF7 ....178 C5
Mead Wy KBTN HD8 ....215 C4
MSTN/BAR LS15 ....104 C5
Meadway WBSY BD6 ....117 K5
Meagill Ri OT LS21 ....33 F1
Meal Hill La HOLM/MEL HD9 ......249 G1
MAR/SLWT HD7 ....188 C8
Meal Hill Rd HOLM/MEL HD9 ......246 E2
Mean La HOLM/MEL HD9 ....231 J1
HWTH BD22 ....231 K7
Meanwood Cl CHAL LS7 ....79 H7
Meanwood Gv HDGY LS6 ....78 E2
Meanwood Rd CHAL LS7 ....79 G6
Meanwood St CHAL LS7 ....7 G1
Meanwood Valley Dr CHAL LS7 ......79 F5
Meanwood Valley Gn CHAL LS7 ....79 F5
Meanwood Valley Gv CHAL LS7 .....79 F5
Meanwood Valley Mt CHAL LS7 .....79 F5
Mearclough Rd RPDN/SBR HX6 ...139 G7
Mears Cl STKB/PEN S36 ....252 D8
Medeway PDSY/CALV LS28 ....98 A1
Medhurst Av GFTH/SHER LS25 ...129 G1
Medley La HIPP HX3 ....116 E7
Medley St CAS WF10 ....153 K4
Medlock Rd HOR/CROF WF4 ....197 G2
Medway CUL/QBY BD13 ....116 E5
HUDE * HD5 ....192 D1
Medway Av GFTH/SHER LS25 .....106 A6
Meeting House La MAR/SLWT HD7 .188 E2
Meggison Gv WBOW BD5 ....95 J7
Meg La HUDW HD3 ....190 B6
Megnaway WBOW BD5 ....96 A7
Melba Rd GTHN BD7 ....95 H8
Melbourne Ms WKFDW/WTN WF2 .149 G8
Melbourne Gv BFDE BD3 ....93 G3
BRAM LS13 ....99 G1
Melbourne Ms WKFDW/WTN WF2 .149 F7
Melbourne Pl WBOW BD5 ....4 B6
Melbourne Rd IDLE OL14 ....159 K2
Melbourne St HBR HX7 ....112 H3
HIPP HX3 ....8 B2
LDSU LS2 ....7 F2
LVSG WF15 ....144 E8
MOR LS27 ....123 G7
PDSY/CALV LS28 ....98 B1
SHPY BD18 ....73 G3
Melbourne Ter WBOW BD5 ....4 B6
Melcombe Wk BOW BD4 ....97 C7
Melford St BOW BD4 ....119 K1
Mellor Brook MAR/SLWT HD7 .....188 D7
Mellor La HOLM/MEL HD9 ....232 B7
Mellor Mill La GTL/HWG HX4 ....166 A7
Mellor St BRIC * HD6 ....168 C1
HFAX HX1 ....8 B6
Mellwood La HEM/SK/SE WF9 ....226 A8
Melrose Cl HUDE HD5 ....192 B5
Melrose Dr ILK LS29 ....32 A1
Melrose Gv HORS LS18 ....77 J3
Melrose Pl HORS LS18 ....77 H3
PDSY/CALV LS28 ....98 B5
Melrose St GTHN BD7 ....95 G7
HIPP HX3 ....8 B2
Melrose Ter ELL * HX5 ....166 E5
Melrose Wk HORS LS18 ....77 H3
Meltham House La
HOLM/MEL HD9 ....234 B7
Meltham Mills Rd HOLM/MEL HD9 .231 K1
HUDS HD4 ....212 B5
MAR/SLWT HD7 ....209 K7
Melton Av EARD/LOFT WF3 ....125 C7
Melton Cl EARD/LOFT WF3 ....125 C6
HEM/SK/SE WF9 ....226 C6
Melton Garth EARD/LOFT WF3 ....125 C7
Melton Ms HWTH 69 F4
Melton Rd HOR/CROF WF4 ....198 C7
Melton St BTLY WF17 ....146 K3
Melton Ter IDLE BD10 ....75 G6
Melton Wy LVSC WF15 ....170 C2
Melville Cl HDGY LS6 ....79 H8
Melville Gdns HDGY LS6 ....79 H8
Melville Gv ILK LS29 ....20 E7
Melville Pl HDGY LS6 ....79 H8
Melville Rd HDGY LS6 ....79 H8
Melville St GTHN BD7 ....4 B1
Memorial Cottages
WOR/ARM * LS12 ....99 H8
Memorial Dr HDGY LS6 ....79 F4
Mendip Av HUDW HD3 ....190 A2
Mendip Cl GFTH/SHER LS25 ....105 K5
Mendip Rd EARL WF12 ....172 E2
Mendip Wy LM/WK BD12 ....118 C5
Menin Dr BAIL BD17 ....51 H6
Menston Dr ILK LS29 ....32 C8
Menstone Gr GIR BD8 ....4 A3
Menston Old La ILK LS29 ....32 B5
Mercer Cl HUDS HD4 ....212 C4

Merchants Ct BOW BD4 ....5 E6
Merchants Quay OSM * LS9 ....7 F4
Mercia Wy MSTN/BAR LS15 ....82 C8
Mercury Rw OT LS21 ....33 J4
Merefield Wy CAS WF10 ....153 K6
Merewood Rd CAS WF10 ....152 E4
Meriden Av GFTH/SHER LS25 .....105 K6
Merlin Cl MOR LS27 ....123 H8
Merlin Ct BTLY WF17 ....145 J3
HUDS HD4 ....212 E4
KGHY BD21 ....2 C5
Merlin Gv GIR BD8 ....94 C4
Merlinwood Dr BAIL BD17 ....51 K7
Merlyn-Rees Av MOR LS27 ....123 F7
Merrion Pl LDSU LS2 ....7 F3
Merrion St LDSU LS2 ....7 E3
Merrion Wy LDSU LS2 ....7 E2
Merrivale Rd WIL/AL BD15 ....94 A3
Merry Bent La RPDN/SBR HX6 ....163 H6
Merrybents St TOD OL14 ....134 C6
Merrydale Rd BOW BD4 ....119 H5
Merton Av PDSY/CALV LS28 ....98 B1
Merton Cl GFTH/SHER LS25 ....129 H1
Merton Dr PDSY/CALV LS28 ....98 A1
Merton Fold WBOW BD5 ....96 A7
Merton Gdns PDSY/CALV LS28 .....98 A1
Merton Rd GTHN BD7 ....4 A6
Merton St HUD HD1 ....12 C5
Merville Av BAIL BD17 ....51 J6
Metcalfe St BOW BD4 ....96 D7
Methley Br RTHW LS26 ....152 E3
Methley Dr CHAL LS7 ....79 K5
Methley Gv CHAL LS7 ....79 J5
Methley La CHAL LS7 ....79 K5
RTHW LS26 ....127 H7
Methley Mt CHAL LS7 ....79 J5
Methley Pl CHAL LS7 ....79 J5
Methley Rd CAS WF10 ....153 F5
Methley Ter CHAL LS7 ....79 J5
Methley Vw CHAL LS7 ....79 K5
Methuen Av LM/WK BD12 ....142 D2
The Mews NORM WF6 ....152 A8
Mews Ct FEA/AMT WF7 ....179 J6
Mexborough Av CHAL LS7 ....79 K7
Mexborough Dr CHAL LS7 ....79 K7
Mexborough Gv CHAL LS7 ....79 K7
Mexborough Pl CHAL LS7 ....79 K8
Mexborough Rd CHAL LS7 ....79 K8
SHPY BD18 ....73 K6
Mexborough St CHAL LS7 ....79 K7
Meynell Ap BEE/HOL LS11 ....6 C6
Meynell Av RTHW LS26 ....126 B6
Meynell Ct MSTN/BAR LS15 ....104 B4
Meynell Hts BEE/HOL LS11 ....6 C6
Meynell Mt RTHW LS26 ....126 C6
Meynell Rd MSTN/BAR LS15 ....104 B5
Meynell Sq BEE/HOL LS11 ....6 C6
Meynell Wk BEE/HOL LS11 ....6 C6
Meyrick Av WBY LS22 ....24 A5
Meyrick Dr DOD/DAR S75 ....239 K4
Miall St HFAX HX1 ....8 B3
Michael Av EARD/LOFT WF3 ....150 B6
Michael's Est CUD/GR S72 ....240 A4
Mickle Ct CAS WF10 ....153 H4
Mickledore Cl GTHN * BD7 ....94 E8
Mickledore Rdg GTHN BD7 ....94 E8
Micklefield Ct YEA LS19 ....53 K7
Micklefield La YEA LS19 ....53 J7
Micklefield Ms YEA * LS19 ....53 J7
Micklefield Rd YEA LS19 ....53 K7
Micklegate PONT WF8 ....180 E2
Micklemoss Dr CUL/QBY BD13 ....116 E1
Micklethwaite Dr CUL/QBY BD13 ..116 D3
Micklethwaite La BGLY BD16 ....49 J5
Micklethwaite Rd HOR/CROF WF4 .198 B8
Micklethwaite Vw WBY LS22 ....23 J7
Micklethorpe Rd RTHW LS26 ......128 B8
Mickley St WOR/ARM LS12 ....100 C4
Middlebrook Cl GIR BD8 ....94 E4
Middlebrook Crs GIR BD8 ....94 D5
Middlebrook Dr GIR BD8 ....94 D4
Middlebrook Hi GIR BD8 ....94 D4
Middlebrook Ri GIR BD8 ....94 D4
Middlebrook Vw GIR BD8 ....94 D4
Middlebrook Wk GIR BD8 ....94 E4
Middlebrook Wy GIR BD8 ....94 D5
Middlecliffe Dr STKB/PEN S36 .....250 A6
Middlecroft Cl RTHW LS26 ....125 G3
Middlecroft Rd RTHW LS26 ....125 G3
Middle Cross St WOR/ARM LS12 ..100 D4
Middle Dean St GTL/HWG HX4 ....166 B4
Middle Field La HOR/CROF WF4 ..220 A5
Middlegate BTLY WF17 ....145 H2
Middlegate Ct BOW BD4 ....119 J3
Middle Hall Cl LVSC WF15 ....144 B8
Middleham Ct BOW * BD4 ....97 G8
Middle La CLAY BD14 ....94 C6
HOR/CROF WF4 ....201 F4
KNOT WF11 ....156 D8
WBY LS22 ....41 G1
Middlemoor SCFT LS14 ....81 K3
Middle Oxford St CAS WF10 ....153 H4
Middle Rd DEWS WF13 ....172 A4
EARL WF12 ....172 D4
OSM LS9 ....103 F8
Middle St BFD BD1 ....4 C4
RPDN/SBR HX6 ....164 B1
Middlethorne Cl AL/HA/HU LS17 ...58 D7
Middlethorne Ct AL/HA/HU LS17 ...58 C6

Middlethorne Ms *AL/HA/HU* LS17 ....58 D6
Middlethorne Ri *AL/HA/HU* LS17 ....58 C7
Middleton Av *ILK* LS29 ....20 B6
  OSM LS9 ....102 B2
  RTHW LS26 ....125 H6
Middleton Cl *MOR* LS27 ....123 D7
Middleton Ct *LVSG* WF15 ....144 B7
Middleton Gv *BEE/HOL* LS11 ....124 C1
  MOR LS27 ....123 C7
Middleton La *EARD/LOFT* WF3 ....148 E1
  RTHW LS26 ....125 H6
Middleton Park Av *MID* LS10 ....124 C7
Middleton Park Cls *MID* LS10 ....124 D7
Middleton Park Gn *MID* LS10 ....124 C7
Middleton Park Grn *MID* LS10 ....124 C6
Middleton Park Mt *MID* LS10 ....124 C7
Middleton Park Pl *MID* LS10 ....124 D7
Middleton Park Rd *MID* LS10 ....124 D6
Middleton Park Ter *MID* LS10 ....124 C7
Middleton St *GIR* BD8 ....95 H2
Middleton Ter *MOR* LS27 ....123 H7
Middleton Wy *KNOT* WF11 ....156 D2
Middleway *AIRE* BD20 ....27 H2
Middle Wy *KGHY* BD21 ....3 F2
Midge Hall Cl *ILK* LS29 ....32 A2
Midgeham Gv *BGLY* BD16 ....70 E2
Midgehole Rd *HBR* HX7 ....112 B5
Midgeley Rd *BAIL* BD17 ....73 C2
Midgley Pl *HDGY* LS6 ....79 H8
Midgley Ri *PONT* WF8 ....154 E8
Midgley Ter *HBR* HX7 ....137 H2
  ILK LS29 ....32 A2
Midgley Ter *HDGY* LS6 ....79 H8
Midland Cl *MID* LS10 ....102 B8
Midland Garth *MID* LS10 ....102 A8
Midland Hl *BGLY* BD16 ....49 K8
Midland Pas *HDGY* LS6 ....79 H8
Midland Rd *BAIL* BD17 ....73 K1
  BSLYN/ROY S71 ....222 B7
  GIR BD8 ....4 B1
  HDGY LS6 ....79 F8
  HTON BD9 ....73 J6
  MID LS10 ....102 A8
  PONT WF8 ....181 F2
Midland St *HUD* HD1 ....13 D2
  RTHW LS26 ....127 F5
Midland Ter *ECHL* BD2 ....4 C1
  HTON BD9 ....73 J6
  KGHY BD21 ....3 D2
Mid Point *BFDE* BD3 ....97 H3
Midway *HUDS* HD4 ....212 A5
Midway Av *BGLY* BD16 ....72 A4
Milan Rd *RHAY* LS8 ....80 B8
Milan St *RHAY* LS8 ....80 C8
Mildred Sylvester Wy *NORM* WF6 ...178 D1
Mile Cross Gdns *HFAX* HX1 ....139 H5
Mile Cross Pl *HFAX* HX1 ....139 H5
Mile Cross Rd *HFAX* HX1 ....139 H5
Mile Cross Ter *HFAX* HX1 ....139 H5
Mile End *HOLM/MEL* HD9 ....231 H2
Miles Garth *AL/HA/HU* LS17 ....40 C1
Miles Hill Av *CHAL* LS7 ....79 H5
Miles Hill Crs *BOW* BD4 ....119 K2
Miles Hill Dr *BOW* BD4 ....119 K2
Miles Hill Gv *CHAL* LS7 ....79 G5
Miles Hill Mt *CHAL* LS7 ....79 H5
Miles Hill Pl *CHAL* LS7 ....79 H5
Miles Hill Rd *CHAL* LS7 ....79 H5
Miles Hill St *CHAL* LS7 ....79 H5
Miles Hill Ter *CHAL* LS7 ....79 H5
Miles Hill Vw *CHAL* LS7 ....79 H5
Mileswood Cl *CUD/GR* S72 ....240 D8
Mile Thorn St *HFAX* HX1 ....8 A4
Milford Gv *CLECK* BD19 ....120 D8
Milford Pl *BULY* LS4 ....100 D1
  HTON BD9 ....73 G8
Milford St *HUD* HD1 ....12 C5
Milgate *BSLYN/ROY* S71 ....222 B7
Millars Wk *HEM/SK/SE* WF9 ....241 G2
Mill Av *HUDE* HD5 ....192 C4
Millbank *PDSY/CALV* LS28 ....98 D6
Mill Bank Cl *RPDN/SBR* HX6 ....163 K4
Millbank Fold *PDSY/CALV* LS28 ....98 D6
Mill Bank Rd *HOLM/MEL* HD9 ....231 J2
  RPDN/SBR HX6 ....163 K4
Mill Banks *AIRE* BD20 ....27 G3
Millbeck Ap *MOR* LS27 ....123 H7
Millbeck Cl *GIR* BD8 ....94 C5
Millbeck Dr *BGLY* BD16 ....70 E2
Millbeck Gn *WBY* LS22 ....40 E3
Millbrook Gdns *DEWS* WF13 ....171 K1
Mill Carr Hill Rd *BOW* BD4 ....119 J5
Mill Cl *FEA/AMT* WF7 ....205 C5
  HEM/SK/SE WF9 ....241 G1
  HOLM/MEL HD9 ....231 H1
Mill Ct *HWTH* BD22 ....90 E1
Mill Cft *MOR* LS27 ....122 C4
Millcroft *EARD/LOFT* WF3 ....150 B5
  OT LS21 ....35 H4
Millcroft Cl *EARD/LOFT* WF3 ....150 A5
Millcroft Ri *EARD/LOFT* WF3 ....150 B5
Mill Dam *BSPA/BRAM* LS23 ....42 E6
Mill Dam La *PONT* WF8 ....181 F1
Millennium Ct *PDSY/CALV* LS28 ....98 D3
Millennium Sq *LDS* LS1 ....7 D2
Millennium Wy *BEE/HOL* LS11 ....124 C2
Miller Av *WKFDW/WTN* WF2 ....199 F1
Miller Ct *WKFDW/WTN* WF2 ....198 D8
Miller Garth *FEA/AMT* WF7 ....203 G6
Millergate *BFD* BD1 ....4 C4
Miller Hl *KBTN* HD8 ....236 E6
Miller Hill Bank *KBTN* HD8 ....236 E6
Millers Ct *LVSG* WF15 ....170 C1
Millers Cft *BTLY* WF17 ....146 A2
Millers Dl *MOR* LS27 ....122 E5
Millersdale Cl *BOW* BD4 ....119 H4
Millfield Crs *HUDW* HD3 ....190 C4
Millfield Crs *PONT* WF8 ....6 B5
Millfield Rd *HOR/CROF* WF4 ....197 J5
Millfields *AIRE* BD20 ....27 F2
  OSS WF5 ....173 H6
Mill Fold Wy *RPDN/SBR* HX6 ....164 A7
Mill Forest Wy *BTLY* WF17 ....146 E7
Mill Garth *MOR* LS27 ....122 C4
Millgarth Ct *WBY* LS22 ....41 F4
Millgarth St *LDSU* LS2 ....7 F3
Millgate *ELL* HX5 ....166 E4
  FEA/AMT WF7 ....203 G6
  HUD HD1 ....12 A5
  HUDS HD4 ....214 D1
Mill Grath *BEE/HOL* LS11 ....6 B5
Mill Gn *BEE/HOL* LS11 ....6 B5
Mill Green Cl *SCFT* LS14 ....82 A6
Mill Green Gdns *SCFT* LS14 ....82 A6
Mill Green Garth *SCFT* LS14 ....82 A6
Mill Green Pl *SCFT* LS14 ....82 A7
Mill Green Rd *SCFT* LS14 ....82 A6
Mill Green Vw *SCFT* LS14 ....81 K9
Mill Gv *BRIG* HD6 ....142 A7
Millhaven Ms *GIR* BD8 ....4 A1
Mill Hey *HWTH* BD22 ....69 F4
Mill Hl *FEA/AMT* WF7 ....203 C5
  HWTH BD22 ....68 E4
  LDS LS1 ....7 E4
  NORM WF6 ....177 K2
  PDSY/CALV LS28 ....98 C6
  RTHW LS26 ....126 B6
Mill Hill Av *PONT* WF8 ....180 C4
Mill Hill Cl *PONT* WF8 ....182 A6
Mill Hill Gn *PONT* WF8 ....126 B6
Mill Hill La *BRIG* HD6 ....142 A7
  BRIG HD6 ....169 G2
  PONT WF8 ....180 C4
Mill Hill Rd *PONT* WF8 ....180 D4
Mill Hill St *RTHW* LS26 ....126 B6
Mill Hill Top *BGLY* BD16 ....71 F3
Mill House La *RPDN/SBR* HX6 ....164 C1
Millhouse La *STKB/PEN* S36 ....251 C8
Mill House Ri *BOW* BD4 ....119 J2
Milligan Av *ECHL* BD2 ....74 B6
Milligan Ct *BGLY* BD16 ....70 E2
Mill La *AIRE* BD20 ....26 E6
  AL/HA/HU LS17 ....40 D8
  BIRK/DRI BD11 ....120 D5
  BOW BD4 ....98 B8
  BRAM LS13 ....76 B8
  BRIG HD6 ....168 C1
  BSPA/BRAM LS23 ....42 E5
  BTLY WF17 ....146 A1
  BTLY WF17 ....146 C7
  CAS WF10 ....152 C7
  CAS WF10 ....153 J2
  CLECK BD19 ....120 A8
  CUL/QBY BD13 ....116 B1
  EARD/LOFT WF3 ....148 E3
  EARL WF12 ....173 F4
  FEA/AMT WF7 ....178 C5
  GSLY LS20 ....51 K3
  GTL/HWG HX4 ....166 B7
  HEM/SK/SE WF9 ....226 D7
  HEM/SK/SE WF9 ....241 G2
  HIPP HX3 ....8 C1
  HIPP HX3 ....117 K5
  HOR/CROF WF4 ....195 H8
  HOR/CROF WF4 ....221 G4
  HOR/CROF WF4 ....223 F2
  HUDE HD5 ....169 J6
  HWTH BD22 ....68 D1
  HWTH BD22 ....68 E8
  LUD/ILL HX2 ....115 F4
  MOR LS27 ....122 C4
  OT LS21 ....33 J3
  OT LS21 ....35 H4
  PONT WF8 ....155 G8
  RTHW LS26 ....128 C8
  STKB/PEN S36 ....251 G3
  STKB/PEN S36 ....251 J8
  WBOW BD5 ....117 H6
Mill Moor Rd *HOLM/MEL* HD9 ....231 G1
Mill Pk *MIRF* WF14 ....193 H5
Mill Pit La *RTHW* LS26 ....126 A4
Mill Pond Cl *HDGY* LS6 ....78 E5
Mill Pond Gv *HDGY* LS6 ....78 E5
Mill Pond La *HDGY* LS6 ....78 E5
Mill Pond Sq *HDGY* LS6 ....78 E4
Mill Race Fold *HOLM/MEL* HD9 ....233 J3
Mill Rd *DEWS* WF13 ....172 B1
Mill Rw *AIRE* BD20 ....26 E5
Mill Royd St *BRIG* HD6 ....168 C1
Mill Shaw La *HOLM/MEL* HD9 ....249 H1
Millshaw Mt *BEE/HOL* LS11 ....123 J2
Millshaw Park Av *MOR* LS27 ....123 J3
Millshaw Park Cl *BEE/HOL* LS11 ....123 J2
Millshaw Park La *BEE/HOL* LS11 ....123 J2
Millshaw Park Wy *BEE/HOL* LS11 ......123 J2
Millshaw Rd *BEE/HOL* LS11 ....123 J2
Millside *CUD/GR* S72 ....223 G8
Millside Wk *CUD/GR* S72 ....223 H8
  MOR LS27 ....123 H7
Millstone Cl *FEA/AMT* WF7 ....203 J5
Millstone Ri *LVSG* WF15 ....170 C2
Mill St *AIRE* BD20 ....5 J6
  BFD BD1 ....5 J6
  BTLY WF17 ....145 K4
  CAS WF10 ....153 J1
  CUL/QBY BD13 ....70 C7
  HEM/SK/SE WF9 ....241 G3
  HIPP HX3 ....165 H4
  HUDS HD4 ....12 D5
  MOR LS27 ....123 H7
  OSM LS9 ....7 J2
  WBSY BD6 ....118 A2
Mill St East *EARL* WF12 ....172 F4
Mill St West *EARL* WF12 ....172 E4
Mill Vw *HEM/SK/SE* WF9 ....224 D5
  ILK LS29 ....32 C6
  KNOT WF11 ....155 F8
Millward St *HOR/CROF* WF4 ....222 C6
Millwater Av *EARL* WF12 ....172 E4
Millwood La *TOD* OL14 ....134 C5
Millwright St *LDSU* LS2 ....7 J4
Milne Ct *MSTN/BAR* LS15 ....104 E1
Milner Av *STKB/PEN* S36 ....252 B5
Milner Bank *OT* LS21 ....33 H3
Milner Cl *GTL/HWG* HX4 ....166 A6
Milner Gdns *OSM* LS9 ....102 E3
Milner Ing *LM/WK* BD12 ....118 B5
Milner La *EARD/LOFT* WF3 ....125 J6
  GTL/HWG HX4 ....166 C6
  SCFT LS14 ....62 C6
Milner Rd *BAIL* BD17 ....73 K1
Milner's La *PONT* WF8 ....182 B1
Milner's Rd *YEA* LS19 ....53 K7
Milner St *HFAX* HX1 ....8 B5
  HUDS HD4 ....190 A7
  OSS WF5 ....173 H6
Milner Wy *OSS* WF5 ....173 H6
Milne's Av *WKFDW/WTN* WF2 ....175 G3
Milnes Gv *CAS* WF10 ....154 A1
Milnes St *WOR/ARM* LS12 ....6 C5
Milne St *GTHN* BD7 ....96 E3
Miln Rd *HUD* HD1 ....13 H2
Milnthorpe Cl *BSPA/BRAM* LS23 ....42 D3
Milnthorpe Crs *WKFDW/WTN* WF2 ...199 F8
Milnthorpe Dr *WKFDW/WTN* WF2 ....199 F8
Milnthorpe Gdns *BSPA/BRAM* LS23 ...42 D3
Milnthorpe Garth *BSPA/BRAM* LS23 ...62 E1
Milnthorpe Gn *WKFDW/WTN* WF2 ...199 F8
Milnthorpe La *BSPA/BRAM* LS23 ....42 D3
Milnthorpe Wy *BSPA/BRAM* LS23 ....42 D3
  WKFDW/WTN WF2 ....199 F8
Milroyd Crs *BTLY* WF17 ....145 J5
Milton Av *LVSG* WF15 ....145 K7
  RPDN/SBR HX6 ....139 H7
Milton Cl *HOR/CROF* WF4 ....197 F1
  LVSG WF15 ....171 K1
Milton Ct *EARD/LOFT* WF3 ....150 A8
Milton Crs *WKFDW/WTN* WF2 ....174 E7
Milton Dr *HEM/SK/SE* WF9 ....224 E2
  LVSG WF15 ....171 K1
  MSTN/BAR LS15 ....82 E4
Milton Gdns *LVSG* WF15 ....145 K8
Milton Gv *DEWS* WF13 ....172 C1
Milton Pl *HFAX* HX1 ....8 A4
  OSS WF5 ....173 H6
Milton Rd *LVSG* WF15 ....145 K8
  WKFDW/WTN WF2 ....174 E7
Milton Sq *HECK* WF16 ....145 J7
Milton St *CAS* WF10 ....153 J1
  CUL/QBY BD13 ....92 E8
  GTHN BD7 ....5 H7
  HECK WF16 ....145 J7
  RPDN/SBR HX6 ....138 E6
  WKFDW/WTN WF2 ....10 A1
Milton Ter *CLECK* BD19 ....143 J1
  HFAX HX1 ....8 A4
  KSTL LS5 ....99 F1
Minden Cl *PONT* WF8 ....181 J4
Minden Wy *PONT* WF8 ....181 J4
Minerva St *HUDS* HD4 ....181 F8
Minnie St *HWTH* BD22 ....6 B3
  KGHY BD21 ....3 C6
Minorca Mt *CUL/QBY* BD13 ....92 E8
Minsthorpe La *HEM/SK/SE* WF9 ....224 E2
  HEM/SK/SE WF9 ....224 E4
Mint St *ECHL* BD2 ....98 C3
  HUDW HD3 ....190 D6
Miramar *HUDN* HD2 ....16 B4
Mirey Butt La *KNOT* WF11 ....150 E7
Mirey La *RPDN/SBR* HX6 ....137 G1
Mirfield Av *ECHL* BD2 ....74 A5
Miry La *HBR* HX7 ....137 F3
  HOLM/MEL HD9 ....169 J7
  LVSG WF15 ....170 E4
  MSTN/BAR LS15 ....84 C6
  YEA LS19 ....54 E5
Mission St *BRIG* HD6 ....157 G7
Mistral Cl *LM/WK* BD12 ....138 A1
Mistral Gv *LVSG* WF15 ....146 A6

Mistress La WOR/ARM LS12 .... 100 C3
Mitcham Dr HTON BD9 .... 95 G1
Mitchell Av HUDE HD5 .... 192 C6
Mitchell Cl IDLE BD10 .... 74 E2
IDLE BD10 .... 74 E2
Mitchell Sq AIRE BD20 .... 27 G2
Mitchell St BRIG HD6 .... 142 B8
HBR HX7 .... 136 B1
KGHY BD21 .... 3 E2
RPDN/SBR HX6 .... 139 F7
TOD OL14 .... 133 H4
Mitchell Ter BGLY BD16 .... 71 K2
Mitchel Sq AIRE BD20 .... 27 G2
Mitford Pl WOR/ARM LS12 .... 100 D4
Mitford Rd WOR/ARM LS12 .... 100 D4
Mitford Ter WOR/ARM LS12 .... 100 D4
Mitford Vw WOR/ARM LS12 .... 100 D4
Moderna Wy HBR HX7 .... 137 G3
Moffat Cl WBSY BD6 .... 118 A4
Moles Head MAR/SLWT HD7 .... 189 G5
Molly Hurst La HOR/CROF WF4 .... 220 B4
Mona St MAR/SLWT HD7 .... 210 D2
WKFDW/WTN WF2 .... 175 K5
Monckton Dr CAS WF10 .... 154 D5
Monckton Rd WKFDW/WTN WF2 .... 198 C1
Mond Av BFDE BD3 .... 97 F2
Monk Barn Cl BGLY * BD16 .... 50 A7
Monk Bridge Av HDGY LS6 .... 78 E5
Monk Bridge Dr HDGY LS6 .... 79 F5
Monk Bridge Pl HDGY LS6 .... 78 E5
Monk Bridge Rd HDGY LS6 .... 78 E5
Monk Bridge Ter HDGY LS6 .... 78 E5
Monkfield MIRF WF14 .... 170 B5
Monkhill Av PONT WF8 .... 180 E1
Monkhill Dr PONT WF8 .... 180 E1
Monkhill La PONT WF8 .... 154 E8
Monkhill Mt PONT WF8 .... 180 E1
Monk Ings BTLY WF17 .... 145 G2
Monk Ings Av BTLY WF17 .... 145 F2
Monkmans Wharfe AIRE BD20 .... 27 F2
Monk St BCTHN BD7 .... 4 A4
WKFDE WF1 .... 11 D4
Monkswood KSTL LS5 .... 77 K5
Monkswood Av SCFT LS14 .... 81 H3
Monkswood Bank SCFT LS14 .... 81 H3
Monkswood Cl SCFT LS14 .... 81 H3
Monkswood Dr SCFT LS14 .... 81 H3
Monkswood Ga SCFT * LS14 .... 81 J3
Monkswood Gn SCFT LS14 .... 81 H3
Monkswood Hl SCFT LS14 .... 81 H3
Monkswood Ri SCFT LS14 .... 81 H3
Monkswood Wk SCFT LS14 .... 81 J3
Monkton Wy BSLYN/ROY S71 .... 222 H4
Monk Wd WKFDE WF1 .... 149 J6
Monson Av PDSY/CALV LS28 .... 75 K5
Mons Rd TOD OL14 .... 133 J4
Montagu Av RHAY LS8 .... 80 D5
Montagu Ct RHAY LS8 .... 80 D5
Montagu Crs RHAY LS8 .... 80 E6
Montagu Dr RHAY LS8 .... 80 D6
Montagu Gv RHAY LS8 .... 80 E6
Montagu Pl RHAY LS8 .... 80 D6
Montagu Ri RHAY LS8 .... 80 E7
Montagu Rd WBY LS22 .... 24 A5
Montagu Vw RHAY LS8 .... 80 D6
Montcalm Crs EARD/LOFT WF3 .... 150 C8
MID LS10 .... 125 F1
Montfort Cl HORS LS18 .... 55 F8
Montpelier Ter HDGY LS6 .... 79 F7
Montreal Av CHAL LS7 .... 79 K5
Montreal St TOD * OL14 .... 159 K2
Montreal Ter BRAM LS13 .... 98 E3
Montrose St ECHL BD2 .... 73 K7
Montserrat Rd BOW BD4 .... 120 C2
Monument La PONT WF8 .... 181 F4
Monument Ms PONT WF8 .... 181 F4
Moody St BOW BD4 .... 5 D6
Moor Allerton Av AL/HA/HU LS17 .... 80 A1
Moor Allerton Crs AL/HA/HU LS17 .... 80 A1
Moor Allerton Dr AL/HA/HU LS17 .... 80 B1
Moor Allerton Gdns AL/HA/HU LS17 .... 79 K1
Moor Av BSPA/BRAM LS23 .... 42 D5
EARD/LOFT WF3 .... 150 B5
MSTN/BAR LS15 .... 103 H4
Moorbottom CLECK BD19 .... 143 J5
Moor Bottom HOLM/MEL HD9 .... 213 F7
Moor Bottom La BGLY BD16 .... 50 A8

GTL/HWG HX4 .... 165 K2
HBR HX7 .... 137 H6
KGHY BD21 .... 69 K1
RPDN/SBR HX6 .... 164 D3
Moor Bottom Rd GTL/HWG HX4 .... 164 C6
LUD/ILL HX2 .... 115 J5
Moorbottom Rd HUD HD1 .... 12 A6
Moorbrow HOLM/MEL HD9 .... 248 D1
Moor Cl HUDS HD4 .... 212 C2
MID LS10 .... 124 E1
Moor Close Av CUL/QBY BD13 .... 116 B3
Moor Close Farm Ms
       CUL/QBY BD13 .... 116 B3
Moor Close La CUL/QBY BD13 .... 116 B3
Moor Close Pde CUL/QBY BD13 .... 116 B3
Moor Close Rd CUL/QBY BD13 .... 116 B3
Moorcock Rd HBR HX7 .... 110 B6
Moor Cottage Cl HUDS HD4 .... 212 D4
Moor Crs BEE/HOL LS11 .... 101 J7
Moor Crescent Cha BEE/HOL LS11 .... 101 J7
Moor Crest Rd HUDS HD4 .... 190 C8
Moor Cft BGLY BD16 .... 50 B6
       BRIF/TINH LS16 .... 56 D7
Moorcroft DEWS WF13 .... 171 J2
Moorcroft Av BFDE BD3 .... 97 F2
       HWTH BD22 .... 47 F8
Moorcroft Avenues
       MAR/SLWT HD7 .... 189 H6
Moorcroft Dr BOW BD4 .... 120 C2
       DEWS WF13 .... 171 J2
Moorcroft Park Dr HOLM/MEL HD9 .... 233 K4
Moorcroft Rd BOW BD4 .... 120 C2
       DEWS WF13 .... 171 J2
Moorcroft Ter BOW BD4 .... 120 C3
Moor Dr HDGY LS6 .... 78 E5
       HWTH BD22 .... 47 F8
       OT LS21 .... 34 B3
       PDSY/CALV LS28 .... 98 D6
Moore Av GTHN BD7 .... 118 A1
Moore Edge High Side BGLY BD16 .... 70 E1
Moorehouse Av OSM LS9 .... 102 A2
Moor End Av LUD/ILL HX2 .... 139 F2
Moor End Gdns LUD/ILL HX2 .... 139 G2
Moor End La DEWS WF13 .... 171 J1
       RPDN/SBR HX6 .... 165 G1
Moor End Rd HUDS HD4 .... 190 E8
       LUD/ILL HX2 .... 114 E8
Moor End Vw LUD/ILL HX2 .... 139 H2
Moore St KGHY BD21 .... 3 D4
Moor Farm Gdns CHAL * LS7 .... 79 J4
Moorfield MOR LS27 .... 122 B4
Moorfield Av BFDE BD3 .... 97 F2
       CLECK BD19 .... 143 F4
       ILK LS29 .... 32 B7
       WOR/ARM LS12 .... 100 A3
Moorfield Cl YEA LS19 .... 54 B5
Moorfield Ct HOR/CROF WF4 .... 194 C7
YEA LS19 .... 54 B5
Moorfield Crs HEM/SK/SE WF9 .... 224 C5
       PDSY/CALV LS28 .... 98 B5
       WOR/ARM LS12 .... 100 A3
       YEA LS19 .... 54 A5
Moorfield Cft YEA LS19 .... 54 B5
Moorfield Dr BAIL BD17 .... 51 J5
       HWTH BD22 .... 47 F8
       YEA LS19 .... 54 B5
Moorfield Gdns PDSY/CALV LS28 .... 98 A5
Moorfield Gv PDSY/CALV LS28 .... 98 A5
       WOR/ARM LS12 .... 100 A3
Moorfield Rd HEM/SK/SE WF9 .... 224 C5
       IDLE BD10 .... 74 D3
Moorfield Rd HUDN HD2 .... 13 D1
       ILK LS29 .... 20 E7
       WOR/ARM LS12 .... 100 A3
       YEA LS19 .... 54 B5
Moorfields AL/HA/HU * LS17 .... 79 K1
       BRAM LS13 .... 77 G8
Moorfield St LDSU * LS2 .... 77 G8
       WOR/ARM LS12 .... 100 A3
Moorfield Vw LVSG WF15 .... 170 B2
Moorfield Wy CLECK BD19 .... 143 F4
Moor Flatts Av MID LS10 .... 124 C6
Moor Flatts Rd MID LS10 .... 124 D6
Moorgarth Av BFDE BD3 .... 97 F2
       GFTH/SHER LS25 .... 106 A8
Moorgate Cl GFTH/SHER LS25 .... 129 F1
Moorgate Dr GFTH/SHER LS25 .... 129 G1
Moorgate Ri GFTH/SHER LS25 .... 129 F1
Moorgate Rd GFTH/SHER LS25 .... 106 A8
Moorgate St HFAX HX1 .... 8 A6
Moor Grange Ri BHP/TINH LS16 .... 78 A3
Moor Grange Vw BHP/TINH LS16 .... 78 A3
Moor Gv EARD/LOFT WF3 .... 150 B5
       HIPP HX3 .... 117 H4
       PDSY/CALV LS28 .... 98 D6
Moorhead Cl HOLM/MEL HD9 .... 231 H1
Moorhead Crs SHPY BD18 .... 72 E4
Moorhead La SHPY BD18 .... 72 E4
Moorhead Ter SHPY BD18 .... 72 E4
Moor Hey La ELL HX5 .... 167 H6
       GTL/HWG HX4 .... 188 C2
Moor Hill Ct HUDW * HD3 .... 189 J3
Moor Hill Rd HUDW HD3 .... 189 K3

Moorhouse Av BEE/HOL LS11 .... 124 A2
       EARD/LOFT WF3 .... 150 E4
       ECHL BD2 .... 74 C6
       WKFDW/WTN WF2 .... 175 G5
Moorhouse Cl EARD/LOFT WF3 .... 150 E4
       HWTH BD22 .... 68 E8
       NORM WF6 .... 152 B8
Moorhouse Ct HEM/SK/SE WF9 .... 242 C2
       HWTH BD22 .... 68 E8
Moorhouse Crs WKFDW/WTN WF2 .... 10 A3
Moorhouse Gap AWLS/ASK DN6 .... 243 H2
Moorhouse Gv EARD/LOFT WF3 .... 150 E4
Moorhouse La AWLS/ASK DN6 .... 242 E5
       DOD/DAR S75 .... 219 J6
       HOR/CROF WF4 .... 201 G7
       HWTH BD22 .... 68 D7
Moorhouse Ter EARD/LOFT WF3 .... 150 E5
Moorhouse Vw EARD/LOFT WF3 .... 150 E5
       HEM/SK/SE WF9 .... 242 D1
The Moorings AL/HA/HU LS17 .... 58 A6
       IDLE BD10 .... 75 F3
       MID LS10 .... 102 D8
Moor Knoll Cl EARD/LOFT WF3 .... 148 E5
Moor Knoll Dr EARD/LOFT WF3 .... 148 D5
Moor Knoll La EARD/LOFT WF3 .... 148 D2
Moorland Av BAIL BD17 .... 51 K7
       BGLY BD16 .... 50 C5
       GSLY LS20 .... 53 C2
       HDGY LS6 .... 6 B1
       MOR LS27 .... 122 A3
Moorland Cl LUD/ILL HX2 .... 115 H8
       MAR/SLWT HD7 .... 211 J4
       MOR LS27 .... 122 B3
Moorland Crs AL/HA/HU LS17 .... 79 J2
       BAIL BD17 .... 51 K7
       GSLY LS20 .... 53 C3
       ILK LS29 .... 32 C6
       ILK LS29 .... 52 D1
       MOR LS27 .... 122 A3
Moorland Dr AL/HA/HU LS17 .... 79 J2
       BIRK/DRI BD11 .... 120 E4
       GSLY LS20 .... 53 C1
       HOR/CROF WF4 .... 220 B1
       PDSY/CALV LS28 .... 97 J3
Moorland Gdns AL/HA/HU LS17 .... 79 K1
Moorland Garth AL/HA/HU LS17 .... 79 J2
Moorland Gv AL/HA/HU LS17 .... 79 J2
       PDSY/CALV LS28 .... 97 J3
Moorland Ings AL/HA/HU LS17 .... 79 J2
Moorland Pl LM/WK BD12 .... 119 F6
Moorland Ri AL/HA/HU LS17 .... 79 J2
       HOLM/MEL HD9 .... 231 G2
Moorland Rd BHP/TINH LS16 .... 55 G1
       BIRK/DRI BD11 .... 121 H5
       HDGY LS6 .... 6 B1
       PDSY/CALV LS28 .... 97 J2
The Moorlands AL/HA/HU LS17 .... 58 A7
       WBY LS22 .... 23 K6
Moorlands Crs HUDW HD3 .... 189 H2
Moorlands Dr LUD/ILL HX2 .... 139 H1
       YEA LS19 .... 54 B5
Moorlands Pl HFAX HX1 .... 8 C5
Moorlands Rd BIRK/DRI BD11 .... 120 D4
       DEWS WF13 .... 172 A3
       GTL/HWG HX4 .... 166 A3
       HUDW HD3 .... 189 H2
Moorlands Vw HFAX HX1 .... 8 C6
       WBY LS22 .... 23 K6
Moorland Ter GFTH/SHER LS25 .... 105 J5
       KGHY BD21 .... 48 D5
Moorland Vw AL/HA/HU LS17 .... 79 J1
       BRAM LS13 .... 77 F7
       BSPA/BRAM LS23 .... 216 E4
       KBTN HD8 .... 238 A1
       LM/WK BD12 .... 119 F6
       RPDN/SBR HX6 .... 138 C8
Moorland Wk AL/HA/HU LS17 .... 79 J1
Moor La AIRE BD20 .... 26 B6
       AL/HA/HU LS17 .... 39 J6
       BSPA/BRAM LS23 .... 24 D6
       BTLY WF17 .... 145 J3
       CLECK BD19 .... 144 E1
       CUD/GR S72 .... 240 E7
       GSLY LS20 .... 53 C1
       HOLM/MEL HD9 .... 232 E4
       HUDS HD4 .... 212 D4
       HUDS HD4 .... 214 A6
       ILK LS29 .... 17 J1
       ILK LS29 .... 18 B3
       ILK LS29 .... 31 K3
       ILK LS29 .... 32 A7
       KBTN HD8 .... 215 H4
       LUD/ILL HX2 .... 115 H7
       PONT WF8 .... 181 F7
       PONT WF8 .... 181 G6
       SKP/WHF BD23 .... 14 B2
       TOD OL14 .... 134 A8

WBY LS22 .... 41 K3
Moorlea Dr BAIL BD17 .... 51 K8
Moorleigh Cl GFTH/SHER LS25 .... 129 G1
Moorleigh Dr GFTH/SHER LS25 .... 129 C1
Moor Park Av HDGY LS6 .... 78 D5
HUDS HD4 .... 212 C2
Moor Park Cl ILK LS29 .... 18 B3
Moor Park Ct EARL * WF12 .... 172 D2
Moor Park Crs ILK LS29 .... 18 B3
Moor Park Dr BFDE BD3 .... 97 F3
HDGY LS6 .... 78 D5
ILK LS29 .... 18 B3
Moor Park Gdns EARL WF12 .... 172 D3
Moor Park Gv ILK LS29 .... 18 C3
Moor Park La EARL WF12 .... 172 D3
Moor Park Mt HDGY LS6 .... 78 D4
Moor Park Rd BFDE * BD3 .... 96 E3
Moor Park Vls HDGY LS6 .... 78 C5
Moor Park Wy ILK LS29 .... 18 C3
Moor Rd BEE/HOL LS11 .... 101 J7
BHP/TINH LS16 .... 55 H1
EARD/LOFT WF3 .... 150 B5
FEA/AMT WF7 .... 179 J6
HDGY LS6 .... 78 D5
ILK LS29 .... 31 F2
MID LS10 .... 124 E1
Moor Royd HIPP HX3 .... 139 K7
HOLM/MEL HD9 .... 212 E8
Moorroyd St OSS WF5 .... 182 C3
Moorshutt Rd HEM/SK/SE WF9 .... 224 C5
Moor Side BSPA/BRAM LS23 .... 42 B3
Moorside BAIL BD17 .... 51 K6
CLECK BD19 .... 143 H5
HTON BD9 .... 94 E1
Moorside Av BIRK/DRI BD11 .... 121 J6
Moorside Av AIRE BD20 .... 26 C6
BIRK/DRI BD11 .... 120 D4
BIRK/DRI BD11 .... 121 J6
DEWS WF13 .... 171 H1
ECHL BD2 .... 78 E8
HUDS HD4 .... 190 D7
Moorside Cl BIRK/DRI BD11 .... 121 J6
ECHL BD2 .... 74 E8
Moorside Crs BIRK/DRI BD11 .... 121 J6
DEWS WF13 .... 171 J1
HOR/CROF WF4 .... 220 B1
Moorside Cft ECHL BD2 .... 96 C1
Moorside Dr BIRK/DRI BD11 .... 121 J6
BRAM LS13 .... 77 G7
Moorside End DEWS WF13 .... 171 J1
Moorside Gdns BIRK/DRI BD11 .... 121 J6
ECHL BD2 .... 74 E8
LUD/ILL HX2 .... 115 J7
Moorside Gn BIRK/DRI BD11 .... 121 J6
Moor Side La HWTH BD22 .... 68 B6
MAR/SLWT HD7 .... 188 B6
Moorside La BFDE BD5 .... 97 F4
ILK LS29 .... 18 C7
Moorside Maltings BEE/HOL LS11 ... 101 J8
Moorside Mt BIRK/DRI BD11 .... 121 H6
Moorside Pde BIRK/DRI BD11 .... 121 J6
Moorside Pl BFDE BD5 .... 97 F4
DEWS WF13 .... 171 J1
Moorside Rd CLECK BD19 .... 143 J4
Moorside Rd BFDE BD3 .... 97 F4
BIRK/DRI BD11 .... 121 H6
DEWS WF13 .... 171 J1
ECHL BD2 .... 74 E8
HOLM/MEL HD9 .... 212 E8
HUDE HD5 .... 192 E1
WIL/AL BD15 .... 71 C7
Moorside Ter BIRK/DRI BD11 .... 121 H6
BRAM LS13 .... 77 G7
ECHL BD2 .... 97 F1
Moorside V BIRK/DRI BD11 .... 121 J6
Moorside Vw BIRK/DRI BD11 .... 121 J6
Moorside Wk BIRK/DRI BD11 .... 121 J6
Moor Stone Pl HIPP * HX3 .... 117 H6
Moor St CUL/QBY * BD13 .... 116 D2
HWTH BD22 .... 47 F8
Moor Ter ECHL BD2 .... 97 F2
Moorthorpe Av BFDE BD3 .... 97 F2
Moorton BIRK/DRI BD11 .... 121 C5
Moor Top BIRK/DRI BD11 .... 121 C6
MIRF WF14 .... 170 B5
OT LS21 .... 33 F6
WOR/ARM LS12 .... 122 B1
Moor Top Av FEA/AMT WF7 .... 202 E6
HUDS HD4 .... 234 B1
Moor Top Dr HEM/SK/SE WF9 .... 224 D6
Moor Top Gdns LUD/ILL HX2 .... 115 H4
Moor Top La HOR/CROF WF4 .... 216 B2
Moor Top Rd HUDE HD5 .... 192 E1
LM/WK BD12 .... 118 C5
LUD/ILL HX2 .... 138 E3
Moor Vw BEE/HOL LS11 .... 6 C6
BOW * BD4 .... 120 D3
HECK WF16 .... 171 H1
HOLM/MEL HD9 .... 211 G8
HOR/CROF WF4 .... 198 B6
MIRF WF14 .... 170 D2
Moor View Av SHPY BD18 .... 73 G3
Moor View Cl CAS WF10 .... 154 A4
Moor View Ct AIRE BD20 .... 49 C4
IDLE * BD10 .... 78 C2
Moorview Cft ILK LS29 .... 32 B6
Moorview Dr BGLY BD16 .... 71 J5

SHPY BD18 .... 74 B4
Moorview Gv KGHY BD21 .... 3 E5
Moorville Av BFDE BD3 .... 97 F2
Moorville Cl BEE/HOL LS11 .... 101 H7
Moorville Ct BEE/HOL * LS11 .... 101 H7
Moorville Dr BIRK/DRI BD11 .... 120 D4
Moorville Gv BEE/HOL LS11 .... 101 G7
Moorville Rd BEE/HOL LS11 .... 101 H7
Moorway GSLY LS20 .... 52 D2
Moor Wy HWTH BD22 .... 46 E8
Moorwell Pl ECHL BD2 .... 74 D7
Moravian Pl WBOW * BD5 .... 95 K7
Morefield Bank HOLM/MEL HD9 ...... 233 J3
Moresby Rd WBSY BD6 .... 117 K5
Moresdale La SCFT LS14 .... 81 H8
Morlands St DEWS WF13 .... 145 J8
Morley Av BFDE BD3 .... 97 F2
KNOT WF11 .... 156 D7
Morley Carr Rd LM/WK BD12 .... 118 E6
Morley Fold WF17 BD8 .... 236 D6
Morley Hall La LUD/ILL HX2 .... 137 K5
Morley La HUDS HD4 .... 190 A7
Morley St GTHN BD7 .... 4 C5
Morningside GIR BD8 .... 95 H2
Morning St KGHY BD21 .... 2 C6
Mornington Rd BGLY BD16 .... 50 A8
ILK LS29 .... 20 C7
Mornington St KGHY BD21 .... 2 C2
Mornington Vls GIR BD8 .... 4 B2
Morpeth Pl OSM * LS9 .... 102 A4
Morpeth St CUL/QBY BD13 .... 116 D2
GTHN BD7 .... 4 A4
Morphet Ter CHAL * LS7 .... 7 E2
Morrell Crs WKFDW/WTN WF2 .... 149 G8
Morris Av KSTL LS5 .... 78 A6
Morris Cl HEM/SK/SE WF9 .... 224 B1
Morris Gv KSTL LS5 .... 78 A7
Morris La KSTL LS5 .... 78 A6
Morris Mt KSTL LS5 .... 78 A7
Morrison St CAS WF10 .... 153 K4
Morris Pl MOR LS27 .... 122 E6
Morris Vw KSTL LS5 .... 78 A7
Morritt Av MSTN/BAR LS15 .... 103 K2
Morritt Dr MSTN/BAR LS15 .... 103 H5
Mortech Pk MSTN/BAR * LS15 .... 83 H4
Mortimer Av BFDE BD3 .... 97 F2
BTLY WF17 .... 145 J6
Mortimer Rl OSS WF5 .... 175 K5
Mortimer Rw BFDE BD3 .... 97 F5
HOR/CROF WF4 .... 197 C7
Mortimer St BTLY WF17 .... 145 J6
CLECK * BD19 .... 144 A4
GIR BD8 .... 95 F3
Mortimer Ter BTLY WF17 .... 145 J6
Morton Crs CAS WF10 .... 154 A4
Morton Gn HUDE HD5 .... 192 C7
Morton Gv AIRE BD20 .... 49 H3
EARL WF12 .... 172 A4
Morton La AIRE BD20 .... 49 H4
Morton Pde WKFDW/WTN WF2 .... 10 A3
Morton Rd BOW BD4 .... 97 F6
The Mortons HUDW * HD3 .... 189 K3
Mortons Cl HIPP HX3 .... 140 D8
Morton Wy HUDW HD3 .... 189 J2
Morton Wood Gv HOLM/MEL HD9 ... 233 K8
Morwick Gv MSTN/BAR LS15 .... 82 C5
Moselden La RPDN/SBR HX6 .... 186 E5
Moseley Pl HDGY LS6 .... 79 H8
Moseley Wood Ap BHP/TINH LS16 ... 55 H7
Moseley Wood Av BHP/TINH LS16 .... 55 H6
Moseley Wood Bank BHP/TINH LS16 55 H6
Moseley Wood Cl BHP/TINH LS16 ..... 55 H7
Moseley Wood Crs BHP/TINH LS16 .. 55 H6
Moseley Wood Cft HORS LS18 .... 55 G7
Moseley Wood Dr BHP/TINH LS16 .... 55 H6
Moseley Wood Gdns BHP/TINH LS16 55 H7
Moseley Wood Gn BHP/TINH LS16 .... 55 H6
Moseley Wood Gv BHP/TINH LS16 .... 55 H6
Moseley Wood La BHP/TINH LS16 ..... 55 J1
Moseley Wood Ri BHP/TINH LS16 ..... 55 G6
Moseley Wood Vw BHP/TINH LS16 ... 55 J5
Moseley Wood Wk BHP/TINH LS16 ... 55 H6
Moseley Wood Wy BHP/TINH LS16 ... 55 H6
Moser Av ECHL BD2 .... 74 C6
Moser Crs ECHL BD2 .... 74 C6
Moss Bridge Rd BRAM LS13 .... 76 D6
Moss Carr Av KGHY BD21 .... 48 D6
Moss Carr Gv KGHY * BD21 .... 48 D6
Moss Carr Rd KGHY BD21 .... 48 D6
Mossdale Av HTON BD9 .... 72 C8
Moss Dr LUD/ILL HX2 .... 115 H5
Moss Edge Rd HOLM/MEL HD9 .... 247 H3
Moss Gdns AL/HA/HU LS17 .... 57 G6
Moss Hall La HBR HX7 .... 110 D7
Moss La HBR * HX7 .... 112 B7
LUD/ILL HX2 .... 115 H5
Moss Ri AL/HA/HU LS17 .... 57 G6
HOLM/MEL HD9 .... 232 E6
Moss Rw WIL/AL BD15 .... 71 C5
Moss Side HTON BD9 .... 94 E1
Moss Side St WHIT OL12 .... 158 B6
Moss St CAS WF10 .... 153 G3
CUL/QBY BD13 .... 93 G4
HUDS HD4 .... 13 D6
HWTH BD22 .... 60 G3
Moss Syke SCFT LS14 .... 60 A2
Mosstree Cl CUL/QBY BD13 .... 116 B1
Moss Va AL/HA/HU LS17 .... 57 G6
Mossy Bank Cl CUL/QBY BD13 .... 116 D1

Mostyn Gv WBSY BD6 .... 118 B3
Mostyn Mt HIPP HX3 .... 115 K8
Mostyn Wk HOR/CROF WF4 .... 198 B8
Motley La GSLY LS20 .... 53 G1
Moule Ri GFTH/SHER LS25 .... 106 B2
Moulson Ct WBOW BD5 .... 96 A8
The Mount AL/HA/HU LS17 .... 57 H5
BTLY WF17 .... 145 H1
CAS WF10 .... 154 D4
GFTH/SHER LS25 .... 129 F2
MSTN/BAR LS15 .... 83 H5
MSTN/BAR LS15 .... 103 K2
PONT WF8 .... 180 D3
TOD OL14 .... 134 B5
WKFDW/WTN WF2 .... 174 E2
WKFDW/WTN WF2 .... 175 G8
YEA * LS19 .... 54 B8
Mountain Crs EARL WF12 .... 195 H1
Mountain Rd EARL WF12 .... 195 H1
Mountain Vw LUD/ILL HX2 .... 115 K5
SHPY BD18 .... 73 K5
Mountain Wy HUDE HD5 .... 192 E4
Mount Av CUD/GR S72 .... 240 A3
ECHL BD2 .... 74 D6
HECK WF16 .... 145 H5
HEM/SK/SE WF9 .... 224 D5
HUDW HD3 .... 189 G2
LUD/ILL HX2 .... 139 F4
WKFDW/WTN WF2 .... 149 G7
Mountbatten Av WKFDE WF1 .... 149 K6
WKFDW/WTN WF2 .... 199 G4
Mountbatten Crs WKFDE WF1 .... 149 K6
Mountbatten Gdns HUDW HD3 .... 190 B4
Mountbatten Gv WKFDE WF1 .... 150 A7
Mountcliffe Vw MOR LS27 .... 121 K5
Mount Ct PDSY/CALV LS28 .... 98 C3
Mount Crs CLECK BD19 .... 144 A3
LUD/ILL HX2 .... 139 F4
WKFDW/WTN WF2 .... 175 G8
Mount Dr AL/HA/HU LS17 .... 57 H5
Mountfield Av HUDE HD5 .... 192 D6
Mountfield Rd HUDE HD5 .... 192 D6
Mountfields HIPP HX3 .... 141 K3
Mountfields Wk HEM/SK/SE WF9 .... 241 H2
Mount Gdns AL/HA/HU LS17 .... 57 H5
CLECK BD19 .... 144 A3
Mount Gv ECHL BD2 .... 74 D6
Mountjoy Rd HUD HD1 .... 12 B3
Mount La BRIG HD6 .... 167 K4
TOD OL14 .... 109 F8
Mountleigh Cl BOW BD4 .... 119 H5
Mount Pellon LUD/ILL HX2 .... 8 A2
Mount Pellon Rd LUD/ILL HX2 .... 139 H3
Mount Pl SHPY BD18 .... 73 H3
Mount Pleasant AIRE BD20 .... 49 G4
BRAM LS13 .... 77 F7
CAS WF10 .... 154 A5
CUD/GR S72 .... 92 B3
CUL/QBY BD13 .... 116 D3
EARL * WF12 .... 172 D4
FEA/AMT WF7 .... 203 F5
GFTH/SHER LS25 .... 129 G3
GIR * BD8 .... 4 A1
GSLY LS20 .... 53 C1
HUD HD1 .... 191 F6
ILK LS29 .... 18 D3
KBTN HD8 .... 217 H4
WBSY BD6 .... 117 K4
Mount Pleasant Av HFAX HX1 .... 8 C4
RHAY LS8 .... 80 B6
Mount Pleasant Dr HBR HX7 .... 137 F2
Mount Pleasant Gdns RHAY * LS8 .... 80 B6
Mount Pleasant La HUDE HD5 .... 192 E1
Mount Pleasant Rd PDSY/CALV LS28 .98 C3
Mount Pleasant St FEA/AMT WF7 .... 179 J5
HUDE * HD5 .... 13 F4
TOD OL14 .... 132 D2
Mount Pleasant Vw TOD OL14 .... 133 K6
Mount Preston St LDSU LS2 .... 6 C2
Mount Ri AL/HA/HU LS17 .... 57 H5
Mount Rd CUD/GR S72 .... 240 A5
EARD/LOFT WF3 .... 150 C5
ECHL BD2 .... 74 D6
HUD HD1 .... 190 D5
MAR/SLWT HD7 .... 228 D2
WBSY BD6 .... 118 B2
Mount Royd GIR BD8 .... 4 A4
Mount Scar Vw HOLM/MEL HD9 .... 233 K7
Mount St BFDE BD3 .... 5 E5
BTLY WF17 .... 146 C8
CLECK BD19 .... 144 A2
ECHL BD2 .... 74 D6
HFAX HX1 .... 9 D4
HUD HD1 .... 191 F6
HUDS * HD4 .... 190 A4
HWTH BD22 .... 2 B8
RPDN/SBR HX6 .... 138 E7
Mount St West LUD/ILL * HX2 .... 139 H7
Mount Tabor Rd LUD/ILL * HX2 .... 114 C7
Mount Tabor St PDSY/CALV * LS28 .... 98 A2
Mount Ter BTLY WF17 .... 146 B8
ECHL BD2 .... 74 D6
LUD/ILL HX2 .... 139 H7
Mount Vernon Rd YEA LS19 .... 54 A1
Mount Vw HWTH BD22 .... 68 D7
LUD/ILL HX2 .... 114 D8
Mount View Ct CLECK BD19 .... 143 K3
Mount View Rd HOLM/MEL HD9 ...... 249 F1
Mount Wk CAS WF10 .... 153 J5

Mou - Nev 323

lount Zion Rd HUDE HD5 .....13 E4
ousehole La MIRF WF14 .....194 B2
overley Flatts PONT WF8 .....181 F4
owat Cl LVSG WF15 .....143 J6
owbray Dr RTHW LS26 .....126 D4
owbray Cl CUL/QBY BD13 .....70 A6
owbray Cl SCFT LS14 .....81 J8
owbray Crs SCFT LS14 .....81 K8
oxon Cl PONT WF8 .....180 E5
oxon Gv WKFDE WF1 .....149 J8
oxon Pl WKFDW/WTN WF2 .....174 D6
oxon Sq WKFDW WF1 .....11 D2
oxon St WKFDE WF1 .....149 K7
oxon Wy WKFDE WF1 .....149 K7
oynihan Cl RHAY LS8 .....80 D7
ozley Dr LUD/ILL HX2 .....115 J5
uddy La WBY LS22 .....23 F8
uffit La CLECK BD19 .....145 G3
uff St BOW BD4 .....5 F6
ug Mill La EARL WF12 .....195 J3
ugup La HOLM/MEL HD9 .....249 F2
uir Ct HDGY LS6 .....78 D7
uirfield Av FEA/AMT WF7 .....179 H2
uirfield Dr WKFDW/WTN WF2 .....198 C1
uirhead Ct BOW BD4 .....120 B1
uirhead Dr BOW BD4 .....120 B1
uirhead Fold BOW BD4 .....120 B1
he Muirlands HUD 169 F6
ulberry Av BHP/TINH LS16 .....56 D7
ulberry Cl MAR/SLWT HD7 .....189 J6
ulberry Garth BHP/TINH LS16 .....56 D8
BSPA/BRAM LS23 .....42 E3
ulberry Pl HOR/CROF WF4 .....223 G2
ulberry Ri HOR/CROF WF4 .....56 D7
ulberry St HUD HD1 .....13 E5
KGHY * BD21 .....3 E2
MID LS10 .....125 F5
ulberry Ter HUD * HD1 .....13 D2
ulberry Vw BHP/TINH LS16 .....56 D8
ulcture Hall Rd HFAX HX1 .....9 E4
ulehouse La HUDW HX1 .....189 F2
ulgrave St BFDE BD3 .....5 F5
ullins Ct OSM LS9 .....102 B5
ullion Av WBOW BD5 .....96 A8
unby St GIR BD8 3
ancaster Rd GFTH/SHER LS25 .....106 B3
unster St BOW BD4 .....96 D8
unton Cl WBSY * BD6 .....117 K5
urdoch St KGHY BD21 .....48 D3
urgatroyd St SHPY BD18 .....73 H3
WBOW BD5 .....96 A8
urray Rd HUDN HD2 .....12 B2
urray St WBOW * BD5 .....95 J8
yers Cft HUDE HD5 .....192 B5
OT LS21 .....33 J4
yers La ECHL BD2 .....74 C7
yrtle Av BGLY * BD16 .....71 K1
DEWS WF13 .....171 H6
LUD/ILL HX2 .....115 H7
yrtle Ct BGLY BD16 .....71 K1
yrtle Dr HWTH BD22 .....69 H2
LUD/ILL HX2 .....115 H7
yrtle Gdns LUD/ILL HX2 .....115 H7
yrtle Gv BGLY BD16 .....71 K1
HUDW HD3 .....190 B5
LUD/ILL HX2 .....115 H7
yrtle Pl BGLY BD16 .....49 K8
LUD/ILL HX2 .....115 H7
yrtle St DEWS * WF13 .....171 H6
ELL HX5 .....116 E6
yrtle St BFDE BD3 .....96 E5
BGLY BD16 .....50 A8
HUD * HD1 .....13 D3
yson Av PONT WF8 .....155 C7
ytholm Bank HBR * HX7 .....111 K8
ytholm Cl HBR HX7 .....112 A8
ytholmes La HWTH BD22 .....68 E4

N

e Nab MIRF WF14 .....170 B5
abbs La MAR/SLWT HD7 .....210 D3
abb Vw HOLM/MEL * HD9 .....233 H7
ab Crs HOLM/MEL HD9 .....231 G1
bcroft La HUDS HD4 .....190 D8

Nabcroft Ri HUDS * HD4 .....190 D7
Nab End La GTL/HWG HX4 .....166 C4
Nab La BTLY WF17 .....145 K1
MIRF WF14 .....170 C5
SHPY BD18 .....72 D4
Naburn Ap SCFT LS14 .....81 K2
Naburn Cl SCFT LS14 .....81 K4
Naburn Dr SCFT LS14 .....81 K4
Naburn Gn SCFT LS14 .....81 K4
Naburn Pl SCFT LS14 .....81 K3
Naburn Rd SCFT LS14 .....81 K4
Naburn Vw SCFT LS14 .....82 A4
Nab Vw AIRE BD20 .....17 H8
Nab Water La HWTH BD22 .....90 E5
Nab Wood Bank SHPY BD18 .....72 D4
Nab Wood * SHPY BD18 .....72 E4
Nab Wood Crs SHPY BD18 .....72 D4
Nab Wood Dr BGLY BD16 .....72 D5
Nab Wood Gdns SHPY BD18 .....72 D4
Nab Wood Mt SHPY BD18 .....72 D4
Nab Wood Pl SHPY BD18 .....72 D4
Nab Wood Ri SHPY BD18 .....72 D4
Nab Wood Rd SHPY BD18 .....72 D5
Nab Wood Ter SHPY BD18 .....72 D4
Nairn Cl HUDS HD4 .....212 C1
Nancroft Crs WOR/ARM LS12 .....100 C4
Nancroft Ter WOR/ARM LS12 .....100 C4
Nancy Crs CUD/GR S72 .....240 B5
Nancy Rd CUD/GR S72 .....240 B5
Nanny Goat La GFTH/SHER LS25 .....105 J3
Nansen Av BRAM LS13 .....99 F1
Nansen Gv BRAM LS13 .....99 F1
Nansen Mt BRAM LS13 .....99 F1
Nansen Pl BRAM LS13 .....99 F1
Nansen St BRAM LS13 .....99 F1
Nansen Ter BRAM LS13 .....99 F1
Nansen Vw BRAM LS13 .....99 F1
Naomi Rd HUDS HD4 .....213 G1
Napier Cl BFDE BD3 .....97 F4
ELL HX5 .....166 D5
Napier St BFDE BD3 .....97 F4
CUL/QBY BD15 .....116 E2
KGHY * BD21 .....3 E4
Napier Ter BFDE BD3 .....97 F4
Naples St GIR BD8 .....95 H2
Nares St HWTH BD22 .....69 G3
KGHY BD21 .....2 C5
Nares St Upper KGHY * BD21 .....2 C5
Narrow La BGLY BD16 .....71 F2
The Narrows BGLY BD16 .....71 F2
Naseby Gdns OSM * LS9 .....102 A3
Naseby Garth OSM LS9 .....102 A3
Naseby Gra OSM LS9 .....102 A3
Naseby Pl OSM LS9 .....102 A3
Naseby Ri CUL/QBY BD13 .....116 E2
Naseby Ter OSM LS9 .....102 A3
Naseby Vw OSM LS9 .....102 A3
Naseby Wk OSM LS9 .....102 A3
Nashville Rd HWTH BD22 .....2 B4
Nashville St HWTH BD22 .....2 B4
Nashville Ter HWTH BD22 .....2 B4
Nassau Pl CHAL LS7 .....80 A8
Nathan La RPDN/SBR HX6 .....163 K4
National Rd MID LS10 .....102 A7
Natty Fields Cl LUD/ILL HX2 .....115 H4
Natty La LUD/ILL HX2 .....115 H4
Nature Wy WBSY BD6 .....117 K4
Navigation Cl ELL HX5 .....167 F3
Navigation Ri HUDS HD4 .....190 B7
Navigation Rd CAS WF10 .....155 J3
EARL WF12 .....172 A7
HIPP HX3 .....9 E5
Navigation Wk MID * LS10 .....7 E4
Navvy La BSLYN/ROY S71 .....222 B4
Naylor Ct DEWS WF13 .....172 C2
Naylor La LUD/ILL HX2 .....137 K3
Naylors Garth HDGY LS6 .....79 F6
Naylor St DEWS WF13 .....172 A1
HFAX HX1 .....8 A4
OSS WF5 .....173 H5
Naze Rd TOD OL14 .....133 J8
Neale Rd HUD HD1 .....191 F6
Neale St HBR HX7 .....136 B1
Neal St WBOW BD5 .....4 C5
Near Bank KBTN HD8 .....235 K1
Nearcliffe Rd HTON BD9 .....95 C1
Near Crook SHPY BD18 .....73 F8
Near La HOLM/MEL HD9 .....231 J1
Neath Gdns OSM LS9 .....81 F8
Necropolis Rd GTHN BD7 .....95 F6
Ned Hill Rd LUD/ILL HX1 .....115 H1
Ned La BOW BD4 .....97 H7
MAR/SLWT HD7 .....210 D3
Needles Inn La RTHW LS26 .....127 F4
Nell Gap Av HOR/CROF WF4 .....196 A4
Nell Gap Crs HOR/CROF WF4 .....196 A4
Nell Gap La HOR/CROF WF4 .....196 B4
Nelson Ct MOR LS27 .....146 E1
Nelson Pl CUL/QBY BD13 .....116 D2
MOR LS27 .....123 F6
Nelson Rd ILK LS29 .....20 B7
Nelson St BFDE BD1 .....4 C5
BTLY WF17 .....145 J2
BTLY * WF17 .....145 K6
CUD/GR S72 .....223 J6
CUL/QBY BD13 .....116 D2
DEWS * WF13 .....172 B3

HUD HD1 .....12 B6
HWTH BD22 .....68 G3
LVSG WF15 .....144 E8
NORM WF6 .....152 B8
OT LS21 .....33 J4
RPDN/SBR HX6 .....139 G7
WIL/AL BD15 .....94 C2
Nene St WBOW BD5 .....95 J7
Nepshaw La MOR LS27 .....122 E6
Nepshaw La North MOR LS27 .....122 D6
Nepshaw La South MOR LS27 .....122 C7
Neptune St OSM LS9 .....7 F4
Nesfield Cl MID LS10 .....125 G5
Nesfield Crs MID LS10 .....125 G5
Nesfield Gdns MID LS10 .....125 F5
Nesfield Garth MID LS10 .....125 F5
Nesfield Rd ILK LS29 .....19 K6
MID LS10 .....125 F5
Nesfield St BFD BD1 .....4 B3
Nesfield Vw ILK LS29 .....19 J7
MID LS10 .....125 F5
Nesfield Wk MID LS10 .....125 F5
Nessfield Dr HWTH BD22 .....2 A5
Nessfield Gv HWTH BD22 .....2 A5
Nessfield Rd HWTH BD22 .....2 A5
Nestfield Cl PONT WF8 .....154 E8
Nest La HBR HX7 .....136 E5
Neston Wy OSS * WF5 .....173 J2
Netherby St BFDE * BD3 .....5 F4
Nethercliffe Rd GSLY LS20 .....53 F1
Nether Cl HUDE HD5 .....192 A3
Nether Crs HUDE HD5 .....192 A3
Netherdale Ct WBY LS22 .....24 A5
Netherend Rd MAR/SLWT HD7 .....210 D2
Netherfield Av HOR/CROF WF4 .....196 D6
Netherfield Cl CAS WF10 .....152 E6
KBTN HD8 .....215 H5
YEA LS19 .....53 K4
Netherfield Crs HOR/CROF WF4 .....196 D6
Netherfield Dr GSLY LS20 .....53 G1
HOLM/MEL HD9 .....233 G4
Netherfield Pl CLECK BD19 .....144 B4
HOR/CROF WF4 .....196 D5
Netherfield Rd DEWS WF13 .....171 H6
ILK LS29 .....32 E8
Nether Hall Av HUDE HD5 .....192 A3
Netherhall Rd BAIL BD17 .....51 K8
Netherhouses HOLM/MEL HD9 .....232 D6
Netherlands Av WBSY BD6 .....118 D4
Netherlea Dr HOLM/MEL HD9 .....233 F8
Nether La HOLM/MEL HD9 .....231 F8
Netherlea Dr HOLM/MEL HD9 .....233 F4
Netherley Dr MAR/SLWT HD7 .....229 C1
Netherly Brow OSS WF5 .....173 K8
Nether Moor Rd HUDS HD4 .....212 B3
Nether Moor Vw BGLY BD16 .....50 A8
Netheroyd FEA/AMT WF7 .....178 B6
Netheroyd Hill Rd HUDN HD2 .....168 A8
Netheroyd Pl HOR/CROF WF4 .....168 A8
Nether St PDSY/CALV LS28 .....76 B7
Netherthong Rd HOLM/MEL HD9 .....231 K3
Netherton Fold HUDS HD4 .....212 C5
Netherton Hall Dr HOR/CROF WF4 .....196 D5
Netherton Hall Gdns
HOR/CROF WF4 .....196 E5
Netherton La HOR/CROF WF4 .....196 D5
Netherton Moor Rd HUDS HD4 .....212 D4
Netherwood Cl HUDN HD2 .....168 B8
Nettle Gv HIPP HX3 .....140 E2
Nettleton Av MIRF WF14 .....170 C6
Nettleton Cha OSS WF5 .....173 H2
Nettleton Cl BOW BD4 .....121 G1
Nettleton Ct MSTN/BAR LS15 .....104 E3
Nettleton Hill Rd MAR/SLWT HD7 .....189 F5
Nettleton Rd HUDE HD5 .....192 C6
MIRF WF14 .....170 C6
Nettleton St EARD/LOFT WF3 .....150 E5
OSS WF5 .....173 H5
Neville Ap OSM LS9 .....102 E5
Neville Av BOW BD4 .....119 J2
OSM LS9 .....102 E5
Neville Cl HEM/SK/SE WF9 .....225 J8
OSM LS9 .....102 E5
Neville Crs OSM LS9 .....103 F3
Neville Garth OSM LS9 .....102 E5
Neville Gv HUDE HD5 .....192 B7
OSM LS9 .....102 E5
RTHW LS26 .....127 K1
Neville Mt OSM LS9 .....102 E5
Neville Pde OSM LS9 .....102 E5
Neville Pl OSM LS9 .....103 F4
Neville Rd BOW BD4 .....96 D7
OSM LS9 .....103 F3
OT LS21 .....33 K4
WKFDW/WTN WF2 .....174 D6
Neville Rw OSM LS9 .....102 E5
Neville Sq OSM LS9 .....103 F4
Neville St CLECK BD19 .....144 B5
KGHY * BD21 .....3 E2
LDS LS1 .....7 D4
NORM WF6 .....178 A2
WKFDE WF1 .....11 E5
Neville Ter OSM LS9 .....102 E5
Neville Vw OSM LS9 .....102 E5
Neville Wk OSM LS9 .....102 E5
Nevill Gv HTON BD9 .....77 D8
Nevins Bd DEWS WF13 .....171 G5
Nevison Av PONT WF8 .....155 F8
New Adel Av BHP/TINH LS16 .....56 A8

ewton Ct *RHAY* LS8	80 E5
WKFDE WF1	149 J7
ewton Dr *CAS* WF10	154 C4
WKFDE WF1	149 J8
ewton Garth *CHAL* LS7	80 A6
ewton Gv *CHAL* LS7	79 K7
TOD OL14	133 J4
ewton Hill Rd *CHAL* LS7	79 K6
ewton La *CAS* WF10	129 J7
WKFDE WF1	149 J8
ewton Lodge Cl *CHAL* LS7	79 J6
ewton Lodge Dr *CHAL* LS7	79 J6
ewton Pde *CHAL* * LS7	79 K6
ewton Pk *BRIG* HD6	142 A5
ewton Park Ct *CHAL* * LS7	80 A6
ewton Park Dr *CHAL* LS7	80 A7
ewton Park Vw *CHAL* LS7	80 A7
ewton Pl *WBOW* BD5	95 K7
ewton Rd *CHAL* LS7	80 A7
ewton St *RPDN/SBR* * HX6	138 E7
WBOW BD5	96 A8
ewton Vw *CHAL* * LS7	79 K6
ewton Vls *CHAL* * LS7	79 J5
ewton Wk *CHAL* LS7	80 A7
ewton Wy *BAIL* * BD17	51 J7
ewtown Av *BSLY/ROY* S71	221 K7
ew Town Ct *HWTH* BD22	2 B3
ew Wk *RHAY* LS8	80 D2
ew Wy *BTLY* WF17	146 B6
GSLY LS20	52 E2
ew Wellgate *CAS* WF10	154 A5
ew Wls *WKFDE* WF1	10 C4
ew Wells Ter *WKFDE* * WF1	10 C4
ew Windsor Dr *RTHW* LS26	126 C5
ew Works Rd *LM/WK* BD12	118 D6
ew York La *YEA* LS19	76 B1
ew York Rd *LDSU* LS2	7 F3
ew York St *LDSU* LS2	7 E4
ibshaw La *CLECK* BD19	144 D3
ibshaw Rd *CLECK* BD19	144 D5
ice Av *RHAY* LS8	80 D7
ice La *RHAY* LS8	80 C1
ice Vw *RHAY* LS8	80 D7
icholas Ct *GTHN* BD7	95 F8
ichols Cl *WBY* LS22	23 G6
icholson Ct *RHAY* * LS8	80 C5
icholson St *CAS* WF10	153 H4
ichols Wy *WBY* LS22	23 F6
ickleby Rd *OSM* LS9	102 C5
icolsons Pl *AIRE* BD20	27 G2
idd Ap *WBY* BD20	23 H5
idd Ct *AIRE* BD20	27 G3
idderdale Cl *GFTH/SHER* LS25	106 B6
idderdale Wk *BAIL* BD17	52 A7
idd St *BFDE*	5 F5
ields Rd *MAR/SLWT* HD7	210 D3
ightborne Av *BFDE* BD3	96 E2
ightingale Crest	
WKFDE/WTN WF2	174 D7
ightingale St *KGHY* BD21	3 D2
ightingale Wk *BGLY* BD16	50 C7
injinsky Wy *MID* LS10	125 J2
ile Crs *HWTH* BD22	2 A4
ile St *HWTH* BD22	2 A4
HWTH BD22	69 G3
LDSU LS2	14 C1
ina Rd *GTHN* BD7	95 F8
inelands *GFTH/SHER* LS25	106 A6
inelands Sp *GFTH/SHER* LS25	105 K5
inelands Vw *GFTH/SHER* LS25	106 A4
HEM/SK/SE WF9	203 K8
inevah La *CAS* WF10	128 E6
ineveh Gdns *BEE/HOL* LS11	6 C6
ineveh Pde *BEE/HOL* LS11	6 C6
ineveh Rd *BEE/HOL* LS11	6 C6
inth Av *LVSG* WF15	143 J6
ippet La *OSM* LS9	102 C5
ixon Av *OSM* LS9	102 D4
ixon St *EARL* WF12	195 K2
oble Ct *HUDS* HD4	212 D5
oble St *HWTH* BD7	95 H6
oble Vw *HWTH* BD7	95 H6
oon Cl *EARD/LOFT* WF3	150 B6
opper Rd *HUDS* HD4	211 K4
ora Pl *BRAM* LS13	76 E8
ora Rd *BRAM* LS13	76 E8
ora Ter *BRAM* LS13	76 E8
orbeck Dr *HWTH* BD22	69 G3
orbury Rd *IDLE* BD10	75 G6
orcliffe La *HIPP* HX3	141 F5
orcroft Brow *GTHN* BD7	4 B5
orcroft La *DOD/DAR* S75	238 D8
orcroft Pl *BFD* BD1	4 A4
orcross Av *HUDW* HD3	190 A4

Norfield *HUDN* HD2	168 B7
Norfolk Av *BTLY* WF17	146 A8
Norfolk Cl *CHAL* LS7	79 K4
KNOT WF11	155 J3
RTHW LS26	127 G6
Norfolk Dr *CHAL* LS7	79 K4
Norfolk Gdns *BFD* BD1	4 C5
CHAL LS7	79 K4
Norfolk Gn *CHAL* LS7	79 K4
Norfolk Mt *CHAL* LS7	79 K4
Norfolk Pl *CHAL* LS7	79 K4
HFAX HX1	8 B5
Norfolk St *BGLY* BD16	50 A4
BTLY WF17	146 A7
HBR HX7	136 B1
Norfolk Ter *CHAL* * LS7	79 K4
Norfolk Vw *CHAL* LS7	79 K4
Norfolk Wk *CHAL* LS7	79 K4
Norgarth Cl *BTLY* WF17	146 E6
Norham Gv *LM/WK* BD12	142 E1
Norland Rd *RPDN/SBR* HX6	138 E8
RPDN/SBR HX6	165 G2
Norland St *GTHN* BD7	95 F8
Norland Town Rd *RPDN/SBR* HX6	165 G1
Norland Vw *RPDN/SBR* HX6	139 G7
Norman Av *ECHL* BD2	74 D6
Norman Crs *ECHL* BD2	74 D6
Norman Dr *MIRF* WF14	170 C5
Norman Gv *ECHL* BD2	74 D6
ELL HX5	167 F5
KSTL LS5	101 K1
Norman La *ECHL* BD2	74 D6
Norman Mt *ECHL* BD2	74 D6
KSTL LS5	78 A7
Normanon Pl *BEE/HOL* LS11	101 G7
Norman Pl *RHAY* LS8	80 C1
Norman Rd *HUDN* HD2	12 C1
KBTN HD8	236 D6
MIRF WF14	170 C5
Norman Rw *KSTL* LS5	78 A7
Norman St *BGLY* * BD16	50 A4
ELL HX5	167 F5
HFAX HX1	8 A6
KSTL LS5	78 A7
SHPY BD18	73 K4
Normans Wy *WKFDW/WTN* WF2	199 H2
Norman Ter *ECHL* BD2	74 D6
ELL HX5	167 F5
RHAY LS8	80 C1
Normanton Gv *BEE/HOL* LS11	101 G7
Normanton Pl *HOR/CROF* WF4	197 J3
Normanton Vw *NORM* WF6	178 A3
Norman Vw *KSTL* LS5	78 A7
Norridge Bottom *HOLM/MEL* HD9	233 G6
Norris Cl *HUDE* HD5	192 C7
Norristhorpe La *LVSG* WF15	170 D1
Nortech Cl *CHAL* LS7	7 F1
Northallerton Rd *BFDE* BD3	5 D2
Northampton St *BFDE* BD3	5 D2
North Ap *TAD* LS24	63 G7
North Av *CAS* WF10	152 E4
HEM/SK/SE WF9	242 B1
HOR/CROF WF4	197 J2
HTON BD9	73 K8
OT LS21	33 J5
PONT WF8	180 B5
WKFDE WF1	10 C1
North Baileygate *PONT* WF8	180 E2
North Bank Rd *BGLY* BD16	72 A6
BTLY WF17	145 K6
HUDN HD2	12 B1
North Bolton *LUD/ILL* HX2	115 G4
North Br *HFAX* HX1	9 D3
North Bridge St *HFAX* HX1	9 D3
North Broadgate La *HORS* LS18	77 G2
Northbrook Cft *CHAL* * LS7	79 K4
Northbrook Pl *CHAL* LS7	79 K4
Northbrook St *CHAL* LS7	79 K4
North Byland *LUD/ILL* HX2	115 H4
North Carr *HUDE* HD5	192 A4
North Ct *LDSU* LS2	7 E3
North Court Gv *WBY* LS22	23 J5
North Crs *HEM/SK/SE* WF9	226 D7
Northcroft *HEM/SK/SE* WF9	226 C8
Northcroft Ri *BGLY* BD16	74 C1
North Croft Grove Rd *ILK* LS29	20 A7
Northcroft Ri *HTON* BD9	94 E2
North Cross Rd *HUDN* HD2	191 F1
North Cut *BRIG* HD6	167 K1
Northdale Av *WBOW* BD5	118 D1
Northdale Crs *WBOW* BD5	118 D1
Northdale Mt *WBOW* BD5	118 D1

Northdale Rd *HTON* BD9	73 H6
North Dean Av *HWTH* BD22	47 G4
North Dean Rd *GTL/HWG* HX4	165 J2
HWTH BD22	2 A3
North Dene Rd *AIRE* BD20	27 G1
North Dr *BHP/TINH* LS16	55 K1
MAR/SLWT HD7	189 J6
Northedge La *HIPP* HX3	141 J2
Northedge Meadow *IDLE* BD10	74 D5
Northedge Pk *HIPP* HX3	141 J5
Northern St *LDS* LS1	6 C4
North Farm Rd *RHAY* LS8	80 D8
Northfield Av *HEM/SK/SE* WF9	225 H7
KNOT WF11	156 C7
OSS WF5	173 J5
RTHW LS26	125 K7
Northfield Cl *AWLS/ASK* DN6	183 J8
ELL * HX5	166 E5
Northfield Crs *BGLY* BD16	72 A4
Northfield Dr *PONT* WF8	181 G2
Northfield Gdns *WBSY* BD6	118 D2
Northfield Gv *HEM/SK/SE* WF9	225 H8
HUD HD1	12 A6
WBSY BD6	118 D2
North Field La *KBTN* HD8	236 E1
Northfield La *HEM/SK/SE* WF9	225 H8
HOR/CROF WF4	197 J2
KBTN HD8	215 G3
KNOT WF11	183 G5
Northfield Pl *DEWS* WF13	172 A2
GIR BD8	4 A2
RTHW LS26	125 J7
WBY LS22	23 J5
North Field Rd *AWLS/ASK* DN6	243 G3
Northfield Rd *DEWS* WF13	172 A2
HOR/CROF WF4	178 A8
KNOT WF11	156 C7
OSS WF5	173 J5
WBSY BD6	118 C2
Northfields *BSPA/BRAM* LS23	25 C8
Northfield St *DEWS* WF13	172 B2
HEM/SK/SE WF9	225 H8
Northfield Ter *CUL/QBY* BD13	117 F2
HOR/CROF * WF4	197 J1
North Fold *IDLE* BD10	74 D3
North Ga *MIRF* WF14	193 F1
Northgate *BAIL* BD17	51 J7
BFD * BD1	4 C4
CLECK BD19	144 B4
CUD/GR S72	223 J5
DEWS WF13	172 C3
ELL HX5	166 E4
GTL/HWG HX4	166 A7
HBR HX7	112 A6
HECK WF16	145 F7
HFAX HX1	9 D4
HOLM/MEL HD9	213 G6
HOLM/MEL HD9	213 H5
HOR/CROF WF4	197 G1
HUD HD1	13 D3
HUDE HD5	192 B8
PONT WF8	180 E2
RTHW LS26	127 F5
WKFDE WF1	10 C3
Northgate Cl *PONT* WF8	180 E2
Northgate La *WBY* LS22	22 E7
WBY LS22	23 F8
Northgate Ldg *WBY* LS22	180 E2
Northgate Ri *WBY* LS22	41 F1
Northgates *WBY* LS22	23 J6
North Grange Ms *HDGY* LS6	79 F7
North Grange Mt *HDGY* LS6	78 E6
North Grange Rd *HDGY* LS6	78 E7
North Gv *WBY* LS22	23 J5
North Grove Av *WBY* LS22	23 J4
North Grove Cl *RHAY* LS8	81 F5
North Grove Crs *WBY* LS22	23 J4
North Grove Dr *RHAY* LS8	81 F5
WBY LS22	23 J4
North Grove Mt *WBY* LS22	23 J5
North Grove Ri *RHAY* LS8	81 F5
North Grove Rd *WBY* LS22	23 J4
North Grove Wy *WBY* LS22	23 J5
North Hall Av *IDLE* BD10	74 C1
North Hl *SCFT* LS14	60 B2
North Hill Cl *RHAY* LS8	80 E5
North Hill Dr *HUDE* HD5	192 E3
North Hill Rd *HDGY* LS6	79 F7
North Holme St *BFD* BD1	4 C3
North King St *BTLY* WF17	146 C7
Northlands *BSLY/ROY* S71	222 A7
North La *MAR/SLWT* HD7	210 B2
RHAY LS8	80 E5
RTHW LS26	127 F6
STKB/PEN S36	252 E1
Northlea Av *IDLE* BD10	74 C2
North Lingwell Rd *MID* LS10	124 D6
North Lodge Fold *DEWS* WF13	145 J8
North Lodge La *PONT* WF8	182 C7
North Md *BHP/TINH* LS16	55 K1
North Moor La *HUDE* HD5	192 E1
Northolme Av *BHP/TINH* LS16	78 B4
Northolme Crs *BHP/TINH* LS16	78 B4
Northorpe La *MIRF* WF14	171 F4
Northorpe La *MIRF* WF14	171 F4
Northowram Gn *HIPP* HX3	117 F7
North Pde *BFD* BD1	4 C4
BHP/TINH LS16	78 A3

HFAX HX1	9 D4
ILK LS29	20 C7
ILK LS29	32 A1
OT LS21	33 J3
WIL/AL BD15	94 A1
North Park Av RHAY LS8	80 B3
North Park Cl RHAY LS8	80 C3
North Park Rd HTON BD9	73 H8
RHAY LS8	80 C3
North Park St DEWS WF13	171 K2
North Park Ter HTON BD9	4 A1
North Pkwy SCFT LS14	81 G6
North Queen St KGHY BD21	3 D5
North Ri HUDN HD2	191 J1
North Rd BSLYN/ROY S71	222 B7
DEWS WF13	171 G5
HORS LS18	55 F8
KBTN HD8	215 G4
KNOT WF11	131 H7
MSTN/BAR LS15	104 A1
OSM LS9	102 E8
WBSY BD6	118 C3
Northrop Cl GIR BD8	95 G2
North Rw KBTN HD8	235 F3
Northside Av GTHN BD7	95 G5
Northside Rd GTHN BD7	95 G5
Northside Ter GTHN BD7	95 F5
North's Pl MIRF WF14	170 D4
Northstead DEWS WF13	171 G5
North St AIRE BD20	27 G1
BFD * BD1	5 D4
CAS WF10	148 C3
CAS WF10	154 D1
CHAL LS7	7 F1
DEWS WF13	172 B2
GTL/HWG HX4	166 A7
GTL/HWG HX4	166 C4
HECK WF16	145 G8
HEM/SK/SE WF9	225 H8
HUD HD1	12 A6
HWTH BD22	68 D4
IDLE BD10	74 D1
ILK LS29	18 E3
KGHY BD21	3 D5
LDSU LS2	7 F2
LM/WK BD12	119 H7
MIRF WF14	170 C3
NORM WF6	177 K3
OT LS21	33 J3
PDSY/CALV LS28	98 C3
WBY LS22	23 J6
YEA LS19	53 K7
North Ter BTLY WF17	145 J2
MSTN/BAR * LS15	104 A1
YEA LS19	53 K4
Northumberland St HUD HD1	13 D4
North Vw AIRE BD20	27 F4
EARL WF12	172 C5
ILK LS29	32 C7
KNOT WF11	156 B6
WIL/AL BD15	71 G6
WIL/AL BD15	94 A2
North View La BFDE BD3	5 D1
BOW BD4	120 D1
North View St KGHY BD21	3 D1
PDSY/CALV LS28	98 C1
North View Ter DEWS * WF13	172 A1
HWTH BD22	2 B6
PDSY/CALV LS28	98 C1
North Wk BGLY BD16	70 E2
North Wy HUDN HD2	169 F7
RHAY LS8	81 F5
Northway MIRF WF14	170 C4
Northway Crs MIRF WF14	170 C4
Northway Gdns MIRF WF14	170 C3
Northwell Ga OT LS21	33 G2
North West Rd LDSU LS2	9 H8
North Wing BFDE BD3	5 C3
Northwood Cl PDSY/CALV LS28	98 D6
RTHW LS26	127 F4
Northwood Crs IDLE BD10	74 E4
Northwood Falls RTHW LS26	127 F4
Northwood Gdns MSTN/BAR LS15	104 C3
Northwood Mt PDSY/CALV LS28	98 D6
Northwood Pk KBTN HD8	215 G4
RTHW LS26	127 F4
Northwood Vw PDSY/CALV LS28	98 D6
Norton Cl ELL HX5	166 E6
LUD/ILL HX2	138 E4
Norton Dr LUD/ILL HX2	138 E4
Norton Fold ECHL * BD2	73 H4
Norton Rd RHAY LS8	58 C8
WKFDE WF1	11 D2
Norton St AIRE BD20	27 F2
ELL HX5	166 E6
WKFDE WF1	11 E5
Norton Wy MOR LS27	122 E5
Norwich Av MID LS10	124 E1
Norwood PONT WF8	181 H6
Norwood Av BIRK/DRI BD11	120 E7
ILK LS29	32 B2
SHPY BD18	73 H5
Norwood Cl ILK LS29	32 B2
Norwood Crs CLECK BD19	120 E7
PDSY/CALV LS28	98 D1
Norwood Dr BIRK/DRI BD11	120 E7
BTLY WF17	145 J3

CUD/GR S72	224 A8
Norwood Green HI HIPP HX3	142 A1
Norwood Gv BIRK/DRI BD11	120 E7
HDGY LS6	78 E8
Norwood La STKB/PEN S36	251 J6
Norwood Mt HDGY LS6	78 E8
Norwood Pk HUDW HD3	190 D2
Norwood Pl HDGY LS6	78 E8
SHPY BD18	73 H5
Nor Wood Rd HEM/SK/SE WF9	224 D6
Norwood Rd HDGY LS6	78 E8
HUDN HD2	190 E1
SHPY BD18	73 H5
Norwood St NORM WF6	152 C8
SHPY BD18	73 H5
WBOW BD5	118 C1
Norwood Ter HDGY LS6	78 E8
ILK LS29	32 B2
SHPY BD18	73 H5
Norwood Vw HDGY * LS6	78 E8
Nostell Cl GIR BD8	4 B3
Nostell La HOR/CROF WF4	223 F1
Noster Gv BEE/HOL LS11	101 F8
Noster HI BEE/HOL LS11	101 F8
Noster Pl BEE/HOL LS11	101 F8
Noster Rd BEE/HOL LS11	101 F8
Noster St BEE/HOL LS11	101 F8
Noster Ter BEE/HOL LS11	101 F8
Noster Vw BEE/HOL LS11	101 F8
Nottingham Cl EARD/LOFT * WF3	125 H8
Nottingham St BFDE BD3	97 G4
Notton La HOR/CROF WF4	222 A4
Nova La BTLY WF17	145 G1
Nowell Ap OSM LS9	102 D2
Nowell Av OSM LS9	102 D2
Nowell Cl OSM LS9	102 D2
Nowell Ct OSM LS9	102 D2
Nowell Crs OSM LS9	102 D2
Nowell End Rw OSM LS9	102 D2
Nowell Gdns OSM LS9	102 D2
Nowell Gv OSM LS9	102 D2
Nowell La OSM LS9	102 D2
Nowell Mt OSM LS9	102 D2
Nowell Pde OSM LS9	102 D2
Nowell Pl HUDE HD5	179 J7
OSM LS9	102 D2
Nowell St DEWS WF13	172 A2
OSM LS9	102 D2
Nowell's Yd DEWS WF13	172 A3
Nowell Ter OSM LS9	102 D2
Nowell Vw OSM * LS9	102 D2
Nowell Wk OSM LS9	102 D2
Nunburnholme Wk IDLE BD10	74 E5
Nunington Av WOR/ARM LS12	100 C3
Nunington St WOR/ARM LS12	100 C3
Nunington Ter WOR/ARM LS12	100 C3
Nunington Vw WOR/ARM LS12	100 C2
Nunlea Royd BRIG HD6	142 B5
Nunnery La WBOW BD5	95 J7
Nunns Av FEA/AMT WF7	179 H8
Nunns Cl FEA/AMT WF7	179 H7
Nunns Ct FEA/AMT WF7	179 H8
Nunn's Cft FEA/AMT WF7	179 J7
Nunn's Gn FEA/AMT WF7	179 J7
Nunn's La FEA/AMT WF7	179 H7
Nunroyd HECK WF16	145 C6
Nunroyd Av AL/HA/HU LS17	79 K2
Nunroyd Gv AL/HA/HU LS17	79 K2
Nunroyd Lawn AL/HA/HU * LS17	79 K2
Nunroyd Rd AL/HA/HU LS17	79 K2
Nunroyd Ter AL/HA/HU LS17	79 K2
Nunthorpe Rd BRAM LS13	76 D6
Nurser La WBOW BD5	95 J7
Nurser Pl WBOW BD5	95 J7
Nursery Av FEA/AMT WF7	179 H7
Nursery Cl AIRE BD20	27 J8
AL/HA/HU LS17	57 J7
BAIL * BD17	72 E1
Nursery Garth WBY LS22	23 K5
Nursery Gv AL/HA/HU LS17	57 J7
LUD/ILL HX2	115 J8
Nursery La AL/HA/HU LS17	57 H7
HIPP HX3	115 J8
ILK LS29	18 E3
RPDN/SBR HX6	163 J8
Nursery Mt MID LS10	125 F2
Nursery Mount Rd MID LS10	125 F2
GTHN BD7	118 A1
Nursery St EARL WF12	172 E7
HUDN HD2	171 G1
Nursery Wy BSPA/BRAM LS23	42 B3
BSPA/BRAM LS23	42 D6
Nursery Wood Rd BTLY WF17	172 C1
Nussey Av BTLY WF17	145 H1
Nutclough Rd HBR HX7	112 C7
Nutfield St TOD OL14	134 A5
Nuttall Rd BFDE BD3	5 E4
Nutter La CLECK BD19	145 F1
Nutter St CLECK BD19	143 K4
Nutting Grove Ter WOR/ARM LS12	99 J6
Nutwood Wk WBSY BD6	117 K5

O

Oak Av BGLY BD16	71 K2
EARD/LOFT WF3	150 C7

GFTH/SHER LS25	105 K
GIR BD8	4 A
HOLM/MEL HD9	211 G
HUDE HD5	192 A
HUDW HD3	189 J
ILK LS29	32 B
MOR LS27	123 G
NORM WF6	177 K
RPDN/SBR HX6	138 E
TOD OL14	133 K
Oak Bank BGLY BD16	71 K
SHPY BD18	73 K
Oakbank Av HWTH BD22	2 A
Oakbank Broadway HWTH BD22	2 A
Oakbank Ct HWTH BD22	2 A
Oakbank Crs HWTH BD22	2 A
Oakbank Dr HWTH BD22	2 A
Oakbank Gv HWTH BD22	2 A
Oakbank La HWTH BD22	2 A
Oakbank Mt HWTH BD22	2 A
Oakburn Rd ILK LS29	20 A
Oak Cl WHIT OL12	158 A
Oak Crs GFTH/SHER LS25	105 K
MSTN/BAR LS15	103 H
Oakdale BGLY BD16	50 A
Oakdale Av SHPY BD18	118 C
WBSY BD6	118 C
Oakdale Cl EARD/LOFT WF3	149 J
HIPP HX3	8 B
IDLE BD10	75 G
Oakdale Crs HUDW HD3	190 A
WBSY BD6	118 C
Oakdale Dr IDLE BD10	75 G
SHPY BD18	74 A
Oakdale Garth SCFT LS14	81 K
Oakdale Gv SHPY BD18	74 A
Oakdale Meadow SCFT LS14	81 K
Oakdale Pk OT LS21	35 H
Oakdale Rd SHPY BD18	74 A
Oakdale Ter WBSY BD6	118 C
Oakdean HUDN HD2	168 B
Oakdene Cl PDSY/CALV LS28	98 D
Oakdene Ct AL/HA/HU LS17	58 C
Oakdene Dr AL/HA/HU LS17	58 C
HOR/CROF WF4	201 F
Oakdene Gdns AL/HA/HU LS17	58 C
Oakdene V AL/HA/HU LS17	58 C
Oakdene Wy AL/HA/HU LS17	58 C
Oak Dr GFTH/SHER LS25	105 K
MAR/SLWT HD7	189 F
Oakenshaw Ct LM/WK BD12	142 C
Oakenshaw La CLECK BD19	119 H
WKFDW/WTN WF2	199 J
Oakenshaw St WKFDE WF1	11 F
Oakes Av HOLM/MEL HD9	233
Oakes Fold KBTN HD8	193
Oakes La HOLM/MEL HD9	233
Oakes Rd South HUDW HD3	190 B
Oakes Rd WKFDW/WTN WF2	174 B
Oakfield HDGY LS6	78 E
Oakfield Av BGLY BD16	72 C
RTHW * LS26	126 B
Oakfield Cl ELL HX5	166 C
GFTH/SHER LS25	105 H
ILK LS29	32 C
Oakfield Crs KNOT WF11	156 C
Oakfield Dr BAIL BD17	73 H
MIRF WF14	170 C
Oakfield Gv HTON BD9	4 A
KBTN HD8	236 E
Oakfield Pk PONT WF8	200 D
Oakfield Rd HUDN HD2	12 A
HWTH BD22	2 B
Oakfield Ter SHPY BD18	73 K
Oak Gv GFTH/SHER LS25	106 A
HWTH BD22	47
MOR LS27	123 G
Oakhall Pk CUL/QBY BD13	93 H
Oak Hall Pk HOR/CROF WF4	197 J
Oakhall Park Av CUL/QBY BD13	93 H
Oakham Wk BOW * BD4	96 C
Oak HI RPDN/SBR HX6	164 C
Oak Hill Rd BRIG HD6	142 C
Oakhill Rd BTLY WF17	145 H
Oakhurst Av BEE/HOL LS11	124 E
Oakhurst Gv BEE/HOL LS11	124 E
Oakhurst Mt BEE/HOL LS11	124 E
Oakhurst Rd BEE/HOL LS11	124 E
Oakhurst St BEE/HOL LS11	124 E
Oakland Ct KBTN HD8	215 H
Oakland Dr HOR/CROF WF4	196 E
Oakland Rd HOR/CROF WF4	196 E
WKFDE WF1	11 E
Oaklands BRIG HD6	168 A
EARD/LOFT WF3	125 J
IDLE BD10	74 D
ILK LS29	29 K
SHPY BD18	72 E
Oaklands Av BHP/TINH LS16	56 E
BRAM LS13	76 E
HIPP HX3	117 F
Oaklands Cl BHP/TINH LS16	56 E
HOLM/MEL HD9	233 F
Oaklands Cft WKFDW/WTN WF2	199 K
Oaklands Dr BHP/TINH LS16	56 E
BTLY WF17	146 E
HUDE HD5	192 B
Oaklands Fold BHP/TINH LS16	56 E
Oaklands Gv BHP/TINH LS16	56 E
Oaklands Rd BRAM LS13	76 E
Oakland St AIRE BD20	27 H

k La GIR BD8 .....4 A1
FAX HX1 .....8 B4
PDN/SBR HX6 .....164 B3
lea Gdns BHP/TINH LS16 .....78 D1
lea Hall Cl BHP/TINH LS16 .....78 D1
lea Rd MSTN/BAR LS15 .....82 D5
Leigh DOD/DAR S75 .....238 E7
leigh Av CLAY BD14 .....94 B8
IPP HX3 .....140 B8
WKFDW/WTN WF2 .....175 F6
leigh Cl CLAY BD14 .....94 B7
OR/CROF WF4 .....178 B7
leigh Gdns CLAY * BD14 .....94 B8
leigh Gv CLAY BD14 .....94 B8
leigh Rd CLAY BD14 .....94 B8
leigh Ter CLAY BD14 .....94 B7
leigh Vw BAIL BD17 .....51 H8
IPP * HX3 .....141 K4
OD OL14 .....134 A5
k GFTH/SHER LS25 .....105 J4
PDN/SBR HX6 .....138 E6
Rdg WBY LS22 .....23 G6
ridge Av ILK LS29 .....32 D7
ridge Ct BGLY BD16 .....50 A7
Ri CLECK BD19 .....144 A1
Rd CHAL LS27 .....79 K6
FTH/SHER LS25 .....105 J4
UDN HD2 .....169 H6
OR LS27 .....146 E1
MSTN/BAR LS15 .....103 H4
OR/ARM LS12 .....6 A4
Royd GFTH/SHER LS25 .....105 K4
royd RTHW LS26 .....126 C7
royd Av WBSY BD6 .....118 D3
royd Cl BIRK/DRI BD11 .....120 D6
RIG HD6 .....142 C6
royd Dr BIRK/DRI BD11 .....120 D7
RIG HD6 .....142 C6
royd Fold MOR * LS27 .....123 H5
royd Mt PDSY/CALV LS28 .....98 C3
royd Rd WBSY BD6 .....118 D3
royd Ter BAIL BD17 .....73 K1
R BD8 .....4 B1
OR * LS27 .....123 H3
DSY/CALV LS28 .....98 C3
royd Vls GIR BD8 .....4 B1
Scar La HOLM/MEL HD9 .....248 E1
Oaks HOR/CROF WF4 .....178 A7
OR LS27 .....123 C4
s Av CHAL S7 .....94 C3
sfield RTHW LS26 .....152 C1
s Fold KBTN * HD8 .....193 J8
BOW BD5 .....96 A8
s Green Mt RHAY HD6 .....168 A4
s La BSPA/BRAM LS23 .....42 D3
R BD8 .....94 C3
St CLAY BD14 .....94 B7
JD/GR S72 .....240 B6
LL HX5 .....166 E5
BR HX7 .....115 F7
ECK WF16 .....145 F7
EM/SK/SE WF9 .....242 A2
OR/CROF WF4 .....200 E4
WTH BD22 .....68 D1
WTH BD22 .....69 F4
OR LS27 .....123 G4
DSY/CALV LS28 .....98 A3
PDN/SBR HX6 .....138 E6
OD OL14 .....133 K7
HIT OL12 .....158 A7
KFDE WF1 .....149 K7
R 8 A4
UDN * HD2 .....13 D1
Tree Av KBTN HD8 .....193 F8
Tree La DOD/DAR S75 .....239 K3
SM LS9 .....80 E8
Tree Cft AIRE BD20 .....27 F1
Tree Crs OSM LS9 .....80 E8
Tree Dr RHAY LS8 .....80 E8
Tree Gv HEM/SK/SE WF9 .....225 F5
SM LS9 .....80 E8
tree La HEM/SK/SE WF9 .....203 J6
Tree Meadow
WKFDW/WTN WF2 .....199 J5
Tree Mt OSM LS9 .....80 E8
Tree Pl OSM LS9 .....80 E8
Tree Rd KBTN HD8 .....193 F8
Tree Ter KBTN HD8 .....193 F8
Tree Wk OSM LS9 .....80 E8
Vw AIRE BD20 .....27 G1
HIT OL12 .....158 A6
Vls GIR BD8 .....4 B1
ville Rd HBR HX7 .....135 J1
way BIRK/DRI BD11 .....120 E7
way Av BTLY WF17 .....145 J5
NT WF8 .....180 D5
HAY LS8 .....80 C5
OR/ARM LS12 .....100 D4
well Cl BIRK/DRI BD11 .....121 K6
THN BD7 .....95 H3
EM/SK/SE WF9 .....224 A1
well Ct BRAM LS13 .....77 F8

Oakwell Crs RHAY LS8 .....80 C5
Oakwell Dr RHAY LS8 .....80 C5
Oakwell Gdns RHAY LS8 .....80 C5
Oakwell Gv BRAM LS13 .....77 F8
Oakwell Mt RHAY LS8 .....80 C5
Oakwell Ov RHAY LS8 .....80 C5
Oakwell Rd BIRK/DRI BD11 .....121 K6
Oakwell Ter PDSY/CALV * LS28 .....76 B8
Oakwell Wy BTLY WF17 .....121 K6
Oakwood WKFDW/WTN * WF2 .....174 E8
Oakwood Av BIRK/DRI BD11 .....120 D6
BSLYN/ROY S71 .....221 K7
ECHL BD2 .....73 K7
RHAY LS8 .....80 D5
WKFDW/WTN WF2 .....174 E6
Oakwood Boundary Rd RHAY LS8 .....80 D5
Oakwood Cl NORM WF6 .....151 J7
Oakwood Cottages BGLY * BD16 .....50 A5
Oakwood Ct GIR BD8 .....4 A3
RHAY LS8 .....80 E5
Oakwood Crs BSLYN/ROY S71 .....221 K8
Oakwood Dr BGLY BD16 .....49 K6
HEM/SK/SE WF9 .....225 F6
NORM WF6 .....151 J7
RHAY LS8 .....80 D5
RTHW LS26 .....126 A4
Oakwood Gdns RHAY LS8 .....80 E5
Oakwood Garth RHAY LS8 .....80 E5
Oakwood Gra RHAY LS8 .....80 E5
Oakwood Grange La RHAY LS8 .....80 E5
Oakwood Gn RHAY LS8 .....80 E5
Oakwood Gv GIR BD8 .....95 G2
HOR/CROF WF4 .....197 J2
RHAY LS8 .....80 D5
Oakwood La OSM LS8 .....81 F8
RHAY LS8 .....80 D5
Oakwood Mt RHAY LS8 .....80 D5
Oakwood Nook RHAY LS8 .....80 D5
Oakwood Pk RHAY LS8 .....80 E6
Oakwood Pl RHAY LS8 .....80 D5
Oakwood Ri RHAY LS8 .....80 E5
Oakwood Rd BSLYN/ROY S71 .....221 K7
BTLY WF17 .....146 D6
Oak Wood Rd WBY LS22 .....23 H4
Oakwood Sq DOD/DAR S75 .....239 H3
Oakwood Ter PDSY/CALV LS28 .....98 C5
Oakwood Vw RHAY * LS8 .....80 D5
Oakwood Wk RHAY * LS8 .....80 D5
Oakworth Hall HWTH BD22 .....68 E1
Oakworth Rd HWTH BD22 .....2 A6
Oasby Cft BOW BD4 .....120 B2
Oast House Cft EARD/LOFT WF3 .....125 J8
Oastler Av HUD HD1 .....12 B4
Oastler Pl LM/WK BD12 .....118 C5
Oastler Rd PDSY/CALV LS28 .....75 K5
SHPY BD18 .....73 F5
Oastler St DEWS WF13 .....172 A3
Oates St DEWS WF13 .....172 C5
Oatland Cl CHAL LS7 .....7 E1
Oatland Ct CHAL LS7 .....7 E1
Oatland Dr CHAL LS7 .....7 E1
Oatland Gdns CHAL LS7 .....7 E1
Oatland Hts CHAL LS7 .....7 E1
Oatland La CHAL LS7 .....7 E1
Oatland Pl CHAL LS7 .....79 J8
Oatland Rd CHAL LS7 .....7 E1
Oatlands Dr OT LS21 .....33 H2
Oat St HWTH * BD22 .....2 B6
Oban Cl EARD/LOFT WF3 .....147 J2
Oban Pl WOR/ARM LS12 .....100 D5
Oban St WOR/ARM LS12 .....100 D5
Oban Ter WOR/ARM LS12 .....100 D5
Occupation La BHP/TINH LS16 .....35 F8
DEWS WF13 .....145 J8
HOLM/MEL HD9 .....233 K2
HWTH BD22 .....47 F2
LUD/ILL HX2 .....115 H5
PDSY/CALV LS28 .....98 A5
TAD LS24 .....62 D7
Occupation Rd HUDN * HD2 .....168 D5
HUDW HD3 .....190 B5
Ochrewell Av HUDN HD2 .....169 F8
Octagon Ter LUD/ILL HX2 .....139 H7
Odda La GSLY LS20 .....52 A2
Oddfellows' Ct BFD * BD1 .....4 C4
Oddfellows St BRIG HD6 .....142 C8
CLECK BD19 .....143 G3
MIRF WF14 .....170 D6
Oddfellows St MOR LS27 .....123 F7
Oddy Pl WBSY BD6 .....118 C2
Oddy's Fold HDGY LS6 .....78 E3
Oddy St BOW BD4 .....120 B2
Odsal Pl WBSY BD6 .....118 D3
Odsal Rd WBSY BD6 .....118 D2
Offley La HEM/SK/SE WF9 .....202 B5
Ogden Crs CUL/QBY BD13 .....92 B1
Ogden La BRIG HD6 .....168 A3
CUL/QBY BD13 .....92 B1
LUD/ILL HX2 .....115 G1
Ogden St RPDN/SBR HX6 .....138 D2
Ogden View Cl LUD/ILL HX2 .....115 G4
Ogilby Ct RTHW LS26 .....126 E4
Ogilby Ms RTHW LS26 .....126 E4
O'Grady Sq OSM LS9 .....102 B4
Old Allen Rd CUL/QBY BD13 .....70 D5
Old Anna La or Long La
STKB/PEN S36 .....251 N2
Old Bank HIPP HX3 .....9 E4
MAR/SLWT HD7 .....210 D3

Old Bank Fold HUDE * HD5 .....13 F5
Old Bank Rd EARL WF12 .....172 D3
MIRF WF14 .....170 D4
Old Bar La HOLM/MEL HD9 .....249 J3
Old Barn Cl AL/HA/HU LS17 .....57 G6
Old Bell Ct HFAX * HX1 .....9 D5
Old Brandon La AL/HA/HU LS17 .....59 G7
Old Bridge Ri ILK LS29 .....20 A7
Old Canal Rd BFD BD1 .....4 C2
Old Cawsey RPDN/SBR HX6 .....139 F7
Old Church St OSS WF5 .....175 J6
Old Cl BEE/HOL LS11 .....123 J3
Old Cock Yd HFAX * HX1 .....9 D4
Old Corn Mill La GTHN * BD7 .....95 C7
Old Crown Rd WKFDW/WTN WF2 .....174 E8
Old Dalton La KGHY BD21 .....3 E3
Old Earth ELL HX5 .....167 G4
Oldfarm Ap BHP/TINH LS16 .....77 K3
Oldfarm Cl BHP/TINH LS16 .....78 A3
Old Farm Crs BOW * BD4 .....96 D8
Oldfarm Cross BHP/TINH LS16 .....78 A3
Oldfarm Dr BHP/TINH LS16 .....78 A3
Oldfarm Garth BHP/TINH LS16 .....78 A3
Oldfarm Pde BHP/TINH LS16 .....78 A3
Oldfarm Wk BHP/TINH LS16 .....77 K3
Oldfield Av WOR/ARM LS12 .....100 C5
Oldfield Ct CHAL LS7 .....80 A5
Old Fieldhouse La HUDN HD2 .....191 K1
Oldfield La HECK WF16 .....145 G8
HWTH BD22 .....67 K3
HWTH BD22 .....68 C4
KBTN HD8 .....187 J1
WBY LS22 .....41 J2
WOR/ARM LS12 .....100 D5
Oldfield Rd HOLM/MEL HD9 .....232 E2
Oldfield St HIPP HX3 .....115 K7
HUDS HD4 .....12 A6
WOR/ARM LS12 .....100 C5
Old Forge Ms BHP/TINH LS16 .....35 H8
Old Garth Cft KNOT WF11 .....131 H7
Old Ga HBR HX7 .....112 B8
HOLM/MEL HD9 .....246 D4
Oldgate HUD HD1 .....13 D4
Old Hall La HIPP HX3 .....9 E5
Old Great North Rd KNOT WF11 .....155 J2
KNOT WF11 .....155 K5
Old Gnd MAR/SLWT HD7 .....209 J3
Old Guy Rd CUL/QBY BD13 .....116 A1
Old Hall Cl HWTH * BD22 .....59 G7
Old Hall La KBTN HD8 .....217 J6
Old Hall Ms BTLY * WF17 .....146 B4
Old Hall Rd BTLY WF17 .....146 B4
EARD/LOFT WF3 .....148 A3
Oldham Rd RPDN/SBR HX6 .....186 A6
Oldham Wy UPML OL3 .....207 J8
Old Haworth La YEA LS19 .....53 K4
Old Hollings Hi BAIL BD17 .....52 E5
Old Laithe La HBR HX7 .....112 D6
Old La BEE/HOL LS11 .....124 A1
BHP/TINH LS16 .....34 E8
BIRK/DRI BD11 .....120 D6
BIRK/DRI BD11 .....121 K4
BRIG HD6 .....142 C8
GSLY LS20 .....52 A3
HBR HX7 .....112 C3
HFAX HX1 .....8 C3
HOLM/MEL HD9 .....231 G7
HUDN HD2 .....168 E7
HWTH BD22 .....44 C1
HWTH BD22 .....67 F4
ILK LS29 .....19 C5
ILK LS29 .....20 D8
LUD/ILL HX2 .....138 A2
MAR/SLWT HD7 .....189 F6
MAR/SLWT HD7 .....210 B4
WHIT OL12 .....158 B5
Old Langley La BAIL BD17 .....51 K7
Old Lee Bank HIPP HX3 .....8 B2
Old Leeds Rd HUD HD1 .....13 D4
Old Lees Rd HBR HX7 .....112 B7
Old Lindley Rd HUDW HD3 .....189 C1
Old Main St BGLY BD16 .....49 K8
Old Manse Cft HWTH * BD22 .....68 B8
Old Market HFAX HX1 .....9 D4
Old Marsh PDSY/CALV LS28 .....98 A4
Old Mill Cl HEM/SK/SE WF9 .....224 C4
ILK LS29 .....32 B1
Old Mill La BSPA/BRAM LS23 .....42 E6
MID LS10 .....102 A7
Old Mill Rd BAIL * BD17 .....73 G5
Old Mill Vw EARL WF12 .....172 A6
Old Mill Yd OSS * WF5 .....173 H8
Old Moll Rd HOLM/MEL HD9 .....212 D6
Old Mount Farm HOR/CROF WF4 .....220 C4
Old Mount Rd MAR/SLWT HD7 .....209 G8
Old Oak Cl BHP/TINH LS16 .....78 A4
Old Oak Dr BHP/TINH LS16 .....77 K4
Old Oak Garth BHP/TINH LS16 .....77 K4
Old Oak Lawn BHP/TINH LS16 .....78 A4
The Old Orch OT LS21 .....35 G4
Old Oxenhope La HWTH BD22 .....68 D6
Old Park Rd IDLE BD10 .....78 C4
RHAY LS8 .....80 C4
Old Pool Bank BHP/TINH LS16 .....35 F7
Old Popplewell La CLECK BD19 .....143 F3
Old Power Wy ELL HX5 .....167 F3
Old Riding La LUD/ILL HX2 .....114 C8
Old Rd AL/HA/HU LS17 .....37 K1
CUL/QBY BD13 .....92 B3

CUL/QBY BD13 ....93 K5
GTHN BD7 ....117 K1
HBR HX7 ....112 B1
HOLM/MEL HD9 ....232 D8
HOR/CROF WF4 ....195 K5
MOR LS27 ....123 H3
Oldroyd Av CUD/GR S72...............240 A5
Oldroyd Crs BEE/HOL LS11 ....123 K1
Oldroyd Rd TOD OL14..................134 C6
Oldroyd Wy DEWS WF13 ....172 A3
Old Run Rd MID LS10 ....124 C1
Old Run Vw MID LS10 ....124 E3
The Old Sawmills RPDN/SBR HX6..186 E1
Old School Ct CAS WF10...............153 H6
Old School La HUD5.....................192 B8
Old School Ms MOR LS27..............123 H3
Old Shaw La HBR HX7..................110 E7
Old Side Ct AIRE BD20..................49 J2
Old Souls Wy BGLY BD16..............49 J5
Old South St HUD HD1 ....1 H4
Old Station Wy ILK LS29 ....18 D3
Old St AWLS/ASK DN6 ....243 H2
Old Town Mill La HBR HX7............112 C6
Old Wakefield Rd HUDE HD5 ....13 F5
Old Well Head HFAX HX1 ....9 D5
Old Westgate EARL WF12 ....172 B3
Old Whack House La YEA LS19 ....53 H5
Old Wood La BGLY BD16 ....51 G1
The Old Woodyard HOR/CROF WF4..218 C1
Old Yew La HOLM/MEL HD9 ....247 K1
Oilcana Pk ILK LS29 ....20 A6
Olive Gv GIR BD8 ....94 E3
Oliver Gdns MIRF WF14 ....170 C4
Oliver Hl HORS LS18 ....77 G4
Oliver Mdw ELL HX5 ....167 F3
Oliver Rd WF16............................145 H6
Olivers Mt PONT WF8...................181 F3
Olive St HUDN HD2 ....13 D1
Olive Ter MAR/SLWT * HD7...........210 A3
Ollerdale Av WIL/AL BD15 ....72 A8
Ollerdale Cl WIL/AL BD15 ....94 A1
Olney St MAR/SLWT HD7..............210 D2
Olympic Pk LM/WK BD12...............119 F6
Omar St HECK WF16 ....145 F7
One St BFD * BD1 ....4 B4
Onslow Pl CHAL LS7 ....79 K5
Ontario Pl CHAL LS7......................79 K5
Opal St HWTH BD22 ....2 B6
Orange St BFDE BD3 ....96 E5
HFAX HX1.....................................9 D4
Orange Hall * HD1 ....13 D2
Orange Tree Gv EARD/LOFT WF3...148 D4
Orchan Rd TOD OL14....................133 J4
The Orchard FEA/AMT WF7 ....179 J2
HOR/CROF WF4 ....200 D2
KGHY BD21 ....208 D4
MIRF WF14 ....170 E4
NORM WF6 ....177 K3
OSS WF5.....................................173 J6
PONT WF8...................................181 C6
WKFDW/WTN WF2 ....149 G8
Orchard Av EARD/LOFT WF3.........150 C6
Orchard Cl EARD/LOFT WF3..........148 E5
HOLM/MEL HD9 ....231 K2
HOR/CROF WF4 ....197 C1
LUD/ILL HX2 ....139 C5
WKFDW/WTN WF2 ....149 F8
Orchard Cft WKFDW/WTN WF2....175 F1
WKFDW/WTN WF2 ....199 J4
Orchard Dr CUD/GR S72................223 H5
FEA/AMT WF7 ....203 C6
HOR/CROF WF4 ....198 B4
KNOT WF11 ....131 K2
WBY LS22 ....23 F8
Orchard Gdns HOR/CROF WF4 ......198 B4
Orchard Gv IDLE BD10 ....75 F4
ILK LS29 ....32 C7
Orchard Head La PONT WF8..........155 F7
Orchard Head Dr PONT WF8..........155 F8
Orchard Head La PONT WF8...........155 F7
Orchard La ILK LS29.......................18 E3
PONT WF8...................................181 K7
Orchard Lees HUDE HD5 ....192 B8
Orchard Mt MSTN/BAR LS15 ....104 A1
Orchard Ri RPDN/SBR HX6............164 C1
Orchard Rd HUDE HD5 ....192 E3
MSTN/BAR LS15 ....103 K1
WKFDW/WTN WF2 ....199 C2
Orchard Sq MSTN/BAR LS15 ....103 K1
RTHW LS26 ....152 B1
Orchard St EARL WF12 ....172 B5
HUDS HD4 ....12 C6
OT LS21 ....33 K4
Orchard St West HUDW HD3 ....190 A6
Orchard Ter DOD/DAR S75 ....239 F7
HUDS HD4 ....13 D6
Orchard Vw HEM/SK/SE * WF9.....241 J1
Orchard Wk HBR HX7 ....137 G2
Orchard Wy BRIG HD6 ....142 B7
RTHW LS26 ....126 B5
Orchid Cl SHPY BD18 ....73 K6
Orchid Ct EARD/LOFT WF3 ....149 J1

Orchid Crest HEM/SK/SE WF9.......226 C4
Oriental St WOR/ARM LS12 ....100 C4
Orion Crs MID LS10 ....125 F4
Orion Dr MID LS10 ....125 F4
Orion Gdns MID LS10 ....125 G4
Orion Vw MID LS10 ....125 G4
Orion Wk MID LS10 ....125 G3
Orlando Cl MIRF WF14 ....170 C4
Orleans St WBSY BD6 ....118 A4
Ormonde Dr WIL/AL BD15 ....94 A3
Ormond Rd WBSY BD6..................118 C3
Ormondroyd Av WBSY BD6...........118 D3
Ormond St GTHN BD7.....................95 C7
Orville Gdns HDGY LS6 ....78 E7
Orwell Cl CAS WF10 ....154 D6
Osborne Av HOR/CROF WF4.........174 D8
Osborne Pl TOD OL14 ....134 B6
Osborne Rd HUD HD1 ....12 B2
Osborne St HBR * HX7 ....112 B8
HFAX HX1......................................8 A3
HUDE HD5 ....13 F5
WBOW BD5 ....4 B6
Osbourne Dr CUL/QBY BD13 ....99 H2
Osbourne Dr CUL/QBY BD13 ....116 C2
Osmondthorpe La OSM LS9...........102 E4
Osmondthorpe Ter OSM LS9 ....102 D3
Osprey Cl GIR * BD8 ....94 C4
Osprey Dr HUDS HD4 ....212 E4
Osprey Cl AL/HA/HU LS17 ....58 B7
Osprey Meadow MOR LS27 ....123 J7
Ossett La EARL WF12 ....172 C4
Osterley Gv IDLE BD10..................75 C6
Oswald St SHPY BD18 ....73 K4
Oswaldthorpe Av BFDE BD3 ....97 F2
Otley La YEA LS19 ....53 K4
Otley Mt AIRE * BD20.....................49 H3
Otley Old Rd BHP/TINH LS16 ....55 J6
HORS LS18 ....54 E2
Otley Rd BAIL BD17 ....52 B8
BFDE BD3 ....5 D4
BGLY BD16....................................51 F2
BGLY BD16....................................51 F2
BHP/TINH LS16............................56 B4
GSLY LS20 ....52 E2
ILK LS29 ....32 C3
OT LS21 ....37 G4
SHPY BD18...................................73 H5
Otley St HFAX HX1 ....8 A4
KGHY BD21 ....2 C4
Ottawa Pl CHAL LS7 ....79 K5
Otterburn Cl WBOW BD5................4 B6
Otterburn Gdns BHP/TINH LS16 .....56 B8
Otterburn St KGHY * BD21..............3 D1
Otter Lee La RPDN/SBR HX6..........163 K5
Otters Holt HOR/CROF WF4..........198 B4
Otterwood Bank WBY LS22 ....23 K4
Ouchthorpe La WKFDE WF1 ....149 K8
Oulton Dr RTHW LS26...................127 F8
Oulton La RTHW LS26 ....126 D6
RTHW LS26 ....127 F4
Oulton Ter GTHN BD7......................4 A6
Ounsworth St BOW BD4..................96 D7
Ouse Dr WBY LS22........................23 H3
Out Gang BRAM LS13 ....77 H8
Outgang La BRAM LS13 ....77 J8
Outlands Ri IDLE BD10 ....75 C5
Out La HOLM/MEL HD9 ....233 F3
KBTN HD8 ....217 G4
Outside La HWTH BD22 ....90 B1
Outwood Av HORS LS18 ....71 H4
Outwood Cha HORS LS18 ....71 H3
Outwood La HORS LS18..................71 H4
Outwood Park Ct WKFDE WF1 ......149 J7
Ouzelwell Crs EARL WF12 ....171 K8
Ouzelwell La EARL WF12...............171 K8
Ouzelwell Rd EARL WF12 ....172 A7
Ouzelwell Gn EARD/LOFT WF3 ......150 A1
The Oval BGLY BD16 ....72 B1
GIR BD8 ....94 E3
GLE DN14 ....157 J6
GSLY LS20 ....52 E3
HOLM/MEL HD9 ....233 F4
HOR/CROF WF4 ....221 K5
LVSG WF15 ....143 K6
MID LS10 ....102 A7
OT LS21 ....33 H2
RTHW LS26 ....126 C7
SCFT LS14 ....8 B1
Ovenden Av HIPP HX3 ....8 B2
Ovenden Cl HIPP * HX3 ....8 B1
Ovenden Crs HIPP HX3 ....8 B1
Ovenden Gn HIPP HX3 ....8 B1
Ovenden Pk LUD/ILL * HX2 ....115 J7
Ovenden Rd HIPP HX3.....................8 C2
Ovenden Road Ter HIPP HX3............8 B1
Ovenden Ter HIPP HX3.....................8 B1
Ovenden Wy HIPP HX3 ....8 A1
Ovenden Wood Rd LUD/ILL HX2....139 F1
Overdale RPDN/SBR HX6...............164 B4
Overdale Av AL/HA/HU LS17 ....58 C6
Overdale Dr SHPY BD18 ....74 B2
Overdale Mt LUD/ILL HX2 ....139 G6
Overdale Ter HWTH * BD22 ....68 E4
MSTN/BAR LS15 ....103 J3
Over Hall Cl MIRF WF14................170 E5

Over Hall Pk MIRF WF14 170
Over Hall Rd MIRF WF14 170
Overland Crs IDLE BD10................75
Over La YEA LS19..........................54
Overthorpe Av EARL WF12 199
Overthorpe Rd EARL WF12 199
Overton Dr WBSY BD6 117
Ovington Dr BOW BD4..................121
Owen Ct BGLY BD16......................51
Owlcotes Dr PDSY/CALV LS28 99
Owlcotes Gdns PDSY/CALV LS28....99
Owlcotes Garth PDSY/CALV LS28....9
Owlcotes La PDSY/CALV LS28 9
Owlcotes Rd PDSY/CALV LS28........9
Owlcotes Ter PDSY/CALV LS28 9
Owler Bars Rd HOLM/MEL HD9 23
Owler Ings Rd BRIG HD6...............16
Owler La BTLY WF17......................12
Owler Mdw HECK WF16................14
Owler Park Rd ILK LS29.................19
Owlers Cl HUDN HD2......................7
Owler's La HEM/SK/SE WF9 20
Owlet Hurst La LVSG WF15 17
Owlet Rd SHPY BD18 7
Owlett Md EARD/LOFT WF3...........14
Owlett Mead Cl EARD/LOFT WF3....14
Owl La EARL WF12........................17
Owl Ms HUDE HD5.........................19
Owl Rdg MOR LS27 12
Owl St KGHY * BD21
Oxfield Ct HUDE HD5 19
Oxford Av GSLY LS20.....................5
Oxford Cl CLECK BD19 14
CUL/QBY BD13 11
Oxford Court Gdns CAS * WF10 15
Oxford Crs CLAY BD14 9
HIPP HX3.....................................14
Oxford Dr CLECK BD19 14
GFTH/SHER LS25..........................12
Oxford La HIPP HX3 14
Oxford Pl BAIL BD17 7
BFDE BD3
HUD HD1 19
LDS LS1
PDSY/CALV LS28...........................9
Oxford Rd CHAL LS7.......................7
CLECK BD19 12
CUL/QBY * BD13 11
DEWS WF13 17
ECHL BD2
GSLY LS20.....................................5
HFAX HX1.
WKFDE WF1 1
Oxford Rw LDS LS1
Oxford St BTLY WF17.....................14
CLAY BD14 9
EARD/LOFT WF3 17
FEA/AMT WF7 17
GSLY LS20.....................................5
HBR HX7 11
HEM/SK/SE WF9 24
HUD HD1.
KGHY BD21
NORM WF6 15
RPDN/SBR HX6............................13
TOD OL14...................................13
WKFDE WF1
Oxford Ter BTLY WF17 14
Oxford Wk CLECK BD19 14
Ox Heys Mdw CUL/QBY BD13 9
Ox Lee La HOLM/MEL HD9............24
Oxley Gdns WBSY BD6..................11
Oxley Rd HUDN HD2 16
Oxley St GIR BD8
OSM LS9.....................................10
Oxspring La STKB/PEN S36 25
Oxton Mt OSM LS9 10
Oxton Wy OSM LS9.......................10
Oyster Cl MOR LS27......................12
Ozar St BEE/HOL LS11

Pacaholme Rd WKFDW/WTN WF2 ...17
Pack Horse Cl KBTN HD8 21
Pack Horse Wk HUD * HD1 14
Padan St HIPP HX3
Pad Cote La HWTH BD22 6
The Paddock AIRE BD20
AL/HA/HU LS17 5
BAIL BD17 5
CAS WF10 15
CLECK * BD19 14
CUL/QBY BD13 11
EARL WF12 17
HDGY LS6
HOR/CROF WF4 22
HUDE HD5 19
ILK * LS29 3
KNOT WF11
NORM WF6 12
RTHW LS26 12
SCFT LS14
WKFDE * WF1 1
Paddock HTON BD9 7
Paddock Br WBY LS22 7

ddock Cl *GFTH/SHER* LS25 **106** A5
.M/WK BD12 **142** D2
ddock Dr *BIRK/DRI* BD11 **121** H6
ddock Foot *HUD* HD1 **12** A5
ddock Gn *AL/HA/HU* LS17 **40** A6
ddock La *BGLY* BD16 **50** D5
.UD/ILL HX2 **139** F3
ddock Rd *HIPP* HX3 **116** D6
(BTN HD8 **215** J4
ddocks Church *BRIG* HD6 **169** F1
ddock Vw *CAS* WF10 **154** C5
ddy Bridge Rd *HBR* * HX7 **136** E2
dgum *BAIL* BD17 **51** J7
dma Cl *GTHN* BD7 **95** H4
dstow Gdns *MID* LS10 **124** B6
ge Hl *LUD/ILL* HX2 **139** H1
ge St *HUD* HD1 **13** D5
get Crs *HUDN* HD2 **190** D2
get St *KGHY* BD21 **2** B3
gewood Ct *IDLE* BD10 **74** C2
nthorpe La *HOR/CROF* WF4 **198** B8
sley Gv *WOR/ARM* * LS12 **100** B3
sley Pl *WOR/ARM* * LS12 **100** B3
sley Rd *WOR/ARM* * LS12 **100** B3
sley St *WOR/ARM* LS12 **100** B3
sley Ter *WOR/ARM* * LS12 **100** B3
kington St *WBOW* BD5 **95** K7
ace House Rd *HBR* HX7 **136** B1
eside La *OSS* WF5 **173** J4
esides Av *OSS* WF5 **173** J3
estine Rd *HBR* HX7 **112** B7
ey Rd *BOW* BD4 **96** C7
ey Ter *BOW* BD4 **96** C7
in Av *BFDE* BD3 **97** F2
ma St *TOD* OL14 **132** E2
m Cl *WBSY* BD6 **118** C3
mer Rd *BFDE* BD3 **5** F3
mer's Av *HEM/SK/SE* WF9 **242** C1
merston St *ECHL* * BD2 **5** F1
m St *HIPP* HX3 **8** C1
'UDS HD4 **13** D6
nelagh Av *IDLE* BD10 **75** G6
nal Av *WKFDE* WF1 **11** E1
nal St *GTHN* BD7 **95** G8
orama Dr *ILK* LS29 **29** J1
Parade *BGLY* BD16 **72** A4
RAM * LS13 **99** G1
TLY * WF17 **121** J8
TLY * WF17 **145** K7
'DGY LS6 **78** D6
'SM LS9 **102** A4
EA * LS19 **53** H5
adise La *LUD/ILL* HX2 **138** E5
AD LS24 **63** H6
adise Rd *HTON* * BD9 **73** F7
adise St *BFD* BD1 **4** B4
'FAX HX1 **8** C5
DSY/CALV LS28 **76** B8
ish Ghyll Dr *ILK* LS29 **19** K8
ish Ghyll La *ILK* LS29 **19** K8
ish Ghyll Rd *ILK* LS29 **20** A8
ish Ghyll Wk *ILK* LS29 **20** A8
s Rd *HOLM/MEL* HD9 **233** K8
Park *DOD/DAR* S75 **238** E7
k Av *BGLY* BD16 **71** K1
'RK/DRI BD11 **121** H5
SLYN/ROY S71 **222** B8
AS WF10 **129** H7
AS WF10 **154** A4
UD/GR S72 **224** B8
UD/GR S72 **240** A3
EWS WF13 **172** A3
ARD/LOFT WF3 **149** K4
.L HX5 **166** D5
'TH/SHER LS25 **129** H2
EM/SK/SE WF9 **241** H1
UD HD1 **12** B4
WTH BD22 **69** F1
'LE BD10 **74** D1
BTN HD8 **215** H8
BTN HD8 **215** J8
BTN HD8 **217** K8
GHY BD21 **2** C4
'SG WF15 **170** D1
'IRF WF14 **170** E7
'OR LS27 **122** E8
'STN/BAR LS15 **104** B1
ORM WF6 **178** A1
ONT WF8 **180** C3
ONT WF8 **181** K6
HAY LS8 **80** D4
THW LS26 **127** K2
HPY BD18 **73** G3
'KB/PEN S36 **252** B8
KFDE WF1 **149** H7
KFDE WF1 **177** G4
KFDW/WTN WF2 **10** B5
OR/ARM LS12 **100** B3
EA LS19 **53** J4
k Cliffe Rd *ECHL* BD2 **5** E1
k Cl *BGLY* BD16 **50** A7
'RK/DRI BD11 **121** H5
RAM LS13 **77** G8
'LY WF17 **146** A8
IL/QBY BD13 **116** C2
PP HX3 **141** K4
OR/CROF WF4 **223** F2
LE BD10 **74** E6
'TN HD8 **215** H8
KGHY * BD21 **3** D5
LUD/ILL HX2 **138** E2
PONT WF8 **181** K6
Park Copse *HORS* LS18 **76** E2
Park Ct *OSS* WF5 **174** A7
OT LS21 **35** H5
Park Crs *BFDE* BD3 **5** E1
BSLYN/ROY S71 **222** B8
CAS WF10 **154** D4
GSLY LS20 **52** E3
HIPP HX3 **8** B2
ILK LS29 **18** E3
MOR LS27 **122** C5
RHAY LS8 **80** D2
RTHW LS26 **126** D5
WOR/ARM LS12 **100** B3
Park Crest *HEM/SK/SE* WF9 **224** D5
Park Cross St *LDS* LS1 **7** D3
Park Cft *BTLY* WF17 **145** K7
DEWS WF13 **171** K3
Parkcroft *PDSY/CALV* LS28 **98** B1
Park Dl *CAS* WF10 **154** D2
ILK LS29 **32** C7
Parkdale Dr *RPDN/SBR* HX6 **164** B4
Park Dene *HFAX* * HX1 **8** B5
Park Dr *BGLY* BD16 **50** B6
BTLY WF17 **145** K4
EARD/LOFT WF3 **149** K4
HORS LS18 **76** D3
HTON BD9 **73** H7
HUD HD1 **12** A3
KBTN HD8 **215** H8
MIRF WF14 **170** E7
Park Drive Rd *KGHY* BD21 **3** D5
Park Dr South *HUD* HD1 **12** A4
Park Edge Cl *RHAY* LS8 **80** E4
Parker Av *NORM* WF6 **151** H7
Parker La *MIRF* WF14 **170** E6
Parker Rd *EARL* WF12 **172** B8
HOR/CROF WF4 **197** J2
Parker's La *AIRE* BD20 **27** J8
Parker St *EARD/LOFT* WF3 **148** D4
LVSG WF15 **145** F8
Park Fld *ILK* LS29 **32** C7
Parkfield Av *BEE/HOL* LS11 **101** G8
ELL HX5 **166** E5
MIRF WF14 **171** F7
Parkfield Cl *GFTH/SHER* LS25 **129** G1
PDSY/CALV LS28 **98** B4
Parkfield Ct *SCFT* * LS14 **81** G8
Parkfield Crs *MIRF* WF14 **170** E7
Parkfield Cft *MIRF* WF14 **171** F7
Parkfield Dr *BSPA/BRAM* LS23 **42** C3
CUL/QBY BD13 **116** C2
RPDN/SBR HX6 **164** D1
Parkfield Gv *BEE/HOL* LS11 **101** G8
Parkfield La *FEA/AMT* WF7 **179** H1
RPDN/SBR HX6 **139** G8
Parkfield Mt *BEE/HOL* LS11 **101** F8
PDSY/CALV LS28 **98** C4
Parkfield Pl *BEE/HOL* LS11 **101** G8
Parkfield Rd *BEE/HOL* * LS11 **101** G8
GIR BD8 **4** B1
SHPY BD18 **72** E3
Parkfield Rw *BEE/HOL* LS11 **101** G8
Park Flds *LUD/ILL* HX2 **138** E1
Parkfield St *BEE/HOL* LS11 **7** E6
Parkfield Ter *PDSY/CALV* LS28 **98** C2
Parkfield Vw *BEE/HOL* LS11 **101** G8
OSS WF5 **174** B6
Parkfield Wy *MIRF* WF14 **170** E7
SCFT LS14 **81** G8
Park Gdns *LUD/ILL* HX2 **139** G6
OSS WF5 **174** A7
Park Ga *BFDE* BD3 **5** D4
Parkgate *HEM/SK/SE* WF9 **241** H2
HUDS HD4 **213** F3
Parkgate Av *WKFDE* WF1 **11** E3
Park Gate Cl *HORS* LS18 **77** F3
Park Gate Rd *MAR/SLWT* HD7 **209** K5
Park Ga West *HIPP* * HX3 **166** D1
Park Gn *AIRE* BD20 **26** E1
NORM WF6 **177** J2
Park Gv *CUL/QBY* BD13 **116** C2
HDGY LS6 **78** D5
HIPP HX3 **140** E2
HOR/CROF WF4 **197** F1
HORS LS18 **76** D3
HTON BD9 **73** J7
HUD HD1 **12** B4
MIRF WF14 **171** F7
MOR LS27 **122** C5
RTHW LS26 **128** A3
SHPY BD18 **73** F3
YEA LS19 **53** J4
Park Grove Rd *WKFDW/WTN* WF2 **10** A4
Parkhead Cl *BSLYN/ROY* S71 **221** J7
Park Head La *HOLM/MEL* HD9 **232** E7
KBTN HD8 **235** H6
Park Hl *DOD/DAR* S75 **219** H8
HUDN HD2 **169** G5
Park Hill Cl *GIR* BD8 **94** D2
Parkhill Crs *WKFDE* WF1 **11** E3
Park Hill Dr *GIR* BD8 **94** D2
Park Hill Gv *WKFDE* WF1 **11** F3
Park Hill La *WKFDE* WF1 **11** E3
Park Holme *CHAL* LS7 **80** A7
Parkhome Est *RTHW* * LS26 **128** A2
Park House Cl *LM/WK* BD12 **119** F4
Park House Ct *STKB/PEN* S36 **251** H3
Park House Crs *LM/WK* BD12 **119** F4
Park House Dr *EARL* WF12 **172** C7
Park House Gn *PBR* HG3 **22** B1
Park House Gv *LM/WK* * BD12 **119** F4
Park House Rd *LM/WK* BD12 **118** E5
Park House Wk *LM/WK* BD12 **119** F4
Parkin Hall La *RPDN/SBR* HX6 **163** J1
Parkin La *IDLE* BD10 **75** H3
TOD OL14 **133** G5
Parkinson Ap *GFTH/SHER* LS25 **105** K3
Parkinson Cl *WKFDE* WF1 **11** E2
Parkinson La *HFAX* HX1 **8** A5
Parkinson Rd *CUL/QBY* BD13 **92** C2
Parkinson St *WBOW* BD5 **95** K7
Parkin St *LVSG* WF15 **143** K6
Parkland Av *MOR* LS27 **122** D8
Parkland Crs *HDGY* LS6 **79** G2
Parkland Dr *HDGY* LS6 **79** G2
IDLE BD10 **74** E4
Parkland Gdns *HDGY* LS6 **79** G3
Parklands *BHP/TINH* LS16 **35** H8
CAS WF10 **153** K4
ILK LS29 **20** D7
OSS WF5 **174** A7
Park Lands *PBR* HG3 **22** A1
Parklands Av *HOR/CROF* WF4 **196** E2
Parklands Ct *HOR/CROF* WF4 **196** E2
Parklands Crs *BHP/TINH* LS16 **35** J8
HOR/CROF WF4 **196** E2
Parklands Dr *HOR/CROF* WF4 **196** E2
RPDN/SBR HX6 **164** B2
Parklands Ga *BHP/TINH* LS16 **35** J8
Parklands Wk *KBTN* HD8 **215** H8
Parkland Ter *HDGY* LS6 **79** F3
Parkland Vw *YEA* LS19 **53** K5
Park La *AWLS/ASK* DN6 **183** K8
BAIL BD17 **52** B7
BVRD LS3 **6** B3
CAS WF10 **129** G6
CLAY BD14 **94** B7
CUD/GR S72 **240** B8
CUL/QBY BD13 **116** E2
GFTH/SHER LS25 **129** H3
GFTH/SHER LS25 **130** D3
GSLY LS20 **52** E4
GTL/HWG HX4 **188** D2
HBR HX7 **136** D3
HIPP HX3 **166** D1
HOLM/MEL * HD9 **231** J1
HOR/CROF WF4 **218** E4
HUDS HD4 **213** G4
KBTN HD8 **216** E6
KBTN HD8 **235** J6
KGHY BD21 **3** D4
MAR/SLWT HD7 **189** H7
PBR HG3 **22** A1
PONT WF8 **179** K2
RHAY LS8 **80** D1
RTHW LS26 **126** C6
RTHW LS26 **151** K2
STKB/PEN S36 **252** C8
WBOW BD5 **95** K7
Park Lane Ms *AL/HA/HU* LS17 **58** D7
Park Lea *HUDN* HD2 **169** G5
MID * LS10 **124** D6
Park Lodge Ct *WKFDE* WF1 **11** E3
Park Lodge Crs *WKFDE* WF1 **11** E3
Park Lodge Gv *WKFDE* WF1 **11** D3
Park Lodge La *WKFDE* WF1 **11** D3
Park Lodge Vw *KBTN* HD8 **236** E2
Park Md *IDLE* BD10 **74** D1
Parkmere Cl *BOW* BD4 **119** J4
Park Ms *OT* LS21 **35** H5
Park Mill La *OSS* WF5 **174** B4
Park Mill Wy *KBTN* HD8 **217** K8
Park Mt *KSTL* LS5 **78** B7
OT LS21 **35** F6
PBR HG3 **22** A1
WOR/ARM LS12 **100** A3
Park Mount Av *BAIL* BD17 **52** A8
Park Pde *DEWS* WF13 **172** A4
MOR * LS27 **122** E8
OSM LS9 **102** C5
Park Pl *HFAX* * HX1 **8** B5
IDLE BD10 **74** D1
LDS LS1 **6** C3
PONT WF8 **180** C3
Park Pl East *HIPP* HX3 **141** K4
Park Pl West *HIPP* HX3 **141** K4
Park Ri *BRAM* LS13 **77** G7
CAS WF10 **154** A4
Park Rd *BGLY* BD16 **49** K8
BRAM LS13 **77** G8
BSPA/BRAM LS23 **42** C3
BTLY WF17 **146** C6
CAS WF10 **154** B6
CUD/GR S72 **224** B8
CUD/GR S72 **240** A4
DEWS WF13 **171** J5
DEWS WF13 **171** K2
EARL WF12 **172** B5
EARL WF12 **172** E4
ELL HX5 **166** E3
GSLY LS20 **52** E4
HECK WF16 **145** G7
HFAX HX1 **8** C5
HUDS HD4 **12** A6
IDLE BD10 **74** D1

IDLE BD10 .... 74 E6
ILK LS29 .... 32 C7
KBTN HUB 217 K8
MSTN/BAR LS15 .... 104 B6
PONT 154 B8
RPDN/SBR HX6 .... 139 F7
SHPY BD18 .... 73 J4
TOD OL14 .... 134 A5
WBOW BD5 .... 4 C6
WBSY BD6 .... 118 D4
WOR/ARM LS12 .... 100 A3
YEA LS19 .... 53 K7
YEA LS19 .... 53 J4
Park Rd West HUDS HD4 .... 190 C7
Park Rw BRIG * HD6 .... 168 C1
LDS LS9 .... 7 D3
PDSY/CALV LS28 .... 98 C2
Park Side CLECK BD19 .... 144 D4
HOLM/MEL HD9 .... 234 A7
HOR/CROF WF4 .... 195 G8
HORS LS18 .... 76 E3
HUDE HD5 .... 192 E2
Parkside BGLY BD16 .... 50 A7
CLECK BD19 .... 144 A4
HOR/CROF WF4 .... 196 B5
Parkside Av CUL/QBY BD13 .... 116 C2
HDGY LS6 .... 79 F4
Parkside Cl HDGY LS6 .... 79 F3
Parkside Ct HWTH BD22 .... 69 G3
Parkside Crs HDGY LS6 .... 79 F3
Parkside Gdns HDGY LS6 .... 79 F4
Parkside Gv HTON BD9 .... 73 G8
Parkside La BEE/HOL LS11 .... 124 D2
EARD/LOFT WF3 .... 176 B1
Parkside Lawns HDGY LS6 .... 79 F4
Parkside Mt BEE/HOL LS11 .... 124 B2
Parkside Pde BEE/HOL LS11 .... 124 B2
Parkside Pl HDGY LS6 .... 79 F3
Parkside Rd HDGY LS6 .... 78 E2
PDSY/CALV LS28 .... 98 B1
TOD OL14 .... 132 E2
WBOW BD5 .... 119 F1
Parkside Rw BEE/HOL LS11 .... 124 B2
Parkside Ter CUL/QBY BD13 .... 70 B5
Parkside Vw HDGY LS6 .... 79 F3
Parkside Wk PDSY/CALV LS28 .... 98 C1
Park Spring Gdns BRAM LS13 .... 99 F3
Park Spring Ri BRAM LS13 .... 99 F3
Park Sq EARD/LOFT WF3 .... 149 K5
OSS WF5 .... 174 A7
OT LS21 .... 35 H5
WBSY BD6 .... 118 A3
Park Sq East LDS LS1 .... 7 D3
Park Sq North LDS LS1 .... 7 D3
Park Sq South LDS LS1 .... 7 D3
Park Sq West LDS LS1 .... 7 D3
Parkstone HUDN HD2 .... 169 G5
Parkstone Av BHP/TINH LS16 .... 78 A2
Parkstone Dr IDLE BD10 .... 74 E6
Parkstone Gn BHP/TINH LS16 .... 78 A2
Parkstone Gv BHP/TINH LS16 .... 78 A2
Parkstone Mt BHP/TINH LS16 .... 78 A2
Parkstone Pl BHP/TINH * LS16 .... 78 A2
Park Stone Ri HIPP HX3 .... 117 G5
Park St BRIG HD6 .... 168 C1
BTLY WF17 .... 145 H3
CLECK BD19 .... 143 J5
CLECK BD19 .... 145 F3
DEWS WF13 .... 172 C2
HECK WF16 .... 160 A7
HOR/CROF WF4 .... 197 G2
HWTH BD22 .... 69 H4
LDS * LS1 .... 7 D3
MAR/SLWT HD7 .... 189 G5
MOR LS27 .... 123 H4
MSTN/BAR LS15 .... 103 K3
OSS WF5 .... 174 A7
RPDN/SBR HX6 .... 139 F7
SHPY BD18 .... 73 G3
WKFDE WF1 .... 11 D4
WOR/ARM LS12 .... 100 A3
YEA LS19 .... 53 J4
Park Ter HDGY LS6 .... 78 D5
HFAX * HX1 .... 8 B4
HIPP HX3 .... 140 E2
KGHY BD21 .... 3 E3
OT LS21 .... 34 E6
SHPY BD18 .... 73 G3
Park Top PDSY/CALV LS28 .... 98 C2
The Park Towngate HIPP HX3 .... 141 F8
Park Vw BEE/HOL LS11 .... 101 G8
BSLYN/ROY S71 .... 222 B7
CAS WF10 .... 154 D5
CLECK BD19 .... 143 K3
CUD/GR S72 .... 223 G8
EARD/LOFT WF3 .... 149 K5
HEM/SK/SE WF9 .... 224 B2
HEM/SK/SE * WF9 .... 225 K8
HFAX HX1 .... 8 B5
HIPP HX3 .... 141 K4
HOLM/MEL HD9 .... 233 F6
MAR/SLWT * HD7 .... 209 J7
PDSY/CALV * LS28 .... 98 C4
RTHW LS26 .... 127 K2
WKFDW/WTN * WF2 .... 175 F5
Park View Av HDGY LS6 .... 78 D8
HIPP HX3 .... 141 F2
HWTH BD22 .... 69 G3
Parkview Crs RHAY LS8 .... 80 D1
SHPY * BD18 .... 73 G4
Park View Gv RHAY LS8 .... 80 D2
Park View Gv BULY LS4 .... 78 D8
Park View Rd BULY LS4 .... 100 D1
HTON BD9 .... 95 H1
Park View Ter HTON BD9 .... 73 H8
YEA LS19 .... 53 K7
Park Vis RHAY LS8 .... 80 C1
Park Villas Dr PONT 180 C2
Parkville Pl BRAM LS13 .... 77 G8
Park Wy BAIL BD17 .... 73 F2
ILK LS29 .... 32 C7
OT LS21 .... 35 H5
Parkway AIRE BD20 .... 26 C6
CUL/QBY BD13 .... 116 C2
HOR/CROF WF4 .... 200 D1
KGHY BD21 .... 3 D5
MOR LS27 .... 122 B5
WBOW BD5 .... 119 G2
Parkway Cl SCFT LS14 .... 81 G7
Parkways RTHW LS26 .... 126 E5
Parkways Av RTHW LS26 .... 126 E6
Parkways Cl RTHW LS26 .... 126 E6
Parkways Ct RTHW LS26 .... 126 E5
Parkways Dr RTHW LS26 .... 126 E5
Parkways Garth RTHW * LS26 .... 126 E6
Park West RTHW LS26 .... 126 C6
Park Willow HIPP HX3 .... 117 J5
Park Wood Av BEE/HOL LS11 .... 124 A4
Parkwood Cl RHAY LS8 .... 80 C3
Parkwood Crs BEE/HOL LS11 .... 124 A4
Park Wood Dr BEE/HOL LS11 .... 124 A5
Parkwood Gdns PDSY/CALV LS28 ... 75 J5
RHAY LS8 .... 80 C4
Parkwood Ri KGHY BD21 .... 3 D5
Park Wood Rd BEE/HOL LS11 ...... 124 A4
Parkwood Rd MAR/SLWT HD7 ...... 189 D1
PDSY/CALV LS28 .... 75 J5
SHPY BD18 .... 73 F4
Parkwood St KGHY BD21 .... 3 E4
Parkwood Vw RHAY LS8 .... 80 C4
Parliament Pl WOR/ARM LS12 ..... 100 D3
Parliament Rd WOR/ARM LS12 ..... 100 D4
Parliament St WKFDW/WTN WF2 ... 10 B3
Parlington Ct MSTN/BAR LS15 .... 83 J4
Parlington Dr GFTH/SHER LS25 .... 84 E4
Parlington La GFTH/SHER LS25 ...... 84 A7
GFTH/SHER LS25 .... 84 E5
Parlington Meadow
MSTN/BAR LS15 .... 83 J1
Parlington Vls GFTH/SHER LS25 ...... 84 E4
Parma St MID LS10 .... 4 C6
Parnaby Av MID LS10 .... 125 G2
Parnaby Rd MID LS10 .... 125 G2
Parnaby St MID LS10 .... 125 G2
Parnaby Ter MID LS10 .... 125 G2
Parratt Rw BFDE BD3 .... 97 F4
Parrock La HBR HX7 .... 112 C5
Parrott St BOW BD4 .... 120 A2
Parry Cl BGLY * BD16 .... 70 E2
Parry La BOW BD4 .... 96 E6
Parsonage La BRIG HD6 .... 142 B8
Parsonage Rd BOW BD4 .... 97 F6
RTHW LS26 .... 128 C8
WBOW BD5 .... 96 A8
Parsonage St HIPP HX3 .... 9 E2
Parson La HOR/CROF WF4 .... 220 C4
Parsons Gn WBY LS22 .... 23 K6
Parson's La ILK LS29 .... 18 A3
Parson Rd HTON BD9 .... 73 G7
Parson St KGHY BD21 .... 3 D1
Partons Pl EARD/LOFT WF3 .... 149 K5
Partridge Cl MOR LS27 .... 123 J7
Partridge Crs EARL WF12 .... 195 K2
Pasture CHAL LS7 .... 79 K4
HWTH BD22 .... 68 C2
Pasture Av WOR/ARM LS12 .... 100 B3
Pasture Crs CHAL LS7 .... 79 K4
Pasture Dr CAS WF10 .... 153 F5
Pasture Fold ILK LS29 .... 32 A1
Pasture Gv CHAL LS7 .... 79 K4
Pasture La CHAL LS7 .... 79 K4
CLAY BD14 .... 94 D7
WBY LS22 .... 39 G2
Pasture Mt WOR/ARM LS12 .... 100 B3
Pasture Pde CHAL LS7 .... 79 K4
Pasture Pl CHAL LS7 .... 79 K4
Pasture Rd CLAY BD14 .... 94 D7
Pasture Rd BAIL BD17 .... 73 K1
RHAY LS8 .... 80 A7
Pasture Side Ter East CLAY BD14 .... 94 B7
Pasture Side Ter West CLAY BD14 ... 94 C7
Pasture St CHAL * LS7 .... 79 K4
Pastures Vw WOR/ARM LS12 .... 100 B3
Pasture Ter CHAL LS7 .... 79 K4
Pasture Vw WOR/ARM LS12 .... 100 B3
Pasture View Rd RTHW LS26 .... 126 A6
Pasture Wk CLAY BD14 .... 94 C7
Pasture Wy CAS WF10 .... 153 F5
Pateley Crs HUDN HD2 .... 191 F1
Patent St HTON BD9 .... 95 H1
Paternoster La GTHN BD7 .... 95 G7

Paterson Av WKFDW/WTN WF2 10
Patience La NORM WF6 151
Patricia Gdns RPDN/SBR * HX6 139
Patterdale Ap WBY LS22 23
Patterdale Dr HUDE HD5 13
Patterdale Rd EARL WF12 172
Patterson Ct WKFDW/WTN WF2 149
Pattie St KGHY BD21 2
Pauline Ter CAS WF10 153
Paul La HOR/CROF WF4 194
HUDE HD5 169
Pavement La LUD/ILL HX2 169
Pavilion Cl CUD/GR S72 224
Pavilion Ms BULY LS4 78
Pavilion Wy HOLM/MEL HD9 211
Paw La CUL/QBY BD13 116
Pawson St BOW BD4 97
EARD/LOFT WF3 149
EARD/LOFT WF3 149
MOR LS27 122
Peabody St HIPP HX3 8
Peace Hall Dr HUDE HD5 192
Peace St BOW BD4 96
Peach Tree Cl PONT * WF8 180
Peacock Av WKFDW/WTN WF2 175
Peacock Ct YEA LS19 54
Peacock Gn MOR LS27 123
Peacock Vw WKFDW/WTN WF2 175
Peak Vw DEWS WF13 171
Pearl St BTLY WF17 145
HWTH BD22 2
Pear Pl TOD OL14 132
Pearson Av HDGY LS6 78
Pearson Gv HDGY LS6 78
Pearson La HTON BD9 94
Pearson Rd WBSY BD6 118
Pearson Rw LM/WK BD12 118
Pearson's La EARL WF12 194
Pearson St BFDE BD3 95
CLECK BD19 143
MID LS10 7
NORM WF6 151
PDSY/CALV LS28 75
Pearson Ter HDGY LS6 78
Pear St HFAX HX1 8
HUDS HD4 12
HWTH BD22 69
HWTH * BD22 90
Pear Tree Acre BSPA/BRAM LS23 42
Pear Tree Cl PONT WF8 180
Pear Tree Ct AIRE BD20 27
Peartree Field La PONT WF8 204
Pear Tree Gdns MSTN/BAR LS15 83
Pear Tree La HEM/SK/SE WF9 224
Peasborough Vw ILK LS29 32
Pease Cl PONT WF8 180
Peasefold GFTH/SHER LS25 129
Peasehill Cl YEA LS19 54
Peasehill Pk YEA LS19 54
Peaseland Av CLECK BD19 143
Peaseland Cl CLECK BD19 144
Peaseland Rd CLECK BD19 144
Peat Ponds HUDW HD3 189
Peckett Cl HUDW HD3 190
Peckover Dr PDSY/CALV LS28 97
Peckover St BFD BD1 5
Peebles Cl HUDW HD3 190
Peel Av BTLY WF17 146
Peel Cl BOW BD4 97
HOR/CROF WF4 197
Peel Cottage Rd TOD OL14 155
Peel Cott St TOD OL14 155
Peel Park Dr ECHL BD2 5
Peel Park Ter ECHL BD2 5
Peel Park Vw BFDE BD3 5
Peel Pl ILK LS29 32
Peel Rw GTHN BD7 95
Peel Sq BFD * BD1 4
Peel St BGLY BD16 50
CUL/QBY BD13 93
CUL/QBY BD13 116
HECK WF16 145
HOR/CROF WF4 197
HUD HD1 12
MAR/SLWT HD7 209
MOR LS27 123
RPDN/SBR * HX6 138
WIL/AL BD15 71
Peep Green Rd LVSG WF15 143
Pegholme Dr OT LS21 33
Pelham Ct EARD/LOFT * WF3 124
ECHL BD2 76
Pelham Pl CHAL LS7 79
Pelham Rd ECHL BD2 74
Pell Ct HOLM/MEL HD9 233
Pell La HOLM/MEL HD9 233
Pellon La HFAX HX1 8
Pellon New Rd LUD/ILL HX2 139
Pellon St TOD OL14 155
Pellon Ter IDLE BD10 74
Pellon Wk IDLE BD10 74
Pemberton Dr GTHN BD7 4
Pemberton Rd CAS WF10 154
Pembroke Cl MOR LS27 122
Pembroke Ct HUDS HD4 12
Pembroke Dr GFTH/SHER LS25 129
Pembroke Ri PDSY/CALV LS28 9
Pembroke St WBOW BD5 9
Pembury Mt MSTN/BAR LS15 8

narth Av *HEM/SK/SE* WF9 ....226 C4
narth Rd *MSTN/BAR* LS15 ....103 K1
narth Ter *HEM/SK/SE* WF9 ....226 C4
nda's Dr *MSTN/BAR* LS15.....................104 B1
nda's Wk *MSTN/BAR* LS15 ....82 B8
nda's Wk *MSTN/BAR* LS15.....................104 B1
nda's Wy *MSTN/BAR* LS15....................104 C1
ndennis Av *HEM/SK/SE* WF9 ....226 A7
ndil Cl *MSTN/BAR* LS15........................104 A3
ndle Rd *CUL/QBY* BD13 ....116 D4
ndle Rd *BGLY* BD16 ....50 B8
ndle Wy *COL* BB8 ....65 C2
ndragon *ECHL* * BD2 ....74 C8
ndragon La *ECHL* BD2...........................74 D8
nfield Gv *CLAY* BD14...............................94 C7
nfield Rd *BIRK/DRI* BD11 ....121 J5
ngarth *BGLY* BD16..................................50 B6
nistone Boundary Wk
STKB/PEN S36 ....250 E6
STKB/PEN S36 ....251 J5
STKB/PEN S36 ....253 F6
STKB/PEN S36 ....253 H3
nistone Ct *STKB/PEN* * S36 ....252 D8
nistone Ms *HWTH* * BD22 ....68 E4
nistone Rd *HOLM/MEL* HD9 ....234 B5
OLM/MEL HD9 ....249 F4
UDE HD5 ....192 D6
BTN HD8 ....235 H1
nlands Av *MSTN/BAR* LS15...................104 B4
nlands Lawn *MSTN/BAR* LS15 ....104 B4
nlington St *STKB/PEN* * S36 ....252 D8
nn Cl *ECHL* BD2 ....74 D8
nn Dr *CLECK* BD19...............................144 A5
nnine Cl *CUL/QBY* BD13 ....116 C4
OLM/MEL HD9 ....232 D6
WKFDW/WTN WF2 ....198 A1
nnine Crs *HUDW* HD3 ....189 J3
nnine Dr *KBTN* HD8 ....237 H1
nnine Gdns *MAR/SLWT* HD7 ....211 H2
nnine Ri *KBTN* HD8...............................237 H1
nnine Rd *EARL* WF12 ....172 D5
nnine Vw *BTLY* WF17 ....121 K8
BR HX7 ....110 E7
EM/SK/SE WF9......................................226 C3
UDE HD5..192 E1
MAR/SLWT HD7....................................211 H2
nnine Wy *HBR* HX7 ....87 H8
BR HX7..111 G5
BR HX7..135 J2
EM/SK/SE WF9 ....225 F4
UDW HD3...207 J5
WTH BD22 ....44 C8
BTN HD8 ....237 H1
T OL15..184 B4
PML OL3 ....207 K8
nnington Gv *HDGY* LS6 ....79 G8
nnington La *RTHW* LS26 ....150 E1
nnington Pl *HDGY* LS6 ....79 G8
nnington St *HDGY* LS6............................79 G8
nnington Ter *HDGY* LS6..........................79 G8
VBOW * BD5 ....95 J7
nnithorne Av *BAIL* BD17 ....51 J7
n St *HFAX* HX1...8 B3
nwell Fold *SCFT* LS14 ....82 C6
nwell Garth *SCFT* LS14..........................82 B6
nwell Gn *SCFT* LS14 ....82 B6
nwell Lawn *SCFT* LS14 ....82 B6
nnygate *BGLY* BD16 ....50 D5
ny Hill Dr *CLAY* BD14 ....94 D7
ny La *HUDE* HD5....................................192 D6
ny Lane Wy *MID* LS10 ....101 K7
ny Spring *HUDE* HD5 ....192 A8
raevon St *CHAL* LS7 ....79 J8
rith Crs *CAS* WF10 ....155 F1
rith Gv *WOR/ARM* LS12 ....100 C5
rose Beck Dr *FEA/AMT* WF7 ....202 E6
rose Dr *CTHN* BD7 ....95 F8
rose Pl *WKFDW/WTN* WF2 ....198 B6
ryn Av *HUDE* HD5 ....192 E3
tland Av *CLAY* BD14 ....94 D7
VOT WF11...156 B7
tland Dr *HWTH* BD22 ....2 B4
tland Dr *GFTH/SHER* LS25 ....105 K6
tland Gv *WKFDW/WTN* WF2 ....175 F8
tland Rd *EARL* WF12..............................172 C5
tland Wy *MOR* LS27 ....123 F8
zance Ct *GIR* BD8 ....95 H5
per Gdns *BRAM* LS13...............................77 J7
per La *BRAM* LS13 ....77 H7
ID LS10 ....102 B8
per Rd *MID* LS10 ....125 G1
per Royd St *DEWS* WF13 ....172 C2
cival Ct *HUDW* HD3 ....189 K5
cival St *BFDE* BD3 ....5 E4
UDW HD3...189 K5
OSU LS2..7 D2
cy St *BGLY* BD16 ....50 A8
EM/SK/SE WF9 ....241 H1
JDH HD2 ....12 C1
GHY BD21 ....2 C6
OR/ARM LS12..100 D5
egrine Av *MOR* LS27 ....123 J7
grine Ct *HUDS* HD4.............................212 E4
grine Wy *WBSY* BD6 ....117 K2
dot Fold *HUDN* HD2 ....191 J1

Per La *LUD/ILL* HX2...............................115 G4
Permain Ct *HUDS* HD4 ....13 D6
Perry Cl *HWTH* BD22 ....47 J8
Perseverance La *GTHN* BD7 ....95 G8
Perseverance Rd *CUL/QBY* BD13 ....92 E4
Perseverance St *BAIL* * BD17 ....51 K7
CAS WF10 ....153 H3
HUDS HD4 ....191 G8
LM/MG BD12 ....118 D7
PDSY/CALV LS28 ....98 A4
RPDN/SBR HX6 ....138 E7
Perseverance Ter *HFAX* HX1 ....8 B6
RTHW LS26 ....126 B7
Perseverance St *HUDS* HD4 ....189 K8
Perth Av *ECHL* BD2 ....74 D8
Perth Dr *EARD/LOFT* WF3 ....148 A3
Perth Mt *HORS* LS18 ....55 F7
Peterborough Pl *ECHL* BD2 ....74 D8
Peterborough Rd *ECHL* BD2 ....5 F1
Peterborough Rd Ter *ECHL* BD2 ....74 D8
Petergate *BFD* * BD1 ....5 D4
Peter Hl *BTLY* WF17 ....172 C1
Peterhouse Dr *OT* LS21 ....34 A4
Peter La *LUD/ILL* HX2...........................138 E4
MOR LS27 ....123 J6
Petersfield Av *MID* LS10 ....125 F4
Peterson Rd *WKFDE* WF1 ....11 D3
Pether Hl *GTL/HWG* HX4 ....165 J3
Petrel Cl *WBSY* BD6..............................117 H2
Petrie Crs *BRAM* LS13 ....76 B6
Petrie Rd *BFDE* BD3.................................97 G4
Petrie St *BRAM* LS13...............................76 B6
Petworth Cft *BSLYN/ROY* S71 ....221 K7
Peverell Cl *BOW* BD4 ....97 G8
Peveril Mt *ECHL* BD2 ....96 E1
Pexwood Rd *TOD* OL14 ....133 J8
Pheasant Dr *BTLY* WF17 ....121 K8
Pheasant St *KGHY* BD21 ....3 E2
Philip Garth *WKFDE* WF1 ....149 J6
Philippa Wy *WOR/ARM* LS12 ....100 C3
Philip's Gv *EARD/LOFT* WF3 ....149 K5
Philip's La *PONT* WF8 ....181 K6
Phillips St *CAS* WF10 ....153 G3
Phil May Ct *WOR/ARM* LS12 ....6 A4
Phoebe La *HIPP* HX3..............................140 C7
Phoenix Av *KBTN* HD8 ....217 H5
Phoenix Ct *BTLY* WF17 ....146 E6
TOD OL14 ....134 C6
WKFDW/WTN WF2 ....10 A3
Phoenix St *BRIG* HD6 ....168 C1
TOD OL14 ....134 C5
Phoenix Wy *BOW* BD4 ....97 G5
Piccadilly *BFD* BD1 ....4 C4
WKFDE WF1 ....10 B3
Packard Bank *HDGY* LS6 ....79 F6
Pickard Ct *MSTN/BAR* LS15 ....104 A3
Pickard La *AIRE* BD20 ....27 G1
Pickard Wy *DEWS* WF13 ....172 A2
Pickering Av *GFTH/SHER* LS25 ....106 B3
Pickering Dr *OSS* WF5............................173 H2
Pickering La *OSS* WF5............................173 G2
Pickering Mt *WOR/ARM* LS12 ....100 D3
The Pickerings *CUL/QBY* BD13 ....116 D3
Pickering St *WOR/ARM* LS12 ....100 D3
Pickersgill St *OSS* WF5..........................173 H3
Pickford St *HUDS* HD4 ....190 A7
Pick Hill Rd *HOLM/MEL* HD9 ....211 H8
Picklesfield *DEWS* WF13 ....172 A1
Pickles La *GTHN* BD7 ....95 F8
KBTN HD8 ....237 F2
Pickles St *DEWS* WF13 ....172 A1
KGHY BD21 ....2 C5
Pickthall Ter *TOD* OL14 ....134 C6
Pickwood La *RPDN/SBR* HX6 ....165 H3
Picton St *GIR* BD8 ....4 B2
Picton Wy *HUDE* HD5 ....192 C4
Pictureville *BFD* * BD1 ....9 E4
Piece Hall *HFAX* * HX1 ....9 H3
Piece Wood Rd *BHP/TINH* LS16 ....55 H8
Pigeon Cote Cl *SCFT* LS14 ....81 J5
Pigeon Cote Rd *SCFT* LS14 ....81 H5
Piggott St *BRIG* HD6 ....142 B8
Pighill Top La *MAR/SLWT* HD7 ....210 B1
Pike End Rd *RPDN/SBR* HX6 ....186 D5
Pike Law La *MAR/SLWT* HD7 ....189 F6
Pike Law Rd *MAR/SLWT* HD7 ....189 F6
Pildacre Brow *OSS* WF5 ....173 H5
Pildacre Cft *OSS* WF5.............................173 H5
Pildacre La *EARL* WF12 ....173 G5
Pilden La *EARD/LOFT* WF3 ....148 D4
Pilgrim Av *DEWS* WF13 ....171 J4
Pilgrim Crs *DEWS* WF13 ....171 J4
Pilgrim Dr *DEWS* WF13 ....171 J4
Pilling La *KBTN* HD8 ....237 F1
Pilling Top La *KBTN* HD8 ....215 K7
Pilmer Rd *WKFDW/WTN* WF2 ....174 E7
Pilot St *OSM* LS9 ....102 A2
Pincheon St *WKFDE* WF1 ....11 D3
Pinder Av *WOR/ARM* LS12 ....99 K7
Pinderfields Rd *WKFDE* WF1 ....10 C2
Pinder Gv *WOR/ARM* LS12 ....99 K6
Pinders Crs *KNOT* WF11 ....155 K6
Pinders Garth *KNOT* WF11 ....155 K6
Pinders Gn *RTHW* LS26 ....152 B2
Pinders Green Dr *RTHW* LS26 ....152 B2
Pinders Green Fold *RTHW* LS26 ....152 B2

Pinder's Gv *WKFDE* WF1 ....11 E1
Pinder St *WOR/ARM* LS12 ....99 K7
Pinebury Dr *CUL/QBY* BD13 ....116 B2
Pine Cl *CAS* WF10 ....153 K5
WBY LS22 ....23 J4
Pine Ct *HUDS* HD4 ....212 D5
LDSU * LS2..9 J1
Pine Cft *KGHY* BD21 ....2 B1
Pinedale *BGLY* BD16 ....49 K6
Pine Gv *BTLY* WF17 ....146 A7
Pine Rd *TOD* OL14 ....133 J4
Pines Gdns *ILK* LS29 ....19 K8
Pine St *BFD* BD1 ....5 D4
HEM/SK/SE WF9 ....242 A2
HUD HD1 ....13 D4
HWTH BD22 ....68 E5
Pine Tree Av *BSPA/BRAM* LS23 ....42 E5
PONT WF8 ....180 C5
Pinewood Av *WKFDW/WTN* WF2 ....174 E5
Pinewood Cl *CUD/GR* S72 ....240 D8
ILK LS29 ....20 A8
Pinewood Gdns *GTL/HWG* HX4 ....166 A7
Pinewood Pl *KNOT* WF11 ....155 J8
Pinfold Cl *EARL* WF12 ....195 J1
GTL/HWG HX4 ....164 D6
HOR/CROF WF4 ....217 G1
KNOT WF11 ....155 K6
MIRF WF14 ....170 E6
WBY LS22 ....25 J2
Pinfold Ct *MSTN/BAR* * LS15 ....103 K3
Pinfold Cft *CLAY* BD14 ....94 C7
Pinfold Gv *MSTN/BAR* LS15 ....103 J3
WKFDW/WTN WF2 ....199 F2
Pinfold Hl *DEWS* WF13 ....172 A4
MSTN/BAR LS15 ....103 K4
Pinfold La *BHP/TINH* LS16 ....55 J5
ELL HX5 ....167 J5
GFTH/SHER LS25 ....105 K4
HOR/CROF WF4 ....217 G1
HUDW HD3 ....188 A6
KBTN HD8 ....193 J8
MAR/SLWT HD7 ....188 E7
MIRF WF14 ....170 E6
MSTN/BAR LS15 ....103 J3
RPDN/SBR HX6 ....138 A7
RTHW LS26 ....152 D1
WKFDW/WTN WF2 ....199 G2
WOR/ARM LS12 ....100 B3
Pinfold Mt *MSTN/BAR* LS15 ....103 K4
Pinfold Ri *GFTH/SHER* LS25 ....85 J5
Pinfold Rd *MSTN/BAR* LS15 ....103 K4
Pinfold Sq *MSTN/BAR* LS15 ....103 J3
Pingle Ri *KBTN* HD8 ....236 E4
Pin Hill La *LUD/ILL* HX2........................138 A2
Pink St *HWTH* BD22 ....68 E5
Pinnacle La *HBR* HX7 ....135 K2
Pinnar La *HIPP* HX3 ....140 E6
Pioneer St *EARL* WF12 ....172 B8
TOD * OL14 ....159 K4
Pioneer Wy *CAS* WF10 ....152 D6
Pipe & Nook La *WOR/ARM* LS12 ....99 K4
Pipercroft *WBSY* BD6 ....117 K5
Piper Hl *KNOT* WF11 ....131 H6
Piper La *HWTH* BD22 ....44 D2
OT LS21 ....33 H4
Piper Well La *KBTN* HD8 ....235 G5
Pipit Meadow *MOR* LS27 ....123 H8
Pippin's Ap *NORM* WF6 ....152 A8
Pippins Green Av
*WF2 ....174 C1
Pirie Cl *ECHL* BD2....................................74 B8
Pitchstone Ct *WOR/ARM* LS12 ....99 H4
Pitcliffe Wy *WBOW* BD5 ....96 A7
Pitfall St *LDS* LS1 ....7 E4
Pit Field Rd *EARD/LOFT* WF3 ....126 A8
Pit Hl *HIPP* * HX3 ....9 E5
Pit La *CLECK* BD19 ....144 E1
CUL/QBY BD13 ....92 A2
CUL/QBY BD13 ....93 G7
DEWS WF13 ....171 J1
GFTH/SHER LS25 ....106 E7
GFTH/SHER LS25 ....107 G5
RTHW LS26 ....128 C8
Pits La *CLECK* BD19 ....143 F5
Pitt Hill La *GTL/HWG* HX4 ....188 A5
Pitt Rw *LDS* LS1 ....7 E4
Pitts St *BOW* BD4 ....97 F7
Pitt St *KGHY* BD21 ....3 E3
LVSG WF15 ....170 D1
TOD OL14 ....134 C6
Place's Rd *OSM* * LS9 ....102 A4
Plaid Row *OSM* * LS9 ....102 A3
Plain La *RPDN/SBR* HX6 ....163 K1
Plains La *ELL* HX5 ....166 E2
MAR/SLWT HD7 ....209 J6
Plane St *HUDS* HD4 ....191 H8
TOD OL14 ....133 H4
Plane Tree Av *AL/HA/HU* LS17 ....58 B7
Plane Tree Cl *AL/HA/HU* LS17 ....58 B7
Plane Tree Cft *AL/HA/HU* LS17 ....58 B7
Plane Tree Gdns *AL/HA/HU* LS17 ....58 B7
Plane Tree Gv *YEA* LS19 ....54 B5
Plane Tree Nest La *LUD/ILL* HX2 ....139 H5
Plane Tree Ri *AL/HA/HU* * LS17 ....58 B7
Plane Tree Rd *RPDN/SBR* HX6 ....138 E6
Plane Trees *LUD/ILL* HX2 ....139 G3
Plane Trees Cl *CLECK* BD19 ....120 A8
Planetrees Rd *BFDE* BD3 ....96 E5
Planetrees St *WIL/AL* BD15 ....94 A2

Plane Tree Vw AL/HA/HU LS17 .....58 B7
Plantation Av AL/HA/HU LS17 .....58 C6
  BSLYN/ROY S71 .....222 B8
  MSTN/BAR LS15 .....103 H4
Plantation Dr HUDS HD4 .....213 G2
Plantation Gdns AL/HA/HU LS17 .....58 C6
Plantation Pl BOW BD4 .....96 E7
Plantation Wy BAIL BD17 .....51 K8
Platt La MAR/SLWT HD7 .....210 E2
Playfair Rd MID LS10 .....124 E1
Playhouse Sq MID * LS9 .....7 F5
The Pleasance RTHW LS26 .....127 K2
Pleasant Ct HDGY * LS6 .....79 G8
Pleasant Mt BEE/HOL LS11 .....6 C6
Pleasant Pl BEE/HOL LS11 .....6 C6
Pleasant St BEE/HOL LS11 .....6 C6
  GTHN BD7 .....95 G7
Pleasant Ter BEE/HOL LS11 .....6 C6
Pledwick Crs WKFDW/WTN WF2 .....199 F5
Pledwick Dr WKFDW/WTN WF2 .....199 F6
Pledwick Gv WKFDW/WTN WF2 .....198 E6
Pledwick La WKFDW/WTN WF2 .....199 F6
Pledwick Ri WKFDW/WTN WF2 .....199 F5
Plevna La BEE/HOL * LS10 .....125 H1
Plevna Ter BTLY BD16 .....49 K7
Plimsoll St BOW BD4 .....96 C7
  HEM/SK/SE WF9 .....224 D4
Ploughcroft La HIPP HX3 .....8 C1
Ploughmans Cft HORS BD2 .....74 A7
Plover Dr BTLY WF17 .....145 J6
Plover Rd HUDW HD3 .....190 B3
Plover St KGHY BD21 .....3 D2
  WBOW BD5 .....95 J8
Plover Wy MOR LS27 .....123 H8
Plumpton Av ECHL BD2 .....74 B5
Plumpton Cl ECHL BD2 .....74 C6
Plumpton Dr ECHL BD2 .....74 B5
Plumpton End ECHL BD2 .....74 C5
Plumpton Gdns ECHL BD2 .....74 B5
Plumpton Lea ECHL BD2 .....74 B5
Plumpton Md ECHL BD2 .....74 B5
Plumpton Pl WKFDW/WTN WF2 .....10 A3
Plumpton Rd WKFDW/WTN WF2 .....10 A3
Plumpton St GIR BD8 .....95 G3
  WKFDW/WTN WF2 .....10 A3
Plumpton Ter WKFDW/WTN WF2 .....10 A4
Plumpton Wk ECHL BD2 .....74 B5
Plum St HFAX HX1 .....8 A5
  NORM WF6 .....47 J8
Plum Tree Cl PONT WF8 .....180 C5
Plymouth Gv HFAX * HX1 .....8 A5
Poet's Pl HORS LS18 .....77 G1
Pohlman St HFAX HX1 .....8 A6
Pole Ga HUDW HD3 .....188 B8
Pole Gate Branch HUDW HD3 .....188 B7
Pole Rd HWTH BD22 .....46 B3
Pollard Av BGLY BD16 .....50 B6
  CLECK BD19 .....144 E2
Pollard Cl CLECK BD19 .....144 E2
Pollard La BFDE BD3 .....5 F2
  BRAM LS13 .....77 K5
Pollard's Flds KNOT WF11 .....155 J6
Pollard St BOW BD4 .....5 D6
  EARD/LOFT WF3 .....149 K6
  HUDN HD2 .....191 H1
  TOD OL14 .....133 H4
Pollard St South HUDW HD3 .....190 B6
Pollard Wy CLECK BD19 .....144 E2
Polperro Cl NORM WF6 .....152 A8
Pomfret Pl GFTH/SHER LS25 .....106 B3
Pond Cl HUDS HD4 .....213 F1
Ponden La HWTH BD22 .....67 C5
Ponderosa Cl RHAY LS8 .....80 B8
Pondfields Cl GFTH/SHER LS25 .....129 G2
Pondfields Crest GFTH/SHER LS25 .....129 G2
Pondfields Dr GFTH/SHER LS25 .....129 G1
Pondfields Pl GFTH/SHER LS25 .....129 G1
Pondfields Ri GFTH/SHER LS25 .....129 G2
Pond St KGHY BD21 .....3 D1
Ponker La KBTN HD8 .....236 C3
Ponker Nook La KBTN HD8 .....236 D2
Pontefract La OSM LS9 .....102 B4
Pontefract La MSTN/BAR LS15 .....127 F1
  OSM LS9 .....102 A3
Pontefract Lane OSM LS9 .....102 B4
Pontefract Rd CAS WF10 .....153 K4
  FEA/AMT WF7 .....179 H7
  FEA/AMT WF7 .....203 G3
  HEM/SK/SE WF9 .....225 F2
  HOR/CROF WF4 .....200 D1
  MID LS10 .....125 H1
  NORM WF6 .....152 C8
  PONT WF8 .....155 H7
Pontefract St OSM LS9 .....102 B4
Pontefract Ter HEM/SK/SE WF9 .....224 E5
Pontey Dr HUDE HD5 .....192 D6
Pontey Mt HUDE HD5 .....192 D6
Ponyfield Cl HUDN HD2 .....12 A1
Pool Bank Cl OT LS21 .....35 H4
Pool Bank Ct OT LS21 .....35 H5
Pool Bank New Rd BHP/TINH LS16 .....35 F7
Pool Br OT LS21 .....35 G3
Pool Ct BFDE BD3 .....5 E3
Poole Crs MSTN/BAR LS15 .....103 K2
Poole Mt MSTN/BAR LS15 .....103 K2
Poole Rd MSTN/BAR LS15 .....103 K2
Poole Sq MSTN/BAR LS15 .....103 K2
Pool Hill La KBTN HD8 .....237 G6

Pool Rd OT LS21 .....34 A3
  OT LS21 .....34 D3
Pools La BSLYN/ROY S71 .....222 C8
Pool St KGHY * BD21 .....3 F1
Popeley Rd HECK WF16 .....145 F5
Pope St KGHY BD21 .....3 E2
  NORM WF6 .....152 A6
Poplar Av CAS WF10 .....154 D4
  GFTH/SHER LS25 .....105 J4
  GTHN BD7 .....118 A1
  HOLM/MEL HD9 .....233 J2
  MSTN/BAR LS15 .....104 B1
  RPDN/SBR HX6 .....138 E6
  SHPY BD18 .....73 J6
  TOD OL14 .....133 K4
  WBY LS22 .....23 J4
  WKFDW/WTN WF2 .....174 E6
Poplar Cft BRAM LS13 .....99 K3
  ILK LS29 .....32 B3
Poplar Cl ELL * LS25 .....166 E5
Poplar Crs EARD/LOFT WF3 .....147 H2
  LUD/ILL HX2 .....115 J4
  SHPY BD18 .....73 J6
Poplar Cft BRAM LS13 .....99 J3
Poplar Dr AIRE BD20 .....49 G4
  HORS LS18 .....76 D7
  NORM WF6 .....151 K6
  SHPY BD18 .....73 J6
Poplar Gdns BRAM LS13 .....99 J3
Poplar Garth BRAM LS13 .....99 J3
Poplar Ga WOR/ARM LS12 .....99 J3
Poplar Gv BGLY BD16 .....70 E2
  CLECK BD19 .....143 K5
  GTHN BD7 .....118 A1
  KNOT WF11 .....171 J4
  PONT WF8 .....180 C3
  SHPY BD18 .....73 J6
Poplar Ri BRAM LS13 .....99 J2
  KBTN HD8 .....237 F2
Poplar Rd GTHN BD7 .....118 B1
  SHPY BD18 .....73 J6
The Poplars BHP/TINH LS16 .....55 K1
  GSLY LS20 .....53 G1
  HDGY LS6 .....78 E7
  HIPP * HX3 .....142 B1
  KNOT WF11 .....182 E1
Poplars Park Rd ECHL BD2 .....73 K7
Poplar Sq PDSY/CALV LS28 .....98 B1
Poplar St CUD/GR S72 .....240 B6
  EARD/LOFT WF3 .....149 K5
  HIPP * HX3 .....9 D3
  HUDE HD5 .....13 E5
  HUDN HD2 .....12 C1
Poplar Ter AIRE BD20 .....49 H4
  BSLYN/ROY S71 .....222 B7
  HEM/SK/SE WF9 .....242 C1
Poplar Vw AL/HA/HU * LS17 .....59 H8
  BRAM LS13 .....99 J3
  BRIC HD6 .....142 B5
  GTHN BD7 .....117 K1
Poplar Wy BRAM LS13 .....99 J3
Poplarwood Gdns IDLE BD10 .....75 G6
Popley Dr HOLM/MEL HD9 .....231 H2
Popples Dr LUD/ILL HX2 .....115 J4
Poppleton Ct EARD/LOFT WF3 .....147 K2
Poppleton Dr EARD/LOFT WF3 .....147 K2
Poppleton Ri EARD/LOFT WF3 .....147 K3
Poppleton Rd EARD/LOFT WF3 .....147 K2
Poppleton Wy EARD/LOFT WF3 .....147 K3
Popple Wells La LUD/ILL HX2 .....138 C4
Poppy Ct WBSY * BD6 .....118 A5
Porritt St CLECK * BD19 .....144 A2
Portage Av MSTN/BAR LS15 .....103 H4
Portage Crs MSTN/BAR LS15 .....103 H4
Portal Cl MIRF WF14 .....170 D3
Portal Dr MIRF WF14 .....170 D3
Portland Av PONT WF8 .....180 C2
Portland Cl HUDW * HD3 .....190 C4
Portland Crs LDSU LS2 .....7 D2
Portland Ga LDSU LS2 .....7 D2
Portland Pl BGLY BD16 .....226 C4
  HEM/SK/SE WF9 .....9 D5
  HFAX HX1 .....9 D5
Portland Rd HIPP HX3 .....9 D3
  WOR/ARM LS12 .....100 C5
Portland St HFAX * HX1 .....9 D4
  HUD HD1 .....12 B4
  HWTH BD22 .....69 F4
  LDS LS1 .....7 D3
  PDSY/CALV LS28 .....98 E4
  WBOW BD5 .....4 C5
  WKFDE WF1 .....11 F6
Portland Wy LDSU LS2 .....7 D2
Portman St PDSY/CALV LS28 .....75 K5
Portobello Gv WKFDW/WTN WF2 .....11 D6
Portobello Rd WKFDW/WTN WF2 .....11 D6
Portsmouth Av BFDE BD3 .....5 D2
Portwood St HTON BD9 .....94 D1
Post Hill Ct WOR/ARM LS12 .....99 H4
  IDLE BD10 .....74 E6
Post Office St CLECK BD19 .....144 C5
Pothouse Rd WBSY BD6 .....118 C3
Pot La AIRE BD20 .....26 D5
Potovens La WKFDW/WTN WF2 .....149 G8
Potter Av WKFDW/WTN WF2 .....175 F7
Potter Brow Rd BAIL BD17 .....51 J4
Potternewton Av CHAL LS7 .....79 H5
Potternewton Ct CHAL LS7 .....79 J5

Potternewton Crs CHAL LS7 .....79 ...
Potternewton Gdns CHAL * LS7 .....79 ...
Potternewton Hts CHAL LS7 .....79 ...
Potternewton La CHAL LS7 .....79 ...
Potternewton Mt CHAL LS7 .....79 ...
Potternewton Vw CHAL * LS7 .....79 ...
Potters Cft EARD/LOFT WF3 149
Potters Ga HOLM/MEL HD9 250
Potters Wk MAR/SLWT HD7 189
Potterton Br MSTN/BAR LS15 83
Potterton Cl MSTN/BAR LS15 83
Potterton La MSTN/BAR LS15 83
Pottery La KNOT WF11 156
  RTHW LS26 127
Pottery Rd MID LS10 101
Potts' Ter NORM WF6 177
Poulton Pl BEE/HOL LS11 101
Poverty La RPDN/SBR HX6 163
Powell Av WBOW BD5 95
Powell Rd BGLY BD16 75
  SHPY BD18 73
Powell St CAS WF10 153
  HECK WF16 145
  HEM/SK/SE WF9 225
Poxton Gv HEM/SK/SE WF9 242
Prail Cl PONT WF8 181
Pratt La MIRF WF14 170
  SHPY BD18 73
Premiere Pk ILK LS29 19
Prescott St WIL/AL BD15 9
Prescott Ter WIL/AL BD15 94
Preston La LUD/ILL HX2 139
  RTHW LS26 128
Preston Pde BEE/HOL LS11 124
Preston Pl HFAX * HX1 8
Preston St BTLY WF17 146
  EARL WF12 172
  GIR BD8 4
Preston Vw RTHW LS26 128
Prestwich Dr HUDN HD2 191
Prestwick Cl OT LS21 33
Prestwick Fold OSS WF5 173
Pretoria St CAS WF10 155
  FEA/AMT WF7 179
  MAR/SLWT HD7 210
  WKFDE WF1 11
Priest Bank Rd AIRE BD20 26
Priest Hill Gdns WBY LS22 23
Priesthorpe Av PDSY/CALV LS28 97
Priesthorpe Ct PDSY/CALV LS28 76
Priesthorpe La PDSY/CALV LS28 75
Priesthorpe Rd PDSY/CALV LS28 75
Priest La RPDN/SBR HX6 164
Priestley Av DOD/DAR S75 239
  HECK WF16 119
  WBSY BD6 118
Priestley Cl PDSY/CALV LS28 98
Priestley Ct PDSY/CALV LS28 98
Priestley Dr PDSY/CALV LS28 98
Priestley Gdns HECK WF16 145
  PDSY/CALV LS28 98
Priestley Gv HUDS HD4 213
Priestley Pl RPDN/SBR HX6 138
Priestley Sq BTLY WF17 145
Priestley St BFD BD1 5
  CUL/QBY BD13 116
Priestley Ter WBSY BD6 118
Priestley Vw PDSY/CALV LS28 98
Priestley Wk PDSY/CALV LS28 98
Priestman Cl GIR BD8 4
Priestman St GIR BD8 4
Priestthorpe Cl BGLY BD16 50
Priestthorpe La BGLY BD16 50
Priestthorpe Rd BGLY BD16 50
Primitive St EARD/LOFT WF3 126
Primley Gdns AL/HA/HU LS17 57
Primley Park Av AL/HA/HU LS17 57
Primley Park Cl AL/HA/HU LS17 57
Primley Park Crs AL/HA/HU LS17 57
Primley Park Dr AL/HA/HU LS17 57
Primley Park Garth AL/HA/HU LS17 57
Primley Park Gn AL/HA/HU LS17 57
Primley Park La AL/HA/HU LS17 57
Primley Park Mt AL/HA/HU LS17 57
Primley Park Ri AL/HA/HU LS17 57
Primley Park Rd AL/HA/HU LS17 57
Primley Park Vw AL/HA/HU LS17 57
Primley Park Wk AL/HA/HU LS17 57
Primley Park Wy AL/HA/HU LS17 57
Primrose Av MSTN/BAR LS15 103
  RTHW LS26 128
Primrose Bank BGLY BD16 50
Primrose Cl MSTN/BAR LS15 103
  PONT WF8 180
Primrose Ct AL/HA/HU * LS17 57
Primrose Crs MSTN/BAR LS15 103
Primrose Dene KNOT WF11 156
Primrose Dr BGLY BD16 50
  CAS WF10 153
  MSTN/BAR LS15 103
Primrose Gdns BTLY WF17 146
  MSTN/BAR LS15 103
Primrose Garth MSTN/BAR LS15 103
Primrose Gv HUDS HD4 19
  KGHY BD21 3
Primrose Hl BTLY WF17 14

...NOT WF11 ....156 D6
...DSY/CALV LS28 ....98 C2
...nrose Hill Cl RTHW LS26 ....128 A2
...nrose Hill Dr RTHW LS26 ....128 A2
...nrose Hill Gn RTHW LS26 ....128 A3
...nrose Hill La HUDS HD4.....................12 C6
...nrose La BEE/HOL LS11 ....101 J8
...BGLY BD16..72 B2
...BSPA/BRAM LS23 ....42 C4
...TCHL BD2 ....73 K7
...OR/CROF WF4 ....197 K5
...BTN HD8 ....215 F3
...VSG WF15 ....144 C7
...MIRF WF14 ....171 F4
...MSTN/BAR LS15 ....103 H4
...nrose Rd MSTN/BAR LS15 ....103 J3
...nrose St GIR BD8 ....4 A3
...HUDS HD4 ....12 C6
...GHY BD21 ....3 F3
...nrose V KNOT WF11 ....156 D7
...nrose Wk MOR LS27 ....123 H3
...nrose Wy HIPP HX3 ....117 J4
...nce Edward La WOR/ARM LS12 ....100 A7
...nce Edward Rd WOR/ARM LS12 ...100 A7
...nce Henry Rd OT LS21....................33 J2
...nceroyd Wy GTHN BD7 ....95 G4
...nce's Av BEE/HOL LS11 ....80 D4
...nce's Ct AL/HA/HU * LS17.............79 J2
...nce's Crs ECHL BD2 ....74 A8
...nce's Ga HIPP HX3 ....140 A7
...nce's Gv HDGY LS6 ....78 D6
...nces Alexandra Wk HUD * HD1 ....135 J3
...ncess Av EARL WF12 ....173 F3
...HEM/SK/SE WF9 ....242 B1
...ncess Cl EARL WF12 ....173 F3
...ncess Ct AL/HA/HU LS17 ....57 K8
...ORM WF6 ....178 D2
...ncess Crs EARL WF12 ....173 F4
...ncess Flds MSTN/BAR LS15 ....104 B5
...ncess La EARL WF12 ....173 F3
...ncess Sq LDS LS1 ....7 D4
...ncess Rd EARL WF12 ....173 F3
...LK LS29 ....20 A8
...ncess St BRIG HD6 ....168 C1
...TLY WF17 ....146 B5
...AS WF10 ....155 K2
...UD/GR S72 ....240 A5
...ARL WF12 ....173 F3
...TL/HWG HX4 ....166 C4
...FAX * HX1 ....9 D4
...UD HD1 ....12 C5
...ORM WF6 ....178 A1
...PDN/SBR HX6 ....139 F7
...WKFDE WF1 ....149 J7
...WKFDE WF1 ....199 F1
...EA LS19 ....53 J7
...nces Wy BFD BD1 ....4 C5
...nceville Rd GTHN BD7 ....95 G4
...nceville St GTHN BD7 ....95 H4
...nce Wood La HUDN HD2 ....190 C1
...ordale Rd FEA/AMT WF7 ....179 G7
...or's La SKP/SMBR BD23 ....14 B4
...ors Ter GTL/HWG * HX4 ....165 J7
...or St BGLY BD21 ....3 F2
...MIRF WF14 ....170 B5
...ORM WF6 ....151 J7
...SS WF5 ....173 J7
...BY LS22 ....23 K5
...ory Cl GIR BD8 ....4 B3
...ory Gv BGLY BD16 ....50 A7
...ory Ms EARD/LOFT WF3 ....150 C5
...ory Pl HUDN HD2 ....169 G6
...ory Rd BRIG HD6 ....168 D2
...EA/AMT WF7 ....179 H7
...ory Sq WKFDW/WTN WF2 ....199 J4
...ory Wk MIRF WF14 ....170 B5
...ory Wy MIRF WF14 ....170 B5
...llege St WOR/ARM LS12 ....100 B5
...ctor St BOW BD4 ....120 A2
...d Ga BAIL * BD17 ....73 F1
...d La BAIL * BD17 ....72 F1
...gress Av BGLY BD16 ....50 A7
...spect Av BRAM LS13 ....77 G8
...JD/ILL HX2 ....139 H7
...ORM WF6 ....152 A8
...DSY/CALV LS28 ....98 B3
...HPY BD18 ....73 J4
...spect Bank BSPA/BRAM LS23 ....42 D8
...spect Cl LUD/ILL HX2 ....139 H7
...HPY BD18 ....73 J4
...spect Crs LUD/ILL HX2 ....138 E3
...ID LS10 ....124 E1
...spect Dr HWTH BD22 ....47 G6
...spect Gdns MSTN/BAR LS15 ....103 J3
...spect Gv PDSY/CALV LS28 ....98 B3

SHPY BD18 ....73 J4
Prospect La BIRK/DRI BD11 ....120 E6
Prospect Mt HWTH BD22 ....47 G6
SHPY BD18 ....73 J4
Prospect Pl BRIG HD6 ....168 B1
EARD/LOFT WF3 ....149 J1
ECHL BD2 ....96 E1
HORS LS18 ....77 F3
HTON BD9 ....95 F2
LUD/ILL HX2 ....115 J8
RPDN/SBR * HX6 ....138 A8
RTHW LS26 ....126 C7
Prospect Rd BFDE BD3 ....5 D3
BGLY BD16 ....50 C6
CLECK BD19 ....144 A3
HECK WF16 ....145 F5
HUDW HD3 ....189 K5
ILK LS29 ....32 B3
LVSG WF15 ....170 A1
OSS WF5 ....173 J6
Prospect Sq PDSY/CALV LS28 ....98 B1
Prospect St BOW BD4 ....5 D6
BTLY * WF17 ....146 B5
CLECK BD19 ....144 A4
CUL/QBY * BD13 ....93 J5
HIPP HX3 ....9 E3
HOR/CROF WF4 ....197 J3
HUD HD1 ....12 B1
HWTH BD22 ....2 A4
HWTH BD22 ....68 E5
IDLE BD10 ....74 E6
PDSY/CALV LS28 ....76 B8
PDSY/CALV * LS28 ....98 A3
SHPY BD18 ....73 J4
WBSY BD6 ....118 A4
YEA LS19 ....54 A8
Prospect Ter BRAM LS13 ....77 G8
CLECK BD19 ....144 A3
GFTH/SHER LS25 ....107 G5
HBR * HX7 ....111 K8
LVSG WF15 ....144 D7
RTHW LS26 ....126 C7
WIL/AL BD15 ....94 C2
Prospect Vw BRAM LS13 ....77 G8
LVSG WF15 ....170 A1
Prospect Wk SHPY BD18 ....73 J4
Prosper St MID LS10 ....102 A7
Providence Av BAIL BD17 ....51 J7
HDGY LS6...79 G8
Providence Ct MOR * LS27 ....123 F6
Providence Crs HWTH BD22 ....68 E1
Providence Gn PONT WF8 ....155 F6
Providence La HWTH BD22 ....68 E1
Providence Pl BRIG * HD6 ....168 D2
GFTH/SHER LS25 ....105 J4
LDSU LS2 ....14 C2
PDSY/CALV * LS28 ....98 C2
RTHW LS26 ....129 G8
Providence Rd HDGY LS6 ....79 G8
Providence Rw BAIL BD17 ....51 J7
LUD/ILL HX2 ....115 J8
Providence St BFD BD1 ....4 B4
BTLY WF17 ....146 B6
CLECK * BD19 ....143 F3
CLECK * BD19 ....144 B3
EARL WF12 ....172 E4
ELL HX5 ....166 E4
OSM LS9 ....102 A4
PDSY/CALV LS28 ....98 B1
TOD OL14..159 K4
WKFDE WF1 ....10 C2
Providence Ter CUL/QBY BD13............93 H5
LDSU * LS2 ....9 K1
Providential St HOR/CROF WF4 ....195 F8
Prune Park La WIL/AL BD15 ....71 J8
Pudding La TOD OL14.........................133 F1
Pudsey Rd BRAM LS13 ....99 F4
TOD OL14..132 E2
Pugneys Rd WKFDW/WTN WF2 ....198 E1
Pule Green La HIPP HX3.....................116 A8
Pullan Av ECHL BD2 ....74 E7
Pullan Dr ECHL BD2 ....74 E7
Pullan Gv ECHL BD2 ....74 E7
Pullan La BAIL BD17 ....52 E6
Pullan St WBOW BD5 ....4 B6
Pumphouse La MIRF WF14 ....170 E5
Pump La DEWS WF13 ....171 J3
EARD/LOFT WF3 ....147 K6
KBTN HD8 ....216 A4
Purbeck Ct BOW * BD4 ....120 B1
Purbeck Gv GFTH/SHER LS25 ....105 K5
Purcell Dr AIRE BD20 ....27 F2
Purley Wk WBSY BD6 ....118 C3
Purlwell Av BTLY WF17 ....146 A8
Purlwell Crs BTLY WF17 ....146 A8
Purlwell Hall Rd BTLY WF17 ....146 B8
Purlwell La BTLY WF17 ....146 A8
Purprise La HBR * HX7 ....112 E2
Purston La FEA/AMT WF7 ....203 F2
Purston Park Ct FEA/AMT WF7 ....179 J7
Pye Nest Av LUD/ILL HX2 ....159 G6
Pye Nest Ct LVSG WF15 ....144 A7
Pye Nest Dr LUD/ILL HX2 ....139 H5
Pye Nest Gdns LUD/ILL HX2 ....159 H6
Pye Nest Gv LUD/ILL HX2 ....139 H5
Pye Nest Ri LUD/ILL HX2 ....139 H7
Pye Nest Rd RPDN/SBR HX6 ....139 G5
Pyenot Av CLECK BD19 ....144 B5
Pyenot Dr CLECK BD19 ....144 B5

Pyenot Gdns CLECK BD19 ....144 B5
Pyenot Hall La CLECK BD19 ....144 B4
Pymont Ct EARD/LOFT WF3 ....149 K2
Pymont Dr RTHW LS26 ....126 E4
Pymont Gv RTHW LS26 ....126 E4
Pymroyd La HUDS HD4 ....190 A8
Pym St MID LS10...................................7 F6
Pynate Rd BTLY WF17 ....145 K5
Pyrah Rd LM/WK BD12 ....118 E4
Pyrah St DEWS WF13 ....172 B2
LM/WK BD12..118 E7

Q

Quail St KGHY BD21...............................3 E2
Quaker La HUD HD1 ....12 A5
LVSG WF15 ....144 A6
WBOW BD5 ....95 H8
Quakers La RPDN/SBR HX6 ....187 F1
YEA LS19 ....53 K6
Quarmby Cft HUDW HD3 ....190 A4
Quarmby Rd HUDW HD3 ....190 B5
Quarrie Dene Ct CHAL * LS7...............79 J5
The Quarry AL/HA/HU LS17 ....57 C5
Quarry Av KNOT WF11 ....156 D8
Quarry Bank Ct KSTL LS5 ....77 K5
Quarry Cl DOD/DAR S75 ....239 K3
HOLM/MEL HD9 ....233 J1
Quarry Ct CAS WF10 ....153 J5
HUDW HD3 ....189 K4
Quarry Dene BHP/TINH LS16...............78 C3
Quarrydene Dr CAS WF10 ....154 C5
Quarry Dene Pk BHP/TINH LS16.........78 C3
Quarry Dr HUDE HD5 ....192 D5
Quarry Farm Rd OT LS21......................34 E6
Quarryfields MIRF WF14 ....170 E4
Quarry Gdns AL/HA/HU LS17...............57 G5
Quarry Hl HOR/CROF WF4 ....197 F2
HUDE HD5 ....192 D7
OSM LS9 ....7 F3
RPDN/SBR HX6.....................................138 E8
RTHW LS26 ....127 F5
Quarry Hill La WBY LS22 ....23 H5
Quarry La BTLY WF17 ....145 J2
HEM/SK/SE WF9 ....226 C3
HUDE HD5 ....192 D5
HUDS HD4 ....212 C4
MOR LS27 ....147 F4
MOR LS27 ....147 C1
Quarry Mt HDGY LS6.............................79 G7
HOR/CROF WF4 ....223 F2
Quarry Mount Pl HDGY LS6.................79 G7
Quarry Mount St HDGY LS6.................79 G7
Quarry Mount Ter HDGY * LS6 ....79 G7
Quarry Pl ECHL BD2 ....5 F1
HDGY LS6..79 G8
MIRF WF14 ....170 A5
Quarry Rd CLECK BD19 ....143 K4
CLECK BD19 ....144 E4
DEWS WF13 ....172 A4
HIPP HX3 ....139 H1
HUD HD1 ....12 A4
HUDS HD4 ....190 B8
LVSG WF15 ....144 D7
OT LS21..34 E6
RTHW LS26 ....127 G5
Quarryside Rd MIRF WF14 ....170 B5
Quarry St FEA/AMT WF7 ....203 F6
HDGY LS6..79 G8
HTON BD9 ....73 G7
KGHY BD21 ....3 E3
WHIT OL12...158 B6
Quarry Vw DEWS WF13 ....171 J2
Quayside BAIL BD17 ....73 H3
Quay St HUD HD1 ....13 D4
Quebec St ELL HX5 ....167 F5
KGHY BD21 ....2 C4
LDS LS1 ....7 D3
TOD * OL14...159 K2
WKFDW/WTN WF2 ....10 B3
Queen Elizabeth Dr NORM WF6 ....177 K3
Queen Elizabeth Gdns HUD HD1 ....12 B4
Queen Elizabeth Gv WKFDE WF1 ....11 E2
Queen Elizabeth Rd WKFDE WF1 ....11 E2
Queen Elizabeth St WKFDE WF1 ....149 H7
Queen Margarets Av KNOT WF11 ....156 A3
Queen Margarets Cl KNOT * WF11 .....156 A3
Queen Margarets Dr KNOT WF11 ....156 A3
Queens Ar LDS LS1 ....7 E3
Queen's Av ECHL BD2 ....74 B8
PONT WF8 ....180 B4
Queensbury Av WKFDE WF1 ....149 K6
Queensbury Ct NORM WF6 ....178 B2
Queensbury Rd HIPP HX3 ....116 A6
Queensbury Sq CUL/QBY * BD13 ......116 D2
Queens Cl BGLY BD16 ....72 B1
CHAL LS7 ....79 J5
Queenscourt MOR * LS27 ....125 F7
Queen's Crs HOR/CROF WF4 ....178 B7
OSS WF5 ....173 J6
Queen's Dr CUD/GR S72 ....223 F8
EARD/LOFT WF3 ....126 A3
HIPP HX3 ....141 F7
ILK LS29 ....19 K8
OSS WF5 ....173 K7
PDSY/CALV LS28 ....98 B3

WKFDW/WTN WF2.....................175 F2
Queens Drive Cl OSS WF5.............174 A7
Queen's Drive La ILK LS29............19 K8
Queen's Gdns ILK LS29.................20 A8
OSS WF5..............................173 J6
Queen's Ga HIPP HX3.................140 A7
Queensgate BFD * BD1..................4 C4
HUD HD1..............................13 D5
Queens Gv KGHY BD21...................2 C5
MOR LS27............................122 E8
Queenshill Av AL/HA/HU LS17..........57 J8
Queenshill Cl AL/HA/HU * LS17........79 J1
Queenshill Crs AL/HA/HU LS17.........79 J1
Queenshill Crs AL/HA/HU LS17.........57 J8
Queenshill Dr AL/HA/HU LS17..........79 J1
Queenshill Gdns AL/HA/HU LS17........79 H1
Queenshill Garth AL/HA/HU LS17.......79 J1
Queenshill Rd AL/HA/HU LS17..........79 J1
Queenshill Vw AL/HA/HU LS17..........79 J1
Queenshill Wk AL/HA/HU LS17..........79 J1
Queenshill Wy AL/HA/HU LS17..........79 J1
Queens Md HIPP * HX3.................117 F8
Queens Mill Rd HUD HD1...............12 C6
Queens Park Cl CAS WF10.............154 C3
Queen's Park Dr CAS WF10............154 B4
Queen's Pr MOR LS27.................123 F7
OT LS21..............................33 J4
SHPY BD18............................73 F3
Queen's Prom MOR LS27...............123 F7
Queen's Ct LDS LS1....................7 E4
Queens Sq HUD HD1....................13 F1
PONT WF8............................180 B4
SHPY BD18............................73 F3
Queens Ter OSS WF5..................173 J6
Queensthorpe Av BRAM LS13............99 H3
Queensthorpe Cl BRAM LS13............99 J3
Queensthorpe Ri BRAM LS13............99 H3
Queen St AIRE BD20...................26 E6
AIRE BD20............................27 G2
BAIL BD17............................73 J2
BGLY BD16............................49 K8
CAS WF10............................153 K2
CLECK BD19..........................144 B5
CLECK BD19..........................144 E1
DEWS WF13..........................171 H5
EARD/LOFT WF3.......................126 A8
EARD/LOFT WF3.......................148 E3
EARL WF12...........................175 F3
GTL/HWG HX4.........................166 B5
HBR * HX7...........................137 F3
HECK WF16...........................145 F8
HEM/SK/SE WF9.......................242 B1
HOR/CROF WF4........................197 G2
HUD HD1.............................13 D4
IDLE BD10...........................75 F4
KBTN HD8............................236 E1
LDS LS1..............................6 C4
MID LS10...........................125 H1
MIRF WF14...........................170 D7
MOR LS27...........................122 E8
NORM WF6............................177 K1
OSS WF5............................173 J6
PONT WF8...........................180 C3
RPDN/SBR HX6........................138 B8
RTHW LS26..........................128 C5
STKB/PEN S36.......................252 D8
TOD OL14...........................134 A6
WBSY BD6...........................117 K4
WIL/AL BD15........................71 C7
WKFDE WF1..........................10 C5
WKFDE WF1..........................149 J7
YEA LS19...........................53 K7
Queen St South HUD * HD1............13 D5
Queens Vw SCFT * LS14...............81 K6
Queen's Wk OSS WF5.................174 A6
Queens Wy KBTN HD8.................215 J6
Queensway BGLY BD16.................72 B1
BSLYN/ROY S71......................222 A7
GFTH/SHER LS25....................105 H4
GSLY LS20..........................53 H2
HFAX HX1............................8 A3
MOR LS27...........................122 E8
MSTN/BAR LS15.....................104 A3
PONT WF8...........................155 G3
RTHW LS26..........................126 B5
Queenswood Cl HDGY LS6.............78 A4
Queenswood Ct HDGY LS6............78 A4
Queenswood Dr HDGY LS6............78 A5
Queenswood Gdns HDGY LS6..........78 C7
Queenswood Gn HDGY LS6............78 A4
Queenswood Hts HDGY LS6...........78 B6
Queenswood Mt HDGY LS6............78 B6
Queenswood Ri HDGY LS6...........78 B7
Queenswood Rd HDGY LS6...........78 B6

Queen Victoria Crs HIPP HX3........117 G8
Queen Victoria St LDS LS1...........7 E3
Quincy Cl ECHL BD2.................74 E7

R

Raby Pk WBY LS22....................23 H6
Raby St CHAL LS7....................79 K8
Racca Av KNOT WF11................156 E7
Racca Gn KNOT WF11................156 D7
Race Moor La HWTH BD22.............46 D8
Rachael St HOR/CROF WF4...........197 F2
Racton St MAR/SLWT HD7.............210 D2
Radcliffe Av ECHL BD2..............74 C4
Radcliffe Gdns PDSY/CALV LS28......98 C4
Radcliffe La LUD/ILL HX2..........137 K1
PDSY/CALV LS28.....................98 C4
Radcliffe Pl WKFDE WF1.............10 C3
Radcliffe Rd HUDS HD4..............190 B7
MAR/SLWT HD7......................210 E2
WKFDW/WTN WF2.....................174 E7
Radcliffe St KBTN HD8.............236 D1
Radfield Dr WBSY BD6..............119 F3
Radford Park Av HEM/SK/SE WF9.....241 H2
Radnor St BFDE BD3.................96 E4
WOR/ARM LS12.......................6 A5
Radwell Dr WBOW BD5................4 C6
Raeburn Dr WBSY BD6..............118 B4
Rae Rd WBSY BD6....................73 G5
Rafborn Av HUDW HD3...............189 J2
Raglan Av HWTH BD22................2 A4
Raglan Cl CAS WF10................155 F3
Raglan Ct HFAX * HX1................8 B4
Raglan Rd HDGY LS6.................79 G8
Raglan St BFDE BD3.................97 F4
CUL/QBY BD13......................116 D2
HFAX HX1............................8 B4
HWTH BD22...........................2 A4
TOD OL14...........................134 A6
Raglan Ter BFDE BD3................97 G4
Raikes La BOW BD4.................120 B4
BOW BD4............................120 D1
BTLY WF17..........................145 H1
Raikes Wood Dr BOW BD4...........120 B4
Railes Cl LUD/ILL HX2.............138 A2
Railgate BCUP OL13................158 A2
Railsfield Mt BRAM LS13...........99 G1
Railsfield Ri BRAM LS13...........99 G2
Railsfield Wy BRAM LS13...........99 G1
Railway Ter BOW BD4...............120 B4
BRIG HD6...........................168 C2
CLECK BD19........................144 A4
DEWS WF13.........................171 J5
EARL WF12.........................172 C3
HECK WF16.........................145 G4
HUD HD1............................12 C4
KGHY * BD21.........................3 D1
TOD OL14...........................134 A5
Railway Ter EARD/LOFT WF3........148 D2
HEM/SK/SE WF9.....................202 A8
HIPP HX3..........................165 K1
NORM WF6..........................177 K1
Railway Vw CAS WF10..............153 G4
Rainbow Ms WBSY * BD6............118 A5
Raincliffe Gv OSM LS9............102 C3
Raincliffe Mt OSM * LS9..........102 C4
Raincliffe Rd OSM LS9...........102 C3
Raincliffe St OSM LS9...........102 C3
Raincliffe Ter OSM * LS9.........102 C4
Rainsborough Av KNOT WF11.........155 K8
Raistrick Av SHPY BD18............73 K3
Rake HBR HX7......................136 A3
Rake Head Barn La TOD OL14.......159 K3
Rake Head Rd HOLM/MEL HD9........246 D4
Rakehill Rd MSTN/BAR LS15.........82 D4
Raleigh St HFAX * HX1...............8 A6
Rampart Rd HDGY LS6...............79 G8
Ramsden Av GTHN BD7...............94 B7
Ramsden Cl KNOT WF11.............155 K3
Ramsden Ct GTHN BD7...............95 G7
Ramsden La TOD OL14..............159 H4
Ramsden Mill Bottom
MAR/SLWT * HD7....................189 K8
Ramsden Mill La MAR/SLWT HD7......189 J8
Ramsden Pl CLAY BD14..............94 B6
Ramsden Rd HOLM/MEL HD9..........247 G4
Ramsden St CAS WF10..............153 H6
GFTH/SHER LS25....................128 C3
HIPP HX3..........................139 H1
MAR/SLWT HD7.....................189 J7
TOD OL14..........................159 H4
Ramsden Wood Rd TOD OL14........159 J4
Ramsey Crs HOR/CROF WF4..........196 B4
Ramsey Rd HOR/CROF WF4..........196 A4
Ramsey St WBOW BD5................95 K8
Ramsey Vw HOR/CROF WF4..........196 A4
Ramsgate EARD/LOFT WF3...........149 J2
Ramsgate Crs EARD/LOFT WF3.......149 J2
Ramsgate St HFAX HX1...............8 A3
Ramshead Ap SCFT LS14.............81 J5
Ramshead Cl SCFT LS14.............81 J4
Ramshead Crs SCFT LS14............81 H4

Ramshead Dr SCFT LS14.............81
Ramshead Gdns SCFT LS14..........81
Ramshead Gv SCFT LS14............81
Ramshead Hl SCFT LS14............81
Ramshead Pl SCFT LS14............81
Ramshead Vw SCFT LS14............81
Randall Pl HTON BD9...............73
Randolph St BFDE BD3..............97
BRAM LS13..........................98
HIPP HX3............................9
Random Cl HWTH BD22................2
Rand Pl GTHN BD7...................4
Rand St GTHN BD7...................4
Ranelagh Av IDLE BD10.............75
Range Bank HIPP HX3................9
Range Bank Top HIPP HX3............9
Range Ct HIPP HX3..................9
Range Gdns HIPP HX3................9
Range La HIPP HX3..................9
Range St HIPP HX3..................9
Ransdale Dr WBOW BD5.............95
Ransdale Gv WBOW BD5.............95
Ransdale Rd WBOW BD5............95
Ranter's Fold HOR/CROF WF4......197
Raper Vw GFTH/SHER LS25..........84
Rapes Hwy UPML OL3...............207
Rashcliffe Hill Rd HUD HD1........12
Rastrick Common BRIG HD6........168
Rathlin Rd EARL WF12.............172
Rathmell Rd MSTN/BAR LS15........103
Rathmell St WBOW BD5.............118
Ratten Row Rd RPDN/SBR HX6.......163
Raven Cl FEA/AMT WF7..............179
Raven La CUD/CR S72...............222
Raven Rd HDGY LS6.................78
Ravens Av DEWS WF13..............171
HUDE HD5..........................192
Ravenscar Av RHAY LS8.............80
Ravenscar Mt RHAY LS8.............80
Ravenscar Ter RHAY LS8............80
Ravenscar Vw RHAY * LS8..........80
Ravenscar Wk RHAY * LS8..........80
Ravenscliffe Av IDLE BD10........75
Ravenscliffe Rd PDSY/CALV LS28...75
Ravens Crs DEWS WF13.............171
Ravensdeane HUDW * HD3............190
Ravensfield Rd DEWS WF13.........171
Ravens Gv DEWS WF13..............171
Ravenshouse Rd DEWS WF13........171
Ravensknowle Rd HUDE HD5.........192
Ravens Lodge Ter * DEWS WF13.....171
Ravensmead FEA/AMT WF7..........180
Ravens Mt PDSY/CALV LS28.........98
Ravens St DEWS WF15.............171
Ravensthorpe Rd EARL WF12.......171
Ravenstone Dr GTL/HWG HX4.......166
Raven St BGLY BD16................50
HFAX HX1...........................8
HUD HD1...........................190
KGHY BD21..........................2
Ravensville AIRE BD20.............26
Ravens Wk DEWS WF13.............171
Ravens Wy HOLM/MEL HD9..........234
Ravenswharf Rd DEWS WF13.........171
Ravenswood GTL/HWG * HX4.........165
Ravensworth Cl MSTN/BAR LS15.....82
Ravensworth Wy MSTN/BAR LS15.....82
Raven Ter GIR BD8.................94
Rawden Hl OT LS21.................36
Rawdon Dr YEA LS19................53
Rawdon Hall Dr YEA LS19...........53
Rawdon Rd HORS LS18...............76
HWTH BD22.........................68
Rawdon St HWTH BD22................2
Raw End Rd LUD/ILL HX2...........138
Rawfield La GFTH/SHER LS25.......131
Rawfolds Av BTLY WF17............145
Rawfolds Wy CLECK BD19...........144
Rawgate Av CAS WF10..............152
Raw Hill BRIG * HD6...............167
Raw La HBR HX7....................112
LUD/ILL HX2.......................115
Rawling St KGHY BD21..............2
Rawling Wy HDGY LS6...............79
Raw Nook LM/WK BD12..............119
Raw Nook Rd HUDH HD3............189
Rawroyds GTL/HWG HX4............166
Rawson Av BFDE BD3................97
HIPP HX3..........................140
Rawson Pl BFD BD1..................5
RPDN/SBR HX6.....................138
Rawson Rd BFD * BD1................4
Rawson Sq BFD BD1..................5
IDLE BD10..........................7
Rawson St HFAX HX1...............11
LM/WK BD12........................118
Rawson St North HIPP HX3...........9
Rawson Ter BEE/HOL * LS11........10
Rawtenstall Bank HBR HX7.........111
Rawthorpe La HUDE HD5............19
Rawthorpe La HUDE HD5.............1
Rawthorpe Ter HUDE HD5............1
Rayfield WKFDW/WTN WF2...........174
Ray Ga HBR HX7....................11
HOLM/MEL HD9......................23
HUDW HD3..........................18
Raygill Cl AL/HA/HU LS17...........5
Raylands Cl MID LS10..............12
Raylands Ct MID LS10..............12

ylands Fold *MID* LS10 ....125 G5
ylands Garth *MID* LS10 ....125 G5
ylands La *MID* LS10 ....125 G5
ylands Pl *MID* LS10 ....125 G5
ylands Rd *MID* LS10 ....125 G5
ylands Wy *MID* LS10 ....125 G6
yleigh St *BOW* BD4 ....96 C7
ymond Av *CUD/GR* S72 ....240 A5
ymond Dr *WBOW* BD5 ....119 F1
ymond St *WBOW* BD5 ....119 F1
ynbron Crs *WBOW* BD5 ....119 G1
ynel Ap *BHP/TINH* LS16 ....55 K8
ynel Cl *BHP/TINH* LS16 ....55 K7
ynel Dr *BHP/TINH* LS16 ....56 A8
ynel Gdns *BHP/TINH* LS16 ....56 A7
ynel Garth *BHP/TINH* LS16 ....56 A8
ynel Gn *BHP/TINH* LS16 ....56 A8
ynel Mt *BHP/TINH* LS16 ....55 K7
ynel Wy *BHP/TINH* LS16 ....55 K7
yner Av *GIR* BD8 ....95 F2
HECK WF16 ....145 G5
yner Dr *BRIG* HD6 ....142 B7
yner Mt *WIL/AL* BD15 ....94 B3
yner Rd *BRIG* HD6 ....142 B7
yners Av *LVSG* WF15 ....143 K7
yner St *HOR/CROF* WF4 ....197 G2
ynham Crs *HWTH* BD22 ....47 G3
ynor Cl *HUDW* HD3 ....190 C4
ynville Ap *BRAM* LS13 ....99 J1
ynville Av *BRAM* LS13 ....77 K8
ynville Crs *WOR/ARM* LS12 ....99 K1
ynville Dr *BRAM* LS13 ....77 J8
ynville Gv *BRAM* LS13 ....77 J8
ynville Mt *BRAM* LS13 ....77 J8
ynville Pl *WOR/ARM* LS12 ....77 J8
ynville Ri *BRAM* LS13 ....99 J1
ynville Rd *WOR/ARM* LS12 ....77 K8
ynville St *BRAM* LS13 ....77 J8
ynville Ter *BRAM* LS13 ....77 J8
ynville Wk *BRAM* LS13 ....99 J1
y St *HUD* HD1 ....13 D3
ywood Cl *YEA* LS19 ....53 J3
ap Hirst Rd *HUDN* HD2 ....190 D1
becca St *GIR* BD8 ....4 B3
creation Crs *BEE/HOL* LS11 ....101 F7
creation Gv *BEE/HOL* LS11 ....101 F7
creation La *ELL* HX5 ....106 D5
creation Mt *BEE/HOL* LS11 ....101 F7
creation Pl *BEE/HOL* LS11 ....101 F7
creation Rd *RPDN/SBR* HX6 ....138 C2
creation Rw *BEE/HOL* LS11 ....101 F7
creation St *BEE/HOL* LS11 ....101 F7
creation Ter *BEE/HOL* LS11 ....101 F7
creation Vw *BEE/HOL* LS11 ....101 F7
ctory Cl *GFTH/SHER* LS25 ....105 K4
MAR/SLWT HD7 ....209 H7
HUDE HD5 ....192 D4
ctory Cdn *KBTN* HD8 ....217 H4
ctory La *KBTN* HD8 ....217 H4
ctory Rw *KGHY* BD21 ....2 C3
ctory St *CAS* WF10 ....153 J3
ctory Vw *EARL* WF12 ....172 D8
d Beck Rd *HIPP* HX3 ....140 C2
d Beck V *SHPY* BD18 ....73 G6
d Brink La *RPDN/SBR* HX6 ....163 J1
dburn Av *SHPY* BD18 ....73 G6
dburn Dr *SHPY* BD18 ....73 G6
dburn Rd *SHPY* BD18 ....73 G6
dcar La *AIRE* BD20 ....48 D1
dcar Rd *IDLE* BD10 ....75 G5
dcliffe Av *KGHY* BD21 ....2 B3
dcliffe Gv *KGHY* BD21 ....2 B3
dcliffe St *KGHY* BD21 ....2 C3
d Deer Park La *HOR/CROF* WF4 .....194 C6
ddisher Rd *MAR/SLWT* HD7 ....209 G7
d Doles La *HUD* HD1 ....13 E1
d Doles St *HUDN* HD3 ....191 J1
ddyshore Scout Ga *TOD* OL14 ......160 A6
ddesdale Gdns *HECK* WF16 ....56 B8
dfearn Av *HECK* WF16 ....145 G6
d Hall Av *SCFT* LS14 ....81 J2
d Hall Av *AL/HA/HU* LS17 ....81 H2
d Hall Cl *BEE/HOL* LS11 ....123 K2
d Hall Ct *SCFT* LS14 ....81 J3
dhall Crs *BEE/HOL* LS11 ....123 K2
d Hall Ctft *SCFT* LS14 ....81 J3
d Hall Dr *SCFT* LS14 ....81 J3
d Hall Gdns *AL/HA/HU* LS17 ....81 H2
d Hall Garth *SCFT* LS14 ....81 J2
dhall Ga *BEE/HOL* LS11 ....123 K2
d Hall Gn *SCFT* LS14 ....81 J2
d Hall La *AL/HA/HU* LS17 ....81 H2
WKFDE WF1 ....175 H2
d Hall Vw *SCFT* LS14 ....81 J2
d Hall Wk *SCFT* LS14 ....81 J2
d Hall Wy *SCFT* LS14 ....81 J2
dhill Av *CAS* WF10 ....154 A5
ARD/LOFT WF3 ....147 K6
dhill Crs *EARD/LOFT* WF3 ....147 K6
dhill Dr *CAS* WF10 ....154 B4
ARD/LOFT WF3 ....147 K6
dhill Gdns *CAS* WF10 ....154 B5
dhill La *GFTH/SHER* LS25 ....131 K2
dhill Mt *CAS* WF10 ....154 B4

Redhill Rd *CAS* WF10 ....154 B4
Redhill Vw *CAS* WF10 ....154 B5
Redhouse La *CHAL* * LS7 ....80 A4
Red Laithes La *DEWS* WF13 ....171 H5
Redland Crs *HEM/SK/SE* WF9 ....224 B1
Redland Dr *KBTN* HD8 ....215 G4
Red La *FEA/AMT* WF7 ....178 D6
HOLM/MEL HD9 ....230 E1
PDSY/CALV LS28 ....76 A8
WKFDE WF1 ....177 H6
Red Lodge Cl *RHAY* LS8 ....81 F7
Redman Garth *HWTH* BD22 ....68 D4
Redmayne Gv *KNOT* WF11 ....156 A7
Redmire Ct *SCFT* LS14 ....81 J7
Redmire Dr *SCFT* LS14 ....81 J7
Redmire St *BFDE* BD3 ....97 G4
Redmire Vw *SCFT* LS14 ....81 J7
Redruth Dr *NORM* WF6 ....152 A8
Redshaw Rd *WOR/ARM* LS12 ....100 D5
Redthorne Wy *CUD/GR* S72 ....223 F8
Red V *CLECK* BD19 ....144 E1
Redvers Cl *BHP/TINH* LS16 ....78 A2
Redwood Av *BSLYN/ROY* S71 ....222 A4
EARD/LOFT WF3 ....148 B3
Redwood Cl *KGHY* BD21 ....3 F5
RTHW LS26 ....127 H5
Redwood Dr *HUDN* HD2 ....168 E6
Redwood Gv *HOR/CROF* WF4 ....178 B7
HUDE HD5 ....13 F4
Redwood Wy *YEA* LS19 ....53 H4
Reedling St *MOR* LS27 ....123 H8
Reed Rd *WOR/ARM* LS12 ....100 D4
Reedsdale Av *MOR* LS27 ....122 B4
Reedsdale Dr *MOR* LS27 ....122 B4
Reedsdale Gdns *MOR* LS27 ....122 B4
Reed St *HUD* HD1 ....190 D4
Rees Wy *BFDE* BD3 ....5 D3
Reeth Rd *BRIG* HD6 ....167 K3
Reevy Av *WBSY* BD6 ....118 A3
Reevy Crs *WBSY* BD6 ....117 K4
Reevy Dr *WBSY* BD6 ....118 B3
Reevylands Dr *WBSY* BD6 ....118 A3
Reevy Rd *WBSY* BD6 ....118 B3
Reevy Rd West *WBSY* BD6 ....117 K3
Reevy St *WBSY* BD6 ....118 B2
Reform St *CLECK* BD19 ....144 E2
Regal Ar *HUDE* * HD5 ....13 F4
Regal Cl *RPDN/SBR* HX6 ....186 E2
Regal Dr *RPDN/SBR* HX6 ....186 E2
Regency Cl *GIR* BD8 ....95 G3
HDGY LS6 ....78 E7
ILK LS29 ....20 A8
Regency Gdns *EARD/LOFT* WF3 ......148 B3
Regency Park Gv *PDSY/CALV* LS28 ..98 C6
Regency Park Rd *PDSY/CALV* LS28 ..98 C6
Regency Pk *MIRF* WF14 ....170 D7
Regency Vw *BFDE* BD3 ....5 E1
Regent Av *HORS* LS18 ....77 G4
Regent Cl *BRIG* HD6 ....167 K5
Regent Ct *LDS* * LS1 ....7 L4
Regent Crs *CUD/GR* S72 ....223 J6
HORS LS18 ....77 F4
Regent Ms *BTLY* WF17 ....146 E7
Regent Pde *RPDN/SBR* * HX6 ....139 F7
Regent Park Cross Av *HDGY* LS6 ...79 F7
Regent Park Ter *HDGY* LS6 ....79 F7
Regent Pl *HBR* HX7 ....112 B8
IDLE BD10 ....74 C2
RPDN/SBR HX6 ....138 E6
dburn Rd *HORS* LS18 ....77 F4
HUDE HD5 ....192 E1
HUDW HD3 ....12 A3
ILK LS29 ....20 A7
Regents Pk *WKFDE* WF1 ....11 E3
Regent St *CAS* WF10 ....153 H4
CHAL LS7 ....79 J4
CUD/GR S72 ....223 J6
CUL/QBY BD13 ....116 E2
FEA/AMT WF7 ....179 J6
HBR HX7 ....112 B8
HEM/SK/SE WF9 ....145 F8
HEM/SK/SE WF9 ....226 A8
HFAX HX1 ....8 C5
HOR/CROF WF4 ....197 F2
IDLE BD10 ....74 C2
IDLE * BD10 ....75 F4
MIRF WF14 ....170 D8
NORM WF6 ....152 B8
OSM LS9 ....7 F3
TOD * OL14 ....159 K2
Regent Ter *HDGY* LS6 ....8 B1
Regina Dr *CHAL* LS7 ....79 K5
HOR/CROF WF4 ....223 G2
Regina Dr *CHAL* LS7 ....79 K5
Reginald Mt *CHAL* LS7 ....79 K7
Reginald Pl *CHAL* LS7 ....79 K7
Reginald Rw *CHAL* LS7 ....79 K7
Reginald St *CHAL* LS7 ....79 K7
WBOW BD5 ....95 K8
Reginald Ter *CHAL* LS7 ....79 K7
Reginald Vw *CHAL* LS7 ....79 K7
Reid Park Av *HOR/CROF* WF4 ....196 E2
Reighton Cft *IDLE* BD10 ....75 G5
The Rein *SCFT* LS14 ....81 H5
Rein Closet *GFTH/SHER* LS25 ......84 E3
Rein Gdns *EARD/LOFT* WF3 ....147 H3
Rein Ms *EARD/LOFT* WF3 ....147 H3
Rein Rd *BRAM* LS13 ....77 G5

EARD/LOFT WF3 ....147 H3
Reins Av *BAIL* BD17 ....73 H2
Reins Rd *BRIG* HD6 ....167 K3
Rein St *MOR* LS27 ....147 H2
Reinwood Av *HUDW* HD3 ....190 B5
RHAY LS8 ....81 F6
Reinwood Rd *HUDW* HD3 ....190 B5
Rembrandt Av *EARD/LOFT* WF3 ......148 A3
Renald La *STKB/PEN* S36 ....252 D4
Renee Cl *BOW* BD4 ....119 K3
Renfield Gv *NORM* WF6 ....152 C8
Renshaw St *IDLE* BD10 ....74 D2
Renton Av *OSLY* LS20 ....53 F2
Renton Dr *OSLY* LS20 ....53 F3
Reservoir Farm Ct
HOR/CROF * WF4 ....223 H1
Reservoir Pl *CUL/QBY* BD13 ......116 E2
Reservoir Rd *HWTH* BD22 ....68 A4
LUD/ILL HX2 ....139 H3
Reservoir Side Rd *MAR/SLWT* HD7 ..211 J4
Reservoir St *DEWS* WF13 ....171 K2
Reservoir Vw *CUL/QBY* BD13 ......93 G5
KBTN HD8 ....38 C1
Restmore Av *OSLY* LS20 ....33 F8
Retford Pl *GTHN* BD7 ....4 A6
Reuben St *LVSG* WF15 ....144 D6
Reva Cl *BGLY* BD16 ....50 B7
Reva Syke Rd *CLAY* BD14 ....94 B8
Revel Garth *KBTN* HD8 ....236 E6
Revie Rd *BEE/HOL* LS11 ....101 F8
Reydon Wk *WBSY* BD6 ....118 A2
Reyhill Gv *WBOW* BD5 ....4 C6
Reyner House Ms *WBOW* BD5 ....4 C6
Reynolds Av *GTHN* BD7 ....94 E6
Rhodes Av *HECK* WF16 ....145 G5
Rhodes Crs *PONT* WF8 ....180 E5
Rhodes Gdns *EARD/LOFT* WF3 ....149 K5
Rhode's Hill La *BSPA/BRAM* LS23 ..42 E8
Rhodesia Av *HIPP* HX3 ....140 B8
WIL/AL BD15 ....94 C3
Rhodes La *BSPA/BRAM* LS23 ....42 B5
Rhodes Pl *SHPY* BD18 ....73 H3
Rhodes St *CAS* WF10 ....153 G4
HFAX HX1 ....8 C4
LVSG WF15 ....145 F7
SHPY BD18 ....73 G3
Rhodes Ter *WOR/ARM* LS12 ....6 A5
Rhodes Wy *GIR* BD8 ....94 D2
Rhodeswy *GIR* BD8 ....94 D4
Rhondda Pl *HFAX* HX1 ....139 H4
Rhum Cl *WBSY* BD6 ....118 A5
Rhyddings Av *FEA/AMT* WF7 ....203 F6
Rhyddings Dr *FEA/AMT* WF7 ....203 F7
Rhylstone St *GTHN* BD7 ....95 F4
Rhyl St *FEA/AMT* WF7 ....179 J5
Ribblesdale Av *GFTH/SHER* LS25 ..106 B5
Ribble St *KGHY* BD21 ....3 F2
Ribbleton Gv *BFDE* BD3 ....5 E3
Ribstone St *HBR* HX7 ....137 F2
Riccall Nook *IDLE* BD10 ....75 F5
Richard Rd *DOD/DAR* S75 ....239 K3
Richardshaw La *PDSY/CALV* LS28 ...98 C2
Richardshaw Rd *PDSY/CALV* LS28 ..98 D2
Richardson Av *WBSY* BD6 ....118 D3
Richardson Crs *OSM* LS9 ....102 D4
Richardson Rd *OSM* LS9 ....102 D4
Richardson Sq *HUD* * HD1 ....12 C4
Richardson St *LM/WK* BD12 ....119 H7
Richard St *BFD* * BD1 ....5 E4
BRIG HD6 ....142 B7
WKFDE * WF1 ....10 C2
Richard Thorpe Av *MIRF* WF14 .....170 E6
Rich Ga *HOLM/MEL* HD9 ....248 A3
Richmond Av *DOD/DAR* S75 ....239 K4
HDGY LS6 ....78 E8
HUDN HD2 ....191 C1
KNOT WF11 ....155 J6
RPDN/SBR HX6 ....138 C8
Richmond Cl *BRAM* LS13 ....98 E1
HFAX HX1 ....8 C3
MOR LS27 ....123 F8
RTHW LS26 ....126 C4
Richmond Ct *HOR/CROF* WF4 ....200 E3
HUDS HD4 ....189 K8
RTHW * LS26 ....126 C4
Richmond Cft *OSM* LS9 ....102 B4
Richmondfield Av *MSTN/BAR* LS15 ..83 J5
Richmondfield Cl *MSTN/BAR* LS15 ..83 J5
Richmondfield Crs *MSTN/BAR* LS15 ..83 J5
Richmondfield Cross
MSTN/BAR LS15 ....83 J5
Richmondfield Dr *MSTN/BAR* LS15 ..83 J5
Richmondfield Garth
MSTN/BAR LS15 ....83 J4
Richmondfield Gv *MSTN/BAR* LS15 ..83 J5
Richmondfield La *MSTN/BAR* LS15 ..83 J5
Richmondfield Mt *MSTN/BAR* LS15 ..83 J5
Richmondfield Wy *MSTN/BAR* LS15 ..83 J5
Richmond Flats *HUD* * HD1 ....13 D3
Richmond Gdns *PDSY/CALV* LS28 ...98 E4
RPDN/SBR HX6 ....138 C8
Richmond Garth *OSS* WF5 ....174 A7
Richmond Green St *OSM* LS9 ......102 A4
Richmond Gv *CLECK* BD19 ....144 E1
Richmond Hill Ap *OSM* LS9 ....102 A4
Richmond Hill Cl *OSM* LS9 ....102 A4
Richmond Lea *MIRF* WF14 ....170 D5
Richmond Ms *SHPY* BD18 ....73 F3

Richmond Mt *HDGY* LS6 .....78 E8
Richmond Park Av *LVSG* WF15 .....144 D8
Richmond Pl *SHPY* BD18 .....73 F3
Richmond Rd *GTHN* BD7 .....4 A5
   HDGY 78 E7
   HECK WF16 .....145 H5
   HEM/SK/SE WF9 .....226 D4
   HFAX HX1 .....8 C3
   PDSY/CALV LS28 .....98 A1
   SHPY BD18 .....73 F3
   WKFDE WF1 .....10 B1
Richmond St *CLECK* BD19 .....144 A4
   HFAX HX1 .....8 C3
   KGHY BD21 .....2 C2
   OSM LS9 .....102 A4
   TOD * OL14 .....134 B6
Richmond Ter *OT* LS21 .....33 H4
   PDSY/CALV LS28 .....98 E4
Richmond Wy *GFTH/SHER* LS25 .....105 K6
Rickard St *WOR/ARM* LS12 .....6 B5
Ridding Ga *OT* LS21 .....33 G2
Riddings Cl *HEM/SK/SE* WF9 .....224 D6
   HUDN 168 C8
Riddings Ri *HUDN* HD2 .....168 E8
Riddings Rd *HUDN* HD2 .....169 F8
Riddlesden St *AIRE* * BD20 .....48 D2
Rider Rd *HDGY* LS6 .....79 H7
Rider St *OSM* LS9 .....102 A3
The Ridge *WBY* LS22 .....23 F8
Ridge Av *HOR/CROF* WF4 .....196 A5
Ridge Bank *TOD* OL14 .....134 A6
Ridge Cl *CSLY* LS20 .....52 E3
   HUDS HD4 .....191 G8
   KBTN HD8 .....236 E2
Ridge Crs *HOR/CROF* WF4 .....196 A5
Ridgedale Mt *PONT* WF8 .....154 D7
Ridgefield St *CAS* WF10 .....153 J4
Ridge Gv *CHAL* LS7 .....79 G7
Ridge Hl *BRIG* HD6 .....167 K2
Ridge Lea *BRIG* HD6 .....168 A2
Ridge Mt *HDGY* LS6 .....79 G7
Ridgemount Rd *AIRE* BD20 .....48 C1
Ridge Rd *GFTH/SHER* LS25 .....129 J1
   HDGY 79 H7
   HOR/CROF WF4 .....196 A4
   TOD OL14 .....134 A6
Ridgestone Av *HEM/SK/SE* WF9 .....224 E4
Ridge St *HUDS* HD4 .....191 G8
Ridge Ter *HDGY* LS6 .....78 E6
Ridge Vw *BRAM* LS13 .....99 G3
Ridge View Dr *HUDN* HD2 .....190 D1
Ridge View Gdns *IDLE* BD10 .....78 E4
Ridge View Rd *BRIG* * HD6 .....168 B2
The Ridgeway *KNOT* WF11 .....156 C8
Ridgeway *BRAM* LS13 .....99 G3
Ridgeway Av *HEM/SK/SE* WF9 .....224 E4
   CSLY LS20 .....52 D3
   HUDE HD5 .....192 A4
   SHPY BD18 .....74 A5
Ridgeway Cl *HUDE* HD5 .....192 A4
   RHAY LS8 .....80 D5
Ridgeway Dr *BTLY* WF17 .....145 K2
Ridgeway Gdns *BRIG* HD6 .....181 K8
Ridgeway Mt *HWTH* BD22 .....2 A5
The Ridgeways *MAR/SLWT* HD7 .....211 H3
Ridgeway Sq *KNOT* WF11 .....156 C8
Ridgeway Ter *HDGY* * LS6 .....79 G7
Ridgewood Cl *BAIL* BD17 .....52 A8
Riding Head La *LUD/ILL* HX2 .....138 D2
Riding Hl *HIPP* HX3 .....117 K5
Riding La *LUD/ILL* HX2 .....115 F8
The Ridings *AIRE* BD20 .....27 K8
Ridings Cl *EARD/LOFT* WF3 .....149 J5
Ridings Ct *EARD/LOFT* WF3 .....149 J5
Ridings Flds *HOLM/MEL* HD9 .....213 J8
   HOLM/MEL HD9 .....233 J1
   MAR/SLWT HD7 .....189 G7
Ridings Gdns *EARD/LOFT* WF3 .....149 J5
Ridings Ms *EARD/LOFT* WF3 .....149 J5
Ridings Rd *EARL* WF12 .....172 C3
Riding St *WOR/ARM* WF17 .....145 H5
Ridings Wy *EARD/LOFT* WF3 .....149 J5
   WBSY BD6 .....117 K3
Ridingwood Ri *KBTN* HD8 .....237 J1
Ridleys Fold *ILK* LS29 .....18 D5
Rievaulx Av *GIR* BD8 .....4 B3
Rievaulx Cl *BSPA/BRAM* LS23 .....42 C4
Rifle Flds *HUD* HD1 .....12 B4
Rigg La *FEA/AMT* WF7 .....203 J1
Rightox Rd *HOLM/MEL* HD9 .....213 J8
Rigton Ap *AL/HA/HU* LS17 .....102 A3
Rigton Bank *AL/HA/HU* LS17 .....40 B7
Rigton Cl *OSM* LS9 .....102 B3
Rigton Dr *OSM* LS9 .....102 A3
Rigton Gn *AL/HA/HU* LS17 .....40 C7
   OSM LS9 .....102 A3
Rigton Lawn *OSM* LS9 .....102 A3
Rigton Ms *OSM* * LS9 .....102 A3
Rigton St *WBOW* BD5 .....95 K8
Riley La *KBTN* HD8 .....215 G6
   LUD/ILL HX2 .....115 J3
Riley Pk *KBTN* HD8 .....215 H5
Riley St *HUDS* HD4 .....13 D6
Rillbank La *BVRD* 6 A2
Rillington Md *IDLE* BD10 .....75 F5
Rillside *KBTN* HD8 .....235 H2
Rills Md *OT* LS21 .....33 J4

Rilston St *GTHN* BD7 .....95 H5
Rimswell Holt *IDLE* BD10 .....75 G5
Ringby La *HIPP* HX3 .....116 A7
Ringby Ter *HIPP* * HX3 .....8 C1
Ring Rd Adel *BHP/TINH* LS16 .....78 E7
Ring Rd Beeston *WOR/ARM* LS12 .....100 C8
Ring Rd Beeston Pk *BEE/HOL* LS11 .....124 A5
Ring Rd Bramley *BRAM* LS13 .....99 H3
Ring Rd Cross Gates
   MSTN/BAR LS15 .....82 A8
Ring Rd Farnley *WOR/ARM* LS12 .....99 H4
Ring Rd Farsley *PDSY/CALV* LS28 .....76 A8
Ring Rd Halton *MSTN/BAR* LS15 .....104 A2
Ring Rd Horsforth *HORS* LS18 .....77 J3
Ring Rd Meanwood *BHP/TINH* LS16 .....78 E1
Ring Rd Middleton *MID* LS10 .....124 E6
Ring Rd Moortown *AL/HA/HU* LS17 .....79 G1
Ring Rd Seacroft *SCFT* LS14 .....81 J3
Ring Rd Shadwell *AL/HA/HU* LS17 .....80 E1
Ring Rd Weetwood *BHP/TINH* LS16 .....78 C2
Ring Rd West Pk *BHP/TINH* LS16 .....78 A2
Ringstone Gv *CUD/GR* S72 .....224 A8
Ringway *GFTH/SHER* LS25 .....105 H5
Ringwood Av *SCFT* LS14 .....81 H3
Ringwood Crs *SCFT* LS14 .....81 J2
Ringwood Dr *SCFT* LS14 .....81 J3
Ringwood Edge *GTL/HWG* HX4 .....166 B5
Ringwood Gdns *SCFT* LS14 .....81 J3
Ringwood Mt *SCFT* LS14 .....81 J3
Ringwood Rd *WBOW* BD5 .....95 H8
Ringwood Wy *HEM/SK/SE* WF9 .....225 H3
Rink St *BTLY* WF17 .....146 C8
Ripley Cl *NORM* WF6 .....178 A3
Ripley Ct *NORM* WF6 .....178 A3
Ripley Dr *NORM* WF6 .....152 C8
Ripley La *GSLY* LS20 .....53 C1
Ripley Rd *BOW* BD4 .....96 B7
   LVSG WF15 .....144 C7
Ripley St *AIRE* BD20 .....48 D2
   HIPP HX3 .....142 B4
   WBOW BD5 .....96 A7
   WIL/AL BD15 .....94 A1
Ripon Av *HUDN* HD2 .....191 G1
Ripon Av *EARL* WF12 .....172 E3
Ripon St *HFAX* HX1 .....139 H5
Ripon Ter *HIPP* HX3 .....8 C1
Ripponden New Bank
   RPDN/SBR HX6 .....164 B7
Ripponden Old Bank
   RPDN/SBR HX6 .....164 B7
Ripponden Old La *RPDN/SBR* HX6 .....163 H8
Ripponden Rd *LIT* OL15 .....206 D5
The Rise *HIPP* HX3 .....141 F1
   KNOT WF11 .....155 K3
   KSTL LS5 .....78 A6
   PONT WF8 .....181 F4
Risedale Av *BTLY* WF17 .....146 A1
Risedale Cl *BTLY* WF17 .....146 A1
Rise La *TOD* OL14 .....133 K6
Rishworth Av *KBTN* HD8 .....217 H5
Rishworth Cl *WKFDW/WTN* WF2 .....175 F1
Rishworth Hall Cl *RPDN/SBR* HX6 .....186 D2
Rishworthian Ct *HIPP* * HX3 .....165 K2
Rishworth Mill La *RPDN/SBR* HX6 .....187 F3
Rishworth New Rd *RPDN/SBR* HX6 .....186 D2
Rishworth St *EARL* WF12 .....172 C5
   GTL/HWG HX4 .....164 D8
   HWTH BD22 .....2 A4
   WKFDE WF1 .....10 B2
Rivadale Vw *ILK* LS29 .....20 B7
Rivelin Rd *CAS* WF10 .....153 H5
Riverdale *CLE* DN14 .....157 K4
   WBY LS22 .....23 K7
Riverdale Av *EARD/LOFT* WF3 .....176 C1
Riverdale Cl *EARD/LOFT* WF3 .....176 C1
Riverdale Crs *EARD/LOFT* WF3 .....176 C1
Riverdale Dr *EARD/LOFT* WF3 .....176 C1
Riverdale Gdns *OT* LS21 .....33 J3
Riverdale Rd *EARD/LOFT* WF3 .....176 C1
   OT LS21 .....33 J3
Riverside Est *BAIL* BD17 .....73 G3
Riverside Pk *OT* LS21 .....33 K2
Riverside Wk *ILK* LS29 .....19 K6
River St *BRIG* HD6 .....168 D2
   HWTH * BD22 .....3 F1
   KGHY BD21 .....3 F1
   TOD OL14 .....134 B6
River Vw *BSPA/BRAM* LS23 .....43 F4
   WF14 .....170 A5
River Wk *BGLY* BD16 .....49 K8
Riverwood Dr *HIPP* HX3 .....166 A1
Riviera Gdns *CHAL* LS7 .....79 J5
Rivock Av *AIRE* BD20 .....27 F5
   AIRE BD20 .....27 H8
Rivock Gv *AIRE* BD20 .....47 H1

Roach Grange Av *GFTH/SHER* LS25 106
Roaine Dr *HOLM/MEL* HD9 233
Roans Brae *IDLE* BD10 75
Robb Av *BEE/HOL* LS11 124
Robbins Ter *FEA/AMT* WF7 179
Robb St *BEE/HOL* LS11 124
Roberson Ter *CLECK* BD19 144
Robert La *HOLM/MEL* HD9 233
Roberts Av *OSM* LS9 102
Roberts Ct *OSM* LS9 102
Robertsgate *EARD/LOFT* WF3 149
Robertshaw Rd *HBR* HX7 112
Robertson Av *BRIG* HD6 168
Roberts Pl *BFD* BD7 4
   OSM LS9 102
Robert's St *CLECK* BD19 143
   HWTH BD22 46
   PDSY/CALV LS28 98
   RTHW * LS26 127
Robert St *BFDE* BD3 5
   HIPP HX3 8
   HWTH BD22 69
Robert St North *HIPP* HX3 9
Roberts Wy *WKFDW/WTN* WF2 199
Roberttown La *LVSG* WF15 170
Robin Cha *PDSY/CALV* LS28 98
Robin Cl *ECHL* BD2 5
   PONT WF8 154
Robin Dr *AIRE* BD20 26
   ECHL BD2 74
Robin Hl *BTLY* WF17 145
Robin Hood Av *BSLYN/ROY* S71 222
   DEWS WF13 145
   HEM/SK/SE WF9 224
   PDSY/CALV LS28 98
Robin Hood Crs *WKFDW/WTN* WF2 174
Robin Hood Gv *HUDN* HD2 168
Robin Hood Hl *HUDS* HD4 213
Robin Hood Rd *HUDN* HD2 168
Robin Hood St *CAS* * WF10 153
Robin Hood Wy *BRIG* HD6 169
Robin La *BSLYN/ROY* S71 222
   DEWS WF13 145
   HEM/SK/SE WF9 224
   PDSY/CALV LS28 98
Robin Rocks *HOLM/MEL* HD9 233
Robin Royd Av *MIRF* WF14 170
Robin Royd Cft *MIRF* WF14 170
Robin Royd Dr *MIRF* WF14 170
Robin Royd Garth *MIRF* * WF14 170
Robin Royd Gv *MIRF* WF14 170
Robin Royd La *MIRF* WF14 170
The Robins *ILK* LS29 126
Robin's Gv *RTHW* LS26 126
Robinson La *GTHN* BD7 95
Robinson La *GFTH/SHER* LS25 129
Robinson St *CAS* WF10 129
   PONT WF8 180
Robin St *HUD* HD1 190
   WBOW * BD5 95
Robin Wk *SHPY* BD18 73
Robson Cl *PONT* WF8 180
Robsons Dr *HUDE* HD5 13
Rochdale Rd *GTL/HWG* HX4 165
   HUDW HD3 188
   LUD/ILL HX2 139
   RPDN/SBR HX6 164
   RPDN/SBR HX6 185
   TOD OL14 159
   UPML OL3 206
Rocheford Cl *MID* LS10 102
Rocheford Gdns *MID* LS10 102
Rocheford Gv *MID* LS10 102
Rocheford Wk *MID* LS10 102
Rochester Ct *HOR/CROF* WF4 174
Rochester Dr *HOR/CROF* WF4 174
Rochester Gdns *BRAM* LS13 76
Rochester Pl *ELL* * HX5 166
Rochester Rd *BTLY* WF17 121
Rochester St *BFDE* BD3 96
   SHPY BD18 73
Rochester Ter *HDGY* LS6 78
Rochester Wynd *AL/HA/HU* LS17 58
The Rock *MAR/SLWT* * HD7 211
Rockcliffe Av *BAIL* BD17 73
Rock Edge *LVSG* WF15 144
Rockery Cft *HORS* LS18 77
Rockery Rd *HORS* LS18 77
Rockery Ter *YEA* LS19 54
Rock Fold *MAR/SLWT* HD7 189
Rock Hl *CAS* WF10 154
Rockhill Cl *BTLY* WF17 145
Rockhill La *BOW* BD4 119
Rock House Dr *DEWS* WF13 172
Rockingham Cl *MSTN/BAR* LS15 82
Rockingham La *HEM/SK/SE* WF9 204
Rockingham Rd *MSTN/BAR* LS15 82
Rockingham St *CUD/GR* * S72 202
   HEM/SK/SE WF9 202
Rockland Crs *GTHN* BD7 94
Rocklands Av *BAIL* BD17 51
Rocklands Pl *BAIL* BD17 51
Rock La *BRAM* LS13 77
   CUL/QBY BD13 93
   MAR/SLWT HD7 188
Rockley Cl *HUDE* HD5 192
Rockley Dr *WKFDW/WTN* WF2 198
Rockley Grange Gdns
   GFTH/SHER LS25 109
Rockley St *EARL* WF12 172
Rockmill Rd *HOLM/MEL* HD9 233

ock Side Rd STKB/PEN S36 ....251 K8
ocks La LUD/ILL HX2.....................115 C3
ocks Vw LUD/ILL HX2.....................139 K8
ck St BRIG HD6...............................142 B8
_ HUDW * HD3....................................189 J4
ock Ter CUL/QBY BD13...................93 H5
EARL * WF12....................................145 C5
GIR BD8...4 B2
_ HUDW HD3......................................190 A1
MOR LS27...123 C6
MSTN/BAR LS15..............................103 H4
ock Vw GTL/HWG HX4...................166 B7
MAR/SLWT HD7...............................209 H8
ockville Ter HFAX HX1...................8 B6
ockwell La IDLE BD10.....................74 E5
ckwood Cl HUDN HD2.....................169 F5
ckwood Crs HOR/CROF WF4.......197 K5
PDSY/CALV LS28..............................75 J8
ckwood Gv PDSY/CALV LS28.........75 K8
ckwood Hill La PDSY/CALV LS28..97 J1
ckwood Ri KBTN HD8.....................236 E4
ckwood Rd PDSY/CALV LS28.........97 J1
derick St WOR/ARM LS12...............100 B4
dger La WKFDW/WTN WF2............175 G1
din Av GIR BD8.................................94 D4
dley La KBTN HD8............................217 H4
_ PDSY/CALV LS28.............................76 A5
dney Wk IDLE BD10.........................10 C3
ds Mills La MOR LS27.......................133 G8
ebuck St BTLY WF17.......................145 J2
ger Ct ECHL BD2...............................5 F2
ger Dr WKFDW/WTN WF2..............199 F2
ger Fold GFTH/SHER LS25..............129 G2
ger Ga HBR HX7..............................136 D2
ger La HUDS HD4.............................191 H8
gers Ct EARD/LOFT WF3.................150 C5
gerson Sq BRIG HD6........................142 B8
gers Pl PDSY/CALV LS28..................98 D3
ils Head Rd LUD/ILL HX2................138 E4
okeby Gdns HDGY LS6.....................78 C6
IDLE BD10..75 G5
oker La PDSY/CALV LS28..................98 D6
man Av HUDW HD3.........................189 H2
RHAY LS8...58 C8
manby Shaw IDLE BD10..................75 F5
man Cl HUDW HD3.........................189 H2
man Crs RHAY LS8............................80 D1
man Dr HUDW HD3.........................189 H2
RHAY LS8...80 D1
man Gdns RHAY LS8........................80 C1
man Pl RHAY LS8..............................80 C1
man Ri PONT WF8............................180 D6
man Rd BTLY WF17..........................145 J3
OOD/DAR S75...................................239 K4
man Ter RHAY LS8.............................80 C1
man Vw RHAY LS8.............................80 D1
mbalds Av WOR/ARM LS12.............100 C3
mbalds Crs AIRE BD20......................27 H3
WOR/ARM LS12.................................100 C2
mbalds Dr BGLY BD16.......................50 B8
mbalds Gv WOR/ARM LS12.............100 C3
mbalds La ILK LS29...........................20 E8
mbalds Pl WOR/ARM LS12..............100 C3
mbalds St WOR/ARM LS12..............100 C3
mbalds Vw ILK LS29.........................20 D6
OT LS21...33 F1
mford Av MOR LS27.........................123 F8
mney Cft PDSY/CALV LS28...............98 E6
msey Hd HUDW HD3.......................189 K2
msey Gdns BOW BD4........................97 F8
msey Ms BOW BD4............................97 F8
na Cft RTHW LS26.............................126 D6
nald Dr GTHN BD7............................95 G4
ods La HOLM/MEL HD9....................232 A8
okery Cottages OSS * WF5...............173 J8
okery La HIPP HX3............................140 C8
okes Av WBSY BD6............................118 D3
okhills HIPP HX3...............................142 B2
okhill Dr PONT WF8........................181 F4
okhill Rd PONT WF8.........................181 G4
ok La BOW BD4.................................119 J1
oks Av CLECK BD19.........................143 K3
oks Cl LM/WK BD12........................142 E2
ok's Nest Rd WKFDE WF1...............149 K7
ok St BGLY BD16...............................49 K8
HUD HD1...12 C3
okwith Pde IDLE BD10.....................75 F5
okwood Av GFTH/SHER LS25.........129 F3
SM LS9...102 E3
okwood Crs OSM LS9......................102 E4
okwood Gdns OSM LS9...................102 E4
okwood Hl OSM LS9........................102 E3
okwood Mt OSM LS9.......................102 E3
okwood Pde OSM LS9......................103 F3
okwood Pl OSM LS9.........................102 E4
okwood Rd OSM LS9........................102 E4
okwood Sq OSM LS9.......................103 F3
okwood St OSM LS9.........................102 E4
okwood V OSM LS9.........................102 E4
okwood Vw OSM LS9.......................102 E3
oley Av WBSY BD6............................118 D3
ey Banks RPDN/SBR HX6................138 B8
ey Cl WBOW BD5..............................119 F2

Rooley Crs WBSY BD6......................119 F3
Rooley Hts RPDN/SBR HX6..............138 A8
Rooley La RPDN/SBR HX6................164 A1
WBOW BD5..118 F2
Roomfield St TOD OL14....................134 A6
Rooms Fold MOR LS27......................123 F5
Rooms La MOR LS27.........................122 E3
Roper Av RHAY LS8............................80 B5
Ropergate PONT WF8.......................180 D5
Ropergate Service Rd PONT WF8....180 D3
Roper Gn LUD/ILL HX2.....................115 G7
Roper Gv RHAY LS8............................80 B5
Roper La LUD/ILL HX2......................115 G3
Ropers St KGHY BD21.......................3 J4
Rope Wk KNOT WF11........................156 D7
LUD/ILL HX2......................................114 C4
Roscoe St CHAL LS7...........................7 F1
Roseate Gn MOR LS27......................123 H8
Rose Av HEM/SK/SE WF9..................226 B4
HORS LS18...76 E3
HUDS HD4..189 K8
HUDW HD3...190 D1
Rose Bank ILK LS29............................32 A3
Rosebank Crs HDGY * LS6.................6 B1
Rosebank Gdns BVRD LS3.................6 B2
Rose Bank Pl GIR BD8........................84 E4
Rosebank Rd BVRD LS3......................6 B2
Rose Bank Rd TOD OL14..................133 K7
Rosebank Rw BVRD LS3......................6 B2
Rosebank St BTLY WF17...................146 A5
Roseberry St HWTH BD22..................69 F1
TOD OL14...132 E2
Rosebery Av HIPP HX3......................140 C7
SHPY BD18...73 J4
Rosebery Mt SHPY BD18....................73 J4
Rosebery Rd GIR BD8..........................4 A1
Rosebery St ELL HX5........................166 C5
HUDN HD2...12 B1
PDSY/CALV LS28.................................98 A3
Rosebery Ter FEA/AMT WF7...............8 B5
PDSY/CALV LS28.................................98 D1
Rosebud Wk RHAY LS8.....................102 A1
Rosechapel Cl WBSY * BD6...............118 A5
Rosecliffe Mt BRAM LS13...................77 F8
Rosecliffe Ter BRAM LS13..................99 F1
Rose Cl HEM/SK/SE WF9..................226 A4
Rose Cottages GTL/HWG * HX4......188 C1
Rose Ct GFTH/SHER LS25.................106 A4
Rose Cft LA/HA/HU LS17.....................40 C5
Rosedale Av LVSG WF15...................170 A1
WIL/AL BD15..93 K1
WKFDW/WTN WF2............................199 G3
Rosedale Bank MID LS10..................124 E2
Rosedale Cl BAIL BD17........................73 G1
HEM/SK/SE WF9................................226 D4
NORM WF6..178 C2
Rosedale Gdns MID LS10..................124 E2
Rosedale Gn MID LS10......................124 E2
Rosedale Ri BSPA/BRAM LS23............42 C4
Rosedale Wk MID LS10.....................124 E2
Rose Farm Ap NORM WF6.................151 J7
Rose Farm Cl NORM WF6..................151 J6
Rose Farm Fold NORM WF6..............151 J6
Rose Farm Ri NORM WF6..................151 J6
Rose Garth HOR/CROF WF4.............200 D2
ILK LS29...31 J4
Rosegarth Av HOLM/MEL HD9........233 J4
Rose Gv HBR HX7..............................137 F3
HEM/SK/SE WF9................................226 C4
RPDN/SBR HX6..................................138 C6
RTHW LS26..126 A5
Rose Heath LUD/ILL HX2..................115 G4
Rose Hl MAR/SLWT * HD7................209 J1
Rose Hl HEM/SK/SE WF9..................224 C5
Rosehill Crs LM/WK BD12.................118 D7
Rose Hill Dr HUDW HD3....................190 D2
Rose La FEA/AMT WF7......................202 D7
Roselee Cl HIPP HX3.........................140 D8
Rosemary Av WOR/ARM LS12.........100 D4
Rosemary La BRIG HD6....................168 B3
HIPP HX3...140 D8
Rose Mdw HWTH BD22......................47 G6
Rosemont Av BRAM * LS13.................99 G1
PDSY/CALV LS28.................................98 D3
Rosemont Dr PDSY/CALV LS28.........98 D5
Rosemont Gv BRAM LS13...................99 F1
Rosemont La BAIL BD17.....................73 K1
Rosemont Pl BRAM LS13....................99 F1
Rosemont St BRAM LS13....................99 G1
PDSY/CALV LS28.................................98 D3
Rosemont Ter BRAM LS13..................98 D3
PDSY/CALV LS28.................................98 D3
Rosemont Vw BRAM LS13..................99 G1
Rosemont Wk BRAM LS13..................99 G1
Rose Mt BOW * BD4..........................120 D3
ECHL BD2...74 C8
HUDN HD2..190 D2
LUD/ILL * HX2.....................................139 K7
Rosemount Av ELL HX5.....................167 F5
Rosemount Cl KGHY * BD21................2 C3
Rosemount Pl WOR/ARM LS12........100 D5
Rosemount Wk KGHY * BD21.............2 C3
Roseneath Pl WOR/ARM LS12.........100 D5
Roseneath St WOR/ARM LS12..........100 D5
Roseneath Ter WOR/ARM LS12........100 D5
Rose Pl LUD/ILL HX2.........................138 B6
Rose St GIR BD8..................................95 H2

HFAX HX1...8 A5
HORS LS18...76 E3
KGHY BD21...48 D4
TOD OL14...134 A6
Rose Ter BTLY * WF17......................145 K1
_ HFAX * HX1..8 B4
HUD * HD1..13 D2
LUD/ILL * HX2....................................139 K7
Roseville Rd OSM LS9.......................102 A2
Roseville St RHAY LS8......................102 A1
Roseville Wy OSM LS9......................102 A1
Rosewood Av GFTH/SHER LS25.......105 K8
KGHY BD21...48 D2
Rosewood Ct RTHW LS26..................126 C4
Rosgill Dr SCFT LS14.........................81 H6
Rosgill Wk SCFT LS14........................81 H6
Rosley Mt WBSY BD6........................118 A5
Roslyn Av HUDS HD4........................212 C4
Roslyn Pl GTHN BD7..........................95 H5
Rossall Gv RHAY * LS8.......................80 B7
Rossall Rd RHAY LS8..........................80 B7
Rossefield Ap BRAM LS13..................99 H2
Rossefield Av BRAM LS13..................99 H1
Rossefield Cha BRAM LS13................99 H1
Rossefield Cl BRAM * LS13................99 H1
Rossefield Dr BRAM LS13...................99 H1
Rossefield Gv BRAM LS13..................99 H1
Rossefield Lawn BRAM LS13..............99 H1
Rossefield Pk HTON BD9....................73 H7
Rossefield Pl BRAM LS13....................99 H1
Rossefield Rd HTON BD9....................73 G7
Rossefield Ter BRAM LS13..................99 H1
Rossendale Pl SHPY BD18..................73 G4
Rossendale Wy WHIT OL12..............158 D8
Rosse St GIR BD8................................95 G4
SHPY BD18...73 H3
Ross Gv BRAM LS13............................77 F7
Rossington Gv RHAY LS8...................80 A7
Rossington Pl RHAY LS8....................80 A7
Rossington Rd RHAY LS8...................80 A7
Rositer Dr KNOT WF11......................156 A8
Rosslyn Av FEA/AMT WF7.................203 F6
Rosslyn Cl FEA/AMT WF7..................203 F6
Rosslyn Ct EARL WF12......................172 E4
FEA/AMT WF7....................................203 F6
Rosslyn Gv FEA/AMT WF7.................203 F6
HWTH BD22...68 E5
Rossmore Dr WIL/AL BD15.................94 C2
Rosy St HWTH BD22...........................69 H3
Rotcher La MAR/SLWT HD7..............210 C3
Rotcher Rd HOLM/MEL HD9.............233 G7
Rothbury Gdns BHP/TINH LS16.........56 B8
Rothery Ct HFAX * HX1........................8 B3
Rothesay Ter GTHN BD7.....................4 A6
Roth St HWTH BD22............................69 G3
Rothwell Dr HFAX HX1.........................8 C6
Rothwell La RTHW LS26....................126 D6
Rothwell Mt HFAX HX1........................8 C6
Rothwell Rd HFAX HX1........................8 C6
Rothwell Rd & Rockwood Ri
_ HFAX HX1..8 C6
Rothwell St HUDE HD5.....................192 A5
Rough Hall La LUD/ILL HX2..............114 B6
Rough Side La TOD OL14..................134 B7
Round Close Rd HOLM/MEL HD9....248 C5
Roundell Av BOW BD4......................119 J3
Roundhay Av RHAY LS8......................80 B6
Roundhay Crs RHAY LS8.....................80 B6
Roundhay Gdns RHAY * LS8..............80 B6
Roundhay Gv RHAY LS8......................80 B6
Roundhay Mt RHAY LS8......................80 B6
Roundhay Park La AL/HA/HU LS17....58 D6
Roundhay Pl RHAY LS8.......................80 B6
Roundhay Rd CHAL LS7........................7 F1
Roundhay Vw RHAY * LS8..................80 B6
Roundhead Fold IDLE BD10................75 G3
Round Hl LUD/ILL HX2......................115 J5
Round Hill Cl CUL/QBY BD13...........117 C1
Roundhill Mt BGLY BD16....................72 B4
Roundhill Pl BFD BD1...........................4 B4
Roundhill Rd CAS WF10....................153 J4
Roundhill St WBOW BD5....................95 K7
Round Ings Rd HUDW HD3...............188 D4
Round St WBOW BD5..........................96 A8
_ WKFDE WF1.....................................11 E5
Round Thorn Pl GIR * BD8.................95 G3
The Roundway MOR LS27..................122 D7
Roundway HOLM/MEL HD9..............213 F8
Roundwell Rd LVSG WF15.................143 K6
Roundwood SHPY BD18......................72 E4
Round Wood Av HUDE HD5..............192 C5
Roundwood Av BAIL BD17...................52 B8
IDLE BD10..75 D7
Roundwood Crs WKFDW/WTN WF2.174 D6
Roundwood Gln IDLE BD10................75 D5
Roundwood Ri WKFDW/WTN WF2...174 E7
Roundwood Rd BAIL BD17..................52 A8
OSS WF5...174 B7
Roundwood Vw IDLE BD10.................75 D5
Rouse Fold BOW BD4............................5 D6
Rouse Mill La BTLY WF17..................147 C2
Rouse St LVSG WF15..........................144 D7
Rowan Av BFDE BD3...........................97 G4
HUDS HD4...212 D5
NORM WF6...177 K3
Rowan Avenue Ms HUDS HD4.........212 D5
Rowanberry Cl ECHL BD2...................74 D7

Rowan Cl *BTLY* WF17 ....145 K1
Rowan Ct *ECHL* * BD2 ....96 E2
  RTHW LS26 ....127 H5
  WKFDW/WTN WF2 ....175 G3
  YEA LS19 ....53 K6
Rowan Dr *BRIG* HD6 ....142 D8
Rowan Pl *GFTH/SHER* LS25 ....106 B5
The Rowans *BAIL* BD17 ....51 F8
  BHP/TINH LS16 ....55 K1
  BRAM LS13 ....98 D3
Rowan St *AIRE* BD20 ....47 J1
Rowantree Av *BAIL* BD17 ....51 H7
Rowantree Dr *IDLE* BD10 ....74 E5
Rowanwood Gdns *IDLE* * BD10 ...75 G6
Row Ga *KBTN* HD8 ....235 F4
Rowgate *KBTN* HD8 ....235 J5
Rowland La *HBR* HX7 ....112 D8
Rowland Pl *BEE/HOL* LS11 ....101 H8
Rowland Rd *BEE/HOL* LS11 ....101 H8
Rowlands Av *HEM/SK/SE* WF9 ...226 C4
  HUDE HD5 ....192 B5
Rowland St *BSLYN/ROY* S71 ....222 B7
Rowland Ter *BEE/HOL* LS11 ....101 H8
Row La *MAR/SLWT* HD7 ....210 A3
  RPDN/SBR HX6 ....138 A8
Rowlestone Ri *IDLE* BD10 ....75 G5
Rowley Dr *ILK* LS29 ....21 F8
  KBTN HD8 ....193 F8
Rowley La *HEM/SK/SE* WF9 ....242 C2
  KBTN HD8 ....215 F1
Rowsley St *KGHY* BD21 ....3 E3
Rowe St *HUDS* HD4 ....12 A6
Rowton Thorpe *IDLE* BD10 ....75 G5
Roxburghe Dl *NORM* WF6 ....178 C2
Roxburgh Gv *WIL/AL* BD15 ....94 B3
Roxby Cl *OSM* LS9 ....102 A2
Roxby St *WBOW* BD5 ....95 K8
Roxholme Av *CHAL* LS7 ....80 A6
Roxholme Gv *CHAL* LS7 ....80 A6
Roxholme Pl *CHAL* LS7 ....80 A6
Roxholme Ter *CHAL* LS7 ....80 A6
Royal Cl *BFDE* BD7 ....95 F8
  MID LS10 ....124 E1
Royal Ct *MID* LS10 ....124 E1
  PONT WF8 ....180 C6
Royal Dr *MID* LS10 ....124 E1
Royal Gdns *MID* LS10 ....124 E1
Royal Park Av *HDGY* LS6 ....6 B1
Royal Park Gv *HDGY* LS6 ....79 F8
Royal Park Mt *HDGY* * LS6 ....79 F8
Royal Park Rd *HDGY* LS6 ....6 A1
Royal Park Ter *HDGY* LS6 ....79 F8
Royal Pl *MID* LS10 ....124 E1
Royal Ter *BSPA/BRAM* LS23 ....42 E3
  HUDW HD3 ....190 A6
Royd Av *BGLY* BD16 ....50 B8
  HECK WF16 ....145 G5
  HUDW HD3 ....167 F8
  HUDW HD3 ....190 A6
  STKB/PEN S36 ....251 G8
Royd Crs *HBR* HX7 ....137 G2
  HFAX * HX1 ....8 A3
Royden Gv *HTON* BD9 ....95 G1
Roydfield Gv *HUDN* HD2 ....191 H1
Royd Head Farm *OSS* WF5 ....173 H6
Royd House Cv *KGHY* BD21 ....3 F5
Royd House La *MAR/SLWT* HD7 ..211 H2
Royd House Rd *KGHY* BD21 ....3 F5
Royd House Wk *KGHY* BD21 ....3 F5
Royd House Wy *KGHY* BD21 ....3 F5
Roydlands St *HIPP* HX3 ....141 H3
Royd La *DOD/DAR* S75 ....239 K8
  HIPP HX3 ....115 K8
  HOLM/MEL HD9 ....247 K1
  KGHY BD21 ....2 C1
  LUD/ILL HX2 ....115 H4
  RPDN/SBR HX6 ....163 K6
  STKB/PEN S36 ....251 G2
  TOD OL14 ....134 A4
Royd Moor La *HEM/SK/SE* WF9 ...225 G2
Royd Moor Rd *BOW* BD4 ....120 C2
  STKB/PEN S36 ....251 G6
Royd Mt *HIPP* HX3 ....9 D1
  HOLM/MEL HD9 ....233 D7
Roydon Cv *HTON* BD9 ....95 G1
Royd Pl *HIPP* HX3 ....9 D1
Royd Rd *HOLM/MEL* HD9 ....231 J3
  TOD OL14 ....133 K5
The Royds *HOLM/MEL* HD9 ....233 G6
  KBTN HD8 ....218 A8
Royds Av *BIRK/DRI* BD11 ....120 E6
  BRIG HD6 ....142 C3
  CAS WF10 ....154 D3
  HOLM/MEL HD9 ....233 K6
  HUDW HD3 ....190 B5
  MAR/SLWT HD7 ....211 H1
  OSS WF5 ....173 H5
Roydscliffe Dr *HTON* BD9 ....73 F7
Roydscliffe Rd *HTON* BD9 ....72 E8
Royds Cl *HOLM/MEL* HD9 ....233 K5
  WOR/ARM LS12 ....100 C7
Royds Crs *BRIG* HD6 ....142 C4
Roydsdale Wy *BOW* BD4 ....119 H5
Royds Dr *HOLM/MEL* HD9 ....233 K6
Royds Farm Rd *BEE/HOL* LS11 ...123 H1
Royds Gv *WKFDE* WF1 ....149 K6
Royds Hall Av *WBSY* BD6 ....118 D3
Royds Hall La *LM/WK* BD12 ....118 B6

Royds Hall Rd *WOR/ARM* LS12 ...100 C7
Royds La *RTHW* LS26 ....126 D7
  WOR/ARM LS12 ....100 C8
Royds Pk *KBTN* HD8 ....236 E6
Royds Park Crs *LM/WK* BD12 ......118 E2
Roydstone Rd *BFDE* BD3 ....97 F3
Roydstone Ter *BFDE* BD3 ....97 F3
Royd St *BTLY* WF17 ....146 D8
  CUL/QBY BD13 ....93 G5
  HUDW HD3 ....190 A6
  KGHY BD21 ....47 K1
  MAR/SLWT HD7 ....210 D2
  TOD OL14 ....133 K5
  WIL/AL BD15 ....71 G4
Royds Vw *MAR/SLWT* HD7 ....211 H2
Royd Ter *HBR* HX7 ....112 B8
Royd Vw *HBR* HX7 ....137 F2
Royd Vls *HBR* * HX7 ....112 B8
Royd Wy *KGHY* BD21 ....3 D1
Roydwood Ter *CUL/QBY* BD13 .....70 B5
Roydwood Ter Back
  CUL/QBY BD13 ....70 B5
Royle Fold *HECK* WF16 ....145 G7
Royles Cl *HEM/SK/SE* WF9 ....241 J1
Royles Head La *HUDW* HD3 ....189 J5
Roy Rd *WBSY* BD6 ....117 J2
Royston Cl *EARD/LOFT* WF3 ......148 E5
Royston Hl *EARD/LOFT* WF3 ......148 E5
Ruby St *BTLY* WF17 ....145 K5
  HWTH BD22 ....3 D1
Rud Broom La *STKB/PEN* S36 .....252 A8
Rudding Av *WIL/AL* BD15 ....94 A2
Rudding Crs *WIL/AL* BD15 ....94 A1
Rudding Dr *BTLY* WF17 ....145 J3
Rudding St *HUDS* HD4 ....190 D7
Rudd St *GTHN* BD7 ....95 G8
Rudgate *TAD* LS24 ....25 J7
  TAD LS24 ....43 K6
Rudgate Pk *BSPA/BRAM* LS23 .....25 G8
Rud La *HBR* HX7 ....136 A8
Ruffield Side *LM/WK* BD12 ....118 C5
Rufford Av *YEA* LS19 ....53 K5
Rufford Bank *YEA* LS19 ....54 A5
Rufford Cl *HOR/CROF* WF4 ....222 E3
  YEA LS19 ....54 A5
Rufford Crs *YEA* LS19 ....54 A5
Rufford Dr *YEA* LS19 ....54 A5
Rufford Pl *HFAX* * HX1 ....140 A7
Rufford Rdg *YEA* LS19 ....54 A5
Rufford Ri *YEA* LS19 ....53 K5
Rufford Rd *ELL* HX5 ....166 D5
  HIPP HX3 ....140 A7
  HIPP HX3 ....189 K6
Rufford St *BFDE* BD3 ....96 E4
  WKFDW/WTN WF2 ....175 G5
Rufford Vls *HIPP* HX3 ....140 A7
Rufus St *KGHY* BD21 ....3 D1
  WBOW BD5 ....95 H8
Rugby Av *HIPP* HX3 ....115 J8
Rugby Dr *HIPP* HX3 ....115 J8
Rugby Gdns *HIPP* HX3 ....115 J8
Rugby Mt *HIPP* HX3 ....115 J8
Rugby Pl *GTHN* BD7 ....95 H5
Rugby Ter *HIPP* HX3 ....115 J8
Rumble Rd *EARL* WF12 ....157 J6
Rumbold Rd *HUDW* HD3 ....190 D4
Rumple Cft *OT* LS21 ....33 G1
Runswick Av *BEE/HOL* LS11 ....6 B6
Runswick Gv *WBOW* BD5 ....118 E2
Runswick Pl *BEE/HOL* LS11 ....6 B6
Runswick St *BEE/HOL* LS11 ....6 B6
  WBOW BD5 ....118 E2
Runswick Ter *BEE/HOL* LS11 ....6 C6
  WBOW BD5 ....118 E2
The Runtlings *OSS* WF5 ....173 G6
Runtlings La *OSS* WF5 ....173 H7
Rupert Rd *ILK* LS29 ....20 A6
Rupert St *HWTH* BD22 ....69 H3
  KGHY * BD21 ....3 D2
Rush Cft *IDLE* BD10 ....74 B2
Rushdene Ct *LM/WK* BD12 ....142 D1
Rushfield V *KBTN* HD8 ....192 E7
Rushmoor Rd *BOW* BD4 ....120 A1
Rusholme Dr *PDSY/CALV* LS28 ....76 A8
Rushton Av *BFDE* BD3 ....97 G3
Rushton Hill Cl *LUD/ILL* HX2 ....139 F2
Rushton Rd *BFDE* BD3 ....97 F3
Rushton St *HFAX* HX1 ....8 A3
  PDSY/CALV LS28 ....75 K5
Rushton Ter *BFDE* BD3 ....97 G3
Rushworth Cl *DOD/DAR* S75 ......239 J3
Rushworth St *HIPP* * HX3 ....8 B2
Ruskin Av *HTON* BD9 ....72 D8
  WKFDE WF1 ....175 H1
Ruskin Cl *CAS* WF10 ....154 C3
Ruskin Ct *WKFDE* WF1 ....175 G1
Ruskin Crs *OSLY* LS20 ....53 H3
Ruskin Dr *CAS* WF10 ....154 C3
Ruskin Gv *HUDN* HD2 ....168 E8
Ruskin Pl *CAS* WF10 ....154 C3
Ruskin St *PDSY/CALV* LS28 ....98 A2
Ruskin Ter *HIPP* HX3 ....8 B2
Russell Av *CUL/QBY* BD13 ....116 D3
  HOR/CROF WF4 ....220 B1
Russell Cl *BTLY* WF17 ....146 B6
  HECK WF16 ....145 H8

Russell Hall La *CUL/QBY* BD13 ...116 C
Russell Rd *CUL/QBY* BD13 ....116 D
Russell St *CUL/QBY* BD13 ....116 C
  DEWS WF13 ....171 H
  HFAX * HX1 ....9 D
  KGHY BD21 ....2 C
  LDS LS1 ....7 D
  SHPY BD18 ....73 G
  TOD OL14 ....134 E
  WBOW BD5 ....5 H
  WKFDE WF1 ....10 C
Russell Wy *BRIG* HD6 ....142 C
The Russets *WKFDW/WTN* WF2 ...199 C
Russett Gv *HUDS* HD4 ....191 H
Rustic Av *HIPP* HX3 ....141 F
Ruswarp Crs *IDLE* BD10 ....75 F
Ruth St *HUDS* HD4 ....213 C
Ruthven Vw *RHAY* LS8 ....80 C
Rutland Av *PONT* WF8 ....180 B
  WKFDW/WTN WF2 ....198 E
Rutland Cl *GFTH/SHER* LS25 ....129 C
  RTHW LS26 ....127 G
Rutland Dr *GFTH/SHER* LS25 ......129 C
  HOR/CROF WF4 ....177 F
Rutland Rd *BTLY* WF17 ....146 C
  HOR/CROF WF4 ....195 G
  HUDW HD3 ....189 H
Rutland St *BOW* BD4 ....96 C
  KGHY BD21 ....2 A
Rutland Ter *BVRD* LS3 ....6 A
Ryan Cv *HWTH* BD22 ....47 H
Ryan Pl *RHAY* LS8 ....80 C
Ryan St *WBOW* BD5 ....95 J
Ryburn Ct *HFAX* HX1 ....8 A
Ryburn La *RPDN/SBR* HX6 ....164 E
Ryburn Pl *WKFDW/WTN* WF2 ......10 B
Ryburn Rd *HUDW* HD3 ....190 E
Ryburn St *RPDN/SBR* HX6 ....138 C
Ryburn Ter *HFAX* HX1 ....8 A
Ryburn Vw *LUD/ILL* HX2 ....139 H
  RPDN/SBR HX6 ....163 H
Rycroft Av *BCLY* BD16 ....72 E
  BRAM LS13 ....98 C
Rycroft Cl *BRAM* LS13 ....99 F
Rycroft Dr *BRAM* LS13 ....99 F
Rycroft Gdns *BRAM* LS13 ....98 D
Rycroft St *SHPY* BD18 ....73 K
Rycroft Towers *BRAM* LS13 ....98 D
Rydal Av *GFTH/SHER* LS25 ....105 G
  HTON BD9 ....73 F
Rydal Cl *STKB/PEN* S36 ....252 E
Rydal Crs *MOR* LS27 ....123 F
  WKFDW/WTN WF2 ....175 H
Rydal Dr *HUDE* HD5 ....171 F
  MOR LS27 ....123 G
  WKFDW/WTN WF2 ....175 H
Rydale Ct *OSS* WF5 ....173 H
Rydale Ms *OSS* WF5 ....173 H
Rydal Gv *LVSG* WF15 ....170 D
Rydall Pl *BEE/HOL* LS11 ....6 C
Rydall St *BEE/HOL* LS11 ....6 C
Rydall Ter *BEE/HOL* LS11 ....6 C
  KGHY BD21 ....2 D
Ryder Cl *PONT* WF8 ....180 A
Ryder Gdns *RHAY* LS8 ....80 E
Rydings Av *BRIG* HD6 ....142 A
Rydings Cl *BRIG* HD6 ....142 B
Rydings Dr *BRIG* HD6 ....142 B
Ryebank *HOLM/MEL* HD9 ....233 H
Ryebread *CAS* WF10 ....153 J
Rye Close La *HOLM/MEL* HD9 .....231 F
Ryecroft *BGLY* BD16 ....70 A
Ryecroft Av *HOR/CROF* WF4 ....223 G
Ryecroft Cl *WKFDE* WF1 ....10 A
Ryecroft Crs *LUD/ILL* HX2 ....139 F
Ryecroft Dr *HUDW* HD3 ....190 C
Ryecroft La *HOLM/MEL* HD9 ....233 H
  LUD/ILL HX2 ....139 F
Ryecroft Rd *BGLY* BD16 ....70 A
Ryecroft St *OSS* WF5 ....173 K
Ryecroft Ter *LUD/ILL* HX2 ....139 F
Ryedale *HUDE* HD5 ....192 C
Ryedale Av *HUDW* HD3 ....182 B
  WOR/ARM LS12 ....100 A
Ryedale Cl *NORM* * WF6 ....151 G
Ryedale Ct *SCFT* LS14 ....85 J
Ryedale Holt *WOR/ARM* LS12 .....100 A
Ryedale Pk *ILK* LS29 ....20 B
Ryedale Pl *NORM* WF6 ....151 G
Ryedale Wy *EARD/LOFT* WF3 ......147 G
  WIL/AL BD15 ....94 A
Ryefield Av *CLAY* BD14 ....94 C
Rye Field La *HUDW* HD3 ....187 H
Rye Field La West *HUDW* HD3 .....187 H
Ryefields Av *HUDW* HD3 ....233 G
Ryefields Rd *MAR/SLWT* HD7 .....189 G
Rye Garth *WBY* LS22 ....29 G
Ryelands Gv *HTON* BD9 ....72 C
Rye La *LUD/ILL* HX2 ....139 G
Rye Pl *SCFT* LS14 ....103 K
Rye St *HWTH* BD22 ....2 C
Ryhill Pits La *HOR/CROF* WF4 .....222 E
Rylands Av *BGLY* BD16 ....50 C
Rylands Meadow *HWTH* BD22 ......69 H
Rylstone Gdns *BFDE* BD3 ....5 G
Rylstone Gv *WKFDE* WF1 ....10 C

ylstone Rd *BAIL* BD17.................................**73** F1
ylstone St *KGHY* BD21...............................**3** E2
yndleside *HUDW* HD3...............................**189** K2
ysworth Av *AIRE* BD20.............................**49** H4
yton Dl *IDLE* BD10....................................**75** G5

S

able Crest *ECHL* BD2.................................**74** B7
ackville Ap *CHAL* LS7................................**79** J8
ackville Rd *AIRE* BD20..............................**27** G1
ackville St *BFD* BD1....................................**4** C4
  CHAL LS7..**7** E1
  DEWS WF13...**171** H5
  HBR HX7..**112** B8
  TOD OL14..**134** B6
addlers Cft *CAS* WF10.............................**154** C5
addlers La *KNOT* WF11............................**155** K2
addler St *LM/AL* BD12.............................**118** D7
addleworth Rd *GTL/HWG* HX4................**164** E6
  GTL/HWG HX4..**166** D4
  HUDW HD3...**208** D7
afron Dr *WIL/AL* BD15..............................**94** A2
agar La *TOD* OL14...................................**133** D2
agar St *CAS* WF10....................................**153** J5
age St *WBOW* BD5.....................................**95** J7
ahara Ct *GIR* BD8...**4** B1
: Abbs Cl *WBSY* BD6...............................**118** D4
: Abbs Dr *WBSY* BD6..............................**118** D4
: Abbs Fold *WBSY* BD6............................**118** D4
: Abbs Ga *WBSY* BD6..............................**118** D4
: Abbs Wk *WBSY* BD6..............................**118** D4
: Abbs Wy *WBSY* BD6..............................**118** D4
  RTHW LS26...**128** D3
: Aidan's Rd *BAIL* BD17.............................**73** K1
: Aiden's Wk *OSS* WF5.............................**174** B6
: Alban Cl *OSM* LS9...................................**102** E2
: Alban Crs *OSM* LS9.................................**102** E2
: Alban Gv *OSM* LS9...................................**102** E2
: Alban Mt *OSM* LS9..................................**102** E2
: Alban Rd *OSM* LS9..................................**102** E2
: Alban's Av *HIPP* HX3..............................**140** B8
  HUDW HD3...**167** F8
: Albans Cft *HUDW* HD3............................**140** C7
: Albans Pl *LDSU* LS2...................................**7** E2
: Alban's Rd *WBSY* BD6............................**140** B8
: Alban Vw *OSM* LS9.................................**102** E2
: Andrew's Av *MOR* LS27...........................**122** D9
: Andrew Cl *BRAM* LS13...............................**76** C6
  MOR LS27..**122** D8
  YEA LS19..**54** A4
: Andrews Cft *BVRD* LS3................................**6** B3
: Andrew's Crs *LM/WK* BD12....................**119** H7
: Andrews Cft *AL/HA/HU* LS17...................**57** H7
: Andrews Dr *AL/HA/HU* LS17......................**57** J7
  BRIG HD6..**142** B7
  FEA/AMT WF7.......................................**179** H2
  HUDE HD5..**192** D3
  KNOT WF11..**155** K6
: Andrew's Gv *MOR* LS27..........................**122** E8
: Andrew's Pl *GTHN* * BD7............................**4** A5
: Andrew's Rd *CAS* WF10.........................**154** D2
  HUDE HD5...**13** E4
  YEA LS19..**54** A4
: Andrews Wk *AL/HA/HU* LS17....................**57** J7
: Andrew's Vls *WF12..................................**172** C4
: Andrews Wk *AL/HA/HU* LS17....................**57** J7
: Anne's Cl *EARL* WF12.............................**172** C7
: Anne's Dr *BULY* LS4.................................**78** C7
: Anne's Gn *BULY* LS4................................**78** C7
: Anne's Rd *HDGY* LS6.................................**78** C6
  HIPP HX3..**166** B1
: Anne's St *HOR/CROF* WF4.....................**223** F2
  LDSU LS2..**7** E3
: Ann's Av *BULY* LS4..................................**100** D1
: Ann's Cl *BULY* LS4....................................**78** C8
: Ann's Gdns *BULY* LS4..............................**78** C8
  KSTL LS5..**78** C8
: Ann's La *KSTL* LS5....................................**78** C8
: Ann's Mt *BULY* LS4...................................**78** B8
: Ann's Ri *BULY* LS4.....................................**78** C8
: Ann's Sq *BULY* LS4...................................**78** C8
  OSM LS9..**102** A3
  RPDN/SBR HX6.....................................**139** F7
: Ann St *LDS* LS1..**7** D3
: Ann's Wy *BULY* LS4...................................**78** C8
: Anthony's Dr *BEE/HOL* LS11..................**124** A1
: Anthony's Pk *BEE/HOL* LS11...................**123** K1
: Anuil *GIR* * BD8..**95** J2
: Augustine's Ter *BFDE* BD3..........................**5** E2
  HFAX HX1..**8** B3
: Barnabas Rd *BEE/HOL* LS11....................**7** D5
  VSG WF15...**143** K2
: Bartholomew's Cl
  WOR/ARM LS12......................................**100** C4
: Bartholomews Ct
  NKFDW/WTN WF2....................................**174** D7
: Benedicts Cha *BRAM* LS13.......................**77** H6
: Benedicts Dr *BRAM* LS13..........................**77** H6
: Bernard's Av *PONT* WF8..........................**180** C3
: Bevan's Rd *HIPP* HX3...............................**140** B8
: Blaise Ct *WBOW* BD5...................................**4** C5
: Blaise Wy *BFD* * BD1....................................**4** C4

St Boltophs Cl *KNOT* * WF11.....................**156** D7
St Catherine's Crs *BRAM* LS13...................**77** H7
St Catherine's Dr *BRAM* LS13.....................**77** H7
St Catherine's Gn *BRAM* LS13.....................**77** H7
St Catherine's Hl *BRAM* LS13......................**77** H7
St Catherine's St *WKFDE* WF1.......................**11** F5
St Catherine's Vls *WKFDE* WF1....................**11** F6
St Catherine's Wk *RHAY* LS8.......................**80** C5
St Chad's Av *BRIG* * HD6............................**141** K6
  HDGY LS6...**78** C5
St Chad's Dr *HDGY* LS6................................**78** C5
St Chad's Ri *HDGY* LS6.................................**78** C5
St Chad's Rd *GIR* BD8...................................**95** H2
  HDGY LS6...**78** C5
St Chad's Vw *HDGY* LS6...............................**78** C6
St Christopher's Av *RTHW* LS26.................**126** C6
St Christophers Dr *ILK* LS29.........................**18** D4
St Clair Gn *NKFDW/WTN* WF2...................**174** E3
St Clair Rd *OT* LS21.......................................**33** K4
St Clair St *OT* LS21..**33** K3
  WKFDE WF1..**11** D3
St Clare's Av *ECHL* BD2................................**97** F1
St Clements Av *RTHW* LS26.......................**126** B6
St Clements Cl *RTHW* LS26........................**126** B6
St Clements Ri *RTHW* LS26.........................**126** A6
St Cuthbert's La *FEA/AMT* * WF7...............**203** G2
St Cyprians Gdns *OSM* * LS9......................**102** D1
St Davids Rd *OT* LS21....................................**33** G1
St Edmunds Cl *CAS* WF10..........................**154** D3
St Edwards Cl *KNOT* WF11.........................**156** B4
St Elmo Gv *OSM* LS9...................................**102** C3
St Eloi Av *BAIL* BD17.....................................**51** J7
St Enoch's Rd *WBSY* BD6...........................**118** C2
St Francis Gdns *HUDN* HD2........................**168** B6
St Francis Pl *BEE/HOL* LS11...........................**7** D5
  RTHW LS26...**125** K4
St George's Av *HUDW* HD3........................**167** F8
  RTHW LS26...**125** K4
St Georges Crs *HOR/CROF* WF4................**223** H1
  RTHW LS26...**125** K4
St Georges Crs *HFAX* HX1...............................**8** B3
St George's Ms *NKFDW/WTN* WF2...........**198** C6
St George's Pl *WBOW* * BD5...........................**4** C6
  HOLM/MEL HD9.....................................**233** K7
  LDS * LS1..**7** D2
  NKFDW/WTN WF2..................................**174** E8
St George's Rd *HBR* * HX7...........................**112** B8
  HUD HD1..**12** C4
St George's St *HBR* HX7..............................**112** B8
  HUD HD1..**12** C4
St Georges Wk *NKFDW/WTN* WF2............**198** D5
St Giles Av *PONT* WF8.................................**180** D5
St Giles Cl *BRIG* HD6..................................**141** K6
St Giles Garth *BHP/TINH* LS16.....................**35** H8
St Giles Rd *HIPP* HX3..................................**141** K5
St Helena Rd *WBSY* BD6.............................**118** C2
  HEM/SK/SE WF9.....................................**224** C4
St Helens Cl *BHP/TINH* LS16........................**56** D8
St Helens Cft *BHP/TINH* LS16......................**56** C8
St Helen's Dr *GFTH/SHER* LS25.................**107** F3
St Helens Fld *HUDS* HD4............................**214** C1
St Helens Gdns *BHP/TINH* LS16..................**56** C8
St Helens Ga *HUDE* HD5.............................**214** C1
St Helens Gv *BHP/TINH* LS16......................**56** C8
  NKFDW/WTN WF2..................................**199** H3
St Helens La *BHP/TINH* LS16.......................**56** B8
St Helen's Pl *CAS* WF10..............................**153** K4
St Helens St *MID* * LS10..................................**7** F6
St Helens Wy *BHP/TINH* LS16......................**56** D8
  ILK LS29...**20** D7
St Helier Gv *BAIL* BD17.................................**51** K7
St Hilda's Av *OSM* LS9................................**102** B5
St Hilda's Crs *OSM* * LS9.............................**102** B5
St Hilda's Gv *OSM* LS9................................**102** B5
St Hilda's Mt *OSM* LS9................................**102** B5
St Hilda's Pl *OSM* LS9.................................**102** B5
St Hilda's Rd *OSM* LS9................................**102** B5
St Hilda's Ter *BFDE* BD3...............................**97** G3
St Ians Cft *ILK* LS29.......................................**18** D4
St Ives Cl *PONT* WF8...................................**180** E8
St Ives Crs *CAS* WF10.................................**154** D6
St Ive's Gdns *HIPP* * HX3...........................**140** B8
St Ives Pl *BGLY* BD16....................................**71** G1
  WOR/ARM LS12.....................................**100** A3
St Ives Mt *WOR/ARM* LS12........................**100** A3
St Ives Pl *BGLY* BD16....................................**71** G1
St Ives Rd *BGLY* BD16...................................**71** G1
  HIPP HX3...**140** A8
St James Ap *SCFT* LS14.................................**81** J7
St James Av *HORS* LS18................................**77** G2
St James Cl *WOR/ARM* LS12........................**99** J3
St James Ct *HFAX* * HX1....................................**8** C6
  HOR/CROF WF4.....................................**223** G2
St James Crs *PDSY/CALV* LS28....................**97** K4
St James Dr *HORS* LS18................................**77** H2
St James Ms *WOR/ARM* LS12.......................**99** K3
St James Ri *NKFDW/WTN* WF2...................**174** D7
St James Rd *HFAX* HX1....................................**8** C6
  ILK LS29...**20** A8
St James's Ct *OSM* LS29.............................**102** A1
  NKFDW/WTN WF2....................................**10** A1
St James's Ms *WOR/ARM* LS12....................**99** K3
St James's Pk *WKFDE* WF1............................**11** E3
St James St *HUD* HD1.................................**190** D4
St James's Sq *WBOW* * BD5............................**4** C6
St James St *WBY* LS22...................................**23** J6
St James St *BTLY* WF17...............................**146** B6
  HECK WF16...**145** G8

HFAX HX1..**9** D4
St James Ter *HORS* LS18...............................**77** H2
St James Wk *HORS* LS18................................**77** H2
St James Wy *HOR/CROF* WF4.....................**198** A6
  HUDE HD5...**13** F3
St John Pde *DEWS* WF13............................**172** A3
St Johns *STKB/PEN* S36..............................**252** E5
St John's Av *HDGY* LS6....................................**6** B1
  HUDE HD5..**192** D2
  HUDS HD4...**213** G1
  ILK LS29...**18** D3
  OSS WF5..**174** B6
  PDSY/CALV LS28......................................**98** B1
  SCFT LS14..**60** D6
  WKFDE WF1..**10** B1
St Johns Cl *CLECK* * BD19..........................**144** B4
  DEWS * WF13..**172** A3
  GFTH/SHER LS25.....................................**84** E2
  HBR * HX7...**112** B8
  HDGY LS6..**6** B1
  OSS WF5..**174** B6
  RPDN/SBR HX6......................................**186** E2
St John's Ct *BAIL* BD17................................**74** A1
  KBTN * HD8...**193** H8
  SCFT LS14...**60** D6
  WKFDE WF1..**10** B2
  YEA LS19...**53** J5
St John's Crs *GIR* BD8...................................**94** E3
  HUD HD1..**12** C2
  NORM WF6...**177** K4
  OSS WF5..**174** B6
St John's Cft *WKFDE* WF1.............................**10** B2
St John's Dr *HUD* HD1.....................................**12** C2
  YEA LS19...**53** J5
St John's Garth *GFTH/SHER* LS25................**84** E3
St John's Gv *HDGY* LS6....................................**6** B1
  WKFDE WF1..**10** C1
St John's La *HFAX* HX1.....................................**9** D5
St Johns Ms *WKFDE* * WF1..........................**10** B1
St John's Mt *WKFDE* WF1.............................**10** A1
St John's North *WKFDE* WF1........................**10** B2
St John's Pk *ILK* LS29....................................**32** B6
St John's Pl *BIRK/DRI* * BD11......................**120** D5
St John's Rd *AIRE* BD20...............................**47** J1
  BSPA/BRAM LS23....................................**42** D5
  BVRD LS3..**6** B2
  HUD HD1..**12** B2
  HUDE HD5..**192** E2
  ILK LS29...**20** E7
  YEA LS19...**53** J5
St John's Sq *WKFDE* WF1.............................**10** B2
St John's St *AIRE* BD20..................................**27** G2
  HOR/CROF WF4.....................................**196** E2
  RTHW LS26...**127** F6
St Johns Ter *HDGY* LS6....................................**6** B1
St John St *BRIG* HD6....................................**168** B2
  DEWS WF13..**172** A3
St John's Vw *BSPA/BRAM* LS23....................**42** C4
St John's Wk *BSLYN/ROY* S71....................**222** B8
St Johns Wy *HWTH* BD22................................**2** A4
  YEA LS19...**53** J5
St John Wk *DEWS* WF13.............................**172** A3
St Joseph's Mt *PONT* WF8.........................**180** C4
St Jude's Pl *GIR* * BD8.....................................**4** B3
St Jude's St *BFD* BD1......................................**4** B3
  HFAX HX1...**8** C6
St Julien's Mt *DOD/DAR* S75......................**238** E7
St Julien's Wy *DOD/DAR* S75......................**238** E7
St Laurence Cl *SHPY* BD18...........................**73** K6
St Lawrence Cl *PDSY/CALV* LS28.................**98** B4
St Lawrence Md *PDSY/CALV* LS28................**98** B5
St Lawrence St *CHAL* * LS7...........................**79** K5
St Lawrence Ter *PDSY/CALV* LS28...............**98** C5
St Leonards Cl *ILK* LS29................................**18** D4
St Leonards Dr *HTON* BD9.............................**95** F2
St Leonard's Gv *GIR* BD8..............................**95** F2
St Leonard's Rd *GIR* BD8..............................**95** F2
St Lucius's Cl *HUDS* HD4............................**214** A5
St Luke's Cl *BSPA/BRAM* LS23......................**42** D6
  BTLY * WF17...**146** D7
  CLECK BD19..**143** J4
  WBOW BD5..**4** D6
St Luke's Crs *BEE/HOL* LS11.......................**101** G7
St Luke's Gn *BEE/HOL* LS11........................**101** G7
St Luke's Rd *BEE/HOL* LS11........................**101** G7
St Luke's St *BEE/HOL* LS11.........................**101** G7
St Luke's Vw *BEE/HOL* * LS11......................**101** G7
St Margaret's Av *BOW* BD4..........................**120** A1
  HORS LS18..**77** F2
  RHAY LS8..**80** C5
  RTHW LS26...**128** C8
St Margaret's Cl *HORS* LS18.........................**77** F1
St Margaret's Dr *HEM/SK/SE* WF9..............**226** D5
St Margaret's Dr *HORS* LS18.........................**77** F1
  RHAY LS8..**80** C5
St Margaret's Gv *RHAY* LS8..........................**80** C5
St Margaret's Pl *GTHN* BD7...........................**95** H6
St Margaret's Rd *GTHN* BD7.........................**95** H5
  HORS LS18..**77** F1
  RTHW LS26...**128** C8
St Margaret's Ter *GTHN* BD7........................**95** H6
  HORS LS18..**20** B8
St Margaret's Vw *RHAY* LS8..........................**80** C5
St Mark's Av *LDSU* LS2...................................**6** C1
  LM/WK BD12...**118** D6
St Mark's Rd *HUDW* HD3.............................**190** A5
  LDSU LS2..**79** C8
St Mark's St *LDSU* LS2.....................................**6** C1

WKFDE WF1 ....11 D1
St Mark's Ter LM/WK BD12 ....118 D6
St Marks Vw HUDW HD3 ....190 A5
St Martin's Av CHAL LS7 ....79 J6
GTHN BD7 ....4 A4
OT LS21 ....33 H1
St Martins Cl FEA/AMT WF7 ....179 H7
St Martin's Crs CHAL LS7 ....79 K6
St Martin's Dr CHAL * LS7 ....79 K5
St Martin's Gdns CHAL LS7 ....79 K6
St Martin's Gv CAS WF10 ....153 C5
CHAL LS7 ....79 K6
St Martin's Rd CHAL LS7 ....79 K6
St Martin's Ter CHAL * LS7 ....79 K6
St Martin's Vw BRIG HD6 ....142 B8
CHAL LS7 ....79 K6
St Mary Magdalenes Cl GIR * BD8 ....4 A3
St Mary's Av BTLY WF17 ....145 K8
HOLM/MEL HD9 ....233 F3
LM/WK BD12 ....142 D1
MIRF WF14 ....171 F5
NORM WF6 ....151 J7
RTHW LS26 ....127 K2
St Mary's Cl CHAL LS7 ....79 K6
EARD/LOFT WF3 ....147 H4
GFTH/SHER LS25 ....105 K5
HEM/SK/SE WF9 ....242 C1
ILK LS29 ....20 C7
LM/WK BD12 ....142 C1
WOR/ARM LS12 ....100 D5
St Mary's Ct CAS WF10 ....129 C7
CHAL LS7 ....79 K6
St Mary's Crs HOLM/MEL HD9 ....233 F3
LM/WK BD12 ....142 C2
St Mary's Dr LM/WK BD12 ....142 D1
St Mary's Gdns LM/WK BD12 ....142 D1
St Mary's Garth AL/HA/HU LS17 ....39 K6
St Marys Ga ELL HX5 ....166 E4
St Mary's La HUDE HD5 ....192 E4
OSM LS9 ....102 A3
St Mary's Mt LM/WK BD12 ....142 C2
St Mary's Park Ap WOR/ARM LS12 .....99 K3
St Mary's Park Ct WOR/ARM * LS12 ...99 K3
St Mary's Park Crs WOR/ARM LS12 ....99 K3
St Mary's Park Gn WOR/ARM LS12 .....99 K3
St Mary's Pl EARL WF12 ....172 B5
St Mary's Ri HOLM/MEL HD9 ....233 F3
St Mary's Rd AIRE BD20 ....97 F6
BOW BD4 ....97 F6
CHAL LS7 ....79 K6
HOLM/MEL HD9 ....213 F6
HOLM/MEL HD9 ....233 F3
HTON BD9 ....4 A1
NORM WF6 ....151 J8
St Mary's Sq HOLM/MEL HD9 ....213 F6
LM/WK BD12 ....142 C1
MOR * LS27 ....123 F7
St Mary's St BSPA/BRAM LS23 ....42 D3
OSM LS9 ....7 F5
STKB/PEN S36 ....252 C8
St Marys Wk GFTH/SHER LS25 ....107 F4
MIRF WF14 ....171 F5
St Mary's Wy HOLM/MEL HD9 ....233 F3
St Matthew Rd DEWS WF13 ....172 A3
St Matthews Cl WIL/AL BD15 ....71 F7
St Matthew's Dr HIPP HX3 ....117 F8
St Matthews Gv WIL/AL BD15 ....71 F7
St Matthew's Rd WBSY BD6 ....118 E2
St Matthew's St BEE/HOL LS11 ....6 C6
St Matthew's Wk CHAL LS7 ....79 J3
St Matthias Ct BULY LS4 ....100 D1
St Matthias' St BULY LS4 ....100 D1
St Matthias Ter BULY LS4 ....100 D1
St Merrion Crs HIPP HX3 ....9 F6
St Michaels Av PONT WF8 ....180 C5
St Michael's Cl CAS WF10 ....153 J4
EARL WF12 ....195 J1
KBTN * HD8 ....217 H4
WKFDW/WTN WF2 ....10 A4
St Michael's Crs CHAL LS7 ....78 D7
St Michaels Gdns KBTN HD8 ....217 G4
St Michaels Gn HDGY LS6 ....177 K2
St Michael's Gv HDGY LS6 ....78 D8
St Michael's La HDGY LS6 ....78 D7
St Michael's Mt EARL WF12 ....195 J1
St Michael's Rd GIR BD8 ....4 A3
HDGY LS6 ....78 D7
St Michael's Ter HDGY LS6 ....78 D7
St Michaels Vls HDGY LS6 ....78 D7
St Michaels Wy ILK LS29 ....18 D3
ILK LS29 ....32 B3
St Nicholas Rd ILK LS29 ....20 A6
St Nicholas St CAS WF10 ....153 J4
St Oswald Av PONT WF8 ....180 C3
St Oswald Rd WKFDW/WTN WF2 .....174 D6
St Oswalds Garth GSLY LS20 ....53 G2
St Oswalds Pl OSS WF5 ....173 K4
St Oswald St CAS * WF10 ....153 J3
St Paulinus Cl DEWS WF13 ....172 A3
St Paul's Av BIRK/DRI BD11 ....120 D5
WBSY BD6 ....118 C3
St Pauls Cl GIR BD8 ....4 A2
HEM/SK/SE * WF9 ....227 F6
St Pauls Ct PONT WF8 ....159 F8
St Pauls Dr WKFDW/WTN WF2 ....174 E3
St Paul's Gv ILK LS29 ....18 C3
WBSY BD6 ....118 C3
St Paul's Pl LDS * LS1 ....7 D3

St Pauls Ri ILK LS29 ....18 D4
St Paul's Rd BIRK/DRI BD11 ....120 D6
GIR BD8 ....4 A1
HFAX HX1 ....8 A6
HUDE HD5 ....192 D3
KGHY BD21 ....3 E4
MIRF WF14 ....170 D7
SHPY BD18 ....73 G4
WBSY BD6 ....118 C3
St Paul's St HUD HD1 ....13 D5
LDS LS1 ....7 D3
MOR * LS27 ....123 F8
St Paul's Ter MIRF WF14 ....170 D7
St Paul's Wk WKFDW/WTN WF2 ....174 E3
St Peg Cl CLECK BD19 ....144 B4
St Peg La CLECK BD19 ....144 B4
St Peter's Av RPDN/SBR HX6 ....138 C8
RTHW LS26 ....126 C6
St Peter's Cl BTLY WF17 ....145 C2
MIRF * WF14 ....170 C6
St Peters Crs BEE/HOL LS11 ....101 J7
BRAM LS13 ....77 H8
HOR/CROF WF4 ....197 Cu1
St Peter's Crs EARD/LOFT WF3 ....150 E5
HUDE HD5 ....192 D5
MOR LS27 ....123 F5
St Peter's Gdns BRAM LS13 ....77 G8
St Peter's Garth SCFT LS14 ....60 E5
St Peters Ga OSS WF5 ....173 K4
St Peter's Gv HOR/CROF * WF4 ....197 H2
St Peter's Mt BRAM LS13 ....99 G1
St Peter's Pl OSM LS9 ....7 F5
St Peter's Sq OSM LS9 ....7 F5
St Peter's St HUD HD1 ....12 C4
LDSU LS2 ....7 F2
St Peter's Wy ILK LS29 ....32 B7
St Philip's Av ILK LS29 ....124 C6
St Philip's Cl DEWS * WF13 ....172 C2
ILK LS29 ....32 B3
MID LS10 ....124 D6
St Philips Ct HUDW HD3 ....190 B1
St Philip's Dr ILK LS29 ....32 B3
St Philip's Wy ILK LS29 ....32 B2
St Phillips Dr GIR BD8 ....95 F2
St Richards Rd OT LS21 ....33 H1
St Stephen's Ct AIRE BD20 ....165 K1
HIPP * HX3 ....9 J3
OSM * LS9 ....102 B3
St Stephen's Rd AIRE BD20 ....26 E6
HUD * HD1 ....12 B6
OSM LS9 ....102 B3
PDSY/CALV LS28 ....75 J4
WBOW BD5 ....95 K8
St Stephen's Ter WBOW * BD5 ....96 A8
Saint St GTHN BD7 ....95 G7
St Swithins Dr EARD/LOFT WF3 ....176 C1
St Swithins Gv EARD/LOFT * WF3 ....176 C1
St Thomas Gdns HUDN HD2 ....169 C5
St Thomas Rd FEA/AMT WF7 ....179 J6
HUD HD1 ....12 B5
St Thomas Rw LDSU LS2 ....7 F2
St Thomas's Rd BFD BD1 ....4 B4
St Vincent Rd PDSY/CALV LS28 ....98 C5
St Wilfred's St PDSY/CALV LS28 ....75 K4
St Wilfrid's Av RHAY LS8 ....80 C7
St Wilfrid's Circ RHAY LS8 ....80 D8
St Wilfrid's Cl GTHN BD7 ....95 F6
St Wilfrid's Crs GTHN BD7 ....95 F6
RHAY LS8 ....80 D7
St Wilfrid's Dr RHAY LS8 ....80 C7
St Wilfrid's Garth RHAY LS8 ....80 D8
St Wilfrid's Gv RHAY LS8 ....80 D7
St Wilfrid's Rd GTHN BD7 ....95 F6
St Winifred's Cl LUD/ILL * HX2 ....115 C6
Salcombe Pl BOW BD4 ....120 B1
Salem Pl GFTH/SHER LS25 ....105 J4
MID LS10 ....7 E5
Salem St BFD BD1 ....4 C3
CUL/QBY * BD13 ....116 C2
HBR HX7 ....112 B8
Salford Wy TOD OL14 ....133 K7
Salisbury Av BAIL BD17 ....51 J8
WOR/ARM LS12 ....100 C3
Salisbury Cl EARL WF12 ....172 E3
NORM WF6 ....152 A8
Salisbury Gv WOR/ARM LS12 ....100 C3
Salisbury Ms HORS LS18 ....77 H1
Salisbury Pl HIPP HX3 ....8 C2
PDSY/CALV LS28 ....75 J5
Salisbury Rd CLECK BD19 ....143 G5
HTON BD9 ....8 C2
HWTH BD22 ....2 B4
LM/WK BD12 ....118 D5
WOR/ARM LS12 ....100 C3
Salisbury St PDSY/CALV LS28 ....75 J5
RPDN/SBR HX6 ....138 D8
YEA LS19 ....53 K7
Salisbury Ter HIPP HX3 ....8 C2
WOR/ARM LS12 ....100 C3
Salisbury Vw WOR/ARM LS12 ....100 C3
Salmon Crs HORS LS18 ....77 G2
Sal Nook Cl LM/WK BD12 ....118 E4
Sal Royd Rd LM/WK BD12 ....119 F6
Saltaire Rd BGLY BD16 ....55 J3
SHPY BD18 ....73 G3
Saltburn Pl HTON BD9 ....95 F1
Saltburn St HFAX HX1 ....8 A4

Salt Drake RPDN/SBR HX6 ....163 J1
Salterhebble Hl HIPP HX3 ....166 C4
Salterlee HIPP HX3 ....9 F1
Salter Rake Ga TOD OL14 ....160 A4
Salter Rw PONT WF8 ....180 E5
Saltersgate Av KNOT WF11 ....156 E5
Salter St DEWS WF13 ....172 A4
Salt Horn Cl LM/WK BD12 ....119 C3
Saltonstall La LUD/ILL HX2 ....114 A4
Salt Pie Aly WKFDW/WTN WF2 ....10 B2
Salts Mill Rd BAIL BD17 ....73 H1
Salt St GIR BD8 ....4 B2
HFAX HX1 ....8 B7
Sampson St LVSG WF15 ....144 E4
Samuel Dr EARD/LOFT WF3 ....150 E5
Samuel St KGHY BD21 ....3 D2
Sandal Av WKFDW/WTN WF2 ....199 C5
Sandal Cliff WKFDW/WTN WF2 ....199 C6
Sandale Wk WBSY BD6 ....118 A3
Sandal Hall Cl WKFDW/WTN WF2 .....199 C4
Sandal Hall Ms WKFDW/WTN WF2 ....199 C5
Sandall Cl GFTH/SHER LS25 ....129 C5
Sandall Magna WBSY BD6 ....117 K5
Sandal Ri PONT WF8 ....204 C8
Sandals Rd BAIL BD17 ....73 ..
Sandal Wy BTLY WF17 ....145 ..
Sandbeck La WBY LS22 ....23 K5
Sandbeck Pk WBY LS22 ....23 K5
Sandbeck Wy WBY LS22 ....23 K5
Sandbed Ct MSTN/BAR LS15 ....82 E6
Sandbed La MSTN/BAR LS15 ....82 E6
Sand Beds CUL/QBY BD13 ....116 C2
Sandbeds HOLM/MEL HD9 ....213 F8
Sandbeds Crs LUD/ILL HX2 ....139 K5
Sandbeds Rd LUD/ILL HX2 ....139 K5
Sandbeds Ter LUD/ILL HX2 ....139 K5
Sandene Av HUDS HD4 ....212 C6
Sandene Dr HUDS HD4 ....212 C6
Sanderling Garth MID LS10 ....124 D5
Sanderling Ct GIR * BD8 ....94 E1
Sanderling Garth MID LS10 ....124 C5
Sanderling Wy MID LS10 ....124 D5
Sanderson Av NORM WF6 ....177 H1
WBSY BD6 ....118 C3
Sanderson La RTHW LS26 ....150 C2
Sanderson St WKFDE WF1 ....11 C6
Sandfield Av HDGY LS6 ....78 E1
Sandfield Garth HDGY LS6 ....78 E1
Sandfield Gv IDLE BD10 ....78 E1
Sandfield Vw HDGY LS6 ....78 E1
Sandford Pl KSTL LS5 ....78 A4
Sandford Rd BFDE BD3 ....96 E8
HEM/SK/SE WF9 ....226 C7
KSTL LS5 ....78 A4
Sandforth Av HIPP HX3 ....9 J3
Sandgate Dr GFTH/SHER LS25 ....129 F5
Sandgate La GFTH/SHER LS25 ....129 F5
Sandgate Ter GFTH/SHER LS25 ....129 F5
Sandhall Av LUD/ILL HX2 ....139 J5
Sandhall Dr LUD/ILL HX2 ....139 J5
Sandhall Gn LUD/ILL HX2 ....139 J5
Sandhall La LUD/ILL HX2 ....139 J5
Sandhill Cl PONT WF8 ....154 E8
Sandhill Crs AL/HA/HU LS17 ....58 E1
Sandhill Dr AL/HA/HU LS17 ....58 E1
Sandhill Fold IDLE BD10 ....74 C1
Sandhill Gv AL/HA/HU LS17 ....58 E1
Sand Hill La AL/HA/HU LS17 ....58 E1
Sandhill Lawn PONT WF8 ....180 C7
Sand Hill Lawns AL/HA/HU LS17 ....57 K1
Sandhill Mt AL/HA/HU LS17 ....57 K1
IDLE BD10 ....74 C1
Sandhill Ov AL/HA/HU LS17 ....58 E1
Sandhill Ri PONT WF8 ....154 E8
Sandholme Crs HIPP HX3 ....141 G8
Sandholme Dr IDLE BD10 ....74 C1
ILK LS29 ....32 B8
OSS WF5 ....173 H5
Sandhurst Av RHAY LS8 ....80 C3
Sandhurst Gv RHAY LS8 ....80 C3
Sandhurst Gr RHAY LS8 ....80 B3
Sandhurst Rd RHAY LS8 ....80 C3
Sandhurst Ter RHAY LS8 ....80 C3
Sandiford Cl MSTN/BAR LS15 ....82 E4
Sandiford Ter MSTN/BAR LS15 ....82 E4
Sandiway Bank EARL WF12 ....172 C2
Sandleas Wy MSTN/BAR LS15 ....104 A3
Sandlewood Cl BEE/HOL LS11 ....6 C6
Sandlewood Gn BEE/HOL LS11 ....6 C6
Sandmead Cl BOW BD4 ....97 J2
MOR LS27 ....141 K2
Sandmead Cft MOR LS27 ....141 K3
Sandmead Wy MOR LS27 ....141 K2
Sandmoor Av AL/HA/HU LS17 ....57 K2
Sandmoor Cha AL/HA/HU LS17 ....57 K1
Sandmoor Cl AL/HA/HU LS17 ....57 K2
CUL/QBY BD13 ....93 K5
Sandmoor Dr AL/HA/HU LS17 ....57 K1
HUDW HD3 ....190 A1
Sandmoor Gdns HIPP HX3 ....117 G1
Sandmoor Garth IDLE BD10 ....74 A3
Sandmoor Gn AL/HA/HU LS17 ....57 K1
Sandmoor La AL/HA/HU LS17 ....57 K2
Sandmoor Ms AL/HA/HU LS17 ....57 K2
Sandon Gv MID * LS10 ....124 C5
Sandon Mt MID LS10 ....124 C5
Sandown Av HOR/CROF WF4 ....200 B5
LUD/ILL HX2 ....115 J5
Sandown Rd LUD/ILL HX2 ....115 J5

andpiper Ap *MOR* LS27 ....123 H8
andpiper Ms *GIR* BD8 ....94 C4
andringham *HUDN* HD2 ....169 F6
andringham Ap *AL/HA/HU* LS17 ....58 A3
andringham Av *KNOT* WF11 ....155 K7
andringham Cl *CLAY* * BD14 ....94 D6
  MOR LS27 ....123 H6
  PONT WF8 ....180 D6
  STKB/PEN S36 ....251 K7
andringham Ct *CLAY* BD14 ....94 D6
andringham Crs *AL/HA/HU* LS17 ....57 K8
  PDSY/CALV LS28 ....98 C5
andringham Dr *AL/HA/HU* LS17 ....57 K8
andringham Gdns *AL/HA/HU* LS17 ....57 K8
andringham La *AL/HA/HU* LS17 ....58 A3
andringham Mt *AL/HA/HU* LS17 ....58 A7
andringham Rd *CLAY* BD14 ....94 D6
  KNOT WF11 ....156 K4
  WBY LS22 ....23 J5
andringham Wy *AL/HA/HU* LS17 ....57 K8
androck Rd *PONT* WF8 ....181 F1
andsend Cl *HTON* BD9 ....72 D8
andside Cl *WBOW* BD5 ....119 G1
ands La *EARL* WF12 ....152 C3
  HUDE HD5 ....193 H5
  MIRF WF14 ....171 G8
ands Rd *EARL* WF12 ....172 D5
ands Ter *HUDN* * HD2 ....192 A1
andstone Cl *HOLM/MEL* HD9 ....213 F8
andstone Dr *WOR/ARM* LS12 ....99 G4
andstone La *HUDS* HD4 ....190 B8
and St *HUD* HD1 ....13 D5
  HWTH BD22 ....68 E5
  KGHY BD21 ....3 D3
andway *MSTN/BAR* LS15 ....103 K1
andway Gdns *MSTN/BAR* LS15 ....103 K1
andway Gv *MSTN/BAR* LS15 ....103 K1
andwell St *MAR/SLWT* HD7 ....210 D2
andwich Crs *HUDN* HD2 ....168 A8
andyacres *RTHW* LS26 ....126 C5
andyacres Crs *RTHW* LS26 ....126 C5
andyacres Dr *RTHW* LS26 ....126 C5
andy Bank Av *RTHW* LS26 ....126 C5
andy Banks *BGLY* BD16 ....71 F3
andy Beck *WIL/AL* BD15 ....72 A8
ndy Dyke La *RPDN/SBR* HX6 ....164 B5
andyfoot *CTL/HWG* HX4 ....164 E7
andy Ga *AL/HA/HU* LS17 ....37 K4
  HBR HX7 ....112 C8
  HOLM/MEL HD9 ....233 J7
andy Lobby *GTL* LS21 ....35 C5
andymoor *WIL/AL* BD15 ....72 A7
andy Wk *BHP/TINH* LS16 ....55 K1
  WKFDE WF1 ....10 B2
ndy Wy *YEA* LS19 ....53 K4
andywood St *KGHY* BD21 ....3 D2
ngster Wy *WBOW* BD5 ....119 H2
nta Monica Crs *IDLE* BD10 ....74 C4
nta Monica Gdns *IDLE* BD10 ....74 C4
nta Monica Rd *IDLE* BD10 ....74 C4
ntingley La *HOR/CROF* WF4 ....200 E5
nworth St *TOD* OL14 ....134 B6
ogate La *CUD/GR* S72 ....223 G5
plin St *GIR* BD8 ....95 H2
pphire Ct *BTLY* WF17 ....145 K5
rah St *EARD/LOFT* WF3 ....148 E3
rdinia St *MID* LS10 ....7 F6
unders Cl *HUDW* HD3 ....190 C4
underson Rd *STKB/PEN* S36 ....252 A7
unters Wy *NORM* WF6 ....151 K7
vile Av *CHAL* * LS7 ....79 K8
  IDLE BD10 ....74 E5
  KBTN HD8 ....217 H4
vile Cl *BRIG* HD6 ....142 E8
vile Ct *MIRF* * WF14 ....170 D5
vile Crs *HFAX* HX1 ....8 C5
vile Dr *CHAL* LS7 ....79 K8
  HFAX HX1 ....8 C6
  HOR/CROF WF4 ....197 G1
vile Gln *HFAX* HX1 ....8 C5
vile Gn *HFAX* HX1 ....9 D5
vile Gv *EARL* WF12 ....172 B4
vile La *BRIG* HD6 ....142 E8
vile Lea *HFAX* HX1 ....8 C5
vile Ms *EARL* WF12 ....172 B6
vile Mt *CHAL* LS7 ....79 K8
vile Pde *HFAX* HX1 ....8 C6
vile Pk *HFAX* HX1 ....8 B6
vile Park Gdns *HFAX* HX1 ....8 C6
vile Park Rd *CLECK* BD19 ....120 A8
  HFAX HX1 ....8 C5
vile Park St *HFAX* HX1 ....8 B6
vile Park Ter *HFAX* * HX1 ....8 B6
vile Pit La *EARL* WF12 ....173 F2
vile Rd *CHAL* LS7 ....79 K8
  MIRF WF14 ....170 D5
vile Rd *CAS* WF10 ....153 H5
  CHAL LS7 ....79 K8
  EARL WF12 ....172 B6

ELL HX5 ....166 E5
HBR HX7 ....111 K8
HFAX HX1 ....8 C5
HUDW HD3 ....190 C3
RTHW LS26 ....128 C8
Savile Royd *HFAX* HX1 ....8 C6
Savile St *BTLY* WF17 ....146 C8
  CLECK BD19 ....144 A2
  DEWS WF13 ....171 J3
  HUDW HD3 ....190 A6
  KBTN HD8 ....217 H4
Savile Ter *HFAX* HX1 ....8 B6
Savile Wy *CUD/GR* S72 ....224 B8
Savile Wy *ELL* HX5 ....167 F5
Saville Cl *EARD/LOFT* WF3 ....149 K2
Saville Ct *OT* LS21 ....33 H4
Saville La *STKB/PEN* S36 ....251 J8
Saville Pk *OSS* WF5 ....174 A7
Saville Park Rd *HFAX* HX1 ....8 C6
Saville Rd *KBTN* HD8 ....236 E1
Saville St *KBTN* * HD8 ....237 H2
  OSS WF5 ....174 A7
  WKFDE WF1 ....10 C2
Savins Mill Wy *KSTL* LS5 ....78 A7
Sawley St *KGHY* BD21 ....2 C4
Sawood La *HWTH* BD22 ....91 H5
Sawrey Pl *WBOW* BD5 ....117 J5
Saw Yd *WKFDE* WF1 ....10 C5
Sawyers Garth *ILK* LS29 ....18 E5
Saxon Av *HEM/SK/SE* WF9 ....241 F1
Saxon Cl *HEM/SK/SE* WF9 ....227 G4
  KBTN HD8 ....217 G5
Saxon Ga *AL/HA/HU* LS17 ....79 H1
Saxon Gn *AL/HA/HU* LS17 ....79 G1
Saxon Gv *AL/HA/HU* LS17 ....79 G1
  HEM/SK/SE WF9 ....241 G2
Saxon Mt *AL/HA/HU* LS17 ....57 H8
  HEM/SK/SE WF9 ....241 F1
Saxon Rd *AL/HA/HU* LS17 ....79 G1
Saxon St *GIR* BD8 ....4 A3
  HFAX HX1 ....8 A4
  TOD OL14 ....159 K2
Saxon Wy *CAS* WF10 ....154 B5
Saxton Av *WBSY* BD6 ....117 G7
Saxton Ct *GFTH/SHER* LS25 ....105 K3
Saxton Gdns *OSM* * LS9 ....102 A4
Saxton La *OSM* LS9 ....7 F4
Saxton Pl *HUDE* HD5 ....192 C7
Saxton St *LVSC* WF15 ....145 F6
Sayers Cl *KSTL* LS5 ....78 B7
Sayle Av *BOW* BD4 ....119 J3
Sayner La *MID* LS10 ....7 F5
Sayner Rd *MID* LS10 ....7 F5
Scalebor Park Cl *ILK* LS29 ....32 A3
Scale Hl *HUDN* HD2 ....191 G1
Scaley Ga *BFDE* BD3 ....97 F4
Scaly Ga *HOLM/MEL* HD9 ....234 C6
  HOLM/MEL HD9 ....249 H1
Scammonden Rd *GTL/HWG* HX4 ....187 H4
  RPDN/SBR HX6 ....164 D5
Scape Vw *MAR/SLWT* HD7 ....189 J7
Scarboro Mdw *MIRF* * WF14 ....170 D6
Scarborough Gv *SHPY* BD18 ....73 C4
Scarborough Rd *EARD/LOFT* WF3 ....147 J3
  SHPY BD18 ....73 C4
Scarborough St *EARD/LOFT* WF3 ....147 J2
  EARL WF12 ....172 C5
Scarborough Ter *EARL* WF12 ....172 C5
Scar Bottom La *GTL/HWG* HX4 ....165 J4
Scarbro' Jct *BRAM* LS13 ....99 H2
Scarcroft Ct *SCFT* LS14 ....60 B5
Scarfold *HOLM/MEL* HD9 ....233 G6
Scargill Cl *OSM* LS9 ....102 B2
Scargill Gra *OSM* LS9 ....102 B3
Scar Gv *HUDS* HD4 ....213 F1
Scar Head Rd *RPDN/SBR* HX6 ....164 E1
Scar Hole La *HOLM/MEL* HD9 ....234 C7
Scarhouse La *MAR/SLWT* HD7 ....189 J7
Scar La *MAR/SLWT* HD7 ....189 K7
Scarlet Hts *CUL/OBY* BD13 ....116 E2
Scarr Bottom Rd *LUD/ILL* HX2 ....139 J7
Scarr End La *DEWS* WF13 ....171 J1
  HFAX HX1 ....172 E6
Scarr End Vw *DEWS* WF13 ....171 J1
Scarsdale La *AL/HA/HU* LS17 ....40 C5
Scarsdale Rdg *AL/HA/HU* LS17 ....40 C5
Scarth Av *OSM* LS9 ....102 C1
Scarth Ter *EARD/LOFT* WF3 ....150 E5
Scar Top *GTL/HWG* * HX4 ....165 J4
Scar Top La *HUDS* HD4 ....212 D5
Scar Top Rd *HWTH* BD22 ....67 F4
Scarwood Cl *BGLY* BD16 ....50 A7
Scatcherd Gv *MOR* LS27 ....122 E7
Scatcherd La *MOR* LS27 ....122 E8
Scatcherd Park Av *MOR* LS27 ....123 F6
Scawthorpe Gv *PONT* WF8 ....181 G2
Sceptone Gv *CUD/GR* S72 ....223 G8
Schofield Ct *MOR* * LS27 ....123 F7
Schofield La *HUDE* HD5 ....193 K2
Scholars Wk *ECHL* BD2 ....74 D8
Schole Av *STKB/PEN* S36 ....252 B8
Scholebrook La *BOW* BD4 ....98 A8
Scholemoor Av *GTHN* BD7 ....94 E6
Scholemoor La *GTHN* BD7 ....94 E6
Scholemoor Rd *GTHN* BD7 ....95 F6
Scholes La *CLECK* BD19 ....143 G3
  GTL/HWG HX4 ....165 K2
  HWTH BD22 ....68 B2
  MSTN/BAR LS15 ....82 C3

Scholes Moor Rd *HOLM/MEL* HD9 ....248 D2
Scholes Rd *CAS* WF10 ....154 E2
  HOLM/MEL HD9 ....234 A7
  HUDN HD2 ....191 G1
Scholes St *WBOW* BD5 ....118 E1
Scholey Av *BRIG* HD6 ....168 B3
Scholey Rd *BRIG* HD6 ....168 B3
Scholfield St *TOD* OL14 ....134 A5
School Av *DEWS* WF13 ....171 J2
  LUD/ILL HX2 ....115 J4
  RPDN/SBR HX6 ....164 B7
  WOR/ARM LS12 ....99 H8
School Cote Brow *LUD/ILL* HX2 ....116 A5
School Crs *DEWS* WF13 ....171 J2
  LUD/ILL HX2 ....115 J4
  WKFDW/WTN WF2 ....174 E7
School Cft *KNOT* WF11 ....155 K3
  RTHW LS26 ....126 B5
School Dr *KNOT* WF11 ....155 K6
Schoolgate *MSTN/BAR* LS15 ....83 J4
School Gn *BHP/TINH* LS16 ....55 J1
  BRIG HD6 ....168 B3
  CUL/OBY BD13 ....94 A5
School Green Av *CUL/OBY* BD13 ....93 K5
School Gv *DEWS* WF13 ....171 J2
School Hl *HUDS* HD4 ....212 A4
  KBTN HD8 ....215 H5
  WKFDW/WTN WF2 ....198 D7
School Houses *HUDW* * HD3 ....189 K3
School Land La *HBR* HX7 ....110 E5
School La *AL/HA/HU* LS17 ....40 A6
  AL/HA/HU LS17 ....58 D3
  BSPA/BRAM LS23 ....25 F7
  CAS WF10 ....154 A5
  CHAL LS7 ....79 J4
  DEWS WF13 ....171 J2
  GFTH/SHER LS25 ....84 E4
  HDGY LS6 ....78 E5
  HIPP HX3 ....141 F8
  HOR/CROF WF4 ....197 G2
  HOR/CROF WF4 ....223 F2
  HUD HD1 ....12 A5
  HUDE HD5 ....192 D4
  HUDS HD4 ....213 F3
  ILK LS29 ....18 C3
  KBTN HD8 ....217 H4
  KBTN HD8 ....236 E5
  LUD/ILL HX2 ....115 J3
  LUD/ILL HX2 ....115 J5
  LVSC WF15 ....170 A1
  MAR/SLWT HD7 ....189 F5
  MAR/SLWT HD7 ....210 A5
  MSTN/BAR LS15 ....103 J3
  MSTN/BAR LS15 ....104 C4
  TOD OL14 ....134 A6
  WBY LS22 ....41 F3
  WKFDW/WTN WF2 ....175 F1
  WKFDW/WTN WF2 ....199 J4
School Pl *LM/WK* * BD12 ....118 D7
School Rd *HWTH* BD22 ....2 A3
  MAR/SLWT HD7 ....189 F5
  PONT WF8 ....181 F4
  WBY LS22 ....23 K5
  WKFDW/WTN WF2 ....174 E8
School Sq *BFDE* BD3 ....97 F4
School St *AIRE* BD20 ....26 E6
  AIRE BD20 ....47 J1
  BGLY BD16 ....72 B4
  BOW BD4 ....96 E8
  BOW BD4 ....119 J3
  BTLY WF17 ....145 J3
  CAS WF10 ....153 J2
  CAS WF10 ....153 K2
  CLAY BD14 ....94 B7
  CLECK BD19 ....143 K5
  CUL/OBY BD13 ....92 D3
  CUL/OBY * BD13 ....92 C3
  DEWS WF13 ....171 G6
  EARD/LOFT WF3 ....147 J6
  EARL WF12 ....172 B3
  EARL WF12 ....173 G3
  GTL/HWG HX4 ....166 A3
  HBR HX7 ....112 B8
  HEM/SK/SE WF9 ....227 F3
  HFAX HX1 ....9 E5
  HOLM/MEL HD9 ....213 F6
  HOLM/MEL HD9 ....233 F3
  HOLM/MEL HD9 ....233 G6
  HUDE HD5 ....13 F5
  LM/WK BD12 ....118 D5
  LM/WK BD12 ....119 H7
  LVSC WF15 ....170 B1
  LVSC WF15 ....170 E1
  MOR LS27 ....123 G7
  MOR LS27 ....123 H3
  OSS WF5 ....173 H2
  PDSY/CALV LS28 ....76 B8
  PDSY/CALV LS28 ....98 B5
  WIL/AL BD15 ....71 G6
School St West *HUDW* HD3 ....190 B3
School Vw *HDGY* LS6 ....78 E8
School Wk *HWTH* BD22 ....2 A3
School Yard Vw *HIPP* HX3 ....9 D2
Sconce La *BAIL* BD17 ....51 C3
Scopsley Gn *EARL* WF12 ....194 C3
Scopsley La *EARL* WF12 ....194 B2
Score Cft *KBTN* HD8 ....236 F1
Score Hl *HIPP* HX3 ....117 F7

Scoresby St *BFD* BD1 ....5 D4
Scotchman Cl *MOR* LS27 ....146 E1
Scotchman La *MOR* LS27 ....146 D3
Scotchman Rd *HTON* BD9 ....95 F1
Scotgate Rd *HOLM/MEL* HD9 .....212 D7
Scotland Cl *HORS* LS18 ....54 E5
Scotland La *HORS* LS18 ....54 E4
Scotland Mill La *BHP/TINH* LS16 ...79 F1
Scotland St *CLECK* BD19 ....145 F2
Scotland Wy *HORS* LS18 ....54 E7
Scotland Wood Rd *AL/HA/HU* LS17 ...79 F1
Scott Av *HECK* WF16 ....145 G5
Scott Cl *HECK* * WF16 ....145 H7
  RTHW LS26 ....127 K2
Scott Dr *HOR/CROF* WF4 ....200 E3
Scott Gn *MOR* LS27 ....122 A3
Scott Green Crs *MOR* LS27 ....122 A3
Scott Green Dr *MOR* LS27 ....122 A3
Scott Green Gv *MOR* LS27 ....122 A3
Scott Green Mt *MOR* LS27 ....122 A3
Scott Green Vw *MOR* LS27 ....122 B3
Scott Hall Av *CHAL* LS7 ....79 J7
Scott Hall Dr *CHAL* LS7 ....79 J6
Scott Hall Gn *CHAL* LS7 ....79 J6
Scott Hall Gv *CHAL* LS7 ....79 J6
Scott Hall Pl *CHAL* LS7 ....79 J6
Scott Hall Rd *CHAL* LS7 ....79 H5
Scott Hall Rw *CHAL* LS7 ....79 J7
Scott Hall Sq *CHAL* LS7 ....79 J6
Scott Hall St *CHAL* LS7 ....79 J7
Scott Hall Ter *CHAL* LS7 ....79 J6
Scott Hall Wk *CHAL* LS7 ....79 J7
Scott Hall Wy *CHAL* LS7 ....79 J5
Scott Hl *KBTN* HD8 ....217 K8
Scott La *AIRE* BD20 ....48 C1
  CLECK BD19 ....144 A3
  CLECK BD19 ....144 E2
  MOR LS27 ....122 D8
  WBY LS22 ....23 J6
Scott La West *AIRE* BD20 ....48 B1
Scott Ms *WBY* LS22 ....23 J6
Scotts Hill Cl *SCFT* LS14 ....60 D6
Scott St *KGHY* BD21 ....2 C3
  PDSY/CALV LS28 ....98 D5
  TOD OL14 ....159 K3
Scott V *HUDN* HD2 ....168 E8
Scott Wood La *CHAL* LS7 ....79 H6
Scotty Bank Brig * HD6 ....168 B1
Scotty Croft La *BRIG* HD6 ....168 B3
Scout Bottom La *HBR* HX7 ....137 G3
Scout Cl *HBR* HX7 ....137 F3
Scout Hill Rd *DEWS* WF13 ....171 K5
Scout La *MAR/SLWT* HD7 ....209 K2
Scout Rd *HBR* HX7 ....137 F3
Scrapers La *TOD* OL14 ....134 A3
Scriftain La *WBY* LS22 ....23 J2
Seacroft Av *SCFT* LS14 ....81 K6
Seacroft Cl *SCFT* LS14 ....81 K6
Seacroft Crs *SCFT* LS14 ....81 K6
Seacroft Ga *SCFT* * LS14 ....81 K6
Seaforth Av *OSM* LS9 ....80 C8
Seaforth Gv *OSM* LS9 ....80 C8
Seaforth Mt *OSM* LS9 ....80 C8
Seaforth Pl *OSM* LS9 ....80 C8
Seaforth Rd *OSM* LS9 ....80 C8
Seaforth Ter *OSM* LS9 ....80 C8
Seagrave Rd *HUDS* HD4 ....190 C6
Seaton St *BFDE* BD3 ....5 F4
Seckar La *HOR/CROF* WF4 ....220 C3
Second Av *AL/HA/HU* LS17 ....40 C6
  BFDE BD3 ....96 E2
  HEM/SK/SE WF9 ....202 A7
  HEM/SK/SE WF9 ....226 C3
  HEM/SK/SE WF9 ....241 F2
  HIPP HX3 ....140 A7
  HOR/CROF WF4 ....197 F2
  HUDE HD5 ....192 B4
  KGHY BD21 ....2 C4
  LVSG WF15 ....143 J7
  RTHW LS26 ....126 C4
  WBY LS22 ....23 K6
  WKFDE WF1 ....175 J1
  WOR/ARM LS12 ....6 A4
  YEA LS19 ....54 A6
Second St *LM/WK* BD12 ....119 F5
Sedbergh Cl *MSTN/BAR* LS15 ....103 F4
Sedbergh Dr *ILK* LS29 ....20 C5
Sedbergh Pk *ILK* LS29 ....20 C8
Sedburgh Rd *HIPP* HX3 ....9 E6
Sedge Gv *HWTH* BD22 ....68 E3
Sedgewick Cl *BTLY* WF17 ....145 H2
Sedgfield Ter *BFD* BD1 ....4 B4
Sedgwick Cl *GIR* BD8 ....4 B3
Seed Hill Ter *LUD/ILL* HX2 ....115 F5
Seed St *LM/WK* BD12 ....118 E5
Sefton Av *BEE/HOL* LS11 ....101 G8
  BRIG HD6 ....157 G6
Sefton Ct *HDGY* LS6 ....78 D5
Sefton Crs *BRIG* HD6 ....142 A6
Sefton Dr *BRIG* HD6 ....142 A6
  ILK LS29 ....20 B8
Sefton Gv *ECHL* BD2 ....74 D7
Sefton La *HOLM/MEL* HD9 ....231 H1
Sefton Pl *KGHY* * BD21 ....3 D2
Sefton Ri *EARL* WF12 ....172 C7
Sefton St *BEE/HOL* LS11 ....101 G8
  HFAX HX1 ....8 B3
  KGHY BD21 ....3 D2
Sefton Ter *BEE/HOL* LS11 ....101 G8

  HFAX HX1 ....8 B3
Selborne Gv *HTON* BD9 ....73 H8
  KGHY BD21 ....2 B5
Selborne Mt *HTON* BD9 ....73 H8
Selborne Ter *HTON* BD9 ....95 H1
  SHPY BD18 ....73 H5
Selborne Vls *CLAY* BD14 ....94 C8
  HTON BD9 ....95 H1
Selbourne Av *EARL* WF12 ....172 B5
Selbourne Dr *EARL* WF12 ....172 B6
Selbourne Rd *EARL* WF12 ....172 B6
Selby *LUD/ILL* HX2 ....115 C4
Selby Av *OSM* LS9 ....103 G3
Selby Rd *SCFT* LS14 ....103 F2
Selby St *WKFDE* WF1 ....10 C2
Seldon St *WBOW* BD5 ....95 H8
Selene Cl *CLECK* BD19 ....145 F1
Sellars Fold *GTHN* * BD7 ....95 G7
Sellerdale Av *LM/WK* BD12 ....142 E2
Sellerdale Dr *LM/WK* BD12 ....142 E1
Sellerdale Ri *LM/WK* BD12 ....142 E1
Sellerdale Wy *LM/WK* BD12 ....142 E2
Selso Rd *EARL* WF12 ....172 E2
Seminary St *LDSU* LS2 ....6 C2
Semon Av *ECHL* BD2 ....74 B6
Senior St *DEWS* WF13 ....172 A4
  HUDE HD5 ....178 B3
Senior Wy *WBOW* BD5 ....4 C5
Sentry *HOLM/MEL* HD9 ....213 F6
Sergeantson St *HUD* * HD1 ....12 C4
Serpentine Rd *CLECK* BD19 ....144 A3
Servia Dr *CHAL* LS7 ....79 H8
Servia Hl *CHAL* LS7 ....79 H8
Servia Rd *CHAL* LS7 ....79 H8
Service Rd *OSM* LS9 ....103 F8
Sessions House Yd *PONT* WF8 ....180 D2
Sevenoaks Md *WIL/AL* BD15 ....94 B2
Seventh Av *LVSG* WF15 ....143 J6
  RTHW LS26 ....126 D5
Severn Dr *GFTH/SHER* LS25 ....106 B6
Severn Rd *ECHL* BD2 ....5 E1
  MID LS10 ....102 B8
Severn Wy *MID* LS10 ....102 B7
Sewage Works Rd *OSM* LS9 ....102 E8
Sewell Rd *BFDE* BD3 ....5 F5
Sewerbridge La *FEA/AMT* WF7 ...178 D2
Seymour St *BFDE* BD3 ....5 E5
  WKFDW/WTN WF2 ....10 C5
Seymour Wk *HOLM/MEL* HD9 ....231 J1
Shackleton St *TOD* OL14 ....133 F2
Shade St *TOD* OL14 ....133 K8
Shadwell La *AL/HA/HU* LS17 ....79 K1
Shadwell Park Av *AL/HA/HU* LS17 ...58 E6
Shadwell Park Cl *AL/HA/HU* LS17 ...58 E6
Shadwell Park Ct *AL/HA/HU* LS17 ...58 E7
Shadwell Park Dr *AL/HA/HU* LS17 ...58 E7
Shadwell Park Gv *AL/HA/HU* LS17 ...58 E6
Shadwell Park Gdns *AL/HA/HU* LS17 ...58 E7
Shadwell Wk *AL/HA/HU* LS17 ....58 A8
Shaftesbury Av *BRIG* HD6 ....168 C4
  CLE DN14 ....157 J6
  HTON BD9 ....94 D1
  RHAY LS8 ....80 C2
  SHPY BD18 ....73 J4
Shaftesbury Pde *OSM* * LS9 ....102 E2
Shaftesbury Rd *RHAY* LS8 ....80 C1
Shafton Hall Dr *CUD/SHP* S72 ....223 F8
Shafton La *BEE/HOL* LS11 ....6 B6
Shafton Pl *BEE/HOL* LS11 ....6 B6
Shafton St *BEE/HOL* LS11 ....6 B6
Shafton Vw *BEE/HOL* LS11 ....6 B6
Shakespeare Ap *OSM* LS9 ....102 B2
Shakespeare Av *NORM* WF6 ....177 K4
  OSM LS9 ....102 B2
  TOD OL14 ....134 C5
Shakespeare Cl *OSM* LS9 ....102 B2
Shakespeare Ct *OSM* LS9 ....102 B2
Shakespeare Crs *CAS* WF10 ....154 E6
Shakespeare Gdns *OSM* LS9 ......102 B2
Shakespeare Gra *OSM* LS9 ....102 B2
Shakespeare Lawn *OSM* LS9 ......102 B2
Shakespeare Rd *GSLY* LS20 ....53 G3
Shakespeare St *HFAX* HX1 ....9 D5
  OSM LS9 ....102 B1
Shakespeare Towers *OSM* LS9 ....102 B1
Shalimar St *HFAX* HX3 ....9 A4
The Shambles *WBY* LS22 ....23 J6
Shann Crs *KGHY* BD21 ....2 A2
Shann La *KGHY* BD21 ....2 A2
Shann St *BRIG* HD6 ....167 K4
  ILK LS29 ....19 K8
Shannon Dr *HUDW* HD3 ....189 H2
Shannon Rd *BRIG* HD6 ....167 K4
  OSM LS9 ....102 A3
Shannon St *OSM* LS9 ....102 A3
Shann St *SHPY* BD18 ....73 K7
Shapla Cl *HWTH* BD22 ....2 B4
Share Hl *MAR/SLWT* HD7 ....189 D7
Sharp Av *WBSY* BD6 ....118 D3
Sharp St *HECK* WF16 ....145 G8
Sharp House Rd *MID* LS10 ....125 F7
Sharp La *HUDS* HD4 ....214 B2
  MID LS10 ....125 F6
Sharp Ms *HDGY* LS6 ....79 F6
Sharp Rw *PDSY/CALV* LS28 ....98 D5
Sharp Royd *HUDE* HD5 ....192 C7
Sharp St *DEWS* WF13 ....172 C5
  WBSY BD6 ....118 D2

Shaw Av *NORM* WF6 ....178 B3
Shaw Barn Cft *WBY* LS22 ....23 C
Shaw Barn La *WBY* LS22 ....23 C
Shaw Booth La *LUD/ILL* HX2 ....114 C
Shaw Cl *GFTH/SHER* LS25 ....106 A
  GTL/HWG HX4 ....166 E
  NORM WF6 ....178 B
Shawfield Av *HOLM/MEL* HD9 ....232 D
Shaw Fields La *MAR/SLWT* HD7 ...210 A
Shaw Fold *WKFDW/WTN* WF2 .....199 C
Shaw Ga *MAR/SLWT* HD7 ....210 C
Shaw Hl *HFAX* HX1 ....9 E
Shaw Hill La *HIPP* HX3 ....9 E
Shaw La *ELL* HX5 ....167 H
  GSLY LS20 ....53 H
  GTL/HWG HX4 ....166 A
  HDGY LS6 ....78 D
  HIPP HX5 ....116 B
  HIPP HX3 ....140 C
  HOLM/MEL HD9 ....232 D
  HUDS HD4 ....190 E
  HUDW HD3 ....189 C
  KGHY BD21 ....48 B
  MAR/SLWT HD7 ....189 F
  MAR/SLWT HD7 209
  RPDN/SBR HX6 ....165 F
  RPDN/SBR HX6 ....186 E
  TOD OL14 ....108 B
Shaw Lane Gdns *GSLY* LS20 ....53 H
Shaw Leys *YEA* LS19 53
Shaw Ri *NORM* * WF6 ....178 B
Shaw Royd *YEA* LS19 53
Shaws *LA* *MSTN/BAR* LS15 ....83 C
  RPDN/SBR HX6 ....163 H
Shaw St *CLECK* * BD19 143
  GTL/HWG HX4 ....166 B
  LM/WK BD12 ....118 C
  MIRF WF14 ....170 C
Shaw Wood Rd *TOD* OL14 ....134 B
Shay Cl *HTON* BD9 ....73 B
Shay Ct *HOR/CROF* WF4 200
  LDSU LS2 79
Shay Crs *HTON* BD9 72
Shay Dr *HTON* BD9 72
Shayfield La *EARD/LOFT* WF3 .....126 A
Shay Fold *HTON* BD9 72
Shay Gap Rd *HWTH* * BD22 46
Shay Ga *WIL/AL* * BD15 71
Shay Gra *HTON* BD9 72
Shay Gv *HTON* BD9 73
Shay La *HOLM/MEL* HD9 231
  HOR/CROF WF4 ....200 A
  HTON BD9 72
  LUD/ILL HX2 115
  WIL/AL BD15 71
Shay St *LDSU* LS2 79
Shay Syke *HFAX* HX1 9
Sheaf St *MID* LS10 7
Shearbridge Gn *GTHN* BD7 4
Shearbridge Rd *GTHN* BD7 4
Shearbridge Ter *GTHN* BD7 4
Sheardale *HOLM/MEL* HD9 212
Shearing Cross Gdns *HUD* * HD1 ...13
Shed St *KGHY* * BD21 3
Sheep Hill La *CUL/QBY* BD13 117
Sheepridge Gv *HUDN* HD2 168
Sheepridge Rd *HUDN* HD2 168
Sheepscar Gv *CHAL* LS7 7
Sheepscar St North *CHAL* LS7 79
Sheepwalk La *CAS* WF10 154
  HEM/SK/SE WF9 227
Sheffield Rd *HOLM/MEL* HD9 234
Sheldon Rdg *BOW* BD4 119
Sheldrake Av *GIR* BD8 94
Sheldrake Rd *CAS* WF10 153
Shelf Hall La *HIPP* HX3 117
Shelf Moor *HIPP* HX3 117
Shelf Moor Rd *HIPP* HX3 117
Shelf Rd *HBR* HX7 112
Shelldrake Dr *MID* LS10 124
Shelley Av *HECK* * WF16 171
Shelley Cl *RTHW* LS26 252
  STKB/PEN S36 252
Shelley Ct *BLY* BD16 50
  HOR/CROF WF4 197
Shelley Crs *RTHW* LS26 127
Shelley Cl *KNOT* WF11 155
Shelley Gv *GIR* BD8 94
Shelley La *KBTN* HD8 215
Shelley Woodhouse La *KBTN* HD8 ...236
Shell La *PDSY/CALV* LS28 75
Shepcote Cl *BHP/TINH* LS16 55
Shepcote Crs *BHP/TINH* LS16 55
Shepherds Gv *HUDN* HD2 168
  RHAY LS8 80
Shepherd's La *CHAL* LS7 80
Shepherd's Pl *RHAY* * LS8 80
Shepherds Thorn La *HUDN* HD2 ...168
Shepley Mt *MIRF* WF14 170
Shepley Rd *HUDS* HD4 234
Shepley St *WKFDE* WF1 11
Shepstye Rd *HOR/CROF* WF4 197
Sherborne Dr *HWTH* BD22 47
Sherborne Rd *GTHN* * BD7 4
  IDLE BD10 78
Sherbrooke Av *MSTN/BAR* LS15 ...103
Sherburn Ap *SCFT* LS14 82
Sherburn Cl *BIRK/DRI* BD11 120
Sherburn Ct *SCFT* LS14 82

herburn Gv BIRK/DRI BD11 ....120 E5
herburn Pl SCFT LS14 ....82 A5
herburn Rd BRIG HD6 ....167 J3
 SCFT LS14 ....82 A5
herburn Rd North SCFT LS14 ....81 K3
heridan Cl PDSY/CALV LS28 ....98 D5
heridan Ct PDSY/CALV * LS28 ....98 D5
heridan La BOW BD4 ....96 C7
 WKFDE WF1 ....150 A6
heridan Wy PDSY/CALV LS28 ....98 C5
heriff La BGLY BD16 ....50 C7
herwell Gv WIL/AL BD15 ....94 C2
herwell Ri WIL/AL BD15 ....94 C2
herwood Av CLECK BD19 ....144 E3
 HUDN HD2 ....169 G6
herwood Cl BGLY BD16 ....50 C6
 CLECK * BD19 ....144 E3
 DEWS WF13 ....145 J8
herwood Dr HUDS HD4 ....212 C5
 WKFDW/WTN WF2 ....198 B6
herwood Gdns EARD/LOFT * WF3 ....149 J1
herwood Gn EARD/LOFT LS12 ....125 H8
herwood Gv SHPY BD18 ....72 E3
 WKFDW/WTN WF2 ....174 E7
herwood Pl ECHL BD2 ....5 F1
herwood Rd BRIG HD6 ....168 D1
hetcliffe La BOW BD4 ....119 K3
hetcliffe Rd BOW BD4 ....119 J3
hetland Cl ECHL BD2 ....74 B7
hibden Dr BTLY WF17 ....145 H5
hibden Garth HIPP HX3 ....141 F3
hibden Grange Dr HIPP HX3 ....140 E2
hibden Hall Cft HIPP HX3 ....140 E3
hibden Hall Rd HIPP HX3 ....140 E3
hibden Head La CUL/QBY BD13 ....116 B4
hibden Vw CUL/QBY BD13 ....116 C4
hielling St WHPT HX3 ....11 D2
hield Cl MSTN/BAR LS15 ....82 C8
hield Hall La BRAM/WRA HX6 ....137 K7
hill Bank Av MIRF WF14 ....171 F5
hill Bank La MIRF WF14 ....171 F5
hillbank Vw MIRF WF14 ....171 F5
hilling St WHPT HX3 ....11 D2
hipley Airedale Rd BFDE BD3 ....5 D3
hipley Fields Rd SHPY BD18 ....73 H5
hip St BRIG HD6 ....168 B1
hipton Ms MOR LS27 ....123 G8
hip Yd WKFDE WF1 ....11 D4
hire Cl WBSY BD6 ....118 A4
hire Oak Rd HDGY LS6 ....78 E6
hire Oak La HDGY LS6 ....78 D6
hires Gv EARD/LOFT WF3 ....150 C6
hirley Av CLECK BD19 ....144 E3
 LM/WK BD12 ....142 C2
hirley Cl OT LS21 ....33 K4
hirley Crs LM/WK BD12 ....142 C2
hirley Dr BRAM LS13 ....77 C7
hirley Gv CLECK BD19 ....144 E3
 HIPP HX3 ....142 B4
hirley Mt CLECK BD19 ....144 E3
hirley Pde CLECK BD19 ....144 D3
hirley Pl CLECK BD19 ....144 D3
 LM/WK BD12 ....142 D2
hirley Rd BOW BD4 ....120 A2
 CLECK BD19 ....144 E3
 GTHN BD7 ....95 H5
hirley St HWTH BD22 ....68 D4
 SHPY BD18 ....73 F5
hirley Ter CLECK BD19 ....144 E3
hirley Wk CLECK BD19 ....144 E3
hoebridge Av AIRE BD20 ....26 B5
hoe Market PONT WF8 ....180 D3
hoebroad La TOD OL14 ....134 A7
hoe New Rd TOD OL14 ....133 F1
hoeref Cl LM/WK BD12 ....118 C6
hort La CHAL * LS7 ....79 J4
hort St EARL WF12 ....173 H4
hrFEA/AMT WF7 ....179 H6
hortway CUL/QBY BD13 ....94 A5
 PDSY/CALV LS28 ....97 J2
hortwood La BTLY DN5 ....241 C7
hrewsbury Pl STKB/PEN LS36 ....252 E8
hrewsbury Rd STKB/PEN LS36 ....252 C8
hroggs Rd HFAX HX1 ....8 B2
hroggs St HFAX HX1 ....8 B3
hroggs Vue Ter HFAX HX1 ....8 B3
he Shutt HOR/CROF WF4 ....197 H3
horeham Rd WOR/ARM LS12 ....100 C5
hort Cl LM/WK BD12 ....118 C6
hort La CHAL * LS7 ....79 J4
hikleholme Ct HUDN HD2 ....169 F6
hkle St CLECK BD19 ....144 B3
hklinghall Rd WBY LS22 ....22 D6
hdal Gv HIPP HX3 ....140 C7
hdal La HIPP HX3 ....140 D7

Siddall St BEE/HOL LS11 ....7 D5
Siddal New Rd HIPP HX3 ....9 E6
Siddal St HIPP HX3 ....140 D8
Siddal Top La HIPP HX3 ....140 D7
Siddon Dr HUDE HD5 ....192 C8
Side Copse OT LS21 ....33 K3
Side La HUDW HD3 ....189 K5
Sides Rd PONT WF8 ....180 E5
The Sidings GSLY LS20 ....53 F2
 SHPY * BD18 ....73 J5
Sidney St LDS LS1 ....7 E3
Siegen Cl MOR LS27 ....123 F7
Siggett La TOD OL14 ....133 J5
Sigott St HUDW HD3 ....189 K5
Sike Cl DOD/DAR S75 ....239 J2
Sike La HOLM/MEL HD9 ....233 K6
 WKFDW/WTN WF2 ....199 K6
Sikes Cl HUDE HD5 ....192 B8
Silcoates Av WKFDW/WTN WF2 ....175 F2
Silcoates Ct WKFDW/WTN WF2 ....175 F3
Silcoates Dr WKFDW/WTN WF2 ....175 F3
Silcoates La WKFDW/WTN WF2 ....174 E2
Silcoates St WKFDW/WTN WF2 ....175 G3
Silk Mill Ap BHP/TINH LS16 ....77 J1
Silk Mill Av BHP/TINH LS16 ....55 H8
Silk Mill Bank BHP/TINH LS16 ....77 H1
Silk Mill Cl BHP/TINH LS16 ....55 H8
Silk Mill Gdns BHP/TINH LS16 ....77 H1
Silk Mill Gn BHP/TINH LS16 ....77 H1
Silk Mill Ms BHP/TINH LS16 ....77 K1
Silk Mill Rd BHP/TINH LS16 ....77 H1
Silk Mill Wy BHP/TINH LS16 ....77 J1
Silkstone Cl GFTH/SHER LS25 ....106 B2
Silkstone Ct MSTN/BAR LS15 ....104 A2
Silkstone Crs NORM * WF6 ....151 J7
 WKFDW/WTN WF2 ....198 E3
Silkstone Wy MSTN/BAR LS15 ....104 A2
Silk St HTON BD9 ....95 G1
Silsbridge St BFD BD1 ....4 B4
Silsden Br AIRE BD20 ....27 F4
Silsden Rd AIRE BD20 ....27 H7
 ILK LS29 ....17 K4
Silson La BAIL BD17 ....52 A7
Silver Birch Av LM/WK BD12 ....142 E1
Silver Birch Cl LM/WK BD12 ....142 E1
Silver Birch Dr LM/WK BD12 ....142 E1
Silver Birch Gv LM/WK BD12 ....142 E1
Silverdale Av AIRE BD20 ....58 D6
 AL/HA/HU LS17 ....58 D6
 GSLY LS20 ....53 G3
Silverdale Cl GSLY LS20 ....53 G4
Silverdale Dr GSLY LS20 ....53 G4
Silverdale Gra GSLY LS20 ....53 G4
Silverdale Gv GSLY LS20 ....53 G4
Silverdale Mt GSLY LS20 ....53 G4
Silverdale Rd GSLY LS20 ....53 F4
 WBOW BD5 ....119 F1
Silverhill Dr BFDE BD3 ....97 F3
Silverhill Rd BFDE BD3 ....96 E2
Silver La YEA LS19 ....53 K4
Silver Mill Hl OT LS21 ....33 K5
Silver Royd Av WOR/ARM LS12 ....99 K5
Silver Royd Cl WOR/ARM LS12 ....99 K5
Silver Royd Garth WOR/ARM LS12 ....99 K5
Silver Royd Dr WOR/ARM LS12 ....99 K5
Silver Royd Gv WOR/ARM LS12 ....99 K5
Silver Royd Hl WOR/ARM LS12 ....99 K5
Silver Royd Pl WOR/ARM LS12 ....99 K5
Silver Royd Rd WOR/ARM LS12 ....99 K5
Silver Royd St WOR/ARM LS12 ....99 K5
Silver Royd Ter WOR/ARM LS12 ....99 K5
Silver St GIR BD8 ....95 H2
 HFAX HX1 ....9 D4
 HUDE HD5 ....13 E4
 KNOT WF11 ....131 H8
 TOD OL14 ....159 K4
 WKFDE WF1 ....149 J8
Silver St East HUD HD1 ....13 E5
Silverwood Av LUD/ILL HX2 ....139 F2
Silwood Dr ECHL BD2 ....74 E8
Simeon St TOD OL14 ....159 K3
Simes St BFD BD1 ....4 B4
Simm Carr La HIPP HX3 ....116 C7
Simmonds La HFAX HX1 ....9 E6
Simmons Ct OSM LS9 ....102 B5
Simmons Wy RHAY LS8 ....82 A7
Simms Dene WIL/AL BD15 ....72 A7
Simon Cl BOW BD4 ....120 C1
Simon Green Rd MAR/SLWT HD7 ....189 F8
Simpson Gv IDLE BD10 ....74 E2
 WOR/ARM LS12 ....100 D4
Simpson Rd HBR * HX7 ....136 E2
 HEM/SK/SE WF9 ....226 D7
Simpsons La KNOT WF11 ....156 A8
Simpson St EARD/LOFT WF3 ....149 F3
 HIPP HX3 ....8 C1
 KGHY BD21 ....3 C2
Sim Royd La STKB/PEN LS36 ....237 H7
Sinclair Garth WKFDW/WTN WF1 ....175 J7
Sinclair Rd ECHL BD2 ....74 B6
Sinden Ms IDLE BD10 ....74 B1
Singleton St BFD BD1 ....4 C3
Sion Hl HIPP HX3 ....140 D8
Sir George Martin Dr BHP/TINH LS16 ....56 D6
Sir Isaac Holden Pl GTHN BD7 ....95 H4
Sir Karl Cohen Sq WOR/ARM LS12 ....100 B4
Sir Wilfred Pl IDLE * BD10 ....74 D3
Siskin Ct MOR LS27 ....123 G8
Sisley La TOD OL14 ....135 F7

Sissons Av MID LS10 ....124 C7
Sissons Crs MID LS10 ....124 C7
Sissons Dr MID LS10 ....124 C7
Sissons Gn MID LS10 ....124 C7
Sissons Gv MID LS10 ....124 C7
Sissons La MID LS10 ....124 C7
Sissons Mt MID LS10 ....124 B8
Sissons Pl MID LS10 ....124 C7
Sissons Rd MID LS10 ....124 C7
Sissons Rw MID LS10 ....124 C7
Sissons St MID LS10 ....124 C7
Sissons Ter MID LS10 ....124 C7
Sissons Vw MID LS10 ....124 B8
Siward St HEM/SK/SE WF9 ....202 K7
Sixth Av BFDE BD3 ....96 E2
 LVSG WF15 ....143 J6
 RTHW LS26 ....126 D4
Sizers Ct YEA LS19 ....53 J6
Skelbrooke Dr PONT WF8 ....180 E6
Skelda Ri ILK LS29 ....20 B8
Skelton Av OSM LS9 ....102 D3
Skelton Crs HUDS HD4 ....190 B8
 OSM LS9 ....102 D3
Skelton Grange Rd MID LS10 ....125 J1
Skelton Mt OSM LS9 ....102 D3
Skelton Pl OSM LS9 ....102 D3
Skelton Rd OSM LS9 ....102 D3
Skeltons La SCFT LS14 ....81 K2
Skelton St OSM LS9 ....102 D3
Skelton Ter OSM LS9 ....102 D3
Skelton Wk IDLE BD10 ....75 F4
Skelwith Ap SCFT LS14 ....103 J1
Skinner La GIR BD8 ....4 A1
 LDSU LS2 ....7 F2
 PONT WF8 ....180 E2
Skinner St LDS LS1 ....6 C3
Skinpit La STKB/PEN S36 ....253 G5
Skipton Av HUDN HD2 ....191 H1
Skipton Ri GFTH/SHER LS25 ....106 B4
Skipton Rd AIRE BD20 ....26 A4
 AIRE BD20 ....26 D2
 AIRE BD20 ....27 H8
 ILK LS29 ....18 B2
 ILK LS29 ....19 H6
 KGHY BD21 ....3 D2
Skipton St BTLY WF17 ....172 B1
Skircoat Gn HIPP HX3 ....166 B1
Skircoat Green Rd HIPP HX3 ....166 B1
Skircoat Moor Cl LUD/ILL * HX2 ....139 K7
Skircoat Moor Rd LUD/ILL HX2 ....139 K7
Skircoat Rd HFAX HX1 ....9 D6
Skirrow St BGLY BD16 ....72 B5
Skye Rd HTON BD9 ....73 G8
Skye Vw RTHW LS26 ....126 C6
Slack Bottom Rd WBSY BD6 ....118 B3
Slack House La HBR HX7 ....112 C5
Slack La CUD/QR S72 ....223 F6
 GTL/HWG HX4 ....164 D8
 HBR HX7 ....113 J7
 HOLM/MEL HD9 ....233 H7
 HOR/CROF WF4 ....200 D3
 HUDW HD3 ....188 E3
 HWTH BD22 ....46 D8
 RPDN/SBR HX6 ....163 G2
 RPDN/SBR HX6 ....163 G6
 WKFDW/WTN WF2 ....198 D7
Slacks La MAR/SLWT HD7 ....209 J3
 MAR/SLWT HD7 ....210 C6
Slack Top La HOLM/MEL HD9 ....249 K2
Sladdin Rw CUL/QBY BD13 ....116 B3
Slade Cl BSPA/BRAM LS23 ....42 D4
Slade La AIRE BD20 ....48 C1
 BRIG HD6 ....168 A5
Sladen Dr KGHY BD21 ....2 B3
Slades La HOLM/MEL HD9 ....211 J7
Slades Rd MAR/SLWT HD7 ....189 F7
Slade Wk BTLY WF17 ....145 J2
Slaithwaite Av EARL WF12 ....172 B7
Slaithwaite Cl EARL WF12 ....172 B7
Slaithwaite Ga MAR/SLWT HD7 ....188 E7
Slaithwaite Rd EARL WF12 ....172 C7
 HOLM/MEL HD9 ....211 F7
Slant Ga KBTN HD8 ....215 G4
 MAR/SLWT HD7 ....211 J1
 STKB/PEN S36 ....251 C7
Slant La TOD OL14 ....134 C5
Slater Av HBR HX7 ....112 B7
Slater Ing La HBR HX7 ....111 H6
Slaters Rd PDSY/CALV LS28 ....98 C2
Slates La ILK LS29 ....20 B4
Slaymaker La HWTH BD22 ....46 E8
Slead Av BRIG HD6 ....142 A7
Slead Ct BRIG HD6 ....142 A7
Slead Crs BRIG HD6 ....142 A7
Slead Gv BRIG HD6 ....142 A7
Slead Royd BRIG HD6 ....142 A7
Sledbrook Crs STKB/PEN S36 ....249 K5
Sledgate La MAR/SLWT HD7 ....210 D2
Sledge Ga HUDW HD3 ....187 H8
Sledmere Cft SCFT LS14 ....82 A5
Sledmere Garth SCFT LS14 ....82 A5
Sledmere La SCFT LS14 ....82 A5
Sledmere Pl SCFT LS14 ....82 A5
Sleep Hill La HEM/SK/SE WF9 ....227 G4
Sleights La AL/HA/HU LS17 ....38 D5
Sleningford Gv SHPY BD18 ....72 E3
Sleningford Ri BGLY BD16 ....49 J6
Sleningford Rd BGLY BD16 ....49 K6
 SHPY BD18 ....72 E3

Slingsby Cl *IDLE* BD10.....................75 F3
Slipper La *MIRF* WF14....................170 B3
Slippery Ford La *HWTH* BD22..........45 J4
Slippy La *LUD/ILL* HX2..................115 F6
Sloan Sq *GIR* BD8...........................95 H3
Slutwell La *PONT* WF8...................180 E3
Smalewell Cl *PDSY/CALV* LS28........98 B5
Smalewell Dr *PDSY/CALV* LS28........98 A5
Smalewell Gdns *PDSY/CALV* LS28....98 A5
Smalewell Gn *PDSY/CALV* LS28........98 B5
Smalewell Rd *PDSY/CALV* LS28........97 K5
Small La *MAR/SLWT* HD7................189 H7
STKB/PEN S36............................253 C3
Small Lees Rd *RPDN/SBR* HX6........164 A8
Small Page Fold *CUL/QBY* * BD13.....116 D2
Smallpage Yd *WKFDE* * WF1.............10 C3
Small Shaw La *HBR* HX7...................112 A2
Smallwood Gdns *EARL* WF12............147 F8
Smallwood Rd *EARL* WF12................147 F8
Smawell La *HOR/CROF* WF4.............221 K4
Smawthorne Av *CAS* WF10...............153 J4
Smawthorne Gv *CAS* WF10...............153 J4
Smawthorne La *CAS* WF10................153 J4
Smeaton Ap *MSTN/BAR* LS15.............82 C8
Smeaton Gv *RTHW* LS26..................127 K1
Smeaton Rd *HEM/SK/SE* WF9...........227 F3
Smiddles La *WBOW* BD5.................117 J3
Smiddy Hl *BSPA/BRAM* LS23.............25 G7
Smirthwaite St *WKFDE* WF1...............10 C1
Smirthwaite Vw *NORM* WF6............177 K2
Smith Av *WBSY* BD6........................118 D3
Smith Crs *BRIG* HD6.......................167 K3
Smitherds St *KGHY* BD21....................2 C4
Smithfield Av *HIPP* HX3..................141 H5
Smith House Crs *BRIG* HD6.............142 A6
Smith House Gv *BRIG* HD6..............142 A6
Smith House La *BRIG* HD6...............142 B6
Smithies La *BTLY* WF17..................145 H3
LVSG WF15...............................171 F1
Smithies Moor Crs *BTLY* WF17.......145 J3
Smithies Moor La *BTLY* WF17.........145 H4
Smithies Moor Ri *BTLY* WF17.........145 J3
Smith La *HTON* BD9..........................94 E1
Smith Rd *DEWS* WF13.....................171 J2
GTHN BD7....................................95 H3
Smiths Av *HUDW* HD3....................190 D4
Smithson Av *CAS* WF10..................154 C5
Smithson St *RTHW* LS26.................126 C7
Smith's Ter *HIPP* HX3.....................141 H5
Smith St *BGLY* BD16........................72 B5
BOW BD4....................................119 J3
CAS WF10.................................130 D8
CAS WF10.................................154 A2
GTHN BD7......................................4 C1
KGHY BD21...................................2 B2
LVSG WF15................................144 E8
Smithville *AIRE* BD20........................48 D2
Smith Wy *OSS* WF5.........................173 K5
Smithwell La *HBR* HX7...................111 K6
Smithy Brook La *EARL* WF12..........195 K2
Smithy Carr La *BRIG* HD6...............142 B7
Smithy Cl *HOR/CROF* WF4..............200 D3
KBTN HD8.................................236 E2
Smithy Clough La *RPDN/SBR* HX6...163 H8
Smithy Hl *CUL/QBY* BD13.................92 C5
KBTN HD8.................................236 D8
WBSY BD6.................................118 D2
Smithy La *AL/HA/HU* LS17.................60 A1
BHP/TINH LS16............................55 J5
EARD/LOFT WF3.........................148 A3
HBR HX7...................................111 F6
HOLM/MEL HD9..........................247 H1
HOR/CROF WF4...........................195 K7
HUDE HD5....................................13 E5
ILK LS29.......................................21 H4
ILK LS29.......................................32 A3
KBTN HD8.................................236 E2
WIL/AL BD15................................71 G5
Smithy Mills La *BHP/TINH* LS16........78 D1
Smithy Pde *EARL* WF12..................195 K2
Smithy Place La *HOLM/MEL* HD9.....233 H1
Smithy St *HFAX* HX1..........................9 J4
Smithy Wk *EARL* WF12..................195 K2
Snail La *HBR* HX7...........................136 C3
Snaith Wood Dr *YEA* LS19................76 A2
Snaith Wood Ms *YEA* LS19...............76 A3
Snape Dr *GTHN* BD7.......................117 J1
Snapes Fold *HUDE* HD5..................192 B7
Snape St *KGHY* BD21..........................3 D6
Snapethorpe Crs
WKFDW/WTN WF2.....................174 E7
Snapethorpe Ga
WKFDW/WTN WF2.....................174 D7
Snapethorpe Rd
WKFDW/WTN WF2.....................174 E7
Snelsins La *CLECK* BD19.................143 K2
Snelsins Rd *CLECK* BD19................143 K3
Snittle Rd *HOLM/MEL* HD9.............248 C4
Snowden Ap *BRAM* LS13....................77 J8
Snowden Cl *BRAM* LS13....................99 H1
Snowden Crs *BRAM* LS13...................99 H1
Snowden Fold *BRAM* LS13.................99 H1
Snowden Gv *BRAM* LS13....................99 H1
Snowden Lawn *BRAM* LS13................99 H1
Snowden Rd *SHPY* BD18.....................73 K5
Snowden Royd *BRAM* LS13................99 H1
Snowden St *BFD* BD1...........................4 C3
Snowdens Wk *CLAY* BD14...................94 D7

Snowden V *BRAM* LS13.....................99 H1
Snowdon Av *KNOT* WF11.................155 K7
Snowdon St *BTLY* WF17...................146 A7
Snowdrop Ms *WIL/AL* BD15................94 B3
Snow Hill Cl *WKFDE* * WF1..............175 H2
Snow Hill Gv *WKFDE* WF1...............175 H2
Snow Hill Vw *WKFDE* WF1.................10 B1
Snug La *HOLM/MEL* HD9.................249 H2
Snydale Av *NORM* WF6...................178 B2
Snydale Cl *NORM* WF6.....................178 B2
Snydale Ct *NORM* WF6.....................178 B2
Snydale Gv *NORM* WF6.....................178 B2
Soaper House La *HIPP* HX3...............141 H1
Soaper La *HIPP* HX3.........................117 J4
Sod House Gn *HIPP* HX3..................115 K8
Soho Gv *WKFDW/WTN* WF2..............10 A3
Soho St *BFD* BD1................................4 B4
HFAX HX1.....................................8 A4
Solid *HUDS* HD4.............................213 F1
Solomon Hl *LUD/ILL* HX2................138 A2
Solway Rd *BTLY* WF17....................146 E6
Somerdale Cl *BRAM* LS13..................99 H2
Somerdale Gdns *BRAM* LS13.............99 H2
Somerdale Gv *BRAM* LS13.................99 H2
Somerdale Wk *BRAM* LS13................99 H2
Somerset Av *BAIL* BD17....................51 H7
BRIG HD6.................................168 C4
Somerset Crs *HUD* HD1.....................13 E5
Somerset Dr *HUD* HD1......................13 E5
PDSY/CALV LS28..........................98 C3
Somers Pl *LDS* * LS1...........................7 D3
Somers St *LDS* LS1............................6 C3
Somerton Dr *BOW* BD4...................120 A1
Somerville Av *SCFT* LS14.................103 H1
WBSY BD6.................................118 C4
Somerville Dr *SCFT* LS14.................103 H1
Somerville Gn *SCFT* LS14..................81 H8
Somerville Gv *SCFT* LS14.................103 H1
Somerville Mt *SCFT* LS14.................103 H1
Somerville Pk *WBSY* BD6.................118 C4
Somerville Vw *SCFT* LS14................103 H1
Sonning Rd *WIL/AL* BD15..................94 B3
Soothill La *BTLY* WF17....................146 E6
Sorbus Wy *KBTN* HD8......................193 G8
Sorrel Cl *PONT* WF8........................180 E4
Sorrin Cl *IDLE* BD10..........................74 C4
Sotheron Cft *PONT* WF8..................181 K6
Soureby Cross Wy *BOW* BD4...........120 C4
Sourhall Cl *TOD* OL14.....................133 G5
Sourhall Rd *TOD* OL14....................133 G6
South Accommodation Rd
MID LS10.......................................7 F6
Southampton St *BFDE* BD3.................5 G1
South Ap *BSPA/BRAM* LS23..............61 K3
GFTH/SHER LS25..........................84 E1
South Av *CAS* WF10........................152 E4
HEM/SK/SE WF9..........................242 A1
HOR/CROF WF4...........................197 J2
HUDS HD4....................................94 B3
PONT WF8.................................180 B4
South Balleygate *PONT* WF8............181 F2
South Bank *AL/HA/HU* LS17..............40 A3
CUL/QBY BD13............................116 E2
South Bank Rd *BTLY* WF17.............145 K5
South Bolton *LUD/ILL* HX2..............115 G4
South Brook Ter *GTHN* BD7.................4 B4
South Cliffe *CUL/QBY* BD13...............93 H5
Southcliffe Dr *BAIL* BD17..................73 H7
Southcliffe Wy *BAIL* BD17.................73 J2
South Cl *GSLY* LS20..........................52 D3
South Clough Head *LUD/ILL* HX2.....138 D4
Southcote Pl *IDLE* BD10....................74 D3
South Cft *CUD/GR* S72.....................223 G8
KBTN HD8.................................236 D8
South Croft Av *BIRK/DRI* BD11........120 D5
South Croft Dr *BIRK/DRI* BD11........120 D4
South Croft Ga *BIRK/DRI* BD11........120 D5
South Cross Rd *HUDN* HD2..............191 F1
Southdale Gdns *OSS* WF5................173 J6
Southdale Rd *OSS* WF5....................173 J7
Southdown Cl *HTON* BD9...................94 E1
Southdown Rd *BAIL* BD17..................73 H2
South Dr *GSLY* LS20..........................52 D3
PDSY/CALV LS28...........................76 B8
WKFDW/WTN WF2......................199 F2
South Edge *KGHY* BD21......................2 B1
SHPY BD18..................................72 E4
Southedge Cl *HIPP* HX3..................141 H1
South End Av *BRAM* LS13..................99 H2
South End Gv *BRAM* LS13..................99 H2
South End Mt *BRAM* LS13..................99 H2
South End Ter *BRAM* LS13.................99 H2
Southern Rd *HUDS* HD4..................190 A8
South Farm Crs *OSM* LS9.................102 E1
South Farm Rd *OSM* LS9..................102 E1
Southfield *BHP/TINH* LS16................55 K1
HBR HX7...................................112 A7
Southfield Av *AIRE* BD20...................48 D1
AL/HA/HU LS17.............................80 A1
FEA/AMT WF7.............................179 G7
WBSY BD6.................................118 D3
Southfield Cl *HOR/CROF* WF4..........197 H2
WKFDW/WTN WF2......................175 F2
Southfield Ct *KBTN* HD8..................215 H4
Southfield Dr *AIRE* BD20...................48 E1
AL/HA/HU LS17.............................80 A1
Southfield Fold *HOR/CROF* WF4.......197 H3
Southfield La *GTHN* BD7....................95 G8

HOR/CROF WF4..........................197 H
ILK LS29.......................................18 D
Southfield Mt *AIRE* BD20...................48 E
WOR/ARM LS12...........................100 C
Southfield Rd *BGLY* BD16..................72 A
HOR/CROF WF4...........................178 A
HUDE HD5.................................192 B
ILK LS29.......................................18 D
ILK LS29.......................................32 A
KNOT WF11...............................156 C
WBOW BD5..................................95 J
Southfield Sq *GIR* BD8..........................4 A
Southfield St *WOR/ARM* LS12...........100 C
Southfields Vw *HOR/CROF* WF4.......196 D
Southfield Ter *BIRK/DRI* BD11..........120 D
HIPP HX3...................................141 H
ILK * LS29....................................18 D
Southfield Wy *AIRE* BD20...................48 E
Southgate *BFD* * BD1...........................4 C
CUD/GR S72.................................223 J
EARL WF12.................................172 B
ELL HX5......................................166 E
GSLY LS20...................................52 D
HFAX HX1.......................................7 D
HOLM/MEL HD9..........................213 F
HUD HD1.......................................12 C
PONT WF8.................................180 E
RTHW LS26................................127 F
WKFDE WF1..................................10 C
South Gv *BRIG* HD6.......................141 J
SHPY BD18..................................72 D
South Hill Cl *MID* LS10...................125 G
South Hill Cft *MID* * LS10................125 C
South Hill Dr *BGLY* BD16...................50 B
South Hill Gdns *RTHW* LS26............125 G
South Hill Ri *MID* LS10....................125 G
South Hill Wy *MID* LS10..................125 G
Southlands *BAIL* BD17........................73 H
HUDE HD5.................................192 D
LUD/ILL HX2................................115
Southlands Av *AIRE* * BD20...............48 E
AL/HA/HU LS17.............................79
BGLY BD16..................................72 A
CUL/QBY BD13..............................94 C
YEA LS19......................................76 B
Southlands Cl *HEM/SK/SE* WF9........226 A
Southlands Crs *AL/HA/HU* LS17........79
Southlands Dr *AIRE* * BD20................48 E
AL/HA/HU LS17.............................79
HUDN HD2.................................168 B
Southlands Gv *AIRE* BD20...................48 E
BGLY BD16..................................71
CUL/QBY BD13..............................94 B
Southlands Gv West *AIRE* BD20........48 E
Southlands Mt *AIRE* BD20...................48 E
Southlands Rd *AIRE* BD20...................48 E
South La *DOD/DAR* S75....................253 C
ELL HX5......................................166 B
HIPP HX3...................................117 C
HOLM/MEL HD9..........................233 C
HOR/CROF WF4...........................196 C
South Lane Gdns *ELL* HX5...............166 B
South Lea *EARD/LOFT* * WF3...........148 A
Southlea Av *HWTH* BD22...................69 C
Southlea Cl *LM/WK* BD12.................119 H
South Lee *HORS* LS18........................77 F
Southleigh Av *BEE/HOL* LS11...........124 C
Southleigh Crs *BEE/HOL* LS11..........124 C
Southleigh Cft *BEE/HOL* LS11..........124 C
Southleigh Dr *BEE/HOL* LS11...........124 C
Southleigh Gdns *BEE/HOL* LS11.......124 C
Southleigh Gra *BEE/HOL* LS11.........124 C
Southleigh Gv *BEE/HOL* LS11...........124 C
Southleigh Rd *BEE/HOL* LS11...........124 C
Southleigh Vw *BEE/HOL* LS11..........124 C
South Md *BHP/TINH* LS16..................55
Southmere Av *GTHN* BD7..................95 C
Southmere Crs *GTHN* BD7.................95 C
Southmere Dr *GTHN* BD7..................95 C
Southmere Gv *GTHN* BD7.................95 C
Southmere Rd *GTHN* BD7..................95 C
Southmere Ter *GTHN* BD7.................95 C
Southmoor Rd *CUD/GR* S72.............240 C
South Mt *AL/HA/HU* LS17...................39
South Nelson St *MOR* LS27..............123
Southolme Cl *KSTL* LS5......................77
Southowram Bank *HIPP* HX3................9
South Pde *CLECK* BD19....................143
ELL HX5......................................166 B
GIR BD8...4
GTL/HWG HX4.............................165
HDGY LS6.....................................78
HFAX HX1.......................................9
ILK LS29.......................................20
LDS * LS1.......................................7
MOR LS27...................................123
OSS WF5....................................174
PDSY/CALV LS28...........................98
WKFDE WF1..................................10
South Parade Cl *PDSY/CALV* LS28......98
South Pkwy *SCFT* LS14.......................81
South Park Wy *WKFDW/WTN* WF2....149
South Parkway Ap *OSM* LS9...............81
South Point *MID* * LS10....................102
South Queen St *MOR* LS27...............123
South Rdg *GFTH/SHER* LS25............129
South Rd *CUL/QBY* BD13...................70

HTON BD9 ....73 J7
OSM LS9 ....102 E8
uth Royd HUDE HD5 ....192 C7
uth Royde Av HIPP HX3 ....140 B8
uthroyd Rd PDSY/CALV LS28 ....98 C6
uth Sq CUL/QBY BD13 ....93 H5
uth St BRIG HD6 ....142 B8
.....................................92 B3
CUL/QBY BD13 ....93 C4
CUL/QBY BD13 ....93 C4
EARL WF12 ....172 B5
EARL WF12 ....172 C5
HEM/SK/SE WF9 ....224 E5
HFAX HX1 ....8 C5
HOLM/MEL HD9 ....233 J5
HOR/CROF WF4 ....223 H2
HUD HD1 ....190 D6
HUD5 HD4 ....212 D5
KGHY BD21 ....2 C4
LM/WK BD12 ....119 H7
LVSG WF15 ....144 E7
MIRF WF14 ....170 C8
MOR LS27 ....123 C7
WORM WF6 ....177 K4
OSS WF5 ....173 J7
WBOW BD5 ....95 J8
WKFDE WF1 ....11 D4
uth Ter OSS WF5 ....173 K8
uth Vw AIRE BD20 ....49 F2
BAIL BD17 ....53 H4
YEA LS19 ....53 H4
uth View Cl BOW BD4 ....120 B4
YEA LS19 ....53 C4
uth View Cottages
AL/HA/HU * LS17 ....59 H8
uth View Ct HIPP HX3 ....141 J5
uth View Dr BOW BD4 ....120 C4
uth View Gdns PONT WF8 ....181 G3
uth View Gv CLECK * BD19 ....144 E4
MID LS10 ....125 F2
YEA LS19 ....53 K4
uth View St TOD OL14 ....133 F2
uth View Ter AIRE BD20 ....27 F2
BAIL * BD17 ....51 J8
HFAX * HX1 ....8 A3
HOR/CROF WF4 ....194 C7
YEA LS19 ....54 A5
uthwaite La SCFT LS14 ....81 H7
uthwaite Pl SCFT LS14 ....81 H7
uth Wk BGLY BD16 ....70 E2
uth Wy BOW BD4 ....120 B4
uthway BGLY BD16 ....50 C6
GSLY LS20 ....58 E8
HORS LS18 ....54 E8
ILK LS29 ....20 D8
MIRF WF14 ....170 C4
uthwell Av HUDW HD3 ....190 B4
uthwell La HOR/CROF WF4 ....197 G3
uthwood Av HOLM/MEL HD9 ......213 H6
uthwood Cl SCFT LS14 ....82 A7
uthwood Crs SCFT LS14 ....82 A7
uthwood Ga MSTN/BAR LS15 ......82 A7
vereign Cl BTLY WF17 ....145 J2
vereign Ct AL/HA/HU LS17 ....58 A5
vereign Gdns NORM WF6 ....177 K1
vereign Quay LDS * LS1 ....7 E4
vereign St HFAX * HX1 ....8 C4
LDS LS1 ....7 E4
/ereign's Wy EARL WF12 ....172 A8
wden Buildings ECHL BD2 ....5 F1
wden Gra CUL/QBY BD13 ....93 H5
wden Rd HTON BD9 ....72 D8
wden St GTHN * BD7 ....95 H8
wden's Yd HDGY * LS6 ....78 D5
werby Croft La RPDN/SBR HX6 ...138 E8
werby La LUD/ILL HX2 ....137 J5
werby New Rd RPDN/SBR HX6 ....138 B8
werby St RPDN/SBR HX6 ....138 B8
wgate La PONT WF8 ....155 H8
wood Av OSS WF5 ....173 K8
wood Ct OSS WF5 ....174 A8
wood Gdns OSS WF5 ....174 A7
wood Gra OSS WF5 ....173 K8
wood La EARL WF12 ....174 A8
OSS WF5 ....174 A8
St BULY LS4 ....100 C1
wood Vw OSS WF5 ....174 A7
nland Town Rd RPDN/SBR HX6 ...164 A5
 Bottom HUDE HD5 ....192 E6
 Croft Rd OSS WF5 ....174 B7
 Flds MAR/SLWT HD7 ....211 F2
 Gv WKFDW/WTN WF2 ....175 F8
ines Rd HUDN HD2 ....12 C1
 La BGLY BD16 ....50 A6

BSPA/BRAM LS23 ....42 E4
MAR/SLWT HD7 ....211 F2
OSS WF5 ....174 B8
Spa Ms BSPA/BRAM LS23 ....42 E4
Sparable La WKFDE WF1 ....11 E6
Spark House La RPDN/SBR HX6 ...139 F8
Sparks Rd HUDW HD3 ....190 B4
Spark St HUDW HD3 ....189 J5
Spartal La GFTH/SHER LS25 ....129 K3
Spartan Rd LM/WK BD12 ....118 E6
Sparth La HOLM/MEL HD9 ....232 B7
Spa St BTLY WF17 ....146 B6
OSS WF5 ....174 C7
Spawd Bone La KNOT WF11 ....156 B8
Spa Well Gv CUD/GR S72 ....224 A8
Speak St WKFDE WF1 ....11 F1
Speakers Ct DEWS WF13 ....172 A3
Spear Fir AL/HA/HU LS17 ....59 J1
Spearhead Wy KGHY BD21 ....3 D2
Speedwell Mt HDGY LS6 ....79 H8
Speedwell Rd CAS WF10 ....168 C5
Speedwell St HUD * HD1 ....190 D6
Speeton Av WBSY BD6 ....117 K1
Speeton Gv GTHN BD7 ....117 J1
Spen Ap BHP/TINH LS16 ....77 K4
Spen Bank BHP/TINH LS16 ....77 K4
CLECK BD19 ....144 C4
Spence La WOR/ARM LS12 ....6 B5
Spenceley St LDSU * LS2 ....79 G8
GTHN BD7 ....95 G6
MOR LS27 ....147 F1
Spencer Av AIRE BD20 ....26 A4
Spencer La HBR HX7 ....136 B2
Spencer Mt RHAY LS8 ....80 A8
Spencer Pl RHAY LS8 ....80 A8
Spencer Rd GSLY LS20 ....53 H3
GTHN BD7 ....95 H6
Spencer St KBTN HD8 ....236 E1
KGHY BD21 ....3 J6
MIRF WF14 ....170 D8
Spen Cl BHP/TINH LS16 ....119 J4
Spen Common La TAD LS24 ....62 E5
Spen Crs BHP/TINH LS16 ....77 K4
Spen Dr BHP/TINH LS16 ....78 A3
Spenfield Ct LVSG WF15 ....170 D1
Spen Gdns BHP/TINH LS16 ....78 B3
Spen Gn BHP/TINH LS16 ....77 K4
Spen La CLECK BD19 ....144 C3
HDGY LS6 ....78 A5
Spen Ms BHP/TINH LS16 ....78 A4
Spennithorne Av BHP/TINH LS16 ...78 A2
Spennithorne Dr BHP/TINH LS16 ...78 A2
Spen Rd BHP/TINH LS16 ....78 B5
Spenser Rd GSLY LS20 ....53 H3
Spenser St GSLY LS20 ....53 H3
Spenslea Gv MOR LS27 ....147 F1
Spen Vale St HECK WF16 ....145 G8
Spen Valley Heritage Trail
BTLY WF17 ....121 G8
CLECK BD19 ....144 B1
Spen Valley Rd DEWS WF13 ....171 H5
Spen Vw DEWS WF13 ....171 H3
Spen Vw La BOW BD4 ....119 J4
Spen Wk BHP/TINH LS16 ....77 K4
Spibey Crs RTHW LS26 ....126 A4
Spibey La RTHW LS26 ....126 A4
Spicer House La STKB/PEN S36 ....250 E4
Spicer St WBOW * BD5 ....95 J8
Spiers Garth WBSY BD6 ....118 C3
The Spindles MID LS10 ....124 E3
Spindle St LUD/ILL HX2 ....115 K6
Spinkfield Rd HUDN HD2 ....12 B2
Spink La PONT WF8 ....180 E2
Spink Pl GIR * BD8 ....4 B3
Spink Well La EARD/LOFT WF3 .....148 A2
Spinkwell Rd DEWS WF13 ....172 B2
The Spinners HWTH BD22 ....68 E5
Spinners Cha PDSY/CALV LS28 .....98 C4
Spinners Wy CLECK BD19 ....143 G3
MIRF WF14 ....170 D8
The Spinney AIRE BD20 ....49 H3
Spinneyfield Ct SHPY BD18 ....118 B1
Spion Kop SCFT LS14 ....60 D6
Spire Ct HUDW HD3 ....12 A3
Spitalgap La PONT WF8 ....181 J4
Spittal Hardwick La CAS WF10 .....154 D6
Spofforth Hl WBY LS22 ....23 G5
Spofforth Wk GFTH/SHER LS25 ...106 B4
Spout Rd HOLM/MEL HD9 ....232 B5
Spout Hl BRIG HD6 ....167 K5
Spout House La BRIG HD6 ....141 K5
Spring Av KGHY BD21 ....3 F4
MOR LS27 ....122 B3
Springbank GFTH/SHER LS25 ......105 G6
Spring Bank HUD * HD1 ....13 B3
LUD/ILL HX2 ....138 B3

Springbank Av MOR LS27 ....122 B4
PDSY/CALV LS28 ....76 C7
Springbank Cl PDSY/CALV LS28 ....76 C8
Springbank Crs GFTH/SHER LS25 .105 G5
Spring Bank Crs HDGY LS6 ....78 E7
Springbank Crs MOR LS27 ....122 B3
Spring Bank Cft HOLM/MEL HD9 .232 D7
Springbank Dr LVSG WF15 ....170 E1
Springbank Dr PDSY/CALV LS28 ...76 C8
Springbank Gv PDSY/CALV LS28 ...76 C8
Springbank Ms HOLM/MEL * HD9 .213 H8
Spring Bank Pl GIR BD8 ....4 B2
Spring Bank Ri KGHY BD21 ....3 D6
Springbank Ri PDSY/CALV LS28 ....76 C8
Springbank Rd HUD HD1 ....13 F1
MOR LS27 ....122 B3
PDSY/CALV LS28 ....76 B8
Springcliffe GIR BD8 ....95 H2
Springcliffe St GIR BD8 ....95 H2
Spring Cl BTLY WF17 ....72 B1
GFTH/SHER LS25 ....106 A3
KGHY BD21 ....3 F4
MOR LS27 ....123 F4
Spring Close Av OSM LS9 ....102 A5
Spring Close Gdns OSM LS9 ....102 A5
Spring Close St OSM LS9 ....102 A5
Spring Close Wk OSM LS9 ....102 A5
Spring Ct WIL/AL * BD15 ....72 A8
Spring Dl HOLM/MEL HD9 ....213 F6
Springdale Av HUD HD1 ....12 B5
Springdale Crs IDLE BD10 ....74 E3
Springdale St HUD HD1 ....12 B6
Spring Dr KGHY BD21 ....3 F4
Spring Edge North HFAX HX1 ....8 B6
Spring Edge South HFAX HX1 ....8 B6
Spring Edge West HFAX HX1 ....8 A6
Spring End Rd OSS WF5 ....174 C8
Spring Farm La BGLY BD16 ....70 E2
Spring Farm Ms WIL/AL BD15 ....71 G6
Springfield BSPA/BRAM LS23 ....42 C3
BSPA/BRAM LS23 ....42 D6
HUDW HD3 ....189 F3
RPDN/SBR HX6 ....138 D8
Springfield Av BTLY WF17 ....146 A6
GTHN BD7 ....95 F6
HEM/SK/SE WF9 ....224 E5
HOLM/MEL HD9 ....213 F8
ILK LS29 ....20 C7
KBTN HD8 ....237 J1
MAR/SLWT HD7 ....210 C2
MOR LS27 ....123 F5
PONT WF8 ....181 F2
Springfield Bungalows
CLECK * BD19 ....144 B4
Springfield Cl HORS LS18 ....77 J2
KBTN HD8 ....237 J1
MID LS10 ....125 H1
Springfield Ct KGHY BD21 ....2 B2
Springfield Crs MOR LS27 ....123 F5
Springfield Dr KBTN HD8 ....235 J7
LVSG WF15 ....143 K6
Springfield Gdns HORS LS18 ....77 H2
KGHY BD21 ....2 B2
Springfield Gra WKFDW/WTN WF2 .174 E5
Springfield Gn MID * LS10 ....125 F1
Springfield Gv BGLY BD16 ....49 K7
BRIG HD6 ....142 B7
Springfield La BOW BD4 ....121 H1
KBTN HD8 ....215 G4
LVSG WF15 ....144 B6
MOR LS27 ....123 F5
Springfield Mt HEM/SK/SE WF9 ...242 A2
HORS LS18 ....77 G2
ILK LS29 ....18 D2
LDSU LS2 ....6 C2
WOR/ARM * LS12 ....100 A4
Springfield Pk MIRF WF14 ....170 E6
Springfield Pl GIR BD8 ....4 B5
MID LS10 ....125 F1
Springfield Ri HORS LS18 ....77 H2
RTHW LS26 ....126 C7
Springfield Rd BAIL BD17 ....51 H7
ELL HX5 ....157 G4
GSLY LS20 ....53 C2
KGHY BD21 ....2 B2
MOR LS27 ....122 E5
Springfields KNOT WF11 ....156 E8
Springfields Av KNOT WF11 ....156 E7
Springfield St CUL/QBY BD13 ....93 J5
GIR BD8 ....4 A3
RTHW LS26 ....126 C7
Springfield Ter CLECK BD19 ....143 G2
DEWS WF13 ....172 B2
GSLY LS20 ....53 C2
PDSY/CALV LS28 ....98 B2
Spring Gdns AL/HA/HU LS17 ....38 C4
BFD BD1 ....4 B3
BIRK/DRI BD11 ....121 J3
BRIG * HD6 ....142 B7
BTLY * WF17 ....146 A6
HOLM/MEL HD9 ....232 E6
MOR LS27 ....123 H4
Spring Gardens Mt KGHY BD21 ......2 C1
Spring Gardens Rd HTON BD9 ....73 C8
Spring Garden St CUL/QBY BD13 .116 D2
Spring Gv HBR HX7 ....112 B7
HFAX HX1 ....139 H4
Spring Grove St HUD HD1 ....12 C5

Spring Grove Vw *HDGY* LS6 ....6 A1
Spring Grove Wk *HDGY* * LS6 ....6 A1
Spring Hall Cl *HIPP* HX3 ....117 G6
Spring Hall Dr *HFAX* HX1 ....139 H5
Spring Hall Gdns *HFAX* HX1 ....139 H1
Spring Hall Gv *LUD/ILL* HX2 ....139 H4
Spring Hall La *HFAX* HX1 ....139 H5
Spring Hall Pl *HFAX* HX1 ....139 H4
Spring Head La *MAR/SLWT* HD7 ....209 H6
Spring Head Rd *CUL/QBY* BD13 ....93 J5
 HWTH BD22 ....68 E3
Springhead Rd *RTHW* LS26 ....126 D5
Spring Hl *BAIL* BD17 ....51 F8
 CHAL LS7 ....79 J7
 SHPY BD18 ....74 A4
Springhill Av *HOR/CROF* WF4 ....200 E2
Springhill Cl *WKFDE* WF1 ....149 H6
Springhill Dr *HOR/CROF* WF4 ....200 E2
Springhill Gv *HOR/CROF* WF4 ....200 E2
Springhill Mt *HOR/CROF* WF4 ....200 E3
Springhills *WKFDE* WF1 ....149 H6
Spring Hill Ter *HDGY* LS6 ....78 E5
Spring Holes La *CUL/QBY* BD13 ....93 F6
Springhurst Rd *SHPY* BD18 ....73 G4
Spring La *BGLY* BD16 ....50 D5
 BTLY WF17 ....146 A4
 DOD/DAR S75 ....220 E7
 GTL/HWG HX4 ....165 K4
 HOLM/MEL HD9 ....232 E7
 HOLM/MEL HD9 ....234 A6
 HOLM/MEL HD9 ....247 J1
 HOR/CROF WF4 ....201 F4
 WBY LS22 ....24 C6
Springlodge Pl *GIR* BD8 ....4 B2
Springmead Dr *GFTH/SHER* LS25 ....105 K3
Spring Mill La *OSS* WF5 ....174 A5
Spring Mill St *WBOW* BD5 ....4 C6
Spring Mt *KGHY* BD21 ....3 F5
Spring Park Rd *WIL/AL* BD15 ....71 G6
Spring Pl *GTHN* BD7 ....4 A6
 KGHY BD21 ....3 F5
 WHIT OL12 ....158 A8
Spring Ri *KGHY* BD21 ....3 F4
 SKP/WHF BD23 ....14 A6
Spring Rd *HDGY* LS6 ....78 D7
Spring Rw *BGLY* BD16 ....77 F2
 KGHY * BD21 ....2 C4
Springroyd Ter *GIR* BD8 ....95 F3
Spring Side *WHIT* OL12 ....158 A7
Spring Side Ri *MAR/SLWT* HD7 ....189 H6
The Springs *WKFDE* WF1 ....10 C3
Springs La *BSPA/BRAM* LS23 ....25 F5
 ILK LS29 ....20 B7
Springs Pavement *ILK* * LS29 ....20 B7
Springs Rd *BAIL* BD17 ....53 G6
 HOLM/MEL HD9 ....231 F8
Springstone Av *HEM/SK/SE* WF9 ....224 E4
 OSS WF5 ....173 J4
Spring St *BRIC* HD6 ....168 B1
 DEWS WF13 ....172 B2
 HUD HD1 ....12 B4
 IDLE BD10 ....74 D5
 KGHY BD21 ....3 D2
 LVSG WF15 ....144 E7
 MAR/SLWT HD7 ....209 H8
 MAR/SLWT HD7 ....210 D3
 RPDN/SBR HX6 ....165 F1
 TOD OL14 ....133 F2
Springswood Av *SHPY* BD18 ....73 G4
Springswood Pl *SHPY* BD18 ....73 G4
Springswood Rd *SHPY* BD18 ....73 G4
Spring Ter *HIPP* HX3 ....9 E3
 KGHY BD21 ....3 F5
 RPDN/SBR HX6 ....165 F1
Springvale *HOR/CROF* WF4 ....178 A8
Springvale Dr *STKB/PEN* S36 ....252 D8
Springvale Gv *HEM/SK/SE* WF9 ....224 D3
Springvale Ri *HEM/SK/SE* WF9 ....224 E4
Spring Vale Rd *HEM/SK/SE* WF9 ....225 J8
Spring Va *PDSY/CALV* LS28 ....98 C2
Spring Valley Av *BRAM* LS13 ....99 G2
Spring Valley Cl *BRAM* LS13 ....99 G2
Spring Valley Cft *BRAM* LS13 ....99 G2
Spring Valley Ct *BRAM* LS13 ....99 G2
Spring Valley Dr *BRAM* LS13 ....99 G2
Spring Valley St *LVSG* WF15 ....144 D6
Spring Valley Vw *BRAM* LS13 ....99 G2
Spring Valley Wk *BRAM* LS13 ....99 G2
Spring Vw *MOR* LS27 ....122 C3
 OSS WF5 ....174 A5
Springville Vls *TOD* OL14 ....132 E2
Springville Gdns *HEM/SK/SE* WF9 ....226 D4
Spring Wy *KGHY* BD21 ....3 F4
Springwell Av *RTHW* LS26 ....127 K2
 YEA LS19 ....54 A5
Springwell Ct *EARD/LOFT* WF3 ....147 K2
 WOR/ARM LS12 ....6 B5
Springwell Dr *WBOW* BD5 ....96 A7
Springwell Rd *RTHW* LS26 ....127 K2
 WOR/ARM LS12 ....6 C5
Springwell Vw *BEE/HOL* LS11 ....6 C5
Spring Wood Av *HIPP* HX3 ....166 A1
Springwood Av *HUD* HD1 ....12 B3
 WBOW BD5 ....96 B8
Spring Wood Dr *HIPP* HX3 ....166 A1
 WBOW BD5 ....119 G1
Springwood Gdns *RHAY* LS8 ....80 D5

Springwood Gv *RHAY* LS8 ....80 E5
Springwood Hall Gdns *HUD* HD1 ....12 A5
Springwood Rd *HOLM/MEL* HD9 ....233 J3
 RHAY LS8 ....80 D5
 YEA LS19 ....53 J8
Springwood Sq *HUD* * HD1 ....12 C4
Springwood St *HUD* HD1 ....12 C5
Springwood Ter *ECHL* BD2 ....4 C1
Sprinkwell Cl *BFDE* BD3 ....5 D2
Spruce Av *BSLYN/ROY* S71 ....221 K8
Spruce Dr *HUDS* HD4 ....212 D5
Spruce Drive Ms *HUDS* HD4 ....212 D5
Spruce Hts *BRIG* HD6 ....142 B5
Spruce St *KGHY* BD21 ....3 E2
Sprutts La *HBR* HX7 ....112 C4
Spry La *CUD/GR* S72 ....241 G8
Spur Dr *MSTN/BAR* LS15 ....82 C8
Spurr Gv *WKFDW/WTN* WF2 ....199 K5
Spurrier's Av *KNOT* WF11 ....155 K8
Spurr St *BTLY* WF17 ....146 C7
The Square *BSPA/BRAM* LS23 ....42 E5
 CAS WF10 ....154 D4
 CUD/GR S72 ....240 B5
 GFTH/SHER LS25 ....129 F7
 GIR BD8 ....94 C4
 KBTN * HD8 ....235 G3
 KNOT WF11 ....155 K5
Square *HFAX* * HX1 ....9 E4
Square Rd *HFAX* * HX1 ....9 E4
Square St *BOW* BD4 ....5 E6
Squire Gn *GIR* BD8 ....95 F2
Squire La *HTON* BD9 ....95 F2
Squirrel Cl *HUDN* HD2 ....190 C1
Squirrel Ditch *HUDS* HD4 ....191 J8
Squirrel Hall Dr *DEWS* WF13 ....145 J8
Squirrels Drey *HOR/CROF* WF4 ....198 B4
Squirrel Wk *DEWS* WF13 ....145 J8
Stable Fold *LM/WK* BD12 ....142 E1
Stableford Gdns *HUDN* HD2 ....190 D1
Stableford Mnr *MAR/SLWT* HD7 ....189 J6
Stable La *HIPP* HX3 ....8 C2
Stablers Wk *NORM* WF6 ....151 K7
The Stables *BSPA/BRAM* LS25 ....42 E4
Stables La *BSPA/BRAM* LS25 ....42 E4
Stackgarth *BRIG* HD6 ....168 B3
Stackhills Rd *TOD* OL14 ....134 B6
Stacks La *HBR* HX7 ....137 G6
Stadium Rd *WBSY* BD6 ....118 E3
Stadium Wy *BEE/HOL* LS11 ....100 E8
 HEM/SK/SE WF9 ....226 D6
 HUDE HD5 ....13 E3
Stafford Av *HIPP* HX3 ....140 B7
Stafford Hill La *HUDE* HD5 ....192 E3
Stafford Pde *HIPP* HX3 ....140 B8
Stafford Rd *HIPP* HX3 ....140 C8
Stafford Sq *HIPP* HX3 ....140 C8
Stafford St *BOW* BD4 ....96 D7
 CAS WF10 ....153 H2
 MID LS10 ....102 A7
Stafford Ter *WKFDW/WTN* WF2 ....175 G5
Stainbeck Av *CHAL* LS7 ....79 F5
Stainbeck Cnr *CHAL* LS7 ....79 J4
Stainbeck Gdns *CHAL* LS7 ....79 H5
 WBSY BD6 ....117 J8
Stainbeck La *CHAL* LS7 ....79 G4
Stainbeck Rd *CHAL* LS7 ....79 H5
Stainbeck Wk *CHAL* LS7 ....79 H5
Stainburn Av *AL/HA/HU* LS17 ....80 A2
 CAS WF10 ....154 B6
Stainburn Cl *OT* LS21 ....34 E1
Stainburn Crs *AL/HA/HU* LS17 ....79 K2
Stainburn Dr *AL/HA/HU* LS17 ....79 K2
Stainburn Gdns *AL/HA/HU* LS17 ....80 A2
Stainburn La *OT* LS21 ....34 E1
Stainburn Mt *AL/HA/HU* LS17 ....80 A3
Stainburn Rd *AL/HA/HU* LS17 ....79 K3
Stainburn Ter *AL/HA/HU* LS17 ....79 K3
Stainburn Vw *AL/HA/HU* LS17 ....80 A2
Staincliffe Cl *DEWS* WF13 ....171 J3
Staincliffe Crs *DEWS* WF15 ....171 J1
Staincliffe Hall Rd *BTLY* WF17 ....145 K8
Staincliffe Mill Yd *DEWS* * WF13 ....145 K8
Staincliffe Rd *DEWS* WF13 ....171 J1
Staincross Av *HUDS* HD4 ....212 C1
Staines Cft *HUDE* HD5 ....192 A5
Stainland Dean *GTL/HWG* HX4 ....188 B2
Stainland Rd *GTL/HWG* HX4 ....164 D7
 GTL/HWG HX4 ....165 J8
 HUDW HD3 ....188 E3
Stainmore Cl *SCFT* LS14 ....81 J8
Stainmore Pl *SCFT* LS14 ....81 J8
Stainton Cl *WBSY* BD6 ....117 K3
Stainton La *EARD/LOFT* WF3 ....126 A7
Staircase La *OT* LS21 ....35 H6
Stairfoot Cl *BHP/TINH* LS16 ....56 D6
Stair Foot La *BHP/TINH* LS16 ....56 D6
Stairfoot Vw *BHP/TINH* LS16 ....56 D6
Staithe Av *MID* LS10 ....124 E6
Staithe Cl *MID* LS10 ....124 E6
Staithe Gdns *MID* LS10 ....124 E6
Staithgate La *WBSY* BD6 ....119 G3
Stake La *HBR* HX7 ....137 F4
Stake Lane Bank *HOLM/MEL* HD9 ....233 H6
Stallabrass St *GIR* BD8 ....4 A3
Stalley Royd La *HOLM/MEL* HD9 ....234 B8
Stamford Av *CAS* WF10 ....153 F5

Stamford St *BOW* BD4 5
Stammergate La *WBY* LS22 41
Stamp Hill Cl *ILK* LS29 18
Stanacre Pl *BFDE* BD3 5
Stanage La *HIPP* HX3 117
Stancliffe Wy *HUDE* HD5 192
Standale Av *PDSY/CALV* LS28 98
Standale Crs *PDSY/CALV* LS28 98
Standale Ri *PDSY/CALV* LS28 98
Standard Dr *HUDS* HD4 212
Standbridge Cl *WKFDW/WTN* WF2 198
Stand Bridge Garth
 HOR/CROF WF4 198
Standbridge La *WKFDW/WTN* WF2 198
 WKFDW/WTN WF2 198
Standedge Trail *MAR/SLWT* HD7 208
 UPML OL3 228
Standiforth La *HUDE* HD5 192
Standiforth Rd *HUDE* HD5 13
Standish Crs *HEM/SK/SE* WF9 225
Stanhall Av *PDSY/CALV* LS28 98
Stanhope Av *DOD/DAR* S75 239
 HORS LS18 77
Stanhope Cl *HORS* LS18 77
Stanhope Dr *HORS* LS18 77
Stanhope Gdns *EARD/LOFT* WF3 149
Stanhope Gv *EARD/LOFT* WF3 149
Stanhope St *KBTN* HD8 237
Stanks Ap *SCFT* LS14 82
Stanks Av *SCFT* LS14 82
Stanks Cl *SCFT* LS14 82
Stanks Cross *SCFT* LS14 82
Stanks Dr *SCFT* LS14 82
Stanks Gdns *SCFT* LS14 82
Stanks Garth *MSTN/BAR* LS15 82
Stanks Gn *SCFT* LS14 82
Stanks Gv *SCFT* LS14 82
Stanks La North *SCFT* LS14 82
Stanks La South *SCFT* LS14 82
Stanks Pde *SCFT* LS14 82
Stanks Ri *SCFT* LS14 82
Stanks Rd *SCFT* LS14 82
Stanks Wy *SCFT* LS14 82
Stanleigh Cft *HBR* HX7 136
Stanley Av *OSM* LS9 102
Stanley Cottages *NORM* WF6 151
Stanley Dr *HAY* LS8 80
Stanley Garth *HECK* * WF16 145
Stanley La *GTL/HWG* HX4 165
 LVSG WF15 144
 WKFDE WF1 150
Stanley Pl *BTLY* WF17 146
 OSM LS9 102
Stanley Rd *ECHL* BD2 73
 HFAX HX1 8
 HUDW HD3 167
 HUDW HD3 190
 HWTH BD22 69
 LVSG WF15 170
 OSM LS9 102
 WKFDE WF1 11
Stanley St *BGLY* BD16 50
 BRIC HD6 142
 CAS WF10 153
 CLECK BD19 144
 FEA/AMT WF7 179
 HUDS HD4 190
 HWTH BD22 69
 IDLE BD10 74
 KGHY * BD21 2
 RPDN/SBR HX6 139
 SHPY BD18 73
 WKFDE WF1 11
Stanley Ter *OSM* LS9 102
Stanley Vw *WOR/ARM* LS12 100
Stanmoor Dr *EARD/LOFT* WF3 150
Stanmore Av *BULY* LS4 78
Stanmore Crs *BULY* LS4 78
Stanmore Gv *BULY* LS4 78
Stanmore Hl *BULY* LS4 78
Stanmore Mt *BULY* LS4 78
Stanmore Pl *BULY* LS4 78
 GTHN BD7 95
Stanmore Rd *BULY* LS4 78
Stanmore St *BULY* LS4 78
Stanmore Ter *BULY* LS4 78
Stanmore Vw *BULY* LS4 78
Stannard Well Dr *HOR/CROF* WF4 197
Stannard Well La *HOR/CROF* WF4 197
Stannary Pl *HFAX* HX1 8
Stannery End La *HBR* HX7 137
Stanningley By-Pass
 PDSY/CALV LS28 98
Stanningley Gv *LUD/ILL* HX2 114
Stanningley Gv *HECK* WF16 145
Stanningley Rd *LUD/ILL* HX2 114
 PDSY/CALV LS28 98
Stansfield Cl *CAS* WF10 154
 HFAX HX1 8
Stansfield Ct *RPDN/SBR* HX6 138
Stansfield Dr *CAS* WF10 154
Stansfield Hall Rd *TOD* OL14 134
Stansfield Mill La *RPDN/SBR* HX6 164
Stansfield Rd *CAS* WF10 134
 TOD OL14 134
Stansfield St *TOD* OL14 134
Stanwell Av *HUDW* HD3 190
Stanwell Av *HUDW* HD3 71
Stapper Gn *WIL/AL* BD15 71

arbeck Rd WKFDE WF1 ....11 E1
arkey La AIRE BD20 ....26 A2
arkie St LUD/ILL HX2 ....2 C4
ar St WBOW BD5 ....95 J8
arwort Cl PONT WF8 ....180 E4
ILK LS29 ....32 A3
TOD OL14 ....134 A6
ation Av BRAM LS13 ....99 F1
ation Ct GSLY * LS20 ....53 F2
ation Crs WOR/ARM LS12 ....100 B4
ation Flds GFTH/SHER LS25 ....105 K4
ation Forecourt BFD * BD1 ....4 C4
ation La BIRK/DRI BD11 ....120 E5
ation Forecourt BFD * BD1 ....4 C4
EARD/LOFT WF3 ....147 K2
EARD/LOFT WF3 ....148 C2
FEA/AMT WF7 ....179 H6
HUDS HD4 ....213 F3
LVSC WF15 ....171 F1
MAR/SLWT HD7 ....188 H8
PONT WF8 ....180 E3
RTHW LS26 ....127 G4
SCFT LS14 ....60 D5
ation Mt BRAM LS13 ....99 G1
ation Pde KSTL LS5 ....78 A7
TOD OL14 ....132 D2
ation Pl BRAM LS13 ....99 G1
ation Rd AIRE BD20 ....27 F5
BAIL BD17 ....51 K8
BAIL BD17 ....52 D5
BFD BD1 ....4 E1
BIRK/DRI BD11 ....121 H5
BOW BD6 ....168 D1
BSLYN/ROY S71 ....221 K7
BTLY WF17 ....146 C7
CAS WF10 ....129 H7
CAS WF10 ....153 J3
CLAY BD14 ....94 C7
CUL/QBY BD13 ....70 A5
CUL/QBY BD13 ....92 C3
CUL/QBY BD13 ....116 D2
EARL WF12 ....172 B6
EARL WF12 ....172 E5
FEA/AMT WF7 ....203 G4
GFTH/SHER LS25 ....128 C8
GSLY LS20 ....53 F2
GTL/HWG HX4 ....166 A7
HBR HX7 ....136 B1
HECK WF16 ....145 F8
HEM/SK/SE WF9 ....224 E4
HEM/SK/SE WF9 ....226 C8
HIPP HX3 ....141 H4
HIPP HX3 ....142 B1
HOLM/MEL HD9 ....213 G6
HOLM/MEL HD9 ....231 J1
HOLM/MEL HD9 ....233 G6
HOR/CROF WF4 ....222 E2
HORS LS18 ....77 C1
HUDN HD2 ....169 H6
HUDS HD4 ....234 E1
HWTH BD22 ....68 E4
HWTH BD22 ....69 F1
HWTH BD22 ....90 E1
ILK LS29 ....20 B7
ILK LS29 ....32 A3
ILK LS29 ....32 C7
KBTN HD8 ....192 E8
KBTN HD8 ....216 E7
KBTN HD8 ....235 G3
KNOT * WF11 ....155 K6
LM/WK BD12 ....119 F6
LUD/ILL HX2 ....138 A4
MAR/SLWT HD7 ....189 H7
MAR/SLWT HD7 ....209 H7
MAR/SLWT HD7 ....210 D2
MIRF WF14 ....170 D7
MOR LS27 ....123 F6
MSTN/BAR LS15 ....82 D4
MSTN/BAR LS15 ....104 A1
NORM WF6 ....151 J8
OSS WF5 ....173 J6
PT LS21 ....33 J4
PT LS21 ....35 K6
RPDN/SBR HX6 ....139 F8
RTHW LS26 ....128 A8
SHPY BD18 ....73 H5
TOD OL14 ....133 F2
VHIT OL12 ....158 A8
WIL/AL BD15 ....70 D8
WOR/ARM LS12 ....100 B4
tion St HOLM/MEL HD9 ....231 H1
HUD HD1 ....17 G7
HDSY/CALV LS28 ....98 B5
WKFDE WF1 ....199 C1
tion Ter BRAM LS13 ....99 H7
AS WF10 ....129 H7
tion to Station Wk
MAR/SLWT HD7 ....207 J6
tion Av BRAM LS13 ....27 F6
WTH BD22 ....68 E8
MSTN/BAR LS15 ....104 A2
tion Wy WOR/ARM LS12 ....100 B4
tion Works KGHY * BD21 ....3 F5
ups La HBR HX7 ....134 E1
JPP HX3 ....140 E2
veley Dr SHPY BD18 ....72 D4
veley Gv HWTH BD22 ....47 J8

Staveley Ms BGLY * BD16 ....50 A7
Staveley Rd BGLY BD16 ....49 K7
GTHN BD7 ....95 H5
HWTH BD22 ....47 J8
SHPY BD18 ....72 D3
Staveley Wy HWTH BD22 ....2 B6
Stavely Ms BGLY * BD16 ....50 A7
Staverton Gv CUL/QBY BD13 ....93 J4
Staverton St LUD/ILL HX2 ....139 H4
Staybrite Av BGLY BD16 ....72 A4
Staygate Gn WBSY BD6 ....119 F2
Staynton Crs HUDN HD2 ....169 G6
Stead Ga KBTN HD8 ....236 B1
Stead Hill Wy IDLE BD10 ....75 H4
Stead La HUDE HD5 ....192 D3
ILK LS29 ....31 H3
RPDN/SBR HX6 ....186 E1
SCFT LS14 ....60 E6
Steadman St BFDE BD3 ....5 F5
Steadman Ter BFDE BD3 ....5 F5
Stead Rd BOW BD4 ....120 B3
Stead St BAIL BD17 ....73 H3
HFAX HX1 ....8 C4
Steanard La MIRF WF14 ....171 F8
Steander OSM LS9 ....7 F4
Steele La GTL/HWG HX4 ....188 A2
Steeplands HUDN HX4 ....169 G5
Steep La HBR HX7 ....137 H7
STKB/PEN S36 ....252 E7
Steeple Av HOR/CROF WF4 ....194 C7
Steep Riding HOLM/MEL HD9 ....213 J8
Steeton Gv AIRE BD20 ....26 E5
Steeton Hall Gdns AIRE BD20 ....26 E5
Stella Gdns PONT WF8 ....181 G1
Stell Hl HIPP HX3 ....47 F6
Stennard Island WKFDE WF1 ....11 D4
Stephen Cl HIPP HX3 ....141 F2
Stephen Crs ECHL BD2 ....74 A8
Stephen Rd WBSY BD6 ....118 A1
Stephenson Dr WOR/ARM LS12 ....99 H8
Stephenson Rd WIL/AL BD15 ....93 H1
Stephenson St GTHN BD7 ....95 H8
Stephenson Wy WKFDW/WTN WF2 ...149 G6
WOR/ARM LS12 ....99 H8
Stepping Stones AIRE BD20 ....49 J3
Steps La RPDN/SBR HX6 ....139 F6
Sterling Ct EARD/LOFT WF3 ....147 K1
Sterling Wy EARD/LOFT WF3 ....147 J1
Sterne Hl LUD/ILL HX2 ....139 J7
Stevenson Av CAS WF10 ....154 D6
Stewart Cl ECHL BD2 ....74 E6
Stewart Royd HECK * WF16 ....145 H7
Stewart St HWTH BD22 ....69 G3
Sticker La BOW BD4 ....96 E8
Stile Common Rd HUDS HD4 ....191 H8
Stile Hill Wy MSTN/BAR LS15 ....104 C4
Stilemoor Ri TOD OL14 ....133 K4
Stile Rd TOD OL14 ....133 K4
Stillwell Dr WKFDW/WTN WF2 ....199 G3
Stillwell Garth WKFDW/WTN WF2 .....199 F2
Stillwell Gv WKFDW/WTN WF2 ....199 F2
Stirling Crs BOW BD4 ....97 G8
HORS LS18 ....54 E7
Stirling Rd ILK LS29 ....31 K2
Stirling St AIRE BD20 ....27 G1
HFAX HX1 ....8 C5
Stirling Wy GFTH/SHER LS25 ....106 B4
Stirrup Gv ECHL BD2 ....74 B7
Stirton St WBOW BD5 ....95 K8
Stithy St OSS WF5 ....173 H5
Stockeld La WBY LS22 ....22 B5
Stockeld Rd ILK LS29 ....20 A7
Stockeld Wy ILK LS29 ....20 A6
Stockerhead La MAR/SLWT HD7 ....210 E3
Stockheld La MSTN/BAR LS15 ....82 D2
Stock Hey La TOD OL14 ....135 G5
Stockhill Fold IDLE BD10 ....75 H4
Stockhill Rd IDLE BD10 ....75 F4
Stockinbridge St DEWS WF13 ....171 K3
Stockingate HEM/SK/SE WF9 ....241 H2
Stockinger La ILK LS29 ....18 D4
Stocking La GFTH/SHER LS25 ....85 F5
KNOT * WF11 ....157 F7
Stock La LUD/ILL HX2 ....138 E5
Stocks Ap SCFT LS14 ....81 K7
Stocks Av HBR HX7 ....136 E3
Stocksbank Rd MIRF WF14 ....170 A5
Stocks Crs HBR HX7 ....136 E3
Stocks Dr KBTN HD8 ....235 F3
Stocks Gdns HBR HX7 ....136 E3
Stocks Hl BEE/HOL LS11 ....6 C6
ILK LS29 ....32 B7
WOR/ARM LS12 ....100 C3
Stocks Hill Cl AIRE * BD20 ....49 H3
Stocks La BTLY WF17 ....146 B6
CUL/QBY BD13 ....117 G2
HBR HX7 ....136 E3
HUDS HD4 ....234 D6
LUD/ILL HX2 ....138 B2
RPDN/SBR HX6 ....138 B8
Stocksmoor Rd HUDS HD4 ....218 C1
Stocks Ri SCFT LS14 ....81 K7
Stocks Rd SCFT LS14 ....81 K7
Stocks St CHAL LS7 ....79 J8

Stocks Wk HUDE HD5 ....192 B8
Stocks Wy KBTN HD8 ....235 F3
Stockwell Dr BTLY WF17 ....146 C5
Stockwell Hl HUDS HD4 ....213 F3
Stod Fold LUD/ILL HX2 ....115 F2
Stone Acre Hts HOLM/MEL * HD9 .....231 K2
Stone Arches WBOW BD5 ....96 A7
Stonebridge Ap WOR/ARM * LS12 ....99 J5
Stonebridge Av WOR/ARM LS12 ....99 J5
Stonebridge Gv WOR/ARM LS12 ....99 K5
Stonebridge La WOR/ARM LS12 ....99 J5
Stonebridge Wk KBTN HD8 ....235 H2
Stone Brig Gn RTHW LS26 ....126 A7
Stone Brig La RTHW LS26 ....126 B7
Stonechat Ri MOR LS27 ....123 H7
Stonecliffe LUD/ILL HX2 ....139 K7
Stonecliffe Crs WOR/ARM LS12 ....99 J5
Stonecliffe Dr HOR/CROF WF4 ....196 B4
WOR/ARM LS12 ....99 J5
Stonecliffe Garth WOR/ARM LS12 ......99 J5
Stonecliffe Gv WOR/ARM LS12 ....99 J5
Stonecliffe Mt WOR/ARM LS12 ....99 H5
Stonecliffe Ter WOR/ARM LS12 ....99 H5
Stonecliffe Wy WOR/ARM LS12 ....99 H5
Stone Ct AIRE BD20 ....23 J6
CUD/OR S72 ....223 J6
Stonecroft EARD/LOFT WF3 ....150 B6
ECHL BD2 ....74 E7
Stonecroft Gdns KBTN HD8 ....235 G3
Stonecroft Mt LUD/ILL HX2 ....139 F6
Stonedale Cl OT LS21 ....35 J5
Stonedene Pk WBY LS22 ....23 J5
Stonefield SCFT LS14 ....60 B3
Stonefield Av HUDS HD4 ....190 B8
Stonefield Cl IDLE BD10 ....74 D6
Stonefield PI BTLY WF17 ....145 J2
Stonefield Rd HUDS HD4 ....190 B8
Stonefield St CLECK BD19 ....143 H5
DEWS WF13 ....172 B2
Stonefleece Ct HOLM/MEL HD9 ....213 F8
Stonegate BGLY BD16 ....50 A6
CHAL LS7 ....79 J8
OSS WF5 ....173 K8
Stonegate Ap CHAL LS7 ....79 F5
Stonegate Cha CHAL LS7 ....79 F4
Stonegate Cl AL/HA/HU LS17 ....57 K8
Stonegate Crs CHAL LS7 ....79 G4
Stonegate Dr PONT WF8 ....180 D5
Stonegate Farm Cl CHAL LS7 ....79 F4
Stonegate Gdns CHAL LS7 ....79 F4
Stonegate Gn CHAL LS7 ....79 F5
Stonegate La CHAL LS7 ....79 F4
FEA/AMT WF7 ....202 E6
Stonegate Ms CHAL LS7 ....79 F5
Stonegate Pl CHAL LS7 ....79 F5
Stonegate Rd AL/HA/HU LS17 ....79 G3
IDLE BD10 ....74 E5
Stonegate Wk CHAL LS7 ....79 G3
Stone Gv AIRE BD20 ....26 E6
Stone Hall Rd ECHL BD2 ....74 D7
Stone Hl BGLY BD16 ....50 B7
Stonehouse Dr CUL/QBY BD13 ....116 B3
Stonehurst MSTN/BAR LS15 ....82 B7
Stonehurst Rd MIRF WF14 ....170 D5
Stonehyrst Av DEWS WF13 ....172 C2
Stone La HWTH BD22 ....90 D1
Stonelea GTL/HWG HX4 ....164 D6
Stonelea Ct CHAL LS7 ....79 G4
HDGY LS6 ....78 D6
Stone Lea Gv HEM/SK/SE * WF9 ....242 C1
Stoneleigh CUL/QBY BD13 ....116 A7
Stoneleigh Ct KBTN HD8 ....215 J8
Stonely Dr TOD OL14 ....159 K4
Stone Mill Ap HDGY LS6 ....78 E4
Stone Mill Ct HDGY LS6 ....78 E4
Stone Mill Wy HDGY LS6 ....78 E4
Stone Pits La MOR LS27 ....122 C6
Stones Dr RPDN/SBR HX6 ....186 D1
Stones Hey Ga HBR * HX7 ....111 H5
Stones La MAR/SLWT HD7 ....189 H6
MAR/SLWT HD7 ....211 G3
TOD OL14 ....133 H7
Stones Rd TOD OL14 ....133 J7
Stones Ter TOD * OL14 ....159 K1
Stone St BAIL BD17 ....74 A1
BFD BD1 ....4 C4
WIL/AL BD15 ....72 A8
Stone Vls FEA/AMT * WF7 ....202 E6
HDGY LS6 ....78 D5
Stone Wood La KBTN HD8 ....234 E2
Stoney Back La HUDS HD4 ....212 E1
Stoney Bank HOR/CROF * WF4 ....197 F2
Stoney Bank La HOLM/MEL HD9 ....233 K3
Stoney Bank St DEWS WF13 ....171 K5
Stoney Battery HFAX HX1 ....9 D5
Stoney Battery Rd HUDW HD3 ....190 D7
Stoneybrook Cl HOR/CROF WF4 ....219 F3
Stoney Cft CLECK BD19 ....144 E4
Stoneycroft La AIRE BD20 ....47 K1
Stoney Cross St HUDS HD4 ....212 E1
Stoney Ford La HUDE HD5 ....192 D2
Stoney Hl BRIG HD6 ....168 B1
Stoneyhurst Sq BOW BD4 ....97 G8
Stoney La AL/HA/HU LS17 ....59 J6
BTLY WF17 ....146 C5
HIPP HX3 ....115 K8
HIPP HX3 ....142 D4
HOR/CROF WF4 ....198 B8
HORS LS18 ....77 F3

HUDW HD3..................................189 K5
ILK LS29.......................................31 J5
WKFDW/WTN WF2..........................148 E6
Stoney Ridge Av WIL/AL BD15...............72 B7
Stoney Ridge Rd BGLY BD16..................59 G3
Stoney Ri HORS LS18..............................77 F5
Stoney Rock Ct OSM LS9....................102 B2
Stoney Rock La OSM LS9.....................102 B2
Stoney Royd Ter HIPP HX3..................140 C7
Stoneys Fold WIL/AL BD15.....................71 F5
Stoney St BGLY BD20.............................47 K1
Stoneythorpe HORS LS18........................77 F3
Stony Croft La GTL/HWG HX4...............164 E7
Stony Ga HOLM/MEL HD9......................247 K1
Stony La ECHL BD2.................................74 E6
  GTL/HWG HX4..................................165 K5
  HBR HX7...135 J1
  HIPP HX3..141 H7
  HOLM/MEL HD9................................213 F7
  RPDN/SBR HX6.................................164 A6
  TOD OL14..133 H2
  WIL/AL BD15......................................93 K1
Stony Royd PDSY/CALV LS28...................76 A8
Stony Royd La HBR HX7.......................136 B7
Stoodley Cl TOD OL14.........................135 F6
Stoodley Gra TOD * OL14....................135 F6
Stoodley La TOD OL14.........................135 H4
Stoodley Ter LUD/ILL HX2....................139 H5
Stopford Av WKFDW/WTN WF2.............199 G3
Stopford Garth WKFDW/WTN WF2........199 G3
Storey Pl SCFT LS14...............................103 G2
Storie Crs WKFDW/WTN WF2...............175 F7
Storiths La SKP/WHF BD23.......................15 K2
Stormer Hill La RPDN/SBR HX6.............165 G1
Storr Hl LM/WK BD12............................118 D7
Storrs La STRB/PEN S36.........................253 H8
Storth Av HUDS HD4...............................189 G8
Storthes Hall La KBTN HD8...................214 D6
Storths Rd HUDN HD2..............................12 B1
Stotfold Rd BTLY DN5.............................241 K8
Stottercliffe Rd STKB/PEN S36..............252 B8
Stott Hl BFD BD1.......................................5 D4
Stott Rd HDGY * LS6................................78 E8
Stott St WOR/ARM LS12........................100 D4
Stott Ter ECHL BD2..................................75 F7
Stourton Rd ILK LS29...............................19 K6
Stowe Gv OSM LS9.................................102 E3
Stowell Mill St WBOW BD5.......................95 K7
Stradmore Rd CUL/QBY BD13..................92 C3
Strafford St DOD/DAR S75....................239 J3
Strafford Wy IDLE BD10...........................75 G3
Straightacres La IDLE BD10......................75 F6
Straight La AWLS/ASK DN6....................227 K7
  ILK LS29..18 B6
  LUD/ILL HX2....................................115 G6
Straits BAIL BD17......................................51 J7
Stralau St BTLY WF17............................146 B5
Strands Ct HOR/CROF WF4....................196 E5
Strangford Ct IDLE BD10..........................75 F5
Stranglands La KNOT WF11...................155 G5
Stratford Av BEE/HOL LS11....................124 B1
Stratford Cl MAR/SLWT HD7..................189 J6
Stratford Rd OSM LS9...............................95 H6
Stratford St BEE/HOL LS11....................124 B1
Stratford Ter BEE/HOL LS11...................101 H8
Strathallan Dr BAIL BD17..........................51 K3
Strathmore Av OSM LS9.........................102 C1
Strathmore Dr BAIL BD17..........................51 H7
  OSM LS9..80 C8
Strathmore Gdns HEM/SK/SE WF9.......226 D7
Strathmore Rd ILK LS29...........................20 E7
Strathmore St OSM LS9.........................102 C1
Strathmore Vw OSM LS9........................102 C1
Stratus Cl FEA/AMT WF7........................203 F7
Strawberry Av GTHN/SHER LS25............105 J5
  LVSG WF15......................................144 D7
Strawberry Bank LVSG WF15................144 D7
Strawberry Fids KGHY BD21.......................3 D2
Strawberry Gdns BSLYN/ROY S71..........222 A7
Strawberry La WOR/ARM LS12...............100 C4
Strawberry Rd WOR/ARM LS12..............100 C4
  KGHY BD21...27 F3
  KGHY BD21..3 D2
Stream Head Rd CUL/QBY BD13..............93 H7
Streamside HDGY LS6................................78 E5
Streamside Fold HBR * HX7...................137 F3
The Street ILK LS29...................................18 B3
Street 1 BSPA/BRAM LS23.........................43 G5
Street 2 BSPA/BRAM LS23.........................43 H3
Street 3 BSPA/BRAM LS23.........................43 H2
Street 5 BSPA/BRAM LS23.........................43 H1
Street 6 BSPA/BRAM LS23.........................25 H8
Street 7 BSPA/BRAM LS23.........................25 H8
Street 8 BSPA/BRAM LS23.........................43 J1
Street Furlong La PONT WF8...................181 J4
Street Head La HWTH BD22.......................68 A2
Street La AIRE BD20.................................29 F8
  AIRE BD20..49 H2
  AL/HA/HU LS17..................................79 K1
  MOR * LS27..122 B4
Strensall Gn WBSY BD6..........................117 K3
Stretchgate La LUD/ILL HX2...................139 H3

Stretton Cl FEA/AMT WF7......................179 F2
Strickland Av AL/HA/HU LS17...................59 H7
Strickland Cl AL/HA/HU LS17....................59 H7
Strickland Crs AL/HA/HU LS17..................59 H7
Strickland Rd HEM/SK/SE WF9...............227 F5
Strikes La AIRE BD20................................26 A8
Strines Moor Rd HOLM/MEL HD9...........248 D4
Strines St TOD OL14..............................159 K4
Stringer House La KBTN HD8...................216 E4
Stringer La HOR/CROF WF4.....................197 H2
Strong Close Gv KGHY BD21.......................3 F3
Strong Close Rd KGHY BD21........................3 F3
Strong Close Wy KGHY BD21........................3 F3
Stuart Gv MAR/SLWT HD7......................210 E3
  NORM WF6...151 K7
Stuart Pl HUDN HD2...............................169 G6
Stuart Rd PONT WF8..............................180 D2
Stuart St CAS WF10................................153 K3
  PONT WF8...180 D2
Stubbin Fold HOLM/MEL HD9.................232 C8
Stubbing Brink HBR HX7.........................111 K8
Stubbing Dr HBR HX7.............................111 K8
Stubbing Holme Rd HBR HX7.................112 A8
Stubbing La GTL/HWG HX4....................165 H6
  RPDN/SBR HX6.................................164 B3
Stubbings Cl HBR HX7............................137 F3
Stubbings Rd BAIL BD17...........................73 F1
Stubbings St HBR HX7...........................137 F3
Stubbin Vly SHPY BD18............................73 F3
Stubbin La HOLM/MEL HD9....................232 C8
  KBTN HD8..237 F5
Stubbin Rd MAR/SLWT HD7...................209 K7
Stubbs Br AWLS/ASK DN6......................243 J1
  KNOT WF11..157 K8
Stubbs Beck La CLECK BD19...................143 K1
  KNOT WF11..182 D4
Stubham Ri ILK LS29................................20 A6
Stubley Farm Rd HECK WF16.................145 H5
Stubley Holme TOD OL14.......................132 D2
Stubley La TOD OL14.............................132 D2
Stubley Rd HECK WF16..........................145 F5
Stubley St WKFDE WF1.............................10 B3
Stubs Beck La CLECK BD19.....................143 K1
Sturdy Gv HUDN HD2.............................169 F6
Sturges Gv HIPP HX3..............................140 E2
Stumpcross Ct PONT WF8.......................155 G8
Stumpcross La PONT WF8......................155 H8
Stumpcross Wy PONT WF8....................155 G8
Stunsteds Rd CLECK BD19......................144 A3
Sturges Gv ECHL BD2.................................5 F1
Sturton Av GFTH/SHER LS25...................106 A3
Sturton Grange La
  GFTH/SHER LS25...............................106 B4
Sturton Gv LUD/ILL HX2.........................115 H4
Sturton La GFTH/SHER LS25...................106 A3
  LUD/ILL HX2....................................115 H5
Stutely Gv HUDN HD2............................169 F6
Styebank La RTHW LS26..........................126 C5
Styes La LUD/ILL HX2.............................138 A7
Sty La BGLY BD16....................................49 K5
Styveton Wy AIRE BD20...........................26 D5
Sude Hl HOLM/MEL HD9.........................234 A5
Sude Hill Ter HOLM/MEL HD9.................234 B5
Sudforth La GLE DN14............................157 K6
Suffield Crs MOR LS27............................122 A3
Suffield Dr MOR LS27.............................122 A3
Suffield Rd MOR LS27.............................122 A3
Suffolk Av BTLY WF17.............................145 K8
Suffolk Ct YEA LS19.................................53 K4
Suffolk Pl ECHL BD2.................................74 B7
Suffolk St BTLY WF17.............................146 A7
Sufton St HUDN HD2................................12 B1
Sugar Hl ILK LS29...................................18 D3
Sugar Hill Cl RTHW LS26.........................127 F8
Sugar La EARL WF12..............................172 D3
Sugar Well Ap CHAL * LS7.......................79 G6
Sugar Well Ct CHAL * LS7........................79 H7
Sugar Well Mt CHAL LS7..........................79 G6
Sugar Well Rd CHAL LS7..........................79 G6
Sugden Cl BRIG HD6..............................168 B3
Sugden St BFD BD1...................................4 A4
  LM/WK BD12....................................119 D7
Sulby Gv IDLE BD10..................................75 G5
Sullivan Cl HUDS HD4.............................190 D8
Sullivan Gv HEM/SK/SE WF9..................241 H2
Summerbank Cl BIRK/DRI BD11.............121 J4
Summerbridge Crs CLECK BD19.............144 E1
  IDLE BD10..75 F6
Summerbridge Dr IDLE BD10.....................75 F6
Summerdale CLECK BD19........................144 E1
Summerfield Av BRAM LS13......................76 E8
  BRIG HD6..142 C5
Summerfield Cl BAIL BD17.........................51 G8
  KNOT WF11..156 B3
Summerfield Dr BAIL BD17.........................51 H8
  BRAM LS13..76 E8
  KNOT WF11..156 A3
Summerfield Gdns BRAM LS13..................76 E8
Summerfield Gn BAIL BD17........................51 H8
  BRAM LS13..76 E8
Summerfield Gv BAIL BD17........................51 G8
  KBTN HD8..215 F1
Summerfield Pk BAIL BD17........................51 H8

Summerfield Pl BRAM LS13.......................76
Summerfield Rd BRAM LS13......................76
  IDLE BD10..74
  TOD OL14..134
Summergate Pl HFAX HX1..........................8
Summergate St HFAX HX1...........................8
Summer Hall Ing LM/WK BD12................118
Summerhill Av AIRE BD20..........................27
Summerhill Dr AIRE BD20...........................27
Summerhill Gdns RHAY LS8.......................58
Summerhill Gv GFTH/SHER LS25.............105
Summerhill La AIRE BD20...........................27
Summerhill Pl RHAY LS8............................58
Summerhill Rd GFTH/SHER LS25.............105
Summer Hill Rd RTHW LS26........................9
Summer Hill St GTHN BD7..........................95
Summerlands Gv WBOW BD5....................119
Summer La BSLYN/ROY S71.....................221
  KBTN HD8...217
Summer Lea IDLE BD10..............................74
Summer Meadow PONT * WF8..................180
Summer Rd BSLYN/ROY S71.....................221
Summerscale St HFAX HX1...........................8
Summerseat Pl GTHN BD7.........................95
Summerset Pl HFAX HX1..............................8
  HUD * HD1...12
  HUDS HD4...212
Summervale HOLM/MEL HD9....................233
Summerville Rd GTHN BD7..........................4
  PDSY/CALV LS28.................................98
Summit St KGHY BD21................................2
Sunbeam Av BEE/HOL LS11.....................101
Sunbeam Gv BEE/HOL LS11.....................101
Sunbeam Pl BEE/HOL LS11.......................101
Sunbeam Ter BEE/HOL LS11.....................101
  EARD/LOFT * WF3.............................147
Sunbridge Rd GIR BD8................................4
Sunbury Gv HUDE HD5.............................192
Sun Ct FEA/AMT WF7...............................179
Sunderland Ct BRIG HD6..........................142
Sunderland Rd HTON BD9...........................95
Sunderland St HFAX HX1.............................8
  HWTH BD22..69
  KGHY BD21...2
Sundown Av GTHN BD7.............................94
Sun Fld PDSY/CALV LS28............................98
Sunfield Dr PDSY/CALV LS28......................98
Sunfield Gdns PDSY/CALV * LS28..............98
Sunfield Pl PDSY/CALV LS28.......................98
Sun Hill Dr BAIL BD17................................68
Sunhurst Cl HWTH BD22............................68
Sunhurst Dr HWTH BD22............................68
Sun La HWTH BD22...................................68
  ILK LS29...31
  WKFDE WF1..11
Sunningdale GFTH/SHER LS25.................107
  GIR BD8..94
Sunningdale Av AL/HA/HU LS17.................57
Sunningdale Crs CUL/QBY BD13................70
Sunningdale Cft HUDN HD2......................168
Sunningdale Dr AL/HA/HU LS17.................57
Sunningdale Gn AL/HA/HU LS17................57
Sunningdale Rd HUDS HD4.......................190
Sunningdale Wy NORM WF6.....................178
Sunny Av HEM/SK/SE WF9.......................226
  HEM/SK/SE WF9................................242
  HBR HX7..137
  HEM/SK/SE WF9................................202
  HOR/CROF WF4..................................222
  KNOT WF11..146
  NORM WF6...177
  SHPY BD18...73
Sunnybank CHAL LS7...............................236
  BFDE BD3..97
  HORS LS18..77
Sunny Bank Av MIRF WF14......................170
  WBOW * BD5.....................................118
Sunnybank Cl CLECK BD19.......................143
Sunnybank Ct YEA LS19.............................54
Sunnybank Crs GTL/HWG HX4.................165
  YEA LS19...54
Sunnybank Dr GTL/HWG HX4...................166
Sunny Bank Dr MIRF WF14.......................170
  RPDN/SBR HX6..................................139
Sunnybank Gv BFDE BD3...........................97
Sunny Bank Gv CHAL LS7..........................80
  MIRF WF14...170
Sunny Bank La BTLY WF17........................146
  HBR HX7..136
  HIPP HX3..141
Sunnybank La BFDE BD3.............................97
  GTL/HWG HX4...................................166
Sunny Bank Pde MIRF WF14....................170
Sunny Bank Rd BRIG HD6.........................142
  BTLY WF17...146
  HOLM/MEL HD9................................231
  LUD/ILL HX2......................................114
  MAR/SLWT HD7.................................189
  MIRF WF14...170
  WBOW BD5.......................................118
Sunnybank Rd GFTH/SHER LS25.............107
  GTL/HWG HX4...................................165
  HORS LS18...77
  HUDW HD3..190
Sunnybank St OSS WF5............................196
Sunny Bank St RPDN/SBR HX6.................139
Sunny Bank Ter HIPP * HX3.........................9

OD OL14.................................132 E2
ny Bank Vw RHAY * LS8............80 B6
ny Bank Wk MIRF WF14............170 D3
nybank Woods BTLY WF17........146 C5
nybrae Crs BGLY BD16................72 B1
ny Brow Crs HUDS HD4............213 F3
ny Brow La HTON BD9................94 D1
nycliffe AIRE BD20....................49 H3
nydale Av BRIG HD6................168 B5
nydale Crt OSS * WF5..............173 K7
nydale Cft OSS * WF5..............173 K7
nydale Gv KGHY BD21................48 D5
nydale Pk AIRE BD20.................49 J2
SS WF5.....................................173 K6
nydale Rdg OT LS21.................33 F5
nydale Rd OSS WF5.................173 K6
nydale Ter OSS WF5................173 K6
nydene SCFT LS14...................103 H2
nyfield EARD/LOFT WF3...........148 D5
nyfield Rd HEM/SK/SE WF9......202 A8
ny Gv MOR LS27......................123 H3
ny Heys Rd HOLM/MEL HD9.....211 H8
ny Heys West HOLM/MEL HD9...211 H8
ny Hl WKFDW/WTN WF2...........174 E1
nyhill Av WKFDW/WTN * WF2.....175 F1
nyhill Crs WKFDW/WTN WF2......174 E1
nyhill Cft WKFDW/WTN WF2.......174 E1
ny Hill Gv HWTH BD22..................2 A5
ny Lea MAR/SLWT * HD7............209 J7
ny Lea Ter WBSY * BD6.............118 E3
nylee Est OT * LS21...................33 J3
ny Mdl HUDE HD5....................192 C5
nymead KBTN HD8.....................237 H1
ny Mt AIRE BD20......................49 G4
GLY BD16.................................71 F2
GHY BD21...................................2 C2
nymount HWTH BD22................47 F3
nyridge Av PDSY/CALV LS28.....97 K4
nyside BRIG HD6.....................168 B5
TL/HWG HX4............................188 D2
ECK WF16................................145 G8
UDW HD3................................12 A2
OD OL14...................................11 K6
nyside Av EARD/LOFT WF3.......147 J5
/SG WF15.................................170 C1
nyside La BFDE BD3....................5 D2
nyside Rd BRAM LS13.................99 F2
ny Side St HIPP * HX3..................9 D2
nyvale Mt HEM/SK/SE WF9........226 A8
nyview EARD/LOFT WF3............148 D4
nyview Av BEE/HOL LS11...........101 F8
ny View Crs HUDN HD2.............168 E8
nyview Gdns BEE/HOL LS11.......101 F8
ny View Ter BEE/HOL LS11.........101 F8
ny View Ter CUL/QBY BD13.......116 B3
nywood House
OLM/MEL * HD9.....................212 D7
royd Av HOR/CROF WF4............197 H1
royd Hl HOR/CROF WF4.............197 H1
set HDGY LS6...........................78 E3
set Dr HDGY LS6......................78 E4
K LS29.....................................20 D6
set Hilltop HDGY LS6...............78 E3
set Mt HDGY LS6......................78 E3
set Ri HDGY LS6........................78 E3
set Rd HDGY LS6......................78 E3
set Vw HDGY LS6.....................78 E3
shine Ct WBSY BD6.................118 A4
St AIRE BD20............................26 B6
FDE BD3....................................5 D3
GHY BD21...................................3 D4
DSY/CALV LS28........................98 B2
EA LS29....................................54 A4
Ter TOD * OL14.......................132 E2
Vale Av TOD OL14..................160 A4
ways MIRF WF14.....................170 D4
Wood Av HIPP HX3..................140 E6
at Rd MAR/SLWT HD7..............210 D1
esnes Rd KGHY BD21................68 E5
gery St HWTH BD22.................68 E5
rey Gv PDSY/CALV LS28..........96 A7
/BOW BD5.................................96 A7
rey Rd PDSY/CALV LS28..........98 C3
rey St BTLY WF17....................146 C6
GHY BD21...................................3 F2
OD * OL14...............................134 A5
sex Av HORS LS18....................55 G8
sex Cl HEM/SK/SE WF9...........224 D3
sex Crs CAS WF10....................155 F4
sex Gdns MID LS10..................102 B8
sex Gn MID LS10......................102 B8
sex Pl MID LS10.......................102 B8
sex St BTLY WF17....................146 C6
GHY BD21...................................3 F2
SM * LS9..................................102 A4
cliffe St LUD/ILL HX2..............139 H5
cliffe Wood La HIPP HX3..........141 H5
nerland Av RHAY LS8.................80 C2
nerland Crs RHAY LS8................80 C1
nerland Dr HUDS HD4..............212 C2
nerland Mt OSM LS9................102 C1
nerland Rd HIPP HX3...............141 K3
SM * LS9.................................102 C1
nerland St WOR/ARM * LS12......6 A5

Sutherland Ter OSM LS9..........102 C1
Sutton Ap SCFT LS14...............103 G2
Sutton Av ECHL BD2..................74 B6
   HUDE HD5...........................192 C3
Sutton Crs BOW BD4.................97 G7
   SCFT LS14..........................103 G2
Sutton Dr CUL/QBY BD13..........70 B6
   HUDE HD5...........................192 C3
Sutton Gv BOW BD4..................97 G6
   MOR * LS27.........................123 F8
Sutton La AIRE BD20..................26 A6
   KNOT WF11.........................156 A4
Sutton Rd BOW BD4..................97 G6
Sutton St WOR/ARM LS12.............6 B5
Suzanne Crs HEM/SK/SE WF9...226 A8
Swaine Hill Crs YEA LS19............53 J4
Swaine Hill St YEA LS19.............53 J4
Swaine Hill Ter YEA LS19............53 J4
Swain House Crs ECHL BD2.........74 C6
Swain House Rd ECHL BD2..........74 C6
Swain Mt ECHL BD2....................74 C6
Swale Crs GFTH/SHER LS25.......106 B5
Swales Moor Rd HIPP HX3.........116 B6
Swales' Yd PONT WF8................180 D3
Swallow Av WOR/ARM LS12......100 A5
   DOD/DAR S75......................239 K3
   OT LS21................................35 H5
Swallow Cl AL/HA/HU * LS17......58 B7
   OT LS21................................35 H5
Swallow Crs WOR/ARM LS12.....100 A5
Swallow Dr AL/HA/HU LS17........58 B7
   OT LS21................................35 H5
Swallow Fold GIR BD8................94 C4
Swallow Garth WKFDW/WTN WF2.199 F6
Swallow Gv HUDS HD4..............212 E5
Swallow Hl BTLY WF17..............145 K2
Swallow La MAR/SLWT HD7......189 C6
Swallow Mt WOR/ARM LS12......100 A4
Swallow St HECK WF16.............145 F8
   KGHY BD21.............................3 E2
Swallow V MOR LS27................123 J7
Swan Av BGLY BD16...................50 C8
Swan Bank HOLM/MEL HD9.......233 C7
Swan Bank La HIPP HX3...............9 E6
   HOLM/MEL HD9....................233 C7
Swanhill La PONT WF8..............180 E4
Swan La HUDS HD4..................190 E8
   HUDW * HD3.......................189 F2
Swan St WBOW * BD5..................4 C5
Swarcliffe Ap SCFT LS14............82 A7
Swarcliffe Av SCFT LS14.............82 A7
Swarcliffe Bank SCFT LS14.........82 A6
Swarcliffe Dr SCFT LS14.............82 A7
Swarcliffe Dr East MSTN/BAR LS15.82 B7
Swarcliffe Gn SCFT LS14............82 B7
Swarcliffe Rd SCFT LS14.............82 A6
Swarcliffe Rd SCFT LS14.............82 A7
Swardale Gn SCFT LS14..............82 A7
Swardale Rd SCFT LS14..............82 A7
Swarland Gv WBOW BD5..............4 C6
Swartha La AIRE BD20.................17 J8
Sweep La HOLM/MEL WF9.........233 H8
Sweet St BEE/HOL LS11................7 D5
Sweet St West BEE/HOL LS11.......6 C5
Swift's Fold HOLM/MEL HD9.......213 F6
Swift Wy WKFDW/WTN WF2.......198 E6
Swillington La RTHW LS26..........127 J3
Swincar Av YEA LS19...................53 K4
Swincliffe Cl CLECK BD19..........120 D7
Swincliffe Crs CLECK BD19........120 D8
Swincroft OSS WF5...................173 K6
Swindon Dr DEWS WF13............172 B3
Swinegate LDS LS1......................7 E4
Swine Lane Br AIRE BD20............49 G3
   HOR/CROF WF4...................201 G3
   HOR/CROF WF4...................201 J5
Swine Market La HBR HX7..........136 B7
Swineshead La TOD OL14...........134 A8
Swineshead Rd TOD OL14..........133 K8
Swinnow Av BRAM LS13..............98 E1
Swinnow Cl BRAM LS13..............98 E2
Swinnow Dr BRAM LS13..............98 E2
Swinnow Gdns BRAM LS13..........98 E1
Swinnow Garth PDSY/CALV LS28..98 E1
Swinnow Gn PDSY/CALV LS28....98 D3
Swinnow Gv BRAM LS13..............98 E1
Swinnow La BRAM LS13...............98 E1
Swinnow Pl PDSY/CALV LS28......98 E1
Swinnow Rd PDSY/CALV LS28.....98 E3
Swinnow Vw BRAM LS13.............98 E2
Swinnow Wk BRAM LS13..............98 E2
Swinton Pl GTHN BD7.................95 H6
Swinton Ter HFAX HX1...................5 A5
Swires Rd ECHL BD2.....................5 F2
   HFAX HX1................................8 C5
Swires Ter HFAX HX1....................8 C5
Swiss St CAS WF10.....................153 K2
Swithenbank Av OSS WF5..........173 H3
Swithenbank St OSS WF5...........173 H2
Swithen Hl DOD/DAR S75..........219 H7
Swithens Ct RTHW LS26.............126 C7
Swithens Dr RTHW LS26.............126 B7
Swithens Gv RTHW LS26............150 C1
Swithen's La RTHW LS26............126 C7
Swithen's St RTHW LS26.............126 C7
Sycamore Av BGLY BD16.............71 K1
   CUD/GR S72........................240 B6
   GFTH/SHER LS25..................128 E1
   GTHN BD7..............................95 F4

HOLM/MEL HD9.....................231 H2
HUDW HD3............................189 K6
KNOT WF11...........................156 A8
MSTN/BAR LS15....................103 J3
RHAY LS8................................80 B6
TOD OL14.............................133 K4
WKFDW/WTN * WF2..............175 C1
WKFDW/WTN WF2................175 C4
Sycamore Cha PDSY/CALV LS28...98 D4
Sycamore Cl BFDE BD3.................5 E3
   BHP/TINH LS16......................55 K2
   CHAL LS7...............................79 F4
   HDGY LS6...............................79 G7
   KBTN * HD8..........................193 H8
   KNOT WF11...........................182 A1
Sycamore Copse
   WKFDW/WTN WF2................175 G6
Sycamore Ct KBTN HD8.............215 H4
   PONT WF8............................181 F1
   RHAY LS8................................80 E5
Sycamore Cft BEE/HOL LS11.......101 H8
Sycamore Dr BRIG HD6..............142 B5
   BSLYN/ROY S71....................221 J8
   CLECK BD19..........................143 J4
   ELL HX5................................166 C5
   ILK LS29................................18 E3
Sycamore Fold BEE/HOL LS11.....101 H8
Sycamore Gn KBTN HD8............236 C4
Sycamore Gv AIRE BD20.............26 B6
   NORM WF6...........................177 K3
   WKFDW/WTN WF2................175 G4
Sycamore La HOR/CROF WF4.....219 F5
Sycamore Ri HOLM/MEL HD9.....233 K4
Sycamore Rd HEM/SK/SE WF9....224 C5
Sycamore Rw BRAM LS13............76 E7
The Sycamores BHP/TINH LS16....55 K2
   DEWS WF13..........................172 A1
   GSLY LS20..............................53 G1
   HOR/CROF WF4.....................197 J2
   WIL/AL * BD15........................71 G7
Sycamore St WKFDE WF1.............11 E5
Sycamore Vw HWTH BD22.............2 A4
Sycamore Wk PDSY/CALV LS28....98 B1
   STKB/PEN S36......................252 C8
Sycamore Wy BTLY WF17...........145 J2
   FEA/AMT WF7.......................179 J5
Sydenham Pl BFDE BD3.................5 E1
Sydenham St BEE/HOL LS11..........6 B5
Sydney St BGLY BD16..................50 A8
   LVSG WF15...........................144 E8
   PDSY/CALV LS28....................98 B1
   RTHW LS26............................127 G5
Syke Av EARD/LOFT WF3...........147 J4
   EARL WF12...........................172 E3
Syke Cl EARD/LOFT WF3............147 H4
Syke Cft BSLYN/ROY S71...........222 A6
Syke Gdns EARD/LOFT WF3.......147 J4
Syke Gn SCFT LS14.....................60 A3
Syke Gv EARL WF12...................172 E3
Syke House La GTL/HWG HX4.....165 J5
Syke Ing Cl EARL WF12..............173 F4
Syke La CUL/QBY BD13.............116 D4
   EARL WF12...........................172 E4
   HIPP HX3..............................141 K2
   LUD/ILL HX2.........................115 C1
   RPDN/SBR HX6....................138 D8
   SCFT LS14.............................59 J5
Syke Pde EARD/LOFT * WF3.......147 H3
Syke Rd EARD/LOFT WF3...........147 J4
   EARL WF12...........................172 E3
   WBY LS22...............................24 A6
Sykes Av MIRF WF14..................171 F5
Sykes Cl BTLY WF17..................146 D5
Sykes Ga HBR HX7....................162 C4
Sykes La AIRE BD20....................27 F3
   EARL WF12...........................147 F7
   HWTH BD22............................47 F8
   LM/WK BD12..........................119 H7
Sykes Rd BTLY WF10................160 D5
Syke St CAS WF10......................153 J3
   CLECK BD19..........................144 A4
Syke St EARL WF12...................172 E4
Syke Ter EARD/LOFT * WF3........147 H4
Syke Vw EARL WF12..................172 E3
Sylhet Cl BFD BD1........................4 B3
Sylvan Av CUL/QBY BD13..........116 C3
Sylvester Av NORM WF6.............177 J4
Symons St WKFDW/WTN WF2.....10 B4
Syringa Av WIL/AL BD15..............72 A7
Syringa St HUDW HD3...............190 D4

T

Tabbs Ct CLECK BD19..............143 G2
Tabbs La CLECK BD19...............143 F2
Tadman St WKFDE WF1...............10 C5
Tagore Ct BOW BD4....................97 F5
Talbot & Falcon Yd WKFDE WF1..10 C3
Talbot Av AL/HA/HU LS17............80 A1
   BULY LS4................................78 C8
   HUDW HD3............................190 C3
Talbot Ct RHAY LS8....................80 B2
Talbot Crs RHAY LS8...................80 B1
Talbot Fold RHAY LS8.................80 B2
Talbot Gdns RHAY LS8................80 B1

Talbot Gv RHAY LS8 ....80 B1
Talbot Mt BULY LS4 ....78 C8
Talbot Ri RHAY LS8 ....80 B1
Talbot Rd RHAY LS8 ....80 B1
 STKB/PEN LS36 ....252 B8
Talbot Rw BTLY WF17 ....146 C6
Talbot St BTLY WF17 ....146 B7
 GTHN BD7 ....95 H4
 KGHY BD21 ....2 B3
 NORM WF6 ....177 K1
Talbot Vw BULY LS4 ....78 C8
Tallow Ms KBTN HD8 ....236 E2
Tall Trees AL/HA/HU LS17 ....57 J8
Tall Trees Dr FEA/AMT WF7 ....179 J3
Tamar St BOW BD5 ....95 J7
Tammy St WKFDE * WF1 ....10 C3
Tamworth St BOW BD4 ....97 G5
Tandem Ms KBTN HD8 ....192 D5
Tanfield Cl BSLYN/ROY S71 ....221 J7
Tanfield Dr ILK LS29 ....32 A1
Tanfield Rd HUDN HD2 ....12 B2
Tanglewood Ct WBSY BD6 ....118 B2
Tanhouse Hill HIPP HX3 ....141 H4
 HORS LS18 ....77 J5
Tan House La FEA/AMT WF7 ....203 H4
 HIPP HX3 ....117 H7
 WIL/AL BD15 ....70 E6
Tanhouse La MIRF WF14 ....193 H4
Tanhouse Pk HIPP HX3 ....141 H4
Tanhouse St DEWS WF13 ....171 J5
Tan La BOW BD4 ....119 J5
Tannerbrook Cl CLAY BD14 ....94 D7
Tanner Hill Rd GTHN BD7 ....94 E8
Tanners MAR/SLWT HD7 ....210 D4
Tanner St LVSG WF15 ....143 J6
Tannery Ct IDLE BD10 ....75 F3
 PDSY/CALV * LS28 ....98 D4
Tannery Sq HDGY LS6 ....78 E4
Tan Pit Cl BTLY DN5 ....241 K7
Tan Pit La BTLY DN5 ....241 K7
Tanpits HBR * HX7 ....112 B8
Tanshelf Dr PONT WF8 ....180 D3
Tanton Crs CLAY BD14 ....94 D7
Tanton Wk CLAY BD14 ....94 D7
Tanyard Av HUDW HD3 ....190 A4
Tanyard Cft CUD/GR S72 ....224 C8
Tanyard Fold HOR/CROF WF4 ....198 C7
Tanyard Rd HUDS HD4 ....190 B7
 HUDW HD3 ....190 A4
Tarn BAIL * BD17 ....52 C7
Tarn Cl CAS WF10 ....155 F2
Tarn Ct HWTH BD22 ....2 A2
 KGHY BD21 ....148 J8
Tarnhill Ms WBOW BD5 ....96 A7
Tarn Hows Wk FEA/AMT WF7 ....202 E5
Tarn La AL/HA/HU LS17 ....59 F4
 HWTH BD22 ....46 E3
Tarn Rd FEA/AMT WF7 ....179 K7
Tarnside Dr SCFT LS14 ....81 H8
Tarn View Rd YEA LS19 ....54 A4
Tarn Vis ILK * LS29 ....20 C8
Tatefield Gv GFTH/SHER LS25 ....129 F3
Tatefield Pl GFTH/SHER LS25 ....129 F3
Tateley Cl OSS WF5 ....173 J2
Tateley La OSS WF5 ....173 H2
Tate Naylor St DEWS * WF13 ....172 A1
Tatham Wy RHAY LS8 ....80 E5
Tatton St WKFDE * WF1 ....11 F6
Taunton St SHPY BD18 ....73 G3
Tavern St BTLY WF1 ....11 D4
Tavistock Wy WKFDW/WTN WF2 ...198 B6
Tavora St WKFDE * WF1 ....10 C2
Tawny Beck WOR/ARM LS12 ....99 G4
Tawny Cl BOW BD4 ....120 B2
 MOR LS27 ....123 J7
Taylor Av AIRE BD20 ....27 F2
Taylor Cl OSS WF5 ....174 A7
Taylor Crs CUD/GR S72 ....240 A6
 OSS WF5 ....174 A7
Taylor Dr OSS WF5 ....174 A7
Taylor Gv WKFDE LS26 ....128 D8
 MIRF WF14 ....170 C4
Taylor Hall La MIRF WF14 ....170 C4
Taylor La LUD/ILL HX2 ....115 K1
 MSTN/BAR LS15 ....83 F5
Taylor Rd WBSY BD6 ....118 E3
Taylors Cl SCFT LS14 ....81 K7
Taylor St BTLY WF17 ....146 B7
 CLECK BD19 ....143 K4
 MAR/SLWT HD7 ....189 J6
Tealbeck Ap OT LS21 ....33 G4
Tealby Cl BHP/TINH LS16 ....77 J1
Teal Cl CAS WF10 ....153 J5
Teal Ct AIRE BD20 ....26 D5
Teal Dr MOR LS27 ....123 J7
Teall Cl OSS WF5 ....174 B6
Teall St OSS WF5 ....174 B7
 WKFDE WF1 ....10 C2
Teal Ms ILK LS10 ....124 E6
Teal St WKFDE WF1 ....10 C3
Teapot Cnr BTLY DN5 ....241 K7
Teasdale St BOW BD4 ....96 D8
Teasel Cl LM/WK BD12 ....119 H7
Tebbet Pl HECK * WF16 ....145 H7

Technology Dr BTLY WF17 ....146 D7
Teddington Av HUDE HD5 ....192 B5
Tees St WBOW BD5 ....95 J8
Telephone Pl CHAL LS7 ....7 F2
Telford Cl AIRE BD20 ....27 H3
 CAS WF10 ....153 C4
 MID LS10 ....125 F1
Telford Pl MID LS10 ....125 F1
Telford Ter BULY LS10 ....102 A8
Telford Wy WKFDW/WTN WF2 ....149 H7
Telscombe Dr BOW BD4 ....120 A1
Temperance Flds CLECK BD19 ...143 C3
Tempest Pl BEE/HOL * LS11 .....101 G8
Tempest Rd BEE/HOL LS11 ....101 G8
 HEM/SK/SE WF9 ....225 J7
Templar Dr HUDE HD5 ....13 F5
Templar Gdns WBY LS22 ....23 H4
Templar La LDSU LS2 ....7 F3
 MSTN/BAR LS15 ....82 B7
Templar Pl LDSU LS2 ....7 F3
Templars Cl GTL/HWG HX4 ......165 K4
Templar St LDSU LS2 ....7 F3
 WKFDE WF1 ....11 F6
Templars Wy GFTH/SHER LS25 ..105 K5
 GIR BD8 ....94 E3
Temple Av MSTN/BAR LS15 .....103 H3
 RTHW LS26 ....126 C4
Temple Bank Flats HTON * BD9 ..94 E2
Temple Cl HUD HD1 ....12 C4
 MSTN/BAR LS15 ....103 J5
Temple Crs BEE/HOL LS11 ......101 G8
Temple Gdns NORM WF6 ....176 J7
Temple Ga MSTN/BAR LS15 ......103 K4
Templegate Av MSTN/BAR LS15 ..103 J5
Templegate Cl MSTN/BAR LS15 ..103 K4
Templegate Crs MSTN/BAR LS15 .103 K4
Temple Gate Dr MSTN/BAR LS15 .103 J5
Templegate Gn MSTN/BAR LS15 ..103 J5
Templegate Ri MSTN/BAR LS15 ...103 J5
Templegate Rd MSTN/BAR LS15 ..103 J5
Templegate Vw MSTN/BAR LS15 ..103 J5
Templegate Wk MSTN/BAR LS15 ..103 K4
Temple Gn RTHW LS26 ....126 D4
Temple Gv MSTN/BAR LS15 ......103 J4
Temple La MSTN/BAR LS15 ......103 K4
Temple Lea MSTN/BAR LS15 .....103 K4
Temple Moor MSTN/BAR * LS15 ..103 K4
Templenewsam Rd
 MSTN/BAR LS15 ....103 H4
Templenewsam Vw
 MSTN/BAR LS15 ....103 H5
Temple Park Cl MSTN/BAR LS15 ..103 J4
Temple Park Gdns MSTN/BAR LS15 103 J4
Temple Park Gn MSTN/BAR LS15 ..103 J4
Temple Rhydding Dr BAIL BD17 ...73 J1
Temple Ri MSTN/BAR LS15 ......103 J5
Temple Rd DEWS WF13 ....171 K4
Temple Row MSTN/BAR LS15 ....104 C5
Templestowe Crs MSTN/BAR LS15 104 A2
Templestowe Dr MSTN/BAR LS15 .104 A3
Templestowe Gdns
 MSTN/BAR LS15 ....103 K3
Templestowe Hi MSTN/BAR LS15 .103 K2
Temple St CAS WF10 ....153 H4
 HTON BD9 ....95 H1
 HUDW HD3 ....190 D2
 KGHY BD21 ....2 C3
Temple Vw EARD/LOFT WF3 .....149 K2
Temple View Gv OSM LS9 ....102 C3
Temple View Pl OSM LS9 ....102 B4
Temple View Rd OSM LS9 ....102 B4
Temple View Ter OSM LS9 ......102 B4
Temple Vue HDGY LS6 ....78 D5
Temple Wk MSTN/BAR LS15 .....103 K3
Tenbury Fold BOW BD4 ....97 G8
Tenby Ter HFAX * HX1 ....8 A3
Ten Lands La HOR/CROF WF4 ...222 D4
Tennis Av BOW BD4 ....120 B2
Tennis Wy BAIL BD17 ....73 G2
Tennyson Av EARD/LOFT WF3 ...150 B5
 RPDN/SBR HX6 ....138 C3
 TOD OL14 ....134 C5
Tennyson Cl PDSY/CALV LS28 ...98 D5
 STKB/PEN S36 ....252 E7
Tennyson Pl BFDE BD3 ....5 F3
 CLECK BD19 ....144 A3
Tennyson Rd WBSY BD6 ....118 C3
Tennyson St GSLY LS20 ....53 H5
 HIPP HX3 ....8 B2
 KGHY BD21 ....2 C5
 MOR LS27 ....123 G7
 PDSY/CALV LS28 ....98 B1
 PDSY/CALV LS28 ....98 D5
Tennyson Ter MOR * LS27 ....123 G7
Tennyson Wy PONT WF8 ....154 E3
Tenter Cl BTLY WF17 ....146 B5
 KBTN HD8 ....236 E1
Tentercroft Ct DEWS WF13 ......172 C2
Tenterden Wy MSTN/BAR LS15 ..82 D8
Tenterfield Ri HIPP HX3 ....141 F7
Tenterfield Rd OSS WF5 ....173 K6
Tenterfields IDLE BD10 ....75 C3
 LUD/ILL HX2 ....138 B6
Tenter Hi BSPA/BRAM LS23 ......62 B7
 CLAY BD14 ....94 B7
 HOLM/MEL HD9 ....234 B7

Tenter Hill La HUDN HD2 168
Tenters Cl KNOT WF11 155
Tenters Gv HUDN HD2 168
Tenth Av LVSG WF15 143
Ten Yards La CUL/QBY BD13 92
Terminus Pde MSTN/BAR * LS15 .104
Ternhill Gv WBOW BD5 4
Tern Pk WBY LS22 40
Tern St WBOW BD5 95
The Terrace PDSY/CALV LS28 98
Terrace Gdns HIPP HX3 ....
Terrington Crest CLAY BD14 94
Terry Rd LM/WK BD12 119
Tetley Dr BIRK/DRI BD11 120
Tetley La HIPP HX3 141
Tetley Pl ECHL BD2 74
Tetley St BFD BD1 ....
Teville Ct BOW BD4 96
Tewit Cl LUD/ILL HX2 115
Tewit Gn LUD/ILL HX2 115
Tewit Hall Gdns LUD/ILL HX2 ...115
Tewit Hall Rd BFDE BD3 ....
Tewit La LUD/ILL HX2 115
Tewitt Cl AIRE BD20 26
Tewitt La BGLY BD16 50
 CUL/QBY BD13 92
Tew St WKFDW/WTN WF2 10
Texas St MOR LS27 147
Thackeray Gv HUDS HD4 190
Thackeray Rd IDLE BD10 75
Thacker Gate Rd HBR HX7 137
Thackley Av IDLE BD10 74
Thackley Ct BAIL BD17 73
Thackley Old Rd SHPY BD18 73
Thackley Rd IDLE BD10 74
Thackley Vw IDLE BD10 74
Thackray Av HECK WF16 145
Thackray La PONT WF8 180
Thackray St LUD/ILL HX2 139
 MOR LS27 123
Thames Dr GFTH/SHER LS25 106
Thanes Cl HUDN HD2 190
Thanet Garth AIRE BD20 27
Thane Wy MSTN/BAR LS15 82
Thatchers Wy CLECK BD19 144
Theakston Md CLAY BD14 94
Thealby Cl OSM * LS9 102
Thealby Lawn OSM LS9 102
Thealby Pl OSM LS9 102
Thearne Gn CLAY BD14 94
Theodore St BEE/HOL LS11 124
Thewlis La HUDS HD4 212
Thick Hollins Dr HOLM/MEL HD9 .231
Thick Hollins Rd HOLM/MEL HD9 231
Third Av BFDE BD3 96
 HEM/SK/SE WF9 226
 HIPP HX3 142
 KGHY BD21 ....
 LVSG WF15 143
 RTHW LS26 126
 WBY LS22 23
 WKFDE WF1 175
 WOR/ARM LS12 100
Third St LM/WK BD12 119
Thirkleby Royd CLAY BD14 94
Thirlmere Av ELL HX5 167
 LM/WK BD12 ....
Thirlmere Cl BEE/HOL LS11 123
Thirlmere Dr CAS WF10 154
 EARD/LOFT WF3 148
 WBY LS22 23
Thirlmere Gdns BEE/HOL LS11 ..123
 ECHL BD2 5
Thirlmere Rd EARL WF12 172
 WKFDW/WTN WF2 175
Thirsk Dr GFTH/SHER LS25 129
Thirsk Gra CLAY BD14 94
Thirsk Gv EARD/LOFT WF3 124
Thirsk Rw LDS LS1 ....
Thirstin Rd HOLM/MEL HD9 212
Thirteenth Av LVSG WF15 143
Thistle Cl HUDN HD2 190
Thistle Dr HEM/SK/SE WF9 226
Thistle Hill Av HUDE HD5 192
Thistle St HUD HD1 13
Thistle Wy MOR LS27 122
Thistlewood Rd EARD/LOFT WF3 150
Thomas Ct WBSY BD6 118
Thomas Dr BRIG HD6 168
Thomas St South HFAX HX1 8
Thomas St West HFAX HX1 8
Thompson Av CAS WF10 155
 ECHL BD2 ....
Thompson Dr WKFDW/WTN WF2 .149
Thompson Gn BAIL BD17 73
Thompson La BAIL BD17 73
Thompson St HFAX HX1 8

...HPY BD18 ....73 G3
ompson's Yd WKFDE WF1 ....10 B3
ong La HOLM/MEL HD9 ....233 G3
oresby Dr CLECK BD19 ....144 E3
oresby Gv GTHN BD7 ....94 E8
oresby Pl LDS LS1 ....7 K5
ornaby Gv BD14 ....94 C7
ornacre Crs SHPY BD18 ....74 A5
ornacre Rd SHPY BD18 ....74 A4
orn Av EARL WF12 ....195 G2
HTON BD9 ....72 C7
orn Bank Av HWTH BD22 ....47 G7
ornberry Dr LVSG WF15 ....143 J6
ornbridge Ms ECHL BD2 ....74 D7
ornbury Av BFDE BD3 ....97 F3
ornbury Crs BFDE BD3 ....97 F3
ornbury Dr BFDE BD3 ....97 F3
ornbury Gv BFDE BD3 ....97 F3
ornbury Pk WKFDW/WTN WF2 ...175 C7
ornbury Rd BFDE BD3 ....97 F4
WKFDW/WTN WF2 ....175 C7
ornbury St BFDE BD3 ....97 F4
orncliffe Rd BTLY WF17 ....145 K3
orncliffe La KBTN HD8 ....217 H4
orncliffe Rd BTLY WF17 ....145 K8
GIR BD8 ....4 B2
HWTH BD22 ....2 A4
orne Cl NORM WF6 ....178 B2
PDSY/CALV LS28 ....97 K3
ornfield Crs EARD/LOFT WF3 .....147 J3
orne Gv RTHW LS26 ....126 C5
orner Gv AIRE BD20 ....27 G1
orner La BSPA/BRAM LS23 ....61 H1
SCFT LS14 ....60 B3
SCFT LS14 ....82 C1
orner Rd HUD HD1 ....12 A6
ornes Farm Av OSM LS9 ....103 F6
ornes Farm Wy OSM LS9 ....103 F6
ornes La WKFDW/WTN WF2 ....10 C5
ornes Lane WH* WKFDE WF1 ......11 D5
ornes Moor Cl WKFDW/WTN WF2 ...10 A6
ornes Moor Rd WKFDW/WTN WF2 ...10 A6
ornes Moor Dr WKFDW/WTN WF2 ...10 A6
ornes Rd WKFDW/WTN WF2 ....10 A6
ornes Pk BRIG HD6 ....168 B2
SHPY BD18 ....73 K6
ornes Park Ct
WKFDW/WTN * WF2 ....10 B6
ornes Rd WKFDW/WTN WF2 ....10 A6
orne St GTL/HWG HX4 ....165 K7
orney La LUD/ILL HX2 ....138 A1
ornfield BGLY BD16 ....49 J7
ornfield Av HUDS HD4 ....190 E8
PDSY/CALV LS28 ....76 A8
ornfield Ct MSTN/BAR LS15 ....103 K1
ornfield Dr MSTN/BAR LS15 ....103 K1
ornfield Ms BGLY BD16 ....49 J4
MSTN/BAR LS15 ....103 K1
ornfield Mt BTLY WF17 ....145 K2
ornfield Pl ECHL BD2 ....74 E8
ornfield Ri GTL/HWG HX4 ....166 A4
ornfield Rd BHP/TINH LS16 ....78 E5
ornfield St GTL/HWG HX4 ....166 A4
orn Garth CLECK BD19 ....143 K5
CHY BD21 ....2 B1
orn Gv HTON BD9 ....72 D7
RHAY LS8 ....80 D8
orn Hl GTL/HWG HX4 ....188 D1
WTH BD22 ....47 G8
HPY BD18 ....73 K6
ornhill Back Rd HUDW HD3 ....190 A5
ornhill Bridge La BRIG HD6 ....142 B8
ornhill Cl HOR/CROF WF4 ....196 B4
PDSY/CALV LS28 ....75 K4
ornhill Cft WKFDW/WTN WF2 ....199 J4
VOR/ARM LS12 ....100 B5
ornhill Dr PDSY/CALV LS28 ....75 K3
HPY BD18 ....73 K6
ornhill Gv AIRE BD20 ....26 D5
PDSY/CALV LS28 ....75 K4
HPY BD18 ....73 K6
ornhill Hey GTL/HWG HX4 ....188 D1
ornhill Park Av EARL WF12 ....172 C7
ornhill Pl BFDE BD3 ....97 G3
VOR/ARM LS12 ....100 B5
ornhill Rd AIRE BD20 ....26 D5
RIG HD6 ....168 A3
AS WF10 ....153 K5
ARL WF12 ....172 A5
ARL WF12 ....196 A2

HUDW HD3 ....190 A5
HUDW HD3 ....190 D3
WOR/ARM LS12 ....100 B5
Thornhills Beck La BRIG HD6 ....142 C7
Thornhills La BRIG HD6 ....142 D7
Thornhill St EARL WF12 ....172 C6
PDSY/CALV LS28 ....75 K5
WKFDE WF1 ....10 C3
WOR/ARM LS12 ....100 B4
Thornhill St Bungalows WKFDE WF1 ...10 C4
Thornhill Ter BFDE BD3 ....97 F3
Thornie Bank EARL * WF12 ....172 D7
Thorn La HTON BD9 ....72 D7
RHAY LS8 ....80 B5
Thorniea Cl YEA LS19 ....53 H6
Thornleigh EARL WF12 ....172 C5
Thornleigh Av WKFDW/WTN WF2 ...10 C6
Thornleigh Cft WKFDW/WTN WF2 ...10 C5
Thornleigh Dr LVSG WF15 ....144 E6
WKFDW/WTN WF2 ....10 C6
Thornleigh Gdns OSM * LS9 ....102 B5
Thornleigh Garth WKFDW/WTN WF2 ...10 C6
Thornleigh Gv OSM LS9 ....102 B5
WKFDW/WTN WF2 ....10 C6
Thornleigh Mt OSM LS9 ....102 B5
Thornleigh Rd HUDS HD4 ....190 B8
WKFDW/WTN WF2 ....10 C5
Thornleigh St OSM LS9 ....102 B5
Thornleigh Vw OSM LS9 ....102 B5
Thormead Rd BAIL BD17 ....73 K1
Thorn Mt RHAY LS8 ....80 E7
Thorn Rd EARL WF12 ....195 G2
Thorn Royd Dr BOW BD4 ....120 C1
Thornsgill Av BOW BD4 ....94 B4
Thorn St BTLY * WF12 ....145 H2
GIR BD8 ....95 F2
HWTH BD22 ....69 G3
Thorn Ter RHAY LS8 ....80 D7
Thornton Av WOR/ARM LS12 ....100 A4
Thornton Cl BTLY WF17 ....121 J8
HEM/SK/SE WF9 ....224 D6
Thornton Ct GIR BD8 ....95 F5
Thornton Gdns WOR/ARM LS12 ...100 A4
Thornton Gv WOR/ARM LS12 ....100 A4
Thornton La WBOW BD5 ....95 J8
Thornton Lodge Rd HUD HD1 ....12 A6
Thornton Moor Rd HWTH BD22 .....91 J4
Thornton Old Rd GIR BD8 ....94 D4
Thornton Rd BRIG HD6 ....167 K3
CUL/QBY BD13 ....92 D6
CUL/QBY BD13 ....93 K5
EARL WF12 ....172 A7
GIR BD8 ....95 H3
Thorntons Ar LDS * LS1 ....7 E5
Thorntons Dl HORS LS18 ....77 F5
Thornton St BFD BD1 ....4 A4
CLECK BD19 ....143 H5
CLECK BD19 ....144 C4
DEWS WF13 ....172 A4
HFAX * HX1 ....8 A1
ILK LS29 ....32 A1
Thornton Ter HFAX HX1 ....8 A6
Thornton View Rd CLAY BD14 ....94 C7
Thorntonville CLECK BD19 ....144 C5
Thorntree Av HOR/CROF WF4 ......200 C2
Thorntree Cl PONT WF8 ....182 A7
Thorntree Ct HOR/CROF WF4 ......200 C2
Thorn Tree St HFAX HX1 ....8 A6
Thorn Vw HBR HX7 ....137 F3
HIPP HX3 ....9 D1
RHAY LS8 ....80 D8
Thornville MOR LS27 ....123 G4
Thornville Av HDGY LS6 ....6 A1
Thornville Cft HDGY * LS6 ....78 E8
Thornville Crs HDGY LS6 ....6 A1
Thornville Gv HDGY LS6 ....78 E8
Thornville Mt DEWS WF13 ....171 K5
HDGY LS6 ....78 E8
Thornville Pl DEWS * WF13 ....171 K5
HDGY LS6 ....6 A1
Thornville Rd HDGY * LS6 ....78 E8
Thornville St DEWS * WF13 ....171 K5
HDGY LS6 ....6 A1
Thornville Ter DEWS * WF13 ....171 K5
HDGY LS6 ....78 E8
Thornville Vw HDGY LS6 ....6 A1
Thornville Wk DEWS WF13 ....171 K5
Thorn Vw RHAY LS8 ....80 E8
Thorp Arch Pk BSPA/BRAM LS23 ...42 E3
Thorp Av HOLM/MEL HD9 ....233 H1
Thorpe Av CUL/QBY BD13 ....94 A3
Thorpe Cl GSLY LS20 ....52 C3
Thorpe Crs MID LS10 ....124 D8
Thorpe Dr GSLY LS20 ....52 D2
Thorpe Gdns MID LS10 ....124 D7
Thorpe Garth MID LS10 ....124 C8
Thorpe Green Dr HUDW HD3 ....189 J5
Thorpe Gv CUL/QBY BD13 ....94 B5
MID LS10 ....124 D7
Thorpe La EARD/LOFT WF3 ....147 K2
GSLY LS20 ....52 C3
HEM/SK/SE WF9 ....204 B8
HUDE HD5 ....192 B8
Thorpe Lower La EARD/LOFT WF3 ...149 G1
Thorpe Mill Ct RPDN/SBR * HX6 ...164 B4
Thorpe Mt MID LS10 ....124 C8
Thorpe Pl MID LS10 ....124 D7

EARD/LOFT WF3 ....148 E4
MID LS10 ....124 D7
PDSY/CALV LS28 ....98 B3
Thorpes Av KBTN HD8 ....236 E4
Thorpes Crs KBTN HD8 ....236 E2
Thorpe Sq MID LS10 ....124 E8
Thorpe St HIPP HX3 ....8 C1
KGHY * BD21 ....3 D2
MID LS10 ....124 D7
MSTN/BAR LS15 ....103 J3
Thorpe Ter MID LS10 ....124 D7
Thorpe Vw EARD/LOFT WF3 ....149 F1
MID LS10 ....124 D8
OSS WF5 ....173 J3
WKFDW/WTN WF2 ....175 C5
Thorp Garth IDLE BD10 ....74 D4
Thorverton Dr BOW BD4 ....120 B3
Thorverton Gv BOW BD4 ....120 B3
Threadneedle St HUD * HD1 ....12 C4
Three Sisters Sq HUD * HD1 ....12 C2
Threshfield Crs BIRK/DRI BD11 ....120 D5
Thrice Fold IDLE BD10 ....74 B2
Thrift Wy BGLY BD16 ....71 K1
Throstle Av MID LS10 ....124 C9
Throstle Bank LUD/ILL HX2 ....8 A6
Throstle Crest FEA/AMT WF7 ....179 F3
Throstle Dr MID LS10 ....124 B8
Throstle Hl MID LS10 ....124 C8
Throstle La MID LS10 ....124 D8
Throstle Mt LUD/ILL HX2 ....138 C6
MID LS10 ....124 C8
Throstle Nest BTLY WF17 ....145 K7
Throstle Nest Cl OT LS21 ....33 F1
Throstle Nest Rd AIRE * BD20 ....27 F1
Throstle Nest Vw HORS LS18 ....77 G4
Throstle Pde MID LS10 ....148 B1
Throstle Pl MID LS10 ....124 C8
Throstle Rd MID LS10 ....124 C8
Throstle Rw MID LS10 ....124 C8
Throstle Sq MID LS10 ....124 C8
Throstle St MID LS10 ....124 C8
Throstle Ter MID LS10 ....124 C8
Throstle Vw MID LS10 ....124 C8
Throstle Wk MID LS10 ....124 C8
Throxenby Wy CLAY BD14 ....94 C7
Thrum Hall Cl HFAX HX1 ....139 F4
Thrum Hall Dr HFAX HX1 ....8 A4
Thrum Hall La HFAX HX1 ....8 A4
Thrush Hill Rd HBR HX7 ....136 E5
Thrush St KGHY BD21 ....3 E2
Thryberg St BFDE BD3 ....5 E4
Thunder Bridge La KBTN HD8 ....215 F8
Thunderton La RPDN/SBR HX6 .....163 J1
Thurgory Ga KBTN HD8 ....193 F8
Thurgory La KBTN HD8 ....193 H7
Thurley Dr BOW BD4 ....119 J1
Thurley Rd BOW BD4 ....119 J1
Thurlstone Rd STKB/PEN S36 ....252 A7
Thurnscoe Rd BFD BD1 ....4 B3
Thurrish La HBR HX7 ....89 H6
Thursby St BFDE BD3 ....5 F4
Thurston Gdns WIL/AL BD15 ....94 B3
Thurstonland Bank Rd
HOLM/MEL HD9 ....233 K2
Thurstonland Rd HUDS HD4 ....214 A6
Thwaite Ga MID LS10 ....102 B8
Thwaite La MID LS10 ....102 D8
Thwaites Av ILK LS29 ....20 C7
Thwaites Br KGHY BD21 ....3 F3
Thwaites Brow Rd KGHY BD21 ....48 C3
Thwaites La KGHY BD21 ....3 F3
Tib Garth WBY LS22 ....23 F8
Tichborne Rd WBOW * BD5 ....96 A8
Tichborne Rd West WBOW BD5 ......96 A8
Tichborne St LVSG WF15 ....144 B7
Tichbourne St BTLY WF17 ....145 J7
Tickhill St BFDE BD3 ....5 F5
Tiding Field La MAR/SLWT HD7 .....210 B1
Tidswell St HECK WF16 ....145 H7
Tilbury Av BEE/HOL * LS11 ....101 F7
Tilbury Gv BEE/HOL * LS11 ....101 F7
Tilbury Mt BEE/HOL * LS11 ....101 F7
Tilbury Pde BEE/HOL * LS11 ....101 F7
Tilbury Rd BEE/HOL LS11 ....101 F7
Tilbury Rw BEE/HOL LS11 ....101 F7
Tilbury Ter BEE/HOL LS11 ....101 F7
Tilbury Vw BEE/HOL * LS11 ....101 F7
Tile La BHP/TINH LS16 ....56 D8
Tile St GIR BD8 ....95 H2
Tiley Sq WBOW BD5 ....96 A7
Till Carr La HIPP HX3 ....142 B4
Tillotson Av RPDN/SBR HX6 ....138 D3
Tillotson St AIRE * BD20 ....27 F1
Timber St ELL HX5 ....166 E5
KGHY BD21 ....3 F2
Timberwood KBTN HD8 ....215 F7
Timble Dr BGLY BD16 ....68 D2
Tim La HWTH BD22 ....47 F5
Timmey La RPDN/SBR HX6 ....138 D6
Timothy La BTLY WF17 ....146 C4
Tinderley Gv HUDE HD5 ....192 A7
Tingley Av EARD/LOFT WF3 ....147 K2
Tingley Common MOR LS27 ....147 G1
Tingley Crs EARD/LOFT WF3 ....147 H2
Tinker La HOLM/MEL HD9 ....231 H2
KBTN HD8 ....215 J1
Tinkingfield La WBY LS22 ....25 J3
Tinkler Stile SHPY BD18 ....74 B3
Tinsel Rd EARL WF12 ....172 E2

Tinshill Av BHP/TINH LS16 .... 55 J8
Tinshill Cl BHP/TINH LS16 .... 55 J8
Tinshill Crs BHP/TINH LS16 .... 55 J7
Tinshill Dr BHP/TINH LS16 .... 55 J8
Tinshill Garth BHP/TINH LS16 .... 55 J7
Tinshill Gv BHP/TINH LS16 .... 55 J7
Tinshill La BHP/TINH LS16 .... 55 H8
Tinshill Mt BHP/TINH LS16 .... 55 J7
Tinshill Rd BHP/TINH LS16 .... 55 H8
Tinshill Vw BHP/TINH LS16 .... 55 J7
Tinsworth Rd WKFDW/WTN WF2 .... 198 C7
Tintagel Ct NORM WF6 .... 152 A8
Tintern Av GIR BD8 .... 94 D4
  HUDW HD3 .... 189 K6
Tippaty La KNOT WF11 .... 156 D4
Tipping La KBTN HD8 .... 217 H4
Tisma Dr BOW BD4 .... 119 K3
Tithe Barn La AL/HA/HU LS17 .... 59 K1
Tithe Barn Rd KNOT WF11 .... 156 D7
Tithe Barn St EARL WF12 .... 172 C3
  HOR/CROF WF4 .... 197 G2
Tithe Barn Vw BRIG HD6 .... 168 D3
Tithe House Wy HUDN HD2 .... 169 F5
Titus La KBTN HD8 .... 216 B5
Titus St SHPY BD18 .... 73 F3
Tivoli Pl ILK LS29 .... 20 C8
  WBOW BD5 .... 95 J8
Tivy Dl DOD/DAR S75 .... 238 E7
Tivy Dale Cl DOD/DAR S75 .... 238 E7
Tivy Dale Dr DOD/DAR S75 .... 238 E7
Toad Carr TOD * OL14 .... 133 K5
Toby La GTHN BD7 .... 95 G6
Toby Wood La KBTN HD8 .... 236 B6
Todd Ter GTHN * BD7 .... 95 H7
Todley Hall Rd HWTH BD22 .... 46 B5
Todmorden Rd TOD OL14 .... 132 C7
Todwell La WBOW BD5 .... 95 J8
Toft La HUDS * HD4a 214 B5
Tofts Gv BRIG HD6 .... 168 A4
Tofts Grove Gdns BRIG HD6 .... 168 A4
Toftshaw Fold BOW BD4 .... 120 A3
Toftshaw La BOW BD4 .... 120 B3
Toftshaw New Rd BOW BD4 .... 120 A3
Tofts House Cl PDSY/CALV LS28 .... 98 CA
Tofts La HUDS * HD4a 214 B5
Tofts Rd CLECK BD19 .... 144 A4
  PDSY/CALV LS28 .... 98 B4
Toft St WOR/ARM LS12 .... 100 C5
Toll Bar La WKFDW/WTN WF2 .... 174 E2
Toll Bar Rd CAS WF10 .... 152 E4
Toller Dr HTON BD9 .... 72 E4
Toller Gv HTON BD9 .... 73 F8
Toller La HTON BD9 .... 73 F8
Toller Pk HTON BD9 .... 73 F8
Tolson Crs HUDE HD5 .... 192 B4
Tolson St DEWS * WF13 .... 172 B2
  OSS WF5 .... 173 C3
Tolsons Yd HUDE HD5 .... 13 F5
Tolworth Fold WIL/AL BD15 .... 94 A3
Tomahawk Trail CAS WF10 .... 154 A6
Tombridge Crs HEM/SK/SE WF9 .... 224 A2
Tom Cat La WBY LS22 .... 25 J2
Tom Dando Cl NORM WF6 .... 178 D1
Tom La HUDS HD4 .... 190 B8
Tomling Cote La AIRE BD20 .... 27 J3
Tomlinson Yd HUD * HD1 .... 13 D4
Tommy La MAR/SLWT HD7 .... 211 J2
Tom Wood Ash La HEM/SK/SE WF9 .... 227 F4
Tonbridge Cl WBSY BD6 .... 118 A3
Tonbridge St LDS LS1 .... 6 C2
Tong Ap WOR/ARM LS12 .... 99 H5
Tong Dr WOR/ARM LS12 .... 99 H4
Tong Ga WOR/ARM LS12 .... 99 H5
Tong Gn WOR/ARM LS12 .... 99 H5
Tong La BOW BD4 .... 121 F3
Tong Rd WOR/ARM LS12 .... 99 F7
Tong St BOW BD4 .... 120 A2
Tongue La HDGY LS6 .... 79 F2
Tong Wy WOR/ARM LS12 .... 99 H4
Tootal St WKFDE WF1 .... 11 D5
Toothill Av BRIG HD6 .... 168 B4
Toothill Bank BRIG HD6 .... 168 B5
Toothill La BRIG HD6 .... 168 B5
Toot Hill La RPDN/SBR HX6 .... 163 J1
Toothill La South HUDN HD2 .... 168 A6
Topaz Cl HUDN HD2 .... 191 J1
Topcliffe Av MOR LS27 .... 123 J7
Topcliffe Gv MOR LS27 .... 147 H1
Topcliffe La MOR LS27 .... 147 H1
Topcliffe Md MOR LS27 .... 123 J7
Topfield Fold MOR LS27 .... 147 H1
Top Fold KNOT WF11 .... 131 H7
Top House Farm Ms KNOT * WF11 .... 131 H7
Top La BTLY DN5 .... 241 H7
  HOR/CROF WF4 .... 218 D2
Top Meadow MIRF WF14 .... 193 H1
Top Orch MIRF WF14 .... 223 F2
Top O' Th' Bank HUDS HD4 .... 234 A2
Top O' Th' Close Rd TOD OL14 .... 160 A5
Top O' Th' Hill Rd TOD OL14 .... 159 K2
Top Rd KBTN HD8 .... 236 C4
Top St HEM/SK/SE WF9 .... 224 C4
Tor Av LM/WK BD12 .... 142 D2
Torcote Crs HUDN HD2 .... 168 D6
Tordoff Av GTHN BD7 .... 94 E6
Tordoff Gn WBSY BD6 .... 118 C3
Tordoff Rd LM/WK BD12 .... 119 F5

Tordoff Ter KSTL * LS5 .... 78 A7
Toronto Pl CHAL LS7 .... 79 K5
Torre Cl OSM LS9 .... 102 C3
  WBSY BD6 .... 117 J2
Torre Dr OSM LS9 .... 102 C2
Torre Gv OSM LS9 .... 102 C2
  WBSY BD6 .... 117 J2
Torre Hl OSM LS9 .... 102 C3
Torre La OSM LS9 .... 102 D3
Torre Mt OSM LS9 .... 102 C2
Torre Pl OSM LS9 .... 102 C3
Torre Rd OSM LS9 .... 102 B3
  WBSY BD6 .... 117 J2
Torre Sq OSM LS9 .... 102 D2
Torre Vw OSM LS9 .... 102 D2
Torre Wk OSM LS9 .... 102 D2
Torridon Crs WBSY BD6 .... 117 K5
Torridon Rd EARL WF12 .... 172 A1
Tor Vw HOLM/MEL HD9 .... 233 J1
Totties La HOLM/MEL HD9 .... 233 K6
Toulston La TAD LS24 .... 63 F1
Tower Av HEM/SK/SE WF9 .... 226 C3
The Tower Dr OT LS21 .... 35 J5
Tower Gdns LUD/ILL HX2 .... 139 J7
Tower Gv WOR/ARM LS12 .... 100 A3
Tower House St LDSU LS2 .... 7 E2
Tower La WOR/ARM LS12 .... 99 K3
Tower Pl WOR/ARM LS12 .... 99 K3
Tower Rd OSM LS9 .... 103 F7
  SHPY BD18 .... 72 E3
The Towers WOR/ARM LS12 .... 100 A3
Towers La HOR/CROF WF4 .... 200 D3
Towers La HOR/CROF WF4 .... 201 F2
Towers Paddock CAS WF10 .... 154 B4
Towers Sq HDGY LS6 .... 79 G3
Tower St ECHL BD2 .... 5 F1
  TOD OL14 .... 132 D2
Towers Wy HDGY LS6 .... 79 G3
Tower Vw HFAX HX1 .... 139 H6
Towlerton La WKFDW/WTN WF2 .... 175 F1
Town Av HUD HD1 .... 13 E2
Town Cl HORS LS18 .... 77 F2
Townclose Vw GFTH/SHER LS25 .... 128 E3
Town Crs HUD HD1 .... 13 E2
Town End GFTH/SHER LS25 .... 105 J3
  GTHN BD7 .... 95 G7
  HUDE HD5 .... 192 A7
  MAR/SLWT HD7 .... 189 H7
  MOR LS27 .... 122 C4
  OSS WF5 .... 173 J6
Town End Av FEA/AMT WF7 .... 203 J4
  HOLM/MEL HD9 .... 233 J5
Town End Crs HOLM/MEL HD9 .... 233 G5
Town End La HEM/SK/SE WF9 .... 193 J7
Townend Pl PDSY/CALV LS28 .... 98 D3
Town End Rd CLAY BD14 .... 94 B6
  HOLM/MEL HD9 .... 233 H5
Townend Rd WOR/ARM LS12 .... 100 B6
Townend Vw HOLM/MEL HD9 .... 233 H5
Towngate BRIG HD6 .... 142 E8
  HIPP HX3 .... 141 F7
  HIPP HX3 .... 141 H3
  HUDS HD4 .... 213 G1
  LM/WK BD12 .... 142 D1
  MIRF WF14 .... 170 E6
  OSS WF5 .... 173 K6
  SHPY BD18 .... 73 J4
  STKB/PEN S36 .... 251 K7
Towngate Av MIRF WF14 .... 170 E6
Towngate Gv MIRF WF14 .... 170 E6
Towngate Rd BTLY WF17 .... 145 K6
Town Hall Sq YEA LS19 .... 53 K4
Town Hall St ELL HX5 .... 166 E5
  HOLM/MEL HD9 .... 233 G6
  KGHY BD21 .... 3 D3
  MIRF * WF14 .... 170 D7
  RPDN/SBR HX6 .... 138 E8
Town Hall St East HFAX * HX1 17
Town Hall Wy EARL * WF12 .... 172 C3
Townhead Fold ILK LS29 .... 18 C3
Town Hl BSPA/BRAM LS23 .... 62 D1
Town Hill St BGLY * BD16 .... 72 B5
Town La IDLE BD10 .... 74 D3
Townley Av HIPP HX3 .... 141 F7
Townley Rd WKFDW/WTN WF2 .... 174 E6
Town Moor HUDS HD4 .... 234 A1

Town Pl HUD HD1 13
Town Rd HUDE HD5 192
Town St BEE/HOL LS11 123
  BIRK/DRI BD11 120
  BRAM LS13 76
  CHAL LS7 79
  DEWS WF13 172
  EARD/LOFT WF3 176
  EARL WF12 172
  GSLY LS20 53
  HEM/SK/SE WF9 224
  HORS LS18 77
  MID LS10 124
  MOR LS27 122
  PDSY/CALV LS28 98
  WOR/ARM LS12 100
  YEA LS19 53
  YEA LS19 54
Town Street Ms CHAL LS7 79
Town Street Vw CHAL LS7 79
Town Ter HUD HD1 13
Town Wells Dr PDSY/CALV LS28 75
Towton Dr CAS WF10 153
Track Mt BTLY WF17 172
Track Rd BTLY WF17 172
Trafalgar Cl HUDN HD2 168
Trafalgar Gdns MOR LS27 123
Trafalgar Rd DEWS WF13 172
  ILK LS29 20
Trafalgar St BFD BD1 4
  BTLY WF17 145
  LDSU LS2 7
Trafford Av OSM LS9 102
Trafford Gv OSM LS9 80
Trafford Ter OSM LS9 102
Traith Ct BTLY * WF17 145
Tramways LM/WK BD12 119
Tranbeck Rd GSLY LS20 52
Tranfield Av GSLY LS20 52
Tranfield Cl GSLY LS20 52
Tranfield Gdns GSLY LS20 52
Tranmere Ct GSLY LS20 52
Tranmere Dr GSLY LS20 52
Tranquility MSTN/BAR LS15 104
Tranquility Ct MSTN/BAR LS15 104
Trans Pennine Trail
  EARD/LOFT WF3 150
  MID LS10 7
  RTHW LS26 127
  RTHW LS26 151
  WKFDE WF1 176
Transpierence Wy LM/WK BD12 119
Transval Ter BTLY WF17 146
Tranter Gv BOW BD4 97
Tranter Pl MSTN/BAR LS15 103
Tredgold Av BHP/TINH LS16 55
Tredgold Cl BHP/TINH LS16 55
Tredgold Crs BHP/TINH LS16 55
Tredgold Garth BHP/TINH LS16 55
Tree La LUD/ILL HX2 114
Trees St GIR BD8 4
Tree Tops Ct RHAY LS8 80
Tree Top Vw CUL/QBY BD13 116
Trelawn Av HDGY LS6 78
Trelawn Pl HDGY LS6 78
Trelawn St HDGY LS6 78
Trelawn Ter HDGY LS6 78
Tremont Gdns MID LS10 125
Trenam Park Dr IDLE BD10 74
Trenance Dr SHPY BD18 73
Trenance Gdns GTL/HWG HX4 165
Trenic Crs HDGY LS6 78
Trenic Dr HDGY LS6 78
Trent Av GFTH/SHER LS25 106
  NORM WF6 7
Trentham Av BEE/HOL LS11 124
Trentham Gv BEE/HOL LS11 124
Trentham Pl BEE/HOL LS11 124
Trentham Rw BEE/HOL LS11 124
Trentham St BEE/HOL LS11 124
Trenton Dr GIR BD8 4
Trenton Rd EARL WF12 172
Trent Rd OSM LS9 102
Trent St BEE/HOL LS11 7
Trescoe Av WOR/ARM LS12 99
Tresham Ct EARL WF12 172
Trevelyan Sq LDS * LS1 9
Trevelyan St BRIG HD6 142
The Triangle HUD * HD1 12
Triath Ct BTLY WF17 145
Trilby St WKFDE WF1 11
Trimmingham La LUD/ILL HX2 139
Trimmingham Rd LUD/ILL HX2 139
Trimmingham Vls LUD/ILL * HX2 139
Trinity Church Ga WKFDE WF1 10
Trinity Cl LUD/ILL HX2 115
Trinity Ct HEM/SK/SE WF9 226
  HOLM/MEL HD9 233
Trinity Dr KBTN HD8 236
Trinity Fold HFAX * HX1 9
Trinity Gv BRIG * HD6 142
Trinity Mt DEWS * WF13 172
Trinity Pl BGLY BD16 72
Trinity Ri OT LS21 33
Trinity Rd HFAX HX1 9
  WBOW BD5 5
Trinity St BTLY WF17 172
  HBR HX7 111

FAX HX1 9 D5
UD HD1 12 A3
GHY * BD21 3 D2
MIRF WF14 170 D7
PONT WF8 180 E2
WKFDE WF1 11 F6
nity Street Ar LDS LS1 7 E3
nity Ter BTLY WF17 145 G2
nity Vw HIPP HX3 9 E5
M/WK BD12 119 F4
OSS WF5 173 J4
nity Wk LM/WK BD12 119 F4
o Garth WBY LS22 41 F1
o La WBY LS22 40 D1
stram Av WBOW BD5 119 H1
umph Cl BEE/HOL LS11 6 C5
on Dr HUDN HD2 168 A8
on Wy WKFDW/WTN WF2 198 C1
oper La HIPP HX3 9 F6
oper Ter HIPP HX3 9 E5
ugh La HEM/SK/SE WF9 226 E8
WTH BD22 91 J2
ugh Well La WKFDW/WTN WF2 149 F8
ydale Gdns PDSY/CALV LS28 99 F6
ydale Gv PDSY/CALV LS28 99 F6
ydale La PDSY/CALV LS28 98 E5
y Hl MOR * LS27 123 F6
y Ri MOR LS27 123 G6
y Rd HORS LS18 77 G1
MOR LS27 123 F6
eman Av HECK WF16 145 H7
eman Ct LM/WK BD12 119 F5
ncliffe WBSY BD6 118 E2
ndles La KNOT WF11 156 E7
ro Dr NORM WF6 152 A8
ro St WOR/ARM LS12 100 C3
ro Wk NORM WF6 152 A8
by La HUDN HD2 13 D1
or Barn Ct SHPY BD18 73 K4
dor Cl PDSY/CALV LS28 98 A1
PONT WF8 180 D6
dor Ct HEM/SK/SE WF9 226 B8
dor Cft HUDN HD2 169 G6
dor Gdns BEE/HOL LS11 123 K1
dor Lawns RHAY LS8 80 D4
WKFDW/WTN WF2 149 F6
dor St MAR/SLWT HD7 210 E3
WBOW BD5 95 K7
dor Wy EARL WF12 172 A8
el La RPDN/SBR HX6 138 E7
ton St AIRE BD20 27 F1
p St HWTH BD22 68 E6
MID LS10 101 K8
mbling Cl OSS WF5 173 K5
mbling Hl PONT WF8 181 H6
mbling Hill St GTHN BD7 4 B5
La CUD/GR S72 223 H4
nacliffe Rd HUDS HD4 191 H8
nel St CUL/QBY BD13 92 B3
UDS HD4 212 C4
nicliffe Pl AIRE BD20 27 F2
stall Gn BOW BD4 97 G8
stall Rd BEE/HOL LS11 101 J8
well La ECHL BD2 74 E7
well St ECHL BD2 74 E7
La HOR/CROF WF4 223 G3
bary Av PDSY/CALV LS28 98 C1
bid La HUDS HD4 212 A5
bury La GTL/HWG HX4 165 H3
f Ct CUL/QBY BD13 70 A6
f La CUL/QBY BD13 70 A5
gate La RPDN/SBR HX6 163 G2
ley Cote La HUDW HD3 189 G2
low Ct OSM LS9 7 F4
nberry Av AL/HA/HU LS17 57 H7
nberry Cl AL/HA/HU LS17 57 H7
nberry Ct AIRE BD20 27 J8
NORM WF6 178 C2
nberry Dr AL/HA/HU LS17 57 H7
ARD/LOFT WF3 147 J3
nberry Gdns EARD/LOFT WF3 147 J3
nberry Gv AL/HA/HU LS17 57 H7
nberry Pl AL/HA/HU LS17 57 H7
nberry Ri AL/HA/HU LS17 57 H7
nberry Vw AL/HA/HU LS17 57 H7
nbridge Rd HUDE HD5 13 E4
ner Av BTLY * WF17 146 B6
THN BD7 95 F6
ner Av North LUD/ILL HX2 115 G6
ner Av South LUD/ILL HX2 115 H7
ner Cl EARD/LOFT WF3 147 K3
ner Crs OT LS21 33 J2
ner Dr EARD/LOFT WF3 147 K3
ner La HIPP HX3 9 E2
K LS29 18 A3
ner Pl GTHN BD7 95 H6
UD/ILL HX2 115 H7
ner's Ct HIPP HX3 8 C1
ner St PDSY/CALV LS28 76 B8
ners Yd PDSY/CALV LS28 76 B8
ner Vw LUD/ILL * HX2 115 H7
ney St HIPP HX3 8 B1
nip La EARL WF12 195 H2
n O' The Nook OSS WF5 173 H5
npike La WBY LS22 25 J2
npike St ELL HX5 167 F4
nshaw Rd HWTH BD22 68 B1
BTN HD8 215 J5
nshaws Av KBTN HD8 215 J4
Turnshaws Cl KBTN HD8 215 J4
Turnsteads Av CLECK BD19 143 J3
Turnsteads Cl CLECK BD19 143 K3
Turnsteads Crs CLECK BD19 143 K3
Turnsteads Dr CLECK BD19 143 K3
Turnsteads Mt CLECK BD19 143 K3
Turnstone Ct MID LS10 124 E6
The Turnways HDGY LS6 78 C7
Turret Hall Rd HBR HX7 135 H1
Turret Royd Rd HBR HX7 135 H1
Turton Gn MOR LS27 122 C4
Turton St WKFDE WF1 11 D3
Turton V MOR LS27 122 C5
Turver's La KNOT WF11 157 H7
Turvin Rd RPDN/SBR HX6 184 D1
Tuscany Wy NORM WF6 151 K5
Twain Crs CAS WF10 154 D6
Tweedale Gdns DEWS WF13 172 A3
Tweedale St DEWS * WF13 172 A3
Tweed Cl BTLY WF17 145 K2
Tweedy St WIL/AL BD15 71 G6
Twelfth Av LVSG WF15 143 J6
Twickenham Ct GIR BD8 4 B1
Twitch Hl HOR/CROF WF4 197 H2
Twivey St CAS WF10 153 H4
Two Laws Rd HWTH BD22 66 C2
Tyas Gv OSM LS9 102 D4
Tyas La MAR/SLWT HD7 209 K1
Tyburn La KBTN HD8 217 F5
Tyersal Av BOW BD4 97 H4
Tyersal Cl BOW BD4 97 H4
Tyersal Crs BOW BD4 97 H5
Tyersal Dr BOW BD4 97 H5
Tyersal Garth BOW BD4 97 H5
Tyersal Gn BOW BD4 97 H5
Tyersal Gv BOW BD4 97 H4
Tyersal La BOW BD4 97 G7
PDSY/CALV LS28 98 A5
Tyersal Pk BOW BD4 97 H5
Tyersal Rd BOW BD4 97 H5
Tyersal Ter BOW BD4 97 G5
Tyersal Vw BOW BD4 97 G5
Tyersal Wk BOW BD4 97 H5
Tyler Cl NORM WF6 178 D1
Tyndale Av HOR/CROF WF4 197 J1
Tyndale Wk BTLY WF17 145 H6
Tynedale Ct CHAL LS7 79 G5
Tyne St BFDE BD3 5 D3
KGHY BD21 3 E3
Tynwald Cl AL/HA/HU * LS17 79 G1
Tynwald Dr AL/HA/HU LS17 57 G8
Tynwald Gn AL/HA/HU LS17 57 G8
Tynwald Hl AL/HA/HU LS17 79 G1
Tynwald Mt AL/HA/HU LS17 57 G8
Tynwald Rd AL/HA/HU LS17 79 G1
Tynwald Wk AL/HA/HU LS17 57 G8
Tyrrell Ct WKFDW/WTN WF2 174 E4
Tyrrel St BFD BD1 4 C4
Tyson St BFD BD1 4 B3
HFAX HX1 139 H5

U

Ullswater Av EARL WF12 146 D8
Ullswater Cl EARL WF12 146 D8
Ullswater Crs MSTN/BAR LS15 103 G5
RTHW LS26 127 F5
Ullswater Dr WBSY BD6 118 A5
WBY LS22 23 G5
Ullswater Ri WBY LS22 23 G5
Ullswater Rd EARL WF12 172 D1
Una Pl HUDN HD2 12 A2
Underbank Av TOD OL14 135 G2
Underbank Old Rd HOLM/MEL HD9 233 H7
Undercliffe La BFDE BD3 5 E2
Undercliffe Old Rd BFDE BD3 5 F2
Undercliffe Ri ILK LS29 30 E1
Undercliffe Rd ECHL BD2 74 D8
Undercliffe St BFDE BD3 5 F2
Underwood Dr YEA LS19 75 K2
Union Bank Yd HUD * HD1 12 C4
Union Cross Yd HFAX * HX1 9 D4
Union Gv LVSG WF15 144 E8
Union House La CLAY BD14 117 H1
Union La LUD/ILL HX2 115 G2
Union Pl BEE/HOL LS11 6 C5
Union Rd GTHN BD7 95 H6
LVSG WF15 144 E8
WBSY BD6 118 D4
Union Sq WKFDE WF1 10 C3
Union St BAIL BD17 73 K1
BGLY BD16 49 J4
BTLY WF17 145 H2
CUL/QBY * BD13 116 D2
DEWS WF13 172 C3
GTL/HWG HX4 166 C4
HEM/SK/SE WF9 224 E5
HFAX HX1 9 D5
HUD HD1 13 D3
HUDW HD3 190 B3
LDSU LS2 7 F3
LVSG WF15 145 F8
MAR/SLWT HD7 210 D2
MOR * LS27 123 H3
OSS WF5 173 J5
OT LS21 33 H4
RPDN/SBR HX6 139 F6
RPDN/SBR HX6 164 B2
WKFDE WF1 10 C2
Union St South HFAX * HX1 9 D5
TOD OL14 134 A6
Union Ter CHAL LS7 79 J5
Union Yd IDLE BD10 74 D3
Unity Cl HDGY LS6 79 H7
Unity Ct DEWS WF13 172 A3
Unity St AIRE BD20 48 D1
EARD/LOFT WF3 126 A8
HBR HX7 112 B7
TOD OL14 159 K3
Unity St North BGLY BD16 71 K1
Unity St South BGLY BD16 71 K1
Unity Ter HFAX HX1 139 H5
University Rd LDSU LS2 6 C1
University St CAS WF10 153 J4
Unwin Pl HTON BD9 94 E1
Upland Crs RHAY LS8 80 C6
Upland Gdns RHAY LS8 80 C7
Upland Gv RHAY LS8 80 C6
Upland Rd RHAY LS8 80 C7
Uplands HUDN HD2 12 A1
KGHY BD21 2 B1
Uplands Av CUL/QBY BD13 117 G1
DOD/DAR S75 239 J3
Uplands Cl CUL/QBY BD13 117 G1
Uplands Crs CUL/QBY BD13 117 G1
Uplands Dr MIRF WF14 170 D5
Uplands Gv CUL/QBY BD13 117 G1
The Uplands PONT WF8 180 D4
Upper Accommodation Rd
OSM LS9 102 A3
Upper Ada St SHPY BD18 73 F3
Upper Addison St BOW BD4 5 D6
Upper Allerton La WIL/AL BD15 93 J3
Upper Ash Gv HEM/SK/SE WF9 226 C8
Upper Ashley La SHPY * BD18 73 H3
Upper Bank End Rd
HOLM/MEL HD9 233 H8
Upper Bank Houses
GTL/HWG * HX4 165 G7
Upper Barker St LVSG WF15 144 D7
Upper Basinghall St LDS LS1 7 D3
Upper Batley La BTLY WF17 146 A3
Upper Batley Low La BTLY WF17 146 A1
Upper Battye St HECK WF16 145 G6
Upper Bell Hall HFAX HX1 8 B6
Upper Bolton Brow
RPDN/SBR HX6 139 G6
Upper Bonegate BRIG HD6 142 C8
Upper Brig Royd RPDN/SBR HX6 164 A7
Upper Brow Rd HUDW HD3 190 D6
Upper Butts CLECK BD19 144 A4
Upper Calton St KGHY BD21 2 C5
Upper Camroyd St DEWS WF13 172 C2
Upper Carr La PDSY/CALV LS28 75 J5
Upper Carr St LVSG WF15 144 D6
Upper Castle St WBOW BD5 4 C6
Upper Chelsea St KGHY BD21 2 C5
Upper Clough Rd MAR/SLWT HD7 211 G3
Upper Commercial St BTLY WF17 146 B6
Upper Common La KBTN HD8 237 K3
Upper Croft Rd BTLY WF17 146 A7
Upper Cross St DEWS * WF13 172 B2
Upper Ellistones Ct GTL/HWG HX4 165 K5
Upper Ferndown Gn WIL/AL * BD15 94 A2
Upperfield Dr MAR/SLWT HD7 189 G7
Upper Field House La
RPDN/SBR HX6 164 A1
Upper Field La DOD/DAR S75 238 D2
Upper Forge HFAX HX1 9 D4
Upper Fountain St RPDN/SBR HX6 138 E7
Upper Fyfe La BAIL BD17 52 A8
Upper Ga HOLM/MEL HD9 249 F1
Upper George St HECK WF16 145 G7
HUD HD1 12 C4
WBSY * BD6 118 C2
Upper Grange Av WIL/AL BD15 94 B3
Upper Green Av CLECK * BD19 143 G3
EARD/LOFT WF3 147 J4
Upper Green La BRIG HD6 141 K6
Upper Green Wy EARD/LOFT WF3 147 J4
Upper Hagg Rd HOLM/MEL HD9 233 H2
Upper Hall Fold GTL/HWG HX4 164 E7
Upper Hall Vw HIPP HX3 117 F8
Upper Hatfield Pl HOR/CROF WF4 223 H1
Upper Haugh Shaw HFAX * HX1 8 B6
Upper Headley CUL/QBY * BD13 93 H6
Upper Heaton La HUDE HD5 169 J8
Upper Heights Rd CUL/QBY BD13 93 G3
Upper Hird St KGHY BD21 2 B5
Upper House La LVSG WF15 143 K7
Upper House Rd HOLM/MEL HD9 248 D3
Upper House St BOW BD4 5 F6
Upper Kirkgate HFAX HX1 9 E4
Upper La CLECK BD19 144 E4
HIPP HX3 116 E7
HOR/CROF WF4 196 C7
KBTN HD8 217 H5
TOD OL14 134 C2
Upper Langwith WBY LS22 40 C3
Upper Lombard St YEA LS19 53 J7
Upper Lumb La HBR HX7 136 D7
Upper Lunns Cl BSLYN/ROY S71 222 C8
Upper Marsh HIPP HX3 140 E6
Upper Marsh La HWTH BD22 68 B6
Upper Martin Gn GTL/HWG HX4 165 K4
Upper Mary St SHPY BD18 73 F3

Upper Maythorn La
  HOLM/MEL HD9 ....250 A3
  HOLM/MEL HD9 ....232 D6
Upper Mdw CUL/QBY BD13 ....116 D3
Uppermoor PDSY/CALV LS28 ....98 A4
Upper Moor Cl PDSY/CALV LS28 .....98 B5
Upper Mosscar St BFDE BD5 ....5 E4
Upper Mount St BTLY WF17 ....146 B8
  HUD HD1 ....12 B6
Upper Nidd St BFDE BD3 ....5 E5
Upper North St BTLY WF17 ....146 A7
  LDSU LS2 ....7 D2
Upper Parish Ghyll La ILK LS29 ......19 K8
Upper Park Ga BFD BD1 ....5 D4
Upper Peel St DEWS * WF13 ....172 C2
Upper Piccadilly BFD * BD1 ....4 C4
Upper Quarry Rd HUDN HD2 ....169 H5
Upper Raglan St TOD * OL14 ....134 A5
Upper Range HIPP HX3 ....9 D2
Upper Rd DEWS WF13 ....172 A1
Upper Royd HIPP * HX3 ....141 H3
Upper Rushton Rd BFDE BD3 ....97 F2
Upper School St AIRE BD20 ....26 E6
Upper Seymour St BFDE BD3 ....5 F4
Upper South St DEWS WF13 ....172 B2
Upper Station Rd BTLY WF17 ....146 C7
Upper St EARD/LOFT * WF3 ....148 A2
Upper Sutherland Rd HIPP HX3 ....141 K1
Upperthong La HOLM/MEL HD9 .....232 D6
Upper Town St BRAM LS13 ....77 G8
Upper Warrengate WKFDE WF1 ....11 D3
Upper Washer La LUD/ILL HX2 ....8 A6
Upper Wellhouse Rd
  MAR/SLWT HD7 ....189 D3
Upper Westlock Av OSM LS9 ....102 C2
Upper West St BTLY * WF17 ....146 D6
Upper Willow Hall LUD/ILL HX2 ......139 G5
Upper Woodlands Rd GIR BD8 ....95 G3
Upper Woodview Pl
  BEE/HOL * LS11 ....124 C1
Upper Wortley Dr
  WOR/ARM * LS12 ....100 B4
Upper Wortley Rd WOR/ARM LS12 ..100 B4
Upper York St WKFDE WF1 ....10 C2
Upton St BTLY WF17 ....146 A5
Upwood La AIRE BD20 ....49 H1
Ure Crs GIR * BD8 ....4 B3
Ure Gv WBY LS22 ....23 H3
Usher St BOW BD4 ....5 E6
Uttley St HIPP * HX3 ....8 C1

V

The Vale HDGY LS6 ....79 F6
  WBY LS22 ....40 E3
Vale Av RTHW WF11 ....156 A7
  RHAY LS8 ....58 C8
Vale Cl HUDE HD5 ....192 B8
Vale Crs KNOT WF11 ....156 A7
Vale Gv AIRE BD20 ....27 F2
  CUL/QBY BD15 ....116 E3
Vale Head Gv KNOT WF11 ....156 A7
Vale Head Mt KNOT WF11 ....156 A7
Vale Mill La HWTH BD22 ....69 F2
Valentine Ct CUL/QBY BD13 ....93 J4
Vale Rd HEM/SK/SE WF9 ....224 B2
Valestone Av HEM/SK/SE WF9 ....224 E4
Vale St BRIG HD6 ....142 B8
  KGHY BD21 ....3 F1
Vale Vw FEA/AMT WF7 ....203 H4
The Valley AL/HA/HU LS17 ....57 G5
  HIPP HX3 ....142 A3
Valley Av HEM/SK/SE WF9 ....226 D8
Valley Cl AL/HA/HU LS17 ....57 G6
Valley Ct AL/HA/HU LS17 ....79 K3
  BFDE BD3 ....4 C2
  CAS WF10 ....153 F6
Valley Crs WKFDW/WTN WF2 ....175 G1
Valley Dr AL/HA/HU LS17 ....79 J2
  ILK LS29 ....20 D7
  MSTN/BAR LS15 ....103 K2
  RTHW LS26 ....128 D3
  WKFDW/WTN WF2 ....175 G1
Valley Farm Rd RTHW LS26 ....125 H2
Valley Farm Wy RTHW LS26 ....125 H2
Valley Fold CUL/QBY BD13 ....116 D3
Valley Gdns CHAL LS7 ....79 J3
  PONT WF8 ....182 B7
Valley Gn PDSY/CALV LS28 ....98 D5
Valley Gv LUD/ILL HX2 ....115 J4
  PDSY/CALV LS28 ....98 D5
Valley Head HUDW HD3 ....190 C1
Valley Mt BRAM LS13 ....98 E3
  GFTH/SHER LS25 ....129 F1
Valley Pde GIR BD8 ....4 B2
Valley Pl BFD BD1 ....4 C1
Valley Rdg GFTH/SHER LS25 ....105 K8
Valley Ri BRAM LS13 ....77 G6
Valley Rd BFD BD1 ....4 C3
  BRAM LS13 ....77 G6
  CLECK BD19 ....144 B3
  EARL WF12 ....172 A7
  GFTH/SHER LS25 ....129 F1
  HBR HX7 ....112 B8
  ILK LS29 ....20 D6

  KGHY BD21 ....3 F3
LVSG WF15 ....144 D6
  MOR LS27 ....123 G6
  OSS WF5 ....173 J7
  PDSY/CALV LS28 ....98 D5
  PONT WF8 ....182 B7
  SHPY BD18 ....73 H5
Valley Sq PDSY/CALV LS28 ....98 D5
Valley St HEM/SK/SE WF9 ....242 B1
Valley Ter AL/HA/HU LS17 ....58 B1
Valley Vw BAIL BD17 ....73 H2
  BGLY BD16 ....70 E2
  HEM/SK/SE WF9 ....226 D8
  LUD/ILL HX2 ....115 J4
  WHIT OL12 ....158 A7
Valley View Cl HWTH BD22 ....47 G8
Valley View Gdns HWTH * BD22 ....69 G5
Valley View Gv ECHL BD2 ....5 E1
Valley View Rd HBR HX7 ....112 A7
  OSS WF5 ....173 J7
Vancouver Pl CHAL LS7 ....80 A5
Varley Rd MAR/SLWT HD7 ....210 D5
Varley St PDSY/CALV LS28 ....98 B2
Vaughan St BFD BD1 ....4 B4
  HFAX HX1 ....8 A6
Venn St HUD * HD1 ....13 D4
Ventnor Cl CLECK BD19 ....144 E1
Ventnor Dr OSS WF5 ....173 J6
Ventnor St BFDE BD3 ....5 E4
Ventnor Ter HIPP HX3 ....140 F7
Ventnor Wy OSS WF5 ....173 J6
Vento Cl WBSY BD6 ....118 C3
Verdun Rd WBSY BD6 ....118 B3
Vere Sq WBOW BD5 ....96 A7
Verity Sp SCFT LS14 ....103 G3
Verity St BOW BD4 ....120 C4
Vermont St BRAM LS13 ....98 E1
Verner St FEA/AMT WF7 ....179 H7
Vernon Av HUD HD1 ....12 B3
Vernon Cl HUD HD1 ....12 B3
Vernon Ct KGHY BD21 ....2 C2
Vernon Pl ECHL BD2 ....5 F1
  PDSY/CALV LS28 ....98 C1
  WKFDW/WTN WF2 ....10 B6
Vernon Rd LDS LS1 ....7 D2
Vernon St HWTH BD22 ....69 H3
  LVSG WF15 ....144 E7
  TOD OL14 ....133 K8
Vesper Cl KSTL LS5 ....77 K5
Vesper Ct KSTL LS5 ....77 J5
Vesper Gdns KSTL LS5 ....77 K6
Vesper Gate Crs KSTL LS5 ....77 K6
Vesper Gate Dr KSTL LS5 ....77 J5
Vesper Gate Mt KSTL LS5 ....77 K5
Vesper Gv KSTL LS5 ....78 A7
Vesper La KSTL LS5 ....77 K6
Vesper Mt KSTL LS5 ....78 A7
Vesper Pl KSTL LS5 ....78 A7
Vesper Ri KSTL LS5 ....77 J5
Vesper Rd KSTL LS5 ....77 J5
Vesper Ter KSTL LS5 ....78 A7
Vesper Wk KSTL LS5 ....77 J5
Vesper Wy KSTL LS5 ....77 H5
Vestry St BOW BD4 ....96 B4
Viaduct Rd WOR/ARM LS12 ....100 D3
Viaduct St HUD HD1 ....12 C3
  MAR/SLWT HD7 ....210 E2
Vicarage Av KSTL LS5 ....78 B7
  MOR LS27 ....122 B5
Vicarage Cl HEM/SK/SE WF9 ....225 J8
  LM/WK BD12 ....142 D1
  WKFDE WF1 ....149 J6
Vicarage Ct CLECK BD19 ....144 A3
Vicarage Dr PDSY/CALV LS28 ....98 B4
Vicarage Gdns BIRK/DRI BD11 ....120 D6
  BRIG HD6 ....168 A3
  FEA/AMT WF7 ....179 J3
  OT LS21 ....33 J4
Vicarage La BSLYN/ROY S71 ....222 A8
  BSPA/BRAM LS23 ....62 D1
  FEA/AMT WF7 ....179 J3
Vicarage Meadow MIRF WF14 ....171 F6
Vicarage Rd EARL WF12 ....172 B6
  EARL WF12 ....172 C3
  HUDW HD3 ....190 A5
  SHPY BD18 ....74 A3
Vicarage St BFD BD1 ....5 D5
  LDS LS1 ....7 J3
  OSS WF5 ....173 K7
Vicarage St North WKFDE WF1 ....11 F6
Vicarage St South WKFDE WF1 ....11 D3
Vicarage Ter KSTL LS5 ....78 B7
Vicarage Vw KSTL LS5 ....78 B7
Vicarage Wk STKB/PEN S36 ....252 C8
Vicar La BFD BD1 ....5 D5
  LDS LS1 ....7 J3
  OSS WF5 ....173 K7
Vicar Park Dr LUD/ILL HX2 ....138 E3
Vicars Rd RHAY LS8 ....80 E7
Vicars Ter CAS WF10 ....129 C7
  RHAY * LS8 ....80 B7
Vickerman Crs HUDS HD4 ....213 F2
Vickerman St HFAX HX1 ....8 A5
Vickers Av HEM/SK/SE WF9 ....242 A2
  KSTL LS5 ....77 K8
Vickersdale PDSY/CALV LS28 ....98 C1
Vickers St CAS WF10 ....153 J4
  MOR LS27 ....122 E8

Victor Dr GSLY LS20 ....53 ..
Victoria Av BRIG HD6 ....142 ..
  BTLY WF17 ....146 ..
  CLECK * BD19 ....144 ..
  ECHL BD2 ....75 ..
  ELL HX5 ....166 ..
  HFAX HX1 ....
  HORS LS18 ....76 ..
  HWTH BD22 ....68 ..
  ILK LS29 ....19 ..
  ILK LS29 ....32 ..
  KGHY BD21 ....3 ..
  MOR LS27 ....123 ..
  OSM LS9 ....102 ..
  RPDN/SBR HX6 ....139 ..
  RTHW LS26 ....126 ..
  SHPY BD18 ....73 ..
  WKFDW/WTN WF2 ....10 ..
  YEA LS19 ....54 ..
Victoria Cl CAS WF10 ....129 ..
  HORS LS18 ....76 ..
  ILK LS29 ....19 ..
  YEA LS19 ....54 ..
Victoria Ct HEM/SK/SE WF9 ....226 ..
  KGHY BD21 ....2 ..
Victoria Court Ms HDGY * LS6 ....79 ..
Victoria Crs DEWS WF13 ....171 ..
  ELL HX5 ....166 ..
  HORS LS18 ....76 ..
  PDSY/CALV LS28 ....98 ..
Victoria Dr EARL WF12 ....172 ..
  ECHL BD2 ....75 ..
  HIPP HX3 ....117 ..
  HORS LS18 ....76 ..
  ILK LS29 ....19 ..
  MOR LS27 ....123 ..
Victoria Gdns HORS LS18 ....76 ..
  ILK LS29 ....19 ..
  PDSY/CALV LS28 ....98 ..
Victoria Grange Dr MOR LS27 ....123 ..
  ILK LS29 ....19 ..
  OSM LS9 ....102 ..
  WKFDW/WTN WF2 ....174 ..
Victoria Houses KSTL * LS5 ....78 ..
Victoria La HUD HD1 ....13 ..
  MAR/SLWT HD7 ....189 ..
Victoria Ms ELL * HX5 ....166 ..
  HORS LS18 ....76 ..
  KGHY BD21 ....2 ..
  MOR LS27 ....123 ..
Victoria Mt HORS LS18 ....76 ..
Victoria Pk HFAX * HX1 ....8 ..
  SHPY BD18 ....73 ..
Victoria Park Av BRAM LS13 ....77 ..
Victoria Park Gv BRAM LS13 ....77 ..
Victoria Park St KGHY BD21 ....3 ..
Victoria Park Vw KGHY BD21 ....3 ..
Victoria Pl BEE/HOL LS11 ....7 ..
  BRIG HD6 ....168 ..
  CAS WF10 ....129 ..
  HUDS HD4 ....212 ..
  MIRF WF14 ....170 ..
  YEA LS19 ....53 ..
Victoria Ri BRAM HD6 ....142 ..
  BSLYN/ROY S71 ....222 ..
  CLECK BD19 ....145 ..
  DEWS WF13 ....172 ..
  EARL WF12 ....172 ..
  ECHL BD2 ....74 ..
  ELL HX5 ....166 ..
  GSLY LS20 ....59 ..
  HBR HX7 ....112 ..
  HDGY LS6 ....78 ..
  HFAX HX1 ....8 ..
  HIPP HX3 ....141 ..
  HOLM/MEL HD9 ....231 ..
  HUD HD1 ....12 ..
  HWTH BD22 ....69 ..
  HWTH BD22 ....69 ..
  ILK LS29 ....19 ..
  KGHY BD21 ....2 ..
  KSTL LS5 ....78 ..
  LVSG WF15 ....144 ..
  MOR LS27 ....123 ..
  PDSY/CALV LS28 ....98 ..
  PDSY/CALV * LS28 ....98 ..
  RPDN/SBR HX6 ....138 ..
  RTHW LS26 ....126 ..
  SHPY BD18 ....73 ..
  TOD OL14 ....134 ..
  WBSY BD6 ....118 ..
Victoria Springs HOLM/MEL HD9 .....232 ..
Victoria Sq LDS LS1 ....7 ..
Victoria St BAIL BD17 ....73 ..
  BFD BD1 ....5 ..
  BRIG HD6 ....168 ..
  BTLY WF17 ....145 ..
  BTLY WF17 ....146 ..
  BVRD LS3 ....6 ..
  CAS WF10 ....129 ..
  CAS WF10 ....153 ..
  CHAL LS7 ....96 ..
  CLAY BD14 ....116 ..
  CLECK BD19 ....144 ..
  CUL/QBY BD13 ....94 ..
  CUL/QBY BD13 ....116 ..
  DEWS WF13 ....171 ..

ECHL BD2 ....96 E1
FEA/AMT WF7 ....179 J6
PONT WF8 ....202 D6
GTL/HWG HX4 ....166 C1
WF16 ....145 G7
HEM/SK/SE WF9 ....224 E5
.......9 D4
HOLM/MEL HD9 ....235 G6
HOR/CROF WF4 ....197 F2
HUD HD11 ....12 C6
HUDE HD5 ....13 F5
HUDN HD2 ....169 F8
HUDW HD3 ....190 C4
DLE BD10 ....74 D1
KBTN HD8 ....237 J1
MAR/SLWT HD7 ....209 H7
MID LS10 ....7 F6
MOR LS27 ....122 E6
MOR LS27 ....123 H4
PDSY/CALV LS28 ....75 J5
PONT WF8 ....154 D8
RPDN/SBR HX6 ....138 E8
STKB/PEN S36 ....252 C8
TOD OL14 ....133 F2
WBY LS22 ....23 J6
WIL/AL BD15 ....71 G7
WIL/AL BD15 ....72 A8
WKFDE WF1 ....149 J7
.......10 A2
toria Ter BVRD LS3 ....6 B2
DGY LS6 ....78 D5
HFAX * HX1 ....8 A5
KGHY BD21 ....3 E3
KSTL LS5 ....78 A7
LUD/ILL HX2 ....138 B6
MAR/SLWT * HD7 ....209 J8
PDSY/CALV LS28 ....98 D1
toria Wk HORS LS18 ....76 E4
tor Rd HEM/SK/SE WF9 ....241 J1
HTON BD9 ....95 H1
tor St BFD BD3 ....97 G4
BTLY WF17 ....146 C6
AS WF10 ....153 H6
HEM/SK/SE WF9 ....242 B1
HTON BD9 ....95 H1
tor Ter HFAX HX1 ....8 B3
HTON BD9 ....95 H1
tory Rd HUDW HD3 ....190 B6
tory La EARD/LOFT WF3 ....176 D1
e View AL/HA/HU LS17 ....57 F5
HAY LS8 ....80 B3
w Croft Rd BAIL BD17 ....73 H5
wlands HUDN HD2 ....168 B7
wlands Ct STKB/PEN S36 ....252 C6
wlands Mt ILK LS29 ....33 F6
w Rd KGHY BD21 ....2 B2
TKB/PEN S36 ....251 K7
w St HUDE HD5 ....13 F5
nola Ter CLAY BD14 ....94 C6
ing Av KBTN HD8 ....217 H5
ing Rd PONT WF8 ....181 F3
e Cl FEA/AMT WF7 ....203 H3
e Village BSPA/BRAM LS23 ....42 E2
HUDS HD4 ....214 B5
HUDS HD4 ....234 A2
age Av BULY LS4 ....100 D1
age Ms WIL/AL * BD15 ....71 G6
age Rd BHP/TINH LS16 ....57 F1
e Village St BULY LS4 ....100 D1
age St HIPP HX3 ....142 A1
age Ter BULY LS4 ....78 D8
a Gv BGLY BD16 ....50 A7
a Mt LM/WK BD12 ....142 A2
a Rd BGLY BD16 ....50 A7
a St RPDN/SBR HX6 ....139 F7
er Ct WIL/AL BD15 ....94 B2
cent Av AIRE BD20 ....26 C6
cent St BFD BD1 ....4 B4
.......8 A5
e Av CLECK BD19 ....143 K3
e Cl BRIG HD6 ....168 E1
e Cl BRIG HD6 ....168 E1
e Crs CLECK BD19 ....143 K3
e Garth BRIG HD6 ....168 E1
e Gv BRIG HD6 ....168 E1
ery Av OSM LS9 ....102 C3
ery Cl KBTN HD8 ....237 K1
ery Mt OSM LS9 ....102 C4
ery Pl OSM LS9 ....102 C4
ery Rd OSM LS9 ....100 D1
ery St OSM LS9 ....102 C4
ery Vw OSM LS9 ....102 C4
e St CLECK BD19 ....144 A3
THN BD7 ....95 H6
UD HD11 ....13 D2
e Ter CUL/QBY BD13 ....93 H5
FAX HX1 ....8 C5
e Ter East GIR BD8 ....94 E3
e Ter West GIR BD8 ....94 E3
et St HFAX HX1 ....8 B3
WTH BD22 ....68 E6
et St North HFAX HX1 ....8 B3
inia Cl EARD/LOFT WF3 ....149 H5
inia Ct EARD/LOFT WF3 ....149 H5
inia Dr EARD/LOFT WF3 ....149 H5

Virginia Gdns EARD/LOFT WF3 ....149 H5
Virginia Rd HUDW HD3 ....190 C4
Virginia St CLAY BD14 ....94 C8
Vissett Cl HEM/SK/SE WF9 ....224 B5
Vissett La HEM/SK/SE WF9 ....224 A5
Vivian Pl GTHN BD7 ....95 G8
Vivien Rd GIR BD8 ....94 C3
Vulcan Cl DEWS WF13 ....172 B3
Vulcan Gdns DEWS * WF13 ....172 B3
Vulcan Rd DEWS WF13 ....172 A3
Vulcan St BOW BD4 ....120 A2
BRIG HD6 ....168 D2
TOD OL14 ....159 K2

W

Waarburton KBTN HD8 ....217 G5
Waddington St KGHY BD21 ....3 D4
Wade House Av HIPP HX3 ....117 H5
Wade House Rd HIPP HX3 ....117 H6
Wade La LDSU LS2 ....7 E3
Wade St BFD * BD1 ....5 G5
HFAX HX1 ....9 D5
PDSY/CALV LS28 ....76 B8
Wadhouse La HOR/CROF WF4 ....198 B3
Wadlands Cl PDSY/CALV LS28 ....76 A7
Wadlands Dr PDSY/CALV LS28 ....76 A8
Wadlands Gv PDSY/CALV LS28 ....76 A7
Wadlands Ri PDSY/CALV LS28 ....76 A8
Wadman Rd HOLM/MEL HD9 ....233 K8
Wadsworth La HBR HX7 ....112 D8
Wadsworth St HFAX HX1 ....8 A3
Waggon La HEM/SK/SE WF9 ....226 D4
Wagon La BGLY BD16 ....72 A2
Wain Brow HUDS HD4 ....213 F3
Waincliffe Crs BEE/HOL LS11 ....124 A2
Waincliffe Dr BEE/HOL LS11 ....124 A3
Waincliffe Garth BEE/HOL LS11 ....123 K2
Waincliffe Mt BEE/HOL LS11 ....124 A3
Waincliffe Pl BEE/HOL LS11 ....124 A3
Waincliffe Ter BEE/HOL LS11 ....124 A3
Waindale Cl LUD/ILL HX2 ....114 D8
Waindale Crs LUD/ILL HX2 ....114 D8
Waindyke Wy NORM WF6 ....178 C1
Waingate MAR/SLWT HD7 ....211 H3
Waingate Pk MAR/SLWT HD7 ....211 H2
Wainhouse Rd HFAX HX1 ....8 A6
Wainman St BAIL BD17 ....51 K7
BAIL BD17 ....73 H5
HFAX HX1 ....8 A4
Wain Pk HUDS HD4 ....213 F3
Wainscott Cl HBR HX7 ....112 C5
Wainsgate HBR HX7 ....112 C5
Wainsgate La HBR HX7 ....112 C5
Wainstalls La LUD/ILL HX2 ....114 B6
Wainstalls Lodge La LUD/ILL HX2 ....114 B6
Wainstalls Rd LUD/ILL HX2 ....114 B6
Waites Cft WKFDW/WTN * WF2 ....174 C1
Waite St WKFDW/WTN WF2 ....175 F5
Wakefield Crs EARL WF12 ....172 E5
Wakefield Ga LUD/ILL HX2 ....139 J7
Wakefield Old Rd EARL * WF12 ....172 C5
Wakefield Rd BFD BD1 ....5 D5
BIRK/DRI BD11 ....121 K6
BOW BD4 ....96 D7
BRIG HD6 ....168 D2
EARL WF12 ....172 E4
FEA/AMT WF7 ....178 E6
FEA/AMT WF7 ....202 D6
GFTH/SHER LS25 ....105 J8
HEM/SK/SE WF9 ....202 A8
HIPP HX3 ....142 A4
HIPP HX3 ....165 K1
HOR/CROF WF4 ....197 J1
HUD HD1 ....13 J4
KBTN HD8 ....217 K8
LVSG WF15 ....144 E7
MID LS10 ....125 C1
MOR LS27 ....122 B6
NORM WF6 ....177 K2
OSS WF5 ....174 C5
PONT WF8 ....180 C4
RPDN/SBR HX6 ....138 C2
RTHW LS26 ....125 J6
RTHW LS26 ....127 J3
Walden Dr HTON BD9 ....72 C8
Walden St CAS WF10 ....153 J4
Waldorf Wy WKFDW/WTN WF2 ....10 C1
Walesby Ct BHP/TINH LS16 ....77 J1
Walford Av OSM LS9 ....102 C3
Walford Gv OSM LS9 ....102 C3
Walford Mt OSM LS9 ....102 C3
Walford Rd OSM LS9 ....102 C3
Walford Ter OSM LS9 ....102 C3
The Walk KGHY BD21 ....3 D4
PDSY/CALV LS28 ....98 A1
Walker Av GTHN BD7 ....94 E6
WKFDW/WTN WF2 ....175 G4
Walker Dr GIR BD8 ....95 G3
Walkergate OT LS21 ....33 J4
PONT WF8 ....181 F2
Walker Gn EARL WF12 ....195 J2
Walker La HBR HX7 ....112 D6
HOR/CROF WF4 ....197 H2
RPDN/SBR HX6 ....139 G7

Walker Pl MOR * LS27 ....123 G4
SHPY BD18 ....73 K3
Walker Rd HORS LS18 ....77 F2
LM/WK BD12 ....119 G7
Walkers Gn WOR/ARM LS12 ....100 C7
WOR/ARM LS12 ....100 C7
Walker's La AIRE BD20 ....17 F4
Walkers Mt BTLY WF17 ....146 B8
HDGY LS6 ....79 F6
Walker's Pl AIRE BD20 ....27 G5
Walkers Rw YEA LS19 ....53 J5
Walker's Ter WKFDE WF1 ....10 B3
Walker St BOW BD4 ....119 J3
CLECK BD19 ....143 G2
CLECK BD19 ....144 A3
DEWS WF13 ....171 G7
EARL WF12 ....172 C7
Walker Ter BOW BD4 ....96 C7
CUL/QBY BD13 ....70 B6
Walker Wd BAIL BD17 ....73 F1
Walkley Av HECK WF16 ....171 G1
Walkley Gv HECK WF16 ....145 G8
Walkley La HECK WF16 ....171 H1
Walkley Ter HECK WF16 ....171 H1
Walk Royd Hl DOD/DAR S75 ....239 H1
Wallace Gdns EARD/LOFT WF3 ....149 J5
Wallace St HFAX HX1 ....8 A5
Wallbank Dr SHPY BD18 ....73 J5
Waller Clough Rd MAR/SLWT HD7 ....188 D7
Wallingford Mt WIL/AL BD15 ....94 B4
Wallis St GIR BD8 ....95 G4
RPDN/SBR HX6 ....138 E7
Wall Nook La KBTN HD8 ....235 F5
Wallroyds KBTN HD8 ....236 C6
Wall St HWTH BD22 ....2 A4
Walmer Gv PDSY/CALV LS28 ....98 D6
Walmer Vls GIR BD8 ....4 B2
Walmsley Dr HEM/SK/SE WF9 ....226 D4
Walmsley Rd HDGY LS6 ....78 E8
Walnut Av EARL WF12 ....173 F4
WKFDW/WTN WF2 ....175 G4
Walnut Cl EARL WF12 ....173 F5
SCFT LS14 ....82 A3
Walnut Crs EARL WF12 ....173 F4
WKFDW/WTN WF2 ....175 G4
Walnut Dr EARL WF12 ....173 G4
NORM WF6 ....177 K4
PONT WF8 ....180 C5
Walnut Gv EARL WF12 ....173 G4
Walnut La EARL WF12 ....173 F5
Walnut Pl EARL WF12 ....173 F4
Walnut Rd EARL WF12 ....173 F4
Walnut St BFDE BD3 ....96 E5
HEM/SK/SE WF9 ....242 B2
HFAX HX1 ....8 B4
KGHY BD21 ....2 C6
Walpole Rd HUDS HD4 ....190 D8
Walsham Dr HUDW HD3 ....189 J2
Walshaw La HBR HX7 ....88 C1
Walshaw St GTHN BD7 ....95 G7
Walsh La BGLY BD16 ....49 K5
HIPP HX3 ....8 C2
WOR/ARM LS12 ....122 B1
Walsh Sq HFAX * HX1 ....8 A4
Walsh St HFAX HX1 ....8 A4
Walter Clough La HIPP HX3 ....141 G6
Walter Crs OSM LS9 ....102 B4
Walter St BULY LS4 ....100 D2
ECHL BD2 ....73 K7
IDLE BD10 ....74 D1
Waltin Rd HOLM/MEL HD9 ....248 A2
Walton Cha BSPA/BRAM LS23 ....25 F8
Walton Cft HUDE HD5 ....192 A5
Walton Dr BIRK/DRI BD11 ....121 J5
Walton Garth BIRK/DRI BD11 ....121 J6
Walton La BRIG HD6 ....143 F6
WKFDW/WTN WF2 ....199 H5
Walton Rd BSPA/BRAM LS23 ....43 F1
HEM/SK/SE WF9 ....227 F3
WBY LS22 ....23 K6
Walton Station La
WKFDW/WTN WF2 ....199 G4
Walton St BEE/HOL LS11 ....6 C5
MID LS10 ....102 A7
RPDN/SBR HX6 ....138 E7
Walton Vw HOR/CROF WF4 ....200 D3
Waltroyd Rd CLECK BD19 ....143 K4
Wansford Cl BOW BD4 ....120 B1
Wanstead Crs WIL/AL BD15 ....94 B3
Wapping Nick La HUDW HD3 ....166 D8
Wapping Rd BFDE BD3 ....5 D3
Ward Bank Rd HOLM/MEL HD9 ....233 G6
Ward Fall HOR/CROF WF4 ....198 B8
Ward La EARD/LOFT WF3 ....176 D1
MID LS10 ....124 E2
Wardle Crs KGHY BD21 ....2 A2
Wardman St KGHY BD21 ....3 F1
Ward Place La HOLM/MEL HD9 ....233 F8
Ward's End HFAX HX1 ....9 D5
Wards Hl BTLY WF17 ....146 B6
Wards Hill Ct BTLY * WF17 ....146 B6
Ward Sq HUD * HD1 ....12 C4
Ward St DEWS WF13 ....172 C2
GTHN BD7 ....95 G8
KGHY BD21 ....2 C4
MID LS10 ....7 F6
Wareham Cnr BOW BD4 ....120 B1
Warehouse Hill Rd MAR/SLWT HD7 ....209 H7
Warehouse St BTLY WF17 ....146 C7

Warhurst Rd ELL HX5 ....167 F3
Waring Wy EARL WF12 ....172 D2
Warlbeck ILK LS29 ....19 K7
Warley Av BFDE BD3 ....97 F3
Warley Dene LUD/ILL HX2 ....138 E5
Warley Dr BFDE BD3 ....97 F4
Warley Edge La LUD/ILL HX2 ....138 E4
Warley Gv BFDE BD3 ....97 F3
  LUD/ILL HX2 ....139 G4
Warley Rd LUD/ILL HX2 ....139 G5
Warley St HFAX HX1 ....8 B5
Warley Town La LUD/ILL HX2 ....138 D4
Warley Vw LUD/ILL HX2 ....139 G4
Warley Wood Av LUD/ILL HX2 ....138 C6
Warley Wood La LUD/ILL HX2 ....138 B5
Warmfield La WKFDE WF1 ....177 H4
Warmfield Vw WKFDE WF1 ....11 F2
Warm La YEA LS19 ....53 J6
Warmleigh Pk CUL/QBY BD13 ....116 A2
Warneford Av OSS WF5 ....173 J4
Warneford Ri HUDS HD4 ....190 A7
Warneford Rd HUDS HD4 ....190 A7
Warrel's Av BRAM LS13 ....99 G1
Warrel's Ct BRAM LS13 ....99 G1
Warrel's Gv BRAM LS13 ....99 G1
Warrel's Mt BRAM LS13 ....99 G1
Warrel's Pl BRAM LS13 ....99 G1
Warrel's Rd BRAM LS13 ....77 G8
Warrel's Rw BRAM * LS13 ....99 G1
Warrel's St BRAM LS13 ....99 G1
Warrel's Ter BRAM LS13 ....99 G1
Warren Av BGLY BD16 ....50 B6
  KNOT WF11 ....156 A8
  WKFDW/WTN WF2 ....199 F1
Warren Ct BSLYN/ROY S71 ....199 K5
  LVSG WF15 ....170 E1
Warren Dr BGLY BD16 ....50 B7
  FEA/AMT WF7 ....179 F3
Warrenfield Ct HUDN HD2 ....168 E8
Warren House La HUDW HD3 ....167 F8
  YEA LS19 ....54 B2
Warren La BGLY BD16 ....50 B7
  DOD/DAR S75 ....220 E7
  OT LS21 ....36 A4
  TAD LS24 ....29 H7
Warren Pk BRIG HD6 ....141 K5
Warren Park Cl BRIG HD6 ....141 K6
Warren Rd FEA/AMT WF7 ....179 G6
Warrenside HUDN HD2 ....169 F7
Warrens La BTLY WF17 ....121 G6
Warren St EARL WF12 ....172 C5
Warrenton Pl GTHN * BD7 ....95 G6
Warton Av BOW BD4 ....119 J2
Warwick Av MAR/SLWT * HD7 ....209 G7
Warwick Cl BOW BD4 ....96 D7
  HFAX * HX1 ....8 C6
Warwick Dr BOW BD4 ....96 D7
Warwick Rd BOW BD4 ....96 D7
  BTLY WF17 ....146 B8
Warwick St WKFDE WF1 ....11 F6
Wasdale Crs WKFDW/WTN WF2 ....175 F4
Wasdale Rd WKFDW/WTN WF2 .....175 F4
Washburn Ct WBY LS22 ....23 H3
Washer La LUD/ILL HX2 ....139 J7
Washfold Rd HBR HX7 ....162 B4
Washington Pl BRAM LS13 ....98 E3
Washington St BRAM LS13 ....98 E3
  BVRD LS3 ....6 A3
  GIR BD8 ....95 F2
  HIPP * HX3 ....8 B2
Washington Ter BRAM LS13 ....98 E3
Washpit New Rd HOLM/MEL HD9 ...248 B1
Wasp Nest Rd HUD HD1 ....12 C1
Waste La HBR HX7 ....89 C6
  HUDE HD5 ....192 M8
  MIRF WF14 ....170 D8
Wastwater Dr WBSY BD6 ....118 A5
Watchit Hole La PONT WF8 ....204 E7
Watercock St BOW BD4 ....5 E6
Watercroft HUDE HD5 ....192 B8
Waterfall Fold PONT WF8 ....155 F7
Waterfront Ms IDLE BD10 ....75 G3
Watergate HIPP HX3 ....141 H4
  HUD HD1 ....13 D4
  PONT WF8 ....180 D3
  RTHW LS26 ....152 A2
Watergate Rd DEWS WF13 ....172 A4
Water Green La RPDN/SBR HX6 .....163 H5
Water Hall La STKB/PEN S36 ....252 C7
Waterhall Vw STKB/PEN S36 ....252 C7
Water Hill La RPDN/SBR HX6 ....138 D6
Waterhouse St HFAX HX1 ....9 D3
  KGHY BD21 ....2 D4
Watering Place Rd STKB/PEN S36 ...251 K8
Water La BEE/HOL LS11 ....6 C5
  BEE/HOL LS11 ....7 E5
  BFD BD1 ....4 B4
  EARD/LOFT WF3 ....150 C7
  EARL WF12 ....172 A5
  FEA/AMT WF7 ....179 F4
  HEM/SK/SE WF9 ....225 F7
  HIPP HX3 ....9 E5
  HOR/CROF WF4 ....196 D3
  HOR/CROF WF4 ....220 C3
  HORS LS18 ....76 C2
  KGHY BD21 ....2 C4

PDSY/CALV LS28 ....76 B8
PONT WF8 ....155 G8
PONT WF8 ....203 K1
WOR/ARM LS12 ....99 H4
Water Lane LM/WK BD12 ....196 D3
Waterloo Cl CAS WF10 ....152 E6
Waterloo Crs BRAM LS13 ....77 H8
  IDLE BD10 ....75 H3
Waterloo Gv PDSY/CALV LS28 ....97 K4
Waterloo La BRAM LS13 ....77 H8
Waterloo Mt PDSY/CALV LS28 ....97 K3
Waterloo Ri HUDE HD5 ....192 C6
  BRIG HD6 ....142 B8
  HUDE HD5 ....192 C4
  PDSY/CALV LS28 ....97 K3
Waterloo St MID LS10 ....7 E4
Waterloo Ter LUD/ILL HX2 ....139 F5
Waterloo Wy BRAM LS13 ....77 H8
Water Rw HOLM/MEL HD9 ....234 A5
Water Royd Av MIRF WF14 ....170 D5
Water Royd Crs MIRF * WF14 ....170 D5
Water Royd Dr MIRF WF14 ....170 D5
Water Royd La MIRF WF14 ....170 D5
Waterside AIRE BD20 ....27 H3
  BGLY BD16 ....49 H6
  HIPP HX3 ....9 E5
  HUD HD1 ....12 B5
  HUDS HD4 ....213 F1
  HIPP HX3 ....9 E5
Waterside Fold HBR HX7 ....112 B7
Waterside La MID LS10 ....125 J1
Waterside Wk HUDE HD5 ....110 A6
Waterside La WBY LS22 ....24 B7
Waters Rd MAR/SLWT HD7 ....208 E6
Water Stalls Rd RPDN/SBR HX6 .....163 F3
Water St BRIG HD6 ....142 C8
  HOLM/MEL HD9 ....232 D8
  HUD HD1 ....12 B5
  KBTN HD8 ....237 H2
  RPDN/SBR HX6 ....138 E8
Waterton Cl HEM/SK/SE WF9 ....226 C4
  WKFDW/WTN WF2 ....199 J5
Waterton Rd WKFDW/WTN WF2 ...174 J7
Water Vw CAS WF10 ....153 F6
Waterwell Ri HUDS HD4 ....212 D1
Waterwood Cl EARD/LOFT WF3 .....148 A4
Waterworks Rd BTLY WF17 ....145 J1
Watery La HOLM/MEL HD9 ....246 E3
Watford Ri HIPP HX3 ....118 A8
Watkin Av CUL/QBY BD13 ....93 K5
Watkinson Dr LUD/ILL HX2 ....115 J7
Watkinson Dr LUD/ILL HX2 ....115 J7
Watkinson Rd LUD/ILL HX2 ....115 J7
Watling Rd CAS WF10 ....154 E2
Watmough St GTHN BD7 ....95 G8
Watroyd La MAR/SLWT HD7 ....189 F8
Watson Av EARL WF12 ....173 G3
Watson Crs WKFDE WF1 ....11 E2
Watson Mill La RPDN/SBR HX6 ......138 E8
Watson St CLAY LS14 ....103 H2
Watson's La TAD LS24 ....43 K6
Watson St MOR LS27 ....122 E8
  NORM WF6 ....177 K1
Wattle Syke WBY LS22 ....41 H2
Watts St CLAY BD14 ....94 B7
Watt St BOW BD4 ....97 J7
Watty Hall Av WBSY BD6 ....118 B1
Watty Hall La WBSY BD6 ....118 C1
Watty Hall Rd WBSY BD6 ....118 B1
Watty La TOD OL14 ....133 J8
Wauchope St WKFDW/WTN WF2 ....10 A3
Wauds Gates BAIL BD17 ....73 J2
Waulkmill Cl HEM/SK/SE WF9 ......226 C4
Wavell Garth WKFDW/WTN WF2 ...199 H4
Wavell Gv WKFDW/WTN WF2 ....199 G4
Waveney Rd WOR/ARM LS12 ....100 C5
Wavell Gv WKFDW/WTN WF2 ....199 G4
Waveney Av AIRE BD20 ....49 F3
  GTHN BD7 ....95 H6
Waverley Crs HIPP HX3 ....141 H4
Waverley Garth BEE/HOL LS11 ......101 H7
Waverley Pl GTHN BD7 ....95 H6
Waverley Rd ELL HX5 ....166 E6
  GTHN BD7 ....95 H6
  HUD HD1 ....12 B3
Waverley St EARL WF12 ....172 B4
  MAR/SLWT HD7 ....210 D2
Waverley Ter GTHN BD7 ....95 H6
  HUD HD1 ....190 D4
Wavell Gn WBSY BD6 ....117 K4
Wavertree Park Gdns
  LM/WK BD12 ....118 D7
Wayland Ap BHP/TINH LS16 ....56 D7
Wayland Dr BHP/TINH LS16 ....56 D7
Wayne Cl BTLY WF17 ....146 B5
Wayside Av SCFT LS14 ....60 B2
Wayside Crs IDLE * BD10 ....74 D6
  SCFT LS14 ....60 B1
Wayside Mt SCFT LS14 ....60 B2
Weardale Cl BOW BD4 ....119 K2
Weardley La AL/HA/HU LS17 ....37 H5
Weatherhead Pl AIRE BD20 ....27 C2
Weatherhill Crs HUDW HD3 ....190 A1
Weather Hill La HBR HX7 ....137 F6
  HOLM/MEL HD9 ....247 K3
Weather Hill Rd HUDW HD3 ....167 F8
Weatherhouse Ter LUD/ILL HX2 .....139 G2

Weaver Cottages HWTH * BD22 90
Weaver Gdns MOR LS27 123
Weavers Ct HOLM/MEL HD9 231
  WOR/ARM LS12 100
Weavers Cft IDLE BD10 74
  PDSY/CALV LS28 98
Weavers Gra GSLY LS20 53
Weavers Hl HWTH BD22 68
Weavers Rd PONT WF8 181
Weavers Rw PDSY/CALV LS28 98
Weaver St BULY LS4 100
Weavers Wk AIRE BD20 27
  KBTN HD8 237
Weaverthorpe Rd BOW BD4 120
Webb Dr ECHL BD2 5
Webb's Ter HIPP HX3 9
Weber Ct BFDE * BD3 96
Webster Hl EARL WF12 172
Webster Pl NORM WF6 177
Webster Rw WOR/ARM LS12 100
Webster St BFDE BD3 5
  DEWS * WF13 172
Wedgemoor Cl LM/WK BD12 118
Wedgewood Dr RHAY LS8 80
Wedgewood Gv RHAY LS8 80
Weeland Av HOR/CROF WF4 178
Weeland Ct KNOT WF11 156
Weeland Crs HOR/CROF WF4 178
Weeland Dr HOR/CROF WF4 178
Weeland Rd HOR/CROF WF4 200
  KNOT WF11 157
Weetlands Cl GFTH/SHER LS25 129
Weetwood Ct BHP/TINH LS16 78
Weetwood Cr BHP/TINH LS16 78
Weetwood Crs BHP/TINH LS16 78
Weetwood Grange Gv
  BHP/TINH LS16 78
Weetwood House Ct
  BHP/TINH LS16 78
Weetwood La BHP/TINH LS16 78
Weetwood Mill La BHP/TINH LS16 ...78
Weetwood Park Dr BHP/TINH LS16 ...78
Weetwood Rd BHP/TINH LS16 78
  GIR BD8 95
Weetwood Wk BHP/TINH LS16 78
Weetworth Av CAS WF10 153
Weetworth Pk CAS WF10 153
Weir Side MAR/SLWT * HD7 209
Weir St TOD OL14 133
Weir Vw CAS WF10 153
Welbeck Dr GTHN BD7 94
Welbeck Ri GTHN BD7 94
Welbeck Rd BTLY WF17 145
  OSM LS9 102
Welbeck St CAS * WF10 153
  WKFDE WF1 11
Welburn Av BHP/TINH LS16 141
  HIPP HX3 141
Welburn Cl WKFDW/WTN WF2 199
Welburn Dr BHP/TINH LS16 78
Welburn Gv BHP/TINH LS16 78
Welburn Mt WBSY BD6 117
Welbury Dr GIR BD8 4
Weldon Ct BOW BD4 97
Weldon Dr HUDW HD3 188
Welfare Av MSTN/BAR LS15 83
Welham Wk BFDE BD3 5
Welland Dr GFTH/SHER LS25 106
Wellands Cn CLECK BD19 143
Wellands La CLECK BD19 143
Wellands Ter BFDE BD3 96
Well Cl RTHW LS26 128
  YEA LS19 54
Well Close Ri LDSU LS2 7
Well Close St BRIG HD6 142
Wellcroft OT LS21 33
Well Cft SHPY BD18 78
Wellcroft Gv EARD/LOFT WF3 148
Wellesley Cn WKFDW/WTN WF2 175
Wellesley Pk LUD/ILL * HX2 139
Wellesley St BFD BD1 5
Wellfield Av HOR/CROF WF4 194
Wellfield Cl HOR/CROF WF4 194
  MAR/SLWT HD7 211
Wellfield Gv STKB/PEN S36 252
Wellfield La ILK LS29 32
Wellfield Rd HUDW HD3 190
Wellfield Ter TOD OL14 134
Wellfield Bank HUDS HD4 212
Wellgarth HFAX HX1 9
Well Garth Bank MSTN/BAR LS15 ...104
Well Garth Bank BRAM LS13 77
Well Garth Mt MSTN/BAR LS15 104
Wellgarth Rd FEA/AMT WF7 177
Well Garth Vw BRAM LS13 99
Wellgate CAS WF10 154
  GTL/HWG HX4 166
  MAR/SLWT HD7 199
Well Green Gdns HOLM/MEL HD9 ..233
Well Green La BRIG HD6 142
Well Gv BRIG HD6 142
  HUDN HD2 169
Wellhead Cl BHP/TINH LS16 35
Well Head Dr HFAX HX1 9
Well Head La HFAX HX1 9
  RPDN/SBR HX6 163
Well Heads CUL/QBY BD13 92
Well Hl HOLM/MEL HD9 213
  OT LS21 33

HOLM/MEL HD9 ...233 F3
MOR ...122 B4
WOR/ARM LS12 ...99 H8
West End Av MOR LS27 ...122 D8
West End Av BSLYN/ROY S71 ...179 J8
  FEA/AMT WF7 ...179 F5
  HOLM/MEL HD9 ...233 J5
  STKB/PEN S36 ...251 D8
West End Cl HORS LS18 ...76 D2
West End Crs BSLYN/ROY S71 ...221 J8
West End Dr CLECK BD19 ...143 J5
  HORS LS18 ...76 C2
West End Gv HORS LS18 ...76 D2
West End La HORS LS18 ...76 D1
West End Pl BEE/HOL LS11 ...6 C6
West End Ri HORS LS18 ...76 D2
West End Rd HFAX HX1 ...139 H5
  MAR/SLWT HD7 ...189 C7
  PDSY/CALV LS28 ...75 K5
Westend St BFD BD1 ...4 B4
West End Ter ECHL BD2 ...74 D6
  GSLY LS20 ...52 E2
  HBR HX7 ...137 F2
  SHPY BD18 ...73 G3
Westercroft La HIPP HX3 ...117 C8
Westercroft Vw HIPP HX3 ...117 C8
Westerley Cl KSTN HD8 ...215 J8
Westerley Crs AIRE BD20 ...26 E2
Westerley La KBTN HD8 ...215 H8
Westerman Rd FEA/AMT * WF7 ...179 J5
Western Av AIRE BD20 ...28 B8
  BTLY WF17 ...145 K2
  PONT WF8 ...181 G2
Western Gales Wy NORM WF6 ...178 C2
Western Gv WOR/ARM LS12 ...100 B6
Western Mt WOR/ARM LS12 ...100 B6
Western Pl CUL/QBY BD13 ...117 C2
Western Rd HUDS HD4 ...190 A7
  WOR/ARM LS12 ...100 B6
Western St WOR/ARM LS12 ...100 B6
Western Wy WBSY BD6 ...118 B4
Westerton Cl EARD/LOFT WF3 ...148 C4
Westerton Ct LM/WK BD12 ...119 J6
Westerton Rd EARD/LOFT WF3 ...147 J4
Westerton Wk EARD/LOFT WF3 ...148 C3
West Farm Av MID LS10 ...124 C6
Westfell Cl HWTH BD22 ...2 A4
Westfell Rd HWTH BD22 ...2 A4
Westfell Wy HWTH BD22 ...2 A4
Westfield CUL/QBY BD13 ...94 A5
  HBR HX7 ...112 D6
  PDSY/CALV LS28 ...98 C2
Westfield Av CAS WF10 ...153 H7
  EARL WF12 ...173 H7
  GFTH/SHER LS25 ...129 F1
  HIPP HX3 ...141 J4
  HOLM/MEL HD9 ...211 G8
  HUDW HD3 ...190 B4
  KBTN HD8 ...236 D2
  KNOT WF11 ...156 C8
  PONT WF8 ...180 D5
  STKB/PEN S36 ...251 K7
  WOR/ARM LS12 ...99 K3
  YEA LS19 ...53 H5
Westfield Cl HECK * WF16 ...145 F6
  RTHW LS26 ...125 K7
  YEA LS19 ...53 H5
Westfield Ct HOR/CROF WF4 ...197 F1
  HUDE HD5 ...13 F4
  MIRF WF14 ...170 D6
  RTHW LS26 ...125 K7
Westfield Crs AIRE BD20 ...48 D2
  BVRD LS3 ...6 B2
  ECHL BD2 ...5 F2
  HOR/CROF WF4 ...222 E2
  OSS WF5 ...173 H6
  WKFDW/WTN WF2 ...174 C1
Westfield Dr AIRE BD20 ...48 D2
  HIPP HX3 ...141 J4
  KBTN HD8 ...236 D2
  OSS WF5 ...173 H6
  YEA LS19 ...53 H5
Westfield Farm OSS WF5 ...173 H5
Westfield Gdns GFTH/SHER LS25 ...128 E1
  HIPP HX3 ...141 J4
Westfield Gv CAS WF10 ...129 F1
  DEWS WF13 ...171 J3
  FEA/AMT WF7 ...203 H3
  IDLE BD10 ...78 A5
  SHPY BD18 ...74 A5
  WKFDE WF1 ...10 C1
West Field La HOLM/MEL HD9 ...233 J8
Westfield La GFTH/SHER LS25 ...128 E1
  HEM/SK/SE WF9 ...242 B2
  IDLE BD10 ...78 B4
  KBTN HD8 ...216 C3
  LM/WK BD12 ...142 E2
  PONT WF8 ...181 K8
  STKB/PEN S36 ...251 K7
Westfield Mt YEA LS19 ...53 G5
Westfield Ov YEA LS19 ...53 G5
Westfield Pk WKFDE WF1 ...10 C1

Westfield Pl CLECK BD19 ...143 F2
  HFAX HX1 ...8 B5
  WKFDW/WTN WF2 ...174 C1
Westfield Rd AIRE BD20 ...48 D2
  BVRD LS3 ...6 B2
  CLAY BD14 ...94 B7
  HECK WF16 ...145 F6
  HEM/SK/SE WF9 ...224 D4
  HOR/CROF WF4 ...197 F1
  HTON BD9 ...95 G1
  KNOT WF11 ...156 C8
  MOR * LS27 ...123 F7
  RTHW LS26 ...125 K7
  WKFDE WF1 ...10 C1
Westfield Ter BAIL BD17 ...51 J7
  BVRD LS3 ...6 B2
  CAS WF10 ...129 F6
  CHAL LS7 ...79 J3
  CLAY BD14 ...94 B7
  ECHL BD2 ...5 F2
  HEM/SK/SE WF9 ...224 C5
  HFAX HX1 ...9 D4
  WKFDE WF1 ...10 C1
Westfield Vw WKFDE WF1 ...175 K2
Westgarth WBY LS22 ...23 F8
West Ga HOLM/MEL HD9 ...248 A3
  WBY LS22 ...23 J6
Westgate BAIL BD17 ...51 J7
  BFD BD1 ...4 B4
  BRIG HD6 ...169 F1
  CLECK BD19 ...143 K4
  EARL WF12 ...172 C5
  ECHL BD2 ...74 E7
  ELL HX5 ...166 E4
  CSLY LS20 ...52 D5
  HEM/SK/SE WF9 ...224 C5
  HFAX HX1 ...9 D4
  HOLM/MEL HD9 ...213 F7
  HOLM/MEL HD9 ...231 H1
  HUD HD1 ...12 C4
  HUDE HD5 ...214 B1
  LDS LS1 ...7 D3
  LVSG WF15 ...145 F7
  OT LS21 ...33 H4
  SHPY BD18 ...73 H3
  WKFDE WF1 ...10 C3
Westgate Cl EARD/LOFT WF3 ...149 J3
Westgate Crs EARD/LOFT WF3 ...149 K3
Westgate End WKFDW/WTN WF2 ...10 A4
Westgate Gdns KGHY BD21 ...2 A4
Westgate Gv EARD/LOFT WF3 ...149 K3
Westgate Hill St BOW BD4 ...120 D3
Westgate La EARD/LOFT WF3 ...149 J3
Westgate Market HFAX * HX1 ...9 D4
Westgate Ter BOW BD4 ...120 D3
West Grange Cl MID LS10 ...124 E2
West Grange Dr MID LS10 ...124 E2
West Grange Fold MID LS10 ...124 E2
West Grange Gdns MID LS10 ...124 E2
West Grange Garth MID LS10 ...124 E2
West Grange Rd MID LS10 ...124 E2
West Grange Wk MID LS10 ...124 E2
West Gv BAIL BD17 ...51 J7
  BSLYN/ROY S71 ...221 J7
West Grove Av HUDE HD5 ...13 F4
Westgrove Ct CLECK BD19 ...143 K5
West Grove St PDSY/CALV * LS28 ...98 B2
West Grove Ter HFAX HX1 ...8 C5
West Hall La ILK LS29 ...18 E1
West Hill Av CHAL LS7 ...79 J4
Westhill Av CUL/QBY BD13 ...70 C6
West Hill St HFAX HX1 ...8 B4
Westholme Rd HFAX HX1 ...8 A4
West Ings Cl KNOT WF11 ...156 E6
West Ings Crs KNOT WF11 ...156 E6
West Ings La KNOT WF11 ...156 E6
West Ings Ms KNOT WF11 ...156 E6
West Ings Wy KNOT WF11 ...156 E6
Westland Ct GBUR LS25 ...
Westland Rd BEE/HOL LS11 ...124 D4
Westlands Dr WIL/AL BD15 ...94 B2
Westlands Gv WIL/AL BD15 ...94 C2
Westland Sq BEE/HOL LS11 ...124 C3
West La BAIL BD17 ...51 J8
  BSPA/BRAM LS23 ...42 C2
  CLECK BD19 ...144 E3
  CUL/QBY BD13 ...93 H5
  HIPP HX3 ...140 E8
  HOR/CROF WF4 ...201 F2
  HWTH BD22 ...68 D4
  KGHY BD21 ...2 A2
Westlea Av KGHY BD21 ...48 D2
West Lea Cl AL/HA/HU ...79 H2
West Lea Crs EARD/LOFT WF3 ...147 J4
  YEA LS19 ...53 H5
West Lea Dr AL/HA/HU LS17 ...79 H2
  EARD/LOFT WF3 ...147 J4
West Lea Garth AL/HA/HU LS17 ...79 H2
West Lea Gdns AL/HA/HU LS17 ...79 H2
West Lea Gv YEA LS19 ...53 H5
West Leeds St HWTH BD22 ...2 C6
Westleigh BGLY BD16 ...50 A7
Westleigh Cl BAIL * BD17 ...73 G1
Westleigh Dr BAIL BD17 ...73 G1

Westleigh Rd BAIL BD17 ...51
Westleigh Wy BAIL BD17 ...73
Westley Av HOLM/MEL HD9 ...233
Westlock Av OSM LS9 ...102
West Ldg ILK * LS29 ...32
West Lodge Av HUDW HD3 ...167
West Lodge Gdns CHAL LS7 ...79
West Md CAS WF10 ...154
Westminster Av CLAY BD14 ...94
Westminster Cl BRAM LS13 ...76
Westminster Crs CLAY BD14 ...94
  MSTN/BAR LS15 ...103
Westminster Cft BRAM * LS13 ...76
Westminster Dr BRAM LS13 ...76
  CLAY BD14 ...94
Westminster Gdns CLAY BD14 ...94
Westminster Pl BFDE BD3 ...5
Westminster Rd BFDE BD3 ...5
Westminster Ter BFDE BD3 ...5
Westmoor Av BAIL BD17 ...51
Westmoor Cl BAIL * BD17 ...51
West Moorlands Av DEWS * WF13 ...172
Westmoor Pl BRAM LS13 ...77
Westmoor Ri BRAM LS13 ...77
West Moor Rd HEM/SK/SE WF9 ...224
Westmoor St BRAM LS13 ...77
Westmoreland Mt BRAM * LS13 ...77
West Mount Pl HFAX * HX1 ...8
West Mount St BEE/HOL * LS11 ...101
Westmount St PONT WF8 ...180
Westoff La CUD/GR S72 ...223
Weston Av CUL/QBY BD13 ...116
Weston Crs OT LS21 ...33
Weston Dr OT LS21 ...33
Weston La OT LS21 ...33
Weston Park Vw OT LS21 ...33
Weston Rdg OT LS21 ...33
Weston St HWTH BD22 ...2
Weston Vale Rd CUL/QBY BD13 ...116
Westover Gdns PDSY/CALV LS28 ...98
Westover Gn BRAM * LS13 ...77
Westover Gv BRAM * LS13 ...77
Westover Mt BRAM * LS13 ...77
Westover Rd BRAM LS13 ...77
Westover St BRAM LS13 ...77
Westover Ter BRAM LS13 ...77
Westover Vw BRAM LS13 ...77
West Pde BHP/TINH LS16 ...78
  HFAX HX1 ...8
  ILK LS29 ...20
  RPDN/SBR HX6 ...139
  RTHW LS26 ...126
  WKFDE * WF1 ...10
West Parade Ct WKFDE WF1 ...10
West Parade Flats HFAX * HX1 ...8
West Parade St WKFDE * WF1 ...10
West Pk BHP/TINH LS16 ...78
  GSLY LS20 ...52
West Park Av RHAY LS8 ...58
West Park Cl RHAY LS8 ...58
West Park Crs RHAY LS8 ...58
West Park Dr BHP/TINH LS16 ...78
  PONT WF8 ...205
West Park Dr East RHAY LS8 ...58
West Park Dr West RHAY LS8 ...58
West Park Gv BTLY WF17 ...145
  RHAY LS8 ...58
West Park Pl RHAY LS8 ...80
West Park Rd BTLY WF17 ...145
  GIR BD8 ...95
West Parks PDSY/CALV LS28 ...98
West Park St BRIG HD6 ...168
  DEWS WF13 ...172
West Park Ter BTLY WF17 ...145
  GIR * BD8 ...95
West Pasture Cl HORS LS18 ...76
West Pinfold BSLYN/ROY S71 ...222
West Pl HUDE HD5 ...13
Westridge Dr HUDS HD4 ...212
West Rd OSM LS9 ...102
West Rd North OSM LS9 ...102
Westroyd PDSY/CALV LS28 ...98
West Royd Av WIL/AL BD15 ...71
West Royd Av ECHL * BD2 ...74
  HFAX HX1 ...8
  MIRF WF14 ...170
  SHPY BD18 ...73
Westroyd Av CLECK BD19 ...120
  PDSY/CALV LS28 ...98
West Royd Cl HFAX HX1 ...73
  SHPY BD18 ...73
Westroyd Crs PDSY/CALV LS28 ...98
West Royd Crs SHPY BD18 ...74
West Royd Dr MIRF WF14 ...170
  SHPY BD18 ...73
Westroyd Gdns PDSY/CALV LS28 ...98
West Royd Gv MIRF WF14 ...170
West Royd Mt SHPY BD18 ...74
West Royd Pk MIRF WF14 ...170
West Royd Rd SHPY BD18 ...74
West Royd Ter SHPY BD18 ...74
West Royd Vis HFAX * HX1 ...8
West Royd Wk SHPY BD18 ...74
West Scausby Pk LUD/ILL HX2 ...111
West Shaw La HWTH BD22 ...6
West Side Ct GIR BD8 ...9
West Slaithwaite Rd
  MAR/SLWT HD7 ...21

est St BAIL BD17	51 J7
BFD BD1	5 D5
BIRK/DRI BD11	121 H6
BRIC HD6	142 B8
BRIG HD6	142 C4
BSLYN/ROY S71	222 B7
BTLY WF17	146 C6
CAS WF10	153 H3
BVRD LS3	6 B3
CLECK BD19	144 A4
CLECK BD19	144 D2
CUD/GR S72	223 J6
EARL WF12	172 B4
ECHL BD2	74 D8
GTL/HWG HX4	166 A7
HECK WF16	145 F7
HOR/CROF WF4	225 G2
HUDW HD3	190 A2
MOR LS27	125 G8
NORM WF6	177 K1
PDSY/CALV LS28	98 C3
RPDN/SBR HX6	138 E8
WKFDW/WTN WF2	175 G6
est V WOR/ARM LS12	6 A6
estvale Ms BRAM LS13	99 J2
est Vw AIRE BD20	27 G1
BEE/HOL LS11	101 G7
BOW BD4	96 C7
DEWS WF13	172 A1
FEA/AMT WF7	202 D6
GFTH/SHER LS25	107 H5
GFTH/SHER LS25	129 G1
GTL/HWG HX4	165 K7
HIPP HX3	8 C1
HUD HD1	190 D6
NORM WF6	151 J6
OT LS21	33 K3
OT LS21	35 K5
RTHW LS26	127 F6
SKP/WHF BD23	14 A6
WKFDW/WTN WF2	174 C1
WEA LS19	53 H4
est View Av CAS WF10	154 B4
HFAX HX1	139 H4
LK LS29	32 A2
SHPY BD18	74 A4
estview Av KGHY BD21	2 C2
est View Dr SHPY BD18	74 A4
estview Ct KGHY BD21	2 B2
est View St YEA * LS19	53 H4
est View Crs HFAX HX1	139 H5
est View Gv LUD/ILL HX2	139 G4
estview Gv KGHY BD21	2 B2
est View Ri HUD HD1	190 D6
est View Rd HIPP * HX3	8 C1
ILK LS29	32 A2
est View Ter GIR * BD8	94 E4
LUD/ILL * HX2	139 H3
estview Wy KGHY BD21	2 A1
est Villa Rd GSLY LS20	53 G2
stville Av ILK LS29	20 A7
stville Cl ILK LS29	20 A7
stville Dr ILK LS29	20 A7
stville Vw CUL/QBY BD13	93 H5
stward Dr HUDW HD3	190 C1
stward Ho HIPP * HX3	8 C1
stway BTLY WF17	146 E8
GFTH/SHER LS25	105 H5
GSLY LS20	52 D3
HTON BD9	94 C1
KGHY BD21	2 A1
MIRF WF14	170 C4
PDSY/CALV LS28	76 A8
st Wd SHPY BD18	72 D4
stways Ct WKFDW/WTN WF2	149 G8
stways Ct WKFDW/WTN WF2	175 G1
stways Dr RHAY LS8	80 E4
st Wells Crs OSS WF5	173 H6
st Wells Rd OSS WF5	173 H6
st Wells Rd OSS WF5	173 H6
stwinn Garth SCFT LS14	82 A3
stwinn Vw SCFT LS14	82 A2
stwood Av ECHL BD2	74 D6
HOLM/MEL HD9	213 J7
stwood Cl FEA/AMT WF7	179 J4
MOR LS27	125 G5
st Wood Dr MID LS10	124 B6
stwood Crs BGLY LS16	72 A3
stwood Dr ILK LS29	29 K1
MOR LS27	125 F5
st Wood Rd MOR LS27	124 A7
stwood Rd CAS WF10	153 G6
SS WF5	174 A6
stwood Side MOR LS27	123 F4
stwoodside MOR LS27	123 G4
stwood St HUDN * HD2	169 H5
stwood Wy BSPA/BRAM LS23	42 D4
therby Grange Pk WBY * LS22	24 A8

Wetherby Gv BULY LS4	100 C1
Wetherby Pl BULY LS4	100 D1
Wetherby Rd AL/HA/HU LS17	40 B7
BSPA/BRAM LS23	24 C1
BSPA/BRAM LS23	42 C8
RHAY LS8	80 D1
SCFT LS14	59 J8
WBY LS22	22 B6
WBY LS22	23 J3
WBY LS22	23 J7
WBY LS22	41 H2
Wetherby Ter BULY LS4	100 C1
Wetherhill St BTLY WF17	146 A6
Wetlands Rd HOLM/MEL HD9	231 J2
Wetton Ct BFDE BD3	97 F4
Weydale Av HUDW HD3	190 A3
Weyhill Dr WIL/AL BD15	94 B3
Weymouth Av HUDW HD3	190 B4
WIL/AL BD15	94 A3
Whack House Cl YEA LS19	53 J5
Whalley La CUL/QBY BD13	92 B1
Wharfe Bank WBY LS22	40 C3
Wharfe Cl BHP/TINH LS16	56 D7
Wharfe Ct AIRE BD20	27 G2
Wharfe Crs OT LS21	35 H4
SCFT LS14	81 H6
Wharfedale Av CHAL LS7	79 H7
Wharfedale Ct OT LS21	35 H4
SCFT LS14	81 H6
Wharfedale Crs GFTH/SHER LS25	105 K6
KBTN HD8	237 F2
Wharfedale Dr ILK LS29	20 C8
NORM WF6	151 K7
Wharfedale Gdns BAIL BD17	52 A7
Wharfedale Gv HDGY LS6	79 H7
Wharfedale Lawns WBY LS22	23 J6
Wharfedale Ms OT LS21	33 K3
Wharfedale Mt HDGY LS6	79 H7
HIPP HX3	117 G5
Wharfedale Pl HDGY LS6	79 H7
Wharfedale Ri EARD/LOFT WF3	147 J4
HTON BD9	94 C1
Wharfedale Rd BOW BD4	119 H4
Wharfedale St HDGY LS6	79 H7
Wharfedale Vw HDGY LS6	79 H7
ILK LS29	18 C3
ILK LS29	32 C7
Wharfe Gra WBY LS22	23 H6
Wharfe Gv WBY LS22	23 H6
Wharfe La WBY LS22	38 E1
Wharfe Ms ILK * LS29	32 D7
WBY * LS22	23 H6
Wharfe Pk ILK LS29	18 E3
Wharfe Rein WBY LS22	40 C3
Wharfeside La ILK LS29	20 C6
Wharfe St OT LS21	33 K3
Wharfe Vw WBY LS22	23 H6
Wharfe View Rd ILK LS29	20 B7
Wharf St BAIL BD17	73 H3
BFDE BD3	5 D3
BRIG HD6	168 C1
EARL WF12	172 C4
LDSU LS2	7 F4
RPDN/SBR HX6	139 F7
TOD OL14	159 K2
Wharncliffe Crs ECHL BD2	75 F7
Wharncliffe Dr ECHL BD2	75 F7
Wharncliffe Gv ECHL BD2	75 F7
SHPY BD18	73 H5
Wharncliffe Rd SHPY BD18	75 F7
WKFDW/WTN WF2	198 C6
The Whartons OT LS21	33 J1
Wharton St LVSG WF15	144 E4
Wheat Cl DEWS WF13	171 J3
HOLM/MEL HD9	247 H1
Wheatcroft CAS WF10	154 C5
Wheatcroft Av BTLY WF17	146 E8
Wheater Rd GTHN * BD7	95 G6
Wheat Field Av HUDW HD3	190 A4
Wheatfield Ct PDSY/CALV LS28	98 B5
Wheathead Crs HWTH BD22	47 G6
Wheat Head Dr HWTH BD22	2 A5
Wheathead La HWTH BD22	47 G6
Wheathouse Rd HUDN HD2	12 B1
Wheathouse Ter HUDN HD2	12 B1
The Wheatings OSS WF5	174 A6
Wheatlands ILK LS29	20 C8
PDSY/CALV LS28	76 A8
Wheatlands Av HTON BD9	94 E1
Wheatlands Crs HTON BD9	94 E1
Wheatlands Dr HTON BD9	94 E1
LVSG * WF15	170 C1
Wheatlands Gv HTON BD9	94 E1
Wheatlands Sq HTON BD9	94 E1
Wheatley Av ILK LS29	20 E8
NORM WF6	178 A2
Wheatley Cl HIPP * HX3	8 B2
Wheatley Dr MIRF WF14	170 D8
Wheatley Gdns ILK LS29	20 E8
Wheatley Gv ILK LS29	20 E8
Wheatley Hill La KBTN HD8	237 J3
Wheatley La HIPP HX3	8 B2
ILK LS29	20 E8
Wheatley Ri ILK LS29	20 E8
Wheatley Rd HIPP HX3	8 A1
ILK LS29	20 C8
Wheaton Av MSTN/BAR LS15	103 J3
Wheatroyd Crs OSS WF5	173 J8
Wheatroyd La HUDE HD5	214 A1
Wheat St HWTH BD22	2 B6

Wheelwright Av WOR/ARM LS12	100 A6
Wheelwright Cl WOR/ARM LS12	100 A6
Wheelwright Dr DEWS WF13	172 A1
Wheelwright St EARL * WF12	172 B3
Wheldale La CAS WF10	155 F1
Wheldon Rd CAS WF10	130 E8
CAS WF10	153 K3
Whernside Mt GTHN BD7	117 K1
Whernside Wy LUD/ILL HX2	114 D8
Wherwell Rd BRIG HD6	168 C2
Whetley Cl GIR BD8	4 A3
Whetley Gv GIR BD8	95 G2
Whetley Hl GIR BD8	95 H2
Whetley La GIR BD8	95 G3
Whetley Ter GIR BD8	4 A3
Whewell St BTLY WF17	145 H2
Whiddon Cft ILK LS29	32 B6
Whimbrel Cl GIR BD8	94 C4
Whimbrel Ms MOR LS27	123 H8
Whinbeck Av NORM WF6	178 C2
Whinberry Pl BTLY WF17	121 J8
Whinbrook Crs AL/HA/HU LS17	79 J2
Whinbrook Gdns AL/HA/HU LS17	79 J2
Whinbrook Gv AL/HA/HU LS17	79 J2
Whin Cl HEM/SK/SE WF9	224 D6
Whincop Av CAS WF10	152 E4
Whincover Cl WOR/ARM LS12	99 K6
Whincover Cross WOR/ARM LS12	99 K6
Whincover Dr WOR/ARM LS12	99 J6
Whincover Gdns WOR/ARM LS12	99 K6
Whincover Gv WOR/ARM LS12	99 K6
Whincover Hl WOR/ARM LS12	99 K6
Whincover Mt WOR/ARM LS12	99 K6
Whincover Rd WOR/ARM LS12	99 J6
Whincover Vw WOR/ARM LS12	99 K6
Whinfield BHP/TINH LS16	56 B7
Whinfield Av HWTH BD22	47 C3
Whinfield Cl HWTH BD22	2 A2
Whinfield Dr HWTH BD22	47 C3
Whingate WOR/ARM LS12	100 A3
Whingate Av WOR/ARM LS12	100 A4
Whingate Cl WOR/ARM LS12	100 A4
Whingate Gn WOR/ARM LS12	100 A4
Whingate Gv WOR/ARM LS12	100 A4
Whingate Rd WOR/ARM LS12	100 A4
Whingrove Av HOLM/MEL HD9	231 G2
Whin Knoll Av KGHY BD21	2 A2
Whinmoor Ct SCFT LS14	81 J2
Whinmoor Crs SCFT LS14	81 J2
Whinmoor Gdns SCFT LS14	81 H2
Whinmoor La AL/HA/HU LS17	59 G8
Whin Moor La DOD/DAR S75	253 H3
Whinmore Gdns CLECK BD19	145 F4
Whin Mt NORM WF6	178 B3
Whinney Brow IDLE BD10	74 B3
Whinney Cl FEA/AMT WF7	178 C6
Whinney Hill Pk BRIG HD6	142 B6
Whinney La FEA/AMT WF7	178 C6
Whinney Moor Av	
WKFDW/WTN WF2	174 E8
Whinney Royd La HIPP HX3	117 F6
Whins La BSPA/BRAM LS23	43 F2
PBR HG3	22 A3
Whin St HWTH BD22	2 B3
Whirlaw Av TOD OL14	133 K4
Whirlaw La TOD OL14	134 A3
Whiskers La HIPP HX3	115 D8
Whisperwood Cl WKFDE * WF1	150 A6
Whisperwood Rd WKFDE WF1	150 A6
Whitacre Cl HUDN HD2	169 F8
Whitacre St HUDN HD2	169 F8
Whitaker Av ECHL BD2	74 E8
Whitaker Cl ECHL BD2	74 E8
Whitaker St BTLY WF17	146 C7
PDSY/CALV LS28	98 B1
Whitaker Wk HWTH * BD22	90 E1
Whitby Av HUDN HD2	191 C1
Whitby Crs EARL WF12	172 E3
Whitby Rd GIR BD8	95 G2
Whitby Ter GIR BD8	95 G2
Whitcliffe Rd CLECK BD19	143 H3
Whitcliffe Sq CLECK BD19	144 A3
White Abbey Rd GIR BD8	4 A3
White Apron St HEM/SK/SE WF9	241 H1
Whitebeam La MID LS10	124 C3
Whitebeam Pk HUDN HD2	190 D1
White Birch Ter HIPP HX3	8 A1
Whitebridge Crs OSM LS9	103 G2
Whitebridge Sp SCFT LS14	103 G2
Whitebridge Vw OSM LS9	103 G2
White Castle Ct CUL/QBY BD13	116 A1
Whitechapel Cl RHAY LS8	80 D5
Whitechapel Gv CLECK BD19	143 H2
Whitechapel Rd CLECK BD19	143 H3
Whitechapel Wy RHAY LS8	80 D5
Whitecliffe Crs RTHW LS26	127 K1
Whitecliffe Dr RTHW LS26	127 K1
Whitecliffe Ri RTHW LS26	127 K1
Whitecote Gdns BRAM LS13	77 F7
Whitecote Hl BRAM LS13	77 F7
Whitecote La BRAM LS13	77 F6
Whitecote Ri BRAM LS13	77 F7
White Ct HOR/CROF WF4	200 E3
White Cross HUDN HD2	169 F6
White Cross Gdns CUD/GR S72	223 H5
White Cross Rd EARL WF12	172 D2
White Field La HBR HX7	136 D3
Whitefield Pl GIR BD8	95 G3
Whitegate AL/HA/HU LS17	40 A5

HIPP HX3	140 C7
White Ga HOLM/MEL HD9	213 F6
LUD/ILL HX2	115 G4
Whitegate Dr HIPP HX5	140 C7
Whitegate La PONT WF8	204 A3
Whitegate Rd WKFDE WF1	9 E6
White Gate Rd HOLM/MEL HD9	247 J2
Whitegate Rd HUDS HD4	13 D6
Whitegates Cl WKFDW/WTN WF2	175 G2
Whitegates Gv KBTN HD8	215 F1
Whitegates Ter HIPP HX3	140 C7
Whitegate Top HIPP HX3	140 D7
White Gv RHAY LS8	80 C3
Whitehall Av LM/WK BD12	142 D2
MIRF WF14	170 D4
WKFDE WF1	175 H2
Whitehall Crs WKFDE WF1	175 H2
Whitehall Cft RTHW LS26	126 C6
Whitehall Est WOR/ARM * LS12	99 K7
Whitehall Gv BIRK/DRI BD11	120 E6
Whitehall Quay LDS LS1	7 D4
White Gv RHAY LS8	80 C3
Whitehall Ri WKFDE WF1	10 A1
Whitehall Rd LM/WK BD12	143 F2
MAR/SLWT HD7	211 C3
WOR/ARM LS12	6 A5
Whitehall Rd East BIRK/DRI BD11	120 E6
Whitehall Rd West CLECK BD19	144 A1
White St HIPP HX3	141 J3
WKFDW/WTN WF2	175 G5
Whitehall Wy DEWS WF13	172 C3
White Hart Dr HUDS HD4	191 G8
White Hart Fold HEM/SK/SE WF9	226 D5
RPDN/SBR HX6	163 K8
Whitehaven Cl WBSY BD6	118 C2
Whitehead Gv ECHL BD2	98 E2
Whitehead La HOLM/MEL HD9	211 K5
HUDS HD4	191 H8
Whitehead Pl ECHL BD2	96 E1
Whitehead's Ter HFAX * HX1	8 A4
Whitehead St BFDE BD3	5 F5
White Hl MAR/SLWT HD7	210 A4
Whitehill Cottages LUD/ILL * HX2	115 H6
Whitehill Crs LUD/ILL HX2	115 H6
Whitehill Dr LUD/ILL HX2	115 H5
Whitehill Gn LUD/ILL HX2	115 J5
Whitehill Rd HBTW BD22	45 J6
LUD/ILL HX2	115 H6
White Holme Dr OT LS21	35 J5
White Horse Fold CAS WF10	146 A1
White Horse Fold CAS WF10	129 K6
White Horse Ms PBR HG3	22 A1
White Horse Yd WKFDE WF1	10 C3
Whitehouse Av RTHW LS26	128 C3
Whitehouse Bungalows	
WKFDW/WTN * WF2	10 B8
Whitehouse Crs RTHW LS26	128 D3
Whitehouse Dr RTHW LS26	128 C3
Whitehouse La RTHW LS26	105 G8
YEA LS19	54 D3
Whitehouse St MID LS10	7 F6
White Laith Av SCFT LS14	81 K3
White Laithe Ap SCFT LS14	81 K3
White Laithe Cl SCFT LS14	81 K3
White Laithe Cft SCFT LS14	81 K3
White Laithe Gdns SCFT * LS14	82 A3
White Laithe Garth SCFT LS14	81 K2
White Laithe Gn SCFT LS14	82 A3
White Laithe La SCFT LS14	82 A3
White Laithe Rd SCFT LS14	81 K3
White Laithe Wk SCFT LS14	82 A3
White Lands YEA LS19	53 J7
Whitelands Crs BAIL BD17	51 K8
Whitelands Rd BAIL BD17	51 K8
White La BTLY DN5	243 G7
HWTH BD22	68 B1
WBSY BD6	118 E3
White Lee AV COL BB8	64 A1
White Lee Cl BTLY WF17	145 H5
White Lee Gdns HBR HX7	137 G2
White Lee Rd BTLY WF17	145 H5
White Lee Side HECK WF16	145 H5
Whiteley Av GFTH/SHER LS25	138 C8
Whiteley Cft OT LS21	33 J4
Whiteley Ley Bank HOLM/MEL HD9	234 B8
Whiteley Croft Ri OT LS21	33 J4
Whiteley Croft Rd OT LS21	33 J4
Whiteley St FEA/AMT WF7	179 K5
HFAX HX1	8 C5
HUDS HD4	190 B7
Whitelock St CHAL LS7	7 F2
White Moss Cl FEA/AMT WF7	203 F5
Whiteplatts St TOD OL14	134 A5
White Rose Av GFTH/SHER LS25	105 K4
HUDE HD5	192 B4
Whiterose Md GFTH/SHER * LS25	106 A4
White Rose Wy GFTH/SHER LS25	106 A4
White Slack Ga TOD OL14	159 J5
White's Rd WKFDE WF1	11 D5
White's Ter GIR BD8	95 H2
Whitestone Crs YEA LS19	53 K4
Whitestone Dr AIRE BD20	49 H2
Whitestone La HUD HD1	13 D2
White St RTHW LS26	127 G5
White's Vw GIR BD8	95 H3
White Walls La HOLM/MEL HD9	231 K8
Whiteways ECHL BD2	74 A8
Whitewell Green La ELL HX5	167 G4

White Wells Gdns HOLM/MEL HD9	233 K8
White Wells Rd HOLM/MEL HD9	233 K8
Whitewood Cl BSLYN/ROY S71	221 K8
Whitfield Av MID LS10	102 A7
Whitfield Gdns MID * LS10	102 A7
Whitfield Pl MID LS10	102 A7
Whitfield Sq MID LS10	102 A7
Whitfield St CLECK BD19	144 A3
RHAY LS8	80 B8
Whitfield Wy MID LS10	102 A7
Whitham Cl BSPA/BRAM LS23	42 D3
Whitkirk Cl MSTN/BAR LS15	104 C3
Whitkirk La MSTN/BAR LS15	104 B3
Whitlam St SHPY BD18	73 F3
Whitley Dr LUD/ILL HX2	115 J5
Whitley Gdns RHAY LS8	80 A8
Whitley La HIPP HX3	141 F6
Whitley Pl CAS WF10	129 G7
Whitley Rd EARL WF12	194 C3
KGHY BD21	2 B5
STKB/PEN S36	250 C5
Whitley Spring Crs OSS WF5	174 A5
Whitley Spring Rd OSS WF5	174 A5
Whitley St BFDE * BD3	5 E4
BGLY BD16	75 K3
Whitley Wy HOR/CROF WF4	194 C6
Whitteron Cl HUDW * HD3	190 B2
Whittle Crs CLAY BD14	94 B6
Whittles St WILL OL12	158 A7
Whittles La LUD/ILL HX2	138 C5
Whitwell Av ELL HX5	167 G4
Whitwell Dr ELL HX5	167 G4
Whitwell Gv ELL HX5	167 G4
Whitwell St BOW BD4	5 E6
Whitwood Common La CAS WF10	152 E6
Whitwood La CAS WF10	152 D5
CLECK BD19	142 D4
Whitworth Rd DEWS * WF13	172 A4
Wholestone Ga MAR/SLWT HD7	189 G6
Whytecote End LM/WK BD12	118 D7
Wibsey Bank WBSY BD6	118 A3
Wibsey Park Av WBSY BD6	118 A3
Wicken Cl IDLE BD10	74 E5
Wicken La CUL/QBY BD13	93 G4
The Wickets BTLY WF17	172 A1
HDGY LS6	79 F4
MSTN/BAR LS15	104 C6
WKFDW/WTN * WF2	199 G3
Wickets Cl WBSY BD6	118 E3
Wickham Av BSPA/BRAM LS23	42 D3
WBSY * BD6	118 D3
Wickham Cl BSPA/BRAM LS23	42 D3
Wickham St CLECK BD19	145 G2
Wicking La RPDN/SBR HX6	163 H3
Wickins La HOLM/MEL HD9	232 D5
Wickleden Ga HOLM/MEL HD9	233 K8
Widdop Rd HBR HX7	111 H4
Wide La HWTH BD22	46 C8
MOR LS27	123 H7
Wigan St BFD BD1	4 B4
Wigeon Ap MOR LS27	123 H7
Wiggan La HUDN HD2	168 E8
Wighill La BSPA/BRAM LS23	43 J1
Wightman St BFDE BD3	5 E1
Wignall St KGHY BD21	2 C1
Wigton Cha AL/HA/HU LS17	58 C6
Wigton Gn AL/HA/HU LS17	58 B5
Wigton Gv AL/HA/HU LS17	58 B5
Wigton La AL/HA/HU LS17	58 A5
Wigton Park Cl AL/HA/HU LS17	58 B5
Wike La AL/HA/HU LS17	58 D8
Wike Ridge Av AL/HA/HU LS17	58 C6
Wike Ridge Cl AL/HA/HU LS17	58 C5
Wike Ridge Ct AL/HA/HU LS17	58 C5
Wike Ridge Fold AL/HA/HU LS17	58 C5
Wike Ridge Gv AL/HA/HU LS17	58 D6
Wike Ridge La AL/HA/HU LS17	58 D6
Wike Ridge Ms AL/HA/HU LS17	58 D6
Wike Ridge Mt AL/HA/HU LS17	58 D6
Wike Ridge Vw AL/HA/HU LS17	58 C6
Wilcock La AIRE BD20	16 B7
Wild Gv PDSY/CALV LS28	97 J4
Wildspur Cottages	
HOLM/MEL * HD9	234 A6
Wildspur Gv HOLM/MEL HD9	234 A7
Wild's Yd WKFDE * WF1	10 C4
Wilfred Av MSTN/BAR LS15	103 K3
Wilfred St CLAY BD14	94 D7
MSTN/BAR LS15	103 K3
Wilfred Ter WOR/ARM LS12	100 A7
Wilkinson Fold LM/WK * BD12	142 D1
Wilkinson Ter GTHN BD7	95 F5
Wilkinson Wy OT LS21	33 G7
Willan's Av RTHW LS26	126 B4
Willan's Rd DEWS WF13	172 B3
Willerton Cl EARL WF12	147 G8
Willgutter La HWTH BD22	68 B2
William Av MSTN/BAR * LS15	103 G3
William Henry St SHPY * HD6	142 B8
SHPY * BD18	73 F5
William Hey Ct OSM * LS9	102 D1
William Horsfall St HUDS HD4	190 C8
William Prince Gv WKFDE WF1	11 E5
William Ri MSTN/BAR LS15	103 G3
William St AIRE BD20	26 D6
Williamson St HFAX HX1	8 B3
Williams Rd AIRE BD20	26 D6

William St BFD BD1	4
BOW BD4	97
BOW BD4	120
BRIG HD6	168
CAS WF10	153
CAS WF10	154
CUL/QBY * BD13	92
DEWS WF13	145
DEWS WF13	171
EARL * WF12	172
HDGY LS6	78
HUD HD1	13
HUDS HD4	190
LVSG WF15	144
MOR LS27	123
PDSY/CALV LS28	98
WBSY BD6	118
WKFDE WF1	11
William Vw MSTN/BAR LS15	103
Willis St OSM LS9	102
Willoughby Ter BEE/HOL LS11	6
Willow Ap BULY LS4	6
Willow Av BSPA/BRAM LS23	42
BULY LS4	6
ECHL BD2	74
Willow Bank HFAX HX1	8
HUDW * HD3	190
TOD OL14	134
Willow Bank Dr PONT WF8	181
Willowbank Gv HUDE HD5	192
Willow Beck HOR/CROF WF4	221
Willowbridge La CAS WF10	152
Willowbridge Wy CAS WF10	152
Willow Cl BULY LS4	6
CLECK BD19	144
ILK LS29	32
LUD/ILL HX2	139
WBSY BD6	118
Willow Clough RPDN/SBR HX6	187
Willow Ct BTLY WF17	146
FEA/AMT WF7	179
OT LS21	35
WKFDW/WTN WF2	174
Willow Crs BSPA/BRAM LS23	42
ECHL BD2	74
MSTN/BAR LS15	104
NORM WF6	177
RPDN/SBR HX6	139
Willow Cft CLECK BD19	143
Willow Dene Av LUD/ILL HX2	139
Willowdene La PONT WF8	154
Willow Dene Rd CUD/GR S72	240
Willow Dr HEM/SK/SE WF9	224
LUD/ILL HX2	139
WBSY BD6	118
Willowfield Av LUD/ILL HX2	139
Willowfield Cl LUD/ILL HX2	139
Willowfield Crs IDLE BD10	74
LUD/ILL HX2	139
Willowfield Dr LUD/ILL HX2	139
Willowfield Rd LUD/ILL HX2	139
Willow Flds KBTN HD8	193
Willowfield St GTHN BD7	95
Willowfield Ter LUD/ILL HX2	139
Willowfield Vw LUD/ILL HX2	139
Willow Gdns CAS WF10	154
ECHL BD2	74
GSLY LS20	37
WKFDW/WTN WF2	174
Willow Garth HEM/SK/SE WF9	42
Willowgarth Cl HOR/CROF WF4	222
Willow Gld BSPA/BRAM LS23	42
Willow Gn WKFDE WF1	149
Willow Gv BSPA/BRAM LS23	42
ECHL BD2	74
GFTH/SHER LS25	105
MAR/SLWT HD7	189
OSS WF5	173
Willow Hall Dr RPDN/SBR HX6	139
Willow Hall La RPDN/SBR HX6	139
Willow La BSPA/BRAM LS23	42
FEA/AMT WF7	179
HUD HD1	12
NORM WF6	177
WKFDW/WTN WF2	174
Willow La East FEA/AMT WF7	179
HUD HD1	13
Willow Ms WKFDW/WTN WF2	174
Willow Mt WKFDW/WTN WF2	174
Willow Pk PONT WF8	181
WKFDE WF1	175
Willow Ri KBTN HD8	236
LUD/ILL HX2	139
Willow Rd BTLY WF17	146
BULY LS4	6
CAS WF10	153
KNOT WF11	156
PDSY/CALV LS28	98
WKFDW/WTN WF2	174
The Willows AL/HA/HU LS17	79
BGLY BD16	71
HOR/CROF WF4	197
LUD/ILL HX2	115
Willow St CLECK BD19	144
GIR BD8	4
HFAX HX1	8
RPDN/SBR HX6	139
Willow Terrace Rd LDSU LS2	6
Willow Tree Cl KGHY BD21	3

illow Tree Gdns *BGLY* BD16 ....50 C6
ILK LS29 ....32 B2
illow V *WBY* LS22 ....23 H4
illow Vls *IDLE* BD10 ....74 C5
illow Well *WK* LVSG WF15 ....144 D8
illow Well Rd *MSTN/BAR* LS15 ....103 H5
ills *GIL* GSLY LS20 ....53 H2
illwood Av *HUDW* HD3 ....190 B4
ilman Dr *OSS* WF5 ....173 H5
ilman Post *OSS* WF5 ....173 H5
ilmer Dr *HTON* BD9 ....73 G7
ilmington Gv *CHAL* LS7 ....79 J8
ilmington St *CHAL* * LS7 ....7 F1
ilmington Ter *CHAL* LS7 ....7 F1
ilmot Rd *ILK* LS29 ....20 C7
ilsden Hill Rd *WIL/AL* BD15 ....71 H6
ilsden Old Rd *BGLY* BD16 ....71 F2
ilsden Rd *BGLY* BD16 ....71 F2
WIL/AL BD15 ....71 J8
ilshaw Mill Rd *HOLM/MEL* HD9 ...232 A3
ilshaw Rd *HOLM/MEL* HD9 ....232 A3
ilson Av *AIRE* BD20 ....26 D5
MIRF WF14 ....170 C6
OSS WF5 ....174 B7
ilson Cl *TOD* OL14 ....133 K4
ilson Ct *WKFDE* WF1 ....149 K7
ilson Dr *WKFDE* WF1 ....149 J7
ilson Rd *BGLY* BD16 ....49 K7
HFAX HX1 ....8 A4
LM/WK BD12 ....118 E2
MIRF WF14 ....170 C6
ilson St *AIRE* BD20 ....26 A6
CAS WF10 ....153 H3
FEA/AMT WF7 ....179 H6
GIR BD8 ....4 A2
PONT * WF8 ....180 E2
ilsons Yd *PDSY/CALV* LS28 ....98 B2
ilson Ter *MIRF* WF14 ....170 C6
ilson Wood St *BTLY* WF17 ....146 A8
ilton Av *HUDN* HD2 ....169 F5
ilton Gv *HUDU* HD3 ....78 E5
ilton Rd *ILK* LS29 ....20 A8
ilton St *BRIG* HD6 ....142 A8
EARL WF12 ....172 C4
ilton Ter *CLECK* BD19 ....144 A4
mborne Dr *HWTH* BD22 ....47 G3
WKFDE WF1 ....4 B5
ilson St *BOW* * BD4 ....5 E6
HEM/SK/SE WF9 ....242 C1
HFAX * HX1 ....9 D5
Windsor Vw *EARL* WF12 ....177 F1
HBR HX7 ....112 B7
Windsor Wk *BRIG* HD6 ....116 A5
Windy Bank La *HIPP* HX3 ....116 A5
LVSG WF15 ....143 J7
Windy Gv *WIL/AL* BD15 ....71 H8
Windy Harbour La *TOD* OL14 ......134 A2
Windy Ridg *CUL/QBY* BD13 ....93 G4
Windyridge St *HOR/CROF* WF4 ...197 F2
Wine St *LDS* LS1 ....7 D3
Wine Tavern La *RPDN/SBR* HX6 ..137 J8
Wine Tavern Rd *RPDN/SBR* HX6 .137 J8
Winfield Dr *HUDW* HD3 ....189 K3
Winfield Gv *LDSU* LS2 ....7 D1
Winfield Pl *LDSU* LS2 ....7 D1
Winfield Rd *BIRK/DRI* BD11 ....120 B5
Winfield Ter *LDSU* * LS2 ....7 D1
Wingate Av *HWTH* BD22 ....2 A4
Wingate Cft *WKFDW/WTN* WF2 .199 H3
Wingate Gv *WKFDW/WTN* WF2 .199 G3
Wingate Wy *HWTH* BD22 ....2 A4
Winget Av *HUDS* HD4 ....189 K8
Wingfield Ct *BGLY* BD16 ....50 A7
Wingfield Mt *BFDE* BD3 ....5 F3
Wingfield St *BFDE* BD3 ....5 F3
Winnard Rw *WBOW* * BD5 ....96 B8
Winney Bank La *HOLM/MEL* HD9 .233 H6
Winnipeg Pl *CHAL* LS7 ....79 K5
Winnow La *BSPA/BRAM* LS23 ....42 B4
Winrose Ap *MID* LS10 ....125 F4
Winrose Av *MID* LS10 ....124 E5
Winrose Cl *LM/WK* BD12 ....118 D7
Winrose Crs *MID* LS10 ....124 E3
Winrose Dr *MID* LS10 ....124 E3
Winrose Garth *MID* LS10 ....124 E3
Winrose Gv *MID* LS10 ....125 F2
Winrose Hl *MID* LS10 ....125 F2
Winsford Dr *HUDE* HD5 ....192 D4
Winslow Av *IDLE* BD10 ....75 G7
Winstanley Ter *HDCY* LS6 ....78 E8
Winston Av *EARD* BD20 ....26 A4
Winston Gdns *HDCY* LS6 ....78 C6
Winston Mt *HDCY* LS6 ....78 C6
Winston Ter *GTHN* BD7 ....95 G6
Winter Av *BSLYN/ROY* S71 ....222 A6
Winterbourne Av *MOR* LS27 ....123 G5
Winterburn La *LUD/ILL* HX2 ....138 D5
Winterburn St *KGHY* BD21 ....3 D2
Winterbutlee Gv *TOD* OL14 ....159 K2
Winterbutlee Rd *TOD* OL14 ....159 K2
Winter Ct *WIL/AL* BD15 ....72 A8
Winter Hl *HUDW* * HD3 ....190 E8
Wintersett La *HOR/CROF* WF4 ....200 E7
Winter's La *HBR* HX7 ....135 H1
Winter St *HFAX* HX1 ....8 A6
Winterton Dr *LM/WK* BD12 ....118 D6
Winthorpe Av *EARD/LOFT* WF3 ...124 E8
Winthorpe Crs *EARD/LOFT* WF3 .148 E1
Winton St *HUD* HD1 ....190 E8
Wintoun St *CHAL* LS7 ....7 F2
Wistons La *ELL* HX5 ....167 F4
Witchfield Hl *HIPP* HX3 ....117 J5
Witham Rd *SHPY* BD18 ....72 E3
Witham Wy *GFTH/SHER* LS25 .....106 A5
Withens End La *GTL/HWG* HX4 ....187 G4
Withens Hill Cft *LUD/ILL* HX2 ......187 H3
Withens La *GTL/HWG* HX4 ....187 H3
HBR HX7 ....136 A8
Withens New Rd *HBR* HX7 ....161 J1
LUD/ILL HX2 ....114 C1
Withens Rd *BTLY* WF17 ....145 H1
LUD/ILL HX2 ....114 C1
Within Flds *HIPP* HX3 ....141 F7
Withins Cl *GTHN* BD7 ....118 C1
Withyside *HUDN* HD8 ....236 E5
Witmore St *HEM/SK/SE* WF9 ......226 C8

MSTN/BAR LS15 ....103 K3
STKB/PEN S36 ....251 K7
Windsor Cl *EARL* WF12 ....147 G8
GFTH/SHER LS25 ....129 F1
NORM WF6 ....178 B2
Windsor Ct *AL/HA/HU* LS17 ....80 A1
Windsor Crs *HWTH* BD22 ....68 D1
LUD/ILL HX2 ....139 H2
RTHW LS26 ....126 B5
WKFDE WF1 ....149 J7
Windsor Dr *HUDE* HD5 ....192 C5
KBTN HD8 ....237 F2
KNOT WF11 ....155 J6
LVSG WF15 ....170 D1
Windsor Gdns *EARL* WF12 ....147 G8
Windsor Gn *GFTH/SHER* LS25 ....106 B4
Windsor Gv *CUL/QBY* BD13 ....93 C5
HWTH BD22 ....68 D1
Windsor Mt *MSTN/BAR* LS15 ......103 K3
Windsor Pl *HUDN* HD2 ....169 F6
Windsor Ri *PONT* WF8 ....180 C6
Windsor Rd *BTLY* WF17 ....145 K2
EARL WF12 ....173 F1
HBR HX7 ....112 B7
HEM/SK/SE WF9 ....225 F5
HUDS HD4 ....189 K8
HWTH BD22 ....68 D1
SHPY * BD18 ....72 E3
TOD OL14 ....133 K5
WKFDE WF1 ....175 G1
Windsor St *BOW* * BD4 ....5 E6
HEM/SK/SE WF9 ....242 C1
HFAX * HX1 ....9 D5

Witton St *WKFDE* WF1 ....10 C2
Woburn Dr *HUDE* HD5 ....192 D5
Woburn Ter *CLAY* BD14 ....94 B7
Wold Cl *CUL/QBY* BD13 ....93 H5
Wolfstones Rd *HOLM/MEL* HD9 ...232 C5
Wolley Av *WOR/ARM* LS12 ....99 H8
Wolley Cl *WOR/ARM* LS12 ....99 H8
Wolley Dr *WOR/ARM* LS12 ....99 H8
Wolley Gdns *WOR/ARM* LS12 ....99 H8
Wolseley Rd *BULY* LS4 ....100 D2
Wolseley St *CLAY* BD14 ....94 C6
Wolseley Ter *HFAX* * HX1 ....8 A3
Wolsey Av *PONT* WF8 ....180 C3
Wolston Cl *BOW* BD4 ....120 B1
Womersley Pl *PDSY/CALV* LS28 .....98 B5
Womersley Rd *KNOT* WF11 ....156 D8
Womersley St *HFAX* HX1 ....8 A4
Wonder St *WKFDE* WF1 ....11 D4
Woodacre Crs *AL/HA/HU* LS17 ......40 A8
Woodacre Gn *AL/HA/HU* LS17 ......40 A7
Woodacre La *AL/HA/HU* LS17 ....40 A7
Woodale Av *HTON* BD9 ....72 D8
Wood Av *HECK* WF16 ....145 G6
Woodbine Av *PONT* WF8 ....180 D3
Woodbine Gv *IDLE* BD10 ....74 D4
Woodbine Rd *HUDN* HD2 ....13 D1
Woodbine St *BFDE* BD3 ....5 E4
HFAX HX1 ....8 E2
OSS WF5 ....173 J4
Woodbine Ter *BRAM* * LS13 ....77 G8
HDGY LS6 ....78 E5
HFAX * HX1 ....8 B6
IDLE BD10 ....74 D4
TOD OL14 ....132 E2
Wood Bottom La *BRIG* HD6 ....141 K6
Wood Bottom Rd *HUDS* HD4 ....212 B6
Woodbourne Av *AL/HA/HU* LS17 ...79 J2
Woodbridge Av *GFTH/SHER* LS25 .106 C2
Woodbridge Cl *HDGY* LS6 ....78 B6
WKFDE WF1 ....11 E3
Woodbridge Crs *HDGY* LS6 ....78 A5
Woodbridge Fold *HDGY* LS6 ....78 A6
Woodbridge Gdns *HDGY* LS6 ....78 A5
Woodbridge Garth *HDGY* LS6 ....78 B6
Woodbridge Gn *HDGY* LS6 ....78 A6
Woodbridge Lawn *HDGY* LS6 ....78 A6
Woodbridge Pl *HDGY* LS6 ....78 A6
Woodbridge Rd *HDGY* LS6 ....78 A6
Woodbridge V *HDGY* LS6 ....78 A6
Woodbrook Av *LUD/ILL* HX2 ....115 F6
Woodbrook Cl *LUD/ILL* HX2 ....115 F6
Woodbrook Pl *LUD/ILL* HX2 ....115 F6
Woodbrook Rd *LUD/ILL* HX2 ....115 F6
Woodburn Av *EARL* WF12 ....172 E6
Woodbury Rd *GIR* BD8 ....95 H1
Woodchurch Vw *HOLM/MEL* HD9 .233 H3
Wood Cl *BAIL* BD17 ....73 H1
BHP/TINH LS16 ....56 D8
CHAL LS7 ....79 J4
HEM/SK/SE WF9 ....224 A1
NORM WF6 ....151 H8
Woodcock St *WKFDE* WF1 ....11 D6
Woodcott Av *BAIL* BD17 ....73 K1
Wood Crs *RTHW* LS26 ....126 A5
Wood Cft *BRIG* HD6 ....168 A2
RPDN/SBR HX6 ....138 B8
Woodcroft *WKFDW/WTN* WF2 ....199 G2
Woodcross *MOR* LS27 ....123 F5
Woodcross End *MOR* LS27 ....123 F4
Woodcross Fold *MOR* LS27 ....123 F5
Woodcross Gdns *MOR* LS27 ....123 F5
Woodcross Garth *MOR* LS27 ....123 F4
Wood Dr *RTHW* LS26 ....125 K5
Woodedge Av *HUDE* HD5 ....192 C5
Woodend *CAS* WF10 ....128 E5
Wood End *HUDS* HD4 ....191 F8
Wood End Cl *HIPP* HX3 ....140 C8
Woodend Cottages *MIRF* * WF14 ..170 C7
Woodend Ct *WBOW* BD5 ....119 G1
Woodend Crs *CAS* WF10 ....128 E6
Wood End Crs *SHPY* BD18 ....73 K3
Wood End La *KBTN* HD8 ....234 E4
Wood End Rd *HUDS* HD4 ....212 E3
Woodend Rd *MIRF* WF14 ....170 C7
Wood Farm La *HOLM/MEL* HD9 ...233 J1
Woodfield Av *BTLY* WF17 ....145 K7
GTL/HWG HX4 ....166 A4
Woodfield Cl *IDLE* BD10 ....74 D3
Woodfield Cottages *HIPP* * HX3 ......8 C2
Woodfield Ct *HUDN* * HD2 ....12 B2
Woodfield Dr *GTL/HWG* HX4 ....166 A5
Woodfield Pk *WKFDW/WTN* WF2 .199 J5
Woodfield Rd *CUL/QBY* BD13 ....70 C4
PONT WF8 ....227 K3
Woodford Av *HIPP* HX3 ....140 C7
Woodford Cl *WIL/AL* BD15 ....94 A3
Woodford Dr *HUDE* HD5 ....192 C4
Woodgarth Gdns *BOW* BD4 ....97 H8
Wood Gn *CAS* WF10 ....152 E6
Wood Gv *OSS* WF5 ....173 J3
WOR/ARM LS12 ....99 G3
Woodhall Av *BFDE* BD3 ....97 G3
KSTL LS5 ....77 J5
Woodhall Cl *HOR/CROF* WF4 ....196 A5
PDSY/CALV LS28 ....97 J1
Woodhall Ct *MSTN/BAR* LS15 .....104 B5
PDSY/CALV LS28 ....75 J6
Woodhall Cft *PDSY/CALV* LS28 ......97 J1

Woodhall Dr *BTLY* WF17	**145** K7
FEA/AMT WF7	**203** F5
KSTL LS5	**77** J5
Woodhall Gv *RTHW* LS26	**128** C8
Woodhall La *AWLS/ASK* DN6	**183** K8
PDSY/CALV LS28	**75** J8
Woodhall Park Av *PDSY/CALV* LS28	**97** J1
Woodhall Park Cft	
PDSY/CALV LS28	**97** J2
Woodhall Park Crs West	
PDSY/CALV LS28	**97** J2
Woodhall Park Cft	
PDSY/CALV * LS28	**97** K2
Woodhall Park Dr *PDSY/CALV* LS28	**97** J2
Woodhall Park Gv *PDSY/CALV* LS28	**97** J2
Woodhall Park Mt *PDSY/CALV* LS28	**97** J1
Woodhall Pl *BFDE* BD3	**97** G2
Woodhall Rd *BFDE* BD3	**97** G3
PDSY/CALV LS28	**75** G8
Woodhall Ter *BFDE* BD3	**97** G3
Woodhall Vw *BFDE* BD3	**97** H2
Woodhead Cl *HUDN* HD2	**168** D8
MOR LS27	**122** B4
Woodhead Rd *BTLY* WF17	**122** A8
GTHN BD7	**95** H5
HOLM/MEL HD9	**215** G8
HOLM/MEL HD9	**233** H3
HOLM/MEL HD9	**246** C6
Woodhead St *CLECK* BD19	**144** B5
LUD/ILL HX2	**139** H3
Wood Hey La *HBR* HX7	**136** C2
Wood Hl *RTHW* LS26	**126** A5
Wood Hill Ct *BHP/TINH* LS16	**55** H7
Wood Hill Crs *BHP/TINH* LS16	**55** G8
Wood Hill Gdns *BHP/TINH* LS16	**55** H7
Wood Hill Ri *BHP/TINH* LS16	**55** H7
Woodhill Rl *IDLE* BD10	**75** G3
Wood Hill Rd *BHP/TINH* LS16	**55** H7
Woodhill Vw *WBY* LS22	**23** J5
Woodhouse Av *HUDN* HD2	**191** J1
KGHY BD21	**3** D5
Woodhouse Cliff *HDGY* LS6	**79** G8
Woodhouse Cl *EARD/LOFT* WF3	**148** C5
KGHY BD21	**3** D5
Woodhouse Crs *NORM* WF6	**178** A3
Woodhouse Dr *KGHY* BD21	**3** D6
Woodhouse Gdns *BRIG* HD6	**168** D3
Woodhouse Gv *HUDN* HD2	**191** H1
KGHY BD21	**3** D5
TOD OL14	**134** C6
Woodhouse Hall Rd *HUDN* HD2	**191** J1
Woodhouse Hl *HUDN* HD2	**191** J1
Woodhouse Hill Av *MID* * LS10	**125** F1
Woodhouse Hill Gv *MID* LS10	**125** F1
Woodhouse Hill Pl *MID* LS10	**125** F1
Woodhouse Hill Rd *MID* LS10	**125** F1
Woodhouse Hill Ter * LS10	**125** F1
Woodhouse La *BRIG* HD6	**168** D3
DOD/DAR S75	**220** D6
HDGY LS6	**79** G8
HIPP HX3	**139** K8
HOLM/MEL HD9	**247** J2
KBTN HD8	**217** K4
LDSU LS2	**7** E2
WKFDW/WTN WF2	**148** B8
Woodhouse Mt *NORM* WF6	**177** K3
Woodhouse Rd *KGHY* BD21	**2** C5
TOD OL14	**134** D6
WKFDE WF1	**11** E3
Woodhouse Sq *BVRD* LS3	**6** C3
Woodhouse St *HDGY* LS6	**79** G8
Woodhouse Ter *WBSY* BD6	**118** E3
Woodhouse Wk *KGHY* BD21	**3** D5
Woodhouse Wy *KGHY* BD21	**3** D5
Woodkirk Av *EARD/LOFT* WF3	**147** H3
Woodkirk Gdns *EARL* WF12	**147** G6
Woodkirk Gv *EARD/LOFT* WF3	**147** J3
LM/WK BD12	**142** D2
Woodland Av *RTHW* LS26	**127** J2
WKFDE WF1	**177** F4
Woodland Ct *HOR/CROF* WF4	**220** B1
HTON BD9	**72** C7
MSTN/BAR LS15	**104** A3
RHAY LS8	**80** B6
Woodland Crs *BGLY* BD16	**49** H6
RTHW LS26	**126** A4
RTHW LS26	**127** K2
Woodland Dr *BRIG* HD6	**142** A8
CHAL LS7	**79** K4
KBTN HD8	**237** F2
LUD/ILL HX2	**139** G6
RTHW LS26	**127** J2
WKFDW/WTN WF2	**199** F5
Woodland Gv *CHAL* LS7	**80** A7
DEWS WF13	**171** J3
FEA/AMT WF7	**203** G2
HTON BD9	**72** C6
RTHW LS26	**127** J2
Woodland Hl *MSTN/BAR* LS15	**103** K3
Woodland La *CHAL* LS7	**79** K4
Woodland Meadow *KBTN* HD8	**215** H4
Woodland Mt *CHAL* * LS7	**80** A7
Woodland Pk *RTHW* LS26	**127** F6
Woodland Park Rd *HDGY* LS6	**78** E6
Woodland Ri *MSTN/BAR* LS15	**104** A3
WKFDW/WTN WF2	**174** E6
Woodland Rd *HUDN* HD2	**192** B1
MSTN/BAR LS15	**103** K3
WKFDW/WTN WF2	**174** E6

Woodlands *BAIL* * BD17	**52** A7
EARD/LOFT WF3	**148** D4
HOR/CROF WF4	**197** J1
HOR/CROF WF4	**200** C1
HWTH * BD22	**68** E1
ILK LS29	**20** D7
OSS WF5	**173** J4
RPDN/SBR HX6	**164** C1
Woodlands Av *CAS* WF10	**154** D5
CLECK BD19	**144** D2
HIPP HX3	**9** D2
HOLM/MEL HD9	**233** J3
PDSY/CALV LS28	**98** A2
TOD OL14	**134** A5
Woodlands Cl *EARD/LOFT* WF3	**148** D4
HUDN HD2	**169** H5
IDLE BD10	**75** H2
ILK LS29	**19** J7
KBTN HD8	**236** E5
SCFT LS14	**60** A3
Woodlands Ct *BHP/TINH* LS16	**78** B2
HEM/SK/SE WF9	**224** E3
Woodlands Cft *GFTH/SHER* LS25	**129** C8
Woodlands Dr *CLECK* BD19	**144** D2
EARD/LOFT WF3	**148** C4
GFTH/SHER LS25	**106** B5
IDLE BD10	**75** H2
MOR LS27	**122** E5
Woodlands Fold *BIRK/DRI* BD11	**120** E6
Woodlands Gv *BAIL* BD17	**73** F1
BGLY BD16	**72** B4
CUL/QBY BD13	**117** F2
GFTH/SHER LS25	**129** H5
HIPP HX3	**9** D2
ILK LS29	**19** J7
PDSY/CALV LS28	**98** A2
Woodlands La *DEWS* WF13	**171** J3
Woodlands Mt *HIPP* HX3	**9** D1
Woodlands Pk *CLECK* BD19	**119** J8
SCFT LS14	**60** A3
Woodlands Park Rd	
PDSY/CALV LS28	**98** B6
The Woodlands *HBR* HX7	**136** B1
PONT WF8	**181** F5
RTHW LS26	**127** F6
Woodland Sq *BRIG* * HD6	**168** D2
WOR/ARM LS12	**99** K3
Woodlands Ri *HWTH* BD22	**68** C5
ILK LS29	**19** J7
Woodlands Rd *BGLY* BD16	**50** C7
BTLY WF17	**145** K3
CLECK BD19	**144** D2
CUL/QBY BD13	**117** F2
ELL HX5	**166** E3
GIR * BD8	**5** D1
HIPP HX3	**9** D2
KBTN HD8	**193** G8
Woodlands Rd East *KBTN* HD8	**193** F8
Woodlands St *GIR* BD8	**4** A3
Woodlands Ter *PDSY/CALV* LS28	**98** A2
Woodlands Vw *GFTH/SHER* LS25	**129** H5
HIPP HX3	**9** D2
Woodland Ter *CHAL* LS7	**79** C4
CUD/GR S72	**240** B6
Woodland Vw *HEM/SK/SE* * WF9	**226** A8
PDSY/CALV LS28	**75** J5
PONT WF8	**181** F5
Woodland Vls *CUD/GR* * S72	**240** A5
Wood La *AL/HA/HU* LS17	**40** B8
BRAM LS13	**77** G7
BRAM LS13	**99** H3
BSPA/BRAM LS23	**24** E8
CAS WF10	**152** E6
CHAL LS7	**79** J4
CUD/GR S72	**240** A5
DEWS WF13	**172** B1
EARL WF12	**195** G3
ECHL BD2	**74** B6
HBR HX7	**113** J5
HDGY LS6	**78** E6
HIPP HX3	**141** G2
HIPP HX3	**167** J1
HOLM/MEL HD9	**233** G5
HOR/CROF WF4	**198** C8
HORS LS18	**77** G4
HUDE HD5	**170** A7
HUDS HD4	**191** H8
HUDS HD4	**191** J8
HUDS HD4	**214** D7
KBTN HD8	**236** E5
LUD/ILL HX2	**139** G2
MAR/SLWT HD7	**210** D6
MSTN/BAR LS15	**82** C5
PDSY/CALV LS28	**75** K4
RPDN/SBR HX6	**138** B7
RTHW LS26	**126** A5
RTHW LS26	**128** D5
WOR/ARM LS12	**122** E1
Wood Lane Ct *HDGY* LS6	**78** E6
Woodlea *BSPA/BRAM* LS23	**42** D3
Wood Lea *KNOT* WF11	**156** A3
TOD OL14	**133** H5
Woodlea Ap *HDGY* LS6	**53** H6
YEA LS19	**53** H5
Woodlea Av *HDGY* LS6	**79** F2
HUDW HD3	**190** D5
Woodlea Cha *HDGY* LS6	**79** F3
Woodlea Cl *YEA* LS19	**53** H6

Woodlea Ct *HDGY* LS6	**79** F
Woodlea Cft *HDGY* LS6	**79** F
Woodlea Dr *HDGY* LS6	**79** F
YEA LS19	**53** H
Woodlea Fold *HDGY* LS6	**79**
Woodlea Gdns *HDGY* LS6	**79**
Woodlea Garth *HDGY* LS6	**79**
Woodlea Ga *HDGY* LS6	**79**
Woodlea Gn *HDGY* LS6	**79**
Woodlea Gv *BEE/HOL* * LS11	**101**
HDGY LS6	**79**
YEA LS19	**53**
Woodlea Holt *HDGY* LS6	**79**
Woodlea La *HDGY* LS6	**79**
Woodlea Lawn *HDGY* LS6	**79**
Woodlea Mt *BEE/HOL* LS11	**101**
YEA LS19	**53**
Woodlea Pk *HDGY* LS6	**79**
Woodlea Pl *BEE/HOL* LS11	**101**
Woodlea Rd *YEA* LS19	**53**
Woodlea Sq *HDGY* * LS6	**79**
Woodlea St *BEE/HOL* LS11	**101**
Woodlea Vw *HDGY* LS6	**79**
Woodleigh *EARL* * WF12	**195**
Woodleigh Av *GFTH/SHER* LS25	**105**
WBOW BD5	**119**
Woodleigh Crs *FEA/AMT* WF7	**203**
Woodleigh Hall Vw *YEA* * LS19	**76**
Woodlesford Crs *LUD/ILL* HX2	**138**
Woodleigh Gv *HUDS* * HD4	**212**
Woodliffe Ct *CHAL* LS7	**79**
Woodliffe Dr *CHAL* LS7	**79**
Woodman Av *ELL* HX5	**166**
HUDN HD2	**169**
Woodman St *MSTN/BAR* LS15	**103**
Woodmoor Cl *HOR/CROF* WF4	**197**
Woodmoor Dr *HOR/CROF* WF4	**197**
Woodmoor Ri *HOR/CROF* WF4	**197**
Wood Moor Rd *HEM/SK/SE* WF9	**225**
Woodmoor Rd *WKFDW/WTN* WF2	**198**
Wood Mt *HOR/CROF* WF4	**195**
RTHW LS26	**125**
Woodnook Cl *BHP/TINH* LS16	**77**
Woodnook Dr *BHP/TINH* LS16	**77**
Woodnook Garth *BHP/TINH* LS16	**77**
Wood Nook La *HOLM/MEL* HD9	**232**
RPDN/SBR HX6	**139**
Woodnook Rd *BHP/TINH* LS16	**55**
Wood Nook Ter *PDSY/CALV* LS28	**98**
Woodpecker Rd *ILK* LS29	**31**
Wood Pl *BEE/HOL* LS11	**101**
GIR BD8	**4**
Wood Rd *HTON* BD9	**73**
WBOW BD5	**96**
Wood Rw *RTHW* LS26	**128**
Woodrow Crs *RTHW* LS26	**127**
Woodrow Dr *LM/WK* BD12	**119**
Woodroyd Av *HOLM/MEL* HD9	**213**
WBOW * BD5	**119**
Woodroyd Dr *HIPP* HX3	**139**
Woodroyd Gdns *ILK* LS29	**21**
RPDN/SBR HX6	**138**
Wood Royd Hill La *HOLM/MEL* HD9	**249**
Woodroyd Rd *WBOW* BD5	**96**
Woodroyd Ter *WBOW* BD5	**96**
Woodside *CAS* WF10	**154**
KBTN HD8	**236**
KGHY BD21	**2**
SHPY BD18	**73**
WKFDW/WTN WF2	**175**
Woodside Av *BGLY* BD16	**71**
BULY LS4	**100**
CHAL LS7	**79**
HOR/CROF WF4	**178**
SHPY BD18	**72**
WKFDW/WTN WF2	**175**
Woodside Cl *MOR* LS27	**123**
Woodside Ct *CUL/QBY* BD13	**70**
HORS LS18	**77**
Woodside Crs *BGLY* BD16	**71**
BTLY WF17	**145**
HIPP HX3	**8**
HOR/CROF WF4	**178**
Woodside Dr *BGLY* BD16	**71**
MOR LS27	**123**
WKFDW/WTN WF2	**175**
Woodside Gdns *MOR* LS27	**123**
Woodside Gv *CAS* WF10	**128**
GTL/HWG HX4	**166**
HIPP HX3	**9**
Woodside Hill Cl *HORS* LS18	**77**
Woodside La *HUDN* HD2	**168**
MOR LS27	**123**
Woodside Ldg *HUDS* HD4	**214**
Woodside Ms *CHAL* LS7	**79**
Woodside Mt *HFAX* HX1	**8**
Woodside Park Av *HORS* LS18	**77**
Woodside Park Dr *HORS* LS18	**77**
Woodside Pl *BULY* LS4	**100**
HIPP HX3	**8**
Woodside Rd *AIRE* BD20	**26**
BSPA/BRAM LS23	**42**
HFAX HX1	**8**
HUDS HD4	**214**
LM/WK BD12	**118**
Woodside St *CAS* WF10	**128**
Woodside Ter *BULY* LS4	**100**

HIPP HX3 .....9 D2
'oodside Veiw HUDS HD4 .....189 K8
'oodside Vw BGLY BD16 .....71 K4
BULY LS4 .....100 C3
HIPP HX3 .....8 C2
HOLM/MEL HD9 .....252 D7
oodsley Gn HDCY LS6 .....6 B1
oodsley Rd BVRD LS3 .....6 A2
IDLE BD10 .....74 C5
oodsley Ter LDSU LS2 .....6 C2
oodsome Av MIRF WF14 .....170 B5
'oodsome Dr KBTN HD8 .....215 F11
MIRF WF14 .....170 C5
oodsome Hall La KBTN HD8 .....214 E2
oodsome Lees La KBTN HD8 .....215 F11
oodsome Pk KBTN HD8 .....214 B4
ood Sq HIPP HX3 .....8 C1
ood's Rw PDSY/CALV LS28 .....98 C2
oodstock Cs HUDW HD3 .....190 B3
oodstock Wk WBOW * BD5 .....4 C6
ood St AIRE BD20 .....26 E6
BAIL BD17 .....73 J2
BGLY BD16 .....49 J5
BRIG HD6 .....168 C1
BTLY WF17 .....146 B7
CAS WF10 .....153 H3
CLECK BD19 .....143 K4
CUD/GR S72 .....223 J5
DEWS WF13 .....172 C2
EARD/LOFT WF3 .....148 E3
ELL HX5 .....167 F5
GIR * BD8 .....4 A3
HOR/CROF WF4 .....178 A7
HUDW HD3 .....189 K5
KBTN HD8 .....236 D1
KBTN HD8 .....237 H2
KGHY BD21 .....3 D4
MAR/SLWT HD7 .....210 D2
MOR LS27 .....122 E6
OSS WF5 .....173 J4
WIL/AL BD15 .....94 C2
WKFDE WF1 .....10 B1
ood St North HIPP * HX3 .....8 C1
ood Ter HUDS HD4 .....191 G8
oodthorpe Ct AL/HA/HU LS17 .....58 B7
oodthorpe Dr WKFDW/WTN WF2 .....199 G4
oodthorpe Dr WKFDW/WTN WF2 .....199 G4
oodthorpe Glades
WKFDW/WTN WF2 .....199 F4
oodthorpe Park Dr
WKFDW/WTN WF2 .....199 F4
oodthorpe Ter HUD HD1 .....12 B5
ood Top BRIG HD6 .....141 K6
ood Top Rd HWTH HX7 .....136 C1
oodvale Cl BOW BD4 .....97 G6
oodvale Gv BGLY BD16 .....50 A6
oodvale Gv GTHN BD7 .....94 E6
oodvale Rd BRIG HD6 .....142 C8
oodvale Wy CLAY BD14 .....94 E6
oodview BIRK/DRI BD11 .....121 G4
ood Vw HUDN HD2 .....190 D1
HWTH * BD22 .....2 A6
MOR LS27 .....123 H5
oodview Av BAIL BD17 .....52 B7
ood View Cl CAS WF10 .....153 H4
ood View Cl HORS LS18 .....77 G1
oodview Cl HORS LS18 .....77 G1
ood View Crs CAS WF10 .....153 H3
ood View Dr ECHL BD2 .....96 E1
oodview Gv BEE/HOL LS11 .....124 C1
ood View Gv HORS LS18 .....142 A7
oodview Mt BEE/HOL LS11 .....124 C1
oodview Rd BEE/HOL LS11 .....124 C1
HWTH BD22 .....2 A6
oodview St BEE/HOL LS11 .....124 C1
oodview Ter BEE/HOL LS11 .....124 C1
ood View Ter KGHY BD21 .....2 C6
oodville Av HORS LS18 .....77 H3
MAR/SLWT * HD7 .....189 J7
odville Ct RHAY LS8 .....80 C2
WKFDW/WTN WF2 .....198 E1
oodville Crs HORS * LS18 .....77 H2
oodville Gv HORS * LS18 .....77 H3
HWTH BD22 .....69 H3
MID * LS10 .....125 F2
oodville Pl HORS LS18 .....77 J2
HTON BD9 .....73 F7
HUDN HD2 .....169 F5
oodville Rd EARL WF12 .....172 C3
CGHY BD21 .....2 C2
oodville Sq MID LS10 .....125 F2
oodville St HIPP HX3 .....8 B2
HORS LS18 .....77 J2
HPY BD18 .....73 K3
oodville Ter HORS LS18 .....77 H3
VBOW BD5 .....4 B6
ood Vine Rd PDSY/CALV LS28 .....98 A2
ood Wk BSLYN/ROY S71 .....222 A6
odward Ct MIRF WF14 .....170 E4
ORS LS18 .....77 G4
oodway Dr HORS LS18 .....77 G4
oodway BGLY BD16 .....71 K4
odworth Gv KGHY BD21 .....47 K8
olcomb Ct HTON BD9 .....95 G1
olcroft Dr HOLM/MEL HD9 .....233 J5
oldale Cliff Rd HOLM/MEL HD9 .....233 H5
oldale Rd HOLM/MEL HD9 .....233 J4

Wooler Av BEE/HOL LS11 .....124 B1
Wooler Dr BEE/HOL LS11 .....124 B1
Wooler Gv BEE/HOL LS11 .....124 B1
Wooler Pl BEE/HOL LS11 .....124 A1
Wooler Rd BEE/HOL * LS11 .....124 A1
Wooler St BEE/HOL LS11 .....124 A1
The Wool Ex BFD * BD1 .....4 C4
Woolford Wy
EARD/LOFT WF3 .....150 A5
Woolgreaves Av WKFDW/WTN WF2 .....199 F5
Woolgreaves Cl WKFDW/WTN WF2 .....199 F4
Woolgreaves Cft
WKFDW/WTN WF2 .....199 F5
Woolgreaves Dr WKFDW/WTN WF2 .....199 F5
Woolgreaves Garth
WKFDW/WTN WF2 .....199 F5
Wooler Rd LM/WK BD12 .....118 E6
Woolley Edge La DOD/DAR S75 .....220 A6
Woolley Low Moor La
HOR/CROF WF4 .....219 K1
Woolley Park Gdns
HOR/CROF WF4 .....220 A1
Woolley Vw HOR/CROF WF4 .....220 B1
Woollin Av EARD/LOFT WF3 .....147 K6
Woollin Crs EARD/LOFT WF3 .....147 K5
Woolmarket PONT WF8 .....180 E3
Woolpack's Yd WKFDE WF1 .....10 B3
Woolrow La BRIG HD6 .....142 D5
Wool Row La KBTN HD8 .....216 A6
Woolshops HFAX * HX1 .....9 E4
Woolstock La DOD/DAR S75 .....238 D8
Wool St HECK WF16 .....145 D8
Wootton St WBOW BD5 .....95 K7
Worcester Av EARD/LOFT WF3 .....125 G7
Worcester Cl EARD/LOFT WF3 .....148 D2
Worcester Dr EARD/LOFT WF3 .....125 G7
Worcester Gv HUDS HD4 .....191 H8
Worcester Pl BOW BD4 .....94 C7
Worden Gv CLAY BD14 .....94 E7
Wordsworth Ap PONT WF8 .....154 E8
Wordsworth Ct RTHW LS26 .....127 F8
Wordsworth St KNOT WF11 .....155 J6
RTHW LS26 .....127 F8
Wordsworth Dr EARD/LOFT WF3 .....150 B6
Work Bank La STKB/PEN S36 .....252 A7
Workhouse La GTL/HWG HX4 .....166 C5
LUD/ILL HX2 .....138 D4
Wormald Rw LDS * LS1 .....7 E3
Wormald St DEWS WF13 .....172 B3
HUDE HD5 .....192 B8
LVSG WF15 .....145 F8
Worrall Rd KFDW/WTN WF2 .....198 C7
Worrall St MOR LS27 .....122 E8
Worsnop Buildings LM/WK BD12 .....118 D7
Worsnop St LM/WK BD12 .....118 E5
Worstead Rd HWTH BD22 .....69 H3
Worth Av KGHY BD21 .....3 F1
Worth Bridge Rd KGHY BD21 .....3 F2
Worthing Head Cl LM/WK BD12 .....118 D8
Worthing Head Rd LM/WK BD12 .....118 D8
Worthing St LM/WK BD12 .....118 D8
Worthington St GIR BD8 .....4 A3
Worthville Cl KGHY BD21 .....3 D5
Wortley Hts HUDW HD3 .....187 K7
HWTH BD22 .....69 J3
KGHY BD21 .....3 D4
Wortley Hts WOR/ARM LS12 .....100 C5
Wortley La WOR/ARM LS12 .....6 B5
Wortley Moor La WOR/ARM LS12 .....100 A4
Wortley Moor Rd WOR/ARM LS12 .....100 A4
Wortley Pk WOR/ARM LS12 .....6 A5
Wortley Pl HEM/SK/SE WF9 .....224 C4
Wortley Rd WOR/ARM LS12 .....100 B4
Wortley St BGLY BD16 .....50 B8
Worts Hill La HUDW HD3 .....187 F2
Worts Hill Side HUDW HD3 .....187 H2
Wrangbrook La HEM/SK/SE WF9 .....226 E5
Wrangbrook Rd HEM/SK/SE WF9 .....227 F3
Wrangthorn Av HDGY LS6 .....79 F8
Wrangthorn Pl HDGY LS6 .....79 F8
Wrangthorn Ter HDGY LS6 .....79 F8
Wrelton Cl BSLYN/ROY S71 .....221 K8
Wren Av GTHN BD7 .....94 E6
Wrenbeck Av OT LS21 .....33 J1
Wrenbeck Cl OT LS21 .....33 J1
Wrenbeck Dr OT LS21 .....33 J1
Wrenbury Av BHP/TINH LS16 .....55 H6
Wrenbury Crs BHP/TINH LS16 .....55 H6
Wrenbury Gv BHP/TINH LS16 .....55 J6
Wren Cft PONT WF8 .....154 E8
Wren Dr MOR LS27 .....123 J8
Wren Garth WKFDW/WTN WF2 .....198 E6
Wren Hl BTLY WF17 .....145 K3
Wren Nest Rd RPDN/SBR HX6 .....163 H7
Wren St HUD HD1 .....190 D6
KGHY BD21 .....3 D4
Wrenthorpe La WKFDW/WTN WF2 .....174 D7
Wrenthorpe Rd WKFDW/WTN WF2 .....175 G2
Wrexhall Rd EARL WF12 .....172 D1
Wrexham Rd ILK LS29 .....31 K2
Wright Av HWTH BD22 .....47 F8
Wrights La KNOT WF11 .....183 G4
Wright St HWTH BD22 .....69 F1
Wrigley Av BOW BD4 .....119 J2
Wrigley Hl LUD/ILL HX2 .....115 H3
Wroe Crs LM/WK BD12 .....118 D8
Wroe Pl LM/WK BD12 .....118 D8
Wroe St DEWS WF13 .....171 J2
Wroe Ter LM/WK BD12 .....118 D8

Wrose Av SHPY BD18 .....73 K5
Wrose Brow Rd SHPY BD18 .....73 K3
Wrosecliffe Gv SHPY BD18 .....74 B3
Wrose Dr SHPY BD18 .....73 K5
Wrose Gv SHPY BD18 .....73 K5
Wrose Hill Pl SHPY BD18 .....73 K6
Wrose Mt SHPY BD18 .....74 A5
Wrose Rd SHPY BD18 .....73 K5
Wrose Vw SHPY BD18 .....73 K5
Wycliffe Cl BRAM LS13 .....76 B6
Wycliffe Dr AL/HA/HU LS17 .....79 K1
Wycliffe Gdns SHPY BD18 .....73 G3
Wycliffe Rd SHPY BD18 .....73 G3
Wycliffe St OSS WF5 .....173 H4
Wycombe Gn BOW BD4 .....97 G8
Wykebeck Av OSM LS9 .....102 E4
Wykebeck Crs OSM LS9 .....103 F3
Wykebeck Gdns OSM LS9 .....103 F3
Wykebeck Gv OSM LS9 .....103 F3
Wykebeck Mt OSM LS9 .....103 F3
Wykebeck Pl OSM LS9 .....103 G3
Wykebeck Rd OSM LS9 .....103 F3
Wykebeck Sq OSM LS9 .....103 F3
Wykebeck St OSM LS9 .....103 F3
Wykebeck Ter OSM LS9 .....103 F3
Wykebeck Valley Rd OSM LS9 .....103 F1
Wykebeck Vw OSM LS9 .....103 F3
Wyke Crs LM/WK BD12 .....142 E1
Wyke La LM/WK BD12 .....142 E1
Wykelea Cl LM/WK BD12 .....142 E1
Wyke Old La BRIG HD6 .....142 C4
Wyncliffe Gdns AL/HA/HU LS17 .....79 K1
Wyncroft Gv BHP/TINH LS16 .....55 K1
Wyncroft Ri SHPY BD18 .....73 K6
Wyndham Av ECHL BD2 .....74 B8
Wynford Av BHP/TINH LS16 .....78 B2
Wynford Dr HEM/SK/SE WF9 .....226 C8
Wynford Gv BHP/TINH LS16 .....78 B2
Wynford Mt BHP/TINH LS16 .....78 A2
Wynford Ri BHP/TINH LS16 .....78 A2
Wynford Ter BHP/TINH LS16 .....78 A2
Wynford Wy WBSY BD6 .....119 F3
Wynmore Av BHP/TINH LS16 .....55 J1
Wynmore Crs BHP/TINH LS16 .....55 K1
Wynmore Dr BHP/TINH LS16 .....55 K1
HUDW HD3 .....189 K2
Wynne St GIR BD8 .....4 B3
Wynthorpe Rd HOR/CROF WF4 .....197 H2
Wynyard Dr MOR LS27 .....122 E7
Wyther La KSTL LS5 .....78 A8
Wyther La KSTL LS5 .....77 K8
Wyther Park Av WOR/ARM LS12 .....99 K2
Wyther Park Cl WOR/ARM LS12 .....99 K2
Wyther Park Crs WOR/ARM LS12 .....99 K2
Wyther Park Gv WOR/ARM LS12 .....99 K1
Wyther Park Hl WOR/ARM LS12 .....99 K1
Wyther Park Mt WOR/ARM LS12 .....99 K1
Wyther Park Rd BRAM LS13 .....99 J2
Wyther Park Sq WOR/ARM LS12 .....99 J1
Wyther Park Ter WOR/ARM LS12 .....99 J2
Wyther Park Vw WOR/ARM LS12 .....99 K1
Wyvern Av HUDW HD3 .....190 C5
Wyvern Cl BTLY WF17 .....146 B5
GTHN BD7 .....95 F5
Wyverne Rd MAR/SLWT HD7 .....189 J7
Wyvern Pl LUD/ILL HX2 .....139 H3
Wyvern Pl LUD/ILL HX2 .....139 H3
Wyvil Crs ILK LS29 .....20 E7
Wyvil Rd ILK LS29 .....20 E6

Y

Yarborough Cft HIPP HX3 .....117 F7
Yardley Wy LM/WK BD12 .....119 F5
Yard No4 BTLY WF17 .....145 J2
Yarn St MID LS10 .....102 A6
Yarwood Gv GTHN BD7 .....94 E8
Yate La HWTH BD22 .....68 E8
Yates Flat SHPY BD18 .....73 K5
Yates La HUDS HD4 .....190 A7
Yeadon Dr HIPP HX3 .....141 F7
Yeadon Moor Rd YEA LS19 .....54 C5
Ye Farre Cl BRIG HD6 .....142 A7
Yewbank Cl ILK LS29 .....20 A7
Yewbank Ter ILK LS29 .....20 A7
Yewdall Rd BRAM LS13 .....76 B6
Yewdall Wy IDLE BD10 .....74 E5
Yew Green Av HUDS HD4 .....190 E8
Yew Green Rd HUDS HD4 .....190 E8
Yew Gv HUDS HD4 .....189 K8
Yew La CFTH/SHER LS25 .....106 B5
Yews Hill Rd HUDS HD4 .....12 A6
Yews Mt HUD HD1 .....12 C1
Yew St HUDN HD2 .....12 C1
Yew Tree Av GIR BD8 .....94 D2
Yew Tree Cl SHPY BD18 .....73 J5
Yew Tree Crs GIR BD8 .....94 E2
Yew Tree Dr RTHW LS26 .....127 H5
Yew Tree La HOLM/MEL HD9 .....232 C8
MAR/SLWT HD7 .....189 K8
MAR/SLWT HD7 .....210 D3
MSTN/BAR LS15 .....104 C4
WIL/AL BD15 .....93 J3
Yew Tree Rd HUDW HD3 .....190 A1

KBTN HD8	235	H2
Yew Trees Av *HIPP* HX3	117	F8
Yew Trees Cft *LUD/ILL* HX2	137	J2
Yew Tree St *WKFDE* WF1	11	E5
Yew Tree Ter *WHIT* * OL12	158	B5
York Av *HUDN* HD2	191	G1
York Crs *BGLY* * BD16	72	A1
HECK WF16	145	G5
York Ga *OT* LS21	33	G7
OT LS21	34	C7
York Gv *BTLY* WF17	146	B5
York Pl *CLECK* BD19	144	A3
FEA/AMT WF7	203	H4
LDS LS1	7	H3
TOD OL14	134	A6
WBY LS22	23	J5
York Rd *BTLY* WF17	146	B5
EARL WF12	172	E2
ILK LS29	32	B2
OSM LS9	102	C3
SCFT LS14	81	K8
SCFT LS14	81	K6

WBY LS22	24	C4
WBY LS22	25	H2
Yorkshire Wy *GTHN* BD7	95	H8
Yorkstone *HUDS* HD4	190	B8
York St *BGLY* BD16	72	A1
BRIG HD6	168	B2
CAS WF10	153	K3
CUL/QBY BD13	116	D2
GIR BD8	94	E4
HBR HX7	136	E1
HEM/SK/SE WF9	224	E6
HFAX HX1	8	C5
NORM * WF6	151	J8
OSM LS9	7	F4
TOD OL14	134	A5
York Ter *HIPP* HX3	8	C2
York Vis *NORM* WF6	178	A1
Young's Ct *GFTH/SHER* LS25	84	E5
Young St *GIR* BD8	95	F4

Z

Zealand St *BOW* BD4	97	F
Zermatt Gv *CHAL* LS7	79	
Zermatt Mt *CHAL* * LS7	79	
Zermatt St *CHAL* LS7	79	K
Zermatt Ter *CHAL* LS7	79	K
Zetland Pl *RHAY* LS8	80	E
Zetland St *HUD* HD1	13	C
WKFDE WF1	10	C
Zion Cl *HUDW* HD3	190	E
Zion Ter *HBR* HX7	137	F
Zoar St *MOR* LS27	123	F

Index - featured places

A1 Business Park
KNOT WF11 ... 155 K8

Abbey Grange CE High School
BHP/TINH LS16 ... 77 K3

Abbey House Museum
KSTL LS5 ... 77 K6

Abbey Park School
LUD/ILL HX2 ... 115 G5

ABC Cinema
HFAX HX1 ... 9 D5

Aberford CE Primary School
GFTH/SHER LS25 ... 84 E4

Abraham Ormerod Day Hospital
TOD OL14 ... 134 A6

Ackton Pastures Primary School
CAS WF10 ... 153 G5

Ackworth Business Park
FEA/AMT WF7 ... 202 E2

Ackworth School
FEA/AMT WF7 ... 203 G4

Acorn Business Park
SCFT LS14 ... 103 G2

Acorn Park Industrial Estate
BAIL BD17 ... 74 A1

Addingham Cricket Club
ILK LS29 ... 18 C3

Addingham Middle School
ILK LS29 ... 18 D2

Addingham Primary School
ILK LS29 ... 18 C2

Adel Primary School
BHP/TINH LS16 ... 56 E8

Adult Education Centre
BRIG HD6 ... 142 B8

Adwalton Cricket Club
BIRK/DRI BD11 ... 121 J6

Adwalton Moor Business Park
BOW BD4 ... 120 E4

Agnes Stewart CE High School
OSM LS9 ... 102 A3

Ainley Industrial Estate
ELL HX5 ... 167 F6

Aireborough Leisure Centre
GSLY LS20 ... 53 G2

Aire & Calder Industrial Park
CAS WF10 ... 153 K2

The Aire & Calder Industrial Park
CAS WF10 ... 153 J2

Airedale Centre
KGHY BD21 ... 3 D3

Airedale Clinic
CAS WF10 ... 154 D4

Airedale Community Business Centre
CAS WF10 ... 154 C3

Airedale Community Campus
CAS WF10 ... 154 E4

Airedale General Hospital
AIRE BD20 ... 26 C5

Airedale Junior School
CAS WF10 ... 154 D4

Aireside Business Centre
LDS LS1 ... 7 D4

Aireside Retail Park
WOR/ARM LS12 ... 6 C4

Aire Valley Business Centre
KGHY BD21 ... 3 D2

Aire Valley Clinic
AIRE BD20 ... 26 E6

Aireview Business Centre
BAIL BD17 ... 73 G3

Aire View Infant School
AIRE BD20 ... 27 F2

Aireview Primary School
BRAM LS13 ... 76 C7

Albion Mills Retail Park
WKFDW/WTN WF2 ... 10 B3

Alhambra Theatre
GTHN BD7 ... 4 B5

Allerton Bywater Business Park
CAS WF10 ... 129 J7

Allerton Bywater Infant School
CAS WF10 ... 129 G7

Allerton Bywater Primary School
CAS WF10 ... 129 G6

Allerton Clinic
WIL/AL BD15 ... 94 B3

Allerton First & Middle School
WIL/AL BD15 ... 94 B2

Allerton Grange High School
AL/HA/HU LS17 ... 80 B2

Allerton High School
AL/HA/HU LS17 ... 57 G7

All Saints CE Infant School
OT LS21 ... 34 A4

All Saints CE Junior School
OT LS21 ... 33 J3

All Saints CE Primary School
BTLY DN5 ... 242 E6

All Saints CE First School
WBOW BD5 ... 95 K7

All Saints CE J & I School
HIPP HX3 ... 166 B1

All Saints First School
ILK LS29 ... 20 B7

All Saints High School
HUDN HD2 ... 168 D6

All Saints Industrial Estate
PONT WF8 ... 181 F2

All Saints Infant School
PONT WF8 ... 181 F2

Almondbury High School
HUDE HD5 ... 192 C7

Almondbury Infant School
HUDE HD5 ... 214 A1

Almondbury Junior School
HUDE HD5 ... 192 C7

Alston Retail Park
KGHY BD21 ... 3 E1

Altofts Middle School
NORM WF6 ... 151 J8

Altofts Sports Club
NORM WF6 ... 151 K6

Alwoodley Golf Club
AL/HA/HU LS17 ... 58 A5

Alwoodley Primary School
AL/HA/HU LS17 ... 57 G8

Amateurs FC
ELL HX5 ... 167 G3

AMF Bowling
LDSU LS2 ... 7 E2

Anglers Country Park
HOR/CROF WF4 ... 200 D6

Apex Business Park
BEE/HOL LS11 ... 7 E

Archbishop Cranmer CE Primary School
AL/HA/HU LS17 ... 57 H

Arlington Business Centre
MOR LS27 ... 123 J

Armley Clinic
WOR/ARM LS12 ... 100 C

Armley Link Trading Estate
WOR/ARM LS12 ... 100 D

Armley Primary School
WOR/ARM LS12 ... 100 E

Armley Sports & Leisure Centre
WOR/ARM LS12 ... 100 E

Armytage Road Industrial Estate
BRIG HD6 ... 168 C

Arndale Centre
HDGY LS6 ... 78 D

Arndale Shopping Centre
SHPY BD18 ... 73 H

A S B & S Sports Club
FEA/AMT WF7 ... 179 H

Ashbrow Junior School
HUDN HD2 ... 168 C

Ashfield Medical Centre
MSTN/BAR LS15 ... 104 A

Ashfield School
IDLE BD10 ... 74 E

Ashlands First School
ILK LS29 ... 20 C

Ashleigh Business Centre
LDSU LS2 ... 7 F

Ashley Industrial Estate
CHAL LS7 ... 79
HUDN HD2 ... 169 H
OSS WF5 ... 173 H

Ashmount Industrial Park
HEM/SK/SE WF9 ... 224 C

Ashton Road Industrial Estate
RHAY LS8 ... 80 C

Ashton View Medical Centre
RHAY LS8 ... 102 E

Ash Tree County Infant School
LUD/ILL HX2 ... 115 H

Astley Lane Industrial Estate
RTHW LS26 ... 128 A

Astra Business Park
BEE/HOL LS11 ... 124 [

Athletic Club
HEM/SK/SE WF9 ... 202 H

Atlas First School
GIR BD8 ... 4

Austhorpe Primary School
MSTN/BAR LS15 ... 104

Automobilia Transport Museum
HBR HX7 ... 112

Aylesham Industrial Estate
LM/WK BD12 ... 118

Badsworth CE J & I School
HEM/SK/SE WF9 ... 226

Bagden Hall Hotel & Golf Club
KBTN HD8 ... 237

Bagshaw Museum
BTLY WF17 ... 146

Baildon CE First School
BAIL BD17 ... 51

aildon Golf Club
BAIL BD17 .... 51 J6
aildon Recreation Centre
BAIL BD17 .... 73 H2
aileygate Industrial Estate
PONT WF8 .... 181 F2
ailiff Bridge Primary School
BRIG HD6 .... 142 C4
alm Road Industrial Estate
MID LS10 .... 101 K8
ankfield Museum
HIPP HX3 .... 9 D2
ankfoot First School
WBOW BD5 .... 118 E1
ankside Primary School
RHAY LS8 .... 80 A8
ardsey Primary School
AL/HA/HU LS17 .... 40 A7
arkerend First School
BFDE BD3 .... 5 E3
arkisland CE J & I School
GTL/HWG HX4 .... 164 D6
arkisland Cricket Club
GTL/HWG HX4 .... 164 D7
arplas Industrial Park
WBOW BD5 .... 96 A8
arras Garth Industrial Estate
WOR/ARM LS12 .... 100 B5
arwick In Elmet CE
Primary School
MSTN/BAR LS15 .... 83 J4
atley Boys High School
BTLY WF17 .... 146 B5
atley Business Centre
BTLY WF17 .... 146 A5
atley Business &
Technology Centre
BTLY WF17 .... 146 D7
atley Bus Station
BTLY WF17 .... 146 B6
atley Grammar School
BTLY WF17 .... 146 A4
atley Parish CE
(A) J I & N School
BTLY WF17 .... 146 A5
atley RLFC
BTLY WF17 .... 146 B7
atley Sports Centre
BTLY WF17 .... 146 A2
attyeford CE (c) J & I School
MIRF WF14 .... 170 B5
atty Street School
HECK WF16 .... 145 G7
C North Studio
BFD BD1 .... 4 C5
C Studios
LDSU LS2 .... 7 D2
acon Business Centre
HIPP HX3 .... 9 F5
e Beaconsfield Centre
HIPP HX3 .... 9 F6
ckett Park Athletics Centre
HDGY LS6 .... 78 A5
ckett Park Primary School
HDGY LS6 .... 78 B6
ckfoot Upper School
BGLY BD16 .... 72 A2
ech County J & I School
MAR/SLWT HD7 .... 189 J6
echi Hill County
Primary School
HFAX HX1 .... 8 C3
echwood Primary School
SCFT LS14 .... 81 J6
eston Hill St Lukes CE
Primary School
BEE/HOL LS11 .... 101 H7
eston Primary School
BEE/HOL LS11 .... 123 K1
eston Royds Industrial Estate
BEE/HOL LS11 .... 100 C8
le Isle Medical Centre
RTHW LS26 .... 125 G3
le Vue Boys School
HTON BD9 .... 72 D7
le Vue Girls Upper School
BGLY BD16 .... 72 C6
l Lane Primary School
EA/AMT WF7 .... 203 F6
mont Business Centre
BFD BD1 .... 5 D4
mont Middle School
BAIL BD17 .... 51 H8

Ben Rhydding Golf Club
ILK LS29 .... 31 F1
Ben Rhydding Sports Club
ILK LS29 .... 21 G6
Bent Ley Industrial Estate
HOLM/MEL HD9 .... 231 H2
Bentley Primary School
HDGY LS6 .... 79 F5
Benton Park School
YEA LS19 .... 53 K6
Bero Bu School
LDSU LS2 .... 7 D2
Berry Brow Infant School
HUDS HD4 .... 213 F3
Bierley CE First School
BOW BD4 .... 119 J2
Bilton Medical Centre
GIR BD8 .... 4 A3
Bingley Grammar School
BGLY BD16 .... 49 J7
Bingley Health Centre
BGLY BD16 .... 49 J8
Bingley Hospital
BGLY BD16 .... 50 A8
Bingley Little Theatre
BGLY BD16 .... 49 K8
Bingley St Ives Golf Club
BGLY BD16 .... 49 G8
Birchfield Primary School
MOR LS27 .... 122 B5
Birch Lane Medical Centre
WBOW BD5 .... 96 A8
Birdsedge First School
KBTN HD8 .... 235 J7
Birkby Infant School
HUDN HD2 .... 12 B2
Birkby Junior School
HUD HD1 .... 12 C1
Birkenshaw CE F & N School
BIRK/DRI BD11 .... 120 D5
Birkenshaw Health Centre
BIRK/DRI BD11 .... 120 D5
Birkenshaw Middle School
BIRK/DRI BD11 .... 120 E7
Birksland Industrial Estate
BOW BD4 .... 5 F5
Birstall Cricket Club
BTLY WF17 .... 145 K2
Birstall J & I School
BTLY WF17 .... 145 J2
Blackgates Infant School
EARD/LOFT WF3 .... 148 A2
Blackgates Junior School
EARD/LOFT WF3 .... 148 A3
Blakehill First School
IDLE BD10 .... 74 C5
Blenheim Primary School
LDSU LS2 .... 7 D1
BMK Industrial Estate
LVSG WF15 .... 144 E7
Bolling Hall
BOW BD4 .... 96 C8
Bolling Road First School
ILK LS29 .... 20 D7
Bolton Abbey (ruined abbey)
SKP/WHF BD23 .... 15 H2
Bolton Brow Primary School
RPDN/SBR HX6 .... 139 G7
Bolton Lane First School
ECHL BD2 .... 74 C8
Bolton Royd College of Further
Education
GIR BD8 .... 4 B1
Bolton Royd Primary School
PDSY/CALV LS28 .... 97 J3
Bolton Villas Cricket Club
IDLE BD10 .... 74 C5
Bolton Woods First School
SHPY BD18 .... 73 K6
Bondgate Industrial Estate
PONT WF8 .... 181 F2
Borough Market
HFAX HX1 .... 9 D4
Boston Spa
Comprehensive School
BSPA/BRAM LS23 .... 42 B4
Bowers Mill Industrial Estate
GTL/HWG HX4 .... 165 G6
Bowling Community College &
Swimming Pool
BOW BD4 .... 96 C8
Bowling Court Industrial Estate
BOW BD4 .... 96 E6

Bowling Green Primary School
GTL/HWG HX4 .... 165 J8
Bowling Park First School
WBOW BD5 .... 96 B8
Bowling Special School
BOW BD4 .... 96 D8
Boyle & Petyts School
SKP/WHF BD23 .... 15 J5
Bracken Edge Primary School
CHAL LS7 .... 80 A6
Brackenhill First School
GTHN BD7 .... 95 F7
Bradford & Bingley RFC
BGLY BD16 .... 72 B2
Bradford Bulls RLFC
(Odsal Stadium)
WBSY BD6 .... 119 F3
Bradford Business Park
BFDE BD3 .... 4 C2
Bradford Cathedral
Community College
BOW BD4 .... 96 D8
Bradford City FC
(Bradford & Bingley Stadium)
GIR BD8 .... 4 B2
Bradford Girls Grammar School
GIR BD8 .... 94 E2
Bradford Golf Club
CSLY LS20 .... 52 C4
Bradford Grammar School
HTON BD9 .... 73 J8
Bradford Ice Rink
WBOW BD5 .... 4 C5
Bradford & Ilkley College
BFD BD1 .... 4 B5
Bradford & Ilkley
Community College
GTHN BD7 .... 4 A5
GTHN BD7 .... 95 H7
ILK LS29 .... 20 B8
Bradford Industrial &
Horses at Work Museum
ECHL BD2 .... 74 E8
Bradford Moor First School
BFDE BD3 .... 96 E3
Bradford Moor Golf Club
BFDE BD3 .... 5 F2
Bradford Royal Infirmary
HTON BD9 .... 95 F1
Bradford Royal Infirmary
Remedial Unit
HTON BD9 .... 94 E1
Bradford Salem RFC
HTON BD9 .... 72 E7
Bradford University
GTHN BD7 .... 4 A5
PDSY/CALV LS28 .... 97 J2
Bradley Junction
Industrial Estate
HUDN HD2 .... 169 G7
Bradley Mills Cricket &
Bowling Club
HUD HD1 .... 13 E1
Bradley Park Golf Club
HUDN HD2 .... 168 E5
Bradshaw School
LUD/ILL HX2 .... 115 H3
Braim Wood
High School For Boys
RHAY LS8 .... 81 F4
Braithwaite Special School
HWTH BD22 .... 47 G3
Bramall Business Park
WBOW BD5 .... 96 A7
Bramham Park
BSPA/BRAM LS23 .... 61 K3
Bramham Primary School
BSPA/BRAM LS23 .... 42 D7
Bramhope Primary School
BHP/TINH LS16 .... 55 J1
Bramley Business Centre
BRAM LS13 .... 99 F2
Bramley Grange College
SCFT LS14 .... 82 A2
Bramley Health Centre
BRAM LS13 .... 77 G8
Bramley RUFC
BRAM LS13 .... 77 G8
Bramley St Peters CE
Primary School
BRAM LS13 .... 99 G1
Brandon Golf Club
AL/HA/HU LS17 .... 59 F6

Branshaw Golf Club
HWTH BD22 .... **47** F8
Branshaw School
HWTH BD22 .... **2** B4
Branxholme Industrial Estate
BRIG HD6 .... 142 D4
Bretton Country Park
HOR/CROF WF4 .... 219 F5
Bretton Hall College
WKFDE WF1 .... **11** D6
Bridge Court Business Park
BEE/HOL LS11 .... **6** C6
Bridge Theatre
HBR HX7 .... 112 A4
Brierley CE Primary School
CUD/GR S72 .... 224 A8
Brighouse High School
BRIG HD6 .... 142 B8
Brighouse Sports Centre
BRIG HD6 .... 142 A6
Brighouse Sports Club
BRIG HD6 .... 142 C8
Brigshaw High School
CAS WF10 .... 128 E4
Britannia Business
Enterprise Centre
EARL WF12 .... 173 G5
Britannia Mills Trading Estate
MAR/SLWT HD7 .... 189 K7
The British Library
Document Supply Centre
BSPA/BRAM LS23 .... **25** H8
Broadfield Industrial Estate
HUD HD1 .... 191 F8
Broadgate Primary School
HORS LS18 .... **77** G2
Broad Lane Business Centre
HEM/SK/SE WF9 .... 242 B2
Broad Oak Cricket &
Athletic Club
MAR/SLWT HD7 .... 211 J1
Brockholes CE School
HOLM/MEL HD9 .... 233 J1
Brockholes Industrial Park
HOLM/MEL HD9 .... 233 H1
Brodetsky Primary School
AL/HA/HU LS17 .... **57** J7
Bronte House School
IDLE BD10 .... **75** H1
Bronte Parsonage Museum
HWTH BD22 .... **68** D4
Bronte School
HWTH BD22 .... **47** G8
Brookfield Infant School
IDLE BD10 .... **75** G5
Brookfoot Industrial Estate
BRIG HD6 .... 168 A1
The Brooksbank School
ELL HX5 .... 166 D6
Brookwoods Industrial Estate
GTL/HWG HX4 .... 166 B6
Broomfield Business Park
HUD HD1 .... **12** C5
Broomwood Middle School
BOW BD4 .... 119 K2
Brotherton & Byram CP School
KNOT WF11 .... 155 K3
Brownhill Infant School
BTLY WF17 .... 145 K2
Brownhill Primary School
OSM LS9 .... 102 C2
Brow Quarry Industrial Estate
HIPP HX3 .... 141 J5
Brudenell Primary School
HDGY LS6 .... **78** E8
Brunswick Industrial Estate
HFAX HX1 .... **8** C5
Bull Royd Industrial Estate
GIR BD8 .... **94** E3
Burley FC
KSTL LS5 .... **77** K5
Burley Hill Trading Estate
BULY LS4 .... **78** C8
Burley In Wharfedale School
ILK LS29 .... **32** A2
Burley Middle School
ILK LS29 .... **32** B3
Burley Park Medical Centre
BULY LS4 .... 100 D1
Burley St Mathias CE
Primary School
BULY LS4 .... 100 D1
Burley Woodhead CE School
ILK LS29 .... **32** B3

Burmantofts Health Centre
OSM LS9 .... 102 A2
Burnley Road Primary School
HBR HX7 .... 136 E2
Burntwood School
HEM/SK/SE WF9 .... 241 J1
Burntwood Sports &
Leisure Centre
CUD/GR S72 .... 240 C1
Butterfield Industrial Estate
BAIL BD17 .... **73** K2
Buttershaw Middle School
WBSY BD6 .... 118 A4
Buttershaw Upper School
WBSY BD6 .... 118 A3
Byram Industrial Park
KNOT WF11 .... 156 A3
Byron Primary School
BFDE BD3 .... **5** F3
Bywell CE Junior School
EARL WF12 .... 172 E1
Calderdale Business Park
LUD/ILL HX2 .... 115 J8
Calderdale Industrial Museum
HFAX HX1 .... **9** E4
The Calderdale Royal Hospital
HIPP HX3 .... 140 B8
Calder High School
HBR HX7 .... 137 G2
Calder Industrial Estate
BRIG HD6 .... 142 C5
Calder Trading Estate
HUDN HD2 .... 169 H5
RPDN/SBR HX6 .... 139 F8
Calverley CE Primary School
PDSY/CALV LS28 .... **75** K4
Calverley Golf Club
PDSY/CALV LS28 .... **75** J8
Calverley Medical Centre
PDSY/CALV LS28 .... **75** J5
Calverley Parkside
Primary School
PDSY/CALV LS28 .... **75** J5
Calversyke Middle School
HWTH BD22 .... **47** G4
Cannon Hall Country Park
DOD/DAR S75 .... 238 C6
Cannon Hall Museum
DOD/DAR S75 .... 238 C6
Cape Industrial Estate
PDSY/CALV LS28 .... **76** C8
Cardigan Trading Estate
BULY LS4 .... 100 D2
Cardinal Heenan RC High School
HDGY LS6 .... **79** F2
Carleton Park Primary School
PONT WF8 .... 180 E5
Carlinghow J I & N School
BTLY WF17 .... 145 K4
Carlisle Mills Business Centre
GIR BD8 .... **4** A2
Carlton Bolling College &
Sports Centre
BFDE BD3 .... **5** E2
Carlton Cricket Club
EARD/LOFT WF3 .... 150 A1
Carlton High School
PONT WF8 .... 181 F6
Carlton J & I School
DEWS WF13 .... 172 A1
Carlton Lanes Shopping Area
CAS WF10 .... 153 J3
Carlton Mills Trading Estate
WOR/ARM LS12 .... 100 D3
Carlton Northfield AFC
EARD/LOFT WF3 .... 150 A1
Carr Gate Hospital
WKFDW/WTN WF2 .... 149 F6
Carr Green County
Primary School
BRIG HD6 .... 168 A4
Carr Manor High School
AL/HA/HU LS17 .... **79** G3
Carr Manor Primary School
AL/HA/HU LS17 .... **79** G3
Carr Wood Industrial Estate
CAS WF10 .... 154 A6
Cartwright Hall Art Gallery
HTON BD9 .... **73** J8
Castlefields Industrial Estate
BGLY BD16 .... **49** H6
Castleford Health Centre
CAS WF10 .... 153 J3

Castleford High School
CAS WF10 .... 153 K
Castleford RUFC
CAS WF10 .... 152 E
Castleford Swimming Pool
CAS WF10 .... 153 G
Castleford Tigers RLFC
(The Jungle)
CAS WF10 .... 154 A
Castle Grove Infant School
WKFDW/WTN WF2 .... 199 G
Castle Hall School
MIRF WF14 .... 170 E
Castle Hill J & I School
TOD OL14 .... 134 C
The Castle Special School
CAS WF10 .... 154 D
Castleton Primary School
WOR/ARM LS12 .... 100 D
Cas Whitwood Mere
Middle School
CAS WF10 .... 153 F
Cathedral Retail Park
WKFDW/WTN WF2 .... **10** B
The Cathedral School
WKFDW/WTN WF2 .... **10** A
Cawley J I & N School
HECK WF16 .... 145 H
Cawthorne CE Primary School
DOD/DAR S75 .... 238 E
Cawthorne Victoria
Jubilee Museum
DOD/DAR S75 .... 238 E
Central Street Infant School
HBR HX7 .... 112 A
Centre 27 Business Park
BTLY WF17 .... 122 A
Chantry Bridge
Industrial Estate
WKFDE WF1 .... **10** C
Chapel Allerton Hospital
CHAL LS7 .... **80** A
Chapel Allerton Medical Centre
CHAL LS7 .... **79** K
Chapel Allerton Primary School
CHAL LS7 .... **79** J
Chapel Grange Special School
GIR BD8 .... **94** C
Chapeltown Business Centre
CHAL LS7 .... **79** J
Chapeltown Health Centre
CHAL LS7 .... **80** A
Chel Business Centre
CHAL LS7 .... **7** F
Chellow Dene Middle School
GIR BD8 .... **94** D
Chequerfield Infant School
PONT WF8 .... 181 C
Chesham Building
GTHN BD7 .... **4** J
Chesney Park Industrial Estate
MID LS10 .... 101 J
Chevet Business Centre
KNOT WF11 .... 155 K
Chevin Forest Park
OT LS21 .... **34** B
Chickenley Community
J & I School
EARL WF12 .... 173 J
Chickenley Medical Clinic &
Health Centre
EARL WF12 .... 173 J
Chippendale Junior School
OT LS21 .... **33** H
Chohan Medical Centre
WBOW BD5 .... **95** J
Christ Church J & I School
LUD/ILL HX2 .... 139 K
Christ Church Junior School
RPDN/SBR HX6 .... 139 J
Christ Church Primary School
WOR/ARM LS12 .... 100 C
Christ Church Woodhouse
J & I School
HUDN HD2 .... 168 A
Christ the King RC
Primary School
BRAM LS13 .... **99** J
Church School
CUL/QBY BD13 .... **93** J
Churwell Primary School
MOR LS27 .... 123 H

heworld
  BFD BD1 .... 5 D4
  WKFDW/WTN WF2 .... 10 B4
y Link Industrial Park
  BOW BD4 .... 97 G4
y of Leeds School
  HDGY LS6 .... 79 G7
y of Wakefield Golf Club
  WKFDW/WTN WF2 .... 198 A1
y Park Industrial Estate
  WOR/ARM LS12 .... 100 C8
apgate Primary School
  MID LS10 .... 125 G6
ayton CE First School
  CLAY BD14 .... 94 C7
ayton Cemetery
  CLAY BD14 .... 94 D6
ayton CE First School
  CLAY BD14 .... 94 B7
yton Golf Club
  CLAY BD14 .... 94 C8
yton Hospital
  WKFDE WF1 .... 10 B2
yton Middle School
  CLAY BD14 .... 94 C7
ckheaton & District Golf Club
  CLECK BD19 .... 143 J1
ckheaton Sports Club
  CLECK BD19 .... 143 K1
vedon House School
  ILK LS29 .... 31 G1
fe Castle Museum & Gallery
  KGHY BD21 .... 2 C1
fe Commercial Business Park
  HUD HD1 .... 12 A5
fe Hill School
  HIPP HX3 .... 142 B5
fe Middle School
  BFDE BD3 .... 5 D2
f School
  WKFDE WF1 .... 10 B1
ton Cemetery
  BRIG HD6 .... 169 F1
ton Forge Business Park
  KNOT WF11 .... 156 B7
ton Infant School
  HOR/CROF WF4 .... 174 A8
ugh Head J & I School
  MAR/SLWT HD7 .... 188 E7
oblers Lane J & I School
  PONT WF8 .... 181 H3
oden Primary School
  WOR/ARM LS12 .... 99 K7
ckburn High School
  BEE/HOL LS11 .... 124 B4
den Primary School
  HBR HX7 .... 111 F6
lege of Technology (Annexe)
  OSM LS9 .... 7 F4
e College
  WKFDE WF1 .... 10 C2
ne Side Business Park
  HUDW HD3 .... 190 B6
ne Valley Business Park
  MAR/SLWT HD7 .... 211 H2
ne Valley High School
  MAR/SLWT HD7 .... 211 J2
ne Valley Leisure Centre
  MAR/SLWT HD7 .... 210 E2
ne Valley Museum
  MAR/SLWT HD7 .... 189 G7
our Museum
  BFD BD1 .... 4 B4
ton Primary School
  MSTN/BAR LS15 .... 104 C5
ton Retail Park
  MSTN/BAR LS15 .... 104 D4
nmon Road Industrial Estate
  LM/WK BD12 .... 118 E5
cert Hall
  HUD HD1 .... 12 C5
way Medical Centre
  RHAY LS8 .... 80 C8
kridge Hall Golf &
  Country Club
  SHP/TINH LS16 .... 55 K5
kridge Hospital
  SHP/TINH LS16 .... 55 J8
kridge Primary School
  SHP/TINH LS16 .... 55 J7
operative Shopping Parade
  HIPP HX3 .... 141 H3
per Lane First School
  WBSY BD6 .... 117 H2

Copley Hill Trading Estate
  WOR/ARM LS12 .... 6 A6
Copley Primary School
  HIPP HX3 .... 166 A2
Copperfields College
  OSM LS9 .... 102 C5
Copthorne First School
  GTHN BD7 .... 4 A6
Copwood Mental Health Clinic
  BOW BD4 .... 97 G7
Corn Exchange
  LDS LS1 .... 7 E4
Cornholme J & I School
  TOD OL14 .... 132 D2
The Coronation Business Centre
  KGHY BD21 .... 3 E1
Corpus Christi Primary School
  OSM LS9 .... 103 F4
Corpus Christi RC High School
  OSM LS9 .... 103 G3
Cottage Road Picture House
  HDGY LS6 .... 78 C5
Cottingley Clinic
  BGLY BD16 .... 72 A4
Cottingley Community
  Health Centre
  BEE/HOL LS11 .... 123 J2
Cottingley First School
  BGLY BD16 .... 72 B4
Cottingley Hall Crematorium
  BEE/HOL LS11 .... 123 J1
Cottingley Primary School
  BEE/HOL LS11 .... 123 H2
Covered Market
  KGHY BD21 .... 3 D3
Craven Road Medical Centre
  HDGY LS6 .... 79 H7
Crawshaw School
  PDSY/CALV LS28 .... 98 D4
Cricket Club
  MIRF WF14 .... 194 A2
Crigglestone Sports Club
  HOR/CROF WF4 .... 198 B7
Crofton Health Centre
  HOR/CROF WF4 .... 200 D3
Crofton High School
  HOR/CROF WF4 .... 200 D3
Crofton Infant School
  HOR/CROF WF4 .... 200 D3
Crofton Junior School
  HOR/CROF WF4 .... 200 E3
Crosland Heath Golf Club
  HUDS HD4 .... 212 A2
Crosland Moor County
  Junior School
  HUDS HD4 .... 190 C8
Crosland Road
  Industrial Estate
  HUDS HD4 .... 212 B6
Crossflatts Cricket Club
  BGLY BD16 .... 49 H5
Crossflatts First School
  BGLY BD16 .... 49 J5
Cross Flatts Park
  Primary School
  BEE/HOL LS11 .... 124 B1
Cross Gates Primary School
  SCFT LS14 .... 103 J1
Crossgates Shopping Centre
  MSTN/BAR LS15 .... 104 A1
Cross Green Light I
  ndustrial Estate
  OSM LS9 .... 102 C6
Cross Hall Infant School
  MOR LS27 .... 122 E8
Cross Lane Business Park
  LVSG WF15 .... 144 D7
Crosslane Industrial Estate
  LVSG WF15 .... 144 D7
Cross Lane Primary School
  ELL HX5 .... 166 D1
Crossley Hall First &
  Middle School
  GIR BD8 .... 94 E4
Crossley Heath School
  HFAX HX1 .... 139 K7
Crossley Retail Park
  HFAX HX1 .... 8 B3
Crossley Street Primary School
  WBY LS22 .... 23 J5
Crowlees CE School
  MIRF WF14 .... 170 D6
Crown Point Retail Park
  MID LS10 .... 7 E5

Crown Point Shopping Park
  MID LS10 .... 7 E6
Cuckoo Nest Industrial Estate
  BTHN BD7 .... 4 A4
Cullingworth First School
  CUL/QBY BD13 .... 70 B5
Cullingworth Medical Centre
  CUL/QBY BD13 .... 70 B5
Cumberworth CE First School
  KBTN HD8 .... 235 K5
Dale Lane Industrial Estate
  HEM/SK/SE WF9 .... 226 D6
Dales Bank Holiday Park
  AIRE BD20 .... 17 F6
Dalton School J I & N
  HUDE HD5 .... 192 B5
Dane Royd J & I School
  HOR/CROF WF4 .... 220 A1
Dansk Way
  ILK LS29 .... 20 C6
Darrington CE J & I School
  PONT WF8 .... 182 A6
Darton High School
  DOD/DAR S75 .... 239 H3
Darton Kexborough
  Infant School
  DOD/DAR S75 .... 239 H3
Deanfield County
  Primary School
  LUD/ILL HX2 .... 115 H8
Dearne Valley Health Centre
  KBTN HD8 .... 237 H2
Delf Hill Middle School
  LM/WK BD12 .... 118 D5
Denby Dale Industrial Park
  KBTN HD8 .... 236 D5
Denby First School
  KBTN HD8 .... 236 C8
Denholme Clinic
  CUL/QBY BD13 .... 92 B2
Denholme First School
  CUL/QBY BD13 .... 92 B2
Dental Institute
  LDSU LS2 .... 6 C2
Dewsbury Bus Station
  EARL WF12 .... 172 B4
Dewsbury Cemetery
  DEWS WF13 .... 171 K4
Dewsbury College
  DEWS WF13 .... 172 A2
Dewsbury District Golf Club
  MIRF WF14 .... 171 G8
Dewsbury & District Hospital
  DEWS WF13 .... 171 K1
Dewsbury Moor Crematorium
  DEWS WF13 .... 171 K3
Dewsbury Moor
  Infant & Nursery School
  DEWS WF13 .... 171 J1
Dewsbury Museum &
  Art Gallery
  DEWS WF13 .... 171 K4
Dewsbury Sports Centre
  EARL WF12 .... 172 C3
Dimplewell Infant School
  OSS WF5 .... 173 J7
District Archives Office
  WKFDE WF1 .... 10 B2
Dixon Lane Medical Centre
  WOR/ARM LS12 .... 100 C7
Dixons City Technology College
  WBOW BD5 .... 96 A7
Dockfield Industrial Estate
  BAIL BD17 .... 73 J3
Domestic Street Industrial Estate
  BEE/HOL LS11 .... 6 B5
Dominion Industrial Park
  HIPP HX3 .... 141 H3
Drakes Industrial Estate
  LUD/ILL HX2 .... 115 K7
Drighlington Junior School
  BIRK/DRI BD11 .... 121 J4
Drug Addiction Clinic
  LDSU LS2 .... 6 C2
Drummond Middle School
  GIR BD8 .... 4 A2
Drummond Trading Estate
  GIR BD8 .... 4 B3
Dudley Hill First School
  BOW BD4 .... 96 E8
Eagles Yard Business Park
  WKFDE WF1 .... 10 C3
Earlsheaton High School
  EARL WF12 .... 172 D3

Earlsheaton Infant School
EARL WF12 .... **172** E4

East Ardsley Health Centre
EARD/LOFT WF3 .... **148** C4

East Ardsley Infant School
EARD/LOFT WF3 .... **148** E3

East Ardsley Primary School
EARD/LOFT WF3 .... **148** E3

East Ardsley United Cricket & Athletic Club
EARD/LOFT WF3 .... **148** D5

East Bierley CE First School
BOW BD4 .... **120** C4

East Bierley Cricket Club
BIRK/DRI BD11 .... **120** B5

East Bierley Golf Club
BOW BD4 .... **120** B4

Eastborough J I & N School
EARL WF12 .... **172** C3

Eastburn J & I School
AIRE BD20 .... **26** B5

East Garforth Primary School
GFTH/SHER LS25 .... **106** B3

East Leeds Clinic
OSM LS9 .... **102** D2

East Leeds Leisure Centre
MSTN/BAR LS15 .... **103** G4

Eastmoor Health Centre
WKFDE WF1 .... **11** F1

East Morton First School
AIRE BD20 .... **49** C2

Eastwood First School
KGHY BD21 .... **3** E2

Eccleshill Clinic & Health Centre
IDLE BD10 .... **75** F5

Eccleshill Cricket Club
IDLE BD10 .... **75** F6

Eccleshill North Middle School
IDLE BD10 .... **75** G5

Eccleshill School
IDLE BD10 .... **75** G6

Eccleshill United Sports Club
ECHL BD2 .... **74** B5

Edgerton Cemetery
HUD HD1 .... **12** B2

Eldwick First School
BGLY BD16 .... **50** C6

Elizabeth Industrial Estate
HFAX HX1 .... **8** B3

Elland CE School
ELL HX5 .... **166** E4

Elland Old Earth School
ELL HX5 .... **167** H4

Elland Road Industrial Park
BEE/HOL LS11 .... **100** D8

Ellen Royde Health Centre
ELL HX5 .... **166** D4

Elmfield Business Park
GFTH/SHER LS25 .... **106** A3

Elmwood Health Centre
HOLM/MEL HD9 .... **233** G4

Embsay & Bolton Abbey Steam Railway
SKP/WHD BD23 .... **14** A5

Emley First School
KBTN HD8 .... **217** H4

Emley Moor Business Park
KBTN HD8 .... **217** F5

Emmanuel Trading Estate
WOR/ARM LS12 .... **6** B5

Empire Business Centre
LUD/ILL HX2 .... **115** K6

England Lane J & I School
KNOT WF11 .... **156** D8

English Martyrs RC Primary School
WKFDW/WTN WF2 .... **174** H4

Enterprise Park Industrial Estate
BEE/HOL LS11 .... **124** A2

Environmental Business Centre
MOR LS27 .... **123** F7

Esholt & Aire Bronians Sports Club
BAIL BD17 .... **52** D6

Essex Park Industrial Estate
BFDE BD3 .... **5** E5

Eureka the Museum for Children
HIPP HX3 .... **9** E5

Euroway Trading Estate
BOW BD4 .... **119** H5

The Eye Clinic
GTHN BD7 .... **4** A5

Fagley First School
ECHL BD2 .... **97** F1

Fairburn Community School
KNOT WF11 .... **131** H7

Fairburn Sports & Recreation Centre
KNOT WF11 .... **131** H7

Fairfield Special School
HECK WF16 .... **145** H6

Fairway Industrial Estate
BTLY WF17 .... **145** J1

Farfield Primary School
PDSY/CALV LS28 .... **98** A1

Farnham First School
GTHN BD7 .... **95** H6

Farnley Park High School
WOR/ARM LS12 .... **99** J7

Farrow Medical Centre
BFDE BD3 .... **5** D3

Farsley Celtic AFC
PDSY/CALV LS28 .... **98** C1

Farsley Community Clinic
PDSY/CALV LS28 .... **76** A8

Fartown Health Centre
HUDN HD2 .... **12** C1

Fartown High School
HUDN HD2 .... **191** J1

Fearnville Sports Centre
RHAY LS8 .... **81** F7

Featherbank Infant School
HORS LS18 .... **77** F3

Featherstone Cemetery
FEA/AMT WF7 .... **179** G1

Featherstone High School
FEA/AMT WF7 .... **180** A6

Featherstone Sports Centre
FEA/AMT WF7 .... **180** A7

Felnex Trading Estate
OSM LS9 .... **102** E6

Fentham Industrial Estate
BRIG HD6 .... **168** B2

Ferniehurst First School
BAIL BD17 .... **73** J1

Fernley Green Industrial Estate
KNOT WF11 .... **156** E7

Ferrybridge Infant School
KNOT WF11 .... **155** K6

Feversham College
BFDE BD3 .... **5** E5

Feversham Street First School
BFDE BD3 .... **5** F4

Fieldhead Business Centre
GTHN BD7 .... **4** A5

Fieldhead Carr Primary School
SCFT LS14 .... **81** K2

Field Head Hospital
WKFDE WF1 .... **176** A1

Fieldhead J & I School
BTLY WF17 .... **121** J8

Field Lane Infant School
BTLY WF17 .... **146** C7

First Avenue Industrial Estate
PDSY/CALV LS28 .... **98** C3

Fir Tree Primary School
AL/HA/HU LS17 .... **57** K8

Fitzwilliam J & I School
HEM/SK/SE WF9 .... **202** B7

Fixby J & I School
HUDN HD2 .... **168** B7

Flanshaw J & I School
WKFDW/WTN WF2 .... **175** G4

Flockton CE School
HOR/CROF WF4 .... **195** G8

Flushdyke Primary School
OSS WF5 .... **174** A4

Forster Square Retail Park
BFD BD1 .... **4** C3

Foundry Industrial Estate
KNOT WF11 .... **155** K6
PDSY/CALV LS28 .... **98** C2

The Fountain Medical Centre
MOR LS27 .... **123** F8

Four Gates End
HBR HX7 .... **110** A5

Four Lanes Business Park
GIR BD8 .... **95** F4

Fowler Street Industrial Estate
BOW BD4 .... **5** F6

Foxhill First School
CUL/QBY BD13 .... **116** C1

Friars Industrial Estate
IDLE BD10 .... **74** D4

Frizinghall First & Middle School
HTON BD9 .... **73** J6

Frizinghall Medical Centre
HTON BD9 .... **73** H7

The Froebelian School
HORS LS18 .... **77** H1

Frost Hill Business Park
LVSG WF15 .... **144** B1

Fulford Grange Hospital
YEA LS19 .... **53** H1

Fulneck Golf Club
PDSY/CALV LS28 .... **98** D8

Fulneck School
PDSY/CALV LS28 .... **98** D8

Garforth Clinic
GFTH/SHER LS25 .... **105** K2

Garforth Community College
GFTH/SHER LS25 .... **105** K2

Garforth Golf Club
GFTH/SHER LS25 .... **83** K8

Garforth Leisure Centre
GFTH/SHER LS25 .... **106** A2

Garforth Medical Centre
GFTH/SHER LS25 .... **105** K2

Gateways School
AL/HA/HU LS17 .... **38** E8

Gawthorpe Primary School
OSS WF5 .... **173** J2

Gelderd Trading Estate
WOR/ARM LS12 .... **6** E6

Gemini Business Park
CHAL LS7 .... **79** K6

Ghyll Royd School
ILK LS29 .... **19** J1

Gibson Lane Junior School
GFTH/SHER LS25 .... **129** H1

Gildersome Junior School
MOR LS27 .... **122** B4

Gilstead Middle School
BGLY BD16 .... **50** E7

Gilthwaites First School
KBTN HD8 .... **236** A4

Girlington First School
GIR BD8 .... **95** K3

Girlington Industrial Centre
GIR BD8 .... **95** K3

Girnhill Infant School
FEA/AMT WF7 .... **179** K2

Glasshoughton Infant School
CAS WF10 .... **153** H4

The Gleddings School
HIPP HX3 .... **139** K4

Gledholt Business Park
HUD HD1 .... **12** B5

Gledhow Primary School
RHAY LS8 .... **80** E5

Glenaire First School
BAIL BD17 .... **73** G1

Glen Cable Tramway
BAIL BD17 .... **73** F3

Glenfield Caravan Park
AL/HA/HU LS17 .... **59** J6

Golcar J & I School
MAR/SLWT HD7 .... **189** K4

Golden Acre Park & Gardens
BHP/TINH LS16 .... **56** D6

Gomersal CE Middle School
CLECK BD19 .... **145** J8

Gomersal First School
CLECK BD19 .... **144** E7

The Good Health Centre
RHAY LS8 .... **80** E4

Gordon Street J & I School
FEA/AMT WF7 .... **179** K3

Gotts Park Golf Club
WOR/ARM LS12 .... **100** A3

Grafton School
HDGY LS6 .... **79** J6

Grand Theatre & Opera House
LDS LS1 .... **7** H4

Grangefield Industrial Estate
PDSY/CALV LS28 .... **98** D4

The Grange Medical Centre
SCFT LS14 .... **81** J4

Grange Middle School
AIRE BD20 .... **3** J5

Grange Road Business Park
BTLY WF17 .... **146** E1

Grange Road Industrial Estate
BTLY WF17 .... **146** E1

Grange Upper School
WBOW BD5 .... **118** A3

Great Horton Cricket Club
GTHN BD7 .... **95** J7

Great Horton Industrial Estate
WBSY BD6 .... **117** G6

Great Horton Middle School
GTHN BD7 .... **95** J8

reat & Little Preston CE
Infants School
RTHW LS26 .... **128** D4
reat & Little Preston
Junior School
RTHW LS26 .... **128** D4
reat Northern Retail Park
HUD HD1 .... **13** D2
reenfield Primary School
GFTH/SHER LS25 .... **129** F1
reenfield School
IDLE BD10 .... **74** D2
reengates First School
IDLE BD10 .... **75** G4
reenhead Athletics Track
KGHY BD21 .... **2** C1
reenhead College
HUD HD1 .... **12** B4
reenhead Grammar School
AIRE BD20 .... **47** J1
reenhill CP School
BRAM LS13 .... **99** H3
reenhill Industrial Estate
HBR HX7 .... **137** F3
reenhill Infant &
Juniors School
WKFDE WF1 .... **11** D2
reen Lane Industrial Estate
FEA/AMT WF7 .... **179** F5
reen Lane Primary School
GFTH/SHER LS25 .... **106** B5
reen Leas School
PONT WF8 .... **181** F6
reen Meadows School
GSLY LS20 .... **52** E2
reenmount Primary School
BEE/HOL LS11 .... **101** H8
reen Mount Retail Park
HFAX HX1 .... **8** C4
reenside Infant &
Nursery School
HUDE HD5 .... **192** B6
reenwood Primary School
BEE/HOL LS11 .... **101** J7
reetland Cricket &
Bowling Club
GTL/HWG HX4 .... **166** B4
reetland J & I School
GTL/HWG HX4 .... **165** K4
reetland Mixed School
GTL/HWG HX4 .... **166** A4
regory Middle School
WBOW BD5 .... **119** H2
resley Road Industrial Estate
KGHY BD21 .... **3** D3
rimethorpe Ladywood
Primary School
CUD/GR S72 .... **240** B5
rove House First School
ECHL BD2 .... **74** C7
rove Lea J & I School
HEM/SK/SE WF9 .... **224** D4
rove Mills Industrial Estate
ELL HX5 .... **167** F4
uiseley AFC
GSLY LS20 .... **52** E2
uiseley Cemetery
ILK LS29 .... **32** E8
uiseley County Infant School
GSLY LS20 .... **53** G2
uiseley School
GSLY LS20 .... **53** F3
ulsyke Medical Centre
MSTN/BAR LS15 .... **103** J4
unthwaite Hall
STKB/PEN S36 .... **252** A1
ade Edge J & I School
HOLM/MEL HD9 .... **248** B3
aigh Hall Medical Centre
IDLE BD10 .... **75** F4
aigh Road Infant School
RTHW LS26 .... **126** B5
ainsworth Moor J & I School
CUL/QBY BD13 .... **116** C3
alf Acres J & I School
CAS WF10 .... **153** H4
alfpenny Lane J & I School
PONT WF8 .... **180** C3
lifax Blue Sox RLFC
(The Shay Stadium)
HFAX HX1 .... **9** D6
lifax Bradley Hall Golf Club
GTL/HWG HX4 .... **165** K6

Halifax Building Society
HFAX HX1 .... **9** D5
Halifax Catholic High School
LUD/ILL HX2 .... **115** K5
Halifax Cricket Ground
HFAX HX1 .... **139** H4
Halifax Golf Club
LUD/ILL HX2 .... **115** F2
Halifax High School
HFAX HX1 .... **9** D5
Halifax Industrial Centre
HFAX HX1 .... **8** B3
Halifax RUFC
LUD/ILL HX2 .... **115** J7
Halifax Swimming Pool
HFAX HX1 .... **9** D5
Halifax Town FC
(The Shay Stadium)
HFAX HX1 .... **9** D6
Hall Bower Athletic Club
HUDS HD4 .... **213** H2
Hall Bower Cricket Club
HUDS HD4 .... **213** H2
Halton Building
GTHN BD7 .... **4** A5
Hambledon First School
BOW BD4 .... **119** J3
Hanging Heaton CE J & I School
BTLY WF17 .... **146** E8
Hanging Heaton Golf Club
EARL WF12 .... **172** D1
Hanson Upper School
ECHL BD2 .... **74** B7
Harden First School
BGLY BD16 .... **70** E2
Harehills Middle School
RHAY LS8 .... **80** B8
Harehills Primary School
RHAY LS8 .... **80** C8
Harewood CE Primary School
AL/HA/HU LS17 .... **38** C4
Harewood House &
Bird Garden
AL/HA/HU LS17 .... **38** A5
Hartington Middle School
HWTH BD22 .... **68** E4
Hartshead J & I School
LVSG WF15 .... **169** K1
Hatfield Hall Golf Club
EARD/LOFT WF3 .... **150** B8
Havercroft Health Centre
HOR/CROF WF4 .... **223** F3
Havercroft J & I School
HOR/CROF WF4 .... **223** F3
Hawksworth CE School
GSLY LS20 .... **52** A3
Hawksworth Wood
Primary School
KSTL LS5 .... **77** J4
Haworth
HWTH BD22 .... **68** E4
Haycliffe Special School
WBSY BD6 .... **118** C1
Headfield CE Junior School
EARL WF12 .... **172** B6
Headingley Golf Club
BHP/TINH LS16 .... **56** D6
Headingley Primary School
HDGY LS6 .... **78** D6
Headlands CE J & I School
LVSG WF15 .... **144** D7
Headley Golf Club
CUL/QBY BD13 .... **93** H6
Headrow Shopping Centre
LDS LS1 .... **7** E3
Headway Business Park
WKFDW/WTN WF2 .... **10** B6
Heady Fields Golf Club
HOLM/MEL HD9 .... **232** A3
Healey J & I School
BTLY WF17 .... **145** J7
Health Studies School
WBOW BD5 .... **4** B6
Heather Grove First School
HTON BD9 .... **72** D8
Heathfield Industrial Estate
ELL HX5 .... **167** F5
Heathfield-Rishworth School
RPDN/SBR HX6 .... **186** E1
Heath View Community School
WKFDE WF1 .... **11** E2
Heaton Middle School
HTON BD9 .... **72** D7

Heaton Royds Hospital
HTON BD9 .... **72** D6
Heaton Royds Special School
SHPY BD18 .... **73** G6
Hebble Brook Business Park
LUD/ILL HX2 .... **115** F4
Hebden Bridge Cinema
HBR HX7 .... **112** B8
Hebden Bridge Golf Club
HBR HX7 .... **112** E8
Hebden Bridge Health Centre
HBR HX7 .... **112** B8
Hebden Royd Cragg Vale
County Primary School
HBR HX7 .... **136** D8
Hebden Royd Primary School
HBR HX7 .... **111** K7
Heckmondwike Grammar School
HECK WF16 .... **145** G7
Heckmondwike Sports Club
HECK WF16 .... **145** G7
Helme CE J & I School
HOLM/MEL HD9 .... **211** H7
Hemsworth High School
HEM/SK/SE WF9 .... **224** E4
Hemsworth RUFC
HEM/SK/SE WF9 .... **225** F4
Hemsworth Sports Complex
HEM/SK/SE WF9 .... **224** E5
Hendal Lane Primary School
WKFDW/WTN WF2 .... **198** D6
Henry Moore Clinic
CAS WF10 .... **153** J4
Heponstall County
Primary School
HBR HX7 .... **112** A6
Hepworth J & I School
HOLM/MEL HD9 .... **249** F2
Highbank First School
LVSG WF15 .... **143** J6
Highburton First School
KBTN HD8 .... **215** G3
Highcliffe Industrial Estate
MOR LS27 .... **122** E6
High Crags First School
SHPY BD18 .... **73** J5
High Fernley First School
LM/WK BD12 .... **118** D8
Highfield Middle School
KGHY BD21 .... **2** B3
Highfield Primary School
AL/HA/HU LS17 .... **58** A7
Highfield School
OSS WF5 .... **173** J2
The Highfields Medical Centre
BRAM LS13 .... **99** H1
Highfields Special School
HUD HD1 .... **12** B3
Highlander Sports Centre
KBTN HD8 .... **193** K8
High Royds Hospital
ILK LS29 .... **52** D1
Hightown School
LVSG WF15 .... **143** K6
High Trees School
BSPA/BRAM LS23 .... **42** E5
Hillcrest Primary School
CHAL LS7 .... **80** A8
Hillside Works
Industrial Estate
CLECK BD19 .... **144** A1
Hill Top CE First School
LM/WK BD12 .... **118** D5
Hill Top Infant School
EARD/LOFT WF3 .... **147** J6
Hinchliffe Mill County School
HOLM/MEL HD9 .... **247** H1
Hipperholme Clinic
HIPP HX3 .... **141** J3
Hipperholme Grammar School
HIPP HX3 .... **141** H3
Hipperholme & Lightcliffe
High School
HIPP HX3 .... **142** A4
HM Prison
BSPA/BRAM LS23 .... **43** G1
WKFDW/WTN WF2 .... **10** A3
HM Prison Service College
WKFDW/WTN WF2 .... **10** B3
HM Young Offender Institution
WBY LS22 .... **24** B4
Hockney Road Industrial Estate
GIR BD8 .... **95** H3
IDLE BD10 .... **74** D6

Hollingwood First School
GTHN BD7 .... **94** E8

Hollybank Natural Health Centre
HUDW HD3 .... **190** B2

Hollywood Bowl
BULY LS4 .... **100** D2

Holmefield First School
BOW BD4 .... **97** H7

Holme J & I School
HOLM/MEL HD9 .... **246** D2

Holme Middle School
BOW BD4 .... **97** F8

Holme Mills Industrial Estate
MAR/SLWT HD7 .... **189** K7

Holme Valley Business Park
HUDS HD4 .... **212** E3

Holme Valley Clinic
HOLM/MEL HD9 .... **213** F6

Holme Wood Health Centre
BOW BD4 .... **97** G8

Holmfield Industrial Estate
LUD/ILL HX2 .... **115** K4

Holmfirth Craft Market
HOLM/MEL HD9 .... **233** F6

Holmfirth J & I School
HOLM/MEL HD9 .... **233** G7

Holmfirth Secondary School
HOLM/MEL HD9 .... **233** J3

Holmfirth Swimming Pool
HOLM/MEL HD9 .... **233** H4

Holycroft First School
KGHY BD21 .... **2** C4

Holy Family RC Primary School
WOR/ARM LS12 .... **100** D4

Holy Family & St Michaels RC
Primary School
PONT WF8 .... **181** H2

Holy Family School
KGHY BD21 .... **2** B1

Holy Name RC Primary School
BHP/TINH LS16 .... **55** K8

Holy Rosary & St Annes RC
Primary School
CHAL LS7 .... **79** K8

Holy Trinity CE First School
BGLY BD16 .... **72** A1

Holy Trinity CE J & I School
OSS WF5 .... **173** J5

Holy Trinity CE Primary School
BHP/TINH LS16 .... **55** H6

Holy Trinity CE Senior School
LUD/ILL HX2 .... **115** J5

Holy Trinity Infant School
HFAX HX1 .... **8** C5

Holy Trinity Junior School
HFAX HX1 .... **8** C5

Holywell Green Primary School
GTL/HWG HX4 .... **166** A7

Homestead Clinic
WKFDW/WTN WF2 .... **175** G5

Honley Business Centre
HOLM/MEL HD9 .... **213** G7

Honley CE Infant School
HOLM/MEL HD9 .... **213** F7

Honley CE Junior School
HOLM/MEL HD9 .... **213** F7

Honley High School
HOLM/MEL HD9 .... **213** G6

Hopton Junior Infant &
Nursery School
MIRF WF14 .... **170** C7

Horbury Junction
Industrial Estate
HOR/CROF WF4 .... **197** J3

Horbury Junior School
HOR/CROF WF4 .... **197** J2

Horbury Primary School
HOR/CROF WF4 .... **197** J2

The Horsefair Centre
WBY LS22 .... **23** J6

Horsfall Stadium
WBSY BD6 .... **118** C4

Horsforth Golf Club
HORS LS18 .... **54** D8

Horsforth Hall Park Cricket Club
HORS LS18 .... **77** J3

Horsforth Newlaithes
Junior School
HORS LS18 .... **76** E5

Horsforth School
HORS LS18 .... **77** F1

Horsforth Village Museum
HORS LS18 .... **76** E3

Horsforth Woodside CE
Primary School
HORS LS18 .... **77** H2

Horton Bank Top First School
GTHN BD7 .... **117** K1

Horton Park First School
WBOW BD5 .... **95** H7

Hothfield Street Junior School
AIRE BD20 .... **27** F2

Hot Shots Ten Pin Bowl & Bar
HUD HD1 .... **12** B5

Hovingham Primary School
RHAY LS8 .... **80** C7

Howards CE J & I School
FEA/AMT WF7 .... **203** H4

Howden Clough High School
BTLY WF17 .... **146** A2

Howden Clough Industrial Estate
BTLY WF17 .... **122** A8

Howland Centre
EARL WF12 .... **172** B3

Howley Hall Golf Club
MOR LS27 .... **146** D4

Howley Park Trading Estate
MOR LS27 .... **147** F1

Hoyers Industrial Estate
HUD HD1 .... **13** F1

Hoyle Court First School
BAIL BD17 .... **52** A8

Hoyle Head Mills
Industrial Estate
EARL WF12 .... **172** E4

Huddersfield Art Gallery
HUD HD1 .... **13** D5

Huddersfield Crematorium
HUDN HD2 .... **168** B5

Huddersfield Giants RLFC
(Alfred McAlpine Stadium)
HUDE HD5 .... **13** E3

Huddersfield Golf Club
HUDN HD2 .... **167** K8

Huddersfield Lawn Tennis
& Squash Club
HUD HD1 .... **12** B3

Huddersfield New College
HUDW HD3 .... **189** K3

Huddersfield Royal Infirmary
HUDW HD3 .... **190** C3

Huddersfield RUFC
HUDS HD4 .... **212** E1

Huddersfield Sports Centre
HUD HD1 .... **13** D4

Huddersfield Technical College
HOLM/MEL HD9 .... **233** C6
HUDN HD2 .... **191** K1
HUDS HD4 .... **213** F1

Huddersfield Town AFC
(Alfred Mcalpine Stadium)
HUD HD1 .... **13** E2

Huddersfield University
HUD HD1 .... **13** D4

Huddersfield University Annexe
HUD HD1 .... **12** B3

Hudds School of Theatre
HUDS HD4 .... **212** E3

Hugh Gaitskell Primary School
BEE/HOL LS11 .... **123** K1

Hunslet Business Park
MID LS10 .... **102** A6

Hunslet Carr Primary School
MID LS10 .... **125** F1

Hunslet Hall Shopping Centre
BEE/HOL LS11 .... **101** H7

Hunslet Health Centre
MID LS10 .... **101** K7

Hunslet Moor Primary School
BEE/HOL LS11 .... **101** J8

Hunslet St Josephs RC
Primary School
MID LS10 .... **102** A7

Hunslet St Marys CE
Primary School
MID LS10 .... **102** A8

Hunslet Trading Estate
MID LS10 .... **102** B8

Hutton J & I School
IDLE BD10 .... **74** E6

Hutton Middle School
ECHL BD2 .... **74** E6

Hyde Park Picture House
HDGY LS6 .... **78** E8

Hyrstmount Junior School
BTLY WF17 .... **146** B8

Ida & Robert Arthington Hospital
BHP/TINH LS16 .... **77** J⁴

Idle CE School
IDLE BD10 .... **74** D²

Idle Cricket Club
IDLE BD10 .... **74** D⁴

Idle Medical Centre
IDLE BD10 .... **74** D³

Ilkley Golf Club
ILK LS29 .... **19** K⁵

Ilkley Grammar School
ILK LS29 .... **20** C⁴

Ilkley Health Centre
ILK LS29 .... **20** C⁴

Ilkley Middle School
ILK LS29 .... **20** E

Ilkley Swimming Baths
ILK LS29 .... **20** B

Immaculate Heart of Mary
Primary School
AL/HA/HU LS17 .... **79** J

Industrial & Commercial Centre
LDSU LS2 .... **7** F

Industrial Avenue
BTLY WF17 .... **145** H

Ingfield Business Centre
HUDN HD2 .... **169** F

Inglebrook School
PONT WF8 .... **180** E

Ingram Road Primary School
BEE/HOL LS11 .... **6** B

Ingrow First & Infant School
HWTH BD22 .... **2** B

Inland Revenue Office
BFD BD1 .... **4** C

Intake High School
BRAM LS13 .... **76** E

Ireland Wood Primary School
BHP/TINH LS16 .... **56** A

Islamia Girls High School
HUD HD1 .... **12** A

Iveson Primary School
BHP/TINH LS16 .... **78** A

Jacksons Estate
OSS WF5 .... **173** K

Jawbone Industrial Estate
RTHW LS26 .... **125** J

Jerry Clay Lane Primary School
WKFDW/WTN WF2 .... **174** E

Joe Dean Recreation Centre
WOR/ARM LS12 .... **99** K

John Jamieson School
RHAY LS8 .... **80** B

John O'Gaunts Trading Estate
RTHW LS26 .... **126** B

John Smeaton High School
MSTN/BAR LS15 .... **82** C

John Smeaton Sports Centre
MSTN/BAR LS15 .... **82** C

John Street Market
BFD BD1 .... **4** C

Joseph Priestley College
MOR LS27 .... **123** C

Junction 25 Business Park
MIRF WF14 .... **170** C

Junction 1 Retail Park
BEE/HOL LS11 .... **123** J

Kayes First School
KBTN HD8 .... **237** K

Keelham First School
CUL/QBY BD13 .... **92** D

Keighley & Worth Valley Railway
HWTH BD22 .... **68** E
HWTH BD22 .... **69** H
KGHY BD21 .... **2** D
KGHY BD21 .... **3** D

Keighley Business Centre
KGHY BD21 .... **2** D

Keighley College
KGHY BD21 .... **3** D

Keighley Crematorium
HWTH BD22 .... **46** D

Keighley Cricket Club
KGHY BD21 .... **3** D

Keighley Golf Club
AIRE BD20 .... **27** F

Keighley Industrial Park
KGHY BD21 .... **3** D

Keighley Leisure Centre
KGHY BD21 .... **3** D

Keighley Retail Park
KGHY BD21 .... **3** D

Keighley RUFC
AIRE BD20 .... **27** F

ighley St Andrew's
Primary School
HWTH BD22 .... 2 B4

nsington Street Health Centre
GIR BD8 .... 95 G3

ents Sports Club
ECHL BD2 .... 74 D7

rr Mackie Primary School
RHAY LS8 .... 80 C4

rshaw Drive Health Centre
LUD/ILL HX2 .... 138 A3

ttlethorpe High School
WKFDW/WTN WF2 .... 198 E5

xborough Primary School
DOD/DAR S75 .... 239 H3

dwick CE Primary School
AIRE BD20 .... 26 A3

lingbeck Retail Park
SCFT LS14 .... 103 H1

linghall First School
BFDE BD3 .... 96 E2

n Hill Industrial Estate
MAR/SLWT HD7 .... 210 E3

ng James School
HUDS HD4 .... 214 C1

ngsgate Shopping Centre
HUD HD1 .... 13 D4

ngs High School
PONT WF8 .... 180 D4

nsley Industrial Estate
HEM/SK/SE WF9 .... 224 C2

ppax Health Centre
GFTH/SHER LS25 .... 129 G1

ppax Infant School
GFTH/SHER LS25 .... 129 F2

ppax Leisure Centre
GFTH/SHER LS25 .... 128 E2

ppax North Primary School
GFTH/SHER LS25 .... 105 K7

rkburton CE First School
KBTN HD8 .... 215 H5

rkburton Cricket Club
KBTN HD8 .... 215 H5

rkburton Middle School
KBTN HD8 .... 215 J4

rkfields Business Centre
YEA LS19 .... 53 J4

rkgate Business Centre
WKFDE WF1 .... 11 D4

rkgate Market
LDS LS1 .... 7 E3

rkgate Shopping
Centre & Market
BFD BD1 .... 4 C4

rkhamgate Primary School
WKFDW/WTN WF2 .... 174 C1

rkheaton Cricket &
Bowling Club
HUDE HD5 .... 192 D2

rkheaton Primary School
HUDE HD5 .... 192 D2

rklees Light Railway
KBTN HD8 .... 237 F1

rklees Music School
HUD HD1 .... 12 C5

rklees Open Market
HUD HD1 .... 13 D3

rkroyd Infant School
HOLM/MEL HD9 .... 233 K4

rkstall Abbey (remains of)
KSTL LS5 .... 77 K6

rkstall Health Clinic
KSTL LS5 .... 78 A7

rkstall Industrial Park
BULY LS4 .... 100 D2

rkstall Leisure Centre
KSTL LS5 .... 78 A7

rkstall Valley Primary School
BULY LS4 .... 100 C1

ottingley CE (C) J & I School
KNOT WF11 .... 156 D7

ottingley Vale J & I School
KNOT WF11 .... 156 A7

owle Spring Industrial Estate
KGHY BD21 .... 2 C5

Bowl
BEE/HOL LS11 .... 7 D6

derbank Middle School
BAIL BD17 .... 52 A7

y Anne Business Park
BTLY WF17 .... 146 C5

y E Hastings CE
Primary School
BSPA/BRAM LS23 .... 42 E2

Lady Elizabeth Hastings CE
Primary School
WBY LS22 .... 40 E2

Lady Lane Park School
BGLY BD16 .... 50 A6

Laisterdyke Clinic
BFDE BD3 .... 97 F4

Laisterdyke Middle School
BFDE BD3 .... 97 F4

Lakeside Industrial Estate
WOR/ARM LS12 .... 99 J4

Langdale Primary School
RTHW LS26 .... 126 E4

Langthwaite Grange
Industrial Estate
HEM/SK/SE WF9 .... 225 K8

Lapage Middle School
BFDE BD3 .... 96 E3

Larks Hill Primary School
PONT WF8 .... 180 C5

Lascelles Hall Cricket Club
HUDE HD5 .... 192 E6

Last of the Summer
Wine Exhibition
HOLM/MEL HD9 .... 233 F6

Latchmore Industrial Park
WOR/ARM LS12 .... 100 C8
WOR/ARM LS12 .... 100 E7

Laura Mitchell Health Centre
HFAX HX1 .... 9 D4

Lawefield Primary School
WKFDW/WTN WF2 .... 10 A4

Lawns Park Primary School
WOR/ARM LS12 .... 99 J6

Lawnswood Business Park
BHP/TINH LS16 .... 78 A2

Lawnswood Cemetery
BHP/TINH LS16 .... 56 B8

Lawnswood Crematorium
BHP/TINH LS16 .... 56 B8

Lawnswood School
BHP/TINH LS16 .... 78 B3

Lawrence Batley Theatre
HUD HD1 .... 13 D4

Laycock First School
HWTH BD22 .... 46 E4

Leaventhorpe Middle School
WIL/AL BD15 .... 94 B4

Lee Bridge Industrial Estate
HFAX HX1 .... 8 B3

Lee Brigg First School
NORM WF6 .... 151 H8

Leeds & Bradford Airport
Industrial Estate
YEA LS19 .... 54 C2

Leeds Bradford
International Airport
YEA LS19 .... 54 D4

The Leeds Business Centre
MOR LS27 .... 122 D7

Leeds City Central Library,
Museum & art Gallery
LDS LS1 .... 7 D3

Leeds College of Art & Design
LDSU LS2 .... 7 D1

Leeds College of Building
CHAL LS7 .... 7 E2

Leeds College of Music
OSM LS9 .... 7 F3

Leeds College of Technology
BEE/HOL LS11 .... 124 B3
LDSU LS2 .... 7 D2

Leeds Community &
Mental Health Services
PDSY/CALV LS28 .... 98 C4

Leeds Community &
Mental Health Services
Teaching NHS Trust
WOR/ARM LS12 .... 6 A5

Leeds General Infirmary
LDSU LS2 .... 6 C2

Leeds Girls High School
HDGY LS6 .... 79 F7

Leeds Golf Centre
AL/HA/HU LS17 .... 58 E2

Leeds Golf Club
RHAY LS8 .... 81 F3

Leeds Grammar Junior School
AL/HA/HU LS17 .... 58 B4

Leeds Grammar School
AL/HA/HU LS17 .... 58 B5

Leeds & Hull Business Centre
LDSU LS2 .... 7 D1

Leeds 27 Industrial Estate
MOR LS27 .... 122 C7

Leeds Industrial Museum
WOR/ARM LS12 .... 100 D3

Leeds Industrial Museum at
Armley Mills
BULY LS4 .... 100 D2

Leeds International
Swimming Pool
LDS LS1 .... 6 C3

Leeds Islamia Girls School
CHAL LS7 .... 79 K5

Leeds Metropolitan University
HDGY LS6 .... 78 C5
KSTL LS5 .... 77 K7
LDS LS1 .... 7 D2

Leeds Rhinos RLFC
(Headingley Stadium)
BULY LS4 .... 78 C7

Leeds Road Hospital
BFDE BD3 .... 5 F4

Leeds Road Retail Park
HUD HD1 .... 13 E2

Leeds Shopping Plaza
LDS LS1 .... 7 E4

The Leeds Teaching Hospitals
NHS Trust
LDS LS1 .... 6 C3

Leeds Tykes RUFC
(Headingley Stadium)
BULY LS4 .... 78 C7

Leeds United AFC (Elland Road)
BEE/HOL LS11 .... 100 E8

Leeds University
LDSU LS2 .... 6 C1

Leeds University
Business School
HDGY LS6 .... 6 B1

Lee Mills Industrial Estate
HFAX HX1 .... 8 C3
HOLM/MEL HD9 .... 233 K6

Lee Mills Industrial Park
HOLM/MEL HD9 .... 233 K7

Lee Mount County
Primary School
HIPP HX3 .... 8 B2

Lees First School
HWTH BD22 .... 69 G3

Leeside J I & N School
HECK WF16 .... 145 H5

Leisure Centre
BGLY BD16 .... 71 F3

Leopold Primary School
CHAL LS7 .... 79 K8

Lepton CE J I & N School
KBTN HD8 .... 193 F8

Library Headquarters
WKFDW/WTN WF2 .... 10 A2

Lidget Green First School
GTHN BD7 .... 95 F5

Lidget Green Middle School
GTHN BD7 .... 95 F5

Lightcliffe CE Primary School
HIPP HX3 .... 141 K4

Lightcliffe Golf Club
HIPP HX3 .... 141 K3

Lightcliffe Preparatory School
HIPP HX3 .... 141 J3

Light Waves Sports Centre
WKFDE WF1 .... 10 C2

Lilycroft First School
HTON BD9 .... 95 H1

Limestone Trail
BRFD/BLYE BB10 .... 108 B5

Lindley County Junior School
HUDW HD3 .... 190 B2

Linthwaite Ardron Memorial CE
Primary School
MAR/SLWT HD7 .... 211 J2

Linthwaite Business Centre
MAR/SLWT HD7 .... 211 H2

Linthwaite Clough J & I School
MAR/SLWT HD7 .... 211 G2

Little London CP School
CHAL LS7 .... 7 E1

Little London Primary School
CHAL LS7 .... 7 E1

Littlemoor Primary School
YEA LS19 .... 54 A7

Littleroyd Mills Business Park
HUD HD1 .... 12 C6

Little Theatre
HBR HX7 .... 112 B8

Littletown J & I School
CLECK BD19 .... 144 D6
Liversedge Cricket Club
LVSG WF15 .... 170 C1
Lofthousegate J & I School
EARD/LOFT WF3 .... 150 A5
Longclose Industrial Estate
OSM LS9 .... 102 A1
Longlands Trading Estate
OSS WF5 .... 173 K5
Long Lee J & I School
KGHY BD21 .... 3 F5
Longley Park Golf Club
HUD HD1 .... 13 E5
Longley School
HUDE HD5 .... 13 E6
Longley Tennis Club
HUDE HD5 .... 13 F6
Longroyde Junior School
BRIG HD6 .... 168 A2
Lorne First School
BOW BD4 .... 96 D7
Lotherton Hall
GFTH/SHER LS25 .... 85 J6
Lounge Cinema
HDGY LS6 .... 78 D6
Low Ash First School
SHPY BD18 .... 73 K5
Lowerfields Middle School
BOW BD4 .... 96 E7
Lower Grange Medical Centre
GIR BD8 .... 94 C4
Lowerhouses CE J & I School
HUDE HD5 .... 13 F6
Lower Wortley CP School
WOR/ARM LS12 .... 100 B6
Lowfields Business Park
ELL HX5 .... 167 G3
Low Laithes Golf Club
OSS WF5 .... 174 C3
Low Mills Industrial Estate
DEWS WF13 .... 171 G7
Low Moor Business Park
LM/WK BD12 .... 119 F5
Low Moor CE First School
LM/WK BD12 .... 118 E5
Low Road Primary School
MID LS10 .... 102 A7
Lowtown Primary School
PDSY/CALV LS28 .... 98 D4
Luddenfoot J & I School
LUD/ILL HX2 .... 138 B6
Luddenden Primary School
LUD/ILL HX2 .... 138 A3
Lupset Group Medical Centre
WKFDW/WTN WF2 .... 174 E8
Lupset Hall (Club House)
WKFDW/WTN WF2 .... 198 B1
Lydgate J & I School
BTLY WF17 .... 146 E6
Lydgate Special School
HOLM/MEL HD9 .... 233 K4
Lynfield Mount Hospital
HTON BD9 .... 94 D1
M1 Industrial Estate
MID LS10 .... 102 A7
Mackie Hill J & I School
HOR/CROF WF4 .... 197 K7
Madni Muslim Girls High School
EARL WF12 .... 172 C5
Magdale Industrial Park
HUDS HD4 .... 213 F5
Mandale Middle School
WBSY BD6 .... 117 J3
Manningham Baths &
Sports Centre
GIR BD8 .... 95 H2
Manningham Clinic
GIR BD8 .... 4 B2
Manningham Middle School
GIR BD8 .... 4 B2
Manorfield Infant School
BTLY WF17 .... 145 K7
Manor House Gallery & Museum
ILK LS29 .... 20 C7
Manor Leisure Centre
YEA LS19 .... 53 J4
Manor Park Industrial Estate
BIRK/DRI BD11 .... 121 H4
Manor Street Industrial Estate
CHAL LS7 .... 102 A1
Manston Primary School
MSTN/BAR LS15 .... 82 A8

Manston St James CE
Primary School
MSTN/BAR LS15 .... 82 B8
Mantra House Business Centre
KGHY BD21 .... 3 D4
Manywells Brow Industrial Estate
CUL/QBY BD13 .... 70 B6
Margaret McMillan First School
HTON BD9 .... 95 G1
Margram Business Centre
HFAX HX1 .... 8 C4
Marriott Hollins Hall Hotel &
Country Club
GSLY LS20 .... 52 C5
Marsden County Junior School
MAR/SLWT HD7 .... 209 J7
Marsden Health Centre
MAR/SLWT HD7 .... 209 H7
Marsden Infant School
MAR/SLWT HD7 .... 209 J7
Marshfield First School
WBOW BD5 .... 95 J8
Martin Frobisher First School
NORM WF6 .... 151 J7
Matthew Murray High School
BEE/HOL LS11 .... 101 F7
Maybrook Industrial Park
WOR/ARM LS12 .... 6 A3
Meanwood CE Primary School
HDGY LS6 .... 78 E4
Meanwood Health Centre
HDGY LS6 .... 79 F5
Meanwood Park Hospital
HDGY LS6 .... 78 E2
Meltham CE J & I School
HOLM/MEL HD9 .... 231 J2
Meltham Cricket & Athletic Club
HOLM/MEL HD9 .... 211 J8
Meltham Golf Club
HOLM/MEL HD9 .... 231 K2
Meltham J & I School
HOLM/MEL HD9 .... 211 G8
Meltham Mills Industrial Estate
HOLM/MEL HD9 .... 231 K1
Menston Cricket Club
ILK LS29 .... 32 D6
Menston Primary School
ILK LS29 .... 32 C7
Merrion Shopping Centre
LDSU LS2 .... 7 E2
Methley Infant School
RTHW LS26 .... 152 B1
Methley Junior School
RTHW LS26 .... 128 D8
Methley Park Hospital
RTHW LS26 .... 127 K8
Methley Road Industrial Park
CAS WF10 .... 153 G4
Micklefield CE Primary School
GFTH/SHER LS25 .... 107 G4
Middlestown Health Centre
HOR/CROF WF4 .... 196 B4
Middlestown Primary School
HOR/CROF WF4 .... 196 B4
Middleton Park High School
MID LS10 .... 124 E7
Middleton Park Leisure Centre
MID LS10 .... 124 E6
Middleton Park Municipal
Golf Club
MID LS10 .... 124 B6
Middleton Primary School
MID LS10 .... 124 C7
Middleton Railway
MID LS10 .... 124 D2
Middleton St Marys CE
Primary School
MID LS10 .... 124 D6
Mid Point Business Park
PDSY/CALV LS28 .... 97 H3
Mid Yorkshire Golf Club
PONT WF8 .... 182 B6
Mid Yorkshire Nuffield Hospital
HORS LS18 .... 77 H3
Miles Hill Primary School
CHAL LS7 .... 79 G4
Milestone School
PDSY/CALV LS28 .... 98 C1
Milford RUFC
KSTL LS5 .... 78 A7
Millbridge J & I School
LVSG WF15 .... 144 E7
Mill Dam J & I School
FEA/AMT WF7 .... 203 C6

Millennium Business Park
AIRE BD20 .... 26 E[]
Mill Hill Community Health Centre
HUDE HD5 .... 192 C[]
Mill Lane J & I School
BTLY WF17 .... 146 C[]
Millshaw Park Trading Estate
MOR LS27 .... 123 K[]
Minerva Industrial Estate
RTHW LS26 .... 127 H[]
Minsthorpe Community College
HEM/SK/SE WF9 .... 226 B[]
Minsthorpe Swimming Pool
HEM/SK/SE WF9 .... 226 []
Mirfield Parish Cricket Club
MIRF WF14 .... 170 C[]
Mixenden Clinic
LUD/ILL HX2 .... 115 []
Mixenden County
Primary School
LUD/ILL HX2 .... 114 E[]
Moderna Business Park
HBR HX7 .... 137 C[]
Moldgreen J & I School
HUDE HD5 .... 13 F[]
Monckton Road Industrial Estate
WKFDW/WTN WF2 .... 198 C[]
Moor Allerton Golf Club
AL/HA/HU LS17 .... 59 C[]
Moor Allerton Hall
Primary School
AL/HA/HU LS17 .... 80 E[]
Moorfield Business Park
YEA LS19 .... 54 E[]
Moorfield First School
BFDE BD3 .... 96 E[]
Moorfield School
ILK LS29 .... 20 C[]
Moorfield Shopping Centre
HUDS HD4 .... 190 D[]
Moorlands School
BHP/TINH LS16 .... 78 D[]
Moorlands Small
Business Centre
CLECK BD19 .... 144 A[]
Moor Lodge Park
AL/HA/HU LS17 59
Moor Park Business Centre
WKFDW/WTN WF2 .... 10 A[]
Moorside School
LUD/ILL HX2 115
The Moors Shopping Centre
ILK LS29 .... 20 A[]
Moorthorpe Primary School
HEM/SK/SE WF9 .... 226 A[]
Moortown Golf Club
AL/HA/HU LS17 .... 57 K[]
Moortown Primary School
AL/HA/HU LS17 .... 79 K[]
Moortown RUFC
AL/HA/HU LS17 .... 57 K[]
Moorview Business Park
IDLE BD10 .... 74 E[]
Morley Bruntcliffe High School
MOR LS27 .... 122 E[]
Morley High School
MOR LS27 .... 122 E[]
Morley Leisure Centre
MOR LS27 .... 122 E[]
Morley Victoria Primary School
MOR LS27 .... 123 E[]
Moslem School
BTLY WF17 .... 146 []
Mountjoy House School
HUD HD1 .... 12 []
The Mount J & I School
WKFDW/WTN WF2 .... 175 []
Mount Pellon J & I School
HFAX HX1 .... 8 []
Mount St Marys High School
OSM LS9 .... 102 []
Mount St Marys RC
Primary School
OSM LS9 .... 102 []
The Mount School
HUDW HD3 .... 12 []
Municipal Baths
BRIG HD6 .... 168 []
Myrtle Park Primary School
BGLY BD16 .... 71 []
Mytholmroyd Health Centre
HBR HX7 .... 137 []
Nab Wood Cemetery
SHPY BD18 .... 72 []

b Wood Grammar School
BGLY BD16 .... **72** C4

b Wood Middle School
BGLY BD16 .... **72** C4

poleon Business Park
BOW BD4 .... **5** F6

tional Coal Mining Museum
for England
HOR/CROF WF4 .... **195** J6

tional Film Theatre North
MID LS10 .... **7** E4

il Hunt Memorial Ground &
Rugby Club
BOW BD4 .... **96** E6

ssfield First School
HWTH BD22 .... **2** A5

therfield Industrial Park
DEWS WF13 .... **171** H6

therleigh School
HTON BD9 .... **95** F1

therthong J & I School
HOLM/MEL HD9 .... **233** G3

therton Infant School
HUDS HD4 .... **212** D4

therton J & I School
HOR/CROF WF4 .... **196** E5

wbridge Industrial Estate
KGHY BD21 .... **3** E3

wby First School
WBOW BD5 .... **95** K8

w College
PONT WF8 .... **180** C2

w Cross Street Health Centre
WBOW BD5 .... **95** K8

whaven Business Park
HUDW HD3 .... **190** A6

w Hold Industrial Estate
GFTH/SHER LS25 .... **106** A3

wlands County Junior School
RPDN/SBR HX6 .... **138** B8

wlands Industrial Estate
BAIL BD17 .... **73** J3

wlands Primary School
MOR LS27 .... **123** J7

w Line Clinic
IDLE BD10 .... **75** G4

wmillerdam Country Park
WKFDW/WTN WF2 .... **220** E1

w Park Spring
CUD/GR S72 .... **240** B7

wsome High School
HUDS HD4 .... **213** F2

wsome Junior School
HUDS HD4 .... **213** G2

wspaper Office
BFD BD1 .... **5** D4

wton Hill Primary School
WKFDE WF1 .... **175** K1

wton Ings
CAS WF10 .... **130** C7

elds Primary School
MAR/SLWT HD7 .... **210** D3

elands Lane Primary School
GFTH/SHER LS25 .... **106** A4

rcroft Industrial Estate
BFD BD1 .... **4** A4

rland CE J & I School
RPDN/SBR HX6 .... **165** G1

rmanton CE First School
NORM WF6 .... **178** A1

rmanton Common First
NORM WF6 .... **152** B7

rmanton Freeston
High School
NORM WF6 .... **178** A2

rmanton Health Centre
NORM WF6 .... **177** K2

rmanton Industrial Estate
NORM WF6 .... **152** C8

rmanton Public Baths
NORM WF6 .... **178** A1

rmanton

Town Middle School
NORM WF6 .... **177** K2

rquest Industrial Park
BTLY WF17 .... **121** K8

risthorpe Primary School
LVSG WF15 .... **170** E1

th Bridge Leisure Centre
HFAX HX1 .... **9** E3

thcliffe Golf Club
SHPY BD18 .... **72** E5

rth Dean Business Park
GTL/HWG HX4 .... **166** C3

North Dean RFC
GTL/HWG HX4 .... **166** C4

Northern Ballet Theatre
BHP/TINH LS16 .... **78** A3
BRAM LS13 .... **77** H7

Northern School
of Contemporary
CHAL LS7 .... **79** K8

Northfield J I & N School
HEM/SK/SE WF9 .... **225** J8

The North Halifax
Grammar School
LUD/ILL HX2 .... **115** J5

North Leeds Cricket Club
RHAY LS8 .... **80** C3

The North of England
Higher Secretarial College
LDS LS1 .... **7** E3

Northowram Hall Hospital
HIPP HX3 .... **117** F7

Northowram School
HIPP HX3 .... **117** F8

Northside Business Park
CHAL LS7 .... **7** F1

Northside Retail Park
CHAL LS7 .... **79** F4

Northwest Business Park
LDSU LS2 .... **79** H8

Norton Thorpe Hall School
HUD HD1 .... **12** B3

Nortonthorpe Hall
Special School
KBTN HD8 .... **237** H2

Nortonthorpe Industrial Estate
KBTN HD8 .... **237** H2

Norwood Business Park
LM/WK BD12 .... **142** C1

Notre Dame C
Sixth Form College
LDSU LS2 .... **79** H8

Nova Scotia Medical Centre
CAS WF10 .... **129** F6

Oakbank School
HWTH BD22 .... **2** A6

Oakdale First School
SHPY BD18 .... **73** K5

Oaktree Business Park
SCFT LS14 .... **81** J4

Oak Tree School
FEA/AMT WF7 .... **203** F7

Oaktree Special School
FEA/AMT WF7 .... **203** F7

Oakwell Hall
BTLY WF17 .... **121** F8

Oakwell Industrial Park
BTLY WF17 .... **121** J7

Oakwood Primary School
RHAY LS8 .... **80** E8

Oakworth Health Centre
HWTH BD22 .... **69** F1

Oakworth J & I School
HWTH BD22 .... **68** E1

Odeon Cinema
BFD BD1 .... **4** C5
BFDE BD3 .... **97** H3
LDS LS1 .... **7** E3

Old Bank Ji & N School
MIRF WF14 .... **170** D4

Oldfield First School
HWTH BD22 .... **67** J3

Old Mill Business Park
MID LS10 .... **102** B7

Old Rishworthians RUFC
HIPP HX3 .... **165** K1

Old Roundhegians RUFC
AL/HA/HU LS17 .... **80** A1

Open Market
KGHY BD21 .... **3** D3

The Open University
LDS LS1 .... **7** E4

Optimax Eye Clinic
LDS LS1 .... **7** D3

Orchard Business Park
HBR HX7 .... **137** F3

Orchard Croft Medical Centre
HOR/CROF WF4 .... **197** H2

Orchard Head Primary School
PONT WF8 .... **155** F7

Osmondthorpe Primary School
OSM LS9 .... **103** F4

Ossett Cricket & Athletic Club
OSS WF5 .... **173** J7

Ossett Dimplewell Junior School
OSS WF5 .... **173** K7

Ossett Health Centre
OSS WF5 .... **173** J6

Ossett School
OSS WF5 .... **173** J8

Otley Golf Club
OT LS21 .... **32** E5

Otley Road Medical Centre
BFDE BD3 .... **5** D2

Otley RUFC
OT LS21 .... **33** K3

Otley Town FC
Old Otliensians RUFC
OT LS21 .... **34** A3

Oulton Health Centre
RTHW LS26 .... **127** F5

Oulton Park Golf Course
RTHW LS26 .... **126** E7

Oulton Primary School
RTHW LS26 .... **126** E5

Our Lady of Lourdes CP School
HUDN HD2 .... **168** D7

Our Lady of Victories
RC J & I School
HWTH BD22 .... **2** A3

Outlane Golf Club
HUDW HD3 .... **188** E4

Outlane J & I School
HUDW HD3 .... **189** H2

Outwood Grange School
WKFDE WF1 .... **149** H7

Outwood Ledger Lane
J & I School
WKFDE WF1 .... **149** J7

Overland Industrial Estate
MOR LS27 .... **122** B6

Overthorpe CE J & I School
EARL WF12 .... **195** G1

The Owlcotes Centre
PDSY/CALV LS28 .... **98** B2

Oxenhope CE First School
HWTH BD22 .... **68** D8

Oyster Park Infant School
CAS WF10 .... **154** E2

Oyster Park Middle School
CAS WF10 .... **154** E3

Paddock Cricket & Bowling Club
HUDW HD3 .... **190** C6

Paddock J & I School
HUD HD1 .... **190** D6

Painthorpe House Golf &
Country Club
HOR/CROF WF4 .... **197** K7

Parkhouse Industrial Estate
LM/WK BD12 .... **119** F5

Parkinson Lane School
HFAX HX1 .... **8** B5

Park Junior School
CAS WF10 .... **153** K4

Parkland First & Middle School
IDLE BD10 .... **75** F4

Parklands County
Primary School
SCFT LS14 .... **81** J7

Parklands Girls High School
SCFT LS14 .... **81** K7

Park Lane College
HORS LS18 .... **76** D4
LDS LS1 .... **7** E3

Park Lane College of
Further Education
BVRD LS3 .... **6** C3
CHAL LS7 .... **80** A6

Park Road J & N School
BTLY WF17 .... **146** C6

Park Road Medical Centre
WBOW BD5 .... **4** C6

Park Road Retail Park
PONT WF8 .... **180** D1

Parkside Industrial Estate
BEE/HOL LS11 .... **124** D2

Parkside Middle School
CUL/QBY BD13 .... **70** C5

The Park Special School
WKFDW/WTN WF2 .... **10** B4

Park Spring CP School
BRAM LS13 .... **99** G3

Park Wood Crematorium
ELL HX5 .... **166** E2

Parkwood First School
KGHY BD21 .... **3** E4

Parkwood Primary School
KGHY BD21 .... **3** E4

Parkwood Street Industrial Estate
KGHY BD21 .... **3** F3

Parl Lane College
PDSY/CALV LS28 .... **98** C3

Pavilion Business Centre
PDSY/CALV LS28 .... **98** D1

Pavilion Business Park
WOR/ARM LS12 .... **100** C8

Pecket Well College
HBR HX7 .... **112** C4

Pecketwell College
HFAX HX1 .... **8** C4

Peel Mill Business Centre
MOR LS27 .... **123** G7

Pellon Industrial Estate
HFAX HX1 .... **8** A3

Penistone Grammar School
STKB/PEN S36 .... **252** B6

Penistone Hill
HWTH BD22 .... **68** C5

Penistone Sports Centre
STKB/PEN S36 .... **252** B7

Penistone Springvale
Primary School
STKB/PEN S36 .... **252** E8

Penistone Thurlstone
Primary School
STKB/PEN S36 .... **251** J7

Pennine Industrial Estate
WOR/ARM LS12 .... **100** B4

Pennine Industrial Park
HBR HX7 .... **112** B7

Penny Field School
HDGY LS6 .... **79** F2

Penraevon Industrial Estate
CHAL LS7 .... **79** J8

Pentland Infant School
EARL WF12 .... **172** C6

Pentland Road Clinic
EARL WF12 .... **172** C5

Percival Whitley
College of Education
(Halifax New College)
HFAX HX1 .... **8** B5

Peter Laycock Industrial Estate
CHAL LS7 .... **79** J8

Phoebe Lane Industrial Estate
HIPP HX3 .... **140** C7

Phoenix Works Estate
HOR/CROF WF4 .... **196** E2

Pickup Business Park
PDSY/CALV LS28 .... **98** C1

Picturedrome Cinema & Museum
HOLM/MEL HD9 .... **233** F6

Picture House Cinema
CHAL LS7 .... **7** F1
NORM WF6 .... **177** K1
WKFDE WF1 .... **11** D2

Piece Hall Art Gallery
HFAX HX1 .... **9** E4

Pilot Theatre
CAS WF10 .... **154** A5

Pinderfield Hospital
WKFDE WF1 .... **176** A2

Pinderfields & Pontefract
Hospital NHS Trust
EARD/LOFT WF3 .... **176** C2

Pioneer Business Centre
CAS WF10 .... **152** E7

Pitt Street Business Centre
KGHY BD21 .... **3** E3

Playhouse & Film Theatre
BFD BD1 .... **5** D5

Police Sports Ground
RHAY LS8 .... **80** B4

Pollard Park Middle School
BFDE BD3 .... **5** F5

Pontefract Castle
PONT WF8 .... **180** E2

Pontefract Crematorium
PONT WF8 .... **180** B5

Pontefract & District Golf Club
PONT WF8 .... **179** K2

Pontefract General Infirmary
PONT WF8 .... **180** E3

Pontefract Museum
PONT WF8 .... **180** D2

Pontefract Racecourse
PONT WF8 .... **180** B2

Pontefract RFC
PONT WF8 .... **181** G7

Pontefract Squash &
Leisure Centre
PONT WF8 .... **180** D2

Pontefract Swimming Pool
PONT WF8 .... **180** D2

Pool CE Primary School
OT LS21 .... **35** H4

Poplars Farm First School
ECHL BD2 .... **74** A7

Potternewton Primary School
CHAL LS7 .... **79** H6

Powerhouse Showcase Theatre
WKFDW/WTN WF2 .... **10** B3

Priesthorpe School
PDSY/CALV LS28 .... **97** K1

Priestley Centre
BFD BD1 .... **5** D4

Priestman Middle School
WBOW BD5 .... **118** D1

Priestthorpe First School
BGLY BD16 .... **50** A8

Priestthorpe Medical Centre
BGLY BD16 .... **49** K7

Primrose High Hill School
OSM LS9 .... **102** A1

Primrose Hill Primary School
PDSY/CALV LS28 .... **98** B2

Primrose Lane Primary School
BSPA/BRAM LS23 .... **42** D4

Prince Henrys Grammar School
OT LS21 .... **33** J2

Prince of Wales Business Park
BRIG HD6 .... **168** C1

Princess Mary Campus
(Halifax New College)
HFAX HX1 .... **8** B5

Princess Mary Stadium
CLECK BD19 .... **144** C6

Princess Royal Health Centre
HUD HD1 .... **12** B4

Princeville First School
GTHN BD7 .... **95** H4

Princeville Road Industrial Estate
GIR BD8 .... **95** G4

Priory Business Park
HEM/SK/SE WF9 .... **202** B7

Prospect Business Centre
HUD HD1 .... **12** C5

Public Baths & Recreation Centre
BTLY WF17 .... **146** B6

Public Health Laboratory Service
Seacroft Hospital
SCFT LS14 .... **103** H1

Pudsey Business Centre
PDSY/CALV LS28 .... **98** D4

Pudsey Grangefield School
PDSY/CALV LS28 .... **98** C3

Pudsey Greenside J & I School
PDSY/CALV LS28 .... **98** B5

Pudsey Leisure Centre
PDSY/CALV LS28 .... **98** C4

Pudsey St Lawrence Cricket Club
PDSY/CALV LS28 .... **98** B4

Pudsey Tyersal Primary School
BOW BD4 .... **97** H6

Pugneys Country Park
WKFDW/WTN WF2 .... **198** D2

Purlwell Infant School
BTLY WF17 .... **146** A7

QBM Business Park
BTLY WF17 .... **145** J1

QF Industrial Estate
BOW BD4 .... **96** D7

Quality Foods Industrial Park
BOW BD4 .... **97** F6

Quarry Hill Industrial Estate
HOR/CROF WF4 .... **196** E2

Quarry House
OSM LS9 .... **7** F3

Quarry Mount Primary School
HDGY LS6 .... **79** G7

Queen Elizabeth Grammar School
WKFDE WF1 .... **10** B2

Queensbury Golf Club
CUL/QBY BD13 .... **116** E3

Queensbury Health Centre
CUL/QBY BD13 .... **116** C2

Queensbury School
CUL/QBY BD13 .... **116** D3

Queensgate Market
HUD HD1 .... **13** D5

Queens Mill Business Centre
HUD HD1 .... **12** C6

Queens Mill Industrial Estate
HUD HD1 .... **12** C6

Queens Road School
HFAX HX1 .... **8** A4

Queens Sports Club
HFAX HX1 .... **8** C6

Queen Street Infant School
MOR LS27 .... **123** I

Queen Street J & I School
NORM WF6 .... **178** A

Queensway Primary School
GSLY LS20 .... **53**

Raglan Industrial Estate
CAS WF10 .... **153** C

Railwaymens Sports Club
BSLYN/ROY S71 .... **222** C

Ralph Thoresby High School
BHP/TINH LS16 .... **55**

Ramgarhia Sikh Sports Centre
CHAL LS7 .... **7**

Rastrick High School
BRIG HD6 .... **168**

Rastrick Squash Centre
BRIG HD6 .... **168**

Ravensbridge Industrial Estate
DEWS WF13 .... **171**

Ravenscliffe First School
IDLE BD10 .... **75**

Ravenscliffe High School
HIPP HX3 .... **166**

Ravensthorpe CE Junior School
DEWS WF13 .... **171** I

Ravensthorpe Infant School
DEWS WF13 .... **171** I

Rawdon CE Primary School
YEA LS19 .... **54**

Rawdon Cricket Club
YEA LS19 .... **54**

Rawdon Golf & Lawn Tennis Club
YEA LS19 .... **53**

Rawfolds Industrial Estate
CLECK BD19 .... **144**

Rawson J & I School
HIPP HX3 .... **8**

Rawson Market
BFD BD1 .... **4**

Rawthorpe High School
HUDE HD5 .... **13**

Rawthorpe Junior School
HUDE HD5 .... **13**

Raynville Primary School
BRAM LS13 .... **99**

Red Doles Industrial Estate
HUD HD1 .... **13**

Redhill Infant School
CAS WF10 .... **154**

Red House
CLECK BD19 .... **144**

Red Ledge Business Centre
HOLM/MEL HD9 .... **233**

Redledge Business Centre
HOLM/MEL HD9 .... **233**

Reevy Hill Primary School
WBSY BD6 .... **118**

Reinwood County J & I School
HUDW HD3 .... **190**

Renji Chinese Medical Centre
HUDN HD2 .... **13**

Revival Industrial Estate
BOW BD4 .... **5**

Rex Cinema
ELL HX5 .... **166**

Rhodesway School
GIR BD8 .... **94**

Richard Dunn Sports Centre
WBOW BD5 .... **118**

Richmond Building
GTHN BD7 .... **4**

Richmond Hill Primary School
OSM LS9 .... **102**

Richmond House School
BHP/TINH LS16 .... **78**

Richmond Medical Centre
OSM LS9 .... **102**

Riddlesden CE School
AIRE BD20 .... **48**

Riddlesden Golf Club
AIRE BD20 .... **27**

Riddlesden Infants School
AIRE BD20 .... **48**

Ridings Business Park
HFAX HX1 .... **8**

The Ridings School
LUD/ILL HX2 .... **115**

Ridings Shopping Centre
WKFDE WF1 .... **10**

RIFFA Business Park
OT LS21 .... **35**

Ringway Industrial Estate
HUD HD1 .... **12**

ponden J & I School
RPDN/SBR HX6 164   B6
verside Business Park
BAIL BD17 73   J3
ILK LS29 20   C6
KBTN HD8 237   H1
verside Industrial Estate
EARL WF12 172   B4
HOR/CROF WF4 196   E3
verside Junior School
HBR HX7 112   B8
verside Medical Centre
CAS WF10 153   H3
ck Hill Sports Club
CAS WF10 154   B5
dillian School
EARD/LOFT WF3 149   K2
dley Primary School
BRAM LS13 76   D6
e Rookeries Carleton
J & I School
PONT WF8 181   G5
oks Nest Primary School
WKFDE WF1 149   K7
sebank Primary School
BVRD LS3 6   B2
semeade School
HUDE HD5 192   A6
seville Business Park
RHAY LS8 102   A1
ssefield School
HTON BD9 73   G7
ssett Business Park
BRAM LS13 77   F7
thwell CE Primary School
RTHW LS26 126   B5
thwell Health Centre
RTHW LS26 126   B6
thwell Methley CP Infant School
RTHW LS26 152   B1
thwell Primary School
RTHW LS26 126   B7
thwell Sports Centre
RTHW LS26 127   F7
thwell West Junior School
RTHW LS26 126   A7
undhay Golf Club
RHAY LS8 80   E1
undhay Park Site
RHAY LS8 81   F4
undhay St Johns
Primary School
RHAY LS8 80   E5
undhay School
RHAY LS8 80   C4
undhill Junior School
KNOT WF11 155   J6
undhouse Business Park
WOR/ARM LS12 6   B4
undwood Industrial Estate
OSS WF5 174   C6
yal Armouries Museum
MID LS10 7   F5
yal Halifax Infirmary
HFAX HX1 9   D6
yal Industrial Park
HFAX HX1 8   C4
e Royal London
Industrial Estate
BEE/HOL LS11 124   A2
yal Park Primary School
HDGY LS6 6   A1
rd Mill Business Park
BRIG HD6 168   C1
rd Mount Middle School
CUL/QBY BD13 93   G5
rds Hall High School
HUDW HD3 190   C5
ds School
RTHW LS26 150   E1
ston Clinic
BSLYN/ROY S71 222   A8
ston High School
BSLYN/ROY S71 222   A7
ston Meadstead
Primary School
BSLYN/ROY S71 221   K8
ston Midland J & I School
BSLYN/ROY S71 222   A7
stons John Baptist CE (A)
Primary School
BSLYN/ROY S71 222   A8

Royston Summerfields
Primary School
BSLYN/ROY S71 221   J7
Rspb Nature Reserve
(Fairburn Ings)
KNOT WF11 130   E7
Russell Hall First School
CUL/QBY BD13 116   D2
Rutland Industrial Estate
WKFDE WF1 11   D5
Ryan Middle School
BOW BD4 96   B8
Ryburn County
Secondary School
RPDN/SBR HX6 164   B1
Ryburn Golf Club
RPDN/SBR HX6 165   F2
Ryecroft First School
BOW BD4 120   C1
Ryecroft Primary School
WOR/ARM LS12 99   J5
Ryhill Industrial Estate
HOR/CROF WF4 222   E2
Ryhill J & I School
HOR/CROF WF4 222   E1
Ryshworth Middle School
BGLY BD16 49   J4
Sacred Heart Catholic
Primary School
BULY LS4 78   B8
Sai Medical Centre
GIR BD8 4   A1
St Agnes PNEU School
HDGY LS6 78   D5
St Aidans CE First School
KBTN HD8 236   E2
St Andrew CE Infant School
BRIG HD6 142   B7
St Andrews CE Junior School
BRIG HD6 142   B8
St Annes Cathedral
LDS LS1 7   D3
St Annes RC School
KGHY BD21 2   C2
St Anthonys RC First School
CLAY BD14 94   D6
St Anthonys RC J & I School
SHPY BD18 74   B3
St Anthonys RC Primary School
BEE/HOL LS11 124   A1
St Augustines CE First School
BFDE BD3 5   E2
St Augustines CE Primary School
HFAX HX1 8   B3
St Augustines RC Primary School
RHAY LS8 80   C8
St Austins RC Primary School
WKFDE WF1 11   D2
St Barnabas CE School
HTON BD9 73   G7
St Bartholomews CE
Primary School
WOR/ARM LS12 100   C4
St Bedes Grammar School
HTON BD9 73   G8
St Benedicts RC Primary School
GFTH/SHER LS25 105   K4
St Catherines Business Complex
BRAM LS13 77   H7
St Chads CE Primary School
BRIG HD6 141   K6
BHP/TINH LS16 78   A4
St Clares Roman Catholic School
ECHL BD2 97   F1
St Columbas RC Primary School
BOW BD4 120   A4
St Cuthberts & First Martyrs
First School
HTON BD9 95   G1
St Edwards RC Primary School
BSPA/BRAM LS23 42   C3
St Francis of Assisi RC
Primary School
BEE/HOL LS11 101   H8
St Francis RC First School
ECHL BD2 74   C7
St Francis RC Primary School
MOR LS27 122   E7
St George's Hall
BFD BD1 4   C5
St Giles CE Va Primary School
PONT WF8 180   E2
St Gregorys RC Primary School
SCFT LS14 82   B6

St Hildas School
HOR/CROF WF4 197   G1
St Ignatius RC Primary School
OSS WF5 173   J8
St James Business Park
BFD BD1 5   D5
St James CE J & I School
HOR/CROF WF4 198   A5
St James CE Primary School
WBY LS22 23   K5
St James Market
BFDE BD3 5   D5
St James's University Hospital
OSM LS9 102   B1
St John Fisher RC High School
DEWS WF13 172   A2
St Johns Catholic School
BSPA/BRAM LS23 42   D4
St Johns CE Infant School
DEWS WF13 171   K3
St Johns CE J & I School
WKFDE WF1 10   B1
St Johns CE Primary School
BRIG HD6 169   F1
RPDN/SBR HX6 186   E2
St Johns CE First School
BOW BD4 120   A2
St Johns CE Primary School
MAR/SLWT HD7 189   H6
St Johns Health Centre
HFAX HX1 8   B4
St Johns Shopping Centre
LDSU LS2 7   E3
St Johns the Baptist
Catholic Primary School
NORM WF6 178   A1
St John the Baptist CE
Primary School
BHP/TINH LS16 56   C7
St John the Evangelist
RC School
WBSY BD6 117   K2
St John with St Michael School
WHIT OL12 158   B6
St Josephs Catholic
Primary School
WBY LS22 23   J5
St Josephs College
HTON BD9 73   J8
St Joseph's Primary School
TOD OL14 134   A6
St Josephs RC First School
WBOW BD5 95   K7
St Josephs RC J I & N School
HUDE HD5 192   B5
St Josephs RC Primary School
CAS WF10 153   K3
DEWS WF13 171   K1
PDSY/CALV LS28 98   D3
PONT WF8 180   D3
TOD OL14 133   K5
St Josephs RC School
BGLY BD16 50   A8
HIPP HX3 9   E3
KGHY BD21 2   C5
St Jospehs RC Primary School
BRIG HD6 142   A6
St Lukes CE First School
CLECK BD19 143   J4
St Lukes Eccleshill CE
First School
ECHL BD2 75   F7
St Lukes Hospital
HUDS HD4 190   C8
WBOW BD5 95   K7
St Malachys RC School
LUD/ILL HX2 115   H8
St Margarets CE Primary School
HORS LS18 77   F2
St Marys Catholic
Primary School
HFAX HX1 8   C5
St Marys Catholic School
ILK LS29 20   D7
St Marys CE J & I School
WKFDE WF1 11   D3
St Marys CE Primary School
RPDN/SBR HX6 163   K4
St Marys Hospital
WOR/ARM LS12 99   K3
St Marys RC Infant School
HFAX HX1 8   C5
St Marys RC J I & N School
BTLY WF17 146   A6

St Marys RC Primary School
BFDE BD3.................................. **5** D4
HORS LS18.............................. **77** G2
RTHW LS26............................ **126** C7

St Marys RC School
ILK LS29................................. **32** E8

St Matthews CE Primary School
CHAL LS7............................... **79** J4

St Matthews CE First School
WBOW BD5............................ **119** F2

St Matthews RC Primary School
WIL/AL BD15.......................... **94** B3

St Michael & All Angels CE Primary School
HIPP HX3............................. **117** J5

St Michaels CE Primary School
HDGY LS6.............................. **78** E6

St Michaels College
BVRD LS3................................. **6** B2

St Nicholas RC Primary School
OSM LS9................................. **81** F8

St Oswald's CE Primary School
WBOW BD5............................. **95** J8

St Oswalds CE Junior School
GSLY LS20............................. **53** G3

St Patricks RC J & I School
HUDW HD3............................. **12** A2

St Patricks RC Primary School
BTLY WF17............................ **145** H1

St Patricks R C Primary School
ELL HX5................................ **166** C5

St Patricks Primary School
OSM LS9............................... **102** C3

St Paulinus RC J & I School
DEWS WF13........................... **171** K4

St Pauls J & I CE School
WKFDW/WTN WF2.................. **174** E3

St Pauls RC Primary School
AL/HA/HU LS17....................... **57** G7

St Peters Cathedral
BFD BD1................................. **5** D4

St Peters CE J & I School
BTLY WF17............................ **145** H1

St Peters CE Primary School
OSM LS9................................. **7** F5

St Peters Infant School
RPDN/SBR HX6...................... **138** B8

St Peters RC First School
BFDE BD3................................ **5** F4

St Philips CE First School
WIL/AL BD15.......................... **94** A1

St Philips RC Primary School
MID LS10.............................. **124** C6

St Saviours CE Junior School
BTLY WF17............................ **145** K2

St Stephens CE Primary School
KSTL LS5................................ **78** A7

St Stephens Special School
WBOW BD5............................. **96** A8

St Theresas RC Primary School
MSTN/BAR LS15...................... **82** A8

St Thomas A Beckett RC Comprehensive School
WKFDW/WTN WF2.................. **199** C2

St Thomas CE Junior School
FEA/AMT WF7........................ **179** H6

St Urbans RC Primary School
HDGY LS6.............................. **79** G2

St Walburgas RC First School
SHPY BD18............................. **73** F4

St Wilfrids Catholic High (VA) School
FEA/AMT WF7........................ **179** H1

St Williams RC Primary School
GIR BD8................................. **95** G4

Salendine Nook High School
HUDW HD3........................... **189** K4

Salford Industrial Estate
TOD OL14............................. **133** K6

Saltaire First School
SHPY BD18............................. **73** F3

Saltaire Medical Centre
SHPY BD18............................. **73** F3

Salterhebble School
HIPP HX3.............................. **140** C8

Salter Lee School
HIPP HX3.............................. **140** E1

Salt Grammar School
BAIL BD17............................. **73** F1

Sandal Castle
WKFDW/WTN WF2.................. **199** F2

Sandal Endowed CE Junior School
WKFDW/WTN WF2.................. **199** G3

Sandal First School
BAIL BD17............................. **51** J8

Sandal Magna J & I School
WKFDE WF1.......................... **199** G1

Sandal Medical Centre
WKFDW/WTN WF2.................. **198** E4

Sandal RUFC
WKFDW/WTN WF2.................. **199** F4

Sandbeck Industrial Estate
WBY LS22.............................. **23** K4

Sandbeck Park Industrial Estate
WBY LS22.............................. **23** K4

Sandbeds Trading Estate
OSS WF5............................... **173** J4

Sand Moor Golf Club
AL/HA/HU LS17....................... **57** J5

Sandy Lane First School
WIL/AL BD15.......................... **72** A7

Savile Business Centre
EARL WF12............................ **172** C4

Savile Park J & I School
HFAX HX1............................... **8** B6

Savile Town CE Infant School & Nursery School
EARL WF12............................ **172** B5

Savoy Squash Club
KBTN HD8............................. **236** E1

Scalebor Park Hospital
ILK LS29................................. **31** K3

Scammonden Sailing Club
HUDW HD3........................... **187** H7

Scapegoat Hill Primary School
MAR/SLWT HD7..................... **189** F5

Scarcroft Golf Club
SCFT LS14.............................. **59** K3

Scarr Hall
BFDE BD3............................... **96** E2

Scholemoor Cemetery
GTHN BD7.............................. **94** E5

Scholemoor Crematorium
GTHN BD7.............................. **94** E5

Scholes Cricket Club
HOLM/MEL HD9..................... **233** K8

Scholes Elmete Junior School
MSTN/BAR LS15...................... **82** C5

Scholes Primary School
HOLM/MEL HD9..................... **233** K8

School Lane Health Centre
DEWS WF13........................... **171** J2

Schreiber Business Centre
WKFDE WF1............................ **11** D5

Scissett Middle School
KBTN HD8............................. **237** H1

Scissett Swimming Baths
KBTN HD8............................. **237** J1

Scotchman Middle School
HTON BD9.............................. **95** G1

Scotch Park Trading Estate
WOR/ARM LS12..................... **100** D3

Scout Road County Primary School
HBR HX7............................... **137** G3

SDH Industrial Estate
RPDN/SBR HX6...................... **138** E8

Seacroft Clinic
SCFT LS14.............................. **81** K6

Seacroft Industrial Estate
SCFT LS14.............................. **81** K4

Seemore Shopping Centre
OSS WF5............................... **173** J5

Selby Gas & Leisure Centre
KNOT WF11........................... **155** K3

Seven Hills Primary School
MOR LS27............................. **123** G7

Shade J & I School
TOD OL14............................. **133** K8

Shadwell Medical Centre
AL/HA/HU LS17....................... **58** A8

Shadwell Primary School
AL/HA/HU LS17....................... **59** H7

Shakespeare Primary School
OSM LS9............................... **102** B2

Sharlston Primary School
HOR/CROF WF4...................... **178** A7

Sharma Park Industrial Estate
RHAY LS8............................. **102** A1

Shaw Business Park
HUDE HD5.............................. **13** E5

Shawcross Business Park
EARL WF12............................ **172** E1

Shaw Cross Health Centre
EARL WF12............................ **147** F8

Shaw Cross Infant School
EARL WF12............................ **147** F8

Shaw House School
HTON BD9.............................. **73** C

Shay Lane Infant School
HOR/CROF WF4...................... **200** C

Sheibarg Industrial Estate
BOW BD4................................ **97** F

Shelf Health Centre
HIPP HX3.............................. **117** H

Shelley First School
KBTN HD8............................. **215**

Shelley High School
KBTN HD8............................. **236**

Shepley First School
KBTN HD8............................. **235** C

Sherwood Industrial Estate
EARD/LOFT WF3..................... **125**

Shibden Hall & Folk Museum
HIPP HX3.............................. **140**

Shibden Head First School
CUL/QBY BD13....................... **116** E

Shipley Baths
SHPY BD18............................. **73** H

Shipley CE First School
SHPY BD18............................. **73** H

Shipley College
SHPY BD18............................. **73** H

Shipley College of Education
SHPY BD18............................. **73** H

Shipley Golf Club
BCLY BD16............................. **71**

Shipley Health Centre
SHPY BD18............................. **73** H

Shipley Hospital
SHPY BD18............................. **73** H

Shires Business Park
GTHN BD7.............................. **95**

Showcase Cinemas
BTLY WF17............................ **122**

Siddal Infant School
HIPP HX3.............................. **140** H

Siddal Junior School
HIPP HX3.............................. **140** H

Sikh Leisure Centre
HUD HD1................................ **12**

Silcoates School
WKFDW/WTN WF2.................. **175**

Silsden Cricket Club
AIRE BD20............................. **27**

Silsden Golf Club
AIRE BD20............................. **27**

Silsden Health Centre
AIRE BD20............................. **27**

Silver Court Industrial Estate
HUD HD1................................ **13**

Simpson Lane J & I School
KNOT WF11........................... **156**

Sirdar Business Park
WKFDW/WTN WF2.................. **175**

Skelmanthorpe Business Park
KBTN HD8............................. **236**

Skelmanthorpe First School
KBTN HD8............................. **237**

Slaithwaite CE Primary School
MAR/SLWT HD7..................... **210**

Slaithwaite Health Centre
MAR/SLWT HD7..................... **210**

Slaithwaite Swimming Baths
MAR/SLWT HD7..................... **210**

Smawthorne Infant School
CAS WF10............................. **153**

Snapethorpe Junior School
WKFDW/WTN WF2.................. **174**

Soothill Cricket Club
BTLY WF17............................ **146**

South Bradford Golf Club
WBSY BD6............................. **119**

South Crosland Junior School
HUDS HD4............................. **212**

Southdale CE Junior School
OSS WF5............................... **173**

South Elmsall Ash Grove J & I School
HEM/SK/SE WF9..................... **226**

South Elmsall Health Centre
HEM/SK/SE WF9..................... **226**

South Halifax High School
HIPP HX3.............................. **166**

South Hiendley J & I School
CUD/GR S72.......................... **223**

South Kirkby Common Road School
HEM/SK/SE WF9..................... **241**

South Leeds Business Park
MID LS10.............................. **101**

uth Leeds Golf Club
 BEE/HOL LS11 .... 124 B4
uth Leeds Sports Centre
 BEE/HOL LS11 .... 101 H7
uth Leeds Stadium
 BEE/HOL LS11 .... 124 D3
uthmere First School
 GTHN BD20 .... 95 C8
uth Ossett Infant School
 OSS WF5 .... 173 K7
uth Parade Junior School
 OSS WF5 .... 174 A7
uthroyd Primary School
 PDSY/CALV LS28 .... 98 C5
uth Side Aviation Centre
 YEA LS19 .... 54 C4
uth View Business Centre
 GSLY LS20 .... 53 G1
uthview Business Park
 GSLY LS20 .... 53 G1
 GSLY LS20 .... 53 G4
uth View Infant School
 YEA LS19 .... 53 K5
uth View Junior School
 YEA LS19 .... 53 K5
vereign Business Centre
 HUDS HD4 .... 191 F8
werby Bridge Clinic
 RPDN/SBR HX6 .... 139 F8
werby Bridge CE
 Junior School
 RPDN/SBR HX6 .... 138 E7
werby Bridge Cricket Club
 RPDN/SBR HX6 .... 138 D7
werby Bridge High School
 RPDN/SBR HX6 .... 139 F6
a Baths
 BSPA/BRAM LS23 .... 42 E3
a Fields Industrial Estate
 MAR/SLWT HD7 .... 211 F2
enborough Industrial Estate
 LVSG WF15 .... 145 F8
enborough Moorend
 CE School
 CLECK BD19 .... 143 K2
enborough Whitcliffe
 Mount School
 CLECK BD19 .... 143 J3
n Trading Estate
 CLECK BD19 .... 144 C4
n Valley High School
 LVSG WF15 .... 144 D8
n Valley Industrial Park
 CLECK BD19 .... 144 B5
n Victoria Cricket
 Bowling & Athletic Club
 CLECK BD19 .... 144 C3
fforth CE Primary School
 PBR HG3 .... 22 A1
ing Bank Industrial Estate
 RPDN/SBR HX6 .... 164 D1
ingbank Junior School
 PDSY/CALV LS28 .... 76 B8
ing Bank Primary School
 HDGY LS6 .... 78 D7
ing Grove Primary School
 HUD HD1 .... 12 B5
ing Ram Business Park
 BTLY WF17 .... 121 K7
 DOD/DAR S75 .... 239 J1
ngwell Health Clinic
 WKFDW/WTN WF2 .... 199 G1
ngwood First School
 GIR BD8 .... 4 A3
ncliffe CE Junior School
 BTLY WF17 .... 145 K8
ndard Industrial Estate
 ECHL BD2 .... 74 E8
ndbridge Primary School
 WKFDW/WTN WF2 .... 198 C6
ndedge Experience
 MAR/SLWT HD7 .... 209 F7
iley Grove J & I School
 ARD/LOFT WF3 .... 150 C8
iley Health Centre
 ARD/LOFT WF3 .... 150 B6
iley Mills Business Park
 MAR/SLWT HD7 .... 189 K7
iley St Peters J & I School
 ARD/LOFT WF3 .... 150 C6
iley Sports & Social Club
 EARD/LOFT WF3 .... 150 C5
nningley Industrial Centre
 PDSY/CALV LS28 .... 98 B2

Stanningley Primary School
 PDSY/CALV LS28 .... 76 D8
Stanningley RLFC
 PDSY/CALV LS28 .... 98 E1
Station Industrial Park
 LUD/ILL HX2 .... 138 A4
Station Road Industrial Estate
 GFTH/SHER LS25 .... 128 E4
Station Works Industrial Park
 KGHY BD21 .... 3 F3
Steed Court Business Park
 HEM/SK/SE WF9 .... 226 E3
Steeton Health Centre
 AIRE BD20 .... 26 E6
Steeton J & I School
 AIRE BD20 .... 27 F6
Steps Industrial Park
 HOLM/MEL HD9 .... 213 G5
Sterling Industrial Park
 CAS WF10 .... 154 A5
Stile Common Infant School
 HUDS HD4 .... 191 H8
Stile Common Junior School
 HUDS HD4 .... 191 G8
Stockingate Junior school
 HEM/SK/SE WF9 .... 241 G2
Stocks Lane First School
 CUL/QBY BD13 .... 117 G1
Stonegate School
 AL/HA/HU LS17 .... 79 G3
Stoney Lee Middle School
 BGLY BD16 .... 72 B5
Stoney Ridge Hospital
 BGLY BD16 .... 72 C6
Stoney Royd Cemetery
 HIPP HX3 .... 9 E6
Stoodley Pike Monument
 TOD OL14 .... 135 H6
Streethouse J & I School
 HOR/CROF WF4 .... 178 B6
Summerfield Primary School
 BRAM LS13 .... 76 D8
Sunday School
 HBR HX7 .... 112 C3
The Sunday School
 HBR HX7 .... 111 J5
Sunfield Medical Centre
 PDSY/CALV LS28 .... 98 B1
Sunny Hill House School
 WKFDW/WTN WF2 .... 175 F2
Surgery Savile Centre
 EARL WF12 .... 195 H1
Swain House Middle School
 ECHL BD2 .... 74 C7
Swillington Primary School
 RTHW LS26 .... 127 K1
Swinnow Primary School
 PDSY/CALV LS28 .... 98 E3
Swinnow Shopping Centre
 BRAM LS13 .... 98 E3
Swire Smith Middle School
 KGHY BD21 .... 3 F3
Sycamore Industrial Estate
 HECK WF16 .... 171 G1
Tadcaster Grammar School
 TAD LS24 .... 63 K1
Tainton Park Trading Estate
 WOR/ARM LS12 .... 6 A5
Taison Industrial Park
 CTHN BD7 .... 95 F8
Takalani Dance Theatre
 RHAY LS8 .... 80 E7
Talbot Primary School
 RHAY LS8 .... 80 B2
Tandem Industrial Estate
 HECK WF16 .... 192 D5
The Tandy Trading Estate
 BULY LS4 .... 100 C2
Tannery Business Park
 HIPP HX3 .... 117 F8
Tanshelf Industrial Estate
 PONT WF8 .... 180 D2
Tanyard Industrial Estate
 HUDW HD3 .... 190 B7
Technical College
 AIRE BD20 .... 27 G2
Temple Bank Special School
 HTON BD9 .... 94 E1
Temple Moor High School
 MSTN/BAR LS15 .... 103 K4
Temple Newsam
 MSTN/BAR LS15 .... 103 K6
Temple Newsam Country Park
 MSTN/BAR LS15 .... 103 K5

Temple Newsam Golf Club
 MSTN/BAR LS15 .... 103 H5
Temple Newsam Halton
 Primary School
 MSTN/BAR LS15 .... 103 J3
Tenterfields Business Park
 LUD/ILL HX2 .... 138 B6
Tetley Brewery Wharf
 MID LS10 .... 7 F4
Thackley AFC
 IDLE BD10 .... 74 C1
Thackley Cricket Club
 IDLE BD10 .... 74 D1
Thackley First School
 IDLE BD10 .... 74 D1
Thackray Medical Museum
 OSM LS9 .... 102 B1
Thomas Danby College
 CHAL LS7 .... 7 F1
Thomas Park Athletics Stadium
 WKFDW/WTN WF2 .... 10 A4
Thongsbridge Tennis Club
 HOLM/MEL HD9 .... 233 H3
Thornbury First School
 BFDE BD3 .... 97 F3
Thornbury Middle School
 BFDE BD3 .... 97 G3
Thorncliffe Square
 Industrial Estate
 GIR BD8 .... 4 B2
Thornes Industrial Estate
 WKFDE WF1 .... 10 C5
Thornhill High School
 EARL WF12 .... 195 J2
Thornhill J & I School
 EARL WF12 .... 195 H2
Thornhill Lees CE Infant School
 EARL WF12 .... 172 B7
Thorn Park School
 HTON BD9 .... 72 D7
Thornton Baths
 CUL/QBY BD13 .... 93 J5
Thornton First School
 CUL/QBY BD13 .... 93 H5
Thornton Lodge Health Centre
 HUD HD1 .... 12 B6
Thornton Medical Centre
 CUL/QBY BD13 .... 93 J5
Thornton Upper School
 CUL/QBY BD13 .... 94 B5
Thorp Arch Trading Estate
 BSPA/BRAM LS23 .... 25 G8
Thorpe First & Middle School
 IDLE BD10 .... 74 D3
Thorpe Primary School
 EARD/LOFT WF3 .... 149 F1
Three Lane Ends
 Business Centre
 CAS WF10 .... 153 F3
Throstle Farm J & I School
 KNOT WF11 .... 182 C1
Thrum Hall Industrial Park
 LUD/ILL HX2 .... 139 H4
Thurstonland Endowed
 Primary School
 HUDS HD4 .... 234 B1
Thwaite Mills Watermill
 OSM LS9 .... 102 D8
Tinshill Primary School
 BHP/TINH LS16 .... 55 J8
Todmorden Community College
 TOD OL14 .... 134 A6
Todmorden Cricket Club
 TOD OL14 .... 133 K5
Todmorden Golf Club
 TOD OL14 .... 134 B4
Todmorden Health Centre
 TOD OL14 .... 134 A6
Todmorden High School
 TOD OL14 .... 133 J5
Tolson Memorial Museum
 HUDE HD5 .... 192 A5
Tong Park First School
 BAIL BD17 .... 52 B7
Tong Sports Centre
 BOW BD4 .... 120 D3
Top Rank Theatre
 HFAX HX1 .... 9 D4
Towngate Primary School
 OSS WF5 .... 173 K5
Tranmere Park Primary School
 GSLY LS20 .... 52 D3
Trawden CP School
 COL BB8 .... 64 A1

Treefield Industrial Estate
MOR LS27...................................... 122 C6

Triangle Business Park
BTLY WF17..................................... 121 K8

Triangle CE Primary School
RPDN/SBR HX6............................... 164 B2

Trinity Business Centre
WKFDE WF1..................................... 11 D4

Trinity Medical Centre
WKFDE WF1..................................... 10 C4

Tropical World
RHAY LS8....................................... 80 D2

Tuel Lane County
Primary School
RPDN/SBR HX6............................... 138 E7

Tulip Street Retail Park
MID LS10....................................... 101 K8

Turnshaws Special School
KBTN HD8...................................... 215 J5

Tyersal Family Clinic
BOW BD4.. 97 H5

Tyersal First School
BOW BD4.. 97 F6

UCI Cinema
HUDE HD5...................................... 13 F2

Undercliffe Cricket Club
ECHL BD2....................................... 96 E1

Undercliffe First School
ECHL BD2... 5 F1

Union Business Centre
ECHL BD2....................................... 75 F7

University of Bradford
GTHN BD7.. 4 A6

University of Huddersfield
HUD HD1.. 13 D5
HUDW HD3..................................... 190 C2
KBTN HD8...................................... 214 E5

University of Leeds
BHP/TINH LS16............................... 78 C2
HDGY LS6....................................... 79 F7
LDSU LS2... 6 C1

University of Leeds
Trinity & All Saints College
HORS LS18...................................... 54 E8

University Sports Centre
LDSU LS2... 6 C2

Upper Abrigg Special School
HOLM/MEL HD9.............................. 233 K5

Upperthong J & I School
HOLM/MEL HD9.............................. 232 E7

Upper Whitley J & I School
HOR/CROF WF4.............................. 194 C7

Upper Wortley Primary School
WOR/ARM LS12............................. 100 B5

Upton ARLFC
HEM/SK/SE WF9............................. 226 D3

Upton Clinic
HEM/SK/SE WF9............................. 227 F3

Usher Street First School
BOW BD4.. 5 E6

Utley J & I School
AIRE BD20...................................... 47 K1

Valley Medical Centre
HBR HX7....................................... 112 B8

Valley Mills Industrial Estate
IDLE BD10...................................... 75 G3

Valley Road Business Park
LVSG WF15.................................... 144 D7

Vehicle Testing Centre
BSPA/BRAM LS23............................ 25 G7

Venlo Industrial Estate
BOW BD4...................................... 119 K1

Victoria Baths
ELL HX5....................................... 167 F5

Victoria Centre
EARL WF12.................................... 172 B3

Victoria Industrial Estate
ECHL BD2....................................... 74 E7

Victoria Industrial Park
SCFT LS14...................................... 81 K3

Victoria Junior School
RTHW LS26.................................... 126 A5

Victoria Park School
BRAM LS13..................................... 77 J8

Victoria Primary School
OSM LS9....................................... 102 D3

Victoria Spring Business Park
LVSG WF15.................................... 144 C6

Vine Industrial Estate
BRIG HD6...................................... 142 A8

Vintage Railway Carriage Museum
HWTH BD22.................................... 68 E4

Wadsworth Old Town
Primary School
HBR HX7....................................... 112 D6

Wainstalls School
LUD/ILL HX2.................................. 114 C6

Wakefield Art Gallery
WKFDE WF1..................................... 10 B2

Wakefield Cathedral
WKFDE WF1..................................... 10 C3

Wakefield City Baths
WKFDE WF1..................................... 11 D3

Wakefield City High School
WKFDE WF1..................................... 11 F2

Wakefield College
CAS WF10..................................... 153 G5
FEA/AMT WF7................................ 179 J6
HEM/SK/SE WF9............................ 224 E4
WKFDE WF1..................................... 10 B2

Wakefield Crematorium
WKFDW/WTN WF2.......................... 198 C5

Wakefield Girls High School
WKFDE WF1..................................... 10 B2

Wakefield Girls
High School (Junior)
WKFDW/WTN WF1.......................... 10 A2

Wakefield Golf Club
WKFDW/WTN WF2.......................... 199 G5

Wakefield Independent
Junior School
HOR/CROF WF4.............................. 201 K5

Wakefield Independent School
HOR/CROF WF4.............................. 201 J3

Wakefield 41 Industrial Park
EARD/LOFT WF3............................. 149 G6

Wakefield Methodist First School
WKFDW/WTN WF2.......................... 10 C6

Wakefield Museum
WKFDE WF1..................................... 10 C3

Wakefield RUFC
WKFDE WF1..................................... 10 C1

Wakefield Superbowl 2000
WKFDE WF1..................................... 11 F6

Wakefield Theatre Royal
& Opera House
WKFDE WF1..................................... 10 B3

Wakefield Trinity RLFC
WKFDE WF1..................................... 11 F6

Wakefield Tutorial
Preparatory School
MOR LS27..................................... 123 F7

Walnut Business Park
HFAX HX1.. 8 A4

Walsden CE (e) Infant School
TOD OL14..................................... 160 A2

Walsden Cricket Club
TOD OL14..................................... 159 K3

Walsden Industrial Estate
TOD OL14..................................... 160 A4

Walsden Junior Mixed School
TOD OL14..................................... 159 K2

Walton Grove Infant School
WKFDW/WTN WF2.......................... 199 K4

Walton Junior School
WKFDW/WTN WF2.......................... 199 J4

Wapping First School
BFDE BD3.. 5 D3

Warley Road J & I School
LUD/ILL HX2.................................. 139 H5

Warley Town School
LUD/ILL HX2.................................. 138 E5

Warner Village
BULY LS4...................................... 100 C2

Warwick Road J & I School
BTLY WF17.................................... 146 B8

Waterloo Infant School
PDSY/CALV LS28............................ 98 A4

Waterloo Junior School
PDSY/CALV LS28............................ 98 A4

Waterside Industrial Park
OSM LS9....................................... 102 D8

Waterton J & I School
WKFDW/WTN WF2.......................... 174 E7

Waterton Park Golf Club
WKFDW/WTN WF2.......................... 200 A5

Waverley Middle School
GTHN BD7...................................... 95 H6

Wax Museum
BFD BD1.. 4 B4

Weetwood Primary School
BHP/TINH LS16............................... 78 D4

Wellhouse J & I School
MAR/SLWT HD7............................. 189 H8

Wellhouse Middle School
MIRF WF14.................................... 170 E4

Wellington Business Centre
ELL HX5....................................... 167 F

Wellington First School
ECHL BD2....................................... 74 D

Wellington Middle School
ECHL BD2....................................... 74 D

Wellington Road
Industrial Estate
WOR/ARM LS12............................... 6 E

Wellington Shopping Arcade
BRIG HD6...................................... 168 E

Wellington Street
Business Park
CAS WF10..................................... 153

Well Lane Business Centre
BTLY WF17.................................... 146 E

Westborough High School
DEWS WF13.................................... 171

West Bowling Golf Club
WBOW BD5.................................... 119 H

West Bradford Golf Club
HTON BD9...................................... 72 E

West Bretton Primary School
HOR/CROF WF4.............................. 219

Westbrook Lane Primary School
HORS LS18..................................... 54 I

Westcliffe Medical Centre
SHPY BD18....................................... 73 C

West End Golf Club (Halifax)
LUD/ILL HX2.................................. 139

West End Industrial Estate
MOR LS27...................................... 122 C

West End Middle School
CLECK BD19.................................. 143

West End Primary School
HORS LS18..................................... 76 I

Westerton Primary School
EARD/LOFT WF3............................. 147

Westfield Industrial Estate
YEA LS19....................................... 53

Westfield Medical Centre
CHAL LS7....................................... 79 I

West Garforth Junior School
GFTH/SHER LS25............................ 105

Westgate Hill First School
BOW BD4...................................... 120 [

Westgate Infant School
OT LS21.. 33

Westgate Retail & Leisure Park
WKFDW/WTN WF2.......................... 10

West Hall Special School
EARD/LOFT WF3............................. 150

West Leeds High School
WOR/ARM LS12............................... 99

Westmoor Junior School
DEWS WF13.................................... 171

West Oaks School
BSPA/BRAM LS23........................... 42

West Park Bramhope RUFC
BHP/TINH LS16............................... 56

West Riding Magistrates Court
BTLY WF17.................................... 145

Westroyd Infant School
PDSY/CALV LS28............................ 98

West Side Retail Park
GSLY LS20...................................... 53

West Vale J & I School
GTL/HWG HX4................................ 166

Westville House
Preparatory School
ILK LS29... 20

Westwood Primary School
MID LS10....................................... 124

West Yorkshire College of
Health Studies
WKFDE WF1................................... 176

West Yorkshire Industrial Estate
BOW BD4...................................... 120

West Yorkshire Playhouse
OSM LS9.. 7

West Yorkshire Retail Park
BTLY WF17.................................... 122

West Yorks Police HQ
WKFDE WF1..................................... 10

Wetherby Business Park
WBY LS22....................................... 23

Wetherby Golf Club
WBY LS22....................................... 23

Wetherby High School
WBY LS22....................................... 23

Wetherby Leisure Centre
WBY LS22....................................... 23

Wetherby Racecourse
WBY LS22....................................... 24

arfebank Business Centre
OT LS21 .... **33** G4
arfedale Business Park
BOW BD4 .... **120** A2
arfedale General Hospital
OT LS21 .... **33** H1
e Whartons Primary School
OT LS21 .... **33** J1
eldon Infant School
CAS WF10 .... **153** K3
etley Middle School
GIR BD8 .... **95** G3
inburn Residential School
AIRE BD20 .... **47** H1
ingate Business Centre
WOR/ARM LS12 .... **100** A4
ingate Business Park
WOR/ARM LS12 .... **100** B4
ingate Primary School
WOR/ARM LS12 .... **100** A4
aitebridge Primary School
MSTN/BAR LS15 .... **103** G4
itechapel Middle School
CLECK BD19 .... **143** K2
itecote Primary School
BRAM LS13 .... **77** G7
itehall Industrial Estate
WOR/ARM LS12 .... **99** K7
itehall Trading Estate
WOR/ARM LS12 .... **99** J7
itehill County Infant School
LUD/ILL HX2 .... **115** H5
ite Horse Leisure Centre
WKFDE WF1 .... **10** C3
ite Laith Primary School
SCFT LS14 .... **82** A4
ite Rose House
WKFDE WF1 .... **10** C4
ite Rose Shopping Centre
MOR LS27 .... **123** K4
itkirk Medical Centre
MSTN/BAR LS15 .... **104** B3
itkirk Primary School
MSTN/BAR LS15 .... **103** K4
itwood Business Centre
CAS WF10 .... **153** F3
itwood Golf Club
CAS WF10 .... **152** D5
sey First School
WBSY BD6 .... **118** C2
sey Middle School
WBSY BD6 .... **118** C2
gan Lane Trading Estate
HUDN HD2 .... **168** E7
ton Moor Primary School
AL/HA/HU LS17 .... **58** B6
berlee J & I School
MAR/SLWT HD7 .... **210** B1
iam Henry Smith School
BRIG HD6 .... **167** K3
ow Industrial Complex
RPDN/SBR HX6 .... **138** E8
e Willows Medical Centre
CUL/QBY BD13 .... **116** D2
ow Valley Golf & Country Club
BRIG HD6 .... **143** F6
sden Primary School
WIL/AL BD15 .... **71** G6

Windhill CE First School
SHPY BD18 .... **73** K3
Windhill Cricket Club
SHPY BD18 .... **73** K2
Windhill Green Medical Centre
SHPY BD18 .... **73** J3
Windmill Primary School
MID LS10 .... **125** F3
Windsor Medical Centre
EARL WF12 .... **172** D3
Wira Business Park
BHP/TINH LS16 .... **77** K2
Withinfields J & I School
HIPP HX3 .... **140** E6
Womersley CE Primary School
AWLS/ASK DN6 .... **183** J8
Woodbank Special School
LUD/ILL HX2 .... **138** B3
Woodhall Hills Golf Club
PDSY/CALV LS28 .... **75** H7
Woodhill Middle School
SHPY BD18 .... **73** K3
Woodhouse Business Centre
NORM WF6 .... **177** K2
Woodhouse Cricket Club
CHAL LS7 .... **79** F5
Woodhouse First School
NORM WF6 .... **177** K3
Woodhouse Grove School
IDLE BD10 .... **75** H2
Woodhouse Health Centre
HDGY LS6 .... **79** H8
Woodhouse Primary School
BRIG HD6 .... **168** C3
Woodkirk High School
EARD/LOFT WF3 .... **147** H2
Woodland Glade Leisure Centre
HUDN HD2 .... **168** E6
Woodlands CE First School
LM/WK BD12 .... **119** H6
Woodlands Cricket Club
LM/WK BD12 .... **119** G6
Woodlands Primary School
OSM LS9 .... **80** D8
Woodroyd Industrial Estate
LM/WK BD12 .... **119** F6
Woodroyd Middle School
WBOW BD5 .... **96** A8
Woodside Clinic
WBSY BD6 .... **118** B5
Woodside First School
WBSY BD6 .... **118** B5
Woodside Middle School
WBSY BD6 .... **118** B5
Woodside Trading Estate
HORS LS18 .... **77** J2
Woodsley Health Centre
HDGY LS6 .... **6** B1
Woodsome Hall Golf Club
KBTN HD8 .... **214** D2
Wooldale Junior School
HOLM/MEL HD9 .... **233** K4
Woolley Hall College
HOR/CROF WF4 .... **220** D4
Woolshops Shopping Centre
HFAX HX1 .... **9** D4
Worthinghead First School
LM/WK BD12 .... **118** E8

Worth Valley Middle School
HWTH BD22 .... **47** J8
Wortley High School
WOR/ARM LS12 .... **99** K5
Wortley Moor Lane
Trading Estate
WOR/ARM LS12 .... **100** B5
WRCC Clinic
MAR/SLWT HD7 .... **211** H2
Wrenthorpe Health Centre
WKFDW/WTN WF2 .... **175** F1
Wrenthorpe Primary School
WKFDW/WTN WF2 .... **175** G1
Wrenthorpe Sports Club
WKFDW/WTN WF2 .... **149** G8
Wrose Health Centre
ECHL BD2 .... **74** B6
Wycliffe Middle School
SHPY BD18 .... **73** G3
Wykebeck Infant School
OSM LS9 .... **103** F1
Wykebeck Primary School
OSM LS9 .... **103** F1
Wyke Manor Upper School
LM/WK BD12 .... **118** E8
Wyke Middle School
LM/WK BD12 .... **118** D8
Wyther Lane Industrial Estate
KSTL LS5 .... **78** A8
Wyther Park Primary School
KSTL LS5 .... **77** K8
Yarnbury RUFC
HORS LS18 .... **54** E8
Yeadon Airport
Industrial Estate
YEA LS19 .... **54** C2
Yeadon Cemetery
YEA LS19 .... **54** A3
Yeadon Cricket Club
YEA LS19 .... **54** A4
Yeadon Health Centre
YEA LS19 .... **53** K4
Yeadon Westfield Junior School
YEA LS19 .... **53** H5
York Road Industrial Estate
WBY LS22 .... **23** K5
Yorkshire Amateurs FC
CHAL LS7 .... **80** B5
Yorkshire Bank Sports Ground
AL/HA/HU LS17 .... **79** K1
Yorkshire CCC
(Headingley Cricket Ground)
HDGY LS6 .... **78** D7
Yorkshire Clinic
BGLY BD16 .... **72** C4
Yorkshire Martyrs
Collegiate School
BOW BD4 .... **120** D3
Yorkshire Post Sports Club
BHP/TINH LS16 .... **78** C4
Yorkshire Sculpture Park
BVRD LS3 .... **218** E4
Yorkshire Television Studios
BVRD LS3 .... **6** A2
Young Street Industrial Estate
GIR BD8 .... **95** F3
Zakaria Muslim Girls High School
BTLY WF17 .... **146** C7